# Newsmakers®

ISSN 0899-0417

# *Newsmakers*®

## *The People Behind Today's Headlines*

**Laura Avery**

Project Editor

# 2005

# Cumulation

Includes Indexes from
1985 through 2005

THOMSON

GALE

Detroit • New York • San Francisco • San Diego • New Haven, Conn. • Waterville, Maine • London • Munich

# THOMSON

### GALE

**Newsmakers 2005, Cumulation**

**Project Editor**
Laura Avery

**Image Research and Acquisitions**
Leitha Etheridge-Sims, Barbara McNeil

**Editorial Support Services**
Emmanuel T. Barrido

**Rights Acquisition and Management**
Margaret Chamberlain, Jackie Jones, Sue Rudolph

**Imaging**
Lezlie Light, Mike Logusz

**Composition and Electronic Capture**
Carolyn A. Roney

**Manufacturing**
Drew Kalasky

*ANF*
*920*
*Newsmakers 2005*
*3748405*
*HQ*

ISBN 0-7876-8081-8
ISSN 0899-0417

Printed in the United States of America
10 9 8 7 6 5 4 3 2 1

# Contents

## Obituaries

# Introduction

*Newsmakers* provides informative profiles of the world's most interesting people in a crisp, concise, contemporary format. Make *Newsmakers* the first place you look for biographical information on the people making today's headlines.

## Important Features

- **Attractive, modern page design** pleases the eye while making it easy to locate the information you need.

- **Coverage of all the newsmakers** you want to know about: people in business, education, technology, law, politics, religion, entertainment, labor, sports, medicine, and other fields.

- **Clearly labeled data sections** allow quick access to vital personal statistics, career information, major awards, and mailing addresses.

- **Informative sidelights essays** include the kind of in-depth analysis you're looking for.

- **Sources for additional information** provide lists of books, magazines, newspapers, and internet sites where you can find out even more about *Newsmakers* listees.

- **Enlightening photographs** are specially selected to further enhance your knowledge of the subject.

- **Separate obituaries section** provides you with concise profiles of recently deceased newsmakers.

- **Publication schedule and price** fit your budget. *Newsmakers* is published in three paperback issues per year, each containing approximately 50 entries, and a hardcover cumulation, containing approximately 200 entries (those from the preceding three paperback issues plus an additional 50 entries), *all at a price you can afford!*

- And much, much more!

## Indexes Provide Easy Access

Familiar and indispensable: The *Newsmakers* indexes! You can easily locate entries in a variety of ways through our four versatile, comprehensive indexes. The Nationality, Occupation, and Subject Indexes list names from the current year's *Newsmakers* issues. These are cumulated in the annual hardbound volume to include all names from the entire *Contemporary Newsmakers* and *Newsmakers* series. The Newsmakers Index is cumulated in all issues as well as the hardbound annuals to provide concise coverage of the entire series.

- **Nationality Index**—Names of newsmakers are arranged alphabetically under their respective nationalities.

- **Occupation Index**—Names are listed alphabetically under broad occupational categories.

- **Subject Index**—Includes key subjects, topical issues, company names, products, organizations, etc., that are discussed in *Newsmakers*. Under each subject heading are listed names of newsmakers associated with that topic. So the unique Subject Index provides access to the information in *Newsmakers* even when readers are unable to connect a name with a particular topic. This index also invites browsing, allowing *Newsmakers* users to discover topics they may wish to explore further.

- **Cumulative Newsmakers Index**—Listee names, along with birth and death dates, when available, are arranged alphabetically followed by the year and issue number in which their entries appear.

## Available in Electronic Formats

**Licensing.** *Newsmakers* is available for licensing. The complete database is provided in a fielded format and is deliverable on such media as disk or CD-ROM. For more information, contact Thomson Gale's Business Development Group at 1-800-877-GALE, or visit our website at www.gale.com/bizdev.

**Online.** *Newsmakers* is available online as part of the Gale Biographies (GALBIO) database accessible through LexisNexis, P.O. Box 933, Dayton, OH 45401-0933; phone: (937) 865-6800, toll-free: 800-227-4908.

## Suggestions Are Appreciated

The editors welcome your comments and suggestions. In fact, many popular *Newsmakers* features were implemented as a result of readers' suggestions. We will continue to shape the series to best meet the needs of the greatest number of users. Send comments or suggestions to:

The Editor
*Newsmakers*
Thomson Gale
27500 Drake Rd.
Farmington Hills, MI 48331-3535

Or, call toll-free at 1-800-877-GALE

# Freddy Adu

**Professional soccer player**

---

**B**orn June 2, 1989, in Ghana; son of Maxwell and Emelia (a hardware store cashier).

**Addresses:** *Office*—D.C. United, RFK Stadium, 2400 E. Capitol St. SE, Washington, DC 20003.

## Career

**J**oined U.S. Under-17 National Team, 2002; joined U.S. Under-20 National Team, 2003; joined major-league soccer team D.C. United, 2004.

**Awards:** U.S. Soccer Chevy Young Male Athlete of the Year, 2003.

## Sidelights

**A**t the age of 14, Freddy Adu became the youngest athlete ever to play major-league soccer. A native of the African country of Ghana who had moved to the United States in 1997, Adu had been recognized as a star in the making since his performance at an under-14 tournament in Italy at the age of ten. His potential was so hyped that some commentators believed he could single-handedly increase soccer's popularity in the United States someday. But his future is very much up in the air after his rookie season as a professional in 2004, which was disappointing but showed he could compete with adults.

Born in Ghana in 1989, Adu played soccer as a kid in pickup games against men three times as old as him. In 1997, the Adu family won a green-card lottery, and Adu left the town of Tema in Ghana to come to the United States with his parents and younger brother, Fro, settling in the Washington, D.C. area. (His father, Maxwell, is now separated from his mother.) A fourth-grade classmate noticed his skills at recess and invited him to a Potomac Soccer Association tournament. He quickly joined the Potomac Cougars, a traveling youth team coached by Arnold Tarzy, who remains a close confidant of Adu and his mother.

At the age of ten, Adu played in an under-14 tournament in Italy for the U.S. Olympic Development Program's team. He was named most valuable player of the tournament. Representatives of the Italian professional team Inter Milan met with his mother in April of 2000, hoping to sign him to a contract. His mother refused, feeling he was too young to sign a professional contract.

She also turned down offers from agents and from the shoe company Adidas, even though she was a single mother working two jobs. In the meantime, her son proved himself to be an exceptional athlete beyond soccer fields, excelling in basketball and golf the first times he played organized games. At school, he also won a fifth-grade art competition.

Adu moved from Potomac, Maryland, to Brandenton, Florida, in the winter of 2002 to join the U.S. Soccer Federation's under-17 residency program, which includes accelerated high-school education. In the spring, when Adu and the rest of the U.S. Under-17 National Team was playing in a full-speed scrimmage with major league soccer's San Jose Earthquakes, Adu, then 12, went up against all-star defender Troy Dayak. "Taking a pass on the left side, Freddy feinted to his right, then swerved like an X-wing fighter to his left with such a sudden and breathtaking *whooosh* that poor Dayak nearly fell over," wrote *Sports Illustrated*'s Grant Wahl. According to Wahl, U.S. coach John Ellinger joked, "I guess Troy hasn't played against a 12-year-old before."

"I love having the ball at my feet and running at the defender one-on-one," Wahl quoted Adu as saying. "That's when I'm at my best, when I can pull some weird move and get by him and everyone goes, *Ohhhhhh*. I *love* that." Adu became an American citizen in February of 2003. He told Wahl of *Sports Illustrated* about his ambitions: "I see myself in a World Cup final for the U.S.A., playing against a top-notch team everyone picks to win. And we just come out and *blast* them."

Because of Adu's skill, some have wondered if he is really as young as he and his birth certificate say he is. Some youth soccer officials quietly suggested he ought to undergo a bone scan to prove his age. *Sports Illustrated* once attempted to confirm his age with sources in Ghana, and produced no evidence challenging his birth certificate.

When he was 13, he and his mother inquired about Adu joining a major league soccer team, but the league replied that 13 was too young. Meanwhile, Adu continued playing with the U.S. Under-17 team, scoring a goal and notching an assist in key wins against Jamaica and Guatemala in March of 2003 that qualified the team for the Under-17 World Cup. In the tournament's first game against South Korea, Adu scored a hat trick, leading the team to a 6-1 victory. Then, against Sierra Leone, he scored the winning goal in the game's 89th minute. That sent the United States team to the quarterfinals, where it lost to Brazil, which went on to win the championship.

In May of 2003, just before he turned 14, Adu signed a $1 million deal with Nike. Later that year, Major League Soccer (MLS) decided he was ready to join the league. He signed a contract with MLS in November of 2003 for $500,000, the league's biggest in

history, and his hometown team, D.C. United, drafted him in January of 2004. In the meantime, the day after signing his professional contract, Adu was called up to the U.S. Under-20 National Team to replace an injured player. He played with the team in the World Youth Championships in the United Arab Emirates in late 2003, starting in four games and assisting on the team's lone goal in its loss to Argentina in the quarterfinals.

When D.C. United's 2004 season began in April, Adu, at 14, became the youngest player ever to appear in a major league soccer game and, on April 17, the youngest player in the league ever to score a goal. Meanwhile, in May of that year, he received his high school diploma, thanks to the accelerated academic program he went through while in the under-17 residency program. D.C. United's home attendance increased by eleven percent as of the end of August, and attendance at its away games increased 45 percent, thanks to Adu. He was named to the league all-star game, as part of an annual commissioner's pick (a player recognized for reasons other than performance on the field). But stardom proved distracting. "Through the end of June, Adu had done hundreds of interviews, chatted up Shaquille O'Neal, dined with Daniel Snyder, taken a cell phone call from Sean 'P. Diddy' Combs, greeted John Ashcroft, mingled with Will Ferrell and Robert Duvall, charmed David Letterman, flirted with FOX starlet Mischa Barton and the Dallas Cowboys cheerleaders, and rocked with David Bowie," wrote Steven Goff in the *Washington Post*.

Adu's play suffered. Though he played in every game of the regular season, he scored only five goals. He found it difficult to play against opponents twice his age. In June of 2004, he seemed to be in a slump, and after one game in which he only played a few minutes, he complained to a reporter about his playing time. His coach told the team not to complain about his decisions through the press. Adu later admitted his comment was a mistake. "When you're 14 and you go and be a pro and get all the media attention in the world, it's a little crazy," he told the *Washington Post*'s Goff. "You're getting pulled in a hundred different directions. It's not the easiest thing." He admitted that it was hard to make his public appearances when he was not satisfied with his play on the field. "I still had to put on a nice face and be a nice person, but inside it didn't feel right because I didn't feel like I deserved it." Eventually, the league changed his schedule, allowing interviews only once every few days, so he could focus more on the game. He scored his first game-winning goal in a 1-0 win over the MetroStars on October 2, 2004. He played in D.C. United's league championship victory in November of that year.

Despite his disappointing first season, most of his fellow players said they thought he would eventually become a star. "I think he has realized how hard the league is," Jaime Moreno, United's all-time leader in points, told the *Washington Post*'s Goff. Moreno, Goff wrote, appeared to be especially frustrated with Adu at times during the season. "He's learning and taking something from each time he has stepped on the field. He's going to be a good player."

During the short off-season, Adu rejoined the U.S. Under-20 National Team. His goal against Panama in January of 2005 helped the team to a 2-0 victory that clinched a berth in the summer of 2005 world championships in the Netherlands. As D.C. United's 2005 exhibition season began in February, Adu told Goff of the *Washington Post* that he had worked hard on the Under-20 team and put on some weight to help his game. "I can't wait," Adu said. "It's been a short winter. Time to get back to work."

Before his rookie season, many soccer commentators expect Adu to join the U.S. World Cup team in 2006. However, as his second professional season began, Adu had yet to live up to the extravagant praise and expectations piled upon him. Whether he could seriously increase soccer's popularity in the United States, a country that has proven stubbornly resistant to embracing soccer for decades, was also uncertain.

## Sources

### Periodicals

*Washington Post,* July 13, 2004, p. D3; August 31, 2004, p. D1; November 15, 2004, p. A1; January 16, 2005, p. E3; January 28, 2005, p. D3.

### Online

"Adu could grow soccer's popularity," ESPN.com, http://espn.go.com/sportsbusiness/s/2003/1119/1665998.html (February 20, 2005).
"Freddy Adu—forward—9," D.C. United, http://dcunited.mlsnet.com (February 20, 2005).
"Who's Next? Freddy Adu," *Sports Illustrated*, http://sportsillustrated.cnn.com/si_online/news/2003/03/03/freddy (February 20, 2005).

*—Erick Trickey*

# Arthur Agatston

## Cardiologist and author

**B**orn in 1947; married Sari. *Education:* Graduate of New York University School of Medicine; specialized medical training at Montefiore Medical Center, Albert Einstein College of Medicine, and New York University.

**Addresses:** *Office*—c/o Author Mail, Rodale, 33 East Minor St., Emmaus, PA 18098-0099.

## Career

**D**octor in private practice, South Florida Cardiology Associates, Miami, FL; University of Miami School of Medicine, associate professor of medicine and director of the Mt. Sinai Non-Invasive Cardiac Lab; expert consultant for the Clinical Trials Committee of the National Institutes of Health; co-director of the annual Symposium on Prevention of Cardiovascular Disease. First book, *The South Beach Diet: The Delicious, Doctor-Designed, Foolproof Plan for Fast and Healthy Weight Loss,* published by Random House, 2003.

## Sidelights

**F**lorida cardiologist Arthur Agatston became America's newest diet guru with his best-selling *South Beach Diet* book in 2003. The Miami doctor had not originally set out to write a weight-loss bible, but instead had devised the healthy-eating plan for his patients to help them avoid heart attacks and strokes. He originally called it a "modified carbohydrate diet," but it became known as the "South Beach diet" on its way to a publishing deal

that would put seven million copies on the market a year later and make it the newest diet craze of the 2000s. A title linked to the fit model types who populate the hedonist-hipster beach spot of Miami worked better than images of his northern Miami waiting room, he admitted to *Time*'s Joel Stein. "My waiting room is not exactly filled with South Beach models."

Born in 1947, Agatston grew up in Roslyn, New York, and earned his medical school degree from New York University. He went on to advanced training in cardiology, and eventually settled in the Miami area and in private practice with South Florida Cardiology Associates. He also served as an associate professor of medicine at the University of Miami School of Medicine and headed the Mt. Sinai Non-Invasive Cardiac Lab.

Agatston was already known in cardiology circles thanks to his research projects. With a radiologist colleague, he devised a way to measure calcium levels in coronary arteries, which predict the risk of a heart attack. Their unique electron beam tomography scan, or EBT, ranks the level of calcium in what is known in medical parlance as the "Agatston Scale." But calcium deposits in the arteries were just one part of the heart-attack equation. Agatston wondered why so many people, himself included, seemed unable to lose that last ten pounds they carried around the midsection. He worked out regularly, and his only indulgence were low-fat chocolate chip cookies, but still he could not shed his "spare tire."

Agatston began to look into research involving insulin resistance and how the body converts calories into glucose. Insulin is a peptide hormone, produced by the islets of Langerhans in the pancreas, which regulates the level of glucose, or sugar, in the blood. Food is converted into energy in the form of glucose, but certain foods have a quick turnaround time, while others take much longer to become fuel for the body's needs. Their rate of conversion is known as the glycemic index, or GI. Its numbers are an indicator of the blood-sugar level and insulin response to various foods. If a food is converted slowly, for example, the GI, which rates items on a scale of zero to 100, will be low.

On the other hand, eating something that converts quickly into glucose—foods that hit the 70s range on the GI scale—means the person will be hungry again sooner because of the insulin response. Agatston wondered if stabilizing the body's insulin levels could end overeating due to hunger and food cravings. Insulin levels could be leveled out by avoiding the foods with the highest GI, which all seemed to be made from refined carbohydrates. Examples are items such as white bread, bagels, and pastries. Agatston devised a diet plan that avoided these foods and included lots of others that had low GI numbers. He tried it on himself, and shed eight pounds in one week.

Agatston then began trying it out on his patients in 1996. They came back, thrilled they had lost weight without increasing their exercise level, and he was pleased to note that their cholesterol and insulin levels had plummeted. When a Miami television station did a story on his plan and followed a group of dieters, Agatston became a local celebrity. Restaurant chefs began offering menu items that adhered to his diet, which advised eating foods with a GI of 55 or lower. He believed that a reliance on a high-carb diet had helped Americans become the fattest nation on the planet. "Nobody in the history of man ever ate complex carbohydrates like we have," he pointed out in an interview with *New York Times* journalist Abby Goodnough.

*The South Beach Diet: The Delicious, Doctor-Designed, Foolproof Plan for Fast and Healthy Weight Loss* was published in April of 2003. It hit the bookstores just

as Dr. Robert Atkins' venerable "no-carbohydrate" diet was enjoying a renewed bout of popularity. But some nutrition experts warned that the famous Atkins no-carb regime, which was heavy on meat and saturated fats, was unhealthy for the heart and arteries. Agatston's modified-carbohydrate plan, on the other hand, promised to keep cholesterol low and help dieters lose those unwanted midsection pounds. It had three phases: during the first one, bread, potatoes, pasta, rice, and even fruit were verboten. During the second phase, carbohydrates that were rich in fiber were permitted, as well as some fruits. The third phase provided suggestions for a healthy-lifestyle eating plan that was meant to be adopted permanently.

Agatston's *South Beach* book remained on the bestseller lists for 26 weeks, with sales boosted by celebrity endorsements that included Bill Clinton and Bette Midler. As with any diet book, there were detractors, who claimed that a food's GI rating had a lot to do with what else had been eaten during a meal. They also pointed out that following a reduced calorie plan—Phase One of Agatston's regime featured a daily calorie intake of just 1,500—would cause anyone to lose weight.

Agatston followed up his immensely successful first book with *The South Beach Diet Cookbook: More Than 200 Delicious Recipes That Fit the Nation's Top Diet* and *The South Beach Diet: Good Fats and Good Carbs Guide.* He was so busy promoting his book in 2003 that he actually regained a few pounds. His wife, Sari, an attorney who handles the financial boon that his book brought in, told him it was time to do something about it. According to her, "I was the only person in the country," Agatston joked in a *People* profile, "*not* on the diet."

## Selected writings

*The South Beach Diet: The Delicious, Doctor-Designed, Foolproof Plan for Fast and Healthy Weight Loss,* Random House (New York, NY), 2003.
*The South Beach Diet: Good Fats and Good Carbs Guide,* Rodale (Emmaus, PA), 2004.
*The South Beach Diet Cookbook: More Than 200 Delicious Recipes That Fit the Nation's Top Diet,* Rodale (Emmaus, PA), 2004.

## Sources

### Periodicals

*Cosmopolitan,* May 2004, p. 220.
*Guardian* (London, England), July 13, 2004, p. 8.
*Independent* (London, England), July 21, 2004, p. 2.
*New York Times,* October 7, 2003, p. F1.

*People,* April 26, 2004, pp. 65-66.

*Publishers Weekly,* January 20, 2003, p. 76; March 1, 2004, p. 65.

*Time,* April 26, 2004, p. 121.

*Tufts University Health and Nutrition Letter,* May 2004, p. 1.

**Online**

*Contemporary Authors Online,* Thomson Gale, 2004.

*—Carol Brennan*

# Chris Albrecht

## Chairman and Chief Executive Officer of HBO

**B**orn c. 1952, in Queens, NY; married (divorced); children: two daughters. *Education:* Hofstra University, degree in dramatic literature.

**Addresses:** *Office*—HBO, 1100 Avenue of the Americas, New York, NY 10036.

## Career

**W**orked as actor on New York stage, c. early 1970s; worked as comedian in New York City, c. early 1970s; manager/owner, The Improvisation Club, New York City and Los Angeles, 1975-80; talent agent, International Creative Management, c. early 1980s; HBO (Home Box Office), senior vice president of original programming, 1985-90, head of HBO Independent Productions, 1990-99, president of original programming, 1995-99, head of all of HBO's original programming, 1999-2002, chairman and chief executive officer, 2002—.

**Member:** Academy of Television Arts & Sciences (board of governors, executive committee).

**Awards:** Television Showmanship Award, Publicists Guild of America, 2001; named Showman of the Year by *Variety,* 2003.

## Sidelights

**A**fter failing to catch on as an actor and a comedian, Chris Albrecht moved into comedy club management and ultimately found his niche in programming. Spending the whole of his executive career with Home Box Office (HBO), the pay cable network, Albrecht helped make HBO a critical favorite, profitable, and full of popular original programming. He authorized many of the network's most successful original shows, movies, and miniseries, including *The Sopranos* and *Angels in America.*

Albrecht was born around 1952, in the borough of Queens in New York City. He grew up in New Jersey, and went to college on Long Island. Albrecht graduated from Hofstra, earning his degree in dramatic literature. When he completed college, Albrecht set his sights on becoming a stage actor. He appeared in a few summer stock productions, but struggled to find work even Off-Broadway.

Turning his focus to comedy, Albrecht was slightly more successful as a comedian. He performed in clubs in New York City, primarily working as a duo with Bob Zmuda. The pair were prop comics. However, their success was limited. Albrecht had to work as a waiter to help support himself.

By 1975, Albrecht had moved from the stage to behind the scenes. He began as a manager for The Improvisation Club (known as The Improv Club) in

New York City, and later moved into management and ownership of the New York and Los Angeles locations. Through his work with clubs, Albrecht developed contacts with many up-and-coming comics, including Larry David, Jerry Seinfeld, Billy Crystal, and Robin Williams.

Albrecht's success with the comedy club led to a new endeavor. He moved into managing talent, becoming an agent with Hollywood powerhouse International Creative Management (ICM). Albrecht's client list included many comic talents including Eddie Murphy, Jim Carrey, and Keenen Ivory Wayans.

In 1985, Albrecht took on a new challenge when he was hired to be senior vice president of original programming for HBO. He worked primarily on HBO shows produced on the West Coast. One show he put together became an annual event; using his comedy connections, Albrecht put together the first Comic Relief benefit for the network.

Albrecht moved into a new position with the network in 1990, when he was named the head of HBO Independent Productions (HIP). This arm of HBO created comedy series for HBO as well as other networks, including the broadcast networks. Among the hits developed by HIP was the long-running CBS comedy *Everybody Loves Raymond*.

Albrecht also helped get hits like *The Larry Sanders Show* on the air. Albrecht began developing what became the HBO mentality toward series television, focusing on adult themes in a realistic manner but with a different twist. These principles guided HBO as they embraced more original series in the 1990s.

While remaining head of HIP, Albrecht added another job at HBO in May of 1995 when he was named president of original programming. At the time, the division was struggling, barely ahead of rival Showtime. Albrecht continued to focus on making quality shows that were bold and went beyond audience expectations. He told A.J. Frutkin of *Mediaweek*, "When we set out to make something, we set out to make it great. Not to make it popular, not to try to figure out what the audience wants, not to be trendy, or hip, or edgy, but just to try to make it great."

Albrecht gave approval to many shows that became hits among audiences and critics alike. They included the prison drama *Oz*, the mob drama *The Sopranos*, and comedies such as *Sex and the City*. Albrecht did not limit HBO's series to scripted shows.

He also was involved with greenlighting talk shows such as *Dennis Miller Live* and variety shows like *The Chris Rock Show*. Albrecht did not choose projects to approve based on what test audiences thought, but by his and his staff's gut feelings about the show.

Two big miniseries also were approved by Albrecht, *From the Earth to the Moon* and *The Corner*. Both were praised by critics, though the latter was somewhat controversial because of its subject matter (inner city drug culture). Controversy did not bother HBO because attracting more subscribers, not pleasing advertisers, was the goal. All these projects, miniseries and series alike, won numerous awards, including Emmys and Golden Globes. The success of such projects also attracted big name talent to the network, including such luminaries as Tom Hanks and Steven Spielberg. Albrecht's reputation as being easy to work with and granting such artists open creative license also helped.

In 1999, Albrecht was given a promotion and more responsibilities. He was put in charge of all the network's original programming including movies, which had been previously done under the guise of HBO Original Movies. This promotion gave Albrecht a significant amount of power at the network.

In that role, Albrecht continued to help develop quality hit shows for HBO. In 2001, he greenlighted *Six Feet Under*, another dramatic show that had long-lasting success. Albrecht also approved the network's costliest venture to date, the World War II-themed *Band of Brothers*. The miniseries cost $120 million to make and took nine months to film. Such moves were risky but paid off. In 2002 alone, the network received 93 Emmy Award nominations.

Albrecht was promoted again to chairman and chief executive officer (CEO) of HBO in 2002. He replaced Jeff Bewkes who was named chief operating officer of the newly created entertainment group of HBO's parent company, AOL Time Warner. Albrecht had much to learn about the operations and financial aspects of running a network, but believed he was up to the task. HBO's earnings were more than $800 million, which is three times more than it was seven years ago when he took over original programming for the network. HBO was more profitable than broadcast networks, due in part to Albrecht's programming choices.

While chairman and CEO of the network, Albrecht still oversaw programming, though his role was not as active as it had been. Instead, he grew the network in other ways. He moved HBO into producing films for theatrical release. For example, he was the co-producer of the 2002 hit *My Big Fat Greek Wedding*. Albrecht also began maximizing profits for HBO by syndicating its original series. Because HBO had no restrictions on language and nudity, its shows had not been previously sold. However, edited versions of HBO shows did work, with *Sex and the City* becoming the first show syndicated. It began airing on TBS in 2004.

Albrecht increased HBO's profits in other ways as well. The network began selling DVDs of its shows as well as putting them on video on demand. Those who subscribed to this service through their cable system paid a fee and could see HBO programming commercial free whenever they wanted. Merchandise such as clothing, food, and books based on the hit programs were available for sale.

Albrecht learned the business aspects of running a network very well, though his tenure was not without challenges. When James Gandolfini, the star of *The Sopranos*, sued HBO, Albrecht stood his ground. Gandolfini wanted a new contract that would pay him more money just before the fifth season of his series started filming. Albrecht threatened to cancel the show, and after two weeks, Gandolfini went to work while a new contract was worked out.

As shows such as *Sex and the City* ended their runs, Albrecht replaced them with new hit such as *Deadwood* and *Carnivale*. He also broadcast another expansive and expensive miniseries, *Angels in America*, which starred Hollywood heavyweights such as Al Pacino and Meryl Streep. The miniseries won eleven Emmy Awards.

In Hollywood, Albrecht had a sterling reputation among both creative types and financial honchos. David Crane, the creator of *The Sopranos*, told Ted Johnson of *Variety*, "I think the thing about Chris is, he is brave. He is not governed by fear. That is not where he works from. He works from enthusiasm and even defiance."

## Sources

*Broadcasting & Cable*, September 9, 2002, p. 12.
*Entertainment Weekly*, October 22, 2004, p. 46.
*Financial Times* (London, England), April 1, 2003, p. 8.
*Mediaweek*, June 16, 2003.
*Multichannel News*, April 19, 1999, p. 10; June 11, 2001, p. 124.
*Newsweek*, March 18, 2002, p. 59.
*New York Times*, December 29, 2002, sec. 3, p. 1; June 3, 2004, p. C6.
*Variety*, October 12, 1998, p. 8; April 19, 1999, p. 27; January 29, 2001, p. 41; July 22, 2002, p. 42; August 25, 2003, p. A3, p. A6.

*—A. Petruso*

# Roger Ames

Bloomberg News/Landov

## Advisor to Time Warner

**B**orn c. 1950 in Trinidad.

**Addresses:** *Office*—Time Warner Inc., One Time Warner Ctr., New York, NY 10019-8016.

## Career

**W**orked at EMI UK, 1975-79; worked for Phonogram Records, PolyGram UK, 1979; worked in A&R dept., then head of London Records, PolyGram UK, 1979-1993; chairman, CEO, PolyGram UK, 1992-96; president, PolyGram Music Group, 1996-98; named executive vice president, PolyGram Group, 1996; president, Warner Music International, 1999; chairman, CEO, Warner Music Group, 1999-2004; advisor to Time Warner, 2004—.

## Sidelights

**A**fter a long career in the music industry, Roger Ames was named chief executive officer of Warner Music Group in 1999. Ames had previously held executive positions at PolyGram and London Records. Though he faced early challenges as Warner's CEO, he enjoyed the confidence of his superiors. However, after a few years with the company, he left to become an advisor to Time Warner.

Ames was born around 1950 in Trinidad, where he received his education. By the mid-1970s, Ames was living in the United Kingdom and working in the music industry. In 1975, he was employed by EMI in the Artists & Repertoire (A&R) department. He also worked for EMI's international department. Four years later, Ames moved on to Phonogram Records, which was part of PolyGram.

By the early 1980s, Ames was working at London Records as the head of A&R. In 1983, he was promoted to general manager. He later became manager-director and, with Tracey Bennett, part owner of the label. During his tenure at London, Ames had a hand in developing important acts including Bronski Beat and its lead singer Jimmy Somerville, Fine Young Cannibals, Bananarama, and Shakespeare's Sister. He also helped artists from the United States, like Los Lobos and Faith No More, gain attention outside their native country.

In 1992, Ames was promoted to chief executive officer and chairman of PolyGram U.K., replacing the retiring Maurice Oberstein, who was stepping down from these positions while retaining his affiliation with PolyGram International. (London Records was part of PolyGram in the United Kingdom.) This marked the first time someone with an background in A&R was put in charge of the label. When Ames took over on January 1, 1993, PolyGram was the leading record company in Britain. Ames was responsible for all of PolyGram's interests in the U.K. and Ireland, including film distribution. Despite the promotion, Ames kept his stake in London Records and constructed his contract so that this would not create a conflict of interest.

Four years later, in the spring of 1996, Ames was named president of the PolyGram Music Group and executive vice president of PolyGram Group. This meant that he was head of all of PolyGram's labels worldwide as well as music publishing, pop marketing, and some financial aspects of PolyGram. Ames remained based in London and continued to retain his interest in London Records. At the time, PolyGram maintained the largest market share of any music company in the world, but was facing competition and did not see its net worth grow in 1995.

Though Ames was picked in part because he already had positive relationships with PolyGram's United States labels, he faced an immediate challenge when he had to integrate the Motown label into the company. This proved difficult to accomplish. During his short tenure in the position, Ames was criticized for his inability to create an effective team and his concern for his own interests. These problems did not matter when Ames was forced out of his post in late 1998, when Seagram purchased PolyGram.

In April of 1999, Ames was hired as part of the senior management group at Warner Music International (WMI). He was hired in part because of his long professional relationship with Ramon Lopez, the chairman and CEO of WMI. They had worked together at EMI and PolyGram. Ames was named president and focused his attention on the European operations. His goal was to improve the overseas operation of the music side of the business that had been faltering. One sticking point of the deal was Ames' financial interest in London Records, which he did not want to relinquish. A deal for distribution of London Records through Warner Music had to be negotiated.

In August of 1999 Ames was named chair and CEO of Warner Music Group, a division of WMI. He relocated to New York City where the new headquarters would be based. Warner Music had a long history of dominance in the United States, but had been suffering from declining market share and management problems for some time. The hiring of Ames marked the first time in nearly 20 years that someone from the music industry headed Warner

Music. Some were surprised by the move, while others thought it was a good choice. When the announcement was made, Andrew Pollack of the *New York Times* wrote, "Some industry executives praised Mr. Ames as having a good mix of creative talent and business acumen, avoiding the extravagant spending that sometimes occurs in the record business."

Ames' affiliation with London Records continued to be something Warner had to deal with until late 1999 when Warner bought the label. London Records was then a part of Warner via Sire Records, a subsidiary of the company. Under the leadership of Ames, Warner began to turn around. By the end of 2000, the label was number four in sales. Early in his tenure, Ames tried to do something radical to improve Warner's status: he worked out a merger between Warner Music and EMI. This shook up the company that had grown staid. However, threats from European regulators related to Time Warner's merging with AOL (America Online) made Time Warner (the parent company of Warner Music Group) back off and the deal never went through.

In 2001, Warner Music began reducing staff, offering early retirements and layoffs. Ames became known for his no-nonsense talk and attention to the bottom line. His strategy seemed to pay off. By late 2001, Warner Music was back to number two in sales.

In 2002, in a continuing attempt to streamline the company, Ames had Warner Music get rid of the Tommy Boy Records imprint. Under the deal's terms, Warner would retain ownership of Tommy Boy's catalog, music publishing rights, and around a dozen acts. Label founder Tom Silverman was given a payout of what was said to be less than $10 million. He retained the label's brand name and several artists. While Ames consolidated or shut down joint-ventures, he also increased spending on "A&R, promotion, and marketing—to improve artist development and exposure," wrote *Variety*'s Justin Oppelaar.

On November 22, 2003, in an effort to reduce its debt load, Time Warner announced that it had agreed to sell Warner Music for $2.6 billion to a group of investors led by Edgar Bronfman Jr. Bronfman would become the head of the new company while Ames was supposed to take the No. 2 spot. However, he was not assigned a formal title, and instead served as a consultant to the company. In

August of 2004, Ames told employees that he would be leaving Warner Music to become an advisor to former employer Time Warner.

## Sources

### Periodicals

*Billboard,* October 3, 1992, p. 6; March 30, 1996, p. 10; April 6, 1996, p. 6; March 20, 1999, p. 6; August 28, 1999, p. 5, p. 99; September 11, 2004, p. 7.

Business Wire, August 16, 1999.

*Daily Variety,* March 5, 2002, p. 9.

*Financial Times,* March 23, 1996, p. 9; January 24, 2000, p. 24.

*Forbes,* July 3, 2000, p. 52.

*Hollywood Reporter,* September 25, 1992.

*New York Times,* August 17, 1999, p. C2; December 7, 2001, p. C4; December 10, 2001, p. C4.

*Variety,* August 23, 1999, p. 25; March 5, 2001, p. 30; May 27, 2002, p. 6.

### Online

"Music official at Warner to step down," *New York Times,* http://www.nytimes.com (December 20, 2004).

"Roger and out," Webpro Wire, http://www.webprowire.com/summaries/675615.html (December 20, 2004).

"Warner Music sold to Bronfman & investors," Rock and Metal, http://www.rockandmetal.com/warnermusic2.html (December 20, 2004).

"Warner Music to be sold for $2.6B," CNNMoney, http://money.cnn.com/2003/11/24/news/companies/warner_music/index.htm (December 20, 2004).

*—A. Petruso*

# Tadao Ando

## Architect

**B**orn September 13, 1941, in Osaka, Japan; married Yumikio.

**Addresses:** *Office*—Tadao Ando Architect & Associates, 5-23 Toyosaki 2-Chome Kita-ku, Osaka 531-0072 Japan.

## Career

**W**orked as a boxer; apprenticed with a carpenter; opened his own architectural practice, 1969. Notable designs include: Azuma House, Osaka, Japan, 1976; Rokko Housing Complex, Japan; Church on the Water, Hokkaido, Japan; Church of Light, Osaka, Japan; Water Temple, Hyogo, Japan; Japan Pavilion, 1992; gallery for Art Institute of Chicago, 1992; seminar house for TOTO, 1999; Yumebutai garden complex, Awaji Island, Japan, 2001; Pulitzer Foundation for the Arts, St. Louis, MO, 2001; Komyo-ji Buddhist temple, Saijo, Japan, 2001; couture house, Milan, Italy, 2002; new building for the Modern Art Museum of Fort Worth, TX, 2002; pavilion at Piccadilly Gardens, Manchester, England, 2002; addition to the Clark Institute, Williamston, MA, 2004; Langen Foundation, Neuss, Germany, 2004. Also taught architecture at Yale, Columbia, and Harvard.

**Awards:** Architectural Institute of Japan Prize, 1979; Japanese Cultural Design Prize, 1983; Alvar Aalto Medal, 1985; Japanese Ministry of Education Prize, 1986; Mainichi Art Prize, 1987; Isoya Yoshida Award, 1988; Medaille d'Or, French Academy of Architecture, 1989; Art Prize, Osaka, 1990; Arnold W. Brun-ner Memorial Prize, American Academy and Institute of Arts and Letters, 1991; Honorary Fellow, American Institute of Architects, 1991; Carlsberg Architectural Prize, 1992; Japan Art Grand Prix, 1994; Pritzker Architecture Prize, 1995; Praemium Imperiale, 1996; British Architects Royal Gold Medal for Architecture, 1997; AIA gold medalist, 2001.

## Sidelights

**T**adao Ando is one of the most renowned contemporary Japanese architects. His designs are often compared to those of Louis Kahn and Le Corbusier and he obviously takes some inspiration from their work. Characteristics of Ando's work include large expanses of unadorned walls combined with wooden or slate floors and large windows. Active natural elements, like sun, rain, and wind are a distinctive inclusion to his contemporary style.

Ando was born a few minutes before his twin brother in Osaka, Japan, in 1941. When he reached the age of two, his family decided that he would be raised by his grandmother while his brother would remain with their parents. Ando's childhood neighborhood contained the workshops of many artisans, including a woodworking shop where he learned the techniques of that craft. As an adult, his earliest design attempts were of small wooden houses and furniture.

Ando told Watanabe Hiroshi in a 1993 article for *Japan Quarterly* that his grandmother "wasn't very strict with regard to school.... But she was strict about me keeping my word." He was a mediocre student, so rather than pursuing an education, Ando followed in the footsteps of his brother to become a professional boxer at the age of 17. A series of boxing matches soon took him to Bangkok, Thailand. While there, he visited Buddhist temples in his spare time and became fascinated by their design. He then spent several years traveling in Japan, Europe, and the United States, observing building design.

Ando abandoned his boxing career to apprentice himself to a carpenter and might have started a career as a builder instead of an architect except that he kept encouraging his clients to accept his unconventional design ideas. He had no formal architectural training. Using a list of the books architecture students were assigned to read in four years, he trained himself within one year. He did not apprentice to another architect because every time he tried, he has explained in interviews, he was fired for "stubbornness and temper."

Ando further demonstrated his independence by refusing to establish an office in Tokyo, which is generally thought to be essential for architectural success in Japan. He opened his practice, in 1969, at the age of 28, in his native Osaka. His firm, which is managed by his wife, Yumikio, is still based in Osaka. Consequently, the great majority of his buildings are in or around Osaka, including several projects in nearby Kobe.

Ando first achieved recognition with the Azuma House which received the Architectural Institute of Japan's annual award in 1979. Completed in 1976, and also known as the Rowhouse in Sumiyoshi, this small house in a working-class section of Osaka introduced all the elements of his later work: smooth concrete walls, large expanses of glass, uncluttered interiors, and an emphasis on bringing nature into contact with the residents. Only two stories high and just over three meters wide, its windowless front wall is made entirely of reinforced concrete with a single recessed area that shelters the entrance. The home is composed of three cubic components. The first cube contains the living room on the ground floor, and the master bedroom above. The third segment contains the kitchen, dining area, and bathroom on the lower floor, and the children's bedroom on the upper floor. The second section, between the other two, is a central courtyard.

The courtyard that lies between the two bedrooms is walled but completely open to the sky above. A bridge spans the courtyard and joins with a side staircase that descends to the courtyard. With the exception of the kitchen/dining/bath grouping, one must go outside to pass between rooms even during the winter and rainy seasons. Ando believes the inconvenience and discomfort are not without recompense. His buildings force an awareness onto their inhabitants of their place in the world. Moreover, the introspective design of the home insulates its occupants from the sound and sights of the city and offers a tranquil space which is still open to the sun, wind, and clouds.

One of Ando's larger well-known housing projects is his Rokko Housing Complex. The complex, which was built in three stages on the sixty degree slope of the Rokko mountains, contains open public spaces and insular private apartments. Each apartment features a terrace with a spectacular view of the port of Kobe and the Bay of Osaka. Ando's Church on the Water, in Hokkaido, is a Christian church which features an artificial lake which comes to the very edge of the building. The cubic concrete chapel has one entirely glass wall that slides completely away in good weather. The pews in the chapel face the lake and overlook a large steel cross standing in the middle of the water. Church of Light, in Osaka, which is recognized as another masterful work, is a rectangular concrete box, intersected at a 15 degree angle by a freestanding wall which defines the entrance. Behind the altar, a clear glass cross-shaped opening in the concrete wall floods the interior with light. Water Temple, in Hyogo, is a Buddhist temple built under a lotus pond. The entrance to the temple is a stairwell which bisects the pond and leads to the temple below.

Ando's four-story Japan Pavilion was considered the most impressive work of architecture at Expo '92 in Seville, Spain. One of the largest wooden buildings in the world, the pavilion measures 60 meters wide, 40 meters deep, and 25 meters high at its tallest point. Unpainted wood, one of the most traditional construction materials in Japan, was juxtaposed with such modern elements as a translucent Teflon-coated screen roof. Though conceptually different from his concrete and glass constructions, the pavilion still exhibits his style by not having front openings save a single breezeway that allows the sun and wind free passage between the two wings. The focus remains internally oriented with an emphasis on tangible natural participation within the defined space.

In 1999, Ando's design for a seminar house for TOTO, a manufacturer of plumbing equipment, was built. Ando had been asked by the firm to "find a site that would be spiritually refreshing," according to Peter Davey of *Architectural Review*. The spot he chose was on the top of a hill that looked down over a forest leading to Osaka Bay. He went on to design his largest project up to that point: a 70-acre garden complex on Awaji Island in Japan. Ando called it yumebutai, which translates to "a place of dreams." He worked hard to get the property transferred to public ownership so that it could be enjoyed by everyone, not just the wealthy. A hotel, conference center, gardens, and water parks were all included in his plan. "Yumebutai cannot be discussed as architecture alone," *Architecture's* Tom Heneghan declared. "It is an overlap between architecture, landscape design, event planning, social programming, and environmental art."

In 2001, the Calder Foundation hired Ando to design its new museum in Philadephia, Pennsylvania, which according to *Interior Design,* would "be dedicated to three successive generations of sculptors who shared both a name—Alexander Calder—and a medium." He was also contracted to design the Francois Pinault Contemporary Art Foundation in Paris, France (scheduled for completion in 2006) and the Clark Institute in Williamston, Massachusetts. His next building, the new Pulitzer Foundation for the Arts in St. Louis, Missouri, opened to the public in October of 2001; it was his first institutional project in the United States. That same year, a Buddhist temple he designed, called Komyo-ji, was built. Replacing a 250-year-old building, the temple incorporated "existing trees, stone walls, gatehouse, and belltower as a memory of the old—a decision that produced a more compressed and engaging complex," wrote *Architectural Review's* Michael Webb. The progressive chief priest had insisted on a light-filled space for the community which was suitable for concerts, lectures, and worship. In 2002, fashion designer Giorgio Armani commissioned Ando to design his world headquarters building. Ando's task was to turn a former chocolate factory in Milan, Italy, into a suitable place for fashion shows and other events. *Architectural Review's* Webb declared that the design demonstrated how Ando "has reinvented the traditional Japanese aesthetic of light and shade, offering linear progression through a walled labyrinth, guiding foot and eye, concealing and selectively revealing to build anticipation for the drama to come. Materials are plain, forms simple, but the effects are thrilling.

From Buddhist temple to European fashion house, Ando finds a common thread between diverse cultures and patterns of human behavior."

Also in 2002, construction was completed on another one of Ando's designs, the Modern Art Museum of Fort Worth, Texas. "In Ft. Worth he's created a rich architectural experience of materials and movement—you feel drawn through galleries that are both logical and mysterious, simple and surprising," wrote *Newsweek's* Cathleen McGuigan. Ando's first British project involved joining a group that relandscaped Manchester's Piccadilly Gardens. Ando's work received mixed reviews, however. Questions were raised "about the value and possible loss of local identity. To what extent is this .... a Japanese garden? And is it at home in central Manchester?," pondered *Building Design's* Steven Morant. In 2004, another of Ando's designs, the Langen Foundation, opened in Neuss, Germany.

Ando has lectured widely and has taught architecture at such American universities as Yale, Columbia, and Harvard. According to Herbert Muschamp in an interview for the *New York Times* in 1995, Ando considers Japan "boring. He prefers the United States because Americans are encouraged to have their own dreams and to pursue them. In Japan, he says, people do not let themselves dream."

## Sources

### Books

Co, Francesco Dal, *Tadao Ando,* Phaidon Press Limited, 1995.
*Contemporary Architects,* 3rd ed., St. James Press, 1994.
Frampton, Kenneth, ed., *Tadao Ando: Buildings, Projects, Writings,* Rizzoli International Publications, Inc., 1984.
Furuyama, Masao, *Tadao Ando,* 3rd ed., Birkhäuser—Verlag Für Architektur, 1996.
Jodidio, Philip, *Tadao Ando,* Benedikt Taschen Verlag GmbH, 1997.

### Periodicals

*Architectural Record,* September 1992, p. 90; November 1995, p. 74.
*Architectural Review,* October 1999, p. 60; October 2001, p. 66; February 2002, p. 74.
*Architecture: The AIA Journal,* May 1995, p. 23; March 2001, p. 96; June 2003, p. 37, p. 48; January 2002, p. 25.

*Art Business News,* September 2004, p. 28.
*Art in America,* April 1, 1990, p. 220; September 2002, p. 31; July 2003, p. 112.
*Building Design,* June 7, 2002, p. 4; September 13, 2002, p. 14.
*Christian Science Monitor,* April 17, 1995, p. 14.
*Concrete Construction,* April 2003, p. 32.
*House Beautiful,* July 1995, p. 33.
*Interior Design,* May 2001, p. 76; October 2001, p. 62.

*Japan Quarterly,* October 1993, p. 426.
*Newsweek,* December 16, 2002, pp. 68-70.
*New York Times,* April 17, 1995, p. C13; April 23, 1995, sec. 2, p. 38; September 21, 1995, p. C1; May 18, 1997, sec. 2, p. 1.
*Time,* March 8, 2005, p. 24.
*W,* December 2002, p. 130.
*Wall Street Journal,* July 23, 1997, p. A16.
*Washington Post,* April 17, 1995, p. C1.

# Lori B. Andrews

## Attorney and ethicist

**B**orn in 1952, in Chicago, IL; married Clem (divorced); children: Christopher. *Education:* Yale University, B.A.; Yale Law School, J.D., 1978.

**Addresses:** *Office*—Chicago-Kent College of Law, 565 West Adams St., Chicago, IL 60661.

## Career

**R**esearch fellow, American Bar Foundation, 1980-1992; senior scholar, Center for Clinical Medical Ethics, University of Chicago, c. 1995—; law professor and director of the Institute of Science, Law and Technology, Chicago-Kent College of Law, c. 1993—.

**Awards:** Named one of the 100 Most Influential Lawyers in America by the *National Law Journal.*

## Sidelights

**W**hen doctors, lawmakers, and reporters need someone to help them navigate the uncertain quandaries of new genetic and reproductive technologies, they frequently call Lori B. Andrews, a top independent expert on bioethics. "I'm interested in the areas where the law has not caught up with medical technology," Andrews told the *Chicago Tribune*'s Charles Leroux. "It's gotten to the point," she added, "where people say, 'If there's no law, call her.'"

Andrews was born in Chicago and grew up in suburban Downers Grove, Illinois. Her legal career began at the same time as the revolution in reproduc-

tive technology: she became a lawyer in 1978, taking the bar exam the same day Louise Brown, the first test-tube baby, was born. To help pay for law school, she had written articles about reproductive technology for women's magazines. She quickly rose to prominence as a bioethicist, because not many people in law and ethics were asking questions about the new ways technology was allowing couples to conceive children with medical help.

At first, she had trouble gaining respect because she was a young woman; she would end up on discussion panels where she was half the age of everyone else. A professional organization once asked her to recommend a male expert to speak on an issue she knew well, then asked her to speak as long as she made herself look authoritative but less glamorous. But she was invited to speak at the First World Congress on in-vitro fertilization and testified before Congress. By the time surrogate motherhood became a major controversy with the "Baby M" case in 1986, Andrews had established herself as an expert, and she took on the issue in her 1989 book, *Between Strangers: Surrogate Mothers, Expectant Fathers, and Brave New Babies.*

In something of a detour in her writing career, Andrews spent much of her spare time from 1989 through 1996 researching and writing a biography of Johnny Spain, a former member of the radical Black Panther party. Spain was a mixed-race child born to a white woman who sent him away at the age of five to a black family his mother did not know. Andrews, who wanted to write a book about how the American justice system treats black defendants, wrote *Black Power, White Blood: The Life and Times of Johnny Spain,* published in 1996, and promoted the book along with Spain, including on *The Oprah Winfrey Show.*

One reason Andrews' opinions are so respected is that she does not work for the biotechnology industry or a religious organization, two major players in the debates over bioethics and the law. Andrews lives only on her academic salary from the Chicago-Kent College of Law, her earnings from her writing, and some grants from public agencies. She handles legal cases, gives speeches, and appears at conferences for free, asking only for expenses, to avoid conflicts of interest. She has written more than 100 articles on biotechnology, genetics, and reproductive technology, is often quoted in news articles on the subjects, and has appeared often on television news shows such as *60 Minutes* and *Today.* "She appears on-camera as aristocratic and self-assured, the fearless female lawyer Hollywood has revered in movies," wrote Stephanie B. Goldberg in *More.* "Off-camera, however, you encounter a very different Andrews: warm, outgoing, self-effacing, giggly and indefatigable."

Her opinions on new biotechnologies are not predictable. Her concern for individual rights makes her sympathetic toward some new procedures, as in the early 1980s, when she urged Congress to allow couples to use new fertility treatments. As new technologies have multiplied, though, she has become more likely to express concern. She is opposed to human cloning, for instance, and helped write legislation introduced by a senator to ban it. That cautious approach places Andrews in conflict with the optimism of many researchers. Joseph D. McInerney, who reviewed her 2001 book *Future Perfect: Confronting Decisions About Genetics* for the *Quarterly Review of Biology,* praised her treatment of the legal issues around genetic medicine and the way it changes people's perceptions of disease. "She has a tendency, however, to downplay the potential benefits of genetics and to focus only on the prospects for harm," he wrote.

Andrews addressed that mindset in her interview with the *Chicago Tribune*'s Leroux. "I'm always dealing with legal cases where things have gone wrong, so I tend to focus on the negative. But I absolutely acknowledge the value of medical research. I just want to be sure the benefits are distributed fairly and there is disclosure of the risks."

On the issue of stem-cell research, she takes a middle ground. A feminist who favors abortion rights, she does not believe in stopping stem-cell research to protect embryos. But she does suggest minimal standards for the research. "There at least should be good rules about getting consent from the couple donating the embryo and making sure that the research being done is important," she told *More*'s Goldberg. In fall of 2004 she spoke out against California's ballot proposal to fund stem cell research, saying it offered public funding to biotechnology research without regulating it or requiring it to provide research benefits to the public.

Andrews argues that the practice of patenting human genes and gene therapies hurts the public. She often notes that one company claims the genes that predispose women to breast cancer as its intellectual property, so it can charge about $2,500 in licensing fees for a lab test that could cost $50. Her 2001 book *The Body Bazaar: The Market for Human Tissue in the Biotechnology Age,* co-authored with Dorothy Nelkin, explains how John Moore, a Seattle businessman with leukemia, began to question why his doctor in California, David Golde, kept insisting he come back for more tests for several years after the doctor cured his cancer by removing his spleen. Eventually Moore learned that Golde had discovered unique antibodies in his blood, grown a cell line from it and patented it. Golde later sold the cell line to a drug company for $15 million. Moore sued for malpractice and property theft in 1988, but the California Supreme Court ruled in 1990 that Moore could not claim his blood or antibodies as property or lay claim to the profits from the cell line.

Writing in the *Chicago Tribune* in November of 2003, Andrews argued that Congress should pass a law barring the patenting of human embryos. "If patents on human embryos are allowed, then biotech companies will market babies with certain traits just like Perdue markets chicken or Ford markets sport-utility vehicles," she warned.

Someday, Andrews may find new ways to tell her story and those of the people who turn to her for advice. She said that she was working on a mystery novel with a female genetic researcher as the main character, and she has talked with the NBC television network about possibly developing a TV show based on her work and the bizarre ethical dilemmas people ask her to resolve.

## Selected writings

*Birth of a Salesman: Lawyer Advertising and Solicitation,* 2nd ed., ABA Press, 1980.

*Deregulating Doctoring: Do Medical Licensing Laws Meet Today's Health Care Needs?*, People's Medical Society, 1983.

*New Conceptions: A Consumer's Guide to the Newest Infertility Treatments, Including In Vitro Fertilization, Artificial Insemination, and Surrogate Motherhood*, St. Martin's Press, 1984.

*Medical Genetics: A Legal Frontier*, American Bar Foundation, 1987.

*Between Strangers: Surrogate Mothers, Expectant Fathers, and Brave New Babies*, HarperCollins, 1989.

*Black Power, White Blood: The Life and Times of Johnny Spain*, Pantheon, 1996.

*The Clone Age: Adventures in the New World of Reproductive Technology*, Henry Holt, 1999.

*Future Perfect: Confronting Decisions About Genetics*, Columbia University Press, 2001.

(Co-author) *The Body Bazaar: The Market for Human Tissue in the Biotechnology Age*, Crown Publishers, 2001.

(Co-author) *Genetics: Ethics, Law and Policy*, West Publishing, 2002.

## Sources

### Periodicals

*Akron Beacon Journal* (Akron, OH), April 7, 2001, p. B1.
*Chicago Tribune*, December 13, 1996, p. 1; October 7, 2001, p. 12; November 9, 2003.
*Cincinnati Post*, October 26, 2004, p. A10.
*More*, November 2001, pp. 68-72.
*Plain Dealer* (Cleveland, OH), January 29, 2000, p. 1F.
*Quarterly Review of Biology*, June 2002, p. 199.

### Online

"Faculty Biographies," Chicago-Kent College of Law, http://www.kentlaw.edu/faculty/Andrews_bio.html (February 21, 2005).
"Faculty Publications," Chicago-Kent College of Law, http://www.kentlaw.edu/faculty/scholarship/Andrews_pubs.html (February 25, 2005).

*—Erick Trickey*

# Louise Arbour

© *Denis Balibouse/Reuters/Corbis*

**United Nations High Commissioner for Human Rights**

**B**orn February 10, 1947, in Montreal, Quebec, Canada; daughter of Ruth Laberge (a retail store owner); partner for 27 years, Larry Taman; children: Emilie, Patrick, Catherine. *Education:* College Regina Assumpta, Montreal, BA, 1967; University of Montreal, LL.L, 1970.

**Addresses:** *Work*—Commission/Sub-Commission Team (1503 Procedure), Support Services Branch, Office of the High Commissioner for Human Rights, United Nations Office at Geneva, 1211 Geneva 10, Switzerland; fax: + 41 22 917 9011; e-mail: 1503ohchr. org.

## Career

**A**rticler, City of Montreal, 1970; law clerk, Supreme Court of Canada, 1971-72; research officer, Law Reform Commission, 1972; lecturer, York University, 1974; assistant professor, York University, 1975; associate professor, York University, 1977-87; associate professor and associate dean, Osgoode Hall School of Law, York University, 1987; high court justice, Supreme Court of Ontario, 1987-90; member, Court of Appeal for Ontario, 1990-96; chief prosecutor, International Criminal Tribunals, 1996-99; judge, Supreme Court of Canada, 1999-2004; high commissioner for human rights, United Nations, 2004—.

**Awards:** Achievement Award, Women's Law Association, 1996; G. Arthur Martin Award, Criminal Lawyers' Association, Toronto, 1998; Medal of Honour, International Association of Prosecutors, 1999; Médaille du mérite, Institut de recherches cliniques de Montréal, 1999; Prix de la Fondation Louise Weiss, Paris, 1999; Second Annual Service to Humanity Award, Pennsylvania Bar Foundation, 2000; Franklin and Eleanor Roosevelt Four Freedoms Medal, Roosevelt Study Centre, the Netherlands, 2000; Women of Distinction Award, Toronto Hadassah-Wizo, 2000; Peace Award, World Federalists of Canada, 2000; Lord Reading Law Society's Human Rights Award, 2000; Wolfgang Freidman Memorial Award, Columbia Law School, 2001; EID-UL-ADHA Award, Association of Progressive Muslims of Ontario, 2001; Médaille du Barreau, Quebec, 2001; National Achievement Award, Jewish Women International of Canada, 2001; Stefan A. Riesenfeld Symposium Award, Berkeley Journal of International Law, 2002; Person of the Year, McGill Center for Research and Teaching on Women, 2002; Justice in the World International Prize, International Association of Judges, 2002; Médaille de la Faculté de droit, University of Montreal, 2003; Hall of Fame, International Women's Forum, 2003.

## Sidelights

**L**ouise Arbour had made it to the pinnacle of any lawyer's dream career: she had a seat on the Supreme Court of Canada. Less than five years into her tenure serving as one of the highest-ranking justices in the country, Arbour stepped down. Instead, she became the fourth person named to the position of United Nations High Commissioner for Human Rights. It was not the first time that Arbour stood in the international spotlight. In 1996, she was chief prosecutor for the International Criminal Tribunal, responsible for bringing to justice major players in the human rights tragedies of both Rwanda and Kosovo. A distinguished career as a lawyer and professor combined with her renowned tenacity and charm have garnered her a reputation as someone who can get the job done while also maintaining civil relationships with her opponents.

Arbour was born on February 10, 1947, in Montreal, Quebec, Canada. Her parents divorced when she was young and her mother, Ruth Laberge, raised Arbour and her brother, Patrick, on her own. While Arbour attended College Regina Assumpta, a strict all-girls Roman Catholic school, her mother ran a store in downtown Montreal. Arbour explained to Allan Thompson of the *Toronto Star* the impact that the school had on her development, "In a sense I was probably manipulated ... to achieve exactly what it is designed to achieve, which is to get you to be a rebel to a point." She attended the school for ten years and received her bachelor's degree from there in 1967.

After graduation she went directly to the University of Montreal where she studied law at the Faculty of Law. She earned her degree, an LL.L, in 1970. During that same year, she later recounted, occurred one of the most influential events in her life and one which directed her in her future career. That year, the Canadian government passed the War Measures Act, which immediately suspended many civil liberties guaranteed by the state in response to kidnappings carried out by French separatists. She told the *Toronto Star*'s Thompson, "In many, many respects this had a very dramatic influence on my outlook on public issues, on the issue of power, abuse of power, the need for information and an element of skepticism towards authority."

After graduating from law school, Arbour held a few minor legal positions before taking a position as a lecturer on criminal procedure for the Osgoode Hall Law School at York University. She had passed the Quebec Bar in 1971 and in 1974 began her long and distinguished career with York University. In 1977, she passed the Ontario Bar. She quickly moved to the position of Assistant Professor, then Associate Professor. In 1987, she was named Associate Dean but only held the position for six months.

In December of 1987, Arbour was appointed as a High Court Justice for the Supreme Court of Ontario. Three years later she was appointed to the Ontario Court of Appeal. In 1995, while still serving on the Court of Appeal, Arbour was named as the sole commissioner to make inquiries into the allegations of abuse at the Prison for Women in Kingston. Her reports, which found institutionalized abuse rampant in the prison, served to help the Canadian government make significant changes in their correctional system, particularly with regard to female inmates.

Perhaps as a result of her effective investigations into prison abuse in Canada, she was asked to join the International Criminal Tribunal for Rwanda and the former Yugoslavia. The appointment, which she accepted, was made by a resolution of the Security Council of the United Nations. Arbour was named to the four-year position of chief prosecutor for what would become known as the War Crimes Tribunal. Her tireless work brought about indictments against former Yugoslavian dictator Slobodan Milosevic and others as well as convictions against 60 people charged with participating in the 1994 massacre in Rwanda.

Unfortunately for the tribunal, Arbour left before her four-year term was finished. In 1999, citing exhaustion, a desire to return to Canada, as well as a desire to accept an appointment to the Supreme Court of Canada, Arbour left the position of chief prosecutor. James Stewart, who worked with Arbour in The Hague described her energy to the *Toronto Star*'s Thompson, "It is as if there is a kind of dynamo there, firing off energy. She wasn't going to take anything from anybody. And yet she was not in any way abrasive. She could disarm through charm."

On September 15, 1999, Arbour took her seat on the highest court in Canada. She served the court for five years, and was part of the deciding vote, which reestablished the right of federal prisoners to vote. Eventually, she was offered another appointment that she found she could not refuse. In 2002, she had been offered the position of United Nations High Commissioner for Human Rights. She turned the job down. The position was eventually filled by Sergio Vieira de Mello, who was subsequently killed in a 2003 bombing while on a mission in Baghdad, Iraq. Kofi Annan, Secretary General of the United Nations, approached Arbour again with the appointment. This time she did not refuse.

For any lawyer, having a seat on the Supreme Court would mark the highest point of one's career. Arbour was not so satisfied and found the possibility of becoming the world's representative for the protection of human rights irresistible. With years of experience working to bring to justice those who would transgress basic human rights, Arbour stepped into this new position boldly on July 1, 2004. She was the fourth person to hold the position, which was established in 1993.

Throughout her career, Arbour has distinguished herself as hardworking. She holds more than 25 honorary degrees from universities around the world. She is fluent in both English and French. Besides court appointments she also wrote extensively on subjects such as criminal procedure, human rights, civil liberties, and gender issues. She was editor for *Criminal Reports, Canadian Human Rights Reporter,* and *Osgoode Hall Law Journal.* Until her first appointment in 1987, she had served as the vice-president of the Canadian Civil Liberties Association. Arbour has three children with Larry Taman, her partner of 27 years.

## Sources

### Periodicals

*Toronto Star,* June 13, 2004, p. A7; July 5, 2004, p. A1.

### Online

"CBC News:Arbour to take UN human rights post," *CBC,* http://www.cbc.ca/stories/2004/02/20/arbour_UN040219 (August 12, 2004).
"Louise Arbour High Commissioner," Office of the United Nations High Commissioner for Human Rights, http://www.ohchr.org/english/about/hc/arbour.htm (August 12, 2004).
"Louise Arbour seeking global justice," *Press Republican,* http://www.pressrepublican.com/Archive/2004/07_2004/07092004pb.htm (August 12, 2004).
"Louise Arbour starts work as new UN High Commissioner for Human Rights," United Nations, http://www.un.org (August 12, 2004).

*—Eve M. B. Hermann*

# Sean Astin

## Actor

**B**orn Sean Patrick Duke, February 25, 1971, in Santa Monica, CA; son of Michael Tell (a rock promoter) and Patty Duke (an actress); raised as the son of John Astin (an actor); married Christine Harrell (an actress and producer), July 11, 1992; children: Alexandra Louise, Elizabeth. *Education:* Attended junior college; University of California at Los Angeles, degree in history and English with honors, c. 1992.

**Addresses:** *Contact*—c/o P.O. Box 57858, Sherman Oaks, CA 91413. *Website*—http://www.seanastin. com.

## Career

**A**ctor in films, including: *The Goonies,* 1985; *The War of the Roses,* 1989; *Staying Together,* 1989; *Memphis Belle,* 1990; *Toy Soldiers,* 1991; *Encino Man,* 1992; *Rudy,* 1993; *Courage Under Fire,* 1996; *Bulworth,* 1998; *Dish Dogs,* 1998; *Deterrence,* 2000; *Lord of the Rings: The Fellowship of the Ring,* 2001; *Lord of the Rings: The Two Towers,* 2002; *Lord of the Rings: The Return of the King,* 2003; *50 First Dates,* 2004; *Smile,* 2004; *Slipstream,* 2004. Works as a film director and producer include: *On My Honor,* 1990; *Kangaroo Court,* 1994; *The Long and Short of It* (also screenwriter), 2003. Television appearances include: "Please, Don't Hit Me," *ABC Afterschool Special,* 1981; *The Rules of Marriage* (miniseries), CBS, 1982; *Just Our Luck* (pilot), 1983; *Kurt Vonnegut's Harrison Bergeron* (movie), 1995; *Perversions of Science,* HBO, 1997; *The Last Producer* (movie), USA, 2001; *Jeremiah,* Showtime, 2003; *Party Wagon* (voice), Cartoon Network, 2004. Works as a television director include:

*Perversions of Science,* HBO, 1997; "Soulless," *Angel,* The WB, 1999; *100 Deeds for Eddie McDowd,* 1999; *Jeremiah,* 2003. Founder, Lava Entertainment, c. 1993.

**Awards:** Best supporting actor award, Seattle Film Critics, for *The Return of the King,* 2003; best supporting actor award, Las Vegas Film Critics Society, for *The Return of the King,* 2003.

## Sidelights

**A**lthough Sean Astin has been an actor since childhood, appearing in such films as 1985's *The Goonies* and the title role in 1993's *Rudy,* he came to international prominence in the early 2000s for his role as Samwise "Sam" Gangee in the film adaptation of author J.R.R. Tolkien's *Lord of the Rings* trilogy. Astin had also appeared in a number of television productions. Not content with just appearing before the camera, Astin is also an aspiring feature filmmaker who has made several short films and directed some episodic television.

Astin was born Sean Patrick Duke on February 25, 1971, in Santa Monica, California. Astin was the son of actress Patty Duke. At the time of his birth, he was assumed to be the son of the man she married soon after, actor John Astin, who had appeared in the 1960s television show *The Addams Family.* The young Astin was raised as the actor's son and took his name, though genetic testing done when Astin was an adult proved that he was the son of Michael Tell, a rock concert promoter to whom his mother was briefly married while also in a relationship with Astin. Astin also has a younger half-brother, Mackenzie, who was the biological son of John Astin and Patty Duke.

Though Astin was exposed to acting from an early age because of his parents, he saw a darker side of life as well. His mother suffered from manic depressive illness. His parents' marriage was troubled, and they separated when he was three years old. They later divorced when he was eight (some sources say this occurred in 1985). Remaining close to both parents, Astin was raised to be normal person instead of a Hollywood tragedy.

Astin began building acting credits by the time he was ten years old, guided by his parents' help and advice. Astin told John Stanley of the *San Francisco Chronicle*, "My parents were also careful that I understood all the classic pitfalls. They embodied in me a real view of the acting world, and not a romantic one. They gave the values you need to succeed and survive."

Astin's first professional acting role came opposite his mother in an episode of the *ABC Afterschool Special* in 1981, called "Please Don't Hit Me." Astin played a child who was the victim of abuse at the hands of his mother, played by Duke. He followed this up with a role in a miniseries on CBS called *The Rules of Marriage* in 1982, and an appearance in a pilot directed by his father, John Astin, in 1983. The pilot was for a situation comedy called *Just Our Luck* for ABC.

While working as a young actor, Astin attended Crossroads School for Arts and Sciences in Santa Monica, California. While there, he excelled in athletics. By the mid-1980s, Astin had moved into film roles. His film debut came in 1985's *The Goonies.* He played Mikey, one of several kids hunting for treasure, in the minor hit. Astin continued to play young roles in the late 1980s. In 1989, he had a role of one of the kids caught in the middle of their parents' testy divorce in the tense comedy *The War of the Roses.* That same year, he played one of three brothers who thought they were inheriting their father's restaurant until he sold it in the drama *Staying Together.*

After Astin graduated from high school in the late 1980s, he attended junior college and later entered the University of California at Los Angeles. Astin graduated with honors with an undergraduate degree in history and English in the early 1990s. Though Astin was a college student, he still played teen roles. In 1991, he had a leading role in *Toy Soldiers* as Billy Tepper, a student at an upscale private school. Astin played the outcast and rebel who helps save students and the school after it is taken over by terrorists. Astin said he really liked the role though the film did not do well with critics or at the box office.

In the early 1990s, Astin was able to transition to more mature roles and he became much more serious about acting. Astin told Marjorie Rosen of *People,* "I have a seemingly reckless abandon in wanting to achieve. My biggest fear in life is that I'm gonna waste time. That's scarier than anything with creepy-crawly legs." In 1990's *Memphis Belle,* Astin played a ball-turret gunner in the World War II film. In 1992, Astin appeared in the comedy *Encino Man.* Astin played a nerd who, with a friend played by Pauly Shore, finds a caveman and digs him up. It was a successful film at the box office, though critics were dismissive.

As Astin began playing adult roles, he also moved into a more adult phase of his life. He married Christine Harrell, an actress and producer, in July of 1992. They later had two daughters together, Alexandra Louise and Elizabeth. One of the biggest roles of his young career came soon after his marriage. Astin was cast in the title role in *Rudy.* The film was based on the true story of Daniel E. Ruettiger, a young man from a down-and-out family who was a student at the University of Notre Dame in the mid-1970s.

Ruettiger, nicknamed Rudy, had learning disabilities and was not very tall or a great athlete. He became a walk-on player for the Notre Dame football team, attending every rough practice for two seasons. Ruettiger was allowed to play in one game during the course of his career. The film depicts Ruettiger's struggles, which Astin tried to live up to. Astin, who was also small in stature, felt compelled to do many of his own stunts on the field because Ruettiger had really played. The film was successful, especially after its video release, and proved popular among sports fans. Astin remained in touch with Ruettiger after the film, participating annually in his charity golf tournament.

In this time period, Astin also moved forward with his own ambitions to make films as he wanted to since childhood. In the early 1990s, he formed a film production company with Milton Justice called Lava Entertainment. Astin made his first film, a short called *On My Honor,* in 1990. It was about a meeting between an American soldier and a Vietnamese soldier. Another filmmaking effort, a 1994 short called *Kangaroo Court,* was nominated for an Academy Award for best short subject—dramatic. Astin later wrote and produced the film *The Long and Short of It* during the filming of the *Lord of the Rings* trilogy. It was an official entry at the Sundance Film Festival.

In the mid-1990s, Astin returned to television roles. In 1995, he appeared in the science fiction satire, *Kurt Vonnegut's Harrison Bergeron.* This was based on the work by author Vonnegut. In the movie, Astin played a teenager named Harrison in mid-2053. While society pressured everyone to be average to fit in as the government mandated, his character was smart and became part of the elite. In 1997, Astin appeared in and directed an episode of *Perversions of Science* for the HBO series. Astin also worked as a director on the hit dramatic series *Angel.* In the early 2000s, Astin played a screenwriter in the USA film *The Last Producer,* provided a voice for an animated show on the Cartoon Network called *Party Wagon,* and appeared in an episode of the science fiction show *Jeremiah* on Showtime.

Though Astin ventured into television roles, he primarily worked in film, appearing in a variety of genres. In 1996, Astin played an enthusiastic soldier in the drama *Courage Under Fire.* Two years later, in the political comedy *Bulworth,* Astin had a role as an employee of the cable network C-SPAN. After appearing in *Dish Dogs,* also released in 1998, Astin was cast as a redneck in Colorado in the heavy-handed *Deterrence.* In the film, which hit theaters in 2000, Astin and other characters are stranded with the United States president in a diner during a snowstorm while a crisis ensues.

Arguably the biggest role of Astin's career came when he was cast as hobbit Samwise "Sam" Gangee in Peter Jackson's ambitious adaptation of J.R.R. Tolkien's *Lord of the Rings* novels. Astin spent more than 18 months in New Zealand filming the three films. His character was one central to the story, the sidekick to main character Frodo Baggins (who had to destroy the ring referred to in the title), and became more important as the trilogy progressed. Astin took a risk by spending the many months in New Zealand filming the trilogy and putting his career on hold with no certain outcome. During the filming, despite such uncertainties, Astin proved himself to be hardworking and generous in his support of his fellow cast members. He gained about 35 pounds to play the pudgy hobbit.

Astin's hard work paid off: the *Lord of the Rings* films proved extremely profitable and popular. They were released over a span of three years. The trilogy began in 2001 with *The Fellowship of the Ring,* followed by *The Two Towers* in 2002 and *The Return of the King* in 2003. The films received numerous awards. There was some buzz about Astin being nominated for an Academy Award for his role in *The Return of the King,* but this never came to fruition. He was honored by the Seattle Film Critics and the Las Vegas Film Critics Society for his role.

The success of the *Lord of the Rings* films led to more roles for Astin. In 2004, he appeared in the comedy *50 First Dates* as the brother of actress Drew Barrymore's character. While Barrymore's character had short-term memory loss, Astin played a bodybuilder with a lisp. He also appeared in *Smile* and *Slipstream* in 2004.

Though Astin continued his successful career as an actor, he still had filmmaking ambitions of his own. His ultimate goal was to direct feature films. To that end, he held the option on a book about the devastating hurricane which hit Galveston, Texas, in 1900. The book was entitled *Isaac's Storm: A Man, a Time, and the Deadliest Hurricane in History.* Astin faced difficulties in getting financing for this film while retaining creative control.

Astin also considered a future outside of acting, perhaps in politics. Astin was a conservative Democrat and thought about running for office, maybe even president. He contemplated going to graduate school to study public policy to achieve that goal. Astin told Toni Ruberto of the *Buffalo News,* "I've acted for more than half of my life, but I'm also a husband, a father and a student. I just try to throw myself passionately into whatever I'm doing. The reason I've endured over time as an actor is that it's not the only thing I'm interested in.... I've always got something on the burner somewhere."

## Sources

### Books

*Celebrity Biographies,* Baseline II, Inc., 2004.

### Periodicals

*Boston Globe,* November 10, 1989, p. 82; May 22, 1992, p. 32.
*Buffalo News* (Buffalo, NY), February 4, 2004, p. A10.

*Chicago Sun-Times,* October 24, 1993, p. 2.
*Columbus Dispatch* (Columbus, OH), June 24, 2004, p. 1B.
*Entertainment Weekly,* January 16, 2004, pp. 30-31.
*Houston Chronicle,* December 17, 2003, p. 1.
*Newsday,* January 18, 2004, p. D7.
*Oregonian,* December 22, 201, p. D1.
*People,* June 15, 1992, p. 59; January 14, 2002, p. 123.
*Pittsburgh Post-Gazette,* October 17, 1993, p. E4.
*San Francisco Chronicle,* April 21, 1991, p. 28.
*Seattle Times,* January 13, 2003, p. E7.
*St. Petersburg Times,* October 10, 1993, p. 11B.
*Tampa Tribune,* December 18, 2001, p. 1.

*Times-Picayune* (New Orleans, LA), March 27, 1995, p. A5; August 13, 1995, p. T7.
*Toronto Star,* April 23, 1991, p. D1.
*USA Today,* October 29, 1993, p. 4D; January 6, 2004, p. 1D.

**Online**

"Sean Astin," IMDB.com, http://www.imdb.com/name/nm0000276/maindetails (August 6, 2004).

—*A. Petruso*

# Alan Ball

*Mike Blake/Reuters/Landov*

## Screenwriter, producer, and director

Born in Georgia, 1957, son of an aircraft inspector and a homemaker. *Education:* Florida State University, bachelor's degree in theater.

**Addresses:** *Agent*—c/o ICM, 40 W. 57th St., New York, NY 10019.

## Career

Wrote for public access television in Sarasota, FL; moved to New York City and worked as a graphic designer for *Adweek* while writing plays on his own time, 1986-1994. Writer for theater, including: *Bachelor Holiday, The M Word, Made for a Woman, Power Lunch, The Amazing Adventures of Tense Guy, Your Mother's Butt,* and *Five Women Wearing the Same Dress.* Writer for television, including: *Grace Under Fire,* 1993- 95; *Cybill,* 1995-98; *Oh Grow Up,* 1999; *Six Feet Under,* 2001—. Writer for film, including: *American Beauty,* 1999.

**Awards:** Academy Award for best original screenplay, Academy for Motion Picture Arts and Sciences, for *American Beauty,* 1999; Directors Guild of America's Award for Outstanding Directorial Achievement in Dramatic Series, for *Six Feet Under,* 2001; Gay and Lesbian Alliance Against Defamation Stephen Kolzak Award, 2002.

## Sidelights

Screenwriter, producer, and director Alan Ball has become one of the most well-known and respected writers in Hollywood. The creator of the television show *Six Feet Under* and the film *American Beauty,* Ball is an Academy Award-winning writer who worked hard to achieve his current position.

Ball was born in Atlanta, Georgia, in 1957, and was raised in that state's city of Marietta. He was the youngest of four children of a homemaker and an aircraft inspector. His family was disrupted by tragedy during his youth: when he was 13, he was in a car accident with his older sister, Mary Ann. He was unhurt, but Mary Ann was killed. He told Dan Snierson in *Entertainment Weekly,* "That really made it impossible for me to ever go home again, because the person I was closest to was gone. My whole family sort of exploded apart." Although his family would later try to reconnect, they would have lasting psychological and spiritual wounds from this experience.

Ball graduated from Florida State University with a degree in theater, then moved to Sarasota, Florida, where he staged plays for the Florida Studio Theatre. With cowriter and college friend Nancy Oliver, Ball wrote comedies and one-act plays for public access television, but their work received little recognition. In 1986, looking for greater opportunities, Ball moved to New York City, where he created the Alarm Dog Repertory Theatre. Like many writers, actors, and artists, he also found a day job, working as a graphic artist for the magazine *Adweek*. He told Kay Kioling in *Sarasota Magazine*, "I was good at the graphics job, and it would have been a career, but to me it was just a day job."

At the time, Ball told Scott Robson in *Variety*, "I never imagined I'd be standing on a stage someday accepting an Oscar or an Emmy. I was pursuing a career as a playwright. I never occurred to me I'd actually be working in Hollywood." His coworkers at *Adweek* did not know much about his dreams of a writing career, but one night a group from the office went to see his play, *Five Women Wearing the Same Dress*. After that, he told Robson, "People around the office looked at me like, 'Oh, wow, you're a person.'" His editor at *Adweek*, Greg Farrell, told Robson that after seeing the play, he frequently asked Ball, "What on Earth are you doing here?" Although the job was not a writing job, Ball found it almost restful not to have to immerse himself in the work, telling Robson, "There's something Zenlike about putting together those graphs."

However, in addition to the accolades of his coworkers, Ball also began to get some recognition outside the office when *Five Women Wearing the Same Dress* was produced at the Manhattan Class Company, starring Thomas Gibson, Ally Walker, and Allison Janney. Ball described the play to *Sarasota Magazine*'s Kioling, noting that it depicted "a big, old-money society wedding" where "five women are the bridesmaids, all wearing the same horrible dress." The play received good reviews and was optioned by Columbia Pictures. While in New York, Ball also wrote *The M Word*—which premiered at the Lucille Ball Festival of New American Comedy in 1991—*Made for a Woman*, *Bachelor Holiday*, *The Amazing Adventures of Tense Guy*, and *Your Mother's Butt*. The attention he received for these plays brought Ball an offer to write for a television situation comedy, *Grace Under Fire*, which starred comedian Brett Butler.

The move to Hollywood was a shock to Ball. In the New York theater world, writers are respected, but in television, he told the *Sarasota Magazine* reporter, they are "just grist for the mill." He added that *Grace Under Fire* was a hit, but Butler "screamed at me, called me [an] amateur in front of people—she was a train wreck.... I spent a year there just morally disgusted."

Ball moved on to another sitcom, *Cybill*, where he was a writer and co-executive producer. Although the emotional tone behind the scenes was much

calmer, Ball told the *Sarasota Magazine* reporter, "[I turned] off my emotions about my writing, to become just a craftsman, a factory worker." He commented to Marc Peyser in *Newsweek* that in both sitcoms, "The stars basically looked at those shows as PR for their own lives. We'd get notes like, 'I would never do that. That makes me look stupid.' And we're like, 'Did [Lucille Ball] ever care about looking stupid [on the *I Love Lucy* show]?'"

While working on the shows, he continually yearned to write "something that meant something, at least to me," as he told *Sarasota Magazine*'s Kioling. He told *Entertainment Weekly*'s Snierson that during these television jobs, he would write his own work late into the night: "I'd come home from work and at like two in the morning, I'd sit down at the computer and just pour stuff out. It was fueled by rage."

This work eventually became the screenplay for *American Beauty*. In addition to his anger, Ball wove in his own experience as a gay man, his childhood awareness of his own father's deep unhappiness, and the awareness of death he had had since his youth. He also drew on his experiences working for *Adweek* to imbue the script with a biting disgust for corporate structure.

*Newsweek*'s David Ansen described the film as "a dreamy black comedy ... narrated by a corpse: Lester Burnham ... who already considers himself among the walking dead." Ansen noted that the film's theme was "the painful gulf between ... fantasies and the reality we can't seem to grasp," and called it "wickedly entertaining." Ball's emotional connection to this work was perhaps part of its success: the film won an Academy Award for Best Original Screenplay in 1999. At the awards ceremony, Ball could not believe it was really happening. He told *Newsweek*'s Peyser, "I usually watch the Oscars at home with friends, drinking martinis and throwing socks at the TV. And all of a sudden, I was there. It was really weird." He keeps the statue representing the award on a shelf in his home—dressed in a pink Barbie jacket. "He [the statue] looks so pretentious. The jacket cuts him down to size a little bit."

Ball told *Newsweek*'s Peyser that after his success with *American Beauty*, people started calling him with ideas, saying he was the "perfect writer" for them, but in most cases, Ball noted, "I would think, that's a movie I would walk out on. Why do you think I'd be the perfect writer for that?" However, one idea did appeal to him. Ball began working on a screenplay for a murder mystery about a 1960s police officer, titled *Mr. Downtown*, with Tom Hanks slated as the star. He told Peyser, "[Tom Hanks] came to me, and I thought it was an interesting notion."

Ball returned to television in 1999 as executive producer of the ABC series *Oh, Grow Up.* However, the series received poor ratings and was soon canceled. Ball returned with another series, *Six Feet Under,* which was set in a funeral home, featured a family of undertakers, and emphasized the dark underside of suburban life. The show was picked up by HBO, and that cable network's freedom, relative to the restrictions placed on broadcast networks, gave Ball the room he wanted to explore his characters' sexuality as well as themes of confronting death. He told *Entertainment Weekly*'s Snierson, "I think our culture tends to deny the reality of death. We're a little bit in the closet about it. This show is trying to demystify the whole process."

In 2001, HBO's president of original programming, Chris Albrecht, noted that death was a risky concept for a show, since "it's provocative, and very little on television is provocative. I'm very curious as to how the public will react to this." The public reacted with outstretched arms, and so did the critics. *Entertainment Weekly*'s Snierson commented, "In a television environment polluted with sameness (six New York cop shows aired this season; three CIA dramas debut this fall), HBO is once again offering up a blast of fresh air. *Six Feet Under* is a frank, trippy, spiritual, witty drama about a fraying L.A. family that runs a funeral home." Peyser, who described the show as "funny, warm, [and] offbeat," detailed the outline of a typical episode: "Each episode opens with a ghoulishly hilarious death. The Fisher family then tends to the survivors, once it gets over its own crises." Ball explained to *Entertainment Weekly*'s Snierson, "This is TV for people who don't really like TV," and added, "It's about people attempting to live an authentic life in a world that's increasingly inauthentic."

In addition to receiving critical acclaim, in 2001 Ball received the Directors Guild of America's Award for Outstanding Directorial Achievement in Dramatic Series, for *Six Feet Under.* In 2002, in recognition of the realistic portrayal of gay characters on the show, he received the Gay and Lesbian Alliance Against Defamation Stephen Kolzak Award. At the awards ceremony, according to Kevin Maynard in *Daily Variety,* Ball noted, "We are the faces of your sons, your daughters. We're not crazy circus freaks—except maybe on the weekend. The face of gay America is really the face of America."

One person who was not a fan of the show was Ball's mother. When he asked her what she thought of it, she replied, "It's filthy, filthy, filthy," Ball told *Newsweek*'s Peyser. "But that's what she says to me. I think she's very proud." His mother did agree to

do a cameo role in the pilot of the series, and as Peyser joked, "Ball was nice enough not to make her into a corpse."

Although Ball works in television, he does not actually watch much of it. At times, this can be a hindrance, as when he comes up with a plotline and discovers that it just appeared on another popular show. Most of the time, however, he feels that this keeps his writing fresh. He told Alan Sepinwell in *Daily Variety,* "I like to hire writers who don't have years and years of TV experience, because they tend not to think in those ironclad paradigms and formulas, which all those scriptwriting books teach." Actor Peter Krause, who stars in the show, added that the show was "less plot-driven and more character-based than a lot of what you see. As an actor, you want to do behavior; you want to get into relationships, and that's really what Alan Ball is interested in."

Ball told *Entertainment Weekly*'s Snierson that in writing for *Six Feet Under,* "I feel very fortunate. For the first time ever in television, I feel like the people who hired me to do this job actually trust me and don't question every little instinct I have...." He noted that although his work may seem dark on the surface, "if you look a little deeper, it's almost shamefully romantic and honest and optimistic."

## Sources

### Periodicals

*Advocate,* January 18, 2000, p. 91; July 3, 2001, p. 50.
*Back Stage,* June 24, 1994, p. 36; March 15, 2002, p. 2.
*Daily Variety,* April 9, 2002, p. A4; August 30, 2002, p. 18.
*Entertainment Weekly,* March 31, 2000, p. 18; June 8, 2001, p. 36.
*Harper's Bazaar,* July 2001, p. 76.
*Newsweek,* September 27, 1999, p. 68; May 28, 2001, p. 62.
*Observer* (London, England), November 2, 2003, p. 13.
*Sarasota Magazine,* February 2000.
*Variety,* December 8, 2003, p. S24.

### Online

"Alan Ball," HBO, http://www.hbo.com/sixfeetunder/cast/crew/alan_ball.shtml (August 3, 2004).
*Biography Resource Center Online,* Gale Group, 2002.

—*Kelly Winters*

# Jason Bateman

## Actor

**B**orn Jason Kent Bateman, January 14, 1969, in Rye, NY; son of Kent (a TV producer) and Victoria (a flight attendant) Bateman; married Amanda Anka (an actress), July 3, 2001.

**Addresses:** *Contact*—20th Century Fox Broadcasting, 10201 West Pico Blvd., Bldg. 88, Rm. 30, Los Angeles, CA 90035. *Home*—Los Angeles, CA.

## Career

**A**ctor on television, including: *Little House: A New Beginning*, 1981-82; *Silver Spoons*, 1982-84; *It's Your Move*, 1984; *Valerie* (renamed *The Hogan Family*), 1986-1991; *Simon*, 1995; *Chicago Sons*, 1997; *George & Leo*, 1997; *Some of My Best Friends*, 2001; *Arrested Development*, 2003—. Appeared in commercials as a child. Film appearances include: *Teen Wolf Too*, 1987; *Necessary Roughness*, 1991; *Breaking the Rules*, 1992; *Love Stinks*, 1999; *The Sweetest Thing*, 2002; *Starsky & Hutch*, 2004; *Dodgeball: A True Underdog Story*, 2004.

**Awards:** Golden Globe award for best performance by an actor in a television musical/comedy series, for *Arrested Development*, 2005; Golden Satellite award for best actor in a comedy series, for *Arrested Development*, 2005.

## Sidelights

**J**ason Bateman made his television debut in commercials at the age of ten, peddling Cheerios and Coke with his cherubic, good-boy charm. He shot to fame a few years later playing Ricky Schroder's mischievous best friend on the 1980s sitcom staple *Silver Spoons*. Bateman's minor *Spoons* character became such a big draw that he was given his own comedy vehicle, *It's Your Move*, in 1984. Several other series followed. Unlike most teen-idol stars of his era, Bateman—and his endearing boyish face—is still around. He became a born-again star in his 30s, playing the central figure on FOX Television's quirky Emmy-winning sitcom *Arrested Development*. "Most people retire after 25 years in this business," Bateman told *People*. "I got to start over."

Bateman was born on January 14, 1969, in Rye, New York, to Kent and Victoria Bateman, who divorced in 1989. It only seems natural that Bateman ended up in television given that his father was a producer, director, and writer of television programs and educational films. His mother worked as a Pan-Am flight attendant. Because of these careers, the Bateman family moved around a lot. During his first dozen years, Bateman spent time in Rye, New York; Winchester, Massachusetts; and Salt Lake City before the family settled in Los Angeles in 1981.

When Bateman was ten, he informed his father that he wanted to star in a commercial. Fulfilling this desire was pretty easy for Bateman. With his winsome, boy-next-door presence—and his father's connections—Bateman found an agent and starred in several commercials, including Cheerios, McDonald's, and Coca Cola. Within a year, Bateman landed his first television role, playing James Cooper, adopted son of the Ingalls clan, on the well-liked *Little House on the Prairie* series. The year Bateman joined the cast the show was renamed *Little House: A New Beginning*. That season, 1981-82, turned out to be its last.

NBC immediately found a new role for Bateman, casting him as child-star Ricky Schroder's misguided sidekick on *Silver Spoons*, which debuted in 1982. Bateman's character, Derek Taylor, was supposed to be a minor foil on the show, but he became a fan favorite. Rumor has it that as the show's second season wore on, Schroder became increasingly jealous of Bateman's popularity and felt he was stealing the show. Though he was barely a teen himself, Bateman broadcast a heartthrob quality young female viewers craved. "Jason was starting to get a lot of mail," show writer Ron Leavitt told *TV Guide*'s Andrea Darvi. Neither side said much about the conflict at the time, but Bateman later told *People*'s Susan Toepfer, "I was 13 and it was my first rude awakening to the dark side of the business. Ricky taught me a lot about what not to do."

NBC resolved the situation by yanking Bateman from *Silver Spoons* and giving him his own show, *It's Your Move*, where he played the conniving-yet-irresistible adolescent Matthew Burton. Though the show only lasted one season, it had better ratings than *Silver Spoons* the year it ran. Bateman's older sister, Justine, was enjoying her own success simultaneously, starring as the ditzy Mallory Keaton on the wildly popular sitcom *Family Ties*.

Like other teen actors, Bateman had an unusual childhood. Keeping up with school was challenging. During his time on *Little House*, Bateman received a progress report with a failing grade—in drama. "Sometimes the teachers are jealous, and you're picked on," Bateman told Darvi in the *TV Guide* interview. On the upside, there were perks to the show business life. Bateman spent his free time hanging out on studio lots, riding bikes with other teen actors. He became particularly close to teen star Glenn Scarpelli, whose *One Day at a Time* set was nearby.

In 1986, Bateman was cast as Valerie Harper's girl-crazy, sharp-tongued son David Hogan on her self-titled situation comedy, *Valerie*. The show followed the antics of the Hogan family. Bateman, playing the oldest son in a family of three boys, brought a huge adolescent following of viewers. Harper played a super-mom stuck raising three boys on her own because her husband was an airline pilot and rarely home. After a couple seasons, Harper clashed with producers, apparently over her salary, and left the show, which was then renamed *Valerie's Family* and later, *The Hogan Family*. Her character was killed off and Sandy Duncan became the matriarch of the clan. The show ran until 1991. Bateman also directed a few of the episodes.

When Bateman turned 18, he went through a period of arrested development himself. He took his show-business earnings and bought his own home, furnishing it in real frat-boy style with a pool table, big-screen television, and indoor basketball court. "I was trying to make up for not going to college," he told *People*. "I *needed* the basketball hoops and the neon beer signs.... But I'm all caught up now." He also traveled a lot, renting ski houses and planes to enjoy with his friends. He also drove race cars and once won the Long Beach celebrity grand prix.

During the 1990s Bateman had plenty of work, though none of it was terribly successful. He appeared in a number of sitcom bombs, including 1995's *Simon*, 1997's *George & Leo*, and *Chicago Sons*, a sitcom that same year about blue-collar brothers. In 2001, he found a role on *Some of My Best Friends* playing a gay writer struggling to overcome a breakup. The show, based on the 1997 gay indie film *Kiss Me, Guido*, lasted just three months on the air. Among other failures was his 1987 feature film debut in *Teen Wolf Too*. The movie was a sequel to the 1995 Michael J. Fox original, *Teen Wolf*. In this film, Bateman played a college co-ed coping with his penchant for changing into a wolf during stressful times. The movie was far too similar to the original and bombed at the box office. Bateman also starred in the failed 1999 feature film *Love Stinks*.

Though he worked steadily through the 1990s, Bateman failed to ignite audiences until he appeared on *Arrested Development* in 2003. This quirky, daringly different FOX show gained critical acclaim from the start. *Arrested Development* explores love and incarceration through the eyes of the Bluths, a dysfunctional, well-to-do family that owns a profitable real-estate development firm. The Bluths fall apart, however, when family patriarch George Bluth (Jeffrey Tambor) is tossed in jail for questionable accounting practices, thus rendering the Bluths bankrupt. The sitcom centers on Bateman's character, Michael Bluth, son of George, who is the only levelheaded one in the family. Other characters include his 13-year-old son, his socialite mother, his Segway-riding magician brother, his perpetual college-student brother, and his twin sister, who uses the company credit card to fund her personal escapades. The clever title refers to two things: literally the arrested real-estate developer as well as the stunted maturity of the family members. The smart-humored show, full of satire concerning upper-middle-class absorption, has a small but faithful following.

While highly scripted, *Arrested Development* has a spur-of-the-moment feel because it is filmed in handheld digital video, giving it the bouncy quality of a real-time documentary. This technique also gives the viewer an intensely personal relationship with each character because the camera has to pan around all the time to catch the action, unlike sitcoms shot with a single, see-all camera. The show's producers also shun canned laugh tracks to cue viewers—this makes the show more intense because there is no pausing for laughter. The fast-paced grittiness also makes it harder to follow punch lines; viewers have to work a bit to get the wit. "The show is unpredictable, and it takes time to get it," Bateman told *USA Today*'s Donna Freydkin. "You miss a word in the first act, and four jokes in the third act aren't going to pay off. That's one of the reasons we are having problems building an audience."

The show is so different from old-school sitcoms that it generated critical acclaim but failed to secure a mass audience its first two seasons. Writing in the *New Yorker,* television critic Nancy Franklin noted that "*Arrested Development* has an energetic, seat-of-the-pants style, which gives its absurdities an air of realism." She also credited Bateman with making his character "appealingly sardonic and smart." Despite all of the encouraging reviews, the show ranked 116th during the 2003-04 season, capturing an average audience of just 6.2 million viewers. Nonetheless, the show was nominated for several Emmy Awards in 2004. It won five: outstanding comedy series, direction, writing, casting, and editing. Winning the outstanding comedy award blew the cast away because they beat out such favorites as *Everybody Loves Raymond* and *Sex and the City.* "I think I blacked out when they said our name," Bateman told the *Los Angeles Times*' Lynn Smith. "I'm glad I TiVo-ed it."

Bateman's co-stars are quick to credit him for the show's award-winning success. Speaking to *People,* co-star Tambor compared Bateman to Johnny

Carson. "He lets the people around him shine, then he has his moment and he just *kills.*"

While critics praised the show as the freshest sitcom to come out of Hollywood in years, ratings dipped to just six million viewers its second season. To grab more viewers, the show has used a steady stream of Hollywood favorites for guest appearances, including Julia Louis-Dreyfus, Liza Minnelli, and Henry Winkler. The show also suffered a slow start to the 2004 season when it should have been gaining viewers on the coattails of its Emmy wins. The show won the Emmys in September, yet stayed off the air until November because FOX had to broadcast the Major League Baseball playoffs and World Series. In February of 2005, FOX announced that it would only go ahead with filming 18 of the show's 22 planned episodes for the season. Industry insiders wondered how much longer the show would go on if viewership did not perk up. Speaking to the *Pittsburgh Post-Gazette*'s Rob Owen, Bateman summed up his frustration, "I think there was some unfortunate timing with us winning the Emmy and not being on the air during ... the first part of the fall, so it was tough to capitalize on that."

Besides his surge in popularity on television, Bateman enjoyed simultaneous success on the big screen as well. He starred as Vince Vaughn's drug-dealing subordinate in 2004's *Starsky & Hutch* and also had a role in Ben Stiller's 2004 comedy *Dodgeball: A True Underdog Story.* When he is not busy filming, Bateman enjoys spending time admiring his backyard Japanese koi pond. He lives in Los Angeles with his wife, Amanda Anka, daughter of pop star Paul Anka. They married in 2001.

While *Arrested Development* has been slow to capture the imagination of the masses, Bateman is enjoying renewed popularity. In 2005, he won a Golden Globe for best actor in a television comedy for his role on the show. Bateman is enjoying his recent success, but he is also smart enough to know that he cannot rest on his laurels—after all, he has spent 25 years of his life reinventing himself for the camera. "Work is tenuous at best," he told the *Hollywood Reporter.* "If you do a perfect job, you are basically fired at the end of it, and you have to find another one."

## Sources

### Periodicals

*Hollywood Reporter,* January 18, 2005, p. 23.
*Los Angeles Times,* September 20, 2004, p. E3.

*New Yorker,* November 10, 2003, p. 124.

*People,* May 16, 1988, p. 101; December 8, 2003, pp. 121-22; November 29, 2004, p. 98.

*Pittsburgh Post-Gazette,* February 11, 2005, p. WE45.

*TV Guide,* February 9-15, 1985, pp. 37-40.

*USA Today,* March 17, 2004, p. 6D.

**Online**

"Jason Bateman: Having a Ball," *USA Weekend Magazine,* http://www.usaweekend.com/04_issues/040613/040613bateman.html (February 22, 2005).

—*Lisa Frick*

# Deron Beal

## Nonprofit executive and website creator

**B**orn c. 1968 in Lancaster, OH; married Jennifer Columbus (a pastry chef), 2003. *Education:* Earned undergraduate and M.B.A degrees from Georgetown University; studied literature in Germany.

**Addresses:** *Office*—c/o RISE, Inc., 82 S. Stone Ave., Tucson, AZ 85701.

## Career

**W**orked as a finance manager for Procter & Gamble; became director of RISE Inc., November, 2002; launched Freecycle.org, May, 2003.

## Sidelights

**D**eron Beal created the Internet phenomenon Freecycle.org in the spring of 2003, and oversaw its growth from a mere e-mail he sent out to a few dozen friends and colleagues into a nearly million-member-strong cyber-marvel over the next two years. Freecycle, which has no membership fees or requirements, allows users to post messages on their local community's Freecycle website about items they would like to discard, and they can also send out a query for various goods which they are seeking for their own households. The *Virginian Pilot* described it as "a sort of virtual curb on the Internet where people can unload everything from hot tubs to seeds to old clothes."

A native of Lancaster, Ohio, Beal was in his mid-thirties when Freecycle.org became the newest eBay-like community in cyberspace. He is a graduate of Georgetown University's rigorous foreign-service studies program, a stepping stone for a career with the U.S. State Department diplomacy corps, and earned a graduate degree in business from Georgetown as well. For a time, he worked as a finance manager at the Cincinnati, Ohio-based consumer-goods giant Procter & Gamble, but left the job to study literature in Germany. From there, he became interested in environmental activism, and eventually wound up in Tucson, Arizona, where he ran a nonprofit recycling organization called RISE Inc.

RISE is a recycling service and employment training group for Tucson-area businesses, and Beal, after taking over in late 2002, was amazed at what companies chucked out the back door every day. "The businesses started giving us all this stuff that's not recyclable but that they don't want to throw away," he recalled in an interview with *People* writer Richard Jerome. "Computers, desks. I didn't know what to do with it, but I couldn't bear to say no." After spending hours on the phone trying to find takers for the used—but still usable—goods that he knew would eventually wind up in a landfill if he could not find them a home, in May of 2003 he came up with the idea for Freecycle and outlined his scheme in an e-mail. "I just sent the information out to my friends and 10 to 15 nonprofits and said, 'Spread the word,'" he told *Christian Science Monitor* writer Tim King. "You get free stuff, and you get to give away the junk in your garage."

Beal created some simple rules for Freecycle.org: users can either post what they have, or what they might like, but their first post must be an offer of something they would like to jettison. All goods must be free to anyone willing to take them, and the taker must make the arrangements for pick-up and transport. The original recipients of that first e-mail did indeed pass it on, and it seemed to click immediately with scores of subsequent e-mail addressees. Nearly everyone, it turned out, had something which they wanted to see vanish from their household or business, and Beal realized he had tapped into an unspoken desire. "We get it drilled into us on television ads: 'Consume, consume, consume. You want more, you need more,' and do we really?" he ventured in an interview with Tina Kelley of the *New York Times*. "I think what's coming out with freecycling is, 'Gee, it's kind of fun not to be into all this.'"

Initially, Beal's Freecycle.org was not even an official website, merely a "listserv" group on the Internet portal Yahoo. The number of users grew exponentially after an article about it in the *Christian Science Monitor* in October of 2003, its first mention in the mainstream print media, and new chapters across the United States seemed to spring up daily. A year after its launch, Beal's cyber-community had grown to more than 500,000 members in 1,500 cities, and by early 2005 had more than 900,000 members.

One of the most popular items for exchange on Freecycle.org was exercise equipment, and the most unusual was a telephone pole, but Beal's personal favorite was a bottle of partially used hair dye, which needs to be applied within a few hours of mixing before self-combusting. There are Freecycle communities in Germany, Japan, and Australia, but in the United States cities like Portland, Oregon, and Austin, Texas, have the highest number of members. Beal estimates that about 20 to 40 tons of goods are traded daily thanks to the site, much of it falling under the "one person's trash is another's

treasure" adage, but he is also proud that individual communities have stepped up to the plate when floods or other disasters strike and victims lose entire households. "We had two elderly people who didn't have insurance when part of their house burned down," he told King in the *Christian Science Monitor* interview. "One of the Freecycle people sent out a note saying they were getting set up at some other place and could use a bed, a couch, and other stuff. Within two days, they had everything they needed."

Beal kept his job at Tucson's RISE, and keeps the Freecycle.org phenomenon running with the help of local listserv moderators, who keep an eye on the posts for rule-breakers or spammers. In time, he plans to make it a freestanding, self-sufficient website. His own household, which he shares with wife Jennifer Columbus, a pastry chef, is furnished with some goods obtained via Freecycle. An idealist at heart still worried about the amount of consumer goods that pile up in landfill mountains across the American landscape, he believes Freecycle.org might someday spark a greater collective consciousness about even larger issues. "When it comes to the Internet and connecting with one another, there are no limitations," he enthused in an interview with Rosemary Barnes of the *San Antonio Express-News*. "We'll continue growing and experiencing the goodness that comes from giving."

## Sources

*Christian Science Monitor*, October 27, 2003, p. 13.
*New York Times*, March 16, 2004, p. B1.
*People*, May 10, 2004, p. 195.
*San Antonio Express-News*, October 30, 2004.
*Virginian Pilot*, January 10, 2005, p. D1.

—*Carol Brennan*

# Jennifer Beals

## Actress

**B**orn December 19, 1963, in Chicago, IL; daughter of Alfred (a supermarket owner) and Jeanne (an elementary school teacher) Beals; married Alexandre Rockwell (a film director), 1986 (divorced, 1996); married Kenneth Dixon (a writer and film technician), 1999. *Education:* Yale University, undergraduate degree with honors in American literature, 1987; studied stage acting at The Goodman School of Drama, DePaul University; studied acting at the Professional Workshop in New York City.

**Addresses:** *Office*—Season II Productions, Inc., 8275 Manitoba St., Vancouver, British Columbia V5X 4L8 Canada.

## Career

**A**ctress in films including: *My Bodyguard,* 1980; *Flashdance,* 1983; *The Bride,* 1985; *Vampire's Kiss,* 1988; *La Partita,* 1988; *Sons,* 1989; *Docteur M.,* 1989; *Le Grande Pardon II,* 1992; *In the Soup,* 1992; *Mrs. Parker and the Vicious Circle,* 1994; *Four Rooms,* 1995; *The Devil in a Blue Dress,* 1995; *The Hunt for One-Eyed Jimmy,* 1996; *The Last Days of Disco,* 1998; *The Anniversary Party,* 2002; *After the Storm,* 2002; *Roger Dodger,* 2002; *Runaway Jury,* 2003. Television movies include: *Terror Stalks the Class Reunion,* syndicated, 1992; *Night Owl,* Lifetime, 1993; *The Twilight of the Golds,* Showtime, 1997; *Let It Be Me,* Starz!, 1998; *Body and Soul,* The Movie Channel, 1999; *A House Divided,* 2000. Television series include: *Faerie Tale Theatre,* Showtime, 1985; *2000 Malibu Road,* CBS, 1992; *Nothing Sacred,* ABC, 1998; *The L Word,* Showtime, 2004—. Stage appearances include: *Macbeth,* 1991. Also worked as a model.

**Awards:** NAACP Award, for *Flashdance*; Golden Satellite Award for best actress in a miniseries or motion picture made for television, for *Twilight of the Golds,* 1997.

## Sidelights

**A**fter beginning her career with the unexpected smash hit film *Flashdance,* actress Jennifer Beals avoided being a one-hit wonder and had an interesting career in film and television. Because of her biracial background and exotic looks, she was able to play roles of various ethnicities and nationalities. Beals did not just appear in Hollywood films, but spent time working in Europe and took roles in a number of independent films. By the 2000s, her unconventional career took her into series television and a starring role in the lesbian-oriented series *The L Word.*

Born December 19, 1963, in Chicago, Illinois, Beals is the daughter of Alfred and Jeanne Beals. Her father was an African-American owner of a supermarket, who died when Beals was nine years old. Her white mother worked as an elementary school teacher. Beals had two older brothers, including Gregory who later became a photographer for *Newsweek.* As a young girl, she received her education at Chicago's Francis Parker School.

Beals' professional career began when she was 16 years old, when she worked as a model. In 1980, she had her first acting role. Though she did not receive a credit, she had a bit role in *My Bodyguard.* Despite this early work, Beals' remained committed to getting a college education. She entered Yale University, where she majored in American literature. Beals also studied acting at the DePaul University's Goodman School of Drama and at the Professional Workshop in New York City.

While a student at Yale, Beals was cast in what was arguably the biggest picture of her career, 1983's *Flashdance.* In the hit Hollywood film, Beals played a woman who works as a welder in a Pittsburgh, Pennsylvania, factory by day, but dances at a bar at night. *Flashdance* unexpectedly became one of the biggest box office smashes of 1983 in the United States, and grossed $150 million worldwide by 1985. The film also started fashion trends such as torn sweatshirts and leg warmers, while clubs started having flashdance contests.

After the film was released, Beals revealed that she did not perform much of the dancing in *Flashdance.* Instead, a double, Marine Jahan, did the dancing in the film. Despite the deception, Beals remained proud of her work. She told the *South China Morning Post* in 2003, "I did it because I loved the character and the story. I never thought I was going to become famous. The culture is different now. People are so dedicated to fame. I never even looked at show business magazines when I was a girl."

After *Flashdance,* Beals returned to Yale to complete her studies. Though she declined to take a role in the follow-up to *Flashdance* (*Flashdance II,* which was never made), she continued to work on her modeling and acting careers. She signed a deal to promote clothing by Marithe and Francois Girbaud. Their line at the time was similar to what was worn in *Flashdance.*

In 1985, Beals appeared in her next film, *The Bride,* which co-starred rock star Sting. In the loose remake of the horror film *The Bride of Frankenstein,* she played Eva, a woman from the nineteenth century being brought back to life by a scientist, played by Sting. Beals was unhappy with the way the final film turned out as she believed that certain scenes that developed her character were cut in the final edit. During the shoot, Beals developed a reputation for being high maintenance as an actress. She took acting seriously, and needed time and space to get into her character.

While still a student, Beals also did a little television work. She appeared as Cinderella in an episode of Showtime's *Faerie Tale Theatre.* However, it was not until Beals graduated from Yale in 1987 that her career really took off. In 1988, she appeared in *Vampire's Kiss,* with co-star Nicolas Cage. The film focused on yuppies in the big city in the 1980s. Cage's character believes he is a vampire, though he is a literary agent in New York. Beals greatly enjoyed the way the film turned out.

In the late 1980s, Beals primarily worked in Europe with a number of leading directors. In 1988, she appeared in the film *La Partita,* directed by Carlo Vanzini. A year later, Beals had a role in the Claude Charbol-directed *Docteur M.* In 1992, she appeared in *Le Grande Pardon II,* which was directed by Alexandre Arcady.

Also in the late 1980s and through the mid-1990s, Beals appeared in films directed by her husband Alexandre Rockwell, whom she married in 1986. Her first film with him was *Sons,* in which she played a transvestite. A bigger success was his 1992 film *In the Soup.* The film was financed by Beals, her mother, and her husband, and won the Sundance Film Festival's Grand Jury Prize. Beals played a Dominican American in the coming-of-age comedy.

Beals' last film directed by Rockwell was his segment of the anthology picture *Four Rooms.* In "The Wrong Man," she played a woman tied to a chair and gagged by her abusive husband, who finally gets a moment to say her piece about the situation. The film was released in 1995, and a year later, Beals and Rockwell divorced.

In the 1990s, Beals worked in films—both mainstream and independent—and television. In 1994, she played Gertrude Benchley in *Mrs. Parker and the Vicious Circle.* The film focused on the famous literary circle of authors who met at the Algonquin Hotel in the 1920s. Beals' character was the disregarded wife of author Robert Benchley. Beals showed she really could dance in the film *Let It Be Me* as her character had to ballroom dance. The film was shot in 1994, but aired on Starz! in 1998. In 1996, Beals appeared in the independent film *The Hunt for One-Eyed Jimmy.*

A bigger film role for Beals came in 1995. She fought to read for the role of Daphne Monet, the femme fatale character in the stylized mystery *The Devil in a Blue Dress,* which starred Denzel Washington. The director, Carl Franklin, originally wanted to cast an unknown actress in the film, which was set in 1940s Los Angeles and based on a novel by Walter Mosely, but Beals won the role. Beals told Ruthe Stein of the *San Francisco Chronicle,* "I love this character. I wanted to hold her hand and take her down this road. It was like she was a real person and I wanted to take care of her. That kind of gave me permission to be much more audacious than I would normally be." Though Beals was intrigued by her role and the film, *The Devil in a Blue Dress* received mixed reviews.

Beals was not afraid to show her range as an actress. In 1998, she had a co-starring role in *The Last Days of Disco,* a drama set at the end of the disco era. Four years later, in 2002, Beals appeared in the drama *The Anniversary Party* as a photographer, a hobby the actress pursues passionately in real life. The film focused on Hollywood types at the anniversary party of an actress and her husband, who is a screenwriter and director. That same year, she had a role in another independent film, *Roger Dodger.* Beals played one of two female friends who met up with the title character and his nephew, a self-conscious, forlorn teen. Hollywood still gave Beals roles in big films. In 2003, she appeared in the mysterious drama *Runaway Jury,* co-starring John Cusack.

Bigger and more varied roles came for Beals on television in the 1990s. In 1993, she had a role in the supernatural television movie *Night Owl* which aired on Lifetime. A bigger role came in the 1997 Showtime movie *The Twilight of the Golds,* based on the 1993 play by Jonathan Tolins. In the movie, Beals played a pregnant woman named Suzanne. Her husband is a genetics researcher and he discovers their baby has a gene that makes him homosexual. Over the course of the movie, her character thinks about ending her pregnancy once she learns this fact, but has to deal with the input of her family and their prejudices.

Beals faced complex issues related to race in another television movie, 2000's *A House Divided.* Based on a true story, the movie was set in the South before, during, and after the Civil War. Beals played a woman of mixed race, Amanda America Dickson, who learns as an adult that her slave owner father, David Dickson, had raped a slave in his household to create her. Amanda's father took her away from her mother after her birth to raise as a white child with the help of his mother. His money protected the child from any questions about her parentage. The slave continued to live in the household, and eventually helped run the plantation. David Dickson's only child, Amanda leaves after she discovers the truth of her heritage, but when her father dies, she inherits his estate. Beals greatly identified with the character and her dilemmas.

Beals also ventured into series television in the 1990s. In 1992, she played Perry Quinn, an attorney with an alcohol problem, on the show *2000 Malibu Road.* The short-lived series was produced by television guru Aaron Spelling and film director Joel Schumacher. Its stories focused on four women, including Beals' character, who lived in a beach house together. Six years later, Beals filmed a recurring role as Justine, the head of religious education in the ABC series *Nothing Sacred,* but her scenes never aired.

As Beals' career continued to grow, especially on television, her personal life also changed. She married her second husband, Canadian Kenneth Dixon, in 1999. He also worked in the film industry as a technician and writer. Around that time, Beals faced some health challenges. Diagnosed with chronic fatigue syndrome, Epstein-Barr virus, and thyroiditis, she used alternative medicines, including healthy diet changes, to cure herself.

In 2004, Beals was cast on the biggest television series of her career, *The L Word.* The Showtime program was one of the first shows to focus on lesbians. Beals played a lesbian named Bette Porter, a museum curator and art dealer in a serious relationship with another woman. The frank show focused on a circle of friends and was a comedy/drama with elements of a soap opera. It was generally critically acclaimed. The year the show debuted, Beals was named one of *People*'s 50 most beautiful people.

Though Beals' career took a number of twists and turns, she was content with its path. In 1997, she told Bill Zwecker of the *Chicago Sun-Times,* "I could have gone in a different direction and done a lot of commercial things. I just wasn't interested, even early on. Career, it's such a bizarre word. Trajectory is probably a better word to describe it, since a trajectory can go at different speeds. I just want mine to be long and steady, rather than one that takes off quickly but then flashes out."

## Sources

### Books

*Celebrity Biographies,* Baseline II, Inc., 2004.

### Periodicals

*Better Nutrition,* March 2004, p. 36.
*Boston Globe,* January 18, 2004, p. N1.
*Chicago Sun-Times,* August 11, 1992, sec. 2, p. 4; November 2, 1997, p. 3; June 22, 2001, p. 31.
*Guardian* (London, England), September 4, 2004, p. 4.

*InStyle,* March 1, 2004, p. 367.

*New York Times,* January 11, 2004, sec. 9, p. 4.

*Organic Style,* September/October 2003, pp. 34-35.

*People,* January 2, 1984, p. 90; September 2, 1985, p. 84; April 12, 2004, p. 35; May 10, 2004, p. 134.

*Plain Dealer* (Cleveland, Ohio), July 30, 2000, p. 6I.

*San Francisco Chronicle,* September 24, 1995, p. 30; September 29, 1995, p. C1; October 24, 1997, p. C4.

*Seattle Times,* June 5, 1991, p. C7.

*South China Morning Post* (Hong Kong), May 22, 2003, p. 8.

*St. Louis Post-Dispatch,* March 7, 1998, p. 38.

*Washington Post,* July 30, 2000, p. G4.

—*A. Petruso*

# Brad Bird

## Director, screenwriter, and animator

**B**orn c. 1956 in Kalispell, Montana; married; children: Nicholas, two other sons. *Education:* Graduated from the California School of Arts, Animation Program.

**Addresses:** *Office*—Pixar Animation Studios, 1200 Park Ave., Emeryville, CA 94608. *Website*—http://www.pixar.com.

## Career

**A**nimator, *Animalympics*, 1979; animator, *The Fox and the Hound*, Disney, 1981; animator, *The Plague Dogs*, 1982; creator, "Family Dog," *Amazing Stories*, CBS, 1985; consultant and guest animator, *The Tracey Ullman Show*, c. 1986; screenwriter, *batteries not included*, Universal, 1987; series storyboard artist and sheet direction, director, character development, *The Simpsons*, FOX, 1990; television executive consultant, *The Simpsons*, FOX, 1990-96; television executive consultant, *The Critic*, FOX, 1994; visual consultant, *King of the Hill*, FOX, 1997; worked at Turner Featured Animation (later merged with Warner Bros.), late 1990s; director and storywriter, *The Iron Giant*, Warner Bros., 1999; hired at Pixar Animation Studios, 2000; director, *The Incredibles*, Pixar Animation, 2004; director, *Jack-Jack Attack* (video), Pixar Animation, 2005.

**Awards:** Annie awards for best animated feature, best directing, and best voice acting for *The Incredibles*, 2004; Academy Awards for best animated feature and best sound editing, Academy of Motion Picture Arts and Sciences, for *The Incredibles*, 2005.

© *Petre Buzoianu/Corbis*

## Sidelights

**B**rad Bird has risen from being a basic unknown in the entertainment business to the stratospheres of the movie world with his 2004 film *The Incredibles*. A precocious child, Bird developed an interest in animation at a very young age and has had quite an impressive career ever since, working for such companies as Disney, Warner Bros., and most recently, Pixar Animation. He has worked on animation shows from *The Simpsons* to *King of the Hill*, and he was the brains behind the cult film favorite *The Iron Giant*. Bird's fans are always eager to see what the animation genius will do next, and he has yet to disappoint, introducing new techniques and fresh ideas into the world of animation.

Bird, who is notoriously reticent about sharing his birth date, was born in Kalispell, Montana. He had three older sisters: Leslie, Susan, and Kathy. Bird's family moved to Oregon when he was still young, and he spent most of his childhood there. Bird became interested in animation very early on in his life, and he started making his first animated film at the age of eleven. He worked on the movie, an adaptation of the old tale about the tortoise and the hare, for four years, finishing it when he was a mere

14 years old. When *The Tortoise and the Hare* was finished he sent the film to Disney, hoping to come to the attention of someone at the famous animation company. This first of Bird's animated films eventually did indeed catch the attention of executives at Walt Disney Studios. They were so impressed that they invited him to enroll in their mentoring program. Bird graduated from Corvallis High School in Corvallis, Oregon, in 1975. Not long after, he was being mentored by the legendary Disney animator Milt Kahl, one of the group known in the industry as the Nine Old Men, the group responsible for most of Walt Disney's early animated movies.

After the stint with Disney, Bird enrolled in the animation program at the California School of Arts. After he got his degree Bird returned to Disney where he had been offered a job as an animator. He was excited about the chance to work at Walt Disney Studios, applying the knowledge he had gained at the California School of Arts, as well as the information he had gleaned from Kahl. He started out his career as an animator on the Disney feature-length film *The Fox and the Hound.* Bird, however, soon became disenchanted with the Disney feature-length animation film department. He thought that the quality in recent years had gone down from what it once was and that they had cheapened the appeal of the films they made by allowing them to become television series. Bird had very strong opinions about maintaining a film's integrity and not corrupting the original story by making sequels just for the sake of making a sequel, and that included turning them into television shows.

Bird left Disney in the mid-1980s. One of the things that brought him fame as an animator in the public eye was the work he did for Steven Spielberg. In 1985 he worked for Spielberg on an episode of *Amazing Stories.* The episode, "Family Dog," was a big hit, and the success of the short had Spielberg asking Bird to write the first draft of the screenplay for *batteries not included.*

After "Family Dog," Bird started working on other television series as a consultant and guest animator. He began on *The Tracey Ullman Show,* which is where *The Simpsons* got its start. He then went on to work as a consultant on *The Simpsons* when it spun off as its own show. He went on to direct several episodes of *The Simpsons* and did most of the animation for the scenes with Krusty the Clown. By the mid-1990s Bird was the consultant on other shows, including *The Critic* from 1994 to 1995, and *King of the Hill* in 1997.

Bird began working at Turner Featured Animation in the late 1990s and was working there when the company merged with Warner Bros. When that hap-

pened Bird began work on his version of *The Iron Giant.* The animated film of *The Iron Giant* was based on a children's book by British writer Ted Hughes. Hughes wrote it in 1968 for his children after his wife, fellow writer Sylvia Plath, killed herself, to help explain the idea of suicide to his children. *The Iron Giant* was released in 1999, and Bird came to the attention of critics immediately with this, his feature film debut. *Newsweek* called the film "beguiling ... at once simple and sophisticated," and they were not the only ones to laud the movie. Unfortunately the film was given very little promotion by Warner Bros. and very few knew of the movie at the time of its release, so the film did rather poorly at the box office, making only $23 million in its first three months of release. However, in this day and age of videotapes and DVDs, the movie has since found a broader fan base and has even become a cult classic. According to the IGN website, "Like another Warner title, *The Shawshank Redemption,* [*The Iron Giant's*] fan base would grow slowly on the home video market and its fan base didn't just like the movie, they adored it. Such is its popularity that every year on Thanksgiving, Cartoon Network runs an *Iron Giant* marathon, replaying the movie for 24 hours straight." Part of the success of the movie has been credited to the fact that it was not strictly a children's movie, as Bird incorporated elements from science fiction and added an emotional honesty and depth that made it attractive to an adult audience as well. Bird told critics that he believes that a good children's film is not directed to children, but is just directed to humans in general. Children, Bird contends, know when you are condescending or talking down to them and are insulted by it. Instead movies should discuss difficult issues in a straight-forward manner, making them interesting to people of all ages. *The Iron Giant* was released in 2005 on a specially packaged DVD.

Bird was next supposed to do a feature-length film based on the *Curious George* books, and even went so far as to write a draft of the film, but it was still in development at Warner Bros. when Bird moved on. Bird next got a job with the innovative Pixar Animation Studios in 2000. He was the first director hired from outside the studio. Bird was hired to create animated, computer-generated features. The first movie he did for Pixar was *The Incredibles,* which was released in November of 2004. It was a departure for Pixar and required an amount of work that might have put off anyone else. Bird wanted the film's characters to look almost real, and so Bird and his group of animators had extras walking around the studio just so they could see and get used to the vision of human motion so they could translate it into animated characters. Bird told the IGN website about the film: "We're doing unrealistic stuff all the way through the film, but we're trying to pay attention to real physics when we do the unreal stuff so you believe it. We had a number of people come up to us and say 'Five minutes into the movie I forgot I was watching an animated film.' I don't think the film looks realistic, I don't think it looks remotely realistic. But it feels realistic." Pixar had never done anything like that before, and there was some nervousness during production, but the end results more than compensated for any extra effort required during the making of the film. The film grossed $256 million at the box office. It also swept the awards at the Annies, an award show for animated features, and won Best Animated Feature and Best Sound Editing at the 2005 Academy Awards.

*The Incredibles* follows the lives of the Parr family, a family whose mother and father are former super-heroes and who, because of a few litigious prob-lems, have gone into the witness protection pro-gram with their children and are not allowed to use their powers outside of the house. During the course of the film the whole family rediscovers the source of their powers and learn to trust and rely on each other. Bird was quoted in the *Birmingham Post* as having said of the film, "My goal was to use the su-perhero theme comment on family archetypes. The dad is always expected to be strong 'for your family's sake', so that was his superpower. Moms are always pulled in a thousand directions, so I had Elastigirl stretch, teenage girls are insecure about themselves so I had Violet be invisible and have de-fensive shields while ten-year-old boys are hyperac-tive energy balls so I gave Dash super rocket speed." Another message in the film that Bird ad-mits to is his irritation at a world that has taken away the "specialness" of being special. He has dis-cussed how he watched boys on his son's soccer team who never tried and slept through practices getting the same trophy that the real performers got. It ticked him off, and so he incorporated that theme into the movie where superheroes are forced to act normal because their "specialness" makes others uncomfortable.

Bird not only directed *The Incredibles,* he also pro-vided the voice for one of the audience's favorite characters: Edna "E" Mode. The *Birmingham Post* quoted Bird as having said about the character Edna: "Here's the thing. Superhero movies always have these flamboyant costumes but they never ex-plain who's making them. Every once in a while they halfheartedly present a scene where the mus-clebound hero is sewing in the basement, but I never really bought it. Suddenly this guy's inter-ested in fabric?" During the planning stages Bird had faked an accent and done E's bits to show a po-tential actor what he would want, but everyone liked his version so much they kept it in, to the de-light of many viewers.

In 2005 Bird was still working at Pixar and said that he would love to do his next film with the company. He has thought for a long time that they are one of the greatest studios around. Bird is married and has three sons. One of his sons, Nicholas, did the voice of Squirt in 2003's *Finding Nemo.* What Bird plans to do next is anyone's guess, but many fans are ea-gerly awaiting his next project.

# Sources

### Books

*Contemporary Theatre, Film and Television,* vol. 27, Gale Group, 2000.

### Periodicals

*Birmingham Post* (Birmingham, England), November 23, 2004, p. 11.
*Denver Post* (Denver, CO), November 11, 2004, p. F7.
*Entertainment Weekly,* August 13, 1999, p. 50.
*Evening Standard* (London, England), January 31, 2005, p. 20.
*Grand Rapids Press* (Grand Rapids, MI), March 18, 2005, p. D3.
*Independent Sunday* (London, England), March 20, 2005, p. 36.
*Liverpool Echo* (Liverpool, England), January 31, 2005, p. 3.
*Newsweek,* August 9, 1999, p. 68; November 8, 2004, p. 52.
*New York Post* (New York, NY), October 31, 2004, p. 88; March 13, 2005, p. 84.
*Seattle Post-Intelligencer* (Seattle, WA), January 3, 2005, p. D3.
*Time,* August 16, 1999, p. 65; October 25, 2004, p. 78.
*Variety,* November 1, 2004, p. 27; January 10, 2005, p. S38.

### Online

"An Interview with Brad Bird," IGN.com, http://dvd.ign.com/articles/594/594806p1.html (March 9, 2005).
*Biography Resource Center Online,* Gale Group, 2004.
"Bird masks his secret identity," *USA Today,* http://www.usatoday.com/life/people/2004/11/02/bird/secret/identity_x.htm (November 2, 2004).
"Brad Bird," Internet Movie Database, http://www.imdb.com/name/nm0083348/ (April 13, 2005).

"Brad Bird," Michael Barrier.com, http://www. michaelbarrier.com/Interviews/Bird/Bird_ Interview.htm (April 22, 2005).

"Brad Bird," *New York Times,* http://movies2. nytimes.com (April 15, 2005).

"The Hot Seat: Brad Bird," *New York Post,* http:// www.nypost.com/entertainment/42371.htm (March 13, 2005).

"Interview," Dark Horizons, http://www. darkhorizons.com/news04/bird.php (April 13, 2005).

"Moriarty Interviews Brad Bird, director of the modern animated masterpiece, The Iron Giant!!!," Ain't It Cool News, http://www.aint-it-cool-news.com/moriarty/bradbird.html (March 10, 2005).

"The 77th Annual Academy Awards," Oscar.com, http://www.oscar.com/oscarnight/winners/ win_34473.html (April 13, 2005).

—*Catherine Victoria Donaldson*

# Zach Braff

## Actor, screenwriter, and director

**B**orn April 6, 1975; son of Hal (an attorney) and Anne Braff (a therapist). *Education:* Northwestern University, B.A., 1997.

**Addresses:** *Office*—c/o NBC, 30 Rockefeller Plaza, New York, NY 10112.

## Career

**A**ctor on television, including: *The Baby-Sitters' Club; My Summer As a Girl* (movie), 1994; *Scrubs,* NBC, 2001—. Film appearances include: *Manhattan Murder Mystery,* 1993; *Getting to Know You,* 1999; *Blue Moon,* 2000; *The Broken Hearts Club,* 2000; *Endsville,* 2000; *Garden State* (also wrote and directed), 2004; *Chicken Little* (voice), 2005. Stage appearances include: *Macbeth,* New York Public Theater, 1998.

## Sidelights

**N**ew Jersey actor Zach Braff parlayed his success as the star of the NBC series *Scrubs* into his first feature film, *Garden State,* in 2004. The novice filmmaker wrote, directed, and starred in the quirky coming-of-age tale filmed on location near many of the same New Jersey haunts he frequented in his teens. "Studios, financiers, production companies, they all passed on it," Braff told *New York Times* writer Lola Ogunnaike about his struggle to see his project to fruition. "They kept saying that the film was 'execution dependent,' which is just fancy lingo for 'We'll believe it when we see it.'"

Braff was born in 1975 and grew up in South Orange, New Jersey. His father, Hal, was an attorney who also taught at Rutgers University law school, but acted on the side in community theater productions. Anne, his mother, was a therapist, and Braff was the last of their four children, but he gained several stepsiblings after his parents' divorce and subsequent remarriages.

A creative child, Braff play-acted at home in elaborate shows with the help of a makeshift theater he set up in the attic. He went to acting camp in the Catskill Mountains one summer when he was eleven, and the experience at Stage Door Manor was a formative one, he told Ogunnaike in the *New York Times* interview. "Because I was in the public school system and had no interest in sports, I always felt really alienated," he explained. "Here was this amazing other world where the cool thing was to be an actor and not a lacrosse player. It was the first time in my life that I felt like I belonged somewhere."

At the camp, Braff and his performances were singled out by a talent manager, who encouraged his parents to let him begin auditioning. He tried out for countless parts, but failed to land anything until three years passed—and that was a pilot for a television series that never aired. It starred a young actress named Gwyneth Paltrow, who was also the producer's daughter. Braff had other brushes with future fame during his teens: he lived near siblings Andrew Shue (*Melrose Place*) and Elizabeth Shue (*Leaving Las Vegas*), and attended the same high school, Maplewood's Columbia High, as Lauryn Hill of the rap/R&B group the Fugees.

Braff's sole credit as a teen actor was in one episode of *The Baby-Sitters' Club* when he was 15. At Columbia High, Braff did not appear in any stage productions, but did serve as a director for its television studio. He proved so skilled at it that he won the school's Excellence in Directing award twice—the only student in Columbia history to do so. When he graduated in 1993, he headed to the Chicago area to enroll at Northwestern University, where he studied film. His first minor break came at just before that, however, when he made his movie debut in *Manhattan Murder Mystery,* the 1993 Woody Allen-Diane Keaton comedy. Braff played their son, and years later told Stephanie Snipes in an interview that appeared on CNN.com about his experience. "I was so wide-eyed and terrified. I would love another shot at it," he enthused. "I was only in one scene but it was in a scene with Woody Allen, Diane Keaton, and Anjelica Houston.... When I play it back now I look like I'm a deer in headlights."

While still at Northwestern, Braff appeared in one other role, a made-for-TV movie called *My Summer As a Girl* that aired in 1994. During his summers off, he returned to the New Jersey-New York area and worked in video production, which he continued for a time after graduating with his film degree in 1997. In 1998, he landed an impressive role in a New York Public Theater production of *Macbeth* that was directed by George C. Wolfe of *Bring in 'Da Noise, Bring in 'Da Funk* fame, but the scarcity of work forced him to try his luck on the West Coast. He moved to Los Angeles, California, in 2000, and found a job waiting tables in a French Vietnamese restaurant.

That same year, three small indie films in which Braff had appeared were released: *Blue Moon, Endsville,* and *The Broken Hearts Club.* The last film, in which he played a wild club kid among a close-knit group of gay men, won him some good reviews. "People would come to the restaurant after seeing the movie and say, 'We just saw your movie,'" he recalled in an interview with *San Francisco Chronicle* journalist Carla Meyer. "I'd be like, 'Thanks, yeah, let me tell you about our specials.'"

Braff finally landed a plum role on a new network series, *Scrubs,* which debuted on NBC's fall 2001 line-up. His turn as medical intern as John "J.D."

Dorian won great reviews, and the show quickly emerged as a standout. Braff's portrayal of the inexperienced, accident-prone future doctor quickly gained a cult following, and series creator Bill Lawrence told one journalist that the part was not that much of a stretch for the novice actor. "His situation in real life is close to his character's," Lawrence asserted to *Entertainment Weekly* television critic Bruce Fretts. "Every day at work, Zach's in way over his head. His inexperience has really worked for us."

Though *Scrubs* finished in 38th place in ratings by the end of its first season, NBC executives recognized its promise and moved the show from Tuesdays to Thursdays. Braff, meanwhile, spent his spare time trying to interest someone in his first screenplay. He had written it just before starting *Scrubs,* but after he had impetuously quit the restaurant job. "I found out we weren't going to be starting *Scrubs* for four months, and I sort of panicked," he told Scott Brown in an *Entertainment Weekly* interview. "I didn't have any money, and I was scared I'd quit too early. But then I figured it was a sign to stop procrastinating and really sit down and write the script."

Braff's script centered on a mostly out-of-work Los Angeles actor named Andrew "Large" Largeman, who returns to his New Jersey home for his mother's funeral. He has been overly medicated by his psychiatrist father, but does not bring the Lithium and other mood-stabilizing pills with him. The plot meanders through the funeral, his various encounters with old high school buddies, and a surprise romance with someone who may be as equally troubled as himself. But Braff did not have much luck in drumming up interest in the project, which became *Garden State.* "Almost everyone had passed on it," he told Joel Stein, a writer for *Time.* "They all said, 'Make it a three-act structure movie.' If I submitted it to a screenwriting class, I would have failed."

Finally actor Danny DeVito's production company, aptly named Jersey Films, showed some interest. Braff managed to strike a deal in which he would both direct the film and star in it, though his sole reel was a 25-minute film he made while at Northwestern. Braff was fortunate to find a financial backer in the person of a onetime mortgage banker who had earned a small fortune in the past few years and was interested in moving into the entertainment industry. The novice film producer allowed Braff to direct it, as long as he promised to keep it cheap. He wanted the lead, he told Snipes in the CNN.com interview, because "a part like this, if

I didn't write it, I never would have gotten a chance to even audition for this.... So, I felt like I wanted to give myself a break in the movie world."

Despite its projected low budget, *Garden State* managed to lure an impressive roster of talent: Natalie Portman as Large's love interest, Ian Holm as his chilly dad, as well as Peter Sarsgaard, Jean Smart, and Method Man. Even Wolfe, Braff's *Macbeth* director, had a cameo in it. Braff shot it on location back in New Jersey—though there were suggestions that Canada might be cheaper, he was adamant that it authentically reflect the "Garden State"—and when it premiered at the Sundance Film Festival in January of 2004, it was an audience favorite and incited a small bidding war. Both Miramax and Fox Searchlight bought it, and split the domestic and international distribution rights.

Critics gave *Garden State* mostly positive reviews. Critiquing it for Salon.com, Stephanie Zacharek noted that the television heartthrob-turned-filmmaker's ambitions in making the film were evident. "But Braff … never comes off as a blowhard—not even a fashionably self-effacing blowhard. His motivation feels genuine, as if he wanted to make a movie because he actually had something to say, instead of just wanting to smear his name around as a career move." Like a few other critics, Zacharek faulted the script for a resolution that seemed forced, but conceded that "Braff does capture the sense of coming home to a place you once loved, and realizing, in spite of any lingering fondness you may have for it, that it's no longer the place for you." *Entertainment Weekly's* Lisa Schwarzbaum noted the significance of its title, which is also the official nickname of New Jersey. "But there's something of the Edenic, lowercase meaning that the writer-director-star is after, too, something gummy that gets at nostalgia for the garden state of childhood—however less-than-perfect that childhood actually was."

Braff had little trouble lining up his next jobs after the success of *Garden State*. He was still charming audiences with the *Scrubs* role, and was serving as the voice of *Chicken Little* in the animated feature film of the same name, set for a 2005 release. With his brother, Adam, he co-wrote a screenplay based on a children's book from the 1960s, which they had loved as kids, called *Andrew Henry's Meadow,*

and Braff would both direct and serve as executive producer of the treehouse-utopia fantasy. The film was scheduled for a 2006 release.

Braff's debut film earned comparisons to *The Graduate,* the acclaimed coming-of-age tale that starred a young Dustin Hoffman. He dismissed such accolades with his characteristic dry wit. "It's flattering," he admitted to Brown in the *Entertainment Weekly* interview. "But I don't want to disappoint people. It's not that good." He did realize, however, that *Garden State* resonated with audiences and critics alike, and reflected in the *New York Times* interview that perhaps it was because the themes were more or less universal for many filmgoers. It was certainly his own story before TV stardom arrived, he told Ogunnaike. "That's where I was, lost and depressed and thinking: 'What's going to be the next chapter of my life? Because I need it to start now.' I felt a lot of people in their twenties could relate to that feeling, praying for an epiphany, praying for some clarity, something that would come along and open their eyes."

## Sources

### Periodicals

*Entertainment Weekly,* November 23, 2001, p. 35; September 13, 2002, p. 86; August 6, 2004, p. 52, p. 59.
*New Jersey Monthly,* August 2004, p. 70.
*New York Times,* July 25, 2004, p. AR13; July 28, 2004, p. E5.
*People,* August 30, 2004, p. 87.
*San Francisco Chronicle,* August 8, 2004, p. 20.
*Star-Ledger* (Newark, NJ), January 11, 2004, p. 1.
*Time,* July 26, 2004, p. 68.
*Vanity Fair,* July 2004, p. 99.

### Online

"Garden State," Salon.com, http://www.salon.com/ent/movies/review/2004/07/28/garden_state/ (November 10, 2004).
"'Scrubs' Star Writes What He Knows," CNN.com, http://www.cnn.com/2004/SHOWBIZ/Movies/08/16/zach.braff/index.html (November 10, 2004).

—*Carol Brennan*

# Rose Marie Bravo

*Bloomberg News/Landov*

## Chief Executive Officer of Burberry

**B**orn Rose Marie La Pila, c. 1951, in the Bronx, New York, NY; daughter of a hair-salon owner and a seamstress; married and divorced; married William Jackey (a retired furniture executive), c. 1983; children: two stepchildren. *Education:* Graduated from Fordham University, c. 1971.

**Addresses:** *Office*—Burberry Ltd., 29-53 Chatham Pl., Hackney, London, B9 6LT, United Kingdom.

## Career

**B**egan career as a trainee buyer for Abraham & Strauss, 1971; hired as assistant buyer, Macy's Department Store chain, 1974; promoted to buyer and then administrator; in 1983 became group vice president for cosmetics, contemporary sportswear, and coats, then senior vice president of merchandising until 1988; served as chief executive of I. Magnin stores, 1988-92; president of Saks Holdings, Inc., 1992-97; joined Burberry as chief executive, 1997.

## Sidelights

**A**merican retail executive Rose Marie Bravo led the British raincoat maker Burberry Ltd. into an unprecedented turnaround since taking over as chief executive officer in 1997. Bravo's talents, which include a savvy marketing expertise and impeccable fashion sense, have served to double sales for the once-beleaguered company and make it into one of the youngest, hippest luxury brands. She is one of the highest-paid executives in Europe, and has been called "a brand name herself in the fashion world" by *Fortune* magazine's Lauren Goldstein.

Born in the early 1950s, Bravo is a native of the New York City borough of the Bronx, where she was grew up as Rose Marie La Pila. Her father ran a hair salon on 181st Street, and while her mother was a seamstress by profession. As a young teen, Bravo won admission to the prestigious Bronx High School of Science, and went on to Fordham University, also in the Bronx. She majored in English literature, and graduated almost two years ahead of schedule by taking summer classes.

Bravo's first job after college had little to do with her choice of major: in 1971, she was hired as a trainee buyer for Abraham & Strauss, a New York City department store chain. Three years later, she moved on to Macy's Department Stores, the landmark Manhattan retailer, with a job as an assistant buyer. She moved up through the ranks to become an administrator, and in 1983 was promoted to the position of group vice president responsible for cosmetics, contemporary sportswear, and coats for Macy's; later in the decade she became senior vice president of merchandising.

In the department-store acquisition mania of the 1980s, Macy's acquired I. Magnin, the California-based retailer with a reputation as the West-Coast home for luxury fashion. Bravo was tapped to head it in 1988, and relocated to Magnin headquarters in San Francisco. Over the next four years, she led the company through an impressive turnaround, despite some immense odds, including the gutting of its recently renovated Los Angeles flagship store in the 1992 riots. That same year, Bravo took over as president of Saks Fifth Avenue, a high-end retailer with a reputation for carrying an impressive international roster of designer goods. Bravo began adding a number of hipper luxury labels with a younger target market to its sales floor, such as Gucci and Prada, and made its cosmetics counters a leading launch space for new fragrance lines from designers.

Bravo was said to be in possession of a fabled personal Rolodex, giving her access to some of the most famous names in fashion, and used it to revitalize Saks and make it a destination for fashionistas and younger shoppers alike. Her impressive turnaround helped the retailer emerge as a publicly traded company in 1996, but there were industry rumors that she and Saks chair Philip Miller did not agree on some issues. In 1997, Bravo shocked the fashion world by taking over at Burberry, the venerable British raincoat manufacturer that had fallen on hard times. Founded in 1856 by Thomas Burberry, the man who invented gabardine, the company was known for its high-end raincoats with a distinctive signature plaid. But its British parent company, Great Universal Stores (GUS), was said to have neglected it over the years, and had sacrificed brand prestige for profit by selling goods in bulk on the so-called "gray market" in Asia.

Once again, Bravo left her hometown for a new job, moving to London and beginning what are known as her trademark 12-hour days in a rather unprepossessing office space above Burberry's London factory. She closed some of the costly raincoat factories that were still in England, installed new computer and manufacturing systems, and secured the services of a young Italian-American designer, Roberto Menichetti, to retool the Burberry look. Menichetti designed a line of Burberry women's clothing that made a stunning runway debut at the ready-to-wear collections in 1999. There was also an ad campaign—once again, likely using Bravo's unerring ability to call in favors—shot by *Vogue* photographer Mario Testino and featuring models Kate Moss and Stella Tennant, whose own ultra-hip, "Cool Britannia"-identities helped reinvigorate the Burberry brand immensely.

Under Bravo's guidance, Burberry morphed into Prorsum, the high fashion line, then a core collec-

tion called Burberry London and, thirdly, a younger, hipper line of clothing with the label "Thomas Burberry." The results were stunning: in 2001, the British journal the *Economist* claimed that the country "is in the grip of Burberry mania. Two years ago, the label was shunned by all but Asian tourists for its naff plaid-lined raincoats that not even dead men would be caught wearing. Today, everyone from Posh Spice to Cherie Blair, who wore Burberry to the state opening of Parliament, is sporting its signature camel, black and red plaid design." Valued as a company worth $360 million in 1997 when Bravo took over, in seven years that figure had increased nearly ten times, to $3.4 billion.

Bravo's London triumph had not been an easy one, she later noted. "Burberry was a mess," she told the *Economist.* "I had many evenings of tears. My parents visited me ... and asked: 'You left Fifth Avenue for this?'" But her faultless sense of what the fashion world wanted next was recognized several times over by her GUS bosses, and she is one of the most well-compensated executives in the retail industry. In 2002, she topped the list of the highest-paid European executives with a $9.2 million salary package. Though Bravo rarely gives interviews, she has said more than once that her rise to the upper echelons of fashion retailing was not that unusual, given her original start in cosmetics. There, she noted, sharp business minds were already commonplace, and her role models were from an earlier generation, such as Estée Lauder and Helena Rubenstein. "If you've been given this road map and you see that others have gone before you and achieved, you never have in your mind the notion of failure," a journalist from Glasgow's *Herald* newspaper, Beth Pearson, quoted Bravo as saying. "You have the notion that you can do it too, if you're good enough and smart enough and make the right decisions."

## Sources

*Economist,* February 3, 2001, p. 7.
*Forbes,* April 3, 2000, p. 84.
*Fortune,* November 9, 1998, p. 154.
*Herald* (Glasgow, Scotland), August 7, 2004, p. 17.
*Time,* February 16, 2004, p. 30.
*WWD,* April 18, 1988, p. 75; September 5, 1997, p. 1.

—*Carol Brennan*

# Berkeley Breathed

**Cartoonist, author, and illustrator**

Born June 21, 1957, in Encino, CA; son of John William and Martha Jane (Martin) Breathed; married Jody Boyman (a psychologist), May 10, 1986; children: two. *Education:* University of Texas at Austin, B.A., 1980.

**Addresses:** *Contact*—c/o Washington Post Writers Group, 1150 15th St. N.W., Washington, D.C. 20071. *Home*—Santa Barbara, CA.

## Career

Syndicated by the Washington Post Writers Group, 1980-95 and 2003—; wrote and illustrated comic *Bloom County,* 1980-89; wrote and illustrated comic *Outland,* 1989-95; wrote and illustrated comic *Opus,* 2003—. Also writer and illustrator of children's books.

**Awards:** Pulitzer Prize for editorial cartooning, for *Bloom County,* 1987.

## Sidelights

Comic-strip artist Berkeley Breathed found himself in the glare of publicity in 1987 when he won the Pulitzer Prize in editorial cartooning for his comic strip *Bloom County.* The controversy stemmed from the fact that his strip appeared not on the editorial page but rather on the comics page, though he used the space to comment on the issues of the day. Traditional editorial cartoonists thought the award belittled their craft. No one could argue,

however, that the strip was not well-read. During its heyday *Bloom County,* with its motley crew of anthropomorphic prairie creatures, children, and eccentric adults, was syndicated in 1,300 newspapers and achieved a cult following. The driving force behind the snicker-inducing cartoon was a big-hearted, tuba-playing, politically astute penguin named Opus, whose neurotic worldview charmed millions of readers each day. Breathed ended the strip in 1989, then created a new one, *Outland,* which ran until 1995. In 2003, Breathed resurrected his famous character in a Sunday-only strip simply titled *Opus.* He has also written and illustrated several whimsical children's books.

Breathed (pronounced BRETH-id) was born June 21, 1957, in Encino, California. He attended high school in Houston, where he was reportedly a cheerleader and was known to peers as "Guy." Next, Breathed headed to the University of Texas (UT) at Austin to study photojournalism. While there, Breathed worked as a photographer for UT's *Daily Texan* and also wrote for the campus magazine. Already, Breathed's unbridled ingenuity was emerging and the student journalist acted in highly unethical ways.

In a rare interview the reclusive artist granted to the online newsmagazine the *Onion,* Breathed admitted to manipulating photographs during this time, once by burning a halo into a photo of a street preacher. He also invented stories that he knew would create a buzz. "I wrote about an unnamed student who secretly released hundreds of baby alligators into nearby Lake Travis, which would have been compelling if I hadn't made it up," he recalled to Tasha Robinson of the *Onion*. Breathed even went so far as to provide the newspaper with a staged photograph of the anonymous student releasing an alligator into the lake. "I was turned in by nearly 200 people," Breathed told *Times-Picayune* reporter Jeff Baker. "My apartment was surrounded by federal game agents. I was tailed, my phones were tapped.... I was driven out of Austin." Breathed's fake story initially caused property values around the lake to drop and he caught the ire of the owners and even endured an arrest. After the incident settled down, someone suggested Breathed might be better suited for the cartooning desk, where his sense of imagination would be better received.

Breathed took the advice and created a comic strip called *Academia Waltz,* which appeared in the *Daily Texan* during the late 1970s. In some ways, the 658-episode strip served as a prequel to *Bloom County.* Some of the characters Breathed conjured up for this strip later appeared in *Bloom County.* They included cigarette-smoking frat boy Steve Dallas and Vietnam vet Cutter John. During this time, Breathed also revealed his passion for commenting on the political through caricatures of then-UT president Peter T. Flawn.

Even in college, Breathed preferred to stay away from the limelight and remained a somewhat elusive figure. The *Texan* "was sort of like family, really," the newspaper's former editor Beth Frerking told the *Star-Telegram*'s Robert Philpot. "Everybody was friends, loved each other, hated each other, dated each other, socialized together. It really was one big group. He wasn't really a part of that, but I never got the feeling that it was a hostile thing." Others remembered Breathed as arrogant; still others said he was simply misunderstood.

Whatever the case, his strip, itself, was well-understood and caught the attention of the Washington Post Writers Group. The group contacted Breathed about syndicating *Academia Waltz.* Instead, Breathed revealed his vision for a new strip called *Bloom County,* and the Washington Post Writers Group picked it up. *Bloom County* debuted on December 8, 1980, in just two dozen papers. By the late 1980s, the strip was syndicated in 1,300 newspapers worldwide.

*Bloom County* featured a lovable maladjusted penguin named Opus, who got his name from a song by the 1970s art-rock band Kansas. In the early years, Breathed endured a lot of criticism from readers who believed the strip was a clone of Garry Trudeau's *Doonesbury.* Admittedly, Breathed said

his gags resembled Trudeau's and the two exchanged heated letters for a while. Like *Doonesbury, Bloom County* helped usher in a new age of cartoons that hinged on both political and pop culture references. At times, Breathed created a ruckus with the social commentary and satire projected in his cartoon. He wrote strips denouncing cosmetic testing on animals and also touched on feminist issues and political patronage. Some managing editors wanted to place *Bloom County* on the editorial page, but he resisted.

This created even more of a stir in 1987 when Breathed won the Pulitzer Prize for editorial cartooning for his comic strip. Traditional editorial cartoonists like Pat Oliphant lashed out in rage, believing that giving the award to an everyday strip cartoonist demeaned their craft. According to the *Star-Telegram*'s Philpot, Oliphant, a 1967 Pulitzer winner, called *Bloom County* a strip of "shrill potty jokes and grade-school sight gags." Breathed retaliated with his pen, introducing to *Bloom County* a new penguin named Ollie Phant. Ollie was portrayed as a begrudging character, jealous of Opus' success. Breathed also got into trouble in the late 1980s for insisting on using the term "that su--s" instead of simply saying "that stinks." Some papers canceled subscriptions. He also explored a gay storyline with one character.

Speaking to the *Onion,* Breathed acknowledged that while doing the strip it was actually hard for him to write about topics he felt passionate about. "One rule: The more pissed-off you are about something, the less funny you are. Never good to get involved. I couldn't, for instance, do justice to animal experimentation. Not funny strips. Effective, though: We got dear Mary Kay to stop squeezing her cold cream into the eyes of rabbits. But not funny." While the strip was highly popular, Breathed, himself, has generally been ambivalent in accepting praise. Years after the strip ended, he said there are many of his own strips he simply does not think are funny and blamed it on his notorious pushing of deadlines. Breathed has said many strips were drawn at 4 a.m. in a sleep-deprived fog.

After a successful nine-year run, Breathed ended *Bloom County* in 1989, saying he wanted to quit while he was ahead. The challenge of turning out a daily cartoon can be draining, acknowledged Ohio State University Cartoon Research Library curator Lucy Caswell. "A lot of people don't realize how hard it is to stare at a blank sheet of paper every day, with no days off and no one else to help," she told Anthony Violanti of the *Buffalo News.*

Breathed returned soon enough. A month after *Bloom County* folded, he began creating a Sunday-only strip called *Outland.* The strip featured new characters, but Opus reigned supreme, and slowly, other characters snuck back into the panels. "They were like in-laws," Breathed told *Psychology Today* writer William Whitney. "You send them home, try to get on with your life, and then wham, doggone if it's not Thanksgiving again." Not that readers minded seeing some of their old favorites. *Outland* ran until 1995. It was never as popular as *Bloom County*, appearing in just 300 newspapers.

When Breathed gave up cartooning in 1995, he turned his attention to writing and illustrating children's books. Over the next decade, he published several, including 1995's *A Wish for Wings That Work: An Opus Christmas Story*, 1997's *Red Ranger Came Calling*, 2000's *Edwurd Fudwupper Fibbed Big*, and 2003's *Flawed Dogs: The Year End Leftovers at the Piddleton "Last Chance" Dog Pound*. This last book was a treatise on animal adoption. Breathed has adopted three dogs from shelters himself. In addition to his book-writing and cartooning, Breathed is an avid activist in People for the Ethical Treatment of Animals (PETA). As such, he drew the cover for PETA's *The Compassionate Cook: Please Don't Eat the Animals!*. He has also been involved with the Sea Shepherd Conservation Society, which works to help endangered whales and other sea creatures.

In 2003, after an eight-year absence from newspaper comic sections, Opus reappeared in a Sunday-only self-titled strip. While fans lauded *Opus,* some in the cartoon industry have been more critical. Newspaper comics page handler Mike Peterson told *Editor & Publisher*'s Dave Astor that *Opus* is "not a bad strip, but there are other people doing equally good work and some doing better work.... I think its main appeal is for people who wish *Bloom County* had never ended." Besides bringing back Opus, several other Breathed staples have slipped into the strip over the past couple years. Among them, Steve Dallas and the anti-Garfield, hairball-spitting Bill the Cat. Breathed said he was partly spurred to return to cartooning because he realized he still had more to say. As he told the Washington Post Writers Group for a profile on its website, "It was painful to sit through the Iraq war without a public voice." Like *Outland, Opus* appears only on Sundays, meaning Breathed has to create just four strips a month as opposed to 30. The demands of a Sunday-only strip fit better with Breathed's life. Married in 1986 to psychologist Jody Boyman, Breathed is busy raising two children.

For die-hard *Bloom County* fans looking for a storyline fix that once-a-week plotlines cannot deliver, Breathed, in late 2004, published *OPUS: 25 Years of His Sunday Best*. The book features Breathed's favorite strips from *Bloom County, Outland* and *Opus*. In reviewing the old strips to decide which ones to include, Breathed told the *Boston Globe*'s Steve Greenlee that they all seemed fresh to him. "I remember virtually none of them. True, if you saw how most of them were actually executed (3 a.m., in a fog of narcotics and caffeine, slapping myself in the face with a ruler to stay awake), you will believe this normally unbelievable claim." In the end, Breathed said he chose only to include the ones that made him chuckle.

During the process, Breathed also tweaked some of the classic cartoons. He acknowledged that his difficulty with deadlines accounted for some of the less profound, more juvenile material. "Traditionally, I've been very rough on my stuff," he told Baker in the *Times-Picayune*. "I never thought it was as good as the readers did, and it pained me to read it. I was appalled at how much overwritten verbiage there was—it was like I didn't trust myself to put across an idea in a few words—so I rewrote a few of them and blamed it on the deadlines."

While some remain critical of Breathed's new *Opus* venture, others in the industry are delighted that he is drawing again. "There's all sorts of cartoonists out there, and there's something nice to be said about every one of them," Washington Post Writers Group comics editor Suzanne Whelton told Philpot in the *Star-Telegram*. "But Berkeley is very unique in my mind. It's good to have him back."

## Selected writings

*The Academia Waltz*, 1979.

*The Academia Waltz: Bowing Out*, 1980.

*Bloom County: Loose Tails*, Little Brown & Co., 1983.

*Toons for Our Times: A Bloom County Book of Heavy Metal Rump 'N Roll*, Little Brown & Co., 1984.

*Penguin Dreams and Stranger Things*, Little Brown & Co., 1985.

*Bloom County Babylon: Five Years of Basic Naughtiness*, Little Brown & Co., 1986.

*Billy and the Boingers Bootleg*, Little Brown & Co., 1987.

*Tales Too Ticklish to Tell: Bloom County*, Little Brown & Co., 1988.

*Night of the Mary Kay Commandos Featuring Smell O-Toons*, Little Brown & Co., 1989.

*Classics of Western Literature: Bloom County 1986-1989*, Little Brown & Co., 1990.

*Politically, Fashionably, and Aerodynamically Incorrect: The First Outland Collection*, Little Brown & Co., 1992.

*His Kisses are Dreamy ... but Those Hairballs Down My Cleavage ... !: Another Tender Outland Collection,* Little Brown & Co., 1994.

*One Last Little Peek, 1980-1995: The Final Strips, the Special Hits, the Inside Tips,* Little, Brown, 1995.

*A Wish for Wings That Work: An Opus Christmas Story,* Little, Brown, 1995.

*Goodnight Opus,* Little, Brown, 1996.

*Red Ranger Came Calling,* Little, Brown, 1997.

*Edwurd Fudwupper Fibbed Big,* Little, Brown, 2000.

*Flawed Dogs: The Year End Leftovers at the Piddleton "Last Chance" Dog Pound,* Little, Brown, 2003.

*OPUS: 25 Years of His Sunday Best,* Little, Brown, 2004.

## Sources

### Periodicals

*Boston Globe,* November 1, 2004, p. B7; December 6, 2004, p. B7.

*Buffalo News* (New York), November 23, 2003, p. E1.

*Editor & Publisher,* June 1, 2004.

*Psychology Today,* January/February 2004, p. 96.

*Times-Picayune* (New Orleans, LA), December 5, 2004, p. 4.

### Online

"Berkeley Breathed," *Onion,* http://avclub.theonion.com/feature/index.php?issue=3728&f=1 (February 21, 2005).

"Berkeley Breathed," Washington Post Writers Group, http://www.postwritersgroup.com/comics/opus/berkleybio.html (February 21, 2005).

"Opus Pocus," *Star-Telegram* (Fort Worth, TX), http://www.dfw.com/mld/dfw/living/7420625.htm?1c (February 20, 2005).

*—Lisa Frick*

# Poppy Z. Brite

Photo by J.K. Potter. Courtesy of Poppy Z. Brite.

## Author

**B**orn Melissa Ann Brite, May 25, 1967, in New Orleans, LA; daughter of Bob and Connie (Burton) Brite; married Chris DeBarr (a chef). *Education:* Attended University of North Carolina, Chapel Hill, 1987.

**Addresses:** *Office*—Three Rivers Press Author Mail, c/o Random House 1745 Broadway, New York, NY 10019.

## Career

**F**irst short story published in *The Horror Show,* c. 1985; worked as candy maker, short-order cook, mouse caretaker, artists' model, and exotic dancer, 1985-91; published first novel, *Lost Souls,* 1992.

## Sidelights

**N**ew Orleans-based writer Poppy Z. Brite garnered a devoted readership for her trio of gory but sensual horror-fiction novels in the early 1990s. Brite was still in her mid-twenties when she debuted as a novelist, and has struggled to break out of the goth-lit genre since then. She earned a small fortune for her biography of rock diva Courtney Love, and in 2004 published *Liquor,* a novel about a cleverly themed New Orleans restaurant. In an interview with Troy Patterson of *Entertainment Weekly,* Brite talked about the difficulties she encountered in transcending the cannibal-vampire- bloodbath realm her readers expected from her. "I need *Liquor* to be—not to be on the *New York Times* best-seller list—but to do respectably well," she reflected. "I really do feel like a first- time novelist."

Brite was a writer from a very early age. Born Melissa Ann Brite in 1967 in New Orleans, she spent her first years there, while her father taught economics at the University of New Orleans. She was reading by the age of three, and was writing and illustrating her own books by kindergarten. When her parents divorced, she moved to Chapel Hill, North Carolina, with her mother. She began sending short stories to magazines and publishers while still in middle school, and in high school launched her own underground newspaper, *The Glass Goblin.*

A small but influential magazine called *The Horror Show* bought Brite's story "Optional Music for Voice and Piano," which became her first published piece. The magazine had a small but influential readership, and subsequent stories of hers that appeared eventually brought an inquiry from Douglas E. Winter, the biographer of horror-fiction master Stephen King. Winter had been hired as a consultant for a planned hardcover line of new horror novels, and contacted Brite while she was enrolled at the University of North Carolina in 1987. As she recalled on her website, Winter had "liked my stories, and he wondered whether I had a novel in the works. I'd just begun my freshman year at the University of North Carolina and was hating it. That letter decided my future. I dropped out of college and began working on what would become *Lost Souls.*"

But the publishing house that hired Winter eventually decided against the hardcover series, and Brite's finished manuscript languished on her desk after she was unable to interest any other publisher. The writer Harlan Ellison had read her short stories, however, and had been bowled over by them; at an industry event where she recalled being too shy to approach her idols, Ellison came up to her and introduced himself. He helped her get a literary agent, who then shopped the *Lost Souls* manuscript around. Dell was interested, and Brite was signed to a three-book deal. In 1992, after solid sales in paperback, *Lost Souls* appeared as the first book in the new Abyss imprint from Delacorte, which was Dell's parent company.

*Lost Souls* was an immense success with younger readers, who loved its modern, decadent, Goth-music-scene milieu. The story was anchored by the story of an adopted teen who learns that his real father is a rock star and vampire named Zillah. A reviewer for *Publishers Weekly* called Brite's debut a "stylishly written, daringly provocative first novel" in which she "creates a convincing, evocative atmosphere in which youthful alienation meets gothic horror." Brite was also hailed as the successor to Anne Rice, another New Orleans-based writer of gothic vampire tales whose "Vampire Lestat" series became a publishing phenomenon and major motion picture.

Thanks to her book deal, Brite was finally able to concentrate solely on her writing after a string of jobs that included stints as a laboratory-mice caretaker, candy maker, and exotic dancer. Her highly anticipated second novel, *Drawing Blood,* appeared in 1993. Its story is set in a haunted North Carolina house where one of its protagonists had lived as a small child before his underground comic-book artist-father murdered the rest of the family and then hanged himself. The now-adult Trevor, also a graphic artist, returns to the small town and falls in love with Zack, a computer hacker and fugitive. Thanks to Zack and the help of psychedelic substances, Trevor is able to enter "Birdland," the bizarre comic world his father created, to confront him about the horrific slayings and exorcise his own demons. A *Publishers Weekly* reviewer, who liked its mix of spooky haunted-house and cybercrime themes, asserted that the second novel from Brite's pen would confirm her place not only "in the horror genre, but also as a singularly talented chronicler of her generation."

*Drawing Blood* was the first of Brite's works to feature two male lovers, which would become a recurring characteristic of her fiction. Its follow-up, her

third in the Dell deal, came after she had published a collection of short stories, *Swamp Foetus,* and served as co-editor of an anthology of vampire erotica. The delay came because of Dell's hesitancy about publishing *Exquisite Corpse,* Brite's third novel. It followed the romance and cannibalistic bloodbath of two serial killers, loosely based on the real-life murderers Jeffrey Dahmer and Dennis Nilsen.

*Exquisite Corpse,* its title borrowed from an old parlor trick of the Surrealist artists' clique of the 1920s, was acquired by Simon & Schuster and appeared in 1996. Reviews were mixed. *New Statesman* journalist Kim Newman felt Brite was maturing as a writer, noting that "the prose here is much shapelier, with convincing and acidly witty talk in between delicately described violence." A review from Robert Armstrong of the Minneapolis *Star Tribune* reminded readers that her work "deals with characters and situations every bit as amoral and terrifying as anything imagined by Bret Easton Ellis in *American Psycho.* Brite is strong stuff and not for the squeamish." A critic for *Publishers Weekly* found some fault with the plotting, but asserted "Brite is a highly competent stylist with a knack for depicting convincing, if monstrous, characters."

That same *Publishers Weekly* article termed Brite "the reigning queen of Generation-X splatterpunks," and she had a serious fan following that even included the occasional stalker. She was prone to making controversial statements in interviews about sexual politics, and was open about her own escapades into the realm. Such fearlessness attracted the interest of Courtney Love of the band Hole, who read Brite's novels and then contacted her. Love talked the fiction writer into penning her first biography, and Brite earned a cool half-million dollars for *Courtney Love: The Real Story,* published by Simon & Schuster in 1997.

Brite had been eager to try her hand at other types of writing, though few authors would have been eager to work with the infamous Love, who was also the oft-maligned widow of Nirvana singer Kurt Cobain. But Love provided Brite with access to journals she had written as a teenager, and Brite uncovered court transcripts that shed light on Love's tragically dysfunctional family. Her mother, for example, had won custody of the child after claiming that Love's father had given her a hallucinogenic drug. "The chilling details of Love's childhood from hell are what save this book from being just another celebrity clip job," wrote *Entertainment Weekly's* Dana Kennedy, and commended Brite for admirably depicting Love's "nightmarish family and her stints in foster homes, reform schools, and strip clubs so effectively that the book briefly transcends its genre. It's a snapshot of a '60s hippie couple and their abysmal child-rearing practices that would be fascinating even if Love weren't famous."

The money that Brite earned from the Love biography enabled her to take some time off. She wrote a few short stories, and worked on a novella that was published by a small imprint in 2000. *Plastic Jesus* was the story of a hugely successful 1960s pop group, an obvious stand-in for and tribute to the Beatles, whose songwriting duo are also carry on a secretive romantic relationship. Years after the group dissolves in rancor, one of the pair is murdered by a homophobic fan.

By the time *Plastic Jesus* appeared, Brite was married and living back in New Orleans after a stint in Athens, Georgia, where she had met her husband, chef Chris DeBarr. As she recalled in the interview with Patterson of *Entertainment Weekly,* she had started to write another full-length horror tale in the summer of 2000, but "I didn't like it." She told her husband one day, she recalled in the interview, "'I'm just so sick of my stupid depressing novel, I'm just gonna go upstairs and write something fun.'"

The result was *Liquor,* a love story set in a New Orleans restaurant, but there was little interest from publishers. Brite was forced to find a new agent to help her land a deal with a company interested in seeing her move out of the goth-horror market. In the interim, she issued a prequel, *The Value of X,* which came out in 2002 and established the early relationship of two teenaged best friends, John Rickey and Gary "G- Man" Stubbs, from *Liquor.* Issued by Three Rivers Press in 2004, the food-centered *Liquor* finds the pair living in New Orleans and on their way to fulfilling a long-cherished dream: their own restaurant.

The twist in *Liquor* is that every item on the menu of their new venue contains some form of booze, and the plot hinges upon some squalid events involving their untrustworthy financial backer. Yet the behind-the-scenes restaurant drama was the real story, many reviewers asserted. "Although Brite rolls her eyes aplenty at the silly dramas and pretensions inherent in any urban restaurant scene, her affection for it is heartfelt," noted a *Publishers Weekly* reviewer. As the spouse of a professional chef, Brite explained why she chose to set the novel in an eatery. "It's just an entire nighttime subculture that completely slips under the radar of people who eat in restaurants," she told *New Orleans Magazine* journalist Katie Block. "They have no idea what's going on behind those kitchen doors."

Brite's latest book did not earn very much attention in the media, save for a sympathetic feature article in *Entertainment Weekly* about her battle to break free of the horror-fiction category. Her admirers seemed divided into two camps: the goth-horror base, and gay readers. From the former group she earned a few death threats for failing to issue another gorefest, while *Gay & Lesbian Review Worldwide* critic Marshall Moore liked it. "Her hallmark lush prose and sometimes overwhelmingly horrific imagery have given way here to a leaner and more realistic approach, yet she also doesn't shortchange the reader on description and setting," wrote Moore.

Brite is a longtime fan of John Kennedy Toole, who wrote a classic novel of New Orleans called *A Confederacy of Dunces* but could not find a publisher for it. He committed suicide in 1969, and the work was published posthumously and went on to win the Pulitzer Prize. She dedicated *Liquor* to Toole's memory, and tends to his grave in Greenwood Cemetery in the city. She hoped her latest novel would bring her new readers, despite the odd trajectory of her themes, from cannibalistic-ritual murders to modern haute cuisine. "I've pretty much lost my interest in writing horror," she told Block in the *New Orleans Magazine* interview. "I love to read it, but it's just not where my interests lie at the current time."

## Selected writings

*Lost Souls,* Delacorte, 1992.
*Drawing Blood,* Delacorte, 1993.
*Swamp Foetus* (stories), Borderland, 1993; later published as *Wormwood: A Collection of Short Stories,* Dell, 1996.
(Editor, with Martin Greenberg) *Love in Vein: Twenty Original Tales of Vampiric Erotica,* HarperPrism, 1994.
*Exquisite Corpse,* Simon & Schuster, 1996.
(Editor, with Martin Greenberg) *Love in Vein II: 18 More Tales of Vampiric Erotica,* HarperPrism, 1997.
*Courtney Love: The Real Story* (biography), Simon & Schuster, 1997.
*The Lazarus Heart* (part of "The Crow" series), HarperPrism, 1998.
*Are You Loathsome Tonight?* (stories), introduction by Peter Straub, afterword by Caitlin R. Kiernan, Gauntlet, 1998.
*Seed of Lost Souls,* Subterranean, 1999.
(And illustrator) *Plastic Jesus* (novella), Subterranean, 2000.

(With Caitlin R. Kiernan) *Wrong Things,* Subterranean, 2001.

(With Caitlin R. Kiernan) *From Weird and Distant Shores,* Subterranean, 2002.

*The Value of X* (limited edition), Subterranean, 2002.

*Liquor,* Three Rivers Press, 2004.

(With Christa Faust) *Triads,* Subterranean, 2004.

## Sources

### Periodicals

*Billboard,* October 11, 1997, p. 85.

*Entertainment Weekly,* October 10, 1997, p. 84; April 30, 2004, pp. 120-122; May 21, 2004, p. 6.

*Gay & Lesbian Review Worldwide,* May-June 2004, p. 44.

*Lambda Book Report,* October 2001, p. 12.

*New Orleans Magazine,* April 2004, p. 22.

*New Statesman,* August 9, 1996, p. 48.

*Publishers Weekly,* September 7, 1992, p. 78; October 4, 1993, p. 65; June 24, 1996, p. 45; September 21, 1998, p. 79; September 4, 2000, p. 88; January 26, 2004, p. 228; April 12, 2004, p. 43.

*Star Tribune* (Minneapolis, MN), August 17, 1997, p. 16F.

### Online

"Biography," Poppy Z. Brite Official Site, http://www.poppyzbrite.com/bio.html (September 2, 2004).

*Contemporary Authors Online,* Gale, 2002.

—Carol Brennan

# James Burrows

*Jeff Vespa/WireImage.com*

## Television director and producer

**B**orn James Edward Burrows, December 30, 1940, in Los Angeles, CA; son of Abe (a writer, composer, and director) and Ruth (maiden name, Levinson) Burrows; married and divorced; married Debbie, 1997; children: three daughters. *Education:* Received undergraduate degree from Oberlin College, 1962; received graduate degree from the Yale School of Drama, 1965.

**Addresses:** *Agent*—Broder Kurland Webb Uffner, 9242 Beverly Blvd., Ste. 200, Beverly Hills, CA 90210-3731.

## Career

**D**rove a truck for a theater company; assistant stage manager for *Holly Golightly* on Broadway, 1967; stage director at Arlington Park Theatre, Arlington Park, IL, early 1970s, and in San Diego; began career as television director on the *The Mary Tyler Moore Show,* CBS, 1974; directed episodes of *The Bob Newhart Show, Rhoda, Laverne & Shirley,* and *Taxi,* among many others, during the 1970s; series co-creator and producer of *Cheers,* NBC, 1982-84, and executive producer, 1984-93; also directed 240 of the show's 275 episodes; television director for numerous other series, including *Wings, Frasier, Friends, 3rd Rock from the Sun, Caroline in the City* and *Dharma & Greg*; executive producer, *Will & Grace,* 1998—, and director.

**Awards:** Emmy Award, National Academy of Television Arts and Sciences, for outstanding direction in a comedy series, for *Taxi,* 1980 and 1981, and for outstanding individual achievement in directing a comedy series, 1991, for *Cheers,* and 1994, for *Frasier*; has also shared Emmys with colleagues in the outstanding comedy series category for *Cheers,* 1983, 1984, 1989, 1991, and *Will & Grace,* 2000; Directors Guild of America award for outstanding directorial achievement in a comedy series for *Cheers,* 1982, 1991, for *Frasier,* 1994, for *Will & Grace,* 2001.

## Sidelights

**T**elevision legend James Burrows has had a hand in perfecting a long list of top-rated sitcoms, from *The Mary Tyler Moore Show* to *Friends* and *Will & Grace.* One of the industry's most highly paid directors, he continues to reap lucrative syndication profits from reruns of the long-running *Cheers,* which he created. His uncanny sense for the timing of an actor's quip have made him, according to *New York Times* television critic Bill Carter, "the man whose visual style and comedic instincts have helped create more comedy hits than anyone else in television."

Burrows comes from a show-business background. Though he was born in Los Angeles in 1940, he grew up in New York City, where his father, Abe, was a noted Broadway VIP as a writer, composer, and director of some of the era's leading stage musicals. The senior Burrows' credits include the books for *Guys and Dolls* and *How to Succeed in Business Without Really Trying,* and his son gained first-hand experience of the craft when he accompanied his father to the office. "I used to suggest jokes all the time," Burrows recalled in the interview with Carter in the *New York Times.* "Abe would be very nice and say, 'I'll think about it.'"

Burrows sang in the Metropolitan Opera Boys Choir during his youth, but chose Oberlin College in Ohio when it came time to leave home. "I had no desire to go into show business! New York was my father's town, and I was just Abe's kid," he explained to *Broadcasting and Cable* writer Caitlin Kelly. His aversion to the arts was so marked by the time he wrote his Oberlin application essay that he asserted, "I don't have any real plans for the future. However, math and science interest me most," according to *Plain Dealer* reporter Sandra Clark.

After majoring in government, Burrows graduated in 1962 and seemed to have a change of heart, winning a spot in the playwriting program at the Yale School of Drama. He started in show business at the relative bottom, as a truck driver for a theater company, and rose to the position of assistant stage manager for a 1967 musical based on the hit movie *Breakfast at Tiffany's. Holly Golightly* was a notable flop, but it did serve to introduce Burrows to Mary Tyler Moore, its star.

By the early 1970s, Burrows was directing theater productions in suburban Chicago and in San Diego. Turning on the television one Saturday evening, he caught the now-famous Moore in her new sitcom, *The Mary Tyler Moore Show* on CBS. "I said, 'Gee, they're doing a little 20-minute play every week and here I am in summer stock doing a two-hour show every week,'" he recalled in an interview for a *Newsweek* profile by Cheech Marin. "If I can do two hours, I can do 20 minutes."

Burrows contacted Grant Tinker, who was both Moore's husband at the time and president of the production company that created the hit show, and asked for a job. The first episode he directed was "Neighbors," which aired on December 7, 1974, and featured Mary's boss, television station manager Lou Grant (Ed Asner) moving into an apartment in the same building as Moore's likable, single-career-girl character. Burrows has called his experience on the show an excellent training ground, noting that Tinker's stable of sitcom writers were a particularly talented, opinionated bunch, and he learned how to cull the best from them as well as translate their ideas into a formula that struck a chord with viewers. Watching veteran director Jay Sandrich—

whose credits included *I Love Lucy*—work with *The Mary Tyler Moore* writing staff was crucial to his own development as a director, Burrows asserted. "You can't teach comedy, but you can teach someone how to feel empowered," he told Kelly in the *Broadcasting and Cable* article. "He taught me to do that."

Burrows earned just $200 week when he began working for Tinker's company, and went on to direct episodes of spin-offs from Moore's show, including *Rhoda* and *Phyllis.* He also directed episodes of the hit ABC sitcom *Laverne & Shirley* before signing on to a quirky new sitcom project set in a New York City taxicab dispatch-center, *Taxi.* In 1980, he won what would be the first of many Emmy Awards.

In the early 1980s, Burrows teamed with brothers Glen and Les Charles, who had been writers on both *The Mary Tyler Moore Show* and *Taxi,* to create a sitcom based on a group of regular patrons at a Boston bar. The series became *Cheers,* which debuted on NBC in 1982. Recalling the moment in the pilot episode when the portly Norm (George Wendt) strode through the bar's entrance, and the bartender said his name—in what would be the signature moment of every episode—and then asked "Whaddaya know?" to which Wendt's character replied, "Not enough," Burrows said the studio audience erupted in laughter. "I said, 'They know who this guy is! They're not laughing at a joke, they're laughing at an attitude!'" Burrows told Josh Wolk in *Entertainment Weekly.* "That was when I knew we had something special."

Few others seemed to agree with that notion, however. *Cheers* suffered dismal ratings during its first weeks on the air as the well-written show struggled to find its audience, but NBC executives failed to move quickly enough to cancel it. "They had nothing to put on in its place," he told Kelly in *Broadcasting and Cable.* The show went on to become one the best-loved and immensely successful sitcoms in television history, and Burrows' role in that achievement was inarguable: he directed all but 35 of its 275-episode run, and won another four Emmys in his capacity as a producer of the series and his third as a sitcom director.

Burrows won another Emmy as a director in 1994 for the *Cheers* spin-off, *Frasier,* and by then had become one of the most sought-after directors in television history for his talent in translating sitcom laughs into ratings gold. In 1995 alone, four of the six pilots he directed for the fall lineup were greenlighted for a full season, including *News Radio* and *Caroline in the City.* He was also involved in another top-rated NBC sitcom by then, *Friends,* in which his production company had also invested. From that point onward, Burrows directed episodes for nearly every hit comedy on the three main broadcast networks for years to come. These included *3rd Rock from the Sun, Dharma & Greg,* and *Will & Grace.*

Any director so prolific must have a few duds on his resume, and Burrows' include *The Tortellis,* an early *Cheers* spin-off, and a 1995 Tony Danza cop comedy called *Hudson Street.* Burrows has also directed one feature film during his long career, a 1982 Ryan O'Neal gay-cop caper, *Partners,* that tanked at the box office. He vowed never to try a feature-length film movie again. "I don't like the two years you have to spend on them," he explained to Carter in the *New York Times.* "I like the instant gratification, the eight-days-and-out of one of these shows. You know when you shoot in front of an audience if it's good."

Burrows has said that his background in theater provided the best training ground for directing sitcoms. He always films before a live studio audience, and rarely watches the camera or the actors, preferring instead to pace—as his father liked to do—and listen. "I listen for the rhythms, I listen for a missed line, for a setup to a joke that's wrong," he told *Electronic Media* journalist Michael Schneider. Every year, about 30 scripts for sitcom pilots land on his desk, and he chooses from these the ones he wants to direct. Not surprisingly, his involvement nearly always ensures a hit—though he does not always stay to direct the entire season; only with the shows to which he is firmly committed—such as *Friends*—does he remain on board. In those cases, his production company, 3 Sisters, which he named after his trio of daughters, antes up a financial stake. Such deals often bring lucrative rewards down the line, when a show enters the profitable syndication phase.

Burrows makes nearly a thousand times what he first earned during his *Mary Tyler Moore Show* days, commanding $200,000 per pilot episode. He also has a hand in casting a new series, and once fired Lisa Kudrow from the pilot of *Frasier,* replacing her radio-producer character Roz with Peri Gilpin instead. "I didn't think she was right," Burrows explained to Wolk in *Entertainment Weekly,* about Kudrow, but he did hire her back a year later when he was working on *Friends*; Kudrow and her five fellow unknowns went on to command $1 million-per-episode salaries on that show, a sitcom-industry record. "She forgave me in about the third year," Burrows joked in the same interview.

Burrows prefers to work with relatively unfamiliar actors when involved in a series pilot, and explained the reasoning behind this in the interview with Kelly in *Broadcasting and Cable.* "Ninety percent of comedy is surprise. If you have a known quantity in a particular role, you're already premeditating and adapting to what you think they'll do," he declared. "I look for people who don't look like they'll be funny."

Burrows made a surprising return to directing live theater in 1998, at the urging of *Frasier* star John Mahoney. He helmed a Chicago stage production of *The Man Who Came to Dinner* at the city's acclaimed Steppenwolf Theatre, and the show went on to a run at London's Barbicon Theatre with Burrows at the helm still. He still strongly believes that the best sitcom experience hits all the same marks as a successful stage play. "I guess what I bring is the sense of the ensemble, the sense that these actors have been with each other for a long time," he reflected in the *New York Times* interview with Carter. "And I do it by creating a lot of stuff that's not necessarily on the page."

In that same interview, Burrows also admitted that he labored under his legendary father's shadow for years. "He was the pre-eminent man on Broadway for years, and I grew up with that," he told the newspaper. "I never thought I could exceed him in anything." As an Emmy-winning television director and recipient of four prestigious Directors Guild of America awards as well, Burrows admits that he may have indeed finally found his niche, and it was not in math or science. "When I was growing up I never thought I'd be as good as my father," he told Marin in the *Newsweek* article. "I'm now coming to terms with the fact that maybe in my field I'm as successful as he was in his."

## Sources

### Books

*Contemporary Theatre, Film and Television,* vol. 36, Gale Group, 2001.

### Periodicals

*Broadcasting and Cable,* January 24, 2005, p. 4A.
*Electronic Media,* September 21, 1998, p. 1; August 20, 2001, p. 1.
*Entertainment Weekly,* March 26, 2004, p. 30.
*Newsweek,* September 11, 1995, p. 73.
*New York Times,* May 14, 1995, p. H1.
*Plain Dealer* (Cleveland, OH), October 11, 1996, p. 1B.

—*Carol Brennan*

# Amanda Bynes

## Actress

**B**orn Amanda Laura Bynes, April 3, 1986, in Thousand Oaks, CA; daughter of Rick (a dentist) and Lynn (an office manager) Bynes.

**Addresses:** *Agent*—c/o Endeavor, 9701 Wilshire Blvd., tenth floor, Beverly Hills, CA 90210. *Office*—c/o Tollin/Robbins Productions, 10960 Ventura Blvd., second floor, Studio City, CA 91604. *Website*—http://www.amandabynes.com.

## Career

**A**ctress in television, including: *All That,* Nickelodeon, 1996-2000; *Figure It Out,* Nickelodeon, 1997-2000; *The Amanda Bynes Show* (pilot), Nickelodeon, 1999; *The Amanda Show,* Nickelodeon, 1999-2002; *Rugrats* (voice), Nickelodeon, 2001; *What I Like About You,* The WB, 2002—. Film appearances include: *Big Fat Liar,* 2002; *What a Girl Wants,* 2003.

**Awards:** Kids' Choice Award for favorite TV actress, Nickelodeon, 2003; Kids' Choice Award for favorite movie actress, Nickelodeon, 2003; two additional Kids' Choice Awards for favorite TV actress, Nickelodeon.

## Sidelights

**A**fter beginning her career as a young comedic actress on the hit Nickelodeon sketch comedy show *All That,* Amanda Bynes soon moved on to her own program, *The Amanda Show,* also on Nickelodeon, before venturing into prime time network television and feature films. From an early age, Bynes was known for her comic timing, and often compared to Lucille Ball, of whom Bynes is a big fan. Her physical comedy was featured in her second feature film, 2003's *What a Girl Wants.*

Born Amanda Laura Bynes on April 3, 1986, in Thousand Oaks, California, Bynes is the daughter of Rick and Lynn Bynes. Her father worked as a dentist while her mother was an office manager who worked at her husband's practice. Bynes has an older brother and sister, Thomas and Jillian. From an early age, Bynes was interested in comedy and acting, pursuits her father encouraged. Bynes would relate her day at school to him as a young child and her father was amused by the way she told her stories.

To that end, Bynes began acting in plays and attending summer comedy camps. When she was seven years old, Bynes played the youngest orphan in *Annie.* Also at seven, she began taking summer comedy classes at the Comedy Store in Hollywood, California, and auditioning for television commercials. She was not pushed, but did it because she wanted to be an entertainer. By the time she was nine years old, Bynes was taking classes at the Laugh Factory in Hollywood, where she learned how to perform stand-up comedy. She loved being on stage there, and often did not want to get off when her time was up. Bynes told Richard Corliss in *Time*, "I was always kind of goofy. And I had all this energy. Getting to put on wigs and props and doing characters was perfect for me."

When Bynes was ten years old, she was discovered by producers at the graduation showcase for her summer class at the Laugh Factory. The producers, Brian Robbins and Dan Schneider, had been young actors themselves on the hit 1980s situation comedy *Head of the Class*. Robbins and Schneider became producers of programming for Nickelodeon and other networks. They were impressed by Bynes' talent, and interviewed her for their show *All That*, which had been airing since 1995.

Bynes nailed the interview for the youth sketch-comedy show. She told Pamela Mitchell of the *Plain Dealer*, "For the interview, I did my comedy act about what it's like to get the same teacher as your wonderful brother. They thought it was funny. I was … so excited when they told me I was going to be on the show."

In 1996, Bynes joined the cast of *All That*, spending the next four years on the show. She soon developed several of her own regular characters, many of whom played off her broad comedy skills and her perky personality. They included her impressions of Barbara Walters as well as Lucille Ball as the character Lucy Ricardo. (Of Ball, Bynes told Jefferson Graham of USA Today, "She's my idol. She made everybody laugh, and made it possible for women to star in their own shows.") Bynes also created the segment "Ask Ashley," playing a somewhat exasperated girl named Ashley who gave sarcastic advice to dim letter writers. For her work on *All That*, Bynes was nominated for a CableACE Award in 1997.

The producers of *All That* saw Bynes as a breakout talent and in 1999, gave the actress her own program. Robbins told *USA Today*'s Graham in 1999, "Amanda is going to be a really big star. She's so young, but tremendously talented beyond her years." In March of 1999, Robbins shot a pilot starring Bynes that was similar to *The Patty Duke Show* in the 1960s called *The Amanda Bynes Show*. Bynes played two characters: a young actress who had been on a situation comedy who goes to live with her cousin after her show was canceled and the actress's cousin, who leads a normal life in Kansas.

When *The Amanda Bynes Show* was not picked up, Robins and Schneider made a second effort at a vehicle for her which was bought by Nickelodeon. In

1999, they created *The Amanda Show,* which ran for three seasons, through 2002. Her variety show, which featured sketch comedy and animation, first aired as an episode of *All That*. Bynes appeared on both shows for one season, leaving *All That* in 2000. On *The Amanda Show,* she played Amanda as well as other characters. Among her regular characters was Penelope Taynt, who was an odd fan obsessed with Amanda, and Miss Elegance, who acted quite the opposite of her name. She also did an impression of Judge Judy, named Judge Trudy, whose rulings always favored kids. The show received good ratings over its run.

While Bynes was an in-demand actress, she still enjoyed a life outside of show business. She liked to play basketball, shop for shoes, and read mystery novels. When she worked on her shows, she attended a private school for one week a month, and worked with an on-set tutor for the rest of the month. She also had experiences that most people her age never did. In the summer of 1999, she was part of the "All That Music & More Festival Tour" with pop and R&B groups as well as sketches from *All That*. The tour covered the United States.

By the end of the run of *The Amanda Show*, Bynes was ready to leave Nickelodeon behind and move into feature films and network television. She told David Hochman of the *New York Times,* "I knew I didn't want to be a Nickelodeon kid when I was 30. I was having fun but at 15, you don't want to be doing what you did when you were 12." The fall after her Nickelodeon show ended, Bynes moved to a prime time network television program that gave her a chance to appeal to a wider audience.

Bynes was cast for a role on *What I Like About You* on The WB, which was produced by Schneider and Wil Calhoun, who had been a writer/producer with the hit NBC sitcom *Friends*. Bynes played teenager Holly Tyler who was sent to live with her adult, rather uptight sister, played by Jennie Garth, in New York City when their father had to move to Japan for work. Bynes and Garth had good chemistry, and Bynes was allowed to use her physical comedy skills, including slapstick. While the show had good ratings in the beginning, they went down in its second season. That season, *What I Like About You* moved away from the sisters' relationship to focusing on Bynes' teen friendships and related dramas.

As Bynes' star continued to rise, her parents tried to keep her life as conventional as possible. She still attended a regular school for at least part of a year, and had no problems with drugs or alcohol. She avoided Hollywood parties. Bynes told Nancy Mills of the *Daily News*, "So many people comment that I'm much more mature than average. But I'm also still a normal kid. I go to regular school. I live only 40 minutes away from Hollywood. I have great friends. I like to draw, see movies, hang out, talk on the phone, and read." In another interview, with Michael Sheldon of the *Daily Telegraph*, "Innocent is who I am. I don't need to watch my image."

Bynes retained her self-assured, clean image as she moved into feature films. She deliberately waited to do films until she was older so that she would be seen as a more adult actress. In 2002, Bynes made her feature film debut in *Big Fat Liar*, written by *All That* and *What I Like About You* producer Schneider. She played a supporting role to *Malcolm in the Middle* situation comedy teen star Frankie Muniz. Muniz played Jason, who had problems telling the truth, while Bynes was cast as his best friend, Kaylee, a more moral character who had a knack for impersonation. The film is set in Michigan where Muniz's character discovers his term paper has been stolen by an unscrupulous producer and made into a hit film. Jason exacts his revenge on the producer with the help of Bynes' Kaylee. Though *Big Fat Liar* was not highly regarded by critics, Bynes' work in the film was praised.

For her next film, Bynes spent the summer in London, England, filming *What a Girl Wants* (originally called *American Girl*). This marked the first time Bynes went abroad, much like the character she played in the film, though her grandmother accompanied her. Somewhat based on the 1950s film *The Reluctant Debutante*, *What a Girl Wants* focused on Bynes' character's journey of self-discovery. She played Daphne Reynolds, an American teenager who discovers her father is a British aristocrat, Lord Henry Dashwood (played by Colin Firth). Daphne was raised by her American hippie singer mother, Libby (played by Kelly Preston), in New York City. Daphne's parents were never married, and her father did not even know she existed.

As *What a Girl Wants* progresses, Daphne meets her father and his stuffy family. She deals with her father's campaign for a seat in the House of Commons, his engagement to a difficult woman with a difficult daughter of her own, and his male adviser who wants to keep Daphne from her father. The themes of being who you are and being true to yourself were underlined in the film. While *What a Girl Wants* tried to appeal to both adults and teenagers, critics believed it was only for a teen audience and were generally unkind.

As Bynes moved into adulthood, she wanted to continue to work as an actress, but she was also interested in fashion design. Bynes also had plans to attend college, perhaps away from her family. Future film roles were already lined up, including a film called *Lovewrecked*. This was a romantic comedy set at a resort where Bynes' character was to work for the summer.

Bynes attributed all her success to her family. She told Rob Salem of the *Toronto Star*, "I owe everything to my family. My mom's artistic and my dad's funny, so I guess that's where I get it from. They've all been so supportive. My friends, too. I guess that's what keeps me grounded. I have a totally normal life. I love to perform, but [at home and at school] I really try not to be too obnoxious."

## Sources

### Books

*Celebrity Biographies*, Baseline II, Inc., 2004.

### Periodicals

*Boston Globe,* February 8, 2002, p. C9; April 4, 2003, p. C8.
*Boston Herald,* April 6, 2003, p. 59; December 13, 2003, p. 23.
*Denver Post,* April 4, 2003, p. F8.
*Daily News* (New York, NY), February 4, 2002, p. 35.
*Daily Telegraph* (London, England), August 5, 2003, p. 13.
*Gazette,* March 28, 2003, p. D14.
*Girls' Life,* October 2002, p. 54.
*Herald Sun* (Melbourne, Australia), April 3, 2003, p. H8.
*Houston Chronicle,* July 15, 1999, p. YO4.
*New York Times,* October 20, 2002, section 2, p. 27.
*People,* February 25, 2002, p. 101.
*Pittsburgh Post-Gazette,* May 7, 2003, p. E1.
*Plain Dealer* (Cleveland, OH), January 2, 1997, p. 9E.
*Time,* April 14, 2003, pp. 76-79.
*Toronto Star,* February 18, 2002, p. C2.
*Toronto Sun,* March 11, 2002, p. 41; April 5, 2003, p. 34; June 24, 2004, p. 81.
*USA Today,* March 5, 1999, p. 10E.
*Variety,* March 31, 2003, p. 29.

—*A. Petruso*

# Santiago Calatrava

## Architect and engineer

**B**orn July 28, 1951, in Valencia, Spain; married Robertina (an office manager and attorney); children: four. *Education:* Earned degree from Institute of Architecture, Valencia, Spain, 1974; earned two Ph.D.s from Federal Institute of Technology, Zürich, Switzerland, 1981.

**Addresses:** *Office*—Santiago Calatrava S.A., Parkring 11, 8002 Zürich, Switzerland.

## Career

**O**pened architectural firm in Zürich, Switzerland, Calatrava Valls S.A., 1981; expanded to offices in Paris, France, and Valencia, Spain; won first major commission for Zürich's Stadelhofen Railway Station, 1982; designed the Lyons Airport Terminal, France, 1994; Campo Volantin footbridge, Bilbao, Spain, 1998; City of Art and Sciences, Valencia, 2000; Quadracci Pavilion, Milwaukee Art Museum, Wisconsin, 2001; roof of Olympic Sports Complex, Athens, Greece, 2004.

## Sidelights

**S**panish architect Santiago Calatrava gained international attention with a number of high-profile projects, and emerged as one of the world's new leading design visionaries. In 2003, his office was selected to design a new commuter-rail transportation terminal to replace the one that was destroyed during the attack on the World Trade Center, and in the summer of 2004 his soaring arches above a re-designed sports complex in Athens, Greece, became

one of the most enduring images of that year's Summer Olympics. Those arches and the new translucent roof over the main Olympic venue featured, like many of Calatrava's earlier projects, a dazzling display of technical bravado.

Both an architect and a structural engineer, Calatrava was already renowned across Europe for his bridges and public buildings, which may be blindingly white, in defiance of physical laws, or just delightfully kinetic. *New York Times* architecture critic Herbert Muschamp had noted back in 1993 that "the appeal of Mr. Calatrava's work rests largely on their resemblance to religious architecture. Immaculately white, accented with tracery of Gothic lightness, these secular projects are imbued with a sacred aura."

Calatrava was born in 1951 in Spain's Mediterranean coastal city of Valencia, and grew up in nearby Benimamet. His mother's family were of Jewish heritage, but had nominally converted during the Spanish Inquisition of the fifteenth century. His Calatrava surname was an old aristocratic one from medieval times, and was once associated with an order of knights in Spain. Both sides of his family were involved in the agricultural export business. Members of his father's family suffered during the turmoil of the 1930s, when a bloody civil war resulted in a military dictatorship, and as a young man Calatrava was eager to leave behind the repressive atmosphere that endured.

Artistically inclined from an early age, Calatrava dreamed of becoming a sculptor, and began to take classes in drawing and painting at the local arts school when he was eight. In his teens, he traveled to Paris as an exchange student, and also visited Switzerland before returning to Valencia to finish high school. In 1968, just weeks after student and workers' riots had disrupted Paris and made international headlines, he arrived to enroll at the city's lauded Ecole des Beaux Arts, but found it impossible to move ahead with his studies because of the lingering turmoil.

Returning to Valencia, Calatrava enrolled at its Institute of Architecture, a course of study he decided upon after having seen a building by modernist master Ludwig Mies van der Rohe that impressed him tremendously. He also studied urban planning at the school. After graduating in 1974, he was still determined to leave Spain, which would remain under Generalissimo Francisco Franco's dictatorial rule for another two years. He traveled to Zürich, Switzerland, to enroll at the city's Federal Institute of Technology, where Albert Einstein had once studied. He earned two Ph.Ds. from the school, the first in structural engineering and the second in technical science. The structural-engineering training was a somewhat unusual choice of study for an architect, for few in either field are trained in both. But Calatrava was fascinated by the construction of large, load-bearing buildings, and the technical expertise he gained would later make his name as an architect.

At the Zürich institute, Calatrava and his fellow students tried to solve unusual gravity and design challenges. They once built a donut-shaped swimming pool in the rotunda of the school, suspended by cables from the ceiling and made of a transparent sheeting material that allowed viewers to watch swimmers from below. His 1981 Ph.D. dissertation was titled "On the Foldability of Space Frames," and after marrying a Zürich law student he decided to remain in the city. In its first year, his small architectural office was hired to do "roofs for a school or entrances to buildings," Calatrava told Smithsonian's Doug Stewart. "Small things."

That changed in 1982, when Calatrava won a competition asking architects to submit a redesign for the Zürich train station, Stadelhofen. His sketches showed curving avenues leading to the various modes of transportation—for the trains, cars, buses, pedestrians—with steel pergolas supporting a skeletal framework above. The entire building, when finished, seemed to resemble a ribcage. These curving spines, usually of poured concrete but still delicate-looking, would become a hallmark of Calatrava's style. They were inspired quite directly by an actual skeleton: while in school in Zürich, he had once helped a veterinary student complete some drawings for a project, and as thanks the student gave him the skeleton of a dog. Calatrava hung it in his office, and his young son named it Fifi.

Calatrava began winning more design competitions: for a factory in Coesfeld, Germany, in 1985, for a concert hall in Suhr, Switzerland three years later. As a structural engineer, he was particularly fascinated by bridges, and began taking on these projects, too, though local authorities did not usually hire architects to design them. Over the next dozen years, he would complete almost 50 spans around the world, but most of them in Europe. Usually suspension bridges, Calatrava's works were often made from white concrete, which reflected the water's light, and steel cables. They often defied the reassuring standard of symmetry in bridge design, and featured a quirk that resembled something organic, such as a bird's wing in flight. "I love being an architect of bridges," Calatrava confessed to Alan Riding of the New York Times. "[E]very bridge has to be different. It is made for different people, above all for different surroundings. It can be in a horrible urban spot, but it can rescue its environs."

In 1991, Calatrava was chosen to design an immense cultural complex in Valencia that would house a science museum, opera house, and other venues under its 95,000 square feet. A Montjuic telecommunications tower finished in time for the 1992 Summer Olympics in Barcelona, Spain, became a noted symbol of that city, and both works earned international attention and advanced his reputation as an architect to watch. In 1993, Calatrava's profile in North America was boosted by a show at the Museum of Modern Art in New York City.

Calatrava went on to complete a number of other impressive projects during the 1990s. These included a train station for Liege, Belgium, an airport-train station in Lyons, France, and the Oriente Station train terminal in Lisbon, Portugal. "Calatrava," noted Time International journalist Rod Usher, "has a peculiarly animal way with concrete and steel, his buildings evoking huge eyes, venus flytraps, giant birds about to take flight, delicate arrangements of human bones. Many have foldable parts; all rely on the eye of an artist and the calculation of an engineer."

Those moveable parts were sometimes derided by Calatrava's detractors among the architectural community, who claimed they were gimmicks that had little to do with the building's function. But Calatrava explained his philosophy to Stewart in the *Smithsonian* interview, noting that "movement gives an added dimension to form. It makes form a living thing. Instead of thinking of a building as something mineral, like a rock, we can start to compare a building to the sea, which has waves that move, or to a flower whose petals open in the morning. This is a new, more poetic understanding of architecture."

Calatrava's first commission for a major American work was very movable, and equally as controversial: Milwaukee visionaries hired him to expand the city's Art Museum. The original structure dated back to the late 1950s and had been designed by renowned Finnish architect Eero Saarinen. For the new Quadracci Pavilion, Calatrava designed a futuristic, two-pronged shade that could open and close according to the atrium's lighting needs. The two fins, called Burke Brise Soleil—*brise soleil* means "movable shade" in French—did not move altogether smoothly from drawing board to completion, however: no company could come up with a working prototype, so Calatrava became a licensed structural engineer in Wisconsin and took over that part of the job himself. He had the pieces made in Spain and shipped over, all 100 tons in total, with the help of a Soviet transport plane.

When the new museum addition formally opened in October of 2001, the *Milwaukee Journal Sentinel* carried a front-page description by Whitney Gould that called the moment "a sight to take your breath away—an exquisite fusion of the natural and built environments and a reminder of architecture's transforming power, its capacity to make life whole." Gould praised other, more prosaic elements of Calatrava's addition, from its parking garage to its lake views. Referring to the architect of New York City's Solomon R. Guggenheim Museum (inarguably the twentieth century's most famous museum design), Gould asserted that Calatrava's "mastery of scale—especially the tension between restraint and grandeur—would do Frank Lloyd Wright proud."

Calatrava went on to complete a number of other breathtaking works, such as an opera house for Santa Cruz de Tenerife, the largest city on Spain's Canary Islands. In homage to the Canaries' link to the Atlantic Ocean that surrounds it, Calatrava came up with a roof with a massive arc that swooped up and over almost like a tidal wave. In 2003, he was selected to design a New York City terminal site for the PATH commuter line, used by commuters to and from New Jersey. The original terminus had been leveled on September 11, 2001, when the towers of the World Trade Center above it fell. Calatrava was also commissioned to rebuild the Roman Catholic cathedral for the diocese of Oakland, California, which had been heavily damaged in an earthquake some years before.

Calatrava still likes to design bridges. His first on American soil was a $23.5 million footbridge of glass and steel over the Sacramento River in a remote part of northern California. The bridge's main pylon, from which cables were connected to the span, was actually a working sundial. His new roof for the Olympic stadium in Athens resembled a bridge of sorts, too, from afar, with its massive arches. On closer view, its curving white beams, connected by transparent tiles, resembled once again a ribcage, and it was a spectacular showpiece building for the 2004 Summer Games.

Bridge projects for the cities of Venice, Jerusalem, and Dallas were next on Calatrava's agenda, and he had also won a commission for a new hall that would be the permanent home of the Atlanta Symphony. His first residential project in the United States was a new high-rise called the 80th South Street Tower in Lower Manhattan, scheduled to open in 2006. The ingenious four-story, cantilevered cubes will rise 835 feet in height, allow residents a four-way view of the city and environs, and are destined to become a skyline landmark.

Calatrava and his family, which includes four children, live in a Park Avenue townhouse in Manhattan. His wife, Tina, the former law student, serves as his business manager, and oversees the details of offices in Zürich, Valencia, and Paris. He continues to be inspired by Fifi, the dog that became a veterinary-school cadaver after a long life as someone's pet. "We see her now without life," Calatrava reflected in the interview with Stewart in the *Smithsonian*, "but once this structure was able to move and run and jump. That to me is almost unbelievable."

## Sources

### Periodicals

*Architectural Review*, February 2001, p. 24.
*Art in America*, March 2001, p. 41.
*House Beautiful*, May 2001, p. 46.
*Independent* (London, England), March 21, 1998, p. 26.

*Milwaukee Journal Sentinel,* October 15, 2001, p. 1.

*New Statesman and Society,* March 18, 1994, p. 49.

*New York Times,* April 9, 1993, p. C26; December 31, 2000, p. 36; October 26, 2003, p. AR1; February 19, 2004, p. F1.

*People,* November 10, 2003, p. 170.

*Smithsonian,* November 1996, p. 76.

*Time International,* January 1, 2001, p. 84.

**Online**

"The Poet of Glass and Steel," *Time,* http://www.time.com/time/2004/innovators/200403/calatrava.html (April 29, 2004).

"Biography," Santiago Calatrava, http://www.calatrava.com/ (August 25, 2004).

*—Carol Brennan*

# Jim Caviezel

*Hubert Boesl/dpa/Landov*

## Actor

**B**orn James Patrick Caviezel, September 26, 1968, in Mount Vernon, WA; son of James (a chiropractor) and Maggie Caviezel; married Kerri Browitt (a teacher), c. 1996. *Religion:* Roman Catholic. *Education:* Attended Bellevue Community College; earned degree in drama from the University of Washington, Seattle; attended the professional acting program at the University of Southern California.

**Addresses:** *Agent*—United Talent Agency, 9560 Wilshire Blvd., 5th Flr., Beverly Hills, CA 90212.

## Career

**A**ctor in films, including: *My Own Private Idaho,* 1991; *Wyatt Earp,* 1994; *Ed,* 1996; *The Rock,* 1996; *G.I. Jane,* 1997; *The Thin Red Line,* 1998; *Ride with the Devil,* 1999; *Frequency,* 2000; *Pay It Forward,* 2000; *Madison,* 2001; *Angel Eyes,* 2001; *The Count of Monte Cristo,* 2002; *High Crimes,* 2002; *Highwayman,* 2003; *The Passion of the Christ,* 2004; *Bobby Jones, Stroke of Genius,* 2004; *The Final Cut,* 2004. Television appearances include: *The Wonder Years,* ABC, 1992; *Children of the Dust* (miniseries), CBS, 1995. Stage appearances include: *The Matchmaker,* Seattle, WA; *Come Blow Your Horn,* Seattle, WA. Also worked as a hay baler, model, and a waiter.

**Member:** Screen Actors Guild.

## Sidelights

**A**lthough Jim Caviezel has been working as a film actor for a number of years, arguably the most prominent role of his career came in 2004 when he played Jesus Christ in the powerful drama *The Passion of the Christ.* Before this film, Caviezel's best known role came in 1998's World War II drama *The Thin Red Line.* As an actor, Caviezel also received press coverage for his refusal to do certain kinds of nude scenes out of respect for his wife and Roman Catholic faith.

Born on September 26, 1968, in Mount Vernon, Washington, Caviezel (pronounced kuh-VEE-zel) is the son of James and Maggie Caviezel. His father was a chiropractor who played college basketball at the University of California at Los Angeles. His mother had studied theater in school. Growing up in Conway, Washington, with his three sisters and one brother, Caviezel was a talented mimic who loved basketball. All five siblings played college basketball. Though Caviezel had the least amount of talent in his family, he also worked the hardest to improve his game.

Caviezel initially attended Mount Vernon High School, then transferred to O'Dea High School, a

Catholic school, because it offered a better chance to play basketball. Caviezel finally graduated from Kennedy High School in Burien, Washington, where he also went to play basketball. After high school, Caviezel spent two years at Bellevue Community College. He attended the school so he could continue to play basketball. The coach of the team said he believed that Caviezel was the hardest worker that he had seen in 30 years.

During his sophomore year, Caviezel suffered an injury which curtailed his basketball playing career. When he transferred to the University of Washington, he was unable to play long term and knew he would never play professional basketball. While recovering from his injury, he stumbled upon acting. Caviezel ended up graduating from the University of Washington with his degree in drama. Basketball, however, informed his career choice. He told Nancy Mills of the *Daily News,* "I never had the talent to be a great basketball player, but basketball took me to college and gave me discipline. It prepared me to be an actor, and it kept me from walking away and quitting when times got tough."

Caviezel began his professional acting career on stage in Seattle. He appeared in productions of plays such as *The Matchmaker* and *Come Blow Your Horn.* Caviezel's first film role came in 1991 in *My Own Private Idaho.* Though he only had two lines in his role as an airline clerk, it led to a Screen Actors Guild card for the young actor.

After *My Own Private Idaho* was completed, Caviezel moved to Los Angeles to further his career. He lived in the home of a friend of a friend for about five years. While Caviezel auditioned for roles, he worked as a waiter at places like Gladstone's. Some of his early roles were on television, including a 1992 guest appearance as a basketball player on *The Wonder Years.*

To further his craft, Caviezel auditioned for and was accepted at Juilliard. He planned on studying there beginning in 1993. But when he was cast in a small role in the film *Wyatt Earp,* he decided to take the role. Around the same time, Caviezel was diagnosed with Attention Deficit and Hyperactivity Disorder. He also had problems with dyslexia.

In *Wyatt Earp,* Caviezel played Warren Earp, the brother of the title character. Though he appeared in only a few scenes of the biographical western, he charmed director Lawrence Kazden and was asked to stay for the whole shoot. Caviezel followed this

up with a television role. In 1995, Caviezel appeared in a miniseries on CBS, *Children of the Dust.* Though he auditioned for many other roles in television and film, including the hit prime-time soap *Melrose Place,* he was considered odd by some casting directors and was often rejected. What attracted some and repelled others was Caviezel's intensity and focus.

As Caviezel's acting career started to build, he married Kerri Browitt around 1996. The couple met on a blind date set up by Caviezel's sisters. A high school English literature teacher, she had played college basketball in Washington. In addition to a love of basketball, the pair shared common, deeply held religious beliefs.

In 1996 and 1997, Caviezel had small roles in Hollywood films of varying quality. In *Ed,* a baseball comedy featuring *Friends* star Matt LeBlanc, Caviezel played a member of the baseball team. The monkey in the film outplayed his character to become the team's third baseman. In the more intense drama *The Rock,* Caviezel played a fighter pilot. The actor only had a few lines in the critically panned *G.I. Jane,* which starred Demi Moore. Caviezel played a rather unintelligent Navy SEALs recruit.

Caviezel received the first big break of his career when he was cast in the 1998 film *The Thin Red Line.* Helmed by acclaimed director Terrence Malick, the film was an adaptation of a popular book about World War II. An ensemble piece, *The Thin Red Line* featured many Hollywood big names as well as relative unknowns like Caviezel. His character, Private Witt, was a native of Kentucky who often went AWOL and did not always understand the war. Though not originally written that way, Caviezel's Witt ended up being the central character in Malick's musings on war after the film was edited.

Because Malick cast Caviezel in his film and enjoyed working with him, more quality rules came the actor's way. Director Ang Lee cast Caviezel as a leader in his Civil War drama *Ride with the Devil.* In 2000, Caviezel had the lead in *Frequency,* a popular dramatic film about time travel. He played John Sullivan, a homicide cop who lives in contemporary New York City. Using a short-wave radio, Caviezel's Sullivan is somehow able to communicate with his fireman father, who has been dead for years, before his death. Caviezel's character tries to stop his father's death, which happened in a warehouse fire 30 years earlier. The actor was attracted to the role in part because eight months before filming started, Caviezel's own father had open heart surgery.

Though Caviezel primarily appeared in dramatic roles, he did not just appear in big-budget films. In 1999, he shot the independent film *Madison,* which was not released until 2001. The film focused on the hydroplaning racing circuit. Caviezel played an engineer in a small town who fought to keep a hydroplaning racing tournament in his community, though San Diego was trying to lure it away.

However, most of Caviezel's roles were in mainstream films. In 2000, he played a homeless heroin addict in *Pay It Forward.* The young lead in the film brings Caviezel's character into his family's home. The following year, Caviezel had the male lead in the thriller *Angel Eyes.* He played a man suffering from amnesia who has a connection to a police officer played by singer/actress Jennifer Lopez. Caviezel gained notoriety for the role because he refused to do a nude love scene with Lopez. He declined because he believed it would disrespect his relationship with his wife.

Despite such stances, Caviezel's acting career continued to progress. In 2002, he played the lead in an adaptation of *The Count of Monte Cristo.* Based on the classic novel by Alexander Dumas, Caviezel's character was the hero Edmond Dantes. Dantes is held in prison under false circumstances for 13 years. His imprisonment is the result of a betrayal by his best friend and after escaping from prison, Dantes exacts his revenge. Caviezel was attracted to the role in part because of his faith and the theme of redemption that underlined the film's action.

Caviezel was known for his intense preparations for his film roles, and *The Count of Monte Cristo* was no exception. In addition to reading the book, he also researched the author, his motivations for writing the book, and what Dumas was interested in. This led Caviezel to Napoleon Bonaparte, the nineteenth century French political and military leader. The actor found what Dumas and Bonaparte had in common, and read related books. Caviezel also learned fencing and other skills.

As an actor, Caviezel took risks, sometimes taking roles out of character. In 2002, he played a supporting role in the thriller *High Crimes.* He played the husband of a character played by actress Ashley Judd. Caviezel's character was a military officer accused of war crimes who switches his identity and is charged with murder. His wife defends him in court. As with *Angel Eyes,* Caviezel would not do certain nude scenes in this film.

Caviezel followed *High Crimes* with another dramatic thriller, 2003's *Highwayman.* The wife of Caviezel's character was killed by a serial killer who uses a 1972 Cadillac El Dorado to murder his victims. Caviezel's character hunts him down to avenge his wife's death.

Caviezel's next film brought him the most attention of his career. When the actor initially met with first-time director Mel Gibson, a well-known actor who appeared in films such as *Mad Max* and *Lethal Weapon,* and his producing partner Stephen McEveety, he was told it was about a role in a surfing film. However, the surfing film was just a ruse to get the actor to talk, while Gibson and McEveety were looking to cast him as Jesus Christ in Gibson's film *The Passion of the Christ.* Though McEveety believed Caviezel was odd, the actor was Gibson's first choice, in part because of his soulful eyes.

Caviezel took the role, which focused on the last hours of Christ's life. He had to learn Aramaic, Hebrew, and Latin for the role, and underwent eight hours of makeup most days of the shoot. But all his preparation for the role could not ready him for the physical suffering he underwent during the production. During scenes in which was beaten, an actor accidentally lashed him twice after missing the boarding that was protecting his back. During the "Sermon on the Mount" scene, he was struck by lightning. Carrying the heavy cross in another scene, he separated his shoulder. The crown of thorns gave him migraines. Shot in Italy in winter, the crucifixion scenes were particularly brutal. A cold wind blew on the actor, who was wearing only a loincloth, and he developed hypothermia.

When *The Passion of the Christ* was released in 2004, Caviezel was praised for his portrayal of Christ. He did not have many lines in the film, but conveyed much of what the character was feeling through his face, body language, and eyes. While Caviezel received accolades, the film itself was controversial among critics. Some critics had problems with the violent, brutal, unflinching look at how Christ was beaten and crucified. Others were unsure how true to the Bible the film really was. Despite the controversy, *The Passion of the Christ* made about $600 million through November of 2004.

Caviezel followed up *The Passion of the Christ* with two other films in 2004. He played another hero, golfer Bobby Jones, in the independent film *Stroke of Genius.* Jones retired at the age of 28 from competitive golf after winning the original Grand Slam of Golf. Though he always played as an amateur, he dominated professional golf. Jones went on to build Augusta National in Georgia, where the Masters

Tournament is still played. Caviezel never played a full round of golf in his life, even after filming ended. Caviezel also appeared as a villain in the science-fiction thriller *The Final Cut* which co-starred Robin Williams and Mira Sorvino.

Of Caviezel's ability to play many types of characters—especially tortured souls—so well, his acting coach, John Kirby, told Richard Seven of the *Seattle Times*, "He has such a soul, such a spiritual center, that it is easier for him to show everything. He's not a cliché. It's real."

## Sources

### Books

*Celebrity Biographies,* Baseline II, 2005.

### Periodicals

*Daily News* (New York, NY), April 23, 2000, p. 14.
*Gazette* (Montreal, Quebec, Canada), January 23, 2002, p. F6.
*Independent* (London, England), March 29, 2002, p. 11.
*Los Angeles Times,* October 15, 2004, p. E10.
*Newsweek,* February 16, 2004, p. 52.
*Observer,* February 29, 2004, p. 5.
*People,* March 22, 2004, pp. 75-76; November 29, 2004, p. 118.
*San Diego Union-Tribune,* April 20, 2004, p. D4.
*San Francisco Chronicle,* December 23, 1998, p. E1.
*Seattle Times,* June 20, 1999, p. 16; April 10, 2000, p. E1; February 22, 2004, p. M1; March 2, 2004, p. D6.
*Star Tribune,* January 25, 2002, p. 10E.

—A. Petruso

# Dave Chappelle

## Comedian, actor, and writer

**B**orn August 24, 1973, in Washington, DC; son of William Chappelle (a voice teacher and college professor) and Yvonne Seon (a Unitarian minister and college instructor); children: two sons.

**Addresses:** *Agent*—United Talent Agency, 9560 Wilshire Blvd., Beverly Hills, CA 90212.

## Career

**B**egan performing in comedy clubs in the Washington, D.C., area, c. 1987; moved to New York City, c. 1990. Television appearances include: *Home Improvement,* ABC, 1995; *Buddies,* ABC, 1996; *Late Night with Conan O'Brien* (guest correspondent), NBC, 1998-99; *Killin' Them Softly* (special), HBO, 2000; *Crank Yankers,* Comedy Central, 2002; *Chappelle's Show,* Comedy Central, 2003—. Film appearances include: *Robin Hood: Men in Tights,* 1993; *Undercover Blues,* 1993; *Getting In,* 1994; *The Nutty Professor,* 1996; *Joe's Apartment* (voice), 1996; *Damn Whitey,* 1997; *Bowl of Pork,* 1997; *Con Air,* 1997; *The Real Blonde,* 1997; *Half Baked,* 1998; *Woo,* 1998; *You've Got Mail,* 1998; *200 Cigarettes,* 1999; *Blue Streak,* 1999; *Undercover Brother,* 2002. Co-author of screenplays, including: *Half Baked,* 1998.

## Sidelights

**D**ave Chappelle hosts the ferocious sketch-comedy series *Chappelle's Show* on cable's Comedy Central Network. On it, he warns viewers that they are watching "America's No. 1 Source for Offensive Comedy," because it features Chappelle and his fellow cast members in daring, often politically incorrect skits that poke fun at racial stereotypes in America. Since its debut in 2003, *Chappelle's Show* has garnered both a cult following and critical accolades. Yet its creator was pragmatic about his success. Referring to the courtroom drama occupying former superstar Michael Jackson, Chappelle noted to an audience in California that "one day people love you more than they've ever loved anything in the world," he reflected, according to a *Sacramento Bee* article by Jim Carnes. "And the next, you're in front of a courthouse dancing on top of a car."

Chappelle was born in 1973, in Washington, D.C., and grew up in one of the tougher areas of the nation's capital. He was the first of three children born to parents who were teachers. They divorced when he was six, but both remained a part of his life and strove to provide him and his siblings with the education and cultural awareness to succeed in life. "We had a picture of Malcolm X over the fireplace," Chappelle told *St. Louis Post-Dispatch* writer Shauna Scott Rhone. "We were like the Huxtables with no money."

Chappelle was referring to television comedian Bill Cosby and the fictional Brooklyn family of Cosby's immensely successful 1980s NBC sitcom, *The Cosby*

*Show.* He once read an article about Cosby's background, not so different in economic status from his own, and that inspired him to make a career out of being the joker in his family and circle of friends. By the time he started high school at the prestigious Duke Ellington School of the Arts in the District of Columbia, he was performing stand-up routines at area comedy clubs. Since he was underage, his mother—who was also an ordained minister—had to accompany him, but he said she had little problem with his hobby. "Crack was king in D.C., and kids my age were getting into incredible trouble," Chappelle explained to the *Plain Dealer*'s Ed Condran. "So it was an easy choice—running the streets doing crack or telling jokes at a nightclub making a little money and getting a lot of experience."

Chappelle's controversial brand of humor did not always win over audiences, and he was once booed offstage during amateur night at New York's famed Apollo Theatre. Forgoing college, he moved to New York City after high school, and found a more receptive audience at a comedy club in Greenwich Village. By the early 1990s, he was being termed one of a new generation of comedians on the scene, and even cited in a 1993 *Time* article in which author Ginia Bellafante wondered if Chappelle was "the brand-new funny Dave," a reference to late-night king David Letterman.

The buzz caused networks and studios to come calling, and Chappelle was offered a number of deals. "I said yes to everything," he told Condran in the *Plain Dealer* interview. "I thought getting a TV show would help make me a star. Little did I know what the reality would be." His first bad experience came with a 1996 ABC sitcom called *Buddies.* The show emphasized the novelty of an interracial friendship between two Chicago guys trying to start their own film-production business, and although 13 episodes were made, only four ever aired.

Chappelle had better luck in films, beginning with roles in comedies like *Robin Hood: Men in Tights* in 1993 and Eddie Murphy's box-office hit of 1996, *The Nutty Professor.* He was eventually signed to a deal with the FOX Network, which gave him executive-producer control of what was slated to be an hour-long show. But network executives allegedly instructed him to diversify his cast, and Chappelle refused. He publicly accused FOX of racism for dictating how many Caucasians they wanted on the series, and the plug was pulled before the untitled project ever went on the air. Closer to home, Chappelle was also experiencing family issues. His father, William, who had become a music professor at

an Ohio college, was ill at the time, debilitated by stroke-related complications that eventually took his life. "It was a lonely, scary time for me. I thought I was done," Chappelle told *New York Times* writer Lola Ogunnaike.

Hollywood remained intrigued by Chappelle's biting, satirical wit, and he wrote a movie with a friend of his from the Greenwich Village comedy-club days, Neal Brennan. Their stoner caper *Half Baked* received predictably lukewarm reviews, but developed a cult following in video and DVD release. In addition to regular appearances as a correspondent on *Late Night with Conan O'Brien,* Chappelle also landed parts in films like *You've Got Mail, Blue Streak,* and *Undercover Brother.* HBO offered him his own special, *Killin' Them Softly,* which aired in 2000.

After Comedy Central offered him his own show, Chappelle returned to work on his original idea for a subversive sketch-comedy series. *Chappelle's Show* premiered on the cable channel in January of 2003, with Chappelle as host and introducing the taped sketches to a live studio audience. They spoofed everything from techno-music car commercials to popular Hollywood movies. One skit was a parody of a wholesome 1950s sitcom, but the family had an unusual name, which forced the actors to utter a controversial racial epithet over and over.

Chappelle's brand of no-holds-barred humor also included his recurring character "Tyrone," an unapologetic crack-cocaine addict. Another recurring joke presented fake-television news updates on the upheavals in the economy caused when reparations checks for slavery began to be issued by the U.S. government. "What fuels this spotty but often funny sketch-comedy series is a kind of laid-back indignation, a refusal to believe that ignoring racial differences will make anyone's life better," wrote *New York Times* critic Elvis Mitchell,

*Chappelle's Show* became the number-one-rated show on Comedy Central, but its popularity proved an obstacle in front of some stand-up audiences. In one Sacramento gig in June of 2004, hecklers kept shouting a punchline from a skit about R&B singer Rick James from the show, and Chappelle walked off the stage for two minutes. When he returned, he chastised the audience, and expressed frustration that his television show was hindering what he really loved: performing stand-up in front of a live audience. In trying to quell the hecklers, he told them that he realized why they liked the show. "Because it's good," *Sacramento Bee* writer Jim Carnes quoted him as saying. "You know why my show is good? Because the network officials say you're not smart enough to get what I'm doing, and every day I fight for you. I tell them how smart you are. Turns out, I was wrong," Chappelle continued.

In May of 2004, Hyperion announced plans to publish Chappelle's first book, *How to Play the Race Card and Win.* He was still working on film projects, including one about a late New York street comic named Charlie Barnett who was an early mentor of his. The Rick James skit was also being shopped around to movie studios in the hopes of turning it into a feature-length film.

In August of 2004, it was announced that Chappelle had signed a $50 million deal with Comedy Central for two more seasons of his show. Under the deal's terms, Chappelle also received a large portion of the series' DVD sales. A collection of the first season of the show became the most successful television-related DVD ever. On September 18 of that year, he hosted a reunion of the R&B/rap group Fugees in Brooklyn, New York. The event was recorded for a concert film/documentary. Later that year, Chappelle hosted the Directors Guild of America Honors and Stevie Wonder's ninth annual House Full of Toys benefit. The start of the third season of *Chappelle's Show* was delayed because Chappelle came down with the flu. The new season was scheduled to debut February 16, 2005, along with the DVD release of the show's second season, but was moved to spring of that year.

Married and the father of two, Chappelle lives in an Ohio farmhouse far from the entertainment-industry epicenters. He credits his own parents for giving him the resources to succeed, including lots of reading materials and a sense of community. "They taught me that if you trust the world, you can do incredible things. I've seen a lot of things and could think the world's a terrible place, but I wasn't raised that way," he told Rhone in the *St. Louis Post-Dispatch* article.

## Sources

### Periodicals

*Billboard,* October 2, 2004, p. 20; December 18, 2004, p. 23.
*Broadcasting & Cable,* July 20, 1998, p. 45.
*Daily Variety,* October 27, 2003, p. 1.
*Entertainment Weekly,* May 10, 1996, p. S8; May 14, 2004, p. 72.
*InStyle,* December 1, 2004, p. 378.
*Jet,* December 21, 1998, p. 55.
*New York Times,* March 23, 2003, p. 24; February 18, 2004, p. E1.
*People,* March 9, 1998, p. 67; March 24, 2003, p. 22.
*Plain Dealer* (Cleveland, OH), April 5, 2003, p. 5.
*Sacramento Bee,* June 17, 2004.
*Seattle Times,* September 27, 2002, p. H5.
*St. Louis Post-Dispatch,* October 1, 1999, p. E3; June 17, 2004.
*Time,* August 2, 1993, p. 63.
*Variety,* January 26, 1998, p. 67.
*Washington Times,* December 23, 2004, p. B6.

### Online

"Chappelle renews for $50 million," CNN.com, http://www.cnn.com/2004/SHOWBIZ/TV/08/03/television.chappelle.reut/index.html (March 2, 2005).

—Carol Brennan

# Patricia Clarkson

## Actress

**B**orn Patricia Davies Clarkson, December 29, 1959, in New Orleans, LA; daughter of Buzz and Jackie (an elected official) Clarkson. *Education:* Attended Louisiana State University, c. 1977-79; Fordham University, B.A. (summa cum laude), 1982; Yale University School of Drama, M.F.A., 1985.

**Addresses:** *Agent*—Gersh Agency, 41 Madison Ave., 33rd Fl., New York, NY 10010.

## Career

**A**ctress in films, including: *The Untouchables,* 1987; *The Dead Pool,* 1988; *Rocket Gibraltar,* 1988; *Everybody's All-American,* 1988; *Tune in Tomorrow,* 1990; *Jumanji,* 1995; *Pharaoh's Army,* 1995; *High Art,* 1998; *Playing by Heart,* 1998; *Simply Irresistible,* 1999; *Wayward Son,* 1999; *The Green Mile,* 1999; *Falling Like This,* 2000; *Joe Gould's Secret,* 2000; *The Pledge,* 2001; *Wendigo,* 2001; *The Safety of Objects,* 2001; *Welcome to Collinwood,* 2002; *Far From Heaven,* 2002; *Heartbreak Hotel,* 2002; *The Baroness and the Pig,* 2002; *Pieces of April,* 2003; *All the Real Girls,* 2003; *The Station Agent,* 2003; *Dogville,* 2003; *Miracle,* 2004; *The Woods,* 2005; *The Dying Gaul,* 2005. Television appearances include: *Spenser: For Hire,* 1985; *The Equalizer,* 1986; *Tales from the Crypt,* 1990; *Law & Order,* 1990; *The Old Man and the Sea* (movie), 1990; *Davis Rules,* 1991; *Blind Man's Bluff* (movie), 1992; *Legacy of Lies* (movie), 1992; *An American Story* (movie), 1992; *Four Eyes and Six-Guns* (movie), 1992; *Queen* (miniseries), 1993; *Caught in the Act* (movie), 1993; *She Led Two Lives* (movie), 1994; *Murder One,* 1995-96; *London Suite* (movie), 1996; *The Wedding* (movie), 1998; *Wonderland,* 2000; *Frasier,* 2001; *The Six Wives of Henry VIII* (miniseries; narrator), 2001; *Carrie* (movie), 2002; *Six Feet Under,* 2002-04. Stage appearances include: *The House of Blue Leaves,* 1986; *Three Days of Rain,* 1997; *A Streetcar Named Desire,* Kennedy Center, Washington, D.C., 2004.

**Awards:** Emmy Award for outstanding guest actress in a drama series, Academy of Television Arts and Sciences, for *Six Feet Under,* 2002; New York Film Critics Circle award for best supporting actress, for *Far From Heaven,* 2002; special jury prize, Sundance Film Festival, 2003.

## Sidelights

**H**ailed as American independent film's newest star, actress Patricia Clarkson won the special jury prize at the 2003 Sundance Film Festival in Park City, Utah. She was honored for her compelling performances in not just one but four different movies, including *The Station Agent,* the acclaimed Tom McCarthy film. Clarkson was also seen in 2002's *Far from Heaven,* Todd Haynes's masterful drama about a faltering marriage in the 1950s.

Clarkson was anything but new to the scene, however. She was 43 years old when she won the Sundance award, and had a career that dated back to New York theater in the mid-1980s. For a time, Clarkson languished in television roles, but her career took off in the late 1990s when individuals who knew her stage work became involved in casting independent films. "Wry, dry, and ruefully self-aware, Patricia Clarkson's performances stand out in current American film like crisp martinis in a soda fountain," asserted Ben Brantley in the *New York Times.* A journalist for London's *Guardian* newspaper, Gareth McLean, also wrote enthusiastically of Clarkson's talents. "She takes on a scarily diverse range of characters and nails every one of them," McLean noted. "Aided by a subtle, willowy beauty, she has a rare talent for transformation" that, he pointed out, also made her one of American cinema's most unrecognized screen stars.

Critics usually note Clarkson's throaty drawl, a by-product of her New Orleans background. She was born the last of Jackie and Buzz Clarkson's five daughters, and had made up her mind that she would become an actress by the time she reached O. Perry Walker High School in the Crescent City. Her mother was a similarly determined woman: she began selling real estate, and was elected to city council in New Orleans; she later went on to a seat in the Louisiana state legislature. Yet Clarkson had inherited the acting talents of her paternal grandfather, who died before she was born. He was a local New Orleans mover and shaker who helped create the city's recreation department, and he also acted in plays at French Quarter theaters. He had even co-founded a theater in the Algiers district of New Orleans.

Like her mother, Clarkson also served a stint in the state capital of Baton Rouge—attending Louisiana State University. She transferred to Fordham University in the New York City borough of the Bronx around 1980, which brought her nearer to the epicenter of American theater. Fordham had an excellent drama program, and for her senior project Clarkson staged a performance of the Henrik Ibsen play *Hedda Gabler.* She graduated summa cum laude in 1982.

Clarkson won a slot at Yale University's prestigious School of Drama, leaving with a graduate fine-arts degree in 1985. That same year, she landed her first television part, as a guest star on the hit ABC series *Spenser: For Hire.* In 1986, she was cast to replace Julie Hagerty (*Airplane!*) in John Guare's *The House of Blue Leaves* on Broadway. The following year, she played the pregnant wife of Kevin Costner's character, Elliott Ness, in the highly anticipated Chicago-mob drama *The Untouchables.* In 1988, she appeared in a little-seen Burt Lancaster film, *Rocket Gibraltar,*

as one of the veteran actor's on-screen daughters. One of her children was played by a then-unknown eight-year-old named Macaulay Culkin.

Roles as moms and wives seemed to make up the bulk of Clarkson's career for the next several years, and she even had a hard time winning new film roles. There was a five-year hiatus between 1990's *Tune in Tomorrow* and her 1995 appearance in the kids' adventure film *Jumanji.* In the interim, Clarkson kept busy with television parts, including the series *Davis Rules* and the miniseries adaptation of the Alex Haley novel *Queen.* That film's title part was played by a young Halle Berry, while Clarkson impressed critics as the vicious wife of the plantation owner who is Queen's secret father.

Clarkson admitted that this was a low point in her life. "I couldn't get a part, and my self-confidence was down. And those two things go hand in hand," she told *Orlando Sentinel* journalist Roger Moore, in a 2003 interview that appeared in the Knight-Ridder/Tribune News Service. "Now, it seems light-years away, like a mere blip in my life. But it wasn't. It was a difficult time."

Just before she turned 40, Clarkson suddenly emerged as the new face in independent cinema. She delivered an impressive performance in *High Art,* a 1998 film written and directed by Lisa Cholodenko (*Laurel Canyon*). Critics commended Clarkson's supporting role as Greta Krause, a heroin addict and German actress who was once a protégé of legendary German filmmaker Rainer Werner Fassbinder. Greta lives in New York with her girlfriend, Lucy, played by Ally Sheedy, an acclaimed photographer who vanished from the art scene after a burst of early promise. Lucy befriends her hesitant, heterosexual neighbor, Syd (Radha Mitchell), and the two begin an affair. Clarkson, noted *New Orleans Magazine* writer Ron Swoboda, "nails Krause cold with a husky Teutonic accent and look, not unlike Marlene Dietrich in slow motion, with the body language to match."

In 1999, Clarkson appeared in *The Green Mile* as Tom Hanks' wife, but began taking small roles in a slew of other films that would be released in 2000 and 2001, including *Joe Gould's Secret, The Pledge,* and the adaptation of the A.M. Homes work of fiction, *The Safety of Objects.* Clarkson also took a part as the flamboyant sister of Ruth, the widow on the acclaimed HBO series *Six Feet Under.* Clarkson's performance earned her an Emmy Award.

In 2002, Clarkson appeared in the heist caper, *Welcome to Collinwood,* and also made what she has called one of her favorite films, *The Baroness and the*

*Pig.* She was cast in the period drama as an American Quaker woman who marries a French baron, settles in Paris, and tries to help a young girl from the countryside. It was never released in theaters.

Clarkson had better luck that year with the critically admired *Far From Heaven,* which starred Julianne Moore as Cathy Whitaker, a 1950s housewife who discovers her husband, played by Dennis Quaid, is gay. Costuming for the film by Todd Haynes (*Velvet Goldmine*) forced both actresses into elaborate period costumes that seemed nearly as constricting as those of an eighteenth-century French aristocrat in Clarkson's previous film. Her part as the best friend and confidante of Moore's character was small, but served to convey the themes that Haynes wanted the story to show: that in middle-class suburban Connecticut, Cathy's attraction to the handsome local florist, who is an African-American man, seems to many a far worse transgression than her husband's furtive sex life.

Clarkson's role as Eleanor Fine in *Far From Heaven* won her a New York Film Critics' Circle award, but she was bypassed for the Academy Award nominations early in 2003. In January, however, she won the unofficial crown of "indie queen" of Sundance, which showcases the best of independent cinema, when she seemed to have a part in nearly every top buzz-worthy entrant of that year's film festival. They were supporting roles, but impressive nonetheless: she was in *All the Real Girls,* a David Gordon Green project in which she portrayed the single parent of a love-struck teenaged son. In some scenes, Clarkson's character gave advice to her son while dressed for her job as a professional clown for children's parties.

Critics also liked Clarkson's performance in *Pieces of April,* an appealing low-budget family drama from Peter Hedges (*About a Boy*'s screenwriter). She played Joy, wife to Oliver Platt's jovial patriarch, and both are en route through Pennsylvania and New Jersey with other family members to spend Thanksgiving with their New Yorker daughter, played by Katie Holmes (*Dawson's Creek*). Mother and daughter have been estranged, but Joy is now terminally ill. *Newsweek* critic Devin Gordon found Clarkson in his film "downright unforgettable. As Joy, a mother with terminal breast cancer, Clarkson is cruel, bitter—and mordantly, marvelously funny." Writing in *Entertainment Weekly,* Owen Gleiberman judged Hedges' efforts unsuccessful, claiming that the filmmaker "shoves his characters into the narrowest of sitcom slots and seals them there.... The one glint of honest comedy in *Pieces of April* comes from Patricia Clarkson's exuberantly hostile performance."

*Pieces of April* finally earned Clarkson her first Oscar nomination, but she lost the Best Supporting Actress statuette to Renée Zellweger for *Cold Mountain.* Clarkson also appeared in yet another Sundance-premiered film that made its way to general release in the fall of 2003, *The Station Agent.* The title character of Fin was played by Peter Dinklage, a rail buff and dwarf who inherits the remote New Jersey station job from a friend. Clarkson's Olivia is a divorced artist, still grieving for her late son, who nearly runs the diminutive Fin over with her car. A quiet bond develops between the pair. Critics commended her portrayal, with the *New York Times'* Elvis Mitchell noting that her entrance into the plot marks a point where the film "takes on a deeper, more tantalizing shape.... Olivia is flushed with pain, and embarrassed by it. The power in Ms. Clarkson's performance comes from Olivia's recognizing parts of herself that she's been suppressing."

Clarkson, who lives in New York City's West Village with her dog, returned to theater in the spring of 2004 in the revival of the Tennessee Williams classic, *A Streetcar Named Desire,* at Kennedy Center in Washington. She was cast as Blanche DuBois, the tragic widow who becomes unglued at any mention of her early, ill-fated marriage. The Southern-belle Blanche comes to live with her sister, Stella, and her ogre-like husband, Stanley, who enjoys taunting Blanche for her airs. Brantley, the *New York Times'* theater critic, lauded "Clarkson's sharp-edged portrayal in this largely spark-free production" and asserted that "her Blanche is unlike any you've seen before."

Several new films—some independent, some mainstream—were next on Clarkson's schedule. They included *The Woods,* a psychological thriller set at a private school in the 1960s, and as the wife of Kurt Russell's coach character in *Miracle,* the story of the 1980 U.S. Olympic hockey team victory over their Soviet counterparts. She was also slated to appear alongside her real-life boyfriend, actor Campbell Scott (*Rodger Dodger*) in *The Dying Gaul,* in 2005. Its story centered on Scott's character, a Hollywood producer who is bisexual. That same year, she filmed *All the King's Men* and signed on to appear in *Goodnight, and Good Luck* and *Conquistadora.*

While admitting that real-life Hollywood is, by reputation, a tough place for a working actress in her early forties, Clarkson is thankful that directors like Cholodenko, Haynes, and Hedges believed in her. "That can be the danger zone, and you're either going to break through or you're going to be struggling," she told *Entertainment Weekly* journalist Gillian Flynn. "And I am lucky, lucky, lucky, that I was able to break through that." Known for tackling roles that often deal with the darker side of life, Clarkson said she refuses to play it safe with lightweight parts. As she explained to *Entertainment Weekly,* "I'm always seeking something that will challenge me, something that will get me going. And frighten me—it's good to be frightened."

## Sources

*Daily Variety,* May 30, 2002, p. 8; January 8, 2003, p. 58; November 12, 2003, p. A1.

*Entertainment Weekly,* November 27, 1992, p. 67; February 12, 1993, p. 45; February 7, 2003, p. 43; June 27/July 4, 2003, p. 41; October 10, 2003, p. 100; October 24, 2003, p. 85; February 6, 2004, p. 68; February 13, 2004, p. 52; March 5, 2004, p. 55.

*Guardian* (London, England), March 24, 2004, p. 24.

*Interview,* November 2003, p. 38.

Knight-Ridder/Tribune News Service, November 14, 2003.

*Los Angeles Magazine,* February 2004, p. 57.

*New Orleans Magazine,* March 2001, p. 38.

*Newsweek,* October 20, 2003, p. 11.

*New York Times,* March 2, 2003, p. 31; October 3, 2003; October 12, 2003, p. ST9; May 18, 2004, p. E1.

*People,* September 12, 1998, p. 17.

*Variety,* November 17, 1997, p. 75; February 2, 1998, p. 29.

*—Carol Brennan*

# Stephen F. Cooper

## Chief Executive Officer of Krispy Kreme Doughnuts

B orn October 23, 1946, in Gary, IN; married Nancie; children: two daughters. *Education:* Occidental College, Los Angeles, CA, B.S., 1968; Wharton School of Business, University of Pennsylvania, M.B.A., 1970.

**Addresses:** *Office*—Kroll Zolfo Cooper, 900 Third Ave., 6th Flr., New York, NY 10022.

## Career

B egan career at Touche Ross & Co., New York City, 1968; helped establish its reorganization advisory group; left c. 1987 to form bankruptcy advisory firm with Frank Zolfo called Zolfo Cooper; firm became Kroll Zolfo Cooper, 2002; also heads Catalyst Equity Partners, a venture fund; has held various executive positions at major corporations, including vice chair and chief restructuring officer of Laidlaw, Inc., 2000, interim chief executive officer of Enron, 2002-04, and chief executive officer of Krispy Kreme Doughnuts, 2005—.

## Sidelights

C orporate-turnaround specialist Stephen F. Cooper became chief executive officer at the troubled Enron Corporation in 2002. Taking over at a crisis-point for the reeling Houston, Texas, energy firm, Cooper created a workable restructuring plan for Enron's bankruptcy process. In early 2005, he moved on to rescue Krispy Kreme Doughnuts. Yet no other mission would ever compare to the complex task he undertook at Enron, whose very name became synonymous with corporate fraud. "Somebody told me that, when they added up the congressional committees and the number of senators or representatives involved in looking at Enron, it's gone well beyond either Watergate or Iran-Contra," Cooper said in a 2003 interview with *Financial Times* writer Alison Maitland, after a year on the job. "This is off the charts."

Cooper was born in 1946 in Gary, Indiana, and earned an undergraduate degree in economics at Occidental College in Los Angeles. He went on to the prestigious Wharton School of Business at the University of Pennsylvania, which granted him his M.B.A. in 1970, but Cooper was already working in finance by then. He had joined the accounting firm Touche Ross & Co. in New York City in the late 1960s, and would spend the next 18 years with it. An emerging bank specialist, he was instrumental in the creation of a reorganization advisory group at Touche Ross, which at the time was one of the world's largest accounting firms.

Cooper's employer belonged to an unofficial group of large United States firms, known as the "Big Eight," that handled the bulk of corporate auditing, the process by which a publicly traded company's books and balance sheets are verified to avert any attempts on the part of corporate officers to defraud investors about the financial health of the company. For decades, Touche Ross, Arthur Andersen, and other Big Eight accounting firms built their business on such contracts, and the independent-auditing process seemed to work as a reliable system to prevent fraud. In 1989, Touche Ross merged with another Big Eight firm, Deloitte Haskins & Sells, to become Deloitte & Touche.

Cooper left Touche Ross in the mid-1980s to start his own corporate-turnaround firm with Frank Zolfo. Over the next several years, Zolfo Cooper emerged as a top bankruptcy consultancy firm, taking on such high-profile clients as Federated Department Stores, the parent company of the Bloomingdale's and Macy's retail chains, in the early 1990s, as well as Trans World Airlines (TWA) and Colt Manufacturing, the vintage Connecticut gun manufacturer. Cooper's team of experts were also involved with the troubled Boston Chicken, and Morrison Knudsen, an Idaho-based engineering and construction firm. Polaroid was another high-profile client for Zolfo Cooper, though the final sale price of $24 million after the camera-maker's bankruptcy earned some criticism for being vastly undervalued.

In most cases, Cooper served merely as a consultant and the frontperson in negotiations with creditors, and not all of the companies headed for bankruptcy court; some could be salvaged by belt-tightening and asset sell-offs before that point. Just before taking over at Enron, Cooper was working with Laidlaw, Inc., and had become its chief restructuring officer and vice chair. Though he had signed on in 2000 to help save Laidlaw—the largest ground transportation company in North America and owner of Greyhound Lines—from bankruptcy, its unwise venture into the healthcare industry via ambulance services a few years before he came aboard had taken the company into a deep financial hole, and Laidlaw was forced to file for bankruptcy anyway in 2001.

The fortunes of Cooper's own firm, which had midtown Manhattan offices, were in far more stable shape. In September of 2002, Zolfo Cooper was sold to Kroll, Inc., a London-based international risk-management firm, in a deal that reportedly netted Cooper some $50 million in cash, and another $50 million to be paid later. He became head of Kroll Zolfo Cooper, a subsidiary of Kroll. By then, Cooper was well-entrenched in the Enron debacle. The company had filed for bankruptcy in early December of 2001, and the widespread nature of its fraudulent business practices dominated news headlines for weeks. Prior to that, it had been the seventh largest company in the United States, and employed some 21,000 workers. It had been formed in the mid-1980s from two other Texas companies, Houston Natural Gas and InterNorth, and gained prominence as one of the first major energy traders. Some of its divisions built power plants and natural-gas and oil pipelines, but it was its impressive trading of commodities on the energy market that secured Enron's reputation in the business press and on Wall Street. *Fortune* magazine even named it the most innovative company in the United States for five years straight between 1996 and 2000.

But Enron's much-ballyhooed vitality was a sham. A lengthy investigation revealed that its corporate officers hid debt, inflated earnings, and moved money around to fool shareholders. Its auditor, Arthur Andersen, was also drawn into the scandal and implicated as well. After rumors that either former New York City Mayor Rudolph Giuliani or onetime General Electric chair Jack Welch would step in to head Enron, Cooper was named the interim chief executive officer (CEO) instead in late January of 2002. He replaced Kenneth L. Lay, who would later be indicted by a federal grand jury on several counts of securities and wire fraud.

Enron's hiring of Zolfo Cooper and the installation of Cooper at the helm was viewed as a good sign for the company's future. Had the U.S. Bankruptcy Court judge appointed a mere bankruptcy trustee instead, it was likely that anything left of Enron would have been sold outright; the appearance of Cooper was considered a portent that the company might be able to right itself. Cooper dismissed any talk that Enron was just a sham company with no real assets. "Our focus is on the future of Enron," a statement issued by his office that first day read, according to a *New York Times* report from Shaila K. Dewan. "Enron has real businesses with real value."

Once he was named the interim CEO, Cooper wasted little time in taking part in the blame game. "The good news is not only do I not know what went wrong, it is literally of no interest to me," he said told reporters in his first hours on the job, according to *Houston Chronicle* journalists Tom Fowler and Eric Berger. "I'm not going to spend my time looking in the rearview mirror, because there are a lot of people here who deserve our best shot of preserving this company." His main challenge was to find ways to repay a mounting debtload that neared $40 billion. His initial task was to devise a reorganization that the bankruptcy-court judge would approve.

Cooper oversaw what went on to be not only the largest bankruptcy case in United States business history, but also the most complex one. Some two-thirds of Enron's staff had been let go, and several investigations were underway: not only was the Securities and Exchange Commission—the federal regulatory agency whose task it is to monitor publicly traded companies to protect investors—investigating the company's fraudulent practices, but there was also a Department of Justice inquiry and even Congressional hearings on the fall of Enron. Even the limousine driver who took Cooper to Enron's lavish high-rise on that first day from the airport demanded that he be paid in cash for the ride.

As interim CEO, Cooper was also there to take some heat. Morale among the remaining employees at the Houston headquarters was abysmal, but the fired employees were even angrier. Many of the thousands who worked or had worked at Enron had 401K savings and retirement plans, in which they were allowed to buy stock in the company, with Enron donating matching shares; when the scope of the financial trickery was revealed in late 2001, the stock price plummeted, and Enron investors suffered heavy losses. Former CEO Lay, however, had dumped a large amount of his Enron stock just before the scandal became public.

In Cooper's first month on the job, he agreed to meet with former employees, many of them irate that their agreed-upon severance payments had been held up by the bankruptcy proceedings; meanwhile, some of the top executives had to be paid bonuses in order to convince them to stay with what appeared to be a sinking ship. At that raucous meeting, one former employee held up a can of shaving cream, and told Cooper that he could no longer afford to buy such luxuries. Cooper did manage, later in 2002, to secure funds from the bankruptcy court in order to help out the fired employees.

In early 2005, several months after Enron finally emerged from bankruptcy, Cooper stepped in to help Krispy Kreme Doughnuts. The North Carolina company dated back to 1937, and for a time was a hot new franchise, especially after a well-received initial public offering of stock in 2000. For a few years thereafter, Krispy Kreme remained a solid performer, according to its quarterly earnings statements, but in May of 2004 it posted its first quarterly loss. Executives blamed the Atkins diet and "no-carb" craze for cutting into donut sales, but then questions were raised about the company's accounting practices. It was revealed that sales had actually been steadily falling since early 2003, but Krispy Kreme executives managed to conceal these by padding figures elsewhere. Once the company admitted that it was under investigation by the SEC, Krispy Kreme's share price plummeted in trading.

Cooper stepped in Krispy Kreme the day after its CEO, chair, and president Scott A. Livengood resigned. Again, he became the interim CEO, but assured employees and investors that the company was not headed for bankruptcy court. "Keeping in mind that I have only been here for eight hours," he said, according to the New York Times's Floyd Norris, "it looks to me that the company has a reasonable level of free cash flow, so I see no reason why this should be a bankruptcy candidate." Three months later, the company was struggling along with a refinancing agreement, and though its stock price had improved little since Cooper took over, the company had not entered bankruptcy.

Despite his talents in helping bring companies out of dire financial straits, Cooper has his share of critics. Many of them are lawyers for shareholders and creditors, and even bankruptcy judges have questioned the fees that he and Kroll Zolfo Cooper receive for their services. At Enron, he earned about $110,000 a month, and his rate at Krispy Kreme was in the neighborhood of $760 an hour. All told, Kroll Zolfo Cooper earned about $20 million annually from Enron. Furthermore, he oversees Catalyst Equity Partners, which is affiliated with Kroll Zolfo Cooper. This is a venture fund that invests in floundering companies, and its clients include some of the biggest names on Wall Street, such as Citibank, J. P. Morgan Chase, and FleetBoston. In some cases, these companies are also creditors of firms in bankruptcy or nearing bankruptcy that have contracted with Kroll Zolfo Cooper for help. Such charges are to be expected in his line of work, he told U.S. News & World Report writer Megan Barnett. "Criticism is bound to turn up somewhere," he asserted. "Our focus is always on the task at hand: maximizing value and returning that to economic stakeholders."

Cooper is married and has two daughters. At his New York office inside Kroll Zolfo Cooper, he keeps a pet lizard in an aquarium on his desk. He is known for his casual dress and sharp sense of humor. He also avoids the word "bankruptcy," preferring "distressed situation" instead. The author of several papers for banking-industry publications that analyze why companies fail, he likes to warn the lay reader that a company's eagerness to please shareholders and institutional investors is a dangerous game. "A lot of the companies we've worked with have gyrated their businesses to meet quarterly or semi-annual or annual expectations about revenues, earnings, balance sheet positioning," he explained in a Financial Times interview with Maitland. "They sacrifice the long-term health of their businesses by jamming steroids into their corporate body every 90 days."

## Sources

### Periodicals

Directors & Boards, Fall 2002, p. 14.
Financial Times, January 30, 2003, p. 12.
Houston Chronicle, January 30, 2002, p. 1; January 31, 2002, p. 1; January 19, 2005.
New York Times, January 30, 2002, p. C7; February 28, 2002, p. C6; January 19, 2005, p. C1.
U.S. News & World Report, May 5, 2003, pp. 26-28.

### Online

"Adventurous Executive Navigates a Tough Job," CareerJournal.com, http://www.careerjournal.com/myc/survive/20030103-pacelle.html (April 13, 2005).

—Carol Brennan

# Jeff Corwin

*Gregg DeGuire/WireImage.com*

## Conservationist, television show host, and biologist

**B**orn Jeffrey S. Corwin, July 11, 1967, in Norwell, MA; married Natasha; children: Maya Rose. *Education:* Graduated from Bridgewater State University with Bachelor of Science degrees in biology and anthropology; graduated from University of Massachusetts at Amherst with master's degree in natural resources conservation.

**Addresses:** *Website*—http://animal.discover y.com/fansites/jeffcorwin/jeffcorwin.html

## Career

**H**elped establish the Emerald Canopy Rainforest Foundation; worked in a field station in Central America; expedition naturalist for the JASON Project, 1994; produced the docudrama *Jaguar Trax*; created and starred in *Going Wild with Jeff Corwin,* Disney Channel, 1997-99; created and starred in *Jeff Corwin Experience,* Animal Planet, 2000—; host of *Jeff Corwin Unleashed,* Discovery Kids, c. 2002—.

**Awards:** Daytime Emmy Award for best performer in a children's series, for *Jeff Corwin Unleashed,* 2004.

## Sidelights

**A**merican conservationist Jeff Corwin never outgrew his childhood fascination with wild animals, when he would routinely bring home salamanders, frogs, and garter snakes. In a 1984 expedition to the Central American country of Bel-

ize, Corwin fell in love with the rain forest and soon began to work as a conservationist, which included the establishment of the Emerald Canopy Rainforest Foundation. After some documentary work and teaching students about wildlife through an interactive computer network project, Corwin helped create and starred in the Disney Channel's *Going Wild with Jeff Corwin.* Since 2000, he has hosted the Animal Planet network's *The Jeff Corwin Experience,* a program that displays Corwin's hammy style as the well-informed animal lover talking about nature and conservation.

Growing up in a small coastal town in Massachusetts, Corwin was fascinated by animals for as long as anyone could remember. At the age of four, a non-venomous garter snake bit him while he was playing in his backyard. When his parents asked him to stay away from snakes, he replied "No." In fact, Corwin eventually started his own menagerie of wild critters. His mother soon learned to frisk him before he could come into the house.

Corwin's love of animals and growing knowledge about them was rewarded when, at the age of 16, he was invited to accompany scientists to the rain forest of Belize in Central America. Corwin's exposure to the rain forest and its teeming animal population led him to become a rain forest conservationist.

After graduating from high school, Corwin attended Bridgewater State University and received Bachelor of Science degrees in biology and anthropology. He also continued his work as an activist to protect the threatened rain forests of South America. He helped establish the Emerald Canopy Rainforest Foundation as a grass-roots organization dedicated to protecting rain forests through habitat conservation and educating the public. Corwin also served as a member of the United Nations Environment Program's Youth Action Committee.

Corwin returned to his beloved rain forests after graduating from college. He lived for three years working in a field station in Central America as he began what he thought would be an academic career in biology. His career goals changed after a documentary film crew came to Belize and asked Corwin to be a part of their project.

"That's when the bell went off," Corwin told Luaine Lee of the Scripps Howard News Service in an article that appeared in the *Pittsburgh Post-Gazette.* "And I said: 'That's what I want to do. People saw it and said, "You might be able to do this, you've got some skills. You could capitalize on it."'"

In 1994, Corwin worked as an expedition naturalist for the JASON Project, which televised live broadcasts from the rain forests of Belize to classrooms. He also produced a docudrama in Costa Rica called *Jaguar Trax.* Nevertheless, Corwin, who was getting married, was struggling to make ends meet. "I gave up a pretty good job working in the field, traveling, on a course of academic research," Corwin told Lee. He added, "I lost my job, lost my security, had to wait tables for five years."

Although Corwin had done television work, like voiceovers, and had learned a lot about the industry, he turned his sights once more to academia and enrolled at the University of Massachusetts at Amherst to work toward a master's degree. Then he got the call. The Disney Channel had seen a demo tape by Corwin and wanted him to create a television show for them.

Corwin made a pilot and Disney picked up the show. The first episode of *Going Wild with Jeff Corwin* was aired in 1997. For the next three years, Corwin co-created, produced and hosted the popular series, which became one of the first computer interactive programs on television.

After *Going Wild with Jeff Corwin* finished its run on the Disney Channel, Corwin completed his master's degree in natural resources conservation and wrote his thesis on Central American bats. But, Corwin's likable personality and infectious enthusiasm for nature and animals were not to be relegated to classrooms and field posts. Instead, he teamed up with the Animal Planet network to create the popular nature show *Jeff Corwin Experience.*

The prime time show premiered in the fall of 2000 and has been one of the network's most successful offerings. Traveling around the globe for ten months of the year, Corwin makes his way through jungles, mountains, rain forests and deserts to reveal animals in their natural habitat and give the audience an education in the process.

Corwin's other efforts at conservation and education include plans to develop a series of books exploring the natural history of endangered species and threatened ecosystems. He is also establishing an interactive museum and environmental education center called the EcoZone. Corwin's alma mater, Bridgewater State College, honored him in 1999 with a doctorate in public education for his efforts to teach the public about sustainable approaches to using natural resources and the importance of conserving endangered species.

Corwin still keeps snakes, a macaw, cats, and a fox as pets at his Massachusetts home, where he lives with his wife, Natasha, who is working on her doctorate in comparative literature. Corwin and his wife welcomed the birth of their daughter, Maya Rose, on July 6, 2003. The high-energy Corwin also finds time to jog between 35 and 40 miles a week. When questioned by Tom Weede in *Men's Fitness* about the importance of staying in good shape for his job, Corwin told about the time he and his film crew were charged by an elephant. "I can't outrun an elephant," Corwin told Weede. "But I sure can outrun the cameraman."

## Sources

### Periodicals

*Men's Fitness,* September 2002.
*People,* July 21, 2003, p. 89.

## Online

"Ellen Earns Daytime Emmy Cred," E! Online, http://www.eonline.com/News/Items/ 0,1,14167,00.html (September 28, 2004).

"Jeff Corwin Experience," Animal Planet, http:// animal.discovery.com/fansites/jeffcorwin/ jeffcorwin.html (September 28, 2004).

"TV Review: Jeff Corwin Stalks Planet's Past and Present Monsters," *Pittsburgh Post-Gazette* Online, http://www.post-gazette.com/tv/20030309 corwin0309fnp4.asp (September 28, 2004).

—*David Petechuk*

# Johnny Damon

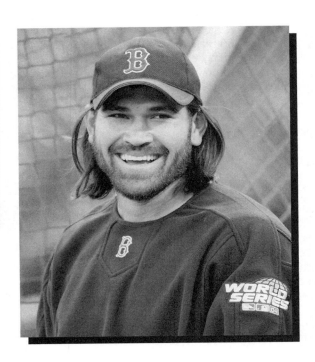

Peter Jones/Reuters/Landov

## Professional baseball player

**B**orn Johnny David Damon, November 5, 1973, in Fort Riley, KS; son of Jimmy (a retired army sergeant) and Yome Damon; married Angie Vannice, 1992 (divorced, 2002); married Michelle Mangan, December 30, 2004; children: Madelyn, Jackson (from first marriage).

**Addresses:** *Home*—Orlando, FL. *Office*—Boston Red Sox, 4 Yawkey Way, Boston, MA 02215-3496.

## Career

**S**igned with Kansas City Royals, 1992; played in minor leagues, 1992-95; played for Kansas City, 1995-2000; played for Oakland A's, 2001; centerfielder, Boston Red Sox, 2002—.

**Awards:** Prospect of the Year, Midwest League managers, 1993; Midwest League All-Star Team, 1993; Player of the Year, Kansas City Royals, 1994; Best Batting Prospect, Best Defensive Outfielder, Most Exciting Player, Carolina League, *Baseball America,* 1994; May Player of the Month, Topps/NAPBL, 1994; Kansas City Royals Organizational Player of the Year, *Baseball America,* 1994, 1995; Player of the Year, Topps/NAPBL's Minor League and Double-A, 1995; Player of the Year, Texas League, 1995; All-Prospect Team, *USA Today,* 1995; Minor League All-Star Team, *Baseball America,* 1995; Double-A All-Star squad, *Baseball America,* 1995; Double-A Player of the Year, *Baseball America,* 1995; named Royals Player of the Month, 1998-2000; won slot on All-Star Team, MLB.com "30th Man Ballot," 2002; Jackie Jensen Spirit Award, Baseball Writers' Association of America, 2004.

## Sidelights

**M**any fans were overjoyed when the Boston Red Sox finally defeated the New York Yankees and went on to win the World Series Championship. This feat had not been done by the Red Sox in 86 years. Most attributed the success to one man, Johnny Damon. The season started with his decision to not cut his hair until they had won. His antics in the locker room helped keep his team loose and stress-free. With each win, the pressure was on for the team's lead-off batter and centerfielder, but Damon was no stranger to pressure.

Damon was born in Fort Riley, Kansas. With his father in the military, the family moved a lot. They settled in Orlando, Florida, where Damon attended Dr. Philips High School. He began his baseball career on the school's baseball team. In his senior year, his coach helped him become one of the best high school players in the country. At each game, the announcer would tout him as "the No. 1 player in the nation on the No. 1 team in the nation." He won a baseball scholarship to the University of Florida, but turned it down and entered the Major League Baseball draft instead. Though many thought he would be acquired in the top ten, Damon, nonetheless, was acquired by the Kansas City Royals at number 35 in 1992.

For the next three years, Damon played in the minor leagues. He received many awards and accolades, including Player of the Year, and impressed the Royals so much that he was thought to be the next George Brett, a former Kansas City Royal and Hall-of-Famer. The two even appeared in a commercial together. In his first seasons with the Royals, Damon did not disappoint. But as far as being the next George Brett, Damon told *Sports Illustrated's* Jeff Pearlman, "I'm no George Brett, and I probably never will be."

Despite posting impressive numbers, and helping his team win many games, Damon, as most other major league players, yearned for the championship ring. A year away from free agency, he announced that he was not looking for a multiyear contract with the Royals. He was traded to the Oakland A's before the start of the 2001 season, but his time with the team was short-lived. His numbers for the season were the lowest of his professional career, but he still managed to lead the club in a couple of records. Damon also ranked high in some of the leagues' yearly records. Many were disappointed as they thought he was the missing component to a championship-winning team. He attributed his poor showing to a couple of things, including adapting to a different form of play and loneliness from being apart from his family, who remained behind in Kansas City. He also lost a former high school teammate, which helped put everything in perspective for him. He told Bob Hohler of *Baseball Digest,* "When you have a friend die young, you realize the game isn't as important as you sometimes make it seem. That's why I'm not that concerned about an O-fer or a tough slump, because I know I have a chance to pull myself out of it."

In December of 2001, Damon signed as a free agent with the Boston Red Sox. In his first season with the Sox, he exploded onto the scene. He led his team with six bunt hits, scored 100 runs, and stole 31 bases, an accomplishment not done by anyone on the Red Sox team since 1994. He was also first in the American League with triples, and second with infield hits, among other accolades. With the addition of Damon, the Boston Red Sox made it to the playoffs, losing only to the New York Yankees.

Damon continued to post remarkable numbers. He averaged .273 with 32 doubles, six triples, 12 homeruns, 67 RBI, 30 steals, and 103 runs scored. Again, the team made to the league championship only to be trounced again by the New York Yankees. Many believed that Damon was behind the team's success. Red Sox hitting coach Ron Jackson told Melissa Segura of *Sports Illustrated,* "People don't realize that he's the guy who makes it all happen here. If Johnny's not rolling, then we don't." However, Damon attributed it to a change in management. He told Pam Lambert of *People,* "When I first got here, it was a bore in the clubhouse. It was like, whoa, no music, no Playstation, no nothing." Under new manager Terry Francona, things changed in the locker room. He continued, "We got the music going.... It's that kind of free style that's propelled us to the next level."

That season was not without its difficulties. Damon suffered from debilitating migraines, and he also sustained a concussion from running into a teammate. However, the concussion helped bring about a symbol that would sustain the team and encourage fans in the next season.

When Damon arrived for spring training in April of 2004, he had allowed his hair to grow to his shoulders, and then vowed he would not cut it until the Red Sox had defeated the New York Yankees, their archrivals. Because of his concussion, it took Damon 20 minutes to shave, so he decided to grow a beard. Again he stated he would not cut his beard until the team had won the American League championship.

Posting his best numbers yet, Damon also helped keep his fellow teammates loose and stress-free by doing nude pull-ups before each game, and dubbing the team "idiots." He told Lambert, "We try not to think when we play, because when we do, we only hurt ourselves." A group of fans began showing up at every game wearing long wigs and fake beards. They were named Damon's Disciples. They led the crowd in chanting, "We believe, Johnny, we believe." They also began sporting shirts that riffed off of the "What Would Jesus Do?" bracelets, stating "What Would Johnny Damon Do?"

In Game One of the American League championship against the New York Yankees, Damon scored a home run, The Yankees did not go down without a fight, but the Red Sox rallied and went down in history when they finally defeated their archrivals. While most fans were ecstatic over this, Damon and the Red Sox still had one more thing to acquire: the World Series championship. A concerted team effort helped sweep the St. Louis Cardinals. After 86 years, the Boston Red Sox were once again World Series champions. Fans celebrated into the night.

Damon, however, just ten hours after winning the major league championship, quietly slipped into his stylist's chair to get his beard trimmed. Later in the week, the team participated in a parade, and Damon appeared on *Late Show with David Letterman.* He also brokered a deal with Crown Publishing to release a book chronicling both his and the team's journey to the championship. His memoir, titled *Idiot,* was published in April of 2005.

Damon has kept very busy post-championship. He let the Fab Five from Bravo Channel's *Queer Eye For The Straight Guy* trim his hair. He had a small part in the feature film *Fever Pitch,* with Drew Barrymore and *Saturday Night Live* alum Jimmy Fallon. Damon was also named to *People* magazine's 50 Sexiest Men's list.

Damon married Michelle Mangan, whom he met two years earlier, on December 30, 2004. This was Mangan's first marriage and Damon's second. He had been previously married to his high school sweetheart, Angie Vannice; they have two children, twins Madelyn and Jackson. They were divorced in 2002.

In May of 2005 Damon stated to Alan Eskew of Redsox.com that he would like to continue with the Red Sox for a few more years, but also thought of retiring. No one can deny that Damon will enter the Hall of Fame, but he will do it in his own creative way.

## Selected writings

*Idiot,* Crown Publishing, 2005.

## Sources

### Periodicals

*Baseball Digest,* July 2002, p. 42-44; July 2003, p. 63.
*Newsweek,* April 11, 2005, p. 83.
*People,* November 15, 2004, pp. 87-88; November 29, 2004, p. 171; January 17, 2005, p. 106.
*Publishers Weekly,* December 6, 2004, p. 12.
*Sports Illustrated,* April 17, 2000, p. 44; January 22, 2001, p. 76; November 10, 2004, p. 40.

### Online

"Johnny Damon," MLB.com, http://mlb.mlb.com/ NASApp/mlb/team/player_career.jsp?/player_ id=113028 (May 16, 2005).
"Notes: Damon ponders the future," Redsox.com, http://boston.redsox.mlb.com/NASApp/mlb/ news/article.jsp?ymd=20050501&content _id= 1034754&vkey=news_bos&fext=.jsp&c_id=bos (May 16, 2005).

*—Ashyia N. Henderson*

# Edwidge Danticat

## Author

**B**orn January 19, 1969, in Port-au-Prince, Haiti; immigrated to United States, 1981; daughter of André Miracin (a cab driver) and Rose Souvenance (a textile worker) Danticat. *Education:* Barnard College, B.A. 1990; Brown University, M.F.A., 1993.

**Addresses:** *Office*—c/o Author Mail, Soho Press, 853 Broadway, No. 1903, New York, NY 10003.

## Career

**A**uthor, educator, and lecturer, 1994—. Professor, New York University, New York, NY, 1996-97; visiting professor of creative writing, University of Miami, Miami, FL, spring, 2000. Also production and research assistant at Clinica Estetico, 1993-94.

**Member:** Phi Beta Kappa, Alpha Kappa Alpha.

**Awards:** Named one of 20 "Best of American Novelists" by *Granta,* 1996; Pushcart Prize for short fiction; American Book Award, Before Columbus Foundation, for *The Farming of Bones;* fiction awards from periodicals, including *Caribbean Writer, Seventeen,* and *Essence;* Lannan Foundation Fellowship, 2004; Story Prize for outstanding collection of short fiction, for *The Dew Breaker,* 2005.

## Sidelights

**F**iction writer Edwidge Danticat (pronounced Ed-WEEDJ Dan-ti-KAH) conjures the history of her native Haiti in award-winning short stories and novels. She is equally at home describing the immigrant experience—what she calls "dyaspora"—and the reality of life in Haiti today. Danticat's fiction "has been devoted to an unflinching examination of her native culture, both on its own terms and in terms of its intersections with American culture," wrote an essayist in *Contemporary Novelists.* "Danticat's work emphasizes in particular the heroism and endurance of Haitian women as they cope with a patriarchal culture that, in its unswerving devotion to tradition and family, both oppresses and enriches them." Readers will find "massacres, rapes, [and] horrible nightmares in Danticat's fiction," wrote an essayist in the *St. James Guide to Young Adult Writers,* "but above all these are the strength, hope, and joy of her poetic vision."

Danticat's first novel, the loosely autobiographical *Breath, Eyes, Memory,* was a 1998 selection of the Oprah Winfrey Book Club, thus assuring its bestseller status. Other Danticat works have won warm praise as well, with some critics expressing surprise that such assured prose has come from an author so young. *Antioch Review* correspondent Grace A. Epstein praised Danticat for "the real courage ... in excavating the romance of nationalism, identity, and home." *Time* reporter Christopher John Farley likewise concluded that Danticat's fiction "never turns purple, never spins wildly into the fantastic, always remains focused, with precise disciplined language, and in doing so, it uncovers moments of raw humanness."

Danticat was born in Haiti and lived there the first 12 years of her life. She came to the United States in 1981, joining her parents who had already begun to build a life for themselves in New York City. When she started attending junior high classes in Brooklyn, she had difficulty fitting in with her classmates because of her Haitian accent, clothing, and hairstyle. Danticat recalled for Garry Pierre-Pierre in the *New York Times* that she took refuge from the isolation she felt by writing about her native land. As an adolescent she began work on what would evolve into her first novel, the acclaimed *Breath, Eyes, Memory*. Danticat followed her debut with a 1995 collection of short stories, *Krik? Krak!*—a volume which became a finalist for that year's National Book Award. According to Pierre-Pierre, the young author has been heralded as "'the voice' of Haitian Americans," but Danticat told him, "I think I have been assigned that role, but I don't really see myself as the voice for the Haitian-American experience. There are many. I'm just one."

Danticat's parents wanted her to pursue a career in medicine, and with the goal of becoming a nurse, she attended a specialized high school in New York City. But she abandoned this aim to devote herself to her writing. An earlier version of *Breath, Eyes, Memory* served as her master of fine arts thesis at Brown University, and the finished version was published shortly thereafter. Like Danticat herself, Sophie Caco—the novel's protagonist—spent her first 12 years in Haiti, several in the care of an aunt, before coming wide-eyed to the United States. But there the similarities end. Sophie is the child of a single mother, conceived by rape. Though she rejoins her mother in the United States, it is too late to save the still-traumatized older woman from self-destruction. Yet women's ties to women are celebrated in the novel, and Sophie draws strength from her mother, her aunt, and herself in order to escape her mother's fate.

*Breath, Eyes, Memory* caused some controversy in the Haitian-American community. Some of Danticat's fellow Haitians felt that some of the practices she documented portrayed them as primitive and abusive. American critics, however, widely lauded *Breath, Eyes, Memory*. Joan Philpott in *Ms.* hailed the book as "intensely lyrical." Pierre-Pierre reported that reviewers "have praised Ms. Danticat's vivid sense of place and her images of fear and pain." Jim Gladstone concluded in the *New York Times Book Review* that the novel "achieves an emo-

tional complexity that lifts it out of the realm of the potboiler and into that of poetry." And Bob Shacochis, in his *Washington Post Book World* review, called the work "a novel that rewards a reader again and again with small but exquisite and unforgettable epiphanies." Shacochis added, "You can actually see Danticat grow and mature, come into her own strength as a writer, throughout the course of this quiet, soul-penetrating story about four generations of women trying to hold on to one another in the Haitian diaspora."

*Krik? Krak!* takes its title from the practice of Haitian storytellers. Danticat told Deborah Gregory of *Essence* that storytelling is a favorite entertainment in Haiti, and a storyteller inquires of his or her audience, "Krik?" to ask if they are ready to listen. The group then replies with an enthusiastic, "Krak!" The tales in this collection include one about a man attempting to flee Haiti in a leaky boat, another about a prostitute who tells her son that the reason she dresses up every night is that she is expecting an angel to descend upon their house, and yet another explores the feelings of a childless housekeeper in a loveless marriage who finds an abandoned baby in the streets. The *New York Times Book Review*'s Robert Houston, citing the fact that some of the stories in *Krik? Krak!* were written while Danticat was still an undergraduate at Barnard College, felt that these pieces were "out of place in a collection presumed to represent polished, mature work." But *Ms.*'s Jordana Hart felt that the tales in *Krik? Krak!* "are textured and deeply personal, as if the 26-year-old Haitian-American author had spilled her own tears over each." Even Houston conceded that readers "weary of stories that deal only with the minutiae of 'relationships' will rejoice that they have found work that is about something, and something that matters."

Danticat's 1998 novel, *The Farming of Bones*, concerns a historical tragedy, the 1937 massacre of Haitian farm workers by soldiers from the Dominican Republic. In the course of less than a week, an estimated 12,000 to 15,000 Haitian workers in the Dominican Republic were slaughtered by the Dominican government or by private citizens in a classic case of "ethnic cleansing." *The Farming of Bones* is narrated by a young Haitian woman, Amabelle Desir, who has grown up in the Dominican Republic after being orphaned. As the nightmare unfolds around her, Amabelle must flee for her life, separated from her lover, Sebastien. In the ensuing decades as she nurses her physical and psychological wounds, Amabelle serves as witness to the suffering of her countrymen and the guilt of her former Dominican employers. The massacre, Danticat told Mallay Charters in *Publishers Weekly*, is "a part of our history, as Haitians, but it's also a part of the history of the world. Writing about it is an act of remembrance."

Dean Peerman wrote in *Christian Century* that "*Breath, Eyes, Memory* was an impressive debut, but *The Farming of Bones* is a richer work, haunting and heartwrenching." In *Nation*, Zia Jaffrey praised Danticat for "blending history and fiction, imparting information, in the manner of nineteenth-century novelists, without seeming to." Jaffrey added: "Danticat's brilliance as a novelist is that she is able to put this event into a credible, human context." *Time*'s Farley also felt that the author was able to endow a horrific episode with a breath of humanity. "Every chapter cuts deep, and you feel it," he stated, continuing on to say that Amabelle's "journey from servitude to slaughter is heartbreaking." In *Americas*, Barbara Mujica concluded that Danticat has written "a gripping novel that exposes an aspect of Dominican-Haitian history rarely represented in Latin American fiction. In spite of the desolation and wretchedness of the people Danticat depicts, *The Farming of Bones* is an inspiring book. It is a hymn to human resilience, faith, and hope in the face of overwhelming adversity." Jaffrey ended her review by concluding that the novel is "a beautifully conceived work, with monumental themes."

The 2002 novel *Behind the Mountains* takes the form of a diary of teenage Haitian Celiane Esperance. Celiane is happy in her home in the mountains of Haiti, but she has not seen her father since he left for the United States years before. She had intended to join him in New York, along with her mother and older brother, but visa applications are inexorably slow. After eight years, the visas are granted, and the family reunites in Brooklyn. After an initially joyful reunion, however, the family begins to slowly unravel. A child when her father left Haiti, Celiane is now a young woman with her own mind and will. Her brother, Moy, a 19-year-old artist, does not quietly slip back into the role of obedient child. Even more universal concerns, such as the freezing New York winters, difficulties at school, and the need to make a living, chip away at the family's unity. Good intentions go awry in a book showcasing "friction among family members" exacerbated by "the separation and adjustment to a new country," but especially by the inevitable maturation of younger family members and the unwillingness of parents to acknowledge it, wrote Diane S. Morton in *School Library Journal*. Hazel Rochman, writing in *Booklist*, praised the "simple, lyrical writing" Danticat demonstrates in the novel. According to *Kliatt*'s Claire Roser, "Danticat brings her formidable skill as a writer and her own firsthand knowledge of Haiti and immigrating to America to this heartfelt story told in the intimate diary format."

In addition to her own works, Danticat has also edited the fiction of others, including 2001's *The Butterfly's Way: Voices from the Haitian Dyaspora in the United States.* This work is a collection of stories, poems, and essays from Haitian writers living in America and Europe, many of whom are concerned about the feeling of displacement that is perhaps an inevitable consequence of emigration. Denolyn Carroll suggested in *Black Issues Book Review* that the pieces in *The Butterfly's Way* "help paint a vivid picture of what it is like to live in two worlds." Carroll also felt that the work added "new dimensions of understanding of Haitian emigrant's realities. This compilation is a source of enlightenment for us all." *Booklist* contributor Donna Seaman found the book "a potent and piercing collection" that will help all Americans understand "the frustrations ... of Haitians who are now outsiders both in Haiti and in their places of refuge."

*After the Dance: A Walk through Carnival in Haiti* is Danticat's 2002 nonfiction account of her first encounter with Carnival, the boisterous, sometimes debauched, sometimes dangerous celebrations that rock Haiti every year. As a child, she did not have the opportunity to attend Carnival. Her family inevitably packed up and left for a remote area in the Haitian mountains each year to escape the celebrations, perpetuating an almost superstitious distrust of the event. At times, though, staying clear has been a good idea. During the regime of Haitian dictator François "Papa Doc" Duvalier, carnival-goers were "subject to beatings and arrest by Duvalier's infamously unregulated militamen," wrote Judith Wynn in the *Boston Herald*. Danticat therefore approaches her first experience of Carnival uneasily. Her trip, however, beginning a week before the actual event, immerses her in the rich culture and history of Haiti, the cultural importance behind Carnival, and the background of the celebration itself. Danticat's "lively narrative" describes a country with a deep history, "influenced by Christianity, voodoo, Europeans, pirates, dictators, past slavery, and an uncertain economy," wrote Linda M. Kaufmann in *Library Journal*. Donna Seaman, writing in *Booklist*, observed that "as in her fiction, Danticat writes about her odyssey with an admirable delicacy and meticulousness," while a *Publishers Weekly* critic noted that the author "offers an enlightening look at the country—and Carnival—through the eyes of one of its finest writers."

In 2004, Danticat's book, *The Dew Breaker*, was published. The nine interrelated short stories move back and forth in time, telling the tale of a sanctioned torturer of dissidents under the regime of Duvalier; he is called the "Dew Breaker" because he arrives before dawn to carry out his task. The unnamed man moves to the United States and raises a family but still feels immense guilt for his deeds. In the book, Danticat brings up the "question of whether forgiveness and redemption are possible in the face of monstrous, unspeakable deeds," according to *Christian Century*. That year, *The Dew Breaker* was nominated for a National Book Critics Circle award; plus, Danticat was awarded the Lannan Foundation Fellowship. In 2005, the book was nominated for the PEN/Faulkner Award and won the Story Prize for outstanding collection of short fiction.

Danticat's 2005 novel, *Anacaona, Golden Flower,* was written for young people. It is the story of Haiti's Queen Anacaona, the wife of one of the island's rulers in the 15th century. When Spaniards began to settle on Haiti, the natives were treated cruelly; when the Haitians revolted, several native nobles were arrested and put to death. According to *Booklist,* the book "adds a vital perspective to the literature about Columbus and European expansion in the Americas."

"In order to create full-fledged, three-dimensional characters, writers often draw on their encounters, observations, collages of images from the everyday world, both theirs and others," Danticat remarked in a biographical essay in *Contemporary Novelists.* "We are like actors, filtering through our emotions what life must be like, or must have been like, for those we write about. Truly we imagine these lives, aggrandize, reduce, or embellish, however we often begin our journey with an emotion close to our gut, whether it be anger, curiosity, joy, or fear."

## Selected writings

*The Creation of Adam* (play), produced in Providence, RI, 1992.

*Dreams Like Me* (play), produced at Brown University New Plays Festival, 1993.

*Breath, Eyes, Memory* (novel), Soho Press (New York, NY), 1994.

*Krik? Krak!* (short stories), Soho Press (New York, NY), 1995.

*Children of the Sea* (play), produced at Roxbury Community College, 1997.

*The Farming of Bones* (novel), Soho Press (New York, NY), 1998.

(With Jonathan Demme) *Odillon Pierre, Artist of Haiti,* Kaliko Press (Nyack, NY), 1999.

(Editor) *The Beacon Best of 2000: Great Writing by Women and Men of All Colors and Cultures,* Beacon Press (Boston, MA), 2000.

(Editor) *The Butterfly's Way: Voices from the Haitian Dyaspora in the United States,* Soho Press (New York, NY), 2001.

(Translator and author of afterword, with Carrol F. Coates) Jackes Stephen Alexis, *In the Flicker of an Eyelid,* University of Virginia Press (Charlottesville, VA), 2002.

*After the Dance: A Walk through Carnival in Haiti,* Crown Publishers (New York, NY), 2002.

*Behind the Mountains* (novel), Orchard Books (New York, NY), 2002.

*The Dew Breaker* (short stories), Knopf (New York, NY), 2004.

*Anacaona, Golden Flower,* Scholastic (New York, NY), 2005.

## Sources

### Books

*Authors and Artists for Young Adults,* vol. 29, Gale, 1999.
*Contemporary Literary Criticism,* vol. 94, Gale, 1996.
*Contemporary Novelists,* 7th ed., St. James Press, 2001.
*St. James Guide to Young Adult Writers,* Gale, 1999.
*Short Stories for Students,* vol. 1, Gale, 1997.

### Periodicals

*America,* November 6, 1999, p. 10.
*Americas,* January 2000, p. 62; May 2000, p. 40.
*Antioch Review,* winter 1999, p. 106.
*Atlanta Journal-Constitution,* October 29, 2000, p. D3.
*Belles Lettres,* fall 1994, p. 36, p. 38; summer 1995, pp. 12-15.
*Black Issues Book Review,* January 1999, p. 20; May 2001, p. 60; July/August 2004, p. 43.
*Bloomsbury Review,* September-October 1994, p. 12.
*Booklist,* January 1, 1999, p. 778; March 15, 1999, p. 1295; June 1, 1999, p. 1796; February 15, 2000, p. 1096; October 15, 2000, p. 416; February 15, 2001, p. 1096; January 1, 2002, p. 763; August 2002, pp. 1895-96; October 1, 2002, p. 312; July 2005.
*Boston Herald,* November 17, 2000, p. 43; September 1, 2002, p. 61.
*Callaloo,* spring 1996, pp. 382-89.
*Christian Century,* September 22, 1999, p. 885; December 14, 2004, p. 22.
*Emerge,* April 1995, p. 58.
*Entertainment Weekly,* September 3, 1999, p. 63; March 19, 2004, p. 69.
*Essence,* November 1993, p. 48; April 1995, p. 56; May 1996.
*Globe and Mail,* June 12, 1999, p. D4.

*Kirkus Reviews,* June 1, 2002, p. 782; September 15, 2002, p. 1387.

*Kliatt,* November 1999, p. 16; November 2002, p. 8.

*Library Journal,* November 1, 2000, p. 80, p. 103; June 15, 2002, p. 83.

*Ms.,* March/April 1994, pp. 77-78; March/April, 1995, p. 75.

*Nation,* November 16, 1998, p. 62.

*Newsday,* March 30, 1995, p. B2, p. B25; May 21, 1995, p. A52.

*New York,* November 20, 1995, p. 50.

*New York Times,* January 26, 1995, p. C1, p. C8; October 23, 1995, p. B3.

*New York Times Book Review,* July 10, 1994, p. 24; April 23, 1995, p. 22; September 27, 1998, p. 18; December 5, 1999, p. 104; December 10, 1999, p. 36.

*New York Times Magazine,* June 21, 1998.

*O,* February 2002, pp. 141-45.

*Off Our Backs,* March 1999, p. 13.

*Organic Style,* April 2004, p. 22.

*People,* September 28, 1998, p. 51; March 29, 2004, p. 53.

*Poets and Writers,* January 1997.

*Progressive,* January 1997, p. 39; December 1998, p. 44.

*Publishers Weekly,* January 24, 1994, pp. 39-40; May 25, 1998; August 17, 1998, p. 42; November 2, 1998, p. 40; September 11, 2000, p. 69; December 18, 2000, p. 65; May 13, 2002, pp. 58-59; October 28, 2002, p. 72.

*Quarterly Black Review,* June 1995, p. 6.

*Reference & User Services Quarterly,* spring 1999, p. 253.

*St. Louis Post-Dispatch,* September 21, 1999, p. D3.

*School Library Journal,* May 1995, p. 135; October 2002, p. 160.

*Time,* September 7, 1998, p. 78.

*Times* (London, England), March 20, 1999, p. 19.

*Times Literary Supplement,* April 28, 2000, p. 23.

*Village Voice Literary Supplement,* July 1995, p. 11.

*Voice of Youth Advocates,* December 1995, p. 299.

*Washington Post Book World,* April 3, 1994, p. 6; May 14, 1995, p. 4.

*World & I,* February 1999, p. 290.

*World Literature Today,* spring 1999, p. 373.

### Online

"Edwidge Danticat," Voices from the Gaps, http://voices.cla.umn.edu/vg/Bios/entries/danticat_edwidge.html (July 5, 2005).

# George David

Bloomberg News/Landov

## Chief executive officer of United Technologies Corporation

**B**orn George Alfred Lawrence David, April 7, 1942, in Bryn Mawr, PA; son of Charles David (a history professor); married Barbara Osborn, September, 1965 (divorced, 1997); married second wife, August, 2003; children: two daughters, one son (from first marriage). *Education:* Harvard University, B.A., 1965; Virginia University, M.B.A., 1967.

**Addresses:** *Office*—United Technologies, Inc., One Financial Plaza, Hartford, CT 06103.

## Career

**W**orked as a technical writer in New York City, early 1960s; began career with Boston Consulting Group, c. 1968; joined Otis Elevator, 1975, became general manager of its Latin American operations, 1977; headed Otis's Asian division and became a senior vice president at United Technologies Corporation (UTC), its parent company; became UTC president, 1992, chief executive officer, 1994, and board chair, 1997.

## Sidelights

**G**eorge David is one of American business's more formidable chief executive officers, though he remains largely under the radar in the mainstream press. As head of United Technologies Corporation (UTC), a large conglomerate with roots in the aerospace industry, David has pursued quietly aggressive and prudent strategies that have brought the Hartford, Connecticut-based Fortune 500 company revenues of $31 billion in 2003.

Born in 1942 in the college town of Bryn Mawr, Pennsylvania, David is the son of a history professor who was nearing retirement age by then. Education and the pursuit of knowledge were stressed when he was growing up. "You don't chuck baseballs with a dad that age," David recalled in an interview with *New York Times* writer Claudia H. Deutsch. "Ours was an intellectual household."

David went on to Harvard University, where he majored in physics and chemistry, but earned such poor grades during his first two years that the school suggested he take a year off. He worked as a technical writer in New York City for a time, but returned to Harvard and graduated in 1965. He went on to earn a graduate business degree from Virginia University two years later, and took a job with the Boston Consulting Group. One of his clients was Otis, the elevator manufacturer, and in 1975 the company offered him a full-time executive position.

Just a year after David joined Otis, the company was bought by United Technologies, formerly the United Aircraft Corporation, which had made rocket engines and jet-propulsion systems. David was convinced that his new UTC bosses would fire him. "I was overtitled, overpaid, and underexperienced," he told Deutsch in the *New York Times* interview.

But instead he was kept on board, and became general manager for Otis in Latin America. He also oversaw the company's Asian operations for a time, and advanced to the post of senior vice president. In 1992, he was made president, and named UTC's chief executive officer in 1994.

UTC had diversified its holdings by then, snapping up Carrier, a pioneer in the air-conditioning business, not long after the Otis purchase. It was still a strong leader in aerospace, reflected by its ownership of Pratt & Whitney, maker of aircraft engines, and helicopter-manufacturer Sikorsky. But UTC was hamstrung in some ways because of its size, and as its new leader David went to work on a series of restructurings over the next decade. He cut costs by downsizing the workforce, decentralizing operations at headquarters, and shedding some of its nonessential businesses, like UTC Automotive. With the extra cash on hand he also began a major acquisition effort, buying up brand names to add to the UTC aerospace stable, like Hamilton Sundstrand, which makes air-pressure systems for airplane cabins. UTC was also a longtime leader in fuel cells, having made the ones used for the Apollo moon landings, and David plowed resources into research and development—a crucial strategy for it to remain on top of the game. It even produced a prototype car with South Korean automaker Hyundai that used a new type of fuel cells, which draw electric current from hydrogen with no byproduct except for water.

After the downturn in the airline industry after the September 11, 2001, terrorist attacks and ongoing recession, David kept UTC financially viable by cutting jobs at Pratt & Whitney, and closing some Carrier plants. He won high marks from Wall Street for pursuing a strategy that kept earnings high on UTC shares. It boasted a traditional 15 percent growth in earnings annually, despite the cautionary remarks that David sometimes delivered to the business press. "We like the philosophy around here of no bad news," he reflected in an interview with *BusinessWeek Online* interview with Diane Brady just weeks after the World Trade Center and Pentagon attacks. "Now, we have bad news.... I hate it. It's management's responsibility not to have bad news. On the other hand, this hasn't changed the fundamental strengths of our company. We're better positioned than we used to be, and we'll come back again. I'm sure of that."

Not all of David's strategies have been a success, however: in 2000, UTC was ready to announce a deal to buy Honeywell, but at the last minute General Electric (GE) put in a higher bid. The move was

the work of GE's high-profile chair, Jack Welch, the darling of Wall Street and the business press at the time. In the end, European regulators nixed the GE-Honeywell deal, thanks in part to David's lobbying efforts. The UTC boss has often been compared to and contrasted with Welch, who became known as "Neutron Jack" for his win-at-all costs corporate ethos. David said the Honeywell deal left no ill will between the two. "I'm not sore. Jack and I are voracious competitors but we have an easy relationship," he told the *New York Times*'s Deutsch, while adding, "It was nice of Mr. Welch to validate our business judgment and to overpay."

David has also been compared to Dennis Kozlowski, once the head of another leading American conglomerate, Tyco, but Kozlowski suffered a drastic fall from grace when revelations surfaced over his misuse of corporate funds. Court records detailed such extravagances as the purchase of a $6,000 shower curtain for a Tyco corporate apartment. Unlike Kozlowski, David is a model of fiscal probity. "I don't have a $6 shower curtain, let alone a $6,000 one," he told *Sunday Times* journalist Dominic O'Connell.

As the son of a professor and one of the first Rhodes scholars, David remains strongly committed to education issues. UTC offers a generous tuition-reimbursement program that provides the option of earning a free college degree for every one of its 205,700 employees. Newly minted college graduates are also rewarded with UTC stock. Twice married, David earns about $3 million annually, and spends his free time competing in yacht races with his 50-foot sloop. He is also a fearless skier and accomplished chef with a penchant for soufflés—one of the trickiest items in any cook's repertoire. When the *New York Times*' Deutsch reminded him that soufflés were prone to fall, he replied, "I like the challenge."

## Sources

### Periodicals

*Black Collegian*, February 1995, p. 56.
*BusinessWeek*, January 12, 2004, p. 60.
*Financial Times*, October 21, 2000, p. 22.
*Forbes*, March 3, 2003, p. 62.
*Money*, November 1, 2003, p. 54.
*New York Times*, November 19, 2000, p. 2.
*Observer* (London, England), July 28, 2002, p. 14.
*Sunday Times* (London, England), October 6, 2002, p. 8.

## Online

"About UTC," United Technologies Corporation, http://www.utc.com/profile/facts/index.htm (September 2, 2004).

"UTC's David: 'We'll Come Back Again,'" *Business-Week Online,* http://www.businessweek.com/bwdaily/dnflash/nov2001/nf2001112_2874.htm (September 2, 2004).

—*Carol Brennan*

# Howard Dean

© *Reuters/Corbis*

## Chair of the Democratic National Committee

Born Howard Brush Dean III, November 17, 1948, in New York, NY; son of Howard Jr. (a stockbroker) and Andree Dean; married Judith Steinberg (a doctor), 1981; children: Anne, one son. *Education:* Yale University, B.A., 1971; attended Columbia University; Albert Einstein College of Medicine, M.D., 1978.

**Addresses:** *Office*—c/o Democratic National Committee, 430 S. Capitol St. SE, Washington, D.C., 20003.

## Career

Started working as an investment banker, Smith Barney, 1972; physician, 1978-91; legislator, Vermont House, 1983-86; elected lieutenant governor of Vermont, 1986, 1988, 1990; assumed governorship, 1991; elected governor of Vermont, 1992, 1994, 1996, 1998, 2000; head of National Governors Association, 1994-95; ran for Democratic U.S. presidential nomination, 2003-04; elected head of the Democratic National Committee, 2005.

## Sidelights

Although he worked as a doctor for many years, Howard Dean was better known for his political activities. After serving in the Vermont legislature and as lieutenant governor, Dean became governor of his adopted home state in 1991. After spending more than a decade in this office, Dean decided to run for the presidential nomination of the Democratic party. Although he did not win the nomination, Dean did become the chair of the Democratic National Committee in early 2005.

Dean was born on November 17, 1948, in New York City, the eldest of four sons born to Howard Brush Dean, Jr., and his wife, Andree. Dean was raised in wealth and privilege in East Hampton, New York. His Republican father worked on Wall Street as a stock broker. Dean received his education at a prep school, St. George's School in Newport, Rhode Island. An athlete who played football and participated in wrestling, Dean graduated in 1966.

After high school, Dean entered Yale University where he studied political science. When he graduated from Yale in 1971, Dean was unsure what career path to choose so he took a year off and skied in Aspen, Colorado. Dean did not serve in the U.S. military during the Vietnam War because he had an unfused vertebra which led to a medical deferment.

When his year off was completed, Dean returned to New York City and a job as an investment banker. But he did not enjoy his life or career and was already thinking about a change. He considered both teaching and medicine, though he also wanted to be outdoors. At the age of 25, Dean decided to go to medical school. To meet the med school requirements, Dean took pre-med classes at Columbia, then entered the Albert Einstein College of Medicine. While a student, he met his future wife, Judith Steinberg, whom he married in 1981.

While a med student, a family tragedy deeply affected Dean. His 23-year-old brother Charlie was an idealist who became involved with the anti-war movement. Charlie Dean was traveling in Laos in the mid-1970s when he disappeared and was murdered. He was probably taken hostage by communists in the area, and the family did not recover his remains for many years. Charlie Dean's death made Dean even more sure of his choice to pursue medicine, and also played a part in his decision to enter politics.

After graduating from medical school in 1978, Dean moved to Vermont. He began practicing medicine as an internist in Shelburne, Vermont, and later shared a practice with his wife. As soon as he moved there, Dean became involved in politics. In 1978, he worked to establish a bicycle path around Lake Champlain. Dean later volunteered on President Jimmy Carter's re-election campaign and went to the Democratic National Convention in 1980.

By 1983, politics drew more of Dean's time and attention. Maintaining his medical practice part-time, Dean ran for office and won a seat in the Vermont legislature, which was also only a part-time job. Dean believed his medical background helped him as a politician. Lawrence K. Altman wrote in the New York Times, "Dean said medical training to ask tough questions about the facts and to analyze them rationally before deciding on a course of action had served him well in politics."

Dean served in Vermont's legislature until 1986 when he ran for lieutenant governor of the state. In Vermont, the governor and lieutenant governor run independently. Dean won his office as a Democrat with 53 percent of the vote, to his Republican opponent Susan Auld's 44 percent. Dean was re-elected two times, in 1988 and 1990. While serving as lieutenant governor, Dean continued his medical practice since the government position was part-time in the small state.

When Vermont's Republican Governor Richard Snelling died after a heart attack in August of 1991, Dean became the state's governor and he was forced to leave medicine behind. Though Dean was not well known in the state, he still managed to win election to the office himself in 1992 by easily defeating Republican Senator John McClaughery. As governor, he promised to keep many Snelling's policies in place, despite the difference in party affiliation. This stance drew some criticism from the Democrats, though Dean openly stated he was a fiscal conservative.

Dean's platform did include such Democratic issues as health care reform, something he fought for in subsequent terms. He also used his position to push for such reform on a national level. He served as the head of a governor's task force on the health care reform. When First Lady Hillary Rodham Clinton had her own task force on the subject, he worked with that group as well. Dean also served as chair of the National Governor's Association, beginning in 1994.

In 1994, Dean was re-elected Vermont's governor, winning 70 percent of the vote and defeating David Kelley. In his second term, Dean managed to get some health care reform passed in his state in 1995. He did face some tough budget problems, including a budget deficit in 1996. Though some Democrats did not support him, he cut many popular programs that Democrats liked such as property tax relief.

Dean's next election was won as easily as the previous one. In 1996, he defeated Republican John L. Gropper with 71 percent of the vote. However, Dean's popularity took a hit with some of the decisions he made. In 1997, he signed into law Act 60, which created a new property tax to support education. The act also forced richer communities to give funds to poorer communities for education.

Dean's fourth run at office in 1998 was not by as wide of a margin, but still significant. He defeated Republican Ruth Dwyer with 56 percent of the vote. Despite the close vote, Dean's term was relatively successful. Vermont's budget improved and by 1999, it had nearly a $90 million surplus. He signed tax cuts into law that year.

A more controversial issue was civil unions. In 2000, he signed into law the right for two people of the same gender to marry in a civil union. This was not just Dean's idea, but something a decision by Vermont's Supreme Court forced on the legislature and Dean. Despite such unpopular stances, Dean considered running for the Democratic presidential nomination in 2000, but did not.

Instead, Dean ran for another term as governor, again against Dwyer. Dean's margin of victory was even closer than his last election. He won with 50.4

percent of the vote to Dwyer's 30 percent. Dean continued to successfully pass social programs such as establishing a child abuse prevention program and expanding health care coverage to cover nearly everyone. He also founded a rainy day fund for the state to draw on when economic problems emerged in the future.

Dean did not seek re-election in 2002, and left the governor's office in January of 2003. He already was set for a new challenge: running for the Democratic presidential nomination in 2004. Dean began his campaign in October of 2002, but was not seen as a serious candidate early on by some observers because he was from such a small state, had no national network, and had little funding. He only raised $85,000 by October of 2002.

Despite the lack of support and visibility, Dean was already polling well in New Hampshire, and already campaigning in New Hampshire, Iowa, and South Carolina. In December of 2002, Todd S. Purdum wrote in the *New York Times,* "his dark horse status and scrappy personality have combined to let him take stands—like his call to roll back almost all of President Bush's $1.3 billion tax cut—that make him stand out."

Dean continued to build steam in his campaign throughout 2003. He became a media darling, in part because of his accessibility. Dean also relished his role as an underdog, something he tried to maintain throughout his campaign as a useful positive. One relatively unique feature of Dean's campaign was attracting supporters through the Internet. While other candidates used the Internet previously, Dean was extremely successful in getting donations through it. In early summer of 2003, Dean raised $7.5 million over three months, more than any other Democratic candidate. Two-thirds of those funds came online. Dean ended up getting more money online in the entire campaign than any other candidate.

Dean continued to press his campaign in Iowa and New Hampshire, where the first primaries were to be held in 2004. As Dean gained momentum through the summer and fall of 2003, his personality became an issue. He had a temper and sometimes displayed an angry side. He had a propensity to make somewhat outrageous statements without thinking, then apologizing for them later. Dean's personality both attracted and repulsed voters. Though his campaign brought in more and more funds—especially from those who were sick of the current state of politics—and the support of many young voters, many

observers believed that if he won the nomination, he could not beat President George W. Bush in the general election.

By early 2004, Dean had the lead among Democrats going into the first primaries and caucuses. However, he did not win the Iowa caucuses in January of 2004, and though he continued to make a push, he never won a primary or caucus. Dean continued his campaign after these defeats for a time, but eventually dropped out of the race. Before he left, however, he founded a grass roots organization that lasted beyond the 2004 election called Democracy for America. This political action group (or PAC) was a progressive Democratic organization that worked to get Democrats elected from the local to the national level.

Though Dean lost, some believed his campaign had not been in vain. His campaign pollster, Paul Maslin, told Mark Z. Barabak of the *Los Angeles Times,* "Howard Dean galvanized the party, awakened the party, got the party going at the grass roots. He showed how we could raise tens of millions of dollars over the Internet. For all our faults, that was a historic campaign."

After the election, Dean started doing commercials for Yahoo!, an Internet search engine and website. But politics remained his primary interest. In January of 2005, he began running for a new office. He wanted to be the chair of the Democratic National Committee (DNC), which ran the Democratic party. Though he was an unexpected candidate because of his criticisms of the insider politics of Washington and major parties, he really wanted the post.

Dean campaigned hard, believing he could draw on his grassroots support to revitalize the Democratic party. Despite potential issues, including his personality and lack of appeal to certain audiences, Dean was elected unanimously by the 450 members of the DNC. His brother, Jim, took over the running of the PAC that Dean had founded.

Dean promised that if he were elected head of the DNC, he would not run for the Democratic nomination in 2008. Instead, he would work on his vision for getting more Democrats elected and winning the White House and control of Congress in 2008, beginning on the local level. One area that Dean had immediate success in was fund-raising. In the three weeks after he was elected, the DNC raised $3.4 million, and a total of $9.6 million in the first seven weeks of the year. These numbers were comparable to what the Republicans raised.

Of Dean's potential to succeed in his new position, former DNC chair David Wilhelm told John Nichols of the *Nation,* "Dean understands that the essence of a good political communicator is somebody who can execute strong message contrasts. Maybe what seemed wild in a presidential candidate will seem much more normal in a chair of a national party."

## Sources

### Periodicals

Associated Press, March 7, 2005.
Associated Press Candidate Biographies, 1996, 2000.
*Campaigns & Elections,* May 2002, p. 18.
*Editor & Publisher,* April 7, 2003, p. 27.
*Los Angeles Times,* November 2, 2004, p. E1; January 28, 2005, p. E1; February 13, 2005, p. A19.
*Nation,* March 7, 2005, p. 13.
*Newsweek,* July 21, 2003, pp. 36-39; August 11, 2003, pp. 22-30; January 12, 2004, p. 18; January 26, 2004, p. 32.
*New York Times,* September 3, 1991, p. C3; December 18, 2002, p. A1.
*Progressive,* June 2004, p. 37.
*Time,* July 14, 2003, p. 40; August 11, 2003, p. 22.
*U.S. News & World Report,* December 29, 2003, p. 48.

### Online

"Dean named Democratic Party Chief," CNN.com, http://www.cnn.com/2005/ALLPOLITICS/02/12/dean.dems/index.html (February 14, 2005).

—*A. Petruso*

# Jaap de Hoop Scheffer

© *Thierry Roge/Reuters/Corbis*

## NATO Secretary General

**B**orn Jakob Gijsbert de Hoop Scheffer, April 3, 1948, in Amsterdam, The Netherlands; son of the general secretary of a stockbrokers' association; married Jeannine de Hoop Scheffer-van Oorschot (a French teacher); children: Caroline, Stephanie. *Politics:* Christian Democratic Alliance. *Religion:* Catholic. *Education:* University of Leiden, law degree, 1974.

**Addresses:** *Office*—NATO Headquarters, Blvd Leopold III, 1110 Brussels, Belgium.

## Career

**J**oined Royal Netherlands Air Force, 1974; worked for Dutch Foreign Ministry, 1976-86; member of Dutch parliament, 1986-2002; leader of Christian Democratic Alliance party, 1997-2001; Dutch Foreign Minister, 2002-03; became NATO Secretary General, 2004.

## Sidelights

**A**s the United States and some of its European allies tried to mend their relationship and fight terrorism together after disagreeing about the Iraq war in the 21st Century, they chose Dutch politician and diplomat Jaap de Hoop Scheffer to head a key trans-Atlantic institution. De Hoop Scheffer, who became secretary-general of the North Atlantic Treaty Organization (NATO) in January of 2004, was chosen because he remained friendly with both the United States and France during the Iraq debate, and because he admires French and other European cultures as well as the American role in Europe's defense. The very personality traits—thoughtfulness, moderation, diplomacy—that may have kept de Hoop Scheffer from being elected leader of the Netherlands have helped him in his foreign-service career. Despite his calm reputation, he is also known for speaking his mind when he has to. That was becoming obvious in his new job: he had pushed, more and more bluntly, for both Europe and the United States to work harder to strengthen NATO and rebuild Afghanistan and Iraq.

Jakob Gijsbert de Hoop Scheffer (who goes by the name Jaap in his private and public life) was born April 3, 1948, in the city of Amsterdam in the Netherlands. His father was general secretary of his country's stockbrokers' association, and his uncle, who shares his name, was the Netherlands' ambassador to NATO in the 1980s. The young de Hoop Scheffer went to the University of Leiden, where he studied law and organized student debates on international relations (and met his wife, Jeannine, who was studying French there). Tellingly, as other students got involved in the protest movements of the 1970s, he wrote his thesis about the United States' military presence in Western Europe. He graduated in 1974 and spent two years in the Royal Netherlands Air Force.

In 1975, de Hoop Scheffer signed up for the Netherlands' one-year training program for aspiring diplomats, and in 1976 the Dutch Foreign Service hired him as a trainee in the information department. That same year, he was sent to the Dutch embassy in Ghana for two years. He was essentially an office manager and fix-it man for the embassy—his tasks included trying to repair the air conditioning, changing the oil in embassy cars, and fighting cockroaches—but he also befriended Jerry Rawlings, a lieutenant who went on to become president of Ghana. Living in Ghana left him with a love of Africa. "Sometimes I can cry when that continent is in the news as a result of mass murder and famine," he said, according to Robert van de Roer in *NATO Review*.

Brussels was de Hoop Scheffer's next assignment, as part of the Netherlands' delegation to NATO. There, while working as a diplomat on defense planning, he showed off his talent as a cabaret performer, singing jazz classics at co-workers' farewell parties. He joined the small local organization of the left-wing Dutch political party D66, but his long-time interest in America's military presence in Europe kept him from fitting in; he was in favor of a deployment of nuclear missiles in Europe, which the party opposed. Back in the Netherlands after 1980, de Hoop Scheffer joined the Christian Democratic Alliance, a center-right party, and worked as the private secretary to the Dutch foreign minister—keeping the job during four different ministers' terms in office, until 1986. The experience demystified diplomacy for him. "It's very pleasant to function quietly in the corridors of power. What struck me was that decision-making takes place in [such] ordinary and clumsy fashion," he said, according to *NATO Review*'s van de Roer.

His work for the foreign ministers and the party was rewarded in 1986. With the help of Hans van den Broek, then the foreign minister, de Hoop Scheffer was elected to the Dutch parliament as a Christian Democrat. He specialized in foreign affairs, and his parliamentary debates made him a rising star. In 1992, for instance, he charged that a member of the opposing party's complaints about Indonesia's human-rights record was hurting van den Broek's diplomacy with Indonesia. The same year, as the war in Bosnia got worse, he forced the parliament to recognize the problem and debate the Netherlands' position on the war.

But de Hoop Scheffer's promising career suffered setbacks in the early 1990s. Many people expected him to become foreign minister when his mentor, van den Broek, left his post in 1993, but he was

passed over. He tried to get elected leader of the Christian Democrats in 1994, but lost. He was named the party's deputy leader in December of 1995 (after the party lost 20 seats in parliament in an election) and finally became its leader in March of 1997. But when he faced his big test with Dutch voters—an election in May of 1998—his party lost five more seats. "[His] perceived dull image failed to ignite public support," Associated Press writer Paul Ames explained.

"Jaap did not seem to be entirely in the right place," van den Broek told van de Roer in *NATO Review*. "He wasn't able to propagate Christian Democratic ideas with an ideological passion. He is much more driven by pragmatism than ideology." De Hoop Scheffer resigned in fall of 2001 after disagreements with other party officials. But his career quickly revived after new Christian Democrat leader Jan Peter Balkenende led the party to victory in the May of 2002 elections. That July, Balkenende named de Hoop Scheffer foreign minister. Finally, he was in his element.

When the U.S. and Great Britain pushed for an invasion of Iraq in winter of 2003, and France and Germany led the opposition to war in the United Nations Security Council, de Hoop Scheffer and Balkenende performed a balancing act. They declared that the Netherlands supported the invasion—defying Dutch public opinion, which was strongly anti-war—but said their support would be political, not military. (The Netherlands did eventually send 1,100 soldiers to Iraq in May, after the invasion was over.) De Hoop Scheffer and Balkenende avoided offending France or Germany. When Britain, Spain, and other European countries signed a letter pledging support for the American position on Iraq, de Hoop Scheffer, true to his diplomatic instincts, refused to sign it, saying it might create further division. In doing so, he was upholding the Netherlands' traditional position of valuing both a united Europe and Europe's alliance with the United States.

That position made de Hoop Scheffer an obvious compromise candidate later in 2003, when it came time for NATO—a military organization made up of the U.S., Canada, and several European nations—to choose its new civilian leader, or secretary general. De Hoop Scheffer was acceptable to the U.S. government because he had supported the Iraq war. Yet he had also maintained good relations with French leaders—not only because of his restraint on Iraq, but also probably because he speaks fluent French and professes a love for French culture. He was unanimously named the new secretary general in September of 2003 and took office in January of 2004.

He took over NATO at a crucial time. Founded in 1949 to provide Western Europe, the United States, and Canada with a common defense against the Soviet Union's military threat, NATO has struggled to stay relevant since the Soviet Union broke up. The alliance reached out to Eastern Europe after the fall of Communism by admitting former Soviet-bloc countries Poland, Hungary, and the Czech Republic as members in 1999, and it fought a successful war against Yugoslavia to stop ethnic cleansing in Kosovo the same year, but it has had trouble reacting to the war on terrorism. Its European members offered to help the United States fight the war in Afghanistan after the September 11, 2001, terrorist attacks, but the Bush Administration declined the offer. Just before the Iraq war, Turkey asked the rest of NATO to defend it in case the war spread over its borders, but France, Germany, and Belgium resisted the idea. But in August of 2003, NATO sent 5,500 peacekeepers to Afghanistan, its first-ever military action outside of Europe.

When de Hoop Scheffer took over as secretary general, everyone knew his biggest challenges would be repairing the damage to the United States-European alliance, increasing NATO's role in Afghanistan, and figuring out what role, if any, NATO would have in rebuilding Iraq. "The primary focus at the moment should be on Afghanistan," he said, according to Ames in the Associated Press. "The world community and NATO cannot afford to lose there." He remained carefully open-minded but non-committal on the Iraq question. As a gesture of unity, he started holding NATO meetings in French as well as English. "I'm a man with both an Atlantic and a European vocation," he told the *Wall Street Journal*'s Marc Champion.

De Hoop Scheffer has had to tap both sides of his personality as secretary general. He is best-known for his calm demeanor, his ability to suppress his emotions and remain pleasant, an essential skill for a diplomat. The Dutch public has known that side of him at least since early 2000, when his daughter, Caroline, cooperated with the television show *Bananasplit,* a Dutch version of *Candid Camera,* to catch her father and mother on camera meeting a strange man she introduced as her new boyfriend. De Hoop Scheffer remained outwardly calm and polite as he met the man, who was older than him, had long hair and an earring, and was supposedly trying to convince Caroline to come with him on a cruise ship where he hoped to make a living as a palm reader. On the other hand, de Hoop Scheffer also "has a crisp tongue and is capable of being vigorous when he needs to be," an anonymous diplomat told BBC News, and he has "carved a reputation for professionalism and straight talking," Lord George

Robertson, the previous secretary general, told BBC News in the same report.

After only a few weeks on the job, de Hoop Scheffer was already showing off his sharp tongue. He told the *Wall Street Journal*'s Champion that if the United States does not work within NATO on its foreign policy goals, it will encourage the European Union to create its own military agreements. He also criticized NATO's member nations for being reluctant to commit the troops, equipment, and money needed to follow through on their political goals. "I have felt like a beggar sometimes, and if the secretary general of NATO feels like a beggar, the system is wrong," he told Champion.

In his first six months on the job, de Hoop Scheffer arranged to send more NATO peacekeepers to Afghanistan. He also presided over NATO's expansion from 19 members to 26, as seven Eastern European countries—Bulgaria, Estonia, Latvia, Lithuania, Romania, Slovakia, and Slovenia—joined the alliance. At NATO's annual conference in Istanbul, Turkey, in late June of 2004, he helped negotiate a plan for NATO to help train Iraq's new army, fulfilling a request from Iraq's new prime minister, Iyad Allawi. But even that limited commitment to Iraq was hard to come by. At the end of the conference, de Hoop Scheffer warned in an interview with the *New York Times*' Elaine Sciolino that Iraq and Afghanistan could easily become failed states, dangerous places that harbor terrorism, if the world does not cooperate better and commit more troops and money to saving them. His remarks were aimed both at European nations who have been reluctant to commit more troops and the United States, which he criticized for neglecting NATO unless it needs the alliance's help. He warned that Afghanistan risked "falling back under the Taliban," the dictatorial regime that harbored the Al-Qaeda terrorist network until the United States overthrew it.

Clearly, de Hoop Scheffer realizes that to accomplish NATO's goals, he will need to show his sharp-spoken side more. "Can we afford two failed states in pivotal regions?" he asked in the interview with the *New York Times*' Sciolino. "It's both undesirable and unacceptable if either Afghanistan or Iraq were to be lost. The international community can't afford to see those countries going up in flames."

## Sources

### Periodicals

*Akron Beacon Journal,* September 11, 2003, p. A9.
Associated Press, September 22, 2003; January 5, 2004.

*Boston Globe,* January 6, 2004, p. A6.
*New York Times,* September 23, 2003, p. A10; January 6, 2004, p. A6; July 3, 2004, p. A8.
*USA Today,* September 22, 2003, p. 17A.
*Wall Street Journal,* January 23, 2004, p. A10.

## Online

"Jaap de Hoop Scheffer: Diplomatic long distance runner," NATO, http://www.nato.int/docu/review/2003/issue4/english/profile.html (September 4, 2004)

"Jaap de Hoop Scheffer," Fact Index, http://www.fact-index.com, http://www.fact-index.com/j/ja/jaap_de_hoop_scheffer.html (September 4, 2004)

"Jaap de Hoop Scheffer," NATO, http://www.nato.int/cv/secgen/scheffer-e.htm (September 4, 2004)

"NATO After Istanbul," Project Syndicate, http://www.project- syndicate.org (September 4, 2004).

"Profile: Jaap de Hoop Scheffer," BBC News, http://news.bbc.co.uk/2/hi/europe/3130410.stm (September 4, 2004).

*—Erick Trickey*

# Oscar de la Renta

Alberto Lowe/Reuters/Landov

## Fashion designer

**B**orn in 1932, in Santo Domingo, Dominican Republic; married Françoise de Langlade (a fashion editor), 1967 (died, 1983); married Annette Engelhard Reed (a philanthropist), January, 1990; children: Moises Oscar (adopted), Eliza (stepchild; from second marriage), two other stepchildren (from second marriage). *Education:* Studied painting at Academia de San Fernando (Madrid, Spain).

**Addresses:** *Office*—550 Seventh Ave., New York, NY 10018-3207.

## Career

**W**orked as a magazine illustrator and illustrator for Balenciaga while an art student; assistant to Antonio del Castillo, Lanvin-Castillo, 1961-63; worked in couture and ready-to-wear at Elizabeth Arden, 1963-65; designer, Jane Derby Designs, 1965-66; founded own company, 1966; introduced first perfume, 1977; began showing his designs in Paris, 1991; signed deal to design two lines for Pierre Balmain, 1992; added Oscar by Oscar de la Renta line, 1996; launched line of lingerie, 1998; launched his first fragrance for men, Oscar for Men, 2000; created furniture line with Century Furniture, 2002; ended deal with Balmain, 2002; launched O Oscar line, 2004; opened first boutique, New York City, 2004.

**Awards:** Coty American Fashion Critics Award, 1967; Women's Wear Designer of the Year Award, 2000; two additional Coty Awards; honor from the government of the Dominican Republic.

## Sidelights

**O**ne of the richest Hispanic Americans, Oscar de la Renta is a very successful and popular fashion designer. Best known for his evening gowns, de la Renta expanded his business to include varying priced lines of women's wear, men's wear, accessories, fragrances, household items, perfume, and furniture. De la Renta's clothes are worn by many society women, and he also provided dresses for many First Ladies of the United States, including Nancy Reagan, Hillary Clinton, and Laura Bush.

Born in 1932, in Santo Domingo in the Dominican Republic, de la Renta was raised in a middle-class household with his six sisters. His father worked as an insurance executive. When de la Renta was 17 years old, he went to Madrid, Spain, to attend art school. He became a student at the Academia de San Fernando, where he studied painting with Vasques Dias. De la Renta's original goal was to become an abstract painter.

While art had its allure, fashion was also of interest to de la Renta. He liked to buy fine suits, and learned the basics of fabrics and fit during his fittings. To buy the suits, de la Renta began doing illustrations for magazines and for a couture house in Spain called Balenciaga. De la Renta created his first dress on a freelance basis for the daughter of a U.S. ambassador. A picture of the debutante in the dress appeared in *Life* magazine.

Of this time in his life, de la Renta told Catherine Patch of the *Toronto Star,* "Soon I found that I was more interested in fashion design than I was in continuing as an illustrator. I think that any experience you have; anything you pay attention to is part of what I call the 'baggage' you carry with you all your life. My early involvement with painting, even the fact that I come from a tropical country, are part of who and what I am today."

De la Renta soon became more interested in designing clothes than painting, and moved into fashion design. While on a working vacation in Paris in 1961, he was hired for his first job at Lanvin-Castillo, where he worked as an assistant to Antonio del Castillo. In 1963, de la Renta moved to the United States to work for Elizabeth Arden. He worked in couture and the ready-to-wear salon.

De la Renta moved to Jane Derby designs in 1965 to work as a designer, though his vision was not fully realized until the end of his tenure with the firm a year later. When Derby retired, de la Renta and colleague Jerry Shaw founded their own company in 1966. De la Renta's first output was a boutique line.

As de la Renta's professional career took off, his personal life also underwent a transformation. He married Françoise de Langlade, the editor of French *Vogue,* in 1967. Her tastes influenced the way her husband designed clothes and ran his business. The couple was also high-profile socially, and their lives were covered regularly in magazines.

As a designer, de la Renta had his first big success with ball gowns. Many of his first clients were married women of leisure. The simple romantic styles of dresses for them often featured ruffles and bows. De la Renta's styles evolved over time. His lines in the 1970s retained the romantic touch, but with exotic influences such as Russian- and gypsy-themed gowns. He struggled a bit in the mid-1970s when androgyny ruled, and his ideas did not fit the times. However, he did bounce back by the end of the decade.

By 1980, de la Renta's company was doing about $200 million worth of business. One very successful product produced by de la Renta was perfume. He introduced his first perfume in 1977, and regularly added new fragrances over the years. They included Oscar de la Renta Esprit de Parfum in 1988, and both Volupte and Ruffles in 1992. In 2000, he launched his first fragrance for men called Oscar for Men. New perfumes for women called Intrusion and Rosamor were introduced in 2002 and 2004, respectively.

De la Renta's personal life evolved in the 1980s. His wife died of bone cancer in 1983. Shortly after her death, de la Renta adopted a son, whom he named Moises Oscar, on his own. He found the boy in his native country though an orphanage/day care center named Casa de Niños that he funded and remained actively involved with. The center gave children who lived in poverty a place to go and parents a place to leave their children in safety. As soon as he saw the boy who became his son, de la Renta became extremely drawn to him and despite the fact that friends were against the adoption, the designer took the child home as his own.

De la Renta's business continued to grow in the 1980s. His evening gowns moved away from the ruffled, romantic look and became even bigger, bejeweled, and full of glamour. However, de la Renta realized that his core audience was changing to career women who need to look good for night and day. While they wanted to be feminine, the clothes had to fit their needs. To that end, he created new styles of day suits for women which became quite colorful. Quilting, close cuts, and bold coloring became trademarks of his pieces in this time period.

By 1985, de la Renta's fashion business was worth $250 million. Part of the increase came from the success of new product lines. He added more day wear and ready-to-wear items as well as a cheaper Miss O line to appeal to less prosperous consumers. The de la Renta name was also put on accessories and linens.

Sales of de la Renta's products greatly increased in the late 1980s. He had one of his best years ever in fashion in 1988, doing about $400 million of business annually. In 1989, his licensed goods alone brought in about $500 million on the retail level. De la Renta did not just dominate in the business sector. In this time period, he served as president of the Council of Fashion Designers of America.

After marrying for a second time in January of 1990 to Annette Engelhard Reed, a philanthropist and socialite, de la Renta continued to grow in business. In 1991, he built on the success he had with fashion in the United States by becoming the first major American designer to show his work in Paris. De la Renta's debut in Paris for the fall 1991 season was a hit. He focused on light, wearable pieces, many of which featured plaids. In 1992, checks dominated his pieces. With this success, de la Renta was essentially on top of the American evening wear market.

De la Renta's business continued to expand in the early 1990s. In 1992, he signed a deal with the Paris-based house of Pierre Balmain to create two lines, couture and a ready-to-wear line called Ivoire. (De la Renta did not have his name on his label.) This deal made de la Renta the first American to design for the fashion house, but did not preclude the continuation of his own business or designing under his own name.

De la Renta was up to the challenge of reviving a house that had always been important but never at the top and that had suffered from major financial losses. Martha Duffy of *Time* wrote, "Oscar, as everybody calls him, fits perfectly into the Balmain aesthetic. He is not an innovator—his few enemies call him a copyist—but he executes gorgeous costumes and with a peerless eye for fabric, detail, and nuance."

De la Renta's first show for Balmain came in February of 1993, featured spring wear, and was well-received. The pieces were very wearable, elegant, contemporary, and sexy with polished touches. De la Renta continued to produce several lines a year for Balmain until 2002.

Though Balmain remained a priority for de la Renta, he did not neglect his own company. He continued to show his own designs in Paris in the early 1990s, but moved his shows back to New York City by the middle of the decade. De la Renta also added more product lines to the company. In 1996, to expand his appeal, he began creating a bridge sportswear line for women called Oscar by Oscar de la Renta. These clothes were less expensive than many other lines produced by him.

While all of de la Renta's lines took on a new, more simple aesthetic in the 1990s to reflect the style of the times, his pieces remained flattering. Though de la Renta's clothes always remained popular, in the late 1990s and early 2000s, his work became the preferred wear of American First Ladies. De la Renta had dressed First Lady Nancy Reagan in the 1980s, then provided the gowns for inaugural events for both Hillary Clinton in 1997 and Laura Bush in 2005. Clinton also wore his designs for other big events during her husband's presidency, including a speech to the Democratic National Convention in 1996, and after she became a senator in 2000.

By 1997, all of de la Renta's businesses were worth $500 million. While his fashions remained profitable, he was making more from his related lines, including accessories and perfumes, than his clothing. In 1998, he launched a line of lingerie, as well as petite division for Oscar by Oscar de la Renta, then plus sizes in 1999, both of which proved very popular. Other products that carried his name included eyewear, swimwear, handbags, and men's accessories. De la Renta continued to design two men's lines, the more expensive Oscar de la Renta Pour Homme, and the less expensive Oscar de la Renta.

In early 2000s, de la Renta entered his seventies, yet remained a vital designer who still enjoyed designing clothes. He continued to show his designs in the United States to good reviews, and his gowns remained in demand. His 2001 fall-winter collection featured some gowns that updated the "Dynasty" gowns from the 1980s in a restrained yet opulent way, while his 2004 collections featured Spanish touches. He always produced feminine clothes that appealed to a higher-end audience. Nancy Kissinger told Julia Reed of *Vogue,* "Oscar is the only one left who makes practical clothes. They fit the times; they fit people's lives."

De la Renta added his name to a whole new business in 2002: furniture, a new frontier for fashion designers. He put together a collection of 100 pieces for Century Furniture that featured dining tables as well as upholstered chairs and couches. He also expanded his fashion lines. In 2004, de la Renta added an even less expensive line of clothing called O Oscar. He wanted to attract new customers, women whom he could not reach before, despite the risk that it could lessen the value of his brand as a whole. The line was sold in mid-level department stores. De la Renta also opened his first boutique, located in New York City, in November of 2004.

As de la Renta grew older, his family became more involved in with his business. His stepdaughter, Eliza Bolen, worked for him overseeing some of the licensed products, while her husband became the company's chief executive officer in 2004. Even de la Renta's son Moises decided on a career as a designer. He dropped out of college and wanted to make his own name in the fashion world. He began with a T-shirt before moving on to a small collection of denim in 2005.

The heart of de la Renta's business remained the designer himself. *InStyle* wrote, "The name Oscar de la Renta is so lushly rhythmic that even women who own nothing more than his perfume spritz it with the confidence of knowing that these six melodious syllables ensure entrance into a world of limitless grace and polish. After more than 30 years on and around Seventh Avenue, his presence is proof that a man can possess impeccable taste and manners without displaying the slightest trace of dandyism and also design unrepentantly feminine clothes without ever misreading the desires of today's women."

## Sources

### Periodicals

*Americas* (English edition), September-October 1990, p. 30.

*Boston Herald,* October 16, 1995, p. 33.

*Cosmetics International Cosmetics Products Report,* March 2000, p. 7; June 2004, p. 3.

*Houston Chronicle,* November 26, 1992, p. 2.

*InStyle,* February 1, 2001, p. 84.

*National Review,* October 13, 1997, p. 48.

*New York Times,* March 26, 1992, p. C1; July 17, 2004, p. C1; January 11, 2005, p. B8.

*People,* September 10, 1985, p. 49.

*Pittsburgh Post-Gazette,* February 15, 2001, p. F1.

PR Newswire, September 1, 2004.

*Rocky Mountain News,* January 7, 1996, p. 19D.

*St. Louis Post-Dispatch,* May 21, 1989, p. 1S.

*St. Petersburg Times,* October 2, 1997, p. 1E.

*Time,* January 8, 1990, p. 68; February 8, 1993, p. 68.

*Time International,* May 24, 1999, p. 80.

*Toronto Star,* March 10, 1988, p. J1; May 7, 1992, p. E3; December 10, 1998, p. H2.

UPI NewsTrack, September 14, 2004.

*USA Today,* March 20, 1991, p. 1D.

*Vogue,* September 2004, p. 738.

*Washington Post,* October 13, 1985, p. K1; November 3, 1993, p. C1; January 15, 1997, p. D1; July 7, 2001, p. C1; October 24, 2002, p. H1.

*Women's Wear Daily,* January 2000, p. 73.

### Online

"Oscar de la Renta's Fashion Dynasty," NewYorkMetro.com, http://www.newyork metro.com/nymetro/shopping/fashion/spring05/11016/index.html (April 12, 2005).

—*A. Petruso*

# Drea de Matteo

## Actress

*Jim Ruymen/UPI/Landov*

Born Andrea Donna de Matteo, January 19, 1973, in New York, NY; daughter of Albert (a furniture manufacturer) and Donna (a playwright) de Matteo. *Education:* Graduated from New York University's Tisch School of the Arts, B.F.A. (film production).

**Addresses:** *Agent*—United Talent Agency, 9560 Wilshire Blvd., 5th Floor, Beverly Hills, CA 90212. *Contact*—Filth Mart, 531 E. 13th St., New York, NY 10009. *Management*—Brillstein-Grey Entertainment, 9150 Wilshire Blvd., Ste. 350, Beverly Hills, CA 90212. *Publicist*—PMK/HBH New York, 650 Fifth Ave., 33rd Flr., New York, NY 10019.

## Career

Actress in films, including: *"M" Word,* 1996; *Meet Prince Charming,* 1999; *Sleepwalk,* 2000; *'R Xmas,* 2001; *Swordfish,* 2001; *Made* (uncredited), 2001; *The Perfect You,* 2002; *Deuces Wild,* 2002; *Love Rome,* 2002; *Prey for Rock & Roll,* 2003; *Beacon Hill,* 2003; *Assault on Precinct 13,* 2005; *Dirty Love,* 2005, *Go-Go Tales,* 2005. Television appearances include: *Swift Justice,* 1996; *The Sopranos,* HBO, 1999-2004; *Joey,* NBC, 2004—. Owns a film and television production company, Great Dane Productions, as well as a New York City vintage-clothing store called Filth Mart.

**Awards:** Emmy Award for best supporting actress in a drama, National Academy of Television Arts and Sciences, for *The Sopranos,* 2004.

## Sidelights

Drea de Matteo snared a devoted television fan base for her portrayal of hapless mob girlfriend Adriana La Cerva on the acclaimed HBO series *The Sopranos.* De Matteo's character was the street-savvy Jersey-girl fiancée of "Chris-tuh-fuh," as she called him, but through a series of judgment errors was forced to become an informant for the Feds. The story arc's predictable outcome won de Matteo a well- deserved Emmy Award in 2004. She went on to take a lead role in a new NBC sitcom and *Friends* spin-off, *Joey.*

De Matteo was born in 1973 and originally grew up in a gated community in Queens, the New York borough. Her mother was a playwright, and her father ran a successful furniture company whose improving fortunes prompted a move to Manhattan's posh Upper East Side when de Matteo was seven. The upheaval traumatized her because she disliked the city, the prissiness of her new Roman Catholic school for girls, and even the home they lived in—a brownstone once owned by singer Aretha Franklin and thought to be haunted. De Matteo's way of coping with the changes was to return to visit her beloved Italian-American grandmother in Queens as often as possible, and to retreat into herself. She became terrifically shy, she told *Esquire*'s Reed Tucker. "I played sick a lot. I missed more school than I attended. I couldn't read out loud in the classroom, and get really shaky and break out in hives."

By her account de Matteo led a turbulent lifestyle during her teens and early-adult years before settling down and earning a degree in film from New York University. She made her film debut in a 1996 project called *"M" Word,* and appeared in two other little-seen films before winning a bit part in the new HBO drama series *The Sopranos* in 1999. She was cast as a restaurant hostess in the pilot episode, but returned as the girlfriend of junior mobster Christopher Moltisanti (Michael Imperioli). The Moltisanti character was originally written as a player, a guy with lots of girlfriends, but series creator David Chase liked de Matteo's performance so much he decided to write her into the series as a regular.

De Matteo's Adriana is a working-class New Jersey-ite with ambition and a taste for the good life. She works as a restaurant hostess, but later Christopher sets her up with her own nightclub to run. One day, while shopping, she is befriended by another gum-snapping, high-heeled Jersey girl, but the woman is an undercover Federal Bureau of Investigation agent. They become fast friends, and de Matteo's incautious statements force her to become a rat. When the agents bring her in for questioning for the first time, the always-excitable and now paralyzed-by-fear Adriana memorably vomits across the conference table.

De Matteo said that her Adriana character resonated back home more than she expected. "My mother loves Adriana because she understands that a life like hers does exist," she told Deborah Sontag in a *New York Times.* interview. "She grew up in that world, where the women cook and clean and get a black eye now and again, and she totally broke out." Adriana spends the rest of the series trying to come to terms with her increasingly untenable position. Her tragic end came near the end of Season Five for *The Sopranos* in 2004, but there were already rumors that her end was imminent, for de Matteo had just signed on for a new NBC sitcom. Still, her final moments—in a series known for its regular episodes of casual, bone-crunching violence—were one of the most heartbreaking in the show's history. Despite the rumors de Matteo was jumping ship, viewers were stunned and her demise incited newspaper articles and a record number of comments on HBO message boards for the show the next day.

Later that year, de Matteo debuted in *Joey,* the new Matt LeBlanc sitcom spun off from the hugely successful *Friends* after it wrapped. She was cast as Gina Tribbiani, the hairdresser sister of LeBlanc's character. In the first episode, Joey moves from New York to Los Angeles to jump-start his acting career, and settles into an apartment with his nephew, Gina's teen-genius son.

*Joey* debuted as the leader for the fall NBC line-up in 2004, and scored both high ratings and excellent reviews. A few weeks later, both de Matteo and Imperioli picked up Emmy awards for Best Supporting Actors in a drama. She still takes the occasional film role, when her schedule permits. She was a lead in *Prey for Rock & Roll,* a 2003 film with Gina Gershon and Lori Petty. In 2005, she made her action-film debut alongside Laurence Fishburne and Ethan Hawke in *Assault on Precinct 13,* a remake of John Carpenter's 1976 thriller. She was also cast in what would be her second film with noted director Abel Ferrara, 2005's *Go-Go Tales,* a strip-club tale that would also star Harvey Keitel and model Eva Herzigova. De Matteo had already appeared in Ferrara's *'R Xmas* in 2001 about an upscale Manhattan couple involved in the heroin trade. She was also developing the feature film *The Waylon Jennings Tribute,* which she will also direct and produce; the film will focus on a large concert.

Over time, de Matteo came to terms with living in the city, and even came to like it. She runs an East Village vintage-clothing store called Filth Mart, which she started with her boyfriend at the time. The relationship ended, but the business was still thriving several years later. She relocated to California for the *Joey* job with the help of her boyfriend Shooter Jennings, son of country singers Jessi Colter and the late Waylon Jennings. Her household also includes the elderly Nicaraguan woman who took care of her when she was a child and her mother was at work. After *Joey* wraps production this year, de Matteo planned to head to New York to star in a play her mother wrote called *The Heart Transplant.*

She finds it somewhat ironic that her greatest professional success has come from portraying a certain kind of woman that lurks in her background back in the more working-class quarters of Queens. "My mother wanted so badly to get me out of that world," de Matteo told Sontag in the *New York Times.* "And now I'm earning a living back in that world!"

## Sources

### Books

*Contemporary Theatre, Film, and Television,* vol. 53, Gale Group, 2004.

**Periodicals**

*Daily Variety,* September 12, 2002, p. 7.
*Esquire,* September 2004, p. 184.
*InStyle,* March 1, 2001, p. 313.
*Interview,* September 2004, p. 186.

Knight Ridder/Tribune News Service, September 20, 2004.
*New York Times,* April 4, 2004, p. AR29.
*People,* October 14, 2002, p. 85.
*Time,* September 13, 2004, p. 82.

—*Carol Brennan*

# Janice Dickinson

## Model, television personality, and author

**B**orn February 15, 1955 (some sources say February 17, 1953); married Ron Levy (a music composer; divorced); married Simon Fields (a film producer; divorced); children: Nathan (with Fields), Savannah (with Michael Birnbaum).

**Addresses:** *Office*—9972 West Wanda Dr., Beverly Hills, CA 90210.

## Career

**B**egan modeling in early 1970s under contract to the Wilhelmina agency in New York City; appeared on the cover of French *Vogue*; worked for designers Gianni Versace, Calvin Klein, and many others in print ads and on the runway; became freelance photographer; *America's Next Top Model* judge, 2003, 2004 seasons.

## Sidelights

**I**n 2003, former model Janice Dickinson began assessing the chances of young modeling hopefuls as a judge on the hit UPN reality-TV/elimination contest *America's Next Top Model.* Not one for sugarcoating opinions, Dickinson has used her experiences in the cutthroat world of modeling to raise awareness of the dangers that lurk for all young women who strive for physical perfection. She herself was once one of the world's highest-paid models, but fell prey to an array of self-abusive habits, detailed with her trademark candid humor in two volumes of memoirs. "I want them to avoid the pitfalls that I've made—bulimia, alcohol addiction,

drug dependency ... shopaholic, and all the other 'aholics' that can occur," she told the London *Mirror*'s Drew Mackenzie just after her second book, *Everything About Me Is Fake—And I'm Perfect,* was published in 2004.

Dickinson provides a birthdate of 1955, though one source claims she is two years older. She grew up in Hollywood, Florida, in a dysfunctional household headed by her father, a merchant marine with a bad temper. The middle of three daughters, she said she was a tall, gawky teenager, "an ironing board with legs," she recalled in an article she wrote for London's *Sunday Times.* "I was tall and dark, with no curves, no nothing, and I took heat for it from everyone around me."

Obsessed with fashion and fashion magazines, Dickinson moved to New York City and tried to break into the modeling business. At the time—in the early 1970s—young women with all-American looks like Cheryl Tiegs set the beauty standard, and Dickinson, with her dark hair and lush lips, was considered too Mediterranean-looking to succeed. She regularly had "the door slammed in my face at every appointment," she told Knight Ridder/Tribune News Service reporter Margaria Fitchtner. "'Sorry. Your face isn't the right shape to sell magazines.'

'Sorry. You're way too ethnic.' 'Excuse me. You don't serve our purposes.' 'You'll never make it in this town. You'll never make it, period.'"

One day, Dickinson went to visit the studio of a fashion photographer unannounced, and found that preparations were underway there for a photo shoot. Thinking quickly, she announced that she was the model that was expected, and the resulting professional shots finally landed her a contract with Wilhelmina, one of the top agencies in New York City. The agency wisely sent her to Europe, believing that she would find work there more easily due to a modeling strike, and Dickinson returned with a slew of excellent credits, including the cover of French *Vogue*. Soon inundated with job offers from American designers, ad agencies, and magazines, Dickinson quickly rose to the top of her profession. For a time in the late 1970s and early '80s, she "appeared in issue after issue of Vogue, and became a beacon of sorts for a wide range of women—Italian, Hispanic, Greek, biracial—who longed to see their own physical features in the big magazines," noted Nara Schoenberg in a Knight Ridder/Tribune News Service report.

Dickinson's career trajectory was copied by a younger model from Philadelphia named Gia Carangi, who was the toast of the fashion world for a time before substance abuse problems resulted in her death from AIDS in 1984. Early in her career, Carangi was sometimes referred to as "the next Janice Dickinson," and a young Cindy Crawford was tagged as "the next Gia Carangi" as the trend toward models who better reflected American demographics became the norm.

Dickinson commanded high rates when she was at the top of her game in the early 1980s, working for such designers as Gianni Versace and Calvin Klein. Her autobiography asserts that she coined the term "supermodel" to describe herself long before it came into common usage, but it had been used at least as early as the mid-1970s to describe Margaux Hemingway and Veruschka von Lehndorrf, who were then segueing into film careers. Supermodel or not, Dickinson maintains she was a pioneer in her field. "I was the first to do editorial, runway, TV commercials, spokesperson and catalogs," she explained to *Newsweek* interview with Nicki Gostin. "Those are five separate categories."

Dickinson worked with some of the world's best photographers, such as Richard Avedon and Irving Penn, and her boyfriend for many years, Michael Reinhardt, was a fashion photographer himself. She eventually picked up a camera herself. "All of our friends were photographers," she recalled years later in an interview with *Petersen's Photographic* writer Jay Jorgensen. "I was eating and sleeping photographs. You'd have to be a moron not to pick it up."

Dickinson thoroughly reveled in the jet-set, decadent lifestyle her fame and fortune begat. She used cocaine to stay slim, and a raft of other drug problems began affecting her work. She once fell off a runway during a Valentino show and into film icon Sophia Loren's lap, and later was a passenger in a car that went off the side of a cliff. The injuries stemming from that accident put her in the hospital for four months. The modeling jobs grew scarcer, and her personal life spiraled downward. There were two failed marriages, a long relationship with actor Sylvester Stallone, and two children. The father of her son, Nathan, was Simon Fields, a film producer to whom she had been married in the late 1980s. The paternity of her daughter, Savannah, however, was disputed for a time before DNA testing proved conclusively that another film producer, Michael Birnbaum, was the father of her daughter, not Stallone.

In July of 2000, Dickinson swore off drugs and alcohol, and began attending regular 12-step meetings. Back in the 1970s, the late makeup artist Way Bandy had suggested she keep a journal as way to attain some personal insight, and she started doing it again early in her recovery period, writing "rooms full. I couldn't stop," she told Fitchtner in the Knight Ridder/Tribune News Service article. Thinking perhaps that she had the makings of a book on her hands, she made a phone call to publisher Judith Regan of ReganBooks. "I just told her from my heart about my life," Dickinson recalled. "She said, after about a minute, 'I'm in.' I didn't turn in one shred of writing sample."

The result was the memoir *No Lifeguard on Duty: The Accidental Life of the World's First Supermodel*, issued in 2002. In it, Dickinson details the more harrowing experiences of her youth—revealing, for example, that her father sexually molested her older sister. Dickinson managed to fend him off when he approached her around the age of nine, but she was thrown across the room for her insolence and then pummeled and verbally abused on a daily basis. He even locked her in the trunk of a car once. Their mother, who died in 1995, was addicted to prescription drugs, and neither Dickinson nor her sister said anything to her to stop the abuse. "That inability to tell anyone, a teacher, a friend, was like a silent prison," she told Mackenzie in the *Mirror* article. "It led me to a lifetime of self-destructive behaviour."

*No Lifeguard on Duty* goes on to recount Dickinson's life in the fast lane during the prime years of her career, when she frequented places like Studio 54 with pals Andy Warhol, Keith Richards, and Jack Nicholson. She reveals some intimate details about famous names, including Mick Jagger and Warren Beatty. "What keeps the book from becoming too tawdry is Dickinson's sense of humor," noted *WWD* journalist Jessica Kerwin. "She applies a healthy dose to both her conquests and disasters alike." Dickinson displayed the same self-deprecating wit in an interview with *Daily Mail* writer Lina Das largely devoted to the affair with Jagger, the Rolling Stones' lead singer and a legendary rake. "It was all about jets and limos and first-class flights to concerts and although he was always wanting me to fly out to see him in concert, I played pretty hard to get, initially," Dickinson recalled about their time together. "Yes, some of the attraction was that he was in one of the biggest rock bands in the world. If that makes me shallow, then I'm shallow."

Dickinson's book caused a bit of a stir, but reviewers commended her courage. "Janice Dickinson is a funny and fluid narrator," asserted *New York Observer* writer Philip Weiss, and though he conceded that some other critics had been less than kind in their reviews, "what makes it interesting is her scathing inventory—from age 47, in Los Angeles—of everyone's desperate behavior, including her own." A *Publishers Weekly* contributor found that the fact that Dickinson comes across as someone prepared to acknowledge and admit "her own flaws makes it easy to relate to her positive message and should inspire readers searching for solutions to career and personal conflicts."

In 2003, Dickinson began appearing on a new reality-television series hosted and created by model Tyra Banks. A model-search contest similar to the talent-show elimination series *American Idol*, *America's Next Top Model* offered the first-prize winner an exclusive modeling contract. As one of the judges, Dickinson's sometimes-acerbic remarks to the young modeling hopefuls helped the show score impressive ratings during its first season, which ended in July of 2003. "I'm brutally honest," she admitted to Mackenzie in the *Mirror* interview. "I feel like I'm saving the girls a lot of time by telling them, 'You're too fat, too skinny, too old or too short.'"

Dickinson's second volume of "brutally honest" revelations came out in 2004: *Everything About Me Is Fake—And I'm Perfect.* True to form, she underwent $60,000 worth of cosmetic-surgery procedures a few months before it was published, and the promotional efforts included a face-lift diary, complete with before-and-after photographs, for *People* magazine. "I'm not doing anything that most people in the entertainment industry aren't doing," the former model pointed out to readers. "I'm just talking about it. People wonder, Why can't I look like that celebrity? This is why."

The dangers of "perfliction"—a term that Dickinson really did coin as a way to describe an unhealthy addiction to perfecting one's appearance—was a topic that Dickinson discussed often. She was fond of warning that magazine images are far, far from reality, telling readers in the article she wrote for the *Sunday Times,* that the women in those photographs "starve themselves for weeks on end, smoke up a storm, scoff diuretics and then, when everyone's still unhappy with their photos, someone sits at a computer and points and clicks them into perfect, unreal sexiness."

Dickinson's first volume of memoirs was acquired as a film property by Warner Brothers in 2004. She is planning a third book, and told *Entertainment Weekly* writer Jennifer Armstrong she had many more stories as yet untold. "I'm like *The Lord of the Rings* of supermodels," she said. "This is only book 2 of the trilogy." A single parent, she lives in the Los Angeles area and appeared on *America's Next Top Model 2,* the 2004 follow-up, where she once again delivered her barbed advice. But Dickinson told one writer that her bravura front was merely a facade. "God granted me this gruff exterior," she told Weiss in the *New York Observer.* "But basically, inside, I'm a piece of fluff."

## Selected writings

### Memoirs

*No Lifeguard on Duty: The Accidental Life of the World's First Supermodel,* ReganBooks (New York City), 2002.
*Everything About Me Is Fake—And I'm Perfect,* Regan-Books, 2004.

## Sources

### Periodicals

*Advocate,* August 17, 2004, p. 93.
*Daily Mail* (London, England), July 29, 2004, p. 54.
*Entertainment Weekly,* February 27, 2004, p. 14; April 30, 2004, p. 168.

Knight Ridder/Tribune News Service, August 31, 2002; September 10, 2002; July 23, 2003.

*Mirror* (London, England), May 25, 2004, p. 38.

*Newsweek,* April 26, 2004, p. 63.

*New York Observer* (New York, NY), September 9, 2002, p. 1.

*People,* May 3, 2004, pp. 87-89.

*Petersen's Photographic,* December 1999, p. 59.

*Publishers Weekly,* July 29, 2002, p. 67.

*Sunday Times* (London, England), August 8, 2004, p. 22.

*WWD,* August 23, 2002, p. 4.

**Online**

*Contemporary Authors Online,* Gale, 2004.

—*Carol Brennan*

# Domenico Dolce and Stefano Gabbana

## Fashion designers

**B**orn Domenico Dolce, August 13, 1958, in Polizzi Generosa, Sicily. Born Stefano Gabbana, November 14, 1962, in Milan, Italy. *Education:* Gabbana attended university in Milan.

**Addresses:** *Office*—Headquarters Via Santa Cecilia, 7 20122 Milan, Italy.

## Career

**F**ounders and fashion designers for Dolce & Gabbana, 1985—; launched Dolce & Gabbana women's collection, 1986; launched beachwear line, 1988; launched lingerie line, 1989; opened first boutique in Japan, 1989; launched Dolce & Gabbana men's collection, 1990; opened first boutique in Milan, 1990; released Dolce & Gabbana perfume, 1992; launched D&G men's collection, D&G women's collection, home collection, and Dolce & Gabbana for men cologne, 1994; launched jeans and eye wear lines, 1996; released By for women and By for men fragrances, 1997; released DG Feminine and DG Masculine fragrances, 1998; released Light Blue for women fragrance, 2001; released Sicily for women fragrance, 2003; opened first stand-alone store, London, England, 2004.

**Awards:** Woolmark Award, 1990.

## Sidelights

**D**omenico Dolce and Stefano Gabbana rose from obscurity to form a partnership that would have them becoming two of the best known designers in the fashion world. They have dressed women like Madonna and Nicole Kidman and men like Tom Cruise. People vie to wear their clothing at public events and to revel in the attention such clothing affords them. According to the Dolce & Gabbana website, their clothes are for a certain type of woman: "The Dolce & Gabbana woman is strong: she likes herself and knows she is liked. A cosmopolitan woman who has toured the world but who doesn't forget her roots." And the same, they say, is true for the man who wears their clothes. "At his ease, he dresses for himself; a little hedonistic, he pays considerable attention to details."

Dolce was born in Polizzi Generosa, a small village near Palermo, Sicily on August 13, 1958. He grew up in fashion, since his father was a tailor. He has always credited this with the reason fashion became his medium of choice for expressing himself, something he felt a deep desire to do from an early age. He studied fashion when he was young and worked in his family's small clothing factory as he was growing up. Deciding to go off and pursue his own career in fashion design, Dolce moved to Milan and got a job there at one of its famous design studios. He knew immediately that he had done the right thing, that he had found the best way to express himself. He told Bruce Weber in *Interview* magazine, "[Design] was the way I was able to do the things I was dreaming about.... As a designer, I see dreams as my job. It's like being a psychologist. I have to capture what people are feeling and translate that into fashion and even provide what people want before they consciously know they want it."

Gabbana, on the other hand, was born in Milan, Italy, on November 14, 1962. Gabbana, unlike his future partner, had never thought about fashion as a child. He grew up away from it and it was not until he was about 15 years old that he became interested in fashion in general for himself, particularly such designers as Fiorucci. Instead, Gabbana studied graphic design at the university because he wanted to go into advertising. He worked in that field for a short time after graduation before he quit, realizing that his heart just was not in it. It was at that time that he turned to fashion. He told Weber in *Interview,* "I was lucky because a designer took me under his wing and helped me understand the world of fashion. But it was ultimately Domenico who taught me the most about fashion. As time went on while I was learning about it, I fell in love with it—with designing, with making clothes, with dressing people."

The pair met in 1980 when they were both assistants at an atelier in Milan. They started their partnership in 1982, although they still did freelance designing for other companies until they had officially started their own company. Fame and fortune, however, did not come immediately to the pair. They struggled to come to the attention of the fashion scene and did everything in their power to show off their designs to bring that about. "I remember our first show," Dolce reminisced to Susannah Frankel of the *Guardian.* "We did it in a small apartment in Milan. We organized it ourselves, me and Stefano, without PR, [with] nothing. My sister and my brother were on the door." According to Allison Adato of *People,* "Using friends as models, they held shows wherever they could—even in a fast-food restaurant. (The invites looked like hamburgers.) The unconventional approach stirred enough buzz to land them a spot in Milan's 1984 fashion week." They made their real world debut at the "New Talent" fashion shows at the Milan collections in October of 1985. They received such acclaim that they launched the Dolce & Gabbana women's collection the very next year, in March of 1986. Not long after, in 1989 they opened their first boutique in Japan.

Their style is a mix of traditionally male and female clothing, as they are known to say that fashion and dressing have nothing to do with being straight or gay, but rather that everyone has a part of the opposite sex inside them and that everyone needs to get in touch with that opposite side of their gender to be whole. They point out that it is only modern fashion that has made men and women so different dress-wise. In the 16th century men wore high heels, make-up, and dandy clothes and they were no less masculine than today's men, and women were seen wearing more manly suit tops and flat shoes. When asked why the two of them collaborated and how it worked, Dolce told Weber in *Interview,* "We have different tastes, which means that together we tap a combination of desires. Sometimes we might create something that is more Gabbana; sometimes it might be more Dolce. But what we create always has to arrive at some kind of agreement." They both love the style and feel of southern Italy and most of their designs pull heavily on that tradition. "We prefer southern people," Gabbana told Frankel of the *Guardian.* "They have more passion. What we hate is when people put up a barrier and try and hide what they feel."

Whatever their likes or dislikes, it became increasingly apparent that the two designers struck a chord with people around the world as their clothing lines became more and more popular. They launched the Dolce & Gabbana men's collection in January of 1990. Then, in that same year they opened their first boutique in Milan. Also in 1990 the pair won the Woolmark Award. They launched the D&G men's collection in January of 1994 and the D&G women's collection in March of that same year. (D&G is their less expensive line of clothing.) Every year their collections change, although each designer has his favorite pieces that remain in the collection each season. Their concern has never been with what is trendy, but what feels right at that moment. Gabbana was quoted by Frankel in the *Guardian* as having said, "We sketch everything from new each season, and it doesn't come out the same, but it has the same feeling. This is better in the end because I have one taste. The customer comes to my shop to buy one taste, not another taste, not what is trendy. Sometimes what's in fashion is good for Dolce & Gabbana, sometimes it's not. But it's better to stay a little outside. Not to try and keep up with it all. It's better to stick with your own style, otherwise, e la morte [death]."

The one thing that really made the designers' career, however, was when their clothes came to the attention of pop sensation Madonna. She has become one of the duo's biggest fans, and the feelings are definitely mutual. There are very few people from whom the two designers will take orders and design clothing specifically for, but for Madonna they will drop everything to help. In 1993, the duo created 1,500 costumes for Madonna's world tour, "The Girlie Show." They expected this to bring them into the eyes of fashion critics and aficionados around the world, but they received even more recognition than they expected. Then, for Madonna's *Music* album, the designers went even further for their favorite pop star; not only did they dress Madonna and her entire ensemble, but they designed and created an entire backdrop for the tour. It was a big success.

In 1995 the book *10 Years of Dolce and Gabbana* was published. The book, which commemorated the first decade of the designers' fashions in photographs had an introduction by Isabella Rossellini, the Italian actress who has been wearing their clothes almost since the pair started designing them. Frankel in the *Guardian* said of the duo's fashions, "There's nothing self-consciously cool about the label. What's more, it suits women (of means, of course) of all shapes and sizes—in many cases, the stick-thin would be hard pushed to fill it. Instead, Dolce & Gabbana's designs are overtly romantic, unashamedly voluptuous, and women the world over love them for it." And their popularity has spread like wildfire. Their clothing has been worn by such famous people as Brian Ferry, Brad Pitt, Bruce Willis, Demi Moore, Victoria Beckham, Kylie Minogue, Beyonce Knowles, Catherine Zeta-Jones, Salma Hayek, and Angelina Jolie, just to name a few.

Although the pair became lovers when they set up their fashion house in 1985, they only announced their relationship publicly in 2000. They bought the Villa Volpe, a 19th-century palazzo in the center of Milan and moved in together. It was a much-talked about house, covered with animal prints, red sofas, and church candles, reflecting the pair's eclectic tastes. In 2003 the pair, who love the glamour and glitz of Hollywood and professedly love it when stars wear their fashions, came out with their second book of photos called *Hollywood.*

In 2004 Dolce and Gabbana opened their first standalone store anywhere in the world on Bond Street in London, England, the D&G emporium, which stocked the duos less-expensive designer collection. Not everyone was excited about the fact, though, just as not everyone was a fan of the duo's styles. A writer for the *Daily Mail* called the Dolce & Gabbana style cheap. "That's not to say D&G clothes can't look good—you just have to be 18 and have a 12-year-old boy's body to wear them. And of course they're fun, but that's usually because the joke's on the person wearing them. One of D&G's few strengths is that they know who they're appealing to and play on that." Although not all felt that way. Lisa Armstrong for the *Times* of London said, "Gabbana's knack for creating just the right degree

of theatrical gorgeousness stops the average shopper dead in her tracks, while Dolce's eye for cut and detail seduces her in a quieter way, usually after she has tried the clothes on. It's a formidable combination."

After 19 years, in February of 2005 Dolce and Gabbana announced that they had split up their personal relationship. They moved into separate apartments, although they both lived in the same block in Milan, and they have said that they will probably still go on vacation together. The break up, they hastened to assure the world, would not affect their famous label. Richard Edwards in the *Evening Standard* quoted Dolce as having said that the separation was friendly. "On a professional level we are still together. We work together wonderfully well, we have a very strong understanding. We have a very strong love which ties us to each other."

## Sources

### Periodicals

*Daily Mail* (London, England), March 4, 2004, p. 57.
*Daily Telegraph* (London, England), February 21, 2005.
*Evening Standard* (London, England), February 2005.
*Guardian* (London, England), October 4, 1997, p. 38; September 23, 2000, p. 26.
*Independent* (London, England), January 10, 2004, p. 19.
*Interview,* September 1995.
*Observer* (London, England), March 4, 2001, p. 1.
*People,* November 10, 2003, pp. 107-10.
*Sunday Mirror* (London, England), February 20, 2005, p. 27.
*Time International,* March 15, 2002, p. 20.
*Times* (London, England), December 4, 2000, p. 12; November 13, 2003, p. 8.

### Online

Dolce & Gabbana, http://eng.dolcegabbana.it/corporate.asp?page=DGProfile (May 15, 2005).
"Dolce and Gabbana Confirm Love Split," *Hello!,* http://www.hellomagazine.com/fashion/2005/02/18/dolcegabbana/ (May 15, 2005).
"Dolce & Gabbana," GLBTQ Encyclopedia, http://www.glbtq.com/arts/dolce_gabbana.html (May 15, 2005).
"Dolce & Gabbana," Webwombat, http://www.webwombat.com.au/lifestyle/fashion_beauty/dolcegabbana.htm (May 15, 2005).

"Santucci at D&G," Fashion United, http://www.fashionunited.co.uk/news/dolcegabbana.htm (May 15, 2005).

"10 Years of Dolce & Gabbana," Abbeville, http://www.abbeville.com/oscar/dg.asp (May 15, 2005).

"Who's who: Stefano Gabbana, fashion designer," Infomat, http://www.infomat.com/whoswho/stefanogabbana.html (May 15, 2005).

—*Catherine Victoria Donaldson*

# Duran Duran

## Pop group

**M**embers include Sterling Campbell (group member, 1990-92), drums; Warren Cuccurullo (born on December 8, 1956; group member, 1986-2001), guitar; Simon Le Bon (born on October 27, 1958, in Bushey, England), vocals; Nick Rhodes (born Nicholas Bates, June 8, 1962, in England), keyboards; Andy Taylor (born on February 16, 1961, in Dolver-Hampton, England; group member, 1978-85, 2001—), guitar, keyboards; John Taylor (born on June 20, 1960, in Birmingham, England; group mem-

ber, 1978-97, 2001—), bass; Roger Taylor (born on April 26, 1960, in Birmingham, England; group member, 1978-85, 2001—), drums.

**Addresses:** *Website*—Duran Duran Official Website: http://www.duranduran.com/.

## Career

Group formed in Birmingham, England, 1978; performed in the Birmingham area, 1980-84; toured internationally, beginning 1984; released debut album *Duran Duran,* 1981; released *Rio,* 1982; released *Seven and the Ragged Tiger,* 1984; split into two side projects, Power Station and Arcadia, 1985; re-formed minus Roger and Andy Taylor, 1986; released *Notorious,* 1987; released *Big Thing!,* 1988; released *Liberty,* 1990; released hits compilation *Decade: Greatest Hits,* 1990; released *Duran Duran (The Wedding Album),* 1993; released *Thank You,* 1995; released *Medazzaland,* 1997; John Taylor left group, 1997; released greatest hits compilation *Greatest,* 1998; group left EMI/Capitol, 1998; signed with Hollywood label, released *Pop Trash,* 2000; Warren Cuccurullo left group, five original members reunited, 2001; Capitol released singles compilation box set *The Singles 81-85,* 2003; toured with original members, 2003-05; released *Astronaut,* 2004.

**Awards:** Grammy Award for best video—short form, Recording Academy, 1983; Grammy Award for best video album, Recording Academy, 1983; Brit Award for best British video, for "Wild Boys," 1985; Ivor Novello Award, 1993; star on the Hollywood Walk of Fame, 1993; MTV Video Music Award for Lifetime Achievement, 2003; *Q Magazine* lifetime achievement award, 2004; Brit Award for outstanding contribution, 2004.

## Sidelights

When MTV dawned in the early 1980s, it changed the face of popular music forever, and the British rock group Duran Duran was one of the first acts to take full advantage of its possibilities. The five-member band of young men, with sculpted faces often adorned with make-up and wearing expensive clothes, saw in the music video the perfect vehicle for propelling their musical abilities to fame, fortune, and good times. Combining the sounds of 1970s British punk and the more upbeat, danceable rhythms of disco, Duran Duran began producing clean, sparkling (if not critically acclaimed) pop tunes. But what set them apart immediately were their videos: somewhat surreal escapist fantasies that took the self-styled playboys to such far-flung locales as Sri Lanka and Antigua. Screaming, record-buying, television-watching teenage girls everywhere ate it up—and no one could have predicted it better than the band members themselves. "Video to us is like stereo was to Pink Floyd," Duran Duran keyboardist Nick Rhodes told Keith L. Thomas in the *Herald.* "It was new, it was just happening. And we saw we could do a lot with it." But, with more than 25 years together and more than 70 million albums sold, the group has proven its significance well beyond the video screen.

While the conservative rock press liked to downplay the success of Duran Duran because of their obvious vanity and lack of attention to "serious" music, it should be noted that some of rock and roll's most time-honored heroes, such as Elvis Presley and even a few members of the Beatles, were never accused of being serious musicians. Success in pop music has always depended upon image at least as much as the music itself. And "serious music" is not necessarily for everyone, as *Rolling Stone*'s James Henke realized when he referred to Duran Duran's eager fans as "young girls who were glued to their television sets watching MTV every waking hour. These girls had little use for the Clash's left-wing politics, or the ranting and raving of that weird-looking Elvis Costello. But Duran Duran, now they were something else. Five extremely good-looking young men. Dream dates."

Duran Duran began coming together in 1978 (some sources say 1977) in the Midlands city of Birmingham, where Rhodes and guitarist John Taylor started performing with a variety of bandmates. The group, which takes its name from a character in the 1968 film *Barbarella,* became complete in 1980 when Simon Le Bon, a drop-out drama student, showed up one day in pink leopard-print leotards and said he wanted to sing in the band. Le Bon joined Rhodes, John Taylor (who switched to bass), drummer Roger Taylor, and guitarist Andy Taylor (none of the Taylors are related), and the quintet began performing in Birmingham, most frequently at a club called Rum Runners which had become established as the home of England's burgeoning New Romantic scene. "Donning the foppish clothes of the movement and playing a slick, if superficial, brand of dance-pop, the band was tailor-made for the style obsessed New Romantics," declared *Encyclopedia of Rock.*

Duran Duran quickly became the headliners of that movement, playing at large clubs and festivals throughout England, and in early 1981 they released their first single, "Planet Earth," which went to number 12 on the United Kingdom charts. Later that year their first album, *Duran Duran,* went to number three on the album charts and spawned two more hit singles, including "Girls on Film." They had already been shunned by the serious music press at this point, but newer, teen-oriented, image-conscious magazines like *Smash Hits* and *The Face* were more than happy to circulate glossy photos of "The Boys," as they had become known. The lavish videos helped transfer this new-found fame to the United States, where "Hungry Like the Wolf" reached number three. Their videos won the group two Grammy Awards in 1983: Best Video—Short Form and Best Video Album. By 1984 Duran Duran was an international phenomenon—their third album, *Seven and a Ragged Tiger,* debuted at number one and suddenly the boys were living the lives they had created for themselves on video, playing sold-out tour dates around the world.

They were dandies, playboys, and their profiles became plastered on teen magazines everywhere. First there was Rhodes (his name was originally Nicholas Bates), the man who probably most personified the band's gaudy image. Rhodes grew up with John Taylor and both found that they liked the music of glittery stars like T. Rex. "We wouldn't buy records by ugly groups," Rhodes told *People,* adding that when he and Taylor decided to start a band they "had vivid ideas of what we wanted to look and sound like, but we looked at the instruments and said, 'Do we have to learn to *play* these things?'" John Taylor was a ladies' man and a huge target for the gossipy British Fleet Street press. His wanderings were well-chronicled there. "Being a rock star is like putting a huge sign in a window, 'For Sale,'" Taylor told *People.* "I did an interview with *Penthouse* and they said, 'What's your idea of a great woman?' I said, 'Someone who could tie me up and whip me and make great bacon sandwiches.'" Le Bon was an unlikely pop star in that he still opened doors for women, had a pensive streak that made him yearn for sailing alone on the sea, and because his bandmates once tagged him with the nickname "Lardo" because of his pudginess. Roger and Andy Taylor rounded out the band and were more known for staying in the shadows while the others baited the screaming girls at center stage.

By 1985 Duran Duran had started suffering from the personality conflicts that hamper many bands. Their production slacked off as the players spent more time apart, getting together only occasionally for certain projects, such as the immensely successful single and video for the James Bond movie *A View To a Kill.* The song was the only Bond theme to go to No. 1 on the charts. John and Andy Taylor began work on an outside project with Robert Palmer in 1985 and formed a band called Power Station, which recorded an album of the same name (which was number 30 that year, according to *Rolling Stone*) and played at the Live Aid benefit concert. In the meantime the remaining "thoughtful" members of the group briefly performed and recorded as Arcadia, spawning the LP *So Red the Rose.* It, too, climbed the charts; *Rolling Stone* found it harmless and bland: "Egan's lubricated bass line contrasts nicely with Simon's hog-calling tenor…. like the Power Station's record, it's proficient, serviceable pop without any unifying drive or purpose. And no matter how obnoxious (or not) you may have found them, personality is one thing Duran Duran never lacked." By 1986 Duran Duran was back intact and recording again, although they would never regain the success of the early 1980s.

Their 1987 effort, *Notorious,* received the usual chilly reception from critics, but the videos were popular on MTV. *Rolling Stone* actually went so far as to call *Notorious* Duran Duran's "most consistently listenable work," but felt the band had lost personality in the search for musical maturity. *Big Thing!* of 1988 had none of the MTV audience and none of the back-handed compliments of earlier reviews. *People* panned the album; "As 'mature' musicians, they're marooned." *Encyclopedia of Rock* summed up Duran Duran's impact on the music world in this way: "Musically, Duran Duran are no more than accomplished studio stylists, skillful welders of a host of disparate elements—hard rock, electro, white soul and, latterly, scratch and hip-hop—into an eminently commercial sound. Far more important was their marketing success, whereby they capitalized on their obvious visual attractions through the media (video and the glossy pop magazines), a technique that became increasingly important in the music industry in the Eighties." Warren Cuccurullo, formerly of the group Missing Persons, began assisting Duran Duran on guitar in 1986; he became a permanent member of the group in 1990.

*Liberty,* released in 1990, was another of Duran Duran's efforts to renew their past success. This time the band combined "everything from disco to guitar rock, … Motown, Philly soul, and new wave," according to Stephen Thomas Erlewine of *All Music Guide,* creating an album that was stylistically confusing and helped to continue the band's falling sales. The greatest hits compilation *Decade: Greatest Hits* was also released that year and would eventually earn platinum sales in May of 1998.

The group's fortunes changed, though, in 1993 with the release of what was considered a comeback album, *Duran Duran (The Wedding Album).* The album topped the charts at number three and went platinum in June of 1993, powered by the hit singles "Ordinary World," which hit number three on the *Billboard* Hot 100 chart, and "Come Undone," which charted in the top ten. The album also achieved broad international success, landing among the top-ten selling records in Japan, the Philippines, Singapore, Malaysia, Hong Kong, Venezuela, Mexico, Brazil, South Africa, New Zealand, Australia, and Argentina. The group toured and was also featured in an *MTV Unplugged* special.

*Thank You,* what *MusicHound Rock: The Essential Album Guide* referred to as a "bizarre" covers album, followed in 1995. Duran Duran's ode to their influences "killed the momentum again," according to *MusicHound Rock,* eroding the resurgent popularity brought about by *Duran Duran (The Wedding Album).* "The idea was to do songs that we wish we'd written," Rhodes told *Entertainment Weekly. Medazzaland* was released in 1997, minus the contribution of John Taylor, who left the group that year to start a new band, Terroristen. Another greatest hits compilation, this one entitled simply *Greatest,* was released in 1998. The group left the EMI/Capitol label that same year.

With Le Bon and Rhodes the only remaining members of the original lineup, the group released *Pop Trash* in 2000 on the Hollywood label. The album "marks a bold departure from Duran Duran's signature dance-oriented pop sound into more avant-garde musical experimentation," said Carly Hay in *Billboard.* "That's what I like about this album: It spans," LeBon told Hay. "This is our statement on how it feels to live a little."

In 2001, Cuccurullo left to re-form Missing Persons, and all five of the original members of Duran Duran reunited to begin work on a new album. At first, Duran Duran had trouble getting signed to a new contract. "Every time we sidled up to a record label, the chief executives would get fired, or the company would be cannibalized by a bigger company," Rhodes explained to Europe Intelligence Wire's Robert Sandall. Duran Duran also had to deal with being considered has-beens. While writing and recording, the band played periodic shows in Japan, the United States, and other countries. On August 28, 2003, the band received a MTV Video Music Award for lifetime achievement. On February 17, 2004, Duran Duran received the BRIT Award for Outstanding Contribution to British Music. At the award ceremony, they played a selection of their hits, receiving resounding applause. In April of that year, the band launched an arena tour of the United Kingdom, their first full-blown tour with the original lineup in 18 years. The concerts were completely sold-out, helping prove that the band still had a faithful fan base. "It says something that 18 years after the original line-up … disbanded, the mere mention of their name can reduce grown women to a state of teenaged hysteria," declared Europe Intelligence Wire's Jeff Magill. "But Duran Duran were the quintessential pop band. They had the good looks, sharp style, and brilliant music required to elevate them to iconic status, where they remain today." After noticing how much public support Duran Duran received, Don Ienner, the head of Sony Music Label Group, signed them to a worldwide contract in 2004. "These guys are very current," Ienner told *Entertainment Weekly*'s Nicholas Fonseca. "They're not just a nostalgia band coming out and playing their history. They want to finish what they started."

In June of 2004, Duran Duran announced plans to release their first new album with this lineup since 1983's *Seven and the Ragged Tiger.* The album's first single, "(Reach Up for the) Sunrise," climbed the charts, prior to the album's release. After working on the album for more than three years, the band released *Astronaut* in October of 2004. Two versions were released: a CD-only version and a limited-edition CD/DVD package that included footage from the band's sold-out April of 2004 show at London's Wembley Arena. Co-produced by Don Gilmore (Linkin Park) and Dallas Austin (Boyz II Men), the album was a return to the band's new-wave sound. "We were very adamant that this has to be classic Duran Duran music," John Taylor told Fonseca in *Entertainment Weekly.* "But it also had to be modern. It took us several years to strike that balance." According to the *Washington Times*' Scott Galupo, the album is "better than anything put out under the band's moniker in more than a decade [and is] among the year's best improbable comeback albums." With the renewed interest in the band, John Taylor told Europe Intelligence Wire's Magill that the band just wants to please the fans. "It's not about the money, you know. We just want to make a difference, I suppose, even if it's just in a few people's lives for one night. That's all a musician can hope for."

## Selected discography

### Duran Duran

*Duran Duran,* Harvest, 1981.
*Rio,* Capitol, 1982.
*Seven and the Ragged Tiger,* Capitol, 1983.
*Arena,* Capitol, 1984.
*Notorious,* Capitol, 1987.
*Big Thing!,* Capitol, 1988.

*Decade: Greatest Hits,* Capitol, 1990.
*Liberty,* Alliance, 1990.
*Duran Duran (The Wedding Album),* Capitol, 1993.
*Thank You,* Capitol, 1995.
*Medazzaland,* Capitol, 1997.
*Night Versions: The Essential Duran Duran* (remixes), EMI/Capitol, 1998.
*Greatest,* Capitol, 1998.
*Pop Trash,* Hollywood, 2000.
*The Singles 81-85* (box set), Capitol, 2003.
*Astronaut,* Epic Records/Sony Music, 2004.
(Contributor) *Queer Eye for the Straight Guy* (soundtrack), Capitol, 2004.
*The Singles, Vol. 2 (1986-1995)* (box set), EMI, 2004.

## Andy Taylor (solo)

*Thunder,* MCA, 1987.
*Dangerous,* A&M, 1990.

## Arcadia

*So Red the Rose,* Capitol, 1985.

## John Taylor (solo)

(Contributor) *9 1/2 Weeks* (soundtrack), Capitol, 1988.
(With Neurotic Outsiders) *Neurotic Outsiders,* Maverick, 1996.
*Feelings Are Good & Other Lies,* Revolver, 1997.
*Techno for Two* (Japanese import), Cutti, 2001.

## Power Station

*The Power Station,* Capitol, 1985.
*Living in Fear,* Chrysalis, 1996.

# Sources

### Books

Graff, Gary, and Daniel Durchholz, editors, *Music-Hound Rock: The Essential Album Guide,* second edition, Visible Ink, 1999.
Hardy, Phil, and Dave Laing, *Encyclopedia of Rock,* Schirmer, 1988.

### Periodicals

*Amusement Business,* November 2, 1998.
*Billboard,* June 26, 1993; May 6, 2000; February 21, 2004, p. 49; February 28, 2004, p. 7; October 2, 2004, p. 5; October 23, 2004, p. 46.
*Billboard Bulletin,* November 25, 2003.
*Entertainment Weekly,* April 14, 1995; August 1, 2003; September 5, 2003; October 15, 2004, pp. 34-37.
*Europe Intelligence Wire,* February 20, 2004; April 5, 2004; September 17, 2004.
*Herald,* August 25, 1984.
*Hollywood Reporter,* August 29, 2003.
Knight Ridder/Tribune News Service, February 10, 2004.
*People,* July 22, 1985; November 7, 1988; October 25, 2004, pp. 128-30; November 1, 2004, p. 37.
*Rolling Stone,* February 2, 1984; January 16, 1986; January 29, 1987.
UPI NewsTrack, June 16, 2004.
*Washington Times,* October 15, 2004, p. D7.

### Online

"Duran Duran," *All Music Guide,* http://www.all music.com (April 5, 2005).
Duran Duran Official Website, http://www.duran duran.com (April 5, 2005).
"Duran Duran," Recording Academy, http://www. grammy.com/awards/search/index.aspx (April 5, 2005).
"Duran Duran," Recording Industry Association of America, http://www.riaa.com/gp/database/ search_results.asp (April 5, 2005).
"Duran Duran to be Honoured with the 'Outstanding Contribution' at the BRIT Awards in 2004," BRIT Awards, http://www.brits.co.uk/2003/ press/release.php?releaseID=32 (April 5, 2005).

*—David Collins*

# James Dyson

## Inventor

**B**orn May 2, 1947, in Cromer, Norfolk, England; son of Alec (a teacher) and Mary (Bolton) Dyson; married Deirdre Hindmarsh (a teacher and painter), 1967; children: Emily, Jacob, Sam. *Education:* Attended Byam Shaw School of Art, London, England, and the Royal College of Art, London, 1966-70.

**Addresses:** *Office*—Dyson Appliances Ltd, Tetbury Hill, Malmesbury, Wiltshire SN16 0RP, United Kingdom.

## Career

**W**ith Rotork Marine, 1970-74; managing director of Kirk-Dyson, 1974-79; founded Dyson Research Ltd., 1979; chair, Dyson Ltd., 1992—. Affiliated with the Design Museum, London, for several years.

**Awards:** Commander of the British Empire, 1998.

## Sidelights

**A**merican consumers first encountered the plummy, authoritative accent of Britain's James Dyson in 2002, in television commercials that starred the maverick inventor and his unique bagless vacuum cleaner. The Dyson Dual Cyclone was already a top-seller in Europe and Japan by then, and Dyson himself was somewhat of a celebrity in Britain, having become known in the 1970s as the man who, quite literally, reinvented the wheel-

barrow. Though his Dyson vacuum cleaner would sell some 12 million units worldwide, the devoted tinkerer was still finessing further improvements to it. "Ideally it should weigh nothing, make no noise, and require no effort," he told *People*. "There's a long way to go before it's perfect."

Born in 1947, Dyson grew up in England's Norfolk countryside. His grandfather had been a headmaster, or school principal, and his father entered the profession as well, but died when Dyson was a child. He was then sent off to a boarding school, where his innate creative inclinations were sometimes discouraged. Once, he was put in charge of the programs to be handed out for a school play, and designed scrolls instead of the usual booklet. The school's headmaster was apoplectic when he saw them, and Dyson later said it was a good early lesson. He "learned that to change things and be an inventor," he told *People*, "you are going to come up against trouble all the time."

Dyson went on to study painting at the Byam Shaw School of Art, but later switched to furniture and interior design at the prestigious Royal College of Art in London. He married a fellow art student, Deirdre Hindmarsh, and eventually settled into a job with Rotork Marine in 1970, which designed and manufactured a high-speed landing craft called the Sea Truck. One version of the flat-bottomed vessel was used by Egyptian troops to get across the Suez Canal during the 1973 Yom Kippur War. In 1974, Dyson struck out on his own, forming a firm with his sister and her husband to make the Ballbarrow. This was the first significant update of the wheelbarrow since the medieval era, and Dyson's innovation was to use a plastic ball instead of a wheel for easier maneuverability.

Like nearly all of Dyson's inventions, the idea for the Ballbarrow had been spurred by personal frustration, when several years earlier his wheelbarrow kept getting stuck in the mud when he was working in the garden. Later that decade, in 1978, he was appalled by the poor performance of his somewhat pricey new vacuum cleaner. Realizing that the "bag" system and the motor that created the suction force had some inherent flaws, he went to work on a new version. It would take him four years, and numerous legal battles. Adding to his troubles, he was ousted from the Ballbarrow company by his partners after management disagreements.

In 1979, the determined tinkerer established Dyson Research Ltd. with the help of one backer, his buy-out funds from Ballbarrow, a second mortgage on his home—which by then also housed three small children—and the support of his wife, who taught school to make ends meet. After building 5,127 prototypes, Dyson finally had a workable vacuum cleaner, which had no bag and relied on centrifugal force to separate the dirt from air. He shopped it around to Black & Decker, Electrolux, and other major vacuum-cleaner manufacturers, and they were all profoundly uninterested. For the companies, the sale of replacement vacuum-cleaner bags was a profitable sideline, and few thought that consumers actually wanted to see the dirt that came off the carpets, as the see-through Dyson chamber revealed in all its filthy glory.

Dyson did manage to begin making and selling what was called the "G-Force" vacuum cleaner in Japan in 1986, and it emerged as a cult favorite, despite its rather high price tag. But then he was forced to begin suing other companies for patent infringement, and the cases dragged on for years and nearly bankrupted him. Finally, in the early 1990s he was able to build a factory in the Wiltshire area of England, after obtaining a business loan from a local bank; several other financial institutions had turned him down, but allegedly the bank manager's

wife had tried his vacuum cleaner and was thrilled with it. The Dyson DC01 vacuum cleaner went on the market in Britain in 1993, and by early 1995 was the best-selling vacuum cleaner in the country. It had so many fans that it eventually entered the permanent collections of the Design Museum of London, the Victoria & Albert Museum, the Design Museum of Zurich, and Paris's Centre Georges Pompidou, and has also collected a long list of industrial-design awards.

When Dyson launched his product in the United States in 2002, he began to appear in television ads for it. At a retail price of $399, the Dyson Dual Cyclone was a hit with American consumers as well, and by early 2005 had captured 20 percent of the vacuum-cleaner sales market. His company, based in Wiltshire, remains a privately held one, and Dyson himself is thought to be worth an estimated $1 billion. He prefers to remain the sole owner of the company, as he explained in an interview with *Management Today*'s Andrew Davidson. "I cannot be bothered with the process of going round convincing other people that what I am doing is right," the man described by his wife as "stubborn" said. "And you have to do that if you don't control all of it."

Perhaps not surprisingly, Dyson's company features an unusual work atmosphere: he prefers to hire recent college graduates who have never worked anywhere else, every employee must begin their training process by building their own Dyson vacuum cleaner, suits and ties are discouraged, and memos are strictly forbidden. The company's next generation of household appliances was launched in 2000 with the Contrarotator washing machine. Dyson is always searching for ways to improve daily life, and knows that his best inspiration comes from sheer daily aggravation. As he told *People*, "almost everything in the house bothers me."

## Sources

*Chicago Tribune*, July 5, 2004.
*HFN: The Weekly Newspaper for the Home Furnishing Network*, February 21, 2005, p. 9.
*Interior Design*, December 2004, p. 74.
*Management Today*, July 1999, p. 72.
*Marketing*, August 1, 2002, p. 21.
*Newsweek International*, January 22, 2001, p. 50.
*New York Times*, August 8, 2004, p. 18.
*People*, December 9, 2002, p. 123.

—*Carol Brennan*

# Louise Erdrich

© Jerry Bauer

## Author

**B**orn June 7, 1954, in Little Falls, MN; daughter of Ralph Louis (a teacher with the Bureau of Indian Affairs) and Rita Joanne (affiliated with the Bureau of Indian Affairs; maiden name, Gourneau) Erdrich; married Michael Anthony Dorris (a writer and professor of Native American studies), October 10, 1981 (died April 11, 1997); children: Reynold Abel (deceased), Jeffrey Sava, Madeline Hannah, Persia Andromeda, Pallas Antigone, Aza Marion, Azure. *Politics:* Democrat. *Education:* Dartmouth College, B.A., 1976; Johns Hopkins University, M.A., 1979.

**Addresses:** *Agent*—Andrew Wylie Agency, 250 West 57th St., Ste. 2114, New York, NY 10107-2199. *Contact*—c/o Author Mail, HarperCollins, 10 East 53rd St., New York, NY 10022.

## Career

**V**isiting poet and teacher, North Dakota State Arts Council, 1976-78; writing instructor, Johns Hopkins University, Baltimore, MD, 1978-79; communications director and editor of the *Circle,* Boston Indian Council, Boston, MA, 1979-80; textbook writer, Charles-Merrill Co., 1980; proprietor, Birch-Bark Books, Minneapolis, MN, 2000—. Previously employed as a beet weeder in Wahpeton, ND, waitress in Wahpeton, Boston, and Syracuse, NY, psychiatric aide in a Vermont hospital, poetry teacher at prisons, lifeguard, and construction flag signaler. Has judged writing contests.

**Member:** International Writers, PEN (member of executive board, 1985-88), Authors Guild, Authors League of America.

**Awards:** Academy of Poets Prize, 1975; Johns Hopkins University teaching fellow, 1978; MacDowell Colony fellow, 1980; Yaddo Colony fellow, 1981; Dartmouth College visiting fellow, 1981; first prize, Nelson Algren fiction competition, for "The World's Greatest Fisherman," 1982; National Endowment for the Arts fellowship, 1982; Pushcart Prize for "Indian Boarding School," 1983; National Magazine Fiction award for "Scales," 1983; Virginia McCormick Scully Prize for best book of the year dealing with Indians or Chicanos, for *Love Medicine,* 1984; National Book Critics Circle Award for fiction, for *Love Medicine,* 1984; *Los Angeles Times* award for best novel, for *Love Medicine,* 1985; Sue Kaufman Prize for Best First Novel from American Academy and Institute of Arts and Letters, for *Love Medicine,* 1985; American Book Award from Before Columbus Foundation, for *Love Medicine,* 1985; fiction award, Great Lakes Colleges Association, for *Love Medicine,* 1985; *Love Medicine* named among *New York Times Book Review*'s best eleven books of the year, 1985; first prize, O. Henry awards, 1985; Guggenheim fellow, 1985-86; *The Beet Queen* was named one of *Publishers Weekly*'s best books, 1986; National Magazine Fiction award, 1987; first prize, O. Henry awards, 1987; first prize, O. Henry awards, 1998; World Fantasy Award for best novel, World Fantasy Convention, for *The Antelope Wife,* 1999; National Book Award finalist, for *The Birchbark House; The Last Re-*

*port on the Miracles at Little No Horse* named one of *Globe & Mail*'s top ten books of the year, 2001; National Book Award finalist, for *The Last Report on the Miracles at Little No Horse,* 2001.

## Sidelights

Once named one of *People* magazine's most beautiful people, Louise Erdrich is a Native American writer with a wide popular appeal. She is no literary lightweight, however, having drawn comparisons to such noted American authors as William Faulkner.

Erdrich (pronounced air-drik) was the first of seven children born to Ralph and Rita Erdrich. Born on June 7, 1954, in Little Falls, Minnesota, she was raised in Wahpeton, North Dakota. Her mother, of Ojibwe descent, was born on the Turtle Mountain Ojibwe Reservation while her father was of German ancestry. Both parents taught at a Bureau of Indian Affairs boarding school.

From childhood, the rich oral tradition of Ojibwe storytelling was a part of Erdrich's life. Her mother and grandparents told her many stories about life on the reservation during the Great Depression of the 1930s, as well as other tales. Erdrich's father also told stories about his relatives and the towns where he grew up. Erdrich maintains that listening to her family's stories has in some ways been her most significant literary influence. Her father introduced her to the works of William Shakespeare and encouraged all of his children to write, paying a nickel apiece for her stories—Erdrich later joked that these nickels were her first royalties. Her mother supported her efforts as well, creating book covers for her daughter's manuscripts out of woven strips of construction paper and staples.

Living in a small town where she and her family were regarded as eccentric, Erdrich became an avid reader. Among her literary influences were Flannery O'Connor, Gabriel García Marquéz, Katherine Anne Porter, Toni Morrison, Willa Cather, Jane Austen, George Eliot, and William Faulkner. Erdrich attended a Catholic school in Wahpeton. Her grandfather, Petrice Gourneau, taught her about culture and religion; tribal chair of the Turtle Mountain Reservation, he worshiped the traditional Ojibwe religion while at the same time was a devout Catholic. Her grandfather's example inspired Erdrich's creation of the character Father Damien who appears in many of her novels.

Indeed, Erdrich has drawn on her roots, both the land and the experiences of her family, for inspiration. As Mark Anthony Rolo wrote in the *Progres-*

*sive,* "Erdrich once mused that Native American literature is often about coming home, returning to the land, the language and love of ancient traditions—a theme opposite of Western literature, which is about embarking on a journey, finding adventures beyond one's beginnings."

In 1972 Erdrich enrolled in Dartmouth College as part of that school's first coeducational graduating class. There she met anthropologist Michael Dorris, chair of the Native American Studies department created at Dartmouth that same year. At Dartmouth Erdrich started writing poems and stories integrating her Ojibwe heritage and in 1975 she was awarded the Academy of Poets Prize. She received her bachelor of arts degree the following year.

Erdrich served as a visiting poet and teacher for the Dakota Arts Council for two years after college graduation. She went on to earn a master of arts in writing from Johns Hopkins University in 1979. While she began sending her work to publishers around this time, most of them sent back rejections. Erdrich served as communications director and editor for one year for the *Circle,* a Boston Indian Council-sponsored newspaper. Following that, she worked as a textbook writer for Charles Merrill Company.

In 1979 Erdrich returned to Dartmouth to do a poetry reading, where she once again met up with Dorris. Dorris became interested in Erdrich's poetry, but even more interested in the poet herself. Although the two went their separate ways for a year—Dorris to New Zealand, Erdrich returning to Dartmouth as a visiting fellow in the Native American Studies department—they continued to exchange manuscripts through the mail. They met back at Dartmouth the next year and were married on October 10, 1981.

Viewed by outsiders as having an idyllic relationship, Erdrich and Dorris collaborated on every project and wrote tender dedications to each other in their books. They had a system worked out: when both wrote comparable amounts of a draft, the work was published under both names, but when one of them wrote the entire first initial draft, that person was the author. Even in the latter case, the final product was always a result of collaboration. They did the research together, developed plot lines and characters—sometimes even drawing them to see what they looked like—and discussed all aspects of the draft before submitting it for publication.

When they were first married and needed money, Erdrich and Dorris published romantic fiction using the pen name Milou North, *Mi* from Michael plus

*Lou* from Louise plus *North* for North Dakota. One of their stories was published in *Redbook,* while others ran in European publications.

Erdrich received the 1982 Nelson Algren Fiction Award for "The World's Greatest Fisherman," a story that became the first chapter of her first novel, *Love Medicine.* Erdrich learned of the contest and started writing just two weeks before the submission deadline. The first draft was completed in just one day, and Dorris collaborated with her on the subsequent drafts. The final product was one of 2,000 entries judged by Donald Barthelme, Studs Terkel, and Kay Boyle.

In 1983 Erdrich was awarded the Pushcart Prize for her poem "Indian Boarding School" and the National Magazine Award for fiction for her short story "Scales." The next year, at the age of 30, Erdrich published *Jacklight,* a book of blank verse poems collected from her graduate thesis work, and *Love Medicine,* her first novel. *Love Medicine* was a runaway success, winning the National Book Critics Circle Award for fiction, the Sue Kaufman Prize for Best First Fiction, and the Virginia McCormick Scully Award. The novel continued to win awards, including the *Los Angeles Times* Award for fiction, the American Book Award from the Before Columbus Foundation, and a fiction award from the Great Lakes Colleges Association.

*Love Medicine* became the first of Erdrich's "Argus" novels covering several generations of three Ojibwe families living in Argus, North Dakota, between from 1912 and the 1980s. Comparisons have been drawn to the work of Southern writer William Faulkner because of Erdrich's use of multi-voice narration and nonchronological storytelling as well as the ties of her characters to the land. Erdrich's fictional town of Argus has also been compared by critics to Faulkner's Yoknapatawpha County.

Erdrich's second novel in the series, *The Beet Queen,* published in 1986, covers a 40-year span beginning in 1932. Through characters like orphans Karl and Mary Adare and Celestine James and her daughter, Erdrich explores the negotiated interactions between the worlds of whites, half-breeds, and Native Americans. She followed this with a prequel, *Tracks.* Gleaned from the manuscript of the first novel she had ever started, *Tracks* explores the tensions between Native American spirituality and Catholicism. Erdrich continued the "Argus" series with *The Bingo Palace, Tales of Burning Love, The Antelope Wife,* and *The Last Report on Miracles at Little No Horse.*

Many of the characters in Erdrich's books grow and develop over time in successive novels. Katy Read in the *Globe & Mail* wrote, "Erdrich's characters do seem to have lives of their own—lives and histories and intricate relationships that meander in and out of nearly all her books." For example, *In the Last Report on Miracles at Little No Horse,* a finalist for the National Book Award, Father Damian Modeste, first introduced in *Love Medicine,* returns. The Father's secret, it unfolds, is that he is really a former nun, Agnes DeWitt, who, through a series of events, ended up posing as a Catholic priest. Agnes spends half a century ministering to the people of an Ojibwe reservation and hiding the fact that she is actually a woman.

Although strange things often happen in her books, Erdrich rejects the "magical realist" label, claiming that even the most unusual events are based on things that really occurred, things she has found documented in newspaper clippings and books. She collects books on strange tales and supernatural happenings and keeps notebooks which she fills with stories of odd events she has heard about. Erdrich has also done a great deal of historical research, especially family history and local history around North Dakota. On the other hand, she admitted to the *Progressive*'s Rolo, "A lot of it is plain made up."

Erdrich's second book of poems, *Baptism of Desire,* was published in 1989. That same year, her husband received the National Book Critics Circle Award for his nonfiction work *The Broken Cord.* The book, with a preface by Erdrich, is a memoir of Dorris' experiences as one of the first single men to adopt children; by the time he married Erdrich he had adopted three Native American children with fetal alcohol syndrome.

In 1991 the couple published their co-authored novel *The Crown of Columbus.* The book is a complicated 400-page story about a love affair between two writers and intellectuals who, at the same time they are trying to define their relationship, are also grappling with the historical figure of Columbus in their research and writing. The couple also co-authored a book of travel essays titled *Route Two.*

Erdrich and Dorris had three children together in addition to the three children Dorris adopted prior to their marriage. The couple separated in 1995 in the wake of allegations of sexual abuse brought against Dorris by some of his children. After an investigation left the accusations unresolved, Dorris committed suicide in 1997. As Erdrich told a National Public Radio *Weekend Edition* commentator that during that time, "All my being was really concentrated on getting our children through it, and that's something you do minute by minute. Then, you know, there's that one day at a time."

Despite the turbulence within her personal life during the 1990s, Erdrich kept writing. In 1995 she published her first nonfiction book, *The Blue Jay's Dance*, in which she records her experience with pregnancy and the birth year of her child. The title, which refers to the way a blue jay will defiantly dance toward an attacking hawk, is a metaphor for "the sort of controlled recklessness that having children always is," Erdrich told Jane Aspinall in an article in *Quill & Quire*. The following year Erdrich wrote the children's book *Grandmother's Pigeon*. Using the same sense of magic found in her novels, she tells the story of an adventurous grandmother who rides to Greenland on a dolphin. The eggs she leaves for her grandchildren hatch into pigeons that can send messages to her.

In 1999 Erdrich and her three youngest children relocated to Minneapolis to be closer to her parents in North Dakota. In July of 2000, she and her sister, Heidi, opened Birchbark Books, Herbs, and Native Arts in the Kenwood neighborhood of Minneapolis. The store, located in a building that was once a meat market, is decorated with a stairway made of birch trees that fell on land owned by friends in Wisconsin; the shop's focal point is an intricately carved Roman Catholic confessional Erdrich found at an architectural salvage store. Dream-catchers hang in the corners of the confessional, along with books with "sin" in the title and a framed copy of the U.S. Government's 1837 treaty with the Chippewa.

Since the late 1990s Erdrich has focused on learning the Ojibwe language and studying her tribe's culture and traditions, including its mysticism. She has also taught her youngest daughter to speak the Ojibwe language. In 2001, *The Last Report on Miracles at Little No Horse* was published. In the book, various characters from some of her previous works reappear. "A few years ago, I finally decided that I was working on one long novel," she told *Time*. "I stopped being concerned about whether the same characters show up or not. I really don't have a choice, anyway. If they show up, they have to show up." That same year, she gave birth to a baby girl; Erdrich declined to name the father, although she said he was of Ojibwe heritage. "Why would I ever talk about the father of my children again?," she told *Time*. "It seems as though to talk about people you love is almost ... what did the Greeks believe? You don't want to incur the wrath of the gods." The following year Erdrich wrote her first novel for young adults, the National Book Award for Young People finalist *The Birchbark House*. The story of a young Ojibwe girl named Omakayas, *The Birchbark House* also features illustrations by Erdrich. Her 2003 novel for adults, *The Master Butchers Singing Club*, returns readers to Argus, North Dakota; its main character is a German butcher named Fidelis Waldvogel, an immigrant to the United States in the 1920s. On July 1, 2004, Erdrich's novel, *Four Souls*, was published. *People*'s Lee Aitken declared, "Erdrich masterfully evokes the clash between Native American psychology and modern values...." The book was a "welcome, if modest, new piece in the ever-expanding Erdrich saga," according to Jennifer Reese in *Entertainment Weekly*.

Speaking with Katie Bacon in the *Atlantic*, Erdrich summed up her writing technique: "Primarily ... I am just a storyteller, and I take ... [stories] where I find them. I love stories whether they function to reclaim old narratives or occur spontaneously. Often, to my surprise, they do both. I'll follow an inner thread of a plot and find that I am actually retelling a very old story, often in a contemporary setting. I usually can't recall whether it is something I heard, or something I dreamed, or read, or imagined on the spot. It all becomes confused and then the characters take over, anyway, and make the piece their own."

## Selected writings

*Imagination* (textbook), C. E. Merrill, 1980.
*Jacklight* (poetry), Holt (New York, NY), 1984.
*Love Medicine*, Holt (New York, NY), 1984; expanded edition, 1993.
*The Beet Queen*, Holt (New York, NY), 1986.
*Louise Erdrich and Michael Dorris Interview with Kay Bonetti* (sound recording), American Audio Prose Library, 1986.
*Tracks*, Harper (New York, NY), 1988.
*Baptism of Desire* (poetry), Harper (New York, NY), 1989.
(Author of preface) Michael Dorris, *The Broken Cord: A Family's Ongoing Struggle with Fetal Alcohol Syndrome*, Harper (New York, NY), 1989.
(Author of preface) Desmond Hogan, *A Link with the River*, Farrar, Straus (New York, NY), 1989.
(With Michael Dorris) *Route Two*, Lord John Press, 1990.
(With Michael Dorris) *The Crown of Columbus*, HarperCollins (New York, NY), 1991.
*The Bingo Palace*, HarperCollins (New York, NY), 1994.
(With Allan Richard Chavkin and Nancy Feyl Chavkin) *Conversations with Louise Erdrich and Michael Dorris*, University Press of Mississippi (Jackson, MS), 1994.
*The Falcon: A Narrative of the Captivity and Adventures of John Tanner*, Penguin (New York, NY), 1994.
*The Blue Jay's Dance: A Birth Year* (memoir), HarperCollins (New York, NY), 1995.

*Grandmother's Pigeon* (children's book), illustrated by Jim LaMarche, Hyperion (New York, NY), 1996.

*Tales of Burning Love,* HarperCollins (New York, NY), 1996.

*The Antelope Wife,* HarperFlamingo (New York, NY), 1998.

(And illustrator) *The Birchbark House* (young adult book), Hyperion (New York, NY), 1999.

*The Last Report on the Miracles at Little No Horse,* HarperCollins (New York, NY), 2001.

(Contributor) *Resurrecting Grace: Remembering Catholic Childhoods,* Beacon Press (Boston, MA), 2001.

*The Master Butchers Singing Club,* HarperCollins (New York, NY), 2003.

*Four Souls,* HarperCollins (New York, NY), 2004.

Author of short story "The World's Greatest Fisherman"; contributor to anthologies, including *Norton Anthology of Poetry; Best American Short Stories,* 1983, 1988; and *Prize Stories: The O. Henry Awards,* 1985 and 1987. Contributor of stories, poems, essays, and book reviews to periodicals, including *New Yorker, New England Review, Chicago, American Indian Quarterly, Frontiers, Atlantic, Kenyon Review, North American Review, New York Times Book Review, Ms., Redbook* (with sister Heidi Erdrich under the joint pseudonym Heidi Louise), and *Woman* (with Dorris, under the joint pseudonym Milou North).

## Sources

### Books

*Conversations with Louise Erdrich and Michael Dorris,* edited by Allan Richard Chavkin and Nancy Feyl Chavkin, University Press of Mississippi, 1994.

### Periodicals

Associated Press Newswires, March 23, 1998; March 25, 1998.
*Entertainment Weekly,* June 25/July 2, 2004, p. 169.
*Globe & Mail* (Toronto, Ontario, Canada), April 21, 2001.
*News & Observer* (Raleigh, NC), April 22, 2001.
*People,* July 19, 2004, p. 45.
*Progressive,* April 1, 2002.
*Quill & Quire,* August 1995.
*Star Tribune* (San Diego, CA), December 30, 2001.
*Time,* April 9, 2001.
*Toronto Star,* April 22, 2001.

### Online

"About Louise Erdrich," Department of English, University of Illinois at Urbana-Champaign, http://www.english.uiuc.edu/maps/poets/a_f/erdrich/about.htm (April 1, 2005).
"An Emissary of the Between-World" *Atlantic,* http://www.theatlantic.com/doc/200101u/int2001-01-17 (April 1, 2005).
"Louise Erdrich," HarperCollins.com, http://www.harpercollins.com/authorintro/index.asp?authorid=2905 (April 1, 2005).
"Louise Erdrich," National Public Radio *Weekend Edition,* http://www.npr.org (April 1, 2005).
"Meet the Writers: Louise Erdrich," http://www.barnesandnoble.com/writers/writer.asp?userid=3B65pq8A4r&cid=929573 (April 1, 2005).
"Voices from the Gaps: Louise Erdrich," http://voices.cla.umn.edu/newsite/authors/ERDRICHlouise.htm (April 1, 2005).

# Janet Evanovich

## Author

**B**orn April 22, 1943, in South River, NJ; married Peter Evanovich; children: Peter, Alex. *Education:* Douglass College, NJ, B.A., 1965.

**Addresses:** *Office*—P.O. Box 5487, Hanover, NH 03755. *E-mail*—janet@evanovich.com.

## Career

**A**uthor. Has also worked in car sales, as an insurance claims adjuster, waitress, and secretary.

**Member:** Romance Writers of America, Sisters in Crime.

**Awards:** John Creasey Memorial Award, British Crime Writer's Association, for *One for the Money,* 1995; Dily Award, Independent Mystery Bookseller's Association, for *One for the Money,* 1995; Last Laugh Award, British Crime Writer's Association, for *Two for the Dough,* 1996; Silver Dagger award, British Crime Writer's Association, for *Three to Get Deadly,* 1997; Lefty award, Left Coast Crime.

## Sidelights

**"W**hat I really write is adventure stories—Indiana Jones in Trenton," mystery writer Janet Evanovich told *Booklist*'s GraceAnne A. DeCandido in an interview. The author of a successful series of humorous detective novels set in Trenton, New Jersey, Evanovich has created what may be "the single hottest character in crime fiction at the moment," wrote Bill Ott in a *Booklist* review of 2001's *Hot Six.* The character Ott refers to is Evanovich's protagonist, Stephanie Plum, a feisty Jersey woman of Hungarian and Italian descent who turns to bounty hunting when she loses her job as a lingerie buyer. Characterized by a flamboyant wardrobe, big hair, and an impertinent manner, Plum tracks bail jumpers for her cousin Vinnie, a bail bondsman. Among the cast of oddball characters Plum gathers around her are retired blond-haired, African-American hooker Lula, mace-toting Grandma Mazur, and Plum's hamster, Rex. The bounty hunter's squeeze of the moment, police officer Joe Morelli, is also often on hand to receive the bail-skippers Plum chases down. Another more enigmatic male in Plum's life is Ricardo Carlos Mafioso, a.k.a. the Ranger, her mentor in the world of bounty hunting. DeCandido described Evanovich's work as a compilation of "romance, cozy, and noir," from which strange brew Evanovich has "created the heady attraction of Nancy Drew grown up." Evanovich's mystery books have crossed over into the mainstream with initial print runs of half a million copies, regularly making it onto the *New York Times* best-seller list. Evanovich likewise has made it into the elite of the whodunit pantheon along with other top names in the genre such as Sue Grafton and Robert B. Parker. Not bad for a writer who started out penning anonymous romance novels.

Born in South River, New Jersey, in 1943, Evanovich spent much of her time in "LaLa Land," as she described her childhood on her author website. "LaLa Land is like an out-of-body experience—while your mouth is eating lunch your mind is conversing with Captain Kirk." Gifted with a rich imagination, Evanovich spent periods of her youth lip-synching opera or galloping about on an imaginary steed, knocking holes into her Aunt Lena's lawn. "Aunt Lena was a good egg," Evanovich wrote on her website. "She understood that the realities of daily existence were lost in the murky shadows of my slightly loony imagination." Evanovich was also a reader. She loved Nancy Drew mysteries as a kid, and enjoyed comic books. As an adult, she still reads about the adventures of Donald Duck and Uncle Scrooge. "Actually, Donald Duck and Uncle Scrooge are the reasons why I am writing books today," she told Jennifer Clarson in *Book.* "They are adventure stories. Uncle Scrooge is always running off looking for Inca treasure or gold in the Klondike, and that is what I'm writing. I love adventure."

After high school graduation Evanovich entered Douglass College, where she studied art, earning her bachelor of arts degree in 1965. She also married her high school sweetheart while at college. Her new husband was a doctoral candidate at Rutgers, and during her first years out of college Evanovich continued to work on her painting while taking a series of temp jobs, waitressing, selling cars, even working as an insurance claims adjuster. The painting eventually got left behind, as "it never felt exactly right," she explained on her website. "It was frustrating at best, excruciating at worst. My audience was too small. Communication was too obscure." She slowly turned to writing as a form of self-expression. Evanovich, the mother of two young children at the time, was a stay-at-home mom. "I loved being a housewife," she told *Time*'s Andrea Sachs. "I thought it was very creative. You got to make things—cooking, baking, sewing. I got to color in coloring books with the kids and build forts out of blocks." At night, once the kids were in bed, she turned to the typewriter in her husband's home office and churned out manuscripts which she dutifully sent out to editors. Just as regularly, she got rejection letters in return, which she saved in a large cardboard box. Once the box got full, she burned it, donned an office uniform, and found a job as a secretary. After four months on the job she received a call from an editor at Second Chance at Love

books who wanted to buy a manuscript she had sent him and promptly forgotten about. With the $2,000 advance from that book, Evanovich quit her secretarial job and took up writing full time.

Evanovich spent five years writing romance titles, both under her own name and as Steffie Hall. One title from that time, *Full House,* has seen a resurrection since Evanovich's subsequent fame as a crime writer, inspiring her to re-enter the romance field with the 2003 *Full Tilt,* written with Charlotte Hughes. But after her half-decade of toil in the romance line, and with a dozen novels under her belt, she tired of the genre. "I ran out of sexual positions and decided to move into the mystery genre," she explained on her website. Speaking with *Book*'s Clarson she noted, "I reached the point where I was very frustrated because I couldn't get anyone to buy the romantic adventure books that I wanted to write. So I just quit. You can reinvent yourself all the time." With mystery and crime, Evanovich figured she could use the skills she had already honed, plus feed her need for more adventure writing. However, it took her two years to research the genre and figure out her main character.

Opting for a female protagonist, she next needed to find the appropriate role. Female private investigators had already been done, and she did not want to make her heroine a cop, "because you really need to know what you're doing to pull off a cop," she told *Book*'s Clarson. Then one night she saw the movie *Midnight Run* on television, with Robert De Niro playing a bounty hunter in a film that is a mix of adventure and goofy comedy. "For Evanovich, it was 'Eureka!' time," wrote Robert Allen Papinchak in *Writer.* "She decided her protagonist would be a bounty hunter." What was still missing, however, was a model for the series she was planning. For that she chose the world of television sit-com, fashioning her books on *Seinfeld.* Her books would become "a series of episodic mysteries with humor," according to Papinchak. The setting would be the "Burg," near Trenton, New Jersey, where she grew up. Stephanie Plum, the protagonist, would be a trash talker, but with snappy dialogue which has an over-the-top noir feel to it. And surrounding her protagonist would be a weird and rather eccentric bunch of characters. The series debuted with 1994's *One for the Money,* the novel in which Plum tackles her first assignment, the capture of Joe Morelli, a police officer and accused murderer who also happens to be the man to whom she lost her virginity when she was 16.

Reviewing *One for the Money,* Marilyn Stasio in the *New York Times Book Review* delighted in a bounty-hunting protagonist "with Bette Midler's mouth and Cher's fashion sense." Stasio concluded that, "with [Plum's] brazen style and dazzling wardrobe, who could resist this doll?" Calling *One for the Money* "funny and ceaselessly inventive," Charles Champlin in the *Los Angeles Times Book Review* applauded Evanovich's use of first-person narration. According to Champlin, "Stephanie's voice, breezy and undauntable, is all her own.... [Her] moral seems to be that when the going gets tough, the tough get funny." But Marvin Lachman, writing in *Armchair Detective,* complained that "Plum's ... voice becomes irritating, largely due to its consistently unsophisticated speech." Calling the plot "minimal," Lachman indicated that the story "cannot sustain a book of two hundred and ninety pages," specifically noting that "reader suspension of disbelief is ... threatened" by Plum's prior relationship with Morelli. Kate Wilson, in a mixed review in *Entertainment Weekly,* suggested that Evanovich's inexperience as a novelist was evident in occasionally contrived dialogue but nevertheless described heroine Plum as "intelligent, cheery and genuine."

Evanovich's follow-up novel, *Two for the Dough,* was published in 1996 and depicts Plum's pursuit of fugitive Kenny Mancuso. The case is complicated by a secondary mystery involving two dozen coffins missing from a local mortuary and intensified by her ongoing relationship with Morelli, who also has an interest in the case. Ultimately, Plum's grandmother gets involved, and, in the words of *Times Literary Supplement* reviewer Natasha Cooper, "does her ham-fisted best to assist Stephanie, falling into coffins, firing off bullets and upsetting the entire neighborhood." In the *New York Times Book Review,* Stasio again praised heroine Plum, whom she described as "the motor-mouthed Jersey girl from Trenton ... with her pepper spray, stun gun, up-to-here hair and out-to-there attitude." An *Entertainment Weekly* reviewer called the "local color ... a bit too forcibly hued" and complained that the "dialogue has a mechanical, insular feel." In the *Times Literary Supplement,* however, Cooper called the work "an entertaining parody of the hard-boiled American crime novel."

The third volume in the series, 1997's *Three to Get Deadly,* details Plum's search for "Uncle Mo," a candy store owner and local hero who skipped out on a concealed weapons charge. A *Publishers Weekly* reviewer appreciated the way the heroine "muddles through another case full of snappy one-liners as well as corpses," and concluded that "the redoubtable Stephanie is a character crying out for a screen debut."

The fourth "Stephanie Plum" mystery, *Four to Score,* was published in 1998. In this novel Plum is called on to find a waitress who has jumped bail after a car-theft charge. *Four to Score* includes some familiar characters as well as a supporting cast of eccentrics. *New York Times Book Review* contributor Stasio called the novel a "brashly funny adventure," while *Booklist* contributor Emily Melton termed it "side-splittingly funny and a fine mystery to boot." A contributor for *Publishers Weekly* also praised the "eccentric" cast of supporting characters, and found that Plum's "brash exterior and high emotionality" provide a "welcome antidote to suave professional PIs."

The first four books in the series proved so successful that Evanovich found herself the recipient of several awards as well as a film option that allowed her family to set up its own business, Evanovich, Inc., with the author's husband in charge of management, her son handling financial affairs, and her daughter handling the author website and fan response. With the fifth title in the series, 1999's *High Five,* Evanovich reached the top of the *New York Times* best-seller list. Subsequent novels have also scored high, reaching the top of the national charts within days of publication. In *High Five,* Plum's romance with Morelli sometimes takes a back seat to the passionate possibilities between her and the mysterious Ranger. In her fifth outing Plum has her hands full tracking her Uncle Fred and a very short computer programmer while trying to avoid being stalked by a rapist and puzzling about what to wear to a Mafia wedding. "Evanovich deftly combines eccentric, colorful characters, wacky humor, and nonstop—if a bit farfetched—action," declared Wilda Williams in a *Library Journal* review.

Plum returns for more adventures in 2000's *Hot Six,* in which Grandma Mazur moves in with her, Ranger goes on the run after being hunted by police for killing a drug dealer, and Plum herself must avoid being kidnaped by the Mafia—all this while figuring out if she can really love Morelli while being so physically attracted to Ranger. "Evanovich spins all these threads, plus more, into a lunatic tapestry of nonstop action peopled by wacky characters," noted a reviewer for *Publishers Weekly.* De-Candido, reviewing the novel in *Booklist,* felt that Evanovich's real strengths are "her sizzling erotic moments" and "her gift of making the grittiest and most terrifying of situations hilarious."

Plum's personal history plays a major part in her seventh outing, 2001's *Seven Up,* when she tries to bring an old character from her neighborhood, Eddie De Chooch, in for trial. Among a panoply of subplots is the arrival of her "perfect" sister, Valerie, after her marriage ends, Grandma Mazur falling in love with her motorcycle, and a pair of fences (criminals who sell stolen property) who get in trouble with the law. "Almost every chapter has a laugh-out-loud moment," noted DeCandido in *Booklist*. A reviewer for *Publishers Weekly* found some things to like in the "zesty" novel, but nonetheless thought it "doesn't quite hit the high marks of her last two." Mark Harris, writing in *Entertainment Weekly*, noted that he likes his mysteries "with more danger and less strenuous comedy."

*Hard Eight*, the 2002 addition to the series, finds Plum on the trail of the granddaughter of her mother's next-door neighbor while also tracking a couple of strange Failure to Appears. Plum is also being trailed by a guy in a bunny suit, has her car blown up, and finds a dead body dumped on her couch. With her sister, Valerie, Valerie's children, and Grandma Mazur camping out in her house, Plum is relegated to sleeping on said couch. A reviewer for *Publishers Weekly* felt that Evanovich delivers "an even more suspenseful and more outrageous turn" in this eighth Plum novel, while Marianne Fitzgerald, writing in *Library Journal*, dubbed the book "great summer reading." However, a critic for *Kirkus Reviews* was less impressed, cautioning against "plot holes big enough to drive that Buick through." Cathy Burke, writing in *People*, also had problems with the plausibility of the plot, but found "the girl mercenary ... as fresh as ever," and the jokes "always perfectly placed."

As a Christmas gift to her fans, Evanovich served up a novella in late 2002 titled *Visions of Sugar Plums*, in which a spectral, blond-haired hunk named Diesel aids Plum in pursuit of her most recent Failure to Appear: a toy-maker named Sandy Klaws. DeCandido called the book a "magical little sweet-meat" in *Booklist*, and a reviewer for *Publishers Weekly* also had praise, concluding, "Throw in some elves, a mad hunt for a Christmas tree, and a few fires and you have a Plum-crazy Christmas classic."

Evanovich kept up her fast writing pace and released *To the Nines* in 2003, which continued Plum's adventures. According to Samantha Miller in *People*, the book was the "sharpest, funniest, sexiest entry in the series since the early days." Her 2004 release in the series, *Ten Big Ones*, proved to be as addictive as the previous books. "Evanovich serves up consistently craveable goodies—and needless to say, they're always perfect for the beach," Miller wrote. With 2004's *Metro Girl*, Evanovich introduced the character Alexandra Barnaby, aka Barney, who is on a mission to find her missing brother. Just as sassy as Plum, Barney finds herself in physical jeopardy dealing with henchmen, lost gold, and many car chases.

Evanovich puts in a 50-hour week, turning out at least a book a year. Guilty habits include eating Cheez Doodles and buying shoes. "Basically," she told Bruce Tierney of *BookPage*, "I'm just a boring workaholic. I motivate myself to write by spending the money I make before it comes in."

## Selected writings

### "Stephanie Plum" series

*One for the Money*, Scribner (New York, NY), 1994.
*Two for the Dough*, Scribner (New York, NY), 1996.
*Three to Get Deadly*, Scribner (New York, NY), 1997.
*Four to Score*, St. Martin's (New York, NY), 1998.
*High Five*, St. Martin's (New York, NY), 1999.
*Hot Six*, St. Martin's (New York, NY), 2000.
*Seven Up*, St. Martin's (New York, NY), 2001.
*Hard Eight*, St. Martin's (New York, NY), 2002.
*Visions of Sugar Plums*, St. Martin's (New York, NY), 2002.
*To the Nines*, St. Martin's (New York, NY), 2003.
*Ten Big Ones*, St. Martin's (New York, NY), 2004.

### Other novels

(As Steffie Hall) *Hero at Large*, Second Chance at Love, 1987.
*The Grand Finale*, Bantam (New York, NY), 1988.
*Thanksgiving*, Bantam (New York, NY), 1988.
*Manhunt*, Bantam (New York, NY), 1988.
(As Steffie Hall) *Full House*, Second Chance at Love, 1989; enlarged edition, St. Martin's (New York, NY), 2002.
(As Steffie Hall) *Foul Play*, Second Chance at Love, 1989.
*Ivan Takes a Wife*, Bantam (New York, NY), 1989.
*Back to the Bedroom*, Bantam (New York, NY), 1989.
*Wife for Hire*, Bantam (New York, NY), 1990.
*Smitten*, Bantam (New York, NY), 1990.
*The Rocky Road to Romance*, Bantam (New York, NY), 1991.
*Naughty Neighbor*, Bantam (New York, NY), 1992.
*Early Evanovich*, Bantam (New York, NY), 2003.
(With Charlotte Hughes) *Full Tilt*, St. Martin's (New York, NY), 2003.
*Metro Girl*, HarperCollins, 2004.

## Sources

### Books

Heising, Willetta A., *Detecting Women 2: A Reader's Guide and Checklist for Mystery Series Written by Women*, Purple Moon Press (Dearborn, MI), 1996.

## Periodicals

*Armchair Detective,* summer 1995, p. 287.

*Belles Lettres,* January 1996, p. 15.

*Book,* May-June 2002, pp. 18-19.

*Booklist,* September 1, 1994; April 15, 1998, p. 1379; May 1, 2000, p. 1622; May 1, 2001, p. 1598, pp. 1628-29; July 2001, p. 2029; December 15, 2001, p. 746; August 2002, p. 1884; October 1, 2002, p. 275; January 1, 2003, p. 803.

*Christian Science Monitor,* July 25, 1996, p. 21.

*Entertainment Weekly,* November 11, 1994, p. 68; February 23, 1996, p. 119; August 10, 2001, p. 66.

*Kirkus Reviews,* May 15, 2002, pp. 706-07; October 1, 2002, p. 1428.

*Library Journal,* December 1996, p. 151; June 1, 1999, p. 186; November 1, 1999, p. 142; March 15, 2000, p. 62; May 1, 2000, p. 158; June 15, 2000, p. 136; June 1, 2001, p. 224; June 15, 2001, p. 122; July 2002, p. 116.

*Los Angeles Times Book Review,* November 20, 1994, p. 8.

*New York Times Book Review,* September 4, 1994, p. 17; January 21, 1996, p. 31; February 16, 1997, p. 28; July 19, 1998, p. 20; June 27, 1999, p. 26; July 22, 2001, p. 22; June 23, 2002, p. 18.

*People,* August 23, 1999, p. 49; June 24, 2002, p. 39; December 2, 2002, p. 51; July 21, 2003, p. 47; June 21, 2004.

*Publishers Weekly,* November 13, 1994; November 25, 1996, p. 59; April 6, 1998, p. 62; June 21, 1999, p. 60; July 5, 1999; August 2, 1999, p. 26; May 1, 2000, p. 52; May 7, 2001, p. 227; May 20, 2002, p. 50; July 1, 2002, p. 18; August 5, 2002, p. 59; October 21, 2002, p. 58.

*Time,* July 22, 2002, p. G4.

*Times Literary Supplement,* March 15, 1996, p. 24.

*Washington Post Book World,* August 28, 1994, p. 6.

*Writer,* August 2002.

## Online

"A Conversation with Janet Evanovich," Writers Write, http://www.writerswrite.com/journal/jan99/evanovch.htm (December 16, 2004).

"Author: Janet Evanovich," BookReporter.com, http://www.bookreporter.com/authors/au-evanovich-janet.asp (December 16, 2004).

"Janet Evanovich: Mystery Maven Keeps Readers Coming Back for More," BookPage, http://www.bookpage.com/0007bp/janet_evanovich.html (December 16, 2004).

Janet Evanovich Online, http://www.evanovich.com (December 16, 2004).

# Dakota Fanning

**Actress**

**B**orn Hannah Dakota Fanning, February 23, 1994, in Conyers, GA; daughter of Steve and Joy Fanning.

**Addresses:** *Home*—Los Angeles, CA.

## Career

**A**ctress in films, including: *Tomcats,* 2001; *I Am Sam,* 2001; *Father Xmas,* 2001; *Trapped,* 2002; *Sweet Home Alabama,* 2002; *Hansel & Gretel,* 2002; *Uptown Girls,* 2003; *The Cat in the Hat,* 2003; *Man on Fire,* 2004; *Hide and Seek,* 2005; *Dreamer,* 2005; *War of the Worlds,* 2005. Television appearances include: *ER,* 2000; *Ally McBeal,* 2000; *Strong Medicine,* 2000; *CSI: Crime Scene Investigation,* 2000; *The Practice,* 2000; *Spin City,* 2000; *Malcolm in the Middle,* 2001; *The Fighting Fitzgeralds,* 2001; *Family Guy* (voice), 2001; *The Ellen Show,* 2001; *Taken* (miniseries), 2002; *Kim Possible: A Sitch in Time* (voice), 2003; *Friends,* 2004; *Justice League* (voice), 2004.

**Awards:** Best young actor/actress, Broadcast Film Critics Association, for *I Am Sam,* 2002.

## Sidelights

**D**akota Fanning delivered an acclaimed performance in the 2001 Sean Penn film *I Am Sam* before her seventh birthday. By 2005, the blond moppet had accrued more major film credits than she had years in age.

Born in February of 1994, Fanning hails from Conyers, Georgia, a suburb of Atlanta. Her father, Steve, had once played minor-league baseball for a St. Louis Cardinals farm team. Her mother, Joy, recognized her first daughter's precocity—Fanning could read before she turned three—and enrolled the kindergartner in an acting workshop. Fanning summed up her career path in an interview with the *Daily Record* of Glasgow, Scotland, telling the newspaper that the acting coaches "all thought I should go with an agency. So my mom got me with an agency in Georgia and they thought I should come out to [Los Angeles] so we did."

Fanning's professional debut was in a television commercial for Tide laundry detergent. The family moved out to Los Angeles in January of 2000, and a slew of roles television roles followed: she made her network debut on an episode of *ER* that aired in April of 2000, played a five-year-old *Ally McBeal* a month later, and won little-kid parts in such top-rated prime-time dramas as *CSI: Crime Scene Investigation* and *The Practice* as well as on comedy staples like *Spin City* and *Malcolm in the Middle.* She also played a part-alien child in the Steven Spielberg miniseries *Taken* in 2002.

By then, however, Fanning had already attracted tremendous notice for her role in *I Am Sam* as the young daughter of a developmentally disabled man who must fight to retain custody of her. Sean Penn played her father, Sam, a Starbucks employee, whose liaison with a homeless woman several years earlier resulted in an unexpected pregnancy. The birth mother abandons her at the hospital and flees, and Sam—an ardent Beatles fan—names her Lucy Diamond and learns to take care of her with the help of a kindly neighbor (Dianne Wiest). But as Fanning's Lucy enters second grade, her teachers begin to suspect she may be deliberately holding herself back as a way to stay at her father's mental level, and the California family-and-children social services agency tries to terminate his parental rights. Penn was nominated for an Academy Award for his portrayal, but Fanning won high marks as well. Terming the youngster "an absolute angel with smarts," in his *Hollywood Reporter* review, Kirk Honeycutt declared she "delivers her lines like a seasoned pro."

Fanning was nominated for a Screen Actors Guild award for the film, becoming the youngest nominee in the award's history. She lost out, however, to Helen Mirren for *Gosford Park*, but Fanning did beat out *Harry Potter* actor Daniel Radcliffe and Haley Joel Osment (*AI: Artificial Intelligence*) for the Best Young Actor honor from the Broadcast Film Critics Association. When she took the stage, there was no step for her nearby so that she might reach the podium's microphone, so award presenter Orlando Bloom picked her up and held her up. She gave a surprisingly long speech.

Suddenly a hot Hollywood name, Fanning went on to appear in a number of other major motion pictures. She had a bit part as the young Melanie, Reese Witherspoon's character, in *Sweet Home Alabama,* and took a starring role opposite Brittany Murphy in the 2003 comedy *Uptown Girls*. Murphy was cast as Molly, the Manhattan party-girl daughter of dead rock royalty who is forced to become a nanny when her accountant absconds with her fortune. The carefree, stalled-adolescent Molly begins taking care of Fanning's Ray, the ultra-serious but largely neglected daughter of a vixenish record-company executive. Ray is bossy, germophobic, devoted to ballet, and a health-food nut—the antithesis of Molly—but the two eventually find a common bond and learn from one another. *Uptown Girls* earned largely negative reviews, however. "Fanning is wonderfully somber and owlish as a tragicomic specimen of precocity, but ... in the end she's just an accessory to Molly's wardrobe of attitudinal poses," wrote *Entertainment Weekly* critic Lisa Schwarzbaum.

The same fate befell Fanning's next project, *The Cat in the Hat,* a lavish adaptation of the beloved Dr. Seuss children's book. She starred as Sally, the little girl whose household is invaded by the mischief-making feline, played by Mike Myers. Nevertheless, her ability to work with top-caliber stars impressed noted action-film director Tony Scott, who cast her in the 2004 vengeance flick *Man on Fire*. This time, Fanning shared crucial screen-time with Denzel Washington, who played a former assassin named Creasy who hires himself out as a bodyguard. She played Pita, whose father hires Washington's character to protect her in Mexico while her parents are gone on a business trip. The unlikely pair bond, but when a shadowy cartel kidnaps her, Washington's character pulls no punches in tracking down the criminals. "Strong work from Washington and his extremely sympathetic co-star Dakota Fanning compensate somewhat for Tony Scott's overbearing direction," noted *Film Journal International* writer Daniel Eagan. The *San Francisco Examiner*'s Edith Alderette noted that the young co-star, "who seems hopelessly typecast as 'the precocious kid,' doesn't do the role disservice. She's adorable, as always, and she provides a good springboard for some witty repartee between Pita and Creasy, but once Pita's kidnapped, her job is done."

Upcoming projects for Fanning included *Hide and Seek* with Robert De Niro, *Dreamer* with Kurt Russell, and as Tom Cruise's daughter in a remake of the infamous alien-invasion drama *The War of the Worlds,* directed by Spielberg. Her younger sister, Elle, is also a budding film star who has appeared in *Daddy Day Care*. Fanning says she has little trouble crying on cue when the script calls for it, and sometimes revisits the day her pet goldfish flopped out of his bowl to get the job done. "I just think about Flounder dying and it makes me sad," she told *People*. Such scenes were not the most challenging part of her career, she said in an interview with the *New York Post*. "You get to know everybody for so long, for two months, and then you have to say goodbye and then you're like 'NO!'" she explained. "That's the hardest part."

## Sources

*Daily Record* (Glasgow, Scotland), October 8, 2004, p. 55.
*Daily Variety,* September 1, 2004, p. 5.
*Entertainment Weekly,* August 22, 2003, p. 110.
*Film Journal International,* June 2004, p. 51.
*Hollywood Reporter,* December 21, 2001, p. 10.
*Independent* (London, England), May 10, 2002, p. 10.
*New York Post,* August 23, 2003, p. 26.
*New York Times,* August 22, 2003, p. E6.
*People,* August 25, 2003, p. 75.
*San Francisco Examiner,* April 23, 2004.

*—Carol Brennan*

# Tovah Feldshuh

## Actress and playwright

**B**orn Terri Sue Feldshuh, December 27, 1952, in New York, NY; daughter of Sidney (an attorney) and Lillian (maiden name, Kaplan) Feldshuh; married Andrew Harris-Levy (an attorney), March 20, 1977; children: Garson Brandon, Amanda Claire. *Education:* Graduated from Sarah Lawrence College; studied acting with Uta Hagen; attended University of Minnesota.

**Addresses:** *Agent*—The Gage Group, 315 West 57th St., Ste. 408, New York, NY 10019. *Contact*—322 Central Park West, #11B, New York, NY 10025. *Management*—Fox-Albert Management, 88 Central Park West, New York, NY 10023.

## Career

**A**ctress on the stage, including: *Cyrano de Bergerac,* Guthrie Theatre, Minneapolis, 1971; *Cyrano,* Palace Theater, New York, NY, 1973; *Yentl, the Yeshiva Boy,* Brooklyn Academy of Music Playhouse, 1974-75; *Yentl,* Eugene O'Neill Theatre, 1975-76; toured United States in *Peter Pan,* 1978; affiliated with the Old Globe Theatre, San Diego, early 1980s; *She Stoops to Conquer,* Roundabout/Triplex Theatre, New York, NY, 1984; *Lend Me a Tenor,* Royale Theater, 1989; *Tallulah's Party,* Kaufman Theatre, 1998; *Tallulah Hallelujah!,* Douglas Fairbanks Theater, New York, NY, 2000; *Golda's Balcony,* Helen Hayes Theatre, 2003-05. One-woman stage shows include: *A Touch of Tovah,* Old Globe Theatre, 1981; *Tovah: Out of Her Mind!,* 1996; *Tovah: Still Out of Her Mind!,* 2002. Film appearances include: *Nunzio,* 1978; *The Idolmaker,* 1980; *Daniel,* 1983; *Brewster's Millions,* 1985; *A Walk on the Moon,* 1999; *Kissing Jessica Stein,* 2001. Television appearances include: *Scream, Pretty Peggy* (movie), ABC, 1973; *Ryan's Hope,* 1976; *Holocaust* (miniseries), NBC, 1978; *Law & Order,* NBC, 1991-2004.

**Awards:** Theatre World Award for *Yentl,* 1976.

## Sidelights

**B**roadway star Tovah Feldshuh has built her career taking on roles that reflect her Jewish heritage. She was the original "Yentl" in the New York theater production of the same name that went on to become a 1983 Barbra Streisand film, and transformed herself into formidable Israeli leader Golda Meir for an acclaimed 2003 play, *Golda's Balcony.* "Feldshuh gives such a fiercely committed performance," noted *New York Times* critic Neil Genzlinger, further asserting "she does more than just resurrect Meir. She embodies an entire country, its hopes and paranoia and anger."

Born Terri Sue Feldshuh in New York City in 1952, the future Broadway star was the daughter of Sidney, an attorney, and Lillian Feldshuh, and grew up in suburban Scarsdale, New York. A talented pianist as a youth, she studied philosophy at Sarah Lawrence College, but took acting classes on the side in New York City with the legendary drama teacher Uta Hagen. At one point, Feldshuh's non-Jewish boyfriend urged her to change first name to the Jewish-sounding "Tovah." As Feldshuh recalled in an interview with *Rocky Mountain News* journalist Lisa Bornstein, "It made no sense. It was ill-advised, it was extremely naive of me to keep the name. I probably should have become Terri Fairchild; it would have changed my whole career."

Still torn between the performing arts or a more traditional career path, Feldshuh was on a waiting list for Harvard Law School when she won a fellowship toward a graduate drama degree at the University of Minnesota. While there, she made her professional stage debut at the Guthrie Theatre in Minneapolis in a 1971 production of *Cyrano de Bergerac,* where she was also the understudy for Dianne Wiest, another future Broadway star. The production morphed into the musical *Cyrano,* and Feldshuh was tapped to appear in it as a foodseller and nun. Before New York City, however, it had a Boston tryout, and the original director was fired. "Heads started to roll," Feldshuh recalled in an interview with Peter Filichia of Newark's *Star-Ledger* newspaper, "and I feared for mine. But then the director wanted someone to do a cartwheel, and that I can do. That little thing kept me in the show." It made it to the Palace Theater in New York City in 1973.

That same year, Feldshuh won a part in a television movie, *Scream, Pretty Peggy,* but returned to the stage with the title role in *Yentl, the Yeshiva Boy* at the Brooklyn Academy of Music Playhouse for a 1974-75 run. That play went on to become *Yentl* at the Eugene O'Neill Theatre for a successful 1975-76 run, which boosted Feldshuh's career immensely and earned her an Antoinette Perry (Tony) nomination. She failed to land the lead in the movie version a few years later, however, which starred Barbra Streisand.

Other television roles for Feldshuh included a 1976 run on the ABC daytime drama *Ryan's Hope,* and one of the leads in the epic NBC miniseries broadcast in 1978, *Holocaust.* She toured in the title role in *Peter Pan* that same year, and also made her feature-film debut in *Nunzio.* In the early 1980s, she spent time in San Diego at the Old Globe Theatre, where she appeared in several Shakespeare classics. That stage was also the site of her first one-woman show *A Touch of Tovah,* in 1981.

Feldshuh remained busy for much of the 1980s. She appeared in the films *Daniel* and *Brewster's Millions,* headed back to the New York stage for a lead in *She Stoops to Conquer* in 1984, and did television work as well. She had a recurring role as Danielle Melnick on NBC's *Law & Order* for several years, and reprised her one-woman act in 1996 with *Tovah: Out of Her Mind!,* which also toured several cities. Yet by then Feldshuh was in her forties, and was beginning to be typecast as a middle-aged Jewish mother-type. Despite this, she claims that one of her favorite roles was in the 1999 Diane Lane-Viggo Mortensen film *A Walk on the Moon.* She was also a sympathetic parent in the 2001 romantic comedy *Kissing Jessica Stein.*

After starring as Broadway legend Tallulah Bankhead in *Tallulah's Party* at the Kaufman Theatre in 1998, Feldshuh both co-wrote and starred in *Tallulah Hallelujah!* at the Douglas Fairbanks Theater in New York City in 2000. Feldshuh delivered several classic songs from the dramatic actress and chanteuse's repertoire, and bantered with the audience as she inhabited the iconic actress known for her fondness for liquor and sexually liberated attitudes in the 1940s and '50s. In 2002, Feldshuh reprised her own solo cabaret act in *Tovah: Still Out of Her Mind!.*

Feldshuh won rave reviews for her role as the late Israeli prime minister Golda Meir in *Golda's Balcony,* which had a successful run at the Helen Hayes Theatre in 2003 and earned the actor her fourth Tony nomination. The one-woman show's focal point is the 1973 Yom Kippur War, when Israel was attacked by its Arab neighbors. Meir's own story—along with that of Israel's—is told in flashbacks by Feldshuh, and its narrative arc hinges upon Meir's decision whether to use nuclear weapons in retaliation. A *Daily Variety* review from Marilyn Stasio gave Feldshuh's stage achievement high marks, calling it "a commanding performance. It acknowledges Meir's stature as a strong-willed politician who, at a time of international crisis, reassured a worried world that she was, indeed, in charge of her country's destiny."

Feldshuh lives in an apartment on Central Park West in New York City with her husband, attorney Andrew Harris-Levy, with whom she has two children. Since her Uta Hagen classes, Feldshuh says she has almost always kept working with others to perfect her craft, and issues the same advice to a future generation of Broadway hopefuls. "You've got a big conveyor belt in New York City, and when you audition, you want to stop the conveyor belt on you," she noted in an interview with *Back Stage* writer Ellas Stimac. "And you want to do that when you're young. So good training is very important."

## Sources

### Books

*Contemporary Theatre, Film and Television,* vol. 45, Gale Group, 2002.

### Periodicals

*Back Stage,* April 10, 1998, p. 13; January 19, 2001, p. A3.
*Daily Variety,* October 16, 2003, p. 5.
*New York Times,* April 1, 2003, p. E5.
*Rocky Mountain News,* November 24, 2003, p. 8D.
*Star-Ledger* (Newark, NJ), November 15, 2002, p. 4.
*Variety,* October 16, 2000, p. 38.

—*Carol Brennan*

# Craig Ferguson

**Television host, actor, and screenwriter**

**B**orn May 17, 1962, in Glasgow, Scotland; married Sascha, July 18, 1998 (divorced); children: Milo.

**Addresses:** *Agent*—William Morris Agency, Inc., 151 South El Camino Dr., Beverly Hills, CA 90212-2775.

## Career

**A**ctor on television, including: *The Ferguson Theory*, 1994; *Freakazoid!*, 1995; *Maybe This Time*, ABC, 1995; *The Drew Carey Show*, ABC, 1996-2000; *Hercules*, syndicated, 1998; *The Late Late Show with Craig Ferguson*, 2005—. Has also appeared on episodes of *Red Dwarf, Chelmsford 1 2 3, Have I Got News for You, The Brain Drain,* and *Almost Perfect.* Film appearances include: *Modern Vampires*, 1998; *The Big Tease*, 1999; *Saving Grace*, 2000; *Chain of Fools*, 2000; *Born Romantic*, 2000. Writer and executive producer of *The Big Tease,* and co-producer and co-writer of *Saving Grace.* Stage appearances include: *Bad Boy Johnny and the Prophets of Doom,* produced at the Theatre at Union Chapel, Islington, London, England, 1994.

## Sidelights

**S**cottish actor Craig Ferguson became the new host of *The Late Late Show* on CBS in 2005, replacing longtime host Craig Kilborn. With his distinct Scottish burr, Ferguson was already known to American audiences as the mildly villainous boss on ABC's long-running sitcom, *The Drew Carey Show.*

He had never contemplated sitting behind a desk and interviewing celebrities before he was invited to do a guest-host tryout for *The Late Late Show* in the fall of 2004, but the minute he stepped onto the set, he told *New York Times* television writer Bill Carter, "I was hooked. I'm like, 'This is it. This is what I do. I'm a talk-show host.'"

Born in the Scottish city of Glasgow in 1962, Ferguson was intoxicated by life in America after spending the summer of 1976 with an aunt and uncle of his who had emigrated to the New York City area years before. By contrast to his own hometown, which was plagued by unemployment and social tensions, even 1976 New York at its grittiest was charming to a 14-year-old outsider. "I went around the whole city that summer," Ferguson told Carter in the *New York Times.* "And I thought, 'This is the greatest country I've even seen in my life. It's unbelievable.' The people were happy. They had jobs. They were friendly. Nobody asked me if I was a Catholic or a Protestant. Nobody hit me the entire summer, not one kid."

The earliest years of Ferguson's entertainment career were spent as a stand-up comic in various Glasgow bars. After moving to London in 1987, he landed the occasional television role and eventually became a regular on *The Brain Drain* and *Have I Got News For You*, two irreverent quiz shows. He also wrote for other television programs, and had a couple of failed pilots. After a few years, Ferguson told Fiona Morrow, a writer for London's *Independent* newspaper, "I found myself merely a drunken minor celebrity in the Groucho Club," referring to a swanky members-only watering hole in London. He stopped drinking with the help of a 12-step recovery program, and moved to the United States in January of 1995. Slightly more than a year later, he had landed the part of Nigel Wick on the second season of *The Drew Carey Show.*

Ferguson continued to write his own comic material on the side, and turned out his first feature film, *The Big Tease,* in 1999, for which he also served as executive producer. He starred in the lead as a Glasgow hairdresser, Crawford MacKenzie, who believes he is on his way to compete in a highly regarded cutting competition in Los Angeles. The movie is structured as a "mockumentary," with Crawford taking a film crew along for the big event, but when he arrives in America he is crushed to find out that he has not technically been invited to compete. He manages to enter it anyway, with the help of a frosty publicist, and Ferguson described his screenplay as a Rocky-type tale in an interview with Stephen Schaefer of the *Boston Herald.* He based the flamboyant, ebullient Crawford, "on a guy I shared an apartment with in Glasgow," he admitted to Schaefer. "He was a waiter in the only posh restaurant in Glasgow and he'd gotten very angry one day because instead of a carafe of wine they'd ask for a 'giraffe' of wine and he'd had them thrown out."

Ferguson also co-wrote and starred in *Saving Grace,* a 2000 comedy set in Cornwall, a picturesque area tucked into Britain's southwest corner. The title character, played by Brenda Blethyn, learns that her recently departed husband has left her no assets, but a mountain of debt. The beleaguered widow teams with Ferguson's character, who is the about-to-be-unemployed gardener on her estate, to start a marijuana farm inside her greenhouse. As a comedy, *Saving Grace* earned mostly mixed reviews, with one critic, A. O. Scott of the *New York Times,* writing that "the movie has a gentle, silly vibe, and it would peter out in triviality if not for Ms. Blethyn's gift for finding the pain and frustration behind Grace's facade of housewifely capability." Scott also remarked that "Ferguson is a leading contender for the title of World's Most Amusing Scot," but termed his performance here "fairly subdued."

After several seasons on *The Drew Carey Show,* Ferguson was invited to try out for the host's slot on *The Late Late Show* after longtime host Craig Kilborn departed in mid-2004. The CBS staple, which follows David Letterman's perennial favorite, runs up against Conan O'Brien's talkfest on NBC as well as part of *Jimmy Kimmel Live,* a relatively newer contender on ABC. More than two dozen comics and actors also tried out, and Ferguson made it to the final four, along with D.L. Hughley, Damien Fahey, and Michael Ian Black. He returned in November to do an entire week as host, and won the job a month later.

*The Late Late Show with Craig Ferguson* began airing the first week of 2005. It was soon pulling in steady ratings numbers—less than O'Brien's show, but more than Kimmel's—thanks in part to Ferguson's rapport with the celebrities who visited. "Ferguson has already proven adept at something most late-show hosts since Johnny Carson never really get a handle on: interviewing guests," noted the *Seattle Times'* Ellen Gray. But Ferguson told the same paper that he came on board with no special training for that. "I don't know how to interview people, and I think that's good," he told Gray. "I know how to talk to people."

In June of 2005, it was announced that Ferguson had completed a darkly comic novel, called *Between the Bridge and the River,* due from Chronicle in spring 2006. Ferguson remains relatively unknown back in Scotland, though some British newspapers do mention that he has earned a small fortune from his *Drew Carey Show* stint. He conceded that he had not always made the best decisions earlier in his career, as he told Morrow in the *Independent* interview, and commented that in his homeland, there seem to be no second acts. "Failure is seen as disgrace, and it's not," he told the London newspaper. "You're not over forever. It's not humiliation. The fear of disgrace stopped me for a long time."

## Sources

*Boston Herald,* February 7, 2000, p. 39.
*Daily Variety,* January 7, 2005, p. 10.
*Entertainment Weekly,* February 4, 2000, p. 48.
*Independent* (London, England), May 19, 2000, p. 11.
*New York Daily News,* December 30, 2004.
*New York Times,* August 4, 2000; December 11, 2004, p. B9.
*People,* June 10, 2005, p. 112.
*Seattle Times,* March 1, 2005, p. E4.
*Television Week,* January 3, 2005, p. 4.
*Variety,* October 9, 2000, p. 27.

—*Carol Brennan*

# Tina Fey

**Writer, comedian, and actress**

© Lisa O'Connor/ZUMA/Corbis

**B**orn May 18, 1970, in Pennsylvania; daughter of Donald (a grant writer) and Jeanne (a brokerage firm worker) Fey; married Jeff Richmond (a director), June, 2001. *Education:* University of Virginia, B.A. (drama), 1992; studied at Second City Training Center, Chicago, IL, and ImprovOlympics, Chicago, IL.

**Addresses:** *Office*—c/o NBC, 30 Rockefeller Plaza, New York, NY 10112.

## Career

**P**erformer, ImprovOlympics; performer and writer, Second City, Chicago, IL, 1994-97; member of company, Inside Vladimir, c. 1990s; childcare registrator at a Chicago-area Y.M.C.A.; *Saturday Night Live,* writer, 1997-99, then head writer, 1999—; wrote and performed show (with Rachel Dratch), *Dratch & Fey,* 1999; "Weekend Update" segment anchor, *Saturday Night Live,* 2000—; screenwriter and actress, *Mean Girls,* 2004.

**Awards:** Writers Guild of America Award (with others), comedy/variety—music, awards, tribute—special any length, for *Saturday Night Live: The 25th Anniversary Special,* 2001; Emmy Award (with others), outstanding writing for a variety, music or comedy program, for *Saturday Night Live,* 2002.

## Sidelights

**A** Second City alum, Tina Fey became the first female head writer in the history of the longtime sketch comedy show *Saturday Night Live.* After writing with the show for several years, Fey also became a performer on *Saturday Night Live.* She primarily appeared on the show's "Weekend Update" segment as a news anchor, but also appeared occasionally in sketches. In 2004, Fey moved to a new medium, film, when she wrote and had a small part in the hit teen comedy, *Mean Girls.*

Fey was born on May 18, 1970, in Pennsylvania, the daughter of Donald and Jeanne Fey. Her father worked as a grant writer at the University of Pennsylvania, and was also employed as a mystery novelist and paramedic. Her mother was of Greek descent and worked at a brokerage firm. Fey and her older brother, Peter, were raised in Pennsylvania. (He also had a career as a writer, working primarily for QVC's website.) As a child, Fey and her brother did comedy routines together. However, she was primarily a shy child, who was very smart and involved in a number of school activities. Fey participated in choir and earned straight A's. By the time she was in middle school, she decided that she wanted to be a comedic performer of some kind.

By the time Fey was in high school at Upper Darby High School, in Upper Darby, Pennsylvania, the honor student was participating in school plays and singing. She also wrote for both the yearbook and the school paper, the *Acorn,* and had a column for the latter. While in high school, Fey was also involved in the local dramatic community by doing publicity and box office work for the Summer Stage in Upper Darby. She graduated from Upper Darby High School in 1988.

After high school, Fey entered the University of Virginia, where she intended to study English. Because she did not like the people in the department, she transferred to the drama department. While a college student, Fey returned to Upper Darby to direct productions at Summer Stage. She also appeared in college stage productions. In 1992, she played Sally Bowles in *Cabaret.* Fey graduated with her degree in drama in 1992.

By the time Fey graduated, she was certain she wanted to be a performer. After graduation, she moved to Chicago, Illinois. Fey intended to do graduate work in drama at De Paul University, but never entered the school. Instead, she trained in comedy at the Second City Training Center and at Chicago's ImprovOlympics. In the early 1990s, she also performed as part of an improvisational group called Inside Vladimir. Fey supported herself by working at a local Y.M.C.A., registering child care customers.

Fey grew to enjoy the improv method she learned at Second City and ImprovOlympics. She told William Booth of the *Washington Post,* "[Improv] tapped into the writer part of my brain and the actor part all at the same time. For me, studying improv was the greatest thing that ever happened to me, and the people I studied with all felt the same way.... It really changed my life."

In 1994, Fey joined Chicago's Second City comedy troupe as both a writer and performer. She wrote and performed in many types of sketches, including one-act works, monologues, and sketches. As a performer, Fey was well-respected for her wide range, but she particularly excelled in satire. While a member of Second City, she worked with Rachel Dratch, a performer who also worked for *Saturday Night Live* (*SNL*).

At the suggestion of a former Second City writer, Adam McKay, who was working at *SNL* in 1997, Fey sent in some sketches to the television show.

This led to a meeting with others at *SNL,* including producer Lorne Michaels, and a job offer. Fey was initially hesitant to take the job because she had achieved a goal by performing and writing with Second City, but soon decided to take the position.

In 1997, Fey joined *SNL* as a writer, but not a regular performer. The move took some adjustment as turnaround was much faster on the television show and sketches were performed differently for television. Among her recurring sketches for *SNL* were a parody of the ABC daytime talk show *The View* and the sketches featuring Boston teens Sully and Denise. The latter started out quite differently than what eventually aired. Fey's original concept was a mother and daughter at dinner, but it became a boyfriend and girlfriend with a mutual friend videotaping them so they could talk to the camera.

After two years on the writing staff, Fey was promoted to head writer. This marked the first time a woman had that role; *Saturday Night Live* had a reputation of being a boy's club. Fey told Ellen Grey in the *San Diego Union-Tribune,* "I think I've been very lucky to get a lot of places at the right time. I don't deny that it probably was harder here at one time. When I got to Second City, everyone said 'Oh, it's a terrible boys' club. It's horrible.' But my experience there was very good … and when I got here, people were saying, 'Oh, it's really hard there for women.' I think I had pretty lucky timing."

As head writer, Fey continued to write sketches, but also oversaw the other writers and their sketches. Throughout the week before the live show aired, Fey also worked with the show's director to make sure the sketches worked and were funny enough. Discussing the process, Virginia Heffernan of the *New Yorker* wrote, "Fey herself tinkers with a line's inflections and implications in a way that befits a Second City alumna. The details of human behavior—minor notes of pomposity, say, in apparently self-effacing speech—make her laugh, and she knows how to introduce those notes into sketches."

While working as a writer on *Saturday Night Live,* Fey also wrote and performed other comedic works. With Dratch, she wrote and performed a show for Second City called *Dratch & Fey* in 1999. It was later performed at the Upright Citizen's Brigade Theater in New York City. This production led to Fey finally performing on *SNL,* beginning in 2000.

Though Fey had been an extra on occasion, as all writers were, she lost 30 pounds by following the Weight Watchers diet system and was soon given a regular on-camera role on the show. She took over as co-anchor of "Weekend Update" in 2000, replacing Colin Quinn. Fey's first co-anchor was Jimmy Fallon. The pair sat on a set not unlike a network news desk, and commented on news and contemporary events. Many of her pithy one-liners were directed at Hollywood types. For the segment, Fey wore a blue suit and glasses, and allowed her personality to come through. Because she rarely wore glasses off-camera, she often went unrecognized outside the studio. Fey's personal life also changed. She married Jeff Richmond in June of 2001, whom she met while part of Second City's touring company. He later became the music director of *SNL*.

With Fey at the helm, *SNL*'s ratings began to rise beginning in 1999. In 2000, Fey and her writing staff were nominated for an Emmy Award. Proving that *SNL* was no longer a "boy's club," five of the show's 18 writers were women. In 2001, three years into her tenure, Fey was still not a demanding person off camera though she had to deal with writing jokes in a more sensitive environment in the post-9-11 landscape. Alex Witchel wrote in the *New York Times* in November of that year, "Comediennes have traditionally been a noisy bunch.... But Ms. Fey, 31, off camera at least, has an unexpected lack of bravado. She is shy, skinny, and seemingly unsure of herself. Maybe it's just her personality and maybe it's the times we're living in, but reconciling life with comedy has been one tough assignment since Sept. 11."

In 2001, Fey was given a co-head writer, Dennis McNicholas, to help with her duties. The following year, *SNL*'s writing staff won an Emmy, the show's first since 1989. NBC and *SNL* wanted to keep Fey under contract. In May of 2003, she signed a deal with the network to ensure that she would continue working on the show. It was a two-year deal for her work on *SNL*, a developmental deal with NBC to develop prime-time programming, and an agreement to option the book that would be her first feature film. The deal was worth about $4 million.

By 2003, Fey was writing an average of two sketches per week for *SNL*. She also ran one of the re-write tables in which everyone's sketches were re-worked. This table helped decide which sketches would air. Fey also had a hand in deciding who would be joining *SNL*'s writing staff. Fey continued to break ground on the show after Fallon left at the end of the 2003-04 season. He was replaced on "Weekend Update" by cast member Amy Poehler. This marked the first time two women served as anchors of the sketch.

Fey moved into a whole new creative venture in 2004 when her first film was released. Called *Mean Girls*, the script Fey wrote was based on a nonfiction book by Rosalind Wiseman called *Queen Bees and Wannabes: Helping Your Daughter Survive Cliques, Gossip, Boyfriends & Other Realities of Adolescents*. Fey also based it on her own experiences in high school. She claimed she had been mean in high school.

Starring popular teen actress Lindsay Lohan as Cady, *Mean Girls* explored the cliques girls form in high school. Cady had been home schooled in Africa where her parents had been working as zoologists. When her family returns to the United States so Cady can attend high school, she learns how mean high school girls can be toward each other and their parents. In addition to writing the screenplay, Fey also had a small role in the film. She played a math teacher with her own problems, including an ongoing divorce. *Mean Girls* received much critical praise. Released in April of 2004, it was the number-one box office draw its first weekend of release. The film proved to be a financial success.

Though Fey acted in *Mean Girls* and on *SNL*, she had no long term plans to work as a performer. However, she did plan to write for *SNL* for some time and work on situation comedy ideas. Of her stamp on *SNL*, Michaels, the show's producer, told Phil Rosenthal of the *Chicago Sun-Times*, "She has a first-rate mind, radiant beauty, and she's very tough-minded, but she's also a worker. She puts in an enormous amount of hours and focus and is uncompromising in her standard, both in what she's writing and what she's supervising or rewriting. That doesn't mean everything she writes gets on the show, but she's always in there."

## Sources

### Books

*Celebrity Biographies*, Baseline II, 2005.

### Periodicals

*Chicago Sun-Times*, December 14, 2001, p. 56; May 7, 2003, p. 69; April 29, 2004, p. 49.
*Entertainment Weekly*, May 7, 2004, pp. 32-34.
*Houston Chronicle*, May 2, 2004, p. 10.
*Newsweek*, April 8, 2002, p. 54.
*New Yorker*, November 3, 2003, p. 42.

*New York Times,* November 25, 2001, sec. 9, p. 1; April 30, 2004, p. E13; October 12, 2004, p. E1.

*People,* May 12, 2003, p. 156; May 3, 2004, pp. 75-76.

*Pittsburgh Post-Gazette,* May 3, 2004, p. D5.

*San Diego Union-Tribune,* December 31, 2000, p. F2; August 25, 2002, p. TV6; April 25, 2004, p. F1.

*Time,* April 26, 2004, p. 139.

*Toronto Sun,* April 25, 2004, p. S10.

*USA Today,* April 23, 2004, p. 1E.

*Washington Post,* April 25, 2004, p. N1.

*—A. Petruso*

# Joschka Fischer

*Andreas Altwein/DPA/Landov*

**Germany's foreign minister**

Born Joseph Martin Fischer, April 12, 1948, in Gerabronn, Baden-Württemberg, Germany; married Edeltraud, 1967 (divorced, 1984); married Inge, 1984 (divorced, 1987); married Claudia, 1987 (divorced, 1999); married Nicola Leske (a journalist), c. 1999 (divorced, 2003).

**Addresses:** *Office*—Foreign Ministry, Werderscher Markt 1, 10117 Berlin-Mitte, Germany.

## Career

Worked as assistant to photographer, mid-1966; factory worker at Opel automobile factory, 1971; taxi driver in Frankfurt, Germany, 1976-81; member of Revolutionary Combat; joined German Green Party, c. 1977; bookstore clerk at the Karl-Marx bookstore, Frankfurt, early 1980s; elected to the Bundestag, 1983; Green Party minister for the environment, state of Hesse, Germany, 1985-87, and 1991-94; Green Party co-chair in the Bundestag, mid-1990s; vice chancellor and foreign minister in the government of Gerhard Schroeder, 1998—.

## Sidelights

In a country not especially known for the colorful personalities of its politicians in the modern era, Germans give their enigmatic and outspoken foreign minister Joschka Fischer high marks. Fischer has served in two consecutive coalition governments headed by Chancellor Gerhard Schroeder, and proved an adept diplomat on the international stage. But his early years as a radical agitator, and evidence thereof, would return later to nearly derail his political career.

The son of a butcher, Joseph Martin Fischer was born in 1948 in Gerabronn, a small town in the Baden-Württemberg state, of which Stuttgart serves as the capital. Fischer grew up in a generation born just after the end of World War II that viewed their parents' era with some suspicion. While many ordinary Germans were innocent of blame for the Nazi period and the crimes of World War II, the pall of shame left over the country was felt sharply by its youth.

Fischer left school at age 15, and settled in Frankfurt as a young man. For a number of years, he held a series of odd jobs, including driving a taxi and working in a Marxist bookstore. His real career, however, was politics, and he was an active participant in one of the extreme-left groups to which many in his generation of West Germans had seemed to gravitate, called Revolutionary Combat. They were known for staging pitched street demonstrations, and Fischer even lived in an illegal "squat," an empty building taken over for living quarters, with members of the group.

Fischer's transition from anti-capitalist leftie to foreign minister of one of Europe's largest countries was not an entirely abrupt one. He was with the Revolutionary Combat group until 1977, when leftist groups began carrying out more deadly attacks in what became known as the notorious *Deutscher Herbst,* or "German Autumn." Spurning violent acts as a tool for change, Fischer joined the emerging Green Party around this time. The Greens—comprised largely of younger West Germans—had an anti-war, pro-environment platform that coalesced around a key issue: opposition to the installation of United States nuclear weapons on West German soil.

The Greens quickly gained political clout and won seats in West Germany's Bundestag, or parliament, in 1983. Fischer was elected in that first wave of new legislators, and proved as skilled at mainstream politics as he had in radical circles. In 1985 he was made the environment minister for the state of Hesse in the first state-level political coalition between the Greens and the Social-Democrat Party (SPD), Germany's leading liberal party. He served in the post for two years, and held the role again in the early 1990s. In the interim, what had been East Germany reunited with West Germany when Eastern bloc communist states fell one by one. It was a long hoped-for reunification, but stirred up other issues, primarily social and economic.

Some of the troubles were blamed on the long-ruling Christian Democrat Party, and German voters ousted it in 1998 in favor of the Social Democrats. SPD leader Gerhard Schroeder became chancellor of Germany, but had to build a coalition with the Green Party in order to secure the post and form a government. He handed out several cabinet positions to Green Party members, and made Fischer his foreign minister. One of Fischer's first controversial moves was to support the sending of 5,000 German troops to Kosovo as part of a North Atlantic Treaty Organization (NATO) mission. Some pacifist Green politicians were so incensed by the decision—it marked the first time since World War II that German soldiers fought on foreign soil—that they resigned from the party.

At times, Fischer's enemies seem to come from all sides. In 2001, the daughter of a famous West German radical who had died in prison claimed that the foreign minister had lived in a house with other members of the Rote Armee Fraktion ("Red Army Faction"), the most notorious of all West German leftist groups in the 1970s, which almost put him in trial for perjury after testifying in a court case

against one of them. Around this same time, the *Stern* ("Star"), a popular German weekly tabloid newspaper, published a 1973 photograph of Fischer in a squatters' battle with the police in which he was clearly enjoying the upper hand. Some Germans called for his resignation, but Schroeder voiced his support for Fischer, who apologized to the police officers' union and to the officer as well, Rainer Marx.

Fischer remained in office, and the SPD won re-election in 2002, but just barely. He was campaigned alongside Schroeder, an unusual move for a minister, but Fischer enjoys high approval ratings among Germans—better even than his boss. As foreign minister, he was a stalwart opponent of the United States plan to invade Iraq in 2003. A month before the war, he spoke at conference in Munich at which U.S. Defense Secretary Donald Rumsfeld had been trying to recruit European support for the American cause. Rumsfeld presented the White House's case, which involved supposed evidence of weapons of mass destruction, and then Fischer stepped to the podium to speak. Rumsfeld did not wear his translation headset, and was chatting with a colleague when Fischer broke from his speech in German to call out to Rumsfeld in English, "Excuse me, I am not convinced. I am not convinced!" according to *Nation* writer Paul Hockenos. He then returned to his native German tongue, saying "We owe our democracy to the United States, but we must be convinced."

Some political pundits see Fischer as a leading candidate for the newly created post of foreign minister for the European Union, which will even have its own diplomatic corps. He will also campaign alongside Schroeder in the 2006 general elections. He has been married four times and owns an Andy Warhol portrait of Willy Brandt, West Germany's Nobel Peace Prize-winning chancellor in the 1970s and longtime SPD chair. Fittingly, only Brandt enjoyed similar popularity in a country which seemed to prefer its politicians bland and decidedly uninspiring for so many years following the Nazi era. But even the evidence of Fischer's slugging of a police officer did little to damage his reputation, in a country were the older generation seems to appreciate the activism of their children. Even Marx, the retired police officer once assaulted by him, told the *New York Times*'s Roger Cohen that "what Fischer did in his youth, many people did. He demonstrated and then it escalated. He has taken all this to heart. He is a very good foreign minister, and should remain."

## Sources

*Guardian* (London, England), February 20, 2001, p. 16; October 15, 2002, p. 12; September 19, 2003, p. 16.

*Independent* (London, England), January 24, 2001, p. 16.

*Maclean's,* March 10, 2003, p. 34.

*Nation,* July 19, 2004, p. 26.

*New York Times,* January 15, 2001, p. A8; February 17, 2001, p. A5.

*Time,* April 26, 2004, p. 104.

—*Carol Brennan*

# Faith Ford

## Actress

**B**orn September 14, 1964, in Alexandria, LA; daughter of Charles (an insurance agent) and Pat (a school teacher) Ford; married Robert Nottingham (an actor), 1989 (divorced, 1996); married Campion Murphy (a fitness consultant and writer), June 27, 1998.

**Addresses:** *Office*—c/o Hope & Faith, Silvercup Studios East, 34-02 Starr Ave., 2nd Flr., Long Island City, NY 11101.

## Career

**A**ctress on television, including: *One Life to Live*, ABC, 1983; *Another World*, NBC, 1984-85; *Hardcastle & McCormick*, 1985; *Webster*, 1986; *Scarecrow and Mrs. King*, 1986; *Cagney & Lacey*, 1986; *The Popcorn Kid*, CBS, 1987; *If It's Tuesday, It Still Must Be Belgium* (movie), 1987; *thirtysomething*, 1987-88; *Murphy Brown*, CBS, 1988-98; *Murder She Wrote*, 1990; *Poisoned by Love: The Kern County Murders* (movie), 1993; *The Hidden Room*, 1993; *A Weekend in the Country* (movie), 1996; *Her Desperate Choice* (movie), Lifetime, 1996; *Night Visitors* (movie), 1996; *Maggie Winters*, CBS, 1998-99; *Norm*, ABC, 1999-2001; *Family Guy* (voice), 2000; *Moms on Strike*, ABC Family, 2002; *Hope & Faith*, ABC, 2003—. Film appearances include: *You Talkin' to Me?*, 1987; *For Goodness Sake*, 1993; *North*, 1994; *Sometimes They Come Back ... For More*, 1999; *Beethoven's 5th* (video), 2003; *The Pacifier*, 2005. Stage appearances include: *Crimes of the Heart*, Los Angeles, CA, 1999.

*Fernando Salas/Landov*

## Sidelights

**A**ctress Faith Ford has starred in a number of television situation comedies, including arguably her best-known role in CBS's long-time hit *Murphy Brown*. Ford also appeared on ABC's *The Norm Show* and *Hope & Faith*. In addition, she had roles in television movies, films, and stage productions.

Born on September 14, 1964, in Alexandria, Louisiana, Ford is the daughter of Charles and Pat Ford. Her father worked as an insurance agent, while her mother taught elementary school. Ford and her older sister were raised in Pineville, Louisiana. Ford's sister was perceived as smarter than Ford, who was voted "Most Spirited" in high school. After completing high school, Ford pursued a career in modeling. She went to a modeling convention in 1982 in New York City, then moved there. Among Ford's accomplishments was becoming a finalist in a modeling search run by *Teen Magazine*. Her success as a model led to an acting career. To prepare, she took voice lessons to lose her Southern accent.

Ford began her acting career on soap operas. Beginning in 1983, she had a recurring role as Muffy Critchlowe on *One Life to Live*. In 1984, she moved to *Another World.* Ford played Julia Schearer from 1984 to 1985. To further her career, Ford moved to Los Angeles and into prime-time acting work. She began by doing guest spots on television series. Her first guest role came in a 1985 episode of *Hardcastle & McCormick.* Ford also appeared in *Cagney & Lacey* and played a secretary on *thirtysomething.* Ford had her first regular role in the short-lived 1987 CBS show *The Popcorn Kid.* That same year, Ford also had her first film role in *You Talkin' to Me?.*

In 1988, Ford received a big career break when she was cast in a supporting role on CBS's *Murphy Brown.* The comedy starred Candice Bergen, and soon became a hit. Ford played Corky Sherwood, a perky, not too bright Miss America-turned-journalist on the fictional newsmagazine *FYI.* Over the course of the show, Ford's character matured and evolved from being a rather simple airhead to a true rival and journalist who was able to compete with Bergen's title character. Ford was nominated five times for Emmy Awards for best supporting actress in a comedy series.

During the ten-year run of *Murphy Brown,* Ford's personal and professional life became transformed. She married her first husband, actor Robert Nottingham, in 1989. The couple divorced in 1996. In 1990, Ford was diagnosed with Graves' disease, an overactive thyroid problem.

Ford also stretched her acting wings. In 1996, she appeared in a dramatic television movie called *Her Desperate Choice.* Ford played Jody Murdoch, a mother who takes her young daughter, Samantha, into hiding because she believes her former husband is molesting the girl. While Ford's Murdoch goes underground and gets rid of evidence related to her old life, she also finds new love. In addition to television movies, Ford also appeared in the 1994 film *North.*

When *Murphy Brown* ended its run in the spring of 1998, Ford was immediately offered a starring role in a new CBS situation comedy called *Maggie Winters.* She told Jefferson Graham of *USA Today,* "I feel like I've already won. What I wanted to achieve was to open up another door in my life and play a different character. It could have been very hard for me to have been accepted in a different role." Ford identified with Winters, who had moved back to her small hometown after the end of her marriage. Though Winters had been voted "Most Likely to Succeed" in high school, she also had no career. Though Ford and the show received positive reviews, it lasted only one season. In addition to the

new, albeit short-lived, situation comedy, Ford also remarried. She and her second husband, fitness consultant and writer Campion Murphy, were wed on June 27, 1998.

After appearing in some television movies, Ford returned to situation comedies in 1999, beginning with ABC's *Norm.* The moderately successful show was a vehicle for comedian Norm McDonald, who played a former hockey player forced to do social work as part of his community service for a tax evasion conviction. In the 1999-2000 season, she had a six-episode appearance on *Norm* as probation officer Shelly Kilmartin. Ford's level-headed character worked as an antithesis to the many oddball characters on the show. Ford was added to the cast full time for the 2000-01 season, but the show was canceled at the end of the season.

After the end of *Norm,* Ford co-starred with Florence Henderson in a short-lived situation comedy for ABC Family called *Moms on Strike* in 2002. In 2003, Ford moved back to New York City for a co-starring role in a more successful situation comedy, ABC's *Hope & Faith.* Ford played Hope, a highly strung housewife in Ohio with three children, who takes in her sister, Faith (played by Kelly Ripa), a soap opera actress whose career is in decline. Though critics were not kind to the show and it was not expected to be renewed for a second season, it proved to have a faithful fanbase and was picked up for the 2004-05 season.

Outside of her acting career, Ford had a long-time interest in cooking and food. She enjoyed it as a hobby from childhood, having learned to cook in the fifth grade. At one point, she wanted to open a restaurant. In 2004, Ford published her first cookbook, written with Melissa Clark, called *Cooking with Faith: 125 Classic and Healthy Southern Recipes.* Of Ford's cooking, former castmate Bergen told *People,* "All of her food is kind of sensuous and it's incredibly comforting, but her cooking is very fresh and light." Though Ford's fascination with cooking led to a successful secondary career, she remained primarily an in-demand actress who continued to work regularly. She went on to appear in the 2005 Vin Diesel vehicle *The Pacifier,* an action comedy, and had other projects lined up.

## Selected writings

(With Melissa Clark) *Cooking with Faith: 125 Classic and Healthy Southern Recipes,* Scribner, 2004.

## Sources

### Books

*Celebrity Biographies,* Baseline II, 2005.

## Periodicals

Associated Press, September 15, 2000; September 23, 2003.

*Baltimore Sun,* August 4, 2004, p. 4F.

*People,* November 14, 1988, p. 19; March 6, 1989, p. 239; October 28, 1996, p. 19; October 19, 1998, p. 29; September 29, 2003, p. 37; June 7, 2004, pp. 105-06; December 3, 2004, p. 42.

*Pittsburgh Post-Gazette,* September 25, 1994, p. TV34.

PR Newswire, April 10, 2003.

*Rocky Mountain News,* September 6, 1998, p. 4.

*St. Petersburg Times,* November 26, 1989, p. 6.

*Times-Picayune* (New Orleans, LA), October 6, 1996, p. T6.

*USA Today,* October 21, 1998, p. 3D; May 28, 2004, p. 6D.

*Variety,* September 28, 1998, p. 86.

—*A. Petruso*

# Claire M. Fraser

## Research scientist and biologist

**B**orn November 5, 1955; married J. Craig Venter (a scientist), 1981. *Education:* Graduated from Rensselaer Polytechnic Institute, 1977; State University of New York at Buffalo, Ph.D, 1981.

**Addresses:** *Office*—The Institute for Genomic Research, 9712 Medical Center Dr., Rockville, MD 20850.

## Career

**R**esearch instructor, SUNY Buffalo, 1981-83; cancer research scientist, Roswell Park Memorial Institute, 1983-85; researcher, National Institutes of Health, 1985; named vice president of research, The Institute for Genomic Research (TIGR), 1992; named president of TIGR, 1998.

## Sidelights

**C**laire M. Fraser, Ph.D, is president of The Institute for Genomic Research (TIGR), a non-profit research institute based in Rockville, Maryland, which is also the leading microbial genomics institution in the United States. *Washington Techway* dubbed Fraser "the quiet revolutionary" whose career has been "spent quietly bucking tradition, pushing boundaries, in search of answers."

Fraser was raised in Saugus, Massachusetts, where her parents were educators. The daughter of a high school principal and an elementary school teacher, she was interested in science from an early age,

which was reinforced by dissecting frogs in high school biology. "I guess it was the idea that was presented that the human body is really a beautiful machine, and this gave me an opportunity to see all the parts, see how they fit together, get a sense of how they might work together," she told *Washington Techway*'s Rob Terry. "To see all of this before me was just enormously exciting."

Fraser had originally planned to enter medical school, but in her senior year of college at Rensselaer Polytechnic Institute (RPI) professor Lenore Clesceri introduced Fraser to the possibility of using her skills in scientific research. She also became Fraser's mentor.

Fraser graduated from Rensselaer Polytechnic Institute with a bachelor of science degree in biology, summa cum laude, in 1977. Barry Martinelli, an RPI hockey player who dated Fraser for several years, said she was not the typical scientist. "She had an unbelievable memory and had a passion for science and research," Martinelli told Paul Raeburn in *BusinessWeek*. "She'd go to the hockey games and go to the parties, and then go back and hit the books for 48 hours straight. Scientists tend to be very rigid. She isn't like that."

Fraser met J. Craig Venter while attending the State University of New York at Buffalo (SUNY) and working on her thesis. Her thesis committee had expressed grave doubts about her intent to study receptor proteins using scientific techniques based on immunology and tissue culture. Venter, who was her lab director and an assistant professor at the time, encouraged her. "It was important for me because I found that I wasn't intimidated enough by my thesis committee to back down, when I suppose that could have been an option," Fraser told *Washington Techway*'s Terry. "I think that was a very important lesson early on, and I learned it from Craig, that you should not be afraid of taking new approaches to try and get at a particular problem. I really consider that a tremendous gift I was given."

She received her Ph.D in pharmacology from SUNY in 1981; the same year, she and Venter married. Together, they worked on several projects, including continuing to work on the biology of G protein-coupled receptors. From 1981 to 1983 Fraser was a research instructor in the biochemistry department at SUNY Buffalo. From there she went to the Roswell Park Memorial Institute as a cancer research scientist for two years. She continued her research on receptors at the National Institutes of Health (NIH) in 1985.

When Venter left the NIH to found TIGR in 1992, Fraser followed as she had been frustrated in the tenure process while at NIH. She was named TIGR's vice president of research. Her first work in genomics was examining genes in human tumors to try to better understand tumor development on a molecular level.

Her marriage and gender have reportedly skewed the perceptions about her professional ability. She dismissed the criticism. "Other than having outside people use this against us or against me somehow, I was never apologetic or embarrassed by the fact that Craig and I have had a long and very successful working relationship," she told a writer for *Washington Techway*. "It's been enormously rewarding to have the opportunity to actually work with my husband. And I don't think I need to make any apologies for that."

She succeeded her husband, who is now Celera Genomics Corporation president, as president of TIGR in 1998. Among the genetic decoding and analysis completed since her appointment as head of the institute are those of various bacteria responsible for diseases such as Lyme disease, syphilis, tuberculosis, meningitis and many others. Of the 65 microbial genes decoded as of July, 2002, TIGR was responsible for about half of those.

*BusinessWeek*'s Raeburn said, "The work has put TIGR at the forefront of the new field of microbial genomics—the foundation for the treatment and prevention of disease in the 21st century.... Fraser

has focused TIGR's efforts on microbes, mostly those that cause disease. Such research is critically important in the quest to develop new drugs. Most current drug research is based on discoveries made in the last century."

Its first success was in 1995 when TIGR staff unraveled the sequence for Haemophilus influenzae, which causes childhood ear infections and meningitis. "It was a landmark—the first time researchers had deciphered the complete genetic code of a free-living organism," wrote a journalist for *BusinessWeek*. Each year following, Fraser and her staff made significant inroads on discovering the causes of disease including Treponema pallidum, which causes syphilis, Vibrio cholerae, which causes cholera, Chlamydia trachomatis, which causes chlamydia, and Streptococcus pneumoniae, responsible for pneumonia and meningitis. In 2002, TIGR examined the anthrax strain used in the bioterrorism attacks in Florida.

"We have more completed sequences available today than anyone would have predicted five years ago," Fraser told a writer for *BusinessWeek*, "and it's going to be enormously important to have this comparative information to help figure out all of the biology that's going on. If you think of the diversity of life on this planet and what is not represented in any of the genomic databases so far, you quickly realize how much there is for us to still understand."

The TIGR staff doubled between 1998 and 2002 to 325 employees, about 30 of whom had Ph.Ds. The budget for the institute is based on winning research grants from organizations including the National Institutes of Health and the National Science Foundation. This amounted to about $50 million in 2002 compared to $24 million in 1998.

Fraser was named one of *Science* magazine's "Hot Scientists" for 1999-2000. She tied for third along with Michael B. Eisen of University of California, Berkeley, Josef M. Penninger and Tak W. Mak of the Amgen Institute/University of Toronto, Antonio Lanzavecchia with the Basel Institute of Immunology, Andrew Wakeham of the Amgen Institute, and TIGR colleague Owen White as one of the most cited scientists during the period. *Science* attributed this to greater interest in genome sequencing.

"If public recognition has been slow in coming, scientific recognition hasn't," commented *BusinessWeek*'s Raeburn. "Fraser has published 130 papers and serves on numerous scientific committees, NIH review boards, and editorial boards. She is one of the few women to run a major research institute. That's more than most scientists achieve in a lifetime."

Fraser has reportedly even thought about returning to school. "I'd like to relearn physics," she told *BusinessWeek*. She also ticked off other interests including nanotechnology and landscape architecture, leading to that publication's opinion that "Fraser is one of those uncommon individuals with a broad intellectual curiosity about the world and how it works. That, more than anything else, may explain her success."

## Sources

### Periodicals

*BusinessWeek*, July 1, 2002, p. 84.
PR Newswire, September 21, 1998; May 15, 2000.
*Science*, March 9, 2001.
*Scientist*, June 2, 2003, p. 13.
*Washington Techway*, September 17, 2001.

—*Linda Dailey Paulson*

# John Galliano

## Fashion designer

Philippe Wojazer/Reuters/Landov

**B**orn Juan Carlos Antonio Galliano-Guillen in 1960 in Gibraltar, Spain. *Education:* Earned design degree from Central Saint Martins College of Art and Design, 1984.

**Addresses:** *Office*—John Galliano, 60 Rue d'Avron, 75020 Paris, France.

## Career

**G**alliano's 1984 design-school graduation collection, "Les Incroyables," sold to Brown's, a London retailer, in its entirety; established fashion house under his own name in London, 1984; worked with various financial backers to produce collections, 1985-95; haute couture and ready-to-wear designer at the House of Givenchy, Paris, France, 1995-96; haute couture and ready-to-wear designer at Christian Dior, Paris, 1996—; opened own shop in Bergdorf Goodman store, 1997; licensed fur line, 1998; opened shop in Saks Fifth Avenue, 2000; launched watch collection, 2001; a partial career retrospective, "John Galliano at Dior," was staged at the Design Museum of London, 2001-02.

**Awards:** British Designer of Year award 1986, 1994, 1995; International Fashion Group, Master of Fashion, 1997; Designer of the Year, Council of Fashion of America, 1998; Commander of Order of the British Empire, 2001.

## Sidelights

**B**ritish fashion designer John Galliano's intricate and provocative clothes, which sometimes teeter on the edge of absurd, have made him one of the leading names in an industry where very few succeed to the top echelon. Usually referred to as fashion's *enfant terrible,* the designer's quixotic vision, exuberant sense of style, and iconoclastic personality have earned him a devoted following among the fashionista set, especially after he took over at the House of Dior in 1996. In a lengthy *New Yorker* profile, journalist Michael Specter noted that some of Galliano's critics claim that "his outfits often seemed more suited to the pageantry of public relations than to profits. Yet his effect on the way women dress is almost impossible to overstate.... More than any other designer working today, Galliano is responsible for the sheer and sexually frank clothing so many women wear."

Galliano emerged from a new generation of daring British designers whose visionary styles began stirring up the somewhat-moribund realm of international haute couture in the 1990s. Along with Alexander McQueen, creative director of Gucci, and

Stella McCartney of Chloe, Galliano was tapped to take over one of France's more venerable design houses, Dior, in the 1990s. Before this generation, few British names had ever had any lasting impact on the French- and Italian-centric world of fashion. But Galliano has continental roots that helped shape his fabulously eccentric vision: his mother was Spanish, and he was born in Gibraltar, an overseas territory of Britain located on the coast of Spain, in 1960. The family moved to London six years later, but Galliano grew up in a household where his mother taught him to flamenco dance and regularly dressed his two sisters and him in formal outfits for Sundays and special occasions.

The Gallianos were working-class, and Galliano's father was a plumber in South London, which is often mentioned in articles about the designer's swift rise in the haute-couture world. "I got so sick of seeing my father called a plumber in every article," he told Specter in the *New Yorker* article, just before his father passed away. "People are always talking about how I am a plumber's son. I am my father's son primarily. What he chose to do as a career was his choice and he did it very, very well."

Galliano was originally drawn to languages, but at school he discovered he had a talent for drawing. His teachers suggested he apply to a fashion college, and he won a slot at Central Saint Martins College of Art and Design, London's top design school. While there, he worked as a dresser at Britain's National Theatre, the eminent theater company in London. As a dresser, it was his job to make sure that the wardrobe worn by some of Britain's most famous thespians was perfect, but Galliano also gained a wealth of experience in the art of spectacle. "That changed my life," he said of the job in the interview with Specter. "I was a good dresser. It helped shape my view of drama, of clothing, of costume--the way people dress."

As a design student, Galliano was often seized by fanciful ideas and schemes. While still in school, he began sketching images of bizarrely modern clothing based on the ideals of the French Revolution. True to form, he sketched them on period-style parchment paper and only by candlelight. When one of his teachers saw them, it was suggested that Galliano turn the sketches of quasi-androgynous gear into his graduation collection at St. Martins. He staged an elaborate spectacle that caused a London fashion-world sensation in 1984. *Harper's Bazaar* writer Colin McDowell was an instructor at the school at the time, and recalled "there was hysteria behind the scenes, with students in tears begging to model for him, and members of the audience, who had already heard the buzz, becoming increasingly excited in anticipation."

Galliano sold the entire collection to the one London retailer, Brown's, that offered forward-minded fashion at the time. "I had to literally wheel my collection up the street to their shop," he said in the *New Yorker* interview. "I couldn't even afford to put the clothes in a cab. And they put one of the coats in the window and it was bought by Diana Ross." Galliano went into business for himself that first year, but struggled financially for the next decade. His clothes remained exuberantly bizarre, often deploying arcane period detail. He liked to visit design museums to examine eighteenth-century frock coats to learn forgotten tailoring secrets, and his collections were staged with increasing theatricality. One 1985 show had a model coming down the runway waving a dead mackerel at the fashion buyers and journalists in the audience.

Galliano was recognized as the British Designer of Year in 1986, but the Danish financial backer he had been working with cut him loose that same year. He quickly found another, Aguecheek, which was a company that owned some of London's priciest designer boutiques. "My next collection will be much more disciplined—it has to be," he told *WWD* journalist James Fallon when Aguecheek agreed to produce his spring 1987 collection. But a year later, Galliano seemed back to his retro-quirk. A *WWD* report on the spring 1988 fashion collections in London described the novelties in his show as "high waists throughout, some over the bust; skirts that are long in front, short in back," and accessories that included "shoulder-length gloves, Twenties-style button-front shoes [and] snoods."

In 1990, Galliano took a leap of faith and moved to Paris. He struggled financially there, too, especially after Aguecheek severed its ties with him. After presenting collections only intermittently for a few years, he was living in reduced circumstances at his tiny atelier. He was known among the fashion-editrix and stylesetter set for his gorgeous and eccentric designs, but was thought to be too outré for the commercial world. That changed when Galliano was befriended by the creative director for the American edition of *Vogue*, Andre Leon Talley. After Talley convinced *Vogue* editor Anna Wintour to give Galliano's newest designs a look, it was decided that Galliano needed to stage a show for the fall 1994 Paris collections to secure some serious financial backing. He had no money to put on a show, but Talley asked Paris socialite Saõ Schlumberger to lend her house, and Galliano filled it with thousands of dead leaves and pumped in dry ice. A roster of top models of the day worked for free, and wore Galliano items cut from the sole bolt of fabric he could afford to buy: black satin-backed crepe, which had a shiny side and matte one.

The show was a sensation, and brought Galliano another British Designer of Year award. He showed an expanded line at Bergdorf Goodman that same year for his American retail debut, but the true turning point was around the corner: in July of 1995, he was announced as the next haute couture and ready-to-wear designer for Givenchy. The classic French house dated back to 1952 and was indelibly associated with actress Audrey Hepburn, the muse of designer Hubert de Givenchy, but in recent years the clothes had lacked excitement and de Givenchy announced he would retire. The parent company, French luxury-goods conglomerate Louis Vuitton-Moët-Hennessy (LVMH), launched a search to replace de Givenchy, and stunned the fashion world by installing Galliano in the post. He became the first British designer to head a French design house since Charles Frederick Worth dressed the Empress Eugenie and France's wealthiest women in the 1850s.

Galliano admitted it caused a bit of a stir. "Understandably, some of the ladies were very loyal to Monsieur de Givenchy," he told *WWD* writers Janet Ozzard and Katherine Weisman. "But we had a lovely tea party for some of them recently, and it was great. I got to talk to them and find out what their needs are, what they want, and they got to meet me." He also asserted he conducted his own method of market research. He began getting pedicures, complete with polish. "I went down to Revlon and lay on the table next to Mrs. So-and-So and had the whole treatment," he said in the same *WWD* interview. "I mean, if you're going to get to know your customer, you have to know what she does. So I went through all that."

Some media sources made much of Galliano's startling rise, and often invoked the "son of a plumber" phrase. Adding to that, Galliano was known as exuberantly, famously eccentric, often sporting long dreadlocks, a pencil mustache, and a roster of ever-changing get-ups that usually featured somewhat of a pirate theme. After a year on the job, Galliano's star rose even further at LVMH when he was named head of Christian Dior, assuredly the most prestigious and vital property in the LVMH stable. Now Galliano had the financial wherewithal to give his creative vision free rein, and LVMH chair Bernard Arnault seemed to let him do as he pleased. His Dior debut at the Paris haute-couture shows was famous for its train-station setting and the models alighting off an antique steam engine that came thundering down the track.

Other Dior shows under Galliano featured models dressed as nuns but also sporting fetish wear, or a theme centered around the idea of Russian aristocrats escaping the 1917 revolution. Critics seemed flummoxed at times to translate Galliano's ideas onto the page and distill what was important and new, but the clothes won their own fans and the Dior name enjoyed an impressive renaissance. The line was suddenly new, sexy, and hip, with its clothes fitting much closer to the body, which Galliano has said he worked diligently to convince its esteemed stable of fitters and seamstresses to do when he took over. Though his runway ideas were sometimes outrageous, in the end they trickled down to the mainstream, and Galliano is credited with bringing dirty denim, camouflage, and even the slip dress to the masses.

Although those priciest haute-couture concoctions remained the province of the immensely wealthy, the more accessible Dior ready-to-wear began to thrive. His dresses became the favorite of trend-setting celebrities, from singer Gwen Stefani to actress Nicole Kidman, and between 1997 and 2001, Dior sales doubled to $312 million. In 2004, he was named to *Time* magazine's 100 list of world trendsetters and visionaries, and while writer Kate Betts hailed him as an immense creative force, she claimed the larger significance of what he introduced was nothing less than "the very proportions of our clothes, cutting dresses and jackets on the bias—against the grain of the fabric—so that they spiral around the body and give women a sinuous, sexier shape."

Galliano still makes his own John Galliano line, and opened an expectedly grandiose retail space in Paris on the Rue Saint-Honore in 2003. He lives in the Marais district of Paris, and adheres to a strenuous fitness regime to keep him toned for the sometimes shirtless catwalk struts he likes to take after presenting his collections. His outrageous costumes are a drastic departure from the well-cut suits of Monsieur Dior, who died in 1957 after revolutionizing women's fashion in a mere decade of innovation. "I don't think if Mr. Dior were here today he'd still be doing what he did back then, redoing things from yesteryear," Galliano told *W*'s Miles Socha in 2002. "Don't forget, he was the first designer to set the standard for the modern fashion show. He was the first to license, the first to look to the United States for sales. He was a leader, and I think the house of Dior should continue to be."

## Sources

### Books

*Contemporary Fashion,* second ed., St. James Press, 2002.

## Periodicals

*Harper's Bazaar,* March 2004, p. 304.
*New Yorker,* September 22, 2003, p. 161.
*New York Times,* October 11, 2000, p. B11; January 20, 2004, p. B8.

*Time,* April 26, 2004, p. 88.
*W,* April 2002, p. 210.
*WWD,* July 1, 1986, p. 6; October 12, 1987, p. 8; September 9, 1996, p. 8.

—*Carol Brennan*

# Amalia García

## Governor and political party leader

Born Amelia García Medina, October 6, 1951, in Zacatecas City, Mexico; daughter of Francisco García Estrada (a politician) and Concepción Medina; children: Claudia Sofia Corichi García. *Education:* Attended college in Zacatecas City, c. late 1960s; earned degrees in sociology from National Autonomous University (Mexico City), 1972, and history from Autonomous University (Puebla), 1976.

**Addresses:** *Office*—c/o Embassy of Mexico, 1911 Pennsylvania Ave. NW, Washington, DC 20006.

## Career

Social and political activist, and active in the Mexican Communist and Socialist parties; founding member of the Democratic Revolution Party (PRD), 1989; at-large congresswoman, then federal senator; elected PRD leader, 1999; elected governor of Zacatecas, 2004.

## Sidelights

Mexican politician Amalia García, elected governor of the state of Zacatecas in 2004, is also the first woman to lead a major political party in her country. Since 1999 she has helmed the Democratic Revolution Party, or PRD, one of her country's three main political parties. Political analysts describe the lifelong activist as a savvy alliance-builder and possible future presidential contender. "She is the model of what a modern Mexican politician ought to be," professor of political science Luis Miguel Rionda told *Dallas Morning News* writer Ricardo Sandoval. "She knows how to dialogue with the different factions of her party and with leaders from other parties. Not many in Mexico can do that today."

García's political skills seem to be inherited ones. Her father, Francisco García Estrada, became governor of Zacatecas in 1956, when she was five years old; prior to that, her grandfather had been mayor of Zacatecas City. When her father became an ambassador, he took the family with him, and García grew up in the capital cities of Guatemala, the Dominican Republic, the Philippines, and then Poland. It was in Warsaw in 1968 when she and her family saw news reports of the Tlatelolco massacre in Mexico City on Polish television. Some 5,000 university students and their supporters had gathered in a large plaza in the Tlatelolco area of the city, but the army fired live rounds into the crowd and scores died. García urged her parents to return home, which they did, and the tragic incident spurred a lifelong commitment to social and political reform for her.

García's college years were spent in Zacatecas City, and then at the National Autonomous University in Mexico City, where she was active in the student-rights movement. She graduated with a degree in sociology in 1972, and went on to earn a history degree from Autonomous University of Puebla in 1976. An active member of the Mexican Communist Party and later the Socialist Party organization, she was involved in various projects, including membership on a committee that worked to call attention to the plight of political prisoners in Mexico.

García came of age in a Mexico that was undergoing tremendous social and political changes. Only in the mid-1970s did the country finally rescind a law that allowed husbands to forbid their wives to work outside the home. Women were still a rare presence inside the political sphere when García was a young woman. But her generation was also moving forward and pushing for more reform, especially in the political arena: her father's party, the Institutional Revolutionary Party (PRI), had controlled the country since 1929, and its members held nearly every important office. Yet the PRI had also gained a reputation for deeply entrenched corruption.

A new political party, the Democratic Revolution Party (PRD) emerged after allegations of widespread voting fraud on the part of the PRI in the 1988 presidential election. García was a founding member of the new party, which quickly gained popular support for its center-left platform that supported both free-market economic reforms and progressive social issues. In the early 1990s, she served as an at-large congresswoman, and then became a federal senator. As a legislator she championed passage of new laws that mandated harsher penalties for assaults on women.

García also successfully urged adoption of a PRD rule stating that no more than 70 percent of a PRD administration could be dominated by any one gender—in effect, an affirmative action policy for women within the party structure. She ran for the party presidency in 1996, but lost to a colleague, and spent the next three years working to build alliances in various electoral districts with the National Action Party, or PAN, the third main party in Mexican politics. In 1999, she stood again for the party leadership post, and this time she won it. Her ballot victory made her the first woman to lead a major political party in Mexican history.

García took over the PRD leadership at a time when the party was bitterly divided into factions led by its two founders, now political adversaries, but she continued to lead efforts to build alliances with PAN. By 2000, PRD governors ruled over four of Mexico's 31 states thanks to that strategy, and the

PRI's control seemed to be eroding. "We are changing an authoritarian regime that's now obliged to talk and dialogue with other powers," she pointed out in an *Austin American-Statesman* interview with Susan Ferriss. "That's new in Mexico."

García stood for election herself in 2004, defeating a PRI candidate for the same governor's office her father once held, and was sworn in for a six-year term. But much had changed in Zacatecas by then: an overwhelming number of its residents leave to seek work in the United States; statistics show that about half of its three million residents are living in the United States, many of them fathers, brothers, and sons. In 2003, they sent back some $480 million to the state of Zacatecas alone to support families there.

García was committed to improving economic conditions and job growth in Zacatecas by encouraging new initiatives. Both before and after her election she traveled regularly to meet with constituents living in cities like Dallas and Los Angeles. While there, she encouraged Mexican-American business leaders there to invest in enterprises back in Zacatecas and other states, but her visits were also in recognition that her official constituency now lived on both sides of the border: a recently enacted Mexican law allowed those living in the United States to return home to vote in elections, and the 2004 balloting that gave her the governorship was the first to include these votes. "I consider Zacatecas as a binational state," she told *New York Times* journalist Ginger Thompson. "Although the reasons our people have migrated are painful, these people have guaranteed our social stability."

"La Gobernadora" García is only the third woman elected to lead a Mexican state since women earned the right to vote in 1953, and observers of Latin American politics predict she may enter the 2012 presidential race. Her daughter, Claudia Sofia Corichi García, is a PRD staffer and also likely to make a run for office someday.

## Sources

*Austin American-Statesman,* February 20, 2000, p. A2.
*Christian Science Monitor,* July 30, 1999, p. 1.
*Dallas Morning News,* October 28, 2004.
*Houston Chronicle,* July 6, 2004, p. 1.
*New York Times,* February 23, 2005.
*Seattle Post-Intelligencer,* January 31, 2000, p. A2.

—*Carol Brennan*

# Gabriel García Márquez

*Henry Romero/Reuters/Landov*

## Author and journalist

**B**orn Gabriel José García Márquez, March 6, 1928, in Aracataca, Colombia; son of Gabriel Eligio Garcia (a telegraph operator) and Luisa Santiaga Márquez Iguaran; married Mercedes Barcha Pardo, 1958; children: two sons. *Education:* Attended Universidad Nacional de Colombia, 1947-48; attended Universidad de Cartagena, 1948-49.

**Addresses:** *Home*—P.O. Box 20736, Mexico City D.F., Mexico.

## Career

**B**egan career as a journalist, 1947; reporter for *Universal,* Cartegena, Colombia, late 1940s, *El heraldo,* Baranquilla, Colombia, 1950-52, and *El espectador,* Bogota, Colombia, until 1955; freelance journalist in Paris, London, and Caracas, Venezuela, 1956-57; worked for *Momento* magazine, Caracas, 1957-59; helped form Prensa Latina news agency, Bogota, 1959, and worked as its correspondent in Havana, Cuba, and New York City, 1961; writer, 1965—; Fundacion Habeas, founder, 1979, president, 1979—; bought *Cambio* newsmagazine, 1999.

**Awards:** Colombian Association of Writers and Artists Award, 1954; Premio Literario Esso (Colombia), 1961; Chianciano Award (Italy), 1969; Prix de Meilleur Livre Etranger (France); 1969, Romulo Gallegos prize (Venezuela), 1971; honorary doctorate, Columbia University, 1971; Books Abroad/Neustadt International Prize for Literature, 1972; Nobel Prize for Literature, 1982; *Los Angeles Times* Book Prize for fiction, 1988; Serfin Prize, 1989.

## Sidelights

**O**ne of the most influential novelists of the twentieth century, Gabriel García Márquez was a key figure in the Latin American literary renaissance of the 1960s and 1970s. His novel *One Hundred Years of Solitude* was read throughout the world, selling millions of copies and introducing enthusiastic readers across the globe to the genre of "magical realism." A prolific journalist as well as a novelist and short story writer, García Márquez has reported from several world capitals and remained active through the 1990s as publisher of the Colombian news magazine *Cambio.*

García Márquez was born on March 6, 1928, in Aracataca, Colombia, a small town on the Caribbean coast to which his mother's family had moved after her father, Colonel Nicolas Marquez Mejfa, had killed a man in a duel. The oldest child of eleven siblings, García Márquez grew up in Aracataca with his maternal grandparents, who nurtured the budding writer's imagination with fascinating stories of local history and family events. The Colonel reminisced frequently about his youth during the country's civil wars, while the boy's grandmother, who claimed to converse with ghosts and spirits, recounted family legends and became the boy's "source of the magical, superstitious and supernatural view of reality," as García Márquez described it in a *New York Times Book Review* article.

Among the more memorable family stories was that of García Márquez's parents' courtship. "This history of their forbidden love was one of the wonders of my youth," he wrote in "Seranade," a piece published in the *New Yorker*. So impassioned were his parents' accounts of the affair, he observed, that when he attempted to write about the subject in his novel *Love in the Time of Cholera*, "I couldn't distinguish between life and poetry." It was the Colonel who disapproved of Gabriel Eligio Garcia as a suitor for his daughter, Luisa Santiaga; the young telegraph operator had a reputation as a womanizer and had been born out of wedlock to a 14-year-old girl who went on to have six other children by three different men. "It is surprising that Colonel Marquez was so disquieted by this irregular conduct," García Márquez wrote, "when the Colonel himself had fathered, in addition to his three official children, nine more by different mothers, both before and after his marriage, and all of them were welcomed by his wife as if they were her own." Gabriel Eligio Garcia was also a political conservative—the party against whom the Colonel had fought in the civil wars—and had few financial prospects. After a passionate courtship that included violin serenades, exile, and even the purchase of a revolver by which Gabriel Eligio Garcia hoped to protect himself from the Colonel's wrath, the couple eloped. When Luisa Santiaga announced her first pregnancy, however, her parents welcomed her and her husband back to Aracataca, where the writer was born in his grandparents' house. García Márquez grew up with ten younger siblings and also has several half siblings from his father's extramarital affairs.

When García Márquez was seven, his grandfather died and the boy returned to his parents in Bogota, the country's capital. During his adolescence the boy developed a love of literature, with such works as Franz Kafka's "The Metamorphosis" inspiring him to dream of becoming a writer. First, though, he planned to obtain a law degree. He entered the Universidad Nacional de Colombia in 1947, the same year he published his first short story in *El Espectador*. In 1948 the country erupted in violence after the assassination of reformist leader Jorge Eliecer Gaitan and the university was damaged by fire and subsequently closed. García Márquez then transferred to the Universidad de Cartagena. There he began writing journalistic pieces for *El Universal*, and also met Ramon Vinyes, who introduced him to the works of Virginia Woolf and William Faulkner. García Márquez abandoned his legal studies in 1949

and moved back to the Caribbean region, to the town of Barranquilla.

During his two years in Barranquilla, García Márquez worked for *El heraldo*, the local paper, writing a regular column that included short stories, fragments, and essays about current issues. He then moved on to a job as correspondent for the Bogota paper *El Espectador*, writing film criticism and investigative reports. In the mid-1950s García Márquez moved to Europe, an environment he considered more amenable to his leftist political views than the regime in his native country. In Paris, where he was based, he continued reporting for *El Espectador* and also for another Colombian paper, *El Independiente*. He also continued to write fiction, publishing his first novel, *Leaf Storm*, in 1955 and completing the novel *El coronel no tiene quien le escriba* in 1957. Though he sometimes lived in poverty during these years, particularly after the Colombian government shut down *El Independiente* and left him without a regular income, García Márquez later noted that his European exile was worthwhile for the fresh perspective it gave him on Latin America.

In 1957 the young journalist moved back to Latin America to help a friend, Plinio Apuleye Mendoza, edit the weekly magazine *Momento* in Caracas, Venezuela. The following year, García Márquez returned to Barranquilla to marry his childhood sweetheart, Mercedes Barcha Pardo, the daughter of a local pharmacist. Soon afterward, García Márquez and Mendoza resigned from *Momento* to protest its tacit support of U.S. foreign policy. The pair traveled to Cuba to document the aftermath of Castro's revolution, and signed on with the new government's news agency, Prensa Latina, to establish branch offices in Bogota and eventually in New York City. In 1961 García Márquez quit Prensa Latina and moved to Mexico City, where he managed to support his family by writing screenplays and doing editorial and advertising work.

Though García Márquez continued a steady production of novellas and short stories during these years, he did not achieve prominence as a writer of fiction until the publication in 1967 of his landmark novel, *One Hundred Years of Solitude*. Based on the author's childhood memories of Aracataca, the novel recounts the founding of the fictional town of Macondo by Jose Arcadio Buendia, and its subsequent rise and fall through several generations from the 1820s to the 1920s. Blending historical events with surrealism and fantasy, the novel includes such characters as Colonel Aureliano Buendia, fomentor of 32 political rebellions and father of 17 illegitimate sons; matriarch Ursula Buendia, who witnesses the town's eventual decline; and the old gypsy scribe, Melquiades, whose mysterious manuscripts are revealed as the novel's text. The complex saga of Macondo and the Buendias, many critics noted, suggests the labyrinthine history of Latin America itself.

The novel caused an immediate sensation, selling out its entire first Spanish printing within one week. So heavy was demand for the book that its publisher could scarcely keep enough copies in print. Critics hailed it as a monumental achievement; Chilean Nobel laureate poet Pablo Neruda was quoted in *Time* as calling the book "the greatest revelation in the Spanish language since the *Don Quixote* of Cervantes." *One Hundred Years of Solitude* went on to sell more than 20 million copies worldwide and to be translated into more than 30 languages. It is widely considered the most popular and influential example of magical realism, a literary style that incorporates supernatural or surreal elements within a realistic narrative. As Faulkner had done with the American South, García Márquez had created in Macondo a world of mythic dimensions.

The success of *One Hundred Years of Solitude* enabled García Márquez to focus full-time on his own writing. In 1975 he published the novel *The Autumn of the Patriarch,* about a tyrant who has held political power for so long that no one can remember his predecessor. After that, however, he vowed not to release any additional fiction until Chilean dictator Augusto Pinochet was removed from office. Though Pinochet was not ousted until 1989, García Márquez published the novel *Crónica de una meuerte anunciada* in 1981. Considered by some critics to be the author's best work, it tells the story of brothers who plot to kill their sister's husband when, after discovering on his wedding night that his bride is not a virgin, he returns her to her family.

In 1982 García Márquez was awarded the Nobel Prize in literature. The Swedish Academy, in bestowing the prize, cited not only the author's narrative gifts but also his demonstrated commitment to social justice. Indeed, the problems of poverty and oppression were the theme of the laureate's acceptance speech. Citing figures that documented thousands of violent deaths and millions of involuntary exiles linked to the political turmoil in Latin America during the 1970s, García Márquez commented that the reality of his native continent nourished in him an "insatiable creativity, full of sorrow and beauty," and made it necessary for Latin Americans to "ask but little of imagination, for our crucial problem has been a lack of conventional means to render our lives believable." Implying that Latin America's cultural remoteness has made it difficult

for European and North American countries to sympathize with the leftist political agendas of many of its inhabitants, he went on to ask, "Why is the originality so readily granted us in literature so mistrustfully denied us in our difficult attempts at social change?"

Criticizing wealthy countries that have "accumulated powers of destruction such as to annihilate, a hundred times over, not only all the human beings that have existed to this day, but also the totality of all living beings that have ever drawn breath on this planet of misfortune," García Márquez ended on a note of hope: "We, the inventors of tales, who will believe anything, feel entitled to believe that it is not yet too late to engage in the creation of ... a new and sweeping utopia of life, where no one will be able to decide for others how they die, where love will prove true and happiness be possible, and where the races condemned to one hundred years of solitude will have, at last and forever, a second opportunity on earth."

García Márquez decided to use his Nobel Prize money to start a newspaper. Yet that venture never materialized, because the author was not satisfied that the independent editorial voice he sought would be respected. More than a decade later, however, he realized his dream to go back to journalism when he bought the Colombian newsmagazine *Cambio* in 1999. "Journalism is the only trade that I like," he commented in the *New York Times,* "and I have always regarded myself as a journalist." The magazine had been struggling, but after García Márquez's purchase its circulation and ad revenues skyrocketed. The writer's international prominence, many observers noted, allowed him access to world leaders who were not always eager to speak to other reporters. "Anyone he calls will pick up the phone," said his American editor, Ash Green, in an Associated Press article. Among the friends and associates about whom García Márquez has written in *Cambio* are Cuban president Fidel Castro, Colombian industrialist Julio Mario Santo Domingo, and U.S. President Bill Clinton, who had once impressed the writer by reciting long passages of Faulkner's *The Sound and the Fury* by heart. When Clinton's affair with Monica Lewinsky was revealed, García Márquez defended the president, according to *New York Times* reporter Larry Rohter, by asking "Is it fair that this rare example of the human species must squander his historic destiny just because he couldn't find a safe place to make love?"

García Márquez's reentry into journalism was not without significant risks. Unlike the more neutral American press, the Colombian media take "a strong position in defense of a democratic state rather than observing from an impartial perch," as *Washington Post* writer Scott Wilson pointed out. "Reporting in Colombia, particularly by Colombians," Wilson noted, "has long been a perilous vocation. But mounting violence, combined with the weakness of public institutions and the blurry line between journalism and advocacy in a country at war with itself, have increasingly placed journalists high on the list of targets." In the first ten months of 2001, nine journalists were killed in Colombia and dozens received death threats. Despite such dangers, García Márquez continued actively reporting on his country's decades-long war between Marxist guerillas and government forces, as well as on controversial issues in other parts of Latin America.

Among García Márquez's political books from this period are *Clandestine in Chile: The Adventures of Miguel Littin,* a nonfiction account of filmmaker Littin's return to Pinochet's Chile after a period of self-imposed exile. The Chilean government, outraged by the book's content, ordered some 15,000 copies of it burned. In 1997 García Márquez published *News of a Kidnapping,* based on his investigation of Colombian drug cartels and their destructive influence on that nation's social fabric. "*News of a Kidnapping* not only provides a fascinating anatomy of 'one episode in the biblical holocaust that has been consuming Colombia for more than 20 years,'" wrote Michiko Kakutani in the *New York Times,* "but also offers the reader new insights into the surreal history of Mr. García Márquez's native country. Indeed, the reader is reminded by this book that the magical realism employed by Mr. García Márquez and other Latin American novelists is in part a narrative strategy for grappling with a social reality so hallucinatory, so irrational that it defies ordinary naturalistic description."

Through the 1980s and 1990s, García Márquez continued to strengthen his reputation as a literary master with publication of the novels *Love in the Time of Cholera,* based partially on the story of his parents' courtship; *The General in His Labyrinth,* a fictional account of the final months in the life of nineteenth-century South American revolutionary Simon Bolivar; and *Of Love and Other Demons,* inspired by the author's recollection of a tomb excavation he had witnessed in 1949, when a centuries-old skeleton of a young girl was discovered with living hair flowing from the skull. García Márquez used this image to create the character of Sierva Maria De Todos Los Angeles, a girl in touch with both the Spanish and the African legacies of her Caribbean heritage. When she is bitten by a mad dog, the area bishop orders an exorcism, but the priest charged with perform-

ing the rite falls in love with the girl. As with many of García Márquez's earlier novels, *Of Love and Other Demons* was hailed for its symbolic commentary on Latin American history. As *Times Literary Supplement* contributor Michael Kerrigan observed, "To excavate the historic vault in which his people lie buried is, for García Márquez, an act not of desecration but of liberation."

Since the summer of 1999, when he was diagnosed with lymphatic cancer, García Márquez has lived in relative seclusion, focusing his attention on completing a planned three-volume memoir. He was quoted in a CNN.com report as hailing his diagnosis as an "enormous stroke of luck" that forced him to put aside less urgent projects. The first volume of the memoir will cover the author's family background and his early life. The second will focus on his writing career, and the third will examine his relationships with world leaders.

In March of 2001, García Márquez swore never to set foot in Spain again unless the government withdrew new rules obliging Colombian visitors to obtain visas. According to the *Guardian*'s Giles Tremlett, García Márquez "said that Colombians grew up thinking of Spain as the 'madre patria,' or mother country, even though Colombia won independence from Spain in 1820." In 2002, the first volume of García Márquez's memoir, *Vivir Para Contarla* (To Live to Tell It) was published. It was later published in the United States under the title *Living to Tell the Tale.* On November 6, 2003, a tribute in honor of the American publication of his memoir was held at the Town Hall Theater in Manhattan. García Márquez did not attend the event, but he sent a statement. In December of that year, the book was named a *New York Times* Editor's Choice for 2003. In 2004, García Márquez received even more recognition when talk-show host Oprah Winfrey chose *One Hundred Years of Solitude* as her January book club selection.

García Márquez continued to stir up controversy in September of 2004 when he was barred from the International Congress of the Spanish Language because he objects to the formal teaching of spelling, a position that angers many of the conference's organizers. On October 18, 2004, his novel *Memorias de Mis Putas Tristes* (Memories of My Sad Whore), was published a week early in Colombia in order to deter people from buying pirated copies. He thwarted bootleggers by changing the last chapter at the last minute, revealing the fact as one million copies of the book shipped to stores throughout Latin America and Spain. With the November 9, 2004, sale of the film rights to his novel *Love in the Time of Cholera,* García Márquez is certain to keep his name in the news.

# Selected writings

## Fiction

*La hojarasca* (novel; title means "Leaf Storm"), Ediciones Sipa, 1955.

*El coronel no tiene quien le escriba* (novella), Aguirre Editor, 1961; translated as *No One Writes to the Colonel*, Harper & Row, 1968.

*La mala hora* (novel), Talleres de Graficas (Madrid, Spain), 1961; reprinted, Bruguera (Barcelona, Spain), 1982; English translation by Gregory Rabassa published as *In Evil Hour*, Harper (New York, NY), 1979.

*Los funerales de la Mamá Grande* (short stories), Editorial Universidad Veracruzana, 1962.

(With Carlos Fuentes) *El Gallo de Oro*, screenplay from novel by Juan Rulfo, 1964.

*Cien años de soledad* (novel), Editorial Sudamericana, 1967; translated as *One Hundred Years of Solitude*, Harper & Row, 1970.

*Isabel viendo llover en Macondo* (novella), Editorial Estuario, 1967.

*La increible y triste historia de la candida Erendira y su abuela desalmada* (short stories), Barral Editores, 1972.

*El negro que hizo esperar a los angeles* (short stories), Ediciones Alfil (Montevideo, Uraguay), 1972.

*Ojos de perro azul* (short stories), Equisditorial, 1972.

*Leaf Storm and Other Stories*, Harper & Row, 1972.

*El otoño del patriarca* (novel), Plaza & Janes Editores, 1975; translated as *The Autumn of the Patriarch*, Harper & Row, 1976.

*Todos los cuentos de Gabriel García Márquez: 1947-1972* (collected short stories), Plaza & Janés Editores, 1975.

*Innocent Eréndira and Other Stories*, Harper & Row, 1978.

*Dos novelas de Macondo*, Casa de las Americas, 1980.

*Crónica de una muerte anunciada* (novel), La Oveja Negra, 1981; translated as *Chronicle of a Death Foretold*, Knopf, 1983.

*El rastro de tu sangre en la nieve: El verano feliz de la senora Forbes*, W. Dampier Editores (Bogota, Colombia), 1982.

*El secuestro: Guion cinematografico* (unfilmed screenplay), Oveja Negra (Bogota, Colombia), 1982.

*Viva Sandino* (play), Editorial Nueva Nicaragua, 1982.

*Eréndira* (film script), Les Films du Triangle, 1983.

*Collected Stories*, Harper & Row, 1984.

*El amor en los tiempos del cólera* (novel), Oveja Negra, 1985; translated as *Love in the Time of Cholera*, Knopf, 1988.

*A Time to Die* (film script), ICA Cinema, 1988.

*Diatribe of Love against a Seated Man* (play, first produced at Cervantes Theater, Buenos Aires, 1988), Arango Editores, 1994.

*El general en su labertino* (novel), Mondadori, 1989; translated as *The General in His Labyrinth*, Knopf, 1990.

*Collected novellas*, HarperCollins, 1990.

*Doce cuentos peregrinos*, Mondadori, 1992; translated as *Strange Pilgrims: Twelve Stories*, Knopf, 1993.

*The Handsomest Drowned Man in the World: A Tale for Children*, Creative Education, 1993.

*Del amor y otros demonios* (novel), Mondador, 1994; translated as *Of Love and Other Demons*, Knopf, 1995.

(Contributor) *The Picador Book of Latin American Stories*, Picador (New York, NY), 1998.

Individually bound series of single stories, including *El verano feliz de la senora Forbes*, illustrated by Carmen Sole Vendrell, Groupo Editorial Norma (Bogota, Colombia), 1999.

*Memorias de Mis Putas Tristes* (Memories of My Sad Whore), Knopf, 2004.

## Nonfiction

(With Mario Vargas Llosa) *La novela en America Latina: Dialogo*, Carlos Milla Batres, 1968.

*Relato de un naufrago* (journalistic pieces), Tusquets Editor, 1970; translated as *The Story of a Shipwrecked Sailor*, Knopf, 1986.

*Cuando era feliz e indocumentado* (journalistic pieces), Ediciones El Ojo de Camello, 1973.

*Operacion Carlota* (essays) 1977.

*Periodismo militante* (journalistic pieces), Son de Maquina (Bogota, Colombia), 1978.

*De viaje por los paises socialistas: 90 dias en la "Cortina de hierro"* (journalistic pieces), Ediciones Macondo (Colombia), 1978.

*Cronicas y reportajes* (journalistic pieces), Oveja Negra, 1978.

(Contributor) *Los sandanistas*, Oveja Negra, 1979.

(Contributor) *Asi es Caracas*, edited by Soledad Mendoza, Editorial Ateneo de Caracas, 1980.

*Obra periodistica* (journalistic pieces), edited by Jacques Gilard, Bruguera, Volume 1: *Textos constenos*, 1981, Volumes 2-3: *Entre cachacos*, 1982, Volume 4: *De Europa y America (1955-1960)*, 1983.

*El olor de la guayaba: Conversaciones con Plinio Apuleyo Mendoza* (interviews), Oveja Negra, 1982; translated as *The Fragrance of Guava*, 1983.

(With Guillermo Nolasco-Juarez) *Persecucion y muerte de minorias: dos perspectives*, Juarez Editor, 1984.

*La aventura de Miguel Littin, clandestino en Chile: Un reportaje*, Editorial Sudamericana, 1986; English translation by Asa Zatz published as *Clandestine in Chile: The Adventures of Miguel Littin*, Holt (New York, NY), 1987.

(Contributor) *La Democracia y la paz en America Latina,* Editorial El Buho, 1986.

*Primeros reportajes,* Consorcio de Ediciones Capriles, 1990.

*Notas de prensa, 1980-1984,* Mondadori (Madrid, Spain), 1991.

(Author of introduction) *An Encounter with Fidel: An Interview,* by Gianni Mina, Ocean Press, 1991.

*Elogio de la utopia: Una entrevista de Nahuel Maciel,* Cronista Ediciones, 1992.

*News of a Kidnapping,* Knopf, 1997.

*For the Sake of a Country Within Reach of the Children,* Villegas Editores, 1998.

(Author of introduction) Castro, Fidel, *My Early Years,* LPC Group, 1998.

(With Reynaldo Gonzales) *Cubano 100%,* Charta, 1998.

*Vivir Para Contarla* (title means "To Live to Tell It") (memoir), Colombia, 2002; published as *Living to Tell the Tale,* Knopf (New York, NY), 2003.

# Sources

### Books

Bell, Michael, *Gabriel García Márquez: Solitude and Solidarity,* St. Martin's Press, 1993.

Bell-Villada, Gene H., *García Márquez: The Man and His Work,* University of North Carolina Press, 1990.

*Contemporary Authors New Revision Series,* vol. 82, Gale, 1999.

*Dictionary of Hispanic Biography,* Gale, 1996.

Dolan, Sean, *Gabriel García Márquez,* Chelsea House, 1994.

Fiddian, Robin W., *García Márquez,* Longman, 1995.

Janes, Regina, *Gabriel García Márquez: Revolutions in Wonderland,* University of Missouri Press, 1981.

McGuirk, Bernard and Richard Cardwell, editors, *Gabriel García Márquez: New Readings,* Cambridge University Press, 1988.

McMurray, George R., *Gabriel García Márquez,* Ungar, 1977.

Wood, Michael, *Gabriel García Márquez: One Hundred Years of Solitude,* Cambridge University Press, 1990.

### Periodicals

*New Yorker,* February 19-26, 2001.

*New York Times,* June 19, 1997; March 3, 1999.

*New York Times Book Review,* September 29, 1968; March 8, 1970; February 20, 1972; October 31, 1976; July 16, 1978; September 16, 1978; November 11, 1979; November 16, 1980; December 5, 1982, p. 7, pp. 60-61; March 27, 1983; April 7, 1985; April 27, 1986; August 9, 1987; April 10, 1988, p. 1, pp. 48-49; September 16, 1990, pp. 1, 30; November 7, 1993, p. 9; May 28, 1995, p. 8; June 15, 1997.

*Time,* March 16, 1970; November 1, 1976; July 10, 1978; November 1, 1982; March 7, 1983; December 31, 1984; April 14, 1986; May 22, 1995; June 2, 1997, p. 79.

*Times Literary Supplement,* July 7, 1995.

*Washington Post,* October 14, 2001, p. A28.

*World Literature Today,* Winter 1982; Winter 1991, p. 85; Autumn 1993, pp. 782-83.

### Online

"Gabriel García Márquez," CNN.com, http://www.cnn.com/2000/books/news (December 14, 2004).

"Gabriel García Márquez" *New York Times,* http://www.nytimes.com (December 14, 2004).

"Gabriel García Márquez," Nobelprize.org, http://nobelprize.org/literature/laureates/1982/index.html (December 14, 2004).

"Gabriel García Márquez," *Publishers Weekly,* http://www.publishersweekly.com (December 14, 2004).

"García Márquez joins protest against new visa rules," *Guardian,* http://books.guardian.co.uk/news/articles/0,,458994,00.html (December 14, 2004).

"Writer stays true to beleaguered Castro," *Guardian,* http://books.guardian.co.uk/news/articles/0,,946285,00.html (December 14, 2004).

*—Elizabeth Shostak*

# Genevieve Gorder

**Television host and interior designer**

---

**B**orn July 26, 1974, in Minneapolis, MN; daughter of Diana Drake. *Education:* Attended Lewis & Clark College, c. 1992-94; earned degree from the School of Visual Arts (New York City).

**Addresses:** *Office*—c/o Town Haul, Discovery Communications, One Discovery Place, Silver Spring, MD 20910.

## Career

**G**raphic design internship with MTV, c. 1994, and permanent position; Duffy Design, Inc., New York City, c. 1998-2000; appeared on *Trading Spaces*, TLC, 2000-04; host of *Town Haul*, 2005—.

## Sidelights

**G**enevieve Gorder attained unlikely fame as one of six designers on the popular interior-design makeover series, *Trading Spaces*, on the cable channel TLC. Trained in the graphic arts, not as an interior designer, Gorder hesitated before taking the job offer back in 2000, as she told *Palm Beach Post* writer Heather Graulich. "They asked me if I want to do this interior design show, and I said no," Gorder said, "because I thought interior design was just super chumpy, you know? Like old ladies with chintz and big hair and bad perfume—totally *Designing Women*; and I was so not that." Gorder's on-screen personality was such a hit with viewers, however, that she went on to host her own show on TLC, *Town Haul*, which debuted in 2005.

Born in 1974, Gorder is a native of Minneapolis, and grew up in the southern section of the city, home to some of the area's oldest housing stock. Her parents bought an old Victorian home, and renovated it themselves, and Gorder became a skilled helper in their projects at an early age. She was the eldest of three children in her family, and the only daughter, and attended the Clara Barton Open School. In her teens, she proved to be a talented violinist, and also played soccer during her years at Minneapolis South High School. Gorder's parents encouraged their children to explore the world, and she spent a year as an exchange student in Barcelona, Spain, which led to a decision to major in international affairs at Lewis & Clark College, an Oregon liberal-arts school.

During Gorder's second year at Lewis & Clark, however, she took a graphic design course, and discovered she loved it. After changing her major, she entered a collage she had made in a competition for an internship at MTV in New York City, and won one of the highly coveted posts. When the stint was over, MTV offered her a job, and she took it and relocated to the city permanently. She eventually earned her design degree from New York's School of Visual Arts, and went on to work in the New York City office of a Minneapolis graphic-arts firm, Duffy Design, where her projects included work for the FAO Schwartz toy-store empire and the label for a new brand of Tanqueray gin.

Given her background in graphic design, Gorder was surprised when someone from Ross Productions contacted her and offered her a tryout for a new reality-TV show. Ross was a Tennessee-based outfit that was planning a series in which neighbors got a chance to redecorate a room in another family's home, and vice versa. "To this day I have no idea how they got my name," Gorder told *Star Tribune* journalist Rosalind Bentley. "I was like, 'Yeah, I'll come for the audition, but I'm not moving to Tennessee.'"

Gorder won a spot as one of six interior designers on *Trading Spaces,* which began airing on TLC in 2000. She was known for working barefoot, a quirk of hers, and for freshening up a room on a budget with smartly framed black and white photography prints. She also created more daring looks for some rooms that were unveiled at each episode's climactic moment, called the "reveal." In some cases, the surprised homeowners were not always thrilled by the results. As Bentley noted in the *Star Tribune,* there had been some "doozies," including an entirely black room, but "until designer Hilda Santo-Tomas glued hay all over a family's living room walls, Gorder created what was arguably one of the most audacious designs: She covered a bedroom wall in moss and built nightstands out of chicken wire."

Thanks to such stunts, *Trading Spaces* garnered a cult following, and became the highest rated TLC show in 2002. Gorder was unnerved to find that fans soon began recognizing her in public. Once, she submitted a call-in diary to Steve Marsh of *MPLS-St. Paul Magazine* in which she revealed the details of one typically hectic week during the show's accelerated taping season. At one point, she and the other cast members discovered that a few hundred fans were waiting outside for them. "I'm hiding behind the door," she told Marsh. "They all want us to sign autographs. They show up on set. It's been a crazy day. They'll find out on the news or on the radio where we're at and then they'll wait for us all day." Later in the article, Gorder said that she and her fellow cast members had to be secreted out of their hiding place inside large garbage cans with the help of the local police force.

Gorder actually wound up reprising the infamous wall of moss—which was faux moss, not real—for several new clients in and around New York City, where she took side projects during the *Trading Spaces* hiatuses. By 2003, with the show's popularity appearing to have peaked, Gorder was ready to move on, and this time became a co-creator of her own show, *Town Haul,* which had its TLC debut in early 2005. The concept was a bit different: Gorder and her team would descend upon a small town and re-do some of its landmarks and businesses. Along with a landscaper, carpenter, and general contractor, Gorder juggled a number of potentially risky reality-television pitfalls, including citizen consensus and zoning codes. Over six episodes in each town, they fixed up a local business or two, came up with a community-friendly new gathering place, and helped out a local resident in need—creating a wheelchair-accessible apartment for one man in Jefferson, New York, for example. The show received mixed reviews, both from viewers and citizens of the towns visited.

Gorder's own home is in New York City, where she has a Tribeca loft. In early 2005, she became engaged to her boyfriend of two years, former TLC *Junkyard Wars* host Tyler Harcott, who went on to host *The Complex: Malibu,* on the FOX network. She liked the fact that *Town Haul* relied more on a do-gooder ethos than the shock factor of seeing what one's neighbor did to a kitchen or living room. "These are small communities across the country that all of us at one point came from," Gorder noted in an interview with the *New York Post,* "and they're slowly disappearing. They're all jewels. We just have to make sure they're cleaned up and shined."

## Sources

*MPLS-St. Paul Magazine,* December 2002, p. 42.
*New York Post,* April 3, 2005, p. 109.
*New York Times,* January 16, 2005, p. AR22.
*Palm Beach Post,* March 22, 2003, p. 1D.
*Post-Standard* (Syracuse, NY), January 22, 2005, p. E1.
*Star Tribune* (Minneapolis, MN), May 2, 2002, p. 1E.
*U.S. News & World Report,* October 21, 2002, p. 12.

—*Carol Brennan*

# Michael Gordon

## Hair stylist and executive

**B**orn c. 1951; son of a hairdresser; married (divorced); children: two. *Education:* Apprenticed at the salons of Rene of Mayfair and Alexandre, both London, England, mid-1960s.

**Addresses:** *Office*—c/o Bumble & bumble, 146 E. 56th St., New York, NY 10022.

## Career

**B**egan career as hairdresser at the House of Leonard, c. 1968-70; Elizabeth Arden salon, creative director, after c. 1970; opened first salon in Johannesburg, South Africa, c. 1972; opened London salon Bumble & bumble, 1977, and New York City salon, 1981; introduced line of hair-care products, 1995; sold stake in company to Estée Lauder, 2000.

## Sidelights

**M**ichael Gordon's Bumble & bumble is a successful Manhattan salon that spawned a cult-favorite line of hair-care products. The British-born stylist became one of a new generation of celebrity hairdressers who began as floorsweepers in the 1960s and went on to become millionaire owners of thriving brand-name salons with a worldwide reputation. In 2004, Gordon opened a posh new salon space in New York that included a school and café.

Born around 1951, Gordon grew up in London. His first unofficial job was helping his mother, a hairdresser, at her job, and by the age of 14 he was de-

termined to leave the Jewish Free School in Camden, a section of west London. His mother found him a spot as an assistant to Rene of Mayfair, one of London's most famous hairdressers at the time. "He had the most glamorous clients in Britain," Gordon recalled in an interview with *Times* of London writer Lisa Grainger. "If they weren't film stars, they had a title—you know, Lady, Countess, Princess, the Right Honourable. It was an incredible world to a teenage boy."

After training under another top London stylist, Alexandre, Gordon was able to land a job with the House of Leonard, a haute-salon of London's ebullient Swinging '60s. He was just 17 when he started, and worked alongside another young hairstylist who would later revolutionize the field, John Frieda. The House of Leonard was a favorite of editors from British and American *Vogue,* and Gordon worked on many daring editorial spreads that highlighted the new, free-spirited or futuristic direction that fashion was taking at the time. By the age of 19, he was made creative director of the Elizabeth Arden salon on Bond Street.

Gordon went to Johannesburg, South Africa, for a vacation, and liked it so much that he decided to stay and take yoga classes. He also married, and by the time he was 21 opened his first salon there. By 1977, he was back in London and had opened a place there. He chose the "Bumble" name, he explained to Grainger in the *Times* of London interview, because "I didn't want something poncy or formal like the places I had worked, but I wanted something English. And because I had set up with my brother (a partnership that lasted three weeks), we thought we'd take the mickey a bit out of British company names like Smith and Smith or Brown's and Sons. So Bumble and bumble we became."

When his marriage ended and he wanted a change of scene in the early 1980s, Gordon headed to New York City. His East 56th Street Bumble salon opened there in 1981, and within a year the American edition of *Vogue* had named it one of the ten best salons in the country. Its stylists, who survived a rigorous, three-year, on-the-job training period, emerged as leading names in the fashion world as coiffeurs for designers' runway shows and magazine layouts.

Gordon began mixing his own hair-care products in the early 1990s for his clients, but did not begin selling them until a few years later. His styling creme quickly became a cult must-have among the fashion crowd, and was notoriously difficult to get outside of New York City or Los Angeles. It was available at his counter, and also at a handful of other salons, which had to submit a lengthy application in order to be considered for membership in the network. Many did not pass muster. "We don't need to be everywhere," Gordon explained to *WWD* writer Julie Naughton. "One of the best things about direct distribution is that we can control where we are—which keeps the brand special."

Gordon's Bumble & bumble line was estimated to be selling about $25 million dollars' worth of styling aids by 1999 with no advertising budget whatsoever—the products had snared a market share merely through word-of- mouth. It was an attractive property, and the cosmetics giant Estée Lauder came calling. Lauder owned a number of prestigious lines, including MAC Cosmetics, and was interested in expanding into the hair-care market. Gordon sold a 60 percent stake in his salon and product line to Lauder for an amount rumored to be around $20 million. Part of the reason he did so, he told *SalonNews*, was to establish a presence outside of North America. "We are in many great prestige doors overseas, but the international arena is not big for us," he told the paper. "Due to our size, we didn't have the resources to deal with it. Lauder has amazing expertise in international—it's really a different world, and it requires a lot of capital and a lot of expertise in many specialized markets."

The new millionaire spent some of his windfall on a New York City apartment and a house on Long Island and took a break. He produced a 2002 book, *Hair Heroes*, which featured interviews with some of the world's top hairdressers. His interviewees include Vidal Sassoon and Gene Shacove, the inspiration for Warren Beatty's Beverly Hills hairdresser character in the 1975 movie *Shampoo*. Shacove died just before the book appeared in print, and Gordon said it was an unforgettable interview. "I realized what a brilliant acting job Beatty had done," Gordon told *New York Times* reporter Penelope Green, "because Gene's way of speaking and his language was exactly like Beatty's in the movie."

Thanks to the Lauder deal, Gordon was also able to fulfill one of his longtime goals with an innovative, impressively luxurious space called the House of Bumble, which opened in New York City in 2004. The eight-story renovated building in the Meatpacking District featured windows that overlook the Hudson River for cut-and-color clients, a school for future hairdressers called Bumble and bumble University, and even a café. Again, he decided to name it "House" in homage to the bygone retail era of his youth. "I'm old enough to remember the old ateliers, where the design, the artisans, the craftsmen, the office people and the shop were all under one roof and were all proud of their craft," he told Grainger in the *Times* interview. "I like the fact we're all now in contact, all working together towards great, creative styling that's based on the best historical styles and the work of the best stylists. If you're a hairdresser, that's nirvana."

## Selected writings

*Hair Heroes,* Bumble & bumble, 2002.

## Sources

*New York Times,* December 22, 2002.
*SalonNews,* April 2000, p. S10; July 2000, p. 2S4.
*Times* (London, England), July 17, 2004, p. 76.
*WWD,* February 18, 2000, p. 10; June 5, 2000, p. 2; July 21, 2000, p. 10.

—*Carol Brennan*

# Topher Grace

## Actor

**B**orn Christopher Grace, July 19, 1978, in New York, NY. *Education:* Attended the University of Southern California, c. 1997-98.

**Addresses:** *Home*—New York, NY.

## Career

**A**ctor on television, including: *That '70s Show,* FOX, 1998-2005. Film appearances include: *Traffic,* 2000; *Ocean's Eleven* (cameo), 2001; *Pinocchio* (voice), 2002; *Mona Lisa Smile,* 2003; *Win a Date with Tad Hamilton!,* 2004; *Ocean's Twelve* (cameo), 2004; *P.S.,* 2004; *In Good Company,* 2004.

**Awards:** Screen Actors Guild Award for Outstanding Performance by the Cast of a Theatrical Motion Picture, for *Traffic,* 2001.

## Sidelights

**T**opher Grace had a year of college and some summer theater-camp experience behind him when he was cast in a new sitcom on FOX, *That '70s Show,* in the late 1990s. Both he and fellow castmate Ashton Kutcher emerged as stars of the hit show, and moved easily into movie careers. Grace made his impressive film debut as the drug-addicted prep-school teen in *Traffic,* the Steven Soderbergh drama from 2000, and has chosen his subsequent film roles carefully. His turn on *That '70s Show* came to an end just after his first starring role in a major Hollywood film, *In Good Company,* hit theaters. It

seemed he had managed to avoid being locked into a teen TV-star slot, and was emerging as a credible new Hollywood talent whom critics were dubbing the next Tom Hanks. Grace had been offered a slew of movie roles, but tried to avoid the teen-comedy genre. "I still feel that I'm more proud of the 18 films I passed on before *Traffic* than actually doing *Traffic,*" he told *International Herald Tribune* writer Alexandra Jacobs.

Grace was born in 1978 in New York City, and grew up in affluent Darien, Connecticut. "Christopher" is his given name, but he disliked its shortened version ("Chris,") so he decided to shorten it himself to "Topher" instead. In his teens, he attended a Massachusetts boarding school, where he appeared in stage productions of *Joseph and the Amazing Technicolored Dreamcoat* and *The Pirates of Penzance,* and spent summer breaks at a youth theater camp, where future starlet Chloë Sevigny was a fellow camper; four years his senior and from Darien as well, Sevigny sometimes babysat Grace back at home.

At his next school, the Brewster Academy in New Hampshire, Grace harbored some ambition to become a tennis pro, but still appeared in school plays. It was his performance in *A Funny Thing Happened on the Way to the Forum* that attracted the attention of husband-and-wife television series creators Bonnie and Terry Turner, whose daughter was also a Brewster student. The Turners were co-writers of the 1992 comedy *Wayne's World,* and had also created the television sitcom *3rd Rock from the Sun.* When introduced to the Turners, Grace mentioned he was heading to the University of Southern California for college, "so they said, 'When you're out in L.A., can we call you?'" Grace recalled in an *Interview* magazine profile in which actress Scarlett Johansson posed the questions. "I said, 'Sure, babe. Hollywood, yeah.' But when they started working on *That '70s Show,* they actually did."

The audition Grace attended for *That '70s Show* was his first ever, and he won the part of Eric Forman for the show's 1998 debut on FOX. Set in Wisconsin in 1976, the sitcom featured Eric's friends Kelso (Ashton Kutcher), Hyde (Danny Masterson), Fez (Wilmer Valderrama), and the girl next door, Donna (Laura Prepon). Eric's slightly overbearing parents, Debra Jo Rupp and Kurtwood Smith, provided some of the comic relief, with *Entertainment Weekly* television critic Ken Tucker asserting that "their cartoonishness—the way they fuss and snipe and worry over their son—would be excessive were it not being played against Eric's poker-faced incredulity." Tucker also gave Grace's work high marks. "Really, I cannot praise enough [his] deftness … this is his first series, and so far, he's uncorrupted by the snarky school of sneery-teen TV acting," Tucker declared.

Grace dropped out of the University of Southern California (USC) when he landed the television job, and admitted to Johansson in *Interview,* "Most of my freshman year at USC I'd just been partying, and I had zero direction. The only reason I'd gone to USC was because it was as far away as I could get from where I grew up. When I got *That '70s Show* it was such a surprise to everyone, even to the people who called me in." He also noted that because he was a complete novice, his first day on the set proved "terrifying," he told Johansson. "Nobody understood why I was there. I had by far the least experience of anyone."

*That '70s Show* made a star out of Kutcher almost immediately, but Grace was leery of the film roles that he was offered when the series' ratings began to soar. He realized it was perhaps risky not to capitalize on the show's popularity, as he told *Entertainment Weekly*'s Josh Rottenberg. "You wonder if you're the guy in the bar who, in 15 years, is going to say, 'They offered me the lead in *Bring It On* and I turned it down,'" he joked. "Which they didn't, by the way—that was just a stupid example."

Instead Grace went after a role he very much wanted—that of Seth Abrahms in *Traffic.* He played the prep-school pal of Erika Christensen's character, Caroline, whose father (Michael Douglas) has become the new federal drug-policy director. Seth introduces Caroline to heroin, and her addiction quickly spirals out of control. Grace's character delivers one of the film's more scathing monologues, a treatise on the class politics of the illegal drug economy, to her father. The film earned the ensemble honor from the Screen Actors Guild awards, Grace's first industry award. He returned to the cast of *That '70s Show,* still a ratings success, and took only minor film work for the next couple of years. He was the voice of Leonardo in the 2002 animated feature *Pinocchio,* and had a supporting role in *Mona Lisa Smile* a year later. In *Win a Date with Tad Hamilton!* he was the torch-carrying pal of Kate Bosworth's supermarket checkout clerk, a girl who lands a date with a movie star (Josh Duhamel) in a publicity contest.

Grace's first lead role was in a little-seen independent film in 2004, *P.S.,* co-written and directed by Dylan Kidd (*Roger Dodger*). The story was based on a novel by Helen Schulman and featured Grace as F. Scott Feinstadt, who hopes to win a spot in Columbia University's graduate-arts program. He chances upon Laura Linney's Louise, a Columbia admissions director, who begins to think he may be a reincarnation of her long-ago love. *New Yorker* film critic Anthony Lane gave *P.S.* a mixed review, but concluded it was worth seeing. "Best of all, there's Topher Grace, who sounds the perfect note of skepticism when, as the kid who sees things more sanely and cloudlessly than the myopic adults around him, he plucks up courage to remonstrate with Louise," Lane wrote. "'Some guy broke your heart, and I get that—that's traumatic,' he tells her, adding, 'but that happens to everybody. It's called'—he pauses—'high school.'"

Grace's next role was also a starring one, and came in a film released later in 2004 that did much better at the box office than *P.S.*; it also boosted his reputation as one of Hollywood's next major players. In *Good Company,* written and directed by Paul Weitz of *American Pie* fame, was a twist on the dating-the-boss's-daughter premise. Grace played Carter Duryea, a rising young executive with a global conglomerate. Dennis Quaid played Dan Foreman, a Manhattan sports magazine ad sales executive with several years of experience, a suburban mortgage, wife, two children, and a third on the way. When the magazine is acquired by a maverick media tycoon, Carter comes aboard and takes Dan's job—but keeps him on as his assistant.

One night, Dan takes Carter home for dinner, where he meets Dan's college-age daughter, played by

Scarlett Johansson, who is about to transfer to New York University. The two begin dating, and Quaid's character is mortally offended by the turn of events—yet powerless to do anything about it. "With Grace's charisma," wrote *Entertainment Weekly*'s Lisa Schwarzbaum in her review of the film, "it's impossible to hate Carter even when he's at his most doltish, telling Dan that the veteran ad guy would make an 'awesome wingman.' ... Indeed, *In Good Company* would go all bad were it not for Grace's valuable ability to play an insensitive jerk and a joke's-on-me good sport simultaneously, with some of the best comic timing in the business."

Other reviews for *In Good Company* were similarly laudatory. "Quaid is particularly convincing as the man who feels his age, and Grace excels as the ambitious animal who exploits it," remarked Doris Toumarkine in *Film Journal International*. Grace played a hotshot wunderkind in the film, but as *Newsweek* writer Devin Gordon noted, he also portrays an upstart who has attained "success way too quickly, and his soul is struggling to keep up. It's a poignant, complex role, and Grace, with shades of Lemmon in *The Apartment*, smacks it out of the park." Gordon was referring to veteran stage and screen star Jack Lemmon, and in the same review mentioned Tom Hanks and Jimmy Stewart as well, predicting Grace might just follow all of the above and "inherit American cinema's Everyman throne."

Both Paul Weitz and Dylan Kidd also commended Grace's strengths and potential. *In Good Company*'s director, who also directed Hugh Grant in *About a Boy*, told Jacobs in the *International Herald Tribune* article that there are not many "young actors who can believably be articulate," Weitz explained, but Grace's "verbal dexterity reminded me to some extent of Hugh Grant. They're both very quick-witted, but there's a slight degree of nihilism behind their wit." The *P.S.* director also found Grace's low-key style appealing. "A lot of young actors are acting with a capital A, begging you to pay attention," Kidd told Jacobs. "Whereas he has a total relaxed thing. He can be himself and do these lightning-fast switches from earnest to funny to mature."

The 2004-05 season of *That '70s Show* was Grace's final one, and he decided to return to the East Coast after many years in Los Angeles. His next film role would be a Harold Ramis comedy centering around online dating and social networks like Friendster. He bought an apartment in New York City, and a dog as well. His personal life remains off the gossip pages, and he credited this to the fact that "I'm just a boring person," he told Los Angeles *Daily News* writer Bob Strauss. "I really am. I'm into board games. I have a Monopoly club.... We recently just bought on the board game black market an unsanctioned by Parker Brothers Triopoly, which is three boards on top of each other. When you hit Free Parking, you actually travel up. There are 50 different states on it. It took us 12 hours to finish it."

In 2005, Grace signed to play a role in *Spider-3*. Though he has just a handful of films to his credit, Grace also made two brief but comic cameos as himself in *Ocean's 11* and its sequel, *Ocean's 12*, both from Soderbergh, who had directed him in *Traffic*. In the first, Grace chats with George Clooney's character during a poker game about his career trajectory. Danny Ocean asks if it was hard to move from television roles into film, but Grace blithely replies, "Not for me, dude." The line was something of an in-joke, for Clooney had had a difficult time making the same transition effectively. Grace realized he was fortunate to have been able to move forward from *That '70s Show*. "There have been a lot of great TV actors who the audience couldn't see outside their character," he told *Entertainment Weekly*'s Rottenberg. "You kind of have one chance."

## Sources

*Daily News* (Los Angeles, CA), January 14, 2005, p. U6.

*Entertainment Weekly*, September 18, 1998, p. 65; June 18, 1999, p. 36; November 12, 2004, p. 37; January 21, 2005, p. 64; April 8, 2005, p. 12.

*Film Journal International*, February 2005, p. 45.

*International Herald Tribune*, October 13, 2004, p. 10.

*Interview*, February 2005, p. 92.

*Newsweek*, January 10, 2005, p. 53.

*New Yorker*, October 18, 2004, p. 214.

*—Carol Brennan*

# Jake Gyllenhaal

AP/Wide World Photos

## Actor

**B**orn Jacob Benjamin Gyllenhaal, December 19, 1980, in Los Angeles, CA; son of Stephen Gyllenhaal (a film director) and Naomi Foner (a screenwriter). *Education:* Attended Columbia University, c. 1998-2000.

**Addresses:** *Home*—Los Angeles, CA.

## Career

**A**ctor in films, including: *City Slickers*, 1991; *A Dangerous Woman*, 1993; *October Sky*, 1999; *Donnie Darko*, 2001; *Bubble Boy*, 2001; *Lovely and Amazing*, 2001; *The Good Girl*, 2002; *Moonlight Mile*, 2002; *The Day After Tomorrow*, 2004; *Brokeback Mountain* 2005; *Proof*, 2005; *Jarhead*, 2005; also appeared in a 1994 episode of the *Homicide: Life on the Street*, NBC, and in the London stage production of *This Is Our Youth*, 2002.

## Sidelights

**A**ctor Jake Gyllenhaal's evolution from playing the troubled anti-hero in small, independent films to the lead in big-budget Hollywood projects was swift and superbly timed. After emerging as the doe-eyed new "It" guy in movies like *Donnie Darko* in 2001 and 2002's *The Good Girl*, Gyllenhaal (pronounced JILL-en-hall) carried the 2004 global-warming disaster flick *The Day After Tomorrow*. He admitted later that the transition was not an easy one, as he told *People*'s Tom Gliatto, but he received some sage advice from co-star Dennis Quaid. "I remember Dennis sitting me down one day," Gyllenhaal recalled, "and just saying, 'You gotta chill out. It's an action movie.'"

Gyllenhaal hails from a show-business family. He was born on December 19, 1980, in Los Angeles, to Stephen Gyllenhaal, a director for film and television, and Naomi Foner, a screenwriter whose credits include *Running on Empty* and *Losing Isaiah*. Gyllenhaal's sister, Maggie, is also a rising star in Hollywood. As youngsters, the siblings had small roles in a 1993 film directed by their father, *A Dangerous Woman*, for which their mother had written the screenplay. It was not Gyllenhaal's first screen appearance, however: that came two years earlier, as the son of Billy Crystal's character in *City Slickers*.

Though Jamie Lee Curtis was Gyllenhaal's unofficial godmother, and he was taken out onto race tracks in hot rods driven by Oscar-winner and racing enthusiast Paul Newman in his teens, both Gyllenhaals were discouraged by their parents from entering show business until they had given college a try. But Gyllenhaal took a couple of parts around the time of his 1998 graduation from the private Harvard-Westlake School in Los Angeles. One was the lead in a small film called *October Sky*, which was released in 1999 to excellent reviews. Its script was based on the life of a real-life aerospace engineer, Homer Hickam, whose father—played by Chris Cooper in the film—tries to discourage his interest in rocketry in a coal mining West Virginia town in 1957.

Though critics lauded Gyllenhaal's *October Sky* performance, the early taste of fame unnerved him, and he followed his sister to New York City and enrolled at Columbia University, as she had done as well. For two years, he studied Eastern religions and worked in restaurants—first as a busboy and later as a sous-chef—before he felt the lure of Hollywood once more. Bypassed for the Ewan McGregor role in *Moulin Rouge,* he took the lead in a small, science-fiction/fantasy movie called *Donnie Darko,* which was released the fall of 2001. The odd movie, directed by Richard Kelly, featured Gyllenhaal as a young high-schooler plagued by visions of giant talking rabbit named Frank, who urges him to commit violent acts and warns that the world will end in four weeks. Drew Barrymore played a sympathetic high-school teacher to Gyllenhaal's character, whom others are convinced is displaying signs of schizophrenia. The film won terrific reviews, but tanked at the box office, earning just $515,000.

Gyllenhaal went on to appear in another box-office dud in 2001, *Bubble Boy,* with this one, by contrast, receiving scathing reviews. Nevertheless, he decided to drop out of Columbia altogether, and he explained why in an interview with Maddy Costa for London's *Guardian* newspaper. "I had gone to school to be intellectual and cerebral, but there isn't an acting programme at my college, and I'm happier when I'm acting." Choosing his next few roles more carefully, Gyllenhaal delivered a string of luminous portrayals and emerged as what *New York Times Magazine* writer David A. Keeps called "the go-to guy for art-house auteurs in search of angst-ridden adolescents." These included *Lovely and Amazing,* a darkly comic family saga from director Nicole Holofcener in which he had a supporting role as a lovestruck photo-processing booth co-worker of Catherine Keener's character, an unhappily married artist.

Gyllenhaal practically reprised that same role in *The Good Girl,* a 2002 film that earned excellent reviews. Again, Gyllenhaal played the co-worker of a depressed, slightly older married woman, this time opposite Jennifer Aniston. Weighed down by her marriage to a chronic pothead and her life in a dusty Texas town, Aniston's Justine falls into a torrid affair with Gyllenhaal's Holden when he begins working at the local Retail Rodeo, but their relationship quickly spirals out of control. Both his and Aniston's performances won high marks from critics, with the *New York Times*'s Elvis Mitchell terming Gyllenhaal "a specialist in sending up infantile narcissism. He satirizes the spaniel-eyed sensitivity that other actors would exploit."

Critics often remarked on Gyllenhaal's beguilingly doe-eyed looks and the sensitivity he seemed to radiate onscreen. Gliatto, the *People* scribe, declared

that Gyllenhaal was beginning to fall into a category of actors known as "geeky but sexy young brooders," while *Entertainment Weekly* critic Owen Gleiberman wrote of his "studied elfin moroseness." Gyllenhaal admitted that at this time of his life he seemed to be choosing films roles that fell into the "misfit" slot, but it was a label he tended to reject. "I find wounded to be a better word, but I don't like it sounding inactive—victim-y," he told Jamie Painter Young in an interview for *Back Stage West.* "I just choose these [roles] because there's stuff to do, whereas other characters are just 'the football jock,' or 'the nerd,' or 'the best friend.'"

The last of these roles seemed to come in *Moonlight Mile,* released in 2002, which starred Gyllenhaal as the fiancé of a young woman who was slain in a random act of violence. He moves in with her grieving parents, played by Susan Sarandon and Dustin Hoffman. Working alongside such illustrious, Academy Award-winning stars was a turning point for Gyllenhaal in his career. Realizing his limitations—he had no formal dramatic training whatsoever—he began working with an acting coach. As he explained to Young in *Back Stage West,* "there are ways of saying and feeling lines that can lead someone to melodrama—bad acting—and I think sometimes I do go there."

Hoffman encouraged Gyllenhaal to test his mettle on the stage, and so in early 2002 Gyllenhaal relocated to London for a stretch to appear in the Kenneth Lonergan play *This Is Our Youth* at the Garrick Theatre. The story of a trio of disaffected young adults is set in New York City in 1982, and Gyllenhaal appeared opposite Anna Paquin and Hayden Christensen. He earned terrific reviews from London theater critics for his stage debut. "Gyllenhaal's performance is perfect—and so rounded that it takes a very long time [until] you even begin to like this Warren, let alone to realise that he's the central character in the play," noted Alastair Macaulay in the *Financial Times.*

Back in Hollywood, Gyllenhaal made a somewhat surprising career move and signed on for his first big-budget action movie, *The Day After Tomorrow.* The $125 million epic was filmed in Montreal during the early part of 2003, but editing and arduous special-effects work delayed its release until May of 2004. It became the biggest box-office opening weekend of Gyllenhaal's career to date. He played high-schooler Sam Hall, who heads to New York City for a school trip and is forced to hide out in the New York Public Library when a freak storm turns into a tidal wave that devastates Manhattan. The global-warming predictions of his on-screen scientist dad, played by Quaid, have gone unheeded, and within hours temperatures in New York descend to Ice-Age levels.

Gyllenhaal did all of his own stunts in *The Day Af-ter Tomorrow,* and turned in an appropriately coura-geous but humble action-hero performance. Critics derided the film for its transparent thrills and schlo-cky dialogue, and even the *New York Times* reviewer, A. O. Scott, commented that "Gyllenhaal has a way of infusing even his most desperate lines with a hint of knowing sarcasm." Gyllenhaal found that appearing in a major Hollywood blockbuster was indeed very different from working in small, inde-pendent films. "I rewrote scenes myself and brought them in, which, much to my dismay, they didn't … really … appreciate," he told *Entertainment Weekly*'s Gillian Flynn. "But they listened. It's nicer to be heard out and then be thrown out than just be thrown out immediately."

After proving himself in such a large-scale Holly-wood project, Gyllenhaal seemed to have his choice of terrific roles offered to him. He was cast in *Proof,* the 2005 screen adaptation of the Pulitzer Prize-winning David Auburn play, which also starred Gwyneth Paltrow and Anthony Hopkins. Alongside Heath Ledger, Gyllenhaal appeared in a literately styled cowboy story, *Brokeback Mountain,* also slated for a 2005 release. But it was his London stage ex-perience back in 2002 that landed him the much-coveted lead in *Jarhead,* a third project with a 2005 release date. The film, based on a best-selling novel by former Marine Anthony Swofford about his Desert Storm experiences, was to be directed by Sam Mendes of *American Beauty* fame, and both Le-onardo DiCaprio and Tobey Maguire had report-edly wanted the part. "The thing that sold me on Jake," Mendes told *Daily Variety,* "was watching him onstage…. He showed amazing range and strength."

Gyllenhaal seems to resist taking part in publicity transactions that might play up the heartthrob angle. Instead, he and Chelsea Clinton discussed their passion for the writings of J.D. Salinger in an *Interview* magazine article; the Hollywood brat and the former First Daughter already knew one an-other from summers spent on Martha's Vineyard with their families. Gyllenhaal has been linked ro-mantically with fellow Hollywood "It" names Na-talie Portman and later Kirsten Dunst, with whom

he lived with for a time. He remains an intensely private person, and even turned down a role in a Bernardo Bertolucci film, *The Dreamers,* because it called for nudity. He was wary of letting his celeb-rity status get in the way of his career, as he told journalist Jeff Strickler of the Minneapolis *Star Tri-bune*—a newspaper for which Gyllenhaal's uncle serves as editor. "Getting your picture on the cover of a magazine is a lot easier than keeping it there," the actor pointed out. "Once you get there, it's all about maintaining the status quo. People get expec-tations, and you have to keep meeting those expectations."

Though Gyllenhaal does admit to harboring ambi-tions to someday follow in his father's footsteps and direct a film, he views the star system as a mixed blessing. Reflecting back on the early buzz that accompanied his swift rise, he later admitted that he felt himself sucked in by the Hollywood fame machine. "I depended on it every day to bring me some sort of happiness and instant gratifica-tion," he told Young in the *Back Stage West* interview. "Just as quickly as it would bring me up, it would let me down. If you recognize that this business chews you up and spits you out, you can't get caught up in it and make it your life. Just see how unhappy people are when they do."

## Sources

*Back Stage West,* August 8, 2002, p. 4.
*Daily Variety,* October 21, 2004, p. 1.
*Entertainment Weekly,* October 4, 2002, p. 121; June 4, 2004, p. 28; June 18, 2004, p. 42.
*Financial Times,* March 19, 2002, p. 22.
*Guardian* (London, England), October 18, 2002, p. 6.
*Interview,* February 2003, p. 142.
*New Statesman,* October 28, 2002, p. 45.
*New York Times,* June 28, 2002; August 7, 2002; May 27, 2004.
*New York Times Magazine,* September 21, 2003, p. 60.
*People,* October 21, 2002, p. 83; June 14, 2004, p. 77.
*Star Tribune* (Minneapolis, MN), October 4, 2002, p. 1E.

—*Carol Brennan*

# Mark Haddon

*Ian West/EPA/Landov*

## Author

**B**orn 1962, in Northampton, England; married Sos Eltis (an educator); children: Alfie. *Education:* Merton College, Oxford, B.A., 1981; Edinburgh University, M.A., 1984.

**Addresses:** *Agent*—c/o Author Mail, Doubleday, 1745 Broadway, New York, NY 10019. *Home*—Oxford, England.

## Career

**A**uthor. During early career, assisted patients with multiple sclerosis and autism, and worked a variety of part-time jobs, including at a theater box office and in a mail order business; worked as an illustrator and cartoonist for periodicals, including cartoon strip "Men—A User's Guide"; creator of and writer for children's television series *Microsoap.*

**Awards:** Smarties Prize shortlist for *The Real Porky Philips,* 1994; Book Trust Teenage Prize for *The Curious Incident of the Dog in the Night-Time,* 2003; Whitbread Book of the Year for *The Curious Incident of the Dog in the Night-Time,* 2003; Art Seidenbaum Award for First Fiction for *The Curious Incident of the Dog in the Night-Time,* 2003; Children's Fiction Prize, *Guardian,* for *The Curious Incident of the Dog in the Night-Time,* 2004; Commonwealth Writers Prize for best first book for *The Curious Incident of the Dog in the Night-Time,* 2004; Los Angeles Times book award for first fiction for *The Curious Incident of the Dog in the Night-Time,* 2004; two British Academy of Film and Television Arts (BAFTA) awards and Best Children's Drama award from the Royal Television Society, all for *Microsoap.*

## Sidelights

**B**ritish author Mark Haddon was enjoying a successful career writing and illustrating children's books, as well as writing for popular children's television shows such as *Microsoap* and *Starstreet* before he surprised even himself with his wildly acclaimed first novel, *The Curious Incident of the Dog in the Night-Time.* Ostensibly a quirky mystery novel about a teenager who investigates the murder of his neighbor's dog, the story gained the most attention for its narrative technique in which Haddon uses the viewpoint of an autistic boy named Christopher. Originally, as the author told Dave Weich in a Powells.com's interview, the idea of the story came from an image in his mind of a poodle that had been killed by a gardening implement. Haddon, who admittedly has a rather dark sense of humor at times, thought beginning a novel this way could be funny, but in order to make it work he would have to tell the incident from a unique viewpoint. "The dog came first," Haddon told Weich, "then the voice. Only after a few pages did I really start to ask, 'Who does the voice belong to?' So Christopher came along, in fact, after the book had already got underway." It was a fortuitous decision that would lead Haddon to win a Whitbread prize, among other honors.

Even though the character of Christopher Boone, who suffers from a disorder known as Asperger's syndrome, is 15 years old, Haddon originally intended the book to be for an adult audience. After having written more than a dozen books for children over the years, he wanted to write about more complex themes. The resulting novel "was definitely for adults," he told Powells.com's Weich, "but maybe I should say more specifically: it was for myself. I've been writing for kids for a long time, and if you're writing for kids you're kind of writing for the kid you used to be at that age.... I felt a great sense of freedom with this book because I felt like I was writing it for me." In presenting the final manuscript to his agent, however, it was decided that it would be marketed to both an adult and a teenage audience.

*The Curious Incident of the Dog in the Night-Time* can be seen, in some ways, as an extension of Haddon's previous books for children, some of which contain a good dose of mystery and, often, humor. For example, his debut children's book, *Gilbert's Gobstopper,* is definitely meant to be humorous and, in its own way, has a touch of adventure. When Gilbert loses his jawbreaker candy, the reader is treated to a trip from the gobstopper's viewpoint as it travels through sewer pipes, enters the ocean, is found by a fisherman, and goes on ever-more surprising turns that include a trip into outer space. "This irreverent entertainment will tickle many a funnybone," asserted Carolyn Polese in a *School Library Journal* review.

Haddon also combines adventure and humor in his "Agent Z" series for children that includes *Agent Z and the Penguin from Mars, Agent Z and the Masked Crusader, Agent Z Goes Wild,* and *Agent Z and the Killer Bananas.* The Agent Z of the title actually refers to a group of three boys, including Jenks, Ben, and Barney, who assume the secret identity as part of their club. The boys get involved in one goofy adventure after another, such as the time they take advantage of Mr. Sidebottom's obsession with UFOs by concocting an alien plot using a penguin and some foil, or the time the boys make a mock movie about killer bananas. Reviewers generally had high praise for these books. *School Librarian* contributor Alicen Geddes-Ward, for one, called *Agent Z Meets the Masked Crusader* a "witty, tight and brilliantly funny book." Adrian Jackson, writing in *Books for Keeps,* similarly felt that *Agent Z and the Penguin from Mars* was "a real hoot of a story, wildly imagined."

But Haddon does not view children as mere material for humorous stories. Some of his children's books show a decidedly more sensitive side to youngsters, such as *The Real Porky Philips* and *Titch Johnson, Almost World Champion.* In a story that *Books for Keeps* critic Gill Roberts called "powerful, poignant and pertinent," *The Real Porky Philips* is about a young, sensitive, overweight boy who finds the courage to finally assert his real personality after he has to play the role of a genie in the school play. *Titch Johnson, Almost World Champion* has a similar theme about self-confidence. Here, Titch, who seems to not be good at anything except balancing forks on his nose, gains a better appreciation of himself after successfully organizing a fund-raising event.

The rich world of dreams and imagination is explored in 1996's *The Sea of Tranquility* and 2002's *Ocean Star Express.* In the former, Haddon draws on his own childhood fascination with the achievement of mankind's first landing on the moon in 1969. The boy in the tale has a picture of the solar system on his wall and fantasizes about what it would be like to be an astronaut. Combined with this storyline are facts about the actual landing, including interesting tidbits; for example, the footprints left there will remain for millions of years because of the lack of wind and rain on the moon. Carolyn Boyd, writing in *School Librarian,* felt that "this book will appeal to those who remember the first moon landing and to young readers who will marvel at it." *Ocean Star Express,* by comparison, is not as grounded in reality. Here, a boy named Joe is becoming bored during his summer holiday when Mr. Robertson, the owner of the hotel where his family is staying, invites him to see his train set. No ordinary toy, apparently, the train takes Joe and the owner on a magical ride around the world in what a *Kirkus Reviews* contributor called a "sweet and simple story that young train enthusiasts will enjoy."

While Haddon received a good deal of praise for many of his children's books, including being short-listed for the Smarties Prize for *The Real Porky Philips,* his book *The Curious Incident of the Dog in the Night-Time* has brought him considerably more critical attention. It combines the humor, sensitivity, and adventure of his earlier books with a highly challenging narrative perspective that impressed many reviewers. The protagonist of the story, Christopher Boone, suffers from Asperger's syndrome, a type of autism that prevents him from being able to accurately perceive and interpret other people's emotions. While he possesses an extremely logical mind, he is dispassionate and unable to empathize with other people whose feelings he cannot comprehend. This makes Christopher both a very reliable narrator, because he is incapable of lying, and an unreliable one, because he cannot fully appreciate the motives behind other people's actions. Making the character even more complicated, Haddon gives Christopher other flaws, including an aversion to being touched, a hatred of the colors brown and yellow, and a sometimes uncontrollable bladder. On the other hand, Christopher is brilliant at math, loves puzzles, and has a photographic memory.

The novel is ostensibly being written by Christopher, whose school counselor has assigned him the task of writing a book as a type of therapy. Haddon becomes his character fully in the story, even numbering the chapters in prime number order rather than sequentially because of Christopher's fascination for prime numbers. The story begins when Christopher discovers the dead poodle, Wellington. A great lover of dogs, as well as a fan of the Sherlock Holmes detective stories, he decides to find out who killed Wellington and why. The chapters then alternate between narratives of Christopher's progress in the investigation and chapters that include mathematical puzzles, charts, and other calculations the 15-year-old uses to try to reason out the information he has gathered. But as his investigation advances, the death of the poodle proves to be a knot that, when untied, reveals much more painful truths involving something terrible that happened between Christopher's parents and their neighbors and what really happened to his supposedly "dead" mother.

Critics appreciated the use of Christopher's dispassionate voice because it forces the author to obey the old writing caveat that authors should always "show and not tell" what is happening in the story. Furthermore, what interested many reviewers is that even though Christopher has autism, Haddon in no way makes this the theme of *The Curious Incident of the Dog in the Night-Time*. Indeed, the word "autism" is never even used. Instead, the novel might best be viewed as an examination of "the process of writing itself," as Daniel J. Glendening put it in *America's Intelligence Wire*. The story's point of view allows considerable latitude for reader interpretation, and indeed Haddon remarked to Powells.com's Weich that people he has talked to have had amazingly disparate reactions to his novel. "People have said to me that it's a desperately sad book and they wept most of the way through it," the author said. "Other people say it's charming and they kept laughing all the time. People say it has a sad ending; people say it has a happy ending. Because Christopher doesn't force the reader to think one thing and another, I get many different reactions."

Although Haddon has had some personal experience in the past working with autistic people, he has admitted to doing very little formal research when creating the character of Christopher. While many critics had no problem buying into the author's portrayal of the boy's condition, one reviewer, Nicholas Barrow of the *Spectator*, found it highly flawed. Barrow considered Haddon's descriptions to be a "total exaggeration of a 15-year-old boy with Asperger's," objecting to the "cliché" of an autistic boy who is a math genius, noting that Christopher is unbelievable as a teenager because he never thinks even once about sex, and finding the boy's problem with incontinence inconsistent with Asperger's patients. In the end, Barrow found the portrayal of Christopher to be "patronizing, inaccurate and not entertaining," and that "some people with Asperger's would be offended by this book." However, if one considers that Haddon's motive is not to discuss the issue of mental or emotional disabilities, but rather to experiment with literary perspective and create an interesting story, then one would fall into the more predominant camp that found Haddon's narrator absorbing. As one *Publishers Weekly* critic put it, "The novel brims with touching, ironic humor. The result is an eye-opening work in a unique and compelling literary voice." *Independent* reviewer Nicholas Tucker concluded, "How Haddon achieves this most delicate of balances is a tribute to his skill as a successful cartoonist as well as novelist." And Glendening called *The Curious Incident of the Dog in the Night-Time* "modern writing at its finest." In August of 2004, it was announced that the novel would be adapted as a film written and directed by Steve Kloves and coproduced by actor Brad Pitt. Haddon's next project is an adult novel, tentatively titled *Blood and Scissors*.

## Selected writings

(And illustrator) *Gilbert's Gobstopper*, Hamish Hamilton (London, England), 1987; Dial Books for Young Readers (New York, NY), 1988.

(And illustrator) *Toni and the Tomato Soup*, Harcourt Brace (San Diego, CA), 1988.

*A Narrow Escape for Princess Sharon*, Hamish Hamilton (London, England), 1989.

*Gridzbi Spudvetch!*, Walker (New York, NY), 1993.

*Titch Johnson, Almost World Champion*, illustrated by Martin Brown, Walker (New York, NY), 1993.

(And illustrator) *The Real Porky Philips*, A & C Black (London, England), 1994.

*Baby Dinosaurs at Home*, Western Publishing (New York, NY), 1994.

*Baby Dinosaurs at Playgroup*, Western Publishing (New York, NY), 1994.

*Baby Dinosaurs in the Garden*, Western Publishing (New York, NY), 1994.

*Baby Dinosaurs on Vacation*, Western Publishing (New York, NY), 1994.

*The Sea of Tranquility*, illustrated by Christian Birmingham, Harcourt Brace (San Diego, CA), 1996.

(And illustrator) *Agent Z and the Penguin from Mars*, Red Fox (London, England), 1996.

(And illustrator) *Agent Z and the Masked Crusader*, Red Fox (London, England), 1996.

(And illustrator) *Agent Z Goes Wild*, Red Fox (London, England), 1999.

*Secret Agent Handbook*, illustrated by Sue Heap, Walker Books (New York, NY), 1999.

(And illustrator) *Agent Z and the Killer Bananas*, Red Fox (London, England), 2001.

*The Ice Bear's Cave*, illustrated by David Axtell, Picture Lions (London, England), 2002.

*Ocean Star Express*, illustrated by Peter Sutton, Picture Lions (London, England), 2002.

*The Curious Incident of the Dog in the Night-Time* (novel), Doubleday (New York, NY), 2003.

Also author of episodes for children's television series, including *Microsoap* and *Starstreet*; contributor to screenplay adaptation of *Fungus and the Bogeyman*, by Raymond Briggs. Contributor of illustrations and cartoons to periodicals, including *New Statesman, Spectator, Guardian, Sunday Telegraph,* and *Private Eye.*

## Sources

### Periodicals

*America's Intelligence Wire*, January 19, 2004.

*Atlanta Journal-Constitution*, June 29, 2003, p. D2; October 26, 2003, p. F3.

*Book,* January-February 2003, p. 43; July-August 2003, p. 76.

*Booklist,* April 1, 2003, p. 1376; January 1, 2004, p. 890.

*Bookseller,* January 24, 2003, p. 29.

*Books for Keeps,* July 1993, p. 28; May 1994, p. 8; July 1995, p. 12; September 1995, p. 12.

*Books for Your Children,* summer 1994, p. 13.

*British Book News,* March 1988, p. 13.

*Daily Variety,* August 2, 2002, p. 5.

*Economist,* May 24, 2003, p. 85.

*Entertainment Weekly,* June 20, 2003, p. 76.

*Florida Times Union,* August 31, 2003, p. D4.

*Growing Point,* July 1989, p. 5197.

*Independent* (London, England), June 6, 2003, p. 15.

*Junior Bookshelf,* June 1993, p. 105; August 1993, p. 135.

*Kirkus Reviews,* January 1, 2003, p. 60; April 15, 2003, p. 557.

*Kliatt,* January 2004, p. 44.

Knight Ridder/Tribune News Service, June 25, 2003, p. K1715.

*Library Journal,* May 1, 2003, p. 155; January 2004, p. 184.

*Magpies,* September 1996, p. 28.

*M2 Best Books,* November 14, 2003; January 26, 2004; January 28, 2004.

*Newsweek,* September 8, 2003, p. 50.

*New York Times Book Review,* June 15, 2003, p. 5.

*Publishers Weekly,* May 13, 1988, p. 273; April 25, 1994, p. 75; September 16, 1996, p. 82; July 1, 2002, p. 14; April 7, 2003, p. 42.

*Reading Teacher,* October 1989, p. 56.

*School Librarian,* August 1989, p. 104; August 1993, p. 109; November 1993, p. 155; February 1997, p. 19; August 2001, p. 136; summer 2002, pp. 74-75.

*School Library Journal,* September 1988, p. 160; October 1989, p. 84; September 1994, p. 185; September 1996, p. 178; October 2003, p. 207.

*Spectator,* May 17, 2003, p. 65.

*Star-Ledger* (Newark, NJ), July 6, 2003, p. 4.

*WWD,* August 7, 2003, p. 4.

### Online

"Mark Haddon," MostlyFiction, http://mostlyfiction.com/contemp/haddon.htm (December 16, 2004).

"The Curiously Irresistible Literary Debut of Mark Haddon," Powell's City of Books, http://www.powells.com/authors/haddon.html (December 16, 2004).

# Zaha Hadid

## Architect

**B**orn in Baghdad, Iraq, October 31, 1950; daughter of a politician/businessman. *Education:* Studied mathematics at the American University of Beirut; Architectural Association School (London), Diploma Prize, 1977.

**Addresses:** *Office*—Zaha Hadid Architects, Studio 9, 10 Bowling Green Lane, London EC1R OBQ, United Kingdom. *Website*—http://www.zaha-hadid.com.

## Career

**G**raduated from the Architectural Association School, 1977; won design competition for Hong Kong's Peak Club, 1983; completed Vitra Fire Station in Germany, 1993; won design competition for Cardiff Bay Opera House in Wales, 1994; designed Bergisel Ski-Jump in Innsbruck, Austria, 1999; completed Rosenthal Center for Contemporary Art in Cincinnati, 2003; two designs chosen for projects in London, 2005.

**Awards:** Mies van der Rohe Award for contemporary architecture from the European Union, 2003; Pritzker Architecture Prize, 2004.

## Sidelights

**Z**aha Hadid, the first woman to win architecture's highest award, spent years on her profession's avant-garde, better known for her wild designs than for built projects. That reputation grew in the 1990s due to a widely publicized rejection in her adopted home country, Great Britain, and her provocative personality. Her professional breakthrough came in 2003 with the successful construction of her challenging design for a museum in Cincinnati, Ohio. The next year, she won the Pritzker Architecture Prize, and several more of her provocative designs were on their way to being realized by early 2005.

Hadid was born in Baghdad, Iraq, in 1950, at a time when the city was considered cosmopolitan and tolerant. Her father embodied that vision: an industrialist who had studied at the London School of Economics, he was the head of the progressive National Democratic Party, which was dedicated to making Iraq secular and more democratic. Her parents sent her to a Catholic school where students spoke French, and Muslim and Jewish students were welcome. "There was never a question that I would be a professional," she told *Newsweek*'s Cathleen McGuigan. The difference between the Baghdad of her childhood and its years of dictatorship, followed by unrest, pains her; interviewers have described her as struggling to talk about Iraq.

After studying mathematics at the American University in Beirut, Hadid came to London in 1972. She has been based there ever since and is now a

British citizen. She studied at the Architectural Association, which was a home for wildly experimental design in the 1970s and 1980s. For her graduation project, called Malevich's Tectonik, she designed a hotel to stand atop the Hungerford Bridge over England's River Thames. After she graduated in 1977, she went to work for one of her teachers, the radical architect Rem Koolhaas.

In 1982 and 1983, she designed a proposed mountainside club, the Peak Club in Hong Kong, and won the design competition. "Her amazing design, a 'horizontal skyscraper,' called for four huge beams to be rammed into a mountainside, yet it looked as sleek as a UFO," wrote McGuigan in *Newsweek.* The design was never built, though it appeared in a show at New York's Museum of Modern Art.

For years afterward, Hadid's designs and her paintings of them challenged other architects, exciting some and alienating others. She was linked with architecture's radical "deconstruction" movement. "The images of Hadid's buildings became staples of the tide of publications about deconstruction which dominated architectural debate in the late 1980s," Edwin Heathcote wrote in the *Financial Times.* "Her seductive paintings of fragmented cityscapes became an antidote to the self-referential pomposity of postmodernism and the crushing banality of British development. But Hadid, despite her influence, was often dismissed as a dreamer, whose work was unrealizable and impractical."

Her next big success came in 1993, when she completed what became her first signature project, the Vitra Fire Station for the Vitra Furniture Company in Weil am Rhein, Germany. The angular building is now a museum. Vitra later brought her back to the town for an exhibition to mark the city's garden festival in 1999.

It appeared that Hadid had scored a triumph in 1994 when her design was chosen for the Cardiff Bay Opera House in Wales. It "called for an inviting glass courtyard around an auditorium within," the *Economist* explained. "It looked on paper angular and explosive—to the casual glance aggressive even. Critics derided it for disregarding the city and its traditions." The design was both inviting to the passer-by and a tribute to opera's refinement, the article said, but local opinion ran against it, and it was rejected. The money was spent on a stadium instead. Hadid still points to the debacle as an example of the disrespect she has suffered in her career. "When I was in Cardiff they didn't talk to me. Literally. They looked at me sideways, or be-

hind me. Not all of them, but some quite specific people." she told *Building Design*'s Zoe Blackler. Hadid's years of struggle to see her designs realized have left her feeling that she faced more obstacles than other architects. "People were patronizing towards me all the time. They didn't know how to behave with me," she told Blackler. "I don't know whether people responded to me in a strange way because they just thought I was one of those eccentric people, or they thought I was a foreigner or behaved funny or I'm a woman."

The other side of that story is that some people believe she is temperamental and difficult. One example of this opinion is Mickey O'Connor, writing in *Architecture* about her appearance at the American Institute of Architects' 2000 convention. He found her "strident" and full of "chutzpah," dismissed as griping her complaints in her keynote speech about the obstacles she had faced, and he recounted her clashes with other members of a panel on American architecture. In confrontational, even crass language, she challenged American architects to be bolder, not be intimidated by zoning laws, and not to defer so much to their clients.

"Beloved by journalists and members of her own profession for what is frequently described as her diva presence, Ms. Hadid has only recently found the clients willing to look beyond her reputation for being difficult," *New York Times* critic Herbert Muschamp wrote in 2004. The reference to her as a diva, a term originally used for female opera stars, can cut both ways. Her critics use it to suggest arrogance, while her admirers adopt it to praise her personal style.

"She cuts a dramatic, voluptuous figure in her black outfits," wrote Mark Irving in the *Financial Times,* "high heels (sometimes these are glass), jewelry (expensive), above which large heavily lidded eyes and purple-painted lips that always seem to be set in a slightly unsatisfied pout, turn on you like the guns of a well-armored battleship." Hadid herself swats away the diva label as sexism. Visitors to a 2003 retrospective of her work in Vienna, Austria, received free T-shirts at the door that read, "Would they call me a diva if I were a guy?," according to the *New York Times*' Muschamp.

Hadid's career really began to take a turn when two of her designs were chosen for construction in 1998 and 1999: the new Rosenthal Center for Contemporary Art in Cincinnati and the Bergisel Ski-Jump on Bergisel Mountain in Innsbruck, Austria. The ski-jump, wrote Richard Lacayo of *Time,* "signs the sky with a swooping slalom."

The Center for Contemporary Art, Hadid's first building in the United States, opened in 2003. "[It is] the most important American building to be completed since the end of the cold war," raved Muschamp in the *New York Times*. "Like Hadid herself, the building links traditional cosmopolitan values with the phenomenon of globalization."

Other writers joined in the praise. McGuigan of *Newsweek* described it this way: "The sidewalk literally continues right into the glassed-in first story, with its concrete floor—the 'urban carpet,' she calls it—inviting passersby to come in and hang out. Then, around the corner, the pavement sweeps up into a curve that ingeniously becomes the building's back wall." *Time*'s Lacayo commented, "This is a building that does not so much sit on its street corner as continuously arrive there."

Hadid explained that variety and surprise are important to her designs. "People don't want to be in the kind of space that they inhabit every day," she told Lacayo in *Time*. He agreed: "[Hadid] treats right angles as something best left to squares." According to Muschamp of the *New York Times*, Hadid's interest in "movement, curvature, porosity, [and] extreme horizontal elongation" have made her a major influence on other architects.

Her sudden breakthrough is partially a result of trends catching up to her, Hadid and critics agree. "In the past few years, fantastic visions have become more familiar," she told Lacayo of *Time*. In other words, radical, challenging architectural designs, such as the Frank Gehry-designed Guggenheim Museum in Bilbao, Spain and Daniel Libeskind's plans for the former site of the World Trade Center in New York City have become accepted and led the way for other ultra-creative designs, including hers. Critics sympathetic to her work have also noted that it has become somewhat less jarring and confrontational than her early work.

A year after the Rosenthal Center opened, Hadid won the Pritzker Prize, architecture's highest honor. "Although her body of work is relatively small, she has achieved great acclaim and her energy and ideas show even greater promise for the future," said Thomas J. Pritzker, president of The Hyatt Foundation, which established the prize, in the press release that announced the award.

Lord Rothschild, chairman of the jury that awards the prize, praised Hadid's "commitment to modernism" and said in the press release that her "always

inventive" designs had "shifted the geometry of buildings." She received the award on May 31, 2004, at the State Hermitage Museum in St. Petersburg, Russia.

Since she is the first woman to win the Pritzker Prize, interviewers have asked Hadid, even more often, what it is like to be a female architect. "I think it shows that you can actually break through the glass ceiling," she told Heathcote in the *Financial Times*. "I don't want to be seen as a woman architect," she added, but she says she is happy if her success helps other women believe they can achieve. "Women would actually come up to me, particularly in New York, in restaurants, to congratulate me. When I lecture all over the world, women come up to me all the time to tell me how encouraged they are."

At the time she won the award, Hadid and the staff of nearly 50 at her London office were working on several new commissions either in construction or design development. They included the BMW Central Building in Leipzig, Germany; the Phaeno Science Center in Wolfsburg, Germany; Maxxi, the National Center for Contemporary Arts in Rome, Italy; a station for high-speed trains in Naples, Italy; a plan for a Science Hub, a huge "science city" development in Singapore; a bridge in Dubai, the United Arab Emirates; and the Price Tower Arts Center addition in Bartlesville, Oklahoma, an addition to a tower designed by legendary architect Frank Lloyd Wright.

As 2005 began, Hadid enjoyed another belated professional triumph. She has never seen one of her designs built in England, her adopted home country, except for temporary pavilions and a temporary exhibit at London's Millennium Dome. But in January of 2005, Britain's Architecture Foundation chose Hadid's design for its new exhibition center in London, which will be one of the first new cultural buildings in central London in decades.

She still had not shaken controversy. Robert Booth, in an editorial in *Building Design*, suggested that "star" architects such as Hadid benefit from a favoritism in competitions that values successful marketing more than pure architectural talent. "Hadid's building hardly stands out as far and away the most fascinating architecture in the context of the competition," he wrote. "However, its presence will bring kudos to the site."

A few weeks later, though, Hadid won a second British competition. Her design was chosen for the Olympic Aquatics Centre, the first sports venue

London will build in hopes of attracting the Olympic Games in 2012. The British used to be reluctant to invest in new ideas, she told the *Financial Times'* Heathcote a few months earlier. "[S]omething has changed radically here recently. There is no resistance to the new any more. Eventually this will filter through into building. England being part of Europe is the most positive thing that could have happened."

## Sources

### Periodicals

*Architecture,* June 2000, p. 31.
*Building Design,* January 21, 2005, p. 11; February 4, 2005, p. 8.
*Economist,* June 19, 1999, p. 85; March 27, 2004, p. 56.
*European Report,* May 24, 2003, p. 479.
*Financial Times,* June 29, 2002, p. 7; May 25, 2004, p. 13.

*Newsweek,* May 19, 2003, p. 78.
*New York Times,* June 8, 2003; March 22, 2004; January 13, 2005, p. E3.
*Time,* April 5, 1999, p. 74; June 23, 2003.

### Online

"On-line Media Kit," Pritzker Prize, http://www.pritzkerprize.com/2004/mediakit.htm (February 20, 2005).
"Profile," Zaha Hadid Architects, http://www.zaha-hadid.com/profile.html (February 20, 2005).
"Zaha Hadid chosen to design first Olympic venue," Greater London Authority, http://www.london.gov.uk/view_press_release.jsp?releaseid=4824 (February 20, 2005).
"Zaha M. Hadid," Archinform, http://www.archinform.net/arch/1186.htm?ID=fQImEVKB9vbe4Qd2 (February 20, 2005).

*—Erick Trickey*

# Paul Hamm

## Gymnast

**B**orn September 24, 1982, in Waukesha, WI; son of Sandy (a farmer) and Cecily Hamm. *Education:* Attended the University of Wisconsin.

**Addresses:** *Agent*—Sheryl Shade, Shade Global, 250 W. 57th St., New York, NY 10019.

## Career

**G**ymnast, 1999—.

**Awards:** Silver medal for men's team competition, Gymnastics World Championship, 2001; bronze medal for individual floor exercise, Gymnastics World Championship, 2002; gold medal for men's all-around, U.S. Gymnastics Championship, 2002; gold medal for men's all-around, U.S. Gymnastics Championship, 2003; gold medal for individual floor exercises, Gymnastics World Championship, 2003; silver for men's team competition, Gymnastics World Championship, 2003; gold medal for men's all-around, Gymnastics World Championship, 2003; gold medal for men's all-around, U.S. Gymnastics Championship, 2004; gold medal for men's all-around, Athens Olympics, 2004; silver medal for high bar, Athens Olympics, 2004; silver medal for team competition, Athens Olympics, 2004.

## Sidelights

**I**n 2003, Olympic gymnast Paul Hamm became the first American male to win the all-around World Championship. In 2004, he competed at the Athens Olympics, where his gold medal win in the all-around competition was the subject of the biggest controversy at those Games.

Born in Washburn, Wisconsin, in 1982, Hamm and his twin brother, Morgan, grew up in an athletic family. His father, Sandy, was an All-American diver, and his sister, Betsy, was a collegiate gymnast at Iowa State. Of watching his sister compete, Hamm remarked to John Meyer in the *Denver Post*, "It just looked like so much fun. My mom put me in it, then Morgan didn't want to be left behind." They started training when they were nine years old, initially practicing on their family's farm using homemade equipment their father made, and have trained and competed together ever since. "Our personalities are very similar," Hamm told a *People* reporter. He told Ellen Labrecque in *Sports Illustrated for Kids* that training together has helped both of them become better gymnasts and achieve in the sport. "We have always helped each other and pushed each other in the gym. If I see him having problems with the skills that I know how to do, I'll go over and teach them to him. He'll do the same for me."

In 2000, both Hamm brothers made the U.S. Olympic team, becoming the first twins to compete in the same Olympics. The U.S. team finished a disappointing fifth in that Olympics, five points behind China, the winner. It was the latest in a string of Olympic disappointments: the United States had not won the Olympic team gold medal since 1984 and had never had an Olympic all-around champion.

At the 2001 World Championships, Hamm literally fell out of individual medal contention when, during the high bar routine, he hit the bar with his lip and fell to the mat. However, the U.S. gymnasts, including Hamm, won a silver medal in team competition. In 2002, he won individual event bronze. He also won a gold medal in all-around competition at the U.S. championships that year.

Things turned around for Hamm at the gymnastics world championships in September of 2003, when he won the U.S. all-around title again and became the first American to win the men's all-around world title. Although he was behind China's Yang Wei when he went into his final high-bar rotation, he made a perfect landing, winning the gold by .064 point. He told Sports Illustrated for Kids' Labrecque that it meant a great deal to him to be the first American to win the all-around title. "My goal as a little boy was, 'Oh, if I could just make it to the Olympics.' Now, having been the best gymnast in the world at one point in time…. I'm so proud of that."

Hamm also won a gold medal in the individual floor exercise and, with his brother Morgan, won a silver medal in the men's team competition. The U.S. team as a whole finished only one point behind China at the World Championships, in contrast to the huge gap between the teams at the Sydney Olympics. Olympic coach Kevin Mazeika told the Denver Post's Meyer, "We've been making tremendous progress. We have great momentum. We have a very strong team, very deep, very talented, very hungry."

Hamm, who had entered the University of Wisconsin as a health and fitness management major, put his education on hold in order to train for the Athens Olympics. In January of 2004, he and Morgan moved from Wisconsin to Ohio to join the Ohio State University gymnastics team. Hamm was looking for a more challenging atmosphere and chose the team because it had other strong contenders for the Olympics; he felt that being around such high-caliber athletes would motivate him even further. One of the coaches at Ohio State, Doug Stibel, told Mike Angell in Investor's Business Daily, "That really helped him, being around other guys [who] were going to push him."

Stibel noted that Hamm is unusually self-motivated. Typically, a gymnast will show up for a workout and wait to hear what the coach's plan for the day is. Hamm, he said, will try to figure out what the day's goals are before the coach tells him. "He takes our plan and goes one step further," he told Investor's Business Daily's Angell. While training and competing, Hamm is unusually focused, thinking of nothing else. Bo Morris, the men's program manager for U.S.A. Gymnastics, told Angell, "He's the hardest working gymnast I've ever seen." Stibel agreed: "He doesn't waste time sitting around." When Hamm fails at a routine, he works even harder to improve it the next time.

As Angell noted in Investor's Business Daily, "Gymnasts toil in obscurity for years to perfect their skills. Gymnastics doesn't offer the same rewards as more popular sports, save for the chance of being in the Olympics and doing one's personal best." Morris told Angell, "Perseverance, hard work, and determination. These are all the clichés you hear about to succeed. But in Paul's case, they are all true."

In 2004, Hamm's hard work paid off when he won his third consecutive U.S. gymnastics all-around title and in doing so, secured a spot on the United States Olympic gymnastics team. He won by 1.7 points, a huge margin in gymnastics. Morgan Hamm told a Houston Chronicle reporter, "He's amazing. It's hard to believe sometimes he's my brother."

Despite the large margin of his win, Hamm told the Houston Chronicle reporter, "There's definitely room for improvement." He added, "There are a lot of little things that will make me look better than other guys in the world." His coach, Miles Avery, commented in the Houston Chronicle, "Paul is the best gymnast in the world," and said, "Even coming into this meet, guys said, 'I want to be second.' Not many will come into this competition and say, 'I'm going to win,' because that's reserved for Paul."

Hamm thus became the first American to go to the Olympics as the reigning United States and world champion, but he tried not to think of himself as defending something. Instead, he told the Denver Post's Meyer, "I'm trying to go into Athens as if I'm trying to achieve something." He noted, "I've never won an Olympic medal before. If I feel like I'm trying to defend something, that will put a little more pressure on myself, and I don't want to be thinking that way."

At the Athens Olympics the United States men's gymnastics team got off to a good start when, led by Hamm, they won a silver medal in team competition. It was the first Olympic medal in 20 years for the American men. During his competition for the team final, Hamm scored a 9.7 or higher on three of his five events in the team finals, and in four out of six events in the qualifying round. He made one mistake, when he did not complete a series of three release moves on his high bar routine in the finals. Other than this error, however, his performance met expectations that he would perform beautifully in individual events at the Olympics. The silver medal left him optimistic about his chances to win gold in the all-around final.

The all-around competition features athletes performing on six different gymnastic apparatuses. Hamm did very well on the floor exercise. In the next two events he received lower scores, but did well enough to be the first in overall scoring. In the fourth event, the vault, he chose a challenging vault, which involved two and a half twists while flipping in midair, with a blind landing. On the landing, he fell off the mat and into the scorers' tables. This dropped him from first place in the competition to twelfth. "Really, in the air I thought I was OK," he told Diane Pucin in the *Cincinnati Post*. But after the disastrous landing, "Honestly, I thought the gold medal was gone. After an error like that, I just wanted to fight for any medal."

However, just as he did in practice, Hamm concentrated on improving his situation. In addition, his opponents also began making mistakes, missing landings or wobbling during their events. Hamm dug deep and performed almost flawlessly on his two remaining events. On the parallel bars, he dismounted without even bending his knees, winning a score of 9.837, and by the time the other competitors had finished with their flawed routines, he had climbed back to fourth place.

On the high bar, his best event, he was the last competitor. He had done poorly in this event during the team competition, almost losing his grip in the middle of a move. But this time, executing his notably difficult routine, he performed perfectly. He needed a score of 9.825 to tie the South Korean athlete who was in first place. The *Cincinnati Post*'s Pucin described his dismount from the bar: "He twisted high toward the lights, toes pointed perfectly, arms stiff at his sides—and when he landed lightly without even a muscle rippling, the crowd exhaled and Hamm pumped his fists."

He thought he had managed to win bronze, but in fact his score, 9.837, showed that he had won gold, by 12/1000ths of a point. He told Juliet Macur in the *International Herald Tribune,* "I still can't believe what happened. I guess I can expect my life to change a little bit now." Avery told Macur, "It's great, but tonight we're back in the gym at 7. He's got more medals to win."

Hamm's life did change, but not in the way he expected. Almost immediately, controversy erupted about his gold medal and about the scoring of the routines for the all-around final. Two days after the event, the South Korean delegation filed a protest, saying that Yang Tae Young, who had been awarded the bronze medal, had been scored incorrectly on his parallel bars routine, and that if this error had not been made by the judges, he would have won the gold. The International Gymnastics Federation, known as F.I.G. viewed a tape of the event and suspended three judges who had been responsible for the error. However, the South Koreans were not satisfied with this, saying they wanted Yang to have a gold medal in recognition of his win. They were willing to have Hamm and Yang share the gold. The U.S. Olympic Committee agreed to consider this, but F.I.G. did not.

Hamm also said he did not believe he should share the medal. According to the *International Herald Tribune*'s Macur, Hamm said, "I'm a gold medalist. Once the meet is over, it's over." This led some observers to accuse him of being a poor sport, since according to the scores, he was not really the winner. However, F.I.G. officials said that according to the rules, scores could not be changed once an event was concluded, so Hamm was technically still the winner. Hamm, in response to the ensuing controversy as well as allegations that his medal was tainted because it was not a clear win, eventually said he would share the medal if necessary, and announced this at a press conference. "I felt really horrible that no one was defending me, not USA Gymnastics, not the F.I.G. who caused the whole thing, nobody. So I just wanted to do it for myself." However, because of the F.I.G. ruling that the case was closed, Hamm was left in a no-win situation. Hamm's situation was not the only scoring controversy in the Games; several other events were the subjects of wrangling over scores.

The controversy affected Hamm's performance in his four remaining events. He came in fifth in the floor exercise, sixth on the pommel horse, and seventh on the parallel bars. On the high bar, he won silver, after a competition disrupted with audience boos and angry gestures about a Russian performer's score, which was subsequently changed. A few spectators booed Hamm when he stepped up on the podium to receive the silver medal. He told the *International Herald Tribune*'s Macur, "I'm very proud of my performance today and all of my performances in the Olympics. I didn't take any of the boos personally. I really think it enhanced my Olympic experience because of the fact that I would perform so well under tough conditions."

Later, the F.I.G. officials changed their minds and sent a letter to Hamm asking him to return his medal so it could be given to Yang. However, they did not actually have the authority to request this or to force Hamm to do so, and the U.S. Olympic Committee intercepted the letter and sent a stinging missive back refusing not only to return Hamm's gold, but also refusing a previous compromise they had been willing to make, which involved Hamm sharing the gold medal with Yang. Peter Ueberroth, chairman of the U.S. Olympic Committee, told Filip Bondy in a Knight Ridder/Tribune News Service article, "[FIG is] deflecting their own incompetence on a young athlete who competed very well and continue to cause him grief. We're not going to let this matter go to Paul." As Bondy pointed out, this left Hamm in a bad situation, where he was "in some sort of medals purgatory where he is neither a champion nor a sportsman. Hamm is the guy who has the gold medal that his gymnastics federation wants back, but can't take away."

Hamm left Athens a day early to escape the bombardment of questions from the press and to get ready for his next event, the Rock & Roll Gymnastics Competition. During the competition, he tried to put the medals controversy behind him. The event featured a mix of gymnastics and music and dance choreography. Hamm was part of a five-man routine called the "Men's Group Matrix." Hamm, who had already received a standing ovation when he was introduced at the beginning of the program, was happy to receive audience cheers with his team. He told a *SFGate.com* reporter, "It was a great feeling when they announced my name and the crowd cheered like that. It was just so amazing to see that." He added, "All this attention is still a little shocking. But it's great for so many people to come out and help our sport grow."

Hamm's stressful medal situation was finally resolved on October 21, 2004. On that date, the Court of Arbitration for Sport (CAS) ruled that he was the rightful champion in the men's all-around gymnastics competition at the Athens Games. The three-judge panel had been asked by Yang to order international gymnastics officials to change the results and adjust the medal rankings so he would get the gold and Hamm the silver. However, CAS rejected the appeal; the verdict was final and could not be appealed. According to *SI.com,* the CAS arbitrators said the Korean protest was submitted too late and the court was not in a position to correct results even if a mistake were admitted. "The solution for error, either way, lies within the framework of the sport's own rules" and does not allow for a judge or arbitrator to step in later, the CAS panel said, according to *SI.com.* In an interview given before the ruling, Hamm said, according to *SI.com,* "I feel like I had to win my medal in three ways, really. Obviously, in competition. Then with the media. Then in court. It really feels like I've been battling this whole time."

## Sources

### Periodicals

*Cincinnati Post,* August 19, 1004, p. B1.
*Denver Post,* June 23, 2004, p. D1.
*Houston Chronicle,* June 5, 2004, p. 10.
*International Herald Tribune,* August 20, 2004, p. 19; August 25, 2004, p. 17.
*Investor's Business Daily,* August 23, 2004, p. A4.
Knight Ridder/Tribune News Service, August 29, 2004, p. K1824; August 29, 2004, p. K1829.
*Newsweek,* August 16, 2004, p. 50; August 30, 2004, p. 21.
*New York Times,* August 25, 2004, p. D1.
*People,* June 28, 2004, p. 92.
*Sports Illustrated,* September 1, 2003, p. Z10.
*Sports Illustrated for Kids,* July 1, 2004, p. T10; August 1, 2004, p. 64.
*Star Tribune,* August 18, 2004, p. 40.
*Time,* August 30, 2004, p. 55.

### Online

"It's Final," *SI.com,* http://sportsillustrated.cnn.com/2004/more/10/21/hamm.medal.ap/index.html (October 21, 2004)
"Paul Hamm Rocks and Rolls in Post-Olympic Exhibition," *SFGate.com,* http://www.sfgate.com/cgi-bin/article.cgi?f=?news/archive/2004/08/31/sports2218RDT0362.DTL (September 3, 2004)
"Paul Hamm," USA Gymnastics, http://www.usagymnastics.org (September 3, 2004).

—*Kelly Winters*

# Teri Hatcher

© Frank Trapper/Corbis

## Actress

**B**orn December 8, 1964, in Sunnyvale, CA; daughter of Owen (an electrical engineer) and Esther (a computer programmer) Hatcher; married Marcus Leithold (a fitness trainer), June 4, 1988 (divorced, 1989); married Jon Tenney (an actor), May 27, 1994 (divorced, 2003); children: Emerson Rose. *Education:* Attended De Anza College, c. 1982-84; took classes at the American Conservatory Theatre, San Francisco, CA.

**Addresses:** *Agent*—William Morris Agency, One William Morris Place, Beverly Hills, CA 90212.

## Career

**A**ctress on television, including: *The Love Boat,* ABC, 1985-86; *Capitol,* 1986-87; *MacGyver,* ABC, 1986-90; *Karen's Song,* 1987; *Night Court,* 1987; *Star Trek: The Next Generation,* 1988; *L.A. Law,* NBC, 1989; *Quantum Leap,* NBC, 1989; *Murphy Brown,* CBS, 1990; *Tales from the Crypt,* HBO, 1990; *The Exile,* 1991; *The Brotherhood* (movie), 1991; *Sunday Dinner,* 1991; *Dead in the Water* (movie), 1991; *Seinfeld,* NBC, 1993; *Lois & Clark: The New Adventures of Superman,* ABC, 1993-97; *Since You've Been Gone* (movie), 1998; *Frasier,* NBC, 1998; *Running Mates* (movie), 2000; *Jane Doe* (movie), 2001; *Momentum* (movie), 2003; *Two and a Half Men,* CBS, 2004; *Desperate Housewives,* ABC, 2004—. Film appearances include: *The Big Picture,* 1989; *Tango & Cash,* 1989; *Soapdish,* 1991; *Straight Talk,* 1992; *The Cool Surface,* 1994; *Heaven's Prisoners,* 1996; *Two Days in the Valley,* 1996; *Tomorrow Never Dies,* 1997; *Fever,* 1999; *Spy Kids,* 2001; *The Chester Story,* 2003. Also wrote an episode of *Lois & Clark,* and starred in the road tour of *Cabaret,* 1999. Member of the "Gold Rush" cheerleading team for the San Francisco 49ers, 1984.

**Awards:** Golden Globe award for best performance by an actress in a television series (musical or comedy), Hollywood Foreign Press Association, for *Desperate Housewives,* 2005.

## Sidelights

**T**elevision star Teri Hatcher won her first Golden Globe Award in 2005 after nearly 20 years in the business—and just a year after she feared her career was finished forever. Hatcher emerged as a celebrity in the early 1990s when she starred as Lois Lane in ABC's *Lois & Clark: The New Adventures of Superman,* but took some time off to become a mother. When her marriage ended, she found that Hollywood roles for women nearing 40 were harder to come by, and worried about her financial future. That changed when she joined the cast of a new ABC series, *Desperate Housewives,* which became the most talked-about new show of the fall 2004 prime-time line-up. Suddenly, Hatcher was appearing on *The Oprah Winfrey Show* and the cover of *Newsweek* alongside her fellow fictional homemakers, but she was still stunned by the show's success, as she admitted in a *Harper's Bazaar* profile. "In my wildest imagination," Hatcher told writer Merle Ginsberg, "I would have said this could never happen."

Born on December 8, 1964, in Sunnyvale, California, Hatcher grew up in the San Francisco Bay area. Her father was an electrical engineer, and her mother worked for much of Hatcher's childhood as a computer programmer. At Fremont High School, Hatcher captained her cheerleading squad, and as her 1982 graduation date neared, her peers voted her the classmate "most likely to become dancer on *Solid Gold*," a popular television show of the era which featured an array of identically-clad dancers grooving to the week's Top-40 hits. But Hatcher had other plans, and began taking math courses at De Anza College in Cupertino, California, with the goal of earning a teaching degree. She also took some acting classes at the prestigious American Conservatory Theatre in San Francisco, and her teaching career was sidetracked when she landed a spot on the 1984 "Gold Rush" cheerleading team for the San Francisco 49ers.

Not long after her National Football League-halftime show appearances had ended with the season, she traveled to Hollywood with a friend in order to provide some moral support during a casting call. Hatcher wound up winning a part herself, as a mermaid dancer on *The Love Boat*, an ABC prime-time staple nearing the end of what had been a hugely successful run. The pay was enormous—$1,000 a week—and after the 1985-86 season finished, Hatcher was able to land a recurring role on another top-rated show, *MacGyver*, as aspiring actor Penny Parker. She also appeared in guest roles on several other series during the late 1980s, including *L.A. Law* and *Star Trek: The Next Generation*.

After her feature-film debut in 1989, *The Big Picture*, a comedy that cast her alongside Kevin Bacon and Martin Short, Hatcher was cast in the Sylvester Stallone-Kurt Russell cop drama, *Tango & Cash*, and made a good impression on critics in 1991's *Soapdish* with Sally Field and Robert Downey Jr. Of all her early roles, however, Hatcher became somewhat legendary for a much-remembered episode of *Seinfeld* from 1993, in which Jerry's friends chastise him for dating a woman—Hatcher's character—who appears to have undergone breast-augmentation surgery. Hatcher gets the last word, exiting with an infamous last line in which she tells Jerry, "They're real and they're spectacular."

Later that same year, Hatcher won a plum role as Lois Lane in *Lois & Clark: The New Adventures of Superman*, an ABC series that paired her with a relatively unknown young actor, Dean Cain. Hatcher's Lane was a newspaper reporter, and the on-screen romance between her and the reluctant superhero anchored the series' plots over the next four seasons and helped make the show a hit. *Lois & Clark* usually topped the Sunday-night ratings, and critics loved it as well. "Much credit must go to Hatcher and Cain for making the show more than a live-action comic book," noted *Entertainment Weekly*'s Ken Tucker. "Hatcher is always working against the good looks that have made her an Internet-downloading favorite, in order to convey both Lois' steely ambition and smitten confusion."

The online popularity to which Tucker referred came at the peak of *Lois & Clark*'s popularity, and just as the number of home Internet users began to surge on a monthly basis. Internet service provider American Online reported that an image of Hatcher clad only in a red "Superman" cape was the most downloaded image on its site for months, logging an average of 250 downloads per day in late 1994. "I hope it's not one guy with a computer and 4,000 pictures of me," Hatcher quipped when told the news, according to *Entertainment Weekly*. Her image as a sirenish, yet girl-next-door pin-up endured, and she earned another inadvertent publicity coup when she appeared alongside comedian Tom Arnold as a presenter at the 1996 Golden Globe Awards. At the podium, Arnold made an unwise remark intended as a compliment, of sorts, and the comment drew a chorus of boos from the audience. Hatcher reacted graciously, and Arnold later apologized profusely.

Hatcher began to explore darker roles in feature films, playing an Olympic-caliber skier who wants her husband dead in the 1996 project *Two Days in the Valley*. That film featured a then-unknown Charlize Theron, with whom Hatcher's character engages in a brutal fistfight. Hatcher also portrayed another schemer in *Heaven's Prisoners*, as the wife of a mob boss played by Eric Roberts; Alec Baldwin also starred in the Louisiana bayou drama. Eager to expand her television career as well, Hatcher wrote an episode of *Lois & Clark*, but felt it was time for a change, as she told *Daily News* writer Bob Strauss in mid-1996. "I've found that I'm less invested in what my opinion is of what should happen on the show," Hatcher admitted. "I have no control, and I've learned that. It's been frustrating to feel like I have ideas that might be good, but that don't get anywhere because there are too many people with agendas in television: networks, studios, producers." The series came to a finale where Hatcher's Lois and Cain's Clark Kent walked down the aisle, and closed with the arrival of an infant—perhaps a future "Superman"—into their household.

After *Lois & Clark* ended, Hatcher took a juicy role in one of the James Bond movies, 1997's *Tomorrow Never Dies*, in which she played Paris Carver, wife of Jonathan Pryce's megalomaniac media tycoon. Paris, true to her unusual name, turned out to be one of a long line of beauties to have dallied with the dashing Bond, in this case played by Pierce Brosnan. After that, Hatcher seemed to vanish from the public eye. Married to a fellow actor, she gave birth to a daughter, Emerson Rose, just weeks before the Bond film premiered, and decided to concentrate on her new role for a time. "To me there's nothing more important than being a mother," she told the *Guardian*'s Dan Glaister. "I always knew that if and when I had a kid I was going to stay at home."

In early 1999, Hatcher took her infant daughter with her and went on tour in *Cabaret*, the saucy musical set in 1930s Berlin whose 1972 film version had made Liza Minnelli a star. Hatcher played the vixenish Sally Bowles in Boston for six months, and earned good reviews for what was her stage debut. She found performing before a live theater audience thrilling, she told the *Boston Herald*'s Alicia Potter. "There's no ego," she reflected. "You feel like all the people in this cast would jump in front of a bus for you, as I would for them. I've never had that experience before working on anything."

Yet Hatcher's career seemed to falter after that. She appeared in the 2001 film *Spy Kids,* did a couple of television movies, and found herself in a series of commercials for Radio Shack alongside former pro football player Howie Long. The ads were clever and well-received, but they were ads nonetheless. When her nine-year marriage ended in 2003, Hatcher began to panic, realizing that she had scarce other means outside of show business to provide an income for herself and her daughter. Afraid she would lose her house, she recalled one trying moment when she sat on her kitchen floor and just cried. "I was feeling I wouldn't be able to pay my mortgage for much longer—there was a lot of money that I'd had that I didn't have anymore," she told *People* writer Tom Gliatto. "That was really a low point."

Hatcher turned to writing once again, and even sold a pilot script about a single mom to ABC. But it was a role as another single parent that would become Hatcher's stunning comeback: that of Susan Mayer on *Desperate Housewives,* which premiered in the ABC fall line-up of 2004. Hatcher's Susan is a children's book author, divorced, with an unusually wise young daughter. Among the five lead female characters on the show, Hatcher's was one of the admired, not loathed, ones. Her Susan was insecure, klutzy, and tentative about a new romance with her handsome neighbor. Coming out of her

own traumatic split, Hatcher quipped in the interview with *Harper's Bazaar,* that in the realm of romance, "I think it's where Susan and I are most alike," she told Ginsberg. "We're both complete failures with men."

*Desperate Housewives*—a mix of drama, comedy, and even murder-mystery—was set on the seemingly idyllic Wisteria Lane, where the quintet of women are neighbors as well as friends and sometimes wary adversaries. All the characters exhibit varying degrees of dysfunction—one is a disturbing perfectionist, another overwhelmed by the pressures of being a stay-at-home mom, the third is carrying on an affair with the teenage landscaper, and one seems to be there just to complicate things for the rest. Hatcher's character, meanwhile, was just the nice, albeit insecure, one. The other actors on the show were Marcia Cross, Felicity Huffman, Eva Longoria, and Nicollette Sheridan, and nearly all of them had reached, as Hatcher had, a crossroads in their careers. No longer cast as vixens, they were heading over to the "motherly" roles, but *Desperate Housewives* seemed to tap into the popular zeitgeist by portraying them as both family-focused and on the prowl.

Hatcher, for her part, was thankful to have landed the role. "I know there are people who didn't get my part because they wanted a bigger trailer," she told *Detroit Free Press* television critic Mike Duffy. "I think, 'Thank God they wanted that bigger trailer.' There are lots of things that fell into place for me to make this happen. I'm not trying to be corny or weird about it. I'm just grateful." Hatcher expressed that gratitude enthusiastically to the world when she won the Best Comedy Show Actress Award at the Golden Globes in early 2005.

Hatcher lives in the San Fernando Valley, and shares joint custody of her daughter with her ex-husband, actor Jon Tenney. With the storylines of *Desperate Housewives* presenting seemingly infinite possibilities for the hit show's longevity, Hatcher was staying on board as Susan Mayer—but she was pragmatic about the pitfalls of the entertainment industry. "Even if it ends tomorrow and I never get another job, I am ready for it," she asserted in an interview with John Harlow of London's *Sunday Times* newspaper. "Life can knock me down but this time I will just get up again. I have stuff to do."

## Sources

*Boston Herald,* May 4, 1999, p. 43.
*Daily News* (Los Angeles, CA), May 12, 1996, p. L3.
*Detroit Free Press,* September 15, 2004.

*Entertainment Weekly,* September 24, 1993, p. 76; December 9, 1994, p. 11; December 8, 1995, p. 53; September 10, 2004, p. 110.
*Guardian* (London, England), February 14, 2005, p. 6.
*Harper's Bazaar,* February 2005, p. 188.
*Herald* (Glasgow, Scotland), January 22, 2005, p. 17.
*InStyle,* October 15, 2004, p. 160.
Knight-Ridder/Tribune News Service, May 15, 1996.

*Newsweek International,* January 17, 2005, p. 50.
*People,* February 14, 2005, p. 70.
*Sunday Times* (London, England), February 13, 2005, p. 6.
*Time,* October 11, 1993, p. 82.

—*Carol Brennan*

# Dustin Hoffman

## Actor

**B**orn August 8, 1937, in Los Angeles, CA; son of Harvey (a set designer, prop supervisor, and furniture designer) and Lillian Hoffman; married Anne Byrne (a ballerina), May 4, 1969 (divorced, October 6, 1980); married Lisa Gottsegen (an attorney), October 21, 1980; children: Karina (stepchild; from first marriage), Jenny (from first marriage); Jacob, Rebecca, Max, Alexandra (from second marriage). *Education:* Attended Santa Monica City College; studied music at Los Angeles Conservatory of Music and Arts; studied acting at Pasadena Playhouse, 1958, and with Barney Brown, Lee Strasberg, and Lonny Chapman.

**Addresses:** *Contact*—540 Madison Ave., Ste. 2700, New York, NY 10022; 9830 Wilshire Blvd., Beverly Hills, CA 90212.

## Career

**A**ctor in films, including: *Tiger Makes Out,* 1967; *The Graduate,* 1967; *Midnight Cowboy,* 1969; *John and Mary,* 1969; *Little Big Man,* 1970; *Straw Dogs,* 1971; *Lenny,* 1974; *All the President's Men,* 1976; *Straight Times,* 1978; *Kramer vs. Kramer,* 1979; *Tootsie,* 1982; *Ishtar,* 1987; *Rain Man,* 1988; *Family Business,* 1989; *Dick Tracy,* 1990; *Billy Bathgate,* 1991; *Hook,* 1991; *Hero,* 1992; *Outbreak,* 1995; *American Buffalo,* 1996; *Sleepers,* 1996; *Wag the Dog,* 1997; *Sphere,* 1998; *Moonlight Mile,* 2002; *Confidence,* 2003; *Runaway Jury,* 2003; *I (Heart) Huckabees,* 2004; *Finding Neverland,* 2004; *Meet the Fockers,* 2005; *Racing Stripes,* 2005. Producer of films, including: *The Blouse Man,* 1999. Stage appearances include: *Yes Is For a Very Young Man,* Sarah Lawrence College, 1960; *A Cook for Mr.*

*General,* Broadway production, 1961; *Endgame,* Theatre Company of Boston, 1964; *The Quare Fellow,* Theatre Company of Boston, 1964; *In the Jungle of Cities,* Theatre Company of Boston, 1964; *Harry, Noon and Night,* American Place Theatre, New York City, 1965; *The Exhaustion of Our Son's Love; Eh?; Jimmy Shine,* 1968; *Death of a Salesman,* Chicago, IL, and Washington, D.C., then Broadhurst Theatre, New York City, 1984; *Merchant of Venice,* London and New York City, 1989. Stage work includes: assistant to the director, *A View from the Bridge,* Off-Broadway production, 1965; stage manager, *The Subject Was Roses,* Broadway production, 1965; director, *Jimmy Shine,* Broadway production, 1968; director, *All Over Town,* Broadway production, 1974. Television appearances include: *Naked City,* 1961; *Marlo Thomas and Friends in Free to Be ... You and Me* (special), 1974; *Death of a Salesman* (special), 1985; *The Simpsons* (voice), 1991. Executive producer of *Death of a Salesman,* 1985. Punch Productions, principal. Also worked as a psychiatric hospital attendant, waiter, dishwasher, typist, janitor, coatchecker, and toy salesperson at Macy's.

**Awards:** Obie Award for best actor, *Village Voice,* for *The Exhaustion of Our Son's Love,* 1966; Drama Desk Vernon Rice Award for performance for *Eh?,* 1967; Theatre World Award for *Eh?,* 1967; Golden Globe Award for most promising newcomer—male, Hollywood Foreign Press Association, for *The Graduate,* 1967; BAFTA award for most promising newcomer, for *The Graduate,* 1968; BAFTA award for best actor, for both *Midnight Cowboy* and *John and Mary,* 1969; Drama Desk Award for outstanding performance, for *Jimmy Shine,* 1969; National Association of Theater Owners Star of the Year Award, 1976; New York Film Critics Circle Award for best actor, for *Kramer vs. Kramer,* 1979; Los Angeles Film Critics Association Award for best actor, for *Kramer vs. Kramer,* 1979; Golden Globe Award for best actor in a motion picture (drama), Hollywood Foreign Press Association, for *Kramer vs. Kramer,* 1979; Academy Award for best actor, Academy of Motion Picture Arts and Sciences, for *Kramer vs. Kramer,* 1979; National Society of Film Critics Award for best actor, for both *Kramer vs. Kramer* and *Agatha*; National Society of Film Critics Award for best actor, for *Tootsie,* 1982; Golden Globe Award, best actor in a motion picture (musical or comedy), Hollywood Foreign Press Association, for *Tootsie,* 1982; BAFTA award for best actor, for *Tootsie,* 1983; Drama Desk Award for outstanding actor in a play, for *Death of Salesman* 1984; Antoinette Perry (Tony) Award for best actor in a play for *Death of Salesman,* 1984; Golden Globe Award for best actor in a television movie, Hollywood Foreign Press Association, for *Death of a Salesman,* 1985; Emmy Award for outstanding lead actor in a miniseries or a special, Academy of Television Arts and Sciences, for *Death of a Salesman,* 1986; Academy Award for best actor, Academy of Motion Picture Arts and Sciences, for *Rain Man,* 1988; People's Choice Award for favorite dramatic movie actor, 1989; Breline Film Festival Golden Bear for Lifetime Achievement, 1989; Honorary Associate of Arts degree, Santa Monica College, 1989; People's Choice Award for world's favorite movie actor, 1990; French Order of Arts and Letters, 1995; Venice Film Festival Golden Lion for Lifetime Achievement, 1996; Cecil B. DeMille Award, Hollywood Foreign Press Association, 1997; BAFTA Britannia Award, 1997; American Film Institute Lifetime Achievement Award, 1999.

## Sidelights

Though not a classically handsome leading man, Dustin Hoffman quickly became a major actor in Hollywood, appearing in many major films produced in the 1960s through early 2000s. Hoffman took roles in films both edgy and commercial, in all genres. He received numerous honors for his work, including several Academy Awards.

Born on August 8, 1937, in Los Angeles, California, Hoffman was the second son of Harvey and Lillian Hoffman. His father worked as a prop supervisor at the Columbia movie lot, and later moved into designing and selling furniture. Raised in Los Angeles with his elder brother Ron, Hoffman was attending Los Angeles High School when he became interested in acting. He told Leslie Bennetts of the *New York Times,* "A big reason I went into acting was social: it was to meet girls. I wasn't athletic, I was a very bad student, there wasn't anything I felt I could do. Acting was the first time in my life when I felt attractive, the first time I felt as though I knew what I was doing. I loved it."

After briefly attending Santa Monica City College and dropping out, Hoffman studied music at the Los Angeles Conservatory of Music and Arts and acting at the Pasadena Playhouse. He also studied acting with Lee Strasberg, Lonny Chapman, and Barney Brown. Hoffman moved from Los Angeles to New York City to further his career and become a stage character actor.

While auditioning for many stage roles, Hoffman held a number of other jobs to support himself. He worked as a janitor in a dance studio, coat checker, dishwasher, and sold toys at Macy's. Hoffman made his stage debut in 1960 in *Yes Is for a Very Young Man* at Sarah Lawrence College. The following year, he made his Broadway debut in *A Cook for Mr. General.* That same year, Hoffman had his television debut in an episode of *Naked City.*

For the first two-thirds of the 1960s, Hoffman concentrated on the stage, appearing in a number of productions in the Northeast. In 1964, he appeared in several productions as a member of the Theatre Company of Boston, including *Endgame* and *In the Jungle of Cities.* In New York City the following year, Hoffman had roles in *Harry, Noon and Night* at the American Place Theatre. Other prominent New York roles for Hoffman included *The Exhaustion of Our Son's Love* and *Eh?.*

Hoffman also ventured into stage work. He worked on two productions for director Ulu Grosbard, serving as his assistant on a 1965 production of *A View from the Bridge* and a stage manager for a production that same year of *The Subject Was Roses.* Hoffman went on to direct at least two Broadway productions, *Jimmy Shine* in 1968 and *All Over Town* in 1974.

While Hoffman found success on stage, film proved to be the medium that made him a star. After making his film debut in 1967's *Tiger Makes Out,* the actor shot to stardom with another film released that year, *The Graduate.* In the film, which became a classic, Hoffman played 21-year-old Benjamin Braddock, a confused young man who is unsure of his future. His performance garnered him an Academy Award nomination and made him a leading man in film despite his short stature and lack of marquee good looks.

Hoffman's next film role was very different, but also went on to become a classic in American cinema. In 1969, he played the physically challenged street hustler Ratso Rizzo in the controversial *Midnight Cowboy*, the first X-rated film to be released by a major studio. His supporting role also led to an Academy Award nomination for best actor, while the film itself won the best picture Oscar. The same year *Midnight Cowboy* was released, Hoffman married his first wife, ballerina Anne Byrne. The couple had two children, Karina, a daughter from Byrne's first marriage whom Hoffman adopted, and Jenny.

As a film actor, Hoffman repeatedly took on challenging, complex roles, though not all of his films were hits. The 1969 film *John and Mary* focused on contemporary courtship, while 1970's *Little Big Man* was a western. In 1971, Hoffman also appeared in *Straw Dogs* as a mathematician who embraces violent solutions to attacks on his home. Seven years later, he played a committed criminal in *Straight Time*.

Hoffman also appeared in more acclaimed films in the 1970s. He received his third Academy Award nomination for his portrayal of comedian Lenny Bruce in 1974's *Lenny*. Hoffman scored another hit with 1976's *All the President's Men*. He played *Washington Post* reporter Carl Bernstein in the drama about the men who helped reveal the Watergate scandal earlier in the decade.

Hoffman continued his reign at the box office with the 1979 hit *Kramer vs. Kramer*. Hoffman played Ted Kramer, an advertising executive with no real connections with his son or wife, played by Meryl Streep, until she walks out on him and their son. Hoffman's character is forced to raise his son alone. Hoffman's portrayal of Kramer won the actor his first Academy Award.

While filming *Kramer vs. Kramer*, Hoffman's own marriage was falling apart, something he drew on emotionally for the role. He divorced his first wife in 1980, and re-married in October of that year. Hoffman's second wife was Lisa Gottsegen, an attorney, and the couple went on to have four children: Jacob, Rebecca, Max, and Alexandra.

After *Kramer vs. Kramer*, Hoffman did not appear in another film for three years. When he returned to acting, he took on another unusual role. In the comedy *Tootsie*, Hoffman played an underemployed actor named Michael Dorsey. Because Dorsey has problems finding roles, he decides to dress as a woman to try out for a soap opera. The woman he creates, a middle-aged Southern actress named Dorothy Michaels, gets the role in the soap and becomes an icon, but the actor playing her falls for a co-star on the soap, played by Jessica Lange.

While *Tootsie* was popular with both critics and audiences, filming had not gone smoothly. Hoffman had a hand in developing the script, but was reportedly difficult on the set. He and director Sydney Pollack often clashed. However, Hoffman was proud of the product and attached to the characters he played. He told Leslie Bennetts of *New York Times*, "I really liked her. I started to feel about her the way I had never felt about a character before. She made me very emotional, very emotional. I still haven't understood it completely."

Though Hoffman had a solid film career, he never forgot his love of the stage. Throughout his career, he continued to appear in stage roles. One role he had coveted for many years was that of Willy Loman in *Death of a Salesman* which he got to play in 1984 in Chicago, Washington, D.C., and New York City to many positive notices. The production was taped for a television special in 1985. In 1989, Hoffman played Shylock in William Shakespeare's *The Merchant of Venice* in London and New York City.

Hoffman occasionally picked some unsuccessful projects. In 1987, he had a co-starring role with Warren Beatty in *Ishtar*, one of the worst film failures of all time. Shot in Morocco and New York City, the film focused on Hoffman and Beatty's characters, two failing singer-songwriters who have to get to Morocco to get work. The film went over budget, and at the time, was the most expensive comedy ever made with a $50 million price tag. After filming, there were many delays before it was finally released. *Ishtar* had to gross $100 million just to break even, but did not come close. The film opened to horrible reviews, and completely failed with critics and film audiences.

Hoffman was able to able to bounce back with his next role, autistic savant Raymond Babbitt in 1988's *Rain Man*. In this challenging role, Hoffman's character is kidnapped from his institution by his younger adult brother Charlie, played by Tom Cruise, so that he can get his hands on their father's estate from his brother's caretakers. Unlike *Ishtar, Rain Man* had critical and box office acclaim. Hoffman won an Academy Award for his performance.

After *Rain Man,* Hoffman did not have much box office success in the early 1990s. While his films had varying degrees of merit, they just did not bring in audiences. For example, Hoffman played the title character in 1991's *Billy Bathgate,* which was a huge box office failure. While 1991's *Hook,* directed by Steven Spielberg, did not fail as badly, another film released the next year flopped completely. In *Hero,* Hoffman played criminal Bernie LaPlanta who saves a number of passengers from a burning plane, risking his life, but does not receive acclaim for what he did because he allowed an imposter to take the credit.

By the mid-1990s, Hoffman began appearing in hits again. He played the lead in the drama *Outbreak* in 1995. Hoffman played Colonel Sam Daniels, a doctor who helps save the world from an infectious disease. He also appeared in quality films like *American Buffalo,* playing the thief in this adaptation of the David Mamet play.

The late 1990s and early 2000s were a time of continued success for Hoffman. At the end of the 1990s, he had starred in three films directed by Barry Levinson. Hoffman played a lawyer with a drug problem in 1996's *Sleepers.* In 1997's *Wag the Dog,* Hoffman played a Hollywood producer who creates a fake war to help make Americans pay less attention to a sex scandal involving their president. Hoffman and the film received many great reviews, with Hoffman being considered one of the best parts of the film. He also nominated for another Academy Award. Hoffman's last film with Levinson was *Sphere,* playing a scientist working under water.

Hoffman's roles in the early 2000s continued to be varied and interesting. In 2002's *Moonlight Mile,* he played the father of an adult daughter who dies, and he and his wife find comfort in their relationship with her fiancé. The following year, Hoffman appeared in *Runaway Jury,* based on a novel by John Grisham. Hoffman played a Southern lawyer named Wendall Rohr. In 2004, Hoffman had one of the lead roles in *I (Heart) Huckabees,* as part of an existential detective duo with his film wife played by Lily Tomlin.

Some of Hoffman's later films were sizable hits. He had a supporting role in 2004's *Finding Neverland,* which starred Johnny Depp as playwright J.M. Barrie; Hoffman played the financier of his plays. Hoffman had a bigger hit in the 2005 comedy *Meet the Fockers.* In the sequel to 2000's *Meet the Parents,* Hoffman played the father of Greg (Gaylord) Focker, with Barbra Streisand as his film wife. That same year, Hoffman provided the voice of Tucker, a Shetland pony, in the family comedy *Racing Stripes.*

Of his drive as an actor and person, Hoffman told Bernard Weinraub of *New York Times,* "I've had to reinvent myself every day. I wasn't in a club in high school, I was never in the 'in' group, and in a way that's stuck with me.... I've always felt like the underdog, right from the get-go, ever since even *The Graduate.* I really believed that was a fluke and I refused to believe I had arrived. And in a way I've been hanging on by my fingertips for the whole ride."

## Sources

### Books

*Celebrity Biographies,* Baseline II, Inc., 2005.

### Periodicals

*Boston Globe,* December 11, 1988, p. B1.
*Entertainment Weekly,* February 4, 2005, pp. 62-68.
*Independent* (London, England), January 28, 2005, pp. 8-9.
*Los Angeles Times,* December 22, 2004, p. E14.
*New York Times,* December 19, 1982, sec. 2, p. 1; December 21, 1982, p. C11; March 18, 1984, sec. 6, p. 37; December 10, 1989, sec. 2, p. 1; September 27, 1992, sec. 2, p. 13; February 17, 1998, p. E1.
*People,* May 25, 1987, p. 102.
*St. Petersburg Times* (Florida), December 16, 1988, p. 19.
*Time,* June 19, 1989, p. 56.
*Vanity Fair,* March 2005, p. 312.
*Washington Post,* December 19, 1979, p. C1.

—*A. Petruso*

# Hale Irwin

### Professional golfer

**B**orn Hale S. Irwin, June 3, 1945, in Joplin, MO; son of Hale S. (an excavation contractor) and Mabel M. (Philipps) Irwin; married Sally Jean Stahlhuth, September 14, 1968; children: Becky, Steven. *Education:* University of Colorado, B.S. (marketing), 1968.

**Addresses:** *Home*—Paradise Valley, AZ. *Office*—Hale Irwin Golf Design, 9909 Clayton Rd., Ste. 209A, St. Louis, MO 63124.

## Career

**G**olfer. Professional Golfers' Association (PGA) Tour wins include: Heritage Classic, 1971, 1973, 1994; U.S. Open, 1974, 1979, 1990; Western Open, 1975; Atlanta Classic, 1975, 1977; Los Angeles Open, 1976; Florida Citrus Open, 1976; Hall of Fame Classic, 1977; San Antonio-Texas Open, 1977; Hawaiian Open, 1981; Buick Open, 1981; Honday-Inverrary Classic, 1982; Memorial Tournament, 1983, 1985; Bing Crosby Pro-Am, 1984; Buick Classic, 1990. Champions Tour victories include: Ameritech Senior Open, 1995, 1998, 1999; Vantage Championship, 1995, 1997; American Express, 1996; PGA Seniors' Championship, 1996, 1997, 1998, 2004; MasterCard Seniors, 1997; LG Championship, 1997; Las Vegas Senior Classic, 1997; Burnet Senior Classic, 1997; Bank of Boston Classic, 1997, 1998; Boone Valley Classic, 1997, 1999; Maui Kaanapali Classic, 1997; Toshiba Senior Classic, 1998, 2002; Las Vegas Senior, 1998; U.S. Senior Open, 1998, 2000; Energizer Senior Tour Championship, 1998; Nationwide Championship, 1999, 2000; Ford Senior Players' Championship, 1999; Coldwell Banker Burnet Se-

nior Classic, 1999; BellSouth Senior Classic at Opryland, 2000; EMC Kaanapali Classic, 2000; Siebel Classic in Silicon Valley, 2001; Bruno's Memorial Classic, 2001; Turtle Bay Championship, 2001, 2002, 2003; ACE Group Classic, 2002; 3M Championship, 2002; Kinko's Classic of Austin, 2003; Liberty Mutual Legends of Golf, 2004. Also founded his own golf-design company, Hale Irwin Golf Services Inc., 1986, later renamed Hale Irwin Golf Design.

**Awards:** PGA World Golf Hall of Fame, 1992; Champions Tour Player of the Year, 1997, 1998, 2002.

## Sidelights

**H**ale Irwin is by no means the most gifted athlete to play on the professional golf circuit. Other players drive the ball longer than he does; they putt better than him, too. Irwin's talent lies in playing nice, clean golf. He drives the ball toward the hole with exceptional accuracy, never having to make up for lost ground. Because of his steadfast consistency, Irwin has remained a force on the pro tour for more than three decades. In this time, he amassed three U.S. Open wins (1974, 1979, and 1990) as well as 17 other Professional Golfers' Association (PGA) Tour victories. Irwin joined the senior golfers' Champions Tour in 1995 and became its most successful player, having won 40 tournaments as of the end of the 2004 season. Golf star Jack Nicklaus summed up Irwin's career this way for Jaime Diaz of the *New York Times*: "Hale is not exceptional in any part of the game, but very good in all parts."

Hale S. Irwin (the "S" does not stand for anything) was born on June 3, 1945, in Joplin, Missouri, to Hale and Mabel Irwin, though he was raised mostly in Kansas and Colorado. Irwin's father was an excavation contractor who spent his weekends on the golf course. As a youngster, Irwin learned the game from him and never took a formal golf lesson. Irwin's first clubs were adult ones cut down to his size and fitted with electrical tape grips. By the age of seven, Irwin could play a nine-hole course.

As a child, one of Irwin's chores was to cut the grass around the family's home. He did this with an old-fashioned scythe, a tool that has a handle like a golf club that is attached to a single-edged blade at the end. While whacking away at the grass with the scythe, Irwin inadvertently mastered the motion of the golf swing.

In the book *Play Better Golf with Hale Irwin*, Irwin explained that using the scythe was good preparation for a golf career. "It was such a long, difficult tool to use that you had to take up a well-balanced footing and move it very easily and rhythmically with a backswing and through swing. Because the golf club is so light and easy to move by comparison, there is so often a tendency to rush the swing.... In no way was that possible with a scythe. I have always carried that image in my mind ... and have added to it over the years because not only is golf a game of smooth rhythm, but also an action of continuous acceleration."

Irwin played football at Boulder High School in Colorado, then enrolled at the University of Colorado—also in Boulder—and was starting quarterback his sophomore year. Though Irwin stood only six feet tall and weighed 175 pounds, he switched to defensive back. Irwin told *Golf Magazine*'s Curt Sampson that he preferred defense because he liked to be "on top of the pile looking like a hero" instead of "on the bottom of the pile getting the hell kicked out of me."

Irwin was voted All-Big Eight free safety in both his junior and senior years. He also excelled at golf, winning the 1967 National Collegiate Athletic Association (NCAA) individual golf championship. The demands of both sports required intense dedication.

Most days, Irwin left football practice and headed to the tee to hit a few hundred balls. After graduating with a marketing degree in 1968, Irwin decided he was too small to continue with football.

Irwin joined the PGA Tour in 1968 and soon made his mark. In 1971, he won the Heritage Classic. He repeated that win in 1973 and in 1974 shot his way to his first of three U.S. Open wins. Irwin continued to dominate tournaments through 1985, then stepped back from the game a bit to spend more time with his family. He had married Sally Jean Stahlhuth in 1968 and they had two children, both born in the 1970s. Besides spending time with family, Irwin dedicated himself to his St. Louis-based golf course design business. Nearly five years passed without a tournament win. By 1990, sports commentators were saying that Irwin's career was over. The rumors rejuvenated his interest in golf.

Irwin committed himself to a comeback and in 1990 won the U.S. Open—a tournament he had not won in eleven years. Irwin was usually calm and collected after his victories, but this time, he celebrated with a high-five lap around the green. At 45, he was the oldest player to win a U.S. Open. Two days later, he arrived at the Buick Classic and won again. Irwin considers these victories some of his sweetest.

"I think my winning brought people pleasure and some identification with my age group and maybe me," he told Diaz in the *New York Times* shortly after the wins. "People said, 'Maybe I can do something like that. Maybe I can extend myself.' I could feel it from people. Those two weeks were easily the most emotional of my career."

Irwin turned 50 in 1995 and joined the Senior Tour, now called the Champions Tour. By 1997, he was on fire. That year, Irwin entered 23 events and ended up with 18 top-ten finishes, including nine victories. He also became the first Champions Tour player to top $2 million in one season. In 1998, he won seven times and earned nearly $3 million. Those two years, Irwin won more money than anyone else in golf. This was a phenomenal accomplishment considering the rewards are higher on the PGA Tour. Irwin was named Champions Tour Player of the Year in 1997, 1998, and 2002.

Irwin said the key to his success has been rest and relaxation. He does not practice much during the off-season so that he can return to the sport with renewed vigor. "I start by analyzing my swing," he told Jerry Potter of *USA Today*. "Then I break it down to the basics: grip, grip pressure, stance."

About ten days before the first game, he starts hitting balls, then plays himself back into shape during the competitions. This technique works. In 2004, Irwin became the winningest player in Champions Tour history when he captured his 40th tournament title. Most players do not last long on the Champions Tour, which they can enter at 50. Before Irwin, most golfers saw their skills diminish by the time they reached 55 or 56 and quit being serious contenders. Irwin, however, has shown that for some, the game can go on.

# Sources

### Books

Mackie, Keith, editor, *Play Better Golf with Hale Irwin*, Octopus Books Limited, 1980.

### Periodicals

*Golf Magazine*, June 1,
*GolfWorld*, April 30, 2004, pp. 20-22.
*New York Times*, June 5, 1991, p. B7.
*Sunday Oregonian*, August 22, 2004, p. 4.
*USA Today*, January 10, 2003, p. F1; August 26, 2004, p. C2.

### Online

"U.S. Senior Open Player Bios: Hale Irwin," U.S. Senior Open, http://www.ussenioropen.com/2004/players/bios/irwin-h.html (November 13, 2004).

*—Lisa Frick*

# B.K.S. Iyengar

**Yoga instructor and author**

---

**B**orn Bellur Krishnamachar Sundararaja Iyengar, December 14, 1918, in Karnataka, India; son of a teacher; married Ramamani, 1943; children: Geeta, Vinita, Suchita, Sunita, Savitha, Prashant (son). *Education:* Studied yoga under T. Krishnamacharya, early 1930s.

**Addresses:** *Office*—Iyengar Yoga Institute, 1107 B/1 Hare Krishna Mandir Rd., Model Colony, Shivaji Nagar, Puna, Maharashtra 411 016, India.

## Career

**T**aught first yoga class, mid-1930s; worked as a traveling yoga instructor in India; began working with classical musicians, 1950s; wrote first book, *Light on Yoga*, 1966; opened yoga institute in Pune, India, 1975.

## Sidelights

**B**.K.S. Iyengar is credited with introducing the practice of yoga, one of the six schools of the ancient Vedic/Hindu philosophy from India, to the Western world. The series of physical postures, or *asanas*, are deemed to be beneficial to the mind, body, and spirit. Iyengar founded his own institute in India, and his devotees went on to open their own schools around the world. Iyengar was named to *Time* magazine's "Time 100" list of heroes and icons for 2004. "Iyengar teaches practitioners to lavish attention on the body," wrote actor Michael Richards in that issue's tribute. "The goal is to tie the mind to the breath and the body, not to an idea."

Iyengar was born in 1918 into a poor family in Karnataka, India, and given the name Bellur Krishnamachar Sundararaja. He was the thirteenth child in his family, and arrived during the global influenza epidemic. His mother had come down with it, and as as a result Iyengar was born weak and frail, and suffered from health problems during his youth. He emerged from bouts of malaria, typhoid, influenza, tuberculosis—all potentially deadly illnesses at the time—even frailer, and doctors claimed he would not live to see his twenty- first birthday. When he was nine years old, his schoolteacher father died, and he went to live with a brother in Bangalore.

As a teenager, Iyengar was stiff as well as frail because he had spent so much time ill in bed. His schoolwork suffered, and he failed his examination in English, which meant he could not go on to college. One of his sisters was married to a famous yoga teacher in India, T. Krishnamacharya, and Iyengar realized that those he knew who practiced yoga seemed much healthier than others who did not. While living with his sister and her husband in Mysore, he asked his brother-in-law to teach him, and Krishnamacharya did so only with reluctance at first, predicting that Iyengar would never be able to meet the physical demands. But Iyengar impressed Krishnamacharya when a favorite student in the household disappeared just before an important demonstration was to take place, and Iyengar quickly learned the postures and executed them perfectly.

Iyengar began to travel with his brother-in-law, giving demonstrations across Karnatak Province. When a group of women requested their own teacher, Krishnamacharya sent Iyengar, though he was the youngest among his students. In time, his health vastly improved, Iyengar would walk from village to village demonstrating yoga. Living like a true ascetic, he ate only rice and water, or sometimes a slice of bread. His family began to worry about him, and a marriage was arranged in 1943, as was the custom. But his new wife, Ramamani, agreed to help him pursue his goal, and he began teaching her yoga.

Due to his intense yoga practice of ten hours a day, Iyengar gained increasing renown in India as a yogi, or yoga master, and famed violinist Yehudi Menuhin heard about his innovative style. In Bombay in 1952, Iyengar received word that Menuhin wanted to meet him, and he traveled seven hours by train to a meeting that was scheduled to last just five minutes. Instead it stretched more than three hours, and eventually led to a series of classes for Menuhin. The health-conscious musician asserted to the media that yoga had improved his concentration and playing. In appreciation of what yoga had done for him, Menuhin presented Iyengar with an Omega wristwatch bearing the inscription "To my best violin teacher—B.K.S. Iyengar." Menuhin also engineered introductions to other musicians in Switzerland and England as well as to Belgium's Queen Mother who became his avid student. In 1956, Iyengar traveled to the United States for the first time, and even demonstrated his asanas for Soviet leader Nikita Khrushchev. He wrote a book, *Light on Yoga,* which was published in 1966 and featured detailed instructions on more than 200 asanas. It would become a standard reference text for the growing number of yoga teachers in the West.

Iyengar was finally able to establish his own institute in Pune, India, in the early 1970s. He named it the Ramamani Iyengar Memorial Institute in honor of his wife, who died in 1973. By the time its doors opened, the Iyengar style of yoga—a strenuous physical workout based on the principles of Patanjali yoga—had caught on with others around the world. Groups began forming in the United States and Europe, and a number of schools and institutes were founded by devotees who had been trained in

Pune. Iyengar's yoga uses props, such as weights, pulleys, stools, and ropes, to help students perfect the postures. Stressing the *pranayama,* or breathing techniques, Iyengar encourages his students to overcome obstacles of the spirit. "The mind is the maker and the mind is the destroyer," he wrote in *Light on Yoga,* according to *Investor's Business Daily* journalist Sonja Carberry. "On one side the mind is making you and on the other side it is destroying you. You must tell the destructive side of the mind to keep quiet—then you will learn."

Iyengar retired from teaching full-time in 1984, when he was 66 years old, but continued the medical classes and the occasional regular class some two decades later. He was still demonstrating his famous headstand, which he could maintain for thirty minutes, well into his eighties. Two of his six children—daughter Geeta and son Prashant—run the school in Pune. His book *Light on Yoga* remained in print nearly 40 years after it was first published, in 18 languages. A new 1995 edition included a foreword by Menuhin. "It's hard to imagine how our yoga would look without Iyengar's contributions," noted *Yoga Journal* writer Fernando Pagés Ruiz, "especially his precisely detailed, systematic articulation of each asana, his research into therapeutic applications, and his multi-tiered, rigorous training system which has produced so many influential teachers."

Yoga vastly increased in popularity in the 1990s, with new schools and styles coming into vogue in the West. Iyengar was dismissive of the trend, especially what he viewed as the yoga-for-profit mindset of some schools. "I think many of my students have followed the advice I gave years ago," he told *New York Times* writer Amy Waldman, "to give more than you take. The commercialism may wash off sometime later." He also recalled in the same interview the prediction of his doctors when he was younger that he would be lucky to reach adulthood. Yoga, he told the newspaper, "has given me a bonus of 65 years."

## Selected writings

*Light on Yoga,* 1966; revised edition, Schocken, 1995.
*Light on Pranayama: The Yogic Art of Breathing,* Crossroad Publishing, 1981.
*Yoga: The Path To Holistic Health,* DK Publishing, 2001.
*The Tree of Yoga,* Shambhala, 2002.

## Sources

### Periodicals

*Investor's Business Daily,* November 30, 2001, p. A4.
*New York Times,* November 22, 1967, p. 49; December 14, 2002, p. A4.
*Time,* April 26, 2004, p. 125.
*Yoga Journal,* May/June 2001.

### Online

"Biography of B.K.S. Iyengar," Iyengar Yoga Resources, http://www.iyengar-yoga.com/bks/biography/ (August 23, 2004).

*—Carol Brennan*

# Jade Jagger

## Jewelry designer

**B**orn Jade Jezebel Jagger, October 21, 1971, in Paris, France; daughter of Mick (a musician) and Bianca Jagger; children: Assisi (daughter), Amba (daughter). *Education:* Studied art history in Florence, Italy.

**Addresses:** *Office*—Garrard & Co., 133 Spring St., 3rd Floor, New York, NY 10012.

## Career

**F**ounded jewelry company, Jade, Inc., 1997; named creative director of Garrard, 2001.

## Sidelights

**J**ade Jagger has led a suitably iconoclastic life as befits the daughter of Rolling Stones lead singer Mick Jagger. Yet she has also forged a career as a successful jewelry designer who serves as the creative director for Garrard, the haute London jewelers. The company, thought to be the world's oldest luxury brand, hired the unmarried, Ibiza-dwelling mother of two for what Shane Watson of London's *Sunday Times* called "her particular flavour of boho bling."

Jagger's very arrival in 1971 was a major international media event. She was born in Paris, France, that October, just a few months after her father wed Nicaraguan beauty Bianca Perez Moreno de Macias. The Stones were at the peak of their fame at the time, and the couple was reportedly already suffering marital issues as a result of lifestyle excesses. Their new daughter went unnamed for two days before they decided on "Jade," because as her father told a reporter, "she is very precious and quite, quite perfect," according to Christopher Andersen's *Jagger Unauthorized.*

Jagger spent her first few years shuttling between her parents' homes in the south of France, New York City, Los Angeles, and London. Though her father was often away on tour or otherwise involved in the business of being a rock star, he was said to have doted on her when she was with him. Jagger saw little of her mother, either, by most accounts, and was often left in the care of nannies. As her daughter grew into a little girl, Bianca Jagger was gaining a reputation as a style-setter and charter member of the jet set, and was regularly photographed at parties and events on both sides of the Atlantic. When Jagger's parents were together, having a child around failed to curb their routine. Parties were the norm, and Jagger grew into a worldly child. The artist Andy Warhol was fascinated by her, according to Andersen's book. "I love Mick and Bianca, but Jade's more my speed," Warhol once said. "I taught her how to color and she taught me how to play Monopoly. She was four and I was forty-four. Mick was jealous. He said I was a bad influence because I gave her champagne."

Jagger's parents divorced by the time she was nine, after an acrimonious financial battle. Custody was awarded to her mother, and her father eventually went on to have several more children with model Jerry Hall. Her mother, meanwhile, became a denizen of New York's famed Studio 54, and once famously entered the storied disco for her thirtieth birthday party astride a white stallion. Jagger's father reportedly removed her from the Spence School in Manhattan when she was 14, worried about the distractions that New York City posed for a teenager. She was installed in an English boarding school outside of London, and her father allegedly insisted upon meeting anyone she dated. Not surprisingly, she chafed at such strictness coming from a parent who had been associated with the worst of rock 'n' roll excesses. In 1988, she was ejected from her $11,000-a-year English school when she was discovered climbing out of room in order to meet her 21-year-old boyfriend, the heir to a British raincoat fortune.

Jagger's father kept watch on her at his Loire Valley chateau before letting her travel to Florence, Italy, to take an art-history course. On the plane, she met Piers Jackson, an art student, and the two became romantically involved. In July of 1992, she gave birth to a daughter, Assisi, followed three years later by a second daughter, whom they named Amba. But Jagger had spoken publicly of her disdain for the institution of marriage, and left Jackson around 1996. She settled on the Spanish resort island of Ibiza, renowned for its heady nightlife, and became involved with another artist, Euan McDonald. For a time, she also dated the great-grandson of a former British prime minister.

Jagger was drawn into jewelry design after serving as an unofficial muse to British designer Matthew Williamson. She began designing her own line of jewelry, and formed a company, Jade, Inc., in 1997. Her Eastern-inspired pieces became a favorite of celebrities and the fashion crowd. After four years in business, Jagger was offered a plum job as creative director for Garrard, a venerable London firm dating back to 1722. It had been the crown jeweler to the British royal family for decades, fashioning tiaras and items like Princess Diana's engagement ring. The company had recently been acquired—along with the clothier Asprey, its sister company—by two Canadian retail moguls, who were interested in making it into a hot new luxury brand.

Jagger does not serve as Garrard's sole designer, but instead works with legendary names in the busi-

ness, including Omar Torres, who was with Van Cleef & Arpels and Bulgari for decades prior. She was eager to give its lines a new verve, but would not be trouncing tradition entirely. "Garrard will be based on classic foundations because this fantastic old brand made some of the most elaborate pieces ever," she said in an interview with *WWD*'s James Fallon. "The jewelry Garrard made for the Queen is outrageous and very avant-garde."

Jagger, whose contract was renewed in 2003 for another two years, approves every line of jewelry the company sells. She also had a say in the design of the Garrard flagship store in London, which features a wall of solid silver and sharkskin display cases. Back home in Ibiza, however, she keeps goats on the property and hangs her laundry on the line to dry. She also has a home in the Kensal Rise area of north London, which her father reportedly bought for her. Disavowing any hints that she has been spoiled by her immensely rich parent, Jagger says she works simply because she has to, she told London's *Guardian* newspaper—and rumors that her father is notoriously frugal with his money seem to bear that out. "We don't have a Jagger salary, you know," she told the paper's Jess Cartner-Morley. "Anyway, what self-respecting 30-year-old would want to be supported by her father, even if he would do it?"

## Sources

### Books

Andersen, Christopher, *Jagger Unauthorized,* Delacorte, 1993.

### Periodicals

*Daily Mail* (London, England), March 16, 2004, p. 26.
*Guardian* (London, England), September 14, 2002, p. 88.
*People,* June 13, 1988, p. 44.
*Sunday Times* (London, England), February 1, 2004, p. 13.
*WWD,* September 20, 2001, p. 6; September 16, 2002, p. 17.

—*Carol Brennan*

# Elfriede Jelinek

## Author and playwright

**B**orn October 20, 1946, in Mürzzuschlag, Steiermark, Austria; daughter of Friedrich (a chemical engineer) and Olga Ilona (Buchner) Jelinek (a personnel director); married Gottfried Hungsberg (an information-systems engineer), June 12, 1974. *Education:* Attended the University of Vienna and Vienna Conservatory of Music, 1960s.

**Addresses:** *Office*—c/o Serpent's Tail Publishing, 4 Blackstock Mews,

## Career

**B**egan writing poetry in the mid-1960s; *Lisas Schatten*, her first collection of verse, published in 1967; first novel, *Wir sind lockvögel baby!*, appeared in 1970; first title to appear in English translation was *The Piano Player*, 1988, which was also made into a 2001 film, *The Piano Teacher*. Has also written extensively for the stage, with works performed regularly in Austria, Germany, and Switzerland.

**Awards:** Austrian Youth Culture award, 1969; Heinrich-Böll Prize, 1986; Heinrich Heine Prize, 2002; Nobel Prize in Literature, 2004; Franz Kafka Prize, Czech Republic, 2004.

## Sidelights

**A**ustrian novelist Elfriede Jelinek was the surprise choice of the Swedish Academy for the 2004 Nobel Prize in Literature. Jelinek's fiction, relatively unknown outside of the German-speaking world, is rife with passages of psychological and physical cruelty, reflecting its author's belief that all humans carry a fair share of inner turmoil, and that the world is a tremendously unjust place as well, especially for women. Elsewhere in her work, Jelinek has been sharply critical of Austrian society and its more conservative elements. "Her charges are carefully researched and laid out in uncompromising and meticulous prose. In the dock are mothers, men, Nazis, the state ... racists and rightwing politicians," asserted Penny Black in a *Financial Times* article. Prior to her Nobel win, Jelinek was perhaps best known as the author of a book that became the 2001 film *The Piano Teacher*, which took a trio of prizes at the Cannes Film Festival.

Jelinek was born on October 20, 1946, when her native Austria was still struggling from the aftereffects of World War II and the country's 1938 annexation by Nazi Germany. Originally from a town in the state of Styria, she grew up in Vienna, where her mother had also been raised. Her mother was a Roman Catholic of mixed Romanian and German heritage, while Jelinek's surname reflected her father's origins in Czechoslovakia. He was Jewish, and had escaped deportation to the Nazi extermination camps because he was a chemist working in a highly sensitive field. Jelinek was their only child, and emerged as a musical prodigy at a young age.

Her childhood years were filled with after-school organ, violin, and flute lessons as well as ballet classes, and she entered the esteemed Vienna Conservatory of Music when she was still in her teens.

By 1964, an 18-year-old Jelinek had completed her Conservatory courses, but suffered a nervous breakdown before her exam date. She later said that writing helped her out of this dark period in her life, and she turned toward a new direction in her studies when she began taking courses in theater and art history at the University of Vienna. She also began to gain a measure of renown for her poetry in Austria, and her first book, a collection of poems titled *Lisas Schatten*, ("Lisa's Shadow") appeared in 1967 and marked her as a rising young literary star.

After completing her Vienna Conservatory of Music exam in the organ, Jelinek began traveling through Europe. She spent time in Berlin and Rome, and worked on her debut novel, *Wir sind lockvögel, baby!* ("We're Decoys, Baby!") Published in 1970, "the novel was heralded in Western Europe as a brilliant literary realization of the aesthetic principles of pop art," noted a *Dictionary of Literary Biography* essay by Frank W. Young. "[It] has neither plot nor characters in the traditional sense. A quartet of metamorphic Viennese proletarians surfaces periodically to mingle with figures from cartoons, comic books, advertisements, and adventure films, and with personalities made famous by the media."

Jelinek's next novel, *Michael. Ein Jugendbuch für de Infantilgesellschaft*, ("Michael: A Young Person's Guide to Infantile Society") came out in 1972. It centers around two teenage girls who are so overly saturated by the media that they seem to become incapable of making decisions for themselves. Two years later, Jelinek had a minor hit in Austria with her play *When the Sun Sinks It's Time to Close Shop*, and also wed an information-systems engineer, Gottfried Hungsberg, that same year.

Jelinek garnered impressive reviews for her 1975 novel, *Die Liebhaberinnen*, which would later be translated into English as *Women as Lovers*. The plot centers around two female friends who head to an Alpine resort town in search of a change of pace and perhaps even romance. But change comes only because of new men in their lives, and does not bring fulfillment in the end. Strongly feminist and even Marxist sentiments about women's roles in contemporary society ran through the novel's subtext.

One of Jelinek's next novels was also hailed as a literary tour-de-force. *Die Ausgesperrten*, published in 1980 and in translation as *Wonderful, Wonderful Times*, follows a group of unhappy teenagers in late 1950s Vienna. Bored with their lives, they commit robberies not for the money, but merely for the thrill. The characters include a twin brother and sister, Rainer and Anna, whose mother is locked in a disturbingly abusive relationship with their father, a former Nazi S.S. guard. Anna is a talented pianist, but falls into lustful relationship with the working-class Hans. Sophie, the fourth member of the group, comes from a well-to-do family. "Chillingly uninvolved, a will-o'-the-wisp … wealthy Sophie is simultaneously the ghost of Austria's past—of the bourgeoisie that welcomed Nazism—and a sign of the prosperous future," noted a review from *Nation* critic Charlotte Innes. "Like fascist acolytes, Rainer and Hans are drawn toward her aura of power."

In the 1980s, Jelinek wrote a number of plays that were performed in Vienna, Germany, and Switzerland, but they also drew a fair amount of criticism for their incendiary themes when they were staged in Austria. These included *Burgtheater: Posse mit Gesang* ("Burgtheater: Satiric Comedy with Music,"), a 1985 work that featured a fictional portrayal of a well-known Austrian actress of a previous generation who had supported the Nazi regime but was quickly forgiven for her transgression after the war. "For all her controversy, Jelinek conforms to a postwar school of exceptional Austrian writers who have urged their countrymen to be honest about themselves," a *Sunday Times* article noted.

In some stagings of Jelinek's plays, boos erupted from the audience, and the merits of her work were usually the subject of ardent debate in the press. Despite the controversial nature of her work, she was awarded West Germany's prestigious Heinrich Böll Prize in 1986. That same year, former United Nations Secretary-General Kurt Waldheim was elected president of Austria, and Jelinek became one of his most vociferous critics. Revelations surfaced that Waldheim had served with a paramilitary unit of the Nazi Party during World War II, though a subsequent investigation cleared him of charges of any war-criminal acts.

Jelinek's plays eventually drew the ire of Austrian cultural authorities, who in 1998 briefly banned their production because of their intense fixation on Austria's Nazi past. Her response was to sharpen her pen even more, and the rise of right-wing politician Jörg Haider and his Freedom Party in 2000 elections prompted Jelinek to declare she would refuse to let any of her plays be performed in Austria as long as he remained in office. Haider had been a staunch critic of her work, and even termed it "degenerate," the term the Nazi regime had attached to modern art back in the 1930s. In December of 2000, Jelinek's monologue *Das Lebewohl* ("The Farewell") was turned into a play by filmmaker Ulrike Ottinger and premiered at the Berliner Ensemble in Berlin. It featured a chorus of 13 actors dressed as Haider in his characteristically exuberant outfits. "They recite the text in stylized Greek-chorus fashion, while performing sporting activities onstage," noted *New York Times* critic Carol Rocamora. "The sight of 13 actors skiing, kayaking, rappelling, and roller-blading, dressed in blinding Kodachrome color, is stunning."

Jelinek came to greater attention outside of German-speaking lands because of her 1983 novel, *Die Klavierspielerin,* which appeared in English translation as *The Piano Player* five years later, and in 2001 was made into a French-language film by Austrian director Michael Haneke. *The Piano Teacher* starred Isabelle Huppert as Erika Kohut, a teacher of advanced piano students at the Vienna Conservatory who descends into an abusive, sadomasochistic relationship with a handsome, arrogant young male student. She lives with her overbearing mother in a small apartment, and the two women argue and even slap one another; at other times, Erika's inner tensions are dramatically depicted in episodes of self-mutilation. Huppert's performance gave Erika a disturbing intensity, and the work took several prizes at the Cannes Film Festival.

*The Piano Teacher* brought Jelinek a measure of international renown, though critics were admittedly confused by the themes in the work, and by what some saw as an autobiographical element—for Jelinek divided her time between a home in Munich with her husband and periods in Vienna with her mother, who was widowed when Jelinek's father died in a psychiatric hospital in 1969. "The book is written in a terse, almost simplistic style, which by the novel's end becomes completely subsumed in obscenity," assessed Ruth Franklin in a *New Republic* article. The filmed images were even more graphic, with the *New Yorker*'s David Denby terming it an "audaciously brilliant" work; Denby admitted that some parts were disturbing indeed, but found it "a seriously scandalous work, beautifully made, and it deserves a sizable audience that might argue over it, appreciate it—even hate it."

Jelinek took another top German literary honor, the Heinrich Heine Prize, in 2002, before her Nobel Prize win was announced in October of 2004. She was only the tenth woman in 103 years of Nobel history to win in the literature category, and there was some surprise in literary circles that a writer whose work was largely unknown outside of the German-speaking world was so honored. Others remarked upon the darkly violent themes in her works, with their sometimes strident strain of feminism. But the Swedish Academy, in bestowing the honor, claimed Jelinek's works deserved merit "for her musical flow of voices and countervoices in novels and plays that with extraordinary linguistic zeal reveal the absurdity of society's clichés and their subjugating power," a *New York Times* article by Alan Riding reported.

Long known for her reclusive nature, Jelinek announced she would not travel to Stockholm for the ceremony because of her agoraphobia. "It doesn't suit me as a person to be put on public display," a *Sunday Times* article quoted her as saying. "I feel threatened by it. I'm not in a mental shape to withstand such ceremonies." Her most recent work at the time, a play titled *Bambiland,* continued her mission to address the injustices in the world. Dealing with the U.S.-led war in Iraq, it contains references to the Abu Ghraib prison-abuse scandal and is intensely critical of American foreign policy. "Unlike others, Jelinek has not calmed down as she has grown older, nor has she sold out," reflected Black in the *Financial Times* critique. "Perhaps her uniquely courageous gaze at what we do not want to see is just what we need."

Jelinek noted that literary fame, even a Nobel Prize, cannot alter the imbalances in the world, especially gender inequalities, which she claims remains similar to that of "master and slave," she told *New York Times* interviewer Deborah Solomon. "A woman's artistic output makes her monstrous to men if she does not know to make herself small at the same time and present herself as a commodity. At best people are afraid of her."

## Selected writings

### Novels

*Lisas Schatten,* Relief Verlag Eilers (Munich), 1967.
*Wir sind lockvögel, baby!,* Rowohlt (Reinbek bei Hamburg), 1970.
*Michael. Ein Jugendbuch für de Infantilgesellschaft,* Rowohlt, 1972.
*Die Liebhaberinnen,* Rowohlt, 1975; translation by Martin Chambers published as *Women as Lovers,* Serpent's Tail, 1994.
*bukolit. hoerroman,* Rhombus (Wien), 1979.
*Die Ausgesperrten,* Rowohlt, 1980; translation by Michael Hulse published as *Wonderful, Wonderful Times,* Serpent's Tail (London), 1990.

*Die Klavierspielerin*, Rowohlt, 1983; translation by Joachim Neugroschel published as *The Piano Player*, Weidenfeld & Nicholson (New York City), 1988.

*Oh Wildnis, oh Schutz vor ihr*, Rowohlt, 1985.

*Lust*, Rowohlt, 1989; translation by Michael Hulse, Serpent's Tail, 1992.

*Totenauberg*, Rowohlt, 1991.

*Die Kinder der Toten*, Rowohlt, 1995.

(With Jutta Heinrich and Adolf-Ernst Meyer) *Sturm und Zwang. Schreiben als Geschlechterkamp*, Klein (Hamburg), 1995.

*Ein Sportstuck*, Rowohlt, 1998.

*Macht Nichts: Eine Kleine Trilogie des Todes*, Rowohlt, 1999.

*Das Lebewohl: 3 kl. Dramen*, Berlin Verlag, 2000.

*Gier: Ein Unterhaltungsroman Elfriede Jelinek*, Rowohlt, 2000.

### Plays

*When the Sun Sinks It's Time to Close Shop*, 1974.

*Was geschah, nachdem Nora ihren Mann verlassen hat*, produced in Graz, 1979.

*Burgtheater: Posse mit Gesang*, 1985.

*Krankheit oder moderne Frauen*, produced in Bonn, 1987.

*Präsident Abendwind, in Anthropophagen im Abendwind*, produced in Berlin, 1988.

*Wolken; Heim*, Steidl (Gottingen), 1993.

*Bambiland*, 2004.

## Sources

### Books

*Dictionary of Literary Biography*, Volume 85: *Austrian Fiction Writers After 1914*, edited by James Hardin and Donald G. Daviau, Gale, 1989, pp. 217-23.

### Periodicals

*Financial Times*, October 11, 2004, p. 13.

*Nation*, March 18, 1991, p. 347.

*New Republic*, November 1, 2004, p. 32.

*New Yorker*, April 1, 2002, p. 98.

*New York Times*, May 13, 2001, p. 10; October 8, 2004, p. A3; November 21, 2004, p. 31.

*Sunday Times* (London, England), October 10, 2004, p. 19.

*Times Literary Supplement*, February 7, 1970, p. 702.

—*Carol Brennan*

# Scarlett Johansson

## Actress

**B**orn November 22, 1984, in New York, NY; daughter of Karsten (an architect) and Melanie (a business manager) Johansson.

**Addresses:** *Agent*—Scott Lambert, William Morris Agency, 151 El Camino Dr., Beverly Hills, CA 90212.

## Career

**A**ctress in films, including: *North,* 1994; *Just Cause,* 1995; *Manny & Lo,* 1996; *If Lucy Fell,* 1996; *Home Alone 3,* 1997; *Fall,* 1997; *The Horse Whisperer,* 1998; *My Brother the Pig,* 1999; *Ghost World,* 2000; *An American Rhapsody,* 2001; *The Man Who Wasn't There,* 2001; *Eight Legged Freaks,* 2002; *Lost in Translation,* 2003; *Girl with a Pearl Earring,* 2003; *In Good Company,* 2004; *The SpongeBob Squarepants Movie* (voice), 2004; *A Good Woman,* 2004; *A Love Song for Bobby Long,* 2004; *The Perfect Score,* 2004; *The Black Dahlia,* 2005; *Match Point,* 2005; *The Island,* 2005. Stage appearances include: *Sophistry,* off-Broadway, 1993.

**Member:** Academy of Motion Picture Arts and Sciences.

## Sidelights

**S**carlett Johansson seemed to be calling the shots in her own impressive career before she could even legally vote. Pacing herself through adolescence with a series of increasingly larger and more complex roles, Johansson was able to choose her own pet projects not long after what critics called an understated but luminous performance in the 2003 hit, *Lost in Translation,* at the age of 19. Far removed from the orbit of most teen actors of her generation, Johansson possesses a slightly cosmopolitan air that comes across in many of her roles, and has been hailed as one of Hollywood's top new-millennium stars. "Johansson's is a sensibility, a cool factor, an instinct for the Zeitgeist, that animates her career, and it's something you either have or you don't," asserted Eve Epstein in a *Variety* article. "Johansson has it; Tara Reid doesn't."

Johansson and her twin brother, Hunter, were born in November of 1984 in New York City. Their father, Karsten, is the Danish-born architect son of Ejner Johansson, a well-known writer in Denmark. Johansson and her brother arrived into a family that already included a stepbrother as well as an older brother and sister. Their parents separated when Johansson was around 13, and her mother, Melanie, would become her manager. Lured into the performing arts at an early age, Johansson's stage debut came at the age of eight when she appeared in an off-Broadway play, *Sophistry,* that featured a young Ethan Hawke. A year later, in 1994, she made her feature film debut in *North,* which starred a young Elijah Wood, years before his *Lord of the Rings* fame.

Johansson attended the Professional Children's School in New York City, which provided her with a more flexible academic schedule so that she could continue to take film roles. Her next came in 1995's *Just Cause*, a thriller with Sean Connery and Laurence Fishburne. But it was her lead as a savvy eleven-year-old girl in *Manny & Lo* in 1996 that earned the preteen her first critical accolades. The small independent film, written and directed by Lisa Krueger, followed the travails of two sisters who run off from their respective foster homes. Aleksa Palladino played Lo, Manny's older sister, who is pregnant, and the two manage to find shelter in an newly built, uninhabited subdivision. Johansson's Manny senses they need a mother figure as Lo's due date nears, and they kidnap a maternity-clothing store saleswoman (Mary Kay Place), and shackle her ankles in the vacation home they have taken over. The *New Republic*'s Stanley Kauffmann gave Johansson one of her first reviews, asserting that the film's "key performance comes from Manny.... She has a lovely core of serenity and concern. It's easy to teach bright children to mimic, but Krueger has evoked a faculty of truth in Johansson. I hope we'll see more of her translucent face."

Johansson even earned a nomination for an industry award from a group of West Coast independent filmmakers for *Manny & Lo*. Though she appeared in a few other films over the next few years, she seemed to choose her parts carefully. After missing out on the *The Parent Trap* lead that went instead to Lindsay Lohan, she was cast by director Robert Redford in *The Horse Whisperer*, a much-anticipated adaptation of a best-selling novel that starred Redford and Kristin Scott Thomas. Johansson played a young teen, Grace, who is out riding horses with a friend in the Connecticut winter when the film opens. They encounter an icy slope leading toward a highway and oncoming traffic, and Grace tries to save her friend from a collision with a truck. The friend—played by an equally young Kate Bosworth—dies, Grace loses her leg, and her beloved horse, Pilgrim, is maimed. Thomas was cast as Grace's brittle mother, a New York magazine editor, who takes Grace and Pilgrim to Montana, where an unofficial equine therapist (Redford), is enlisted to help both horse and teenager recover. The film earned near-unanimous bad reviews, with *Newsweek*'s Jeff Giles remarking that the "opening scenes are brutal and beautifully choreographed. Then Grace and the mother she hates go West, and the movie goes south—it's punishingly dull for fully half of its two hours and 45 minutes."

Thanks to her performance as the sullen Grace, Johansson was offered a number of big roles, few of which appealed to her. She characterized them as "the deformed ballet dancer who becomes a cheerleader who marries a prom king and decides to work for a Third World country," she joked in an interview with Leslie Felperin for London's *Independent* newspaper. "But I was in school the whole time after that. I didn't have to support myself, so I didn't have to take those roles, I could let other people do them."

Johansson's first almost-adult role came in *Ghost World,* a well-received 2000 film based on a cult-comic series by Daniel Clowes. Johansson played Rebecca, the best friend and fellow loner to Thora Birch's Enid, both recent high-school graduates. The girls seem to loathe everything in their suburban Southern California landscape, and dream of escape. Their friendship seems to falter when Rebecca, less proud than Enid, takes a low-end job in order to move out of the house. Though Johansson's part was overshadowed by Birch's, whose relationship with a geeky middle-aged record collector moves the plot forward, critics gave *Ghost World* high marks and took notice of Johansson's pitch-perfect portrayal of the droll outsider.

Johansson made two films that were released in 2001. *An American Rhapsody* centered around another at-odds teenage girl, this one separated from her parents during the Cold War, and reunited with them at the age of six in America. Johansson's Suzanne then returns to Budapest to discover her roots. Also in 2001 Johansson played a vixenish teen who seduces Billy Bob Thornton in *The Man Who Wasn't There*, a film by the Coen brothers. The sole film she did for 2002 was *Eight Legged Freaks*, a spider-horror flick that also starred David Arquette.

In 2002, Johansson graduated from the Professional Children's School, and took what would become her most significant role to date: as Charlotte in *Lost in Translation*. The acclaimed film, which won writer/director Sofia Coppola an Academy Award for Best Screenplay, featured Johansson as a young newlywed, a Yale-degreed philosophy major, who finds herself left alone a great deal when she travels to Tokyo with her photographer husband, played by Giovanni Ribisi, for his assignment. Drinking in the hotel bar, Charlotte strikes up an unusual friendship with a famous American actor, played by Bill Murray, whose faltering career has brought him there to collect a princely sum for appearing in a Japanese whiskey commercial. Coppola had written the part of Charlotte with Johansson in mind, though they had met just once.

*Lost in Translation* made Johansson a bona-fide Hollywood star. Critics delivered enthusiastic reviews for her performance, with *Rolling Stone*'s Peter

Travers asserting she had "matured into an actress of smashing loveliness and subtle grace." Even the veteran comic actor Murray, noted David Ansen in *Newsweek,* has "never been better, and part of the credit goes to Johansson. They're oddly but perfectly matched. Her directness opens him up, pierces his solitude, softens him. Their connection is what this small, unforgettable movie is about: a transient, magical, restorative meeting of souls."

Filmmakers seemed eager to cast Johansson for her ability to dominate a scene, even in the absence of dialogue, and this was showcased to maximum effect in *Girl with a Pearl Earring,* released for the Christmas 2003 season. Based on the Tracy Chevalier novel of the same name, the story takes place in the household of renowned Dutch painter Johannes Vermeer, and imagines the backstory behind one of his most famous works. Johansson played Griet, the servant who is drafted into sitting for the portrait of the title, a turn of events which greatly upsets Vermeer's wife. Colin Firth was cast as the brooding Vermeer, and though the production and cinematography won immense praise, critics found the story slim and predictable. "It's to Johansson's credit that she alone pulls something plausible out of her character," declared Erica Abeel in a *Film Journal International* review. "Her haunting beauty is a throwback to an earlier century, her screen presence luminous, her stillness and intelligence mesmerizing."

On screen, older men seemed to fall easily for Johansson's characters, and comments she made in some interviews were misinterpreted as an assertion that she disliked dating men her own age. "I never said that," she clarified to *Esquire* writer Chris Jones. "I've just been fortunate enough to work with some incredible older male actors. And that's turned into, 'I can only date men over 30.' Now I'm stuck with the geezers." However, she has been romantically linked with Benicio del Toro, 17 years her senior, and Jared Leto, who was 13 when Johansson was born. Her next film role, however, had her romancing Topher Grace, just six years her senior. Their relationship complicated the plot of *In Good Company,* which starred Dennis Quaid as her father and Grace as her father's whiz-kid new boss.

Johansson's famously husky voice served to capture the character of Mindy in *The SpongeBob Squarepants Movie* in 2004, and she also appeared in *A Love Song for Bobby Long* that same year. It was a film she had wanted to make since she was 15 years old, and told her agent so when she signed with the prestigious William Morris Agency. The moody New Orleans-set drama, which also starred John Travolta, was little seen and took in just over $28,000 on its opening weekend on eight United States screens in January of 2005.

Johansson's next projects were likely to fare better: she was set to appear in *The Black Dahlia* in 2005, a Brian DePalma film based on the James Ellroy novel about a notorious Hollywood murder in the 1940s. She also took on a sci-fi thriller, *The Island,* opposite Ewan McGregor and directed by Michael Bay (*Pearl Harbor*), and a Woody Allen film, *Match Point.* Another project she hopes to be able to bring to the screen is a remake of the 1958 Natalie Wood film, *Marjorie Morningstar.*

Johansson's bee-stung lips, voluptuous figure, and glamorous red-carpet gowns have given her some secondary fame as one of Hollywood's newest fashion icons. In 2004, she signed with Calvin Klein's Eternity Moment fragrance to appear in its ad campaign, and was the subject of flattering profiles in fashion magazines like *InStyle* and *Harper's Bazaar,* which put her on its January 2005 cover. Savvy enough to realize the pitfalls of celebrity, Johansson tries to keep the two realms separate. "Being a movie star is a quality that somebody sort of embodies, and being a celebrity is something that people give to you," she told Graham Fuller in an *Interview* profile. "It has to do with being recognizable, as opposed to something that people recognize in you. I just hope to make good movies."

Johansson had actually applied to New York University's Tisch School of the Arts for the fall 2003 semester, but her application was rejected. Her ambitions lie elsewhere, however, and she has told more than one journalist that she someday hopes to move behind the camera. "I definitely want to make a big epic film, not necessarily *Gladiator,* but a larger-than-life subject," she told the *Independent*'s Felperin, "and also a story I've had experience in, like a New York story, a coming-of-age sort of thing.... I want to make all kinds of movies, I'm totally ambitious."

## Sources

*Esquire,* February 2005, p. 64.
*Film Journal International,* November 2003, p. 55.
*Harper's Bazaar,* January 2005, p. 72.
*Independent* (London, England), January 9, 2004, p. 8.
*Interview,* September 2003, p. 188.
*New Republic,* August 12, 1996, p. 26.
*Newsweek,* May 18, 1998, p. 74; September 15, 2003, p. 64.
*New York Times,* September 7, 2003, p. AR39; December 12, 2003, p. E19.
*Philadelphia Inquirer,* August 23, 2001.
*Rolling Stone,* September 8, 2003.
*Time,* August 19, 1996, p. 68.
*Variety,* December 8, 2003, p. S38.

—*Carol Brennan*

# Abigail Johnson

**President of Fidelity's Employer Services Company**

**B**orn Abigail Pierrepont Johnson, December 19, 1961, in Boston, MA; daughter of Edward C. (Ned) Johnson III (an investment-services company executive); married to Christopher J. McKown (a company president); children: two daughters. *Education:* Hobart and William Smith College, B.A., 1984; Harvard University, M.B.A., 1988.

**Addresses:** *Office*—Fidelity Investments, 82 Devonshire St., Boston, MA 02109-3605.

## Career

**A**nswered phones in the customer-service department of Fidelity Investments, 1980; research associate with Booz, Allen and Hamilton; joined Fidelity Investments as a stock analyst, 1988; became a portfolio manager; became associate director, 1994; named senior vice president, 1998; became president of investment services, 2001; named president of Fidelity's Employer Services Company, 2005.

## Sidelights

**F**ew outside the financial world know Abigail Johnson's name, and that is by design. Johnson runs the employer services division of Fidelity Investments, the Boston-based powerhouse founded by her grandfather. In 2004, her company managed a staggering $893 billion in assets on the mutual-fund market, and thanks to that she is considered the most influential woman among the ranks of American financial executives. Despite her status, Johnson shuns publicity and rarely gives interviews.

"Anyone who has run money knows that blowing your own horn is usually a way of calling a top on your own performance," she told *BusinessWeek* writer Geoffrey Smith.

Born on December 19, 1961, in Boston, Abigail Pierrepont Johnson is descended from an old Boston Brahmin family whose roots in New England commerce date back to the early 1800s. In 1946, her grandfather, Edward C. Johnson II, founded Fidelity Management and Research (FMR) as a mutual-fund firm. Mutual funds are groups of stock-market investors whose money is pooled and managed by a professional portfolio manager, or team of managers. Fidelity emerged as one of the leading firms in this finance sector, which enjoyed phenomenal growth alongside the general boom in stock-market investing during the 1980s and '90s.

Johnson's father, Edward C. (Ned) Johnson III, took over the company in 1977, when the elder Johnson retired. Her first job at the company came when she was just out of high school in 1980, answering phones in its customer-service department. At Hobart and William Smith College, she majored in art history, but went on to Harvard Business School, from which she earned her M.B.A. in 1988. She joined Fidelity Investments full-time as lowly stock analyst that same year, just as her father had once done, and was assigned to the Select Industrial Equipment Fund, a decidedly unglamorous division. Johnson was eventually promoted to port-folio manager, and proved herself an able fund over-seer who achieved solid, though not extravagant, results for Fidelity's thousands of clients.

In 1994, Johnson was made an associate director of the company, and a year later, her father divested himself of a large chunk of voting shares, handing them over to FMR, the parent company. This left Johnson as the largest shareholder—though the company is still a privately held one—and the busi-ness media predicted that her father's move was a sign that she was now in line to someday succeed him as company chair. In 1998, she was promoted to senior vice president. By this time she was also married and a mother of two; her husband, Christo-pher J. McKown, is a health-care information com-pany co-founder and president.

In May of 2001, Fidelity announced that Johnson was succeeding Robert C. Pozen as president of Fidelity's mutual-fund division. There were rumors of personality conflicts between Pozen and some of the company's fund managers, and the news came as somewhat of a surprise to Wall Street. Johnson's position made her number three at the company, af-ter her father and chief operating officer Robert L. Reynolds, but she was in charge of a significant area, investment operations. The 280 mutual funds run by Fidelity were in trouble at the time, with a bear market—when the value of stocks traded de-clines at a steady rate, and investors struggle to earn money instead of lose it—in full swing by then, with little sign of abating.

Fidelity had been losing market share over the past few years, with a slew of competitors like the Van-guard Group gaining new customers via savvy mar-keting strategies. Still, Johnson's company remained an industry powerhouse. It was a $1.4 trillion em-pire, holding nearly $900 billion of the American mutual-fund business, plus another $100 billion in fund business from overseas, for some 17 million investors. "Its investment decisions are felt in the stockmarket, and at companies in which it holds shares," an article in the *Economist* noted. "Fidelity's voice is heard in the proxy motions that are filed by disgruntled investors, and in the reorganisations that follow bankruptcies."

Johnson's approach was likely to vary from her father's, some industry analysts theorized; Ned Johnson, a collector of Asian art, was a follower of *kaizen,* a Japanese management philosophy that ad-vised growth in small increments—a direct contrast to the American penchant for growth by mergers and acquisitions. Johnson, by contrast, liked con-temporary art, and voiced a different view on the matter in a rare interview. "Sometimes you can gradually improve things," she reflected in the *Busi-nessWeek* article by Smith. "But sometimes, they don't work, and you've just got to just say: Let's grind this baby to a halt."

Fidelity also differentiated itself from other mutual fund companies by letting its portfolio managers buy and sell more aggressively on the market, rather than just following the stock market indices, as many of its competitors did. Johnson encouraged her managers to be even more aggressive—though she admitted it was a chancier strategy, she told *BusinessWeek*'s Smith. "It's never obvious what a smart risk is, which is why we hire smart people." Yet the mutual-fund business was just the part of Fidelity by then, thanks to her father's aggressive expansion. It was involved in venture capital, real estate, temporary employment, and even a motor-coach business. Johnson's younger brother, Edward C. Johnson, is an executive with the real-estate divi-sion, and her sister's husband also holds a manage-ment position. On May 2, 2005, Johnson was named president of Fidelity's Employer Services Company, which provides retirement, benefit, and human re-sources services to companies.

Johnson is one of a handful of women to run a mutual-fund company, among the 400-plus firms that make up the market. She rarely gives inter-views, but is a well-known figure at Fidelity's Bos-ton headquarters, where she is called "Abby." After eleven-hour days at the office, she heads home to her grandfather's former abode, located on a subur-ban Boston road. She and her family also spend time on Nantucket Island in the off-duty hours. Thanks to her family's Fidelity fortune, *Forbes* esti-mated her net worth at $10 billion, which made her the fourth-richest woman in United States in 2001. Her company is so powerful that it has spawned its own independent press, such as the *Fidelity Insight* newsletter. Its editor, Eric Kobren, gave Johnson high marks for her old-fashioned Yankee values and aversion to publicity. "She's cool and calm, and she works hard every day," Kobren told *Time* journalist Daniel Kadlec. "She doesn't have that air of being one of the richest people in the world."

## Sources

*BusinessWeek,* July 8, 2002, p. 56.
*Economist,* May 26, 2001, p. 2.
*Money,* October 1995, p. 52.
*New York Times,* May 22, 2001, p. C1; May 3, 2005.
*Time,* April 26, 2004, p. 81.

—*Carol Brennan*

# Beverly Johnson

## Fashion model, actress, and activist

**B**orn October 13, 1952, in Buffalo, NY; daughter of an electrician father and Gloria (a surgical technician) Johnson; married Billy Potter, 1971 (divorced, 1973); married Danny Sims (a music producer and publisher), 1977 (divorced); children: Anansa (from second marriage). *Education:* Studied criminal justice at Northeastern University, c. 1969-72; studied acting with Lee Strasberg.

**Addresses:** *Office*—c/o Warner Books, 1271 Avenue of the Americas, New York, NY 10020.

## Career

**W**orked as a fashion model, 1971—; appeared in *Glamour*, 1971; first African-American model to appear on the cover of American *Vogue*, 1974, and French *Elle*, 1975; appeared in television commercials and print advertisements; worked as an actress, c. 1977—. Film appearances include: *Deadly Hero*, 1976; *The Baron*, 1977; *Ashanti*, 1979; *The Meteor Man*, 1993; *National Lampoon's Loaded Weapon*, 1993; *A Brilliant Disguise*, 1994; *Crossworlds*, 1996; *True Vengeance* (video release), 1997; *How to Be a Player*, 1997; *54*, 1998; *Down 'n' Dirty*, 2000; *Crossroads*, 2002; *Red Shoe Diaries 15: Forbidden Zone* (video release), 2002. Television movie appearances include: *Crisis in Sun Valley*, 1978; *The Sky is Gray*, 1980; *The Cover Girl Murders*, 1993; *Perry Mason Mystery: The Case of the Wicked Wives*, 1993; *Ray Alexander: A Menu for Murder*, 1995. Television episodic appearances include: *Emergency!*, 1976; *Hunter*, 1990; *Law & Order*, 1992, 1993; *Martin*, 1993; *Lois & Clark*, 1994; *The Wayans Bros.*, 1995; *The Red Shoe Diaries*, 1996; *The Parent 'Hood*, 1996; *Arli$$*, 1996; *Sabrina,*

*the Teenage Witch*, 1997; *3rd Rock from the Sun*, 1998. Wrote *True Beauty: Secrets of Radiant Beauty for Women of Every Age and Color*, 1994. Served as spokesperson for Marine Optical, 1995; designed a line of costume jewelry, 1998; designed a line of wigs, The Beverly Johnson Skin Care System, her own doll, and other products; spokesperson for uterine health, 1999—.

## Sidelights

**O**ne of the first successful African-American fashion models, Beverly Johnson became a celebrity because of her success in the 1970s and 1980s. The 5'9" Johnson was the first black woman to appear on the cover of American *Vogue* and French *Elle* magazines. Over the course of her career, she was featured on more than 500 magazine covers and in numerous advertising campaigns. Johnson used her success as a model to launch a second career as an actress and to become an advocate for several social issues.

Johnson was born on October 13, 1952, in Buffalo, New York, where she was raised. She was the daughter of an electrician father and his wife, Gloria, who worked as a surgical technician. Johnson received her education at School 74, Fillmore Junior High, and Bennett High School in Buffalo. As a child, she was gawky and tall, and believed her younger sister was far more beautiful. Johnson became very interested in sports, including swimming. She won a number of swimming championships, and nearly made the U.S. national team in the 100-yard freestyle for the 1968 Summer Olympics in Mexico City, Mexico.

After graduating from high school, Johnson moved to Boston, Massachusetts, to enter Northeastern University around 1969. She had a full scholarship and studied criminal justice, with the intention of becoming a lawyer. While still a college student, she started modeling with the encouragement of friends. Johnson also had somewhat tumultuous personal life, marrying her first husband, Billy Potter, in 1971. The couple divorced in 1973.

In the early 1970s, Johnson gave up her studies at Northeastern to focus on modeling full time in New York City. This phase of her modeling career began with much difficulty. She applied to the famous Ford modeling agency, but was turned down. Johnson then turned to a modeling agency that specialized in African-American models called Black Beauty. This company was also not interested in signing her. Finally, Johnson went to *Glamour* magazine in 1971. She walked into the office and was immediately hired for a shoot. The issue went on to set sales records. However, from the first big job, Johnson was told to lose weight. She weighed about 135 pounds at the time, and by not eating, got her weight as low as 103 pounds.

Johnson built on this success, appearing on the cover of *Glamour* five more times over the next two years. By the mid-1970s, she was an in-demand magazine model. One highlight of her career was her appearance as the first African-American cover model for *Vogue* in the United States. Johnson appeared on the cover of the August 1974 issue, also a best-selling issue. She was quoted on the website for clothing line Peter Nygard Signature as saying, "Becoming the first African American to grace the cover of *Vogue* magazine in August 1974 was a historical movement in time, the color barrier was broken...." Johnson again appeared on the cover of *Vogue* in June of 1975.

Johnson broke the barrier again for the French edition of *Elle*, in 1975. Over the course of her career, Johnson appeared on more than 500 magazine covers, including other leading magazines such as *Cosmopolitan* and *Essence*. Johnson's career was not lim-

ited to print work. She also worked as a runway model for designers such as Halston, and appeared in television commercials. For example, Johnson had a role in ads for National Airlines, singing a well-known jingle of the time, "Come On and Fly Me." In addition, she appeared in print ads for Virginia Slims cigarettes and was a spokesperson for Avon cosmetics.

In the mid-1970s, Johnson was part of a trend where black models were considered hot, and she was regarded as arguably the most successful African-American female model of the time. At the time, she told *Newsweek*, "I see the inspiration of black women being lifted up all over when they look at me and that's a super feeling." Johnson wanted to build on her popularity with black women by creating her own brand of cosmetics targeted at them. She also thought about making her own doll. Both ideas came to fruition years later.

Johnson's success in the 1970s, however, transcended race. She signed with the Ford agency, and was one of the highest-paid models in the industry making about $100 per hour for advertising work and $125 per hour for editorial modeling. Johnson saw herself as more than just a black model. She told Ted Morgan in the *New York Times Magazine*, "I've in the business for four years. There's not a model, black or white, who's done what I've done in such a short time. It's so, and I think I should say it."

As Johnson's modeling career reached its height in the mid-1970s, she wanted to move into acting as well. To that end, she studied acting with Lee Strasberg, a well-known acting teacher. Her future in feature films looked bright. She appeared in several in the late 1970s, including 1976's *Deadly Hero*, 1977's *The Baron*, and 1979's *Ashanti*. In the last film, she played Dr. Anansa Linderby. Johnson also had roles in television movies including 1978's *Crisis in Sun Valley* and a guest-starring role on *Emergency!* in 1976.

Johnson's acting career stalled in the 1980s as her personal life became more complicated. In 1977, she married her second husband, Danny Sims, a music producer and publisher. The couple had a daughter, Anansa, before separating in 1979. When the couple's divorce became final, Johnson lost custody of her daughter to her former husband. While Johnson had some visitation rights, she felt restricted from seeing her daughter. Johnson fought for custody of her daughter for nearly a decade, spending nearly all her money and causing her much emotional distress. She also had some health concerns, including thyroid problems, perhaps caused by dieting to keep her weight down. Johnson later admitted that she was anorexic and bulimic. To address these issues, she joined Overeaters Anonymous in 1986.

By the end of the 1980s, Johnson had moved to Los Angeles to further her acting career. She soon gained custody of her daughter without a fight. When Sims moved to London, England, in the late 1980s for business reasons, Johnson's daughter began spending long periods of time with her mother in Los Angeles, beginning in 1990. Anansa soon decided she wanted to live with her mother full time in 1992. Sims agreed because his business situation had changed and his work required much travel and living abroad. By the age of 13, Anansa Sims decided she wanted a modeling career as well. She signed with the same agency which then represented her mother, Wilhelmina.

Johnson's acting career took off again in the late 1980s, and into the 1990s and 2000s. She appeared in small roles in feature films including 1993's *Meteor Man* and *National Lampoon's Loaded Weapon*, playing Doris Luger in the latter. Johnson went on to appear in 1997's *How to Be a Player*. She played Sandra Collins in *Down 'n' Dirty* and Kit's mother in the Britney Spears film *Crossroads*, both in 2000.

Johnson also worked in television in this time period. In 1993, she appeared in two television movies, *The Cover Girl Murders*, as Michaela and as Jane Marlowe Morrison in a *Perry Mason Mystery: The Case of the Wicked Wives*. In addition to guest-starring appearances on shows like *Law & Order*, *Martin*, and *Lois & Clark*, Johnson also appeared on the hit NBC situation comedy *3rd Rock from the Sun* with other former models in 1998. She played a character named Prell. Johnson's ambitions were not limited to acting. Summing up her career at the time, she told Karen Brady of *Buffalo News*, "I love comedy. I have been working on a lot of auditions for films. I would like to do more in the line of producing. I know how to get people together."

In the mid to late 1990s, Johnson also became an author. In 1994, she published a book called *True Beauty: Secrets of Radiant Beauty for Women of Every Age and Color*. This tome was a guide to inner and outer beauty targeted at minority audiences, including African Americans and others. Johnson wrote it to address self-esteem issues as well as outward appearance topics specific to minority women, including bleaching and skin issues. Johnson included

pictures of many of the women in her life, including her daughter and her mother. In the late 1990s, she also wrote a novel *Top Model*, though she could not find a publisher.

Business ventures also consumed some of Johnson's focus in this time period. In 1995, she licensed her name to be featured on a line of eyewear. Though Johnson did not create the glasses, she approved the designs. The line of eyewear was primarily intended for women of color, and Johnson served as spokesperson for the company, Marine Optical. The glasses were sold at Montgomery Ward and Sears. In addition to eyewear, Johnson also had her own line of cosmetics called The Beverly Johnson Skin Care System that was sold on a home shopping channel. She also had a line of wigs and extensions that featured her name and were sold through beauty shops and other supply houses. In 1998, Johnson added a line of costume jewelry. Johnson also had her own doll as part of the Real Model Collection sold by Matchbox Toys.

Throughout her career, Johnson had been very active in charity work and speaking out about health issues. Beginning in the 1980s, she worked as an AIDS activist. Some of her activism was related to her own health problems. In 1997, she went public with the fact that she had been suffering from panic attacks for many years, beginning in college. In the early 2000s, Johnson announced that she had had a hysterectomy that she probably did not need. She became a paid spokesperson for Johnson & Johnson during a uterine health information campaign. Johnson shared that she had problems with fibroids as early as 1997, but continued pain led to the hysterectomy. She wanted other women to become informed about their choices, including the fact that a hysterectomy would led to full-blown menopause. Recognizing her contributions to the world of fashion and activism, President Bill Clinton named her goodwill ambassador to the fashion industry in the late 1990s.

Despite her many ups and downs professionally and personally, Johnson remained self-assured. She told *More* magazine, "I had my midlife crisis at twenty-six. It's the age at which a model starts to feel the pressure of being past her prime. So while women who are turning forty or fifty may be feeling it now, I've done it already."

## Selected writings

*True Beauty: Secrets of Radiant Beauty for Women of Every Age and Color*, Warner Books, 1994.

# Sources

## Periodicals

*Buffalo News* (New York), November 24, 1997, p. 1B.
*Chicago Sun-Times,* May 18, 1994, sec. 2, p. 46; December 27, 1995, p. 43.
*Daily News* (New York), January 2, 1996, p. 14.
*Ebony,* July 2003, p. 69.
*More,* October 2002, p. 40.
*Newsweek,* May 5, 1975, p. 68.
*New York Times Magazine,* August 17, 1975, pp. 1014-18.
*People,* August 10, 1992, p. 85; January 11, 1993, p. 80; July 31, 2000, p. 88; June 2, 2003, pp. 123-24.
*Record* (Bergen County, NJ), January 25, 1998, p. Y2.

*Rocky Mountain News* (Denver, CO), February 13, 1997, p. 54A.
*USA Today,* July 2, 1997, p. 2D.

## Online

"Beverly Johnson," Internet Movie Database, http://www.imdb.com/name/nm0424588/ (November 2, 2004).
"Beverly Johnson—Portrait of a Lady," Nygard.com, http://www3.nygard.com/corporate/news/beverly_johnson.html (November 4, 2004).
"Beverly Johnson Spotlights Hysterectomy Awareness," DrDonnica.com, http://www.drdonnica.com/celebrities/00006539.htm (November 3, 2004).

*—A. Petruso*

# Edward P. Jones

*AP/Wide World Photos*

## Author and professor

Born Edward Paul Jones, October 5, 1950, in Arlington, VA. *Education:* Holy Cross College, BA, 1972; University of Virginia, MFA, 1981.

**Addresses:** *Home*—4300 Old Dominion Dr., No. 914, Arlington, VA 22207.

## Career

Worked for *Science* magazine; worked at the American Association for the Advancement of Science; sold his first story to *Essence,* 1975; columnist and proofreader for *Tax Notes,* 1990-2002; author, 1992—; guest instructor at George Washington University, University of Maryland, and Princeton University, 2000s.

**Awards:** National Book Foundation Award, for *Lost in the City,* 1992; Ernest Hemingway Foundation/ PEN Award, for *Lost in the City,* 1992; grant, Lannan Foundation; grant, National Endowment for the Arts; National Book Critics Circle for *The Known World,* 2004; Pulitzer Prize for fiction, for *The Known World,* 2004.

## Sidelights

In 1992 Edward P. Jones burst on the literary scene with his much-hailed collection of short stories called *Lost in the City,* which was nominated for a National Book Award. Then after a decade-long silence, Jones published his first novel, *The Known World.* Initially catching reviewers' attention for its unusual subject matter—the ownership of slaves by a black master in the antebellum South—the novel soon demonstrated its literary qualities as well. Reviewers lauded Jones for the novel's epic grandeur, vernacular, and lyrical prose, fully realized characters, and lively dialogue. Comparing Jones favorably with William Faulkner and Toni Morrison, several critics went so far as to dub Jones a major new force in Southern writing. For his novel *The Known World,* Jones won the Pulitzer Prize.

Edward Paul Jones was born on October 5, 1950, in Arlington, Virginia. The only son of an illiterate hotel maid and kitchen worker, Jones grew up in his mother's sphere because his father had drifted out of his life when he was a preschooler. After attending Catholic school for kindergarten and part of first grade, Jones was educated in Washington public schools. His interest in literature was sparked early, yet it was some time before he realized that African Americans, like their white counterparts, were writing works of literary merit. "I always loved reading," Jones recalled to Robert Fleming of *Publishers Weekly.* Comic books formed the mainstay of his reading until as a 13 year old, he discovered novels. "When I started reading black writers, I discovered two books that had a great impact on me: Ethel Waters' *His Eye Is on the Sparrow* and Richard Wright's *Native Son.* I felt as if they were talking to me, since both books had people in them that I knew in my own life. I was shocked to learn black people could write such things."

On a scholarship, Jones studied at Holy Cross College, in Worcester, Massachusetts. Many writers begin writing seriously during their college years, and Jones was no exception, writing his first fiction during his sophomore year. Although a professor encouraged his efforts, Jones did not consider writing as a possible career then, or even after his graduation in 1972, when he returned to Washington, D.C. Living with his terminally ill mother, he worked in various positions, including a stint with *Science* magazine. Once upon reading a short story in his sister's copy of *Essence*, Jones decided he could write better stories, and during the after-work hours at the American Association for the Advancement of Science, he typed them up. In 1975 he sold his first story to *Essence* at a particularly difficult time in his life—after his mother's death and when he was between jobs and living in a city mission.

After reading *Dubliners,* a collection of short stories by James Joyce, Jones decided to give Washington, D.C., a similar treatment with *Lost in the City.* As he told Carole Burns in an interview for the *Washington Post,* "I went away to college and people have a very narrow idea of what Washington is like. They don't know that it's a place of neighborhoods, for example, and I set out to give a better picture of what the city is like—the other city." While working at various jobs and attending graduate school at the University of Virginia, Jones wrote these realistic and personal stories over a period of three years, although he had been thinking about them for years before then. He wanted each story to be unique in its characters and situations, rather than linked to each other. "Every major character, and even most minor characters, would be different, so that each story would be distinct from the others," he recalled to Lawrence P. Jackson of *African American Review.* "I didn't want someone to come along and be able to say that the stories are taken out of the same bag. I suppose that is one of the reasons that it has taken me so long."

With stories bearing such titles as "The First Day," about a girl's first day of kindergarten, "The Girl Who Raised Pigeons," about a girl's relationship with her birds, "The Store," which tells of a man who tries to make a success of a neighborhood grocery, "His Mother's House," which recounts how a mother takes care of a home her son has bought by selling crack, and "Young Lions," about the criminal element in the District of Columbia, Jones clearly showed his talent. Although only one story, "The

First Day," has a clearly autobiographical element, the others recapture the life Jones knew growing up in the 1950s and 1960s, especially the rich vernacular of his mother and her associates. "I remember black people's poetic language," he told *African American Review*'s Jackson. "Over years and years you absorb all of this stuff." Yet, according to Jones, writers must use such language judiciously: "I grew up with this wonderful way of talking. One of the things I remember about reading Zora Neale Hurston was that in certain novels you hear it too much. If you have lines like that in every paragraph, it's too rich."

Even the city itself, with its palpable presence, plays a character's role in the stories. As the title indicates, some of the characters in these stories become lost, engulfed in the city, while others "eventually find their way a bit." For these "insightful portraits" and "unsensationalized depictions of horrifying social ills," to quote a *Publishers Weekly* critic, Jones earned a National Book Award nomination.

Even with the prestigious nomination to his name, Jones struggled to earn a living, and when a steady, if dry, job presented itself, he did not refuse. For more than a decade Jones, a confirmed bachelor who has never owned a car, worked full time as a freelance columnist and proofreader for *Tax Notes,* a newsletter for tax professionals. It was tedious work and thus left room for his imagination to wander to other topics. After publishing his short story collection, Jones had pondered his subjects for future pieces. He had even bought and read portions of more than a dozen books on slavery. However, it was an obscure fact that remained with him since his college days that charged his imagination—the fact that some free blacks had become slaveowners. Yet because he was not planning to become a writer at that time, he had mentally filed away this information.

Finally Jones let his imagination run free and started mentally plotting in intricate detail the story of Henry Townsend, a Virginia slave who buys his freedom and then becomes a slave owner himself. However, this novel, told in omniscient point of view and in a nonlinear form, is more than the tale of Townsend. Townsend is the pivotal character around which the stories of myriad other characters revolve. In concrete terms, there is no main character in *The Known World.* Yet in the abstract, the reader may consider the inhumane institution of slavery to be the novel's central "character." Structurally *The Known World* recalls *Lost in the City* because in both works various characters gather to tell a number of tales and consider the repercussions on the lives of those people somehow involved.

When Jones started writing *The Known World* after being laid off from *Tax Notes* in 2002, he began with the 12 pages he had at one time written down. He believed that he was writing a short story and was unaware that he was going to write a novel until he did. As Jones explained in a Bookbrowse interview, the novel's structure developed as he committed it to paper: "I always thought I had a linear story. Something happened between the time I began the real work in January [of] 2002 of taking it all out of my head and when I finished months later. It might be that because I, as the 'god' of the people in the book, could see their first days and their last days and all that was in between, and those people did not have linear lives as I saw all that they had lived." Compared with the years he had spent plotting the novel in his head, the actual writing of *The Known World* required a very short time, a mere two and a half months. After the work had been accepted for publication, Jones again spent that much time shortening it at the publisher's request.

When it rolled off presses in 2003, *The Known World* quickly earned accolades from reviewers. Critics praised Jones for his use of language, well-drawn characterizations, and historical accuracy, nominating the novel for a National Book Award. While some readers may be drawn to the novel for the "hook" of its unusual subject matter, Jones did not have an agenda, an intent to say something particular about race. Rather, "It's about a person deciding to control another," he explained to the *Washington Post*'s Burns. "If someone reading it goes into it they'll see that I'm just not stuck on that topic. There are other things going on. There are relationships among people, of various kinds." Jones worked diligently to avoid creating stereotypical characters, a quality of the work that was not lost on reviewers.

Like he had in *Lost in the City,* Jones employed the colorful language that is a heritage of black Americans. He also enlivened the narrative with hints of humor and superstitions of his forebears. And although he wrote of some horrific events about slavery, he was able to remain emotionally detached from them because he had dealt with them during the novel's lengthy gestation period. "I had enough time to come to grips with what was going to be in the novel, so it didn't have that kind of immediacy," Jones told Edward Guthmann of the *San Francisco Chronicle.* This detachment is evident in Jones' narration, noted *Washington Post Book World* reviewer Jonathan Yardley: "The pace of the novel is leisurely and measured, and Jones' lovely but unobtrusive prose is tuned accordingly." It is this "patient, insistent, sometimes softly sardonic, always wise" narrative thread that entices the reader to turn the next page, and the next.

While one reviewer pointed out several errors in fact in *The Known World*, many cited the work's verisimilitude as one of its strengths, praising Jones for his copious research. For his part, Jones admitted that the novel's setting, the fictional Manchester County, Virginia, is just that—fictional—and that his research efforts were limited. Originally he had planned to visit Lynchburg, Virginia. "But I never got around to going down there, and so I was forced to create my own place," he told the *San Francisco Chronicle*'s Guthmann. "One can pick at its [the novel's] small faults without detracting from its overall importance," remarked Claude Crowley in a Knight Ridder/Tribune News Service review. What is the work's importance? Although only the passage of time will provide the ultimate answer, *Washington Post Book World*'s Yardley concluded: "Jones has woven nothing less than a tapestry of slavery, an artifact as vast and complex as anything to be found in the [world-famous French museum, the] Louvre. Every thread is perfectly in place, every thread connects with every other. The first paragraph connects, nearly 400 pages later, with the last. Against all the evidence to the contrary that American fiction has given us over the past quarter-century, *The Known World* affirms that the novel does matter, that it can still speak to us as nothing else can."

In 2004, *The Known World* won the Pulitzer Prize for fiction and the National Book Critics Circle Award for fiction. That same year, Jones was working on another anthology of short fiction. Still intent on writing fiction "that matters," he told *Publisher's Weekly*: "I want to write about the things which helped us to survive: the love, grace, intelligence, and strength for us as a people."

## Selected writings

*Lost in the City*, photographs by Amos Chan, Morrow, 1992.
*The Known World*, Amistad, 2003.

## Sources

### Periodicals

*African American Review,* spring 2000, p. 95.
*American Statesman* (Austin, TX), September 21, 2003, p. K5.
*Book,* September-October 2003, pp. 87-88.
*Booklist,* September 15, 2003, p. 211.
*Entertainment Weekly,* October 30, 1992, p. 80; August 22, 2003, p. 134.
*Globe & Mail* (Toronto, Canada), November 15, 2003, p. D8.

*Journal* (Winston Salem, NC), September 7, 2003, p. A24.

Knight Ridder/Tribune News Service, September 17, 2003, p. K3969; October 8, 2003, p. K1755.

*Library Journal,* May 15, 1992, p. 122; August 2003, pp. 131-32.

*Los Angeles Times Book Review,* July 12, 1992, p. 6.

*Newsweek,* September 8, 2003, p. 57.

*New York Times,* June 11, 1992, p. C18; August 23, 1992, sec. 7, p. 16.

*New York Times Book Review,* August 23, 1992, p. 16; August 31, 2003, p. 9.

*People,* September 29, 2003, p. 45.

*Post* (Cincinnati, OH), August 21, 2003, p. B3.

*Publishers Weekly,* March 23, 1992, p. 59; August 11, 2003, pp. 253-55.

*San Francisco Chronicle,* October 30, 2003, p. E1.

*School Library Journal,* January 1993, p. 144.

*Times Literary Supplement,* October 10, 2003, p. 24.

*Washington Post,* July 22, 1992, p. G1; October 6, 1992, p. B4.

*Washington Post Book World,* June 21, 1992, p. 3; August 29, 2003.

**Online**

"Edward P. Jones," BookBrowse, http://www.bookbrowse.com/index.cfm?page=author&authorID=930 (September 30, 2004).

*"Known World, Gulag* win Pulitzers," CNN.com, http://www.cnn.com/2004/SHOWBIZ/books/04/05/pulitzers.arts.ap/index.html (September 30, 2004).

"Off the Page," *Washington Post,* http://www.washingtonpost.com/wp-dyn/articles/A11797-2003Oct24.html (September 30, 2004).

**Transcripts**

"Fresh Air," interview with Edward P. Jones, National Public Radio, November 11, 2003.

—*Jeanne M. Lesinski*

# Sarah Jones

## Poet and playwright

**B**orn c. 1974, in Baltimore, MD; daughter of a physician. *Education:* Attended Bryn Mawr College, c. 1992-95.

**Addresses:** *Agent*—Creative Artists Agency, 9830 Wilshire Blvd., Beverly Hills, CA 90212-1825.

## Career

**D**ebuted first solo performance piece, *Surface Transit,* in 1998 at the Nuyorican Poets Café, New York City, and later performed it at the American Place Theater; *Women Can't Wait,* commissioned by Equality NOW, debuted at the P.S. 122 in New York City, 2000, and was later performed at a United Nations conference; third one- woman show, *Bridge & Tunnel,* premiered at 45 Bleecker, 2004; signed with Creative Artists Agency, 2004; *Bridge & Tunnel* performed on Broadway, 2005.

**Awards:** Nuyorican Poets Cafe's Grand Slam Championship, 1997.

## Sidelights

**S**poken-word performance artist Sarah Jones and her one woman-show, *Bridge & Tunnel,* drew effusive reviews from theater critics in 2004 and helped land its author and star a Hollywood agent. *Bridge & Tunnel* is a 14-character study—with all parts inhabited by the energetic, versatile Jones— and deals with themes of intolerance and injustice in the melting-pot microcosm of the Greater New York area. Jones has said that writing about the immigrant experience has been relatively easy for her, because ultimately her source material is so rich. "It's such a poetic story," she told *Vanity Fair* writer Anne Fulenwider, "to pick up everything you can gather with you and against incredible odds manage to find your way to this country."

Jones was around 30 years old the year *Bridge & Tunnel* premiered in New York City. She was born in Baltimore, the city where her parents had first met as Johns Hopkins University students, but the family later settled in Boston and finally New York because of her father's work as a physician. She was from a biracial family, and sometimes felt uncomfortable as a child, especially when they lived in Roxbury, a predominantly African-American section of Boston. "From a very early age I had a profound sense of justice," she recalled in an interview with Mazi Gaillard for *Harper's Bazaar.* "I wanted to fix the fact that I felt uncomfortable when my mother and I went into certain places together."

When the Joneses settled in New York City, they did so in the richly multicultural borough of Queens. She was sent to the prestigious United Nations School, and it was there she discovered she had an unusual talent for mimicry. "There were all these kids, something like 150 nationalities, and everybody had these gorgeous accents, and I would listen all day," she recalled in an article by *New York Times* journalist Barbara Crossette. "The U.N. school opened up so much for me. It really broadened my horizons. As a kid I was suddenly aware of the plights of people not only in my own backyard but all over the place."

Jones landed at an equally prestigious women's college in Pennsylvania, Bryn Mawr, but left after her junior year. Returning to New York City, she drifted through a series of jobs for a time, and then her career as a writer began with a tragedy: in 1997, her younger sister, Naomi, died after her first intravenous heroin use experience. She was just 18 years old. Jones' grief came through in her writing, and that output found a forum in the downtown poetry-slam scene. She won the Nuyorican Poets Cafe's Grand Slam Championship that same year.

In 1998, Jones' first solo show, *Surface Transit,* had its premiere at the same venue. Its character study of eight compelling New Yorkers, created entirely in Jones' head and deftly characterized by her onstage, was such a success that it enjoyed a run at the American Place Theater. As with her subsequent work, *Surface Transit* deals with injustice and intolerance. One of the monologues features a rapper named Rasheed who discourses for ten minutes on contemporary urban slang. "The vast list of references he drops could be an encyclopedic dictionary of hip-hop," asserted *New York Times* theater reviewer D.J.R. Bruckner about Jones' talents onstage, "and the rhythm of his patter is so finely modulated that his ten-minute speech sounds like a grand aria of rap."

*Surface Transit* earned other high-profile reviews, and Jones was tagged as a rising new name in performance art. Spike Lee offered her a part in his next film, *Bamboozled,* but by the time it was released in 2000 most of her scenes had been excised. She also briefly joined an MTV sketch comedy series, *The Lyricist Lounge Show,* but was disappointed by the themes the spoken-word show was presenting. "I didn't realize that I didn't have the power to say to an executive that 'Puerto Rican woman pregnant with nine kids in the kitchen let's make rice and beans' jokes are not funny to me," she told *New York Times* writer Jason Zinoman about the experience.

Jones' next solo show was a work commissioned by Equality NOW, an international women's advocacy group. In *Women Can't Wait,* which debuted in 2000, she played eight different women who deliver monologues about injustice and oppression in their respective countries. Jones becomes each character with the help of a simple shawl, and they include an abused wife in India and a little girl facing mutilation per tribal custom in Kenya. But Jones' work also comes closer to home, showing how the justice system or unfair laws penalize women in more "modern" places: her New Yorker Bonita is a teen jailed for killing her abusive boyfriend, while another, Emeraude, is a French woman who disdains and disobeys a vintage law that prohibits women from working at night.

In 2004, Jones scored once again with *Bridge & Tunnel,* her solo show built around several immigrant characters making their way and settling down in the New York area. They run the gamut from a Jewish grandmother on Long Island to a Pakistani who runs a poetry slam night at a South Queens club. Reviews were once again near-unanimous in their praise of Jones and her talent when the show began at the 45 Bleecker theater space. *Entertainment Weekly* writer Karen Valby noted that her impressive repertoire of accents and seemingly facile physical transformations "would all be just a neat trick if Jones weren't such an intelligent writer and actress. But she's funny and empathetic, in complete control of the slightest gestures and tics and inflections."

In 2005, *Bridge & Tunnel* moved to Broadway and Jones was also in talks with the cable network Bravo. Her next work would deal with the immigrant experience again, but in a post-9/11 world, and she planned to call it *Waking the American Dream.* She asserted that she never feared running out of material for her shows. "It's easy to find good stories in New York," she told the *New York Times*'s Zinoman. "Go downstairs and buy your newspaper, there's somebody to talk to…. [Y]ou're just as likely to find someone from South Asia or West Africa as someone who was born here. And it always feels fresh because no one talks about it. These people are not on television."

## Sources

*American Theatre,* September 2002, p. 40.
*Entertainment Weekly,* April 9, 2004, p. 94; December 17, 2004, p. 40.
*Harper's Bazaar,* October 2000, p. 260.
*Mother Jones,* July-August 2004, p. 82.
*New York Times,* June 7, 2000, p. E1; July 28, 2000, p. E3; July 12, 2001, p. B2; February 8, 2004, p. AR6; March 5, 2004, p. E2.
*Vanity Fair,* July 2004, p. 60.

—Carol Brennan

# Eric Kandel

*Ezio Petersen/UPI/Landov*

**Neurobiologist and professor**

---

**B**orn Eric Richard Kandel, November 7, 1929, in Vienna, Austria; son of Herman Kandel and Charlotte Zimels; married Denise Bystryn, c. 1956; children: Paul, Minouche (daughter). *Education:* Graduated from Harvard College (history and literature), 1952; New York University School of Medicine, MD, 1956; attended Columbia University.

**Addresses:** *Office*—Center for Neurobiology and Behavior, Columbia University, 1051 Riverside Dr., New York, NY 10032. *E-mail*—erk5@columbia.edu.

## Career

**R**esearcher, National Institutes of Health Laboratory of Neurophysiology, 1957; resident in psychiatry, Harvard Medical School, 1960-64; staff psychiatrist, Harvard Medical School, 1964-65; associate professor, department of physiology and psychiatry, New York University, 1965-68; professor, New York University, 1968-74; professor, department of physiology and psychiatry, New York University, 1974—; director, Center for Neurobiology and Behavior, Columbia University, 1974-84; professor, Columbia University, 1983—; senior investigator, Howard Hughes Medical Institute, Columbia University, 1984—; co-founded Memory Pharmaceuticals, 1998.

**Member:** National Academy of Sciences.

**Awards:** Henry L. Moses Research Award, Montefiore Hospital, 1959; Lester N. Hofheimer Prize for Research, 1977; Lucy G. Moses Prize for Research in

Basic Neurology, 1977; Solomon A. Berson Medical Alumni Achievement Award, 1979; Karl Spencer Lashley Prize in Neurobiology, 1981; The Dickson Prize in Biology and Medicine. 1982; Albert Lasker Basic Medical Research Award (shared with V.B. Mountcastle), 1983; Lewis S. Rosenstiel Award for Distinguished Work (shared with D. Koshland), 1984; Howard Crosby Warren Medal, 1984; American Association of Medical Colleges Award, 1985; Gairdner International Award for Outstanding Achievements in Medical Science, 1987; National Medal of Science, 1988; Gold Medal for Scientific Merit, 1988; Distinguished Service Award of the American Psychiatric Association, 1989; Award in Basic Science, American College of Physicians, 1989; Robert J. and Clarie Pasarow Foundation Award in Neuroscience, 1989; Diploma Internacional Cajal, 1990; Bristol-Myers Squibb Award for Distinguished Achievement in Neuroscience Research (shared with T.V.M. Bliss), 1991; Warren Triennial Prize, 1992; Jean-Louis Signoret's Prize on Memory, 1992; Harvey Prize, 1993; F.O. Schmitt Medal and Prize in Neuroscience, 1993; Stevens Triennial Prize, 1995; New York Academy of Medicine Award, 1996; Gerard Prize for Outstanding Achievement in Neuroscience, 1997; Charles A. Dana Award for Pioneering Achievement in Health (shared with Paul Greengard), 1997; Wolf Prize in Biology and Medicine, Israel, 1999; A.H. Heineken Prize for medicine, Royal Netherlands Academy of Arts and Sciences, 2000; Nobel Prize in Physiology or Medicine (shared with Arvid Carlsson and Paul Greengard), 2000.

## Sidelights

Eric Kandel's groundbreaking research revealed what happens to the brain when memories are formed. Kandel explored how nerve cells (neurons) change during learning. His research involving the sea slug *Aplysia* and mice uncovered the basis of short and long-term memory. Kandel shared the 2000 Nobel Prize for physiology or medicine with fellow neuroscientists Arvid Carlsson and Paul Greengard. Kandel's research could lead to the development of treatments for Alzheimer's disease and other conditions related to memory loss.

Eric Richard Kandel is the youngest of two sons born to Herman Kandel and Charlotte Zimels. He was born November 7, 1929, in Vienna, Austria, five years after his brother, Lewis. His father owned a toy store where both parents worked. His experiences as a Jewish boy later sparked a fascination with "the mind, how people behave, the unpredictability of emotion, and the persistence of memory," according to Kandel's autobiography, which is posted on the Nobel Prize website. Kandel was eight years old when Adolf Hitler marched into Austria on March 14, 1938. The leader of the Nazi Party received an "enthusiastic greeting" from thousands of people. Mobs attacked Jews and destroyed their property. The next day, only one classmate talked to Kandel. When he went to the park to play, boys roughed him up. Kandel acknowledged that his was a "mild example" of what Jewish people experienced when Hitler was in power.

Kandel's ninth birthday was the day before *Kristallnacht,* an intense night of violence against Jewish people. Police arrested Jewish men, including Kandel's father. Jewish families were temporarily evicted from their homes. Kandel's father, who had served in World War I, was released several days later. After about a week, the family received permission to return home. Everything valuable had been stolen.

In 1939, the Kandels left Austria and moved to Brooklyn, New York, where they lived with Charlotte's parents. Herman worked in a toothbrush factory and then opened a clothing store. Their sons

attended the Yeshiva of Flatbush, a Jewish elementary school. Kandel graduated from the elementary school in 1944 and became a United States citizen during the mid-1940s. He attended Erasmus Hall High School in Brooklyn. Encouraged by a history teacher, Kandel applied to Harvard. The university accepted Kandel and gave him a scholarship. At Harvard, Kandel majored in 19th and 20th century European history and literature. He intended to do graduate research on European intellectual history but his plan changed when he met Anna Kris, a student from Vienna. Her parents, Ernest and Marianne, were psychoanalysts who knew Sigmund Freud. Kandel began to think psychoanalysis offered another approach to understanding the mind and memory. He decided to become a psychoanalyst.

After graduating from Harvard in 1952, Kandel entered New York University's medical school. By his senior year there, Kandel's career direction changed again. He felt he needed to learn more about the biology of the mind. NYU did not have a faculty member working with basic neural science, so Kandel studied that subject at Columbia University in New York City. In 1955, he began working in the Columbia lab with Harry Grundfest. Kandel was encouraged in that work by a new Jewish friend whose family fled the Nazis. Denise Bystryn was a French woman who met Kandel while she studied at Columbia for a doctorate in medical sociology. Kandel graduated from medical school in 1956 and married Bystryn. He then divided his time between a medical residency at Montefiore Hospital and work at the lab. In 1957, Kandel began doing research at the National Institutes of Health Laboratory of Neurophysiology.

Kandel's early research focused on the biology of cells in the hippocampus, the part of the brain related to memory. After working with mammals, Kandel wanted to take a biological approach and do a less complicated study. That work would initially involve invertebrates, creatures with no backbones. Some neurobiologists and psychologists thought Kandel was making a mistake, one that would hurt his career. They believed that a mammal's brain was so complex that research results could not be compared with studies involving invertebrates. Kandel knew that some comparative behavior researchers like Konrad Lorenz discovered that humans and simple animals sometimes behaved the same way when they learned. Kandel reasoned that since nothing was known about the cell biology of learning, that any insight would be highly informative. After researching subjects including crayfish, lobsters, and snails, Kandel decided to concentrate on *Aplysia*. While the human brain contains billions of nerve cells, the sea slug only has 20,000.

Kandel arranged to study in Paris, France, with Ladislav Tauc, one of two researchers working with *Aplysia*. Before going to France, Kandel needed to complete a two-year residency in psychiatry. In 1960, he began residency training at the Massachusetts Mental Health Center of Harvard Medical School. The following year, Denise gave birth to Paul, the Kandels' first child. In September of 1962, Kandel took his family to Paris.

In France, Kandel and Tauc started research on the gill-withdrawal reflex of the sea slug. *Aplysia,* which are five inches long, breathe through gills. If the slug is touched on or near the gill, it instinctively protects itself by withdrawing and covering the gill area with a skin flap. Stimulus used to cause the reflex included touching the tail or injecting a needle. Repeatedly touching the *Aplysia* eventually caused the slug to withdraw less. After 16 months in Paris, Kandel returned to Harvard Medical School. He served on the faculty of the Department of Psychiatry until 1965. That year, he joined the faculty of New York University as an associate professor. Furthermore, his daughter, Minouche, was born in 1965. Three years later, Kandel was named a professor at NYU.

In 1974, Kandel was invited to serve as founding director of the Columbia University's Center for Neurobiology and Behavior. In addition to work as a professor, Kandel would research memory. Kandel wanted to know how *Aplysia* learned to avoid the reflex. At Columbia, his gill-withdrawal research showed that memory and learning were the result of changes in the synapse, the place where there is contact between adjacent neurons. The lab showed that cells communicate by signal transduction, meaning a message is sent from one cell to another through chemical transmitters. The signal transfer occurs at the synapse. A weaker stimulus in slugs resulted in short-term memory that lasted several hours or days. Short-term memory involved a process called adenosine monophosphate (AMP). A stronger stimulus produced long-term memory that lasted weeks. Kandel's lab discovered that memory was triggered by variations of a molecule called CREB (cyclic-AMP-response element-binding protein). CREB changes the short-term memory into a long-term memory that in humans can last months or years. In that process, the shape of the synapse changes.

Kandel left the lab in 1984 to become a senior investigator at Howard Hughes Medical Institute at Columbia. He continued to research and teach. During the 1990s, Kandel broadened his research to include mice. The mice experienced many of the changes that *Aplysia* did, indicating that findings about memory applied to mammals. Mouse research showed that a process called long-term potentiation (LTP) increased the efficiency of signals that neurons send to the brain. LTP is essential in the area of the brain that holds memories of people, places, and things. Kandel's research could lead to the development of treatments for memory-related conditions like Alzheimer's disease.

In 1998, Kandel co-founded Memory Pharmaceuticals with Dr. Walter Gilbert, a Nobel Laureate and Harvard professor specializing in molecular genetics. The company, licensed in agreement with Columbia University, explores drug treatments for memory disorders.

In 2000, the Nobel Prize for Physiology or Medicine was awarded to Kandel, American Paul Greengard, and Arvin Carlsson of Sweden. They were honored for career achievements in research related to "signal transduction in the nervous system." Kandel's other honors include the National Medal of Science and the Lasker Prize.

In March of 2003, Memory Pharmaceuticals announced that the drug company Roche would do clinical studies on MEM1414, a compound discovered by Memory Pharmaceuticals. Studies on the chemical mixture targeted for the treatment of Alzheimer's could lead to the development of drugs to treat the condition. While there was no pill to improve memory on the market as of December of 2004, hope was in sight. The drugs were in the early stages of clinical trials that could be finished in as little as "two years, if we're lucky," Kandel told *Newsweek*'s Mary Carmichael.

## Selected writings

(With Thomas M. Jessell and James H. Schwartz) *Essentials of Neural Science and Behavior,* McGraw Hill, 1995.

(Editor with Thomas M. Jessell and James H. Schwartz) *Principles of Neural Science,* McGraw Hill, 2000.

(With Larry R. Squire) *Memory: From Mind to Molecules,* W.H. Henry Holt, 2000.

# Sources

## Books

Bolhuis, Johan J., editor, *Brain, Perception, Memory: Advances in Cognitive Neuroscience,* Oxford University Press, 2000.

Czerner, Thomas B., *What makes you tick? The brain in plain English,* Wiley, 2001.

## Periodicals

*BusinessWeek,* October 25, 2004.

*Newsweek,* December 6, 2004, p. 44.

*New York Times,* October 10, 2000.

## Online

"Eric Kandel," Nobelprize.org, http://nobelprize.org/medicine/laureates/2000/kandel-cv.html (December 9, 2004).

"Making Memories," Web MD, http://my.webmd.com/Content/Article/50/40389.htm (December 9, 2004).

*—Liz Swain*

# M. Farooq Kathwari

## Chief Executive Officer of Ethan Allen and philanthropist

**B**orn August 16, 1944, in Srinagar, Kashmir; married Farida Khan, 1968; children: three (one deceased). *Education:* Earned degree from Kashmir University, 1965; New York University, M.B.A., 1968.

**Addresses:** *Office*—Ethan Allen, Inc., P.O. Box 1966, Danbury, CT 06813-1966.

## Career

**W**orked as a bookkeeper in New York City, mid-1960s, and ran a handicraft-import business out of his apartment; financial analyst with Bear Stearns after 1968, and with New Court Securities, where he rose to vice president; formed KEA International, 1973; sold KEA to Ethan Allen, Inc., 1980; Ethan Allen, Inc., vice president, 1980, executive vice president, 1983, president and chief operating officer, 1985, board chair and chief executive officer, 1988. Elected president of the American Furniture Manufacturers Association, 2002. Established the Irfan Kathwari Foundation and the Kashmir Study Group.

## Sidelights

**M**. Farooq Kathwari has headed Ethan Allen, Inc., the venerable American furniture-maker based in Danbury, Connecticut, since 1985. As chief executive officer and board chair, he has been credited with guiding the company whose brand name was once synonymous with staid, American Colonial styles into an unprecedented turnaround. Kath-

wari also has a sideline career, however—that of philanthropist and potential peacemaker for his troubled homeland, Kashmir. "To a great degree, politicians and the diplomats have failed in regions of conflict and war," Kathwari contended in an article he wrote for *Chief Executive.* "The reason CEOs can contribute is that they have a different mind set."

Kathwari was born in 1944 into a longtime merchant family in Srinagar, an ancient city in the Indian-controlled part of Kashmir known for its houseboats and canals along Dal Lake. Even his own family was torn apart by the political trouble: when he was five years old, Kathwari's father traveled to the Pakistan-controlled area on business and was detained there. A year passed before Kathwari, his mother, and two other siblings were allowed to join him; an older brother and sister remained behind. They assumed the split was merely a temporary one, but instead they stayed for ten years, living on a mountain whose peak reached 8,000 feet. "Going to school was a hike," Kathwari wrote in a *New York Times* profile in 2004. "I'd pass trees and rocks and a spring. At the end of October it started snowing. The mountain is a great teacher. It teaches you to pace yourself."

Kathwari's family was able to return to Srinagar in 1960, but without their father. In his teens, Kathwari became a top cricketeer, and went on to captain his Kashmir University team. He majored in literature and political science, but was also active in the student protest movement, and was jailed briefly after speaking to a foreign journalist. By the time he graduated in 1965, his father was already in

New York, working at the 1964 World's Fair, and had been sending him college applications and encouraging him to leave.

Kathwari arrived in the United States as a political-asylum seeker. Career-wise, he suffered a somewhat inauspicious start for a future American CEO. He was hired at a factory in Queens, which he thought may have made shower stalls; he did not last very long and was told not to return when he was given his first paycheck. After that, he answered an ad for bookkeeper, and assured the interviewer that he knew the rudiments. That was not true, but the secretary managed to give him a crash course on his first day while the others were away at lunch.

Kathwari earned his graduate business degree from New York University in 1968, and fared better in his job prospects after that. He worked on Wall Street as a financial analyst at Bear Stearns, and went on to another firm, New Court Securities, where he rose to vice president. He also had a lucrative side career as an importer of Kashmir-made handicrafts, sent by his family, which he sold wholesale to Bloomingdale's department store. One day in the early 1970s, he met Ethan Allen's board chair, who admitted that his company's American furniture factories were having a hard time obtaining enough top-notch Kashmiri crewelwork for its upholstery fabrics. Kathwari set up a business with his cousins to provide a steady supply for Ethan Allen.

Kathwari called his new company KEA International, which stood for "Kathwari Ethan Allen," and when Ethan Allen decided to buy it outright in 1980, they offered Kathwari a vice presidency. Three years later, he became an executive vice president at the company, and was named president and chief operating officer in 1985. His control over Ethan Allen's future direction was complete when he was made board chair and chief executive officer in 1988. At the time, the company had steady but unimpressive sales. In business since the 1930s, it had once been an innovator in its field, pioneering the gallery-style showroom in which furniture was displayed in different rooms that mimicked an actual American home. The company dominated the market in the post-World War II years, when mass-market tastes ran to the vaguely colonial, and Ethan Allen's styles remained firmly in the traditional category long thereafter.

Kathwari's vision was to modernize the furniture lines, and the stores as well. There was some resistance from within the company, as well as external

pressure, and he managed to successfully fend off a 1989 buyout attempt. After he took the company public again in 1993, its fortunes began to improve considerably. When he had taken over in 1985, Ethan Allen had been posting sales figures of about $200 million annually for past seven years; by 2002, when Kathwari was elected president of the American Furniture Manufacturers Association, Ethan Allen was selling about $200 million each quarter.

Kathwari's own home was not far from Ethan Allen's Danbury, Connecticut, headquarters, across the state line in New Rochelle, New York. He had married his wife, Farida, by telephone in 1968, since he could not return to Kashmir for the ceremony because of his political-refugee status. She joined him several months later, and in suburban New York the couple raised three children. The elder of their two sons, Irfan, went to Afghanistan as a young man, over his family's objections, to join the mujahadeen fighters. He died in 1992 during the battle to take Kabul. Kathwari established the Irfan Kathwari Foundation in his name, which works to promote understanding between the Muslim world and the West.

In 1996, Kathwari founded the Kashmir Study Group, which he also underwrites. Comprised of scholars and experts from both sides of the Indian-Pakistani dispute, it has conducted studies and offered a framework to end the bloodshed, which escalated in the late 1990s. The group's recommendations have been moderately well received, and its work has even earned tacit support from the United States government. Though Kathwari hopes the conflict might be resolved in his lifetime, he recalls the lessons he learned from the mountain as a schoolboy. "If your nation's been fighting for self-governance since 1586," he reflected in an article that appeared in the business magazine *Inc.*, "you realize that to change things sometimes takes a long time."

## Sources

*BusinessWeek*, October 22, 2001, p. 68.
*Chief Executive*, December 2003, p. 38.
*Forbes*, July 27, 1998, p. 20.
*HR Magazine*, May 1994, p. 61.
*Inc.*, November 1999, p. 119.
*New York Times*, December 26, 2004, p. BU11.

—*Carol Brennan*

# Charlie Kaufman

## Screenwriter and producer

**B**orn Charles Stewart Kaufman, November, 1958, in New York; son of Myron (an engineer) and Helen (a homemaker) Kaufman; married Denise; children: two. *Education:* Attended Boston University and New York University.

**Addresses:** *Agent*—c/o Marty Bowen, United Talent Agency, 9560 Wilshire Blvd., 5th Floor, Beverly Hills, CA 90212.

## Career

**P**roducer and author of screenplays for film and television. Worked in circulation department of the Minneapolis *Star Tribune* and the Minneapolis Institute of Arts. Staff writer for television shows, including: *Get a Life!*, 1990-92; *The Trouble with Larry*, 1993; *The Dana Carvey Show*, 1996; *Ned and Stacey*, 1996-97. Producer of television shows, including: *Ned and Stacey* and *Misery Loves Company*. Author of screenplays, including: *Being John Malkovich*, 1999; *Human Nature*, 2001; *Confessions of a Dangerous Mind*, 2002; *Adaptation*, 2002; *Eternal Sunshine of the Spotless Mind*, 2003. Producer of films, including: *Being John Malkovich*, *Human Nature*, and *Adaptation*.

**Awards:** Best screenplay, National Society of Film Critics, for *Being John Malkovich*, 2000; Saturn Award for best writer, American Academy of Science Fiction, Fantasy, and Horror Films, for *Being John Malkovich*, 2000; best screenplay, New York Film Critics Circle Awards, for *Adaptation*, 2002. Both films also won numerous other film-festival and critics' honors.

## Sidelights

**C**harlie Kaufman became one of Hollywood's hottest screenwriters by penning daring stories featuring a socially inept and often rather slovenly male protagonist struggling to make his way in the world on his own terms. Kaufman waited several years to make *Being John Malkovich* with director Spike Jonze in 1999, and the collaboration between the two has also yielded the Academy Award nominated *Adaptation*. Both films, while unconventional by Hollywood standards, were nevertheless box-office successes, and critics have lauded Kaufman's work as simultaneously entertaining and profound. These screenplays, noted *Time* writer Joel Stein, "up-end time, logic, and the laws of physics, and in the process of writing them, he has upended many of the conventions of Hollywood films."

Kaufman is also famously publicity-shy, which has become part of the legend surrounding the success of this most unlikely of Hollywood creative talents. Certain facts are known: that he was born in 1958, grew up in Massapequa, New York, and finished high school in West Hartford, Connecticut. He appeared in high-school plays and liked to make Super-8 movies during his teens. After a stint at

Boston University, he studied filmmaking at New York University, but never finished his degree. At one point in the late 1980s, he lived in the Twin Cities area and worked for the circulation department of the Minneapolis *Star Tribune*. He also worked at the Minneapolis Institute of Arts, delivering the standard "the museum will be closing soon" announcement over the public-address system.

Kaufman's writing credits were limited to a couple of articles that appeared in *National Lampoon*, the humor magazine whose staff roster included many notable *Saturday Night Live* alumni, when he decided to move to Los Angeles, California, to break into the television-comedy business. In 1991, he drove his old Volkswagen cross-country, and managed to land a writing job for *Get a Life!*, the Chris Elliott sitcom with a cult following. Elliott had gained fame on David Letterman's late-night show with his bizarre antics, and *Get a Life!* featured him as a 30-year-old paperboy who still lived at home with his parents. Kaufman and Elliott also made some short films that aired on *Late Night with David Letterman*

Kaufman came up with an idea for his own sitcom, with the unappealing title *Depressed Roomies*. He shopped its script around, but network executives turned him down repeatedly, and Kaufman took other writing jobs instead, including one on a short-lived sitcom called *The Trouble with Larry*. It starred Bronson Pinchot (of *Beverly Hills Cop* fame) as a man who is dragged off by a giant baboon during his honeymoon and is presumed dead. He returns a decade later to his wife, played by Courteney Cox, who has since remarried.

Kaufman also wrote for *The Dana Carvey Show*, and scored what was perhaps his biggest hit when he landed on the critically acclaimed Debra Messing sitcom *Ned and Stacey* during its second and final season in 1996-97. *Ned and Stacey* was also Kaufman's first screen credit as a producer, which gave him a degree of creative control. He insisted upon the same when he shopped his first script around Hollywood during this era, too. It was the story of a timid New York City puppeteer named Craig, whose street-theater vignettes contain themes unsuitable for children. Unhappy at home as well, he takes a job as a file clerk, and at the office discovers a door that allows him to enter the head of actor John Malkovich for 15 minutes at a time.

Not surprisingly, there were few studios interested in *Being John Malkovich*; some who were intrigued by the premise also wanted to make some major re-visions to Kaufman's script, which he refused to do. He would only sign on if he was given executive-producer credit as well, and five long years later, the movie finally made it to screens thanks to a collaboration between Kaufman and director Spike Jonze. The 1999 film starred John Cusack as well as the real John Malkovich—a terrific but crucial casting coup—Cameron Diaz, and Catherine Keener. *Newsweek* critic David Ansen termed it "a teemingly imaginative screenplay.... I don't know how a movie this original got made today, but thank God for wonderful aberrations."

Kaufman even earned an Academy Award nomination for the screenplay, which cemented his reputation as a daring new creative talent in Hollywood. Abandoning television altogether, Kaufman completed another screenplay, *Human Nature,* that failed to achieve the commercial success of the *Malkovich* movie. Directed by Michel Gondry, a former music-video director, the 2001 film starred Patricia Arquette as an extremely hirsute woman and Tim Robbins as her behavioral-scientist beau. The plot involves a man they discover, who has been raised as an ape, and the romantic intrigues that ensnare the trio and others. A farce that explores what differentiates humans from animals, the film delved heavily into psychology and seemed to have a murder-mystery subplot tacked on to lend it a narrative arc. Critics were mostly baffled, though some conceded it featured some hilariously written scenes.

The story surrounding *Adaptation,* the 2002 film that also earned Kaufman an Oscar nomination, is in itself part of the plot and made him the anti-hero of the "plot." In short, Kaufman had been hired to write the screenplay for *The Orchid Thief: A True Story of Beauty and Obsession,* a nonfiction bestseller by *New Yorker* writer Susan Orlean. It involved the rare-orchid trade and an eccentric Florida horticulturist who landed in legal trouble for his shady dealings on the market. Yet Orlean's story was a reflective one, more about the nature of obsession and what compels others to attach to an object, movement, or person, and Kaufman found it difficult to create a plot around it. To make matters worse, he also had another deadline looming, this one for an original story idea about a memory-erasing institute that helps mend broken hearts. "I was getting nothing done," Kaufman explained in an interview with *Esquire*'s Mike Sager. "I was going out of my mind. And then I came up with this idea to include myself in the story, because it seemed that my energy was in the paralysis of not being able to write. But I didn't want to tell anybody my idea because I thought they would say no. And I didn't have any other ideas. None."

In the end, Jonze agreed to direct *Adaptation,* and it hit theaters in late 2002. The plot featured a screenwriter named Charlie Kaufman, played by Nicholas Cage, who begins to panic when he cannot come up with a working screenplay for a book about ... an orchid thief. In the movie, he stalks the author (Meryl Streep), and is horrified when his twin brother Donald (also played by Cage) comes to stay with him and decides to bang out a screenplay of his own. Donald's hugely successful script is a typical Hollywood blockbuster, with chase scenes and formulaic plot twists, and in the end the two scripts seem to merge, with *Adaptation* devolving into an action movie. "With subversive wit, *Adaptation* works in all the devices Charlie swore he'd never resort to, from drugs to violence to romance," noted *Maclean's* film critic Brian D. Johnson. "And a movie about nothing becomes a movie about everything."

Critics wrote reams on the hidden messages that surfaced in *Adaptation.* Was there really a Kaufman twin, or was this simply Kaufman's alter ego? Did Kaufman really stalk Orlean? What about casting Cage, whose career started with some impressive early performances but devolved into a long, nearly unbroken string of action films in the 1990s? Kaufman would say little about his immediate family, Orlean told one interviewer there were indeed some eerie similarities on the screen that hinted Kaufman may have been observing her unbeknownst, and Cage said that he just liked the challenge of the script.

Nearly all of *Adaptation*'s reviewers had nothing but accolades for it. "What makes the movie so accessible is that its expressionist devices—the twin brother gambit, the fantasies, Charlie's woebegone distress—don't exactly have a fancy pedigree," pondered *Esquire* writer Tom Carson. "They're poetic extrapolations of sitcom ploys.... [Kaufman] may be the first artist to grasp the fluky profundity of nutso TV." The *New Yorker*'s David Denby theorized that "Kaufman and Jonze portray Charlie as a sweating loser because, in the big- money environment of Hollywood, that's inevitably how he would appear to himself—no matter how high-minded you are, you really can't mock the monetary success exploding all around you. The filmmakers are expressing their own anger and ambivalence about the movie business, and *Adaptation,* for most of its length, is a furious act of rebellion."

Famously reticent about giving interviews, Kaufman grudgingly participated in press rounds for the film, but perversely would not answer questions about his personal life or the screenplay. The mystery surrounding Kaufman prompted *Esquire*'s Sager to note that "not since Woody Allen has an American filmmaker seemed so self-consciously uncomfortable in the spotlight, nor produced such bizarre and original work." A long *Los Angeles Magazine* profile that seemed to involve an evasive interview session prompted Dave Gardetta to summarize the Kaufman mystique. "*Adaptation* had, of course, completed once and for all the shell that Kaufman now bumps around inside of," Gardetta asserted. "A movie about a fabricator fabricating the story of the fabricator's own fabrication."

Kaufman's next work, *Confessions of a Dangerous Mind,* followed close on the heels of *Adaptation,* but it was based on a script he had written some years earlier. No studio was interested in the property until actor George Clooney acquired it for his directorial debut. The film's plot centers around the bizarre exploits of real-life game-show czar Chuck Barris, who created such hits as *The Dating Game, The Newlywed Game,* and *The Gong Show,* all staples of 1970s daytime television. Kaufman based the script on Barris's "unauthorized" 1982 autobiography, in which he claimed to have worked as a hit man for the Central Intelligence Agency while at the height of his television fame. As played by Sam Rockwell, Barris comes across as grasping and self-loathing, making yet another Kaufman film in which the hero is a decidedly unlikable character. *Entertainment Weekly* critic Owen Gleiberman called the movie a "sharp, funny, unreasonably compelling adaptation," but most reviewers were baffled by it.

Kaufman's *Eternal Sunshine of the Spotless Mind* reunited him with director Gondry once again. Jim Carrey played Joel, a shy loner who undergoes a radical new experiment to erase the memory of his ex-girlfriend, Clementine, played by Kate Winslet, after learning she has had the same done to her. Characteristic of Kaufman's scripts, the story is rife with romantic yearnings and odd plot twists, and some decidedly surreal scenes. Kaufman, wrote Graham Fuller in *Interview,* "knows it's better to have loved and lost than never to have loved, but better still when you can remember it, for all that rejection costs us in dignity, self-esteem, and peace of mind."

There are rumors in Hollywood that Kaufman has sometimes hired actors to stand in for him at public appearances. Few photographs of him exist, but it is known that he is married, lives in Pasadena, and has two children with his wife, Denise. He continues to dislike discussing his work, his work habits, his ingenious ideas and how difficult it is to translate them for the screen, or anything about his personal life. He did once try to explain to *Newsweek* writer Devin Gordon why he was uncomfortable in the spotlight. "People want to paint me in a very specific way," he asserted. "A nebbish. Socially awkward. That seems to be the thing. You go, 'OK, I get this guy, he's the nerd who made good.' I mean, look, I read this stuff. I don't want to be a caricature."

## Sources

### Periodicals

*Book,* January-February 2003, p. 13.
*Entertainment Weekly,* January 10, 2003, p. 49.
*Esquire,* April 2002, p. 30; December 2002, p. 139; January 2003, p. 36.

*Interview,* April 2004, p. 100.
*Los Angeles Magazine,* March 2003, p. 98.
*Maclean's,* December 9, 2002, p. 78.
*Newsweek,* November 1, 1999, p. 85; April 15, 2002, p. 56; December 9, 2002, pp. 82-83.
*New Yorker,* December 9, 2002, p. 142.
*New York Times Magazine,* March 19, 2000, p. 80.
*Time,* April 29, 2002, p. 16; April 26, 2004, p. 83.

### Online

*Contemporary Authors Online,* Gale, 2003.

—*Carol Brennan*

# John Kerry

*AP/Wide World Photos*

## Politician

**B**orn John Forbes Kerry, December 11, 1943, in Denver, CO; son of Richard (a foreign service officer) and Rosemary (a homemaker and community service volunteer); married Julia Thorne, 1970 (divorced, 1988); married Teresa Heinz, 1995; children: Alexandra, Vanessa (from first marriage). *Politics:* Democrat. *Religion:* Catholic. *Education:* Yale University, B.A., 1966; Boston College, J.D., 1976.

**Addresses:** *Office*—U.S. Capitol, 304 Russell Bldg., Third Flr., Washington, DC 20510; One Bowdoin Sq., Tenth Flr., Boston, MA 02114. *Website*—http://www.johnkerry.com; http://kerry.senate.gov.

## Career

**S**erved in the U.S. Navy in Vietnam, 1967-69; ran unsuccessfully for U.S. Congress, 1970 and 1972; organized Vietnam Veterans Against the War's march on Washington and testified before the Senate Foreign Relations Committee, 1971; assistant district attorney, Middlesex County, Massachusetts, 1976-79; private law practice, 1979-82; elected lieutenant governor of Massachusetts, 1982; elected to the U.S. Senate, 1984; appointed to the Foreign Relations Committee, 1986; Democratic nominee for U.S. president, 2004.

## Sidelights

**J**ohn Kerry, the Democratic party's nominee for president in 2004, became a nationally prominent figure almost overnight in 1971, when he testified before the United States Senate as a spokesman for Vietnam veterans who opposed the Vietnam War. Though his 1972 campaign for Congress ended in defeat, Kerry took a more patient path to the political power he always longed for, becoming a prosecutor, then lieutenant governor of Massachusetts before getting elected to the Senate in 1984. After 20 years developing a reputation as an authority on foreign policy, he ran for the presidency in 2004, but lost to incumbent George W. Bush.

Kerry was born December 11, 1943, in Denver, Colorado, at an Army base where his father, Richard, a test pilot for the Army Air Corps, was recovering from tuberculosis. He grew up in Massachusetts, where his father and mother, Rosemary, were from, but by the time Kerry was seven, they were living in Washington, D.C., and politics was often part of family conversation. His father became a foreign service officer when Kerry was eleven, so Kerry was educated in boarding schools, first in Switzerland, then in New England.

Politically liberal from an early age, Kerry volunteered for Edward Kennedy's campaign for the United States Senate in the summer of 1962, just after he graduated from high school. He briefly dated Janet Auchincloss, the half-sister of President John F. Kennedy's wife, Jacqueline, and one day in August of 1962, Auchincloss invited Kerry to the family estate, where Kerry met the president and went sailing with him. That fall, Kerry enrolled at Yale University, where his father had gone to college. While there, he joined the debate and soccer teams, and his political ambitions grew. He told his debate team partner that his dream was to become president of the United States.

The 1963 assassination of President Kennedy deeply upset Kerry. As a result, it left an impression when William Bundy, an assistant secretary of state under Kennedy, came to Yale to defend the Vietnam War, visited his nephew (Kerry's roommate), and implored Kerry and his friends to go to Vietnam as officers. When Kerry's 1966 graduation neared, he decided to enlist in the Navy—realizing he might well be drafted anyway, and aware that military service had helped the career of his idol, President Kennedy. Yet when he was chosen to give the class oration at graduation, he used it to criticize American foreign policy, including the Vietnam War.

For his first six months in the war, starting in December of 1967, Kerry served uneventfully on a guided-missile frigate. Then, after five months in port in California, Kerry spent December of 1968 to April of 1969 captaining a small patrol boat, known as a "swift boat." At first, the swift boats patrolled the Vietnamese coast, but soon after he signed up for the duty, the boats' mission was changed to patrolling the Mekong River Delta and drawing fire from the enemy so that the boats could counterattack. While commanding the boat, Kerry received three Purple Heart medals for combat wounds. He was also awarded a Silver Star, which honors bravery in action, for a fight in which he ordered his boat's pilot to steer into enemy fire and land. Kerry jumped out of the boat and shot and killed a young Viet Cong guerrilla who was carrying a grenade launcher. He also earned a Bronze Star for pulling a member of his crew out of the water after he had fallen off the boat, even though enemy snipers were shooting at the man and Kerry had just been wounded in the arm by shrapnel from a mine. After that incident, since a rule allowed soldiers to return home after three Purple Hearts, Kerry applied successfully for a transfer to New York, where he became an admiral's aide.

Fighting in Vietnam left Kerry feeling certain that the war was wrong. He and several dozen other boat captains had even confronted the American commander of the war in January of 1969, protesting the policy of "free fire zones," which authorized naval forces to shoot anyone violating a curfew, civilians as well as guerrillas. Also, five of Kerry's friends, including a Yale classmate, had died in the war. Kerry received an early discharge in January of 1970 to run for Congress in a district in Massachusetts, but he was not well-known, and he dropped out after he saw another anti-war candidate would win. That year, he married Julia Thorne, his best friend David's sister, who he had met and started dating six years earlier. He soon joined the protest group Vietnam Veterans Against the War, and argued that it should attract attention by staging a rally in Washington. He became the organizer of the rally, and since his educated, clean-cut image helped refute the then-common stereotype that anti-war protestors were hippie radicals, Kerry quickly became a leading spokesman for the group.

In April of 1971, the day before the rally, Kerry testified before the Senate Foreign Relations Committee. According to the *Boston Globe*'s Michael Kranish, Kerry said, "How do you ask a man to be the last man to die for a mistake?" He also asserted that some American soldiers in Vietnam had committed atrocities during the war, citing soldiers' testimony during a conference his group had held on the subject. The speech immediately made him a celebrity. He spoke the next day at the rally, which drew 250,000 people to the Mall in Washington. Weeks later, Kerry was profiled on the television program *60 Minutes*. "Do you want to be president of the United States?" the interviewer asked him, according to Kranish. "No," Kerry said, but he added, "That's such a crazy question when there are so many things to be done and I don't know whether I could do them." He began traveling the country to speak at protests, including an appearance with singer John Lennon in New York City.

However, when Kerry ran for Congress again in Massachusetts in 1972, his success stalled. Before the election, he moved twice in two months, looking for the best congressional district to run in. He won the Democratic primary in the district he settled on, but a conservative newspaper there attacked Kerry's patriotism and questioned his loyalty to the area's voters. Kerry lost to the Republican in the general election.

The year 1973 marked a turning point in Kerry's life. He enrolled in Boston College Law School days after his wife gave birth to their first daughter, Alexandra. After graduating in 1976 (the same year their second daughter, Vanessa, was born), he became a prosecutor in Middlesex County. The district attorney, John Droney, who suffered from Lou Gehrig's disease, quickly made Kerry his first assistant, shocking the veteran lawyers on his staff. Droney let Kerry run, expand, and modernize the office. As a prosecutor, Kerry fought organized crime and created a crisis unit for rape victims. When Droney's health improved in 1979, and he took back some of his old responsibilities, Kerry started a private law practice. But his years as a prosecutor positioned him well politically, and when the office of lieutenant governor of Massachusetts opened up in 1982, Kerry ran for it and won. (He and his wife separated the same year; they finally divorced in 1988.) He spent much of his time in the office fighting acid rain, which again won him national attention.

Issues of war and peace were still Kerry's greatest passion, though. So when U.S. Senator Paul Tsongas of Massachusetts announced in 1984 that he would not run for re-election, Kerry ran to replace him. Kerry made a freeze on building nuclear weapons a major campaign issue, which helped him in liberal, anti-war Massachusetts, and he won. In the Senate, he specialized in foreign policy; he was appointed in 1986 to the Foreign Relations Committee, where he had testified 15 years earlier. He also made his mark as an investigator; he and his staff uncovered some of the early evidence that President Ronald Reagan's administration was illegally sending aid to the Contra rebels in Nicaragua. Later, Kerry chaired a committee that investigated the fates of American soldiers still missing in Vietnam, Cambodia, and Laos. The task was politically dangerous because at the time, because rumors and conspiracy theories were circulating that soldiers who had fought in the Vietnam War were still being held prisoner there. But Kerry's committee refuted the suspicions, which allowed the United States to normalize its relations with Vietnam in 1995.

On the domestic side, Kerry successfully pushed to include funding for 100,000 more police in a 1994 crime bill and helped write several environmental laws. Though his voting record was mostly liberal, he also defied many fellow Democrats by becoming an early supporter of the landmark Gramm-Rudman-Hollings bill that forced spending cuts to control the federal deficit. Kerry found it harder to make a major impact after the Democrats lost control of the Senate in the 1994 elections, but he developed a reputation for working well with Republicans on some issues. Meanwhile, in 1995, Kerry remarried. His second wife was Teresa Heinz, widow of another senator, Pennsylvania's John Heinz, who had left her his fortune of about $500 million. The next year, Massachusetts' governor, William Weld, tried to unseat him and put up a tough fight, but Kerry beat him by seven percentage points.

In late 2002, Kerry declared that he would run for president in the 2004 election. He was expected to be the Democratic front-runner, but throughout 2003, former Vermont governor Howard Dean attracted more attention, passion, and support. Dean was running as a clear opponent of the war President George W. Bush had started with Iraq in March of 2003. Kerry was stuck in the middle on the issue; he had voted to authorize the use of force against Iraq in 2002 but was critical of the president's decision to go to war without more allies. After a disappointing year, Kerry fired his campaign manager in November of 2003 and started giving tougher speeches. In January of 2004, Kerry surprised political observers by beating Dean in the Iowa caucuses. Days later came a win in the key New Hampshire primary. By March, Kerry had clinched the Democratic nomination.

Kerry campaigned on a domestic policy that included cutting the budget deficit, increasing access to health care, and changing the tax code to discourage companies from moving jobs to other countries. He continued to criticize the president for going to war in Iraq without a stronger coalition of other nations involved, but Kerry's attempts to claim a middle ground on the Iraq issue continued to haunt him, especially his 2003 vote against an $87 billion funding package for the occupation of Iraq, which he explained as a protest vote against a failed policy.

At the Democratic convention in July of 2004 Kerry relied heavily on his service in Vietnam to assert that he could defend the country from terrorists, a major concern of Americans since the September 11, 2001, terrorist attacks. But afterward, a group of Vietnam veterans attacked his war record and his anti-war protests of the 1970s in television commercials. The press declared that the veterans' ads were misleading, but the Kerry campaign was slow to respond. Speakers at the Republican convention in August and September also attacked Kerry's national security record. Polls, which had shown Kerry and Bush in a close race for most of the year, showed Kerry behind in September.

The campaign tightened again after the presidential debates in September and October. Kerry showed off his debating skills and command of foreign policy in the first debate, and commentators and polls overwhelmingly judged him the winner. Kerry's performances in the next two debates were also strong, though Bush held his own better. Polls began to show the candidates nearly tied again. As Election Day approached, it appeared to be a very close election. But on November 2, 2004, Bush beat Kerry 51 to 48 percent in the popular vote and 286 to 252 in the electoral vote. Kerry won all the states in the Northeast and on the West Coast, plus some of the upper Midwest, but Bush dominated the South and West.

Still a senator, Kerry sent an e-mail to his supporters in late November asking them to rally against parts of Bush's second-term agenda and promising to introduce a bill in January of 2005 to extend health care coverage to all children in the United States. Aides say Kerry is considering running for president again in 2008.

## Sources

### Periodicals

*Boston Globe,* June 15-16, 18-21, 2003.
*Newsweek,* November 15, 2004, pp. 42-53.
*Washington Post,* July 25, 2004, p. A1; July 26, 2004, p. A1; November 20, 2004, p. A2.

### Online

"Biography," John Kerry for President, http://www.johnkerry.com/about/john_kerry/bio.html (November 29, 2004).

"Biography," John Kerry's Online Office, http://kerry.senate.gov/bandwidth/about/biography.html (November 29, 2004).

"The Race for President," *New York Times,* http://www.nytimes.com/ref/elections2004/2004President.html (November 29, 2004).

*—Erick Trickey*

# Barbara Kingsolver

## Author

**B**orn April 8, 1955, in Annapolis, MD; daughter of Wendell R. (a doctor) and Virginia (a homemaker; maiden name, Henry) Kingsolver; married Joseph Hoffmann (a chemistry professor), April 15, 1985 (divorced, 1993); married Steven Hopp (a ornithologist), c. 1995; children: Camille (from first marriage), Lily (from second marriage). *Education:* DePauw, B.A. (magna cum laude), 1977; University of Arizona, M.S., 1981; additional graduate study.

**Addresses:** *Office*—c/o HarperCollins Publishers, 10 East 53rd St., New York, NY 10022.

## Career

**R**esearch assistant, department of physiology at University of Arizona, Tucson, 1977-79, technical writer in office of arid lands studies, 1981-85; freelance journalist, 1985-87; author, 1987—; also worked as copy editor, typesetter, medical document translator, X-ray technician, and biological researcher.

**Member:** Amnesty International, National Writers Union, National TV Turnoff, Environmental Defense, PEN West, Phi Beta Kappa.

**Awards:** Feature-writing award, Arizona Press Club, 1986; American Library Association Award for *The Bean Trees*, 1988; American Library Association Award for *Homeland*, 1990; Citation of Accomplishment, United Nations National Council of Women, 1989; PEN Fiction Prize for *Animal Dreams*, 1991; Edward Abbey Ecofiction Award for *Animal Dreams*, 1991; Woodrow Wilson Foundation/Lila Wallace fellow, 1992-93; D.Litt, DePauw University, 1994; Book Sense Book of the Year Award for *The Poisonwood Bible*, 2000; National Humanities Medal, 2001.

## Sidelights

**D**ubbed "the Woody Guthrie of contemporary American fiction" by Matthew Gilbert of the *Boston Globe*, Barbara Kingsolver is an author and social activist. Many of her writings, both fiction and nonfiction, feature social commentary on some level. Through the years, Kingsolver slowly built a following and by the early 2000s, her novels often sold in millions of copies as she fulfilled her goal of both entertaining and informing her readers. Kingsolver told Lisa See of *Publishers Weekly*, "I like to remind people that there's nothing wrong with living where we are. We're not living 'lives of quiet desperation,' but living in the joyful noise of trying to get through life."

Kingsolver was born on April 8, 1955, in Annapolis, Maryland, the daughter of Dr. Wendell R. Kingsolver, a physician, and his wife, Virginia. She grew up in rural Kentucky, specifically Carlisle, where her father was the only doctor in Nicholas County. Her childhood home was located in an alfalfa field. Her father grew a garden, which became one of her interests as she grew up. Kingsolver spent the whole of her childhood in Kentucky, save a year that her father took the family to Central Africa to work as a doctor in a village that needed medical help in 1963. While in Africa, Kingsolver missed second grade.

Because of the rural environment that Kingsolver grew up in, she was not exposed to many things. For example, she did not see a tennis court until she attended college. A sensitive, intelligent child, Kingsolver was an outcast socially. She was interested in writing and reading from an early age, and was a fan of the writings of Carson McCullers and Flannery O'Connor when she was young. Though she did not receive a great high school education, her parents expected her to go to college. Kingsolver's experiences in Kentucky later influenced the topics and characters she explored as an adult author.

After high school, Kingsolver entered DePauw University. Kingsolver had a music scholarship for classical piano, but majored in biology because of the career limitations for someone with a music degree. Though she knew she wanted to be a writer, she took only one creative writing course. She often wrote poems in the margins of her textbooks. She also participated in the protests against the Vietnam War at its end. When Kingsolver graduated, she wanted to be a writer, but did not know how to make a living at it.

When Kingsolver graduated, she traveled to Europe for a time, living in Greece and France. She worked on the fringes of publishing, working as a copy editor, typesetter, and medical document translator. Kingsolver also worked as an X-ray technician and biological researcher. Upon her return to the United States, Kingsolver entered the University of Arizona where she earned her master's degree in biology (some sources say environmental technology). As a graduate student, she studied the social life of termites. She also took another writing class.

After obtaining her master's degree, Kingsolver worked as a science writer for the university's arid lands studies department. She did not pursue a career as a biologist nor complete the Ph.D. program she was entered in because the demands of academia were not to her liking. Many of her advisors thought she was wasting her talents in the sciences. By this time, Kingsolver was writing poems and short stories on her own time, but not showing them to anyone. Kingsolver began thinking about becoming a fiction writer in 1982, after winning a contest in a Phoenix newspaper.

In the early to mid-1980s, Kingsolver worked primarily for the university, but by 1985, was a full-time freelance journalist. She first sold articles to journals such as the *Progressive* and *Smithsonian*. Kingsolver later progressed into doing short fiction works for *Redbook* and *Mademoiselle.*

While attending school and working in Arizona, Kingsolver continued to be a political and social activist. Her first book, which she began writing in the early 1980s, was an extension of this interest. It was about the strike of unionized copper workers against the Phelps Dodge Corporation in Arizona. Kingsolver's focus was on the female union workers as she documented their struggles and growth over the course of the strike. After her agent could not sell Kingsolver's half-completed manuscript that she wrote over two years, Kingsolver temporarily gave up writing the nonfiction work.

In 1985, Kingsolver married Joe Hoffman, a chemistry professor at the University of Arizona. While pregnant with their daughter, Camille, she suffered from insomnia, a condition which actually helped her write her first novel, *The Bean Trees*. Somewhat based on her own life, it was about a woman, Taylor Greer, who leaves behind a rural life in Kentucky for the more urban Tucson, Arizona. There, she encounters the sanctuary movement. Over the course of the novel, she adopts a young Cherokee girl named Turtle, and hits the road.

Kingsolver's agent successfully auctioned the book, and Kingsolver used her advance to finish her book about the female miners. Entitled *Holding the Line: Women in the Great Arizona Mine Strike of 1983*, it was published in 1989. That same year, Kingsolver published a collection of short stories, *Homeland and Other Stories*. Like the mining book, many of the stories were political and it was set in the Southwest, but with a variety of characters, many of whom were different than herself and those found in her first novel.

While Kingsolver published nonfiction works and short story collections, novels remained her primary publications. She carefully planned her novels, focusing on themes and craft. In these aspects, she was greatly influenced by Doris Lessing, Margaret Atwood, Alice Walker, and John Steinbeck. One novel by Kingsolver that was carefully constructed was her second, 1990's *Animal Dreams*. The novel focused on Codi Noline, a character who is rather lost at the beginning of the book. Her sister has left to go to Nicaragua to engage in battle for social justice. Noline goes to her hometown where she deals with past pains, her father's struggle with

Alzheimer's disease, and family and environmental problems. Despite these struggles, she grows in her family life, her community, and the world at large. Kingsolver found the novel hard to write because the issues were close to her heart, yet she developed a following of readers for her combination of politics and social activism in a fictional milieu.

As Kingsolver was publishing her third novel in the early 1990s, her personal life was undergoing some changes. Her marriage to Hoffman ended in divorce in 1993. Within a few years, she was remarried to Steven Hopp, an ornithologist, with whom she had another daughter, Lily, in 1996. The same year as her divorce, Kingsolver published her third novel, *Pigs in Heaven.* This was a continuation of the story she told in *The Bean Trees.* In the novel, Taylor Greer has to fight the Cherokee Nation to retain custody of her adopted daughter, Turtle. The nation's lawyers believe the girl should be raised among her own people and tries legal means to get her back. Kingsolver explores issues of community and different points of view on a difficult issue. She was compelled to address the Native American point of view she felt she left out in *The Bean Trees.*

*Pigs in Heaven* became a best-seller for months, and the first book by Kingsolver to reach the *New York Times* best-sellers list. Kingsolver followed this two years later with a collection of essays called *High Tide in Tucson.* In the essays, many of which were written specifically for the book, she addressed issues such as activism, love, motherhood, and her relationship with her daughter and the world around her. This book also sold well, and its popularity gave her hope.

Kingsolver's biggest and best-selling book to date was published in 1997, the novel *The Poisonwood Bible.* Drawing somewhat from her experiences in Africa as a child, the novel was primarily set in Africa's Belgian Congo in the late 1950s and early 1960s just as the Republic of Congo was being established. She focused on the lives of a family of evangelical Baptist missionaries headed by Nathan Price over a span of 30 years. Price wants to civilize the Africans, though his efforts do not turn out the way he expected and profoundly affects him and his family. The story is told by the five women in his life, his wife and four daughters, each of whom offers their own point of view and voice. Kingsolver had wanted to write this book since her childhood, and when she finally did, it was with a new maturity in its breadth, tone, and themes. The sweeping epic was also the longest book she had written, nearly 550 pages.

The book proved extremely popular. While it was a best-seller soon after publication, sales of *The Poisonwood Bible* zoomed after talk show host Oprah Winfrey selected it for her book club in 2000. The novel sold at least two million copies. After this success, Kingsolver was unsure what to do next creatively. One thing she did was found and endow the Bellwether Prize for Fiction. She did this to support and promote literature of social change. While benefiting other writers, Kingsolver continued to write herself.

In 2000, Kingsolver published her next novel, *Prodigal Summer,* which was also a best-seller. Unlike any of her previous novels, this book explored themes of relationships and sex and was set in the Appalachias. *Prodigal Summer* had a complex narrative structure in that the stories were linked together through Deanna, a naturalist who lived with a man named Eddie Bono. In addition to looking at sex, it was also about biology, the preservation of wilderness, small farmers, and the challenges they face.

While Kingsolver was becoming a very successful novelist, she continued her political activism. She participated in the dissent against the American war in Afghanistan, and published many outspoken editorials and essays critical of U.S. President George W. Bush after the September 11, 2001, terrorist attacks on the United States. Because she supported her country, but was critical of its leaders, some critics pushed booksellers to remove her books from their shelves. Kingsolver's writings about politics and America, as well as nature and humanity, were published in a collection of essays called *Small Wonder* in 2002.

Over the years, many critics praised Kingsolver's ability to balance social and political concerns with the demands of a novel's narrative. Yet because many of her readers were women, many male critics were accused of giving her negative reviews because they did not understand her writing the way women did. As she explained to the *Boston Globe*'s Gilbert, "The power of fiction is that it creates empathy. It differs from nonfiction in that way.... If I write a novel, I'm not just informing you, I'm inviting you into someone's life. And fiction takes place in real time. So you put your own life away and you put on this other life and you hear the things she hears and sees the things she sees and you feel her feelings.... And then you close the book and go back to your own life, but that set of feelings is embedded in you somewhere. I think creating empathy is a political act. It's the antithesis of bigotry and meanness of spirit."

## Selected writings

*The Bean Trees,* HarperCollins (New York City), 1988.
*Holding the Line: Women in the Great Arizona Mine Strike of 1983,* ILR Press (Ithaca, NY), 1989.

*Animal Dreams,* HarperCollins (New York City), 1990.

*Another America/Otra America,* Seal Press (Seal Beach, CA), 1992.

*Pigs In Heaven,* HarperCollins (New York City), 1993.

*High Tide in Tucson,* HarperCollins (New York City), 1995.

*The Poisonwood Bible,* HarperCollins (New York City), 1997.

*Homeland and Other Stories,* Buccaneer Books, 1999.

*Prodigal Summer,* HarperCollins (New York City), 2000.

*Small Wonder,* HarperCollins (New York City), 2002.

# Sources

## Books

*Dictionary of Literary Biography: Volume 206: Twentieth Century American Western Writers, First Series,* Gale Group, 1999, pp. 180-90.

## Periodicals

*Boston Globe,* June 23, 1993, p. 25.
*Denver Post,* May 30, 2004, p. F12.
*Guardian* (London, England), November 18, 2000, p. 48; June 22, 2002, p. 10.
*Independent on Sunday* (London, England), July 8, 2001, p. 17.
*Nation,* January 8, 2001, p. 7.
*Newsweek,* November 13, 2001, p. 66.
*New York Times,* September 1, 1993, p. C1; October 11, 1998, sec. 6, p. 53.
*Organic Style,* May/June 2003, p. 83.
*People,* October 11, 1993, p. 109.
*Progressive,* February 1996, p. 33.
*Publishers Weekly,* August 31, 1990, p. 46; February 10, 1997, p. 19; June 26, 2000, p. 20; October 9, 2000, p. 22.
*Rocky Mountain News,* October 18, 1998, p. 1E.
*St. Louis Post-Dispatch,* December 17, 1995, p. 3D.
*Washington Post,* July 14, 1993, p. D1.
*Women's Review of Books,* July 2002, pp. 10-11.
*World and I,* April 1999, p. 254.

## Online

*Contemporary Authors Online,* Gale, 2002.

—A. Petruso

# Sophie Kinsella

AP/Wide World Photos

## Author

**B**orn in 1969, in England; married Henry (a teacher), c. 1990; children: Freddy, Hugo. *Education:* Earned degree from Oxford University, c. 1991.

**Addresses:** *Agent*—c/o Author Mail, Transworld Publishers Ltd./Black Swan, 61-63 Uxbridge Rd., Ealing, London W5 5SA, England.

## Career

**A**ccompanied her vocalist husband on the piano in musical recitals, early 1990s; financial journalist in England until c. 1995; published first novel, *The Tennis Party,* under name Madeleine Wickham, 1995; wrote four others before *The Secret Dreamworld of a Shopaholic,* published under pen name Sophie Kinsella, 2000, and in the United States as *Confessions of a Shopaholic,* 2001.

## Sidelights

**B**ritish author Sophie Kinsella is the pseudonymous creator of the immensely successful "Shopaholic" novels. The lighthearted tales center around one woman's struggle to rein in her madcap spending habits, find professional achievement, and snag the man of her dreams. The first book to feature Becky "Shopaholic" Bloomwood was published in the United Kingdom in 2000, and sold so well on both sides of the Atlantic that Kinsella created an entire mini-genre featuring her heroine, and some three million copies of the series were in print four years later. Kinsella believed that the financial woes chronicled in the books were part of their appeal.

"Money is an emotional subject, which affects people's lives, even though they think it shouldn't," she told *Sunday Times* journalist Samita Talati. "I find that interesting."

But few knew that the "Shopaholic" books were not actually Kinsella's literary debut. She had written several others under her real name, Madeleine Wickham, before deciding to try to write something new when she was nearing 30 years old. Like her heroine, Kinsella had worked as a financial journalist. She grew up in the Wimbledon area, the southwest London suburb, in a home where both parents were educators. A talented pianist as a teen, she attended the Sherbourne School for Girls in Dorset, and entered Oxford University to pursue a degree in music. She decided, however, that musical studies were not for her and switched instead to the politics, philosophy, and economics program at New College of Oxford.

In a real-life romantic twist, Kinsella met her future husband on her first night at Oxford. He was an aspiring musician, too, but eventually earned his degree in classics. They married when she was 21 years old, and for a time even toured together giving recitals. But by 1993 or so Kinsella had settled into a career as a financial journalist, which she found uninspiring. She confessed in an interview with CNN.com that she had a bad habit of "taking the longest lunch hours known to mankind." She began to write fiction on the side, and her first novel, published under her real name, was 1995's *The Tennis Party*. Its story centered around a group of well-to-do friends—with some veiled enmities against one another—who gather for a country-estate weekend. One tries to lure the others into a spurious investment scheme, and there is a hint of future "Shopaholic" themes when one of the husbands discovers that his wife is deeply in debt.

Kinsella had written her first novel during her lunch hours and in the evenings, and was stunned to land a large advance for three more books when an agent found a publisher for *The Tennis Party*. "I wasn't sure what I wanted to do as a career, but didn't have any expectations of becoming a full-time novelist," she recalled in the interview with the *Sunday Times'* Talati. That first book, and Kinsella's subsequent novels under her Wickham name, fit neatly into what is sometimes dismissively referred to as the "Aga sagas" of contemporary British popular fiction. Named after the classic kitchen stove common to many middle-class households in Britain, their plots hinge upon some family- and friends-drama among well-educated suburbanites. Kinsella's second book, *A Desirable Residence,* was an interconnected tale of three suburban London families at personal and real-estate crossroads, which a *Publishers Weekly* reviewer found "entertainingly related, for Wickham has a clever eye that renders her characters' emotions and fears universal rather than stereotypical."

Kinsella's third novel under her Wickham name was *Swimming Pool Sunday* in 1997, in which tragedy befalls a little girl at a pool party. The ensuing drama complicates her mother's already-troubled relationships with both her husband and paramour. "In less brisk hands than Wickham's this could all descend into queasy sentimentality," noted a *Times* of London review from Sally Baker, "but instead rattles along at a good pace, assisted by subplots concerning other people's hopes and dreams."

Kinsella wrote *The Gatecrasher* and *The Wedding Girl* as Madeleine Wickham before deciding to try her hand at a lighter style of fiction. She settled on a new pen name, taken from her middle name and her mother's maiden name, and called herself Sophie Kinsella. "Writing under a different name meant that it didn't matter if the book was a disaster," she told Karyn Miller for a *Mail on Sunday* profile. "I could always go back to my other books."

*The Secret Dreamworld of a Shopaholic* was published by the London company Corgi in 2000, and the following year in the United States as *Confessions of a Shopaholic*. Its heroine, Rebecca "Becky" Bloomwood, is a 25-year-old financial journalist with some terrible personal-finance habits of her own. She lives in a posh London neighborhood she can ill afford, overspends on clothes, and then buries her bank statements and credit-card bills in a drawer. Seeking an avenue out of her mounting crisis, she settles upon a plan to snag a successful advertising mogul as her future husband. A series of comic mishaps followed by a few revelatory moments bring the plot to a satisfying end.

*Confessions of a Shopaholic* caught on with readers via word-of-mouth, and sold extremely well. Critics were not always kind, however. "Rebecca is so unremittingly shallow and Luke is so wonderful that readers may find themselves rooting for the heroine not to get the man," noted a *Publishers Weekly* reviewer, who conceded that some passages have "a certain degree of madcap fun." But Becky's real-life counterpart in the United States, *Money* magazine advisor and television personality Jean Sherman Chatzky called it "an entertaining read" and admitted the ultimate message of the plot seemed to be "it's not always about the money."

Kinsella said that the idea for *Shopaholic* came relatively easily to her. It was the initial "Visa bill scene" that spurred her, she told *San Francisco Chronicle* writer Laurel Wellman. "It came into my head, opening a Visa bill and being in total denial about the whole thing. And once that happened I could see the character, I could see where it was going, and I could see the potential for comedy." Setting Becky out on more adventures came easily after the success of the first. The sequel *Shopaholic Abroad*—changed to *Shopaholic Takes Manhattan* for its American publication in 2002—finds Becky with a better-paying television job and the ad-exec Luke as her steady boyfriend. When his career takes him to Manhattan and she follows, however, a whole new world of high-end shopping tempts her. Before long, she has been exposed in the press back in England as a questionable financial-advice giver, and Luke breaks up with her. The setbacks dissipate, however, before the conclusion, and Becky triumphs once again.

Kinsella continued to write soberer fare under her own name, and in 2000's *Cocktails for Three* she moved out of the Aga-saga realm and set her characters in the world of magazine publishing. She returned to Shopaholic Becky in 2002 with *Shopaholic Ties the Knot*, which begins with Becky in perhaps the ideal job, finally: as a personal shopper for Barneys, the upscale Manhattan retailer. Predictable chaos ensues as plans to wed Luke get underway.

"I think, what would be the most cringing, toe-curling thing that could happen to this person and will create ultimate tension in the story?" Kinsella told Talati in the *Sunday Times* about how she devises Becky's often-comical mishaps.

It was only with the 2004 publication of her first non-Shopaholic book under the Kinsella pseudonym that she finally revealed her identity as Madeleine Wickham. *Can You Keep a Secret?* features a Becky-like heroine named Emma Corrigan, who desperately hopes for a promotion in the marketing department of the beverage giant where she works. Coming back from a client meeting that went badly, Emma blurts out several secrets—including the fact that she doesn't really like her job all that much anyway—to the handsome stranger seated next to her on a bumpy business flight. On Monday morning, she sees the man again, but this time at the office: he is the company's American owner. A *Publishers Weekly* review termed the plot somewhat transparent, but conceded that "Kinsella's down-to-earth protagonist is sure to have readers sympathizing and doubled over in laughter." The title landed on the *New York Times* best-seller list and Kinsella even wrote the screenplay for the film version, in which Kate Hudson would star as Emma.

*Shopaholic & Sister,* published in 2004, features a now-married Becky still struggling with her personal-finance demons. But more complex problems arise when her parents reveal that a long-ago relationship her father had produced a long-lost sibling. Kinsella imagines the fun sisterly shopping trips she and Jessica will embark upon, but Jessica turns out to be a stodgy environmentalist with a distaste for frivolous consumerist pursuits.

Kinsella's Shopaholic series has been such a success that the titles have been translated into nearly three dozen languages, a testament to the universal themes she addressed about finance and romance. The story has even been optioned by Disney for a possible movie. Though she admits to being somewhat of a free-spender on clothes, Kinsella is a suburban mother of two boys who lives near where she herself grew up. Having left her journalism job behind many years ago, she writes novels full-time, and keeps to a regular schedule. She has been sidetracked from her writing only once when poor ergonomics brought on sudden, intense pain in her arms and an inability to write.

"The pain was bad enough," Kinsella recalled in an article she wrote about the experience for the *Evening Standard.* "But it was nothing compared to the panic I felt.... Writing is my livelihood." Diagnosed with repetitive strain injury from poor posture at her desk and long working hours, she began to manage the condition with a combination of Pilates, physiotherapy, and some new office furniture. "I still slouch, I still forget to stretch, and I constantly forget to take regular breaks," she admitted in the *Evening Standard.* "It's very hard to wrench myself away from the middle of a scene—especially if my fictional lovers are on the brink of kissing. But then, it would be harder still if my hands seized up ... and they never got to kiss at all."

Kinsella is thrilled that she hit upon a literary heroine who resonated with millions of readers. She had not planned to write the fourth in the series, *Shopaholic & Sister,* "but I kept getting letters from readers asking, 'Where's Becky?' 'What's she doing?' 'How's her honeymoon going?'" Kinsella said in the CNN.com interview. "It was like being asked about a mutual friend. So I started thinking, 'How is she? How's the honeymoon going? What did she buy?'" Though some critics have dismissed the books as frothy "chick-lit" in the vein of *Bridget Jones' Diary,* Kinsella noted that the sales speak for themselves. "If you look back at books of the '80s," she told CNN.com, "they were all about women in shoulder pads, often coming from a poverty-stricken background, forming a multinational company and taking over the world while having sex in lots of glamorous locations, sometimes with goldfish. You gobbled them up, but you didn't think, 'Oh, this is like me.' It was like reading about aliens."

## Selected writings

### Novels (as Madeleine Wickham)

*The Tennis Party,* Black Swan (London, England), 1995.
*A Desirable Residence,* Black Swan, 1996; St. Martin's, 1997.
*Swimming Pool Sunday,* Black Swan, 1997.
*The Gatecrasher,* Black Swan, 1998.
*The Wedding Girl,* Black Swan, 1999.
*Sleeping Arrangements,* Black Swan, 2001.
*Cocktails for Three,* Black Swan, 2000; St. Martin's/ Dunne, 2001.

### Novels (as Sophie Kinsella)

*The Secret Dreamworld of a Shopaholic,* Corgi (London, England), 2000; published as *Confessions of a Shopaholic,* Bantam Dell/Delta (New York City), 2001.

*Shopaholic Abroad,* Black Swan (London, England), 2001; published as *Shopaholic Takes Manhattan,* Dell (New York City), 2002.
*Shopaholic Ties the Knot,* Black Swan, 2002; Bantam Dell/Delta, 2003.
*Can You Keep a Secret?,* Dial (New York City), 2004.
*Shopaholic & Sister,* Dial, 2004.

## Sources

### Periodicals

*Booklist,* January 1, 2001, p. 918; February 15, 2004, p. 1037; April 5, 2004, p. 15.
*Bookseller,* June 18, 2004, p. 62.
*Evening Standard* (London, England), May 4, 2003, p. 18; June 17, 2003, p. 24.
*Library Journal,* March 1, 1998, p. 130.
*Mail on Sunday* (London, England), May 4, 2003, p. 18; June 20, 2004, p. 21.
*Money,* July 1, 2001, p. 121.

*People,* October 11, 2004, p. 56.
*Publishers Weekly,* February 26, 1996, p. 86; January 20, 1997, p. 394; December 18, 2000, p. 53; June 25, 2001, p. 46; December 10, 2001, p. 49; January 5, 2004, p. 37; April 5, 2004, p. 15; August 30, 2004, p. 32; October 11, 2004, p. 17.
*Times* (London, England), June 10, 1995, p. 15; May 3, 1997, p. 12.
*WWD,* October 7, 2004, p. 4.

### Online

"Confessions of a 'Shopaholic' Enabler," CNN.com, http://www.cnn.com/2004/SHOWBIZ/books/10/13/books.shopaholic.ap/ (November 16, 2004).
"Sophie Kinsella," *Contemporary Authors Online,* Thomson Gale, 2004.

—*Carol Brennan*

# Keira Knightley

Francis Specker/Landov

## Actress

**B**orn March 26, 1985, in Teddington, Middlesex, England; daughter of Will Knightley (an actor) and Sharman Macdonald (a playwright).

**Addresses:** *Agent*—PFD, Drury House, 34-43 Russell St., London, England, WC2B 5HA.

## Career

**A**ctress in films, including: *Star Wars: Episode I—The Phantom Menace,* 1999; *Bend It Like Beckham,* 2002; *Pirates of the Caribbean: The Curse of the Black Pearl,* 2003; *Love Actually,* 2003; *King Arthur,* 2004. Television appearances include: *Oliver Twist* (British miniseries), 1999; *Dr. Zhivago* (British miniseries), 2002.

**Awards:** London Critics Circle award for best newcomer, 2003; best international actress award, Irish Film and Television Festival, 2004; breakthrough award, Hollywood Film Festival, 2004.

## Sidelights

**W**hen people talk and write about British actress Keira Knightley, they usually start by mentioning her beauty, but Knightley's personality and background add dimension to her appeal and her life story. Her best early roles, in action-adventure and sports films, show off her tough, tomboy side. She comes from a family of dramatists, who have given her a realistic, cautious outlook about the film industry and her own career. As 2004 came to a close, Knightley had just filmed her first serious, dramatic role, a big test of how seriously she will be taken as an actress in the future.

Knightley grew up in suburban London, England, the daughter of actor Will Knightley and playwright Sharman Macdonald. The theater has been in the family's blood for a long time. A great-grandmother was in a dance troupe called the Tiller Girls, and a great-grandfather, after trying to make it as a Shakespearean actor, ended up as a ringmaster for the European version of Buffalo Bill's Wild West show. Knightley's older brother, Caleb, is also an actor.

"I was born on a bet," Knightley told *Vanity Fair*'s Steven Daly. "My dad said to my mum, 'If you sell a script, we can have another child.' She wrote a play called *When I Was A Girl, I Used to Scream and Shout,* and she won various awards for it. And I was the child." The play ran for eight years in London.

When Knightley was three years old, she got jealous of the phone calls her father got from his agent, and begged her parents for an agent of her own. They got her one when she was six, as a reward for her hard work trying to overcome dyslexia, a learning disability that makes it difficult to read. She has been a professional actress since age seven, working in television and commercials, but her parents never enrolled her in any formal acting training. Today, Knightley still brings her mother with her on many of her acting travels. People remark on their closeness and similarities. As a sign of their informal relationship, she calls her mother "Shar."

In 1999, Knightley appeared in her first blockbuster film, though it hardly made her famous, because the role kept her from standing out. In *Star Wars: Episode I—The Phantom Menace,* she played a handmaiden to Natalie Portman's character Queen Amidala. At one point, her character becomes a decoy, standing in for the queen. Though no one would confuse Portman and Knightley today, at age 12, Knightley looked enough like Portman that, with makeup on, even their mothers could not tell them apart.

Stardom came a few years later, after Knightley turned 16 and her parents let her become a full-time actress. She was chosen for a major role in *Bend It Like Beckham,* a British film released in 2002 about teenage girls on a soccer team. (The movie's title refers to British soccer star David Beckham and his ability to kick a ball so that it curves instead of going in a straight line.)

To look convincing as a soccer player, Knightley trained for about five months. "I was very sporty at school," she told *Cosmopolitan*'s Lesley Goober. "I was captain of the girls' soccer team, but I still had to learn to play for *Beckham,* because my version of playing soccer was being fast and kicking people in the shins."

Knightley's character, Jules Paxton, becomes good friends with the main character, played by Parminder Nagra, a teen of Indian descent whose traditional parents are not sure they want their daughter playing a sport. Knightley was planning to return to college and work at a skateboard shop after filming the movie. But it became an unlikely hit—the number-one movie in Great Britain, popular and critically acclaimed in the United States.

Moving quickly to a new project while she had Hollywood's attention, Knightley appeared in 2003's *Pirates of the Caribbean: The Curse of the Black Pearl,* based on the Disney amusement park ride. Her co-stars were established leading man Johnny Depp and young star Orlando Bloom. (Knightley has often repeated the story of meeting Depp for

the first time and being shocked by the gold caps he had had put on his teeth so he could look more pirate-like.) In the movie, Knightley plays Elizabeth Swann, a governor's daughter, snobby and disapproving of Depp's rakish ways, but also falling in love with Bloom's character.

"She took an underwritten, damsel-in-distress character and turns her into a full-blooded, damsel-doing-just-fine-thank-you," Carla Power of *Newsweek* noted approvingly after the movie came out. In one of Knightley's most talked-about scenes, her character attacks a pirate with a metal pole and quips, "You like pain? Try wearing a corset." Her corset complaints were included in the movie's trailer, and she repeated them off-camera, telling one interviewer that the constricting wardrobe—which helped give her a 19-inch waist—almost made her faint one day.

Moviegoers got another chance to see Knightley in 2003 when she appeared in the Christmastime film *Love Actually,* with an ensemble cast full of well-known British actors. She played a young bride who discovers that her husband's best friend has a secret crush on her. The role pretty much only called for her to look beautiful and seem sweet, but it got her a lot of attention.

"There are a lot of beautiful girls around the world," Jerry Bruckheimer, producer of *Pirates of the Caribbean* and her next film, *King Arthur,* told *Vanity Fair*'s Daly. "But the problem is, they can't turn off who they are when the camera turns on. Keira is very natural in front of the camera—when she becomes the character, you don't see any of the acting wheels turning."

Bruckheimer cast Knightley as Guinevere in his retelling of the King Arthur legend, giving her a chance to play an action heroine. The movie aimed to tell a gritty, authentic version of Arthur's story, so Knightley played a tougher Guinevere than people are used to. "British women used to fight alongside the men, so it is historically accurate," she told *Cosmopolitan*'s Goober. "I got to use swords and knives and axes and garrotes and bows and arrows," she enthused to *Vanity Fair*'s Daly.

Knightley trained four days a week for three months, then almost every day during the five months of filming, to meet the script's physical demands. On a typical day, she lifted weights for an hour and a half or more, then spent three hours boxing or horseback-riding. Director Antoine Fuqua got rid of Knightley's stunt double once he saw she could wield a sword herself. She bragged that she was better at archery than her male co-stars. She kept up with the guys off-camera too, joining them out at the bars and drinking Guinness with them after a day of filming. "I would describe her as the most beautiful tomboy you will ever come across," Ioan Gruffudd, an actor in the film, told *People*.

Josh Tyrangiel of *Time* summed up Knightley's acting talents this way: "[She] has a refined look, brisk comic timing and a brawler's instinct for knowing when to shut up and throw a punch." But Knightley expressed skepticism about her accomplishments. Of her *King Arthur* role, she told Tyrangiel, "I had to work out physically quite a bit, but pretty much it's scream a lot and enjoy being painted blue." About her career, she added, "I don't think I can call myself an actress yet.... Until I'm good, I can say I'm trying to be an actor, but I don't think I've completely made it." *Newsweek*'s Power, visiting Knightley while she was filming *King Arthur*, noticed a video entitled "Acting for Film" in her trailer.

Writers marvel at Knightley's lack of pretension. They note that unlike many of her young acting peers, she does not have a personal assistant. She explained that she needs to learn how to be an adult and take care of herself. Her skepticism about Hollywood also makes an impression. "I love to visit L.A., but I couldn't live there," she told *Vanity Fair*'s Daly. "As an actor you're supposed to be simulating reality, and L.A. is based on unreality. Personally, I don't know how I could 'grow artistically' in a place like that." She seemed very conscious of being judged on her looks in Los Angeles. *Cosmopolitan*'s Goober asked her to name something very British about her. "I haven't had my teeth straightened," she replied. "Aren't British people known for having crooked teeth? It's funny, when I was in L.A., people were like, 'Wow, your teeth aren't actually that bad.'" She stays true to her roots while in California by getting up at 6:30 a.m. to watch her favorite British soccer team, West Ham, at a bar in Santa Monica. One writer noted that even her love for West Ham shows a lack of pretension; she is rooting for her father's favorite team, a working-class team that does not make a lot of money, while most London celebrities root for flashy teams such as Arsenal or Manchester United.

In 2004, Knightley was dating Irish model Jamie Dornan, whom she met during a photo shoot in New York City in August of 2003, the same year a two-year relationship with British actor Del Synnott ended. In April of 2004, *Vanity Fair* reported that she was still living with her parents, but *People* reported in July 2004 that she had recently bought a flat in London.

To some, Knightley still has a lot to prove. In England (where she had appeared in two nude scenes, including one in the 2002 miniseries Dr. Zhivago), the famously snarky tabloid press has called her "English Rose," a nickname meant to suggest that she is mostly famous for being a blushing beauty. She has used the term herself, to describe the roles she wants to get away from. "I'd been doing very English Rose, 'I'm pretty' roles," she told *Vanity Fair*'s Daly. Now, she adds, she's trying to avoid "pretty girl in corset gets into trouble" films.

Instead, Knightley spent part of 2004 filming *The Jacket*, a drama in which she plays the alcoholic American wife of a Gulf War veteran. She says she admired director John Maybury for telling her right away that he was not sure she was right for the role and making her prove herself before she was cast. She is also set to appear in a dramatization of the classic English novel *Pride and Prejudice* in 2005. Her parents, who sometimes had trouble finding steady work in their famously fickle professions, have taught her to work hard while she is in demand. "My five-year plan is to take every job I can," she told Tyrangiel in *Time*. "I know for a fact the work is going to dry up, and people will get bored of me. That's not bitterness, just the truth."

## Sources

### Periodicals

*Cosmopolitan*, August 2004, p. 44.
*Elle*, August 2003, pp. 130-38.
*Entertainment Weekly*, June 27/July 4, 2003, p. 56.
*Hollywood Reporter*, October 11, 2004, p. S8.
*Newsweek*, December 29, 2003, p. 102.
*People*, July 19, 2004, pp. 65-66.
*Time*, July 5, 2004, p. 84.
*Vanity Fair*, February 2003, p. 111; April 2004, p. 314.

### Online

"Keira Knightley," Internet Movie Database, http://www.imdb.com/name/nm0461136/ (November 28, 2004).
"Keira Knightley," PFD, http://www.pfd.co.uk/scripts/get.py/actors/?actors20KNIGHTLK (November 28, 2004).

—*Erick Trickey*

# Bernard Kouchner

## Physician and humanitarian aid worker

**B**orn November 1, 1939, in Avignon, France; married Christine Ockrent (a television journalist); children: one son. *Education:* Earned medical degree in France, c. 1968.

**Addresses:** *Office*—Médecins du Monde, 62 rue Marcadet, 75018 Paris, France.

## Career

**W**orked as a gastroenterologist at Cochin Hospital; volunteer doctor with the International Red Cross, late 1960s; founded Médecins Sans Frontières (Doctors Without Borders), 1971, and served as president until 1978; founded Médecins du Monde (Doctors of the World), 1979, and served as president, 1980-88; became French Minister of State with the Ministry of Social Affairs and Employment, 1988-91; became Minister of State for humanitarian action with the office of the Prime Minister, 1988-91; Minister of State for humanitarian action in the Ministry of Foreign Affairs, 1991-93; Minister of Health and Humanitarian Action, March 1993-99; chief of the United Nations Administration Mission in Kosovo (UNMIK), July 1999-January 2001.

**Awards:** Dag Hammarskjold Prize for Human Rights, 1979; Prix Europa, 1984.

## Sidelights

**A** household name in France, Bernard Kouchner is the physician who founded the humanitarian-relief group Médecins Sans Frontières, or

Doctors Without Borders, in 1971. Known for his high-profile French government posts, Kouchner also directed the United Nations mission in war-torn Kosovo between 1999 and 2001. His publicity-savvy tactics have sometimes made him the target of criticism, but his zeal in helping the world's most helpless is unmatched. "It is Kouchner, more than anyone else, who taught nongovernmental aid agencies to use the political and fund-raising power of the media," asserted Michael Ignatieff in a *New York Times* profile. "Where Kouchner led with Doctors Without Borders, all modern humanitarian agencies now follow."

Kouchner was born in the southern French city of Avignon in 1939. His Jewish father's parents perished a few years later in Nazi German concentration camps, and Kouchner has said that it was this terrible crime of the Holocaust, perpetrated on the soil of a civilized Europe, which fueled a sense of personal injustice that brought him to humanitarian work. As a young man, he was naturally drawn to medicine, and became a gastroenterology specialist. Like many of his age, however, he was also active in the street demonstrations and strikes that rocked France in the spring of 1968.

After a stint at Cochin Hospital, Kouchner answered a newspaper advertisement placed by the International Red Cross that called for volunteer doctors to work in Biafra. The small nation in the Horn of Africa enjoyed a brief period of sovereignty from Nigeria at the time, but was also engaged in a vicious war to maintain it. The Red Cross needed medical personnel to help civilians caught in the crossfire. But the international aid organization also had an official policy of "silent" neutrality, refusing to comment on human-rights abuses they witnessed from either side, be it at the hands of rebels or government troops. That same policy, Kouchner knew, meant that Red Cross aid workers were among the few outsiders to witness the horrors of the Nazi extermination camps firsthand during World War II, but the organization did little to alert Germany's foes at the time. The experience in Biafra, he told *Financial Times* writer Robert Graham, forced him to reevaluate his belief system. "Medical school never prepared me for this: it was only about caring for patients," he told Graham. "But in Biafra I was confronted with basic questions of human justice. You couldn't stand by or remain silent about the broader context in which the humanitarian disaster was happening."

In response, Kouchner founded Doctors Without Borders with other like-minded visionaries in 1971. It was committed to providing humanitarian aid in the midst of armed conflicts, but also stepped in when natural disasters struck. One of its first full-scale missions was to the Nicaraguan capital of Managua, where some 10,000 perished as a result of a devastating earthquake in December of 1972. French physicians with both an adventurous and a humanitarian streak signed up in droves, and were sent off to some of the world's most troubled spots, including Lebanon, El Salvador, Somalia, Vietnam, Cambodia, Honduras, Peru, and Guatemala. In many of those cases, the suffering was the direct result of political conflict, and Doctors Without Borders did not hesitate to alert the media to human-rights abuses committed by any of the involved parties.

Kouchner served as president of Doctors Without Borders until 1978. The following year, he organized hospital ships to aid the scores of Vietnamese refugees who were fleeing the country in rickety, over-crowded vessels and perishing in the South China Sea as a result of their quest for asylum. Aboard Kouchner's "Boat for Vietnam" were noted French philosophers Jean-Paul Sartre and Raymond Aron, who had been longtime foes, but the mission came under fire for the publicity Kouchner courted; the project was even derided as the "Boat for St. Germain des Pres," a reference to the fashionable quarter of Paris where many of France's liberal elite resided. The event caused Kouchner to break with

Doctors Without Borders, and he founded a similar group, Doctors of the World, in 1979. Again, he led humanitarian aid workers to some of the world's most troubled areas, and back in France worked to call attention to the plight of victims of political strife everywhere.

By then, Kouchner was so well-known a figure in France that he decided to enter politics. In 1988, he ran for a seat in the French parliament from Valenciennes, but lost. Instead, French President François Mitterrand appointed him to serve as Minister of State with the Ministry of Social Affairs and Employment, a cabinet department. There, Kouchner was responsible for social integration, and also took a second post, attached to the office of the Prime Minister and with responsibility for humanitarian action, that same year. In 1991, he moved over to the Ministry of Foreign Affairs, again holding a post that made him the country's humanitarian-action watchdog. The French press nicknamed him the "minister of indignation" for his scathing pronouncements, but Kouchner had the support of many for his missions, including that of Danielle Mitterrand, the French First Lady. Kouchner even took Madame Mitterrand to the Kurdish province of Iraq—which he had first visited with Doctors Without Borders back in 1974—in July of 1992 to show her the plight of Kurds under Iraqi leader Saddam Hussein. There, their convoy was the target of a bomb that killed four, and which their own vehicle narrowly escaped.

The attack was thought to have been on orders of Hussein, and may have been in retribution for what some have viewed as Kouchner's greatest achievement: in 1991, he argued successfully for United Nations Resolution 688, by which U.N. peacekeeping forces were sent to protect Iraq's Kurdish minority. Until that time, the concept of national sovereignty had been the guiding objective in United Nations peacekeeping missions, but this one was the first in which the U.N. took a different approach. From that point forward, U.N. "humanitarian corridors" were established by peacekeeping forces in troubled regions where refugees or other victims of authoritarian regimes needed help.

Kouchner launched a national "Rice for Somalia" program in France in the early 1990s, and was credited with bringing the world's attention to the wide-spread famine there. His campaign asked French schoolchildren to donate packets of rice for Somalians, and Kouchner and other aid workers landed on a beach in Mogadishu with television cameras, with Kouchner carrying a sack of rice on his back. "The resulting spectacle looked less like a humanitarian rescue than an MTV video starring Kouchner," noted *Sunday Times* correspondent Tony Allen-Mills. "His political rivals were appalled but, once again, the French public seemed to be thrilled." Kouchner has a different approach to the subject, believing that "without photography, massacres would not exist," the *New York Times* profile by Ignatieff quoted him as saying. "Nothing can be done without pressure on politicians."

Kouchner continued to serve in the French cabinet, in March of 1993 taking a post as Minister of Health and Humanitarian Action. Over the next few years, he made the troubles in the former Yugoslavia his pet project, working to publicize the horrors of the ethnic-cleansing atrocities that were taking place there on a large scale. He traveled regularly to the Bosnian capital of Sarajevo, which suffered tremendous damage in the Balkans war during those years. His work led United Nations Secretary-General Kofi Annan to appoint him to serve as chief of the United Nations Administration Mission in Kosovo (UNMIK) in July of 1999. The post made him the highest-ranking non-military authority in Kosovo, and Kouchner's task was to restore order to the troubled southern Serbia region, which had been the site of a brutal war the year before that was quelled only when military forces of the North Atlantic Treaty Organization (NATO) stepped in. The United Nations established a formal mission there to set up a workable local government, and broker an end to the bloodshed between Kosovo's Albanian majority and the Serb minority.

International political analysts noted that Kouchner's job was a tough one, and his tenure in Kosovo lasted just 18 months. As an administrator, he was responsible for procuring and delivering aid to some 1.4 million displaced persons, but as the head of the U.N. mission he also met regularly—under the most dangerous of conditions at times—with Kosovo Liberation Army rebels and Serb police and paramilitary groups in an effort to end the violence. Several months after taking over, he admitted it was indeed a difficult task. "How can you solve the problems of this region in eight months?" he said in an interview with *Newsweek International*'s Michael Glennon and Joshua Hammer. "Serbs, Albanians, and Turks have been fighting one another in this area for centuries." In the same interview, the eternally optimistic Kouchner recognized that change was not impossible. "Fifty years ago it was unimaginable that my own country and Germany would ever cooperate," he reflected.

Kouchner departed his office in the Kosovo city of Pristina and returned to France in early 2001. He continued his work as the gadfly of French foreign policy, regularly commenting on international matters and bringing media attention to the plight of the world's refugees and displaced persons. Still unofficially known as the Minister of Indignation, Kouchner admitted that he indeed took politics too personally at times. "Of course I do," he responded when Ignatieff asked him about it in the *New York Times* article. "I've been a human rights activist for 30 years, and here I am unable to stop people being massacred."

Though Kouchner is considered the founder of Doctors Without Borders, he took no part in the ceremony when the group earned the 1999 Nobel Peace Prize for its humanitarian work. Married to Christine Ockrent, a well-known French television journalist, he has long been the subject of rumors that he may one day make another electoral bid in France, this one for the president's office. He is the author of several books, including one that has appeared in English translation, *Blood and Honey: A Balkan War Journal*. In early 2003, when many in Europe objected to the United States' plan for military intervention to oust Saddam Hussein in Iraq, Kouchner took what was viewed as a surprising stance for a lifelong French leftist, and supported the idea. In the *Financial Times* interview with Graham conducted in early 2004, he termed Hussein "a monster. The case for going to war to get rid of him was not one of weapons of mass destruction—they probably weren't there anyway. It was a question of overthrowing an evil dictator and it was right to intervene."

Indefatigable, energetic, and impressively media-savvy, Kouchner is also a runner whose morning route varies from Paris's delightful Luxembourg Gardens to some of the world's most devastated landscapes. When he ran the New York City Marathon in 1993, *Runner's World* profiled him, and he asserted that his dual passions—running and humanitarian work—were, in theory, not entirely incompatible. "When I see runners gathered like this today, it seems to me a symbol of what could be done," he told the magazine's John Hanc. "War is the worst side of humanity. Running is the best. And let me tell you, most of the people making war are not runners. It would be a better world if they were."

## Sources

### Books

*Notable Scientists: From 1900 to the Present*, Gale Group, 2001.

## Periodicals

*Economist,* October 13, 1990, p. 43; July 10, 1999, p. 48.

*Financial Times,* September 16, 2000, p. 3; January 17, 2004, p. 14.

*Independent* (London, England), July 26, 1999, p. 4; October 16, 1999, p. 17.

*Newsweek International,* May 15, 2000, p. 74.

*New York Times,* August 6, 2000, p. 42.

*Runner's World,* December 1993, p. 36.

*Sunday Times* (London, England), January 10, 1993, p. 19.

*Time,* April 26, 2004, p. 121.

*Times* (London, England), July 27, 1992, p. 5; October 17, 1992, p. 14.

—*Carol Brennan*

# John Agyekum Kufuor

## President of Ghana

**B**orn December 8, 1938, in Kumasi, Ghana; son of Nana Kwadwo Agyekum (a clan leader) and Ama Paa (a political activist); married Theresa Mensah; children: five. *Education:* Oxford University, B.A. and M.A., 1964.

**Addresses:** *Office*—Office of The President, P.O. Box 1627, Castle Osu, Accra, Ghana. *Website*—http://www.jakufuor2004.org. *E-mail*—jakjakufuor2004.org.

## Career

**N**amed chief legal officer and town clerk of Kumasi, Ghana, 1967; member of Ghana's constituent assemblies (constitutional conventions), 1968-69 and 1979; served as deputy foreign minister and led Ghana's United Nations delegation, 1969-71; elected to parliament, 1969 and 1979; secretary for local government in Ghana's national government, 1982; unsuccessful candidate for president, 1996; won presidential elections, 2000 and 2004; president of Ghana, 2001—; elected chairman of the Economic Community of West African States, 2003.

## Sidelights

**J**ohn Agyekum Kufuor helped bring democracy back to Ghana after a long history of coups and military rulers. His defeat of longtime president Jerry Rawlings in elections in 2000, and the peaceful transfer of power that followed, Ghana's first, marked a significant triumph for democracy in Africa. His diplomacy across West Africa has pro-

*Larry Downing/Reuters/Landov*

moted peace in the region, and his reforms at home have improved Ghana's economy and won the respect of other world leaders. Tall but quiet, he is nicknamed "The Gentle Giant," and his 2004 re-election cemented his reputation as one of Africa's most prominent elected leaders.

Kufuor was born in 1938 in Kumasi, Ghana's second-largest city. His father was the Oyokohene of Kumasi, a powerful clan leader, and his mother was a strong supporter of a party opposed to prime minister and president Kwame Nkrumah in the 1950s and 1960s. Kufuor was such a star pupil at a school in Kumasi that he was admitted to study law at the prestigious Exeter College at Oxford University in England in 1961, and was admitted to the bar as a lawyer in England and Ghana in 1962. (He met his wife, Theresa, who was studying midwifery at Oxford, in 1961 and married her in 1962.) He then earned bachelor's and master's degrees from Oxford in 1964.

Once he graduated, Kufuor returned to Ghana, and was appointed town clerk and chief legal officer of Kumasi in 1967. His political stature increased quickly. He was a member of the assembly that drafted the constitution for Ghana's second republic in 1968-69, then was elected to parliament in 1969.

The prime minister, K. A. Busia (a former Oxford professor who had encouraged Kufuor to study there), named Kufuor deputy foreign minister; Kufuor also headed Ghana's United Nations delegation from 1969 to 1971. However, the government was overthrown in a 1972 coup, and Kufuor spent time in political detention. Once released, he worked as a lawyer and businessman until civilian government returned in 1979, when he again attended the constitutional assembly and was elected to parliament.

Jerry Rawlings, president of Ghana throughout the 1980s and 1990s, was Kufuor's great rival. Rawlings twice took power in Ghana through coups, in 1979 and on the last day of 1981. After the second coup, Kufuor was one of the members of the opposition invited to take part in the government. Kufuor served as the secretary for local government in Rawlings' cabinet for seven months, but resigned. "The regime started committing brutalities. I wrote Rawlings that I disagreed and resigned," Kufuor told a Reuters reporter, according to a *Chicago Tribune* article. "The murder of three magistrates was for me the main reason to resign."

Rawlings ruled Ghana for 18 years, first as a Marxist military dictator, but during the 1990s, he embraced capitalism and responded to pressure for democratic reforms. Meanwhile, Kufuor pursued success in business and helped found the New Patriotic Party, built on a pro-capitalist, moderate-conservative ideology. His party won about a third of the vote in 1992, and Kufuor challenged Rawlings in the 1996 presidential elections, but lost.

In 2000, however, Ghana's constitution prohibited Rawlings from running for re-election, and very high inflation and unemployment had made him and his party less popular. Kufuor ran for president again, this time against Rawlings' vice-president, John Atta Mills, and beat him, 48 to 45 percent in the first round of voting and 57 percent to 43 percent in the runoff election in late December. Mills promised a smooth transition, and in early January of 2001, Ghana saw its first peaceful, democratic change of leaders. "With these elections, Ghana has demonstrated that democracy and its institutions continue to take root in Africa," United Nations Secretary General Kofi Annan, a native of Ghana, commented, as quoted by Kwaku Sakyi-Addo in the *Washington Post*. "The international community should rejoice at this orderly and democratic transfer of power."

Kufuor promised free-market reforms to attract foreign investment and trade. He hoped to improve Ghana's economy enough to pay off the massive domestic and foreign debt accumulated during the Rawlings era. His reforms, he promised, would go deeper than Rawlings' lip service to capitalism. "If this means my being unpopular, it's just unfortunate. I'm ready to be very tough, but tough for a purpose," he told George B.N. Ayittey of the *Wall Street Journal*. While Rawlings' government had often used price controls, Kufuor raised the prices of fuel, electricity, and water in his first year in office. Rawlings, in opposition, loudly criticized Kufuor. He also suggested that Kufuor did not have the military's confidence, a remark that was considered a threat of another coup, but the military declared it supported Kufuor.

In his first year in office, Kufuor and his government entered into the World Bank and International Monetary Fund's Heavily Indebted Poor Countries (HIPC) Initiative, a decision the opposition criticized. Entering the HIPC requires carrying out reforms that countries often find painful. However, the end result is that some of its foreign debt is cancelled as long as the money that would have been spent on debt relief goes to social programs such as poverty reduction. Kufuor's government not only submitted to the program's requirements, it successfully argued that it should be able to use 20 percent of the money freed by foreign debt relief to pay down its domestic debt.

By 2004, Ghana's foreign creditors had agreed to write off more than half of the country's foreign debt over the following 20 years. Ghana also received funding from the United States' Millennium Challenge Account, which only gives money to countries that have shown a commitment to economic freedom and investing in their people. In June of 2004, John B. Taylor, the United States undersecretary of international affairs, visited Ghana to see the impact of its reforms. "We are impressed with Ghana's democracy and [the] government's policies on governance, education, health and freedom of the press. We are also impressed to see inflation down," Taylor said, according to George Frank Asmah of *African Business*.

During his first term, Kufuor became a diplomat who pressed for more democracy and peace in Africa, especially in Ghana's West African neighbors. He and the presidents of Mali and Senegal visited the White House in 2001 and joined United States President George W. Bush in a statement opposing governments that take or hold on to power by unconstitutional means, a remark that was considered a criticism of Zimbabwe's longtime president, Robert Mugabe. When a civil war ended in Sierra Leone in 2002, Kufuor commemorated the moment by joining Sierra Leone's president in setting fire to a pile of thousands of rifles and automatic weapons.

In early 2003, Kufuor was elected chairman of the Economic Community of West African States (ECOWAS), a group that not only promotes economic cooperation in West Africa, but has also worked as a peace-maker, mediating military disputes and sometimes deploying peacekeeping troops. That year, Kufuor brought the Ivory Coast's prime minister and rebel leaders together for peace talks in Accra, Ghana's capital. His efforts could not end the war there. But as the world pressed for an end to the civil war in Liberia in 2003, Kufuor pledged that West African nations would send a peacekeeping force there once the fighting ceased. When Liberian president Charles Taylor stepped down later that year, ending the civil war, Kufuor spoke at the ceremony at which Taylor handed over power.

Kufuor faced some criticism for two foreign policy decisions toward the end of his first term. One was signing an agreement to exempt American citizens from prosecution by the new International Criminal Court, which the United States does not recognize. The other was his support for suspending Zimbabwe from the Commonwealth, an international organization composed of former members of the British Empire. Critics said Kufuor was trying too hard to please Western nations, but his stance on Zimbabwe, at least, was consistent with his opposition to undemocratic governments.

When Ghana's next elections came in December of 2004, Kufuor again faced Mills in the presidential contest. He ran on a platform of having improved Ghana's economy. "Judge me by my works," he told voters at campaign appearances, according to Asmah in *African Business*. Mills accused Kufuor's government of being too dependent on foreign donors and called for a more self-sufficient economy. But Kufuor won almost 53 percent of the vote in the election to Mills' 44 percent.

In his State of the Nation speech in February of 2005, Kufuor pointed to a declining inflation rate and increased stability in Ghana's national currency as signs the country's economy was improving. He promised to improve education in Ghana, support business growth, and pass laws to increase the flow of government information and protect government whistleblowers. "Let's work together to make this nation the just, humane, and prosperous one it can be," he said, according to Kwadwo Mensah of the *New African*.

## Sources

### Periodicals

*African Business*, December 2004, p. 44.
*Akron Beacon Journal* (Akron, OH), June 29, 2003, p. A6.
*Chicago Tribune*, December 8, 1996, p. 17; February 16, 2003, p. 8; December 10, 2004, p. 27.
*New African*, February 1, 2004, p. 42; March 2005, p. 47.
*New York Times*, December 30, 2000, p. A4; May 4, 2001, p. A25.
*Philadelphia Inquirer*, August 12, 2003, p. A1.
*Wall Street Journal*, January 4, 2001, p. A18.
*Washington Post*, December 30, 2000, p. A19; June 29, 2001, p. A5.

### Online

"Biography of J.A. Kufuor," 4 More Years for JAKufuor, http://www.jakufuor2004.org/html/jak_biography.htm (May 21, 2005).
"Debt Relief Under the Heavily Indebted Poor Countries (HIPC) Initiative," International Monetary Fund, http://www.imf.org/external/np/exr/facts/hipc.htm (May 30, 2005).
"ECOWAS elects Niger's Tandja as new head, slams Cote d'Ivoire," IRINNews.org, http://64.233.161.104/search?q=cache:QAa0GQH9eZYJ:www.irinnews.org/report.asp3FReportID3D4516026SelectRegion3DWest_Africa26SelectCountry3DWEST_AFRICA+ecowas+kufuor&hl=en (May 30, 2005).

—*Erick Trickey*

# Ken Kutaragi

**Group Executive Officer of Sony Computer Entertainment**

---

**B**orn in August of 1950 in Tokyo, Japan; son of a printing plant owner.

**Addresses:** *Office*—6-7-35 Kitashinagawa, Shinagawa-ku, Tokyo 141-0001, Japan.

*Kyodo/Landov*

## Career

**J**oined Sony Corporation, 1975; named manager for PlayStation project, Sony, 1991; named assistant general manager, computer entertainment project, Home Video Group, Sony, April, 1993; named director and general manager, research and development, Sony, November, 1993; named executive vice president, research and development, Sony, 1996; named chairman and chief executive officer, Sony Computer Entertainment America, April, 1997; named group executive and executive vice president, Sony Computer Entertainment, June, 1997; named co-chief organization officer, Sony Computer Entertainment, October, 1997; named group executive officer, Sony Corporation, 1998; named president and chief executive officer, Sony Computer Entertainment, 1999; resigned from board and named group executive officer, Sony Computer Entertainment, 2005.

## Sidelights

**K**en Kutaragi is a hero to video-game fans for his role in inventing the Sony PlayStation, and people who admire innovative business leaders get excited about him, too. His battles within Sony to value new invention and compete in the home-video-game market have been well-publicized, and many speculated he would take over leadership of Sony someday. However, in 2005, it was announced that the reins had been handed to Howard Stringer, the first non-Japanese chief executive officer in the company's history. In the meantime, though, as the company struggles, it looked to Kutaragi's newest products to help it turn around.

Born in Tokyo in 1950, Kutaragi is the son of a businessman from the Japanese island of Kyushu who came to Japan's capital to start his own printing company. Kutaragi learned about business while watching his father, and listened when his father, ill with cancer, told him not to take over the family business but to strike out on his own. Trained as an electrical engineer, Kutaragi joined Sony in 1975. He designed a liquid-crystal-display projector in the 1970s, but Sony did not use his design, losing out to other companies who marketed similar technology with success. He developed a reputation as one of Sony's most talented engineers.

The turning point in Kutaragi's career came in 1990, when a partnership between Sony and Nintendo to create a new home-video-game system broke down. Many Sony executives wanted to give up on the home-gaming market. But Kutaragi insisted that Sony could develop its own system. He even threatened to leave Sony if it did not pursue his goal. In 1991, he won his battle: he was named project manager of a group that built a new game system, the PlayStation. The gaming console went on the market in December of 1994 and was a huge hit. It is the most popular video-game console in the world. By the end of the 1990s, it was so popular, it alone was generating 40 percent of Sony's profit.

Kutaragi's charisma, daring, and eagerness to question authority are unusual in Japanese corporate culture. In 1995, he once tried to settle a debate over the PlayStation's design by arm-wrestling a coworker. "Kutaragi is a rare breed in Corporate Japan: an engineer with vision and marketing smarts," said journalist for *BusinessWeek*. Winning the respect of other Sony executives took a long time. "They used to say I was merely lucky with the PlayStation," he told the magazine.

At a 1999 meeting of Sony executives, Kutaragi shocked the crowd by saying Sony needed to be shaken up. "The old guys should step aside to make way for the young," he declared, according to Robert A. Guth in the *Wall Street Journal*. "For years he has reveled in his role as Sony's precocious bad boy—a visionary who pitched spitballs at the company's rulers from his own unassailable perch at Sony Computer Entertainment, the wildly profitable house that his PlayStation built," wrote Steven Levy in *Newsweek*.

Most Japanese companies are secretive about their internal decision-making, but Sony chairman Nobuyuki Idei has often talked about Kutaragi's position in the company, acknowledging him as an important talent while saying he needs to work well with the rest of the company. It is a sign that Sony succeeds in part because it tolerates idealists and rebels more than other companies.

Kutaragi convinced the company to take another big risk on his vision when it began work on PlayStation 2. Instead of using already built components, everything in the PlayStation 2 was designed from scratch. The cost of developing it grew and grew. Other Sony executives, feeling Kutaragi needed a partner, encouraged him to enter a deal with Microsoft to produce an online video game business. Kutaragi met with Microsoft chairman Bill Gates in 1999, but no deal resulted.

When the PlayStation 2 debuted in April of 2000, it sold very well, but Sony found it difficult to mass-produce the chips inside it. The company had to

pour more money into the project, bringing the development cost up to $2.5 billion. Meanwhile, Microsoft announced it would release a competing game console, the Xbox. Sony Computer Entertainment (SCE) lost money that year, nearly dragging all of Sony below the break-even point. Speculation arose in the company that Kutaragi would be nudged out. But PlayStation 2 sales rallied as more games came out for it, and SCE began making money again. The PlayStation 2 took over about 70 percent of the home-gaming market. Within a few years, SCE was generating 60 percent of Sony's profits. Kutaragi's work became even more important to Sony as the company's profits and stock price declined in 2003. Some commentators pointed to Kutaragi's new PSX, a combination digital video recorder, TV, and game player as a possible bright spot, but it ended up having disappointing sales.

As 2005 began, Kutaragi was the center of attention at Sony again. Another new product from his branch of Sony, the PlayStation Portable (or PSP), a nine-ounce gaming machine that can also play movies and music, was released in Japan in December of 2004 and sold 800,000 copies in its first six weeks on the market. Again, Sony was making a big bet on a Kutaragi product; it is producing many of the parts for the PSP itself, which kept the device's retail price down and could make producing it less expensive if it is a hit. But if it flops, the financial cost for the company could be steep. January of that year found Kutaragi at a press conference promoting the PSP, which was scheduled to be released in the United States in spring of 2005. The PSP uses flash memory and a new technology, Universal Media Disc: discs that are only six centimeters in diameter but can store up to 1.8 gigabytes of data. Kutaragi confidently predicted that portable entertainment that uses Universal Media Discs will win out over hard-drive-based devices such as Apple's iPod.

Kutaragi was talking up the PSP as Sony reported that its sales and profits for the year would probably miss their targets, in part because of tough competition from portable entertainment devices such as the iPod. Kutaragi admitted to reporters that Sony had missed out on opportunities in the portable entertainment market by not releasing a device similar to the iPod earlier. (Sony's first music players had not supported the popular MP3 format, and would only play files with Sony's format, Atrac.) Sony management had hesitated because its music and movie divisions were worried about content rights, he said. In the meantime, Kutaragi and his division worked on another innovation: developing powerful microprocessors that could take various kinds of input from broadband networks and run several products, including an upcoming PlayStation 3 home media center.

Sony's innovative spirit had become "diluted," and the company needed to "concentrate on our original nature—challenging and creating," Kutaragi said at the January press conference, as quoted by Yuri Kageyama in the *Washington Post*. His admission of such a mistake and his revelation of an internal company dispute were considered surprising, unusual remarks.

Journalists often suggested that Kutaragi would become chairman of Sony someday. Kutaragi disdained the idea while talking with the *Wall Street Journal*'s Guth. "I would need to sacrifice myself endlessly for the coming years," he says. "My health would be ruined. Some people may find it interesting. But not me." However, Guth pointed out that Sony had a history of elevating mavericks like Kutaragi to top positions to make sure the company is periodically reinvented. However, on March 7, 2005, it was announced that Howard Stringer would become the new chairman and chief executive officer of the company. Kutaragi was scheduled to resign his spot on the board on June 22, 2005, and lose his position as executive in charge of semiconductors and home electronics. He was to remain on top of the game division and take on the new title of group executive officer on April 1, 2005.

## Sources

### Periodicals

*BusinessWeek*, January 13, 2003, p. 64.
*Hollywood Reporter*, January 25, 2005, p. 40.
*New York Times*, May 4, 1999, p. C1; October 29, 2003, p. W1; January 21, 2005, p. C2.
*Newsweek*, October 25, 2004, p. 82.
*Time*, April 26, 2004, p. 93.
*Wall Street Journal*, November 18, 2002, p. A1; October 8, 2003, p. B5; December 10, 2004, p. B3.
*Washington Post*, January 21, 2005, p. E05.

### Online

"Corporate Information," Sony Global, http://www.sony.net/SonyInfo/CorporateInfo (February 21, 2005).
"Ken Kutaragi," Sony Global, http://media.corporate-ir.net/media_files/nys/sne/custom/5-09-02/pdf_bio/kutaragi.pdf (February 21, 2005).
"Sony taps foreigner for CEO," CNN Money, http://money.cnn.com/2005/03/07/news/international/sony.reut/index.htm (March 7, 2005).

*—Erick Trickey*

# Christian Lacroix

AP/Wide World Photos

## Fashion designer

**B**orn Christian Marie Lacroix in 1951 in Arles, France; married Francoise Rosenthiel (a boutique manager), c. 1991. *Education:* University of Montpellier, arts degree, 1973; attended the Sorbonne; received museum curator training at Ecole du Louvre.

**Addresses:** *Office*—Christian Lacroix, 73, rue du Faulbourg Saint-Honoré 75008 Paris, France. *Website*—http://www.christianlacroix.fr.

## Career

**B**egan as a fashion assistant at Hermes; assistant in accessories, Guy Paulin; worked in the office of Jean-Jacques Picart; worked for a haute couture firm in Tokyo, Japan; fashion designer, house of Jean Patou, 1981-86; fashion designer, house of Christian Lacroix, 1987—; costume designer for theater, opera, stage, and film, 1985—; founder, XCLX, 2001; head designer, Pucci, 2002—.

**Awards:** Golden Thimble Award, 1986; Most Influential Foreign Designer Award, Council of Fashion Designers of America, 1987; Golden Thimble Award, 1988; Moliere Award, best costumes, 1996, for *Phedre.*

## Sidelights

**F**rench fashion designer Christian Lacroix made a splash in the mid-1980s with his haute couture line created first for the house of Patou then under his own name. Though he could not come close to

repeating his success until the late 1990s and early 2000s, Lacroix remained an important fashion designer in France and among fashionistas. Lacroix also had an interest in costume design, and designed costumes for a number of ballets, stage productions, and operas beginning in 1985.

Born in 1951 in Arles, France, Lacroix is the son of an engineer father who helped design equipment used in oil drilling. Raised in a bourgeois household in Arles, a community located in the south of France region of Camargue, Lacroix liked to draw as a child. Many of his sketches were of clothing. He also enjoyed the old fashion magazines he found in his grandmother's attic, some from the 1800s. When asked at one point about his future career, the young Lacroix said he wanted to be Christian Dior, the famous French designer. Lacroix also had an interest in costumes, and greatly enjoyed regular visits to Arles' Museon Arlaten, a small museum dedicated to costumes and customs of the area.

While a student, Lacroix built on these interests. He studied art history and the classics at the University of Montpellier. After graduating with his arts degree in 1973, Lacroix went to study at the Sorbonne in Paris. His goal was to become a museum curator, perhaps working at a costume museum like the one he enjoyed as a child. To reach this goal, Lacroix did some additional training at the Ecole du Louvre. However, despite this training, he could not find a job in the field.

The influence of Francoise Rosenthiel, a boutique manager who also worked in other aspects of the fashion industry, changed the course of Lacroix's career. The pair met at a party in 1973 and soon became romantically involved. (They were married around 1991.) At the time, she worked in the office of Jean- Jacques Picart, a freelance image consultant and powerful public relations consultant. Lacroix soon began working in the fashion industry himself.

Lacroix began by working as an assistant for several fashion firms. He started out at Hermes as a fashion assistant. Lacroix then worked at Guy Paulin as his assistant working on accessories. Lacroix moved on to the employ of Picart's offices, where he showed his superior some the fashion sketches he continued to make on the side. Lacroix moved to Tokyo after a time to work for a haute couture firm for a year. Soon after his return, Lacroix was given a job as a head designer at a leading French fashion house.

Lacroix's hiring in 1981 at Jean Patou as a designer was to help the company improve its clothing sales. He was hired by Jean de Mouy, the grandnephew of the company's founder, who wanted to ensure that the company could continue to exist if not be profitable after a time. At the time Lacroix came aboard, the firm sold more of its popular perfumes, such as Joy, than its clothing. De Mouy gave Lacroix the freedom to create two collections per year of couture for women in any way he wanted to do them.

One reason Lacroix was given the chance to design for Patou was his connection to Picart. Picart helped him get the job, and he was involved with the revitalization of Patou. During his early tenure there, Lacroix initially produced designs inspired by what Patou had done in the past. Over time, he slowly developed what would become his signature style. By 1984, his out-there designs attracted a following among fashionable women. He finally broke out with a 1985 collection influenced by his childhood in the south of France.

Lacroix became a star with his 1986 collections for Patou. The collections included a short bubble dress and a pouf dress, both of which were very influential on other designers and changed the face of fashion for a time. Lacroix took many chances with his haute couture looks, including placing bustles on strapless evening dresses. Many observers believed he made modern couture, an industry some considered a dying art, fun again. *People* called his spring/summer 1986 collection "a madcap mix of elegance and razzle-dazzle."

By 1987, Lacroix was considered the toast of Paris because he pushed the envelope of what fashion could be. Many of his designs of the period had an element of fantasy. Lacroix created wide-based skirts, dresses that had a small crinoline in the back but a traditional-looking front, taffeta eyelet skirts, and short, stiff crinolines. Many pieces had a "poufy" element to them. He told Martha Duffy of *Time*, "I am very sure that haute couture should be fun, foolish, almost unwearable. We are like a beautiful Christmas window in a store. We have to make dreams."

Though Lacroix was happy to create haute couture for the house of Patou, he also wanted to create ready-to-wear lines. However, de Mouy would not let Lacroix do this. By the end of 1986, Lacroix was open to offers from other companies. After showing his spring/summer collection for 1987, Lacroix signed a contract to open his own couture company and quit Patou. He was able to just walk because he was only an employee of the company. De Mouy was not happy about the abrupt departure and sued him. De Mouy accused Lacroix, as well as Picart, of planning to leave for months before the designer left his employ. Upon his departure, de Mouy closed down the couture arm of Patou.

Lacroix was able to do both couture and ready-to-wear for his own fashion house, Christian Lacroix. With the deal signed in January of 1987, the company that bore his name was funded with eight million dollars from Financiere Agache, a French company that owned other fashion houses including Dior and a textile manufacturer, Boussac. Financiere Agache was owned by Bernard Arnault, who was interested in what Lacroix had done with fashion. Lacroix signed a 99-year deal with the company. With the founding of his own fashion house, Lacroix was free to design what he wanted, including ready-to-wear, in any manner that suited him. He also had final approval of all products with his name on it. American companies and others lined up to sell Lacroix's work.

For Lacroix's first collections under his own name in 1987, he remained focused on haute couture. He wanted to establish his own identity away from what he did for Patou, including moving away from bustles. Many of his clothes were inspired by the south of France and the costumes that were worn there. The pieces featured bright and deep colors, touches of embroidery, and trims of jewels, fur, and lace. The dresses were not all short as in past collections; the collection included long lengths as well. Lacroix continued to impress with his spring-summer 1988 collection, again influenced by the south of France. Lacroix's success put him at the top of the fashion world. Duffy wrote in *Time,* "Since he opened his own couture house a year ago, his ideas have become the most visible in the field, a rare combination of wit, frivolity, and knowing thefts from both past designers and the great ages in clothing history."

By March of 1988, Lacroix had his first full ready-to-wear collection for fall completed. It was inspired by his couture creations, but was much more simple. The pieces included knits, leathers, and different fabrics. Lacroix also introduced a second ready-to-wear collection that was more expensive and more high-end than the first. To increase the company's profitability, as the couture collections actually did not generate much profit, the Lacroix name was used on a line of furs, fabrics, eyewear, costume jewelry, and men's clothing. By 1990, he also added his own perfume, C'est la vie, and expected to add other cosmetics.

While Lacroix continued to be an influential couture designer in the late 1980s, critics were not as impressed with his creations. Other designers were emerging and becoming more important, and while his celebrity status remained intact, his outrageous designs began to look out of place in a world plagued by economic insecurity after the stock market crash of 1987. As 1990s wore on and fashion became more minimalist, Lacroix's work seemed to better reflect the 1980s than current trends. Even his ready-to-wear collections were not particularly popular as they did not mesh with what was hot in the market at the time. Lacroix still had his fans among fashion critics, but the public was often not in step with him.

Lacroix tried to find his niche in the 1990s, especially in the ready-to-wear market. He introduced Bazaar, a collection of casual clothes, in 1994. Lacroix moved into home products like bed linens in 1995 and blue jeans in 1996. None of these lines did particularly well, though his haute couture line always had a steady core clientele. However, by the late 1990s and early 2000s, the fashion world and the fashion public embraced fantasy and Lacroix became somewhat popular again. In response, Lacroix hired new people to help him revamp his im-

age and provide input into collections in 2000. Around the same time, he signed a new contract with the owners of the house of Lacroix, Louis Vuitton-Moët Hennessy. Lacroix was given the freedom to split his time between his work at his fashion houses and other projects.

While Lacroix's couture collections gained popularity in the early 2000s, his career was especially relaunched by creating wedding dresses, primarily in Europe. This business grew after he designed a wedding dress for the marriage of actress Catherine Zeta-Jones to actor Michael Douglas. Lacroix made wedding dresses for a number of celebrities and other clients. His couture collections moved beyond his obsession with the south of France, but stayed challenging with stripes, animal prints, and other big, bright flourishes. Lacroix expanded his business in other ways as well. He opened a flagship store in Tokyo in 2002, and planned a second in London, England.

Though Lacroix's design career picked up in the early 2000s, his other projects also brought him much joy. Since 1985, he had been designing costumes for stage productions, opera, and ballets. One of his first experiences as a costume designer came with the American Ballet Theatre's production of *Gaiete Parisienne.* By 2001, he had designed costumes for more than 20 shows for companies all over the world. That same year, Lacroix designed costumes for his first film, *Les Enfants du Siecle.* Also during that year, he founded a new company, XCLX, to work in contemporary art, writing, editing, music, and publishing, and design. Lacroix focused on projects and ideas that interested him including redesigning the interior of a high-speed train, releasing a compact disc, and creating installations for an Avignon, France, exhibition.

Side projects aside, Lacroix remained a fashion force. In 2002, he added an additional designing job to his plate. He agreed to become the head designer for the house of Pucci. Lacroix had been influenced by the label in his career, and wanted to help further develop Pucci. Pucci had its heyday a few decades earlier, and was stumbling as a company, but its new owner wanted to keep the name alive. Lacroix had to work within the Pucci aesthetic which worked well with his own approach to fashion. Pucci was big and bold, but with a slightly more stylized look. For his own label and other work, Lacroix looked to a new source of inspiration. He told Jess Cartner-Morley of the *Guardian,* "Today, I feel more than ever connected to the future. Ten years ago, my work was connected with the past, with nostalgia, but now the engine driving me is my life here now and the future."

## Sources

*Australian,* July 25, 2003.

*Guardian* (London, England), March 10, 2001, p. 24; July 7, 2004, p. 9.

*Independent* (London, England), April 18, 2002, pp. 10-11; July 15, 2004, pp. 12-13.

*Independent on Sunday* (London, England), July 1, 2001, p. 12, p. 14.

*InStyle,* June 1998, p. 68.

*Interior Designer,* April 2002, p. 216.

*Los Angeles Times,* July 9, 2004, p. E18.

*Newsweek International,* February 24, 2003, p. 49.

*New York Times,* March 27, 1987, p. A22; September 6, 1987, sec. 6, p. 23; October 17, 1987, sec. 1, p. 11; April 22, 1988, p. B4.

*People,* May 19, 1986, p. 138; December 28, 1987, p. 50.

*Time,* February 9, 1987, p. 76; February 8, 1988, p. 62; March 28, 1988, p. 64.

*Time International,* October 8, 2002, p. 8.

*Times* (London, England), November 24, 2003, p. 10.

—*A. Petruso*

# Ricardo Lagos

## President of Chile

**B**orn Ricardo Lagos Escobar, March 2, 1938, in Santiago, Chile; son of Don Froilán Lagos (a landowner) and Emma Escobar (a teacher); married Carmen Weber, early 1960s (divorced, c. 1967); married Luisa Durán de La Fuente, 1971; children: Ricardo, Ximena (from first marriage), Francisca, two stepchildren (from second marriage). *Education:* Earned law degree from the University of Chile, 1960; earned Ph.D. (economics), Duke University, 1966.

**Addresses:** *Office*—c/o Embassy of Chile, 1732 Massachusetts Ave. NW, Washington, DC 20036.

## Career

**B**egan career at the Institute of the Economy at the University of Chile; director of the university's School of Political and Administrative Sciences, 1967-69; University of Chile, secretary-general, 1970-73, and professor of economics; also served as director of the Institute of the Economy, 1971-72; appointed Chile's ambassador to the Soviet Union, 1972, but not confirmed for the post; Secretary-General of the Latin American Faculty of Social Sciences in Buenos Aires, Argentina, 1973-74; visiting professor, University of North Carolina, Chapel Hill, 1974-75; consultant and economist for United Nations agencies, 1978-83; co-founder, Alianza Democratica (Alliance for Democracy), early 1980s, and president, 1983-84; founded the Party for Democracy, 1987; Minister of Education, 1990-94; Minister of Public Works, 1994-99; elected president of Chile, January, 2000.

*AP/Wide World Photos*

## Sidelights

**C**hileans elected a veteran political operative, Ricardo Lagos Escobar, as their president in 2000. An ardent socialist earlier in his career, Lagos spent years working to unite Chile's fractured left during the country's repressive era of military dictatorship. He is also the first Socialist Party politician to lead the country since President Salvador Allende Gossens died in the 1973 coup that ended democracy for a generation in Chile.

Lagos was born on March 2, 1938, in Santiago, Chile's capital city. His father, Don Froilán Lagos, was a landowner, while his mother Emma Escobar was a teacher by profession. She became a young widow after Don Froilán died when Lagos was eight. At the age of 16, the future politician entered the University of Chile, where he studied law and became active in student politics. He joined Chile's Radical Party during this period, and concluded his studies with a paper on economic theories that gained him a small measure of notoriety and even an interview in *Time* magazine. He went on to earn a doctorate in economics from Duke University in 1966. An early marriage, which produced a son and daughter, ended in annulment after his return from the United States.

The first years of Lagos' career were spent at the University of Chile. He served as director of its School of Political and Administrative Sciences, taught economics courses, and was named Secretary-General of the university by Allende. Elected in 1970, Allende instituted a bold socialist-centered reform program in Chile, which included nationalizing the copper and banking sectors—moves that threatened the country's firmly entrenched middle class. It also made the U.S. presidential administration of Richard M. Nixon wary, and the Central Intelligence Agency worked covertly to destabilize the Allende government, though it had been legitimately elected. On September 11, 1973, after a week of national strikes that paralyzed the country, Allende's presidential palace was hit with aerial fire, and then Army personnel stormed in. After a gunfight, Allende allegedly committed suicide with a weapon given to him as a gift from Cuban leader Fidel Castro, but other sources claim he was slain in a shootout.

That day's cataclysmic events, engineered by a group of conservative, top-ranking Chilean military officers, left a scar on the nation that would prove difficult to heal even three decades later. Socialists and other Allende supporters were rounded up by the Army and detained at the main Santiago sports stadium, and a period of brutal political repression followed. Thousands were jailed, tortured, or disappeared altogether. Within a year, one of the coup leaders, General Augusto Pinochet Ugarte—the country's commander-in-chief of the army—emerged from the junta and proclaimed himself president. Pinochet banned political activities, dissolved congress, and severely curtailed freedom of the press.

As a result, many more fled the country, including Lagos, whom Allende had named Chile's new ambassador to the Soviet Union before the coup; the Chilean Congress, however, had not yet ratified the appointment. Lagos went first to Argentina, where he became Secretary-General of the Latin American Faculty of Social Sciences in Buenos Aires, and then to the United States, where he served as a visiting professor of Latin American studies at the University of North Carolina in Chapel Hill. Back in Chile, the ruthless campaign against the left continued, and it was to this bleak climate that Lagos returned in 1978 to Santiago with his family, which by then included a young daughter with his second wife, Luisa Durán de La Fuente, as well as two children from his first marriage and Durán's two children. He took a post as a consultant and economist for a United Nations regional development agency.

The Pinochet regime began to relax certain restrictions on political activities after a new 1980 constitution that nevertheless served to firmly entrench the military dictatorship. Lagos became involved in politics once again, forming the Alianza Democratica (Alliance for Democracy) with several other progressives; its goal was to foment opposition to the Pinochet regime. After leaving his United Nations post in 1983, he served as the Alianza's president for a year, and emerged as one of the leaders of the country's Socialist Party.

Chile's political thaw ended in September of 1986, when Pinochet was the target of an assassination attempt. Along with 44 other prominent leftists, Lagos was arrested and held for nearly three weeks, though he had no role in the event. His detention only further incited his determination to help Chile return to democracy, and in 1987 he founded a new political organization, Party for Democracy (PPD). Finally, in 1988 international pressure and growing internal unrest forced Pinochet to hold a plebiscite vote on whether or not he should remain in office. Back in 1980, Pinochet had pledged to serve as president for only eight years. In a climate where dissent was dangerous, Lagos was interviewed on television and roundly excoriated Pinochet for going back on his word, and urged Chileans to vote "no" to what he predicted would be another 25 years of human-rights abuses.

Lagos' brave act stunned the nation, and voters turned out in droves to reject another eight-year term for Pinochet in the plebiscite. Free elections were held the following year, in December of 1989, and Lagos ran for a seat in the Senate from a Santiago district, but lost. A new government was installed in early 1990, a Christian Democratic-Socialist coalition, and President Patricio Aylwin Azocar named Lagos to serve in the cabinet as minister of education. Lagos instituted several significant reforms in this post, including a lifting of the ban on female students from their schools if they became pregnant.

Lagos made his own presidential bid in the 1993 race, as a candidate of the Concertación para la Democracia (Concert of Parties for Democracy), which he had worked to bring together. He lost in the primaries to another Concertación candidate, Eduardo Frei Ruiz-Tagle, who won the election, and Frei made Lagos minister of public works after taking office. Pinochet was still around, with a seat in the Senate granted to him for life according to the 1980 constitution, and he remained commander-in-chief of the army. But by then, Chile's economy was flourishing, with rapid growth and impressive international trade revenues, and internal dissent against military rule grew along with it.

In late 1998, Pinochet, who had traveled to Britain for medical treatment, was arrested thanks to a joint effort by Spain—a center of opposition to the Pinochet regime—and British authorities. He was charged with a number of human-rights violations, and the situation threatened to destabilize Chile once again, with the immensely powerful military cabal—which retained unprecedented independence thanks to the 1980 constitution—pressuring Frei to break off formal relations with both European nations. In the end, Pinochet remained under house arrest for more than a year, and was then released on health and humanitarian grounds.

By that point, Chile was gearing up for another presidential race, and Lagos entered the fray once again, this time as a Socialist Party candidate. After doing well in the primary, he faced off with Joaquín Lavín, an early Pinochet supporter and newspaper editor who had authored books lauding Pinochet's economic programs. It was a tight race, and though Lagos finished slightly ahead, he failed to achieve the necessary 51 percent majority to win the election. He squeaked by in the runoff election held in January of 2000 with 51.3 percent of the vote. Before the final count was in, Lagos addressed a crowd of some 20,000 at Santiago's Plaza de la Constitución (Constitution Plaza), and made a special mention of Allende's widow, who was among them. The first elected Socialist president since the slain Allende, Lagos told the crowd that "a new spirit is spreading across our territory," *New York Times* journalist Clifford Krauss quoted him as saying. "I want to resolve the pains of our past. There is space here for everyone. I haven't forgotten the past, but my eyes are open to the future."

Later, Lagos appeared with Lavín on a balcony, and embraced him, a move that was unprecedented in Chilean politics and cemented Lagos' promise to reconcile Chile's right and left. Lavín, in his concession speech, promised to support Lagos and his administration's policies, another surprising turn of events. Lagos was inaugurated in March of 2000, and a disgraced Pinochet returned to Chile days later. There were calls to put the former dictator on trial in Chile, and Lagos promised that he would let the courts decide the matter.

During the first years of his six-year term, Lagos worked to initiate many reforms, both social and economic. He took steps to improve conditions in small Andean mountain towns that were once de-

pendent on mining, and courted American support, from both the government and investment community. He also continued to deal with the Pinochet issue, albeit from a distance. The need to resolve Chile's abysmal human-rights record of the recent past was of particular importance for Lagos' government, and he established a commission, headed by Santiago's archbishop emeritus, Sergio Valech, that began investigating the tragic post-coup years. Some 35,000 Chileans testified, and an official list of 28,000 victims of torture was released in November of 2004. In his statement that day, Lagos professed his sorrow over the findings, but concluded with the phrase *nunca mas* or "never again," which had been a familiar piece of political graffiti in Chile for many years.

The Valech commission recommended life pensions for the victims of torture, and Lagos' government approved the benefit plan, which grants each of the 28,000 a monthly stipend equal to about half of the average monthly wage in Chile. Human-rights groups were still pressuring the military to release information about the missing, but details were slow in coming forth, and there was an amnesty law in place since late 1970s that protected military and police personnel from prosecution. Some argued that Lagos' government should rescind that amnesty law, but instead judicial proceedings against some 300 officers began anyway during the latter half of his six-year term.

Lagos' other achievements in office are similarly historic. In May of 2004, he signed into law a new decree that lifted the country's prohibition on divorce. He also opened the doors of the Palacio de La Moneda, the official seat of the presidency, to the public for the first time in decades. Known as La Moneda, the palace dates back to 1805 and is considered one of the grandest buildings built by the Spanish in South America. It was also the place that the Chilean army stormed in 1973, and where Allende died. Perhaps tellingly, on an official presidential website that reports extensively on Lagos' daily activities, there is also a Web camera feature that provides a number of exterior shots.

Known for his lack of impulsiveness and reasoned approach to reach political consensus, Lagos enjoys high public-approval ratings. He is a weekend gardener and occasional rock climber, and reads histories and listens to Mozart in his spare hours as well. As his country's first Socialist president since the 1973 coup, he does not dispute that his once ardently leftist views have been accordingly adjusted for the 21st century. In a 2002 *Newsweek International* interview with Joseph Contreras, he was asked if he was still a socialist. "Of course," Lagos replied. "Socialism is still guided by a vision of a just society. The tools that are used to achieve that goal are different today because the world has changed. But the search for greater equality is still just as important as the search for greater freedom."

## Sources

### Books

*Worldmark Encyclopedia of the Nations: World Leaders,* Gale, 2003.

### Periodicals

*Guardian* (London, England), January 18, 2000, p. 14; November 30, 2004, p. 14.

*Newsweek International,* August 12, 2002, p. 28.

*New York Times,* January 17, 2000, p. P1; January 18, 2000, p. P3; January 22, 2000, p. P2; December 10, 2001, p. A3; September 7, 2003, p. A3.

*—Carol Brennan*

# Avril Lavigne

AP/Wide World Photos

**Singer and songwriter**

---

**B**orn Avril Ramona Lavigne, September 27, 1984, in Belleville, Ontario, Canada; daughter of John and Judy Lavigne.

**Addresses:** *Management*—Nettwerk Management, 8730 Wilshire Blvd., Ste. 304, Beverly Hills, CA 90211. *Record company*—Arista Records, 6 W. 57th St., New York, NY 10019. *Website*—Avril Lavigne Official Website: http://www.avril-lavigne.com.

## Career

**W**on contest to perform with Shania Twain, 1999; signed with Arista Records, 2002; released *Let Go,* 2002; released *Under My Skin,* 2004.

**Awards:** MTV Music Video Award, Best New Artist, 2003; Juno Award, Single of the Year for "Complicated," 2003; Juno Award, Album of the Year for *Let Go,* 2003; Juno Award, New Artist of the Year, 2003; SOCAN Awards for "Complicated," "Sk8er Boi," and "I'm With You," 2003.

## Sidelights

**T**he rebellious Avril Lavigne has led the way for teenybopper mall shoppers to find a new path to music that is different from the sex-oriented pop released by such performers as Britney Spears, Jennifer Lopez, Christina Aguilera and other singers popular with the MTV crowd.

Lavigne was born in Belleville, Ontario, Canada, and raised in Napanee, a town with a population of roughly 5,000 people located 100 miles southwest of Ottawa. It was a strong Christian home with a stay-at-home mother, Judy, and a father, John, who worked for Bell Canada. Avril was the second of three children, including older brother, Matt, and younger sister, Michelle. As a youngster, Lavigne loved to follow her older brother around. "If he played hockey, I had to play hockey. He played baseball, I wanted to," she told *Entertainment Weekly.* The family enjoyed camping and canoeing trips, dirt-biking and four- wheeling. They attended church at Evangel Temple, and when she was ten years old, Lavigne sang a solo in the Christmas pageant. "They really had no choice," her father told *Maclean's,* "she hogged the mike anyway. She had such a big voice."

Lavigne began taking her talent beyond the church, singing at local fairs and festivals, and even a Canadian Tire celebration. She was discovered singing in a bookstore when she was 14 by her first manager, Cliff Fabri. Fabri recalled to *Entertainment Weekly,* "When I first saw her, I liked her voice, and obviously the looks. But it was the attitude. She goes hunting all the time with her brother and dad.

Here's this sweet little thing, and I said to her one time, 'What about when a little doe comes out and starts nudging up to the mother? What do you do?' And she goes"—Fabri makes the sound of a shotgun blast—"'Dinner.'"

In 1999 Lavigne won a contest to sing with Shania Twain at the Corel Centre in Ottawa. "As soon as I walked out in front of 20,000 people, I'd never smiled so much in my life—it was like perma-smile," she told *Entertainment Weekly.* "And I thought, 'This is what I'm going to do with my life, walk out on stage, have my own band, and be doing my own concert with my own songs.' I'm serious—this was meant to happen to me."

This event helped Lavigne move beyond local performances. Soon the chief executive officer of Arista Records, Antonio "L.A." Reid, noticed her. He signed her to a $1.25 million contract when she was 16. Lavigne, seeing a bright career before her, proceeded to drop out of high school. Arista provided her with country music to record, but after six months of working with co-writers it became clear that Lavigne was more interested in rock music. Arista sent her to Los Angeles, California, to work with some writing teams, including The Matrix. Lavigne poured all her teenage feelings into her lyrics and quickly worked to write "Complicated." Shortly thereafter, Lavigne transferred management allegiances from Fabri to the powerful Canadian management group Nettwerk. Nettwerk provided Lavigne with a touring band consisting of young musicians including guitarist Jesse Colburn, drummer Matt Brann, bassist Charles Moniz, and lead guitarist Evan Taubenfeld. Shauna Gold, Lavigne's manager, told *Maclean's,* "She's young, her music's young, we needed a band that would fit well with who she is as a person."

Lavigne's debut album, *Let Go,* was released in June of 2002, and within six months it had sold more than eight million copies worldwide. "Complicated" and "Sk8er Boi" topped the charts at number one. Lavigne and her band were off to tour through Europe, Asia, Australia, and North America. It was the third biggest-selling album of 2003, and garnered the MTV Video Music Award for Best New Artist.

With her tomboy looks and tough attitude, Lavigne's skategirl pop music gained in popularity with parents as well as teens. Her signature necktie look suddenly sprouted on girls around the world. When Lavigne changed from the necktie to camouflage, her fans followed suit. She was often called the "anti-Britney," referring to Britney Spears' re-vealing outfits and suggestive music and videos. Lavigne was uncomfortable with the comparison. "I don't like that term—'the anti-Britney.' It's stupid," Lavigne told *Entertainment Weekly.* "I don't believe in that. She's a human being.... Leave her alone."

Lavigne earned even greater recognition during 2003. In April of that year she received several Juno Awards, winning Single of the Year for "Complicated," Album of the Year for *Let Go,* and New Artist of the Year. In May, Paramount Pictures optioned the song "Sk8er Boi," planning to adapt the words into a feature film. In June, the ABC Family cable network aired the television special *Avril Lavigne: Anything But Ordinary.* And in November of 2003, the Society of Composers, Authors and Music Publishers of Canada (SOCAN) Awards honored Lavigne for "Complicated," as well as for "Sk8er Boi" and "I'm with You." In addition, the song "I'm with You" was showcased in the feature film *Bruce Almighty* starring Jim Carrey.

Lavigne began work on her second album, this time choosing to bypass the writing machine teams and to work on the lyrics and melodies herself. Her second album reflected Lavigne's own growth. "It's a more serious album in [some] ways," she told *Newsweek.* The album included a song, "Slipped Away," about the death of her grandfather. She worked with Canadian singer and songwriter Chantal Kreviazuk to write some of the new music. "She's one of my best friends," Lavigne told *Billboard.* "We understand the same stuff, and writing with another girl is easier." In addition, Lavigne co-wrote the song "Don't Tell Me" with Taubenfeld, her guitar player. It was her self-proclaimed "girl-power" song about resisting pressure to have sex. She wrote another song with Ben Moody, who had previously played guitar for the band Evanescence. Lavigne did not allow anyone at Arista to hear any of her music until after it was recorded. "There was no way I was gonna write songs and send them to people to re-write them like I did last time," she told *Newsweek.* "I need to feel I'm doing this on my own." *Under My Skin* was released in the spring of 2004.

In order to promote her new release, Lavigne performed a series of concerts at large malls across the country, starting with the Mall of America in Minneapolis, Minnesota. "We thought it would be cool to put on a free show and give back to fans," Lavigne told *Billboard.* "It was more than I expected. The crowds ranged from a few thousand to 10,000. Some of [the events] were moved outside. It's been great."

Late in 2004, Lavigne gained an even younger audience when she sang the "SpongeBob SquarePants theme" for the film based on the hit Nickelodeon cartoon. According to Heather Phares of *All Music Guide,* the album was "both a witty soundtrack and a hip children's album with wide-ranging appeal."

## Selected discography

*Let Go,* Arista, 2002.
*Under My Skin,* Arista, 2004.
(Contributor) *The SpongeBob SquarePants Movie: Music from the movie and more* (soundtrack) Sire, 2004.

## Sources

### Periodicals

*Billboard,* May 22, 2004, p. 1.

*Entertainment Weekly,* November 1, 2002, p. 22.
*Maclean's,* January 13, 2003, p. 22.
*Newsweek,* December 30, 2002; March 22, 2004, p. 58.
*People,* April 5, 2004; May 31, 2004.

### Online

Avril Lavigne Official Website, http://www.avril-lavigne.com (December 7, 2004).
*The SpongeBob SquarePants Movie: Music from the movie and more, All Music Guide,* http://www.all music.com (December 7, 2004).

—*Carol Brennan*

# Matt LeBlanc

## Actor

**B**orn July 25, 1967, in Newton, MA; son of Paul LeBlanc (a mechanic) and Pat Grossman (an office manager); married Melissa McKnight (a model), May 3, 2003; children: Jacki (stepchild), Tyler (stepchild), Marina. *Education:* Attended Wentworth Institute of Technology.

**Addresses:** *Office*—NBC Studio Fan Mail, 1122 South Robertson Blvd., #15, Los Angeles, CA 90035. *Publicist*—PMK/HBH, 8500 Wilshire Blvd., Ste. 700, Beverly Hills, CA 90211.

## Career

**A**ctor in television, including: *TV 101,* CBS, 1988-89; *Anything to Survive* (movie), ABC, 1990; *Top of the Heap,* FOX, 1990-91; *Rebel Highway,* Showtime, c. 1991; *Vinnie and Bobby,* FOX, 1992; *Friends,* NBC, 1994-2004; *Joey,* NBC, 2004—. Film appearances include: *Ed,* 1996; *Lost in Space,* 1998; *Charlie's Angels,* 2000; *All the Queen's Men,* 2002; *Charlie's Angels 2: Full Throttle,* 2003. Also appeared in numerous television commercials for products such as Coca-Cola, Levi's, Heinz Ketchup, and Doritos, and worked as a model.

**Awards:** The Actor Award (with others), outstanding ensemble performance in a comedy series, 1995, for *Friends.*

## Sidelights

**A**fter appearing on several failed series, actor Matt LeBlanc had his breakout role when he was cast as Joey Tribbiani on *Friends.* This ensemble

situation comedy became a major hit for NBC, airing on Thursday nights for ten years. Unlike other stars of the show, LeBlanc was unable to capitalize on his success by starring in popular and/or profitable films. However, LeBlanc's character on *Friends* was given his own spin-off beginning in the fall of 2004. *Joey* could not match the audience of *Friends,* at least initially, but attracted a solid fanbase.

LeBlanc was born on July 25, 1967, in Newton, Massachusetts, the only child of Paul LeBlanc and his wife, Pat Grossman. His father worked as a marine diesel mechanic, while his mother was an office manager who worked in the business of manufacturing circuit breakers at one time. His parents divorced in 1974, and LeBlanc was raised primarily by his mother in a working-class household.

By the time LeBlanc was a student at Newton North High School, he seemed destined for a working-class life himself. He studied carpentry in high school, and after graduating in 1985, continued his studies at a trade school. LeBlanc spent one semester studying building construction technology at the Wentworth Institute of Technology. He planned on becoming a carpenter.

However, LeBlanc also had bigger ambitions. When he was 17 years old, he moved to New York City with the intention of becoming an actor. He also found work as a model while appearing in television commercials. LeBlanc appeared in spots for Doritos, Coca-Cola, Levi's, and Heinz Ketchup. His Heinz commercial was his first and aired for four years.

In the late 1980s, LeBlanc broke into television roles. His first regular role came on the short-lived CBS drama, *TV 101*. The show only lasted for 13 episodes and aired from 1988 to 1989. LeBlanc's next roles came primarily in situation comedies.

In 1990, LeBlanc had one of the leads in FOX's *Top of the Heap*. The show was a spin-off of FOX's hit comedy *Married ... With Children*, but did not have the same fate as that long-running show. *Top of the Heap* focused on a father-son relationship. LeBlanc played the son, named Vinnie Verducci, who lived with his father, a building superintendent played by Joseph Bologna. The father tried to get LeBlanc's character married to a rich woman, and both had a con-artist aspect to their personalities.

LeBlanc's character on *Top of the Heap* was similar to his Joey on *Friends* in that both used their good looks and rather dim, naïve personality to great comic effect. However, *Top of the Heap* was slammed by critics and lasted for only seven episodes.

Though *Top of the Heap* did not make it, LeBlanc's character had a second chance. LeBlanc's Vinnie was featured in a second show called *Vinnie and Bobby*. In this show, Vinnie's father was dropped and a roommate named Bobby (played by Robert Torti) was added. Bobby was even less intelligent than Vinnie, and both worked in construction. *Vinnie and Bobby* also failed to impress critics during its trial run. Only seven episodes aired in the summer of 1992.

After these shows tanked, LeBlanc struggled as an actor for a time. He could not find much work and had to move to a smaller apartment in Los Angeles. However, within two years LeBlanc was on a hit show. In 1994, he was cast as Joey Tribbiani on *Friends*. The show focused on six twentysomething friends who lived in New York City. *Friends* featured witty dialogue and a balanced ensemble. LeBlanc's character was a struggling actor who was not particularly bright but very loyal to his friends.

Though *Friends* initially received mixed reviews from critics, the show built an audience in its first season and soon became a massive hit that aired through 2004. The six stars of the show became regulars on magazine covers and often had their lives scrutinized. In 1995, LeBlanc told Traci Grant of the *Boston Globe,* "It blows my mind. It's like somebody strapped a jet pack on my back and lit the fuse and off I went. It's been a wild ride." One of the first things LeBlanc did with his newfound wealth was buy a home for his mother.

As LeBlanc's acting career in sitcoms took off, he showed his range by taking on dramatic roles from time to time. In 1990, he appeared in the ABC television movie *Anything to Survive.* The movie focused on a family surviving in nature. LeBlanc later appeared in two episodes of the Showtime series *Rebel Highway,* "Motorcycle Gang" and "Reform School Girl." Both were remakes of films that originally appeared in drive-in theaters.

During the run of *Friends,* all six stars worked in feature films with varying degrees of success. While LeBlanc was one of the first to make the move, his output was not memorable. He made his film debut in 1996's *Ed,* a comedy about a minor league baseball team. LeBlanc played pitcher Jack Cooper who had a great arm but could not handle pressure. His team hires a chimp, Ed, to be a mascot, but the animal proves to be a good fielder so the team plays him at third base as a way to attract crowds to the ballpark. The chimp also becomes LeBlanc's character's roommate.

While *Ed* bombed at the box office, not all critics attacked LeBlanc's performance. Doug Hamilton of the *Atlanta Journal and Constitution* wrote, "LeBlanc, who retains the affable charm he displays on his show, shouldn't really be faulted for the movie's awfulness (beyond agreeing to appear in such drivel in the first place). Even the most established star would be capsized by a role that primarily consists of reacting to monkey flatulence."

Two years later, LeBlanc had a featured role in a very different kind of film, *Lost in Space.* The science-fiction drama was based on the campy 1960s show of the same name. LeBlanc played Major Don West, the driver/astronaut of the crew. The rest of the group included the Robinson family—scientist parents and their three kids—as well as a male scientist and a large robot. Set in 2058, they all leave Earth aboard the ship Jupiter II and are headed toward a colony in outer space. Though LeBlanc and the film received better reviews than *Ed, Lost in Space* was not really a hit. Around the time of the film's release, LeBlanc faced another challenge: rumors of his death, one of the many tabloid-hyped stories with which he had to deal.

LeBlanc did appear in two successful films, though only in cameo roles. In 2000, he appeared briefly in the huge hit film *Charlie's Angels,* which was based on the 1970s television show. LeBlanc played an actor in the film, one who shared many qualities of his character on *Friends*. The character was the boyfriend of the character played by Lucy Liu. LeBlanc reprised the role in the sequel to *Charlie's Angels*, 2003's *Charlie's Angels 2: Full Throttle*. Though the film did well at the box office, the sequel could not match the success of the first.

LeBlanc tried different kinds of film roles, but his starring roles often did not connect with audiences. In 2002, he challenged his acting persona by taking a starring role in the war comedy *All the Queen's Men*. LeBlanc played O'Rourke, an American soldier working with the British during World War II. LeBlanc's character dresses as a woman to infiltrate a factory—which only employed women—in order to get a coding device. *All the Queen's Men* was screened at festival's such as the Mill Valley Film Festival but was not well-received by audiences.

Though LeBlanc's film career did not take off, his role on *Friends* unexpectedly grew. Though Joey was initially a sweet but rather superficial character who usually provided comic relief to other story lines, especially the romantic ones, his character evolved in the early 2000s. Beginning in 2002, Joey had a surprising romance with Rachel, played by actress Jennifer Aniston, and his character became deeper. LeBlanc's Joey helped revitalize *Friends*, which had declining ratings as it aged.

LeBlanc's work as Joey late in the series' run led to numerous major award nominations. In 2002 and 2003, he was nominated for a Golden Globe as best actor in a musical or comedy. In 2002, LeBlanc was also nominated for a Screen Actors Guild Award for outstanding performance by a male actor in a comedy series. An Emmy Award nomination for best actor in a comedy series came LeBlanc's way in 2004, the same year that *Friends* ended its run.

However, before the end of *Friends*, it was decided that LeBlanc's character would star in his own show on NBC the following season. Entitled *Joey*, the show featured Joey moving from New York City to Los Angeles to further his acting career. There, he was close to his sister, Gina, who lives there with her young adult son, Michael, who is very intelligent. The relationship between Joey and Gina added depth to LeBlanc's character's background, something which was not explored on *Friends* as much as other characters on the show. *Joey* also featured his agent, Bobbie, and had a love interest/neighbor for Joey, attorney Alex Garrett. The show was produced by several writers from *Friends*.

When *Joey* began airing in the fall of 2004, it took over the time slot previously occupied by *Friends*. However, *Joey* could not match the ratings of *Friends*, at least in the first season. The first episode of *Joey* attracted 18 million viewers, but lost six million of those viewers by December. The show did have high ratings relative to other new comedies on the broadcast networks.

Though some observers believed that *Joey* was failing to attract a huge audience because of its own problems, NBC believed that it was often compared to *Friends*. Kevin Reilly, the president of NBC Entertainment, told Scott Collins of the *Los Angeles Times*, "Were *Joey* not a *Friends* spinoff, it would be called an unequivocal hit. But being held to the standard of a *Friends* spinoff, it somehow seems as if its underperforming." Despite the numbers, LeBlanc was nominated for a Golden Globe award for best actor in a musical or comedy in 2004. *Joey* was renewed for the 2005-06 television season. However, changes were expected to be made to the show.

Near the end of the run of *Friends*, LeBlanc's personal life also changed. He married longtime girlfriend Melissa McKnight, a model, on May 3, 2003, in Hawaii. LeBlanc became the stepfather to her two children from a previous marriage, Jacki and Tyler, and together the couple had a daughter named Marina. LeBlanc appreciated his life and his success, telling Robert Bianco of *USA Today*, "I come from a very blue-collar background. I'm not carrying anything heavy. I'm not working in the rain. [Acting is] a cakewalk."

## Sources

### Books

*Celebrity Biographies*, Baseline II, Inc., 2005.

### Periodicals

*Atlanta Journal and Constitution*, March 15, 1996, p. 7P.
*Boston Globe*, April 28, 1995, p. 84; April 3, 1998, p. D7.
*Buffalo News*, July 12, 2004, p. C1.
*Daily News* (New York, NY), September 5, 2004, p. 2.
*InStyle*, November 1998, p. 137.
*Los Angeles Times*, December 13, 2004, p. E1.
*People*, April 29, 1991, p. 12; June 15, 1992, p. 9; April 20, 1998, p. 140; May 19, 2003, p. 64; February 9, 2004, p. 86; September 13, 2004, p. 39.
*Time*, September 13, 2004, p. 82.
*USA Today*, January 17, 2002, p. 1D.
*Variety*, April 6, 1998, p. 46.

—A. Petruso

# Chang-rae Lee

## Author and professor

**B**orn July 29, 1965, in Seoul, South Korea; immigrated to the United States, 1968; son of Young Yong (a psychiatrist) and Inja (Hong) Lee; married Michelle Branca (an architect), June 19, 1993; children: Annika, Eva. *Education:* Yale University, B.A., 1987; University of Oregon, M.F.A., 1993.

**Addresses:** *Agent*—International Creative Management, 40 West 57th St., New York, NY 10019.

## Career

**E**quities analyst, Donaldson, Lufkin & Jenrette, c. 1987; assistant professor of creative writing, University of Oregon at Eugene, 1993-98; professor of writing, Hunter College, City University of New York, 1998-2002; professor of creative writing and humanities council member, Princeton University, 2002—.

**Awards:** "New Voices" Award, Quality Paperback Club, c. 1995; Barnes & Noble Discover Great New Writers Award; Oregon Books Award; American Library Association Notable Book of the Year Award for *Native Speaker,* 1995; American Book Award, Before Columbus Foundation, for *Native Speaker,* 1995; Hemingway Foundation/PEN Award for *Native Speaker,* 1996; named one of the 20 best American writers under the age of 40 by the *New Yorker,* 1999.

## Sidelights

**K**orean-American novelist Chang-rae Lee published several books in the late 1990s and early 2000s which explored themes of identity and

*AP/Wide World Photos*

isolation. Often praised by critics for his ability to write deep, heartfelt characters, Lee's first novel, *Native Speaker,* was the first novel by a Korean American to be published by a mainstream publisher, G.P. Putnam's Sons' imprint Riverhead. In addition to being a very successful and popular novelist, Lee was also a professor of creative writing who worked at the University of Oregon, Hunter College, and Princeton.

Lee was born on July 29, 1965, in Seoul, South Korea, the son of Young Yong Lee and his wife, Inja. Young Yong Lee had attended medical school in Korea, and went to the United States when Lee was a toddler for additional training to become a psychiatrist. After Young Yong Lee established himself in Pittsburgh, Pennsylvania, he brought his family to the United States, including his wife, Lee, and Lee's older sister, Eunei. Lee was three years old when he immigrated to the United States. The family lived in Pittsburgh for approximately six months, before moving to New York City. His father eventually found a position at Bellevue.

Lee's parents wanted him to assimilate to his new country and to that end, would only speak to him in Korean at home so that he would learn English without a Korean accent. His mother did not learn

English right away, and though she had a full life in Korea, she did not have as much of one in the United States. She pushed her son to do better. After living in Manhattan while he was a small child, Lee and his family moved to the suburbs, where he spent the rest of his childhood.

As a child, Lee inhabited both cultures and languages. He did not speak in kindergarten, but linked English and Korean in his head. His family was greatly involved with a Korean Presbyterian church in Flushing, New York, where he got to be around other Korean kids. By the time he was ten years old, Lee translated for his mother when she had to deal with English-speaking people. He also was an avid reader as a child.

Lee did not always take the expected route for Korean-American children, which "tends more toward law and medicine," according to Charles McGrath of the *New York Times*. He applied for admission to and was accepted at Phillips Exeter Academy, a high-profile East Coast prep school. After graduating from Exeter, Lee entered Yale University in 1983. He majored in English, and while he wrote short stories on his own time, he did not show them to anyone.

When Lee graduated in 1987, he found a job working as an equities analyst on Wall Street at Donaldson Lufkin & Jenrette, an investment bank. As in college, he wrote fiction on the side. He soon realized that his job was not fulfilling and that he wanted to write full time. Lee was also inspired by his roommate and friend from prep school, Brooks Hansen, who was working as a novelist. Lee soon quit his job at the investment bank to work on a novel.

Lee completed an unpublished novel, *Agnew Belittlehead*, which he used to gain entrance and a scholarship to the creative writing program at the University of Oregon. Lee earned his M.F.A. in 1993, and was then hired as an assistant writing professor by the University of Oregon. That same year, Lee married an architecture graduate student named Michelle Branca, with whom he later had two daughters.

In 1995, Lee published his first novel, *Native Speaker,* a complex book with many plots and themes. At its center was the character Henry Park, a young Korean American who works for a private surveillance company as a spy for hire. Park has self-identity issues, and has recently suffered from personal tragedies. Park's young son died unexpectedly and

his wife, a white woman who works as a speech therapist, has left him at the beginning of the novel. Before she departed, she gave him a list of his faults, including his emotional distance.

Park also reflects on his father, an immigrant to the United States who works as a grocer, and the values he imparted to his son. Park does not fit fully into the culture of his father's world nor that of mainstream America, and disavows who he is. He must confront his conflict and pain in the two cultures. Despite these problems, Lee's character is a good observer, especially about language and its power. He uses these skills to infiltrate the campaign of a Korean American running for office as a New York City councilman.

Lee received generally good reviews for *Native Speaker,* which sold well. The novel received a number of honors, including being selected as a finalist for the Quality Paperback Club's "New Voices" Award. Pam Belluck of the *New York Times* wrote, "The book has been acclaimed as a lyrical, edgy, and perceptive tale of the second-generation foreigner, the child of immigrants stranded in a no-man's-land between the old culture and the new."

While Lee appreciated the positive attention for him and his book, he did not want it to be regarded as an autobiographical statement nor as an author who was hot for the moment. He told Maureen Dezell of the *Boston Globe* that he felt some pressure "to represent Koreans and speak to all things Korean. There's this essentialist attitude that ethnic American writers must speak to their 'true' ethnic experience. Otherwise, people don't think it works. In my case, people have told me the book isn't believable because it isn't thought out like an Amy Tan story…. Well, Amy Tan and I are from different generations. I'm Korean-American, not Chinese." Yet the novel deeply affected other Asian-American readers, including Korean Americans, for its exploration of truths about identity and assimilation, and related sacrifices.

As *Native Speaker* continued to do well, Lee signed a contract for his second novel in 1995. He had his topic already chosen. The book was to be about Korean comfort women, the 200,000 sexual slaves for the Japanese military personnel during World War II. Such women were not treated humanely, and were forced to have multiple sex partners per day. Lee saw that these women could have been related to him, members of his grandmother's generation. To do research for this novel, he went to Korea and met with women who had survived the experience.

Lee wrote a portion of the book and realized that what he had written was not living up to the comfort women's stories and the women he met. He put this idea aside and wrote another novel related to his original concept. Lee focused on a minor character in the unfinished work, a Japanese soldier who came to visit the comfort women and just talk to them. As he was working on these novels, Lee left Oregon to take a job at Hunter College in New York City. In 1998, he was hired to set up a graduate writing program at the college. Lee and his family settled in Bergen County, New Jersey.

Lee's novel, *A Gesture Life,* was published in 1999 and it again focused on issues of assimilation, immigration, and identity. The central character was Doc Hata, who had been a soldier in the Japanese army in World War II. Hata was Korean and a very intelligent child. He was adopted by rich Japanese parents when he was young. Hata was very concerned with pleasing his parents and living up to their expectations, as well as that of the army when he joined. He was also in love with a comfort woman.

The focus of the novel was Hata's current life in the United States, where he came as an adult. He is now an older gentleman who struggles with his past and present. While Hata seems to fit in suburban American since he is respected by his neighbors and is the former owner of a successful medical supply business, Hata is unable to connect emotionally with people nor know himself fully. One person Hata is unable to connect with is his mixed-race daughter, Sunny, whom he adopted when she was seven years old. She is rebellious and becomes pregnant as a teenager, though Hata forces her to have an abortion late in her pregnancy so she can do what she wants in life. Hata also fails at romance with a local widow because of opportunities missed.

Lee's exploration of Hata's outsider status and the effect of traumas on people was praised by critics and sold well, though some believed its nonlinear plot sometimes dragged. Some newspapers named *A Gesture Life* as one of the best books written in 1999.

As Lee worked on his next novel, he left Hunter College when he was hired by Princeton as a professor of creative writing in 2002. Lee tried to lead a normal life, not traveling in literary circles. He was very involved in his daughters' lives, and enjoyed playing golf. Some believed that he was too nice and concealed his feelings, not unlike the main characters of his novels thus far.

Lee's third novel, 2004's *Aloft,* also featured an older gentleman who is lost in life. This time, his character was a white man named Jerry Battle, who was about 60 years old; the character was loosely based on Lee's father-in-law. Battle was retired from his family landscaping business, which he ceded to his son. His son was trying to transform it into a home renovation business. While Battle worked as a travel agent on the side, he did not have great relationships with his children, his elderly father, or his girlfriend, who leaves him. Battle's wife was a manic depressive who accidentally drowned when their children were young. Battle was able to escape from his reality by flying his small plane and looking down on the orderly landscape below. The novel was full of metaphors and Lee's meaningful character nuances.

As with Lee's other novels, critics praised his prose and how he was able to get into the heads of his characters. *Aloft* did well even before it was published: the movie rights were sold while it was still a manuscript. Many of the reviews for *Aloft* were positive. Michiko Kakutani wrote in the *New York Times,* "Although the plot ... often strains credulity, he writes with such uncommon grace, such complete understanding of his hero's inner life that the reader is happy to overlook the story's occasional lurches."

Though Lee often wrote about alienated men, he claimed they were not based on himself. Peter Greer, a teacher of Lee's from Exeter, told the *New York Times'* McGrath, "There's this undiscovered country in Chang that's a source of a lot of what comes out in the books. To a certain extent, I think Chang has internalized the experience of his parents. It's out of sympathy with them that he's able to project that sense of alienation."

## Selected writings

*Native Speaker,* Riverhead (New York City), 1995.
*A Gesture Life,* Riverhead (New York City), 1999.
*Aloft,* Riverhead (New York City), 2004.

## Sources

### Periodicals

*Boston Globe,* May 11, 1995, p. 65.
*Daily Telegraph* (London, England), June 19, 2004, p. 12.
*Entertainment Weekly,* March 12, 2004, p. 117.

*Houston Chronicle,* March 28, 2004, p. 19.

*Independent* (London, England), July 16, 2004, p. 23.

*Los Angeles Times,* March 9, 2004, p. E10.

*Newsday* (New York, NY), March 22, 2004, p. B2.

*New Statesman,* March 20, 2000.

*New York Times,* July 10, 1995, p. B1; August 31, 1999, p. E8; September 5, 1999, sec. 7, p. 6; February 29, 2004, sec. 6, p. 44; March 9, 2004, p. E1.

*Ottawa Citizen,* July 11, 2004, p. C9.

*Rocky Mountain News* (Denver, CO), March 19, 2004, p. 29D.

**Online**

*Contemporary Authors Online,* Gale, 2004.

—*A. Petruso*

# Lee Jong-Wook

*AP/Wide World Photos*

**Director-general of the World Health Organization**

---

**B**orn in 1945 in Seoul, Korea; married Reiko; children: Tad. *Education:* Seoul National University's College of Medicine, medical degree; University of Hawaii, master's degree (epidemiology and public health), 1981.

**Addresses:** *Office*—World Health Organization, Avenue Appia 20, CH-1211 Geneva 27 Switzerland.

## Career

**W**orked with lepers in South Korea; leprosy control team consultant, World Health Organization (WHO), 1983-86; director of disease prevention and control, WHO's Western Pacific Regional office, Manila, the Philippines, 1986-94; head of global program on vaccines and immunizations, and executive secretary of the children's vaccine initiative, WHO, Geneva, Switzerland, 1994-98; senior policy advisor and special representative, WHO, 1998-2000; head of Stop TB program, WHO, 2000-03; director general, WHO, 2003—.

## Sidelights

**I**n 2003, South Korean native Dr. Lee Jong-Wook was named the head of the World Health Organization (WHO), the public health arm of the United Nations (UN). He was the first South Korean to head an agency at the UN. Lee was trained as a physician and was an expert on the treatment of leprosy. He spent much of his professional career at WHO working on a number of health issues such as immunization and disease prevention.

Lee was born in 1945, the son of a civil servant father. The family suffered greatly during the Korean War in the early 1950s. Lee, his two brothers, and his mother had to walk from Seoul to Taegu, approximately 400 miles, around 1950 to meet his father at his post during the early days of the conflict. The 60-day trek gave Lee an understanding of the plight of refugees, which served him well later when he worked for the WHO. After the war, Lee's father held political office, and both of his brothers also became politicians. Lee's mother urged him to become a doctor to have a more stable income, while he thought it would attract the attention of women.

Lee earned his medical degree from Seoul National University's College of Medicine. After graduating, he started training to become a practicing doctor. Though his mother wanted him to become a plastic surgeon to make a good living, Lee was already interested in the disease of leprosy. Even as a medical student, Lee was fascinated with leprosy because it was still very feared by the general public and left a lifetime stigma on those who suffered from it. Lee began working in a leper colony in South Korea. He then decided to switch his focus from a private practice to public health despite the fact that he could have made more money in the former. Lee was attracted to the fact that he could positively affect many more lives in public health.

While working with lepers, he met his wife, a Japanese woman named Reiko, who worked on leprosy in South Korea for a Catholic organization. They later had a son named Tad. In addition to his training in leprosy and related public health issues, Lee also gained expertise in tuberculosis and vaccines in Korea.

Lee and his family left South Korea to continue his education in the United States. In 1981, he earned his master's degree in epidemiology and public health from the University of Hawaii's School of Public Health. While a student there, Lee specialized in tropical diseases and also focused on leprosy. After graduation, he began a preventive medicine residency program because he landed a job with WHO. When he took the job, Lee did not intend for it to be long term, though he ended up spending much of the rest of his career there.

In 1983, Lee was hired by WHO as a consultant on the leprosy control team for the South Pacific. During the week, he visited villages and provided his expertise to them. On the weekends, Lee would enjoy his surroundings and snorkel in the ocean. Three years later, Lee was selected by WHO to be their director of disease prevention and control in its Western Pacific Regional office. There, he served as a regional advisor on chronic diseases. As a manager of others, Lee did not micromanage, but encouraged his underlings to push their own good ideas.

Lee's work was noticed by WHO's home office in Geneva, Switzerland. In 1994, he was selected to head the Global Program on Vaccines and Immunizations, and worked out of WHO's Geneva office. He also was the executive secretary of the Children's Vaccine Initiative. While holding this office, Lee had the goal of increasing access to the basic childhood vaccinations for all children. He also wanted to help eradicate worldwide poliomyelitis (polio) and other childhood diseases that were preventable via vaccines.

Lee made forward progress in these matters. One of his accomplishments was discussing with drug companies what it would take for them to begin to de-velop vaccines specifically for diseases that primarily affected developing nations. Lee was the first to open such discussions. Previously, organizations such as WHO asked the companies to give what drugs they had for free to such programs or made deals that would allow the companies to make a profit. Lee's work in polio eradication had a positive effect in the western Pacific. The numbers of those affected went from 6,000 cases per year in 1990 to nearly none by 2004.

When Norwegian Dr. Gro Brundtland took office as the head of WHO in 1998, she selected Lee to be a senior policy advisor and her special representative. Lee held both posts until 2000, when Brundtland put Lee in charge of WHO's Stop TB program. As the head of the Stop TB program, Lee was charged with ending the spread of tuberculosis across the globe. When he took over, the program was in disarray. There were big organizational problems in the field as well as much infighting. The program also suffered from a lack of consensus on a comprehensive global strategy.

Lee worked to change these problems. First, he made sure that WHO was at the center of the Stop TB program, but did not dominate. He also helped put into more common practice treatments that were proven to save lives from the disease. These treatments included a health care worker directly observing each patient as he or she takes medication daily for half a year. Lee also supervised the creation of an anti-TB partnership which had 250 members, including government health centers, charities, pharmaceutical companies, and others. Despite his improvements, the coverage for eradicating TB did not reach WHO's goals.

In January of 2003, Lee left his post as the head of the Stop TB program when he was unexpectedly elected the director-general of WHO by an executive committee of the UN. Bruntland's five-year term was ending on July 21, and she did not seek a second term. Lee was one of five candidates for the post, and he was regarded as a dark horse as he was the only one without experience as a minister in a government department or head of a UN agency. Lee was also not expected to win because he was not regarded as politically strong enough to work with heads of state and promoting a world agenda. Lee proved his detractors wrong when he was able to convince 53 members of the U.S. Congress to write letters of support for his bid to Colin Powell and Tommy Thompson, two members of President George W. Bush's cabinet. U.S. Representative Sherrod Brown, an Ohio Democrat, told John

Donnelly of the *Boston Globe*, "He's one of those guys who checks his ego at the door and comes in and listens to the people. He puts the information together and acts skillfully as a result." Lee won the post by a narrow margin, marking the first time a native of South Korea headed an agency at the UN.

For his five-year term, Lee set a number of goals. He wanted to improve the international monitoring of infectious diseases to help control outbreaks of diseases such as SARS (severe acute respiratory syndrome). To that end, he sought more funding from certain countries to make disease monitoring better with additional staff and training. The fight against three specific diseases also important to Lee. To work on the spread of the spread of HIV/AIDS, malaria, and tuberculosis in poor countries, he created a team that focused on improving WHO's role in the fight against these diseases, especially in Africa. Lee also wanted a new plan to be developed for fighting AIDS. He was especially sensitive to such public health issues in underprivileged countries whose health care systems were tenuous at best. He believed in programs that benefited poorer populations because vulnerability to disease was linked to the level of poverty. Lee also had concerns that affected both wealthy and poor countries. He pushed for an anti-tobacco treaty so that tobacco products would have a higher tax and fewer people would use them. In addition, Lee wanted to increase the number of smoke-free areas in the world.

Another priority was working on the Millennium Development Goals set out by the UN in 2000. Among them was reducing childhood malnutrition by half as well as reducing to 15 percent the proportion of the world's population that survived on less than one dollar per day by 2015. Lee was quoted by Gretchen Vogel in *Science* as saying "The problem is that people setting the goals believe the day of reckoning will never come. We cannot behave like that. There are concrete steps to take to achieve the lofty goals. We need to be accountable."

To that end, Lee also wanted to increase the WHO's relevancy in the world. By 2005, he hoped to get 75 percent of WHO's staff (which numbered about 4,000 when he took over) and resources to be working on regional and country levels. To emphasize such field programs, Lee implemented several new programs including one in which a group of epidemiologists were trained to battle outbreaks of disease. It was based on a program run by the U.S. government's Centers for Disease Control and Prevention and to be called the Epidemic Intelligence Service. Some of its workers would go to world-wide schools of public health, and the health departments of developing countries. They would be specially trained to be able to go out in the field to help countries with epidemics like AIDS and Ebola virus outbreaks.

In addition, Lee also wanted to pay attention not just to the policy experts and health officials, but also organizations based in the community that work with the poor. Lee told Lawrence K. Altman and Alison Langley of *New York Times,* "Curing someone of tuberculosis is a hollow victory if the person goes on to die of an untreated heart condition or of obstetric complications to which an inadequate health system is unable to respond."

While Lee wanted to continue the reforms of his predecessor, some wondered if he had the ability to be creative with WHO's budget of one to two billion dollars to achieve the goals. There was also some controversy over whether his insider status was good or bad for WHO, and if he could use his position to encourage political change. In addition, Lee had to deal with newly emerging issues of public health, including advances in biotechnology and cloning.

Lee's five-year term as director general of WHO was renewable, but he could only head the organization for a total of ten years. Lee's abilities as a manager were seen as a positive step forward for WHO since he listened to others for a collective clear vision. The dean of the Harvard School of Public Health, Barry R. Bloom, told David Brown of the *Washington Post,* "Whatever his ego may be, it is under control of a greater commitment to do the right thing and to share the credit with everyone who makes things happen. In a bureaucracy, that is tremendously unusual." Lee himself was quoted in the *New York Times* as saying, "We have to find ways to unite our strengths as a global community to shape a healthier future."

## Sources

### Periodicals

*Associated Press,* July 21, 2003.
*Boston Globe,* January 29, 2003, p. A6; May 22, 2003, p. A19.
*British Medical Journal,* February 1, 2003, p. 241.
*Bulletin of the World Health Organization,* March-April 2003, p. 154; August 2003, p. 628.
*Indian Journal of Medical Sciences,* August 2003.

*International Midwifery,* May 2003, p. 27.

*Lancet,* January 18, 2003, p. 235; February 1, 2003, p. 399; May 31, 2003, p. 1874.

*Medical Letter on the CDC & FDA,* February 23, 2003, p. 10.

*Newsweek International,* July 28, 2003, p. 58.

*New York Times,* January 29, 2003, p. A9; May 22, 2003, p. A6; July 21, 2003, p. A3; July 22, 2003, p. F3; December 18, 2003, p. A1.

*Science,* February 7, 2003, p. 809.

*Time,* April 26, 2004, p. 105.

*Washington Post,* January 29, 2003, p. A5.

**Online**

"Director-General—Biography," World Health Organization, http://www.who.int/dg/lee/biography/en/print.html (August 6, 2004).

*—A. Petruso*

# Sandy Lerner

**Founder of Urban Decay and philanthropist**

**B**orn c. 1955; married Leonard Bosack, 1980 (divorced). *Education:* Earned undergraduate degree from California State University—Chico, c. 1971; Claremont Graduate School, M.A., econometrics; Stanford University, M.S., statistics and computer science.

**Addresses:** *Office*—Ayrshire Farm, 21846 Trappe Rd., Upperville, VA 20184.

## Career

**D**irector of computer facility, Stanford University Graduate School of Business, early 1980s; co-founder, Cisco Systems, Inc., c. 1984, vice president for customer service, 1988-90; founded Urban Decay, Inc., 1995.

## Sidelights

**S**andy Lerner co-founded Cisco Systems, Inc., maker of the first commercially viable router that allowed computers to "network" to one another. Lerner and her husband began their company out of their living room back in the 1980s, and it grew explosively over the next few years. Within a decade, both had stepped away from it and began cashing in their stock in order to pursue other interests. Lerner's own Cisco windfall made her the first female philanthropist to emerge from the Silicon Valley boom era, and she has since gone on to fund a number of unusual pet projects, including the cosmetics company Urban Decay. Its name reflects her iconoclastic vision. "A number of people have tried to get me to grow up," she once joked with James Sterngold of the *New York Times.*

Born in the mid-1950s, Lerner was four years old when her parents divorced, and she spent her childhood divided between the homes of two aunts. One had a cattle ranch in the California Sierras, while the other lived in Beverly Hills. Both lifestyles would influence her in ways both obvious and subtle, but it was on the Clipper Gap ranch that she first exercised her entrepreneurial instincts. At the age of nine, Lerner bought her first steer, selling it for a profit two years later; with those proceeds she acquired two more head of cattle. By the time she entered college, she owned a registered livestock herd of 30 head of cattle, and it provided an income stream that paid for her college tuition.

Lerner breezed through an undergraduate degree in political science at California State University in Chico, finishing in two years. For a time, she considered academia as a career, and began graduate school at Claremont College outside of Los Angeles. She was particularly fascinated by comparative political studies, but came to realize there was likely little financial gain in it. In 1975, she stumbled into the school's nascent computer lab, and was intrigued by what she saw. She began visiting it so frequently that she was eventually made its manager. Still at work on her degree, she enlisted the computers to do quantitative data analysis for her research in social-science topics. This was uncharted academic waters, she explained to San Jose's

*Business Journal* writer Genevieve Leone. "People left you alone because they thought you were weird, and nobody knew anything about what you were doing."

After earning her master's in econometrics from Claremont, Lerner entered Stanford University's graduate program for statistics and computer science. Such graduate programs were relatively new at the time, and a female student was a rarity. But as Lerner told *Business Journal*'s Leone, "Stanford was dying to get graduate students back then who could bail out the faculty who didn't know anything about computers. If you had all these hacker-type graduate students, you'd moved into the computer age. So they let me in."

Lerner actually married a fellow "hacker type" from Stanford, Leonard Bosack, in 1980. He eventually became director of computer facilities for Stanford's Computer Science Department, while Lerner had found a job running the computer facility for the Graduate School of Business at Stanford. Their offices were just 500 yards apart, but their computers were separate entities, as were all the departments' computer rooms across the campus. Lerner and Bosack wanted to share software and databases with one another without resorting to time-consuming disk transfers; it was a time when floppy disks were actually floppy, measuring more than five inches across, and software purchases came in a box containing a dozen or more of them. They created a local area network, or LAN, using a router that Bosack had made, first between their offices, and then linking the entirety of the school's computer system.

Lerner and her husband were at the cutting edge of computer technology at the time, having linked 5,000 computers across a 16-square-mile campus area single-handedly. Some computer makers were offering networking capabilities, but their systems could only be used with their own particular products. By contrast, the router that Lerner and Bosack had come up with was a unique "multiprotocol" bit of hardware and software that could work with many different kinds of computers. Venture capitalists who provided start-up money for new businesses that were still in the idea stage claimed this would never sell, however, and told the couple that in the future, companies would each market their own LAN systems.

Lerner and Bosack thought otherwise. Schools like the University of Chicago had heard about the Stanford network and were begging them to share their expertise. But Stanford administrators were leery of

licensing the technology, and Lerner and Bosack grew tired of arguing with them. They decided to strike out on their own, and quit their jobs. They began Cisco in the living room of their Atherton, California, home and sold their first router in 1986. Early on they realized there were much larger possibilities for networking, Lerner told *Forbes* journalist Julie Pitta. "We suspected that Procter & Gamble in Des Moines was going to want to talk to Procter & Gamble in San Francisco."

During their first month in operation, Cisco landed contracts worth more than $200,000. The university, irate, eventually demanded $11 million in licensing fees, but settled instead for a tenth of that plus free product and tech support from Cisco forever. Lerner and Bosack hired friends and neighbors, and asked them to work for deferred salaries or stock options, and they also mortgaged their home and went into credit-card debt to keep their business afloat. At one point, they ran so low on funds that Lerner took a job as a corporate data-processing manager.

Finally, in late 1987 a venture capitalist firm came on board, and Cisco began to thrive. Yet the backer, Donald Valentine, wasn't happy with Lerner and Bosack's management style, and installed John Morgridge as chief executive officer. This was a bad start, Lerner recalled in the *Forbes* interview. "The first time I met John Morgridge he had already been hired," she told Pitta. The new senior management also began replacing some employees who had been with Cisco from the start, such as the retired physicist in his seventies who served as their plant manager.

For a time, Lerner served as vice president for customer services, but clashes with Morgridge forced her out in August of 1990. Her husband resigned as well from his post as Cisco's chief scientist. Their company was taken public that same year, after previous year's revenues of an astonishing $25 million, and its stock quickly became the darling of Wall Street analysts. For much of the 1990s, it was one of the most popular of all tech stocks.

When Cisco went public, Lerner and her husband suddenly found themselves in possession of $85 million in stock. They began to sell it off, and with the bulk of it created a charitable foundation and trust that would fund their pet projects. These included animal-welfare issues and the search for extraterrestrial life. Their marriage, however, had suffered. Both worked extremely long hours, Lerner told Leone in the *Business Journal* article. "What do married people do together? Watch TV, go to the opera, mow the lawn? We didn't do any of that."

Still eager to manage a company, Lerner looked for another market void to fill, and came up with an idea for a cosmetics line that steered clear of the standard girlish pinks and reds in nail polish and lipstick. Inspired in part by the dark-red, nearly black "Vamp" nail color introduced by Chanel that was selling out at makeup counters across North America, Lerner decided to create a line of alternative shades of lipstick and nail color. In mid-1995, she founded the company, which she called Urban Decay, and installed her accountant as its president. This left her free to concentrate on the creative side of the business.

Urban Decay products came on the market in January of 1996 and were an instant smash. Its nail-varnish palette had punk-rock names like Bruise, Pallor, Smog, and Roach, and stayed in the blue-green-purple-black spectrum, with a few odd white choices thrown in. Its marketing campaign garnered instant attention with the tag line, "Does Pink Make You Puke?" and the products were packaged in aluminum shells that resembled pipe bombs or even gun shell casings. In its first year in business, Lerner's new venture took in $9 million. Male celebrities, from rock stars to athletes, even liked the nail lacquers, and Urban Decay was said to have helped launch the nail polish-on-men trend.

Lerner was also busy with her philanthropic ventures. She helped create PetLink, a database system of missing and up-for-adoption cats and dogs that linked local shelters to one another. She bought an 800-acre property in Loudoun County, Virginia, called Ayrshire Farm that was home to her own impressive collection of cats, cattle, and English Shire horses, which she sometimes rode in Elizabethan jousting contests. It also became a working farm dedicated to promoting the virtues of organically grown produce. She had a Harley-Davidson motorcycle and was a rare-book collector, spurred in part by her love of the Jane Austen novels of the early 1800s. She had read Austen's *Persuasion* some 60 times, she once admitted, having discovered Austen during her graduate-school days. Her time at Stanford involved "a pretty hellish computer science-mathematics" curriculum, she recalled in an *Independent Sunday* article by Laura Tennant, and she found the Austen works "a wonderful escape into a kind of civilized, humorous world, a thinking person's escape."

Lerner's passion for Austen's work eventually led to her purchase of Chawton House, a manor dating back to the 1580s in Hampshire, England. It had once been owned by a well-to-do family who adopted Austen's brother as their heir. Though Edward Austen did not use it as his primary residence, he spent regular intervals there, and installed his mother, Austen, and another sister in the nearby village of Chawton. They were regular visitors to the estate, which is considered the model for the "Great House" mentioned in Austen's fiction. By the twentieth century, however, it had fallen into disrepair, and a consortium was established to turn it into a golf resort. The group succeeded in buying back the 275 acres surrounding the manor house before it went bankrupt. Lerner acquired the house and land on a 125-year lease, and turned it into a research facility for early English women writers.

Lerner donated to the Chawton House Library her 7,000-volume collection of tomes by and about early English female writers. These are works that came before Austen, whose handful of novels published in a few short years before her 1817 death established her as the first significant female novelist in English. Lerner's library includes works by other female writers dating all the way back to the early 1600s, and Lerner had said that tracing the genesis of English women's fiction deepened her appreciation for her favorite writer. "All of a sudden, Jane Austen made a whole lot more sense," she said in the *Independent Sunday* interview with Tennant. "It wasn't like she'd dropped in from outer space with six of the best novels in the English language and left. You could see her in the context of things she'd read."

## Sources

*Business Journal* (San Jose, CA), July 31, 1989, p. 12; April 28, 1997, p. 1.

*Forbes,* March 16, 1992, p. 136; August 25, 1997, p. 58.

*Independent Sunday* (London, England), April 26, 1998, p. 7; July 20, 2003.

*More,* February 2002, p. 76.

*New York Times,* November 12, 1995, p. F8.

*San Francisco Chronicle,* September 20, 1996, p. P1.

*Success,* October 1997, p. 68.

*Times* (London, England), November 23, 1996, p. 42.

—*Carol Brennan*

# Jet Li

*AP/Wide World Photos*

## Actor

**B**orn Li Lian Jie, April 26, 1963, in Hebei, China; married Qiuyan Huang, 1987 (divorced, 1990); married Nina Chi Li, September 19, 1999; children: two daughters (from first marriage), two daughters (from second marriage).

**Addresses:** *Contact*—Jet Li Autographs, 1411 5th St., Ste. 405, Los Angeles, CA 90401. *Publicist*—Wolf, Kasteler & Associates, 132 S. Rodeo Dr., Ste. 300, Beverly Hills, CA 90212. *Website*—http://jetli.com.

## Career

**M**ember of Beijing Wushu Team, 1970s. Actor in films, including the Chinese-language films *Shaolin Temple,* 1979; *Kids from Shaolin,* 1983; *Born to Defend,* 1986; *Martial Arts of Shaolin,* 1986; *This Is Kung Fu,* 1987; *Abbot Hai Teng of Shaolin,* 1988; *Dragon Fight,* 1988; *The Master,* 1989; *The Legend of the Swordsman,* 1991; *Once Upon A Time In China,* 1991; *Once Upon A Time In China II,* 1992; *Lord of the Wu Tang,* 1993; *The Invincible Shaolin,* 1993; *Deadly China Hero,* 1993; *The Legend,* 1993; *The Legend II,* 1993; *Twin Warriors,* 1993; *The Defender,* 1994; *Fist of Legend,* 1994; *Meltdown,* 1995; *Jet Li's The Enforcer,* 1995; *Adventure King,* 1996; *Black Mask,* 1996; *Once Upon A Time In China and America,* 1996; *The Contract Killer,* 1998; and *Hero,* 2002 (released in North America, 2004); and the English-language films *Lethal Weapon 4,* 1998; *Romeo Must Die,* 2000; *Kiss of the Dragon,* 2001; *The One,* 2001; *Cradle 2 the Grave,* 2003; *Unleashed,* 2005. Directed *Born to Defend,* 1986.

**Awards:** All-Around National Wushu Champion of China, 1974-79.

## Sidelights

**J**et Li is a former martial arts star in his native China and one of Asia's biggest movie stars. Li has made the successful move to Hollywood movies, introducing himself to American audiences as a villain in *Lethal Weapon 4* and going on to star as the good guy in several action films. On-screen, Li projects an image as a fearless, efficient, yet stylish fighter. Off-screen, Li has an aura of calm and often talks about his Buddhist beliefs, hoping to spread spiritual wisdom as well as the physical thrill of martial arts.

Born in 1963, Li is the youngest of five children. His father died when he was two years old. Li was enrolled in the Beijing Amateur Sports School in the summer of 1971 at the age of eight and began studying the art of wushu, or martial arts, as a summer program. He was one of the few students, and the youngest student, picked to continue wushu in the fall after school. Apparently the teachers had already noticed his budding talent for martial arts; at the age of nine, he won an award for excellence at the national wushu championships.

Two years later, he won his first national championship. He went on a world tour in 1974 and performed in a fight on the lawn of the White House for U.S. President Richard Nixon. At age 12, he won first place in China's National Games despite cutting his head with his saber. He held the title of All-Around National Wushu Champion of China until 1979.

Li retired from wushu at 17 and pursued a film career. His first film, *Shaolin Temple,* released in 1979, quickly made him a movie star in China and sparked the kung-fu boom there. He later filmed two sequels. He directed a film in 1986, *Born to Defend,* but it was not considered a success.

In 1988, Li tried to break into American movies, but because his English was not very good and he was not offered strong scripts, he did not succeed right away. Instead, he relocated to Hong Kong, where kung fu went through a surge of popularity in the early 1990s. He gained a huge following through films such as the 1991 epic *Once Upon A Time in China* and the *Fong Sai-Yuk* series.

By the mid-1990s, Li has told interviewers, he felt burned out and ready to retire. At the time, the Hong Kong film industry was faltering, in part because of Asia's weak economy and partly because of Hong Kong's impending takeover by communist China. He focused on his spiritual life and studied Tibetan Buddhism. But a Buddhist teacher told him he had a responsibility to continue his work.

Coincidentally, Li soon got an offer to play a crime boss in the American film *Lethal Weapon 4.* He moved to Los Angeles and spent four hours a day with an English-language tutor to prepare. *Lethal Weapon 4* became Li's debut in English-language films. He played the villain opposite Mel Gibson and Danny Glover and, by most accounts, stole the show.

Next, he starred in the film *Romeo Must Die,* a sort of urban take on William Shakespeare's Romeo and Juliet. The film, which blended martial arts and hip-hop, starred the rapper DMX and the singer Aaliyah. Li played a member of a Chinese crime family from San Francisco at war with a black crime family. Li falls in love with Aaliyah, daughter of the black family's leader. A review of the movie in *Time* praised Li's martial-arts moves: "He hangs by one foot from a rope in a Hong Kong prison cell, and presto, four guards are zapped into electric skeletons. He twirls a water hose to subdue some villains, spins in the air to kick five guys at once, strips the belt off one oaf and hog-ties him with it, and goes spectacularly hand-to-hand with Asian-

American lookers Russell Wong and Francoise Yip. In the battle with Yip, Li uses Aaliyah as a human nunchaku." The film made $100 million.

In September of 1999, Li married his longtime girlfriend, Nina Li. He told a reporter he turned down a role in the film *Crouching Tiger, Hidden Dragon,* which became enormously popular and moved martial arts films into the mainstream, because he had promised his wife that he would take a break from working when she became pregnant.

Instead, Li traveled to Paris after his daughter was born to star in *Kiss of the Dragon* with Bridget Fonda. In the film, written and produced by Luc Besson, Li played a Chinese police officer who fights corruption in the French police. Richard Corliss of *Time International* described his action highlights this way: "Watch him defeat bad guys with the tools of domesticity: a mop, a bale of laundry and (ouch) an iron. Gasp as he kicks a billiard ball out of an end pocket, then swats it, cricket-bat-style, into a villain's cranium.... He sneaks past a sentry's guardhouse outside the evil inspecteur's police station and, just to show he can, he rams his foot through his guardhouse door, neatly kicking the sentry in the groin. Inside, he chances upon 20 martial-arts students armed with clubs. Not a problem: he levels five of them with five quicker-than-the-eye maneuvers." Before the film came out, Li posted a note on his website warning parents that the R-rated movie—which was more graphic than his other films, with adult themes involving sex and drug use—was not appropriate for children. He said his next film, *The One,* would be more family friendly.

In 2001's *The One,* directed by James Wong, Li played two characters, one good, one evil. Owen Gleiberman, reviewing the film for *Entertainment Weekly,* criticized Li and his performance. "It's standard operating procedure in a review of a movie like this one to proclaim that the star, however trashy his surroundings, is a veritable fireball of charisma. I'm here to offer a heretical view: Jet Li is not charismatic." Gleiberman found neither the movie's good Li nor its bad Li compelling. But Christopher Noxon, writing in the *Los Angeles Times,* took a more generous view of Li while comparing him to Asia's other top action hero. "Unlike Jackie Chan, who is known for his comic pratfalls and elaborate stunts, Li has fashioned a persona that's sexy and potent," he wrote. "While Chan is constantly scuttling away from danger, mugging for the camera as he blocks the attacks of enemies, Li walks solemnly into even the most dangerous trap, dispatching all comers with economic flourish. If Chan is the exuberant jokester of Hong Kong imports, Li is the ace fighter, sleek and dangerous."

Next, Li returned to China to film the movie *Hero* with acclaimed director Zhang Yi Mou. In it, Li played a warrior in China in the 3rd century B.C. The film begins with a king congratulating Li for killing three assassins, but flashbacks show what really happened through many perspectives. The film, which opened in China in 2002, was nominated for an Oscar in the foreign language film category in 2003. It debuted in North America in August of 2004, was released in more than 2,000 theaters, and set a new record for an Asian film, earning $17.8 million in its first week in theaters. It was also a critical success. Leah Rozen of *People* praised its "superb fight sequences" as well as its "satisfyingly complex plot, passionate romance, cool special effects, and strong performances by a handful of China's top actors."

In 2003, Li provided voice-overs in both English and Mandarin Chinese for the Sony PlayStation 2 video game *Rise to Honor.* He also performed fight scenes that were added to the game using motion-capture technology. Meanwhile, the 2003 film *Cradle 2 the Grave* reunited him with producer Joel Silver and DMX from *Romeo Must Die.* The movie was a remake of the 1931 Fritz Lang film *M.* Scott Brown of *Entertainment Weekly* gave the film a B- but praised Li's performance: "Li—refreshingly unfettered by the overdone computer effects that marred his performance in *Romeo [Must Die]*—brutalizes enemy upon enemy with chill dispatch and increasingly baroque gore, weaponizing everything around him, from his jacket collar to an unlucky dwarf. He's the aloof yin to DMX's impassioned yang." His next film, *Unleashed,* another collaboration with Luc Besson, was scheduled for release in 2005.

Li, who meditates for an hour a day or more, says he is looking for ways to communicate the message of Buddhism and the wisdom behind martial arts to Americans. "Whenever I work in the United States, the young people say, 'Yeah, Jet Li! You kick [butt], blah, blah, blah.' Sometimes I feel sad, because I've only shown them that martial arts hurt people," Li told Mike Zimmerman of *Men's Health.* "I haven't had the opportunity to show them that the important thing is not kicking people's [butts]. If you understand Eastern and Western culture, you will understand the yin-and-yang balance. Maybe you will grow up." There are three levels of martial arts, he explained to Zimmerman. The first is physical, making your body a weapon; the second is using psychology to help win battles; the third is achieving an inner peace.

When *People* named him one of its "men we love," a runner-up in its "Sexiest Man Alive" issue for 2003, it found him meditating and studying Buddhism at his home in San Gabriel Valley, California. The magazine reported that he had recently spent three months in Asia to learn more about Buddhism. "In Tibet I was not able to shower for two weeks," he told the magazine. "There was no hot running water. But while I was there, I was truly happy."

Li was vacationing in the Maldives, a chain of islands in the Indian Ocean, when a massive tsunami struck southern Asia on December 26, 2004. He and his four-year-old daughter were in their hotel's lobby when the wave hit, and he injured his foot on a piece of furniture while running for safety. He later posted a message on his website assuring his fans he was okay, thanking the staff of the hospital for keeping the guests safe, and encouraging his fans to donate to tsunami relief efforts.

Thanks to his spiritual beliefs, Li has told interviewers, he does not fear death, and says thoughts of it can make living in the present more precious. Likewise, he can handle either further success or commercial failure. "In Buddhism, nothing is permanent. This flower is very beautiful now, but a few months later, no flower," Li told the *Los Angeles Times'* Noxon. He explained that martial arts movies are hot now but there are no guarantees that their popularity will last. "You hope your movie becomes successful, but all you can do is your best and keep your responsibility to yourself," he said.

## Sources

### Periodicals

*Entertainment Weekly,* July 13, 2001, p. 44; November 9, 2001, p. 83; March 7, 2003, p. 51; September 3, 2004, p. 56.
*Hollywood Reporter,* December 29, 2004, p. 3.
*Los Angeles Times,* July 4, 2001.
*Men's Health,* September 2004, p. 176.
*Newsweek,* March 27, 2000, p. 74.
*People,* August 3, 1998, p. 25; December 1, 2003, p. 125; September 6, 2004, p. 31.
*Time,* April 3, 2000, p. 80.
*Time International,* July 30, 2001, p. 48.
*Video Business,* February 25, 2002, p. 17; August 18, 2003, p. 39.

### Online

"Chinese film 'Hero' tops North American box office," CNN.com, http://www.cnn.com/2004/SHOWBIZ/Movies/08/29/boxoffice.reut/index.html (February 20, 2005).

"Jet Li," All Movie Guide, http://www.allmovie.com/cg/avg.dll?p=avg&sql=2:42291~C (February 20, 2005).

"Jet Li," Internet Movie Database, http://www.imdb.com/name/nm0001472 (February 20, 2005).

"Life: Biography," Official Jet Li Website, http://jetli.com/jet/index.php?s=life&ss=biography&p=0 (February 20, 2005).

*—Erick Trickey*

# Peter Liguori

© Ciniglio Lorenzo/Corbis Sygma

## President and Chief Executive Officer of FX Networks

---

**B**orn July 6, 1960, in the Bronx, NY; married Hannah; children: Jackson, Susannah. *Education:* Yale University, B.A. (history), 1982; attended Northwestern University.

**Addresses:** *Office*—10000 Santa Monica Blvd., Rm. 464, Los Angeles, CA 90067.

## Career

**B**rand assistant, Richardson-Vicks (division of Procter & Gamble), 1982-83; account executive, Saatchi & Saatchi, 1983-86; account supervisor and director of account-management training, Ogilvy & Mather, 1986-88; director of marketing, vice president of marketing, senior vice president, HBO Video, 1988-94; vice president of marketing, HBO, 1994-96; senior vice president of marketing and promotion, Fox-Liberty Networks, 1996-98; president, FX Networks, 1998—; chief executive officer of FX Networks, 2001—.

**Awards:** Leaders of Vision Award, RP International, 2004.

## Sidelights

**P**eter Liguori took over the reins of the FX television network in 1998. Since then he has worked tirelessly to create a niche for the small cable channel as it attempts to find a place in the competitive world of ad-supported cable networks. As a member of the much larger Fox-Liberty Networks group of media outlets, FX has been able to take its time finding a share of the audience. When he first joined the station, like its competitors USA, TNT, and TBS, FX was the final resting ground for popular reruns. Liguori had a different vision for FX. His goal was to increase viewership, particularly among men in their mid-20s to late-30s, in order to compete with established networks. With that goal in mind, Liguori went in search for original programming produced by and for the station that would intrigue and delight viewers.

After a couple years of false starts, Liguori found the right combination of violence, intrigue, and creativity in the police drama *The Shield.* Audiences either loved or hated the show. Critics praised the gritty drama about a police officer who most often operates on the wrong side of the law. Advertisers feared the public backlash against the violent content, and in its first year, ads were pulled. But Liguori had confidence in the show and kept with it. That confidence paid off in 2002 when the show's star, Michael Chiklis, won an Emmy for Best Actor in a Series. The award was the most prestigious ever given to a basic-cable show. The following year Chiklis won a Golden Globe for best actor, and the series won for best drama. Liguori was beginning to reap huge benefits for his risk. Speaking to *Media-*

*week,* Liguori commented on the success of *The Shield* and what it meant for the future of FX, "It takes a long time to entrench a brand in TV, and I have no illusions that we have cemented one. We have just taken the first few steps, but it's a damn shame if we don't use this opportunity."

Born on July 6, 1960, Liguori grew up in the Bronx, New York, with his parents and members of his extended family. He told Joe Schlosser of *Broadcasting & Cable,* "It was the quintessential extended immigrant family. It was a warm, fun environment." His father worked two jobs until his death when Liguori was 16. Liguori's father was committed to having his son go to college and emphasized academic achievement. Liguori explained to Schlosser, "There were few things that were uncompromised in our family, but one thing was absolute: grades." At Harry S. Truman High School, Liguori made the grades and ended up graduating valedictorian of his class.

Possessed of an interest and ability in business, Liguori went to college at Yale University. By his sophomore year, he was running the on-campus laundry service. He graduated in 1982 with a degree in history. When he graduated he was hired by Procter & Gamble, for whom he worked for about a year. The job at Procter & Gamble proved boring and unchallenging and was located in the suburb of Wilton, Connecticut. Liguori grew tired of working on projects for products like denture adhesives and left the job after only a year. He was drawn to New York and moved there to work for the advertising agency of Saatchi & Saatchi.

Because his father had wanted him to be a lawyer, Liguori moved to Chicago in 1985 to attend Northwestern University's law school. He dropped out after only one semester because he realized he wanted to be in the film business. Just before his finals he had seen the film *Once Upon a Time in America.* He explained to *Broadcasting & Cable*'s Schlosser, "I fell in love with the movie and found a bit of a calling." Liguori finished his semester at Northwestern and then returned to New York hoping to get into movies.

Liguori did not get into the film business immediately upon his return to New York; he spent a few more years in advertising, including a return to Saatchi & Saatchi and a stint at Ogilvy & Mather, another large advertising firm. In 1988, his chance to get into the film business came when he was of-

fered a position with HBO in the marketing department of their newly formed home video division. He started out as director of marketing and by 1994, he had become senior vice president of marketing. In 1994, he moved to the position of vice president of marketing for all of HBO. He held the position for two years before Fox-Liberty Networks hired him as senior vice president of marketing and promotion.

In 1998, Liguori was named president of FX Networks. Three years later, in 2001, during one the most dismal years for the entertainment industry, in the midst of layoffs and cutbacks, Liguori was named chief executive officer and given a five-year contract. That year FX was in the top 10 of favorite cable stations among adults between 18 and 49. By 2004, Tim Goodman of the *San Francisco Chronicle* argued that FX ranked as the number five network in television, coming in after ABC, CBS, Fox, and NBC. Using well-performing shows such as *The Shield, Nip/Tuck,* and *Rescue Me* as examples, Goodman stated, "[T]here is no more wondering out loud about whether FX has been extremely lucky ... and stumbled upon two quality dramas in some fluke-filled guessing game. Three is a trend...."

In 2003, Liguori was listed as one of *Entertainment Weekly*'s most powerful people in the entertainment industry in their 14th annual Power Issue. The magazine cited his ability to transform FX from a rerun station to a presenter of high-quality, envelope-pushing weekly drama series. As he has risen to prominence and power in the entertainment industry, Liguori—who is married and has two kids—claims that he tries to always remember his roots. He explained to Schlosser, "[P]art of what I am in terms of being a programmer is rooted in my experiences growing up in the Bronx."

## Sources

*Broadcasting & Cable,* July 17, 2000, p. 38; January 29, 2001, p. 64.
*Cable World,* October 15, 2001, p. 42.
*Daily Variety,* October 15, 2001, p. 4; June 8, 2004, p. B1.
*Entertainment Weekly,* October 24, 2003, p. 26.
*Hollywood Reporter,* June 4, 2004.
*Mediaweek,* May 19, 2003.
*Multichannel News,* May 8, 2000, p. 78.
*San Francisco Chronicle,* July 19, 2004, p. C1.

—*Eve M. B. Hermann*

# Lindsay Lohan

### Actress and singer

*Michael Germana/UPI/Landov*

**B**orn Lindsay Morgan Lohan, July 2, 1986, in Long Island, NY; daughter of Michael (a salesman and actor) and Dina (an actress, dancer, analyst, and talent manager) Lohan.

**Addresses:** *Office*—LL Rocks, Inc., PMB 179, 223 Wall St., Huntington, NY 11743-2060. *Website*—http://www.llrocks.com.

## Career

**A**ctress in films, including: *The Parent Trap,* 1998; *Freaky Friday,* 2003; *Confessions of a Teenage Drama Queen,* 2004; *Mean Girls,* 2004; *Herbie: Fully Loaded,* 2005; *Just My Luck,* 2005. Television appearances include: *Another World,* NBC, 1996-97; *Guiding Light,* CBS; *Healthy Kids,* The Family Channel; *Life-Size* (movie), 2000; *Bette,* CBS, 2000; *Get a Clue* (movie), Disney Channel, 2002; *King of the Hill* (voice), 2004; *MTV Movie Awards* (host), 2004; *Saturday Night Live* (host), NBC, 2004; *That '70s Show,* Fox, 2004. Signed five-album production deal with Emilio Estefan, Jr., 2002; signed record contract with Casablanca Records, 2004; released *Speak,* 2004. Appeared in television commercials as a child for companies such as The Gap, Jell-O, and Pizza Hut; modeled for Abercrombie & Fitch Kids and Calvin Klein Kids.

**Awards:** Young Artist award for best leading young actress in a feature film, for *The Parent Trap,* c. 1998; MTV Movie Award, breakthrough female, for *Freaky Friday,* 2004.

## Sidelights

**W**ith her first film as a child actress, 1998's *The Parent Trap,* Lindsay Lohan (pronounced LOW-han) had box office success. After appearing in a number of television productions as she made the transition from child to teenager, she made several successful films as a teen actress. They included *Freaky Friday* and *Mean Girls,* both hits at the box office. Lohan also tried to launch a career as a singer, signing a recording contract with music guru Tommy Mottola. After contributing tracks to several film soundtracks, she released her first album, *Speak,* in 2004.

Born July 2, 1986, in Long Island, New York, she is the oldest child of Michael and Dina Lohan. Her father is a one-time Wall Street trader who also worked as an entrepreneur and in food sales, selling products like pasta. Her mother had been an actress, dancer, and one-time Rockette, who later worked as a Wall Street analyst. When her daughter's career took off, Dina Lohan became her manager. Lohan's younger siblings—two brothers, Michael and Dakota, known as Cody, and a sister Aliana—also had acting and modeling careers.

Growing up in Cold Spring Harbor, New York, Lohan began her modeling career when she was a toddler. She signed to the Ford Modeling Agency at the age of three in 1989, allegedly the first red-headed child model taken on by the agency. She modeled for companies such as Calvin Klein Kids and Abercrombie & Fitch Kids. As a youngster, Lohan also appeared in more than 60 television commercials. She appeared with Bill Cosby in a commercial for Jell-O, as well as commercials for The Gap, Wendy's, and Pizza Hut.

By the time Lohan was ten years old, she was transitioning into acting roles, though she never took an acting class or studied the craft. In 1996, she landed a recurring role on the daytime soap opera *Another World*; Lohan spent a year playing Ali Fowler. She also had a role on *Guiding Light* and appeared with her mother on the Family Channel series *Healthy Kids*.

Lohan had her first big break in 1998 when she had the starring role in the film remake of *The Parent Trap*. The original was made in 1961 and starred Hayley Mills. As Mills did, Lohan played both leads, identical twins Hallie and Annie Parker. The Parker twins were separated at birth by their parents when they divorced, and raised in different countries. One was raised in Great Britain, the other in the United States. Each did not know about the other's existence until they meet up at a summer camp. After overcoming an initial dislike and then realizing they are twins, the girls try to get their parents back together by switching their identities and living with their non-custodial parent. They reveal the deception before their father gets engaged to another woman, but continue their quest.

Lohan beat out 4,000 other actresses to get the role. Her whole family came along when she did the six-month shoot to keep her life as normal as possible. Each member of her family had a cameo role in *The Parent Trap*. The shoot was demanding since Lohan had to remember both characters' lines and do movements exactly the same twice in each scene the twins appeared in to create the illusion. The dual images were put together with a computer to complete the scene. All of Lohan's hard work paid off since the film made more than $66 million in the United States alone.

After the success of *The Parent Trap*, Lohan focused on school. She continued to attend public schools, including Cold Spring Harbor High School. Eventually the demands of her career compelled her to turn to home schooling to complete her education. Though her education took up much of her time for several years, she continued to work as an actress.

Much of Lohan's work from 2000 to 2003 was in television. In 2000, she had a leading role in the television movie *Life-Size*. It co-starred model Tyra Banks, whose Barbie-doll character comes to life. The movie originally aired as part of *The Wonderful World of Disney*, and was later released on home video. In 2002, Lohan appeared in another television movie. She played Lexy Gold on a Disney Channel movie called *Get a Clue*.

Lohan also tried to move into series television. In the 2000 pilot for the CBS situation comedy *Bette*, a vehicle for actress and singer Bette Midler, Lohan played her daughter. The pilot was shot in New York City and the show was picked up by the network. However, when producers decided to move the production to Los Angeles, Lohan did not want to move with it, so she gave up the role. Lohan's part was taken over by another actress, but the situation comedy was soon canceled.

In 2003, Lohan returned to features. Her next film, *Freaky Friday*, was also a remake. Based on a novel published in 1972, the original film was made in 1976 and starred Jodie Foster in the role Lohan would play. In the film, Lohan played Annabelle (Anna), a teenager who wants to be a rock star. Her psychotherapist mother Tess Coleman, played by Jamie Lee Curtis, is about to re-marry. Suffering from communication problems, the pair somehow switch bodies for a day. The switch forces them to walk in the other person's shoes and creates many comic situations. The film was praised by critics, and earned more than $100 million at the box office. *Freaky Friday* also marked the debut of Lohan as professional singer. Her song, "Ultimate," appeared on the *Freaky Friday* soundtrack.

Lohan had two feature films released in 2004, both teen comedies. The first was *Confessions of a Teenage Drama Queen*, based on the novel by Dyan Sheldon. Lohan played Mary, a teenager who moves from New York City to New Jersey after her parents' divorce. Lohan's character changes her name to Lola and creates a number of schemes to get attention, including befriending a famous rock star and helping her new best friend deal with bullying girls at school. Lohan also contributed four songs to the film's soundtrack. *Confessions* was not particularly well-received.

Lohan had a bigger hit with *Mean Girls*, penned by *Saturday Night Live* head writer Tina Fey. The screenplay was based on the book *Queen Bees & Wannabes* by Rosalind Wiseman. Lohan played Cady Heron, a naïve girl who was home schooled in Africa by her zoologist parents. The family comes back to the United States so that Cady can attend high school. She finds herself dealing with the intricacies of high school cliques. As part of an experiment, she becomes part of the popular set of girls, dubbed "The Plastics." However, Cady gets caught up in her newfound popularity and, for a time, becomes just as mean as the rest of the popular girls.

*Mean Girls* received much critical praise and was a hit at the box office. The number-one film in the United States the week it opened, it went on to earn more than $86 million. Lohan's performance as Cady was particularly praised, and she was seen as a film star. Industry expert Paul Dergarabedian told *People,* "This really puts her on the map as far as being a box office draw."

After the release of *Mean Girls,* Lohan remained in the public eye. In 2004, she became the youngest person ever to host the MTV Movie Awards. At the ceremony, she also showed she could dance. Later in the year, she was the guest host in an episode of *Saturday Night Live.* Dating actor Wilmer Valderrama of the hit situation comedy *That '70s Show* for several months brought Lohan tabloid press attention.

The tabloids also followed Lohan around for other reasons. She allegedly had a public feud with another young actress/singer, Hilary Duff, over a common boyfriend both had. There was also speculation on whether Lohan had plastic surgery, including breast augmentation. Lohan's family situation was also tense and drew press attention. Her father had served time in prison for securities fraud, and had been arrested several times in the early 2000s for assault. Dina Lohan took out a restraining order against her husband and filed for divorce in 2005. Lohan told Gill Pringle of the *Observer,* "People try and dramatize every little thing I do, and it's hard dealing with stuff and having my friends read about me and them calling and being like, 'OK, I know this isn't true, but I just have to ask....' It's weird, but you deal with it."

Lohan also focused on her singing career. She contributed a song, "I Decide," to the *Princess Diaries 2* soundtrack, and looked to record a full album. After signing a five-album production deal with Emilio Estefan, Jr. in 2002, and recording several demos, she signed with Casablanca Records in 2004. Casablanca was run by the former head of Sony Records, Tommy Mottola, who took charge of Lohan's recording career. In addition to singing, Lohan wanted to write her own songs and had a publishing deal arranged by Mottola as well.

In December of 2004, Lohan released her first record, *Speak,* which had a rock, pop, and urban feel. She co-wrote five of the songs on the record, with lyrics inspired by her life. Though the first single "Rumors" reached number 23 on *Billboard*'s Top 40 charts, the album and single were not highly regarded by critics. While some believed that Lohan could sing well enough, they found the material generic, second rate, and not fitting with her personality. As Jim Farber of the *Daily News* wrote, "What Lohan's album really needed was more of the sass—not to mention the tune—of Ashley Simpson's CD, a worthy album regardless of Simpson's actual input. After all, you don't need great talent to make a fun teen-pop album. You just need to have fun."

Having a singing career remained secondary to Lohan's acting career. In 2004 and early 2005, she shot several more films including a remake of Disney's *Herbie the Love Bug* called *Herbie: Fully Loaded.* Lohan also appeared in *Just My Luck,* as the title character. She played the luckiest woman in the world who loses this touch. Lohan remained in demand as an actress and had many other film roles lined up, including *Fashionistas, Dramarama,* and *Gossip Girl.*

Lohan also had a life outside of work. Having completed high school by home schooling, Lohan moved to Los Angeles by 2004 and lived with fellow young star Raven for a time before buying her own home. She also talked about going to college, perhaps to study entertainment law. But for the immediate future, Lohan remained focused on acting, and hoped to move beyond the teen roles she was currently doing. Lohan told Jamie Portman of the *Ottawa Citizen,* "This, acting, is what I aspired to do. It's what I want to do in life. It's what I want my career to be. So to just kind of put it aside right now and leave it to go to college when this is what I want to do ... I can't do that yet."

## Selected discography

(Contributor) *Freaky Friday* (soundtrack), Hollywood Records, 2003.
(Contributor) *Confessions of a Teenage Drama Queen* (soundtrack), Hollywood Records, 2004.
(Contributor) *The Princess Diaries 2: Royal Engagement* (soundtrack), Disney, 2004.
*Speak,* Casablanca Records, 2004.

## Sources

### Books

*Celebrity Biographies,* Baseline II, 2005.

## Periodicals

Associated Press, January 19, 2005.

*Billboard,* December 18, 2004.

*Daily News* (New York, NY), May 26, 2004, p. 32; June 20, 2004, p. 3; December 7, 2004, p. 49.

*Los Angeles Times,* December 7, 2004, p. E8; December 7, 2004, p. E1.

*Observer* (London, England), June 13, 2004, p. 32.

*Ottawa Citizen,* April 28, 2004, p. E6.

*People,* August 24, 1998, p. 70; May 24, 2004, pp. 79-80; July 12, 2004, p. 51; September 6, 2004, p. 70; November 8, 2004, p. 26; November 22, 2004, p. 21; December 13, 2004, p. 46; December 20, 2004, p. 70.

*Sacramento Bee,* June 7, 2004, p. E1.

*Star Tribune* (Minneapolis, MN), August 2, 1998, p. 6F.

*Toronto Star,* August 10, 2003, p. D4.

*USA Today,* December 6, 2004, p. 1D.

*Variety,* July 27, 1998, p. 51; July 28, 2003, p. 27; February 23, 2004, p. 34.

—*A. Petruso*

# Derek Lovley

## Scientist and professor

**B**orn c. 1954; married Marie; children: Erika, Zak, Cole. *Education:* University of Connecticut, B.A. (biological sciences); Clark University, M.A. (biological sciences); Michigan State University, Ph.D. (microbiology), 1982.

**Addresses:** *Office*—Department of Microbiology, 203 Morrill Science Center IVN, University of Massachusetts, 639 North Pleasant St., Amherst, MA 01003. *E-mail*—dlovleymicrobio.umass.edu.

## Career

**U**.S. Geological Survey, water quality, then groundwater studies, 1984-95; discovered class of bacteria named Geobacter, 1987; hired as professor at University of Massachusetts, Amherst, 1995; named microbiology department head at University of Massachusetts, Amherst, 1997; named a distinguished professor at University of Massachusetts, Amherst, 2000; discovered (with others) Rhodoferax ferrireducens, 2003; received numerous grants from both private and public sources over the course his career. Also worked as a lifeguard.

**Awards:** Grand Prize Winner, *Popular Science*'s "best of What's New in Environmental Technology," 1992; Proctor & Gamble Award, American Society for Microbiology, 2004.

## Sidelights

**U**niversity of Massachusetts scientist Derek Lovley helped create a new field of study around a microorganism he discovered, Geobacter. Since the mid-1980s, he has studied Geobacter and related anaerobic microorganisms. Lovley and his team of researchers found a number of uses for such bacteria, telling Robert S. Boyd in the *Milwaukee Journal Sentinel*, "Geobacter gives us a cheap and simple alternative to a cleaner, safer environment and the generation of cleaner forms of energy."

Raised in northwest Connecticut, Lovley was interested in water-based environments and the outdoors from an early age. While young, he worked as a lifeguard during summers out of school. By the 1970s, Lovley was a student at the University of Connecticut where he studied biological sciences. Within that field, he focused on environmental sciences and hoped to find employment that kept him in the outdoors.

While an undergraduate student, Lovley had an epiphany that drew him to microbiology. He believed that microbiology could be more than just medical-related and disease-related research as many scientists believed. Lovley realized that microbiology included microscopic life that also helped the ecosystem and the planet. He became interested in the microorganisms that lived in water, especially microbes which processed material in the water. Lovley studied these areas in graduate school. He earned an M.A. in biological sciences in from Clark University, then a Ph.D. in microbiology from Michigan State University in 1982.

In 1984, Lovley joined the U.S. Geological Survey, where he focused on water resources. He first worked on water quality in the Chesapeake Bay, but later moved into groundwater studies. By 1987, Lovley believed that certain microbes existed which could eat metals or breathe metals since the Earth has elements such as iron on which such microbes could live. However, not many of Lovley's colleagues agreed with him.

Lovley soon proved his fellow scientists were wrong. While looking through sediments in the Potomac River in 1987, Lovley made his discovery. He found a previously unknown type of bacteria that survived by living off metals, which he called Geobacter metallireducens. He dubbed their class Geobacter. Geobacter metallireducens converted insoluble ferric oxide in non-oxygen environments into soluble iron. The iron was then able to travel in the environment, become re-oxidized, and return to its original insoluble state.

Around the same time that Lovley made his discovery, another scientist, Kenneth Nealson, discovered a microbe that worked in similar fashion. Nealson called his discovery Shewanella. Though the findings of both scientists were controversial, both were proven correct and important in geological history. Lovley and Nealson had a long-lived rivalry as each continued to learn more about the microbes they had found.

Lovley located at least 70 types of Geobacter, some of which had far-reaching implications. Some types of the bacteria had a role in forming magnetite, a magnetic mineral. Magnetite comprises a vast percentage of the rocks from 500 million years ago. In the early 1990s, Lovley and his team applied their theories about Geobacter to gold and uranium, proving certain types of the microbe could process those metals as well. He believed that Geobacter could be used to clean up toxic waste, such as in water systems with oil problems. The microbe was also believed to be able to break down benzene and toluene. By the early 2000s, Geobacter was used to decontaminate a uranium mine as well as an oil spill, proving Lovley's theory correct.

In 1995, Lovley left the Geological Survey to take a professorship at the University of Massachusetts at Amherst. The scientist had offers from Ivy League schools, but chose the University of Massachusetts

because it allowed him an opportunity to continue doing field work. However, by taking the post, he did spend more time in the laboratory. He focused his research on the life of Geobacter and its biochemical composition. By 1997, Lovley was the head of the department, and in 2000, was named to a distinguished professorship. He also helmed what became known as the Geobacter Project.

Lovley was a very successful professor at the University of Massachusetts in that he was able to obtain a significant amount of grant money for Geobacter-related research. Lovley and his team were granted funds for many different kinds of projects and companies. The funds came from both private and government sources.

Several projects were done in conjunction with the U.S. Navy. In 2000, the Navy found sea muck that was electrified, and Lovley and his lab created sediment batteries. The researchers discovered that Geobacters could donate electrons to an electrode as well as iron. This process created an electrical current, which could power such batteries.

Lovley and his team continued to work on this idea for the U.S. Department of Energy, Naval Research, and the Defense Advanced Research Projects Agency. In 2003, Lovley and one of his scientists discovered Rhodoferax ferrireducens, which had the potential to be a long-term source of energy. That same year, Lovley and his team built a fuel cell, or battery, that used bacteria to turn garbage into energy. The Rhodoferax ferrireducens bacteria in the battery creates the current by feeding on sugars found in carbohydrates. Though the initial fuel cell did not have a lot of power, there was much potential for growth of this idea.

Lovley and his researchers worked on other Geobacter-related projects as well. In 2000, they discovered a bacteria that lived below the surface of the Earth that when placed in oil-rich soil, could quickly convert the oil to methane gas. This discovery had applications in the oil industry, making exploration safer than it had been previously. In 2002, Lovley received an $8.9 million grant over three years from the U.S. Department of Energy to research microbes that could be used to revitalize soil polluted by uranium and to create electricity. In 2003, he received two $900,000 grants from the U.S. Department of Energy to use a type of Geobacter to decontaminate water polluted with uranium because of mining.

Lovley's work was not limited to applications of Geobacter bacteria. He and his team also wanted to learn exactly how the microbes did this work. In conjunction with the Institute of Genomic Research, Lovley studied the genome sequence of the Geobacter as it was being completed. By 2002, they learned that Geobacter metallireducens could find and focus on the metal that keeps it alive. The bacteria could literally swim toward its food source, primarily metal oxides as found in the natural environment. Of his current research, Lovley told Mary Wiltenburg of the *Christian Science Monitor,* "It's a great time to be a microbiologist. I've got a team of 50 people working with me; almost every day somebody discovers something that changes the way we think about how things work."

## Sources

### Periodicals

Ascribe Newswire, April 12, 2000.
Associated Press State & Local Wire, December 8, 2002.
*Boston Globe,* September 8, 2003.
*Christian Science Monitor,* October 16, 2003, p. 16.
*Milwaukee Journal Sentinel,* July 25, 2004, p. 23A.
*Science,* May 10, 2002, p. 1058.
University Wire, October 14, 2003.
*USA Today,* September 8, 2003, p. 6D.

### Online

"Derek Lovley receives 2004 Proctor & Gamble Award from American Society for Microbiology," http://www.eurekalert.org/pub_releases/2004-04/asfm-drl043004.php (February 1, 2005).
"Derek Lovley," UMass Amherst Microbiology—Faculty, http://www.bio.umass.edu/micro/faculty/Lovley.html (February 1, 2005).
"Geobacter: A Bacterium with Surprising Survival Tactics," Office of Science, Department of Energy, http://www.er.doe.gov/Science_News/feature_articles_2002/June/Geobacter/UMass-Geobacter.htm (February 1, 2005).
"Lovley lands $8.9m grant for microbial studies," *Campus Chronicle,* http://www.umass.edu/chronicle/archives/02/07-26/Lovley.htm (February 1, 2005).
"The Microbe Master Getting a Charge out of Mud," *Time,* http://www.time.com/time/2004/innovaters/200401/story.html (February 1, 2005).
"The pervasive presence of microbes," UMass Magazine Online, http://www.umassmag.com/Summer_2003/The_pervasive_presence_of_microbes_508.html (February 1, 2005).
"UMass Faculty Member Receives Federal Funds to Continue Research on Water Cleanup," University of Massachusetts Amherst, http://www.umass.edu/newsoffice/archive/2003/072303Lovley.html (February 1, 2005).

—A. Petruso

# Susan Lyne

**Chief Executive Officer of Martha Stewart Living Omnimedia**

**B**orn April 30, 1950, in Boston, MA; married George Crile (a television producer); children: two daughters. *Education:* Attended the University of California, Berkeley.

**Addresses:** *Office*—Martha Stewart Living Omnimedia, 11 W. 42nd St., New York, NY 10036.

## Career

**B**egan career in journalism with a San Francisco alternative weekly, *City,* c. 1970; moved on to the *Village Voice,* and rose to managing editor, 1978; vice president, IPC, 1982-86; founding editor of *Premiere* magazine, 1987; joined Walt Disney Pictures & Television as executive vice-president, 1996; with ABC Entertainment after 1998, first put in charge of movies and miniseries, and as president, 2002-04; joined board of Martha Stewart Living Omnimedia, June, 2004; named chief executive officer of Martha Stewart Living Omnimedia, November, 2004.

## Sidelights

**J**ust a few months after being ousted from her post as president of the ABC television network's entertainment division, Susan Lyne became the newest chief executive officer of Martha Stewart Living Omnimedia. The challenges Lyne faced when she took over the once-thriving lifestyle and media conglomerate were both numerous and novel, and nowhere in Lyne's long and impressive resume had

her duties included visiting the company founder at Camp Cupcake, the minimum-security prison where Martha Stewart was serving a five-month jail sentence.

Born in 1950, Lyne grew up in a traditional Irish-Catholic family in Boston. Eager for a change of scenery, she spent her college years at a hotbed of 1960s West-Coast radicalism, the Berkeley campus of the University of California. She abandoned her political-science studies, however, when she was hired at a San Francisco alternative weekly, *City,* owned by future filmmaker Francis Ford Coppola. From there, Lyne moved on to a post at the nation's top alternative newspaper, New York's *Village Voice,* where she served as managing editor from 1978 to 1982.

Lyne's first foray into the entertainment business came when the *Voice* did a story on a murdered *Playboy* centerfold, Dorothy Stratten, and the article won a Pulitzer Prize for the paper. It also led to a movie deal, and Lyne eventually signed on with a production company owned by Jane Fonda, IPC, where her job entailed looking for new film projects based on true-life stories. Lyne spent the years between 1982 and 1986 as an IPC company vice president, and in 1987 ventured back into journalism full-scale with the launch of *Premiere,* a much-lauded entertainment-industry periodical. She spent several years as its editor, until Walt Disney Pictures & Television hired her in 1996 as an executive vice-president. In that capacity, Lyne helped bring some impressive feature films to the big screen, including the 2003 story of a slain Irish journalist, *Veronica Guerin.*

Lyne moved over to the ABC network, which was a Disney company, and its entertainment division in 1998. She presided over ABC TV's movies and miniseries, and brought such notable projects as *Tuesdays with Morrie* and *Life with Judy Garland* to fruition. Her track record paved the way for her elevation to the presidency of ABC Entertainment in early 2002, which gave her responsibility for nearly all of its all prime-time programming. At the time, however, ABC's line-up was in terrible shape, and tied with the FOX network for third place in overall ratings. Lyne's three predecessors on the job had not lasted long, and industry gossip claimed that Disney executives liked to meddle. For the past few years, ABC had been determined to cull a younger, edgier audience, but had failed miserably. Its sole success story had been the quiz show *Who Wants to Be a Millionaire*—which pulled in huge ratings at first, but then other ABC executives decided to put in on the air four nights a week, and viewers quickly lost interest.

Lyne believed that family-friendly fare was ABC's best bet for maintaining an audience. Sitcoms like *8 Simple Rules for Dating My Teenage Daughter* and *George Lopez* were both greenlighted by her for the fall 2002 season, and proved a hit with critics and viewers. Lyne was also determined to decrease reliance on reality-television programming, but a year after she took the job, in the February 2003 sweeps period, ABC foisted six reality shows on viewers, nearly all of which tanked. *Are You Hot?* was a particularly notable failure, and even Lyne admitted in a *Business Week* interview with Ronald Grover, "I was embarrassed watching that. When it was pitched to us it sounded like fun. It was a little tongue-in-cheek. On some level it was going to make fun of or comment on the whole beauty-pageant genre. In reality, once we watched it we were mortified."

Despite Lyne's best creative efforts, ABC continued to suffer ratings and thus advertising-revenue losses; in the spring of 2004 there was yet another management reshuffle, and she lost her seat. "I was surprised, but I understood," she diplomatically told *Broadcasting & Cable*'s Jim Finkle when asked several months later about her reaction to being fired. "They felt they needed to make a larger change than they anticipated." Somewhat ironically, two of the following season's shows that Lyne had greenlighted, *Desperate Housewives* and *Lost,* went on to become two of the biggest hits of the year.

Lyne was invited to join the board of Martha Stewart Living Omnimedia in June of 2004, a troubled time for the once-mighty lifestyle and media empire. Stewart, its namesake and founder, had recently been convicted of lying to federal investigators about the sale of some stock in a biomedical company owned by her friend, and was facing prison time. Stewart no longer had a title at the company, but was still the majority shareholder. In November of 2004, with Stewart already serving her sentence at a Alderson, West Virginia, facility, the board replaced a longtime executive with Lyne as the new CEO.

Lyne faced a daunting array of challenges, as she had at ABC, but these were truly unique: Martha Stewart Living Omnimedia was charting unknown waters, with its founder and image-bearer in jail. The stock price had been plummeting, and the magazine's advertisers had been decamping in droves. Still, its share price climbed a bit the day the announcement was made that Lyne was in charge, and she moved quickly to branch out and bolster revenue.

Lyne retreated from the spotlight some when Stewart was released in March of 2005. She likely helped engineer the company's deal with the Sirius satellite radio network, which would launch a 24-hour Martha Stewart Living channel featuring lifestyle news and information. Lyne seemed to have more than a few similarities with her indefatigable boss. A former colleague from *Premiere,* Cyndi Stivers, told *Advertising Age* reporter Jon Fine that Lyne is "unflappable." Stivers recounted about a pregnant Lyne, who drove "a bunch of the staff to a screening, dropped them off, and drove herself to the hospital and had the baby in the hallway or something. No one had any idea she was about to give birth." When asked to verify the incident, Lyne said she had actually been in a taxi, and that she did actually make it into a delivery room, but just barely.

## Sources

*Advertising Age,* February 21, 2005, p. 42.
*Broadcasting & Cable,* January 24, 2005, p. 16.

*BusinessWeek,* May 12, 2003, p. 74; November 12, 2004.

*MediaWeek,* May 11, 1998, p. 8; April 12, 2004, p. 23.

*Newsweek,* January 21, 2002, p. 59; May 20, 2002, p. 46.

*New York Observer,* February 4, 2002, p. 1.

*New York Times,* November 12, 2004, p. C3.

*Variety,* January 14, 2002, p. 6.

—*Carol Brennan*

# Wangari Maathai

*Ulrich Perrey/dpa/Landov*

**Environmental activist, educator, and government official**

---

**B**orn Wangari Muta Maathai, April 1, 1940, in Nyeri, Kenya; married (divorced, c. 1984); children: three. *Education:* Mount St. Scholastica College, Atchison, Kansas, BA (biology), 1964; University of Pittsburgh, MS, 1965; University of Nairobi, PhD.

**Addresses:** *Office*—Old Treasury Building, Harambee Avenue, P.O. Box 30551, Nairobi, Kenya.

## Career

**M**ade research assistant, department of veterinary medicine, University of Nairobi, 1966; joined National Council of Women of Kenya; lecturer, then assistant professor, then head of the faculty of veterinary medicine, University of Nairobi, 1970s; chair of veterinary anatomy, 1976; professor of veterinary anatomy, 1977—; founder and president, Green Belt Movement (formally Envirocare), 1977—; chair, National Council of Women of Kenya, 1981-87; Forum for Restoration of Democracy, founder with others, and member, 1991—; named co-chair for Jubilee 2000 Africa Campaign, 1998; elected member of parliament; Deputy Minister of the Environment, Natural Resources, and Wildlife, Kenyan Parliament, 2002—; named McCluskey Visiting Fellow in Conservation, Yale University, 2002.

**Awards:** Woman of the Year Award, 1983; Better World Society Award, 1986; Windstar Award for the Environment, 1988; Woman of the Year Award, 1989; Woman of the World, 1989; Honorary Doctor of Law, William's College, Massachusetts, 1990; Goldman Environmental Foundation Award, San Francisco, CA, 1991; laureate, Africa Prize for Leadership, the United Nations, 1991; Hunger Project Prize (with others), 1991; Honorary Doctor of Veterinary Medicine, 1992; Edinburgh Medal, 1993; Jane Adams Conference Leadership Award, 1993; Golden Ark Award, 1994; *Utne Reader*'s Top 100 Visionaries Award, 1995; listed in the United Nation's Environment Program Global 500 Hall of Fame, 1997; Honorary Doctor of Agriculture, University of Norway, 1997; named one of 100 persons in the world who have made a difference in the environmental arena, *Earth Times,* 1997; *Time* magazine's "Hero of the Planet" Award, 1998; Excellence Award, Kenyan Community Abroad, 2001; Outstanding Vision and Commitment Award, 2002; WANGO Environment Award, 2003; Sophie Prize, 2004; Petra Kelly Prize for Environment, 2004; J. Sterling Morton Award, Arbor Day Foundation, 2004; Conservation Scientist Award, 2004; Nobel Peace Prize, 2004.

## Sidelights

**A** visionary environmentalist, Wangari Maathai created a successful reforestation program that began in Kenya and was adopted in other African nations and the United States. Maathai continues to be recognized worldwide for her achievements, although she is denounced as a traitor and a rebel in her home country.

Maathai (pronounced MATH-eye) is perhaps best known for creating the Green Belt Movement of Kenya, a program recognized all over the world for combining community development and reforestation to combat environmental and poverty issues. Maathai excelled at mobilizing people for a very simple goal—reforestation—which also impacted poverty and community development in Kenya. Maathai believed that people needed to help with environmental issues and should not rely upon the government. Maathai clashed with the Kenyan government, often at risk to her own life, when she opposed destructive governmental initiatives and when she forayed into politics personally.

Maathai was born in Kenya in 1940. Attending college in the United States, she went on to earn a B.S. from Mount St. Scholastica University, in Kansas and a M.S. from University of Pittsburgh, in Pennsylvania. She then earned a Ph.D. from the University of Nairobi. She was the first woman in Kenya to earn a Ph.D. and at age 38, she held the first female professorship (in Animal Science) at the University of Nairobi. She credited her education with giving her the ability to see the difference between right and wrong, and with giving her the impetus to be strong.

Maathai's life was not without turmoil and hurdles, which she described as God-given. She married a politician who unknowingly provided the basis for her future environmental activities when he ran for office in 1974 and promised to plant trees in a poor area of the district he represented. Maathai's husband abandoned her and their three children later, filing and receiving a divorce on the grounds that she was "too educated, too strong, too successful, too stubborn and too hard to control," according to the *Mail & Guardian.* Maathai maintained that it was particularly important for African women to know that they could be strong, and to liberate themselves from fear and silence.

In 1977 Maathai left her professor position at the University of Nairobi and founded the Green Belt Movement on World Environment Day by planting nine trees in her backyard. The Movement grew into a program run by women with the goal of reforesting Africa and preventing the poverty that deforestation caused. Deforestation was a significant environmental issue in Africa and was resulting in the encroachment of desert where forests had stood.

According to the United Nations in 1989, only nine trees were replanted in Africa for every 100 trees that were cut down. Not only did deforestation cause environmental problems such as soil runoff and subsequent water pollution, but lack of trees near villages meant that villagers had to walk great distances for firewood. Village livestock also suffered from not having vegetation to graze on.

Women in the Kenyan villages were the people who first implemented Maathai's Green Belt Movement. "Women," Maathai explained at *National Geographic. com,* "are responsible for their children, they cannot sit back, waste time, and see them starve." The program was carried out with the women establishing nurseries in their villages, and persuading farmers to plant the seedlings. The movement paid the women for each tree planted that lived past three months. Under Maathai's direction in its first 15 years, the program employed more than 50,000 women and planted more than 10 million trees. Other African nations adopted similar programs based on the Green Belt Movement model. Additionally, the government stepped up its tree planting efforts by 20 times.

The Greenbelt Movement that Maathai conceived was not limited solely to tree planting. The program worked in concert with the National Council of Women of Kenya to provide such services and training to Kenyan women and villages as family planning, nutrition using traditional foods, and leadership skills to improve the status of the women. By 1997 the Movement had resulted in the planting of 15 million trees, had spread to 30 African countries as well as the United States, and had provided income for 80,000 people.

Maathai had strong beliefs about how she carried out environmental activism. She warned that educated women should avoid becoming an elite, and instead, should do work for the planet. Nobody could afford to divorce themselves from the earth, she believed, because all human had to eat and depend on the soil. Activism, she felt, was most effective when done in groups rather than alone. She credited her success with the Green Belt Movement to keeping the goal simple. The program provided a ready answer for those who asked, "What can I do?" Planting trees, in this case, was the simple solution.

Maathai continued to oppose modernization that collided with her environmental beliefs; this often put her at odds with the government. As an example, she was thrown out of her state office in 1989 when she opposed the construction of a 60-story skyscraper in Uhuru Park in Nairobi. Maathai claimed that the building, which was to house government offices and a 24-hour TV station, would cost $200 million. The money, she claimed, could be better spent addressing serious poverty, hunger, and education needs in the country. Her opposition succeeded in frightening off foreign investors and they withdrew their support; the skyscraper was never built. In Nairobi, Maathai also opposed the deforestation of 50 acres of land outside the city limits to be used for growing roses for export.

Politics and environmental activism continued to interweave in Maathai's life even before she attempted to run for office. In 1991, she helped found the Forum for the Restoration of Democracy, a group that was opposed to the leadership of then-president Daniel arap Moi. She advocated for the release of political prisoners and led a hunger strike on 1992 with the mothers of these prisoners. During one of these protests, she was beaten by police until she lost consciousness.

In January of 1992 she was arrested for her political protest activities when more than 100 police raided her Nairobi residence. Later in 1992, she was charged with spreading rumors that then-president Moi planned to turn government power over to the military in order to prevent multi-party elections. While Maathai awaited trial for the latter charge, she was refused medical treatment in jail; even though she was experiencing difficulties due to a history of heart problems and arthritis.

In 1992 Maathai was approached to run for the Presidency by a cross section of the Kenyan population. She declined, preferring to try and unite the fractured opposition parties against President Moi. Her efforts failed and Moi was again elected.

In 1997 Maathai responded to encouragement from supporters and friends and announced that she was running not only for a Parliament seat, but for the presidency under the Liberal Party of Kenya (LPK) in an attempt to defeat Moi. She got a late start in the process and did not announce her intentions until a month before the election. She denounced the current corruption in the government, and urged that the time had come to restore Kenyan people's dignity, self respect, and human rights. The government that she proposed was a people centered operation, or an "enabling political environment to facilitate development." Central to her vision was a Kenyan society where people acknowledged their cultural and spiritual background as they participated in government.

However, Maathai released no party manifesto prior to the election, claiming that the Green Belt Movement would provide the direction for her platform. At least one political analyst of the Africa News Service, saw this as troubling, claiming that Maathai might focus only on environmental issues and that the LPK already had a manifesto. Maathai countered such fears by claiming that her leadership would focus not only on the environment (which was, in her mind, tied to other issues like hunger), but on infrastructure issues, poverty, disease, and the empowerment of the oppressed.

Maathai found fault with the current political system, which required candidates to acquire extremely large amounts of money in order to carry out campaigns. This situation, she claimed, made it difficult for many visionary hopefuls like herself to even have a chance at making a difference in Kenya. A few days prior to the December 1997 election, the LPK leaders withdrew Maathai's candidacy without notifying her. Her bid for a Parliament seat was also defeated in the election; she came in third. Moi again emerged as the presidential victor. She continues to be admired worldwide, however, for her visionary work in the environmental arena.

In January of 1999, Wangari was hospitalized for a head wound and concussion she suffered during a government-arranged attack while she and some supporters were planting trees in the Karura Public Forest in Nairobi. The plantings were part of a protest against the land being approved for clearing and development. She immediately reported the incident to Amnesty International and other agencies, which publicized it through the world media as Wangari lay in her hospital bed. Accustomed to such treatment, however, Wangari has continued her environmental campaign undaunted.

In 2001, the Green Belt Movement filed suit to prevent a forest clearance project by the Kenya government that included a plan to clear 69,000 hectares of woodland to house homeless squatters. Maathai believed that it was the government's deliberate ploy to gain support in the coming elections. Planet Ark. com reported that she commented, "It's a matter of life and death for this country, we are extremely worried. The Kenyan forests are facing extinction and it is a man-made problem."

Maathai's future plans include another worthy cause: she hopes to establish a center to house battered women and children. This is an enormous undertaking that will require a lot of support, education, and resources. Many African men will need to be persuaded as they might see this as an intrusion into their culture. Oftentimes they treat women as personal property, especially among those who have paid exorbitant amounts of money for the bride price. Successful programs in Europe and the United States include components for counseling both the victims and the perpetrators. Many Africans will have to change their mind-set and treat men who abuse women and children as law-breakers. On the other hand, African women should not be content to remain as victims; they should be aware that they have choices and human rights. Moi left office in December of 2002, after a constitutional ban prevented him from seeking reelection.

Maathai was elected a member of parliament and appointed Deputy Minister of the Environment, Natural Resources, and Wildlife. Now as she serves as a lawmaker, she is in a good position to support or enact laws that will protect women's rights as human rights. She also began an appointment as the fifth McCluskey Visiting Fellow in Conservation at Yale University's prestigious Global Institute for Sustainable Forestry, where she co-taught a course titled "Environment and Livelihoods: Governance, Donors, and Debt."

Such commitment has earned Maathai many accolades and acclaim. Among the many prizes and recognitions bestowed upon her is the 1991 Goldman Environmental Prize, one of the most prestigious in the world. She received the Edinburgh Medal in 1993, and in 1997, she was elected by *Earth Times* as one of 100 persons in the world who have made a difference in the field of environmentalism. On March 30, 2004, Maathai won the 2004 Sophie Prize, founded by Norwegian writers Jostein Gaardner and Siri Dannevig. The $100,000 award recognized Maathai's work on environmental issues.

Maathai's name became even more well-known when she was awarded the Nobel Peace Prize, the first ever given to an African woman. She was honored for aiding democracy and attempting to save Africa's forests. At the ceremony, Maathai stated, according to CNN.com, "The environment is very important in the aspects of peace because when we destroy our resources and our resources become scarce, we fight over that. I am working to make sure we don't only protect the environment, we also improve governance." According to the *Mail & Guardian,* the money that goes with the Nobel Peace Prize received a lot of attention from the Kenyan media. After being asked frequently about what she planned to do with the money—and giving the standard answer, about funding environmental programs—Maathai finally declared, "I could indulge, yes, but how many cups of tea can I drink?"

## Selected writings

*The Green Belt Movement: Sharing the Approach and the Experience,* International Environmental Liaison Center (Nairobi, Kenya), 1988.
"Foresters Without Diplomas," *Ms. Magazine,* March-April 1991, p. 74.
"Kenya's Green Belt Movement," *UNESCO Courier,* March 1992, p. 23.

## Sources

### Periodicals

Africa News Service, October 27, 1997; January 5, 1998.
*E Magazine,* January 11, 1997.
Inter Press Service English News Wire, December 10, 1997.
*People,* October 25, 2004, pp. 71-72.
*Time,* April 23, 1990; April 29, 1991; April 27, 1992.
*Women in Action,* January 1, 1992.

### Online

"Acceptance Address by Professor Wangari Maathai," The Hunger Project, http://www.thp.org/prize/91/wm991.htm (March 18, 2005).
"Africa Prize Laureates, Professor Wangari Muta Maathai," The Hunger Project, http://www.thp.org/prize/91/maathai.htm (March 18, 2005).
"A long way to Oslo for the Mother of Trees," *Mail & Guardian,* http://www.mg.co.za (April 20, 2005).
"Bottle-Necks of Development in Africa," Gifts of Speech, http://gos.sbc.edu/m/maathai.html (March 18, 2005).
"Dr. Wangari Maathai," Africa Society Profile, http://www.ualberta.ca/~afso/documents/maathai.pdf (March 18, 2005).
"Environmental Hero: Wangari Maathai," Environmental News Network, http://www.enn.com/arch.html?id=30047 (March 18, 2005).
"Kenyan environmentalist to teach as McCluskey fellow," Yale University, http://www.yale.edu/opa/v30.n17/story19.html (March 18, 2005).
"Kenyan Greens File Suit to Stop Forest Clearance," Planet Ark, http://www.planetark.com/dailynewsstory.cfm/newsid/13379/newsDate/20-Nov-2001/story.htm (March 18, 2005).
"Kenyan's Painful Path to Nobel Peace Prize," *National Geographic.com,* http://news.nationalgeographic.com/news/2004/10/1019_04041019_peace_prize.html (April 20, 2005).

"Kenya: Wangari Maathai Attacked," Africa Action, http://www.africaaction.org/docs99/ken9901.htm (March 18, 2005).

"Maathai: Fighter for the forests," CNN.com, http://www.cnn.com/2004/WORLD/europe/10/08/nobel.maathai.profile/index.html (March 18, 2005).

"Wangari Maathai," Goldman Environmental Prize, www.goldmanprize.org/recipients/recipientProfile.cfm?recipientID=29 (March 18, 2005).

"Wangari Maathai: Saving the Earth, Tree by Tree," State of the World Forum, http://www.simulconference.com/clients/sowf/dispatches/dispatch27.html (March 18, 2005).

# Ellen MacArthur

## Yachtswoman

**B**orn July 8, 1976, in Derbyshire, England; daughter of Ken (a teacher) and Avril (a teacher) MacArthur.

**Addresses:** *Office*—Offshore Challenges Group, Cowes Waterfront, Venture Quays, Castle St., East Cowes PO32 6EZ, Isle of Wight, United Kingdom.

## Career

**C**ompleted solo sail around the British Isles, 1995; finished in seventeenth place in a transatlantic race, 1997; won first place in her class in the France-to-Guadeloupe Route du Rhum challenge, 1998; placed second in the Vendée Globe race, 2001; set new world record in the Route du Rhum race, 2002; set new world record for fastest circumnavigation of the globe as solo sailor, 2005.

**Awards:** Member of the Order of the British Empire, 2002; created dame by Queen Elizabeth II, 2005.

## Sidelights

**A** crowd of thousands greeted 28-year-old Ellen MacArthur on a chilly February day in 2005 when she and her boat, the *B&Q*, arrived in Falmouth, England, after completing a 71-day around-the-world solo voyage. MacArthur's achievement made her the youngest woman ever to circumnavigate the globe on a solo sail, but she also set a new world record for the feat. "There were some times out there that were excruciatingly difficult," a *New York Times* report quoted her as saying. "I have never in my life had to dig as deep as I did in this trip, and not just once or twice, but over consecutive weeks."

Born in July of 1976, MacArthur grew up in a land-locked part of England's north, Derbyshire, in a town called Whatstandwell. The middle child of two schoolteachers, she was four years old when she experienced her first sea voyage, out on a dinghy with her aunt, and she was entranced from that point onward. Over the next several years, MacArthur read anything she could find about sailing and the oceans of the world. By saving her lunch money she managed to buy her own dinghy at the age of 13, which she kept in her bedroom. Though she had considered becoming a veterinarian, just before her high-school finishing exams she fell ill with glandular fever and was confined to bed; she spent hours watching the progress of the Whitbread Round the World Yacht Race, and decided to pursue yachting as a career instead.

At the age of 18, MacArthur made a historic solo trip around the British Isles. Two years later, in 1997, she took part in a solo race across the Atlantic Ocean, in which she made a respectable seventeenth-place finish. In February of 2001, she made a stunning finish in what is known as one of the world's toughest sailing challenges, the solo Vendée Globe race. With a time of 94 days and a second-place win, she was the youngest person ever to finish it, and also set a new women's world record in yachting for solo circumnavigation. One of her preparations for the trip was teaching herself to sew on a piece of pigskin, for MacArthur knew of a sailor who had bitten off his tongue during a solo race when the boat's boom struck him; she wanted to be prepared to sew hers back on in the event that the same happened to her.

MacArthur's boat in the Vendée Globe was a monohull named the *Kingfisher* in honor of her generous sponsor, a British retail group. In 2002, she won the Route du Rhum, a solo transatlantic race from St. Malo, France, to the archipelago of Guadeloupe in the French West Indies. The following year, she attempted to break the world record for fastest nonstop circumnavigation in the Jules Verne Trophy race, but her boat's mast snapped in the Indian Ocean and she was forced to drop out.

Back on land, MacArthur became a partner in the Offshore Challenges Group, a project management company in adventure sports. It was her sponsor for her solo trip, which began on November 28, 2004. This time, her boat was a 75-foot multihull, which is faster on the high seas, but also prone to capsizing. Only one other solo sailor had circumnavigated the globe in a multihull, Francis Joyon of France, and he had done it just the year before. MacArthur's voyage would last 71 days, 14 hours, 18 minutes, 33 seconds, and she survived on stores of freeze-dried meals and desalinated sea water. The trip was an arduous one, with tremendous physical and mental hardships, but perhaps worst of all was the need to keep constant watch on the unpredictable sea: MacArthur could sleep only in 15- to 30-minute intervals. The *B&Q* was regularly buffeted by wind gusts that could reach 65 miles per hour, and twice she was forced to scale her boat's 98-foot mast to repair the main sail.

Fans of MacArthur's avidly followed her progress on a Web site, www.teamellen.com. For a time, she lost her lead over Joyon's voyage because of wind conditions, but then a storm pushed her ahead and she began to make excellent progress. In an online diary she kept, excerpts from which were reprinted in London's *Guardian* newspaper, she wrote of South Atlantic storms on January 15. "Everything is creaking and groaning and smashing and grinding ... it's just terrible, and you go over three waves and you close your eyes and hope it's okay, then the fourth one ... whack. I'm sure something is going to break." Two weeks later, she reported a near-collision. "I saw a whale very, very close to the boat ... it was just in front of us, and we sailed right over it," she wrote on January 29. "It went underneath our starboard float and, as it went underneath us, it blew its air tanks out and its nose came out of the water."

On Monday, February 7, MacArthur and her boat crossed an imaginary finish line between Ushant, France, and the Lizard peninsula of the southwest coast of England. After a journey of 27,353 miles, she arrived at the Cornwall port of Falmouth the following day, and was met by a crowd of 8,000 well-wishers. She beat Joyon's record by an entire day, and was informed that Queen Elizabeth II had bestowed the title "Dame" on her for her achievement.

MacArthur lives in Cowes, the epicenter of British yachting, on the Isle of Wight. Her achievement was the latest in a long line of notable record-breaking sails by British sailors, which dates back to Sir Francis Drake's journey around the world in 1580. Thrilled to be back on land and with people after her long solo experience, she nevertheless admitted that her trip had its joys. "Some days you have a huge rolling sea and the boat is sailing beautifully," a report in the *Guardian* quoted her as saying, "and then there is no better place to be on Earth."

## Sources

### Periodicals

*Guardian* (London, England), February 8, 2005; February 9, 2005.
*Independent* (London, England), March 21, 2003, p. 4.
*New York Times*, February 9, 2005.

### Online

"MacArthur Sails into Record Books," BBC News. com, http://news.bbc.co.uk/sport1/hi/other_sports/sailing/4229079.stm (February 10, 2005)
"Swift Sailing," *SI.com*, http://sportsillustrated.cnn.com/2005/more/02/07/bc.eu.spt.sai.macarthur.ap/index.html (February 9, 2005).

—*Carol Brennan*

# Julien Macdonald

© Reuters/Corbis

## Fashion designer

**B**orn c. 1973 in Merthyr Tydfil, Wales; son of a factory worker and a homemaker. *Education:* Earned undergraduate degree in textiles from Brighton University; earned graduate degree in fashion from the Royal College of Art, 1997.

**Addresses:** *Office*—65 Goldborne Rd., London W10 5NT, United Kingdom.

## Career

**I**nternship with designer Koji Tatsuno in Paris, c. 1993; launched own line, Brother Julien's Ghetto Couture, 1994; head knitwear designer for Chanel, c. 1994-97; launched Julien Macdonald label, 1997; entered partnership with Gruppo Lineapiu, 2000; women's artistic director for House of Givenchy Haute Couture, 2001-04.

## Sidelights

**W**hen British designer Julien Macdonald was named the newest designer for Paris's venerable House of Givenchy in 2001, the announcement was received with some degree of alacrity by the fashion world. In business for himself for just four short years prior to that, Macdonald's claims to fame included a stint at Chanel and the creation of the stage outfits for the Spice Girls on their first world tour in 1997. His three-year run at Givenchy was a difficult one, marked by scathing press reviews and charges that he had irreparably damaged the design house known for the cool, understated elegance long associated with its unofficial muse,

Audrey Hepburn. "Look, nobody was more surprised than I was when I got the job," Macdonald told a writer for London's *Independent* newspaper, James Sherwood. "I was told that they wanted to change the image: make it sexy and fun—and very Julien Macdonald."

An exuberant personality along the lines of fellow Brit designers John Galliano and Alexander McQueen, whose fortunes were also made in Paris early in their careers and at the helm of Givenchy, Macdonald was barely 30 years old when he took the job. Born in a small town in Wales called Merthyr Tydfil, he inherited a love of sequins and sparkly things from his mother, a former swimsuit model who made an art of dressing up for an evening out. Pop culture was another important influence on him during his adolescent years in the mid-1980s. "I had a very isolated upbringing," he told the *Independent* in another article. "I aspired to the things I saw on TV." He credited flamboyant androgyne Boy George as an early fashion inspiration, and found that making his own clothes was an excellent way to express himself. He asked for a sewing machine for his sixteenth birthday, but had never planned to pursue fashion as a career—instead he took ballet and acting classes, and was accepted at the Royal Academy of Dramatic Arts, Britain's top training ground for thespians. He opted instead to earn a textiles degree from Brighton University.

After that, Macdonald won a spot at London's Royal College of Art in its graduate fashion design program. He did an internship with designer Koji Tatsuno in Paris and wound up designing the fabrics for one of Tatsuno's 1993 collections. Back in London at school, Macdonald entered a student design competition and his work was noticed by Karl Lagerfeld, Chanel's chief designer and a couture legend. Lagerfeld mentored him and eventually made him head knitwear designer for Chanel, and in the mid-1990s the daring sweaters and other outfits Macdonald designed for the label won rave reviews and sold extremely well.

Eager to strike out on his own, Macdonald left Chanel to launch his own label in 1997. His work was heavy on the glitz and sequins, and his first major coup came when he was asked to design the tour outfits for the Spice Girls at the height of their fame. Fashion-conscious celebrities began to favor his dresses for the red carpet, among them Elizabeth Hurley, Nicole Kidman, and Madonna. His London fashion shows became a sought-after ticket for their over-the-top themes, and a roster of pop stars was usually in attendance in the first row.

However, like many independent designers, Macdonald struggled to stay afloat financially. Relief came when he signed a partnership deal with Italian yarn and clothing manufacturer Gruppo Lineapiu in the fall of 2000, and it was at an Italian showroom that an executive with Louis Vuitton-Moët Hennessy (LVMH), the luxury-brands group, chanced upon Macdonald's line. The Paris-based company, which owns a dazzling array of the world's top designer labels and prestige companies, quietly brought Macdonald to its headquarters for a round of interviews. In March of 2001, the company announced that Macdonald was to be the new women's artistic director for House of Givenchy Haute Couture. The news, noted Rachel Cooke in London's *Observer*, "was greeted with surprise and even horror. He was, it is fair to say, the last person anyone expected to get the job." Other candidates were rumored to have been Stella McCartney, Olivier Theyskens, and Alber Elbaz.

Even Macdonald himself was stunned, according to Cooke, given his relative lack of experience and reputation for exuberantly styled frocks. "Even when they asked me to go over to Paris for the in-

terviews, I had no idea which job I was being considered for," he recalled. "I mean, at the time, they were looking for someone for Pucci, too. It was all very James Bond." Givenchy had an older customer base, and had struggled along since its founder, Hubert de Givenchy, retired in 1995. Monsieur Givenchy's muse had been his longtime friend, film star Audrey Hepburn, and the elegant, chic designs created with her in mind were the company's trademark look for years. Both John Galliano and then Alexander McQueen preceded Macdonald at Givenchy in what was viewed as LVMH's determined strategy to inject some much-needed verve and sexiness into designs coming out of the somewhat moribund atelier.

Macdonald did well with his first ready-to-wear collection at Givenchy, and it sold well, but his couture designs were greeted with scorn by the fashion press. He had been given the job with a mission to shake things up, he noted in the interview with Sherwood for the *Independent*, "but, as time went on, we realised that the customers and the press didn't want Givenchy to change... I don't find a black dress with three holes exciting. I don't find the black cashmere pencil-skirt suit fun. But I kept quiet and did my job."

LVMH did not renew Macdonald's contract in 2004, but he had continued to produce his own line during his Givenchy stint, and returned full-time to it in London when his Paris role came to an end. Other ventures include a limited-edition Barbie he did for Mattel, and a mass-market line, "Star by Julien Macdonald," launched at Debenhams, a leading British retailer. He was relieved, in the end, to finish his last Givenchy collection, after which he headed back to London and "cried for half an hour with sheer happiness," he told Sherwood. "I'm not bruised by the experience, and I am glad I did it. I could have been set up for life if I'd been happy. But I wasn't."

## Sources

*Independent* (London, England), February 15, 2003, p. 7; December 8, 2004, p. 2.
*Interview*, April 1994, p. 20.
*Newsweek International*, July 16, 2001, p. 66.
*Observer* (London, England), February 10, 2002, p. 3.
*WWD*, March 15, 2001, p. 1; March 16, 2001, p. 7; July 5, 2001, p. 1.

—*Carol Brennan*

# Alexander McCall Smith

## Author and professor

Juda Ngwenya/Reuters/Landov

**B**orn August 24, 1948, in Bulawayo, Rhodesia (later Zimbabwe); married Elizabeth Parry (a physician), 1982; children: Lucy, Emily. Religion: Scottish Presbyterian. *Education:* University of Edinburgh, LLB and Ph.D.

**Addresses:** *Contact*—16A Napier Rd., Edinburgh EH10 5AY Scotland. *Website*—http://www.random house.com/features/mccallsmith/.

## Career

**P**rofessor, Queens University, Belfast, Northern Ireland; taught in Swaziland Africa; helped found the law school at the University of Botswana, c. 1980, then served as law professor there; professor of medical law, University of Edinburgh; fiction author, c. 1984—; deputy chairman of Human Genetics Commission for the British government; served as Great Britain's representative on the bioethics commission for the United Nations Educational, Scientific, and Cultural Organization (UNESCO).

**Awards:** Chambers award in children's fiction; SAGA Award for Wit, 2003; Author of the Year, British Books Awards, 2004.

## Sidelights

**A**lthough he is a worldwide recognized expert on issues of medical ethics, Alexander McCall Smith became better known as the author of best-selling adult mysteries. His 1998 book *The No. 1 Ladies' Detective Agency,* focusing on a female investigator in the African country of Botswana, launched his fiction-writing career into international fame and acclaim. The growing success of his books led him to take a leave of absence from his professorship at the University of Edinburgh and give up his advisory posts related to medical ethics to focus on writing full-time.

McCall Smith was born on August 24, 1948, in Bulawayo, Rhodesia (later known as Zimbabwe), where his father worked as a public prosecutor in what was then a British colony. His mother wrote a number of unpublished manuscripts. The youngest of four children, McCall Smith spent the whole of his childhood in that African country. He attended the Christian Brothers College in Bulawayo. McCall Smith left Africa when he was 17 years old to continue his education in Scotland.

Entering the University of Edinburgh, McCall Smith studied law and earned two degrees, first an LLB, then a Ph.D. After completing his education, he began teaching law. His first teaching job was at Belfast, Northern Ireland's Queens University. McCall Smith then went back to Africa. He first went to

Swaziland to teach, and by 1980, he went to Botswana. There, he helped found the law school and taught law at the University of Botswana. While in Botswana, he also put together and wrote Botswana's criminal code. Though McCall's codification was not put into law, it was later published as *The Criminal Law of Botswana* and still proved to be very important to legal issues in that country.

McCall Smith eventually returned to Scotland where he became a professor in medical law at the University of Edinburgh. Over the years, he wrote a number of significant articles and books about the law and related medical ethics questions. In 1983, he co-wrote with Ken Mason *Law and Medical Ethics* which was updated every few years. In 1987, McCall Smith co-authored *Butterworths Medico-Legal Encyclopedia* with John Kenyon Mason. One interesting title was *Forensic Aspects of Sleep* which considered, among other topics, the legal culpability of those who were sleepwalking while committing an alleged crime.

As McCall Smith's stature as an expert in medical legal ethics increased, he was given many prestigious positions. He did several year-long professorships abroad including a stint at the law school at Southern Methodist University. McCall also served as the deputy chairman of Human Genetics Commission for the British government and served as Great Britain's representative on the bioethics commission for the United Nations Educational, Scientific, and Cultural Organization (UNESCO). He regularly traveled to London to advise the British government and other places around the globe in his UNESCO position. McCall Smith helped answer hard questions on issues such as how to manage DNA databases and protect the information therein.

While McCall Smith was becoming a highly respected professor and ethics expert, he began a secondary career as an author of fiction. His interest in such writing began in childhood. When McCall Smith was eight years old, he wrote his first book and tried to get it published. In his twenties, he began writing children's books almost by accident. He entered a contest run by Chambers with pieces of children's fiction and adult fiction. McCall Smith won the literary prize for his children's fiction manuscript, and went on to publish about 30 such works. His titles included *Film Boy, Suzy Magician,* and *Children of Wax,* a collection of short stories about Africa. The latter was later made into a television series.

By the late 1990s, McCall Smith branched out into adult fiction. After a visit to Botswana, he was inspired to write 1998's *The No. 1 Ladies' Detective*

*Agency.* Of the inspirational incident, McCall Smith told Marcel Berlins of the *Guardian,* "We were going to have chicken for lunch, and there was this woman in a red dress who chased and chased the chicken and eventually caught it, and wrung its neck. I thought to myself: I would like to write about an enterprising woman like that." The character he created was named Precious Ramotswe. She used an inheritance of 180 heads of cattle from her father to found the first all-female detective agency in Gaborone, Botswana.

In *The No. 1 Ladies' Detective Agency,* McCall Smith had his detective investigate everyday human crimes related to distresses within families. Most had nothing to do with murder, though one missing husband was found to have been eaten by a crocodile. However, American critics often compared Ramotswe to the Miss Marple character in Agatha Christie's seminal mystery novels. McCall Smith wanted to do more than write about an interesting female character. He also wanted to show the positive side of Africa and Botswana, a country that impressed him with its democracy, high moral standards, and human decency. McCall Smith used real people and locations from Botswana in his books.

Although *The No. 1 Ladies' Detective Agency* was originally published in 1998, it took several years to find an audience. It received some critical acclaim in Scotland, before word of mouth at independent bookstores in the United States helped the book become a success a short time later. As McCall Smith's book became a best-seller in the United States, its popularity spread to Canada, Australia, and New Zealand, and into England, Europe, and beyond. Although some readers found it hard to believe that a white Scottish man could understand African women so well, the book and its follow-ups received much critical praise.

After *The No. 1 Ladies' Detective Agency,* McCall Smith wrote more books featuring Ramotswe and other central characters. *The No. 1 Ladies' Detective Agency* was followed by 2000's *Tears of the Giraffe,* 2001's *Morality for Beautiful Girls,* 2002's *The Kalahari Typing School for Men,* 2003's *The Full Cupboard of Life,* and 2004's *In the Company of Cheerful Ladies.* All the books focused on Ramotswe's investigations into problems in people's lives instead of hard-core crimes. McCall Smith was able to publish a novel a year in the series because he could write at least 4,000 words a day, and, if inspired, as much as 1,000 words an hour.

Because of the popularity of the series, the books were translated into at least 26 other languages and sold millions of copies. Their popularity led to a profitable deal with Random House, a large publishing company, for McCall Smith in 2003. Random House acquired the United States rights to the series and also published other projects by the author. McCall Smith also sold the television rights to at least one of the books to a production company in Africa, where the books also sold well. Film rights were also sold with director Anthony Minghella attached to direct and/or produce.

Because of the gentle humor and focus on human nature, the books' success in the United States seemed unexpected. Some critics believed that they were popular in the United States because of the decay of society and the stress living in a post-9/11 world. McCall Smith told Rodney Chester of the *Courier Mail,* "We've had enough of mayhem and aggressive social realism and in-your-face stuff. I think people actually want something that deals with the little events in life and drinking tea."

While the success of *The No. 1 Ladies' Detective Agency* and the rest of the series were satisfying for McCall Smith, he also began other adult fiction series. Another female detective was at the center of one series. Isabelle Dalhousie lived in the suburbs of Edinburgh, Scotland, and worked as the editor of *The Review of Applied Ethics.* She approached getting involved in other people's crimes from the point of view of a moral philosopher. The first book in the series, *The Sunday Philosophy Club,* focused on a death Dalhousie investigates after she witnesses it. The more traditional mystery novel was generally praised, and the BBC (British Broadcasting Corporation) bought the rights to turn it into a television series.

Intellectual concerns were also part of another series written by McCall Smith that came out in the early 2000s. Originally written in 1997 and self-published at that time, *Portuguese Irregular Verbs* was a collection of short stories focused on the rather odd world of three German professors and their inability to function in the everyday world. The primary one was Professor Von Igelfeld, who lived in his academic milieu of Romance languages and worked as a philologist (a person who studies literature and language). McCall Smith wrote the book after being inspired by a German professor he met a conference in the mid-1980s. McCall Smith wrote it to poke fun at academics. The original work was passed around among these intellectuals who appreciated the joke. McCall Smith wrote two other books using these characters: *The Finer Points of Sausage Dogs* and *At the Villa of Reduced Circumstances.*

The prolific McCall Smith had other ideas for series, some of which came to immediate fruition. He wrote a book about an American tourist called *Fatty O'Leary's Dinner Party,* published in 2004. The primary character would be used in subsequent books. Another series was less traditional. Late in 2003, the *Scotsman* commissioned McCall Smith to write a serialized novel to be published five days a week for six months in 2004. With a story set in Edinburgh, *44 Scotland Street* featured 800-word chapters and reader input into the direction of the narrative. McCall Smith wanted the work to be unlike the original works of British author Charles Dickens in the nineteenth century, which also began as newspaper serials.

As McCall Smith became a more popular author, he still maintained his first career as a professor and ethics expert despite the many demands on his time to do book tours abroad and the like. Late in 2003, he cut down his professorship to part-time, and in early 2004, decided to take an unpaid leave of absence for the next three years. McCall Smith also gave up being the vice chairman of the Human Genetics Commission in 2004 and later, his work with UNESCO. McCall Smith's book contracts called for him to produce a certain number of books a year, and despite his prolific writing abilities, he needed the focus to get his work done. However, his success as an author allowed him to give to charities. He gave some money to support families affected by AIDS in Botswana and to Book Aid, which sent books to third world countries.

Although a few critics dismissed his works as too gentle and unassuming, McCall Smith believed in his work. He told Sarah Lyall of *New York Times,* "There is a role for books that say to people that life is potentially amusing and that there are possibilities of goodness and kindness—that kindness needn't be dull, that it can also be elevating and moving."

## Selected writings

### Nonfiction

(With Ken Mason) *Law and Medical Ethics,* 1983.
*Butterworths Medico-Legal Encyclopedia,* Butterworths, 1987.
(With Kwame Frimpong) *The Criminal Law of Botswana,* 1992.
*Scots Criminal Law,* 1992.
*The Duty to Rescue,* 1994.

*Forensic Aspects of Sleep*, Wiley, 1997.
(With Daniel W. Shuman) *Justice and the Prosecution of Old Crimes: Balancing Legal, Psychological, and Moral Concerns*, American Psychological Association, 2000.
(With Alan Merry) *Errors, Medicine and the Law*, Cambridge University Press, 2001.

### Children's fiction

*The Perfect Hamburger*, 1984.
*Alix and the Tigers*, 1988.
*Film Boy*, Methuen, 1988.
*Mike's Magic Seeds*, Random House, 1988.
*Children of Wax: African Folk Tales*, 1989.
*Suzy Magician*, Random House, 1990.
*The Five Lost Aunts of Harriet Bean*, Blackie, 1990.
*The Tin Dog*, 1990.
*The Girl Who Married A Lion and Other Stories*, Pantheon, 2004.

### Novels

*Portuguese Irregular Verbs*, self-published, 1997; Polygon, 2003.
*The No. 1 Ladies' Detective Agency*, Polygon, 1998.
*Tears of the Giraffe*, Polygon, 2000.
*Morality for Beautiful Girls*, Polygon, 2001.
*The Kalahari Typing School for Men*, Polygon, 2002.
*The Full Cupboard of Life*, Polygon, 2003.
*At the Villa of Reduced Circumstances*, 2003.
*The Finer Points of Sausage Dogs*, 2003; Anchor, 2004.
*In the Company of Cheerful Ladies*, Polygon, 2004.
*The Sunday Philosophy Club*, Polygon, 2004.
*The 2 Pillars of Wisdom*, 2004.
*Fatty O'Leary's Dinner Party*, Polygon, 2004.

# Sources

### Books

*Debrett's People of Today*, Debrett's Peerage, Ltd., 2004.

### Periodicals

*Booklist*, August 2004, p. 1872.
*Boston Globe*, June 17, 2003, p. E1.
*Boston Herald*, October 4, 2002, p. 39.
*Commentary*, October 2004, p. 86.
*Courier Mail* (Queensland, Australia), September 27, 2003, p. M3.
*Daily Telegraph* (London, England), January 2, 2003, p. 19.
*Financial Times* (London, England), August 21, 2004, p. 14.
*Guardian* (London), January 21, 2003, p. 8.
*Herald* (London), March 3, 2003, p. 11.
*Independent* (London), August 14, 2004, pp. 40-41.
*New York Times*, September 27, 2004, p. E3; October 6, 2004, p. E1.
*Observer*, May 2, 2004, p. 25.
*People*, May 10, 2004, p. 59.
*Publishers Weekly*, July 22, 2002, p. 75.
*Scotsman*, May 1, 2002, p. 8; May 7, 2002, p. 8; January 24, 2004, p. 1.
*Sunday Telegraph* (London, England), December 21, 2003, p. 3.
*Sunday Times* (London, England), March 12, 2000; February 16, 2003, p. 1.
*Time*, April 26, 2004, p. 143.

—A. Petruso

# Phil McGraw

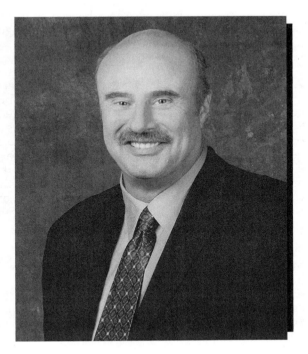

## Talk-show host, psychologist, and author

**B**orn Phillip C. McGraw, September 1, 1950, in Vinita, OK; son of Joe (an oilrig equipment supplier turned psychologist) and Jerry McGraw; married first wife (divorced); married Robin, c. 1976; children: Jay, Jordan. *Education:* Attended University of Tulsa; Midwestern State University, B.S. (psychology), 1975; University of North Texas, M.S. (psychology), 1976; University of North Texas, Ph.D. (psychology), 1979.

**Addresses:** *Home*—Beverly Hills, CA. *Office*—5482 Wilshire Blvd., No. 1902, Los Angeles, CA 90036.

## Career

**W**orked in private psychology practice with father, 1979-89; co-founded Courtroom Sciences Inc., 1989; regular guest on *The Oprah Winfrey Show,* 1998-2002; host of *The Dr. Phil Show,* 2002—.

## Sidelights

**D**r. Phil—aka Phillip McGraw—burst onto the talk-show circuit in the late 1990s as a regular guest on *The Oprah Winfrey Show.* He immediately captured a fan base with his blunt-fire style of therapy and folksy Texas twang. McGraw proved so popular that in 2002, he launched his own program, *The Dr. Phil Show,* which earned the highest ratings for a new talk show since Winfrey started hers in 1986. Part showman, part psychologist, McGraw draws six million daily viewers to his pro-

gram, where he urges people to "get real" about their lives. His self-help books are also popular, topping the *New York Times'* best-seller list.

McGraw was born September 1, 1950, in Vinita, Oklahoma, to Joe and Jerry McGraw. He and his three sisters spent most of their childhoods in rural Oklahoma and Texas, where their father worked as an oilrig equipment supplier. McGraw's father taught him early on the importance of doing whatever it takes to make your dreams come true. "[Our] dad said, 'Successful people will do what unsuccessful people won't,'" McGraw's sister, Deana, recalled to Marc Peyser of *Newsweek.* What Joe McGraw did was quit his job in the booming oil business and uproot his family so he could pursue a doctorate in psychology. The family was so poor that McGraw, his parents, and younger sisters had to move in with his older, married sister.

McGraw took an early interest in football and it was through this sport that he first became interested in psychology. Speaking to *Newsweek's* Peyser, he recalled a time in junior high when his team lost to an unlikely bunch of ragamuffins from the Salvation Army. McGraw said his team felt invincible, decked out in their black jerseys and matching helmets. The Salvation Army team showed up to play in rolled-up jeans and loafers. "They beat us like they were clapping for a barn dance," McGraw recalled. "At that point I really got interested in why some people, with all the advantages in the world, don't do well, and those with no advantages can be absolute champions."

As a six-foot-four-inch linebacker, McGraw earned a football scholarship to the University of Tulsa, but got injured and quit. He transferred to Midwestern State University in Wichita Falls, Texas, earning a bachelor's degree in psychology in 1975. From there, he headed to the University of North Texas to earn a master's and a doctorate in psychology with the aim of joining his father's private practice. Over the course of this time, McGraw married twice. He married straight out of high school and soon divorced. Around 1976, he married his current wife, Robin.

McGraw spent ten years working side-by-side with his father, then decided he did not have the patience for therapy. According to his book *Self Matters*, McGraw finally broke down and told his wife: "I hate my career. I hate where we are living. I hate what I am doing.... I have one shot at this, one shot, and I'm choking, I'm blowing it. I'm now almost forty years old. I've wasted ten years of my life and I can't get them back no matter what I do.... I'm tired of not waking up excited in the morning. I'm tired of not being proud of what I do or who I am."

Just like his father before him, McGraw quit his job and uprooted his wife and two sons to pursue other opportunities. McGraw drew upon his expertise in the field of human behavior to co-found Courtroom Sciences Inc. in 1989 with neighbor and attorney Gary Dobbs. The Irving, Texas-based company helps defendants with court strategy and jury selection. It was through this business that McGraw met Winfrey in the late 1990s when some West Texas cattle ranchers sued her for defamation after she broadcast a show on mad-cow disease. With the help of McGraw, Winfrey won her case. McGraw's straight talk so impressed Winfrey that she invited him to appear weekly on her show, beginning in 1998.

In 2002, McGraw left Winfrey's show to produce his own daily self-help show, which has proved enormously popular. The format is simple. Each show typically features a couple of troubled guests. McGraw introduces each one to the audience through a short segment taped from the guest's home, where the guest asks for help. The guest then appears on the show to speak with McGraw. He is quick to identify the problem and provide his guest with a solution, which generally involves trying to alter the person's way of thinking. The show has covered such issues as money, obesity, spoiled children, and disgruntled spouses. Since starting his own show, McGraw moved his family from Texas to Beverly Hills, California, where he bought a home for a reported $7.5 million. He also sold his stake in Courtroom Sciences.

McGraw has also written several books, most of which top the best-seller lists. One of his most popular was *The Ultimate Weight Solution: The Seven Keys to Weight Loss Freedom*, which garnered a reported $10 million advance. The topic is close to McGraw's heart. "I've had obesity obliterate my family—it took my father early, and I've got two nephews over 500 pounds," he told *Time*'s Jeffrey Ressner. "I feel a sense of urgency to shake people up about that."

McGraw himself has struggled with weight issues. He said he keeps the pounds off through strenuous workouts and near-daily tennis matches. McGraw believes success in weight loss involves healing your feelings. "If you're overweight, you're using food for other than nutritional purposes," he told *Good Housekeeping*'s Lily Bosch. "You're not feeding your body, you're feeding your need."

McGraw has his detractors. Some psychologists think his "tell-it-like-it-is" style is too harsh. Some marketing experts question his staying power. "I'm not sure [he'll be] around in five or ten years," marketing professor Peter Sealey told *BusinessWeek*. "I have a sense he knows that and is milking it at every step." However, McGraw's straightforward brand of psychology has been popular in the United States. Six million people tune in daily and his website gets 14 million page visits a month.

## Selected writings

*Life Strategies: Doing What Works, Doing What Matters,* Hyperion, 2000.
*Relationship Rescue: A Seven-Step Strategy for Reconnecting with Your Partner,* Hyperion, 2001.
*Self Matters: Creating Your Life from the Inside Out,* Free Press, 2003.
*The Ultimate Weight Solution: The Seven Keys to Weight Loss Freedom,* Free Press, 2003.
*Family First: Your Step-by-Step Plan for Creating a Phenomenal Family,* Free Press, 2004.

## Sources

### Books

McGraw, Phillip C., *Self Matters: Creating Your Life from the Inside Out,* Simon & Schuster, 2001.

## Periodicals

*BusinessWeek,* June 21, 2004, p. 108.
*Good Housekeeping,* November 2003, p. 146; March 2004, p. 118.
*Newsweek,* September 2 2002, p. 50.
*Texas Monthly,* September 2003, p. 120.
*Time,* September 13, 2004, p. 8.

## Online

"About Dr. Phil," DrPhil.com, http://www.drphil.com/about/about_landing.jhtml (October 30, 2004).

*—Lisa Frick*

# James McGreevey

**Politician**

---

**B**orn James Edward McGreevey, August 6, 1957; son of Jack (a trucking company director) and Veronica (a nurse) McGreevey; married Kari Schutz (a librarian), c. 1991 (divorced, c. 1995); married Dina Matos (a public relations executive), 2000; children: Morag (daughter from first marriage), one other daughter (from second marriage). *Politics:* Democrat. *Religion:* Catholic. *Education:* Attended Catholic University; Columbia University, B.A., 1978; Georgetown University, J.D., 1981; Harvard University, M.A. (education), 1982.

**Addresses:** *Home*—New Jersey.

## Career

**W**orked as an assistant prosecutor, 1982-83; worked as an attorney for the Democrats in the state assembly; became director of the state parole board; became a lobbyist for Merck; elected to New Jersey state assembly, 1989; elected mayor of Woodbridge, NJ, 1991; elected to the state senate, 1993; ran unsuccessfully for governor of New Jersey, 1997; elected governor, 2001; resigned as governor, 2004.

## Sidelights

**J**ames McGreevey, former governor of New Jersey, became America's first openly gay state governor in August of 2004 when he revealed he had engaged in an affair with another man. But that distinction was short-lived, and did not tell his whole story: in the same speech, he announced he would resign as governor three months later. His private life caused the last of several scandals that marred his governorship and sabotaged his reputation and his huge political ambitions.

Growing up in small-town Cateret, New Jersey, the young McGreevey seemed ambitious from the start. His father, Jack, director of a trucking company and a former drill instructor in the Marines, is said to have given him two pieces of advice, according to Jason Fagone of *Philadelphia Magazine*: "Plan your work, work your plan," and "Don't worry about being liked. Worry about being respected." (Once McGreevey's term as governor went downhill, writers and fellow politicians lamented that he did not take the second piece of advice.) His high school teachers predicted he would be governor someday.

McGreevey attended Catholic University for a while, then transferred to the more prestigious Columbia University, where he earned a bachelor's degree. He studied law at Georgetown University and earned a master's degree in education at Harvard University. He returned to New Jersey in 1982, spent a year as an assistant prosecutor, then worked as an attorney for the Democrats in the state assembly, became director of the state parole board, and became a lobbyist for the pharmaceutical company Merck.

After moving to Woodbridge, New Jersey's sixth-largest city, he began his political career in 1989 by running for state assemblyman. He won, and joined the assembly at age 32. The next year, he met his first wife, Kari Schutz, a librarian from Vancouver, on a cruise. They eventually had a daughter, Morag, but separated in 1995 and later divorced. The mayor of Woodbridge, Joseph DeMarino, took McGreevey under his wing, but in 1991, after DeMarino was indicted on a bribery charge (he was never convicted), McGreevey decided to run for mayor against his former mentor; McGreevey won.

Styling himself in the then-popular mold of President Bill Clinton, as a socially and fiscally moderate "New Democrat," McGreevey made political friends across New Jersey. He was elected to the state senate in 1993, holding that job and the Woodbridge mayor's office at the same time. He ran for governor in 1997, won the Democratic primary, and ran in the general election on a platform of property tax and auto-insurance reform. Though he was running against Christine Whitman, an incumbent governor with a moderate platform and national stature, McGreevey lost to her by around 25,000 votes. He made it clear he wanted to run for governor again in 2001, and he wrapped up the Democratic nomination with some furious politicking in late 2000. U.S. Senator Bob Torricelli announced that he wanted to be the Democratic nominee for governor, and for a moment it seemed like Torricelli would eclipse McGreevey's second effort. But McGreevey drove around the state, asking everyone he knew for support. When Sharpe James, the powerful mayor of Newark, endorsed McGreevey, Torricelli bailed out of the race after only 12 days.

Soon after, McGreevey married his second wife, Dina Matos, a public-relations executive (with whom he also has a child). They held their wedding in Washington, D.C., even though neither of them are from there. That puzzled the wedding guests until they got to the reception at the Hay-Adams Hotel, went up to the hotel's rooftop deck, and discovered the hotel's dramatic view of the White House. McGreevey's friends took it as a sign of his ambitions.

The path to the governor's office was much clearer for McGreevey the second time around. Instead of Whitman, his opponent was a conservative Repub-

lican, Bret Schundler, which made McGreevey the favorite, since New Jersey is a Democratic state. McGreevey won the election by 14 percentage points and became governor at age 44. In his January of 2002 inauguration speech, he quoted Abraham Lincoln and Martin Luther King Jr. and promised (according to Fagone in *Philadelphia Magazine*) to "change the way Trenton does business" (referring to the capital of New Jersey)—a promise that disillusioned critics would soon hold against him.

Scandal dragged McGreevey's administration down almost from the start. His chief counsel and chief of staff resigned while under investigation for allegedly using their positions working for McGreevey to generate profits for their billboard company. The governor's commerce secretary and chief of the state police—the latter a candidate McGreevey picked as a favor to Newark mayor James—also left because of conflict-of-interest questions.

"It seemed like [McGreevey's] loyalty was blind loyalty," David Rebovich, a political science professor at Rider University, told David Kocieniewski of the *New York Times* as McGreevey's governorship drew to a close. Republicans went further, saying McGreevey tried to do too many favors for donors and political bosses, with little or no attention to ethics. "Jim McGreevey put a 'For Sale' sign on New Jersey government," Larry Weitzner, a Republican political consultant, told Kocieniewski. A trip McGreevey took to Ireland got him in more trouble with voters. It cost the taxpayers $105,000, including the cost of an expensive hotel room, a rented Mercedes-Benz, and a family reunion.

McGreevey's worst mistake, however, was the hiring of Israeli poet and public relations specialist Golan Cipel; it would eventually destroy his career. McGreevey met Cipel, a former spokesman at the Israeli consulate in New York City, in 2000 on a trip to Israel. Soon after, Cipel moved to New Jersey and took a job as the McGreevey campaign's liaison with the state's Jewish community. When McGreevey became governor—mere months after the September 11, 2001, terrorist attacks killed hundreds of New Jersey residents—he named Cipel his special assistant on homeland security. Cipel was clearly unqualified. As a non-citizen, he could not even get federal security clearance. Reporters and Republican lawmakers severely questioned the hire, and McGreevey changed Cipel's responsibilities, renaming him a "special counsel." By August of 2002, Cipel had left state government for a lobbying job.

The constant scandal news hurt McGreevey's popularity. A July of 2003 poll showed only 35 percent of New Jersey residents approved of the job he was doing. The questions about McGreevey's activities kept coming. The next year, the governor was implicated in a bribery scheme. The Federal Bureau of Investigation was looking into allegations that a trash hauler and McGreevey supporter was trying to extort money and contributions from a landowner. Agents taped McGreevey talking to the landowner and mentioning the 16th-century Italian philosopher Niccolo Machiavelli. Prosecutors claimed they had been told that Machiavelli was a code word meant to show the governor was part of a bribery plot, but McGreevey insisted it was merely a literary reference.

Soon after came the final scandal. McGreevey called a press conference in August of 2004 and announced that he was gay and would resign. "My truth is that I am a gay American," he said in his speech, according to John Cloud in *Time*. He added that he had had a consensual affair with another man and that he would resign three months later, on November 15, 2004, to protect the governor's office from "false allegations and threats of disclosure," according to *Newsweek*.

The dramatic "gay American" part of the speech seemed meant to focus attention on McGreevey's coming out of the closet. Some people did sympathize with him for that reason. But there was more to the story. His advisers soon told reporters that the man he had the affair with was Cipel, the former homeland security adviser, and that Cipel had threatened to sue McGreevey for sexual harassment. Cipel's lawyers soon held a press conference and read a statement from their client claiming he was "the victim of repeated sexual advances" by the governor, wrote *Time*'s Cloud. Cipel also alleged that McGreevey and his aides retaliated against him "when I finally dared to reject Governor McGreevey's advances." McGreevey's aides retorted that Cipel and his lawyers had attempted to extort either a financial settlement or political favors in return for his silence.

The acknowledgement that McGreevey had either sexually harassed an aide or installed someone he had had a romantic relationship with in an important position struck many people as the last and perhaps worst of McGreevey's scandals. Political observers also attacked McGreevey for waiting three months to resign. It was, they said, clearly timed to avoid a special election for governor in November

of 2004 and ensure that state senate president Richard Codey, a Democrat, would automatically become governor.

In his last three months in office, McGreevey became bolder. He issued an executive order that bans those who have contracts with state government from making campaign contributions. He also approved a controversial needle-exchange program for drug addicts, meant to fight the spread of AIDS, that he had avoided supporting earlier in his term. Critics noted sadly that McGreevey had lacked the courage to take those stands until he knew his political career was almost over.

In a farewell address in November of 2004, a few days before his resignation, McGreevey said his proudest accomplishments included reforming New Jersey's child welfare system, enacting a land-preservation plan, and signing a domestic partnership law to protect gay couples. But the *New York Times*' Kocieniewski, summing up McGreevey's legacy on his last day in office, declared that until McGreevey announced he was going to resign, "he never managed to free himself from the contributors and party bosses who orchestrated his election" and instead indulged "his instinct to accommodate whoever he was talking to."

For someone who had campaigned as a moderate, Kocieniewski added, McGreevey had "embraced a surprisingly liberal agenda: doling out fat contracts to union supporters, indulging in a torrent of borrowing and spending, and enacting laws that legalized stem cell research and domestic partnerships for gay couples." The writer gave McGreevey credit for improving state government's efficiency, as he had promised. Despite the catastrophic hiring of Cipel, Kocieniewski added, McGreevey had improved New Jersey's counterterrorism work. But his environmental record was mixed; at the same time he had supported an ambitious land-preservation plan, he also rolled back development rules in a way that was considered likely to worsen suburban sprawl. (At the end of his time in office, he suspended the rollback for a few months.)

Just before McGreevey left office, he moved from the governor's mansion to an apartment in the town of Rahway, while his wife bought a house in another town. Friends of McGreevey said he was joining Weiner Lesniak, the law firm of his friend, state senator Raymond J. Lesniak, but this had not been confirmed at the time of his resignation. The press speculated that he might rehabilitate his image by promoting causes he believes in, such as stem cell research and gay rights. Still, he may never escape his reputation as a politician who gave too many favors to friends and only took principled stands when he had nothing left to lose.

## Sources

### Periodicals

*Newsweek,* August 23, 2004, p. 24.

*New York Times,* November 9, 2004, p. B1; November 15, 2004, p. B1; November 16, 2004, p. B1.
*Philadelphia Magazine,* September 2003, p. 84.
*Time,* August 23, 2004, p. 22.

### Online

"Jim McGreevey," Wikipedia, http://en.wikipedia.org/wiki/James_McGreevey (November 28, 2004).

*—Erick Trickey*

# Aaron McGruder

## Cartoonist

**B**orn Aaron Vincent McGruder in 1974, in Chicago, IL; son of Bill (a communications specialist) and Elaine (a homemaker) McGruder. *Education:* University of Maryland, Afro-American studies, 1997.

**Addresses:** *Home*—Los Angeles, CA. *Office*—Universal Press Syndicate, 4520 Main St., Kansas City, MO 64111-7701.

## Career

**D**ebuted *The Boondocks* on The Hotlist website, 1996; moved strip to University of Maryland's college newspaper, *The Diamondback*, 1996; switched strip to *The Source*, 1997; signed with Universal Press syndicate, and *The Boondocks* began running in newspapers, 1998—; released *Boondocks: Because I Know You Don't Read The Newspaper*, 2000; *Fresh for '01 ... You Suckas: A Boondocks Collection*, 2001; *A Right To Be Hostile: The Boondocks Treasury*, 2003; co-released *Birth of A Nation: A Comic Novel*, 2004; *Public Enemy #2: An All-New Boondocks Collection*, 2005; turned comic strip into cartoon, 2005.

**Awards:** Chairman Award, National Association for the Advancement of Colored People, 2000.

## Sidelights

**W**hen Aaron McGruder created *The Boondocks* comic strip, he wanted to shock the masses. Since the strip began, he has outraged readers, poli-

ticians, even A-list celebrities. The strips printed after the September 11th terrorist attacks on the United States helped him truly achieve his goal. With *The Boondocks* also airing as a television show in the fall of 2005, McGruder seems to be taking his shock to a higher level.

McGruder was born in 1974 in Chicago, Illinois. His parents moved shortly after he was born, and finally settled in Columbia, Maryland. McGruder and his brother, Dedric, found themselves living in predominately white surroundings. His was a typical childhood filled with kung fu movies, rap music, and video games. He attended a majority-white Jesuit school that repressed and liberated him. If it was not for the restrictions the school imposed, he would not have begun using his creativity to deal with the oppression. He switched to a predominately black high school, and became a true fan of the rap music of the late 1980s and early 1990s, with groups that concerned themselves more about raising the consciousness of black youth. It was during this time that he began to formulate his opinions, and also turned into an "angry black man," who wanted to challenge mainstream society's way of thinking in a manner that would bring about real reform.

After graduating from high school, McGruder began his studies at the University of Maryland. While he pursued a degree in Afro-American studies, he began laying the groundwork for *The Boondocks*. The comic strip made its debut on *The Hotlist Online* in 1996. The strip was also run in the University of Maryland's newspaper, *The Diamondback*. Ironically, the person who is credited for allowing the strip to run in *The Diamondback* is none other than Jayson Blair, the former *New York Times* reporter who was fired for fabricating stories.

Things fell apart between McGruder and the college newspaper, and he removed his strip. *The Boondocks* was later printed in *The Source*, a magazine geared toward the hip-hop audience. The partnership was short, but a chance meeting with Harriet Choice of Universal Press Syndicate at the National Association of Black Journalists Convention proved fruitful. Universal Press Syndicate had been keeping an eye on the comic strip, so a deal was made. *The Boondocks* began running in 160 newspapers in late 1998. By February of 1999, the strip was running in 195 newspapers. As of 2005, *The Boondocks* ran in 250 newspapers.

The premise of *The Boondocks* centered around two children, Huey and Riley Freeman, who moved from the urban city to the boondocks (slang for the suburbs) and how they and their neighbors dealt with the transition. Huey, named after Black Panther co-founder Huey Newton, is a black nationalist who questions authority at every given chance. Riley, his younger brother, is a young thug-in-training. The two live with their cantankerous grandfather. McGruder saw the three main characters as three sides to the angry black man.

Other characters who appear in the strip include Caesar, a friend of Huey's, a former Brooklynite who wants to be a rapper; and neighbors Thomas and Sara Dubois, an interracial couple with a daughter, Jazmine. Huey tries to help Thomas get in touch with his blackness so he can help his daughter accept hers. There were also two other characters, Cindy and Hiro Otomo, but they have all but disappeared.

There was much fanfare when *The Boondocks* first appeared. McGruder was only one of a handful of African-American cartoonists with strips in major newspapers. The number of African-American cartoonists in the past was still a paltry few dozen. So, McGruder was met with praise for this accomplishment alone. *The Boondocks*, which began as a critical, and sometimes, scathing, review of race relations in America, was also praised for originality. The comic was drawn in the manga style, a popular Japanese comic form, which also set it apart from other comic strips. Pulitzer Prize-winning cartoonist Joel Pett told John Nichols of the *Nation*, "I think that not only is [McGruder] doing good stuff, the fact that he is on the comic pages makes it important in a way that none of the rest of us could accomplish. He's hooking a whole group of people. He's getting ideas out to people who don't always read the opinion pages." No matter how thought provoking the comic strip was, there were many dissenters. White readers felt the strip made jokes at their expense. Black readers felt the strip should not air the race's "dirty laundry." While some newspapers moved the strip from the comics section to the editorial pages, a few removed the strip altogether. That did not deter McGruder, who as child, was a fan of *Doonesbury* and *Bloom County*, *The Boondock's* comic predecessors. If anything, McGruder upped his shock value; no one was safe.

In the years after its debut, the strip has poked fun at a wide variety of people, including President George W. Bush, former presidents Ronald Reagan, Bill Clinton, and George H.W. Bush, the CIA, the FBI, cable channel BET, the founder of BET and the first African-American billionaire Robert L. Johnson, Cuba Gooding Jr., Will Smith, Vivica A. Fox, and the rappers of today whose bling-bling lifestyle he frowns upon. He stated to the *New Yorker's* Ben Mcgrath, "I've never understood all the obsession over diamonds and jewelry and designer clothes—that just seems female to me."

McGruder's criticism of Robert L. Johnson led the billionaire to take out a two-page ad in *Emerge* magazine, criticizing the cartoonist for not having respect for the accomplishments of BET and Johnson. McGruder fired back in *The Boondocks*, and expressed to Monica Hogan of *Multichannel News*, "The worst thing about BET is it is taking up space and preventing another black station from coming along and doing it right."

He also drew the ire of conservative talk show host Larry Elder who in an op-ed piece suggested (according to the *New Yorker*) that the award for the "Dumbest, Most Vulgar, Most Offensive Things Uttered By Black Public Figures" be named the McGruder. Even the *National Review* wrote a short article condemning the comic strip and its creator in 2005.

But not all of McGruder's foes hate him. He has openly discussed his hatred of Secretary of State Condoleezza Rice and told her she was a mass murderer when they met while both received awards from the National Association for the Advancement of Colored People. She, however, holds no ill will toward him and asked him to incorporate her into his comic strip. McGruder finally obliged in October of 2004, having characters Huey and Caesar attempt to locate a boyfriend for Rice so she would not destroy the world.

As the comic strip gained in popularity, McGruder was named one of *People*'s "25 Most intriguing People" in 1999. He is a sought-after lecturer, speaking at a variety of places, including college campuses, conventions, and banquets, though one particular group regretted having him speak: at the 138th birthday celebration of the left-leaning political magazine, *The Nation,* he blasted the liberals for not doing enough.

As shocking to readers as *The Boondocks* was, no one was prepared for what was to come in the days and weeks following the September 11th attacks on the United States. While all of the editorial cartoonists, left-wing political pundits, comedians, and even late-night talk show hosts steered clear of attacking the president as well as questioning the government, McGruder and political dissident Huey went on a rampage. McGruder noticed that no one was asking the tough questions, and decided to use his strip to do so, even if it meant the end of his career. In the strip Huey decried the actions of Bush, the Defense Department, Attorney General John Ashcroft, the Democrats, and overzealous patriotic Americans. In one strip, Huey calls the FBI and asks if he can give the names of Americans who financed terrorists. When the agent says yes, Huey gives him Ronald Reagan's name.

Though the amount of outrage was huge, only a handful of newspapers removed the strip, and only for a small amount of time. In October of 2001, McGruder poked fun at the controversy surrounding *The Boondocks* by replacing it with a strip titled "The Adventures of Flagee and Ribbon." This pseudo-strip's characters were the patriotic symbols that appeared everywhere after the attacks. Of course, the new strip was pure satire, poking fun at the fear Americans were feeling and the enormous surge of patriotism. When "The Adventures of Flagee and Ribbon" appeared, readers of the *Akron Beacon Journal* in Akron, Ohio, praised the paper for removing *The Boondocks* and replacing it with the new strip.

McGruder and his friend, Reginald Hudlin, director of the popular *House Party* films, teamed up to turn *The Boondocks* into a television show and a motion picture. A deal was made with Sony Entertainment and episodes of *The Boondocks* were scheduled to began airing in the fall of 2005 during Cartoon Network's Adult Swim time block. Adult Swim is known to air popular Japanese anime, including *Inu Yasha, Ghost In The Shell,* and *Cowboy Bebop,* and also satiric shows such as *Family Guy, Space Ghost Coast to Coast,* and *Home Movies. The Boondocks* should be a perfect fit, and it would bring the strip and its creator full circle as Adult Swim's dominant audience is college-age. The show features the voices of actress Regina King of *Jerry Maguire* and comedian John Witherspoon, who was one of the stars of the film *Friday.*

McGruder and Hudlin co-wrote a script about the 2000 presidential election irregularities, but could not find any takers. They turned the script into a graphic novel, enlisting the help of artist Kyle Baker. *Birth of A Nation* was released in 2004. In the book, the black citizens of East St. Louis are denied the right to vote in the presidential elections, the city decides to secede from the United States and names the new country Blackland. *Time* stated that new readers "will appreciate [the novel's] readability. And though it lacks the racial zings of, say, Dave Chappelle, it manages to land some clever social jabs." While *Booklist* said the book was "highly entertaining," *Publishers Weekly* panned the novel stating that though the concept was terrific, and the talent behind it was impressive, there was "not enough follow-through to make it completely satisfying."

In addition to putting out *The Boondocks* daily, McGruder has released a few collections of the strip: *Boondocks: Because I Know You Don't Read The Newspaper, Fresh for '01 … You Suckas: A Boondocks Collection, A Right To Be Hostile: The Boondocks Treasury,* and 2005's *Public Enemy #2: An All-New Boondocks Collection.* He has also overseen the drawing of the television show in Seoul, Korea. McGruder has begun writing other scripts, and is penning a book, tentatively titled *Profits of Rage,* and a coffee-table book, *Huey Hate Book.*

Throughout the comic strip's run, McGruder has become ill several times trying to keep up with the hectic pace. With so many projects in the air, and his plate overflowing, he turned over the day-to-day drawing of *The Boondocks,* to a Boston-based artist. The future of the comic strip version of *The Boondocks* is uncertain. However, it is certain that McGruder will not fade into history, but will continue to provoke America into looking at its societal ills.

## Selected writings

*Boondocks: Because I Know You Don't Read The Newspaper,* Andrews McMeel Publishing, 2000.

*Fresh for '01 ... You Suckas: A Boondocks Collection,* Andrews McMeel Publishing, 2001.

*A Right To Be Hostile: The Boondocks Treasury,* Three Rivers Press, 2003.

(With Reginald Hudlin and Kyle Baker) *Birth of A Nation: A Comic Novel,* Crown, 2004.

*Public Enemy #2: An All-New Boondocks Collection,* Three Rivers Press, 2005.

## Sources

### Books

*Contemporary Black Biography,* vol. 28, Gale Group, 2001.

### Periodicals

*Black Enterprise,* July 2000, p. 64.

*Black Issues Book Review,* September-October 2003, pp. 36-42.

*Booklist,* July 2004, p. 1831.

*Editor & Publisher,* August 14, 1999, p. 29; October 9, 1999, p. 47; December 10, 2001, p. 12; July 14, 2003, p. 7.

*Entertainment Weekly,* October 19, 2001, p. 16; July 23, 2004, p. 81; January 21, 2005, p. 51.

*Library Journal,* September 1, 2004, p. 128.

*Multichannel News,* November 29, 1999, p. 10.

*Nation,* January 28, 2002, p. 11.

*National Review,* February 14, 2005, p. 14.

*Newsweek,* July 5, 1999, p. 59.

*New Yorker,* April 19, 2004, p. 153.

*New York Times Upfront,* November 26, 2001, p. 7.

*People,* July 26, 1999, p. 125.

*Publishers Weekly,* June 28, 2004, p. 33.

*Time,* July 5, 1999, p. 78; August 2, 2004, p. 83.

*—Ashyia N. Henderson*

# Brad Meltzer

## Author

**B**orn in 1970; married Cori (an attorney); children: one son. *Education:* University of Michigan, B.A., 1993; Columbia Law School, J.D., 1996.

**Addresses:** *Office*—3389 Sheridan St. #267, Hollywood, FL 33021. *Website*—http://www.bradmeltzer.com.

## Career

**A**uthor of novels, including: *The Tenth Justice,* 1997; *Dead Even,* 1998; *The First Counsel,* 2001; *The Millionaires,* 2002; *The Zero Game,* 2004. Co-creator and a writer and producer on *Jack & Bobby,* WB Network, 2004-05. Actor in the Woody Allen film *Celebrity,* 1998. Writer of *Green Arrow: The Archer's Quest,* book version of issues of the comic book *Green Arrow,* 2003; wrote the comic book series *Identity Crisis,* 2004.

## Sidelights

**I**n 2004, Brad Meltzer proved the breadth of his writing talent with three very different successes: his fifth novel, the thriller *The Zero Game,* was released; he wrote a comic-book series for DC Comics; and he saw a television show he co-created, *Jack & Bobby,* debut on the WB television network. His thrillers, with well-researched details and often set in Washington, D.C. politics, have attracted such attention that a United States Senator wrote the introduction to the book version of another of his comic-book projects.

Meltzer grew up in Brooklyn and Miami. His father, the son of a Jewish immigrant, worked in the garment industry until 1983, when the family moved to Florida. There, his father started selling insurance, and his mother got work in a furniture store. Writing was always a big part of Meltzer's life, even if he did not quite realize it. He got into the University of Michigan in part by writing his application letter as a love letter to the school. He told the *Chicago Tribune*'s Web Behrens, "Even when I was in junior high school, high school, college, anytime I had to write an essay, I would always go up to the teacher and say, 'You know what? Rather than comparing Freud and Erikson in an expository essay, can I send them on a picnic and let them get in a fight with each other and just write the dialogue?' Invariably, every teacher would say yes. I did that all the time."

At age 19, while in college, Meltzer went to Washington, D.C. for an internship on Capitol Hill, an experience that would influence much of his future writing. When he graduated in 1993, he got a job offer from *Games* magazine and moved to Boston to take it, but the publisher he had wanted to work with soon left the magazine, so Meltzer put his energies into writing a novel instead. That novel, called *Fraternity,* was rejected 24 times and never published. But Meltzer resolved to write a second novel, and he did so while going to Columbia Law School. (Attending law school with him was his high-school sweetheart, Cori, whom he married.)

The new book, *The Tenth Justice,* about a Supreme Court clerk who accidentally reveals an important decision before it is announced, was published in 1997 and became a best-seller, so Meltzer continued with his writing career and never practiced law. *People* reviewer Pam Lambert noted that Meltzer's characters were not as rich as his plot but declared that Meltzer showed "a veteran's panache with plot and pacing" and had "earned the right to belly up to the bar in the company of John Grisham, Scott Turow, and David Baldacci, and join the growing ranks of attorneys making their cases on the best-seller list."

Meltzer says research is key to his writing. "You can invent all the stuff you want, but if it doesn't smell real, readers will know in a nanosecond," he said in a question-and-answer page on his website. "To me, fiction is at its best when it has one foot in reality." When he decided one of the characters in his 2004 novel *The Zero Game* would be a young, black, female Senate page, he spent months researching, interviewing people, and talking with friends, trying to perfect the character. He spent so much time researching what it was like to be one of the president's children for *The First Counsel,* his 2001 novel about a White House lawyer who dates the president's daughter, that he also wrote an article of advice for President George W. Bush's daughters Jenna and Barbara for *USA Weekend.* As part of his research, Meltzer contacted every living daughter of a president, and one (he will not say who) agreed to talk with him. Friends who worked in the White House let him in and showed him around, and a former Secret Service agent who had enjoyed *The Tenth Justice* also helped him.

In the book, the lawyer and First Daughter slip into tunnels under the White House to evade Secret Service agents who are supposed to watch her. Such details about Washington landmarks in his books are probably one reason he was consulted by the Department of Homeland Security's Analytic Red Cell office, which brings together people from outside the department to brainstorm about how to prevent possible future terrorist tactics. "When I got the call, I was floored," Meltzer told the *Washington Post*'s John Mintz. "They said, 'We want people who think differently from the ones we have on staff.'" Meltzer signed an agreement not to talk about the hypothetical situation he helped discuss, but he told the newspaper that his panel also included FBI and CIA employees, a psychologist, a professor who studies Middle Eastern terrorism, and a philosopher.

In his 2002 book *The Millionaires,* Meltzer veered away from Washington thrillers to tell a bank-robbing story. The millionaires in the title are two brothers who work at a bank, Oliver and Charlie, one responsible and ambitious, the other a free spirit. They decide to transfer an unclaimed $3 million into their bank account, triggering a chase and intrigue involving Secret Service agents, an insurance investigator, and a mysterious woman. Reviewer Ron Bernas, writing in the *Chicago Tribune,* declared that the brothers' relationship lifted the book above the average thriller.

Meanwhile, Meltzer also wrote some issues of the comic book *Green Arrow.* "I thought about saying no. My wife reminded me I'd been waiting my whole life to do this," he said in an interview with the website BookReporter.com. Comic books influenced his writing, much as classic mystery and thriller writers Agatha Christie and Alfred Hitchcock did, he explained. "I was raised on comic books," Meltzer told the *Chicago Tribune*'s Behrens. "Those were my first serials. You had 22 pages and you had a cliffhanger. So it's no shock to me that [in novels] I like to write a chapter, tell a story, leave a cliffhanger and go to the next chapter. It's not a conscious choice; it's second nature." His issues of *Green Arrow* were published in graphic novel form as *Green Arrow: The Archer's Quest* in 2003; United States Senator Patrick Leahy of Vermont wrote the introduction.

Meltzer's career peak in 2004 included a return to Washington thrillers with *The Zero Game,* a novel about a betting pool on votes in Congress that grows into a murder story. Scenes take place in the United States Capitol, including its basement and hidden rooms for senators and congressmen—all of which were inspired by his explorations of the Capitol during his college internship. During his research, he also explored an 8,000-feet deep gold mine. In addition, he asked uncomfortable questions about a connection between plutonium, the radioactive element often used in nuclear weapons, and the neutrino, a subatomic particle. Because of the questions, a good source of his at a government scientific facility stopped calling him back and asked Meltzer to take his name out of the book's acknowledgements.

Not everyone liked *The Zero Game.* "Meltzer's description of how items get into an appropriations bill and the power of congressional staffers to make things happen is informative," reviewer Ann Hellmuth wrote in the *Chicago Tribune.* "But once the bodies start falling, it is all downhill for *The Zero Game.* It's a stereotypical chase story, where the protagonists escape death by inches, foil villains and keep moving non-stop through the pages with little rhyme or reason."

Also in 2004, the WB Network debuted a television series Meltzer developed with his friend Steven "Scoop" Cohen. The series, *Jack & Bobby,* was about two teenage brothers, one of whom will grow up to be president. It showed Bobby (the future president) as a solitary kid, interspersed with documentary-style glimpses from the future, in which people commenting about Bobby's time as president look back on his early life. (The series attracted some critical acclaim and a Golden Globe nomination, but was cancelled after one season.) At the same time, DC Comics was publishing the comic-book series *Identity Crisis,* a murder mystery written by Meltzer that included an all-star lineup of DC Comics characters, including Superman, Batman, and Wonder Woman. *Wizard* magazine called it the "most anticipated comic book project for 2004," according to Meltzer's website.

"I want to explore the emotional cost of putting on a cape," Meltzer told *Entertainment Weekly.* The magazine was impressed with the results. Reviewer Tom Russo noted that most "event" projects in comics featuring big-name writers or several comic heroes sacrifice character development for extreme action. But Meltzer, Russo wrote, "seems quite willing to resist the temptation to have big, loud, pointless fun with the legends at his disposal. *Identity Crisis* focuses on lesser-known DC characters, including the Elongated Man, and shows how they react when some of the superheroes' loved ones are murdered. "The effect is to underscore that these are very human characters engaged in a very risky business," Russo noted approvingly.

Meltzer, who lived for years in Montgomery County, Maryland, near Washington, D.C, now lives in Miami with his wife, Cori, and their son.

## Selected writings

*The Tenth Justice,* William Morrow & Co., 1997.
*Dead Even,* Rob Weisbach Books, 1998.
*The First Counsel,* Warner Books, 2001.
*The Millionaires,* Warner Books, 2002.
*Green Arrow: The Archer's Quest* (graphic novel), DC Comics, 2003.
*The Zero Game,* Warner Books, 2004.
*Identity Crisis* (comic book series), DC Comics, 2004.
*Jack & Bobby* (television show), WB Network, 2004-05.

## Sources

### Periodicals

*Chicago Tribune,* January 29, 2002, p. 7; February 20, 2004, p. 5; November 23, 2004, p. 1.
*Entertainment Weekly,* June 25/July 2, 2004, p. 23, p. 108.
*People,* May 19, 1997, p. 50.
*Publishers Weekly,* May 3, 2004, p. 29.
*Washington Post,* March 14, 2004, p. T10; June 18, 2004, p. A27.

### Online

"About Brad Meltzer," Brad Meltzer.com, http://www.bradmeltzer.com/author/index.html (May 21, 2005).
"Author Profile: Brad Meltzer," Bookreporter.com, http://www.bookreporter.com/authors/au-meltzer-brad.asp (May 21, 2005).
"Jack & Bobby," TV Tome, http://www.tvtome.com/tvtome/servlet/ShowMainServlet/showid-21658 (May 23, 2005).
"Other Works," Brad Meltzer.com, http://www.bradmeltzer.com/other/index.html (May 22, 2005).
"Profiles and Praise," Brad Meltzer.com, http://www.bradmeltzer.com/author/homeland.html (May 21, 2005).
"Q & A," Brad Meltzer.com, http://www.bradmeltzer.com/author/qa.html (May 21, 2005).

*—Erick Trickey*

# Stipe Mesic

## President of Croatia

**B**orn Stjepan Mesic, December 24, 1934; married Milka Dudunic; children: two daughters. *Education:* University of Zagreb, law degree, 1961.

**Addresses:** *Office*—Office of The President, Pantovcak 241, 10,000 Zagreb, Croatia. *Website*—http:// www.predsjednik.hr.

## Career

**E**lected to the parliament of the Socialist Republic of Croatia, 1967; elected mayor of Orahovica, 1967; sentenced to one year in prison for political activities, 1970s; became member of the Croatian Democratic Union, 1990; elected to Croatia's parliament, 1990; first prime minister of the Republic of Croatia, 1990-91; president of Yugoslavia, 1991; speaker of the parliament of the Republic of Croatia, 1992-94; founded the political party Independent Croatian Democrats, 1994; president of Croatia, 2000—.

## Sidelights

**C**roatia's election of Stipe Mesic as its president in 2000 signified an embrace of liberal democracy and a rejection of a decade of war and extreme nationalism. Mesic, who was jailed in the 1970s by the Communist regime in what was then Yugoslavia, emerged as a major political figure in 1990 and briefly served as Yugoslavia's president in 1991 as the country was splintering during civil war. A prominent leader in newly independent Croatia, he broke with its strongman president in 1994 and opposed the war in nearby Bosnia. Since his election as president, he has been Croatia's conscience, cooperating with an international war crimes tribunal, reaching out to neighbors to repair the wounds of the wars in the former Yugoslavia, and apologizing for the crimes of Croatia's World War II government.

Mesic, whose first name, Stjepan, is usually shortened to Stipe in English, was born in the town of Orahovica in Croatia when it was part of Yugoslavia. He studied law at the University of Zagreb, where (according to his official biography) he was a prominent student leader. He was elected mayor of Orahovica and to the Croatian parliament in 1967. But in 1971, he supported the Croatian Spring movement, which advocated equality for Croatia within Yugoslavia. The country's Communist government opposed the movement, and Mesic was sentenced to a year in the Stara Gradiska prison for his participation in it. He did not participate in politics again until free elections replaced Yugoslavia's Communist regime.

In 1990, Mesic became a member of the Croatian Democratic Union (HDZ), was elected to Croatia's parliament, and named Croatia's prime minister. He also became Croatia's representative in Yugoslavia's presidency. At the time, Yugoslavia had a collective presidency made up of representatives from the nation's six republics and two provinces, and the position of president rotated among the eight members. But with the Communist regime gone, the tensions among the different republics were set loose. In 1991, when it was Croatia's turn to take over the presidency for a year, members of the presidency who were loyal to Serbia blocked Mesic from becoming president.

That action started a civil war among the Yugoslav republics. Slovenia declared it would secede from Yugoslavia in June of 1991, and Croatians voted to do the same. The Yugoslav army, dominated by Serbs, began fighting the secessionists, and the Serb-influenced members of the presidency vetoed attempts for Mesic to establish control over the army. The disintegration of Yugoslavia was postponed in July when the deadlock broke, Mesic was elected president, and Slovenia and Croatia agreed to postpone secession for three months.

But the day that agreement expired, the Yugoslav army, no longer controlled by the federal government, attacked Croatia's presidential palace while Mesic and Croatia's president were inside. The navy blockaded the Croatian resort town of Dubrovnik, and Serb-led forces fired mortars and grenades at it. At the end of October of 1991, Mesic and Croatian Prime Minister Franjo Greguric led a fleet of boats to break the siege of the city, in order to call worldwide attention to it, and were allowed to land there.

In December of that year, Mesic resigned as president, saying the federation of Yugoslavia no longer existed. (Yugoslavia actually carried on for another eleven years, but with only two republics, Serbia and Montenegro, left in it.) Croatia and the Serb-led forces reached a cease-fire in 1992, but Serbs retained control of parts of Croatia for years afterward, and Croatia soon became involved in the war in the neighboring former Yugoslav republic of Bosnia-Herzegovina.

In 1992, Mesic was elected to Croatia's parliament and named speaker of its lower house. However, in 1994, he and Josip Manolic, speaker of the upper house, broke with the HDZ party and Croatian President Franjo Tudjman over several issues, most importantly the Bosnian war. The two speakers accused the president of abusing his power, not respecting freedom of the press or the rights of minorities, and allowing only people completely loyal

to him to hold any power. They formed a new political party, the Independent Democrats. Mesic and Manolic argued, in a letter to Tudjman, that his main goal was to "intimidate and silence the HDZ membership, government administration officials, and the Croatian political public, and to prevent democratic discussion on the current issues essential for the democratic future of Croatia," according to the *Christian Science Monitor*.

Mesic and Manolic charged that Tudjman was trying to expand Croatia by taking over parts of Bosnia. (Starting in 1993, Tudjman had supported separatist ethnic Croats in Bosnia who were fighting the Muslim-led Bosnian government. International pressure later led him to endorse a Croat-Muslim federation dedicated to fighting the two groups' common enemy, Bosnian Serb forces supported by Serbia. Mesic and Manolic charged that Tudjman's support of the federation was not genuine.)

Tudjman remained president until his death in December of 1999. Elections were called for January, and Mesic declared himself a candidate for president. Frank criticism of Tudjman had been rare while he was alive, but Mesic quickly impressed Croatians with his candor. He declared that the war in Bosnia had been a mistake and that Croatia should cooperate with the international tribunal looking into war crimes committed in the former Yugoslavia. He also charged that Croatian politicians had stolen millions of dollars while in power. He promised to cut off Croatia's financial support to Bosnian Croats and their army and to no longer allow them to vote in Croatian elections. "I sent the blunt message to the Croats in Bosnia-Herzegovina that they have to turn toward Sarajevo," Mesic told Steven Erlanger of the *New York Times,* referring to the capital of Bosnia. "They must lose all illusions that they will one day be part of Croatia."

Tudjman had been fond of wearing white military uniforms decorated with braids and sashes, and he had required every member of his cabinet to come to the airport to see him off whenever he left the country. To make himself seem as different as possible from Tudjman, Mesic held a series of chats with voters in coffeehouses as part of his campaign. "Fancy a coffee with the president? Let's go," his campaign ads said, according to R. Jeffrey Smith of the *Washington Post*. "With bushy black eyebrows, a close-cropped beard, and a bristle haircut, Mesic appears more avuncular and jolly than most of his eight opponents," Smith wrote. "Mesic speaks in broad terms, gently waves his hands, and swats away criticism with irreverent humor. He says he is proud of driving a four-year-old Volkswagen Golf and promises his net worth won't be any greater after he leaves office." Mesic also promised to pare down the vast presidential powers Tudjman had accumulated.

Mesic came in first in the first round of presidential elections, with 42 percent of the vote, then won the second round in February with 56 percent. "We want to convince the world that Croatia is a part of Europe and that Europe is in Croatia, too," Mesic told his supporters after his election, according to Smith of the *Washington Post*. "We want to fulfill our strategic goals of entering the European Union and NATO as soon as possible." At his inauguration later that month, Mesic pledged to support human rights, the war crimes tribunal, and free markets. Western leaders and diplomats, including United States Secretary of State Madeleine Albright, who attended the ceremony and immediately invited Mesic to visit Washington, expressed hope that Bosnia and Yugoslavia might also become more democratic.

By April of 2000, Mesic told *Chicago Tribune* reporter Tom Hundley that he had already cut the number of presidential staff members. The country was about to switch from a semi-presidential system to a parliamentary system, which meant the president would retain authority over defense and foreign policy, but parliament would be the major decision-maker. Mesic also promised to investigate possible theft by members of the previous government and their cronies. "We must prosecute all of those people who have emptied the treasury, or who permitted or took active part in the capital drain from Croatia," he told Hundley. "We must also prosecute all of those who abused their offices in the process of privatization or took part in the Mafia-like destruction of the Croatian economy. The difference between the Croatian mafia and Italian Mafia is that the Italian still operates underground."

The new government quickly cooperated with the war crimes tribunal. In March of 2000, it turned over suspect Mladan Naletilic, whom the previous government had avoided extraditing for two years. It also shared some files with the tribunal and allowed it to investigate inside Croatia. When seven generals protested the government's cooperation with the tribunal that October, Mesic retired them. The pressure got more intense after reformers were elected in Yugoslavia and turned over former Yugoslav President Slobodan Milosevic to the war crimes court. (Serbs in Yugoslavia were complaining that Croatia had not extradited any Croatian citizens to the court, only Bosnian Croats.) In July of 2001, the Croatian cabinet voted to extradite any Croatian indicted by the court, a decision which caused four dissenting ministers to quit. Mesic stuck to his commitment, though, and even testified at the trial of Milosevic in 2002. He told the court that Milosevic repeatedly tried to divide Yugoslavia ethnically in order to create a Greater Serbia. "I never saw any sign of feeling in him, ever," Mesic told the judges, according to the *Washington Post*'s Katie Nguyen. "All he had was goals he was implementing."

Abroad, Mesic often played the role of a diplomatic healer. He visited Israel in 2001 and apologized for the crimes of Croatia's World War II-era Nazi puppet government, which ran concentration camps where Jews and others were executed. When he met with Yugoslavia's new president, Vojislav Kostunica, and the three members of Bosnia's presidency in 2002, the first meeting of the three countries' leaders since the 1991 war, they promised to repair their relations and cooperate to return war refugees home. A year later, after Yugoslavia renamed itself Serbia-Montenegro, Mesic visited its capital, Belgrade. Serbia-Montenegro's new president, Svetozar Marovic, apologized "for all the evils any citizen of Serbia and Montenegro has committed against any citizen of Croatia," according to Alissa J. Rubin and Zoran Cirjakovic of the *Los Angeles Times'*). "In my name I also apologize to all those who have suffered pain or damage at any time from citizens of Croatia who misused or acted against the law," Mesic responded.

Croatia moved back to the right politically in late 2003, when the HDZ, now positioning itself in the political center-right under new leader Ivo Sanader, won parliamentary elections. That made Western observers nervous, even though the HDZ had recently abandoned Tudjman's defiant nationalism. When Mesic's term as president was about to expire, the deputy prime minister, Jadranka Kosor, ran against him as the HDZ candidate. But Mesic won re-election easily, with 66 percent of the vote, in January of 2005. Even though the presidency did not have nearly as much power as it once had, Western diplomats were relieved. "In many respects, Mesic had been the moral correction in this country," an unnamed senior European diplomat stationed in Croatia told CNN.com.

"I'm proud of the maturity of Croatia's democracy," said Mesic after his re-election, according to the *Chicago Tribune*. "It has been recognized by the world and Europe. That is why we are at the doors of Europe." Mesic was referring to Croatia's attempt to enter the European Union, a goal he had not accomplished in his first term.

As 2005 began, Croatia had aimed to open negotiations about joining the EU that March. However, many EU nations were skeptical that Croatia was still complying fully with the war crimes tribunal. One man was at the center of the debate: Ante Gotovina, the last Croatian war crimes suspect still on the loose. An army general, Gotovina was indicted in connection with the deaths of 150 Serbs and the expulsion of 150,000 others during a 1995 offensive that reclaimed Croatian land from Serb forces. The EU demanded that Croatia hand over Gotovina.

During the election, Mesic had said more than his opponent about what he would do to arrest Gotovina. But by March, Mesic was trying to convince the EU that Gotovina was no longer in Croatia. Meanwhile, a wave of nationalism swept through the country. Many Croatians thought of Gotovina as a hero for his role in the war with the Serbs. To try to fight the trend, Mesic declared that the government had to cooperate better with the tribunal. (He also reiterated his refusal to sign an agreement exempting Americans from prosecution by the International Criminal Court, which the United States does not recognize, explaining that Croatians could not agree to exempt the United States from an obligation Croatia was respecting.) In April of 2005, Mesic also accused Gotovina and another general (now deceased) of being responsible for the deaths of their own soldiers during a 1993 offensive. The same month, Croatian police arrested two people they suspected of giving Gotovina a false passport to help him flee the country. Meanwhile, Mesic atoned once more for Croatians' World War II crimes, by speaking at Croatia's most infamous concentration camp.

## Selected writings

*The Demise of Yugoslavia: A Political Memoir,* Central European University Press, 2003.

## Sources

### Periodicals

AP Worldstream, March 10, 2005; April 22, 2005; April 25, 2005; April 26, 2005; April 29, 2005; May 5, 2005.
*Chicago Tribune,* April 16, 2000; October 1, 2000, p. 19; July 16, 2002, p. 6; January 17, 2005, p. 7.
*Christian Science Monitor,* May 6, 1994; February 7, 2000, p. 8.
*International Herald Tribune,* April 5, 2005.
*Los Angeles Times,* May 16, 1991, p. 1; July 1, 1991, p. 1; October 8, 1991, p. 1; October 31, 1991, p. 4; December 6, 1991, p. 21; February 19, 2000, p. 9; July 9, 2001, p. A3; November 1, 2001, p. A22; September 11, 2003, p. A3.
*New York Times,* February 7, 2000, p. A10; February 8, 2000, p. A12.
*Plain Dealer* (Cleveland, OH), May 31, 2000, p. 4A.
*Washington Post,* January 22, 2000, p. A13; February 13, 2000, p. A23; October 2, 2002, p. A18; November 24, 2003, p. A17.

### Online

"Croatia," Encyclopedia Brittanica Online, http://www.search.eb.com/eb/article?tocid=223957 (May 30, 2005).
"Mesic takes victory in Croatia," CNN.com, http://www.cnn.com/2005/WORLD/europe/01/16/croatia.result.reut/index.html (January 19, 2005).
"Stjepan Mesic—biography," Office of the President of the Republic of Croatia, http://www.predsjednik.hr/default.asp?ru=101&sid=&akcija=&jezik=2 (May 30, 2005).

—Erick Trickey

# Helen Mirren

## Actress

**B**orn Ilyena Lydia Mironoff, July 26, 1945, in Hammersmith, London, England; married Taylor Hackford (a film producer and director), December 31, 1997.

**Addresses:** *Agent*—c/o Toni Howard, International Creative Management, 8942 Wilshire Blvd., Beverly Hills, CA 90211.

## Career

**A**ctress on stage, including: National Youth Theatre, c. 1960; joined the Royal Shakespeare Company, c. 1964; appeared in London stage productions with the Lyric Theatre Company, 1970s; *Dance of Death*, 2001. Film appearances include: *Herostratus*, 1967; *A Midsummer Night's Dream*, 1968; *Age of Consent*,1969; *Savage Messiah*, 1972; *Miss Julie*, 1972; *O Lucky Man!*, 1973; *Hamlet*, 1976; *Caligula*, 1979; *The Quiz Kid*, 1979; *Hussy*, 1980; *The Fiendish Plot of Dr. Fu Manchu*, 1980; *The Long Good Friday*, 1980; *Excalibur*, 1981; *Cal*, 1984; *2010*, 1984; *White Nights*, 1985; *Heavenly Pursuits*, 1985; *Coming Through*, 1985; *The Mosquito Coast*, 1986; *Pascali's Island*, 1988; *When the Whales Came*, 1989; *The Cook, The Thief, His Wife and Her Lover*, 1989; *The Comfort of Strangers*, 1990; *Bethune: The Making of a Hero*, 1990; *The Hawk*, 1993; *Prince of Jutland*, 1994; *The Madness of King George*, 1994; *Some Mother's Son*, 1996; *Critical Care*, 1997; *The Prince of Egypt* (voice), 1998; *Teaching Mrs. Tingle*, 1999; *Greenfingers*, 2000; *Happy Birthday*, 2000; *The Pledge*, 2001; *No Such Thing*, 2001; *Last Orders*, 2001; *Gosford Park*, 2001; *Calendar Girls*, 2003; *The Clearing*, 2004; *Raising Helen*, 2004. Television appearances include: *Cousin Bette* (miniseries), 1971; *The Changeling* (movie), 1974; *Coffin for the Bride* (movie), 1974; *The Applecart* (movie), 1975; *Caesar and Claretta* (movie), 1975; *The Philanthropist* (movie), 1975; *The Little Minister* (movie), 1975; *The Collection* (movie), 1976; *The Country Wife* (movie), 1977; *As You Like It*, (movie), 1978; *Blue Remembered Hills* (movie), 1979; *Oresteia* (miniseries), 1979; *S.O.S. Titanic* (movie), 1979; *Mrs. Reinhardt* (movie), 1981; *Soft Targets* (movie), 1982; *Cymbeline* (movie), 1982; *Cause célèbre* (movie), 1987; *Red King, White Knight* (movie), 1989; *Prime Suspect*, 1992-96, 2004; *Losing Chase* (movie), 1996; *Painted Lady* (miniseries), 1997; *The Passion of Ayn Rand* (movie), 1999; *Door to Door* (movie), 2002; *Georgetown*, 2002; *The Roman Spring of Mrs. Stone* (movie), 2003; *Pride* (movie; voice), 2004.

**Awards:** Best actress award, Cannes Film Festival, for *Cal*, 1984; BAFTA Award, British Academy of Film and Television Arts, 1992, 1993, and 1994, all for *Prime Suspect*; Emmy Award for outstanding lead actress in a miniseries or a movie, National Academy of Television Arts and Sciences, for *The Passion of Ayn Rand*, 1999; created Dame of the British Empire, 2003.

## Sidelights

**B**ritish actress Helen Mirren delighted fans when she returned to the role of London police detective Jane Tennison in the cult-favorite *Prime Suspect* miniseries in 2003 after a seven-year hiatus. The original episodes ran from 1992 to 1996, and Mirren decided to take a break from the grisly plots and dour characters for a while. Notoriously tough and whip-smart, Mirren's Tennison is one of the most compelling crime- solvers in small screen history. "Scrappy, irritable, acerbic, and impassioned—a workaholic woman fighting for respect in a male domain," noted *Maclean's* writer Brian D. Johnson, "Tennison is one of the most brilliantly nuanced heroines ever created for television."

Mirren was born in 1945 in London. Her mother came from a long line of butchers in the city, but her given name, Ilyena Lydia Mironoff, betrays her half-Russian heritage from a line of landed gentry and military officials. Her father's father had come to England to negotiate an arms deal during the Russo-Japanese War of 1905, and there had even been a mention of an ancestor in Leo Tolstoy's 1865-69 classic *War and Peace.* In their adopted land, however, Mirren's family was anything but noble. Her father had played viola with the London Philharmonic Orchestra before working as a cabdriver and later a driver's-license examiner. Her parents, who Anglicized their "Mironoff" surname to Mirren, settled in Ilford, Essex, where a teenage Mirren worked summers at an amusement park.

Mirren was educated at a convent school, where she discovered the plays of William Shakespeare and became engrossed in their intricate plots and well-drawn characters during her teen years. When the school received notice that the National Youth Theatre was holding tryouts, Mirren decided to audition, and won a spot in the esteemed government-funded drama program whose alumni include some of the best-known names in British theater and film.

Mirren's parents initially discouraged her ambitions, thinking it wiser that she choose a career in teaching instead, but she was determined to become an actress. At the age of 19, she joined the Royal Shakespeare Company, and became one of its newest stars, thanks in part to some daring new productions of classics like *Antony and Cleopatra.* Early on, Mirren won press attention for low-cut costumes that highlighted her buxom figure, but critics also commended her solid, somewhat smoldering performances.

In the mid-1970s, Mirren left England for a time. She joined an experimental theater troupe run by Peter Brook, a renowned stage director, and visited parts of Africa and even a Native American reservation with it. Because she had never taken a formal drama course, she hoped to expand her horizons through the experience. "It wasn't something that you walk away from with a few quick, easy tricks that you've learned," she said of her time with the Brook group in an interview with *Back Stage West*'s Rob Kendt. "It was much more to do with understanding yourself as a person, and, it seemed at the time, constantly confronting your failures as an actor and as a person." A legacy of that time in her life is visible between her thumb and forefinger in the form of a small tattoo, which she had done on the Minnesota reservation. The design translates as "love thy neighbor."

Mirren began her career in film with a forgotten 1967 black comedy called *Herostratus,* about a man who sells the rights to his suicide jump to an advertising agency in exchange for a bout of luxury living. During the 1970s, she appeared in a number of feature films and television productions, but emerged as a leading actress to watch in the controversial 1979 film *Caligula.* It was produced by Bob Guccione, Sr., the publisher of *Penthouse* magazine, and retold the story of one of the Roman Empire's most debauched leaders, Emperor Gaius Germanicus Caesar, also known as Caligula. Mirren was cast in one of the female leads alongside Malcolm McDowell and Peter O'Toole in the near-pornographic epic. On her first day on the set, Mirren arrived in Rome and was scheduled to meet with O'Toole. "So I'm taken to Peter's trailer to be introduced," she recalled in interview with *New York Times* writer Ted Loos. "But he's wrapped in his costume—bandages that were oozing with fake sores, pus and blood. I went outside and I threw up in a field."

*Caligula* was a legendary debacle, and a film that interviewers still asked Mirren about years later. It was reportedly the first film to charge an admission price of $7.50, and there were rumors that its gory scenes even caused audience members to throw up. Critics were scathing in their indictments, but Mirren was pragmatic about the experience. "I was pretty young when I made that—not physically young as much as inexperienced in film," she told Loos. "And you know what? It was a great experience. It was like being sent down to Dante's Inferno in many ways."

Mirren took a more solid role as a gangster's moll opposite Bob Hoskins in the acclaimed drama *The Long Good Friday* in 1980, and began to win impressive leading roles afterward. She was cast as Morgana in the 1981 King Arthur epic *Excalibur,* and won a best actress award at the Cannes Film Festival for her part in the contemporary Irish drama *Cal,* as the widow of a slain police officer. Her first true Hollywood job came in *White Nights* in 1985, the Mikhail Baryshnikov ballet drama, as an aging Russian ballerina named Galina Ivanova.

Mirren also had a memorable part in the 1989 Peter Greenaway film *The Cook, The Thief, His Wife and Her Lover.* She played Georgina, the wife of a ruthless mob boss. The lavish, big-budget production took place almost exclusively inside a modernist, extremely expensive restaurant at which Georgina, her loathsome husband played by Michael Gambon, and his entourage dine nightly. She carries on a torrid affair behind the scenes with a lone, bookish diner, and the revenge that her husband extracts when he discovers her transgression is suitably gastronomic and brutal. The Greenaway film called for several scenes of full-frontal nudity, and Mirren gained a reputation as being rather fearless about such requirements in the roles she took. She admitted later, however, that the first time she had to disrobe it was tough. "I just wanted to die," she told *New York Times* writer Bernard Weinraub. "I wanted the earth to open and swallow me up. But then you get on with it and it becomes absolutely fine."

In 1992, Mirren took on the role that would earn her legions of new fans: that of Detective Superintendent Jane Tennison in *Prime Suspect.* The clever but gritty mystery miniseries was set in London, and captured fans on both sides of the Atlantic when it became a *Masterpiece Theater* staple on Public Broadcasting Service (PBS) in the United States. Tennison regularly solved some of the toughest, most gruesome cases, while challenging her male colleagues' gender biases and overcoming troubles in her personal life. The fifth installment aired in 1996, and Mirren decided to leave it behind—though she refused to allow the writers to kill off her character.

Mirren returned to her film career during the late 1990s in earnest, appearing in a slew of works. She had already earned her first Academy Award nomination for best supporting actress as Queen Charlotte in 1994's *The Madness of King George.* In 1999, she won an Emmy award for her title part in *The Passion of Ayn Rand,* the story of the feted writer. She also took the occasional fun role, such as the title character in the movie *Teaching Mrs. Tingle,* a dark teen comedy that featured Katie Holmes as her young nemesis in a film that gave Mirren an entirely new generation of fans.

Mirren earned her second Oscar nomination for her part of the prim housekeeper in Robert Altman's *Gosford Park* in 2001. Her Mrs. Wilson was just one member of Altman's ensemble cast, who gather at an English country manor in 1932 for a hunting party. As *Observer* critic Ed Vulliamy noted, "Mirren's lines are few, but in a film of few sharp edges, the intensity of her taut control, giving way to an outpouring of grief at the end, gives her the commanding role."

Finally, Mirren decided to return to *Prime Suspect* as Jane Tennison. *Prime Suspect 6: The Last Witness* began airing in the spring of 2004 with a story about a murdered Bosnian woman that Tennison begins investigating just as her bosses are pressuring her to retire. Mirren initially agreed to return to the role after believing that enough time had passed, but on her first day on the set, "there I am putting on what looks like exactly the same costume I wore seven years ago," she recalled in an interview with *Times of London* journalist Paul Hoggart. "My heart just dropped and I thought 'My God! What am I doing? I'm going backwards!'" After a few days, however, Mirren watched the footage that had been shot. "I thought: 'This is going to be great. You're an idiot.'"

Mirren still likes the stage, telling *W*'s Peter Braunstein that "I've made a conscious decision to keep doing theater, to stay viable, because you lose your courage if you don't." She has worked regularly in London over the years, and has also appeared on Broadway, most notably in the August Strindberg revival of *Dance of Death* during the 2001 season. The play, a gripping, claustrophobic marital drama, featured fellow British stage veteran Ian McKellen as her spouse.

Regularly hailed on lists of Britain's most enticing actresses in fan polls, Mirren remained unhesitant about disrobing on-screen. She starred in *Calendar Girls* in 2003, based on a true story of a group of English women who decided to pose nude for a charity calendar for their local hospital. She has also been known to take on romantic lead roles opposite younger men, and was slated to appear in a British television production as Queen Elizabeth I in the tale of the regent's romance with the much-younger Earl of Essex. In an intriguing royal twist, Mirren—who was created a dame by Prince Charles in 2003—was also set to appear as the second Queen Elizabeth, the mother of the Prince, in another British telefilm fictionalizing the British royal family's reaction to events following the 1997 car-crash death of Diana, the Princess of Wales.

Mirren was once romantically linked with the actor Liam Neeson, but in 1997 wed her longtime boyfriend, American director Taylor Hackford, whom she had met on the set of *White Nights*. She has said that she would love to play America's most famous housewares doyenne on screen. "I don't understand the vilification of Martha Stewart," Mirren told Loos in the *New York Times* interview just after Stewart was found guilty of obstructing a federal investigation. "She doesn't deserve Lady Macbeth. In a way, she's more like Rosalind from *As You Like It*. She's mouthy, pushy and opinionated—kind of wonderful and kind of difficult."

Mirren spent some early years in her career wondering if she should have heeded her parents' warnings about her choice of vocation. She admitted there was a time in her life in her mid-twenties when she "was really depressed.... I went to a hand-reader, this Indian guy in a funky neighbourhood," she told Vulliamy in the *Observer* article. "He said: 'The height of your success won't happen until you're in your late forties.'"

## Sources

*Back Stage West,* February 21, 2002, p. 1.
*Entertainment Weekly,* January 22, 1993, p. 30; September 15, 1995, p. 116; January 9, 2004, p. 61; April 23, 2004, p. 70.
*Independent* (London, England), September 20, 2001, p. 7; November 5, 2003, p. 14.
*Maclean's,* January 20, 1997, p. 70.
*Mirror* (London, England), July 23, 2004, p. 11.
*New Republic,* April 23, 1990, p. 26.
*New York Times,* April 23, 1995, p. H5; April 11, 2004, p. AR8.
*Observer* (London, England), January 20, 2002, p. 3.
*People,* March 16, 1992, p. 16.
*Sunday Times* (London, England), November 7, 1999, p. 4.
*Time,* December 30, 1996, p. 148.
*Times* (London, England), October 23, 1975, p. 11; November 8, 2003, p. 10.
*W,* January 2002, p. 30.

—*Carol Brennan*

# Alfred Molina

## Actor

**B**orn May 24, 1953, in London, England; married Jill Gascoine (an actress and novelist); children: Rachel. *Education:* Guildhall School of Music and Drama, London.

**Addresses:** *Agent*—United Talent Agency, 9650 Wilshire Blvd., Ste. 500, Beverly Hills, CA 90212.

## Career

**A**ctor in television, including: *The Losers*, 1978; *Reilly: The Ace of Spies*, 1983; *Cats Eyes*, 1985; *Casualty*, 1986; *Miami Vice*, 1987; *Nativity Blues*, 1989; *The Accountant*, 1989; *El C.I.D.*, 1989; *The Trials of Oz*, 1991; *Typhon's People*, 1993; *A Year in Providence*, 1993; *Requiem Apache*, 1994; *The Place of Lions*, 1997; *Rescuers: Stories of Courage: Two Couples*, 1998; *Ladies Man*, 1999; *The Miracle Maker* (voice), 2000; *Murder on the Orient Express*, 2001; *Bram and Alice*, 2002. Film appearances include: *Raiders of the Lost Ark*, 1981; *Ladyhawke*, 1985; *Number One*, 1985; *Water*, 1985; *Letter to Brezhnev*, 1985; *Prick up Your Ears*, 1987; *Manifesto*, 1988; *American Friends*, 1991; *Not Without My Daughter*, 1991; *When Pigs Fly*, 1993; *The Trial*, 1993; *Maverick*, 1994; *The Steal*, 1994; *White Fang II: Myth of the White Wolf*, 1994; *Dead Man*, 1995; *Species*, 1995; *The Perez Family*, 1995; *Hideaway*, 1995; *Mojave Moon*, 1996; *Before and After*, 1996; *The Man Who Knew Too Little*, 1997; *Boogie Nights*, 1997; *Anna Karenina*, 1997; *Scorpion Spring*, 1997; *A Further Gesture*, 1997; *Pete's Meteor*, 1998; *The Impostors*, 1998; *Dudley Do-Right*, 1999; *Chocolat*, 2000; *Frida*, 2002; *Coffee and Cigarettes*, 2003; *Spider-Man 2*, 2004. Stage appearances include: *Accidental Death of an Anarchist*, London, 1979; *Serious Money*, Royal Court Theatre, London; *Taming of the Shrew*, Royal Shakespeare Company, London, 1985; *Destry Rides Again*, Donmar Theatre, London; *Night of the Iguana*, Royal National Theatre, London; *Speed the Plow*, Royal National Theatre, London; *Oklahoma!*, Palace Theatre, Greensburg, PA; *Molly Sweeney*, Roundabout Theatre, NY, 1995-96; *Art*, New York, NY, 1998; *Fiddler on the Roof*, New York, NY, 2004.

**Awards:** UK Royal Television Society, best male actor, for *The Accountant*, 1990; Imagen Foundation Award, for *Frida*, 2003; Visual Effects Society Award for outstanding performance by an actor or actress in a visual effects film, for *Spider-Man 2*, 2005.

## Sidelights

**A**lfred Molina has more than 50 film, television and stage credits to his name yet remains a sideline figure in Hollywood. Moviegoers recognize Molina's face but can seldom come up with his name because he melds into each role so completely that his own ego and personality disappear. Over the course of his 30-year career, Molina has earned praise for his uncanny ability to nail character-driven roles. Show-biz insiders liken Molina to a chameleon for his ability to mold himself into nearly every character imaginable, no matter their nationality. Molina played the perpetually unfaithful Mexican painter Diego Rivera in the biopic *Frida* as well as a close-minded, fretful French mayor in *Chocolat.* Likewise, he mastered the role of a deranged drug-dealer in *Boogie Nights* as well as that of comic-book villain Doctor Octopus in *Spider-Man 2.* "He's great in just about everything," filmmaker Sam Raimi told the *Detroit Free-Press,* "but he disappears so completely in the roles you forget where you've seen him before."

Molina—friends call him Fred—was born on May 24, 1953, in London, England. His father, a Spaniard and waiter, left Madrid just before World War II. His mother, a cook and housekeeper, left Italy just after the war. Together, they settled in one of London's working-class, immigrant neighborhoods, providing Molina with a rich foundation of friends. His neighborhood friends hailed from all over Europe, the West Indies and Africa. Like Molina, most of his playmates were first-generation Brits. He said this exposure helped him master the different accents he has needed in his roles. "So I kind of grew up in this whole environment where I heard all these different rhythms and accents," Molina told Katherine A. Diaz in *Hispanic* magazine. "I think I just soaked it up unconsciously, and when I became an actor I had it all there stowed away."

Although Molina's parents were thankful for the opportunity to start a new life in England, they were mindful of keeping their heritage alive—both Spanish and Italian were spoken in the home. But no matter what language Molina was speaking, early on, he was a boisterous kid. "I think I was quite unpleasant," he told Eleanor Blau in the *New York Times.* "My father used to put me on a chair and make me sing. I didn't want to, but I did because I knew I was pleasing him."

Molina caught the stage bug at age nine after seeing a production of *Spartacus,* announcing to his parents that he intended to become an actor. Trips with the school drama club to see live performances solidified his desire. At first, his father was unsupportive, figuring it was just a phase. In 1969, Molina put his talents to the test and joined the London-based National Youth Theater company. He returned for two more seasons, then went on to study at London's Guildhall School of Music and Drama. Next, he joined the repertory circuit before securing a spot with the Royal Shakespeare Company in 1977. Molina also polished his skills as part of a street-corner comedy act. In 1979, Molina captured the attention of the play-going British public with his portrayal of The Maniac in a stage production of *Accidental Death of an Anarchist.*

Molina brought his skills across the Atlantic in the 1980s and made his Hollywood debut in spine-tingling style, playing Indiana Jones' double-crossing South American tour guide Satipo in the 1981 action-adventure *Raiders of the Lost Ark.* Molina had his glory moment in the film's opening scenes when he led Indiana Jones (Harrison Ford) astray in an ancient temple treasure hunt and uttered his famous line, "Throw me the idol, and I'll throw you the whip." Molina's character eventually leaves Indy for dead, only to come to his own demise, courtesy of a booby trap.

One scene required Molina to endure tarantulas crawling on his body. Before filming the tarantula sequence, Molina was told that tarantulas, though venomous, were really harmless creatures who had earned a bad reputation for their size and hairy facade. Two suitcases of tarantulas arrived on the set and were let loose. The creatures refused to move, stunned by the bright lights, so the film crew paired up two female tarantulas on Molina's back and a fight ensued. Recalling this first introduction to Hollywood filmmaking, Molina told the *New York Times'* Blau that director Steven Spielberg kept calling out, "Look scared, Alfred." Molina put on a scared face, but it had nothing to do with acting.

Molina returned to Britain's Royal Shakespeare Company in 1985 and appeared in a production of Shakespeare's *Taming of the Shrew.* He received high marks for his portrayal of Petruchio. He followed up with several minor film roles through the mid-1980s, then really turned up the heat in 1987, playing Kenneth Halliwell, the homicidal lover of playwright Joe Orton, in *Prick Up Your Ears,* a film based loosely on Orton's life. Bald and deranged, Molina's Halliwell was both terrifying and pathetic at the same time, even as he hammered his lover to death. Speaking to the *New York Times* Molina acknowledged the sympathy he felt for his horrid character, noting he understood "what it's like to be jealous, to feel betrayed, to be lonely. I really latched on to those feelings."

Over the next several years, Molina gave solid film performances playing characters with accents from all over the world. In 1991, he played a tyrannical Iranian husband to Sally Field in the heart-churning flick *Not Without My Daughter.* In 1995 he appeared in *The Perez Family,* as the patriarch of an immigrant Cuban family trying to find its way in Florida. In 1996 he played Panos Demeris, a Greek-American attorney in *Before and After.* In a *New York Times* review, Janet Maslin had nothing but accolades for Molina's performance. "In his showiest screen performance, Mr. Molina turns this wily, entertaining figure into something more than just another legal eagle."

In each of these roles, Molina nailed the nationality of his character with an impeccable accent. "I have always enjoyed working with different accents," Molina told Diaz in *Hispanic*. "It's become sort of a trademark of mine. It's not because of any special skills; it's a happy accident of nature and nurture that I am able to do it."

Though he was busy with film productions, Molina also kept up his stage acting and moved as fluidly between stage and film as he did in his varied roles. Molina's New York stage debut came in 1995 in *Molly Sweeney*, where he played a gentle companion to a blind woman. In 1998, he made his Broadway debut alongside Alan Alda and Victor Garber in playwright Yasmina Reza's *Art*, earning a Tony nomination. This dialogue-driven play revolved around three friends in conflict over their disparate views surrounding a piece of modern art.

Because he appears in both film and stage productions, Molina often finds himself acting two roles simultaneously—playing one character during the day for a film and appearing onstage at night in a completely different personality. In 1996, for instance, he was busy filming on the streets of various New York boroughs during the day for *A Further Gesture*, which was released in 1997. At night, he appeared on stage in New York City in *Molly Sweeney*. "I was playing an Irishman in the evening and a Guatemalan dissident during the day," he recalled to the *New York Times*. "That's the usual for me. I think I've been almost every nationality under the sun now. Well, I haven't been a South African yet."

For the most part, Molina enjoys pushing himself into new territory with new roles. "I always look for something that is as different and as diametrically opposed to what I did last time," Molina told Diaz in *Hispanic*. "I try to make each job as different as I can from the last job. And that's really my only criteria."

The summer of 2004 found Molina appearing in several places at once. At the box office, he was featured in the movie *Spider-Man 2* and also appeared onstage in the Broadway production of *Fiddler on the Roof*. Molina's role in *Fiddler* was quite different from the villainous men he had been portraying on film. In *Fiddler*, Molina played the mild-mannered Jewish milkman Tevye who is on a mission to find suitable husbands for his daughters in pre-Revolutionary Russia. He was successful in the role even though he had not done a musical in nearly two decades. "I know it sounds perverse, but in the 20 years that I haven't been singing, I think my singing has improved," he told *Entertainment Weekly*. He

joked that this improvement was not because he had improved, but because he recognized his limitations.

In *Spiderman 2*, Molina tried a new role—that of the maniacal comic-book super-villain Dr. Otto Octavius, Spider Man's latest onscreen nemesis. Octavius is a gentle genius who makes a mistake in an energy fusion experiment and ends up permanently attached to an octopus-like apparatus he created. With four independent-thinking tentacles bonded to his body, Doc Ock, as he becomes known, loses his mind and becomes an enemy foil to Spider Man, bent on blowing up New York City. Much of the film's success was linked to Molina's over-the-top character.

Playing the role required Molina to act with a 75-pound tentacle costume strapped onto his back. It taxed even Molina's rugged 6-foot-3 frame. Molina required the assistance of a team of more than a dozen puppeteers in order to maneuver the hulking suit. Speaking to Stephen Schaefer in the *Boston Herald*, Molina said that over the course of filming, he and the team developed their own language of movement so they could make his character do destructive things like "push a hole through a building." At the same time, they had to work in concert with each other to do smaller movments, like removing a pair of glasses. "In one shot—and I don't think that we ever used it—we actually had one of the tentacles come and wipe away a tear."

For the most part, Molina has been successful because he approaches each new role with a sense of wonder. "I'm always scared," he told *Newsweek*. "Any actor who doesn't walk into a job without a certain sense of trepidation is either lying or very highly medicated."

## Sources

### Periodicals

*Boston Herald*, June 25, 2004.
*Detroit Free Press*, July 5, 2004.
*Entertainment Weekly*, January 23/30, 2004, p. 76.
*Hispanic*, July/August 2004, p. 46.
*Newsweek*, March 1, 2004, p. 14.
*New York Times*, May 15, 1987, p. C11; March 3, 1996, p. B11.

### Online

"Biography," Alfred-Molina.com, http://www. alfred-molina.com/bio/html (February 26, 2004).

—*Lisa Frick*

# Arturo Moreno

## Owner of the Anaheim Angels

**B**orn in August of 1946, in Tucson, AZ; son of Art and Mary Moreno; married (divorced); married Carole; children: Bryan (from first marriage), Rico, Nikki (from second marriage). *Military:* U.S. Army, 1966-68. *Education:* University of Arizona, B.S. (marketing), 1973.

**Addresses:** *Office*—Angels Baseball, 2000 Gene Autry Way, Anaheim, CA 92806.

## Career

**S**alesperson for a billboard company, 1973-84; became principal and chief executive officer of Outdoor Systems, Phoenix, AZ, 1984; owned share of the Salt Lake City Trappers, a Class A baseball team, 1985-92; original investor in the Arizona Diamondbacks, 1998; bought Anaheim Angels, 2003.

## Sidelights

**I**n 2003, Arturo "Arte" Moreno made sports history when he bought the Anaheim Angels, and became major league baseball's first-ever minority team owner. Ranked no. 244 on *Forbes* magazine's rankings of the richest 400 people in the world thanks to the outdoor-advertising empire he created, Moreno saw his new job as just another chief executive officer's post, he told *USA Today* writer Greg Boeck in a rare interview. "The fans own the team," he asserted. "I'm the economic caretaker."

Born in 1946, Moreno is a fourth-generation Mexican-American with roots in Tucson, Arizona. His grandfather founded a printing company there,

and his father was the publisher of the city's Spanish-language newspaper, *El Tucsonense*. But Moreno grew up in circumstances that were anything but comfortable: he was the first of eleven children in a family that lived in a two-bedroom, one-bathroom home. After high school, he worked in the family's print shop, and took classes at the local community college. Drafted into the U.S. Army in 1966, he served two years, including a stint in Vietnam. While there, he later noted, he decided to set down some goals for his future. One was to finish college, and the other to become a millionaire by the time he turned 40.

Back in civilian clothes, Moreno enrolled at the University of Arizona, and earned his marketing degree in 1973. He landed a sales job with a local billboard company that was later bought by Gannett, an outdoor-advertising powerhouse, and advanced up the corporate ladder. His millionaire goal still in mind, Moreno had an epiphany at one point. "I was generating x amount of profit," he told *Fortune* writer David Whitford, "and I knew that if I could have a small company generating even just a percentage of that profit I could reach my goals much faster. Like I once told somebody, I became very dangerous when I learned how to add."

In 1984, Moreno entered into a partnership deal with an 80-billboard business in Phoenix called Outdoor Systems. As chief executive officer, he took the company on a strategic expansion plan that involved acquiring larger and larger competitors. Revenues went from $500,000 to $90 million over the next dozen years, and Outdoor Systems became a publicly traded company in 1996. Three years later, he and his original partner sold the business to Infinity Broadcast Co. for more than $8 billion.

Buying the Anaheim Angels was not Moreno's first venture into baseball: a lifelong fan of the game, he served as a coach for youth teams in Phoenix, including his son's, for a decade, and in the late 1980s and early '90s was one of several owners of a Class A team, the Salt Lake City Trappers. He was also an original investor in the Arizona Diamondbacks baseball team. In the spring of 2003, he emerged as one of three contenders to become the newest owner of the Angels. Multimedia giant Disney had owned it in full since 1999, and the team even won the World Series in 2002, but it remained a money-losing franchise in the Disney portfolio. Moreno's bid package won out, and he put $182.5 million on the table in a cash deal. It made him the first person of color to own a Major League Baseball team, ever. But Moreno avoided dwelling on his historic achievement as baseball's first Hispanic team owner. "I'm proud of being a Mexican American," *New York Times* journalist Murray Chass quoted him as saying at the news conference to announce the deal, but stressed that "we're all Americans. Most of us are immigrants from someplace, and I think we always try to do our best being an American."

Moreno's first official act as team owner was to lower the price of beer at the Anaheim home field, from $8 to $6.75. He also slashed ticket prices to as low as $3 and $5 for some seats on certain nights, halved the price of souvenir "A" baseballs, and initiated a family friendly package deal for tickets and food. The end result was that the team took in $2.5 million more in revenue for 2003 from concession sales than it had the previous—and championship—year, and souvenir-sales revenues came to $1.25 million as well.

Yet the world-championship Angels fared poorly on the field that first year of Moreno's stewardship, finishing near the bottom of the American League West standings. Their new boss, however, began spending heavily on adding fresh talent to the team roster. He signed four new players, all of them Hispanic: pitcher Bartolo Colon, who accepted a four-year, $51 million deal; outfielder Vladimir Guerrero for $70 million for five years; and Kelvim Escobar and Jose Guillen. Moreno was also committed to increasing diversity within every facet of organization, and made the stadium more bilingual-friendly in its signs and personnel. Hoping to lure more Latino fans in a sport where an overwhelming number of players are of Hispanic heritage, Moreno has not had to look very far: nearby the Angels Stadium is the city of Santa Ana, which has proportionately more Spanish speakers than any other city in the United States.

Thanks to the new blood, the Angels did better in 2004, finishing with a 92-70 record and even making it into the playoffs, where they were ousted by eventual World Series pennant winners the Boston Red Sox. This feat, and his family friendly policies, has made Moreno a popular figure at Angels Stadium, where youngsters ask him for autographs. His home, however, remains back in Phoenix, where he lives with his wife, Carole, and their two teenage children. He has a son from a previous marriage, and also keeps a home in the California oceanside town of La Jolla, near San Diego. He has a net worth of $1 billion, and made sure to give out raises in the front office, too, when he increased his team's payroll past the $100-million mark. "It all comes down to people," he told *Boston Herald* journalist Howard Bryant. "This is an outstanding organization with outstanding people, and I can only say that I'm fortunate to be a part of it."

## Sources

*Arizona Daily Star,* April 17, 2003, p. A1.
*Boston Herald,* October 5, 2004, p. 91.
*BusinessWeek,* June 2, 2003, p. 85.
*Fortune,* October 13, 2003, p. 181.
Knight Ridder/Tribune News Service, May 24, 2003; March 1, 2004.
*New York Times,* May 16, 2003, p. D3; October 10, 2004, p. SP2.
*USA Today,* February 24, 2004.

—*Carol Brennan*

# Doug Morris

**Record company executive, songwriter, and producer**

**B**orn November 23, 1938, in New York; married. *Education:* Columbia University, undergraduate degree.

**Addresses:** *Office*—Universal Music Group, 2220 Colorado Ave., Santa Monica, CA 90404; 1755 Broadway, New York, NY 10019.

## Career

**S**taff songwriter, Robert Mellin, Inc.; songwriter and producer, Laurie Records, 1965, then vice president and general manager; founder and owner, Big Tree Records, 1970-78; president, ATCO Records, 1978-81; president, Atlantic Records, 1981-90, chief operating officer, 1989-90, named co-chairman and co-chief executive officer, 1990; chairman, Atlantic Group, c. 1991; president and chief operating officer, Warner Music Group, 1994, chairman and chief executive officer U.S. division, c. 1994-95; chairman and chief executive officer, Rising Tide Entertainment (later known as Universal), 1995; chairman and chief executive officer, MCA Entertainment Group's music division (known as Universal Music Group after 1996), 1995—.

**Awards:** Record Company Executive of the year, *The Gavin Report,* 1991.

## Sidelights

**A**fter beginning his career as a somewhat sucessful songwriter and producer, Doug Morris moved into the business end of the music industry.

© *James Leynse/Corbis*

Morris served as an executive for Atlantic Records, and later, the Warner Music Group after the companies merged. When he was fired from his leading post with the company, he went to MCA/Universal (later known as the Universal Music Group) and helped rebuild the floundering record company into a international power that beat his former employer in world-wide market share. Many believed that some of Morris' success could be attributed to his credibility with musicians and ability to relate to them because of his own beginnings in the business.

Morris was born on November 23, 1938, in New York, the son of an attorney father and ballet instructor mother. He grew up on Long Island, New York. For college, Morris won a scholarship to attend Columbia University. He was already working as a songwriter while studying at the university. After he graduated, he served in the U.S. Army for a time and was stationed in France.

When Morris was discharged from the Army, he went to New York City and found a job as a staff songwriter for Robert Mellin, Inc., a music publisher. In 1965, Morris joined Laurie Records, working as both a songwriter and producer. Within a short amount of time, he was named vice president and general manager of the label. He wrote the biggest hit of his career in 1966, the Chiffons' song "Sweet Talkin' Guy." Morris also produced the 1970 hit single, "Smokin' in the Boys' Room," which was written by Cub Koda of the band Brownsville Station.

In 1970, Morris ventured out on his own in the music business. He founded his own label, Big Tree Records. The small label soon had a distribution deal with Atlantic Records. In 1978, Morris sold the label to Atlantic (some sources say Warner Music, Atlantic's parent company).

After the sale of Big Tree Records, Morris joined Atlantic Records as the president of their ATCO Records subsidiary. Three years later, he was promoted to president of Atlantic Records. At the time, the label did not do well creatively or economically. Yet Morris was able to sign good acts to the label including Pete Townsend and Stevie Nicks. Because of his success, in 1989, he was given additional duties, serving as chief operating officer in addition to president.

In 1990, Morris was named co-chairman and co-chief executive officer of Atlantic Records. He was hand-picked by the head of the Warner Music Group, Robert J. Morgado. Atlantic was doing well, with a solid market in rock, R&B, dance, and other genres. The label had rebounded from the problems it had in the 1980s. A rival record executive, David Geffen, told Ron Stodghill II of *BusinessWeek,* "Until recently, this was a company that was doing very badly and it was doing badly because it wasn't doing all the things that Doug is doing: signing labels, taking risks."

Morris was able to expand Atlantic by taking such chances. He helped create and/or buy smaller labels to give Atlantic a hipper edge. EastWest Records was one such label that proved valuable, as was Atlantic Nashville, which was created to exploit the growing lucrative country music market. Though Atlantic lost money in 1992, it soon proved profitable. In 1993, Atlantic scored a big coup when it acquired Rhino Records, a label which repackaged older hits into new sets for release. Such releases were very profitable since they consisted of a known quantity that was already produced and popular.

By 1994, Morris was serving as the chairman of the Atlantic Group, an overseeing company of Atlantic Records. The company also produced fitness videos and other products. He took over from Ahmet Ertegun, the founder of Atlantic Records. When Morris was in charge, the company remained successful. Atlantic had a number of hits on the charts and saw a vast increase in revenues. In 1990, revenues were $400 million, and by 1994, they had reached $900 million. Atlantic also had the largest market share of all the labels in the United States with 9.4 percent.

In July of 1994, Morris was again promoted to the head of the Warner Music Group, serving as president and chief operating officer. The Warner Music Group owned Atlantic as well as the Elektra and Warner Bros. labels. Morris oversaw all three labels and directed the shuffling and mergers of other imprints. Morris had to work with Morgado, who was the chairman and chief executive officer of Warner Music Group. Morris was given the position because the company as a whole did not do well financially in 1993. He was expected to do for Warner Music Group what he had done for Atlantic.

Morris's promotion led to the resignation of the other executives. He feuded with Morgado, but won out when he was named the chairman and chief executive officer of the U.S. division of the Warner Group. Morgado was later fired as chairman of the Warner Group. In Morgado's place, Michael J. Fuchs was hired in 1995, though Fuchs had no experience in the music business. Initially, Morris was to handle day-to-day operations while Fuchs focused on the big picture. However, Fuchs believed that Morris and his minions were trying to destabilize the company so that Morris could be named chief executive officer of Warner Music. Morris had also wanted the international division and music publishing arm of Warner Music to report to him.

Morris was also controversial at Warner because he wanted to buy an equity stake in Priority, a gangsta rap label. By this time, gangsta rap was a controversial music form because of its harsh, sometimes offensive lyrics. Morris had already convinced Warner Music to buy a 50 percent stake in Interscope, a label which featured many rappers. Warner was taking a beating in the public eye because of its support and profiting from gangsta rap, though Morris was unwavering in his support of it. Because of such problems, Morris was ousted by Fuchs on June 21, 1995. Some observers believed that Warner erred in getting rid of Morris, who was popular among artists and their managers.

After his firing, Morris sued Warner Music Group for breach of contract and asked for $50 million in damages and compensation. Though it was not initially a reason for his dismissal, he was countersued for $10 million by his former employers for improper sales practices. This was related to a scandal in which there were allegations of newly pressed discs being stolen and sold to wholesalers and retailers. The suit claimed Morris was fired because he did not let his superiors know about the scheme, which involved Atlantic employees.

Within weeks of his firing, Morris went into business with one of Warner's main rivals, MCA, Inc., which owned MCA Records and Geffen Records, as well as distributing DreamWorks SKG. Morris was given a multi-year contract to form a joint company with MCA called Rising Tide Entertainment. Morris and MCA each owned 50 percent of the company. Morris served as chairman and chief executive officer of the new company.

While Morris continued to work with Rising Tide, he was named chairman and chief executive officer of the MCA Entertainment Group's music division in November of 1995. Its former head, Al Teller, quit because of differences with management. Morris's label was renamed Universal, and Morris hoped to make MCA into a success like Atlantic. Among Morris's first moves was remaking the A&R (Artists and Repertoire) department, and putting a Rising Tide imprint in Nashville. MCA's strength was in country music at the time.

Under Morris's leadership, MCA and Morris's Universal label were doing well in the 1990s. In 1996, MCA changed its name to the Universal Music Group, and Morris continued to serve as chairman and chief executive officer. That December, Morris's company had artists at the top three slots of the *Billboard* charts. Soon after, when Warner ended its deal with Interscope, Morris bought a 50 percent stake in the company for Universal. This brought many artists in whom Morris believed into the Universal fold. While he still personally struggled with the tone and tenor of gangsta rap, he believed in marketing and profiting from cutting-edge music.

As Morris had done with Atlantic, he conducted phone surveys of radio stations and retailers to discover new talent. This lead to the successful launch of signer Erykah Badu. Despite Morris's hands-on touch, Universal Music Group faced monetary loses the first few years he ran it, primarily because of the cost of investments. However, sales continued to increase, and in 1996 and 1997, market share did as well. Universal was on its way to becoming an important player in the American music scene.

In 1998, Universal Music Group got even bigger when it acquired PolyGram, a large global music company. Though the acquisition cost $10.6 billion,

after the merger, Morris's company sold about a quarter of all music in the United States. Although up to this point in his career Morris had focused on the American scene and hiring others to handle the international market, he took charge of the whole company, including overseeing international markets, as the merger was being completed. The merger took some time as the companies consolidated their distribution and labels. The merger also negatively affected Universal's ability to sign artists who were uncertain about the attention they would receive during the consolidation process.

Morris remained chairman and chief executive officer of the merged company, which retained the name Universal Music Group. In 2000, because of his success, he was given a new five-year deal. Universal's parent company, Seagram, was still expanding. It soon merged with Vivendi SA and Canal Plus which were large, European-based operations. After the merger, the Universal Music Group was a division of Vivendi Universal as the parent company was now known. By 2003, the Universal Music Group was the largest record company in the world, selling 25 to 30 percent of the records sold around the globe. Morris remained respected by artists, and was known for his ear for talent.

Morris still faced many challenges. Online music piracy cut into the company's profits, and the number of employees and acts signed to Universal Music Group's labels decreased. But Morris moved the company into new areas, such as concert tours, career management, and merchandising, to increase profits. In 2003, he signed Tommy Mottola, who had been the head of Sony, to a joint venture. Universal hoped to survive the slump in the music industry by adding executives like Mottola who had ties to talent. Despite such hires, Morris had to cut jobs in the company because of internet pirates. While the company saved money by restructuring and still controlled a huge part of the United States market, Universal Music Group had operating losses in 2003. Morris tried to adapt to doing business in this tense environment by reducing prices of some compact discs and making inexpensive downloads available.

Despite such problems, Morris remained upbeat about the music industry. In 2003, he told Sathnam Sanghera of the *Financial Times*, "This is an incredible industry. It's never been as good.... I think about the challenges that the industry faces in relation to digital delivery, and I get really excited. I still get a real kick out of running this group—and I'll be around for a while."

# Sources

Associated Press, July 10, 1995; November 16, 1995.

Associated Press State & Local Wire, January 17, 2003.

*Billboard,* July 23, 1994, p. 1; July 1, 1995, p. 1; July 15, 1995, p. 3; December 9, 1995, p. 6; June 20, 1998, p. 1; July 4, 1998, p. 1; December 23, 2000, p. 1; July 19, 2003, p. 1; October 25, 2003, p. 7.

*BusinessWeek,* June 20, 1994, p. 176.

Business Wire, February 21, 1991; July 11, 1994; June 23, 1998.

*Daily News* (New York), June 1, 1998, p. 30.

*Financial Times* (London, England), June 11, 1998, p. 35; January 7, 2003, p. 8; January 7, 2003, p. 10.

*Music Business International,* February 1997, p. 17.

*Music Week,* October 25, 2003, p. 4.

*New York Times,* June 22, 1995, p. D1; June 24, 1998, p. D8.

*Variety,* June 22, 1998, p. 7.

—*A. Petruso*

# Morrissey

© Ethan Miller/Reuters/Corbis

## Singer and songwriter

Born Steven Patrick Morrissey, May 22, 1959, in Manchester, England; son of Peter Aloysius (a security guard) and Elizabeth (Betty) Ann (a librarian; maiden name, Dwyer) Morrissey. *Education:* Attended Stretford Technical School, Stretford, England, 1975-76.

**Addresses:** *Record company*—Attack/Sanctuary Records Group, Sanctuary House, 43-53 Sinclair Rd., London W14 ONS, England, website: http://www.sanctuaryrecordsgroup.com. *Website*—Morrissey Official Website: http://www.morrisseymusic.com.

## Career

Worked as civil-service clerk, hospital porter, record-store salesman, c. 1976; singer, songwriter with the Smiths, 1982-88; solo artist, 1988—; released solo debut *Viva Hate*, 1988; released solo albums throughout 1990s; released *You Are the Quarry*, 2004.

**Awards:** O2 Silver Clef Award, 2004; *Mojo* Icon Award, 2004.

## Sidelights

From his debut as lead singer of the Smiths in the early 1980s, Morrissey has been—to critics and fans alike—an enigma. Although his hearing is fine, he often wears a hearing aid; his eyesight, on the other hand, is poor, but he cannot stand wearing his contact lenses on stage. This self-proclaimed "prophet for the fourth gender" has hinted at being gay, but prefers to discuss his celibacy, dismissing strictly defined sexual orientation as too limiting of people's potential. Morrissey's subtle, sardonic wit constantly confuses those interviewers who probe too far, making it particularly difficult to tell who the real Morrissey is: the morose and lonely lyricist or the passionate and engaging performer.

Steven Patrick Morrissey was born on May 22, 1959, in Manchester, England. Son of Peter, a night security guard, and Elizabeth, a librarian, Morrissey recalls his childhood as being morbid, with undercurrents of violence, elements later reflected in his often humorously black lyrics. His parents divorced when he was 17. "I literally never, ever met people," he told James Henke in *Rolling Stone*. "I wouldn't set foot outside of the house for three weeks on a run." To *Spin* magazine, Morrissey admitted, "There was no sense of frivolity in my young life at all, ever. There was no such thing as going crazy, or getting drunk, or falling over, or going to a beach.... Everything in my life was just hopelessly premeditated."

Morrissey passed the days reading, writing pages of poetry, and listening to music. "The power of the written word really stung me, and I was also entirely immersed in popular music... [Actor James

Dean and nineteenth-century Irish wit Oscar Wilde] were the only two companions I had as a distraught teenager. Every line that Wilde ever wrote affected me so enormously. And James Dean's lifestyle was always terribly important. It was almost as if I knew these people quite intimately and they provided quite a refuge from everyday slovenly life," he revealed to *Rolling Stone*'s Henke. Morrissey also found refuge in the feminist writings of Susan Brownmiller and Molly Haskell, as well as the "terribly gloomy" and "terribly embittered" British novelist Charles Dickens. Where music was concerned, Morrissey lost himself in mid-1960s British pop hits and later, the androgynous glitter rock of the New York Dolls and David Bowie.

Morrissey left school at 17. Jobs as civil-service clerk, hospital porter, and record-store salesman did not interest him past the first paycheck. It was guitarist Johnny Marr's 1982 invitation to join a band that finally got him out of the house. Within months, the Smiths burst onto the British music scene. As the result of several BBC radio broadcasts, the band landed a contract with Rough Trade Records along with an impressive and enthusiastic following—this even before the release of their debut album, *The Smiths*. *Stereo Review*'s Steve Simels referred to the album as "mostly midtempo love ballads with a not-so-subtle homoerotic ambiguity.... Morrissey has a vocal style that manages to walk the tightrope between being affectingly plaintive and cloyingly sensitive." With the 1985 album *Meat Is Murder* entering the British charts at number one and going gold within a week, the Smiths had made their mark. Writing for the *Nation*, Frank Rose described their sound as "a difficult but strangely compelling amalgam of American blues and British folk set to a spinning beat.... Morrissey doesn't sing with the tune, he sings all around it, and the resulting tension is as hypnotic as it is disorienting." The release of 1986's *The Queen Is Dead* further deepened their impression on the music world. Johnny Rogan, author of *Morrissey & Marr: The Severed Alliance*, hailed them as the most critically acclaimed and musically accomplished ensemble of the decade.

Yet, by the time *Strangeways, Here We Come* was released, in 1988, the Smiths had disbanded; Marr had decided to work with other artists, and the group simply dissolved. What would become of Morrissey was a mystery to critics who assumed he would be nothing without Marr. "The general opinion was that once Johnny Marr unplugged that umbilical cord I would just kind of deflate like a paddling pool," Morrissey told *Spin*'s Steven Daly. Mark Peel, for example, declared in *Stereo Review*, "Morrissey seemed headed over the abyss."

Morrissey defied them with his first solo release, *Viva Hate*. *Melody Maker* called the album "implausi-

bly fresh: the music's breathing again, free of a certain stuffiness and laboriousness that had set in seemingly irreversibly in the Smith's twilight period." *Stereo Review*'s Peel wrote of the singer's triumph, "Morrissey's band may have deserted him, but fortunately for us, his muse didn't." However, reviews for his second solo release were not as kind. Rachel Felder of *Rolling Stone* characterized his second release, *Bona Drag*, as "a choppy compilation of British B sides." Although critics on both sides of the Atlantic appeared to dismiss this collection, in a not-so-favorable *Melody Maker* review, Dave Jennings did concede that "Morrissey still asks awkward questions, gets under skins, touches nerves."

Critics seemed to lose faith in Morrissey with the 1991 release of *Kill Uncle*. Excerpts from several *Melody Maker* reviews clearly define their position: "devoid of magic, melodies and memorability"; "Morrissey revelling in mundanity"; "such a tragic, turgid pathetic record one can only assume it's an act of spite"; and finally, "Morrissey's future probably lies in America.... Over there, [it] was critically acclaimed, his gigs were received rapturously and he even made it onto the *Johnny Carson Show*." And although a bigger American audience was discovering Morrissey through *Kill Uncle, Rolling Stone* felt it "only hints at the achievement of the earlier album.... What *Kill Uncle* lacks is the musical coherence, let alone the stick-in-your head charisma, that would lend the album the consistency of the singer's previous work.... [I]t plays more like a fragmented collection of polished studio outtakes than a finished album."

*Melody Maker* was correct in noting that reception of Morrissey in Britain and the United States diverged. The most notable example of this being—no matter how critics and fans rave—Morrissey just cannot get a hit in America. "As far as I can tell, any fool can have a hit record in America—except me," he lamented to David Browne in *Entertainment Weekly*. "I don't want to be the biggest star in the universe, but I do feel deliberately slighted." He could sell out New York City's Madison Square Garden, but he couldn't get a spot on MTV. "Everything I've achieved, I've earned, and nobody has handed it to me, and that kind of existence is hard to understand for the music industry. They don't understand the language of being your own person. Don't get me wrong, I wouldn't change it. But I just feel anger, because when you repeatedly do things against what seems like all the odds there comes a time when the size of your audience should be recognized and you should be treated accordingly," he complained to *Spin*'s David Thomas.

Morrissey's fans would certainly be the first to point out this glaring omission on the pop charts; they are an almost unnervingly ardent group. The singer's love of Oscar Wilde had prompted him to carry flowers in concert, which in turn inspired fans to heap the stage with his favorite, gladiolus. Dozens of fanzines devote their pages to "Mozz," as they call him, and fans regularly almost crush him when they practice the traditional concert group hug. Describing a Morrissey concert, Bill Flanagan of *Musician* called it "strange, the wimpy kids stood on their chairs and pumped their fists in the air and screamed and the wimpy singer ripped off his shirt. All the people who usually mock the big hairy-chested rock show had a big hairy-chested rock show of their own. It was touching. Like the Special Olympics." When Morrissey does meet his fans outside the concert hall, wrote *Spin*'s Thomas, "he treats them with kindness and consideration. He talks to them, hugs them, and bashfully accepts the flowers, books, and little presents that they always want to give him."

"So why is Morrissey held a rock hero in the hearts of half the population of England's disaffected bohos and America's freshman dorms?" asked *Musician*'s Flanagan. Partly because of his overwhelming fan identification and partly because "Morrissey, who in his lyrics, on his albums and in his interviews shows self-immolating weariness with the insensitivity of the world, comes alive in concert as a stomping, rocking, posing, sweating, handsome and scream-inducing star."

Morrissey's fans were at last vindicated in 1992 with the release of *Your Arsenal*; although *they* had never given up hope in his ability, his critics were beginning to. "But on *Your Arsenal*," wrote Jeremey Helligar in *People*, "he pulls back from the brink of self-parody and delivers some of his strongest tunes yet ... bless his bummed-out soul." Mark Coleman of *Rolling Stone* called *Arsenal* "the most direct—and outwardly directed—statement he's made since disbanding the Smiths. Buoyed by the conversational grace of his lyric writing, Morrissey rides high atop this album's rip-roaring guitar tide.... His penchant for maudlin balladry held firmly in check by taut arrangements and riff-driven melodies ... *Your Arsenal* is stockpiled with the rock and roll equivalent of smart bombs: compact missives that zoom in on their targets with devastating precision. The repercussions last long after the rubble is cleared." According to *New York Times* contributor Jon Pareles, "The band can also strut and stomp with the brawn and moxie of a rockabilly band. The contrast between the introversion of Morrissey's smooth, vibrato-rounded croon and rock's brashest tradition only heightens the piquancy, and Morrissey knows it."

Morrissey continued releasing a steady stream of material through the mid-nineties, but only 1994's *Vauxhall and I* elicited the same excitement as *Your Arsenal*. A single from *Vauxhall and I*—"The More You Ignore Me, the Closer I Get"—played on MTV and reached the top 50 singles chart, introducing the singer to an American audience. Bolstered by his success in the United States, Morrissey moved from Dublin to Los Angeles where he began work on a new album for Mercury in 1996.

If fans had greeted Morrissey's *Kill Uncle* with anger, they greeted 1997's *Maladjusted* with indifference. "The last album was not a showstopper," Morrissey recalled to Marc Spitz in *Spin*. "The sleeve was dreadful. I look like a mushroom or a leprechaun. It was designed by the record company, and they were collapsing." Following the album, the singer dropped out of public view (with the exception of sightings at Libertines and Sex Pistols' concerts) for the next seven years. During this period he devoted a great deal of time to People for the Ethical Treatment of Animals (PETA) and working in coordination with the Los Angeles Animal Police.

In 2004 Morrissey returned to the music scene with the release of *You Are the Quarry*. Speaking of his long absence, he told *Spin*'s Spitz: "It was very frustrating. But I absolutely believe in fate and I knew that it would end. I felt like I was being carried along by something, and perhaps it's all the better that there was a gap." Critics and fans, meanwhile, warmly embraced the new album, calling it a return to form. "At its best," wrote Allison Stewart in the *Washington Post*, "it pulls off the near-impossible trick of being both a good wallow and a sharp stick in the eye. Even at its worst, it's simply irreproducible, the rare record that's actually about something." Morrissey launched a tour in support of the album, which included an appearance at Radio City Music Hall in New York City. In reviewing that appearance, Frank Scheck of the *Hollywood Reporter* declared that the singer was "in fine voice and as bitterly ironic as ever."

Morrissey claims to know a lot; he is notorious for his forthright opinions: "Michael Jackson has outlived his usefulness," he said in *People*, "Prince and Madonna are of no earthly value whatsoever." While he's fond of British singer-songwriter Paul Weller and Prefab Sprout's Paddy McAloon, he told *Entertainment Weekly* that "I certainly think Britney Spears is ... the devil. The way she projects herself and the fact that she is so obviously vacuous. I think it's such a shame that she became so influential to very small children. Most of the faces I see on the covers of American music magazines are just dreadful—people with nothing to offer the world at all."

"Many people underestimate [rock] as a force; this is dramatically wrong," Morrissey told *People*. "It is the last refuge for young people; no other platform has so much exposure." It is a platform on which Morrissey will more than likely remain. Life, as well, will apparently continue much as it has before; he told *Spin*'s Thomas, "The day always ends the same way, with exactly the same scenario. I'm closing the door and putting the lights out and fumbling for a book. And that's it. I find that very unfortunate, but then, I could have a wooden leg."

## Selected discography

### Solo albums

*Viva Hate,* Sire/Reprise, 1988.
*Bona Drag,* Sire/Reprise, 1990.
*Kill Uncle,* Sire/Reprise, 1991.
*Your Arsenal,* Sire/Reprise, 1992.
*Beethoven Was Deaf,* EMI, 1993.
(Contributor) *Alternative Energy,* Hollywood/ Greenpeace, 1993.
*Vauxhall and I,* Sire/Reprise, 1994.
*Southpaw Grammar,* Sire/Reprise, 1995.
*Maladjusted,* Mercury, 1997.
*You Are the Quarry,* Attack/Sanctuary, 2004.

### With the Smiths

*The Smiths,* Rough Trade, 1984.
*Hatful of Hollow,* Rough Trade, 1984.
*Meat Is Murder,* Sire, 1985.
*The Queen Is Dead,* Sire, 1986.
*The World Won't Listen,* Sire, 1987.
*Louder Than Bombs,* Sire, 1987.
*Strangeways, Here We Come,* Sire, 1988.
"Rank," Sire, 1988.

## Sources

### Books

Rogan, Johnny, *Morrissey & Marr: The Severed Alliance,* Omnibus Press, 1992.

### Periodicals

*Advocate,* July 16, 1991.
*Billboard,* May 7, 1988; June 22, 1991.
*Cash Box,* November 16, 1991.
*Entertainment Weekly,* August 14, 1992; October 16, 1992; May 21, 2004.
*GQ,* April 2004.
*Hollywood Reporter,* October 12, 2004, p. 45.
*Los Angeles Times,* November 3, 1991.
*Melody Maker,* September 12, 1987; February 20, 1988; January 7, 1989; February 4, 1989; April 15, 1989; April 22, 1989; May 26, 1990; November 3, 1990; May 4, 1991; October 5, 1991; December 21, 1991.
*Musician,* May 1988; June 1991; December 1992.
*Nation,* August 3, 1985.
*New York Times,* July 15, 1991; July 17, 1991; July 21, 1991; February 23, 1992; September 22, 1992.
*People,* June 24, 1985; August 19, 1991; October 5, 1992.
*Pulse!,* April 1993.
*Rolling Stone,* June 7, 1984; October 9, 1986; May 19, 1988; December 15, 1988; August 23, 1990; August 22, 1991; October 29, 1992; January 21, 1993.
*Spin,* April 1990; July 1990; February 1991; April 1991; November 1992; April 2004.
*Stereo Review,* October 1986; July 1984; July 1985; July 1988; October 1988.
*Time,* May 31, 2004.
*Village Voice,* April 5, 1988; May 3, 1988; July 12, 1988; July 18, 1989; April 2, 1991.
*Washington Post,* May 19, 2004, p. C05.

Additional information for this profile was obtained from a Sire/Reprise Records press release on *Kill Uncle,* 1991.

—*Joanna Rubiner and Ronnie D. Lankford, Jr.*

# Mos Def

© Terry Kane/ZUMA/Corbis

## Actor and rap artist

**B**orn Dante Terrell Smith, December 11, 1973, in Brooklyn, NY; son of Abdul (Abi) Rahman and Sheron (Umi) Smith.

**Addresses:** *Record company*—Geffen Records, 2220 Colorado Ave., Santa Monica, CA 90404.

## Career

**A**ctor on television, including: *God Bless the Child* (movie), ABC, c. 1988; *You Take the Kids*, CBS, 1990-91; *The Cosby Mysteries*, NBC, 1994; *NYPD Blue*, ABC, 1997; *Brooklyn South*, 1997; *Spin City*, 1998; *Carmen: A Hip- Hopera* (movie), MTV, 2001; *My Wife and Kids*, ABC, 2002; *Chappelle's Show*, Comedy Central, 2003-04; *Something The Lord Made* (movie), HBO, 2004; *Lackawanna Blues* (movie), HBO, 2005. Album releases include: *Mos Def And Talib Kweli Are ... Black Star*, 1998; *Black on Both Sides* (solo), 1999; *The New Danger* (solo), 2004. Stage appearances include: *Topdog/Underdog*, Broadway, 2002. Film appearances include: *The Hard Way*, 1991; *Where's Marlowe?*, 1991; *Bamboozled*, 2000; *Monster's Ball*, 2001; *Showtime*, 2002; *Civil Brand*, 2002; *Brown Sugar*, 2002; *The Italian Job*, 2003; *The Woodsman*, 2004; *The Hitchhiker's Guide to the Galaxy*, 2005.

**Awards:** Black Reel Award for best actor in an independent film, for *The Woodsman*, 2005.

## Sidelights

**I**n the entertainment industry there are plenty of performers who dabble in both music and film. Few, however, move so fluidly between the two as actor-rapper Mos Def, who has been hot on both

scenes at nearly the same time. For example, during the first weekend of May of 2005, his sci-fi spoof *The Hitchhiker's Guide to the Galaxy* opened at number one at the box office, raking in $21.7 million in ticket sales. Not seven months earlier, his second solo hip-hop album, *The New Danger*, debuted at number five on the *Billboard* album chart.

Speaking to *New York* magazine's Chris Norris, *Hitchhiker* film director Garth Jennings described the Mos Def enigma this way: "He's got this odd quality about him. A Zen-like presence that can be cool and weird and everything all at once. He'll have hit records one moment, then doing some live jazz thing one evening, then doing furniture design, then appearing in terrific plays—he just struck me as this extraordinary bloke that doesn't seem to be tied by anything."

Mos Def was born Dante Terrell Smith on December 11, 1973, in the Brooklyn borough of New York City. The oldest of 12 kids (some sources say nine), Mos Def was raised by his mother, Sheron, whom he calls Umi, in Brooklyn's rough-and-tumble Roosevelt housing project. His father, Abdul Rahman, whom he calls Abi, lived in neighboring New Jersey. Growing up, Mos Def made the most of his surroundings. Speaking to Richard Cromelin of the

*Los Angeles Times,* Mos Def characterized his neighborhood as "a bright valley with dark prospects." He said he believed his neighbors were good people with bad habits. Early on, Mos Def decided he would work hard and make a better life for himself. At one time, Mos Def thought about becoming a doctor or a minister. Filled with initiative, he filled his spare time reading. "I wanted to be informed..... I had a curious mind, so I wanted to do things that activated that challenge," he told Cromelin. "I wanted to get involved, I didn't want to just sit around and accept my surroundings."

Mos Def made his stage debut in fifth grade in a production of Marlo Thomas's *Free to Be ... You and Me.* He loved the experience and when he reached high school, he enrolled at a New York City performing arts magnet school. When Mos Def was a freshman, he landed his first real acting gig, starring in an ABC movie of the week called *God Bless the Child* in the late 1980s. At the age of 16 he earned the part of Nell Carter's son on the sitcom *You Take the Kids,* which ran from 1990 to 1991. Fresh out of high school Mos Def earned a role on the short-lived 1994 TV show *The Cosby Mysteries.* He later made appearances on *NYPD Blue* in 1997 and *Spin City* in 1998. Mos Def landed a few other roles as well and during this time used the name Dante Beze. After high school, his mom worked as his manager.

Though Mos Def was earning sporadic film and television roles, he began turning his attention toward music, which had also been a childhood passion. Mos Def began writing rhymes in grade school, at first as a desperate act of survival. Speaking to *Entertainment Weekly*'s Daniel Fierman, Mos Def acknowledged that he was a small and nerdy child who could barely hold his own on the basketball court. "I was a 99-punch kid," he joked. "If you hit on me 100 times, I'd be like, 'Okay, now I'm gonna break you.' So I had to do somethin' to be able to just survive around my neighbors, you know?" Entertaining would-be bullies with his witty rhymes offered some form of protection. When he was ten years old, Mos Def was enthralled by rap group Run-DMC's song "It's Like That." From that moment on, hip-hop played a significant role in Mos Def's life.

In his early 20s, he changed his name to Mos Def, which is short for his favorite affirmation—"most definitely"—which was his typical response when friends asked him if he wanted to hang out. Around this time Mos Def launched his first group, called Urban Thermal Dynamics, along with his siblings. They signed with a local label but never produced a record. Mos Def, however, began to carve out a name for himself among the Brooklyn hip-hop scene. In 1995, he met De La Soul's lyrical genius Maseo and was invited to perform on De La Soul's album *Stakes Is High* on the track "Big Brother Beat" in 1996. Mos Def also sang on 1996's "S.O.S.," a song produced by da Bush Babees. This exposure led to a record deal with Rawkus Records. At the time, Mos Def was working at a Brooklyn bookstore called N'kiru Books, alongside another aspiring rapper named Talib Kweli. They spent their time browsing the literature and later became co-owners of the bookstore.

The pair also worked together creating rhymes and in 1998 released a political yet playful album called *Mos Def And Talib Kweli Are ... Black Star*; the space entity of the title is a cosmic phenomenon. It became a classic of the hip-hop underground. Just a year later, Mos Def released a solo album, *Black on Both Sides,* which had a jazzy, R&B flavor. The releases heightened Mos Def's notoriety and established him as a socially conscious, introspective, and insightful rap artist. In *Black on Both Sides,* which was certified gold, Mos Def makes references to the insults and injuries black men often feel at the hands of police officers. He also took time to question the amount of money allocated in the U.S. defense budget. The albums established Mos Def as a master of the art of conscious rap.

The reaction surprised Mos Def himself. "I was in L.A. right after the album came out and I'm on stage performing and I'm lookin' at people reciting words of the songs off the album," he told *Entertainment Weekly*'s Fierman. "And I'm like, 'Am I seein' this right? I know this record has not been out that long.'"

The albums created quite a buzz in the hip-hop world, but Mos Def left them behind to concentrate on acting once again. He earned roles in 2000's *Bamboozled,* which was directed by Spike Lee, 2001's *Monster's Ball,* starring Halle Berry, 2002's *Brown Sugar,* and 2004's *The Woodsman.* For his role in *The Woodsman,* Mos Def earned a Black Reel Award for best actor in an independent film.

All of the roles, though small, worked together to broaden and mature his acting skills. They also afforded him the opportunity to brush shoulders with industry heavyweights. In 2004 Mos Def established himself as a multidimensional actor in the HBO flick *Something The Lord Made,* playing pioneer heart surgeon Dr. Vivien Thomas. Mos Def earned critical acclaim for the role, along with Golden Globe and Emmy nominations.

In 2002 Mos Def became a theater star after landing on Broadway in a production of *Topdog/Underdog.* Starring in the production allowed him to work with renowned director George C. Wolfe in a play that won the author, Suzan-Lori Parks, a Pulitzer Prize. Mos Def starred opposite Jeffrey Wright in the two-man show with the duo playing con-artist brothers. Even Mos Def realized this was a turning point in his career. "Actors would give their eye-teeth to work with people of this level," Mos Def acknowledged to the *New York Times's* Robin Finn. "This is a major, major, major turning point, not just for me, but for the culture … [T]his is one of those rare instances where something of a high artistic order is like at ground level, at street level, where Jay-Z and Puffy have come to the theater, where kids are coming to Broadway to watch this play." He was proud to inspire fellow African Americans to attend the play.

The play also showcased some of Mos Def's unseen talents. In one act, he had to do a striptease to a James Brown piece while removing several stolen suits lifted as part of his day's work. The play itself was filled with gritty lyricism, and Mos Def, with his background in smooth rap-delivery, nailed the lines. The playwright herself could not have been more pleased. "What's really cool about watching Mos onstage is that there's such a freedom to him," Parks told *Rolling Stone's* Mark Binelli. "I'd guess it comes from a real inner strength—not a conceited-pride … but a strong heart-center, like you say in yoga. A warrior spirit." For Mos Def, rapping and acting are almost the same thing. "I enjoy telling a story with all that I have—my mind, my body," he told Ebonny Fowler of *Essence*. For him, it is about connecting with the crowd, whether he is singing or acting.

During his spare time between performances Mos Def worked on a recording with his band Black Jack Johnson, named after the first African-American boxing champion, Jack Johnson. The group is composed of artists from Living Colour, Bad Brains, and Parliament-Funkadelic. Mos Def wants the group to make an album that is hip-hop rock.

In October of 2004 Mos Def released his long-awaited second solo album, *The New Danger*. It debuted on the *Billboard* album chart at number five. One *Vibe* magazine reviewer called the album "explosive, creative, political, experimental, [and] soulful." The reviewer went on to say, "Lyrically, the *New Danger* has cemented Mos in the upper eschelon of wordsmiths and album makers in this art that we call rap." Overall, reviews were mixed. The album featured backup from his new band venture, Black Jack Johnson. One single from the album, "Sex, Love & Money," earned a Grammy nomination for best alternative/urban performance.

The year 2005 found Mos Def back on the big screen, this time in a lead role, playing alien journalist Ford Prefect in the sci-fi comedy *The Hitchhiker's Guide to the Galaxy*, based on the Dou-

glas Adams book of the same name. In a discussion with *Jet's* Marti Yarbrough, Mos Def said that he was excited about his clever, imaginative, and playful character. "I get a chance to play a character that transcends certain boundaries whether it be racial or cosmic. He's a character that could have been played by any actor, black or white. I'm just grateful that I got a chance to do it, and I'm really excited and interested to see how people are going to receive it."

In an interview for *Entertainment Weekly's* Must List in 2005, Mos Def said a new album was in the works. That year, he began filming the real-time action thriller, *16 Blocks*, which co-starred Bruce Willis. Also in 2005, a 20-foot-tall image of Mos Def was unveiled in Brooklyn outside the Restoration Plaza shopping center as part of a cultural heritage exhibit to honor noteworthy natives who have found success. By being part of the display, Mos Def's image helps remind others that they, too, can rise above their circumstances. "I respect Mos Def," Brooklyn resident Naim Martin told the *New York Times's* Jennifer Bleyer shortly after Mos Def's image appeared. "He shows that if you use your talent properly, you'll be all right."

## Selected discography

*Mos Def And Talib Kweli Are … Black Star*, Rawkus Records, 1998.
*Black on Both Sides*, Rawkus Records, 1999.
*The New Danger*, Geffen Records, 2004.

## Sources

### Periodicals

*Entertainment Weekly*, April 12, 2002, p. 32; June 24/July 1, 2005, pp. 96-97.
*Essence*, July 2002, p. 74.
*Jet*, May 2, 2005, pp. 58-62.
*Los Angeles Times*, November 28, 2004, p. E45.
*New York*, May 2, 2005, pp. 85-86.
*New York Times*, April 19, 2002, p. B2; March 20, 2005, p. 146; May 2, 2005, p. E2.
*Rolling Stone*, May 23, 2002, p. 51.
*Washington Post*, October 13, 2004, p. C1.

### Online

"Mos Def: Biography," VH1.com, http://www.vh1.com/artists/az/mos_def/bio.jhtml (April 23, 2005).
"Mos Def's New Danger," *Vibe*, http://www.vibe.com/modules.php?op=modload&name=News&file=article&sid =529 (April 23, 2005).

—*Lisa Frick*

# Brittany Murphy

## Actress

**B**orn November 10, 1977, in Atlanta, GA; daughter of Sharon Murphy (in advertising).

**Addresses:** *Office*—c/o Dimension Films, 375 Greenwich St., 4th Fl., New York, NY 10013.

## Career

**B**egan career as a child actor in television commercials. Television appearances include: *Drexell's Class*, 1991-92; *Murphy Brown*, 1991; *Kids Incorporated*, 1992; *Parker Lewis Can't Lose*, 1992; *Blossom*, 1993; *Almost Home*, 1993; *Sister, Sister*, 1994-95; *Frasier*, 1994; *Party of Five*, 1994; *Boy Meets World*, 1995; *Murder One*, 1995; *The Marshall*, 1995; *SeaQuest DSV*, 1995; *Double Jeopardy* (movie), 1996; *Nash Bridges*, 1996; *Clueless*, 1996; *Disney's Pepper Ann* (voice), 1997; *King of the Hill* (voice), 1997—; *David and Lisa* (movie), 1998; *The Devil's Arithmatic* (movie), 1999; *Common Ground* (movie), 2000. Film appearances include: *Family Prayers*, 1993; *Clueless*, 1995; *Freeway*, 1996; *Drive*, 1997; *The Prophecy II* (straight-to-video), 1998; *Bongwater*, 1998; *Phoenix* (straight-to-video), 1998; *Zack and Reba*, 1998; *Falling Sky*, 1998; *Drop Dead Gorgeous*, 1999; *Girl, Interrupted*, 1999; *Angels!*, 2000; *Trixie*, 2000; *Cherry Falls*, 2000; *The Audition*, 2000; *Summer Catch*, 2001; *Riding in Cars with Boys*, 2001; *Sidewalks of New York*, 2001; *Don't Say a Word*, 2001; *Spun*, 2002; *8 Mile*, 2002; *Just Married*, 2003; *Uptown Girls*, 2003; *Good Boy*, 2003; *Little Black Book*, 2004. Stage appearances include: *Really Rosie*, c. 1986; *A View from the Bridge*, New York, NY, 1997-98.

*Brendan McDermid/EPA/Landov*

## Sidelights

**B**lond screen vixen Brittany Murphy emerged as one of Hollywood's leading names after her appearance in the 2002 Eminem biopic *8 Mile*. Prior to that, Murphy had logged an impressive roster of rather tough roles, and earned high marks despite her lack of formal dramatic training. She segued easily from supporting parts to leading ones, though some of her films have tanked at the box office; critics seem to like the bit of edginess she brings to her characters. Writing in *Newsweek*, journalist Devin Gordon asserted that Murphy "has specialized in taking one-note parts and shaping them into memorable creations."

Murphy was born in 1977 in Atlanta, Georgia, and grew up an only child in a single-parent household. After her parents divorced when she was a toddler, her mother, Sharon, took her to New Jersey, where they had relatives. They settled in the town of Edison, and the young Murphy emerged as a born performer. Her mother struggled to make ends meet and pay for her dance classes as well. "Financially, I don't know how she swung it," Murphy said of her mom, who held various advertising and sales jobs, in an interview with *Marie Claire*'s David A. Keeps.

"But the most important thing she did was teach me that 'poor' is a state of mind—and that we were rich in love. It's been my mom and me against the world for as long as I can remember. And it still is."

Murphy had a hard time in regular school, she also told *Keeps*. "They made fun of my size, because I was always the shortest, and the clothes that I wore," she recalled. "I was picked on to death in school." Her first taste of fame came when she appeared in a community theater production at the age of nine, and was interviewed by the local television news outlet. She asserted that she hoped to become a film actress, work on Broadway, and become a singing star, too. "If someone had asked me when I was young what I wanted to be when I grew up, I would have said Madonna," she told *Cosmopolitan* writer Lesley Goober. "I hate to admit it, but I always wanted to be famous."

After appearing in television commercials for Pizza Hut and Skittles, the 13-year-old Murphy went to Los Angeles, California, with a chaperone to try to break into show business there. She endured many auditions, but did not land any parts at all. Depressed and distressed, she called her mother and asked her if they could just move there permanently. Sharon Murphy acquiesced, and just a week later Murphy was cast in her first role in *Drexell's Class*, a 1991-92 FOX series that also featured a young Jason Biggs. The sitcom starred Dabney Coleman as a disgraced stockbroker who becomes an elementary school teacher. Murphy played one of his two daughters, who try to help their dad in his drastic career transition.

After *Drexell's Class* was not picked up again by the network for the 1992-93 season, Murphy did not land another steady part until 1993, when she appeared in another short-lived series called *Almost Home*. The show was based on earlier sitcom, *The Torkelsons*, about a single mom in Oklahoma with three kids. The name change reflected a change of venue for the family, when they relocated to Seattle so that the mother can take a job as a nanny for the two children of an attorney. Murphy played one of the rich, spoiled new kids.

Murphy's breakout role came in the 1995 film *Clueless*, an Alicia Silverstone comedy. Loosely based on the plotline of the Jane Austen novel *Emma*, the film skewered Beverly Hills teens and their devotion to fashion and fun. Murphy was cast as Tai, the hapless, style-challenged pal whom Silverstone's character decides to make over. Murphy returned to the FOX Network in 1997 for a new animated series

that year, *King of the Hill*. She was the voice of Luanne Platter, and later said she modeled the beauty-school student's Texas twang on Jessica Lange's character in the 1994 film *Blue Sky*.

In 1997, a 20-year-old Murphy realized her Broadway ambitions when she appeared in a revival of an Arthur Miller play, *A View from the Bridge*. She starred in it alongside Anthony LaPaglia and Allison Janney, who played the aunt and uncle who have raised her as their own daughter. But LaPaglia's Eddie, a Brooklyn dockworker, finds himself pathologically attracted to Murphy's character, Catherine. When two young men, distant relatives from Italy, come to visit, Eddie becomes jealous and sets in motion a tragic chain of events.

A television executive who saw the Broadway play offered Murphy her next role, in the 1998 television film *David and Lisa*. The love story, set in a school for troubled teens, was a remake of an acclaimed 1962 film, and was produced by Oprah Winfrey's company. Murphy appeared alongside Lukas Haas, playing a girl who speaks only in rhyme. Ray Richmond reviewed it in *Variety* and, citing her earlier work in *Clueless*, termed her "terrific here as well, turning in sparkling work as a complex lost soul. She pulls off the difficult trick of blending coquettish sensuality with aimless angst, in the process supplying the film's true backbone."

Murphy was next cast in 1999's *Girl, Interrupted* alongside Winona Ryder and Angelina Jolie. The film, based on a true story, was set in a Massachusetts psychiatric hospital in the late 1960s. Murphy was riveting as Daisy, a fellow patient who keeps whole roasted chicken carcasses under her bed and talks about the apartment her father will pay for when she leaves the hospital. Shortly afterward, she was asked by *Interview*'s Graham Fuller about the difficulties in taking on such roles. "I don't take my characters home," she reflected, "but they stay inside you. I'm not eloquent talking about acting and I never intellectualize a script. Sometimes I just know how to do a character, but I don't know why. It's as if you know what the spirit of the person is, though not consciously, and everything else floats into you."

The number of roles began multiplying for Murphy after that point. In 2000, she appeared in *Trixie*, an Alan Rudolph film that starred Emily Watson, and went on to make a horror-flick spoof called *Cherry Falls* that was not released in theaters. She also appeared in another little-seen work, the female cop-caper *Angels!*. The following year proved a bit more rewarding: she had a supporting role in the Freddie Prinze Jr. movie *Summer Catch,* and turned in a solid performance as the teenage best friend of Drew Barrymore in *Riding in Cars with Boys.* Next, writer-director Ed Burns cast her as a likable waitress who tries to extricate herself from an affair with a married man in *Sidewalks of New York,* and she chilled moviegoers with her portrayal of a razor-wielding psychiatric patient in the Michael Douglas thriller *Don't Say a Word.* Douglas played a New York City psychiatrist whose young daughter is kidnapped, and the ransom involves a jewel heist and a murder-gone-awry. Bent on vengeance, the kidnappers give the doting father just a day to unlock the secret, to which only Murphy's disturbed character can provide the clues to solve.

Murphy took another memorable part as a member of a circle of methamphetamine addicts in the 2002 dark comedy *Spun.* That same year she also appeared in the immensely successful Eminem biopic, *8 Mile.* She was cast as Alex, the love interest and aspiring model who betrays the working-class rapper. There were rumors that she and Eminem were romantically involved off the set as well, to which her co-star, whose real name is Marshall Mathers, would reply to press inquiries by delivering her famous line from *Don't Say a Word*: "I'll never tell."

After the success of *8 Mile,* Murphy began winning more leading roles. She starred in *Just Married,* a ditzy romantic comedy that paired her with heart-throb Ashton Kutcher. They play newlyweds who have married despite vastly dissimilar backgrounds and interests, and set off on a predictably disastrous European honeymoon. Murphy and Kutcher also began dating off-screen, but only after the film had wrapped. There was certainly chemistry beforehand, though: when *Cosmopolitan*'s Goober asked Murphy about her vision of a dream wedding, she replied that the one in that film "will always be my first wedding, and Ashton will always be my first husband … [W]e both had meltdowns before we walked down the aisle. I was crying hysterically in my trailer because my mom wasn't there. I didn't want her to miss the wedding in case I never got married again!" While the film was dismissed by critics, it did respectable numbers at the box office.

Murphy also starred in *Uptown Girls* in 2003, which critics trounced on. She was cast as a young New York City party girl who learns that her accountant has embezzled the small fortune left to her when her father, a rock legend, died in a plane crash with her mother. To make ends meet, Murphy's character must take a job as a nanny to the daughter of a brittle record executive. Her charge, played by Dakota Fanning, is a decidedly serious and no-nonsense youngster, but the pair manage to bring out each other's better halves.

In 2004, Murphy appeared in another quickly vanished box-office disaster, *Little Black Book.* She played the nosy girlfriend of Ron Livingston (*Sex and the City*), a worrier who suspects he may be seeing his ex-girlfriends. When he departs on a business trip, she snoops through the PDA (personal digital assistant) he mistakenly left behind. Her co-worker at the schlock-shock television show encourages her to phone some of the exes listed and use her skills as a producer to interview them for a possible show.

Murphy was slated to appear in *Sin City,* scheduled for 2005 release, a noir story that put her alongside a roster of all-star acting names, including Elijah Wood and Benicio del Toro. She was also doing another voice-over, this time for a project titled *Happy Feet* in which she served as a singing penguin. Though critics have not always liked the fare in which she appeared, Murphy usually earns positive reviews. *Film Journal International* writer David Noh commented that she remains "perhaps too distinctive a talent to be squeezed into a leading-lady mold," and noticed "something a bit raffish and unseemly about her raspy voice, thin physique, and huge, dissipated-looking features in that tiny face." Noh compared her instead to Ann-Margret, the kittenish lead in several films from the 1960s. *Entertainment Weekly* critic Owen Gleiberman, on the other hand, asserted she could be a younger Meg Ryan. "Up until now, she has made a calling card of her baby-doll lewdness," Gleiberman declared, "but if Murphy wants a future in mainstream romantic comedy, she appears to have the chops for it."

Realizing her final ambition, to make a record, Murphy spent much of 2004 in the studio. There are rumors that she has appeared, uncredited, on singles from more than one rap act, but she refuses to divulge which ones. Known for her boundless energy and affectionate enthusiasm in person, Murphy works with Dress for Success, a charity organization that helps women prepare to return to the job market after difficult times. For the *Marie Claire* article, Keeps accompanied her to one event where she spoke with the women who were receiving some new job-interview clothes and grooming tips. Listening to their stories, Murphy said she felt a kinship with them. "I was always told, 'You'll never be in movies—you're not talented enough, you're not pretty enough,'" Keeps quoted Murphy as saying to them. "It hurt, but it was ammunition, fuel for my fire."

## Sources

*Cosmopolitan,* June 2003, p. 236.

*Entertainment Weekly,* February 5, 1993, p. 43; July 14, 2000, p. 54; October 5, 2001, p. 110; October 12, 2001, p. 54; January 17, 2003, p. 54; August 22, 2003, p. 110; June 25, 2004, p. 119; August 13, 2004, p. 60.

*Film Journal International,* September 2003, p. 36.

*Interview,* May 2000, p. 152; October 2002, p. 60; December 2002, p. 100.

*Marie Claire,* September 2003, p. 122.

*Newsweek,* November 4, 2002, p. 56.

*New Yorker,* November 11, 2002.

*People,* November 2, 1998, p. 127.

*Time,* July 31, 1995, p. 65.

*Variety,* December 15, 1997, p. 68; October 26, 1998, p. 79.

—*Carol Brennan*

# Andrew S. Natsios

**Administrator for the U.S. Agency for International Development**

**B**orn September 22, 1949, in Philadelphia, PA; son of Basil and Eta Natsios; married Elizabeth; children: Emily, Alexander, Philip. *Education:* Georgetown University (bachelor's degree); Harvard University Kennedy School of Government (master's degree in public administration), 1979.

**Addresses:** *Office*—U.S Agency for International Development, 1300 Pennsylvania Ave. NW, Washington, DC 20523.

## Career

**M**assachusetts House of Representatives, 1975-1987; executive director, Northeast Public Power Association of Milford, Massachusetts, 1987-89; director of USAID Office of Foreign Disaster Assistance, 1989-91; assistant administrator, USAID Bureau for Food and Humanitarian Assistance, 1991-93; vice president, World Vision Inc., 1993-98; secretary for administration and finance, Commonwealth of Massachusetts, 1999-2000; chief executive officer, Massachusetts Turnpike Authority, 2000-01; administrator, U.S. Agency for International Development, 2001—.

**Awards:** Massachusetts Municipal Association Legislator of the Year, 1978; Massachusetts Association of School Committees Legislator of the Year, 1986; Citizens for Limited Taxation Legislator of the Year, 1986.

*AP/Wide World Photos*

## Sidelights

**A**ndrew S. Natsios is administrator of the U.S. Agency for International Development (USAID). He served in the Massachusetts State Legislature from 1975 to 1987, and has held various offices at USAID, with the state of Massachusetts, and with World Vision, a Christian organization. He is the author of numerous articles on foreign policy as well as two books. He served for 23 years in the U.S Army Reserves and retired from military life in 1995 with the rank of lieutenant colonel. He is also a veteran of the Gulf War.

Natsios' grandparents were Greek immigrants who found work in the mills of Massachusetts; he grew up in Holliston, Massachusetts. His grandparents were avid Democrats, as was his mother, Eta; however, Natsios followed the lead of his father, Basil, who was politically conservative.

Natsios earned a bachelor's degree at Georgetown University. While at Georgetown, he joined the Army ROTC. He went on to receive a master's degree in public administration from Harvard University in 1979. While still at Harvard, he began his political career, serving in the Massachusetts House of Representatives from 1975-1987. He was named Legislator of the Year by the Massachusetts Municipal Association, the Massachusetts Association of School Committees, and the Citizens for Limited Taxation. He also served as chair of the Massachusetts Republican State Committee for seven years.

His service to the Republican party did not go unnoticed, and in 1989, under the first Bush administration, Natsios was appointed director of the US-AID Office of Foreign Disaster Assistance. The job proved to be a baptism by fire, since during his first week in office, he had to respond to the Chinese massacre of protestors in Tiananmen Square. Other incidents occurring during his tenure included the worst train accident in Soviet history and a massive famine in the Sudan. Despite these challenges, or perhaps because of them, he found that he loved the work. He remained with USAID until 1993, when the Clinton Democrats came into power. Natsios then became vice president of World Vision, a Christian antipoverty organization. A few years later, he was appointed Massachusetts secretary for administration and finance.

In 2000, Natsios was called in to become chief executive of the "Big Dig," a mammoth project in downtown Boston, Massachusetts. The largest public works project in American history, the Big Dig involved burying a major highway under downtown Boston in order to reduce traffic congestion in the city. The project had gone over its budget and suffered from disorganization. Natsios focused on five areas of the project's management system: procurement, personnel, financial management, computer services, and administrative services. He replaced an 18-year-old contract-writing system with a new electronic one, and replaced paper with computers in hiring and other areas. He did not particularly like this job, as his true interest was in foreign affairs.

In May of 2001, President George W. Bush brought Natsios back to foreign affairs when he offered him the position of administrator of USAID. Natsios faced various minor controversies, such as his decision to combat AIDS by doubling the number of condoms provided to poor countries where the disease was rampant. This decision brought fire from other Republicans who were against birth control. On the other hand, Natsios was attacked by some liberals when he commented that rural Africans had no concept of time.

These troubles appeared trivial when terrorists attacked the United States in September of 2001. The United States subsequently attacked Afghanistan, where many terrorists were hiding, and Natsios was the first U.S. civilian official to arrive in Afghanistan after the attacks. The country suffered from decades of war, disease, poverty, illiteracy, and the threat of famine. In response, Natsios moved a large amount of money through USAID in a very short time to help with these problems.

Natsios also faced a heavy load of responsibility in administering part of the rebuilding of Iraq after the United States' destruction of that country that began in 2002. He commented to Kris Frieswick in *CFO*, "No one's life was at risk on the Big Dig. There are millions of lives at stake in Iraq." In addition, Natsios' predecessors in the job had not been as interested in management and finance as he was, so some of the administrative systems within the agency were not efficient.

In his new position, Natsios quickly stirred up controversy. Critics charged that he gave preferential treatment to Bechtel Group Inc., which won the contract to rebuild Iraq's infrastructure. Natsios had previously worked with Bechtel, which was one of the contractors that worked on the Big Dig. According to *CFO*'s Frieswick, Natsios said that Bechtel had been working on the Big Dig for more than a decade when he entered the project. He also said that when bidding for the project, Bechtel had put in the lowest price of seven bidders and also had the highest technical score. To further counteract the criticism, Natsios ordered a review of the bidding process by the Inspector General. However, in an interview on ABC's *Nightline*, Ted Koppel pointed out that when Natsios took over, Bechtel was under investigation for excessive charges of more than a billion dollars in the Big Dig. Natsios told Koppel that when he took the job, he fired his predecessor and was asked by the governor of Massachusetts to "clean up the mess." However, he did not comment on the charges against Bechtel, repeating that the company had the highest quality and the lowest bid.

In addition to criticizing his choice of Bechtel in the rebuilding process, some observers were also angry because the lucrative rebuilding contracts in Iraq were only given to American companies, and because the contracts were awarded before any attacks on Iraq ever took place, leading some to believe that the decision to bomb Iraq was tied into the fact that certain companies could profit greatly from the war. In the *Nightline* interview, Natsios admitted to Koppel that the planning for Iraq's postwar reconstruction began six months before the country was attacked. He also said that because of the logistics of the planning process, it was easier to remain with American companies. He also claimed that the entire rebuilding process would cost American taxpayers no more than $1.7 billion, a figure that was met with widespread skepticism.

Despite these controversies, Natsios focused on improving USAID. In the *Foreign Service Journal*, Natsios told Ben Barber that he wanted to reform the agency's "personnel, the financial management system, computers, the procurement system and the system of grants and contracts." He also noted that the agency needed to look carefully at why some foreign aid projects worked and others did not: "If there are venal and predatory governments, foreign aid can keep people alive but the country won't develop," he told Barber.

In an interview with *Newsweek*'s Michael Hirsh, Natsios commented on the perception that the United States was not doing enough to help other countries, noting that the nation applies only 0.1 percent of its gross domestic product, or $10 billion per year, to foreign aid. If the United States spent, for example, 0.7 percent, this would amount to $70 billion. Natsios said that if this occurred, "We would be bigger than all the banks put together. It would distort the economies in the Third World to an extraordinary degree."

Despite the criticisms that are inevitable with any high-profile position, Natsios loves his job. He told Chris Black in *Boston Magazine*, "On any given day at (USAID), you save hundreds of thousands of people's lives. It must be nice on your deathbed to look back on your life and realize you did something."

## Selected writings

*U.S. Foreign Policy and the Four Horsemen of the Apocalypse,* Center for Strategic and International Studies, 1997.
*The Great North Korean Famine,* U.S Institute of Peace, 2001.

## Sources

### Books

*Carroll's Federal Directory,* Carroll Publishing, 2004.

### Periodicals

*CFO,* June 2003, p. 80.
*Foreign Service Journal,* September 2002, pp. 20-27.
*Newsweek,* December 30, 2002/January 6, 2003, p. 8.

### Online

"Andrew Natsios," World Food Prize, http://www.worldfoodprize.org/Symposium/speakers/natsios.htm (August 3, 2004).
"Biography of Andrew S. Natsios," USAID, http://www.usaid.gov/about_usaid/bios/bio_asn.html (August 3, 2004).
*Biography Resource Center Online,* Gale Group, 2003.
"Interview with Andrew Natsios," *Nightline,* http://www.mtholyoke.edu/acad/intel/iraq/koppel.htm (August 3, 2004).
"Our Man in Afghanistan," *Boston Magazine,* http://www.bostonmagazine.com/ArticleDisplay.php?id=124 (August 3, 2004).

*—Kelly Winters*

# Ryan Newman

## Professional race car driver

**B**orn December 8, 1977, in South Bend, IN; son of Greg and Diana Newman. *Education:* Purdue University, bachelor's degree in vehicle structural engineering, 2001.

**Addresses:** *Office*—c/o Penske Racing, 136 Knob Hill Rd., Mooresville, NC 28117.

## Career

**B**ecame a champion midget racer at the age of 17; raced USAC sprint cars and won USAC sprint car Silver Crown championship, 1999; signed to Roger Penske's NASCAR team, 2000.

**Awards:** Michigan State Midget Championship, 1993; AAMS Midget Series Rookie of the Year, 1993; USAC Midget Rookie of the Year, 1995; USAC Silver Crown; USAC Silver Bullet National Championship, 1999; Winston Cup Rookie of the Year, 2002; Speed Channel Driver of the Year, 2003; Quarter Midget Hall of Fame.

## Sidelights

**N**ASCAR driver Ryan Newman started driving when he was four years old and has not stopped since. He is the first driver to win all three USAC divisions and was named Winston Cup Rookie of the Year in 2002.

Newman's interest in driving may have come from his father, Greg, who had wanted to drive race cars but never had the chance to do so. He ran an auto repair business, and encouraged his son to become a race car driver. Newman's mother also loved racing—the couple drove all night after their wedding in order to make it to a race the next day. When Newman was four and a half years old, he drove in his first quarter midget race. The sport filled his childhood; his father told Stephen Cannella in *Sports Illustrated* that throughout his childhood, Newman "didn't do much of anything else." By the time he was seven years old, his family saw that he did have a talent for driving, and Newman was a champion midget racer by the age of 17. In all, he had more than 100 victories, and was eventually inducted into the Quarter Midget Hall of Fame.

After graduating with honors from South Bend La-Salle High School in 1996, Newman studied engineering at Purdue University but at the same time, continued to race. He raced USAC sprint cars during the 1999 season, and won the USAC Silver Bullet Series title, making him the first driver to win all three USAC divisions (midget, sprint, and Silver Bullet). Although he had previously only competed in open wheel racing, he decided during the 1999 season that he wanted to race in NASCAR on the Winston Cup circuit.

This was not an easy goal to reach, since in order to drive in NASCAR, Newman had to learn to drive stock cars. However, because he had displayed such potential as a driver, he was signed to Roger Penske's team in 2000. In that year, he drove in five ARCA stock car races, winning three of them. At one race, the EasyCare 100, he led every lap after setting an all-time stock-car qualifying mark at Loew's Motor Speedway. In the same year, he also competed in some NASCAR Busch Series and Winston Cup races.

In 2001, Newman continued to drive part-time for Penske. He drove in the ARCA, Busch, and Winston Cup races, winning his first Busch race in Michigan in August of that year. In addition, he won the ARCO 200 at Daytona International Speedway. During this season, he concentrated on gaining experience, improving his driving, and getting a feel for the length of the races and the way the heavier stock cars handled. However, his wins gave him confidence that he was on the right track.

In August of 2001, he graduated from Purdue, having earned a degree in vehicle structural engineering. That next year was Newman's official Winston Cup rookie year; he continued to drive for Penske and was sponsored by Alltel in the No. 12 Ford. The first half of the season was difficult for him, but he did manage to win the New Hampshire 300. He also set a record for the number of poles won in a rookie year, winning at least six. He won the Winston in Charlotte, North Carolina, and was named the Winston Cup Rookie of the Year. According to the NASCAR website, Newman said of this honor, "It was unbelievable. I feel like I have some of the best people you could ask for on my team. No matter what I've done or what mistakes I've made, they've always stood behind me."

In 2003, the Penske team switched from Ford cars to Dodge vehicles, and Newman drove the No. 12 Dodge for Penske. He was not hurt in a rollover crash at Daytona, and did not finish above seventh place until he won the Samsung/Radio Shack 500. He went on to win the MBNA 400, the Tropicana 400, and the GFS Marketplace 400. In all, he won twice as many races as any other driver did that year, and came close to taking the Winston Cup, ending only 311 points behind champion Matt Kenseth.

One thing that sets Newman and his team apart from many other teams is their use of computerized technology. While other teams make mechanical adjustments to their cars and then test them on the track, Newman and his crew chief, Matt Borland, who is a mechanical engineer, use computer simulations, wind tunnel tests, and computer modeling to examine what effect various changes might have on the Dodge. As veteran driver Bobby Labonte told *Sports Illustrated*'s Cannella, "Nowadays the cars have gotten so much more sophisticated. There are a lot of smart people working on race teams lately. People are looking at all different ways to win." The Penske shop, in Mooresville, North Carolina, has nine engineers on staff.

Perhaps because of this technology, Newman has become known for his amazing fuel economy, which has allowed him to win more races. For example, in the Banquet 400 at Kansas Speedway in October of 2003, Newman ran a poor qualifier and started 11th. However, he raced the last 117 miles on a single tank of gas, allowing him to pass competitors who had to stop for a fill-up. Most teams drive 4 miles per gallon; Newman, by precisely calculating his car's performance, drove 5.3 miles per gallon in that 177-mile stretch.

Newman's crew also praises his down-to-earth ability to work on cars and the fact that unlike some drivers, he does not mind getting his hands dirty. Mechanic Chad Norris told *Sports Illustrated*'s Cannella, "If he had to, Ryan could work on his own car. He's pretty mechanically inclined."

After his stellar year in 2003, Newman told Monte Dutton in *Auto Racing Digest*, "I've gained a lot of experience in the past year and a half. I think that has made a big difference for me personally. There are things you learn at one race track that you can carry over to the other, and there are things that are still specific to certain tracks." On June 20, 2004, Newman won the DHL 400 in Brooklyn, Michigan, and on September 26 of that year, he won the MBNA American 400 in Dover, Delaware.

Newman, who does not usually discuss his personal life with the press, told Bob Myers in *Circle Track* that although he has many female friends, he is not looking for a relationship and no intention of marrying. He would rather focus his attention and energy on racing. And, he commented, "By the time I'm 40, people will be living to 120. So I can get married when I am 60 and have kids when I'm 80." When Newman is not racing, he spends much of his free time tinkering with old cars, including a 1928 Ford Roadster, a 1939 Hudson, and a 1957 Thunderbird.

## Sources

### Periodicals

*Auto Racing Digest*, December 2003, p. 22.
*Circle Track*, April 2002, p. 66.

*Sporting News,* May 19, 2003, p. 42; November 3, 2003, p. 14.
*Sports Illustrated,* December 17, 2003, p. 74.

**Online**

*Biography Resource Center Online,* Gale Group, 2003.
"Driver profile," NASCAR.com, http://www.nascar.com/drivers/dps/rnewman00/bio.html (August 3, 2004).

"Newman dominates Dover; Gordon takes lead," *Sports Illustrated,* http://sportsillustrated.cnn.com/2004/racing/09/26/bc.car.nascar.dover.ap/index.html (October 11, 2004).
"Newman gets first win of season," *Sports Illustrated,* http://sportsillustrated.cnn.com/2004/racing/06/20/bc.car.nascar.michigan.ap/index.html (October 11, 2004).

*—Kelly Winters*

# Sean O'Keefe

NASA/Bill Ingalls

**Chancellor at Louisiana State University and former NASA admistrator**

Born Sean Charles O'Keefe, January 27, 1956, in Monterey, CA; son of Patrick Gordon (a U.S. Navy nuclear submarine engineer) and Patricia Carlin O'Keefe; married Laura Jean McCarthy, October 7, 1978; children: Lindsey, Jonathan, Kevin. *Education:* Loyola University, B.A., 1977; Syracuse University, M.P.A., 1978.

**Addresses:** *Office*—Louisiana State University, Office of the Chancellor, 156 Thomas Boyd Hall, Baton Rouge, LA 70803.

## Career

Presidential Management Intern, 1978-80; member, Senate Appropriations Subcommittee on Defense, 1981-86; staff director, Senate Appropriations Subcommittee on Defense, 1986-89; comptroller, Department of Defense, 1989-92; chief financial officer, Department of Defense, 1991-92; acting Secretary of the Navy, 1992; professor of business and federal policy, Pennsylvania State University and Syracuse University, 1992-2000; deputy director, Office of Management and Budget, 2000-02; administrator, National Aeronautics and Space Administration, 2002-04; chancellor, Louisiana State University, 2005—.

**Awards:** U.S. Distinguished Public Service Award, 1993; Syracuse University's Chancellor's Award for Public Service, 1999; Department of the Navy's Public Service Award, 2000.

## Sidelights

Sean O'Keefe received a cool welcome from the National Aeronautics and Space Administration (NASA) when he was named administrator of the agency in 2001. O'Keefe, a hard-nosed accountant and federal budget analyst, had no scientific background. Agency insiders feared he would dampen the pioneering spirit of NASA with his legendary sleight-of-hand budget cuts. No one could deny, however, that NASA was a financial and managerial mess when O'Keefe took over. Because of chronic cost overruns in the billions, the agency had lost its credibility with Congress, which was reluctant to keep handing over money. O'Keefe, however, got costs under control and improved fiscal management, opening the door for a new mission involving human exploration.

"There were skeptics when he was named," House Science Committee Chairman Sherwood L. Boehlert told the *Washington Post*'s Eric Pianin and Guy Gugliotta. "The claim was that he was a budgeteer, not a rocketeer, [but] he earned the respect of the workforce and the space community." In 2004, however, it was announced that O'Keefe was resigning to take a position at Louisiana State University.

O'Keefe was born on January 27, 1956, in Monterey, California, to Patrick and Patricia O'Keefe. His father was a nuclear submarine engineer with the U.S. Navy. Consequently, O'Keefe spent his childhood on military bases located all over, from Hawaii to Connecticut. He grew up in an Irish-Catholic family that was no stranger to politics. O'Keefe's great-grandfather was once mayor of New Orleans and his grandfather a judge. Older brother Patrick O'Keefe told the *New York Times'* Eric Schmitt that O'Keefe, early on, displayed a natural, personal charm, even when engaged in heated debates. "We had very, very long family dinners on Sunday where Sean developed a fine sense of getting his point across without leaving any visceral animosity." This skill would serve him well later on in Washington, D.C.

As a teenager, O'Keefe lived in Connecticut and attended North Stonington's Wheeler High School, graduating in 1973. After high school, O'Keefe headed to Loyola University in New Orleans. At Loyola, O'Keefe got his first taste of politics and his first try at managing a public budget when he was elected student government president and charged with supervising an annual campus activities budget of $50,000. To support himself during his college years, O'Keefe installed sheetrock and did other construction work. He also developed a fondness for bass fishing and alligator hunting on the Louisiana bayous. O'Keefe graduated from Loyola in 1977, then studied public administration at Syracuse University's Maxwell School of Citizenship and Public Affairs. He earned his master's degree in 1978.

On October 7, 1978, O'Keefe married Laura Jean McCarthy. That same year, he landed a job as a presidential management intern. From the start, O'Keefe worked on budgetary matters. One of his first tasks involved scrutinizing troop pay for the White House's Office of Management and Budget. He also helped the Navy put together its submarine budget.

By 1981, O'Keefe was working his budgetary magic as a member of the Senate Appropriations Subcommittee on Defense. His outstanding number-crunching talents put him in the spotlight and in 1986, O'Keefe, just 30, became staff director of the committee, which was ruled over by Washington insiders much older than him. In 1989, O'Keefe was appointed Department of Defense comptroller. He was the youngest person to ever hold that position in the Pentagon. In 1991, he became the Pentagon's chief financial officer, too. In this capacity, O'Keefe managed a staff of more than 130 accountants and

analysts charged with assessing military needs and figuring out how to make them work within budget limitations. "Not exactly sexy stuff," O'Keefe said in summing up his duties for the *New York Times'* Schmitt.

At the Pentagon, O'Keefe worked hand-in-hand with Department of Defense Secretary Dick Cheney, who later became vice president of the United States. O'Keefe logged 14-hour days, seven days a week, while preparing the defense budget, which in 1992 was about $280 billion. O'Keefe became an expert in military budgets, programs, and weapons systems.

As the Department of Defense's leading accountant and hatchet man, O'Keefe upset a lot of people on Capitol Hill when he trimmed programs, particularly when he felt like something had outlived its need. O'Keefe's influence led to the cancellation of the Navy's A-12 attack plane, as well as the M1-A1 tank and F-15 fighter. "There's no question that in a time of dramatic decline ... the least popular guy around has been the bean counter, but that comes with the territory," O'Keefe told the *New York Times'* Schmitt. O'Keefe said a lot of Congressional leaders blamed him instead of rationalizing why their program was no longer needed.

In July of 1992, President George H.W. Bush named O'Keefe acting Secretary of the Navy after secretary H. Lawrence Garrett III resigned amidst the infamous Tailhook scandal. The incident involved the sexual harassment of 26 women at a convention of naval aviators in Las Vegas in 1991. Just 36, O'Keefe became the second-youngest Navy secretary in history and was charged with the tall order of restoring discipline to the Navy in terms of budget, missions, and behavior.

O'Keefe received mixed reviews for his job performance as Navy secretary. He worked to restore order quickly, handling the resignations of two admirals involved in the Tailhook cover-up. Some service members, however, said he failed to restore confidence in the establishment.

Co-workers, however, lauded O'Keefe's performance and compassion for others. O'Keefe often worked long hours, but instead of making aides stay until he finished, O'Keefe took it upon himself to lock up the office so staffers could go home. This was a big change from how previous Navy secretaries had acted. Another time, when Navy officials visited New Orleans, O'Keefe insisted on driving since it was his hometown; previous Navy secretaries always used chauffeurs.

After Bush lost the 1992 presidential election to Democrat Bill Clinton, O'Keefe retreated from Washington along with other Republican officials as the new administration took over. He found work as a professor of business and federal policy, first at Pennsylvania State University and later at Syracuse, his alma mater.

O'Keefe returned to Washington eight years later after Republican Texas Gov. George W. Bush won the 2000 presidential election. Bush offered O'Keefe the job of deputy director of the Office of Management and Budget. In this capacity, he oversaw the preparation and management of the federal budget. He also represented the administration during heated spending negotiations with Congress.

O'Keefe wrangled with the federal budget until December of 2001, when Bush appointed him NASA administrator. Because O'Keefe's background lay in budgets and public policy, not science, agency insiders questioned the appointment. It was clear, however, that Bush had appointed O'Keefe because he wanted fiscal responsibility restored within the agency. "It's great for the nation and it's great for NASA," Syracuse professor Robert McClure told the *Post-Standard*'s Mark Libbon. "The problems with NASA are not engineering, but in public and political management and they just haven't functioned well. Sean has a long and effective track record at being able to manage difficult public and political environments."

During his swearing-in ceremony in January of 2002, O'Keefe acknowledged the awesome mission before him. Speaking to the crowd, O'Keefe said he was "astonished that I have been given this dream assignment," according to an article on SpaceRef.com. O'Keefe also noted that his children had been teasing him, telling him he could not possibly handle the job, saying, "'Hey, Dad, I thought you had to be smart to run NASA. You know, you're NO rocket scientist, Dad.'"

During O'Keefe's first weeks on the job, he proved himself to be a different kind of administrator when he invited reporters to breakfast and let them fire away with questions. This openness with the press was something new. According to Keith Cowing and Frank Sietzen's book *New Moon Rising,* reporters dogged O'Keefe with questions about whether a budget man should be running a technical branch of government. Asked if he had a burning passion to be NASA's top dog, O'Keefe replied that "whatever you do, you do it right."

Facing intense scrutiny, O'Keefe went to work. There were sore feelings to mend. During his time in the budget office, O'Keefe had been critical of the agency. Now he had to win over the trust of its employees. O'Keefe made himself open and available to NASA staffers by visiting all ten NASA centers early on. He also broke from decades of tradition by leaving the executive office doors unlocked. *New Moon Rising* author Cowing, a former NASA employee and longtime critic of the agency, had nothing but praise for O'Keefe's first year on the job. "If you're looking for something negative to say about O'Keefe, you end up making fun of his haircut," he told *U.S. News & World Report*'s Thomas Hayden. "So far there's just nothing else."

Things went smoothly the first two years. Then, in February of 2003, the space shuttle Columbia broke apart over Texas, killing the seven astronauts on board. Instantly, O'Keefe came under scrutiny—and blame. After all, he was not a technical guy, so he had no business running the agency, critics said. Once again, O'Keefe turned on the charm to maintain credibility for himself and the department. In handling the situation, O'Keefe won praise for his openness. In the month that followed the tragedy, he willingly testified before Congress several times and made himself accessible to both lawmakers and reporters. The agency did, however, limit public access to internal documents and e-mails concerning the tragedy, which upset some critics.

Confidence in O'Keefe, however, remained high. "I think he's conducting himself well," Senate science, technology, and space subcommittee chairman Sam Brownback told *Washington Post* staff writers Pianin and Gugliotta. "The biggest [danger] in something like this is to try to hide or slow the release of information. He's not doing that. He's getting it out as soon as possible."

In the months that followed the disaster, O'Keefe replaced eleven of 15 top shuttle managers. Some Congressional leaders thought this was good enough, while others said O'Keefe simply shuffled people around or let them retire without being held responsible for their missteps that led to the disaster.

Columbia Accident Investigation Board consultant Karlene Roberts told the *Orlando Sentinel* that O'Keefe had to be careful in his reprimands. "It's very tricky what the balance is between accountability and creating a system in which people feel they can speak up from the very bottom." Roberts said that many lower-level engineers were too intimidated to voice their concerns. O'Keefe was working to change that.

Despite the tragedy, O'Keefe showed potential for rebuilding NASA into a bolder, more aggressive agency. During his tenure, O'Keefe restored fiscal credibility to the agency by getting its budget under control. With the new credibility came more responsibility. In January of 2004, President George W. Bush unveiled a new vision for the space agency with a focus on human exploration. Bush specifically called for returning humans to the moon and launching them on toward Mars. O'Keefe also got approval to develop the first all-new human orbiter in three decades.

The new vision—and the new trust—were reflected in the budget. In 2004, NASA received a budget increase of $469 million, whereas the agency had seen decreases in six of the previous eight years. Despite his lack of technical skills, O'Keefe had a huge impact on NASA because of his budgetary prowess.

On December 13, 2004, O'Keefe announced his resignation from NASA. He had accepted an offer from Louisiana State University to be its chancellor. He was expected to assume the new position in early February of 2005.

## Sources

### Books

Cowing, Keith L. and Frank Sietzen, *New Moon Rising: The Making of America's new Space Vision and the Remaking of NASA,* Apogee Books, 2004.

### Periodicals

*New York Times,* May 7, 1992, p. D1.
*Orlando Sentinel,* September 13, 2003.
*Post-Standard* (Syracuse, NY), November 15, 2001, p. A2.
*San Diego Union-Tribune,* September 30, 2004, p. B2.
*Science,* January 30, 2004, pp. 610-19.
*U.S. News & World Report,* May 5, 2003, p. 44.
*Washington Post,* March 23, 2003, p. A6.

### Online

"LSU Board of Supervisors votes to approve the hiring of O'Keefe," LSU News, http://app1003. lsu.edu/unv002.nsf/PressReleases/PR3005 (December 22, 2004).
"NASA Administrator Honorable Sean O'Keefe," NASA, http://www.nasa.gov/about/highlights/ AN_Feature_Administrator.html (November 1, 2004).
"Sean O'Keefe Sworn in Amidst the Rockets," SpaceRef.com, http://www.spaceref.com/news/ viewnews.html (November 1, 2004).
"Sources: NASA chief to resign," CNN.com, http:// www.cnn.com/2004/TECH/space/12/12/ okeefe.resign/index.html (December 14, 2004).

*—Lisa Frick*

# Rafael Palmeiro

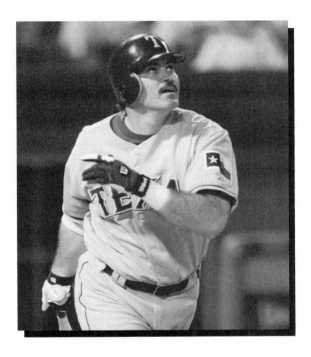

## Professional baseball player

**B**orn Rafael Corrales Palmeiro, September 24, 1964, in Havana, Cuba; married Lynne; children: Patrick, Preston. *Education:* Attended Mississippi State University.

**Addresses:** *Office*—Baltimore Orioles, 333 W. Camden St., Baltimore, MD 21201.

## Career

**S**igned with Chicago Cubs, 1986; traded to Texas Rangers, 1988; signed with Baltimore Orioles, 1993; returned to Rangers as a free agent, 1999; returned to Baltimore Orioles, 2004.

**Awards:** Gold Glove Award, 1997; Silver Slugger Award, 1998; Gold Glove Award, 1998; Associated Press Major League All-Star Team, 1999; Gold Glove Award, 1999; *Sporting News* Player of the Year, 1999.

## Sidelights

**R**afael Palmeiro (pronounced pahl-MARE-oh) is one of only 19 players in baseball history to hit 500 home runs. Throughout the end of the twentieth century and the beginning of the twenty-first, he has been one of the greatest players in the sport. From 1993 through 2002, Palmeiro hit 395 home runs, the third most in baseball history, only behind Sammy Sosa's 462 and Barry Bonds' 437. During that same period, Sosa was the only player to drive in more runs than Palmeiro, with 1,206 to Palmeiro's

1,154, and Sosa and Palmeiro are tied with the longest streak of 100-plus RBI seasons, with eight each. Surprisingly, however, Palmeiro has not been as well-known as these statistics might make him.

Palmeiro was born in Havana, Cuba in 1964, and had an excellent amateur career at Mississippi State University before moving to the major leagues. He signed with the Chicago Cubs in 1986, but after 1988, his first full year in the big leagues, he was traded to the Texas Rangers. Although he had a decent batting average, he had hit only eight home runs, which led to the Cubs concluding that he was not a strong hitter. Palmeiro told *Sports Illustrated*'s Josh Elliott that although this quick trade left him feeling bitter, like the Cubs had not given him a chance, "It was a wake-up call for me. I realized that I'd have to produce more runs to stay in the big leagues." In response, he began working out, lifting weights and strengthening his upper body, arms, and wrists. He also stopped swinging at pitchers' first strikes, preferring to wait for ones that would more reliably lead to good hits.

Despite all this hard work, when Palmeiro's contract ran out after the 1993 season, the Rangers traded him to the Orioles. Palmeiro was shocked by this, but made the best of it. "Those years in Baltimore were great," he told *Sports Illustrated*'s Elliott. While in Baltimore, he hit his 300th home run, and began dreaming of someday hitting his 500th.

In 1999, Palmeiro returned to the Rangers as a free agent, a move that he worked hard to get, since his wife, Lynne, and his sons, Patrick and Preston, were still living in Texas. By this time, all his hard work in Baltimore had paid off; while playing for the Orioles, he had hit a home run every 15.7 at bats, and with the Rangers he was able to continue that success. In addition, Palmeiro became a leader among his teammates; his leadership was based on the quiet strength of his personality as well as his knowledge of the game. In *Sports Illustrated,* Jeff Pearlman characterized Palmeiro as "sensitive, quiet, careful with his words." He quoted Palmeiro, who said, "I don't say things just to say them. But if I see a situation where I can help out, I do."

Palmeiro's success comes at least partly from his rigorous training regimen. When he does hitting drills, he swings bats with five-pound weights attached to them. He strengthens his knees and ankles in the off-season with deep-water running, and throughout the year, he spends many hours in the batting cage.

In *Sports Illustrated,* Elliott noted that one reason Palmeiro's career has remained relatively unnoticed is because on every team he played with, there was another player who received more media attention. With the Cubs, it was Ryne Sandberg; with the Rangers, it was Ruben Sierra and then Juan Gonzales; when Palmeiro signed with Baltimore, he was eclipsed by Cal Ripken. When he returned to the Rangers, he was overshadowed by the American League MVP season of catcher Ivan Rodriguez. Famed player Alex Rodriguez joined the Rangers two years later.

In addition, Palmeiro has never won an MVP award or finished above fifth place in the MVP voting, has never led the league in home runs or hit 50 in a season, and has never been voted to the All-Star Game starting lineup or played in a World Series. In response to these facts, Palmeiro told *Sports Illustrated*'s Elliott, "I've been damn lucky to play with the teammates I've had.... They've made me a better player. I just try to use it as a positive."

However, Palmeiro seems destined to become a much more notable figure. His status began to rise in 1997 and 1998, when he won Gold Glove Awards;

in 1998 he won the Silver Slugger Award as the best-hitting American League first baseman, and in 1999 he won another Gold Glove Award. Also in 1999, he was named the *Sporting News* Player of the Year in a vote by his peers.

On May 18, 2003, Palmeiro became the 19th player in baseball history to hit 500 home runs. During the game, he told *Sports Illustrated*'s Elliott, "I tried not to think about [hitting the 500th home run] too much, but it's hard not to when you have a sign that's about 600 feet long staring at you from behind the pitcher's release point." The sign in question read 499 HR RAFAEL PALMEIRO. At his final at-bat of a six- game home stand against the Toronto Blue Jays and the Cleveland Indians, Palmeiro took an inside fastball for a strike, hitting it high along the rightfield line. Initially he feared the crosswind would make the hit a foul, but it stayed true, taking Palmeiro into baseball history.

The sign that Palmeiro had tried to avoid looking at was immediately changed to read 500 HR RAFAEL PALMEIRO, fireworks filled the sky, and the crowd went wild. Palmeiro's family, gathered in a private box, cried with joy. Palmeiro, unaware of any of this, later told Elliott that he didn't remember anything after he rounded the first base. He also said that the achievement would not change who he was. "I've never been a guy who does any look-at-me stuff. I'm not fancy." He added that his role models were some of the most famous players of the past: "I look at videos of Mantle and Maris and DiMaggio—those guys weren't flashy. I don't try to attract attention."

According to Elliott, "If he plays three more years—as he expects to—Palmeiro ... has a good shot to join Hank Aaron as the only players with 3,000 hits, 600 doubles, and 500 home runs." Palmeiro told *Sports Illustrated*'s Elliott that he had a bigger goal: "As long as I keep my best shape for three or four more years, 600 [home runs] isn't at all out of the question. It's a matter of time."

In 2004, Palmeiro rejoined the Orioles with a one-year, $4.5 million free-agent contract with a club option for 2005. However, his batting average suffered in 2004, and he told Bruce Lowitt in the *Tampa Tribune,* "I'm frustrated because I feel like I'm not producing the way I should." He noted that although other players were having stellar seasons with the Orioles, "The rest of us need to step it up." The team's manager, Lee Mazzilli, told Joe Christensen in the *Grand Rapids Press,* "You want to see him do well. You're talking about a great ballplayer. You're talking about a Hall of Fame player. But this is also part of the job, I guess, the business and the personal."

Palmeiro finished the season with only 128 games; he needed to play in 140 games in order to trigger the $4.5 million option on his contract for 2005. While he could have gotten angry and left the team, Palmeiro decided he did not want to go to another team. On October 27, 2004, Palmeiro took a pay cut and accepted a one-year, $3 million contract. "I'm very happy. Otherwise, I wouldn't be returning. What happened last year is in the past. I'm not going to worry about it. I'm more concerned with moving forward," Palmeiro told *SI.com.* He further explained to *SI.com,* "I wanted to show the fans in Baltimore and [Orioles owner] Peter Angelos that I was serious when I said I wanted to end my career here and, if I'm fortunate enough to get elected to the Hall of Fame, that I want to go in as an Oriole."

## Sources

### Periodicals

*Grand Rapids Press,* September 12, 2004, p. C16.
*Sporting News,* September 13, 1999, p. 48; October 25, 1999, p. 10.
*Sports Illustrated,* April 25, 1994, p. 66; July 19, 1999, p. 46; May 19, 2003, p. 52.
*Tampa Tribune,* July 15, 2004, p. 4.

### Online

*Biography Resource Center Online,* Gale Group, 2000.
"Palmeiro signs one-year contract with Orioles," *SI. com,* http://sportsillustrated.cnn.com/2004/baseball/mlb/10/27/bc.bba.orioles.palmeiro.ap/index.html (October 28, 2004).

—*Kelly Winters*

# Violet Palmer

**Professional basketball referee**

Born c. 1964, in Compton, CA; daughter of James and Gussie Palmer. *Education:* Attended California State Polytechnic University, Pomona, CA.

**Addresses:** *Home*—Los Angeles, CA.

*Jeff Christensen/Reuters/Landov*

## Career

Coached high school basketball; referee for recreation leagues, high schools, and colleges; referee for the Women's National Basketball Association; began training to be a National Basketball Association referee, 1994; referee for National Basketball Association, 1997—.

## Sidelights

As a rarity in professional sports, a female referee, Violet Palmer had her critics when she began in the National Basketball Association in 1997. One of them was Charles Barkley. "This is a man's game. It should stay that way," said Barkley, then of the Houston Rockets, today an analyst with Turner Network Television, and under any circumstance one of the mouthier subjects in professional sports.

But later her first season, she encountered Barkley after working a game in Houston. "Violet, I was wrong about you. I apologize," he said. "You're all right with me." Barkley then pointed to the two male officials. "You're better than him and him," he said.

Out of uniform, Palmer looks unassuming, Vanessa Juarez wrote in *Newsweek*. "She reminds you of Sandra Bullock or Julia Roberts, a pal you'd like to hang out with. But once the curtain goes up, she's all business. Palmer's curtain is a basketball tipoff, her stage is the court and her craft is to make sure the ten giants stampeding around her aren't out of bounds. She keeps them in line with a stern poker face and an encyclopedic knowledge of the rules."

Palmer broke into the NBA as one of two female referees. (The NBA has since fired the other, Dee Kantner, for what it said was substandard performance; she now works in the Women's National Basketball Association). By then, Palmer's grounding in basketball was solid. She grew up in a sports family in the hard-edged Compton section of Los Angeles, played for two NCAA Division II women's basketball championship teams at California State Polytechnic University, Pomona (Cal Poly-Pomona), and worked her way up the ranks, from city recreation ball to NCAA Division I to summer pro men's league.

She credits her strong family background for giving her a start. "My friends say, 'Violet, you grew up in Compton, but your family was like Little House on the Prairie,'" she said, according to Referee.com. The daughter of James and Gussie Palmer, who have been married for more than 50 years, Palmer is one of four children. She held the point guard position at Compton High School, where she also played softball and ran track. She was captain for three years at Cal Poly-Pomona under the late coach Darlene May, and she helped the Broncos win national titles in 1985 and 1986. May also nurtured her interest in officiating.

Palmer briefly coached high school basketball but didn't like it. "Oh, my God, the kids needed so much attention," Palmer told Juarez. "I had migraines. I was just so tense and stressed out. I said, 'This ain't for me.'"

It took seven years, three fewer than the norm, for Palmer to get her first NBA assignment. By then she had a thick enough skin, a thorough grasp of the game and its rules, and enough experience at the lower levels. She took the floor with peers Bill Oakes and Mark Wunderlich on October 31, 1997—Halloween night—in Vancouver, British Columbia, as the Vancouver Grizzlies played host to the Dallas Mavericks. "I will never, ever forget the moment I put that jacket on and walked onto that floor," she said. "It was like, 'Wow, you're telling me I'm going to do this every single night!' It was more than nervous, I was going to pee in my pants."

"Her eyes were as big as saucers," Dallas player Michael Finley told *Sports Illustrated,* speaking about Palmer's first game. "I know she was as nervous as any of us players." Palmer was unwavering in her calls, and working as the "third official" took some of the pressure off. NBA vice president Rod Thorn after the game was praiseworthy. "She did her job, like the other two officials on the court," Thorn said. "The better she performs, the more anonymous she'll become."

Early in her career a player offered her a date if she changed a foul call against him, Palmer told Referee. com. "We can't go out on a date," she said. "And you still got the foul." Players and coaches stopped making sexist remarks, said Palmer, although fans were slower to accept her. Meanwhile, she earned

the admiration of her co-workers and supervisors. "She is very well liked amongst the staff," said director of officials Ronnie Nunn, a former peer of Palmer, in *Newsweek*. "They don't have to circle the wagons around her, either. She stands on her own, which is beautiful."

Palmer has not hesitated to eject a player when the situation called for it. In January of 2004, she tossed guard Raja Bell of the Utah Jazz for punting the ball, football-style, after Palmer ruled that Bell had shot after the buzzer sounded to end the first quarter. And she made a habit of evaluating her own performances, as well. She and her fellow officials have reviewed their performances on film after each game. After each game and a quick snack, the trio of referees has watched the game video until about 1 a.m., "a brutal routine they repeat as many as 75 times a season," Juarez wrote.

Palmer, who is single and lives in Los Angeles, said the most difficult part of her job is traveling 23 days a month during the eight-month season. Her next goal? Some playoff assignments, she told *Newsweek*. "Then they're really going to go, 'Wow, she has arrived.'"

## Sources

### Periodicals

*Deseret Morning News* (Salt Lake City, UT), January 23, 2004.
*Ebony*, February 1998.
*Newsweek*, March 8, 2004.
*Sports Illustrated,* November 10, 1997.

### Online

"Her Call," ESPN.com, http://insider.espn.go.com/insider/story?id=1511196 (December 21, 2004).
"Ultra Violet," Referee.com, http://www.referee.com/sampleArticles/2000/SampleArticle0100/samplisting.htm (December 21, 2004).

*—Paul Burton*

# Alexander Payne

© Neal Preston/Corbis

**Director and screenwriter**

**B**orn February 10, 1961, in Omaha, NE; married Sandra Oh (an actress), January 1, 2003 (separated). *Education:* Earned undergraduate degree from Stanford University, and M.F.A. from the University of California—Los Angeles, 1990.

**Addresses:** *Agent*—Endeavor Agency, 9701 Wilshire Blvd., 10th Flr., Beverly Hills, CA 90212-2020.

## Career

**S**igned to picture deal with Universal Studios based on his 50-minute graduate thesis film, *The Passion of Martin,* 1990; collaborated with screenwriter Jim Taylor on *Citizen Ruth,* 1996, *Election,* 1999, *About Schmidt,* 2002, and *Sideways,* 2004, all of which Payne also directed; also credited as screenwriter on *Jurassic Park III,* 2001.

**Awards:** New York Film Critics Circle award for best screenplay, 1999, for *Election,* and 2004, for *Sideways* (with Jim Taylor); *Sideways* won several other honors, including the best picture, best screenplay, best actor, and best supporting actor prizes from the New York Film Critics Circle Awards, the Academy Awards, and Writers' Guild of America prize for best screenplay based on material previously produced or published, and two Golden Globes from the Hollywood Foreign Press Association for best picture and best screenplay.

## Sidelights

**A**merican filmmaker Alexander Payne won his first Academy Award for *Sideways,* the darkly comic California road-trip story that was the surprise hit of 2004. The work was nominated in five Academy Award categories, and Payne and his screenplay co-author, Jim Taylor, took home one of the Best Screenplay statuettes. But Payne's films had long enjoyed top critical accolades for their darkly comic humor, credible characters simultaneously compelling and unlikable, and their ability to capture the more banal details of modern American middlebrow culture. Jack Nicholson, the star of Payne's third movie, extolled Payne's skills as a director and screenwriter. "Black humor is a tough sell," Nicholson told the *New York Times'* John Hodgman in a lengthy profile on the Nebraska-born maverick. "If you're not making essentially youthful films, you're taking chances. Alexander is a real throwback to the kinds of moviemakers I started with."

Born in 1961, Payne grew up in the Nebraska city of Omaha, which would become the integral setting for his first three films before *Sideways.* His parents were of Greek heritage, and the family name had been changed from "Papadopoulos." A good student, he earned his undergraduate degree from Stanford University, where he studied Spanish and history, and went on to film school at the University of California's Los Angeles campus but first had to choose between film and journalism, because he had also been accepted into another esteemed graduate program, the journalism school at Columbia University. He chose filmmaking over a career as a foreign correspondent, and when he graduated in 1990, his thesis film, *The Passion of Martin,* earned him notoriety for its bleak 50-minute chronicle of a photographer obsessed with a woman. Within a few weeks of its first screening at UCLA, Payne had been signed to a picture deal with Universal Studios.

From the start, Payne's moviemaking plans were greeted with some degree of skepticism in Hollywood. He had written a screenplay called "The Coward," about a middle-aged Nebraska man who leaves his wife and begins a journey of self-discovery, but Universal was deeply uninterested in committing to the project. Payne had better luck making his feature-film debut, though its subject matter was one Hollywood studios generally avoided: the debate over reproductive rights. In *Citizen Ruth,* released in 1996, Laura Dern played a glue-sniffing wastrel, pregnant for the fifth time, who is caught huffing patio sealant by the cops. She has already lost custody of her other four children for being an unfit parent, and this time, the judge makes Ruth an offer: if she terminates the pregnancy, the court will drop the charges. Anti-abortion activists step in to help, and so do pro-choice advocates, each of whom attempts to make the hapless Ruth their *cause celebre.* "Payne has a good eye for the character traits of zealots who feel the call to run other people's lives," assessed Roger Ebert in his *Chicago Sun-Times* review, and noted that the script's conclusion shows neither side—nor even Ruth—in a favorable light. "The movie illuminates the ways in which mainstream films train us to expect formula endings," Ebert reflected.

Payne set the film in Omaha partly because, as he explained to Hodgman in the *New York Times* article, "if you're trying to recreate life, the life that you best know is the one you grew up with. I hadn't seen the Midwest in a movie. I'd never seen it." By that, Payne meant the real Midwest, not the sanitized version depicted in most Hollywood films. He also returned to his hometown to shoot *Election,* a darkly satiric look at a high school student-government contest. He wrote the screenplay with

Jim Taylor, with whom he had also co-written *Citizen Ruth,* from a novel by Tom Perrotta that was actually set in New Jersey. Perrotta, in turn, based his story on 1992's three-way American presidential race.

A cult favorite of 1999, *Election* is a battle of wills between beloved high-school civics teacher Jim McAllister (Matthew Broderick) and desperate overachiever Tracy Flick (Reese Witherspoon). In contrast to the depressed, repressed "Mister M.," Tracy, noted *Cineaste*'s Thomas Doherty "has what he doesn't: a promising future. Chirpy, clipped, coiled like a rattlesnake, Tracy is that most-likely-to-succeed-and-[tick]-off-her-peer-group overachiever issued one-per-graduating class, the girl with complete homework, perfect hair, and sensible clothes who always thrusts her hand into the air like a Hitler salute when teacher asks a question." Prior to the election, Tracy had been involved in an affair with a teacher, McAllister's best friend, but emerged unscathed when it was discovered.

When Tracy runs unopposed for the presidency of the Student Government Association, Broderick's character convinces popular student-athlete Paul Metzler (Chris Klein) to run against her; Paul's loose-cannon sister, a closet lesbian, then enters the ring as the spoiler candidate when her girlfriend dumps her for Paul. In the end, Mr. M's career is ruined, like that of the shamed teacher's, but Tracy manages to enter the college of her choice, the ultimate goal of all her extracurricular activities.

*Election* earned such positive critical accolades—and an Oscar nomination for best adapted screenplay—that Payne was offered a slew of potentially big projects, including the first *Charlie's Angels* movie. He was uninterested, he told Liese Spencer in an interview that appeared in London's *Independent.* "It was a ton of money but I just couldn't do it." Instead he and Taylor adapted another novel, with some similarities to his "Coward" project from years before, and snagged Jack Nicholson as the lead. Released in 2002, *About Schmidt* was based on a novel by Louis Begley, which was actually set in the Hamptons, the posh summer resort part of Long Island populated by wealthy New Yorkers. In the novel, Schmidt was a Manhattan attorney at the end of his career, but in this case Payne and Taylor set the story in Omaha and had Nicholson's Schmidt as a recently retired insurance actuary. When he is suddenly widowed—and learns that his wife may have had an affair with his best friend—he sets off in a Winnebago to visit his daughter Jeannie (Hope Davis). Secretly, he hopes to prevent her marriage to waterbed salesman Randall Hertzel (Dermot Mulroney), and is drawn into the odd aging-hippie world of Randall's parents. Meanwhile, Schmidt writes long letters to the unseen Ndugu, a six-year-old Nigerian orphan boy he signed on to sponsor after capitulating to a television-commercial plea.

*About Schmidt* was chosen as the opening-night entry for the 2002 New York Film Festival, and earned both strong critical plaudits and good box-office receipts. The *New Yorker*'s film critic, Anthony Lane, noted that the film at first seems to have a self-discovery theme, but conceded that such a construct requires "a self to begin with, and Schmidt is hard to call. Is he a hollow man, or a fully fledged soul who has been plucked and spatchcocked by the attrition of modern life? It is to Payne's credit that the question arises at all, for not many directors can be bothered to approach what is still the most taxing of dramatic subjects."

Payne's next film would be his first to be set somewhere other than Omaha. *Sideways* generated an industry buzz when it debuted at film festivals in the fall of 2004, and won Payne critical accolades that hailed it as a masterpiece, a tour de force, and predicted that it would sweep the Academy Awards. Again, he and Taylor adapted the story from a novel, this one an unpublished work by Rex Pickett, which had been titled "Two Guys on Wine." Pickett never managed to find a publisher for his book—mirroring a subplot that nearly sinks one of the two leads in *Sideways*—and the road-trip buddy-tale about two men, nearing middle age, who head off for a weekend of golf and vineyard-hopping in California's Santa Ynez Valley, did not exactly appeal to Hollywood studio executives, either. Despite Payne's excellent track record, they balked at his plan to recreate Pickett's book for the big screen, and one studio even dangled a much larger budget if Payne would agree to let them suggest who would be cast. It was a game he was uninterested in playing along with any longer. "With *Election,* I had to first offer it to Tom Cruise and Tom Hanks, who were never going to take it in a million years," he revealed to *Entertainment Weekly*'s Josh Rottenberg. "That's a process I didn't want to repeat."

Because of Payne's reputation, several leading actors reportedly wanted one of the *Sideways* roles, but Payne cast Paul Giamatti—previously seen as Harvey Pekar in *American Splendor*—as the nebbish

Miles, a frustrated novelist and tedious wine snob, and Thomas Haden Church, who once starred on the sitcoms *Wings* and *Ned and Stacey,* as the callow Jack, a onetime soap opera actor about to marry. Miles takes Jack on a road trip north to celebrate his final weeks as a bachelor, and Jack plans to use the time to his maximum advantage. Jack also believes that all Miles needs to lift him out of his long-term, post-divorce funk is some female attention. They meet two women, one of them played by Sandra Oh, Payne's real-life wife, but the outcome is predictably disastrous.

The immense critical plaudits showered upon *Sideways* even inspired a *New York Times* article about why critics loved it so much, with one line of reasoning concluding that many critics—who might be characterized as a slightly nebbish, sometimes pedantic group—saw themselves in Miles. A review from the *New York Observer*'s Andrew Sarris was one example of the superlatives heaped upon Payne's latest project. "*Sideways* is quasi-Chekhovian in the moving vitality of its ever-hopeful prisoners exploring their lost aspirations. It could turn out to be the best English-language picture of the year." Stanley Kauffmann, the *New Republic* film critic, conceded the story had a couple of Hollywood-type attention-getters, but "otherwise, Payne's directing is alert, warm, patient. He knows that the surface must keep us interested until we go below it, and his confidence holds us." Writing in *Time,* Joel Stein called it "a quiet, sad, beautiful story about how ego obstructs work and love," while Lisa Schwarzbaum, the *Entertainment Weekly* critic, mused that "it's an intoxicating feeling when a movie excites and enlivens us like this—and there's a particular giddiness to be had in thinking about what movies can (but don't often) do for one's soul after imbibing such a fine vintage."

*Sideways,* though Payne's first to be filmed outside of Omaha, still managed to capture that grittier, decidedly un-picture-perfect side of life. In this case, details included a visit to Miles' mother's home, a typical southern California condo development, and an entire town, Solvang, built to resemble an authentic Danish village. His next project, however, would return him to his home state. *Nebraska* was another road-trip movie, this one about a Montana man who is convinced he has won the Nebraska lottery and convinces his son to drive him there to claim the winnings.

Payne has sometimes criticized the American entertainment industry in interviews, and spoken of his deep respect for the bygone zenith of the 1970s, when "studios [financed] personal, risky and political cinema," he wrote in a manifesto-style piece that appeared in *Daily Variety* in 2004. "For 25 years we've largely been making not films but rather glorified cartoons which can be as easily digested in Omaha as on a bus in Thailand; films whose principal message is, 'We need your money to keep our stock price up.'" He clarified his own expectations of the medium, asserting that he hoped for American "cinema that is intelligent, uplifting, and human, and that serves—as good art should—as a mirror, not as an impossible or fraudulent consumer-oriented projection."

## Selected writings

### Screenplays

*The Passion of Martin* (thesis film), 1989.
(With Jim Taylor) *Citizen Ruth*, Miramax, 1996.
(With Taylor) *Election*, Paramount, 1999.
(With Taylor) *About Schmidt*, New Line, 2002.
(With Taylor) *Sideways*, Fox Searchlight, 2004.

## Sources

*Back Stage West*, October 14, 2004, p. 12.
*Chicago Sun-Times*, April 4, 1997.
*Cineaste*, Fall 1999, p. 36.
*Daily Variety*, September 8, 2004, p. S7.
*Entertainment Weekly*, October 29, 2004, p. 36, p. 46; December 3, 2004, p. 43.
*Esquire*, January 2003, p. 20.
*Independent* (London, England), September 24, 1999, p. 14.
*New Republic*, November 15, 2004, p. 24.
*New Yorker*, December 16, 2002, p. 106.
*New York Observer*, October 25, 2004, p. 23.
*New York Times*, December 8, 2002, p. 88; January 2, 2005, p. AR18.
*Time*, October 25, 2004, p. 90.

—*Carol Brennan*

# Holly Robinson Peete

*Fred Prouser/Reuters/Landov*

## Actress

Born Holly Robinson, September 18, 1964, in Philadelphia, PA; daughter of Matthew (a television actor, producer, and writer) and Dolores (a school teacher, television station publicist, and talent manager) Robinson; married Rodney Peete (a professional football player), June 10, 1995; children: Ryan Elizabeth, Rodney Jackson, Robinson James. *Education:* Sarah Lawrence College, undergraduate degree in French and psychology, 1986.

**Addresses:** *Office*—HollyRod Foundation, 9250 Wilshire Blvd., Ste. 300, Beverly Hills, CA 90212. *Website*—http://www.hollyrobinsonpeete.com/.

## Career

Actress in television, including: *Kidsworld,* c. 1975; *This Is Your Life,* 1975; *21 Jump Street,* FOX, 1986-91 (also theme song singer); *Hangin' With Mr. Cooper,* ABC, 1992-97; *For Your Love,* NBC, 1998, then The WB, 1998-2001; *One on One,* 2001-02; *Like Family,* The WB, 2003-04. Television movies include: *Dummy,* 1979; *Killers in the House,* 1998. Miniseries include: *The Jacksons: An American Dream,* 1992. Film appearances include: *Lorea and the Outlaws,* 1985; *Howard the Duck,* 1986. Signed recording deal with Atlantic Records, 1988; performed in night clubs and at Club Med; founded the HollyRod Foundation, 1997; designer of maternity clothing and spokesperson for Mervyn's, 2003—; author of *Get Your Own Damn Beer, I'm Watching the Game,* 2005.

## Sidelights

With the help of her talent manager mother, Holly Robinson Peete has had a successful acting career, appearing in a succession of television series. Peete's career was launched on the FOX hit drama *21 Jump Street,* and she also appeared on the situation comedy *Hangin' With Mr. Cooper* and several television programs. In addition to acting, Peete longed for a singing career, though she was never able to match the success she found in acting. She did, however, use her fame for charitable causes, including the founding of the HollyRod Foundation.

Born on September 18, 1964, in Philadelphia, Pennsylvania, she is the daughter of Matthew and Dolores Robinson. Her father was a local television writer and producer, while her mother worked as a school teacher, and later for a Philadelphia television station doing public relations. In 1968, Peete's father nabbed a career-defining role in a new PBS children's show, *Sesame Street.* Matthew Robinson was cast as Gordon, a friendly grown-up on the show. He later returned to producing and writing for television, including work on *The Cosby Show.*

After her parents divorced in the early 1970s, Peete moved with her mother and older brother, also named Matthew, to Malibu, California. The transition from Philadelphia to Malibu was not easy for the family, but Dolores Robinson's career was enhanced, which later helped when Peete pursued acting. Dolores Robinson found employment at a talent agency and went on to become a manager for actors and actresses. Some of them quite high profile; one of her first clients was actor LeVar Burton. Dolores Robinson was one of the few black women to succeed in a business dominated by white men.

Peete already had entertainment industry ambitions of her own. As a small child, she had tried to be on *Sesame Street* with her father, but repeatedly flubbed her line and her appearance was never completed. After Peete moved to Malibu, where she attended Malibu Park Junior High School, she had her own job on television. At the age of eleven, Peete worked for the children-oriented show *Kidsworld* as a celebrity correspondent. She interviewed many actors and actresses for the show. Peete wanted to have her own career as an actress and singer, but her parents insisted she finish school.

Though Peete excelled in school, she had a few acting roles as a child and teenager. In 1975, she had a guest-starring role in *This Is Your Life.* Four years later, her mother also helped her win a role in a television movie called *Dummy.* The movie starred Burton, and Peete played his character's sister, Genettia Long.

While Peete's mother helped her secure roles, she also helped her daughter understand the business by allowing her to come to the sets of television shows. Peete told Margena A. Christian of *Jet,* "This gave me an unbelievable advantage to understand what show business was and how I needed to be and remain a professional when I got my shot. It was a real edge. I was watching what people did wrong and right. Ultimately this contributed to the longevity I've had on television. I'm real proud of that."

After graduating from high school, Peete entered Sarah Lawrence College in New York. She majored in psychology and French, and could speak four languages. During her time as an undergraduate, she spent a year abroad at the Sorbonne in Paris, France. After she graduated in 1986, she considered attending graduate school and perhaps working in languages for the U.S. State Department. However,

her love of acting contributed to her decision to give an acting career a chance for a few months first. Within a short time, Peete found roles on a television series and in two films, and thoughts of graduate school were left behind.

When Peete decided to try and establish her acting career, it was with her mother's help. Dolores Robinson ended up acting as her manager for much of her career. Peete appeared in her first film, *Lorea and the Outlaws,* in 1985. In 1986, Peete played a member of a band Cherry Bomb in the box office disaster *Howard the Duck.* These two films did not do much to further her career, but a role on a hit television series did.

Shortly after Peete's college graduation, she was cast on *21 Jump Street,* one of the first casting calls she had attended. On the show, she played Judy Hoffs, one of several young detectives who went on undercover investigations in high schools. Originally, the role called for a white actress, but Robinson impressed producers enough to win the role despite her relative inexperience as an actress. The show became one of the first hits on FOX, then a young fourth network. Though Peete was learning much about acting, she was not sure she still wanted to be an actress. Peete left the show in 1991, before the end of its run.

One reason Peete was not yet committed to an acting career was her continued interest in singing. She provided the vocals to the theme song of *21 Jump Street.* During the show's run, she also signed a recording deal with Atlantic Records in 1988. Although she recorded tracks under the contract, she was not happy with the results and nothing was ever released. She continued to sing in nightclubs in New York City and at Club Med, and once also appeared with Lionel Hampton.

Of her problems in establishing a singing career, Peete told Aldore Collier of *Ebony,* "What I found was that in Hollywood, once you establish yourself as a television person, they put up barriers in the recording business. You get pigeonholed. For a minute, it was tough for me letting go of that dream but I had to. I still want to sing, but it's not do or die. Now, I have different priorities."

Peete still tried to take roles that involved singing. In 1992, she appeared in the miniseries *The Jacksons: An American Dream.* The miniseries focused on the musical Jackson family, including the rise of the

Jackson 5 and Michael Jackson. Peete had a small part as Diana Ross, the Motown singer who was once a member of the Supremes. Ross played a very small part in the start of the group's career.

The same year that Peete appeared in the miniseries, she was cast in her second television series, ABC's *Hangin' With Mr. Cooper.* The show starred comedian Mark Curry as Mr. Cooper, and Peete played Vanessa Russell, his rather airheaded housemate who worked as a secretary. *Hanging' With Mr. Cooper* marked the first time she worked on a comedic show and she enjoyed the experience. However, the fact that the show's focus changed several times, from a comedy focusing on African-American professionals, to a more urban *Three's Company,* to a more kid-oriented show, bothered Peete. She also did not like the fact that her character did not evolve, but acted inconsistently and went in several different directions like the show did. *Hangin' With Mr. Cooper* went off the air in 1997.

During the run of *Hangin' With Mr. Cooper,* Peete's personal life was transformed. On June 10, 1995, she married Rodney Peete, a professional football player. Peete played quarterback for a number of National Football League teams, including the Detroit Lions, Dallas Cowboys, Philadelphia Eagles, and the Carolina Panthers. Their wedding was officiated by the Reverend Jesse Jackson, a civil rights activist, one-time U.S. presidential candidate, and family friend.

Because of the nature of Rodney Peete's job, and the fact that Holly Robinson Peete had to be based in California to work in television, the couple spent a lot of time apart during football season. This situation provided drama when Peete was ready to deliver the couple's first children, a set of fraternal twins, in 1997. When Ryan Elizabeth and Rodney Jackson were ready to be born, their father finished a game halfway across the country, received a police escort to the airport, and flew to California in time to see them born by caesarean section. The couple later had another child named Robinson James.

Though Peete would often bring their children to their father's football games on Sundays, her work on television also allowed her to bring them with her to her job. In 1998, Peete was cast in the situation comedy *For Your Love.* The show spent part of its first season on NBC, before moving to The WB for the rest of its run. Peete played psychiatrist

Malena Ellis, who has just married an attorney named Mel and played by James Lesure. *For Your Love* focused on their relationship, the relationships of two other couples, one black and one white, and their interactions.

Peete enjoyed working on the romantic situation comedy, especially as *For Your Love* discussed race in a positive way. She wrote in a biography on her website, "This is a dream show and I hope it lasts forever! I only wish more network programmers would give us more shows like *For Your Love*—multi-ethnic romantic comedy with humor that can appeal to everyone, celebrating the things we have in common instead of highlighting our differences as so many other shows do."

After *For Your Love* ended its run in 2001, Peete went for a season without a lead on a television series. She had a recurring role on the show *One on One.* She also had pilots and talk shows in development. Peete also took time to focus attention on her charitable foundation, the HollyRod Foundation, which she and her husband had founded in 1997. Robinson's father had been diagnosed with Parkinson's while she was a college student, and died of the disease in 2002. The HollyRod Foundation provided financial support for low-income sufferers of the disease as well as those with cancers of the breast and ovaries. Peete also served as a spokesperson for respiratory syncytial virus (RSV) awareness, a respiratory infection infants can suffer from.

In 2003, Peete was cast in a lead role in her fourth situation comedy, *Like Family.* On The WB show, she played Tanya Ward, a wife and mother who lives in suburban New Jersey and decides to spend more time at home. She and her family open their home to her long-time friend, a white single mother who lived in New York City, and her teenaged son. The situation comedy focused on how the families lived and blended together, and Peete had taken the role in part because race was just there, not a major issue. *Like Family* lasted for only one season.

While Peete worked on *Like Family,* she had moved into new business ventures. In 2003, she signed a deal with the Mervyn's department store to design a line of maternity clothing and serve as a spokesperson for the retailer. The clothing was introduced in the fall of 2004 and was meant to be affordable yet fashionable. It was announced that she would be publishing a woman's guide to football in the fall of 2005 with Daniel Pasiner, *Get Your Own Damn Beer, I'm Watching the Game.*

From the beginning of her career, Peete worked to ensure her success. She wrote in *Black Enterprise,* "You're not guaranteed anything in this business. You get this one little shot. When you get your first shot, whatever you do with it basically sets up what's going to happen in the future.... I was fortunate that I took my shot and made the best of it. I think that's why I've been able to sustain a consistent career in television to this point."

## Sources

### Books

*Celebrity Biographies,* Baseline II, Inc., 2004.

### Periodicals

*Black Enterprise,* December 2001, p. 123.
*Black Issues Book Review,* September-October 2004, p. 11.
*Boston Globe,* September 19, 2003, p. D18.
*Boston Herald,* March 17, 1998, p. 40.
*Business Wire,* November 18, 2003.
*Ebony,* September 1995, p. 132; April 1998, p. 30; December 2002, p. 52.
*Herald,* August 29, 1988, p. 6.
*Jet,* July 10, 1995, p. 32; March 22, 2004, p. 54.
*Knight Ridder/Tribune News Service,* August 15, 2003, p. K1467.

*Toronto Star,* March 17, 1998, p. B8.
*USA Today,* November 12, 1992, p. 3D.

### Online

"Holly Robinson Peete," Internet Movie Database, http://www.imdb.com/name/nm0005372/ (November 2, 2004).
"Holly Robinson Peete—My Story," http://www.hollyrobinsonpeete.com/story.html (November 3, 2004).
*"Like Family,"* Internet Movie Database, http://www.imdb.com/title/tt0374412/combined (November 2, 2004).
*"Like Family,"* The WB 16, WRWB TV Rochester, http://www.wb16.com./shows_details.asp?ID=351 (November 3, 2004).
"Looking good: A new line from a mother-to-be," sacbee.com, http://www.sacbee.com/content/lifestyle/story/10160990p-11081749c.html (November 3, 2004).
"Mom of the Month: Holly Robinson Peete," iParenting.com, http://iparenting.com/mom/0802.htm (November 3, 2004).
"Whatever happened to Holly Robinson?," CNN.com, http://www.cnn.com/2003/SHOWBIZ/TV/12/10/apontv.hollyrobinson.ap/index.html (November 3, 2004).

—*A. Petruso*

# Ty Pennington

## Television show host and carpenter

**B**orn October 19, 1965, in Atlanta, GA. *Education:* Attended Kennesaw College, Atlanta, GA; Art Institute of Atlanta, B.A.; Atlanta College of Art, studied art and sculpture.

**Addresses:** *Home*—Los Angeles, CA. *Office*—Lock and Key Productions, 1149 South Gower St., Ste. 10, Los Angeles, CA 90038. *Website*—http://www.tythehandyguy.com.

## Career

**T**ook carpentry jobs to pay for college; became a model, working with various companies; purchased a piano factory and turned it into loft-style apartments; founded Furniture Unlimited; built sets for film *Leaving Las Vegas;* carpenter, *Trading Spaces,* 2000-04; actor, *The Adventures of Ociee Nash,* 2002; wrote book, *Ty's Tricks,* 2003; host and head designer, *Extreme Makeover: Home Edition,* 2003—; spokesperson, Sears, 2004—; host and head designer, *Extreme Makeover: Home Edition—How'd They Do That?,* 2005—; designer of Ty Pennington Style, Sears, 2005—.

## Sidelights

**W**hen cable channel TLC's show *Trading Spaces* first aired, no one dreamed of the phenomenon it would help start. Nor did anyone expect that one of the show's breakout stars would be a carpenter. But with his model looks and goofy personality, Ty Pennington turned from simple carpenter into television icon.

As a child, Pennington learned woodworking from his father. He would tear apart furniture and turn them into toys. His mother sent him outside to build something that he could then destroy. He gathered up the neighborhood kids, negotiated pay at three comic books per hour, borrowed tools from their parents, and then constructed a three-story tree house.

While visiting his father, the young Pennington was asked what he wanted to do. He chose to build something. He and his father began construction on a boat, which was sea-worthy three days later. When he entered Kennesaw College, he majored in art and history. He told Alma E. Hill of the *Atlanta Journal-Constitution* that carpentry was "not something I wanted to do professionally." On the advice of one of his professors, Pennington transferred to the Art Institute of Atlanta to study graphic design. To pay for college expenses, he continued taking carpentry jobs. He graduated with a bachelor's degree, and continued his studies at the Atlanta College of Art.

He also became a model, where he traveled the world. He modeled for a variety of companies, including J. Crew, Swatch, Body Glove, Macy's, and Land's End. He appeared in television commercials for Diet Coke and Levi's. He helped construct the sets for the 1995 film *Leaving Las Vegas*. He also purchased an old factory with his brother, and renovated the place, turning it into loft-style apartments. Pennington also started a company called Furniture Unlimited, where he designed and constructed furniture in the modern primitive style. Pennington then purchased a home in the Grant Park section of his native Atlanta. He renovated the three-bedroom, two-bath house for only $10,000. He added some special touches, including using a metal salad bowl as a sink, and using a plunger as a lighting fixture.

Pennington joined *Trading Spaces,* a show that was based on a popular BBC program, in 2000. The premise of the television program is two neighbors (working in pairs) swap houses and renovate one room in the house on a $1,000 budget in two days. They receive help from designers and a carpenter. Pennington was one of two carpenters for the show. He and fellow carpenter Amy Wynn Pastor shared an assistant to help meet the show's tight deadlines.

The show was a success and Pennington was a hit, especially with women. His comedic antics and occasional bare chest quickly made him a star. In addition to his role on *Trading Spaces,* he traveled around the country making appearances at home and garden shows. His fans would line up for hours, traveling long distances just to see the hunky carpenter. Pennington aimed to please, using the time to answer questions and dish on his co-stars.

Though Pennington had lived in Atlanta most of his life, he and his girlfriend, Drea Bock (who is also his manager), moved to Los Angeles so he could begin his acting career. Hyperion also released his do-it-yourself book, titled *Ty's Tricks: Home Repair Secrets Plus Cheap and Easy Projects to Transform Any Room* in 2003. The book featured the renovation of his Grant Park residence. In addition to tips and how-to guides, he also included humorous anecdotes that would set his book apart from the others. He toured to promote the book, and it also landed on the *New York Times* best-seller list.

Pennington signed a multiyear contract with the Sears department store chain in 2004. He began appearing in ads that were aimed at families. In addition to being a spokesperson, he also acts as an ambassador for the Sears American Dream Campaign. He has also developed a line of products for the home titled Ty Pennington Style. Products were available for sale in the spring of 2005. "I wanted to show you can create a fun, casual, and quality living space, and you don't have to break the bank," he told *People.*

During this time, he signed with ABC to do *Extreme Makeover: Home Edition. Home Edition* was a spin-off of the *Extreme Makeover* program that gave a chosen few the chance to be made over physically with plastic surgery. Both television programs were similar to the 1950s show, *Queen For A Day.* In the case of *Home Edition,* a well-deserving family would have their home renovated, and in some cases, rebuilt, for free. Pennington led a group of designers to design the house, and they would use local construction companies to renovate the home in seven days while the family was sent away on vacation. As the hour-long show progressed, viewers watched as the designers sometimes bickered, and Pennington would playfully tease the family with misinformation. In each show, he would also take on special projects for one of the family members. *Extreme Makeover: Home Edition* would turn a two-bedroom house into a mini-mansion. Companies such as Sears and Home Depot donated appliances, furniture, and building materials. The house would be revealed to the family, and many times, a few extras were thrown in.

In the middle of the second season, Pennington was preparing for a shoot when he needed an emergency appendectomy. Not one to shirk his duties, he had the surgery, and camera crews were with him in the hospital as he tried to lead the renovation from the hospital bed. Later in the week, he was able to film some scenes for the episode. In a statement obtained by CNN.com, Pennington expressed, "I don't want to let the family down, and all of us with the show want to give them the new house they deserve."

*Extreme Makeover: Home Edition* became a popular show, one that continued to grow in popularity. Applications to be on the program come by the thousands each week. Fans line up for hours at the shoots waiting to catch a glimpse of the star. One female fan showed up in a wedding dress, so Pennington dropped to one knee for a picture. In addition to *Home Edition,* there have been two spin-offs: *EMHE: How'd They Do That?* and *Extreme Makeover: Wedding Edition.* Both shows began airing in 2005.

In addition to being a carpentry whiz and home design guru, Pennington is also a painter, which he studied at the Atlanta College of Art along with sculpture. He also has a one-man band named Barney. He has released a demo CD, and performs reggae, country, and hip-hop while wearing a leisure suit made of Christmas lights. He loves to surf and skateboard. Though currently enjoying all that he does, he told Mary Beth Breckenridge of Newark, New Jersey's *Star-Ledger,* "when my 15 minutes are over with, I can go back and do carpentry, and be happy."

## Selected writings

*Ty's Tricks: Home Repair Secrets Plus Cheap and Easy Projects to Transform Any Room,* Hyperion, 2003.

## Sources

### Periodicals

*Atlanta Journal-Constitution,* November 29, 2002, p. B2; September 14, 2003, p. LS1; November 3, 2003, p. E2; January 19, 2005, p. E2.
*Booklist,* September 15, 2003, p. 190.
*Budget Living,* October/November 2003, p. 36.
*Home Textiles Today,* September 27, 2004, p. 2.
*Library Journal,* December 2003, p. 161.
*New York Times,* April 14, 2005, p. F3.
*People,* November 29, 2004, p. 113; April 18, 2005, p. 40.
*Publishers Weekly,* October 21, 2002, p. 14.
*Redbook,* September 2004, p. 58.
*Star-Ledger* (Newark, NJ), March 13, 2003, p. 67.
*Time,* December 20, 2004, p. 159.

### Online

*Biography Resource Center Online,* Gale Group, 2003.
"Makeover's Ty has appendectomy," CNN.com, http://www.cnn.com/2005/SHOWBIZ/TV/01/19/people.pennington.ap/index.html (January 19, 2005).
"News," Ty the Handy Guy, http://www.tythehandyguy.com/news_set.html (May 21, 2005).
"Ty Pennington," ABC.com, http://abc.go.com/primetime/xtremehome/bios/ty_pennington.html (May 21, 2005).
"Ty's Biography," Ty the Handy Guy, http://www.tythehandyguy.com/bio_set.html (May 21, 2005).

—*Ashyia N. Henderson*

# Elizabeth Plater-Zyberk

## Architect and urban planner

**B**orn in 1950 in Bryn Mawr, PA; daughter of an architect and a landscape architect; married Andres Duany (an architect and urban planner), 1976. *Education:* Earned undergraduate degree in architect from Princeton University, 1972; Yale University, M.Arch., 1976.

**Addresses:** *Office*—Duany Plater-Zyberk & Company, 1023 SW 25 Ave., Miami, FL 33135.

## Career

**B**egan teaching architecture at the University of Miami, 1976; worked for Miami firm Arquitectonica, c. 1976-80; founded Duany Plater-Zyberk & Company, 1980; dean of the University of Miami School of Architecture, 1995—.

**Awards:** Co-recipient of Vincent J. Scully Prize, National Building Museum, 2001.

## Sidelights

**A**rchitect and urban planner Elizabeth Plater-Zyberk is one half of a two-person revolution in American town planning. With her husband, Andres Duany, Plater-Zyberk has pioneered the "New Urbanism" movement, which urges local officials, regional planners, and architects to jettison the cookie-cutter suburb, the exclusive gated community, and the McMansion in favor of more pedestrian-friendly, community-oriented residential spaces. Plater-Zyberk and Duany are best known as the designers of Seaside, the Florida town used as the fictional setting in the 1999 film *The Truman Show,* but it was merely one of more than 200 immensely successful communities their firm had helped create, each with their own design vernacular. "The fence, the walkway, the screen porch," she listed in an interview with *Smithsonian* writer Phil Patton, "create an elaboration of ceremony. You have a choice of realms ranging in increments from the public to the most private."

Born in 1950 in Bryn Mawr, Pennsylvania, Plater-Zyberk grew up in nearby Paoli. Her parents were immigrants from Poland, where her father had been an architect; her mother a landscape architect. At Princeton University in the late 1960s, where Plater-Zyberk studied architecture, she met Andres Duany, who is of Cuban heritage, and the pair met once again when both were enrolled at the Yale Graduate School of Architecture by 1972. They wed in 1976, not long after finishing the prestigious graduate program, and soon took dual teaching posts at the University of Miami in Florida.

Plater-Zyberk and Duany were affiliated with the prominent Miami architectural firm Arquitectonica, known for its fresh new designs that drew upon Miami's Art Deco past, but were becoming increasingly intrigued by larger urban-planning issues. A developer named Robert Davis approached them about designing a new town he was hoping to create from a parcel of land he had inherited in the Florida Panhandle. Plater-Zyberk and her husband put together a plan that encouraged more of a sense of community and contact, rather than elevating the ideals of individualism and isolation. All houses, for example, were located within walking distance of commercial area. Newer building materials, such as vinyl windows and aluminum siding, were prohibited. Houses were required to have a front porch, and the property a picket fence—though homeowners had to come up with their own design for the fence.

Construction began in 1982 for what would become the town of Seaside, Florida, and though it was considered somewhat experimental at the time, real-estate prices continued to rise steadily for its parcels over the next decade. It became a phenomenon and even a tourist destination, and in 1999 Hollywood arrived to use its pastel, picture-perfect streets as the setting for *The Truman Show,* which starred Jim Carrey as a man who learns that his entire life is a fictional television show.

Seaside became the most well-known of the projects done by Plater-Zyberk and Duany's eponymous firm, founded in Miami in 1980, but it spawned a number of new projects across the United States. These included Charleston Place in Boca Raton, Florida; Kentlands, Maryland; Blount Springs, Alabama; and Middleton Hills in Middleton, Wisconsin. As she explained in an interview with *Index* magazine's Peter Halley, many of the new communities are located in the southern United States, because "in the North, government is usually organized by township. In the newer Sunbelt states, it's organized by county. Townships are characteristically small and inexpert, and they don't have enough money to spend on things. The officials are almost always volunteers. The county structure is usually far more professional and forward-looking."

Plater-Zyberk does not design houses; instead other professionals adhere to her firm's residential architecture guidelines, which usually specify an updated version of older American styles, like Victorian. The communities she plans often feature such attributes as narrower streets, which slows driving speeds, and a commercial center within 1,300 feet, which studies had shown was the maximum distance that an average person will walk to a store rather than drive.

Plater-Zyberk and Duany were hailed as visionaries in the mainstream media early on, with a 1990 *People* magazine profile asserting that "in the '90s, when their plans come to fruition, they will be recognized

as the most influential American town planners in decades—or ever." In 1993, Plater-Zyberk took part in a conference with other architects, urban planners, and similar cohorts, out of which arose the Congress for the New Urbanism (CNU). The group set forth the principles of the movement, and advocated "mixed-use" development over the "single-use" zoning rules that most American suburbs had deployed since the 1950s. This meant that areas could have both residential *and* commercial districts, enabling those who lived there easy access to stores and possibly even their workplace, in contrast to the current standard, which was biased toward cars and drivers.

Many of these principles were laid out in Plater-Zyberk's 2000 book, written with Duany and Jeff Speck, *Suburban Nation: The Rise of Sprawl and the Decline of the American Dream.* She has been a vocal opponent of the gated community concept, which restricts access to residents only. "There are lots of reasons why they shouldn't exist," she told Halley in the *Index* interview. "There's the idea of exclusion. And there are traffic reasons. The gate dictates that you're only going to come and go by car. Gated communities always let out onto the big roads, so there are no smaller interconnections."

Since 1995 Plater-Zyberk has served as dean at the University of Miami School of Architecture, to which a new generation of future architects interested in the New Urbanism movement have flocked. She founded the school's master of architecture program in Suburb and Town Design, and serves as director for the Center for Urban and Community Design. In 2001 she and Duany were co-recipients of the Vincent J. Scully Prize from the National Building Museum, named after their onetime Yale professor upon whose ideas the New Urbanism movement was built. She predicted that movement toward more pedestrian-friendly communities "will intensify," she told *South Florida Business Journal's* Darcie Lunsford. "One big thing that bothers people is traffic congestion. Until we start reorganizing the bigger picture so that we don't have to do so much driving, the conditions we complain about in our cities and suburbs are only going to get worse."

## Selected writings

(With Andres Duany and Jeff Speck) *Suburban Nation: The Rise of Sprawl and the Decline of the American Dream,* North Point Press (New York City), 2000.

# Sources

## Periodicals

*Architecture,* January 2002, p. 27; July 2003, p. 23.
*Florida Trend,* July 1992, p. 32.
*Index,* June/July 2003, pp. 56-61.
*New York Times,* January 7, 2001, p. 7.

*People,* Spring 1990, Special Issue, p. 72.
*Publishers Weekly,* January 31, 2000, p. 88.
*Smithsonian,* January 1991, p. 82.
*South Florida Business Journal,* September 25, 1998, p. 3A.
*U.S. News & World Report,* March 20, 2000, p. 64.

*—Carol Brennan*

# Carolyn Porco

© *Space Science Institute*

**Planetary scientist**

**B**orn Carolyn C. Porco in 1953, in New York, NY. *Education:* State University of New York at Stony Brook, B.S. in physics and astronomy, c. 1976; California Institute of Technology, Ph.D. in planetary sciences, 1983.

**Addresses:** *Office*—Space Science Institute, 4750 Walnut St., Ste. 205, Boulder, CO 80301.

## Career

**B**egan work as a planetary scientist as a graduate student at the California Institute of Technology, early 1980s; joined the faculty of the Planetary Sciences Department at the University of Arizona, 1983, and simultaneously worked as imaging team member for Voyager mission to Uranus, 1986, and Neptune, 1989; imaging team leader for the Cassini-Huygens mission to Saturn, 1990—; senior researcher, Space Science Institute, Boulder, CO, 2003—.

**Awards:** "Asteroid 7231 Porco" named in her honor for contributions to the field of planetary science, 1998.

## Sidelights

**C**arolyn Porco may walk upon the earth, but as a planetary scientist her mind is far away. Captivated by the vastness of space, Porco has dedicated her life to studying the mysteries it holds. "I enjoy my career because it allows me to live my life on a plane different than most people do," Porco told *Tucson Citizen* reporter Mitch Tobin. "My mental life is spent elsewhere—it's spent in the outer solar system."

In 1990 Porco became the imaging team leader for the Cassini-Huygens mission, which is charged with exploring earth's planetary sibling Saturn. As such, Porco helped design the most complex camera system sent into space, complete with 200- and 2,000-millimeter lenses capable of taking black and white, color, infrared, and ultraviolet pictures. The $3.4 billion, camera-bearing Cassini spacecraft was launched in 1997 and reached Saturn in July of 2004, providing Porco and her scientist pals with close-ups of the planet, its many moons and rings. The craft was to send back images for four years, keeping Porco busy with analysis.

Porco was born into an Italian working-class family in New York City in 1953. She grew up alongside four brothers in the Bronx. Her interest in astronomy came about during an adolescent spiritual quest, which led her to study eastern religions and philosophy. According to *Newsday*'s Earl Lane, as Porco pondered these topics, she began to wonder, "what are we doing here and what's out there." These ruminations led to a fascination with planets and galaxies. "In a figurative and a literal sense, I was looking from inside to outside," she told Lane.

By the time Porco entered the Catholic Cardinal Spellman High School in the Bronx in the mid-1960s, she knew she wanted to study planets. Following graduation, Porco enrolled at the State University of New York at Stony Brook, where she earned an undergraduate degree in physics and astronomy. By 1976, Porco was a graduate student in the Division of Geological and Planetary Sciences at the California Institute of Technology, where NASA's Jet Propulsion Laboratory is based. While Porco was at the university, the Voyager I spacecraft flew past Saturn, sending the lab thousands of images and vast amounts of data. The sheer amount of information streaming in was too much for the imaging team to handle, so Porco was handed the data on Saturn's ring system. Highly intuitive and able to synthesize information effectively, Porco made some significant discoveries concerning the rings and the planet's magnetic field.

Porco earned her doctorate in 1983 and joined the University of Arizona planetary sciences department. After Porco received her graduate degree, she became an official member of the Voyager imaging team and analyzed data from Voyager II's 1986 pass by Uranus and 1989 pass by Neptune. Among the main 178 scientists working on the Voyager mission, only seven were female. Porco has said that she is glad she can be a role model to other women and girls interested in science, though she tends to downplay the topic when it arises. Porco explained it this way to the *Boston Globe*'s David L. Chandler, "The beauty to me of science is that what we are really after is the truth.... So if a person, male or female, is good at what they do, and competent, and it's obvious they're competent, in the end everyone is going to pay attention."

In 1990, Porco became imaging team leader for the Cassini mission to Saturn, beating out applicants with more experience. Clearly, Porco had already earned a reputation as a promising solar system scholar. "As an undergraduate, she was bright-eyed, feisty and full of enthusiasm," Stony Brook astronomer Michal Simon told *Newsday*, "and that's exactly what she became as an astronomer."

Through the Cassini mission, scientists hope to obtain new data that might tell them how the solar system was formed, or how life on earth began. "We are attempting to understand our own planet as one of a family of planets all born of the same parent, of the same material, at the same time," Porco told Carolyn Niethammer of the *New York Times*. "We enhance our chances of understanding what makes this complex system work by having another example to study."

Launched in 1997, the bus-sized Cassini spacecraft traveled nearly seven years and more than two billion miles before it began orbiting Saturn in 2004. The spacecraft was expected to take some 500,000 images. In addition, a European-built probe dove from the spacecraft into Saturn's largest moon, Titan. Porco breathed a sigh of relief when the spacecraft reached Saturn and began sending back images, but her work was far from over. As the spacecraft orbits the planet, new moons and other phenomena are discovered, forcing the imaging crew to write new commands for the spacecraft. "We do retargetable observations of such objects," Porco told CNN's Bjorn Carey. "We find a new moon, determine its orbit and then use that information to predict where the moon will be at a later time so that we can take a closer look at it. It's a very deadline-driven activity."

When the Cassini mission comes to an end, Porco will focus her energies on Pluto as a member of the imaging team for the New Horizons mission, which will give scientists the first close-ups of Pluto. Arrival is expected around 2015. In 2003, Porco became a senior researcher at the Boulder, Colorado-based Space Science Institute. In other pursuits, Porco worked as an advisor for movie producers for 1997's *Contact,* a film that starred Jodie Foster as an extraterrestrial-seeking scientist. Porco's other passion is the Beatles. Porco, who has every album the Fab Four ever released, says one of her greatest disappointments is not getting to see them perform live.

Over the years, Porco has appeared on many major network television newscasts talking about astronomy. Highly charismatic, Porco has a gift for conveying the joys of astronomy to the average person. For all of her accomplishments in the field of planetary exploration, Porco was honored in 1998 when "Asteroid 7231 Porco" was named for her.

Porco is aware that some people scoff at her projects as another example of government largess; however, she believes exploring new frontiers is inevitable for humans, who may one day colonize other planets. "It's in us; it's part of our genetic makeup," Porco told the *Tucson Citizen.* "Dogs don't seem to do it, giraffes don't do it, fish don't do it ... but humans do. It's what we're made of. We explore because exploring must convey an evolutionary advantage to us. You have to prevent us from doing it."

## Sources

### Periodicals

*Boston Globe,* October 2, 1989, p. 41.
*Daily Camera* (Boulder, Colorado), June 28, 2004, p. A1.
*New York Times,* August 17, 1999, p. 3.
*Tucson Citizen,* January 19, 2001.

### Online

"Astronomer's 'Cosmic Connection' to Saturn," CNN.com, http://www.cnn.com/2005/TECH/ space/02/15/saturn.astronomer/index.html (February 16, 2005).

"Mission Operations," Space Science Institute, http://www.spacescience.org/missionops/ index_more.html (April 22, 2005).

"She's the Ringleader: Stony Brook Grad will Lead Team Running the Cameras, Studying Pictures when Cassini Enters Orbit this Week," *Newsday,* http://www.newsday.com/news/health/ny-hsporc273870395jun28,0,4544007,print.story?c (April 22, 2005).

*—Lisa Frick*

# Nora Pouillon

## Chef, restaurateur, and author

**B**orn Nora Aschenbrenner in 1943, in Vienna, Austria; married Pierre Pouillon (a journalist; divorced); companion of Steven Damato; children: Alexis, Olivier (from first marriage), Nina, Nadia (with Damato).

**Addresses:** *Office*—Nora, 2132 Florida Ave. NW, Washington, DC; Asia Nora, 2213 M Street NW, Washington, DC.

## Career

**C**hef, restaurant at Tabard Inn, c. 1976; founder, co-owner, and chef, Restaurant Nora (organic restaurant), Washington, D.C., 1979—; opened second restaurant City Café, 1986, revamped as Asia Nora (Asian fusion), 1994; published cookbook *Nora: Cooking in a Healthy Way,* 1994, published as *Cooking with Nora: Seasonal Menus from Restaurant Nora,* 1996; lobbyist, Public Voice for Food and Health Policy, 1998; spokesperson for "Give North Atlantic Swordfish a Break" campaign for NRDC/SeaWeb, 1998-2000; Restaurant Nora certified organic, 1999; created organic frozen dinners with Green Circle Organics, late 1990s-early 2000s; consultant, Fresh Fields Wholefoods Market and Walnut Acres Organic Foods.

**Member:** Les Dames d'Escoffier, Washington, D.C. chapter; International Association of Women Chefs and Restaurateurs; Chefs Collaborative 2000 (founding board member); International Committee on Alternative and Complementary Medicine.

**Awards:** U.S.A. Chef of the Year, American Tasting Institute, 1996; Catherine B. Sweeney Award, Ameri-can Horticultural Society, 2003; Chief of the Year Award, Excellence by the International Association of Culinary Professionals.

## Sidelights

**A**ustria-born chef and restaurateur Nora Pouillon owns the first certified organic restaurant in the United States, Restaurant Nora, located in Washington, D.C. Pouillon had sought out the certification as she was an active supporter of organic foods. Pouillon later opened a second restaurant, Asia Nora, in the same city, which was as organic as possible. An activist in food-related causes and education, she also published a cookbook full of recipes inspired by her organic cooking. As Pouillon was quoted as saying in *Art Culinaire,* "Organic is not about diet but about agriculture. My customers come for the good food. They don't have to understand it, but for me it is the only food that is good to eat."

Pouillon was born in Vienna, Austria, in 1943. Living in post-World War II Europe, fresh food supplies were limited, so the family grew their own. Her parents got her interested in cooking. Meals were often simple with fresh ingredients, instead of eating in the rich French tradition that was common at the time. Though Pouillon was raised in Austria, she attended a French boarding school in Vienna with her sisters. There, she learned manners and how to eat formally. Pouillon spent her summers in a village in the Alps, where many farmers were self-sufficient, another aspect of food that intrigued Pouillon as an adult.

Though Pouillon was a student of interior design, food and cooking soon became the focus of her life. In 1965, when she was 21 years old, she moved to the United States with her journalist husband, a Frenchman named Pierre Pouillon. The couple had two sons, Alexis and Olivier. Pouillon enjoyed cooking for her family. Because of her flair for cooking, friends of her husband began asking her to help out with their parties. Pouillon soon had several home-based businesses including hosting and teaching cooking classes, and later, a catering business.

In the course of doing these businesses, Pouillon became very familiar with the kinds of produce available in American supermarkets and was disappointed by the quality. She also learned that American beef and chicken was often full of growth hormones, and vegetables were covered with pesticides. For these reasons, Pouillon became interested in organic meat and vegetable products. She wanted to buy only organic food products, but sometimes had to make an extra effort to get them. For example, Pouillon would drive to places like Virginia to pick up produce, since many organic farmers did not deliver.

Around 1976, Pouillon was hired to help open the restaurant at Tabard Inn, serving as its chef, though she had no formal training. She separated from her husband that year and began what became a long-time relationship with Steven Damato, the manager of the restaurant. (The pair eventually had a daughter, Nina, and adopted another, Nadia.) With the help of Damato and his brother, Thomas, Pouillon opened her own restaurant in 1979 called Restaurant Nora. Together, the three raised money among friends and associates to fund the new restaurant. The focus of Restaurant Nora's menu was healthful, European-influenced American organic cooking.

Pouillon's concept for Restaurant Nora was seen as far outside of the mainstream when it opened. At the time, healthy cooking meant tofu and bad hippie fare that had no flavor, the opposite of what Pouillon offered on her menu. This idea persisted for many years, even as attitudes changed. In 1996, she told Jerry Shriver of USA Today, "People have this fear of healthy food. They automatically think it tastes disgusting and looks disgusting, and that you have to eat it in some sort of little hippie place.... I wanted to tell them, 'Look, health food is the best way to eat, and I give it to you in an environment I want to eat in myself.'"

Restaurant Nora was located in what was once a nineteenth-century grocery store. The store front had been a failed Yugoslavian restaurant before Pouillon and her partners took over. The interior was decorated with Mennonite and Amish quilts for baby's cribs that were of museum quality. In addition to decorating the restaurant herself, Pouillon did much of the cooking, serving, and bussing of tables in the early days. She even planted the flowers and herbs near the building. As the restaurant grew and more employees were hired, Pouillon sometimes had problems retaining staff, especially chefs, because she was demanding and a perfectionist. Also, her emphasis on organic meant certain ingredients were off limits, pushing the bounds of what chefs were trained to work with.

Over the years, Restaurant Nora received many good reviews. One reason for Pouillon's success was her insistence on the best ingredients, including meats and vegetables. She did business with organic growers as much as possible. Though the process was time consuming, she developed relationships with organic farmers that produced the ingredients she wanted. Because Pouillon would only work with in-season fresh ingredients, her menu changed daily based on what was available. When the produce arrived at the restaurant, one employee was dedicated to cleaning it with a special sophisticated water filtration system. Even the water she served to customers was filtered three times before it appeared on their table. Though such processes sometimes made for high costs, other restaurants soon followed Pouillon's lead to obtain and serve the best ingredients possible.

Restaurant Nora's amount of business continued to grow on annual basis. However, it did take time for Pouillon's take on cooking to really catch on, though Restaurant Nora always had a devoted patronage. By the early 1990s, it was a very popular spot in D.C. During the two terms of Bill Clinton's presidency, many members of his administration, including the President himself, dined at Pouillon's restaurant. Pouillon was even considered for the post of White House chef during Clinton's second term.

While Restaurant Nora was on its way to becoming a success, Pouillon and her partners opened a second restaurant, City Café, in 1986. It was a more casual and inexpensive version of Restaurant Nora. Despite the fact that City Café was popular, in 1994, Pouillon turned it into a very different restaurant called Asia Nora. As the name suggests, it served Asian cuisine, featuring dishes from China, Vietnam, India, Thailand, and Japan, but with an organic, Western interpretation. Before opening Asia Nora, Pouillon took private lessons from a number of Asian chefs to get her menu right.

As with Restaurant Nora, Pouillon tried to make Asia Nora as organic as possible. However, because many ingredients used in Asian dishes were not available in organic form, her goal became to use organic when available. While Asia Nora received some good reviews early on, the restaurant's reputation greatly improved in 1995 after Pouillon began working with a new chef to revamp the menu and the restaurant's organization.

When Pouillon began working in food and establishing her successful restaurants, she had a goal of publishing a cookbook. She was rejected three times over a 20-year period, and was often told that restaurant cookbooks were not good sellers. In 1994, Pouillon finally reached her goal. Originally published in Japan by Shibata Publishing, *Nora: Cooking in a Healthy Way,* focused on cooking healthy with menus and recipes. Two years later, the cookbook was published in English in the United States as *Cooking with Nora: Seasonal Menus from Restaurant Nora* by Park Lane Press. After receiving a number of positive reviews, the book was a finalist in the Julia Child Cookbook Awards, in the "First Book" category. In 1996, Pouillon was also named U.S.A. chef of the year from the American Tasting Institute. This marked the first time a woman was given this award.

In the late 1990s, Pouillon pursued another goal. She wanted to get Restaurant Nora certified organic by one of the six private organic certifiers in the United States, Oregon Tilth. (At the time, the federal government had no standards for what constituted certified organic. Such standards were developed in the early 2000s.) Because no other restaurant had wanted such a certification before, Pouillon spent two years documenting how organic her restaurant was as Oregon Tilth developed this standard for restaurants. To gain the certification, Pouillon had to prove that at least 95 percent of the ingredients used—including meats, vegetables, dairy, flour, coffee, chocolate, and oils—were from farmers and suppliers that were certified organic.

Pouillon's efforts paid off in 1999, when Restaurant Nora received this organic certification. Being certified organic gave Restaurant Nora an even wider

audience. In a CNN.com chat from 2000, Pouillon said of her certification, "I think what it does is give an enormous amount of confidence to my customers and makes my claim to being organic credible and gives them trust in what they eat in my restaurant—because it has been certified and not just because it says so on the menu, but because I have legal proof. And it brings awareness to the food consumer in general that there is actually something out there that they can feel safe in eating."

As Pouillon became a well-known chef, she began using her skills and name in other related areas. With Damato, she began working with Green Circle Organics to help create a certified organic line of products in the late 1990s and early 2000s. Such products included frozen burgers, and pre-cooked ready-to-eat foods like meatloaf and roasts. Pouillon also worked as a consultant for Fresh Fields Wholefoods Market and Walnut Acres Organic Foods, which sold organic foods through catalogs.

From 1998 to 2000, Pouillon was also a spokesperson for "Give North Atlantic Swordfish a Break" campaign for NRDC/SeaWeb. She had stopped serving swordfish in her restaurants in the mid-1990s after she learned that swordfish were being overfished. With the group, she asked for a moratorium so that the swordfish population could be replenished. This was not the only dish she would not serve in her restaurants. She also stayed away from foie gras and fish from the Gulf of Mexico as it was too polluted.

Pouillon also was involved with promoting culinary education. As a member of Chefs Collaborative 2000, she worked with the Adopt a School program to teach children about good nutritional choices, world cuisine, and how to cook. In addition, Pouillon was involved with similar programs sponsored by the Federal Agricultural Department and served as a lecturer to adult education students.

Pouillon's future included perhaps opening a third restaurant, an idea that had been floating around for several years. In the early 2000s, she continued the challenges of being a power chef. She told Catherine S. Gregory of *Yoga Journal,* "Many people don't realize how complicated it is to be a professional chef. You have to be creative; you have to be an economist; you have to be like a mechanic to realize your ideas; you have to be an artist to make it look pretty on the plate. That complexity makes it very satisfying for me."

## Selected writings

*Nora: Cooking in a Healthy Way,* Shibata Publishing (Japan), 1994; published as *Cooking with Nora: Seasonal Menus from Restaurant Nora,* Park Lane Press (United States), 1996.

## Sources

### Periodicals

*New York Times,* May 10, 1998, sec. 6, p. 51; May 14, 2003, p. F6.
*Organic Style,* November/December 2002, pp. 58-62.
*Publishers Weekly,* February 19, 1996, p. 211.
*Restaurants & Institutions,* February 15, 2003, p. S13.
*USA Today,* March 11, 1994, p. 1D; May 24, 1996, p. 8D.
*Washingtonian,* May 2001, p. 147.
*Washington Post,* September 22, 1993, p. E1; December 11, 1994, p. W21; November 3, 1995, p. N28; December 3, 1995, p. W43; March 10, 1996, p. X15; November 19, 1998, p. J1; February 10, 1999, p. F1; June 23, 1999, p. F1; July 3, 2002, p. F1; January 4, 2004, p. W5.
*Washington Times,* May 1, 1996, p. 3.

### Online

"A Pioneer in Organic Cuisine," AHS Great American Gardeners Awards, http://www.ahs.org/publications/the_american_gardener/ pdf/0307/GAG_Award_Winner_12.pdf (July 21, 2004).

"Chef Nora Pouillon," The O'Mama Report, http://www.theorganicreport.com/pages/315_chef_nora_pouillon.cfm (July 21, 2004).
"Chefs @ Home," http://www.foodfit.com/cooking/archive/chefsAtHome_sept04.asp (July 21, 2004).
"Eating out organic, a new challenge for natural food connoisseurs," CNN.com, http://www.cnn.com/FOOD/specials/2000/organic.restaurants/ (July 21, 2004).
"Nora Pouillon," Nora, http://www.noras.com/pouillon/index.shtm (July 21, 2004).
"Nora Pouillon," NRDC, http://www.nrdc.org/reference/qa/intnora.asp (July 21, 2004).
"Nora Pouillon," Seafood Choices Alliance, http://www.seafoodchoices.com/feature/pouillon_feature.shtml (July 21, 2004).
"Organic Chemistry," Yoga Journal, http://www.yogajournal.com/views/1275.cfm (July 21, 2004).
"Profiles of chefs," Art Culinaire, http://www.findarticles.com/p/articles/mi_m0JAW/is_2001_Summer/ai_76445718/pg_3 (July 21, 2004).
"Restaurateur Nora Pouillon on organic food," CNN.com, http://www.cnn.com/COMMUNITY/transcripts/2000/12/20/pouillon/ (July 21, 2004).
"The Quiet Invasion Continues ... Nora Pouillon—A Purist in the Nation's Capital," Austrian Information, http://www.austria.org/oldsite/mar99/nora.html (July 21, 2004).

—*A. Petruso*

# Samantha Power

## Author and journalist

**B**orn in 1970, in Ireland; daughter of a physician; emigrated to the United States, 1979. *Education:* Attended Yale University and Harvard Law School.

**Addresses:** *Home*—Winthrop, MA. *Office*—Carr Center for Human Rights Policy, Harvard University, 79 J. F. Kennedy St., Cambridge, MA 02138.

## Career

**A**uthor, journalist, and educator. Reporter, *U.S. News and World Report* and *Economist,* 1993-96; political analyst, International Crisis Group, 1996; adjunct lecturer in public policy and executive director, Carr Center for Human Rights Policy, John F. Kennedy School of Government, Harvard University. Contributor to publications such as *New Republic, New Yorker,* and *Atlantic Monthly.*

**Awards:** Pulitzer Prize, for *A Problem from Hell: America and the Age of Genocide,* 2003.

## Sidelights

**J**ournalist and human-rights crusader Samantha Power won a 2003 Pulitzer Prize for *A Problem from Hell: America and the Age of Genocide.* Power's treatise examined American foreign policy in the modern era, in particular what appeared to be a reticence to become involved in situations where the horrific slaughter of civilians was occurring. Once, she writes in her book, she had believed that U.S. foreign policy was a "failure" because of this

skittishness, but then conceded it was instead "ruthlessly effective: No U.S. president has ever made genocide prevention a priority, and no U.S. president has ever suffered politically for his indifference to its occurrence," she writes.

Power was born in Dublin, Ireland, in 1970. Her father died when she was still quite young, and her mother, one of Ireland's leading female tennis players, eventually remarried. Power's mother went on to earn a doctorate in biochemistry and became a kidney transplant specialist in the United States after the family emigrated in the late 1970s. As a youngster, Power initially harbored an ambition to become a sports broadcaster, but her interest in the political was awakened by the footage of the 1989 Tiananmen Square demonstrations in Beijing, when Chinese authorities cracked down on student demonstrations in front of the world's television cameras.

That significant event occurred just as Power began her undergraduate education at Yale University. She eventually won an internship with a Washington, D.C. foundation that shared an address with the magazine offices of *U.S. News and World Report.* She was about to embark on a trip to a republic of the former Yugoslavia, and "one day, I introduced myself to an editor, said I was heading over to Bosnia, and asked if I could call him with stories," she recalled in an interview with *Cosmopolitan* writer Ruth Davis. The editor agreed, and thus Power began her career as a war correspondent. She wrote for *U.S. News and World Report* and the *Economist,* and her articles chronicled the ethnic-cleansing atrocities taking place across Serbian-held Bosnia. After a time, however, she grew perplexed by the fact that while most Americans back home agreed the violence against civilians in the Balkans was horrific, no one seemed willing to step in to help.

Power's first book, *Breakdown in the Balkans: A Chronicle of Events, January, 1989 to May, 1993,* was published in 1993. Her next title, co-edited with Graham Allison, was *Realizing Human Rights: Moving from Inspiration to Impact,* which featured an impressive list of contributors on the topic, including U.N. Secretary-General Kofi Annan and former U.S. president Jimmy Carter. By then, Random House had signed Power to a book deal, and she worked on what would become her Pulitzer-Prize-winning volume while studying for her degree from Harvard Law School. She finished both, and took a position as the founding executive director of the Carr Center for Human Rights Policy at Harvard's John F. Kennedy School of Government. Random House rejected her first manuscript, however, suggesting it should perhaps be a less political, more personal tale, but Power found another publisher and *A Problem from Hell: America and the Age of Genocide* appeared in 2002.

Power borrowed the title of her book from the words of former U.S. Secretary of State Warren Christopher, of the first Clinton Administration, but devotes a large section to the life and work of a Polish attorney, Raphael Lemkin, who coined the term "genocide" in 1943. Power notes that most of Lemkin's family perished in the Holocaust, and he dedicated himself to petitioning international policy-makers at the United Nations to formally define and recognize similar acts of murder. Power goes on to chronicle the various incidences of this around the world since the landmark 1948 U.N. Convention on genocide, and the failure of U.S. administrations to deal with what seems to be a fight in someone else's backyard.

Power's book earned laudatory reviews, as well as the 2003 Pulitzer Prize in the general nonfiction category. At 32, she was one of the youngest writers ever to win the prestigious honor, and was frequently interviewed in the lead-up to the U.S. inva-

sion of Iraq in March of 2003. *A Problem from Hell,* noted *New York Times* journalist Celestine Bohlen, "has stirred debate in foreign policy circles as diplomats and experts deal with the question of when and how American power, military and diplomatic, should be deployed on behalf of humanitarian goals."

Yet that same *New York Times* piece also revealed that in some circles, "Power's book was cited as an example of how humanitarian intervention as embraced by American liberals helped lay the groundwork for the Bush administration's policy of preemptive intervention, as now foreseen for Iraq," Bohlen wrote a few weeks before U.S.-led invasion to oust Saddam Hussein occurred. A year later, Power continued to respond to such charges, telling Paige Williams of London's *Financial Times* that "it causes me great discomfort when my book is read in its most narrow sense, which is that, 'The United States should intervene militarily when it feels like it.'"

Power has discussed in the media the 1988 incident in which Saddam Hussein deployed chemical weapons against the Kurds in northern Iraq. A year later, the first President Bush doubled U.S. foreign aid to Iraq. The time to have intervened in Iraqi atrocities, Power has argued, was back then, when nearly 100,000 Kurds were thought to have been killed by Hussein's genocidal act. "The unfortunate part of the relationship about human rights and security is that now we view the welfare of foreign citizens as valuable and relevant only in so far as it advances our security," she contended in the *Financial Times* interview.

Power is planning a work on the ideas of Hannah Arendt, the German-American writer who wrote extensively on politics and authoritarianism. She views her work as a continuation of Lemkin's crusade, and believes that the best defense against preventing future Holocausts is to make human rights an integral part of U.S. foreign policy. Had that happened during the first Bush Administration, she argues, the 2003 invasion might not have been necessary. "You can't allow these kinds of crimes to go unnoticed," she pointed out in the *New York Times* interview with Bohlen, "and not have them come back and reflect on us."

## Selected writings

*Breakdown in the Balkans: A Chronicle of Events, January, 1989 to May, 1993,* preface by Morton Abramowitz, Carnegie Endowment for International Peace (Washington, DC), 1993.

(Editor with Graham Allison) *Realizing Human Rights: Moving from Inspiration to Impact,* St. Martin's Press (New York, NY), 2000.

*A Problem from Hell: America and the Age of Genocide,* Basic Books (New York, NY), 2002.

# Sources

**Periodicals**

*Atlantic Monthly,* September 2001, p. 8.
*Commonweal,* May 3, 2002, p. 21.
*Cosmopolitan,* August 2003, p. 62.
*Financial Times,* March 13, 2004, p. 14.
*New Statesman,* July 21, 2003, p. 48.
*New York Times,* February 5, 2003, p. E1.
*Time,* October 4, 2004, p. 63.
*U.S. News and World Report,* April 11, 1994, p. 15.

**Online**

*Contemporary Authors Online,* Gale, 2003.

—*Carol Brennan*

# Larry Probst

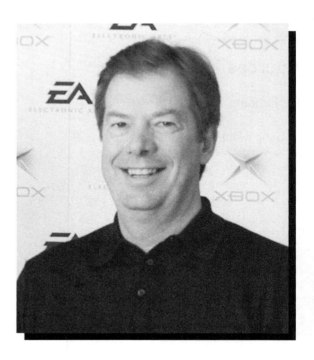

AP/Wide World Photos

## Chief Executive Officer of Electronic Arts

**B**orn Lawrence F. Probst III, c. 1951; married Nancy; children: Scott, Chip. *Education:* Received undergraduate degree from University of Delaware.

**Addresses:** *Office*—Electronic Arts, 209 Redwood Shores Pkwy., Redwood City, CA 94065-1175.

## Career

**H**eld sales positions with Johnson & Johnson and Clorox; worked for Activision, 1982-84; joined Electronic Arts, September, 1984, as vice president of sales; senior vice president of distribution, after January, 1987, president, 1990—, chief executive officer, 1991—; chair, 1994—.

## Sidelights

**L**arry Probst helms Electronic Arts (EA), the largest independent videogame publisher in the world. Chief executive officer of the company since the early 1990s, Probst has led EA to dominance in the highly competitive field of interactive entertainment. By 2002, it was No. 1 in American sales and took in some $2.5 billion in revenues worldwide. "Under Probst," declared *Newsweek* journalist N'Gai Croal, "EA took what was an unpredictable hit-driven business dominated by iconoclastic Japanese creators and turned it into a machine that relentlessly delivers high-quality blockbusters, like clockwork, aimed primarily at mainstream North American and European audiences."

Born in the early 1950s, Probst studied business administration at the University of Delaware, and spent several years in sales at Johnson & Johnson, the personal-care products maker. He moved on to a similar position with Clorox, but was recruited in 1982 by Activision, the leading videogame software maker at the time. Activision was thriving as the developer of games for the popular Atari system back then, and Probst learned the business before jumping ship to rival company Electronic Arts.

Probst had been hand-picked for the job of sales vice president by EA's enigmatic founder, Trip Hawkins. He was given carte blanche to hire a direct sales team, which was a first in the gaming industry. This helped EA increase its market position considerably over the next few years. In early 1987, Probst became a senior vice president for distribution, and was made company president three years later when Hawkins departed to launch his new venture, 3DO. 3DO was a hardware gaming console, and the first to use the compact-disc format, but it retailed for nearly $700 and had some technical issues. EA was a major shareholder in 3DO, and made games for it as well, and Probst was faulted at the time for not pulling the plug on the 3DO strategy soon enough.

Probst was named EA's chief executive officer in 1991, which gave him the freedom to pursue a new corporate plan to conquer the console gaming market. Until then, EA had mainly made games for PCs, but a new generation of Sega and Nintendo players was capturing large numbers of devotees. Probst oversaw a massive expansion of EA over the next decade. It went from $100 million in annual sales in 1991 to six times that five years later. He bought out eight other game-makers, and invested in several more. EA became the leader in domestic sales in United States, in part by putting out popular releases in all formats, from PlayStation to Nintendo. In the mid-1990s, it moved into valuable new Internet territory with Ultima Online, a multi-player subscription game that can accommodate up to 3,000 players at a time.

EA's top sellers were the Madden NFL Football game, and its "Sims" series, which had a number of popular PC titles. Company revenues skyrocketed in 2002, though the company had actually issued fewer titles than the year before. "We do fewer things, and we do them better," Probst conceded in an interview with *Time International* writer Chris Taylor. "We don't just throw something at the wall and hope it sticks."

Probst is the boss of some 5,000 employees worldwide from his office at EA's Redwood City, California, headquarters. By 2004, EA's sales figures were nearing $3 billion, and the company's stock was also performing well after posting profits of $577 million. Even he confessed to a bit of astonishment when he reviewed his career. When he joined EA, he told a writer for the *San Francisco Chronicle,* "we had about 40 or 50 employees and $8 million in revenue, and it was a pretty different thing. I don't think any of us could have imagined that we would have this kind of growth and this kind of success over the past 20 years. It's been phenomenal."

Probst had continued to lead the company into new and lucrative strategies, including tie-ins with major movie studios for games that mimicked blockbuster films, such as *The Lord of the Rings* and the *Harry Potter* franchise. The internal structure at EA has sometimes been compared to that of the famed Hogwarts academy for young wizards that the fictional Potter attends. There are several teams at the company, and each is responsible for their own game development and sales. Each tries to outdo one another, though they do share some of technical leaps—the same highly realistic blade of grass on the field of *Madden NFL 2003,* for example, can also be found in the next Harry Potter title.

As for the future of the gaming industry, Probst was hesitant to make concrete predictions. "I can't give you a vision ten years out," he told the interviewer for the *San Francisco Chronicle* in 2004. "Anybody that pretends that they can, get as far away from them as you can get because they're making it up. Five years, in terms of what are the products going to look like, imagine Nemo-like graphics with much more realistic characters and animation."

Recognizing the growth of the industry since he joined EA in 1984, Probst has led the company into educational ventures with the film school at the University of Southern California and another with high-tech leader, Pittsburgh's Carnegie Mellon University. The *San Francisco Chronicle* journalist asked him a few obvious questions near the interview's close. "No, I don't know the cheat codes," Probst replied. "And to be very honest, I don't spend a lot of time playing games. I spend a lot of time watching people play games. My most favorite games tend to be the ones selling the best at that moment." He did admit to one memorable Atari title, a game that came out in 1983. "My favorite is [an] Activision-published [game] called Seaquest," he told the newspaper. "I was really good at it, really good."

## Sources

*Newsweek,* December 29, 2003, p. 101.
*New York Times,* May 8, 1995, p. D7.
*San Francisco Business Times,* September 26, 1997, p. 8A.
*San Francisco Chronicle,* May 9, 2004, p. J1.
*Time International,* July 7, 2003, p. 46.

—*Carol Brennan*

# Albert Pujols

AP/Wide World Photos

## Professional baseball player

**B**orn Jose Albert Pujols, January 16, 1980; son of Bienvenido Pujols (a minor league pitcher); married Deidre (a secretary), January 1, 2000; children: Isabella (stepdaughter), A.J. (Albert Jose). *Religion:* Born-again Christian. *Education:* Attended Maple Woods Community College, Kansas City, MO.

**Addresses:** *Office*—c/o St. Louis Cardinals, 250 Stadium Plaza, St. Louis, MO 63102.

## Career

**D**rafted by St. Louis Cardinals, 1999; played for Class A Peoria Chiefs, A Potomac Cannons, and AAA Memphis Redbirds, 2000; played third base, outfield, and first base for St. Louis Cardinals, 2001—.

**Awards:** National League Rookie of the Year, 2001; St. Louis Baseball Man of the Year, 2002-05; Most Valuable Player Award, National League Championship Series, 2004; Silver Slugger Award, 2004; two additional Silver Slugger Awards.

## Sidelights

**D**rafted by the St. Louis Cardinals at the age of 19, Albert Pujols spent only one full season in the minor leagues before joining the Cardinals' major league roster. The 6'3", 225 lb. baseball player soon proved his worth, emerging as one of St. Louis's most versatile players. A strong hitter who often got on base, Pujols played third base, first base, and two outfield positions for the team. Despite his early success, Pujols remained humble and focused much of his off-field energy on his family.

Born Jose Albert Pujols on January 16, 1980, he is the son of Bienvenido Pujols, who had been a pitcher in the minor leagues in the Dominican Republic. Pujols spent his youth in the Dominican Republic, raised in poverty primarily by his grandmother, named America. He had little contact with his parents, who had divorced when he was very young. When Pujols was about 16 years old, he moved to the United States with his father and other family members. They settled in Independence, Missouri, where a small Dominican community existed and his grandmother already lived. He later studied to become an American citizen.

When Pujols arrived in Missouri, he did not speak English, but picked it up while attending Fort Osage High School. He also played baseball and proved to be a natural at the sport. Pujols played for two years and was named all-state twice. Even as a high school player, he possessed a sense of discipline that would serve him well as a professional player. After high school, Pujols attended Maple Woods Community College in Kansas City, Missouri, for one season. That year, he posted a .461 batting average on the school's team.

In 1999, Pujols was drafted by the St. Louis Cardinals in the 13th round. He was the 402nd overall pick in the draft. Pujols soon signed with the team for $60,000. The Cardinals believed they were putting a good hitter under contract, but had no real idea of the talent they were obtaining. Before the start of Pujols' professional playing career, he married his girlfriend, Deidre, a woman he had been dating since he was 18 years old. She already had a toddler daughter named Isabella who had Down syndrome. The couple became very active in associations related to the disease. They later had a son together named A.J.

Pujols played one season of minor league baseball, in 2000. He spent much of the season with St. Louis's A club, the Peoria Chiefs. Pujols posted a .314 batting average, with 19 homeruns and 96 runs batted in (RBIs). Both he and his wife also worked as waiters at a local country club to help support themselves. Over the course of the season, Pujols moved up, playing for the A Potomac Cannons for 21 games and ended the season with AAA Memphis Redbirds for three games. He also played in the AAA world series.

In 2001, Pujols went to spring training with the Cardinals and though he was expected to spend the season with AAA Memphis, an injury to a teammate opened up a spot for him with the Cardinals. Two of the team's best players, Jim Edmonds and Mark McGwire, were soon injured, and Pujols became a regular player. Though Pujols primarily played third base, the team already had a third baseman and needed outfielders. Thus, he played both right field and left field during the season. He also proved that he was the skilled hitter the team thought he was when they drafted him.

Though no one really knew Pujols, his calm, professional play on the field brought him attention and praise, and not just from his team. With Pujols playing a significant role in the Cardinals' success, the team moved into contention for a wild card playoff berth. Lloyd McClendon, manager of the Pittsburgh Pirates, told Tom Verducci of *Sports Illustrated*, "I've never seen anything like it. He's quick to the ball with his bat, he hits to all fields, he rarely goes outside the strike zone, and no situation seems to rattle him. This young man has a chance to be quite a force for some time in this league."

Pujols finished the year with a .329 batting average, 194 hits, and 37 home runs. He was the most productive offensive player for St. Louis and helped revitalize the team. Because of his success, Pujols was unanimously voted National League Rookie of the Year. Some observers believed that he should have won the National League Most Valuable Player Award. Pujols received a new contract with the Cardinals in the off-season, a one-year deal worth at least $600,000.

Pujols proved his 2001 season was not a fluke from 2002 through 2004. In 2002, he had a batting average of .314, with 185 hits and 34 homeruns. Pujols still led the Cardinals offensively, when other players like Edmonds were injured. Pujols also continued to field where needed, playing both third base and left field again. St. Louis reached the National League Championship series, before losing. Pujols was runner up for the National League Most Valuable Player Award.

The 2003 season showed marked improvement for Pujols. Playing both first base and left field, he went on an offensive tear, with a 30-game hitting streak during the season. His numbers went even higher, with a batting average of .359, with 212 hits and 43 homeruns. He was consistent like the great players in baseball to which he was often compared. William Gildea wrote in the *Washington Post,* "No player has achieved what Pujols has in the first three years of his major league career. None: not Ruth or Cobb, DiMaggio or Williams, Mays or Mantle, Brett or Gwynn. No one before Pujols ... amassed at least 30 home runs, 100 runs scored, and 100 RBI during each of his first three seasons."

One reason for Pujols' success was his hard work in the off season. He spent a lot of time in batting cages and lifting weights to improve his forearm strength. He also worked on his swing. Such work led to financial rewards. Before the 2004 season, Pujols signed a seven-year contract worth $100 million with the Cardinals. However, the 2004 season was frustrating for Pujols. Throughout the season, he suffered from a painful heel injury—a plantar fasciitis—which prevented him from playing his best. He also suffered from elbow problems. Despite these issues, Pujols' season was productive. He still hit on a consistent basis, producing a hit in nearly every game. Pujols had 46 homeruns and 123 RBIs. Pujols also had a new position, first base. He was named the team's first baseman during the season, in part because of his elbow problems.

St. Louis still won their division and then a tough National League Championship series. The Cardinals defeated the Houston Astros in seven games. Pujols had four home runs and a .500 batting average in the series. Though St. Louis made it to World Series, they lost in four straight games to the Boston

Red Sox. Pujols still had a .333 batting average, but only five hits and did not play as well as he had earlier in the season.

Though Pujols faced continued problems with his heel in 2005, he was still regarded as a player with unlimited potential. He was only in his mid-twenties. Pujols believed that his natural abilities combined with hard work led to his success. He told Jack Etkin of the *Rocky Mountain News,* "I've been blessed. I don't know how. The main thing is I can read a pitcher. I can make adjustments. People wonder how I'm able to do that. I don't know. I can't explain.... I try to see the ball and have a plan. That's how you become a good hitter, when you tell yourself what's you're doing wrong and correct it the next at-bat."

## Sources

### Periodicals

*Los Angeles Times,* October 27, 2004, p. D1.
*People,* October 11, 2004, pp. 81-82.

*Rocky Mountain News,* September 8, 2003, p. 4H.
*San Diego Union-Tribune,* October 26, 2004, p. D1.
*Sports Illustrated,* April 16, 2001, p. 48; October 1, 2001, p. 44; October 25, 2004, p. 48.
*St. Louis Post-Dispatch,* March 3, 2002, p. D1; June 18, 2002, p. E1; November 3, 2004, p. D2; February 27, 2004, p. D1; October 24, 2004, p. O2; January 18, 2005, p. C1.
*Washington Post,* August 24, 2003, p. E1.

### Online

"Albert Pujols," ESPN.com, http://sports.espn.go.com/mlb/players/profile?statsId-6619 (February 1, 2005).
"Albert Pujols Player Page," *SI.com,* http://sports illustrated.cnn.com/baseball/mlb/players/6619/ (February 1, 2005).

*—A. Petruso*

# Manny Ramirez

*Daniel Bersak/Ai Wire/Landov*

## Professional baseball player

**B**orn Manuel Aristides Ramirez, May 30, 1972, in Santo Domingo, Dominican Republic; son of Aristides (a cab driver) and Onelcidad (a seamstress) Ramirez; married to Juliana Monterio (October, 2001); children: Manuel, Manny Jr.

**Addresses:** *Contact*—Boston Red Sox, 4 Yawkey Way, Boston, MA 02215-3496. *Home*—Fort Lauderdale, FL.

## Career

**D**rafted out of high school by the Cleveland Indians to play in the Appalachian League, 1991; promoted to Class-A Carolina League, 1992; played in Class-AA Eastern League and Class-AAA International League, 1993; made major league debut for the Indians, September, 1993; became a free agent, 2000; joined Boston Red Sox, 2001.

**Awards:** New York City Public Schools High School Player of the Year, 1991; named to American League All-Star team, 1995, 1998-2004; American League Hank Aaron Award, 1999, 2004; Major League Baseball World Series Most Valuable Player award, 2004.

## Sidelights

**B**oston Red Sox leftfielder Manny Ramirez started the 2004 season as an outcast after the franchise spent the off-season trying to give him away. While Ramirez shone as an RBI machine, his eccentricities and fielding mishaps had become too much to bear.

No one else wanted him either, so Ramirez stayed in Boston. However, he turned his fortune around, becoming an unstoppable force from the batter's box. Ramirez's super slugging propelled the Red Sox to a 2004 World Series championship and earned him World Series MVP honors.

Manuel Aristides Ramirez was born on May 30, 1972, in Santo Domingo, Dominican Republic, to Aristides and Onelcidad Ramirez. The family relocated to New York City in 1985 hoping to build a better life than their poverty-stricken island could provide. They settled in the Washington Heights area of Manhattan, a place filled with Dominican immigrants, though plagued by drugs and violence. Ramirez's father drove cabs while his mother found work as a seamstress.

When Ramirez started playing little league baseball he was often benched. A coach suggested he become a pitcher because his batting skills were so poor. Ramirez, however, was determined to master the game and follow in the footsteps of his hero, Jorge Bell, a Dominican-born American League MVP who played for the Toronto Blue Jays in the 1980s. To improve his game, Ramirez awoke at 4:30 a.m. to practice before school.

Ramirez's dedication paid off. By high school, he was the star third baseman and outfielder at George Washington High School. In 1991, his last year in school, Ramirez hit .643 and was named High School Player of the Year for all of New York City's public schools. Ramirez left high school a few credits shy of graduation, entered the 1991 draft and was picked by the Cleveland Indians in the first round. Ramirez's first season in the minors, playing in Burlington, North Carolina, proved tough. Ramirez grew so depressed and homesick that one night, after going hitless, he told his roommate he was leaving. This teammate persuaded Ramirez to tough it out and advised him to relax and try to have fun. Since then Ramirez has made a career of not taking himself too seriously, though this attitude sometimes frustrates teammates.

After the pep talk, he burned his way through the minor league divisions and in September of 1993 was called up to the majors. Ramirez went hitless his first game, then headed to play at Yankee Stadium in his hometown. Friends and family flocked to the game and Ramirez produced, smacking a double his first at-bat, followed by two homers. With his quicksilver swing, Ramirez showed enormous potential as a hitter and remained on the Indians' roster at the start of the next season.

Lacking focus and maturity, Ramirez earned a reputation as one of baseball's most oblivious players. At times, he left the batter's box for first base on the third ball instead of waiting for the fourth. Once, a batter smacked a ball under the bullpen bench and Ramirez refused to dig it out, handing the hitter an in-the-park homer. When the Indians made it to the 1995 World Series, Ramirez infuriated teammates when he got picked off first base, then pranced smiling to the dugout. Teammates found his personal habits odd, too. He dyed his hair orange and borrowed pants from other players. Despite his downfalls, Ramirez's slugging kept him in the lineup. During his seven full seasons with the Indians, Ramirez batted .319 and averaged 36 homers and 123 RBI a year. Four of those seasons, he made the All-Star team.

After becoming a free agent in 2000, Ramirez, who had proven himself a true slugging machine, set off a bidding war and signed with the Boston Red Sox in 2001. From the batter's box, Ramirez gave the Sox the help they needed. In 2002, Ramirez won the American League batting title with his .349 average. His immature antics, however, continued. In 2001, Ramirez skipped the All-Star workouts, claiming his grandmother had died, though he provided no details. In 2002, he showed up late for spring training, broke a finger during a foolish headfirst slide and was demoted to the minor leagues for rehab. While there he halted a game to search for a diamond earring he had lost. Ramirez rejoined the Red Sox and while his hitting was hot, his behavior enraged teammates. In one game, Ramirez hit a grounder and headed straight for the dugout instead of running it out.

Ramirez proved productive at times, but his strange behavior grated on teammates, fans, and coaches alike. In 2003 Ramirez caused an outrage when he refused to play in a game because of a sore throat. That night, he was spotted at the Boston Ritz-Carlton meeting a friend. Though he hit .325 in 2003—second in the American League—the Red Sox placed him on irrevocable waivers at the season's end. In other words, instead of trading him, the Red Sox were willing to give him away to anyone willing to take over the rest of his eight-year, $160 million contract.

During the off-season, Ramirez seemed to undergo a transformation. At the start of the 2004 season, he made himself more available to the media and showed fans a long-hidden friendly side. Ramirez grew out his hair and became more carefree, encouraging his teammates to do the same. Ramirez's play was startling as well and he went from "unwanted to unstoppable," according to Charles P. Pierce in *Sports Illustrated*. During regular-season play, Ramirez hit .308 and had 43 homers and 130 RBI. With help from Ramirez's bat, the Red Sox won the American League championship and faced the St. Louis Cardinals in the World Series.

In Game One, Ramirez made an error in left field that cost his team a run, followed by a second one that nearly cost the game. Teammates, however, brushed his blunders aside. As Pedro Martinez remarked to the *Boston Herald*'s Howard Bryant, "That was just Manny being Manny. You know at some point during the game, however, that he's going to do something good to help you win."

That is exactly what Ramirez did. From the batter's box, Ramirez was relentless and his batting prowess helped the underdog Red Sox to a four-game sweep. In sum Ramirez hit .412 in the series, going 7-for-17 with four RBI to earn the World Series's Most Valuable Player award and help the Sox break a curse that gave them their first championship in 86 years.

## Sources

### Books

Vascellaro, Charlie, *Latinos in Baseball: Manny Ramirez*, Mitchell Lane Publishers, Inc., 2000.

## Periodicals

*Boston Herald,* October 30, 2004, Sports, p. 148.

*New York Times,* June 18, 1995, sec. 8, p. 7; September 23, 1997, p. C1.

*Sports Illustrated,* July 5, 2004, p. 56; November 10, 2004, p. 80.

## Online

"Manny Ramirez," Baseball-Reference.com, http://www.baseball-reference.com/r/ramirma02.shtml (May 9, 2005).

*—Lisa Frick*

# Raven

## Actress and singer

**B**orn Raven-Symone Christina Pearman, December 10, 1985, in Atlanta, GA; daughter of Christoper (a manager) and Lydia (Gaulden) Pearman.

**Addresses:** *Agent*—International Creative Management, 8942 Wilshire Blvd., Beverly Hills, CA 90211-1934.

## Career

**M**odel, 1986-89; appeared in television commercials for Cool Whip, Ritz Crackers, and other products, 1986-89. Recording artist, 1993—. Television appearances include: *The Cosby Show,* 1989-1992; *A Different World,* 1989; *The Muppets at Walt Disney World* (movie), 1990; *The Fresh Prince of Bel-Air,* 1992; *Queen* (miniseries; uncredited) 1993; *Hangin' with Mr. Cooper,* 1993-97; *Happily Ever After: Fairy Tales for Every Child* (voice), 1995; *Space Ghost Coast to Coast,* 1997; *Zenon: Girl of the 21st Century* (movie), 1999; *My Wife and Kids,* 2001; *The Proud Family* (voice), 2001; *Kim Possible* (voice), 2002; *That's So Raven,* 2002—; *The Cheetah Girls* (movie), 2003; *Kim Possible: A Sitch in Time* (movie; voice), 2003; *Zenon: Z3* (movie), 2004. Film appearances include: *Little Rascals,* 1994; *Doctor Dolittle,* 1998; *Dr. Dolittle 2,* 2001; *Princess Diaries 2: Royal Engagement,* 2004; *Fat Albert* (voice), 2004.

**Awards:** Young Artists Award for Exceptional Performance by a Young Artist Under Nine, for *The Cosby Show,* 1991; Image Award for Outstanding Performance in a Youth/Children's Program, for *That's So Raven,* 2004.

AP/Wide World Photos

## Sidelights

**A**lthough most child stars fade in popularity as they get older, Raven is one of the few whose fame has grown through the years. She began her career as a three year old on the hit television sitcom *The Cosby Show,* continued to act on the show *Hangin' With Mr. Cooper,* and since has branched out into film roles and recording contracts, largely with Disney, which considers her to be its next big star.

Born Raven-Symone Christina Pearman in Atlanta, Georgia, in 1985, Raven is the daughter of Christopher Pearman, who continues to work as her manager, and his wife, Lydia. Her parents signed her up to model before she was two years old, and she was so successful at it that they decided to move to New York City, the hub of modeling and television commercial work. Raven was soon acting in commercials. Although she was young, she had a quick mind and the ability to memorize lines. She and her parents liked to watch *The Cosby Show,* starring Bill Cosby and featuring an educated, middle-class African-American family, the Huxtables, living in Brooklyn. Raven observed the girl playing the youngest daughter, Rudy, and as her father told Douglas C. Lyons in *Ebony,* often said, "I can do that. Why can't I be on *The Cosby Show?*"

Raven did audition for a role in the Bill Cosby film *Ghost Dad,* but instead, he offered her a role on the show. She began appearing on the show during its sixth season in 1989, playing a toddler named Olivia, the stepchild of the second Huxtable daughter, Denise, who had married Martin, a naval officer. Raven was a hit with viewers, and did so well in this role that she stayed until the show's final episode in 1992. She told CNN.com's David Haffenreffer that because she was so young when she did the show, the details of her work there are "fading very slowly. The one thing I do remember is working with the people and how wonderful they were to me and I was very fortunate to go onto a set at such a young age with so many veterans in such a wonderful atmosphere. It was something good to start the business off at."

Raven told Jessica Shevlin and Katie Nappi in the *Houston Chronicle* that she still sometimes sees reruns of *The Cosby Show.* "It's kind of cool seeing yourself that young. I'm not able to remember much of it, so it's kind of like looking at someone else." She commented to Michael A. Lipton in *People,* "I'll always be known as a Cosby kid. And it doesn't bother me. I get to keep that fan base."

In addition to her acting aspirations, Raven also wanted a singing career. She told her father about her dream, and he began looking for a deal for her. Eventually he found one, and when she was five years old, Raven signed with MCA, the youngest artist ever to join the label. She released her debut single, "That's What Little Girls Are Made Of," in 1993 as part of the LP *Here's to New Dreams,* which featured a medley of R&B, pop, and dance tunes. In *Jet,* a reviewer commented that the album was "getting a lot of airplay."

During the early 1990s, Raven made appearances in various television shows, including *The Muppets at Walt Disney World, The Fresh Prince of Bel-Air, Queen,* and *Space Ghost Coast to Coast.* In 1993 Raven won a part on the sitcom *Hangin' with Mr. Cooper,* playing Nicole, the daughter of Cooper's cousin. At the time, the seven- year-old Raven told a *Jet* interviewer, "I love this show. It was the second show that I saw and wanted to be on." She added, "There are a lot of great writers and producers on this show." She also said that her character was different from the one she played on *Cosby*: "For one, I'm a lot older here. Olivia was a lot younger. Olivia has grown into Nicole. I'm in a new city and trying to learn new things."

In 1994, Raven made her debut on film in a remake of the 1930s series *Little Rascals,* playing Stymie's girlfriend. She continued to work in the latter half of the 1990s, providing her voice for the role of Goldilocks in the animated television series *Happily Ever After: Fairy Tales for Every Child* in 1995. In 1998 she appeared in the film *Dr. Dolittle,* which starred Eddie Murphy playing a vet who can talk to animals; she played one of his daughters. She appeared in the same role in the film's sequel in 2001.

When Raven released her second LP, *Undeniable,* in 1999, it did well enough to earn her an opening spot for the teen pop band N'Sync's tour. However, while she was on tour, she still had to complete her schoolwork. As she explained in a *Jet* interview, her parents warned her, "You can be in the business all you want but you better graduate with honors." She continued to juggle acting and schoolwork when she landed a role on the animated series *Kim Possible,* providing the voice of Monique. When she got this role, she dropped "Symone" from her name, using only "Raven."

In 2002, she landed a major role when Disney chose her to star in her own sitcom, *That's So Raven.* The series featured Raven as a psychic teenager who can see a few seconds into the future, but no farther, an ability that gets her into various wacky situations. Raven told CNN.com's Haffenreffer, "It has a lot of physical comedy." The series soon had 1.9 million viewers each week, and Raven was considered to be Disney's next famous face, according to Disney Channel entertainment president Rich Ross, who told Nicholas Fonseca in *Entertainment Weekly,* "We expect her to be a big star for this company." Fans of the show, many of whom were children, believed wholeheartedly in the show's premise that she was psychic, and as she told a *Jet* interviewer, "Little kids are coming up to me asking me, ' What's my future?' I [tell them], 'I'm not really psychic.' And they are like, 'No, what's my future?' And I am like, 'OK, you are going to have a good future.'"

In addition to working on the television show, Raven also appeared in a Disney television movie in 2003: *The Cheetah Girls.* The film told the story of an all-female pop group that hoped to make it big by winning their high-school talent contest. In *Daily Variety,* Laura Fries wrote that the film "aspires to be a culturally diverse morality lesson disguised as musical fantasy. Instead, it's a diva training film." She also panned the movie's unmemorable plot, noting, "The pic is all about the hair, the look, the attitude. And like hungry cheetahs on the prowl, teen audiences will probably eat it up." However, she noted that the film "does have a few things going for it, namely Raven, an appealing and versatile young actress who has charm and skill."

Raven also sang on the film's soundtrack—which eventually went platinum despite the critics' comments about the film. She was thinking about enrolling in culinary school after she graduated from high school, but she also had more film roles in her future. She was slated to appear in a remake of a 1976 film, *Sparkle*, about a singing group that resembled the Supremes. It was originally supposed to star singer Aaliyah, but was temporarily shelved when that singer was killed in a plane crash. Raven was cast as the youngest in the three-sister group, which would undergo conflict and tragedy in their pursuit of success. She planned to watch the original version only once, she told *Entertainment Weekly*'s Fonseca, "Just to make sure I'm on the right track. I don't want to follow in anybody else's footsteps." She would do all her own singing in the film.

Disney also planned to have Raven star in *All American Girl*, a feature film about a girl who inadvertently rescues the president of the United States. In the film, she would play a part that was originally written for a white girl; the script would be adapted to reflect an African-American sensibility. The film was slated to be released in 2005. Raven also planned to release another album, with the aid of a variety of producers, which would feature hip-hop, alternative, and neo-soul tracks. She told *Entertainment Weekly*'s Fonseca that she was influenced by a wide range of performers: "I listen to everything from Jay-Z to Bjork to Avril Lavigne to Mary J. Blige."

In addition to her onscreen film roles, Raven found work providing voices for animated productions. Having worked on the television show *Kim Possible*, she provided the voice of Monique for the television movies *Kim Possible: The Secret Files* and *Kim Possible: A Stitch in Time*. She also provided the voice of Danielle in *Fat Albert*, released in 2004.

In 2004, Raven graduated from high school, but she was immediately bored by the lack of work to do and the abundance of free time. Nevertheless, she told CNN.com's Haffenreffer that she was "still having fun. I just turned 18 in December. So I'm having a wonderful time being a teenager. I'm just sitting back and enjoying it all." In addition to her acting, she contributed to the CD *Disney Mania 2*. She told Haffenreffer that the success of the Disney CDs came from the public's "familiarity with the songs and the people singing the songs." On September 21, 2004, Raven released the album *This Is My Time*, which included a mix of pop and R&B songs. She co-wrote five of the songs.

Raven is still thinking about going to culinary school, but only when her busy schedule subsides. "I don't want to worry about skipping spaghetti class because I have to make a movie," she told Michael Moses in *Teen People*. She has also thought about moving into the fashion world, with her own line of clothing. She told Julee Greenberg in *WWD*, "I would do it for girls who are built like me. When I shop for myself it's very hard to find clothes. I'm curvy and there should be more clothes out there for curvy girls." For now, Raven plans to concentrate on acting and singing. She told *Entertainment Weekly*'s Fonseca, "I'm very comfortable with what I do. I like entertaining people and making them laugh."

## Selected discography

*Here's to New Dreams*, MCA, 1993.
*Undeniable*, Crash, 1999.
(Contributor) *Disney Mania 2*, Disney, 2004.
*This Is My Time*, Hollywood, 2004.

## Sources

### Books

*Contemporary Black Biography*, vol. 44, Gale Group, 2004.

### Periodicals

*Daily Variety*, August 15, 2003, p. 8; August 18, 2003, p. 5.
*Ebony*, May 1990, p. 106.
*Entertainment Weekly*, October 17, 2003, pp. 42-43.
*Houston Chronicle*, November 27, 2003, p. 2.
*Jet*, July 5, 1993, p. 61; November 8, 1993, p. 58; September 8, 2003, p. 60.
*People*, May 20, 2002, p. 140; October 18, 2004, p. 46.
*Teen People*, February 1, 2004, p. 93.
*WWD*, August 7, 2003, p. 12.

### Online

"Getting the Scoop on Disney TV's Raven," CNN. com, http://www.cnn.com (August 30, 2004).
"Raven," Internet Movie Database, http://www.imbd.com/name/nm0712368/ (August 30, 2004).
"That's So Raven," TV Tome, http://www.tvtome.com/tvtome/serlet/ShowMainServlet/showed-8257/ (August 30, 2004).

*—Kelly Winters*

# Joan Rivers

**Comedian, writer, actress, and television show host**

Born Joan Alexandra Molinsky, June 8, 1933, in Brooklyn, NY; daughter of Meyer C. (a physician) and Beatrice Molinsky; married James Sanger (an heir to a department store fortune), 1957 (annulled, 1958); married Edgar Rosenberg (a manager, executive, and producer), 1964 (committed suicide, August 14, 1987); children: Melissa (from second marriage). *Education:* Attended Connecticut College for Women; Barnard College, B.A. (English and anthropology), 1954.

**Addresses:** *Agent*—William Morris Agency, 151 El Camino Dr., Beverly Hills, CA 90212. *Office*—c/o QVC, 1200 Wilson Dr. at Studio Park, Westchester, PA 19380. *Website*—http://www.joanrivers.com.

## Career

Worked as fashion coordinator for Bond Clothing Store and as publicist in New York department store Lord & Taylor, 1950s; actress in Off Broadway plays; worked as a comedian touring United States, billed as Pepper January; appeared with Second City improvisational troupe, 1961-62; wrote for television show *Candid Camera*; first appearance on *The Tonight Show*, NBC, 1965; released album *Joan Rivers Presents Mr. Phyllis and Other Funny Stories*, Warner Bros., 1965; first appearance on *The Ed Sullivan Show*, 1966; continued to tour as a comedian, 1960s-1970s; had own talk show, *That Show Starring Joan Rivers*, 1968; made big-screen debut in *The Swimmer*, 1968; wrote and starred in Broadway play, *Fun City*, 1972; co-wrote television

movie, *The Girl Most Likely To ...*, ABC, 1973; wrote syndicated column for *Chicago Tribune*; wrote and directed feature film *Rabbit Test*, 1977; co-creator of television series *Husbands, Wives, and Lovers*, CBS, 1978; worked as substitute host for *The Tonight Show*, through early 1980s; signed contract to be permanent co-host for Carson on *The Tonight Show*, 1983; released album *What Becomes a Semi-Legend Most*, Geffen, 1983; appeared as guest host, *Saturday Night Live*, NBC; signed to be host of *The Late Show*, FOX, 1985; center square on *Hollywood Squares* game show, 1987; had role in *Broadway Bound*, 1988; had own daytime talk show, *The Joan Rivers Show*, 1988-93; had talk show *Joan Rivers' Gossip! Gossip! Gossip!*, USA, 1992-93; sold line of jewelry on QVC home shopping network, 1992—; had talk show *Can We Shop?*, syndicated, 1994; co-wrote the stage show *Sally Marr ... and Her Escorts*, 1994; co-wrote and appeared in *Tears and Laughter: The Joan and Melissa Rivers Story*, NBC, 1994; hostess of pre-award show programs for E! Entertainment Television, 1995-2004; made guest appearances on *Another World*, NBC, 1997; radio talk-show host, WOR, 1997-2002; performed *Broke and Alone in London* (solo show), West End, London, 2002; guest appearance on *Nip/Tuck*, F/X, 2004; provided voice for animated film *Shrek 2*, 2004; host of pre-award show programs for TV Guide Channel, 2004—.

**Awards:** Georgie Award for best comedian, American Guild of Variety Artists, 1975; Clio Awards, best performance in a TV commercial, 1976, 1982; Daytime Emmy Award for best talk show host, for *The Joan Rivers Show,* 1990; Marymount Manhattan College, honorary doctorate, 1996.

## Sidelights

In the early 2000s, Joan Rivers was best known for her work as a red carpet fashion commentator for the Academy Awards, Emmys, and other major awards shows. However, she has had a varied career, working on stage, film, and television. Rivers began her career as a touring comedian before her big break on *The Tonight Show* in the 1960s. In the 1970s, she wrote and/or starred in films, plays, and television movies. By the 1980s, Rivers had a high profile, first as the permanent guest host of *The Tonight Show* then as the host of her own, usually short-lived talk shows. Rivers re-invented herself in the mid-1990s as a fashion commentator who often appeared with her daughter, Melissa.

Rivers was born Joan Alexandra Molinsky on June 8, 1933, in the borough of Brooklyn in New York City. She was the daughter of Meyer and Beatrice Molinsky. Her father was a doctor, while her mother had been born to wealth in Imperial Russia, but her family had become impoverished during the Russian Revolution. Rivers was raised in wealth with an older sister, Barbara, who became an attorney and was seen as better and more accomplished than her younger sister.

Rivers attended Connecticut College for Women, then Barnard College. As a student, she appeared in college productions of *Othello* and *An Ideal Husband.* Rivers earned her B.A. in English and anthropology from Barnard College in 1954. She then worked for Lord & Taylor, a New York City-based department store, as a publicist, as well as a fashion coordinator for Bond Clothing Stores in the 1950s. Rivers married for the first time to James Sanger, the heir to the Bond Stores fortune, in 1957. The marriage was short-lived, and annulled the following year.

When her marriage to Sanger ended, Rivers went home for a time and decided that she wanted to be an actress. She studied the craft and appeared in some Off Broadway plays. Rivers soon turned to comedy when she was told that was where her talents laid. She did not really have the support of her family, who wanted Rivers to marry. Instead, Rivers supported herself by becoming a comedian touring the United States under the name Pepper January.

From 1961 to 1962, Rivers worked with Second City, the well-known improvisational comedy troupe. After this run, she continued to perform as a comedian, primarily working in New York City. Her comedy focused on politics and society. Rivers had one immediate goal: appearing on *The Tonight Show with Johnny Carson.* After a number of unsuccessful attempts, she finally made her debut on the show in 1965. Carson said he enjoyed her act and stated she would be successful. This marked Rivers' first big break. She soon appeared on *The Ed Sullivan Show,* a popular variety show, for the first time.

As Rivers' professional career began to soar, her personal life also improved. In 1964, she married her second husband, Edgar Rosenberg, a British producer. Together, they had one child, a daughter named Melissa. Rosenberg supported his wife's career and helped her hone her comedy act. He also helped her work through her fears about performing. Rivers' comedy focus gradually changed as she began talking about herself instead of others. Drawing on her Jewish, middle-class background, she made light of herself as an obese child, an adult who liked to shop, and a wife who could not cook.

In 1968, Rivers had her first shot at a talk show, the short-lived *That Show Starring Joan Rivers.* She also tried to break into films, with a small role in *The Swimmer.* Most of her success still came as a touring comedian, including stints in Las Vegas throughout the 1970s. Rivers also appeared on a number of television variety shows, as well as *The Tonight Show* on a regular basis.

In the 1970s, Rivers' career expanded beyond comedy and television as she moved into other genres. In 1972, she wrote and starred in her own Broadway play, *Fun City.* The following year, she co-wrote a television movie that aired on ABC, *The Girl Most Likely To.* During this same time period, she was writing a nationally syndicated column for the *Chicago Tribune.* In 1977, Rivers wrote and directed her first feature film, *Rabbit Test.* Starring comedian Billy Crystal, the film focuses on the first man to become pregnant and give birth. The film was panned by critics.

After the failure of *Husband, Wives, and Lovers,* a 1978 television situation comedy that Rivers cocreated, she continued working on screenplay and television script ideas through the early 1980s. However, Rivers primarily focused on developing her own comic material and performing live. By this time, her comedy made fun of celebrities and other people, such as Elizabeth Taylor, Queen Elizabeth II, and First Lady Nancy Reagan. Rivers also focused on her own appearance, promoting plastic surgery, and the promiscuity of a made-up best friend. Of her take on comedy, she told Gerald Clarke of *Time*, "Comedy should always be on that very fine line of going too far. It should always be on the brink of disaster. Otherwise, it's pap and who cares? It's boring. Then you become the grand old lady...."

Rivers' frequent appearances on *The Tonight Show* led to her being a frequent substitute host for Carson. In 1983, she signed a contract making her the permanent substitute for Carson, essentially his co-host. Rivers hosted *The Tonight Show* on a weekly basis as Carson often went on vacation and worked many shortened weeks by this time period. Though sometimes controversial—especially among those she skewered with her comedy—she did well in the ratings. She sometimes drew better ratings than Carson himself. However, Rivers soon feuded with NBC over *The Tonight Show* because she allegedly was not being considered to replace Carson when he retired.

The situation with *The Tonight Show* soon worsened. In 1985, Rivers signed with the new FOX network to host her own talk show, *The Late Show*. The move was considered a stab in the back to Carson, who had helped her career in so many ways, because she worked on the deal without telling him about it. After she signed the three-year, $15 million deal, Carson and Rivers became rivals. *The Late Show* premiered in the fall of 1986, and only had low ratings and mostly negative reviews. Rivers was fired in the spring of 1987, and replaced by guest hosts.

One potential reason for the failure of *The Late Show* was tension between FOX and Rivers. The network wanted her to be more pleasant to guests and not the hard interviewer she had been on *The Tonight Show*. She also believed that she could not get great guests to appear. Rivers' husband acted as the show's executive producer and ran it behind the scenes. Rosenberg and FOX had major disagreements about *The Late Show*, and the network fired Rivers primarily because of him. It was believed that FOX would have kept her if she would have gotten rid of him.

The failure of *The Late Show* weighed heavily on Rosenberg. Soon after its end, he killed himself in a hotel room in Philadelphia, Pennsylvania. However, the show's demise was probably not the only reason for his suicide. He had suffered two heart at-

tacks and heart failure in 1984, and had to have bypass surgery. He and Rivers had also separated. After his death, the general perception by the public was that Rivers did not particularly care about her husband's suicide. This happened despite the fact that she had called him her strength and stability in print three years earlier and considered suicide herself for a time after his passing.

As Rivers pulled her life back together, she found she was no longer in demand as she had been. For a time, she was not booked in the same clubs as before because of her show's failure and husband's death. To continue to earn a leaving, she served as the center square on the game show *Hollywood Squares* for a time in 1987. Rivers also moved back to New York City, where she returned to the stage. She appeared as Kate in *Broadway Bound*, a critical and box office success.

Television still had its allure for Rivers, and she soon had new talk shows. Beginning in 1988, she had a gossipy syndicated daytime talk show, *The Joan Rivers Show*, which lasted for several years. On this show, she was open about herself—her surgeries, her husband's death, her relationship with her daughter—and tried to get her guests to be as honest about themselves. Rivers told Joanne Kaufman of *People*, "If I had seen myself as this real failure, I wouldn't have done this. But this was a case of getting back on the horse. I know I can do a talk show as well as some and better than others. And don't dare anyone tell me I cannot do something. I had to prove to myself I could." Rivers won a Daytime Emmy Award for her work on the show.

While *The Joan Rivers Show* was still on the air, Rivers began doing another show as well. In 1992, she did *Joan Rivers' Gossip! Gossip! Gossip!* for the USA network. Both shows were canceled in 1993. By this time, Rivers had another source of income. Since 1992, she had been selling her own line of jewelry on QVC. She later added other products to her line, including clothing. By early 1994, she had sold $60 million in jewelry and fashion. Rivers owned her own company to create these products called Joan Rivers Worldwide, of which she served as chief executive officer and president.

Rivers also continued to write and act in television and on stage. In 1994, she co-wrote a stage show with Lonny Price and Erin Sanders called *Sally Marr ... and Her Escorts*. It was loosely based on the life of comic Lenny Bruce's mother. When the show made it to Broadway, Rivers played the title role. That same year, Rivers and her daughter co-wrote the autobiographical television movie, *Tears and Laughter: The Joan and Melissa Rivers Story,* for NBC. The pair also starred in the movie, which focused on their relationship and Rivers' professional career after the death of her husband. *Tears and Laughter* did well in the ratings.

In 1995, Rivers started a new line of work, providing commentary on what celebrities wore to awards shows and related pre-awards shows with her daughter. The pair had a contract with E! Entertainment Television to do this commentary before the Emmys, Academy Awards, Golden Globes, and other events. Rivers and her daughter also interviewed attendees about all aspects of their lives when they walked on the red carpet. After several years, they also added a special after the Academy Awards to talk about who wore what to the ceremony.

While continuing her commentary shows, Rivers also began a new job. In 1997, she began hosting a syndicated talk show on WOR, a New York City-based radio station. It was eventually syndicated to about 50 other radio stations. On the show, Rivers interviewed guests, talked about the news, discussed both sides of a current issue, and did some comedy. The show ended its run in 2002.

Rivers continued to work as an actress on occasion. In 1997, she had a role for a few episodes on the soap opera *Another World.* In 2002, Rivers performed a solo show in England, *Broke and Alone in London.* Two years later, she had a guest appearance on the F/X show *Nip/Tuck* and provided a voice in the animated feature *Shrek 2.*

In 2004, Rivers and her daughter ended their relationship with E! and joined the *TV Guide* Channel for the same kind of commentary shows in June of that year. Rivers' three-year deal was worth $8 million. In addition to doing the award show programming, Rivers and her daughter also planned to do holiday specials and other shows for the *TV Guide* Channel. Of Rivers' importance to awards shows, Rose Apodaca Jones told Clarissa Cruz of *Entertainment Weekly,* "The red carpet is what it is because of Joan."

## Selected discography

*Joan Rivers Presents Mr. Phyllis and Other Funny Stories,* Warner Bros., 1965.
*What Becomes a Semi-Legend Most,* Geffen, 1983.

## Sources

### Books

*Celebrity Biographies,* Baseline II, 2005.

### Periodicals

*Broadcasting,* October 20, 1986, p. 33; May 25, 1987, p. 34.
*Broadcasting & Cable,* June 9, 1997, p. 24; February 23, 2004, p. 3.
*Entertainment Weekly,* October 1, 2004, pp. 34-37.
*Forbes,* March 22, 1999, p. 228.
*Inc.,* June 1999, p. 107.
*Los Angeles Times,* January 15, 2005.
*Mediaweek,* March 25, 2002, p. 5.
*Multichannel News,* July 5, 2004, p. 35.
*New York Times,* August 30, 1990, p. C1; May 1, 1994, sec. 2, p. 1.
*People,* January 2, 1984, p. 49; December 10, 1984, p. 130; June 1, 1987, p. 28; February 19, 1990, p. 67; June 21, 1993, p. 70; February 7, 1994, p. 100; May 16, 1994, p. 65; November 12, 2001, p. 22.
*Time,* April 11, 1983, p. 85; May 19, 1986, p. 98; May 16, 1994, p. 79; May 24, 2004, p. 86.
UPI NewsTrack, June 22, 2004.

—*A. Petruso*

# Narciso Rodriguez

## Fashion designer

**B**orn January of 1961, in New Jersey; son of Narciso, Sr. (a longshoreman) and Rawedia Maria (a homemaker) Rodriguez. *Education:* Parsons School of Design, graduated in 1982.

**Addresses:** *Office*—50 Bond St., New York, NY 10012. *Website*—www.narcisorodriguez.com.

## Career

**F**reelance fashion designer, c. 1982-85; fashion designer, Anne Klein, 1985-91; design assistant for women's wear, Calvin Klein, 1991-94; women's wear and men's wear designer, Tse, 1994-95; fashion designer and consultant, Nino Cerruti, 1995-97; designed wedding dresses for Dina Ruiz and Carolyn Bessette, 1996; designed own fashion line, 1997—; designed fur collection for Goldin Feldman, c. 1997; named design director for women's wear, LVMH's Loewe, 1997.

**Awards:** Designer of the year, Hispanic Society, 1997; VH1 Fashion Award, new designer of the year, 1997; Council of Fashion Designers of America Award, 1998; best womenswear designer of the year award, Council of Fashion Designers of America, 2002; best womenswear designer of the year award, Council of Fashion Designers of America, 2003.

## Sidelights

**T**hough American fashion designer Narciso (pronounced Nar-SEE-so) Rodriguez had toiled for years for such upscale companies as Anne Klein

*AP/Wide World Photos*

and Nino Cerruti, his career took off when he designed the wedding dress for former Calvin Klein colleague Carolyn Bessette for her wedding to John F. Kennedy, Jr., the son of former president John F. Kennedy. With this success in 1996, Rodriguez received many offers to start his own women's wear fashion line, which he started in 1997. He also held a contract to work as the design director for women's wear produced by LVMH's Loewe, a Spain-based luxury leather company, for several years. By the early 2000s, Rodriguez concentrated only on his own line of clothing and based his business in New York City. His dresses were especially popular among actresses.

Rodriguez was born in January of 1961, in New Jersey, the son of Narciso, Sr. a longshoreman, and Rawedia Maria, a homemaker. His parents were immigrants from Cuba, and the future designer was the oldest of three children. Rodriguez and his two sisters were raised in Kearny, New Jersey, and in his neighborhood, he was around many women who sewed. By the time he was in elementary school, he liked to sketch. In high school, Rodriguez took art classes and apprenticed with a tailor. While his parents supported his sketching, they were less than encouraging of his interest in sewing and making clothes until he was successful later in life.

After high school, Rodriguez entered Parsons School of Design in New York City. As a student, he was known as much for his cooking as his fashion sense. When he graduated from Parsons, he worked as a freelance designer for several years. In 1985, Rodriguez was hired as an anonymous designer for Anne Klein. During his first year there, he worked under Donna Karan, who later launched her own successful line of women's wear. After Karan left, Rodriguez worked under Louis Dell'Olio. At Anne Klein, Rodriguez had a variety of experiences, including designing shoes and bags, and going to factories where he learned technical aspects of the business.

Rodriguez left Anne Klein in 1991 when he moved to Calvin Klein as a design assistant. He worked on tailored pieces in Calvin Klein's women's collection. While at Calvin Klein, he met Bessette, who was a publicist for the label. The pair became close friends. In 1994, Rodriguez moved on again, this time to Tse, an American-based company that created designer cashmere pieces. At Tse, he designed for both the men's and women's collections.

In 1995, Rodriguez left the United States and moved to Paris, France, to work as a designer and consultant for Nino Cerruti, a master couturier. For the Cerruti label, Rodriguez helped design the women's line. Until this point, Cerruti had been successful with its men's wear line, but not its women's wear. Rodriguez helped revitalize Cerruti's women's line with his alluring and uncomplicated designs.

While still working for Cerruti, Rodriguez designed several wedding gowns on a freelance basis. For the March of 1996 wedding of Dina Ruiz to acclaimed actor Clint Eastwood, Rodriguez designed her dress. An even bigger splash came with the simple gown he created for the wedding of Bessette and Kennedy later that year. The simple off-white silk dress featured a train and a bias cut. Rodriguez also designed the dress Bessette wore to the rehearsal dinner. Both dresses were his gifts for the bride. After the wedding photos came out for the high profile couple, Rodriguez became a celebrity in his own right. As the knock-offs of the dress sold well, he was soon besieged with offers to start his own label. Rodriguez told Allison Adato of *People,* "I wasn't prepared for the impact. [Carolyn] warned me. It was overwhelming."

The success of the gown Rodriguez designed for Bessette affected his status at Nino Cerruti. The fame was too much for the company since Rodriguez was given more attention than the label because of the

dress. After a well-received Autumn/Winter 1997 show in March of that year, Rodriguez was forced out of the company when he would not sign a two-year contract.

Rodriguez then sorted through a number of job offers. In 1997, he signed with Aeffe, an Italian manufacturing company that was owned by fashion designer Alberta Ferretti, to manufacture his women's wear including gowns, shoes, and handbags, as well as casual wear, suits, and dresses. He told Suzanne C. Ryan of the *Boston Globe* that working on his own was not easy. He said, "It's a very romantic fantasy when you're young. But when you see how much it takes, how draining it is—at the end of the day, it's a business. I was quite fine where I was. I don't think my personality is such that I need to be the one taking the bow but the one creating the clothes."

Despite the fact that Rodriguez did not seek the spotlight, his first fashion show ever, in Milan, Italy, in October of 1997 for the spring 1998 season, was a success and fun for the designer who was coming into his own. He received good reviews for his women's clothes which flattered the models with clean, modern, simple lines. Reviewing the show, Tamsin Blanchard of the *Independent* wrote, "He is not trying to challenge women, stun the world with his intellect or shock us with see-through underwear. All he wants is for women to look at his sequined slips and camisoles and sporty, luxurious separates on the rail, and want to wear them there and then...."

In addition to producing his own line of fashion, Rodriguez also designed for other companies. He designed a fur collection that was licensed to Goldin Feldman. Rodriguez had a contract with LVMH's (Louis Vuitton Moet Hennessey) Loewe (pronounced Lo-a-vey), a Spain-based luxury leather company. He served as design director for women's wear, and created evening dresses. His first collection made its debut in March of 1998. All of his work paid off when Rodriguez began being considered for awards. In 1998, he was nominated for the Perry Ellis Award for the best new designer of women's wear.

Balancing the demands of his label with his work for Loewe proved difficult for Rodriguez. He did shows for his own collection four times a year, often to positive reviews. His clothing was very popular, and was carried by retailers such as Neiman Marcus, Saks Fifth Avenue, and Barneys New York, among others. Many in the fashion world liked

Rodriguez's clothes and supported the man himself, so he did not suffer from the same backstabbing that left other designers feeling undermined by their peers.

Rodriguez had to travel to Madrid for Loewe, but did not get as much support for his work there. The company was once important, but it had faded creatively over time; he hoped to revive it. Rodriguez created two collections a year for the company, though his employment there was often stressful. He told Vanessa Friedman of the *Financial Times,* "There was a lot of suffering. Trips to factories in the middle of nowhere, living out of a suitcase. I completely lost my focus, and didn't know why I was doing what I was doing or where I was doing it. But I did learn how much I could endure...."

By the early 2000s, Rodriguez ended his relationship with Loewe and focused on his own line. He also made his full-time home in New York City, and built his own studio that reflected his style as a designer. Rodriguez had his first show in New York City in February of 2001, showing his fall 2001 collection. It featured many tailored pieces. Fitted pieces that flattered women's figures were also found in his spring 2003 collection which debuted in September of 2002. His sophisticated but wearable clothing became a staple of the New York fashion scene. Rodriguez told Alev Aktar of the *Daily News,* "I want my clothes to be worn. I want women in the audience at my shows to see really desirable things. That's my success."

As Rodriguez conquered New York in the early 2000s, he continued to win awards. He was named best women's wear designer of the year by the Council of Fashion Designers of America two years running, in 2002 and 2003. Rodriguez was the first designer of the year to win the award twice in a row. His business also prospered financially. In 2002, the sales of his line were about $20 million per year. The number was that high despite the fact that there was no advertising budget nor a chief financial officer. In fact, only 12 people worked at the studio. Rodriguez planned to expand his sales, staff, and his company over time.

Some critics believed that Rodriguez's collection continued to improve as he was less distracted and drained by his previous travel demands. He developed a reputation as a leading American designer. By spring of 2003, his gowns, which had already been favored by some Hollywood types, became very fashionable, chosen by actresses such as Sarah Jessica Parker and Salma Hayek to be worn on the red carpet. Some of his designs also appeared on the hit HBO show *Sex and the City.* This led to him creating clothing specifically for some of the actresses, including Parker.

Rodriguez also moved beyond women's wear to grow his company. He introduced a perfume in 2003 called narciso rodriguez for her, also known as For Her, which was developed with Beaute Prestige International. It was combination of musky, vanilla, amber, vetiver, and orange blossom scents. In addition, Rodriguez opened a store in New York City and planned to open one in Milan, Italy. He also considered doing some advertising.

Rodriguez's shows remained hits for spring 2004 and fall-winter 2004, with fitted dresses and corset details inspired by his trip to Carnival in Rio de Janeiro, Brazil. His fashion shows became the ones that everyone looked forward to during fashion week. The high profile of his shows was heightened by the number of big names in the audience. Critics noted that he stuck with the same basic styles and fabrics with different color palates over the years. This led some to ask why he did not try to innovate more, though others understood that Rodriguez stuck with what worked.

Because of Rodriguez's success, he was considered for other jobs. When head women's wear designer Tom Ford left Gucci in 2004, Rodriguez's name was mentioned as a possible replacement. Although he was not chosen, it was clear that Rodriguez was considered a world-class designer. Rodriguez remained focused on the clothes and the women who wore them instead of his status in the fashion world and unnecessary theatrics. He told Constance C.R. White of the *New York Times,* "What I'm trying to capture with the look is something more sensual, more feminine. For me, designing is such a personal thing. It's really emotional—that's part of my Latin upbringing."

## Sources

Associated Press, September 17, 2003.

*Boston Globe,* December 4, 2000, p. E1.

*Cosmetics International Cosmetic Products Report,* July 2003, p. 5.

*Daily News* (New York City), February 8, 2001, p. 51; February 11, 2004, p. 28.

*Daily Telegraph* (London), February 18, 2004, p. 23.

*Financial Times* (London, England), September 13, 2003, p. 5.

*Guardian* (London), February 28, 1998, p. 40; February 12, 2004, p. 11.

*Houston Chronicle,* February 12, 2004, p. 1.

*Independent,* October 8, 1997, p. 19; March 18, 2004.

*Interior Design,* April 1, 2003, p. 174.

*Newsday* (New York City), February 12, 2004, p. A12.

*New York Times,* December 30, 1997, p. B7; May 6, 2003, p. B8; November 2, 2003, sec. 6, p. 78, p. 86.

*Ottawa Citizen,* March 24, 1998, p. E7.

*People,* October 14, 1996, p. 65; June 23, 2003, pp. 97-98.

*San Francisco Chronicle,* February 12, 1998, p. E6.

*South China Morning Post* (Hong Kong), April 22, 1998, p. 23.

*Toronto Star,* December 11, 2003, p. H4.

*Washington Post,* September 21, 2002, p. C1; June 4, 2003, p. C10.

*—A. Petruso*

# Robert Rodriguez

## Filmmaker

**B**orn Robert Anthony Rodriguez, June 20, 1968, in San Antonio, TX; son of Cecilio (a cookware sales manager) and Rebecca (a nurse) Rodriguez; married Elizabeth Avellan, c. 1991; children: Rocket Valentino, Racer Maximiliano, Rebel Antonio. *Education:* University of Texas at Austin, B.A.

**Addresses:** *Office*—Troublemaker Studios, 4900 Old Manor Rd., Austin, TX 78723. *Contact*—c/o P.O. Box 608, Spicewood, TX 78669.

## Career

**W**orked as a file clerk in the University of Texas at Austin's Provost office; participated in clinical drug research trials. Filmmaker for feature films, including: director, screenwriter, editor, camera operator, still photographer, producer, music editor, sound editor, cinematographer, and special effects, *El Mariachi,* 1993; director, editor, and screenwriter, "The Misbehavers," *Four Rooms,* 1995; producer, screenwriter, director, steadicam operator, and editor, *Desperado,* 1995; director, editor, camera operator, steadicam operator, executive producer, and sound re-recording mixer, *From Dusk Till Dawn,* 1996; director, editor, camera operator, producer, and sound re-rerecording mixer, *The Faculty,* 1998; director, editor, camera operator, producer, screenwriter, composer, sound re-recording mixer, and visual effects supervisor, *Spy Kids,* 2001; director, editor, producer, writer, composer, sound effects editor, cinematographer, visual effects supervisor, and production designer, *Spy Kids 2: The Island of Lost Dreams,* 2002; screenwriter, cinematographer, director, production designer, editor, camera operator,

producer, visual effects supervisor, and composer, *Once Upon a Time in Mexico,* 2003; director, editor, producer, screenwriter, composer, cinematographer, visual effects supervisor, and production designer, *Spy Kids 3-D: Game Over,* 2003. Film shorts include: director, editor, animator, writer, composer, sound effects, cinematographer, *Bedhead,* 1991. Television work includes: director, screenwriter, editor, and songwriter, *Roadracers,* Showtime, 1994.

**Awards:** *Bedhead* won awards including first place at Atlanta Film and Video Competition, the Amarin County Film Festival, the 11th Annual Edison Black Maria Film Festival, the Charlotte Film Festival, the 9th annual Third Coast Film Festival, and the Melbourne International Film Festival and Fine Arts Film and Video Competition; won two Columbia University Awards for strip "Los Hooligans" and for his political cartoons; Sundance Film Festival Audience Award for best feature, for *El Mariachi,* 1993; Independent Spirit Award for best first feature, for *El Mariachi,* 1993.

## Sidelights

**B**eginning with *El Mariachi* in 1993, Robert Rodriguez has established himself as a filmmaker with unique vision and innovation who can also deliver box office success. Though he moved from independent films to Hollywood-financed productions, he remained true to his roots and worked primarily out of his home near Austin, Texas. While Rodriguez's early films were often violent adult features, later in his career he made a successful trilogy of children's action films, the *Spy Kids* series.

Born Robert Anthony Rodriguez on June 20, 1968, in San Antonio, Texas, he was the third of ten children born to Cecilio, a sales manager for a cookware firm, and his wife, Rebecca, a nurse. Rodriguez was interested in making films from an early age. He began by making little animated flip films in the margins of books. By the time he was 13 years old, he was making Super 8 movies at home using his many siblings as actors. He also used a video camera—which his father had bought to make presentation videos for the cookware he sold—to make short films.

Rodriguez realized that he was not a great student at a San Antonio junior seminary boarding school. He told Rita Kempley of the *Washington Post,* "I accepted the fact that I would never be a rocket scientist. I knew that if I could just draw cartoons or make little movies on the side, just to keep myself alive, I would be happy the rest of my life." He also liked studying music; he learned how to play the guitar, piano, and saxophone. Rodriguez would later use these skills to write songs and score some of his films.

After high school, Rodriguez attended the University of Texas at Austin. There, he was a cartoonist for the university's newspaper for three years. The strip, called "Los Hooligans," was based on the antics of his younger siblings. Rodriguez wanted to enter the University of Texas's film program, but was rejected because of his low grade point average. Even though he was not in the program, he made film and video shorts on the side with equipment he managed to borrow. He put together a video reel he called *Austin Stories.* This won several film competitions and won him entry into the University of Texas's film program.

To help finance his first 16mm film short, Rodriguez was a participant in a clinical research trial for a local company. He used the money he made as a human guinea pig to make *Bedhead* in 1991. This eight-minute film was about a young girl who finds out that she has telekinesis and uses her skill to get back at her older brother. The film featured four of his siblings, and won awards at 14 film festivals. Because of this success, Rodriguez soon left school,

though he later finished his B.A. He did meet his future wife, Elizabeth Avellan, at the University of Texas before he left. She serves as a producer on all of her husband's films. They also have three sons together: Rocket, Racer, and Rebel.

While on a summer break from the University of Texas in 1991, Rodriguez went back to a local research center to serve as a test subject for a new drug. He used the time to write a script for what was going to be his first feature film, *El Mariachi.* Using the money he made as a lab rat, Rodriguez and his friend Carlos Gallardo—who helped write the script—shot the film in two weeks in a Mexican border town with a hand-held 16mm camera. Most of the actors were amateurs who came from the town and worked for free. The film cost a total of $7,000 to shoot. Rodriguez did a cheap edit on video to hold costs down.

Rodriguez and Gallardo intended for *El Mariachi* to be sold on the lucrative Spanish-language video market targeting Mexicans. They learned that cheap videos were often made for this market. *El Mariachi* was a take-off of Mexican action films, westerns, and other genre films. At its center was a mariachi singer who accidentally gets mixed up with an assassin while trying to find work in Acuna, Mexico. The mariachi ends up living the tragedies he sings about in his songs. *El Mariachi* was violent, but also was intended to be humorous.

While in negotiations for selling *El Mariachi* to the American and Mexican video markets, Rodriguez sent a trailer for the film and *Bedhead* to Robert Newman, an agent for International Creative Management (ICM), in 1992. Newman thought the trailer had such promise that he decided to represent Rodriguez. This led to a two-year, two-picture development deal with Columbia Pictures. Rodriguez only agreed to the contract if he could work from Texas, where he felt freer and more inspired.

Columbia chose to release the subtitled *El Mariachi* with improved sound after blowing it up to 35mm in 1993. When it was released, it was one of the most inexpensive films ever released by a Hollywood studio. The film made about $5 million at the box office, though this only recouped the costs of post-production and marketing.

Though Rodriguez did not want to leave Texas, he briefly lived in Los Angeles, California, in the mid-1990s. In 1994, he made a television movie for Showtime called *Roadracers.* This was a remake of a 1959 film, and marked the first time Rodriguez worked in 35mm. In this homage to 1950s drive-in movies, he served as director, screenwriter, editor, and songwriter. At its heart, the film was about smoking cigarettes and looking cool.

For his next project, Rodriguez filmed a sequel to *El Mariachi* called *Desperado*. Though the film was made for a very low budget by Hollywood standards, only about $7 million, it was a leap forward in terms of quality of actors. He used more established stars such as Spanish film star Antonio Banderas and Mexican actress Salma Hayek, but shot it in the same place, Acuna, Mexico. The stylish, violent action film was a success for Rodriguez.

Hayek appeared in two more films that Rodriguez made. The first was a segment in the anthology film, *Four Rooms*. Each segment in the 1995 film was directed by a hot young director. Rodriguez's was entitled "The Misbehavers." Hayek also had a leading role in Rodriguez's next feature, 1996's *From Dusk Till Dawn*. This violent horror film about vampires also featured Quentin Tarantino and George Clooney.

In this time period, Rodriguez returned to Texas to live full time. By this point, he was considered an important director, one of several prominent Latino directors. His return to Texas happened after he was unable to make a deal to direct a new version of *Zorro* because of some differences with the film company. Rodriguez later turned down the chance to direct other high profile projects such as *X-Men*, *Superman Lives*, and *Planet of the Apes*.

Working in Texas, Rodriguez was convinced to direct *The Faculty*, written by then-popular screenwriter Kevin Williamson (the creator of the hit television show *Dawson's Creek*, and writer of *Scream* and *Scream 2*). This horror/teen/science fiction film is about a group of high school students who have to fight teachers—who are inhabited by space aliens—in order to save the world. Like most Rodriguez projects, it was inexpensive, costing only $15 million to make.

After *The Faculty*, Rodriguez took several years off from filmmaking to raise his young sons. When he returned to filmmaking in the early 2000s, his next film was intended for a much younger audience than his previous works. Released in 2001, *Spy Kids* was a kids' film focusing on the adventures of the children of retired international spies. The spys, played by Carla Gugino and Banderas, are forced out of retirement but are captured by the bad guy; the children, Carmen and Juni, have to save their parents and the world.

While the film was laden with gadgets not unlike a James Bond film, Rodriguez put the family at the heart of the story. *Spy Kids* cost only $36 million to make, despite the many special effects, but was a hit at the box office and made more than $100 million worldwide. Even Rodriguez's parents were proud. He told Joshua Mooney of the *San Diego Union-Tribune*, "This is the first movie my parents can see and say, 'That's my boy!' I think they were wondering when I was going to make something more representative of what I grew up as and the messages my parents gave us and what I learned from them. It's been such a strong portion of my life."

Rodriguez followed up *Spy Kids* with an adult film shot in 2001, but not released until 2003. *Once Upon a Time in Mexico* was another sequel to *El Mariachi*. Rodriguez again held multiple jobs on the film, including screenwriter, cinematographer, director, production designer, editor, and composer. The film was an experiment in some ways for the filmmaker. While doing a sound mix for *Spy Kids* at *Star Wars* creator George Lucas's Skywalker Ranch, Lucas introduced Rodriguez to the high-definition (HD) digital format as an alternative to shooting on film stock. Rodriguez shot *Once Upon a Time in Mexico* in the format, using cameras he bought for the shoot. By the time the shoot ended, Rodriguez had recouped his costs, as the format was much cheaper and more efficient than film. The film cost only $29 million to make, and was number one at the box office for at least one week when originally released in the United States.

Another aspect that made high definition appealing for Rodriguez was that it allowed him to edit films at home. In his home in the Hill Country of central Texas, he had his own studio from which to work, allowing him to be very involved with his family's life. Rodriguez planned on shooting all his films in the high definition format, including his follow-ups to *Spy Kids*. *Spy Kids 2: The Island of Lost Dreams* was released in 2002. Rodriguez found another advantage to shooting in high definition while making this film. It was easier to work with his younger actors because he did have to stop and wait while film was reloaded while shooting in HD. The kids remained focused and the shoot went much more quickly. The film only cost about $30 to $35 million to make, despite the fact that there were more than 1,000 special effects shots.

In *Spy Kids 2: The Island of Lost Dreams*, the family of spies again saves the world from bad guys. While the film featured cool new gadgets and a similar plot to the first, it did not do as well at the box office. A similar fate befell the third *Spy Kids* movie, which also was a critical failure. *Spy Kids 3-D: Game Over* was released in 2003 as a 3-D film. More than the other films in the series, special effects dominated *Spy Kids 3-D: Game Over*. In the plot, Carmen gets stuck in a video game and her younger brother, Juni, has to save her. He is aided in his quest by their grandfather, played by Ricardo Montalban.

Though Rodriguez liked to work on his home turf of Texas, he used Hollywood actors and had big projects lined up for the mid-2000s. Future releases included *Sin City,* based on the graphic noir crime novel series by Frank Miller, and *A Princess of Mars,* a science fiction epic based on the first volume in the *John Carter of Mars* series by Edgar Rice Burroughs. Rodriguez told Will Hodgkinson of the *Guardian,* "I'm probably the only guy who really enjoys being in the business, because I get to make my own rules. I cut my own trailers, make my own ads, live and work at home in Texas. It's ridiculous. What did I do in a past life?"

## Sources

### Books

*Celebrity Biographies,* Baseline II, Inc., 2004.

### Periodicals

*Billboard,* August 23, 2003.
*Entertainment Weekly,* August 9, 2002, pp. 40-41; August 1, 2003, p. 82.

*Guardian* (London, England), April 11, 2001, p. 16.
*Houston Chronicle,* August 11, 2002, p. 8.
*Millimeter,* August 2002, p. 8.
*Milwaukee Journal Sentinel,* January 1, 1999, p. 10.
*Newsweek,* August 12, 2002, p. 62.
*People,* August 7, 1995, p. 14; August 4, 2003, pp. 101-02.
*Plain Dealer* (Cleveland, OH), April 11, 1993, p. 1H.
*San Antonio Express-News,* May 10, 2004, p. 2C.
*San Diego Union-Tribune,* April 1, 2002, p. A2.
*Texas Monthly,* May 1998, p. 108.
*Time,* July 28, 2003, p. 60.
*Times* (London, England), September 25, 2003, p. 1.
*Toronto Sun,* September 7, 2003, p. S14.
*Variety,* March 1, 2004, p. 2; March 8, 2004, p. 5.
*Washington Post,* April 3, 1993, p. C1; September 15, 2003, p. C1.

### Online

"Do-it-all director Robert Rodriguez," CNN.com, http://www.cnn.com/2003/SHOWBIZ/Movies/09/15/sprj.caf03.rodriguez.ap/index.html (September 16, 2003).
"Robert Rodriguez," Internet Movie Database, http://www.imdb.com/name/nm0001675/filmoyear (August 6, 2004).

—A. Petruso

# Roh Moo-hyun

**President of South Korea**

Born August 6, 1946, in Kimhae, South Korea; married Kwon Yang Sook; children: Geon-ho, Jeong-yeon. *Education:* Studied on his own to become an attorney.

**Addresses:** *Office*—c/o Embassy of Korea, 2450 Massachusetts Ave. N.W., Washington, DC 20008.

## Career

Passed South Korean bar examination to become an attorney, 1976; Taejon Regional Court judge; worked as a tax lawyer and then human-rights attorney; won a seat in the National Assembly representing Pusan, 1988; served as Minister of Fisheries in the Millennium Party government, August 2000-April 2001; supreme council member for the Millennium Party, 2001; standing advisor for the Millennium Party, 2001; elected president of South Korea, December, 2002; became leader of new Uri Party, May, 2004.

## Sidelights

Roh Moo-hyun's victory in close national elections in South Korea in 2002 heralded a changing of the guard for this Asian economic power of 48 million people. Sworn in at the age of 56, the onetime human-rights lawyer rode the wave of a grass-roots political movement that prompted one news source to call him the Howard Dean of South Korea, referring to the Vermont governor who became an early favorite in the 2004 American presidential race thanks to Internet websites.

*AP/Wide World Photos*

Roh made it to South Korea's highest office despite his lack of foreign-policy credentials, and arrived there at a time of increased tensions with neighboring North Korea. "Roh the President is a symbol of a South Korea that's now emerging as a major economic power in the region," asserted *Time International*'s Michael Schuman, "and is eager to be treated as an equal partner with the U.S. on security matters, not as the protectorate it's been since the end of the Korean War."

Roh has sometimes said that his political role model is Abraham Lincoln, the United States president who ended slavery. Like Lincoln, he is a self-taught lawyer from humble beginnings. He was born in 1946 in Kimhae, in southeastern Korea, and grew up in a village called Bonsan. The nearest city was Pusan, a major shipping port and the second-largest city in the South. His family were simple farmers who grew peaches and raised poultry.

Just a year before Roh was born, the Allied victors of World War II divided the Korean peninsula into two sections. It had been a colony of Japan since 1910, and Soviet and American forces shared responsibility for administering it and helping it return to independence. But tensions arose in the late 1940s over the future unification of the two halves, and worries about an entirely communist Korean peninsula began to preoccupy the American administrators in the southern half. War erupted in 1950, with the North Korean side backed by Soviet and Chinese troops, while an immense influx of American and United Nations forces arrived in the South.

In 1953, the year Roh turned seven years old, a stalemate and armistice resulted in a Demilitarized Zone, or DMZ, a large swath of border between the two Koreas that became the most heavily guarded frontier in the world. An ardent anti-Communist, Syngman Rhee, led South Korea for the next several years, thanks in part to support from the United States, now South Korea's most important ally. Rhee ruthlessly suppressed dissent, won elections widely suspected of being rigged, and even changed the constitution to allow him to seek another term in 1960.

Imbued with a sense of moral justice from an early age, Roh was an outspoken student in school at times. One annual class assignment for every South Korean schoolchild during his youth involved writing an essay about the achievements of President Rhee. Roh persuaded his entire seventh-grade class to turn in blank pieces of paper, an incident that earned him a suspension. He went on to Pusan Commercial High School, and was a good student when he applied himself. At other times, he skipped class and drank heavily. After finishing in 1966, he was unable to go on to college, since his family could not afford it, and instead did a mandatory stint in the military. He worked menial jobs after being discharged in 1971, such as making fishing nets, and built a small mud hut overlooking Bonsan. In his spare time, he studied to become a lawyer, and passed the bar examination in 1976 on his third try.

Roh became a judge at Taejon Regional Court, and then a tax lawyer. He continued to drink, however, and spent his money on bars, women, and sailboats. He had married a childhood friend, Kwon Yang Sook, by then, but later said that for many years he treated his wife badly, and even hit her. Their marital problems were detailed in a 1994 autobiography, *Dear Wife, Please Help Me*. Meanwhile, South Korea remained under the control of autocratic leaders. A military dictatorship under Chun Doo Hwan held power from 1980 to 1988 after dissolving the National Assembly and declaring martial law. Chun's government was tough on dissenters as well, and there were widespread human-rights violations. In the 1981 "Boolim Incident," 12 students were arrested in Pusan and detained for two months for possessing banned literature; they were tortured while in custody.

Roh was convinced to take the students' case against the government by his mentor, an attorney named Kim Guang Il. Though he had little interest in human rights, Roh said that he went to see the jailed students, and "when I saw their horrified eyes and their missing toenails, my comfortable life as a lawyer came to an end," a British Broadcasting Corporation report quoted him as saying. He also recalled that his old iconoclast spirit reared itself, noting he "felt ashamed," as he told *Time International* writer Donald Macintyre. "There were 100 lawyers in Pusan and not one was willing to stick his neck out."

Roh went on to become a leading figure in the pro-democracy movement during the rest of the decade, and was even jailed for three weeks and charged with giving aid to labor-union strikers. Despite the absence of democracy, South Korea became an economic powerhouse during the 1980s, with companies such as Samsung and Hyundai enjoying success first in Asia and then in the greater global market. But the growing middle class took up the protest banner from the students, and the government was pressured to reform. In June of 1987, news that Chun's handpicked successor would succeed him and discussion of constitutional reform would be tabled for the time sparked a wave of massive demonstrations across South Korea. The successor, Roh Tae Woo, began a series of democratic reforms within weeks.

In 1988, Roh decided to enter politics formally with the Unification Democratic Party, a pro-democracy group, and won a seat in the National Assembly representing a district of Pusan. He also came to prominence that same year thanks to televised parliamentary hearings on government corruption and human-rights abuses, during which he relentlessly grilled discredited officials. But he failed to keep his seat in the National Assembly, and also lost his bid for the mayor's office of Pusan a few years later. He had better luck with Seoul voters in a parliamentary elections in 1998, returning to the National Assembly as a representative of the capital city, but lost again in 2000.

Roh had immense name recognition, however, and younger voters liked his reputation as an iconoclast. Many of this generation were calling for a re-evaluation of their country's ties to the United States, and he had once said that the 30,000-plus U.S. troops should go home. A grass-roots movement arose to return Roh to politics, with a large number of supporters connecting over the Internet; the influential "OhmyNews" website emerged as a particularly popular information source that did not hesitate to criticize South Korea's old guard and the continuing U.S. military presence. By this time Roh had moved over to the Millennium Democratic Party (MDP), another liberal political group, and his supporters managed to successfully petition the party, which was in power at the time, to recognize Roh after his 2000 election loss. Thanks to that effort, he was named a supreme council member and standing advisor in the MDP, and also served a stint as Minister of Maritime Affairs and Fisheries, his only government post before being elected to the presidency.

Roh became the MDP candidate in South Korea's 2002 presidential election, in part with the help of a new system whereby the candidates were chosen by popular vote rather than the whims of party officials. South Korean politics had been rocked by countless scandals in recent years, thanks to the sticky ties between politicians and the huge business conglomerates like Hyundai and Samsung, called *chaebols*. Roh garnered popular support as the outsider candidate, one who had no links to the political elite or the business community. He won the December of 2002 balloting, narrowly beating the Grand National Party candidate Lee Hoi Chang.

Just before his inauguration on February 25, 2003, North Korea fired a short-range missile into the sea in one of the belligerent gestures it made on occasion. Roh did not mention it in his half-hour speech that day, but did note that the North Korean nuclear program was a threat to world peace. His predecessor, Kim Dae Jung, had launched a new effort to improve relations with the North in the late 1990s that he termed South Korea's "sunshine policy." A stunning 2000 summit between Kim and North Korean leader Kim Jong Il had given the South Korean Kim a Nobel Peace Prize. Just before Roh's inauguration, however, it was revealed that the summit only took place thanks to $500 million secretly donated by Hyundai to the North Korean government. At a time when millions of North Koreans were said to be starving as a result of its government's relentless spending on military defense, South Koreans were outraged.

Roh sent emissaries to Washington to meet with U.S. State Department officials soon after taking office, but the talks over the North Korean situation stalled. There were worse problems at home, however: a series of campaign-finance scandals came to light during his first year in office, with some of Roh's aides and staff implicated. A wave of resignations and firings swept through the Blue House (the presidential residence); the opposition parties, who still dominated the National Assembly, called for

Roh to step down. On March 12, 2004, his foes in the National Assembly gathered enough votes to impeach him on the grounds that he voiced support for the new Uri Party, to which his MDP supporters had decamped, in the run-up to legislative elections scheduled for April.

Roh stayed in the official residence for the next two months as he appealed the decision in the courts, while thousands of South Koreans protested the National Assembly impeachment vote. In the April elections, South Koreans voiced their support further by tripling the Uri Party's number of seats in the National Assembly and ousting many opposition politicians. On May 14, 2004, Roh's impeachment edict was lifted by South Korea's Constitutional Court, and he returned to the business of governing.

Roh's government continued to suffer blows during his second year of a five-year term. There was a national pension-fund crisis, a plan to move the capital city from Seoul to the Chungcheong area, and protests over the deployment of 3,600 South Korean troops as part of the United States-led coalition forces in Iraq. Roh had arrived in office by hinting that the time had come to re-evaluate South Korea's relationship with the United States. In response, an Islamic militant group in Iraq kidnapped a Korean man working there as an interpreter and beheaded him in June.

Despite the political turmoil, Roh is considered a harbinger of new era for his country. South Korean society, heavily influenced by Confucian principles, had placed a premium on age. But at 57 years old, he was one of the younger presidents in South Korean history, and was said to have been helped immensely by his popularity among what is called the "386 Generation"—with the trio of numbers referring to voters who are in their 30s, took part in student protests of the 1980s, and were born in the 1960s.

Among his other political heroes, Roh also cites West German chancellor Konrad Adenauer, who ruled from 1949 to 1963 as his country experienced what became the permanent separation with its Soviet-controlled former half to the East, but forged ahead with wider plans for a European alliance that laid the groundwork for the immensely successful European Union. Roh has spoken of his hope to unite Asia along the same lines, with a future in which "North-east Asia will be the centre of the world, and we will stand at its heart," *Times* of London writer Richard Lloyd Parry quoted him as saying. "America has New York, Europe has London, and Asia will have Seoul."

# Sources

## Periodicals

*Economist,* April 24, 2004, p. 40.
*Newsweek International,* March 3, 2003, p. 26; August 4, 2003, p. 28; May 31, 2004, p. 53.
*New York Times,* March 6, 2003, p. A3.
*New York Times Magazine,* January 19, 2003, p. 20.
*Time International,* May 6, 2002, p. 19; March 3, 2003, p. 36; July 5, 2004, p. 10.
*Times* (London, England), March 7, 2003, p. 6.

## Online

*Biography Resource Center Online,* Gale Group, 2003.
"Profile: Roh Moo-hyun," BBC News, http://news.bbc.co.uk/2/hi/asia-pacific/2535143.stm (August 20, 2004).
"S. Korean president sworn in," CNN.com, http://www.cnn.com/2003/WORLD/asiapcf/east/02/24/skorea.inauguration.reut/index.html (February 25, 2003).

*—Carol Brennan*

# Dave Rosgen

## Hydrologist

**B**orn c. 1942. *Education:* Ph.D. in fluvial geomorphology.

**Addresses:** *Office*—Wildland Hydrology, 11210 N. County Rd. 19, Fort Collins, CO 80524. *Website*—http://www.wildlandhydrology.com.

## Career

**J**oined U.S. Forest Service, 1960s; left Forest Service, 1985; started Wildland Hydrology Consultants, c. 1985; published paper in *Catena,* 1994; published book, *Applied River Morphology,* 1996.

**Awards:** Outstanding Achievement Award from the U.S. Environmental Protection Agency, 1993; Leopold Conservation Award from the Federation of Fly Fishers, 2001.

## Sidelights

**I**f you have ever seen a stream confined in a man-made channel, or walked along a river and discovered a crazy quilt of concrete lining the bank, you can understand why Dave Rosgen and his ideas are so popular. He has become the leading figure in the science of restoring rivers. "People think we have natural, stable rivers all over the place," he told writer Jessica Snyder Sachs of *National Wildlife.* "In fact, we've altered most of them in one way or another." Rosgen's mission is to alter them once more, but in ways that mimic their natural behavior.

His methods have become very popular, although he has critics who question whether those methods are really as effective as he claims.

Born in northern Idaho and raised on a ranch, Rosgen went to college in the early 1960s, then went to work for the U.S. Forest Service as a watershed forester in the mountains of his home state. What he saw made him angry. "The valleys I knew as a kid had been trashed by logging. My trout streams were filled with sand," he recalled to David Malakoff, a writer for *Science.* He suspected logging and road-building were harming streams, but he had no measurements to prove it, so his bosses did not listen. He studied soil types and water flows in the streams, and he noticed that some types of streams resisted damage better than others.

Starting in the late 1960s, Rosgen teamed up with a leading river science researcher, Luna Leopold of the University of California, Berkeley, and used Leopold and others' work to develop a system for classifying rivers. Rosgen's system looks at rivers' width, depth, slope, sediment and other aspects, then puts them into nine major categories. The system, he decided, could identify natural, stable channel shapes—and rivers could be restored to those shapes even after erosion or re-engineering had altered them.

Rosgen left the Forest Service in 1985 over a disagreement about a dam he opposed, and retreated to his cattle ranch near Fort Collins, Colorado. It ended up being a turning point in his life, because it freed him to work on his ideas full-time. He founded Wildland Hydrology Consultants, a company that restores rivers and offers classes based on his methods.

A previous generation of river engineers would try to prevent flooding and fix eroded river banks by running rivers into narrow concrete channels, or by installing rip-rap along the banks—usually ugly piles of concrete, sometimes even junked cars. Rosgen, instead, will drop dead trees or boulders in strategic places to help direct the stream's flow. He may also run a bulldozer through a stream bed, trying to get the stream to flow at just the right angle, or grade, so that it flows fast. He might even out an unnaturally steep bank, or plant small trees on the bank to fight erosion or the effects of cattle-grazing. If all goes well, grass will grow on the banks, fish will return, and the river will flood less often. "I try to copy what works in nature," he explained to *Time*'s Pat Dawson. His methods can also cost as little as one-fourth the prices of most structures built to control floods.

The idea of making a river more "natural" by running a bulldozer through it horrified some. But when Rosgen rebuilt stretches of the troubled San Juan and Blanco rivers in southern Colorado, his methods seemed to work, and they caught on. The National Research Council issued a report on river restoration in 1992 that essentially endorsed his methods. Two years later, Rosgen published a paper describing his system in the prestigious journal *Catena*. It declared that there were seven major types of streams and dozens of subtypes, such as Type A streams (steep, narrow and rocky) or E channels (gentle, wide, and meandering). The article also explained how restorers could forecast how a stream's shape might change due to erosion or other stresses, and it explained how to alter a stream so it returned to a stable state often seen in untouched rivers. Rosgen expanded his ideas into a book, *Applied River Morphology*, published in 1996.

Since then, Rosgen has taught his methods to more than 12,000 people, including many natural resource managers for government agencies and nonprofits. The pricey classes promise to teach students "how to think like a river," according to Malakoff's profile of Rosgen in *Science*. "Your job is to help the river be what it wants to be," Malakoff quoted Rosgen as telling his students. Rosgen himself has reconstructed about 100 miles of rivers, and others have used his methods to reconstruct many more. Many

government agencies are so impressed, they now refuse to fund river-restoration projects unless they use Rosgen methods.

Critics of Rosgen and his effect on river restoration question whether his methods are really based on good science. Some say his system oversimplifies how rivers behave. In 2003, two government researchers concluded that a competing method of analyzing streams did better than Rosgen's methods in analyzing a Wisconsin river. (Rosgen says the researchers did not really understand his method.)

Some projects that followed Rosgen's methods have failed, leaving streams eroded and full of silt. "There are tremendous doubts about what's being done in Rosgen's name. But the people who hold the purse strings often require the use of his methods," Peter Wilcock, a geomorpologist who specializes in river dynamics at Johns Hopkins University, told *Science*'s Malakoff. Some criticism is not aimed at Rosgen's work exactly, but more at the way others use it. Detractors of his methods say they are so simple, they give people the feeling that they know more about rivers than they really do, and that Rosgen's inspiring charisma can make people too zealous about his system. (Rosgen admits his ideas have been misused, and he says he has increased the amount of training he offers.)

A glowing profile in *Time* in 2004 helped increase Rosgen's stature. River restorers, whether they love or hate his work, say he is the dominant figure in their field. "It's almost impossible to talk about the subject without his name coming up," David Montgomery, a geomorphologist at the University of Washington, Seattle, told *Science*'s Malakoff.

## Selected writings

*Applied River Morphology*, Wildland Hydrology, 1996.

## Sources

### Periodicals

*American City & County*, January 1, 1996.
*National Wildlife*, June/July 2002, p. 10.
*Science*, August 13, 2004.
*Whole Earth*, Summer 1998, p. 37.

## Online

"Dave Rosgen," Federation of Fly Fishers, http://www.fedflyfishers.org/Conserve/Leopold.htm (November 28, 2004).

"The Stream Saver," *Time,* http://www.time.com/time/2004/innovators/200404/rosgen.html (November 28, 2004).

Wildland Hydrology Consultants, http://www.wildlandhydrology.com/index.htm (November 28, 2004).

Additional information was obtained from a press release from Wildland Hydrology Consultants.

—*Erick Trickey*

# Renzo Rosso

*AP/Wide World Photos/Fashion Wire Daily*

## Fashion designer

**B**orn in 1955 in Brugine, Italy; married; children: Stefano, Andrea (son), four others.

**Addresses:** *Office*—Diesel, Molvena, Italy. *Office*—Diesel USA, 770 Lexington Ave., 9th Flr., New York, NY 10021.

## Career

**W**orked for Moltex; bought part of the company and changed the name to Diesel, 1978; bought out the Diesel name, 1985; created website, 1995; opened first flagship store in New York, NY, 1996.

**Awards:** Premio Risultati award, Bocconi Institute, for Best Italian Company of the Year, 1996.

## Sidelights

**R**enzo Rosso is the president and powerhouse behind Diesel, the Italian-based international fashion brand with more than 10,000 points of sale and more than 200 privately owned stores in over 50 countries. Rosso created the brand name in 1978 while part owner of a small clothing manufacturing company, of which he became sole proprietor in 1985. By 2003, Diesel's worldwide revenue rose above $760 million. While the luxury brand's primary product is denim—particularly jeans—it designs, manufactures, and markets trendy consumer products from sunglasses to underwear. Rosso's motto is "Diesel is not my company, it's my life."

Growing up, Rosso lived in northeastern Italy on a farm near a village of about 2,000 people where there was only one car and one television set. Rosso told Brad Goldfarb of *Interview,* "I think this experience of growing up in a little town, of doing farmwork, was important for me because I learned to respect the value of things.... These sorts of experiences give you a real sense of the value of money, and over the years this has helped keep my feet on the floor."

At the age of 15, not liking to study, he decided to attend a newly established Italian industrial textile manufacturing and fashion school where he thought graduation would be easier. Here, he discovered he loved the fashion business and, after graduating in 1975, made clothes for himself and his friends. He dreamed of one day owning his own small business.

He took a job with a small trouser manufacturing company called Moltex. He told *Interview*'s Goldfarb that once he had money in his pocket, he bought a car, a motorcycle, and "went out too much." Then, he got a letter from the owner, "You're a nice guy but I don't want to work with you any more." He pleaded for a second chance and was re-employed with a salary based on how much volume the company did. "This gave me an incredible incentive," he told Goldfarb. "The company completely turned around."

Beginning to comprehend his potential, Rosso decided to move on. The company's owner enticed him to stay by offering him the opportunity to purchase 40 percent of the company. Rosso borrowed the money from his father and changed the company's name to Diesel because, he told Goldfarb, "It's short. It's easy to remember. And it was already a word that was pronounceable—the same way everywhere—and understood worldwide." Rosso's dream was bigger now. In 1985, he bought the entire business, and this would be the beginning of Diesel's remarkable growth.

Rosso then went in search of an international design team. "When I started my first job," he told *Interview*'s Goldfarb, "I would pass through the offices of one of the sister companies on the way home, and I'd meet a lot of people there from all over the world. We would share information, our different mentalities, different ways in which we'd all been brought up." Through this experience, he understood the importance of multicultural input, a component now vital to Diesel's success. At first, Rosso hired every Diesel employee himself, believing it was important he feel a connection with each one. "This doesn't mean we're not professional," he said, "but we maintain this incredible team spirit by working together." By 2003, Rosso left most of the recruitment to his Human Resources department, but still had a final say. "I look for people who can work in a team. I don't want the star, I want the number two," he explained to Sara Manuelli in *Design Week*. Rosso encourages freedom of expression and design, "hoping they could create a line of clothing perfect for people who follow their own independent path in life," reads the description on the company's website. "The company now views the world as a single, border-less macro-culture."

In 1991, Diesel went international. In 1996, they opened the first U.S. store—on New York's Lexington Avenue; in 2001, their third New York store opened on Union Square making it the twelfth store in the United States. In December of 2002, Rosso flew to the United States to celebrate $100 million of sales with his New York staff, then on to Miami, Florida, to the opening night party of a store in South Beach—his 23rd U.S. store with five more U.S. openings planned for 2003. By February of 2003, the total number of stores worldwide numbered 203.

While 85 percent of the company's business flows from outside Italy, the small Italian town of Molvena is the hub of the organization. From here the business is run, and the team of 40 young international designers produces 3,000 new designs every six months. While Diesel is known for its denim, that fabric constitutes only about half of those designs.

Rosso told Thomas Cunningham of the *Daily News Record*, "We have [many] different items each season, including shoes, watches, shades, and Diesel Style Lab and 55-DSL. We don't look for big production of key items. Instead we divide the production more evenly. That makes each item more exclusive and more appealing."

When the Union Square store opened, a separate space became the first boutique for 55-DSL, Diesel's board sport brand, the creative force behind which is Rosso's son, Andrea (Rosso has six children total). Catering to the skateboard and snowboard crew, the boutique includes couches and video screens showing boarding videos with dressing rooms designed as toilet and shower rooms, "adding a dose of Diesel wit to the decor," commented the *Daily News Record*'s Cunningham. In addition to the Diesel, Diesel Style Lab, and 55-DSL lines, the company also manufactures a children's line. In 2000, Rosso purchased Staff International, an Italian fashion manufacturing and distributing company that produces the NewYorkIndustrie brand and licensed brands such as Vivienne Westwood, Martin Margiela, and Dsquared.

Rosso envisioned customizing each store to the culture in which it is located. "It's quite impossible, but it's a dream," he told the *Daily News Record*'s Cunningham. "Because the customers [at our Union Square store] are kids, they are fashionable and trendy, and at Lexington Avenue they are richer, more interested in the upper end." Rosso makes sure every Diesel store is stocked with merchandise unique to that store and its clients. "Different stores, different displays, create interest.... Companies like Gucci, Prada, and Armani always have the same display in all their stores. Our policy is much more difficult to manage and we really have to have people that know how to do more than just read a manual but that are actually creative," he explained to the *Daily News Record*'s Courtney Colavita.

Rosso, for now, has decided to keep the company private. A businessman with his feet on the ground, he has been twice tempted to put it on the stock exchange, but decided that is too much of a headache and can cause too many mistakes. Rather than rewarding his employees with shares—he reason he considered going public—he decided to reward them with bonuses based on sales volume.

In the 21st century, Rosso moved beyond just working in fashion. He supported the Online Flash Film Festival, which was held in May of 2002 in Barcelona, Spain. The company also runs events such as the Diesel U Music awards. Rosso published a nightlife guide in partnership with the Little Black

Book. However, he did not leave fashion far behind. In November of 2003, the company launched a jewelry collection for men and women.

When asked whether he fears the increasing competition from high-end denim companies like Lucky Jeans and Paper Denim & Cloth, Rosso scoffed. He explained to Colavita in the *Daily News Record,* "In the past 25 years, we've seen many ups and downs in denim, but actually I like when there's a crisis in the denim market because only the true professionals remain.... I don't really think there are other [denim] companies out there that really have as much know-how and experience as Diesel."

## Sources

### Periodicals

*BusinessWeek,* February 10, 2003, p. 64.

*Daily News Record,* July 30, 2001; December 9, 2002; September 15, 2003, p. 14.
*Design Week,* July 10, 2003, p. 15.
*Interview,* November 1998.

### Online

"Renzo Russo, The Man Behind Diesel," Diesel, http://www.diesel.com/companyinfo/renzorosso/ (December 7, 2004).

### Transcripts

Africa News Service, December 9, 2002.

—*Marie L. Thompson*

# Jack Rowe

*Mike Fuentes/Bloomberg News/Landov*

**Chairman and Chief Executive Officer of Aetna**

**B**orn John Wallis Rowe, June 20, 1944, in Jersey City, NJ; son of Albert Wallis (a professional soccer player and factory worker) and Elizabeth (a hospital clerk; maiden name, Lynch) Rowe; married Valerie Ann DelTufo, August 10, 1968; children: Meredith, Abigail, Rebecca. *Religion:* Roman Catholic. *Education:* Canisius College, B.S., 1966; University of Rochester, M.D., 1970.

**Addresses:** *Office*—Aetna, 151 Farmington Ave., Hartford, CT 06156.

## Career

**C**ompleted residency, Harvard Medical School and Beth Israel Hospital, Boston, 1970-72; worked as an instructor, then professor, Harvard Medical School, 1976-88; founded the Harvard Medical School's Division of Aging, 1979; chief of gerontology, Beth Israel Hospital, c. 1982; president, Mount Sinai Hospital and School of Medicine, 1988-98; president and chief executive officer, Mount Sinai NYU Health, 1998-2000; chairman and chief executive officer, Aetna Inc., 2000—.

**Member:** Council for Affordable Quality Healthcare; National Academy of Sciences' Institute of Medicine; Medicare Payment Advisory Commission; NY Yacht Club.

## Sidelights

**J**ack Rowe is a turnaround king, credited with saving insurance industry giant Aetna Inc. from the brink of extinction. When Rowe joined Aetna as chairman and chief executive officer (CEO) in 2000, the company was deep in trouble. Doctors and patients alike were fed up with its policies. In fact, more than 700,000 practitioners nationwide had filed a class-action lawsuit against the insurer, citing dubious billing practices and patient-care interference because doctors had to get permission for even the most basic procedures. Financially, the company was a mess, too. But none of that scared Rowe, who came in with an ambitious plan for restoration. Rowe laid off thousands of workers and trimmed the customer base. He sought ways to practice good medicine and good business. As a physician himself who once considered suing Aetna, Rowe concentrated efforts on improving relationships with doctors. The hard work paid off. In just three years, Rowe's leadership transformed Aetna "from being a poorly run company with very few prospects to an intriguing one with very solid growth," Lehman Brothers Inc. senior analyst Joshua Raskin told *BusinessWeek's* Diane Brady.

Rowe was born on June 20, 1944, in Jersey City, New Jersey. His father, Albert, played professional soccer in Britain, then worked in a pencil factory. His mother, Elizabeth, worked as a hospital clerk. An Irish Catholic, Rowe attended Jesuit-based Canisius College, located in Buffalo. He graduated in 1966, then studied medicine at the University of Rochester in New York, earning his medical degree in 1970. From 1970-72, Rowe completed a residency in internal medicine at Harvard Medical School and Beth Israel Hospital, located in Boston. By 1976, Rowe was an instructor at Harvard and later became a professor. He specialized in gerontology (the study of the aging process). At Harvard, Rowe founded and directed the medical school's Division of Aging. He also served as chief of gerontology at Beth Israel Hospital.

In 1988, New York City's Mount Sinai Hospital and School of Medicine lured Rowe away from Harvard to become its president. The position saddled Rowe with a lot of administrative work, but he still found time to maintain a small practice and spent one month each year rounding with medical students. Under Rowe, the Mount Sinai medical school also received a lot of money in research grants from the National Institutes of Health.

Things went smoothly for Rowe until the late 1990s, when managed-care cutbacks made money tight. Government reimbursement money dwindled, making the hospital's required care of the poor more costly. Rowe worried about keeping the hospital afloat. He thought a merger with the New York University (NYU) Medical Center would fix the fiscal mess. The plan was announced in 1997. Rowe figured Mount Sinai could save money by combining office operations and sharing high-priced medical equipment with NYU. He also thought the merger would give the institutions better bargaining power with insurers. NYU faculty opposed the merger and formed an opposition group called the Committee of Concerned Physicians. The group published fiery memos, according to the *Wall Street Journal*'s Lucette Lagnado, warning that their medical school was about to be taken over by Rowe, "the aggressive 'czar' of Mount Sinai Medical Center."

After a year of talks, Rowe pushed the merger through, gaining prominence as an administrator who could get tough things done. He reportedly appeared on then-President Bill Clinton's list of candidates for FDA Commissioner, though he was never called. With the merger complete, Rowe, in 1998, became president and CEO of the not-for-

profit Mount Sinai NYU Health. In this capacity, Rowe formed partnerships with dozens of neighboring hospitals to turn the institution into one of the nation's leading academic health-care centers. Mount Sinai NYU Health also became New York's largest employer, with 31,000 employees and revenues of $1.8 billion—all under Rowe's direction. By the summer of 2000, however, Rowe was losing support as the merger continued to be a sore spot for faculty. When Aetna asked Rowe to become its CEO, he jumped at the chance, eager to attack a new challenge.

When Rowe took over Aetna, the company was in a shambles. Patients, doctors, and shareholders were all fed up with the insurer. As one analyst remarked to *BusinessWeek*'s Brady: "Aetna came close to blowing itself up." Wall Street hardly gave Rowe a vote of confidence. Share prices dropped 0.7 percent after the announcement, but that is not surprising, given the enormity of the task before him: keeping costs under control and making peace with physicians at the same time.

Rowe brought in a new management team and developed a three-pronged attack to restore the insurance company's health. First, Rowe cut costs by eliminating 15,000 jobs. He shrank the customer base from 19 million to 13 million by abandoning unprofitable markets. Secondly, Rowe made peace with physicians in May of 2003 by settling a massive class-action lawsuit claiming unfair billing practices. Aetna became the first insurer to settle the suit. The deal paid 700,000 practitioners up to $150 million. Some of Rowe's moves proved good for the bottom line, but not for customers. He raised annual rates more than 16 percent, he said, to better reflect the actual costs of health care. Though the company suffered losses of more than $265 million in 2001, by 2003, it had turned a profit.

As part of the class-action lawsuit, Aetna agreed to contribute $20 million to establish a foundation to study issues such as childhood obesity, end-of-life care, racial disparities in health care, and the uninsured. Aetna also began offering customer-driven products and gave patients more say over their care. Speaking to *BusinessWeek*'s Brady, Connecticut State Medical Society executive director Tim Norbeck praised Rowe's performance: "Aetna has become the physician-friendliest and user-friendliest company in America." It is a model Rowe hopes other insurance companies will follow.

## Sources

### Periodicals

*BusinessWeek,* June 9, 2003, pp. 98-102; December 8, 2003, p. 86.
*New York Times,* April 7, 2003, p. F1.
*USA Today,* September 7, 2004, p. B4.
*Wall Street Journal,* November 21, 1997, p. 1.

### Online

"Aetna Aims to be Friendly to at Least One Physician," American Medical Association News, http://www.ama-assn.org/amednews/2000/09/25/bisa0925.htm (November 4, 2004).

"Aetna Names Dr. John W. Rowe President and CEO of Aetna U.S. Healthcare," Aetna, http://www.aetna.com/news/2000/prtpr_20000905.htm (November 4, 2004).

"Aetna's New CEO can 'Rowe' Through Choppy Waters," American Medical Association News, http://www.ama-assn.org/amednews/2000/10/16/bica1016.htm (November 4, 2004).

—*Lisa Frick*

# Katey Sagal

Steve Granitz/WireImage.com

## Actress and singer

**B**orn Catherine Louise Sagal, January 19, 1954, in Los Angeles, California; daughter of Boris Sagal (a television director and producer) and Sara Zwilling (also known as Sara Macon; a singer and television director, producer, and writer); married Freddie Beckmeyer, 1978 (divorced, 1981); married Jack White (a country music drummer), November 27, 1993 (divorced, 2000); married Kurt Sutter (a television writer and producer), October 2, 2004; children: Sarah Grace, Jackson James (from second marriage). *Education:* Attended California Institute of the Arts.

**Addresses:** *Office*—Touchstone Television, 500 S. Buena Vista St., Stage 6, 5th Flr., Ste. 514, Burbank, CA 91521. *Website*—http://www.kateysagal.net.

## Career

**A**ctress in television series, including: *Mary*, CBS, 1985; *Married ... With Children*, FOX, 1987-97; *Futurama* (animated), FOX, 1999-2002; *Tucker*, NBC, 2000; *Imagine That*, NBC, 2002; *8 Simple Rules*, ABC, 2002—. Television movies: *The Failing of Raymond*, 1971; *The Dream Makers*, NBC, 1975; *She Says She's Innocent*, NBC, 1991; *Trail of Tears*, NBC, 1995; *Mr. Headmistress*, ABC, 1998; *Chance of a Lifetime*, CBS, 1998; *God's New Plan*, CBS, 1999. Television pilots: *Earth Scum*, ABC, 1998. Film appearances include: *Maid to Order*, 1987. Stage appearances include: *Two Gentlemen of Verona*, mid-1970s; *The Beautiful Lady*, Los Angeles, CA, early 1980s. Film song performer for *The Silent Rage*, 1982. Worked as a singing waitress at the Great American Food and Beverage Company, Santa Monica, CA; appeared as back-up singer on tours of Olivia Newton-John, Etta James, and Tanya Tucker; a member of Bette Midler's Harlettes, c. 1978-81; recorded solo albums including, *Well*, 1995, and *Room*, 2004.

## Sidelights

**B**est known for her role as Peg Bundy on the long-running FOX situation comedy *Married ... With Children*, actress Katey Sagal also had prominent roles in other television shows including the animated *Futurama* and ABC's *8 Simple Rules*. Sagal began her career in show business as a back-up singer for musical acts in the 1970s and 1980s, and released several records after her acting career took off. In addition to her roles on television series and her singing career, Sagal also appeared in a number of television movies, sometimes in dramatic roles.

Born Catherine Louise Sagal on January 19, 1954, in Los Angeles, California, she is the daughter of Boris Sagal and Sara Zwilling (also known as Sara Macon). Her mother, who worked as a singer and was one of the first women to work in television as a director and producer, died of heart disease when Sagal was 19 years old. Her father was a film and television director and producer, who died tragically in 1981. When Sagal's mother became ill and died, Sagal helped care for her four younger siblings, three of whom also worked as professional actors. Raised primarily in Los Angeles, she attended Pacific Palisades High School. After graduation, Sagal was a student at the California Institute of the Arts, located in Valencia, California, for a time.

From an early age, Sagal liked to sing, and she taught herself how to play the piano when she was a teenager. While she wanted to pursue singing, Sagal focused her attention on acting first, with encouragement from her father. Sagal had several early acting roles. In 1971, she appeared in the television movie *The Failing of Raymond* as a mental patient. A few years later, Sagal had a role in the nine-month run in a touring stage show *Two Gentleman of Verona* by Joe Papp. When she returned, she worked at the Great American Food and Beverage Company in Santa Monica, California, as a singing waitress. She later appeared in a television movie directed and produced by her father, *The Dream Makers*, but disliked the experience and decided to focus on singing.

Sagal spent the rest of the 1970s primarily working as a singer. She performed as a back-up singer on the concert tours of many singing artists including Olivia Newton-John, Etta James, and Tanya Tucker. One of Sagal's longest-running gigs as a singer was with Bette Midler. She was one of Midler's "Harlettes" from about 1978 to 1981. Though Sagal had success as a back-up singer, her attempts to succeed with her own band in Los Angeles' music industry failed. She was able to perform some songs that appeared in films, including 1982's *Silent Rage.*

Acting lured Sagal back by the early 1980s. She first appeared in a Los Angeles stage production of *The Beautiful Lady.* Sagal's performance caught the eye of television producers and helped launch her career as an actress in that medium. It led to a role in the situation comedy *Mary,* which starred Mary Tyler Moore. Sagal played Jo Tucker, a reporter with attitude. Though Sagal was beginning her acting career, she struggled with personal problems. After her father's death, she began using drugs. She finally sought treatment in 1986, and conquered her addiction.

In 1987, Sagal was cast in her second television series, in what became arguably the biggest role of her career. On FOX's *Married ... With Children,* she played Peg Bundy, the wife of long-suffering shoe salesman Al Bundy, and mother to two teenage children. Sagal's Peg had big red hair, dressed in tawdry clothes, and liked to do little more than sit on the couch and watch television or cut her husband down. However, the Bundys pulled together when threatened by others. While *Married ... With Children* was considered crass by some critics, within a season it became a hit show and had a loyal following.

When Sagal joined the show, she did not have much experience in the industry and, despite some initial nervousness, learned on the job. The success of *Married ... With Children* gave Sagal the chance to expand her acting career. In 1987, she made her film debut with a role in *Maid to Order.* She also appeared in several television movies including 1991's *She Says She's Innocent* and 1995's *Trail of Tears.*

Both television movies gave Sagal a chance to demonstrate her ability to do drama. In *She Says She's Innocent,* she played Susan, a pregnant mother of a teenage girl who was accused of murdering a friend. In *Trail of Tears,* Sagal and co-star Pam Dawber portrayed mothers whose children are kidnapped by their former spouses.

Tragedy also struck Sagal's own life. In 1991, she became pregnant by boyfriend Jack White, a country music drummer, and the pregnancy was worked into the *Married ... With Children.* However, Sagal's child was stillborn in her eighth month of pregnancy. To explain the loss on the show, her character's pregnancy was explained as a dream and all the related episodes were fantasies that did not happen. In Sagal's real life, she married White in 1993 and had two children with him, Sarah Grace and Jackson James, before the marriage ended in divorce in 2000.

Music continued to play a role in Sagal's life while her acting career and personal life continued to grow. In 1987, she formed a R&B (rhythm & blues) band called Katey Sagal. While she achieved little success with the band, she was given a solo recording deal in the early 1990s. In 1995, after 18 months of work, she released *Well.* Sagal wrote or co-wrote nearly all the tracks on the album, which featured an adult contemporary/R&B sound.

When *Married ... With Children* ended its run in 1997, Sagal did not regret her time on the show. She told Ed Bark of *St. Louis Post-Dispatch,* "I'm so proud to have been on *Married ... With Children* and to have been Peg Bundy. I can't imagine my recoiling from it or not wanting it mentioned... I don't have any negative things to say about it, so you won't find me hiding my head."

Professionally, Sagal had several options. After *Married ... With Children,* she signed a development deal with CBS to create a situation comedy and appear in television movies. The situation comedy pilot did not make it air, but she did appear in the ABC pilot for *Earth Scum* in 1998. Sagal also appeared in several television movies.

In 1998, Sagal appeared in a comedic role in the ABC television movie *Mr. Headmistress.* Set at a girl's school, the title refers to a con artist who dresses like a woman and takes charge of the school. Sagal portrayed his assistant, "Dirty" Harriet Magnum, who wanted his job. It was one of the few times Sagal played a truly bad character. Later that year, she took on a completely different kind of role on the CBS television movie, *Chance of a Lifetime.* In the drama, she played Irene Duncan, a character who was overweight. She had to wear a padded suit to play the role. Sagal's Duncan was editor at a newspaper who helps her reporter colleague, played by actor John Ritter, when he suffers from health problems. In 1999, Sagal appeared in the dramatic film *God's New Plan* on CBS. She played a woman who becomes close to a nurse who helps her and her husband after the premature birth of their child, then prevails upon the nurse to take care of the child and her husband a short time later when she learns she is dying.

In addition to appearing in such television movies, Sagal also soon returned to series television. In 1999, she provided a voice for the animated series *Futurama,* created by Matt Groening who also devised the long-running animated series *The Simpsons.* Sagal's character was named Leela, who had only one eye and was an alien. The animated show lasted through 2002 on Fox. Several of Sagal's live-action roles were not as long-lived. In 2000, she had a role on *Tucker,* an NBC situation comedy. Sagal also appeared in another short-lived series on NBC, *Imagine That.* This program lasted only two episodes in 2002 before being cancelled.

Sagal finally found television gold when she won a role on *8 Simple Rules,* known as *8 Simple Rules for Dating My Teenage Daughter* when it first hit the air. Sagal had to fight to be cast as Cate Hennessey, a role that was originally quite small, so she could work with Ritter again. The family situation comedy primarily focused on the relationship between Cate's husband Paul, played by Ritter, and his two teenage daughters, with their son and the couple's relationship only minor concerns. In the premise of the show, Paul is a newspaper columnist who works at home, while Sagal's character has returned to the work place, putting her husband in a bigger role in his children's lives.

When *8 Simple Rules* began airing in 2002, ABC desperately needed a hit. The show was a success in the first season, and as its popularity grew, so did Sagal's role. Sagal unexpectedly became the lead during the second season of *8 Simple Rules* when Ritter died on September 11, 2003, while shooting one of the first episodes of the season. After his death, the show was retooled to focus on how the family dealt with the sudden death of their television father. Relatives of Sagal's character were brought in to support her in her loss. *8 Simple Rules* remained a popular show and continued into a third season, with Sagal playing a leading role in its success.

As Sagal's professional life remained strong, her personal life and secondary careers also grew. On October 2, 2004, Sagal married her third husband, a television writer and producer named Kurt Sutter. That same year, Sagal released her second album, *Room.* As with her first album, this record featured many of her own songs as well as covers of classic tunes.

Though Sagal never had the singing career she originally wanted, acting, especially in comedies, proved to be a satisfying career choice for her. She told Dan Yakir of BPI Entertainment News Wire, "Acting offers you the opportunity to explore different features of yourself, which is always illuminating, to put yourself in a situation you've never been in.... I have a special feel for comedy, but I didn't know I was funny. I first found out when I went to auditions and the network told me, 'You're funny. You have a gift. You've got the job.'"

## Selected discography

*Well,* Virgin, 1995.
*Room,* Valley Entertainment, 2004.

## Sources

### Books

*Celebrity Biographies,* Baseline II, Inc., 2004.

### Periodicals

Associated Press, May 2, 2003.
*Billboard,* March 12, 1994, p. 15.
BPI Entertainment News Wire, March 11, 1998.
*Buffalo News,* February 14, 1999, p. 10TV.
*Daily News* (New York, NY), May 20, 2004, p. 44.

*Entertainment Weekly,* November 21, 2003, pp. 30-33.

*Gazette* (Montreal, Quebec, Canada), September 17, 2002, p. D5.

*People,* April 18, 1994, p. 109.

*Plain Dealer* (Cleveland, OH), July 28, 2002, p. J1.

*St. Louis Post-Dispatch,* November 15, 1989, p. 3; March 28, 1998, p. 38.

*Toronto Star,* July 18, 1987, p. S6; May 29, 1994, p. F2.

*Toronto Sun,* October 5, 2004, p. 29SUN.

*USA Today,* October 28, 1991, p. 1D; September 17, 2004, p. 4E.

*Washington Post,* October 28, 1991, p. D1.

—A. Petruso

# Michael Schumacher

**Professional race car driver**

Born January 3, 1969, in Huerth-Hermuelheim, Germany; son of Rolf (a bricklayer and go-kart track worker) and Elisabeth (a go-kart track worker); married Corinna Betsch (an office worker), 1995; children: Gina-Maria, Mick.

**Addresses:** *Management*—Weber Management GmbH, Traenkestrasse 11, Stuttgart, DE 70597, Germany.

## Career

Joined Benetton's Formula One racing team, 1991; won first race, 1992; won first two Formula One championships, 1994 and 1995; joined Ferrari's Formula One team, 1996; won five straight championships, 2000-04.

**Awards:** Formula One champion, 1994, 1995, 2000, 2001, 2002, 2003, 2004.

## Sidelights

One of the world's richest, most famous athletes, Michael Schumacher has won more Formula One auto-racing championships than any other driver. Some fans enjoy hating Schumacher because of his controversial racing tactics, but he has a lot of fans too, and his success has won him grudging respect from others. He may not be well-known in the United States, but that is only because American car-racing fans prefer Indianapolis 500 racing to the European-dominated Formula One. Outside America, he is the popular sport's biggest star.

Ever since he was a little boy, Schumacher has been racing. His father, Rolf, a bricklayer, also worked part-time at a go-kart track with his mother, Elisabeth. They would let Michael ride a go-kart around the track on off hours while they worked, and by the time he was five, they noticed that he was very good at it. He won his first club championship at age six. Though his family was not well-off, he would keep his often inferior karts going by scavenging parts from other boys' wrecked karts.

As he got older, Schumacher began racing sports cars. In 1988, race team sponsor Wilhelm Weber noticed his talent and invited him to join his team. In a sign of how certain Weber was that Schumacher would be a star, he allowed the young racer to come on the team without providing a sponsor to fund his car, which was a rare move. Weber has been Schumacher's manager ever since. Three years later, Weber convinced Formula One team owner Eddie Jordan to let Schumacher race for Jordan's team once as a substitute. He made his debut in the 1991 Belgian Grand Prix, and quickly proved his skill.

Within a week, he signed a contract—with a different team, Benetton.

Schumacher won his first Formula One race in 1992 and another the next year. He won the world championship in 1994, becoming the first German champion. He dedicated his win to his mentor Ayrton Senna, the champion racer who had died that year in the San Marino Grand Prix. Schumacher won eight races on the way to the title, even though he was banned from two for breaking two minor rules.

The 1994 championship was decided in the season's final race, in a dramatic fashion that gave Schumacher a reputation in some circles as a poor sport. He was two points ahead of rival Damon Hill in the championship standings when the last race began. Seconds ahead of Hill in the race, Schumacher brushed against the racetrack's wall, and Hill moved to pass him. Schumacher swerved and crashed into Hill, knocking both drivers out of the race—which preserved Schumacher's lead and gave him the championship. Schumacher claimed he had lost control of his car, but much of the racing press believed he had crashed into Hill on purpose. The rivalry between Schumacher and Hill lasted into 1995, when Schumacher repeated as champion, this time unsullied by controversy.

For the 1996 season, Schumacher left Benetton for the Ferrari team and a rumored base salary of $25 million. It was Ferrari's attempt to make a comeback, since the team's last championship had been in 1979. Schumacher, hobbled by a car that broke down a lot, lost the title to Hill in 1996. But the next year, he vied for the championship with a new rival, Jacques Villeneuve. In what seemed like a repeat of his 1994 season, he began the last race slightly ahead of Villeneuve in the standings, and again, when his rival tried to pass him, he crashed into him. But Villeneuve's car shrugged off the crash, while Schumacher was knocked out of the race. This time, Schumacher was punished for a deliberate collision; his second-place finish was officially deleted from the standings.

Bad luck plagued Schumacher the next two seasons. In 1998 he again went into the last race with a chance to win the championship, but he punctured a tire and lost. In 1999, he severely broke a leg in a crash during the British Grand Prix and finished fifth in the final season standings.

Then, Schumacher made a comeback, winning the championship in 2000, 2001, and 2002 by taking first place in nine races each of the first two years

and eleven races the third. "Schumacher's combination of raw speed, racecraft, tactical awareness and sublime skill in the rain sets him apart from the pack," wrote Kate Noble of *Time International.*

With his success, Schumacher's controversial racing style became somewhat more accepted. "By the end of last season," quipped *Sports Illustrated* writer Jeff MacGregor in a 2003 profile, "what had formerly been referred to as Michael Schumacher's 'willingness to commit the professional foul' was being extolled by backpedaling journalists as his 'canny race craft.' " Still, in 2002, Formula One began changing its rules to try to limit Schumacher's runaway success.

It did not work. Schumacher won the championships in 2003 and 2004 as well, for a total of seven championships, including five straight. He won 13 races in 2004, for a total of 83 wins in his career. He and his Ferrari teammate, Rubens Barrichello, so completely dominate Formula One that the sport is commonly criticized for no longer being competitive enough to interest fans. In 2005, Formula One will again change its rules to try to rein in Schumacher. But he insists he has not made the sport boring. "Something very special is happening with Ferrari," Terry McCarthy of *Time* quoted him as saying. "I think people want to see who is going to be the first to beat us, too."

Schumacher is now the most successful Formula One driver ever. He makes about $80 million per year (half in salary, half in sponsorships and endorsements), and he is one of the two highest-paid athletes in the world, behind only golfer Tiger Woods. The racing press in Great Britain and France often nicknames him the "Red Baron" and caricatures him as an unfeeling German, but others say he has shown a wide range of emotion, seeming ecstatic after big wins or weeping in 2000 after he tied the number of wins (41) achieved by his idol, Senna.

Five feet, eight inches tall and weighing 164 pounds in 2003, Schumacher works out obsessively, giving him a stamina that may account for much of his success in his physically demanding sport. His brother, Ralf, is also a Formula One driver. Schumacher and his wife, Corinna, have two children and live in Vufflens, Switzerland.

## Sources

### Periodicals

AP Worldstream, October 26, 2004.

*Halifax Daily News,* October 28, 2004.

*Sports Illustrated,* July 17, 1995; April 28, 2003, pp. 55-62.

*Sunday Telegraph* (London, England), October 24, 2004.

*Time,* July 26, 2004, p. 56.

*Time International,* September 3, 2001, p. 52.

**Online**

"Michael Schumacher Biography," mSchumacher. com, http://www.mschumacher.com/biography. html (November 28, 2004).

*—Erick Trickey*

# Alice Sebold

AP/Wide World Photos

## Author

**B**orn c. 1963, in Madison, WI; daughter of a Spanish professor and a journalist; married Glen David Gold (an author), November, 2001. *Education:* Earned degree from Syracuse University, 1984; attended the University of Houston, c. 1984-85; University of California—Irvine, M.F.A., 1998.

**Addresses:** *Office*—c/o Author Mail, Little, Brown & Company/Warner Books, 1271 Avenue of the Americas, New York, NY 10020.

## Career

**A**djunct instructor in English at Hunter College, and research analyst in New York City, c. 1985-93; published a memoir, *Lucky,* 1999; debut novel *The Lovely Bones* published, 2002; film rights to *The Lovely Bones* sold for a film project set to be released in 2007.

**Awards:** Bram Stoker Award for best first novel for *The Lovely Bones,* 2002.

## Sidelights

**A**lice Sebold's debut novel, *The Lovely Bones,* dominated the best-seller lists for several months in 2002. The story of a murdered teenager who observes her grieving family and the impact the crime had on everyone involved, Sebold's literary tour-de-force struck a chord with readers, garnered impressive reviews, and sold 2.5 million copies in hardcover—a new record for a first-time novelist.

In an article solely devoted to this publishing phenomenon of the year, *New York Times* writer Bill Goldstein called Sebold's novel "the literary equivalent of that other word-of-mouth success *My Big Fat Greek Wedding,"* and included it in a roster of several other recent novels, more literary in spirit than purely potboiler, that had also climbed to the top of the best-seller lists. Such books, Goldstein asserted, were "a trend that appears to be blurring the boundaries of literary and commercial fiction." Sebold, for her part, was elated by all the attention. "I've been such a miserable failure my whole life," she enthused in an *Entertainment Weekly* interview with Karen Valby, "this feels great!"

Born in the early 1960s, Sebold spent her formative years in suburban Philadelphia. Her mother was a journalist for a local paper, while her father was a professor of Spanish at the Ivy-League University of Pennsylvania. She had an older sister who excelled in school, and while Sebold was also a good student, she was the self-admitted joker in her family. It was a way of coping with the stress inside the household, which she dissected years later in her memoir, *Lucky.* Her parents were undemonstrative, and her mother suffered from panic attacks and endured a secret drinking problem for a number of years. Because her parents were more intellectual than their neighbors in their upper-middle-class world, Sebold recalled that they were considered somewhat "weird," a tag that followed her into college.

Sebold chose to attend Syracuse University—in part to distance herself from her family—and it was there, near the end of her freshman year, that she was attacked while walking back to her dormitory on the evening of the last day of school for the year. She struggled with her assailant, but was badly beaten and bloodied. After sexually assaulting her in a tunnel that was once the stage entrance to a now-closed amphitheater, he let her go. She managed to make it back to her dorm, and was taken from there to a local hospital. When she gave the police her account of the rape, one cop told her that the tunnel had been the site of where a young woman was once murdered and dismembered, and made the offhand remark that Sebold was "lucky" to have walked away.

Sebold's rapist was caught, convicted, and given a maximum prison sentence, but the ordeal was far from over. She recounts in *Lucky,* her 1999 memoir centered around the experience, that she lost friends over it, and that even her father was disdainful that she had not put up more enough of a struggle. Somewhat surprisingly, Sebold returned to school in Syracuse, and after graduating headed to the University of Houston for a brief attempt at graduate school. She eventually settled in New York City, where she planned to become a writer. For years, she lived in the East Village—during its rattiest period, before it was an acceptable post-college, bar-and-restaurant-filled enclave—while working as a research analyst and teaching English as an adjunct instructor at Hunter College on the side. She wrote fiction and poetry, but her submissions were met with rejection. It took her several years to emerge from her post-assault experience, she admitted, and recalled her 20s as a period in which she dated the wrong men, drank too much, snorted heroin for three years, and took part in daring stunts like climbing to the top of the Manhattan Bridge.

Finally, Sebold wrote a *New York Times* article about her rape, which led to an appearance on *The Oprah Winfrey Show.* A sentence from her article was quoted a few years later in a book called *Trauma and Recovery,* about post-traumatic stress disorder. As she explained in an interview with the *Guardian*'s Katharine Viner, reading that book was a turning point in her life. "I was failing miserably in New York, I'd written two novels that weren't published," she recalled. "And I realized I was quoted

in the 'trauma' section of the book, but not in 'recovery.'" She found a therapist, and spent the next three years coming to terms with the assault. Finally, she decided to leave New York City after nearly a decade there. This was around 1994, and her plan was to move to California. "I couldn't handle the rejection and the failure anymore ... and the 'almost' of it all," she told Valby in the *Entertainment Weekly* interview about her decision. "Everybody from New York has their almost-but-not-quite story, and I just felt like I don't want to be walking around on the planet trotting out mine."

Sebold applied to graduate school in California, but was determined to relocate no matter what. "If I didn't get in I was going to buy a dozen nude-colored panty hose and get an office job in Temecula, California," she said in the interview with Valby. Accepted into the master of fine arts writing program at the University of California's Irvine campus, she took out a student loan, and met her future husband on the first day of school. She earned her M.F.A. in 1998, and a year later *Lucky* was published by Scribner. Its title, of course, was the word that the police officer had used in an attempt to console her. The work earned good reviews, with *Publishers Weekly* describing it as a "fiercely observed memoir about how an incident of such profound violence can change the course of one's life," but failed to catch on with readers. After disappointing sales of about 14,000 in hardcover, it was not even released in paperback.

Yet Sebold had already started the manuscript that would become her first published novel, *The Lovely Bones.* She felt compelled to chronicle her own traumatic experience first, she told Christina Patterson in an interview that appeared in London's *Independent.* "When I felt a sense of polemic entering the novel, I realised that I had to get myself out of there," she admitted. Finally, she finished *The Lovely Bones* manuscript, and it netted her a two-book deal with Little, Brown. As advance copies began circulating in the months prior to its June of 2002 publication date, a publishing-industry and bookseller buzz began to attach to it.

*The Lovely Bones* is told in the first-person voice of Susie Salmon, who tells readers in the book's second sentence, "I was fourteen when I was murdered on December 6, 1973." She recounts the crime in horrific detail: being lured by a sinister neighbor to a field, then sexually assaulted. She fought back, but was no match for the man she knew as Mr. Harvey. "I wept," Susie recalls. "I began to leave my body; I began to inhabit the air and silence. I wept and struggled so I would not feel."

Police never find Susie's remains, save for an elbow, for Harvey had put her body inside a safe and buried it in quicksand. Susie chronicles the posthumous events from above—the police investigation, her father's belief that the culprit was indeed their neighbor, the grief and detachment that drives her mother into an adulterous affair and abandonment of Susie's teenage sister and very young brother. In heaven, Sebold reveals, "life" is somewhat better. Apparently the afterlife is tailored to the desires of the individual, and Susie's is a teenage girl's version of heaven: she goes to school, but there are no teachers, and the textbooks are fashion magazines. She lives in duplex with a friend, has unlimited access to peppermint ice cream, and there are also lots of dogs around. An "intake counselor" serves as her new mentor in the afterlife, and Franny helps Susie realize that she is not in heaven quite yet, and must first break the chains to her earthly relationships. The Salmons eventually reknit the fabric of their family together, Harvey comes to a violent end, and Susie's best friend discovers she has a strong ability to connect with the departed.

Reviewing *The Lovely Bones* in the *New York Times,* Michiko Kakutani gave it high praise. "What might play as a sentimental melodrama in the hands of a lesser writer becomes in this volume a keenly observed portrait of familial love," Kakutani noted, "and how it endures and changes over time." The *Times'* notoriously frank critic did concede that the plot falters toward the end, but "even these lapses do not diminish Ms. Sebold's achievements: her ability to capture both the ordinary and the extraordinary, the banal and the horrific, in lyrical, unsentimental prose; her instinctive understanding of the mathematics of love between parents and children; her gift for making palpable the dreams, regrets, and unstilled hopes of one girl and one family," Kakutani concluded.

Sebold's debut novel spent weeks on the best-seller list, and Little, Brown even ponied up funds for a television advertising campaign—a rare occurrence for a first-time fiction writer. For several weeks, *The Lovely Bones* outsold competition that included titles from Nicholas Sparks, Stephen King, and Tom Clancy, and was selling at the rate of a million copies a month at one point. Perhaps more impressively, it had not even enjoyed the boost of being included in television personality Oprah Winfrey's hitmaking book club, either. A writer for London's *Guardian* newspaper, Ali Smith, theorized about the appeal of Sebold's book for American readers. "Perhaps the reason," Smith noted, "is something to do with the aftermath of public mourning after [the 2001 terrorist attacks], the reassurance and satisfaction of being able to hear the voice of the gone and to piece together the future after cataclysm."

*The Lovely Bones* was optioned for film, and in early 2005 the director of the *Lord of the Rings* trilogy, Peter Jackson, signed on to the project. Creating the "heaven" from which Susie tells her story was a challenge for any filmmaker without resorting to fluffy clouds or other potentially ludicrous imagery, but Jackson had also done *Heavenly Creatures,* a cult-classic New Zealand film from earlier in his career based on a true story of two teenage girls whose elaborate fantasy life seems to propel them to commit murder. The film version of *The Lovely Bones* was slated for a late 2007 release.

Sebold spent some of her best-seller earnings on retiling the bathroom of the home she shares with her husband, Glen David Gold, whose first novel, *Carter Beats the Devil,* was also a literary sensation. They live in Long Beach, California, where Sebold rises at 3 in the morning to write. She even managed to make a success out of the disappointing first book, *Lucky* which was reissued in paperback and racked up impressive sales in 2003, thanks to the success of *The Lovely Bones.* Sebold hoped that, in the end, the aura of shame, of victimhood, that attached to women who had experienced a traumatic sexual assault would dissipate. Such an event, she noted, is "a story of survival, which is actually heroic," she pointed out in the interview with Viner in the *Guardian.* "The stereotype is that you're always weak or passive or falling apart—so you don't talk about it because if you do, people will change their opinion of what you're capable of. When the truth is that you're probably capable of a lot more if you survived rape."

## Selected writings

*Lucky* (memoir), Scribner (New York, NY), 1999.
*The Lovely Bones: A Novel,* Little, Brown (Boston, MA), 2002.

## Sources

### Periodicals

*Book,* July/August 2002, p. 64.
*Booklist,* July 1999, p. 1903.
*Christian Science Monitor,* July 25, 2002, p. 15.
*Daily Variety,* January 19, 2005, p. 1.

*Economist,* September 7, 2002.

*Entertainment Weekly,* July 12, 2002, p. 74; August 16, 2002, p. 39.

*Guardian* (London, England), August 17, 2002, p. 21; August 24, 2002, p. 18.

*Independent* (London, England), June 6, 2003, p. 4.

*New Statesman,* August 19, 2002, p. 39; June 30, 2003, p. 51.

*New York Times,* June 18, 2002, p. E1; July 14, 2002, p. 14; October 21, 2002, p. C7.

*Publishers Weekly,* June 21, 1999, p. 44; June 17, 2002, p. 41; July 29, 2002, p. 22; December 23, 2002, p. 15.

*Time,* July 1, 2002, p. 62.

**Online**

*Contemporary Authors Online,* Gale, 2003.

—*Carol Brennan*

# David Sedaris

## Radio commentator and author

**B**orn in 1957, in New York; partner of Hugh Hamrick (a painter). *Education:* Attended Kent State University; graduated from School of the Art Institute of Chicago, 1987.

**Addresses:** *Agent*—Steven Barclay, 321 Pleasant St., Petaluma, CA 94952. *Home*—New York, NY; Paris, France; and Normandy, France.

## Career

**W**orked variously as a moving company worker, an office worker, an elf in SantaLand at Macy's department store, and an apartment cleaner. Has taught writing at School of the Art Institute of Chicago. Also author of commentaries for National Public Radio, 1992—, and of satirical plays, co-written with Amy Sedaris.

**Awards:** James Thurber Prize for *Me Talk Pretty One Day,* 2001.

## Sidelights

**H**umorist David Sedaris does not pull any punches when he writes about his family's quirks, but he also "mocks himself and explores cross-cultural absurdities," wrote *People*'s Sean Daly. Sedaris (pronounced seh-DAR-iss) once took an IQ test to see if he could join the ranks of Mensa. As he reported in his essay collection *Me Talk Pretty One Day,* Sedaris did not really give those heavyweights a run for their money: "There are cats that weigh more than my IQ score." But as many reviewers have pointed out, it is humor and not brains that sells Sedaris' work.

Sedaris is the master of spin, turning the quotidian into the stuff of laugh-out-loud humor. His wry and insightful observations about daily life, tales of growing up and the alienated angst of feeling different have won radio audiences and book readers alike. He talks of his foul-mouthed younger brother, of family foibles and foils, and of his own misguided attempts to adapt to his adopted home in Paris, France. As Bob Hoover noted in an article in the *Post-Gazette,* Sedaris is an "elfin figure" with a "faintly nasal deadpan delivery." Hoover also noted that Sedaris is "one of life's true outsiders, a Northerner transplanted to the South, a gay man in a society of male role models, a sensitive soul in a dumb culture." Sedaris uses painful bits from his family history as well as the flotsam he finds all around him. "I'm just the friendly junk man," Sedaris told Hoover. "I take pieces of junk and make my stories out of them."

Born in New York, the second of six children in a Greek-American family, Sedaris grew up in Raleigh, North Carolina. Neva Chonin, writing in the *San Francisco Chronicle,* described him as an "obsessive-compulsive child [who] spent his days licking light switches and hitting himself over the head with his shoe." He dropped out of Kent State University in 1977 to travel around the country, working for a time as a field laborer in California. He moved to Chicago while in his twenties, where he attended the Art Institute, and performed readings from his diaries for audiences. After his move to New York

City in 1991, Sedaris began reading excerpts from his diaries on National Public Radio (NPR), where his "nicely nerdy, quavering voice," in the words of *Newsweek* commentator Jeff Giles, delivered monologues praised for their acerbic wit and dead-pan delivery. His "SantaLand Diaries," recounting his misadventures as an elf at Macy's, was an instant hit and ensured further appearances on NPR. John Marchese commented in the *New York Times,* "In the five radio pieces that he has done, Mr. Sedaris has shown remarkable skill as a mimic and the ability to mix the sweet and the bitter: to be naive and vulnerable and at the same time, jaded and wickedly funny." *Entertainment Weekly* contributor Margot Mifflin remarked, "Sedaris is a crackpot in the best sense of the word."

Sedaris' comic, and often satirical, monologues draw primarily on his experiences in the odd day jobs he held before his work with NPR heated up his artistic career. Of his long-standing position as an apartment cleaner, Sedaris told Marchese in the *New York Times,* "I can only write when it's dark, so basically, my whole day is spent waiting for it to get dark. Cleaning apartments gives me something to do when I get up. Otherwise, I'd feel like a bum." As a result of his appearances on NPR, Sedaris has received numerous job offers, both for cleaning and for writing—as well as a multi-book contract with Little, Brown which in 1994 published *Barrel Fever,* a collection of Sedaris' essays and short stories.

*Barrel Fever* includes several of the pieces that brought Sedaris to national attention when he read them on the radio, including "Diary of a Smoker," in which the author declares that the efforts of non-smokers to extend his life by not allowing him to smoke in front of them only gives him more time to hate nonsmokers, and "SantaLand Diaries," a "minor classic," according to *Booklist*'s Benjamin Segedin, in which the author chronicles his amorous and aggravating experiences playing one of Santa's elves in Macy's one Christmas. Critics remarked on the humorously exaggerated self-delusion of Sedaris' narrators in the short stories, including a man who brags on talk-shows about his affairs with such stars as rock singer Bruce Springsteen and boxer Mike Tyson, and a gay man with a persecution complex who "bemoans his suffering at the hands of society in a style so over-the-top as to be laughable," according to a critic in *Kirkus Reviews.*

Critical response to *Barrel Fever* was generally positive, with reviewers appreciating Sedaris' humorous yet accurate portrayal of such American foibles as the commercialism of Christmas and the self-righteousness of health fanatics. "Without slapping the reader in the face with a political diatribe," wrote the critic for *Kirkus Reviews,* "the author skewers our ridiculous fascination with other people's tedious everyday lives." A contributor to *Publishers Weekly* commented, "Sedaris ekes humor from the blackest of scenarios, peppering his narrative with memorable turns of phrase and repeatedly surprising with his double-edged wit." *Booklist*'s Segedin compared Sedaris' humor to Dorothy Parker, in which he demonstrates "low tolerance for human foibles." To the *Booklist* critic, Sedaris' humor can be "vindictive and nasty," but also "extremely, relentlessly funny." Allison Levin, however, reviewing the collection in *Whole Earth Review,* found it "uplifting, nasty, sweet, and frightening but at the heart of Sedaris' storytelling is humor born of compassion." And although *Newsweek* critic Giles found some of Sedaris' commentary relatively shallow, he nonetheless concluded, "This is a writer who's cleaned our toilets and will never look at us the same way."

Sedaris' second collection of essays, *Naked,* appeared in 1997. These essays, according to a reviewer for *Publishers Weekly,* revealed that "he can hardly be called a humorist in the ordinary sense.... Sedaris is instead an essayist who happens to be very funny. In his characteristic deadpan style, Sedaris tells stories "about nutty or bizarre experiences, like volunteering at a hospital for the insane," Craig Seligman observed in the *New York Times Book Review.* Other essays include Sedaris on hitchhiking, working in Oregon, his personal battle with his childhood nervous disorders, and the title piece about his sojourn at a nudist colony. In still others, the essayist turns his eye on his family, especially his mother. In these autobiographical tales, wrote Mifflin in *Entertainment Weekly,* "Sedaris covers a impressive emotional range ... from the comically corrosive title piece ... to 'Ashes,' his account of his mother's death from cancer—a direct, unsentimental hit to the heart." The essays that go beyond the sarcastic to touch the heart, suggested Seligman, reveal an evolution in the essayist. "He's in the process of figuring out how to go beyond the short humor piece," noted Seligman, "and the essays in *Naked* feel transitional." As Ira Glass, the producer for Sedaris' NPR commentaries and the host of Public Radio International's *This American Life,* to which Sedaris frequently contributes, told Peter Ames Carlin in a *People* profile, "People come to his work because he's funny.... But there's a complicated moral vision there."

Sedaris reprised some sketches from his first two collections along with some new ones for his 1997 collection, *Holidays on Ice.* According to a reviewer for *Publishers Weekly,* the three best stories of the collection come from *Barrel Fever* and *Naked:* "Dinah, the Christmas Whore," "Season's Greetings," and the ever-popular "SantaLand Diaries." The newer sketches "look very thin indeed" by comparison, thought the same critic, who concluded that "flashes of … customary brilliance" will keep this gift book from being disappointing.

Sedaris moved to Paris with his partner in the late 1990s, initially to escape the disruption of renovations on his New York apartment. However, he liked the city of light well enough to settle down there, and his attempts at navigating the treacherous shoals of French culture have provided him with more material for his self-deprecating tales of humorous misadventure. "A sequel of sorts to *Naked*, [Sedaris'] … 2000 book, *Me Talk Pretty One Day*, amplifies the antic family portrait he created in the earlier book, while recounting his adventures in New York and Paris," summarized Michiko Kakutani in the *New York Times Book Review*. "Although amusing, Sedaris' tales of life in France now that he's happy don't have the bite of those in the first half of the book, many of them dealing with his eccentric father, an IBM engineer who ruins miniature golf with dissertations on wind trajectory," wrote Nancy Pate in Knight-Ridder/Tribune News Service. As Glass observed in *Esquire*, "A lot of people think they love David for his acidic tongue—which is still there, believe me—but I think it's his empathetic side, his skill in evoking real affection and sadness in his stories, that from the beginning brought people back for more." Kakutani largely agreed, but argued that "Sedaris' bitchiness can easily wear thin … in the slighter pieces…. Indeed, the stronger chapters in this book tend to be the ones that mix satire with sentiment, brazenness with rumination. Those pieces reveal a writer who is capable not only of being funny, but touching, even tender, too." A critic for *Publishers Weekly* felt that Sedaris is "Garrison Keillor's evil twin," focusing on the "icy patches that mar life's sidewalk." The same reviewer also commented that Sedaris will exhaust readers of the new book "with helpless laughter." Lisa Schwarzbaum concluded in *Entertainment Weekly*, "These days Sedaris glitters as one of the wittiest writers around, an essayist and radio commentator who only appears to be telling simple then-what-happened anecdotes."

In June of 2004, Sedaris' book, *Dress Your Family in Corduroy and Denim*, was published. "You'd think that the best-selling storyteller … would have run out of dish by now, but Sedaris has a few juicy ones left, and each is told with stand-up precision," declared Daly in *People*. Sedaris remains a master in turning personal and overheard tragedy and pathos into the material of comedy. He told Knight Ridder/Tribune News Service correspondent Robert K. El-

der that he is not interested if he merely hears laughter in a hotel where he is staying. "I don't want to see what someone in a hotel finds funny," Sedaris commented. "But if they are screaming in pain or terror, I'm interested. I want to see what is so horrible. I want to see if I think it's horrible too." Elder commented that Sedaris is an "unapologetic voyeur of human behavior" with a talent for "finding laughter in the macabre, beauty in oddity." Writing in *Time*, Walter Kirn noted that Sedaris' target with his humor is most often himself, "vulnerable, vain, afflicted with bad habits and perpetually defending his right to self-destruct in peace." Kirn concluded that the "humor in Sedaris is transgressive, but it never feels contrived to be so. It's his legitimate, warped view of his legitimate, warped life."

## Selected writings

*Origins of the Underclass, and Other Stories*, Amethyst Press (Washington, DC).
*Barrel Fever: Stories and Essays*, Little, Brown (Boston, MA), 1994.
*The SantaLand Diaries* (play), produced off-Broadway at the Atlantic Theater, New York, NY, 1996.
*Naked* (autobiographical essays), Little, Brown (Boston, MA), 1997.
(With Amy Sedaris) *Little Freida Mysteries* (play), produced at La Mama, New York, NY, 1997.
*Holidays on Ice* (short stories), Little, Brown (Boston, MA), 1997.
*Me Talk Pretty One Day* (autobiographical essays), Little, Brown (Boston, MA), 2000.
(With Amy Sedaris) *The Book of Liz* (play), produced at Greenwich House, New York, NY, 2001.
*Dress Your Family in Corduroy and Denim*, Little, Brown (Boston, MA), 2004.

## Sources

### Books

Sedaris, David, *Me Talk Pretty One Day* (autobiographical essays), Little, Brown (Boston, MA), 2000.

### Periodicals

*Advocate*, December 10, 1996, p. 54; June 20, 2000, p. 133.
*Booklist*, June 1, 1994, p. 1762; June 1, 2001, p. 1907.
*Entertainment Weekly*, July 29, 1994, p. 55; December 13, 1996, p. S10; March 21, 1997, p. 68; June 2, 2000, p. 72.

*Esquire,* June 2000, p. 38.

*Fortune,* June 12, 2000, p. 358.

*Kirkus Reviews,* April 1, 1994, p. 430.

Knight Ridder/Tribune News Service, June 20, 2001, p. K6846; July 18, 2001, p. K2674.

*Library Journal,* May 1, 1994, p. 104; April 1, 1997, p. 93; July 1997, p. 143; October 15, 2000, p. 124.

*Los Angeles Times Book Review,* October 16, 1994, p. 6; July 2, 1995, p. 11.

*Newsweek,* August 15, 1994, pp. 66-67.

*New Yorker,* August 1, 1994, p. 81.

*New York Times,* July 4, 1993, p. V5; February 19, 1997, p. C14.

*New York Times Book Review,* March 16, 1997, p. 10; June 16, 2000.

*Orlando Sentinel,* June 28, 2000.

*People,* March 24, 1997, pp. 35-37; October 20, 1997, p. 129; June 26, 2000, p. 20; June 7, 2004, p. 50.

*Publishers Weekly,* April 25, 1994, p. 58; January 27, 1997, p. 88; April 7, 1997, p. 22; November 24, 1997, p. 55; May 8, 2000, p. 212; June 19, 2000, p. 54; June 18, 2001, p. 20.

*San Francisco Chronicle,* March 14, 1999.

*Time,* June 19, 2000, p. 139; September 17, 2001, p. 86.

*Tribune Books* (Chicago, IL), February 2, 1996, p. 2.

*Variety,* November 11, 1996, p. 66.

*Wall Street Journal,* June 2, 2000, p. W10.

*Washington Post,* March 22, 1997, p. B1.

*Whole Earth Review,* winter 1995, p. 63.

## Online

"Book Review: Sedaris' Wit Entertains at Byham." *Post-Gazette.com* (Pittsburgh, PA), http://www.post-gazette.com/books/20011023sedaris1023fnp2.asp (March 31, 2005).

"David Sedaris," *January Magazine,* http://www.januarymagazine.com/profiles/sedaris.html (March 31, 2005).

"David Sedaris," Steven Barclay Agency, http://www.barclayagency.com/sedaris.html (March 31, 2005).

"This American Icon," *Tucson Weekly,* http://www.tucsonweekly.com/gbase/arts/Content?oid=oid:42574 (March 31, 2005).

# Shelli Segal

## Fashion designer

**B**orn c. 1955, in Dallas, TX; daughter of Jerry (a comedy writer) and Ann (a nightclub singer; maiden name, Benson) Segal; married Moshe Elimelech (a graphic designer), c. 1987; children: Dena, Sam (twin daughters). *Education:* Attended the State University of New York—Purchase, 1972, and the Mayer School of Fashion Design, c. 1972-74.

**Addresses:** *Office*—Laundry by Shelli Segal, 5835 Southeastern Ave., Commerce, CA 90040.

## Career

**B**egan at a junior dress company, Ruth Manchester, 1974; also worked for two other New York City apparel firms, St. Michel and Andre Bini, before 1981; during the 1980s and early 1990s, designed clothing for Leon Max, La Blanca sportswear, TKO, Leo, and Jolie Madame; had signature line for JM Studio; hired as chief designer for the Laundry label, 1992; company acquired by the Liz Claiborne apparel group, 1999.

## Sidelights

**S**helli Segal is the press-shy designer behind the contemporary sportswear and dress label "Laundry by Shelli Segal." One of the top-selling women's lines in scores of American department stores, Segal's Laundry is known for its cutting-edge design and appealing colors and prints. She is a design veteran of both New York's Seventh Avenue Garment District and its more exuberant Los Angeles cousin, and possesses a sharp eye for the kind of casual but sexy clothing that best exemplifies California chic.

Segal is the sister of actor and director Robby Benson, who uses their mother's maiden name as his professional one. Born in the mid-1950s in Dallas, Texas, the future brand name grew up in a show-business family: her father, Jerry Segal, was a comedy writer, while mother Ann Benson Segal continued to work as a nightclub singer even when she was a full-time parent. "I grew up in nightclubs," Segal recalled in an interview with Dan Jewel for *People.* "My childhood memories are of seeing my mother onstage in sexy costumes looking like Marilyn Monroe."

Segal's family eventually relocated to New York City, and settled on Manhattan's Upper West Side. She entered the entertainment business herself at the age of six, when she was cast in a summer-stock production of the musical *The King and I.* She told Jewel, however, that she "would get hysterical crying when the king would die every night," she said in the *People* article. "So I knew showbiz wasn't for me." She sewed from an early age, but ventured back into entertainment when she was accepted at the prestigious High School of Music and Art in New York City. She graduated in 1972, and went on to the State University of New York at Purchase. An accident with a circular saw in woodworking class finally compelled her to choose between career paths, however: she lost part of her left index finger, and had to quit school. She underwent plastic surgery on it, and the forced recuperative lull, she later admitted to Jewel, "gave me a sense of immediacy and urgency. I was always interested in fashion—so I went for it."

Enrolling at the Mayer School of Fashion Design in New York City, Segal did a nine-month course and found a job with a company called Ruth Manchester in 1974, which made a junior dress line out of the slinky new synthetic fabrics that were relatively recent arrivals in the fashion industry. Show business remained near, however, because Manchester was the mother of singer Melissa Manchester. Segal went on to jobs with two other New York City companies that made women's clothing, St. Michel and Andre Bini. In 1981, when her brother—now a full-fledged star—and parents moved once again, this time to Los Angeles, she followed.

Segal easily found design jobs in the burgeoning fashion industry in southern California. She worked for a sportswear line, and designed children's togs as well. Companies she was affiliated with during this era include Leon Max, La Blanca sportswear, TKO, and JM Studio, which let her do a signature line for its contemporary division. She later designed for two other companies, Leo, which made junior-contemporary gear, and Jolie Madame, a dress manufacturer. Since the clothes were made in the Los Angeles area, Segal no longer was forced to travel regularly to Asia, as she had with the New York jobs. In a *WWD* article from 1986 about up-and-coming American designers, she told Maureen Sajbel that "the most obvious advantage to making my line here in Los Angeles is that when there is a problem.... I don't have to solve it with a telex and a prayer."

Segal was hired at Laundry in 1992 as its head designer. Launched a few years earlier, Laundry was a contemporary dress and sportswear line that was a division of a junior sportswear firm owned by entrepreneur Anthony Podell. Its first designer had been Katayone Adeli, who went on to her own successful ready-to-wear career. The company was thriving by the time Segal joined, with $12 million in sales, but her spirited, fashion-forward designs soon made the company an industry powerhouse. A year later, Laundry posted $28 million in sales, and five years after "Laundry by Shelli Segal" debuted, the company hit the $75-million sales mark. Laundry became so successful that Podell closed down the company's other divisions and transferred all employees over to Segal's Laundry offices. Laundry eventually morphed into a five lines: sports-

wear, contemporary dresses, social occasion and bridal, knitwear, and weekend sportswear. Each had its own designer, but all reported to Segal.

Segal's Laundry line, with its trendy, slim-fitting designs, became a major seller for all department stores that carried it, including Lord & Taylor, Macy's, and Bloomingdale's. There had never been a major ad campaign, but the company did hire a firm to place its designs on female stars of top-rated television shows. Segal's clothing was worn on-screen by *Buffy the Vampire Slayer*'s Sarah Michelle Gellar, Jennifer Aniston's character on *Friends,* and *X-Files* star Gillian Anderson.

In 1997, Segal's line opened a flagship store on Wooster Street in New York City's SoHo neighborhood, and by then it also had premium retail space inside stores like Bloomingdale's. Two years later, it was acquired by Liz Claiborne Inc., which owns or holds licenses for a number of top women's clothing labels, including DKNY and Lucky Brand. The deal was reportedly struck for a purchase price in the neighborhood of $40 to $50 million. "We've had Laundry on our radar screen for a long time," Liz Claiborne chair Paul R. Charron told *WWD* when the deal was announced. "We have admired the creativity of Shelli Segal. She is a talented designer."

Despite the fact that Segal's Laundry line came under a major corporate umbrella, she remains its Los Angeles-based designer. She is married to a graphic designer, with whom she has twin daughters, Dena and Sam, born in 1996. They were toddlers when she gave the *People* interview, in which she told Jewel that she liked to outfit them as "little biker chicks," in tough boots and tank tops. "I can't stand frills," Segal joked.

## Sources

*People,* January 12, 1998, p. 105.
*WWD,* May 28, 1986, p. S38; May 7, 1997, p. 12; August 4, 1998, p. 1; October 8, 1999, p. 2.

—Carol Brennan

# Maria Sharapova

## Professional tennis player

**B**orn April 19, 1987, in Nyagan, Siberia, Russian Federation; daughter of Yuri and Yelena Sharapova.

**Addresses:** *Agent*—International Management Group, IMG Center, 1360 E. 9th St., Ste. 100, Cleveland, OH 44114.

## Career

**S**igned with sports agency division of the International Management Group, c. 1996; won endorsement contracts with racket-maker Prince and Nike; turned professional in April of 2001 and joined the Women's Tennis Association tour; ranked No. 4 women's player in the world, November, 2004.

**Awards:** Holds the 2003 women's singles titles for the DFS Classic (Birmingham, England), Japan Open, and Bell Challenge (Quebec City, Canada); holds 2004 women's singles title from The Championships at Wimbledon, Japan Open, and WTA Championships (Los Angeles, CA).

## Sidelights

**M**aria Sharapova's stunning victory over Serena Williams at Wimbledon in July of 2004 for the women's singles title in tennis prompted predictions that the lithe, 17-year-old Russian would dominate women's tennis in the coming decade.

*Andy Rain/EPA/Landov*

Known for her intense focus and mastery of the psychological nuances of the game, Sharapova has earned nicknames like "the iron maiden" and "Russian steel." Even Williams commended her opponent afterward. "She's kind of like me," the two-time Wimbledon champ said after the match, according to *New York Times* writer Christopher Clarey. "She doesn't back off. She keeps giving it her all."

Sharapova's story has all the elements of a sports-legend-in-the-making. She was born in 1987 in Nyagan, Siberia, an area known for its oil fields and refineries, but her parents Yuri and Yelena were originally from Belarus. Just a year before she was born, the Chernobyl nuclear reactor in the Ukraine exploded, and the disaster sent families from the area, including Belarus, eastward to escape the toxic fallout. In 1989, the Sharapovas relocated once again, but this time to Sochi, a city in a more temperate south Russian climate and noted Black Sea resort town.

Sharapova began playing tennis at a very young age. By the time she was five, her parents took her to a tennis event in Moscow, where she was hitting balls around at a children's clinic when tennis legend Martina Navratilova, the event's big draw, saw her play and had a word with the Sharapovas. "What I saw in Sharapova was not just in the way she played tennis," the Czech-born holder of nine Wimbledon titles wrote in an article for London's *Guardian* newspaper some years later. "It was there in the way she moved, in the way she walked and the way she would kick a ball or pick it up and throw it. You cannot teach that fluidity or that ease of movement," Navratilova declared.

When she was seven, the Sharapovas decided to send their tennis prodigy to a famous tennis camp in Bradenton, Florida. Run by Nick Bollettieri, the Bollettieri Tennis Academy was known for grooming several major players, from Andre Agassi to Venus and Serena Williams, to championship-caliber play. There were two issues, however: the family was only able to get an exit visa for one parent, and they had no invitation from Bollettieri. But Yuri Sharapova made his way from the Miami airport with his daughter, and she was given a tryout the day they showed up. The coach was so impressed by her nascent skills that he immediately phoned Bollettieri. Sharapova began training there, and did not see her mother for the next two years. That same year, when she was nine years old, she won a scholarship spot at the academy, and a contract with the International Management Group, a top sports agency.

Though it may have seemed that Sharapova came out of nowhere to capture the Wimbledon title in 2004, the teenager had actually made it to the fourth round at the venerable English contest the year before. She then went on to win three tournaments over the next year—the DFS Classic in Birmingham, England, the Japan Open, and Quebec City's Bell Challenge—before advancing to the quarterfinals of the French Open in May of 2004. When the Wimbledon matches began a month later, she was ranked 13th in the world and bested her opponents all the way to the finals. Serena Williams was a tough challenge for even the most experienced of players, but midway through the second set, the American champion "found herself sprawling in the dust beyond the baseline," noted a sportswriter for the *Guardian,* Richard Williams. "Chasing a deep crosscourt forehand at the end of a long rally in which she had been pulled from side to side and lured fore and aft by the guile and power of Sharapova's driving from both wings, finally one attempt to apply the brakes and shift her weight had proved too much."

Sharapova beat Williams in straight sets, 6-1, 6-4, to become the first Russian player ever to win Wimbledon. She was also one of the youngest players in tournament history to capture what is known as one of the sport's four Grand Slam titles, which refer to Wimbledon, and the French, U.S., and Australian Opens. Even she was a bit stunned by her victory, she confessed to reporters in the post-game press conference. "To tell you the truth, I don't know what happened in the match," the *New York Times*'s Clarey quoted her as saying. "I don't know what the tactics were. I was just out there. I was just playing. I could really not care less what was going on outside me. I was in my own little world."

Sharapova's rise marked the first time since 1999 that neither Serena nor Venus Williams was holding a Grand Slam singles title. There were high expectations for Sharapova's next big match, the U.S. Open in Flushing Meadows, New York, but she barely beat the no. 68-ranked player, Laura Granville, in the opening round, and lost to veteran player Mary Pierce in the third round. She won her second Japan Open title later that year, however, and bested Williams once again at the WTA Championships in Los Angeles in November of 2004.

The U.S. Open loss, despite the major hype surrounding Sharapova's appearance, did little to dampen enthusiasm for what some journalists had dubbed "Maria Mania." Sharapova possesses endorsement contracts from Prince rackets, Nike, and even Motorola cellular phones, and signed with IMG's modeling division. Her earning potential sometimes prompts comparisons to Anna Kournikova, another attractive blonde Russian player who won many lucrative endorsement contracts despite a lack of Grand Slam titles. Sharapova displays a barely concealed weariness in interviews when asked about Kournikova, but delivers polite retorts—in near-flawless English—on the subject of letting her early promise become eclipsed by her celebrity. "Being a tennis babe doesn't do it for me," Sharapova told *Miami Herald* writer Michelle Kaufman. "If that's what people are hoping for, then I'm afraid they're going to be disappointed. Of course I like to look good on court, but I'm there for business, to play tennis and win, not to look sexy."

## Sources

### Periodicals

*Guardian* (London, England), July 3, 2004, p. 2; July 5, 2004, p. 12.
*Miami Herald,* June 28, 2004.

*New York Times,* June 29, 2004, p. D1; July 4, 2004, p. SP1, p. SP3; September 1, 2004, p. D1; November 16, 2004, p. D4.

*Sports Illustrated,* July 7, 2003, p. 72; July 26, 2004, p. 58.

**Online**

"Maria Mania: No Stopping Her Now," CNN Money, http://money.cnn.com/2004/08/27/ commentary/column_sportsbiz/sportsbiz/ index.htm (December 18, 2004).

"Sharapova Wins Japan Open," *USA Today.com,* http://www.usatoday.com/sports/tennis/2004-10-09-roundup_x.htm (December 18, 2004).

"Stunning Sharapova Wins the Title," CNN.com, www.cnn.com/2004/SPORT/07/03/tennis.sharapova.reut/index.html (December 18, 2004).

*—Carol Brennan*

# Lou Anna K. Simon

## President of Michigan State University

**B**orn Lou Anna Kimsey in 1947, in Sullivan, IN; married Roy Simon (a school administrator). *Education:* Indiana State University, B.A., 1969, M.A., 1970; Michigan State University, Ph.D., 1974.

**Addresses:** *Office*—Office of the President, Michigan State University, 450 Administration Building, East Lansing, MI 48824-1046.

## Career

**M**ichigan State University, assistant director for Office of Institutional Research, 1974, assistant provost for general academic administration, c. 1980, professor, Educational Administration department, 1984—, associate provost, c. 1990, provost, MSU College of Law, interim provost, associate and assistant provost, assistant to the president, provost and vice president of academic affairs, 1993-2003, interim president, 2003, president, 2005—.

**Member:** Executive Committee of the Committee on Institutional Cooperation.

## Sidelights

**L**ou Anna K. Simon rose through the ranks of academia to become the first female president of Michigan State University (MSU). She took over the reins of control during MSU's 150th year celebrations and received much attention as people eagerly watched to see how the new president would fare. Doug Guthrie for the *Detroit News* said of the new president, "Simon ... plans to quickly establish her own leadership style. She intends to show early in her administration how her academic background is likely to lend a different style of leadership in East Lansing."

Simon was born in 1947 into a blue collar family. Her maternal grandfather ran a lumber yard, and her paternal grandfather, who died from black lung disease, worked in a factory. Simon's father was a World War II vet. When he finished his tour of duty he worked at the American Electrical Power Company plant. Simon grew up and went to high school in Sullivan, Indiana. She was the first person in her family to go to college and the fact that she went happened by chance, as she really had not considered the idea until she was given a scholarship by her father's company. She was not sure where to go and went to her high school counselor for help. He suggested Indiana State University in Terre Haute because it was only 30 minutes away from her home. She went there and obtained a bachelor's in mathematics in 1969 and a master's in student personnel and counseling in 1970.

One of Simon's master's professors sent her to MSU after graduation to see Paul Dressel, the director of the Office of Institutional Research at the university; Dressel was known nationally as a higher education researcher. He was impressed by Simon and offered her a job in institutional research. She quickly accepted and while there obtained a doctorate, in 1974, in administration and higher education. She met her husband, Roy Simon, while they were both graduate students.

In 1984 Simon took on a professorship in the Educational Administration department. She worked also as interim provost, associate and assistant provost, and assistant to the president. She became provost and vice president of academic affairs in 1993. She was seen as indispensable to MSU's administration, and therefore she was chosen to take on the position of interim president in May of 2003 for five months when then-president M. Peter McPherson was in the Middle East helping to rebuild Iraq's monetary system.

In 2004, McPherson announced his plans to retire. In January of 2005, Simon began a three-year term as president of MSU, making her the 20th person to hold the post and the first woman to do so. The decision was made quickly because the MSU Board of Trustees wanted a known person to replace McPherson. She was an easy choice because eleven years earlier Simon almost got the presidency—she was a finalist for the position—but the job went to someone else. The *Grand Rapids Press* said of the appointment, "Ms. Simon will provide the continuity MSU seeks as it pursues major initiatives that will impact the university's future into the 21st century." Some thought that there should have been a wider, national search, perhaps bringing in new blood with new ideas and perspectives. Board President Dave Porteous, according to Judy Putnam in the *Grand Rapids Press,* defended their decision, arguing that "the board did do a national search—eleven years ago—and came up with Simon as one of four finalists. She's even more qualified now." The board will determine over the three years of Simon's term if they should renew her contract or do another search.

Simon garnered many skills during her time at MSU that were thought to be a great asset in a president. She has taught education courses on evaluation, planning, and budgeting. She is actively involved in the academic governance of the institution, encouraging faculty and student participation in their courses, departments, and even on a whole university level. Simon belongs to the Executive Committee of the Committee on Institutional Cooperation (CIC), an academic consortium that involves the eleven universities of the Big Ten, along with the University of Chicago. And, of course, she has a progressively more responsible background in leadership at MSU. Also, McPherson wanted to move the medical school to Grand Rapids, something that Simon was overseeing and that was considered one of the benefits of having her become president: she would continue with the process, even making it one of her first priorities.

She took on the position of president at an important, if rather daunting time—2005 marks MSU's 150th anniversary. Students and faculty alike are looking to Simon with great expectation to see how she will handle such an auspicious event. A journalist for MSU's *Big Green* paper wrote, "As the new president of MSU, you have big shoes to fill. I'm sure that you don't need me to remind you that moving in on MSU's 150th anniversary comes with much anticipation. Students' minds have already formed lists of expectations of you and your staff during this presidency.... [T]here is the need for State to be a better and safer place for everyone." Women's rights advocates were also watching Simon with great anticipation, as there was a great hope for change involved with a woman becoming president of the university. There had been an increase in rape cases on the campus at the end of McPherson's reign and it was hoped by many that Simon, as a woman, would make the abolition of such violence a priority in her upcoming years as president.

When she is not involved in the running of MSU, Simon loves to golf. She and her husband are also actively involved in their community, so much so that she decided not to move into Cowles House, the president's house on campus. Instead she and her husband intended to keep their own home in East Lansing and use Cowles for entertaining.

## Sources

### Periodicals

*Grand Rapids Press* (Grand Rapids, MI), June 22, 2004, p. A12; December 12, 2004, B3.
*MSU Today,* Fall 2004, p. 3.
PR Newswire, January 27, 2005; March 11, 2005.
*Women in Higher Education,* August 2004, p. 20.

### Online

"Biography & MSU History," Office of the President-MSU, http://president.msu.edu/biography.html (June 18, 2005).
"Dear Lou Anna," *Big Green,* http://www.thebiggreen.net/article.php?id=216 (June 18, 2005).
"New MSU president has plans to establish own style, agenda," *Detroit News,* http://www.detnews.com/2005/editorial/0501/03/A16/47258.htm (June 18, 2005).
"Statement from Lou Anna K. Simon," Special Reports, MSU, http://special.newsroom.msu.edu/new_president/simon_statement.html (June 18, 2004).

—*Catherine Victoria Donaldson*

# Pam Skaist-Levy and Gela Taylor

AP/Wide World Photos

## Fashion designers

Born Pamela Skaist, c. 1964; married Jeff Levy (a musician, film director, and producer), c. 1986; children: Noah. Born Gela Jacobson, c. 1959; married Chris Nash (a musician; divorced); married John Taylor (a musician), March 16, 1999; children: Travis, Zoe (from first marriage). *Education:* Skaist-Levy: Studied at Fashion Institute of Design & Merchandising, Los Angeles, CA, late 1980s. Taylor: Earned drama degree from Carnegie-Mellon University, c. 1983.

**Addresses:** *Office*—Juicy Couture, Inc., 12720 Wentworth St., Pacoima, CA 91331.

## Career

Skaist-Levy had a millinery business in the late 1980s called Helmet and also worked as a film stylist; Taylor appeared on Broadway in the late 1970s and went on to become a film and television actress in the 1980s; the duo launched a line of maternity wear, Travis Jeans, c. 1989; created Juicy line of T-shirts, 1994, and Juicy Couture, 1997.

## Sidelights

Pam Skaist-Levy and Gela Taylor founded their hugely successful Juicy Couture clothing company out of a one-bedroom apartment in Los Angeles, California. Friends, Hollywood scenesters, and inveterate shoppers both, Skaist-Levy and Taylor created a company that became a major international player in fashion thanks solely to their shared vision and business sense. Their stylish velour track suits, in particular, virtually revolutionized the casual- wear market for women in 2002. "Before Juicy, women either looked sexy or casual," theorized *Sunday Times* writer Claudia Croft a year later. "After Juicy, they could pull off both looks at the same time. Every era has its defining fashion moment, and, right now, that moment belongs to Taylor and Skaist-Levy."

Skaist-Levy is the younger of the duo, and the more punk-rock-oriented. She gravitated to Los Angeles' thriving underground music scene in the late 1970s, and waited tables at the once-popular Sushi on Sunset. She married a musician-turned-director, Jeff Levy, whose credits include episodes of *Roswell* and *CSI: Crime Scene Investigation*. In the late 1980s, Skaist-Levy took courses at the Fashion Institute of Design & Merchandising, and one class project required her to make a hat. That led to her own line of millinery, which she sold under the name Helmet at stores like Barneys New York and Fred Segal, the top Los Angeles fashion retailer.

Skaist-Levy also worked as a film stylist and knew former model/hipster boutique owner Tracey Ross, who introduced her to Taylor around 1988. About five years older than Skaist-Levy, Taylor had a drama degree from Pittsburgh's Carnegie Mellon

University and lived in New York City after graduation. There she landed a role in the original Broadway production of *Zoot Suit* in 1979. She also appeared on television series like *Taxi* and *Hill Street Blues,* and had a bit part as a secretary in the 1984 Melanie Griffith thriller *Body Double.*

When Skaist-Levy and Taylor met, Taylor was expecting a child with her first husband, a musician named Chris Nash. Frustrated at the lack of stylish maternity wear in stores, she cut a pair of her pre-pregnancy jeans and sewed a panel into the waist-line instead. The two women, whose friendship had been cemented by their love of fashion, decided to start a maternity-clothing line with just $200 each. They called it Travis, after Taylor's infant son, and their fledgling company thrived in the early 1990s with nearly $1 million in sales annually. But Skaist-Levy and Taylor were vexed by the relationship with store buyers. Once, they designed a catsuit in shades of red, white, and blue, but their major store account balked. "They took one of these colour predictives," Taylor explained in a *Times* of London interview with Grace Bradberry. "Predictives" are what trend-alert companies send out, forecasting hot new colors for the coming seasons. "Then they recoloured it in lime green, tangerine and yellow checked—on a pregnant woman! We freaked out."

Skaist-Levy and Taylor decided to license the Travis name to someone else and let them take over the maternity sector. They turned their sights to another forgotten segment of the fashion industry. "The Hanes t-shirt really is an amazing product," Skaist-Levy explained in an interview with Larry Kanter of the *Los Angeles Business Journal,* "but it wasn't quite sexy enough. We made it sexy." Working in Taylor's one-bedroom Los Angeles-area apartment, they began designing a line of T-shirts in good, form-fitting fabrics and enticing colors; they named the business Juicy. The line sold between $21 and $30 a piece, and quickly began selling out at the specialty boutiques that carried them. Soon they had to recruit Taylor's cleaning woman to help with their shipping demands.

Early on, the "Juicys," as the pair became known, knew they were going to design simply what they themselves wanted to wear. They steered clear of ideas about trends or new fall colors. As Skaist-Levy told *Times* of London journalist Bradberry, "The designers who stay close to their philosophy are the designers you go out and buy. When it gets watered down by people telling you what you should think, and by lists that say, 'You should be making this, doing that,' it doesn't work. That's why so much fashion is the same—you look at predictives and everyone is filtering the same information."

Eventually the business duo moved their enterprise into a rather unglamorous section of Los Angeles, in a San Fernando Valley industrial park. It was a bare-bones operation, and Skaist-Levy joked in the *Los Angeles Business Journal* profile that "the only people who come here are our bankers—and they like to see that we keep our overhead low." Their sole extravagance was to keep the items manufactured at home—not overseas, as many clothing manufacturers do because labor costs in Asia or Central America are so much cheaper. From the start, Juicy T-shirts sported a label that read "Made in the Glamourous U.S.A." Taylor also explained their business strategy in the *Times* of London article. "We have a revolving line of credit that you have to have," she told Bradberry, "but we always pay down zero because we never want to owe anybody anything.... Instead, we took our profits and put them back in. We didn't take a salary for probably the first two years."

The Juicy line sold $1 million in its first year, and soon began appearing in department stores like Bloomingdale's and Nordstrom. Skaist-Levy and Taylor expanded the line to include dresses, skirts, and other casual wear. By 1996, they had $5 million in sales, which helped bankroll their higher-end, cheekily named "Juicy Couture" line in fall of 1997. The line expanded to an entire range of casual wear for women and then men, too, and added jeans and even yoga wear, but the Juicy velour track suit remained the staple and the fashion must-have of the millennial era.

The Juicy track suit was photographed on the likes of Madonna, Gwen Stefani, Kate Moss, Cameron Diaz, and other style-setters, and appeared in some infamous shots, too: Mariah Carey wore one on her way into the hospital for nervous exhaustion, and Lizzie Grubman, the vilified Manhattan public-relations executive convicted of running over a Hamptons nightclub crowd with her SUV, wore one on her way to jail. Its was widely copied by lower-end manufacturers, but Taylor told Croft in the *Sunday Times* article that the knockoffs were not an issue. "You can't be put off by it, otherwise you become bitter and exhausted," she said.

Juicy Couture opened a boutique inside posh British fashion retailer Harvey Nichols in early 2003, and items were selling at a steady pace in more than a thousand stores. Skaist-Levy and Taylor, noted Bradberry in the *Times,* "have probably had more impact on the way women dress in their everyday lives than any catwalk designer in Paris or Milan." Even *Vogue* magazine did a lengthy feature for its April 2003 issue on the Juicy Couture phenomenon, taking Skaist-Levy and Taylor backstage to meet all their favorite designers at the real European couture shows. "A craze is upon us," enthused writer Sally Singer, "one that validates the lifestyle of the yoga-practicing, self-employed, cheerful, rock-'n'-roll soccer mom.... It's nonfashion at its most fashionable, and it may be a moment, or it may be the future of the way we dress." Singer went on to note that Skaist-Levy and Taylor's Hollywood insider status and fun-loving personalities made their clothes the ultimate hipster wear. "What makes Juicy special is that, although the clothes are not fashion, they are the perfect complement to fashion," she asserted in the *Vogue* article. "They are worn by, and made by, women who follow the trends, the couture, the whole deal, and who know the difference between a silhouette or fabric that works, and one that just gets you by."

Skaist-Levy and Taylor's company had clocked sales of an astonishing $47 million in 2002, and the industry's heavy-hitters were courting them. Just as that *Vogue* article was going to press, Skaist-Levy and Taylor were signing with apparel powerhouse Liz Claiborne, Inc. The deal was rumored to be in the $90 million range, with Skaist-Levy and Taylor receiving an up-front cash payment of $39 million to split. Their company joined a stable of stylish labels acquired by Claiborne, including Laundry and Lucky Brand, and they remained co-presidents. "We got to a point with all these things we started adding to our line, from flip-flops to fur parkas, and we just wanted a sugar daddy to help finance what we want to do," Skaist-Levy explained to *WWD*'s Rose Apodaca Jones about the decision to sell. Separate Juicy lines of handbags, fragrance, footwear, and even home furnishings were planned.

As with anything in fashion, once the Juicy label became too popular, there was a bit of a backlash. In the late summer of 2003, a writer for London's *Independent* newspaper, Clare Dwyer Hogg, declared the still-ubiquitous Juicy velour track suit over, noting that what she termed "D-list" celebs were now wearing them. She spoke to one of those trend-predicting experts, who seemed to extract a bit of revenge on Skaist-Levy and Taylor for their independence of mind. "Juicy Couture is almost sneering at working class fashion and making fun of a lot of people," Martin Raymond of The Future Laboratory told Dwyer Hogg. "It's the slightly offensive ... approach to reality: looking at people's dreariness, buying into it and making a fad means that if you wear it, you are being a bit disingenuous and ironic."

With their entirely unironic business strategy, Skaist-Levy and Taylor's Juicy offices are still located in unfashionable Pacoima, California. Taylor's cleaning woman became their warehouse manager, and her teenage son, Travis, is now a future rock musician himself. Her surname, which went from Jacobson during her television career to Nash during her first marriage, became Taylor in 1999 when she wed musician John Taylor of Duran Duran. The legendary British group of the 1980s even reunited to help Skaist-Levy and Taylor out for the 1999 launch of Juicy Jeans.

Skaist-Levy and Taylor are sometimes called by another nickname they share in addition to "the Juicys"—"Fluffy." They were tagged with it when both showed up once to the same party wearing fluffy white fur pieces. Both like to dress in identical outfits, even for press opportunities, and each has a home in the Hollywood Hills. In addition to her son, Travis, Taylor is also the mother of a daughter, Zoe. Skaist-Levy became one of those Juicy-track-suit-sporting moms when her son, Noah, arrived in 2001. "My single girlfriends always ask me how to start a business," Taylor told Singer in the *Vogue* article. "Men tell them they have to go to a bank, do a business plan, borrow $60,000 to $100,000. If I'd started a business $60,000 in debt, I wouldn't have been able to get up in the morning. We learned from our experiences, and we were lucky." To which her best friend and business partner added, "We weren't lucky. We worked our [tails] off."

## Sources

### Periodicals

*Evening Standard* (London, England), July 30, 2001.
*Financial Times,* July 5, 2003, p. 4.
*Independent* (London, England), September 16, 2003, p. 4.
*Los Angeles Business Journal,* January 27, 1997, p. 8.
*Sunday Times* (London, England), June 8, 2003, p. 27.
*Times* (London, England), April 11, 2003, p. 6.
*WWD,* April 17, 2003, p. 10.

### Online

"Juicy Couture," Style.com, http://www.style.com/vogue/feature/040703/page2.html (August 25, 2004).

—*Carol Brennan*

# Margaret Spellings

## U.S. Secretary of Education

**B**orn in 1957 in Michigan; married (divorced, 1997); married Robert Spellings, 2001; children: Mary, Grace. *Education:* University of Houston, B.A., 1979.

**Addresses:** *Office*—U.S. Department of Education, 400 Maryland Ave. SW, Washington, DC, 20202.

## Career

**A**ide to the Texas legislature; director of select committee on education for Texas Gov. William P. Clements Jr.; associate executive director, Texas Association of School Boards; political director, George W. Bush's campaign for governor, 1994; senior advisor to Texas Governor George W. Bush, 1995-2000; assistant to the president for domestic policy, 2001-04, U.S. Secretary of Education, 2005—.

## Sidelights

**A**fter years as a behind-the-scenes aide to President George W. Bush, Margaret Spellings became secretary of education in January of 2005. She immediately threw herself into the country's culture wars by pressuring public television not to broadcast an episode of a children's show that included lesbian mothers. But she is usually considered a pragmatist, not a conservative ideologue. Her main goal is to fully implement the controversial standards of Bush's signature education reform, the No Child Left Behind Act, allowing more flexibility in how the act is enforced without bargaining away its essential parts.

Spellings was born in Michigan in 1957, but her family moved to Houston, Texas, when she was in third grade. Spellings is the oldest of four daughters. She graduated from the University of Houston, helping to pay for her education by working at a grocery store.

In the 1980s, Spellings worked as an aide in the Texas legislature and was a lobbyist for the state school boards association. Karl Rove, a political adviser to George W. Bush, introduced Bush to Spellings, figuring Bush, who was thinking of running for governor, needed advice on education issues. Bush was impressed with her, and made her political director of his successful 1994 campaign for governor.

Once Bush took office, he made Spellings his chief education adviser. She became known for working toward ending "social promotion," the practice of automatically passing students to the next grade to keep them in class with students their age. For instance, she ordered schools to keep third-graders in third grade for another year if they failed a state reading test.

When Bush became president in 2001, he brought Spellings to Washington with him, naming her assistant to the president for domestic policy. She worked on health care, immigration, and job training issues as well as education. Her biggest accomplishment was helping to draft the No Child Left Behind Act, which passed in January of 2002. It requires states to develop strong reading, math and science standards and tests in order to create more accountability for schools. The law has been controversial: some critics claimed it was too ambitious or too bureaucratic, while other critics have claimed it is under-funded.

Bush nominated Spellings to become the new secretary of education in November of 2004, after his re-election. She was considered a moderate choice who would be easily confirmed by the Senate. At her confirmation hearings in January of 2005, as Democrats such as Sen. Edward Kennedy of Massachusetts praised her, she promised to be pragmatic in the way the administration applied the No Child Left Behind Act. Critics of the law had been afraid it would be applied inflexibly, even though half the schools in some states failed their first round of federally required testing, which could have eventually required them to close.

The nomination of Spellings was also expected to improve the Bush Administration's relations with teachers. Spellings' predecessor as secretary of education, Roderick Paige, had called the National Education Association, the country's largest teachers union, a "terrorist organization" for opposing the No Child Left Behind law. When Spellings' appointment was announced, the NEA called it "a great opportunity" for the Bush Administration to "change the tone" of its conversation with educators, according to CNN.com. Conservative groups that support sweeping education reforms such as school choice and school vouchers were disappointed. "The emphasis will be on standards and accountability rather than choice-based reform," Frederick M. Hess of the American Enterprise Institute complained to the *Washington Post*'s Michael Dobbs.

However, as soon as Spellings became education secretary, she stepped into the sort of cultural clash more often associated with conservatives than moderates. On her second day on the job, she sent a letter to Pat Mitchell, chief executive officer of the Public Broadcasting System (PBS), warning the network not to air an episode of the children's program *Postcards From Buster* that showed two pairs of lesbian mothers. PBS had just decided not to air the episode a few hours before it received Spellings' letter, a network spokesperson said.

*Postcards From Buster*, a mix of animation and live action, features an animated young rabbit who crosses the country with a video camera and talks to real people of different cultural backgrounds about local attractions. An episode called "Sugartime!" had Buster learning how maple syrup and cheese are made in Vermont, and along the way, he meets a pair of families that are each headed by two women. One child introduces one of the couples to Buster as her mother and stepmother. "Many parents would not want their young children exposed to the life-styles portrayed in this episode," Spellings wrote to PBS, according to the *Washington Post*. Spellings added that Congress's intent in funding children's programming "certainly was not to introduce this kind of subject matter to children."

The warning proved controversial. When Mitchell announced her resignation from PBS a few weeks later, she had to stress that she had previously planned to step down and that Spellings' Buster letter played no part in her decision. Public television station WGBH in Boston decided to broadcast "Sugartime!" and make it available to any other PBS station that wanted to air it; at least 40 announced they would. Conservative groups applauded Spellings' stance. "At its heart, the issue before us is the 'sexual reorientation' and brainwashing of children by homosexual advocacy groups," James Dobson, founder of Focus on the Family, wrote on his website, while Donald Wildmon of the American Family Association wrote that "the homosexual community has long used PBS ... to promote their agenda," according to an article by Frazier Moore on CNN.com.

However, Moore, in his commentary, wrote sarcastically that the episode was truly dangerous because the two lesbian couples in the show "come across as perilously likable people and loving parents," making it hard for them to "be demonized for being who they are." Spellings' decision also attracted an angry letter from openly gay Congressman Barney Frank. "You have said that families should not have to deal with the reality of the existence of same-sex couples, and the strong implication is that this is something from which young children should be shielded," Frank wrote, as quoted by Lisa de Moraes in the *Washington Post*. Frank added that he has not usually had to explain to his younger relatives why he lives with a man, "because young people, not exposed to the kind of distaste for us that you embody, did not demand explanations."

That Spellings sparked the controversy was surprising for two reasons. She had a reputation for avoiding attention, not seeking it. "I don't like to be in the limelight," Dobbs of the *Washington Post* quoted her as saying. "I like to be under the radar." The other reason was that the divorced Spellings has not always followed a conservative line on social issues. Early in Bush's first term, she appeared on C-SPAN, where she was asked for her reaction to census figures that showed traditional families were in decline. She declined to express concern, noting that she was a single mom and that there were "lots of different types of family," Dobbs noted in 2004. (Spellings married her second husband, Robert Spellings, an Austin lawyer and lobbyist who favored school vouchers, in 2001.)

As commentators batted the Buster controversy around, Spellings focused most of her energy on defending and improving No Child Left Behind. Both Bush and Spellings mentioned the law at her formal swearing-in at the end of January of 2005. "When you signed No Child Left Behind into law three years ago," Spellings told Bush, as quoted by *Washington Post* reporter Peter Baker, "it was more than an act, it was an attitude—an attitude that says it's right to measure our children's progress from year to year so we can help them before it's too late, an attitude that says expecting students to read and do math at grade level or better is not too much to ask." Bush and Spellings indicated they would expand the law to include high school and also work to increase access to college by improving loan programs. Spellings noted she is the first education secretary who is the mother of school-age children. "In carrying out my duties to the American people, I will be carrying out my duties as a mom," the *Washington Post* quoted her as saying.

Quickly, though, Spellings demonstrated flexibility on the No Child Left Behind law. In February of 2005, she declared that school districts did not have to accept students from schools that had scored badly on tests if it would cause overcrowding, a decision that saved schools in New York from upheaval. She also settled a dispute about teacher certifications in North Dakota, signaling an end to the rigid interpretations of her predecessor, Paige, that had left 31 state legislatures challenging parts of the law. In April, she followed up by declaring that states that already have strong systems for accountability could opt out of certain provisions of No Child Left Behind. However, she also said she would not be flexible about the law's requirement that students be tested every year between grades 3 and 8 and also once in high school.

"In her four months as education secretary, Margaret Spellings has made it clear that her top priority is to fix problems with the No Child Left Behind Act," Dobbs of the *Washington Post* summarized in May of 2005. By then, Spellings was facing tougher challenges from states such as Utah and Connecticut that wanted to disregard core parts of the law.

## Sources

### Periodicals

*New York Times,* February 14, 2005, p. A18.
*Washington Post,* November 18, 2004, p. A37; January 7, 2005, p. A5; January 27, 2005, p. C1; February 1, 2005, p. A15; February 17, 2005, p. C1; February 18, 2005, p. C7; April 24, 2005, p. B6; May 18, 2005, p. A15.

### Online

"Bush has chosen education nominee, official says," CNN.com, http://www.cnn.com/2004/ALLPOLITICS/11/16/education.secretary (May 21, 2005).
"Commentary: Buster and the lesbians," CNN.com, http://www.cnn.com/2005/SHOWBIZ/TV/02/15/apontv.buster.busted.ap/index.html (February 15, 2005).
"Margaret Spellings, U.S. Secretary of Education—Biography," ED.gov, http://www.ed.gov/print/news/staff/bios/spellings.html (May 21, 2005).
"President Bush Nominates Margaret Spellings as Secretary of Education," The White House, http://www.whitehouse.gov/news/releases/2004/11/print/20041117-4.html (May 21, 2005).
"Profile: Secretary of Education Margaret Spellings," ABCNews.com, http://abcnews.go.com/Politics/print?id=263257 (May 21, 2005).

*—Erick Trickey*

# Gwen Stefani

**Singer, songwriter, and fashion designer**

**B**orn Gwendolyn Renee Stefani, October 3, 1969, in Anaheim, CA; daughter of Dennis (a marketing consultant) and Patricia (a homemaker) Stefani; married Gavin Rossdale (a musician), September 14, 2002.

**Addresses:** *Record company*—Interscope Records, 2220 Colorado Ave., Santa Monica, CA 90404.

## Career

**B**egan singing back-up vocals with No Doubt, 1986; became lead singer, c. 1988; band signed with Interscope Records, 1991, and released first LP, *No Doubt*, 1992; introduced own clothing line, L.A. M.B., 2004; released solo record, *Love. Angel. Music. Baby.*, 2004; made film debut in *The Aviator*, 2004.

**Awards:** Grammy Award for best rap/sung collaboration (with Eve), Recording Academy, for "Let Me Blow Ya Mind," 2001; Grammy Award for best pop performance by a duo or group with vocal (with No Doubt), Recording Academy, for "Hey Baby," 2002; Grammy Award for best pop performance by a duo or group with vocal (with No Doubt), Recording Academy, for "Underneath It All," 2003.

## Sidelights

**A**fter spending nearly all of her adult life as frontwoman for the ska-pop band No Doubt, Gwen Stefani emerged with her first solo release,

*Love. Angel. Music. Baby.*, in 2004. A rock-star fashion trendsetter since No Doubt released its multiplatinum-selling *Tragic Kingdom* in the mid-1990s, the energetic singer/songwriter also launched her own line of clothing in 2004 under the "L.A.M.B." label, and even made her film debut later that year as 1930s screen siren Jean Harlow in Martin Scorsese's Howard Hughes biopic, *The Aviator*. "In one of those unpredictable pop transformations, Stefani started the 21st century as the squeaky-voiced wacko from No Doubt," wrote Caroline Sullivan of London's *Guardian* newspaper, "but enters 2004 a hard-currency 'celebrity' whom fashion designers seat in the front row of their shows. More mysteriously, she has achieved this without losing a corresponding amount of musical credibility."

Born in 1969, Stefani is a product of the Southern California world later made famous in the hit teen-drama series on FOX, *The O.C.* Yet unlike the fictional teens in the more upscale oceanside Newport Beach community, Stefani grew up in sprawling Anaheim, the city that is also home to Disneyland. Her father, Dennis, worked in marketing for Japanese motorcycle-maker Yamaha, while her mother, Patricia, was a stay-at-home mom to Stefani, her sister, Jill, and a pair of brothers. Pat Stefani was a talented seamstress who made her children elaborate Halloween costumes, and Stefani took up the hobby as well by the time she reached Loara High School. "I couldn't stand to have the same thing as everyone else," she told *WWD*'s Karen Parr. "I always made my own clothes—and had many disasters."

In 1986, the year she turned 17, Stefani was recruited to sing back-up for an eight-member ska band her older brother, Eric, had started with a friend from his Dairy Queen job, John Spence. The band, which settled on the name No Doubt after the charismatic Spence's favorite phrase, played their first show in January of 1987 at Fender's, a Long Beach venue. Over the next several months, the group quickly gained an ardent following, with Spence's on-stage backflips a particular crowd favorite, and were booked for a gig at the Roxy, a top Los Angeles showcase, for late December. Stefani, her brother, and the other band members were devastated when Stefani shot himself in an Anaheim parking lot four days before Christmas of 1987.

Stefani and the rest of the band nearly called it quits, but decided to soldier on without the beloved singer and showman. By then Stefani was dating Tony Kanal, No Doubt's bassist, and their relationship would last eight years. After several changes in line-up, the final roster was Stefani, who took over the lead vocals, guitarist Tom Dumont, drummer Adrian Young, and Stefani's brother, Eric, who was the band's keyboard player. Though she was the frontperson for the still-popular Southern California act, Stefani was shy and remained somewhat in the background when they were not playing live. "At first it was my brother's songwriting and I was just doing what everyone told me," she told *Newsweek*'s Lorraine Ali. "I was completely passive, no goals. I was in love with Tony and just happy to be in the band."

In 1991, No Doubt signed with Interscope, and their self-titled debut came out the following year. Sales were lackluster, and by 1994 Stefani's brother had quit to take a job as an animator for *The Simpsons*. Around the same time, Kanal broke it off with Stefani, and she was devastated. At the time, they were working on songs for a follow-up, and Stefani began writing some lyrics herself. The result was "Don't Speak," which would become the band's breakout single and exposed to the world her feelings about the split with Kanal. "I told the story of us, not ever knowing 16 million people would hear it," she recalled in another interview with Ali for *Newsweek* in 2001. "Then the record just blew up. Now we regret being so open about it 'cause it was so painful. Imagine every day sitting in interviews talking about it, and we still do."

"Don't Speak" and another hit song, "Just a Girl," appeared on *Tragic Kingdom,* which was released in October of 1995. The band was still with Interscope, but the label had so little faith in their future by that point that the record was farmed it out to one of Interscope's subsidiaries, Trauma. But the record was a huge hit, and went on to a nine-week run in the No. 1 spot on the Billboard 200 chart; it would eventually sell 15 million copies worldwide. *Entertainment Weekly*'s music critic David Browne called it "a virtual Cuisinart of the last two decades of pop: a hefty chunk of new-wave party bounce and Chili Peppers-style white-boy funk, with dashes of reggae, squealing hair-metal guitar, disco, ska-band horns, and Pat Benatar, whom Stefani occasionally resembles vocally…. Rarely have a band called alternative sounded like such savvy, lounge-bred pros."

Stefani's energetic stage presence, platinum-blond hair, and trademark siren-red lipstick made her a distinctive presence that quickly propelled the band toward stardom. Her eye-catching outfits, which ran to zippered punk-rock-style trousers and plaid during these early years, were widely copied by female fans. The success that had come out of heartbreak also opened other doors for Stefani: during a touring spell that went on for more than two years, she met Gavin Rossdale, lead singer for the British grunge band Bush, which was huge at the time. The two began dating, though the relationship was a long-distance one for several years.

In early 1998, No Doubt stopped touring in order to settle in and come up with a new record. That process would take two long years, and Stefani once again penned some personal lyrics that brought the band another hit. In this case, "Ex-Girlfriend" highlighted some of the problems she had with Rossdale, with its first line, "I kinda always knew I'd end up your ex-girlfriend." The track appeared on *Return of Saturn,* released in 2000, which also featured "Marry Me" and "Simple Kind of Life," in both of which Stefani seemed to be confessing a desire to settle down and become a wife and mother. It was a far more reflective album, less ska in feel than their earlier music. Browne, the *Entertainment Weekly* critic, called its "smoother, layered mid-tempo ballads as creamily textured as extra-thick napoleon pastries." Yet once again, the music journalist gave it a mixed review, in particular finding that some of "Stefani's lyrics incessantly circle around the same theme: terminal insecurity and docility."

Stefani dismissed the lovestruck-co-dependent tag that some felt came through too strongly in songs like "Marry Me." The sentiments expressed were not a sign that she was nearing 30 and ready to get married, as she told *Entertainment Weekly* writer Chris Willman. "I have to clarify this, because everybody gets it wrong," she said. "It's more about how I used to think that's all I ever wanted, and the confusion of realizing that I am more faithful to my freedom than I ever thought I could be. And that's scary."

Stefani and her bandmates emerged from the recording studio more quickly for their next effort, which was 2001's *Rock Steady*. To help out, a roster of producers and collaborators joined in, among them funk and pop legend Prince, British techno producer William Orbit, and reggae stars Sly & Robbie. Stefani also did a pair of side projects, with rapper Eve in "Let Me Blow Ya Mind" and "South Side" with Moby, which garnered serious radio airplay. But once again, the biggest single for No Doubt was another dissection of Stefani's love life, in this case "Underneath It All." It was also the album's sleeper hit, reaching the No. 1 spot in 2002 on the Billboard Top 40 Mainstream chart. The song also netted the group their second Grammy Award for Best Pop Performance by a Duo or Group with Vocal (the first was for "Hey Baby" the previous year).

Stefani, by then, had married Rossdale in a lavish Anglican service in London in September of 2002, for which she wore pink and white silk faille gown created for her by one of her favorite designers, John Galliano of Dior. There was also a second ceremony, a Roman Catholic one, held in California two weeks later. Taking a hiatus from the music business, the new bride ventured into a related career: as designer for her own clothing line, which she called "L.A.M.B." The acronym stood for "Love. Angel. Music. Baby." and was introduced in 2003 with a line of purses Stefani designed for LeSportsac. A full line of clothing and accessories hit department stores in the spring of 2004.

*Love. Angel. Music. Baby.* was also the title of Stefani's first solo record, released in late 2004. There were rumors that her band's most recent single—a remake of an '80s alternative hit from Talk Talk, "It's My Life"—would be their final recording, but Stefani assured fans that they were just taking a break. "We were pretty much married to each other for 17 years," she told journalist Ben Wener for her hometown daily, the *Orange County Register*. "It's healthy for us to take time for ourselves. We've had our cake and eaten it so many times, we can't believe it."

The album *Love. Angel. Music. Baby.* was an homage to the '80s dance music that Stefani loved as a teen, and its all-star production team included Andre

3000 of OutKast and Dr. Dre. "I was not looking to make an art record," she asserted to *Billboard* writer Michael Paoletta. "I was looking to make a specific record that would be everyone's guilty pleasure." Its first single, "What You Waiting For?," was doing well on the charts just as Stefani was conquering another realm: the big screen. Martin Scorsese cast her alongside Leonardo DiCaprio in *The Aviator* as Jean Harlow, the Hollywood bombshell who dated aviation pioneer Howard Hughes.

With the transition to film, and her sideline career as a trendsetting style icon, Stefani has often been compared to Madonna, whose over-the-top image also belies a more traditional Italian-American/Roman Catholic heritage. Like her predecessor, Stefani has made Los Angeles' Los Feliz neighborhood her home, but also has a place in London and an Englishman for a husband. And like Madonna, Stefani has also been the subject of her share of British tabloid stories, especially when London papers revealed that Rossdale was the father of a teenage daughter—now a runway model—he never knew he had.

There were rumors that Stefani was devastated by the news, partly because her own oft-stated desire to become a mother was still unfulfilled. In a 2004 interview with Ali in *Newsweek*, Stefani remembered what Interscope label president Jimmy Iovine had told a decade earlier, before the success of *Tragic Kingdom*. "'You're gonna be a star in six years.'" Stefani recalled Iovine as telling her that day. "I was like, 'Yeah, right. First off, I won't be with my band then; second, I'll have, like, five kids, and third, there's just no way.'"

## Selected discography

### No Doubt

*No Doubt*, Interscope, 1992.
*Tragic Kingdom*, Trauma/Interscope, 1995.
*Return of Saturn*, Interscope, 2000.
*Rock Steady*, Interscope, 2001.
*Everything in Time* (B-sides, rarities, and remixes), Interscope, 2004.

### Solo

*Love. Angel. Music. Baby.*, Interscope, 2004.

## Sources

*Billboard*, November 6, 2004, p. 1.
*Cosmopolitan*, June 2004, p. 60.

*Entertainment Weekly,* August 2, 1996, p. 56; April 14, 2000, p. 71; May 12, 2000, p. 32; December 14, 2001, p. 81; December 3, 2004, p. 83.

*Guardian* (London, England), February 27, 2004, p. 8.

*Harper's Bazaar,* March 2005, pp. 322-28.

*InStyle,* February 1, 2003, p. 264; November 1, 2004, p. 60.

*Newsweek,* December 17, 2001, p. 67; August 30, 2004, p. 47.

*Orange County Register,* November 24, 2004.

*People,* May 19, 1997, p. 105.

*WWD,* September 5, 1996, p. 13.

—*Carol Brennan*

# Yoshio Taniguchi

## Architect

**B**orn in 1937 in Japan; son of Yoshiro Taniguchi (an architect); married Kumi. *Education:* Earned engineering degree from Keio University, 1960; Harvard University Graduate School of Design, M.Arch., 1964.

**Addresses:** *Office*—c/o Museum of Modern Art, 44 W. 53rd St., New York, NY 10019.

## Career

**A**ffiliated with the architecture studios of Walter Gropius, and Kenzo Tange in Japan; established own practice, 1975.

## Sidelights

**A**rt-world denizens and architecture critics were stunned when New York City's esteemed Museum of Modern Art (MoMA) chose a relatively unknown Japanese architect, Yoshio Taniguchi, to design a much-needed expansion for the midtown Manhattan landmark. The modernist-minded Taniguchi was a somewhat controversial choice for the project, but in 2004, when the MoMA officially reopened, critics bestowed ardent accolades on the coolly Zen-like new design. "In an era of glamorously expressionist architecture," asserted *Time*'s art scribe Richard Lacayo, the New York art treasurehouse "has opted for a work of what you might call old-fashioned Modernism, clean-lined and rectilinear, a subtly updated version of the glass-and-steel box that the museum first championed in the 1930s, years before that style was adopted for corporate headquarters everywhere."

Taniguchi was born in 1937, and is the son of a wellknown architect, Yoshiro Taniguchi. The elder Taniguchi belonged to the first wave of modernist architects in Japan, following the dictates of a German-Russian axis of innovators of the 1920s who believed in creating structures in which clean design lines and an absence of extraneous detail were paramount. The Taniguchi family lived in Tokyo, and as a young man Taniguchi studied at the city's prestigious Keio University, where he earned his mechanical engineering degree in 1960. From there, he went directly to Harvard University and its Graduate School of Design, which granted him a degree in architecture in 1964.

For a short time, Taniguchi worked in the studio of one of the founders of modernism in architecture, Walter Gropius. Back in Japan, he spent several years working for the architect Kenzo Tange, who was a key figure in the reconstruction of Hiroshima after World War II. Taniguchi's years at that studio coincided with the era when Tange's office was seeing Tokyo Olympic Complex to completion, and also St. Mary's Cathedral, a Tokyo Roman Catholic landmark. By 1975, Taniguchi had opened his own practice, and began taking on design jobs for schools, libraries, and other public-use buildings throughout Japan. He limited the number of projects his firm accepted, so that he might better oversee the numerous details himself, rather than delegating such decisions.

Taniguchi emerged as one of Japan's leading museum architects in the 1980s and '90s. His projects included the Shiseido Museum of Art, Marugame Museum of Contemporary Art, Toyota Municipal Museum of Art, and Tokyo National Museum's Gallery of Horyuji Treasures. But his design for a less austere destination site, the Tokyo Sea Life Park, earned high marks from *Architecture*'s Dana Buntrock. "The skillful way in which Taniguchi manipulated the landscape of this site to establish a series of horizontal planes merging with the sea, and the dramatic beauty of the entry pavilion, make this park one of Tokyo's most popular spots," the writer assessed.

Taniguchi's buildings had a cool minimalism to them, and often used luxurious construction materials. He preferred to let the wood or stone convey the building's aesthetic grace. "A lot of architects design a lot of details," he explained to *Newsweek* writer Cathleen McGuigan. "I try to conceal details." When he took part in the design competition for the Museum of Modern Art expansion, he reportedly told the MoMA trustees and curator of architecture, Terence Riley, that "if we were to raise a lot of money for the project, he would make very good architecture," Riley recalled in an interview with *Financial Times* journalist Edwin Heathcote. "However, if we were to raise a real lot of money, he would make the architecture disappear." Taniguchi showed them a model that featured glass, aluminum and black slate, but recalled that his presentation before the trustees went so poorly that he headed to a nearby watering hole to drink afterward. Despite his misgivings, he was chosen as the architect of choice for the MoMA project in late 1997.

Taniguchi was a controversial choice for the museum re-design. He beat out several other more well-known names—including Dutch star Rem Koolhaas—with his small box that mirrored the original MoMA building, but with a new entrance atrium. Some derided Taniguchi's style as overly "corporate," and not a good match for the museum, which houses the world's best collection of modern art and sculpture under one roof. Its treasures include Pablo Picasso's "Les Demoiselles d'Avignon," Andy Warhol's soup cans, and a long list of other seminal works from, among others, Henri Matisse, Willem deKooning, and Jackson Pollock. MoMA opened its doors in 1939 as one of New York City's first Bauhaus-style structures. Later additions were done by renowned architects Philip Johnson and Cesar Pelli, but the place was still cramped.

When Taniguchi's name was announced as the winner of the MoMA competition, the museum's trustees had not yet raised the money for the expansion, and that figure rose to an astonishing $425 million. Moreover, the building had to be closed for more than two years and its collection relocated to a temporary museum space in Queens. Taniguchi himself did not relocate from Japan, but instead spent long stretches in New York to oversee the project. When the MoMA reopened to the public in late 2004, Taniguchi's once-questioned design was judged a perfect fit for the famed museum. Visitors entered through a stunning 110-foot-high new atrium, which connected nearly all the galleries, and his addition raised the existing 85,000 square feet of space to 125,000. Some of the galleries were large, while others were more intimate in scale. "In Taniguchi's subtly tailored galleries you have room to wander, to enjoy MoMA's greatest hits in a variety of sequences and to get a clear look at everything," remarked *Newsweek* art critic Peter Plagens. Many critics commented on how the familiar masterpieces now seemed to shine, and that seemed to have been Taniguchi's intention from the start. "Without art, museum architecture should look unfinished," he told *New York Times* writer Robin Pogrebin. "If it looks finished, it's a very bad museum."

Late in 2004, Taniguchi won another high-profile U.S. commission, this one for a new site for the Houston outpost of the Asia Society, to be situated in the city's Museum District. The MoMA project, which took up eight years of his career, remains his proudest achievement. He and his wife, Kumi, "don't have any children," he explained to Pogrebin in the *New York Times*. "So this is like my daughter." He also added that the MoMA administration "made me an honorary trustee, so I can watch how my daughter will grow."

## Sources

*Architectural Review*, November 1999, p. 96.
*Architecture*, October 1996, p. 96; June 1998, p. 104.
*Financial Times*, November 15, 2004, p. 15.
*Houston Chronicle*, November 11, 2004.
*Newsweek*, October 11, 2004, p. 50; November 22, 2004, p. 74.
*New York Times*, November 16, 2004, p. E1.
*Time*, October 11, 2004, p. 86.

—*Carol Brennan*

# Graham Taylor

**Author and reverend**

Born c. 1958 in Scarborough, England; married Kathy (a nurse), c. 1983; children: Lydia, Hannah, Abigail.

**Addresses:** *Office*—Penguin Publicity, 345 Hudson St., New York, NY 10014.

## Career

Roadie for musical acts such as the Sex Pistols and Elvis Costello, c. 1974-79; worked as a glass washer at a nightclub in Yorkshire, c. 1979; worked as a social worker in Yorkshire, c. early 1980s; beat officer, North Yorkshire police, 1986-96; vicar, Church of England, 1995-2004; author, 2002—.

## Sidelights

The Reverend Graham Taylor was a vicar in the Church of England when he decided to write and publish a children's novel about witchcraft, a response to the popular "Harry Potter" series by J.K. Rowling. After self-publishing *Shadowmancer* and distributing it in his community, the book was picked up first by a big publisher in England and then by one in the United States. Taylor's book, which was published under the name G.P. Taylor, became an international publishing phenomenon, and the author signed a large deal for future novels.

Taylor was born around 1958 in Scarborough, England, to deaf parents. His father was employed as a cobbler and shoe repairer while his mother worked as an assistant at a canteen. The family often communicated using sign language. Taylor was not a great student as a teenager. At school, he earned four GCEs, sub-O-levels. When he was 16 years old, Taylor felt called to become a clergyman. Instead of following that impulse, he ran away from home. He went to London where he got involved with the punk scene and worked in the music business. He worked as a roadie for the musical acts such as the Sex Pistols and Elvis Costello.

When Taylor was 21 years old, he left London and eventually returned to Yorkshire. While working as a glass washer in a night club, he received some training and became a social worker. Through work, Taylor came into contact with other Christians and found his Christian faith again. Taylor soon moved into a new profession. He became a police officer for the North Yorkshire police. From 1986 to 1996, he worked as a beat officer.

Taylor's career in law enforcement ended after he was attacked by 35 drunken people. The attack left him deaf in one ear. He also had been kicked in his throat, among other parts of his body, and left with a growth there because of the attack. By this time, Taylor was already training to become an Anglican minister. In 1995, he entered the clergy and soon became the vicar in Whitby. Taylor later transferred to Cloughton, near his birthplace of Scarborough, where he was the vicar of St. Mary's. The church soon developed a well-known ministry of healing that focused on prayer. He became known for his exorcism-like activities in homes, something he called "house prayers."

Around 2002, a woman heard Taylor speak at his church and suggested that he write a book. Inspired by her words and his interest in the occult, he wrote what became *Shadowmancer* in about nine months. Set in the 1750s in the Yorkshire coast in England, the novel's story focused on two children, Kate and Thomas, who become friends with an Ethiopian teen who is in England looking for a fragment of the Ark of the Covenant taken from his tribe. Major characters also included a reverend, Obadiah Demurrel, who made a deal with the Devil and wanted to take over the world beginning in Scarborough.

Taylor filled *Shadowmancer* with ghosts, demons, and other such characters. He told Jane Dickson of the *Times* of London, "I believe in a personal power of evil and his name is Satan or the Devil or whatever you want to call him. You see that power manifested in people's lives. *Shadowmancer* is a book about that power and the struggle between good and evil. But it's not a big, waggy-finger moralistic book. It's not even a specifically Christian story. I just wanted to write a scary story for kids with characters who do odd things."

After completing his draft of *Shadowmancer,* one of Taylor's parishioners, who had been a secretary to author T.S. Eliot and a reader for a publishing house, helped him edit it. He hired a local artist to create a cover, then printed it though a writer's cooperative in the area. Because Taylor self-published the novel, he had to sell his beloved motorcycle to cover the cost of printing 2,500 copies. Taylor distributed *Shadowmancer* at his church, targeting the children in his parish. He expected to sell about 200 copies at his church and through a local bookstore. Sales were much better than expected: He sold 3,500 copies in about six weeks. This led to word-of-mouth sales around Great Britain, and various branches of one national bookseller put it on their shelves.

One of Taylor's parishioners especially enjoyed *Shadowmancer* and gave it to a relative, David Reynolds. Reynolds had founded the publishing company that published the Harry Potter books. Reynolds sent *Shadowmancer* on to an agent. The book caught the attention of Faber & Faber, a large British publishing house, and Taylor signed a five-figure deal to publish the book in Great Britain. Published by Faber in June of 2003, *Shadowmancer* was an immediate hit and sold more than 300,000 copies in the United Kingdom alone. In July of 2003, Taylor signed a deal with Penguin Putnam to publish the book in North America and elsewhere. *Shadowmancer* was eventually translated into 20 languages.

While Taylor was becoming an internationally acclaimed author, his health was suffering. He suffered from a blood clot in his heart and an irregular heartbeat, as well as a deep-vein thrombosis, pneumonia, and pleurisy. Doctors advised him to give up his primary job as a vicar. Taylor was a perfectionist who often worked 70 to 90 hours per week and never took time off. He decided to leave his position in November of 2003, though he remained the church's vicar until October of 2004. Taylor then moved to the village of Scalby, where he was going to buy a house and continue writing.

Taylor insisted the success of his book had nothing to do with his decision to leave his position in the church. Instead, he looked for new opportunities to reach out to people. He planned to use his new position to minister to the celebrities and other people he met as he did publicity for his books and related film projects.

Early in 2004, Taylor signed a $6 million film deal with Fortitude Films. He sold the rights to the relatively unknown company because they agreed to make the film in Yorkshire using locals and other clauses that Taylor asked for. *Shadowmancer* was published in the United States in April of 2004. The novel also sold well there, with 600,000 copies moved in the first six months. That same month, Taylor signed a new, multi-book deal with Penguin Young Readers Group and Faber. He was to publish a book a year simultaneously for both companies beginning in 2005.

Taylor's second novel, *Wormwood,* was published in 2004. Also set in the 1700s, the novel's action took place in London, where a scientist and kabbalah master help save the city. Taylor soon sold the film rights to this book as well.

Though Taylor's third novel was scheduled for publication in 2005, an accident put him a little behind. While moving out of his vicarage in the fall of 2004, he accidentally threw the hand-edited manuscript of his next novel, *Tersias,* in the fire. Set in the 1700s, the story focused on a boy whose parents take away his sight so he can beg, but he overcomes his circumstances by becoming a sought-after oracle. Taylor had an original to work off for that book, but he also accidentally burned his original manuscript of *Shadowmancer.* Taylor was burning his papers because people had been stealing bits and pieces of his writing from his office because of his new-found popularity. He was also working on a fourth book, a ghostly murder mystery.

Despite acclaim, Taylor was still in awe of his success as an author. He told Troy Patterson of *Entertainment Weekly,* "I do get very nervous when people come saying 'You're going to be the next J.K. Rowling, you're going to be the next C.S. Lewis, the next Roald Dahl.' It's not a false modesty. It's terror more than anything. I woke up this morning and thought, 'Crumbs, what am I doing here?'"

## Selected writings

*Shadowmancer.* self-published, c. 2002; Faber & Faber, 2003; Penguin, 2004.

*Wormwood.* Faber & Faber, 2004; Penguin, 2004.

## Sources

*Christianity Today,* October 2004, p. 98.
*Daily Telegraph* (London), November 8, 2003, p. 3; April 20, 2004, p. 7; October 14, 2004, p. 10.
*Entertainment Weekly,* May 28, 2004, pp. 78-79.
*Guardian* (London, England), July 24, 2003, p. 6.
*Independent on Sunday* (London, England), February 16, 2003, p. 13.
*Northern Echo,* June 4, 2004, p. 12.
*People,* June 21, 2004, p. 51.
PR Newswire, April 15, 2004.
*Times* (London, England), June 14, 2003, p. 3; May 29, 2004, p. 42.
*Writer,* September 2004, p. 8.

*—A. Petruso*

# Thaksin Shinawatra

*Sukree Sukplang/Getty Images*

## Prime minister of Thailand

**B**orn July 26, 1949, in Chiang Mai, Thailand; son of Boonlert (a silk businessman); married Potjaman; children: Parthongtae (son), Praethongtarn (daughter), Pintongta (daughter). *Religion:* Buddhism. *Education:* Graduated from the Police Cadet Academy in Thailand, 1973; Eastern Kentucky University, M.A. in criminal justice, 1975; Sam Houston State University, Ph.D. in criminal justice, 1978.

**Addresses:** *Office*—Government House, Thanon Pissanulok, Dusit, Bangkok 10300, Thailand. *Website*—http://www.thaigov.go.th.

## Career

**J**oined the Royal Thai Police Department, 1973; promoted to lieutenant colonel, 1987; founder and chairman of Shinawatra Computer and Communications Group, 1987-94; minister of foreign affairs, 1994-95; deputy prime minister, 1997; founded Thai Rak Thai party, 1998; member of parliament, 1998-2001; prime minister of Thailand, 2001—.

**Awards:** ASEAN Businessman of the Year, 1992; 1993 Outstanding Telecom Man of the Year Award, 1994; Leading Asian Businessman, *Singapore Business Times,* 1994; Outstanding Criminal Justice Alumnus Award and Distinguished Alumni Award, Sam Houston State University, 1996; Outstanding Politician Award, Mass Media Photographer Association of Thailand, 1997.

## Sidelights

**F**irst a policeman, then a billionaire telecommunications executive, now prime minister of Thailand, Thaksin Shinawatra (pronounced Chin-a-what) is a strong leader in a country not known for strong leaders. He has delivered on his promises to help Thailand's rural poor—at the risk of letting them go into more debt—and his policies and decisive style have won over most Thais—though some have complained that he has an autocratic streak and that his law-and-order campaigns have come at the expense of human rights. His strong leadership served him well after a devastating tsunami hit Thailand at the end of 2004, when he toured the damaged coastal lands and promised swift relief. Those pledges helped him win an unprecedented second term.

Thaksin was born in the city of Chiang Mai in northern Thailand. He worked in the family business—a silk business that had grown into a bus line and movie theaters—with his father, Boonlert. Thaksin studied to become a police officer, graduated at the top of his police cadet class, and won a government scholarship to study abroad. He got a master's degree and doctorate in criminal justice at universities in Kentucky and Texas. When he returned to Thailand, he advanced to the rank of lieutenant colonel in the police force. He began supplying the police department with computer software in 1982.

In 1987, he left the police force to market a movie, *Bann Sai Thong,* and started his telecommunications company, the Shinawatra Company, which sold computer software and soon expanded into pager services, cable television, satellites, data communications networks, and mobile phone services. The company went public on the Bangkok Stock Exchange in 1990, the same year he made a successful bid for a 20-year deal with the Telephone Organization of Thailand. Eventually, his company, now named Shin Corporation, made him one of Thailand's richest men.

Thaksin left the company in 1994 to enter politics, becoming minister of foreign affairs as part of the Palang Dharma Party. His goal, he proclaimed, was to clean up politics in his country. He founded the Thai Rak Thai (Thai Love Thai) party in 1998, and it quickly came to dominate Thai elections.

Thaksin was elected prime minister in 2001 on promises to offer loans to help the poor and provide health care for only 30 bhat (less than $1). His politics were proudly nationalistic, and in his northern Thai accent, he often criticized the "Bangkok elite." Yet businesspeople liked his leadership style, often considered similar to a company chief executive officer's, and his economic policies. "Thaksin is an effortless campaigner," wrote *Time Asia's* Karl Taro Greenfeld in a mostly skeptical profile, "his languorous walk, the gradual coming together of his palms in a Buddhist greeting, the soft grip of his handshake, all his movements coalesce to communicate equilibrium, an almost soothing presence."

Early in his first term, Thaksin faced an investigation by Thailand's Corruption Commission; he was charged with failing to reveal all his wealth while he was a deputy prime minister in 1997 and with giving Shin Corp. shares to his drivers and maids when he had to give up his stock. However, the Constitutional Court acquitted him of corruption charges in an 8-7 vote. To follow Thai law aimed at preventing conflicts of interest, he gave stock in most of his companies to his son and teenage daughters. Today, his family controls about 39 percent of Shin, and the market considers the company's fortunes as still linked to Thaksin's, since Shin's stock rises and falls along with Thaksin's approval ratings, the *Wall Street Journal* reported in 2005. *Forbes* magazine estimates that the prime minister's family has accumulated about $1.9 billion in wealth.

When Thaksin took office, Thailand was recovering from the Asian financial crisis of the late 1990s and needed to adjust to the changing global economy. The country had relied on exports to countries such as the United States to keep its economy going, but it was growing difficult for Thailand to compete with China. So Thaksin's focus on the countryside and the poor had the benefit of building a more self-sufficient economy, less dependent on the export market.

Thaksin quickly delivered on his promise of cheap health care. He also helped the rural poor with a $2 billion Village Fund that gave $25,000 each to Thailand's 80,000 small towns to fund low-cost loans to villagers. His economic policies, known as Thaksinomics, have helped the economy boom: Thailand's gross domestic product jumped by 22 percent in the first four years he was in office, and incomes in the countryside have increased even faster. Critics have warned that Thais were becoming debt-ridden and dependent on government handouts, but when Thaksin ran for another term in early 2005, the economy was continuing to grow and the middle class, originally skeptical of him, largely supported him. "Thaksin's policies have turned him into something of a popular hero, hailed by his fans as the decisive, no-nonsense leader who has lifted Thailand from the doldrums of the Asian financial crisis, restored Thai pride, and lavished cash on the forgotten backcountry," Michael Schuman of *Time Asia* summed up.

Thai liberals have often warned that Thaksin has an authoritarian streak. More than 2,500 people died during a Thaksin-led crackdown on drugs in 2003, and human-rights groups complained that suspects' due-process rights had been violated and that people innocent of crimes may have died. The government's reaction to violence by Islamic separatists in southern Thailand has attracted similar criticism. In 2004, the militants stepped up their attacks, and police were accused of responding brutally. In October of 2004, about 80 suspected militants held prisoner by the government died, most of them suffocated inside trucks. Thaksin apologized for the deaths, saying authorities had not handled the prisoners correctly.

In December of 2004, Thaksin offered an unusual peace gesture: he had the Thai air force drop millions of paper cranes on the southern provinces on the king of Thailand's birthday. The cranes were folded, origami-style, by troops, students, volunteers, and even Thaksin and his cabinet. Paper cranes, in Japanese tradition, are supposed to bring people peace and hope. However, Thaksin proposed tougher security laws at the same time, such as the ability to tap phones without warrants and hold suspects without a charge for a week. The cranes, the *New York Times* quoted him as saying, would "have a psychological effect on moderate people ... but it will not work with people who are leading the vicious acts."

Late that month, a giant tsunami struck the coasts of Thailand and several other Asian nations. It was the region's biggest natural disaster in a century. Thailand responded more quickly than other Asian nations, moving food and first-aid teams into coastal areas right away. Several factors helped Thailand respond, including better medical and transportation networks than other countries and less widespread damage, but observers credited Thaksin's strong leadership as another factor. Thaksin visited the resort areas hit by the tsunami several times in the days after the disaster, promising immediate relief for local residents and foreign tourists alike and the construction of an early-warning system for future tsunamis.

Political observers had already expected Thaksin's party to win the 2005 elections, but his strong response to the tsunami undoubtedly helped his popularity. It also helped him put a less impressive response to a natural disaster behind him; he had to admit in January of 2004 that his government, fearing panic, had failed to alert people to a bird flu outbreak.

So it was no surprise that Thaksin's Thai Rak Thai party won about 375 of the 500 seats in the Thai parliament in February of 2005. That made Thaksin the first prime minister to lead an elected government through a full four-year term (Thailand has a history of shaky coalitions and the occasional overthrow of democratically elected leaders by coups).

It was also the first Thai election won outright by one party, without the need for a coalition partner. With his broad mandate, Thaksin was expected to pursue education reform and to expand his credit program for rural areas into a program to create banks in his second term.

## Sources

### Periodicals

*Economist,* February 12, 2005, p. 40.
*New York Times,* December 3, 2004, p. A11; February 7, 2005, p. A8.
*Time Asia,* August 4, 2001; October 20, 2003; January 31, 2005.
*Wall Street Journal,* December 2, 2004, p. A1; December 30, 2004, p. A7; January 6, 2005, p. A10; January 19, 2005, p. C18.

### Online

"Mr. Thaksin Shinawatra (23rd Prime Minister)," Royal Thai Embassy, Washington, D.C., http://www.thaiembdc.org/bio/pms/thaksin.html (May 21, 2005).
"Profile: Thaksin Shinawatra," BBC News, http://newsvote.bbc.co.uk/mpapps/pagetools/print/news.bbc.co.uk/2/hi/asia-pacific/1108114.stm (May 21, 2005).
"Royals & Rulers," *Forbes,* http://www.forbes.com/billionaires/2005/03/07/cz_bill05_royalsslide_4.html (May 21, 2005).
"Thaksin Shinawatra—a biography," *Bangkok Post,* http://www.bangkokpost.net/election2001/thaksinprofile.html (May 21, 2005).

—*Erick Trickey*

# Edmond J. Thomas

**Chief of the Office of Engineering and Technology at the Federal Communications Commission**

**B**orn c. 1943. *Education:* Rensselaer Polytechnic University, B.S. and M.S.; Pace University, M.B.A.

**Addresses:** *Office*—Office of Engineering & Technology, Federal Communications Commission, 445 12th St. SW, Washington, DC 20554.

## Career

**P**resident of science and technology for Bell Atlantic; president and CEO of telecommunications company RSL USA; chief of the Federal Communications Commission's Office of Engineering and Technology, 2002—.

**Awards:** Named one of the 50 most influential people in long distance by *Phone Plus Magazine,* 1998; included in *Forbes* magazine's E-Gang of luminaries in wireless communication, 2003.

## Sidelights

**I**nnovators trying to develop new, faster, easier ways for people and their computers to communicate have a friend in government. Edmond J. Thomas, engineering and technology chief for the Federal Communications Commission (FCC), is trying to clear away technical barriers and open more of the broadcast airwaves to new technologies. He is a former executive for telecommunications compa-

nies, so he is as far as possible from the stereotype of the government regulator whose old rules get in the way of fast-paced change. Thomas tries to throw the old rules out the window when he can.

"I want to start creating places where American innovation can go forward," Thomas told *Forbes* magazine's Scott Woolley. "[I'm] a techie businessman in regulator's clothing." New-technology companies love him for that, but older, established industries and organizations are rising up in opposition to Thomas' efforts, afraid his efforts might cause interference on the parts of the broadcast spectrum they used to have to themselves.

His history in business is part of Thomas' appeal: he wants to clear the way for new invention because he is an innovator himself. Thomas, who has bachelor's and master's degrees from Rensselaer Polytechnic University and a masters in business administration from Pace University, holds several patents in data and voice communications and developed the first telephony-based speech recognition system. He spent 35 years at technology and telecommunications companies, serving as president of science and technology for Bell Atlantic (now Verizon), in charge of developing new products and services. In his last job before joining the federal government, he was president and chief executive officer of telecommunications company RSL USA. Under his leadership, RSL USA grew five-fold in one year, to $500 million in revenue, up from $120 million.

FCC chairman Michael K. Powell offered a clue about what he expected from Thomas when he named him chief of the commission's Office of Engineering and Technology (OET) in January of 2002. Thomas, Powell said, would prepare the OET "to take on sweeping, fast-paced changes that characterize the industries we regulate...." Soon, it became clear that Powell expected Thomas' office itself to make sweeping, fast-paced changes. Powell and Thomas began rewriting FCC rules to open up the airwaves.

In February of 2002, Thomas helped institute new rules on ultrawideband technology. Ultrawideband spreads its low-power radio signals across many frequencies, including a lot that are already being used. Cell phone companies, airlines, and the military all protested to Thomas, but he insisted that studies showed ultrawideband's pulsing signals were so faint that they would not interfere with other signals. "The reason we got it through is we had good science to back it," Thomas told Woolley of *Forbes*. "I don't want to hurt the incumbents [those who were already using a frequency] but I'm not going to accept subjective arguments." In August of 2003, when Thomas took reporters on a rare tour of the FCC's engineering lab, he was still promoting ultrawideband. He showed off ultrawideband devices the FCC was testing, including radar devices that can look into the ground, and he used a global positioning system device right in front of one, to show that ultrawideband did not cause any interference.

Thomas often argues that longtime users of the airwaves are overreacting, protecting their turf, and ignoring evidence that new technology can share their space on the broadcast spectrum without interference. For instance, Thomas and the FCC also increased the amount of the spectrum available to Wi-Fi, or wireless fidelity technology, which gives computer users fast, wireless Internet access in places such as cafes and airports. The new frequencies were taken from the military and from unused parts of the spectrum. By 2004, the FCC was moving to let wireless Internet services take over unused television frequencies between Channels 5 and 51, and Thomas was helping Powell justify the idea. When television broadcasters complained that Wi-Fi could interfere with their signals, Thomas told the *Chicago Tribune*'s Jon Van that smart Wi-Fi technology can sense other signals and move to unused frequencies.

In June of 2004, the FCC cleared the way for another innovation: broadband over power lines (BPL), which lets computer users access the Internet through high-speed modems plugged into their electrical outlets. Some observers say BPL could be a cheaper alternative than high-speed cable and tele-phone Internet connections, especially in rural areas where cable TV is not offered. Thomas raved about BPL's possibilities to the *Christian Science Monitor*'s Brad Rosenberg, in the sort of speculation usually heard from young, hopeful tech-geek visionaries, not regulators in their sixties. "If every power plug in your house becomes a broadband connection, that means that almost anything you plug into the wall can connect to the Internet," he said. "That means that your refrigerator can have a meaningful conversation with the supermarket and say, 'Hi, I need milk.' Or you could call your house and say, 'I'm coming home in two hours, turn the air conditioner on.' It's only restricted by imagination."

Amateur radio operators, also known as hams, said BPL interferes with their signals, because power lines have less shielding than phone and cable lines, so more signals spill out. They pointed to other countries where BPL was rejected for interfering with existing signals. Thomas insisted they did not have their facts straight. "What was banned in Japan is very old technology," he told the *Christian Science Monitor*'s Rosenberg.

While he fights those battles, Thomas is lending his office's expertise to a much more literal war. He told Bloomberg.com's Neil Roland that the FCC will help the Defense Department try to invent technology to interfere with remote-controlled bombs in Iraq. Small bombs detonated by cell phones or electrical charges are killing more United States soldiers in Iraq than any other weapons, according to the Army. A congressman asked Powell to get the FCC to help the military build a device, to be placed on military vehicles, that could interfere with signals between cell phones and bombs. Thomas says the FCC is willing to try. "I certainly don't know how to design that device. But people are looking into it to see what we can do," he told Roland.

## Sources

### Periodicals

*BusinessWeek,* April 22, 2002; December 15, 2003.
*Chicago Tribune,* March 21, 2004, p. 1.
*Christian Science Monitor,* April 26, 2004, p. 16.
*Forbes,* September 1, 2003, p. 103; September 6, 2004, p. 52.
*USA Today,* May 13, 2004.
*Wall Street Journal,* March 23, 2004, p. A1; May 14, 2004, p. A1.
*Washington Post,* November 14, 2003, p. E1.

### Online

"Edmond J. Thomas to be Appointed Chief of the Office of Engineering and Technology," Federal Communications Commission, http://www.fcc.

gov/Bureaus/Engineering_Technology/News_Releases/2002/nret0201.htm l (September 4, 2004)

"FCC Joins DoD to Devise Ways to Counter Iraq Bombings," Bloomberg.com, http://quote.bloomberg.com (September 6, 2004).

"Official touts FCC's UWB work," RCR News, http://rcrnews.com (September 6, 2004)

"Prepared Witness Testimony," House Committee on Energy and Commerce, http://energy commerce.house.gov/108/Hearings/06112003hearing951/Thomas1528.htm (September 6, 2004).

"Report: Fourth Meeting of FCC Technological Advisory Council II," FCC Technological Advisory Council, http://www.fcc.gov/oet/tac/april26-02-docs/tac4-26report.pdf (September 6, 2004)

*—Erick Trickey*

# John W. Thompson

## Chief Executive Officer of Symantec

**B**orn John Wendell Thompson, April 24, 1949, in Fort Dix, NJ; married (divorced); married Sandi Thompson (an attorney), 1998; children: a son and a daughter (from first marriage). *Education:* Florida A&M University, B. A., 1971; Massachusetts Institute of Technology, M.S., 1983.

**Addresses:** *Office*—World Headquarters, Symantec Corporation, 20330 Stevens Creek Blvd., Cupertino, CA 95014.

## Career

**S**alesman for IBM, 1971; general manager for development and marketing OS/2, Intel-based server products, and communication product distribution; general manager IBM Americas, 1993-1999; president, CEO, chair, Symantec, 1999-2002; CEO and chair, 2002—.

**Awards:** Digital 50, *Time*, 1999; 50 Most Important African-Americans in Technology, *BlackEngineer.com*, 2001; top manager, *BusinessWeek*, 2002.

## Sidelights

**A**fter 28 years with IBM, one of the world's leading companies, John W. Thompson chose to take a daring risk. Instead of waiting for retirement, which was only a couple years away, he accepted an offer to become head of Symantec—a leading software company located in California's Silicon Valley. It was the kind of challenge that he was ready to tackle. While his first years had their ups and downs, through his vision and determination the company renewed its focus and goals.

Thompson was born April 24, 1949, in Fort Dix, New Jersey, and raised in West Palm Beach, Florida. His father was a postal worker and his mother was a teacher. Thompson claims to have had an early education in business when he accompanied his father as he collected rent on some apartments the family owned. His parents inspired a strong work ethic in Thompson. He described his family when he talked to Anne Saita of *Information Security*, "My mom and dad believed very much in the concepts of working hard for what you want and making sure you're properly prepared for what your pursuits are. We were a loving bunch, but a very competitive bunch."

Thompson went to college on a music scholarship at Florida A&M University, where he studied business administration. Although he played clarinet and saxophone, he did not want to become a musician. His goal was to become a businessman, he just did not know what kind of business he wanted to pursue. Toward the end of his college career, during which he had married and had a child, Thompson was encouraged by one of his professors to apply to IBM.

He started out in 1971 as a salesman for the company. In the beginning, he was determined to be his own person. He eschewed the traditional look of corporate culture and sported a mustache, a large afro hairstyle, and wore leisure suits. The plan that

Thompson had laid out for himself was to work for IBM for two years and then apply to law school. As it happened, he and his wife at the time had a second child and he was promoted several times. His winning and charismatic style helped him work his way up the corporate ladder.

He worked as general manager to develop and market IBM's operating system OS/2. He also helped market the company's server products and communication product distribution. Midway through his career, Thompson took a leave-of-absence to earn a master's degree in management science from the Sloan School of Management at MIT. By 1993, he was general manager of IBM Americas, a division of IBM worth $37 billion with 30,000 employees.

In 1999, R.S. Miller, CEO of Bethlehem Steel and a board member for Symantec came calling at Thompson's door. Founder Gordon Eubanks was stepping down as head of the company and a search was on for a new leader, one who had to be from outside the company. At the time, Symantec was strong but lacked focus and did not seem to know what direction in which to head. Thompson seemed like the best candidate and he was up for the task.

Thompson and his second wife, Sandi, relocated from Connecticut to California and began another phase in their lives. Sandi, who had worked for IBM as well, returned to school and earned a law degree. Thompson took on the mantle of chairman, president, and chief executive officer of Symantec. He wasted no time implementing changes at the floundering company. One of his first moves was to replace two-thirds of the senior executives. He also increased the number of employees by 40 percent. As part of a new focus on corporate customers, Thompson sold off several divisions including Internet Tools and its Visual Cafe as well as ACT contact manager software.

Besides the challenges he faced within the company, Thompson was faced with other challenges. In 1999, Reverend Jesse Jackson came to Silicon Valley with his Rainbow/PUSH Coalition to address the issue of diversity in the high-tech industry. The coincidental event ended up creating a great deal of speculation on whether or not Thompson had been hired because he was African American. Thompson was upset by the conjecture. He explained to Karl Schoenberger of the *New York Times*, "I'm not here to create an image of myself as some black messiah in Silicon Valley. But ... I've learned some things I'm willing to share, as long as I don't miss a beat in my No. 1 priority of running a company.... They will never say I failed because I was distracted. And they'll never be able to say I succeeded because I

was black." Thompson worked with Jackson to change the name of the conference from "Digital Divide" to "Digital Connections," with the hope of switching its focus to inclusiveness.

Many of the changes that took place when Thompson took over Symantec made his investors nervous. In his first couple years, he faced criticism and concern over his decisions. In order to shore up Symantec's resources for corporate customers, the company bought many smaller companies during a time when most other software companies had withdrawn from such acquisitions. But by 2001, Symantec had hit a revenue goal of having 60 percent of its sales coming from corporate accounts, a switch from its previous focus on individual users. Symantec's health was given a boost by Thompson's extensive list of contacts from his former IBM associates, who had always considered him trustworthy.

In his personal life, Thompson enjoys both the finer things in life as well as simple pleasures. His father taught him to shoot a gun when he was a child. On one hand Thompson is an avid hunter who owns three hunting dogs. He primarily hunts duck, which he then takes home and prepares in gourmet fashion. Speaking to George V. Hulme of *Information Week*, Thompson had this to say about his hobbies, "I enjoy hunting, and what I catch gives us something to cook. Hunting ties together my two hobbies." On the other hand, he owns a BMW and a Porsche and has his suits tailor-made by designer Ermenegildo Zegna.

Thompson took a bold step in 1999, leaving the comfort and security of IBM, to take the helm of Symantec. His efforts have helped the company achieve sales in 2003 that reached $1.4 billion. He credits his success to his determination and focus as well as mentoring. He explained to *Information Security's* Saita, "It's a combination of hard work and good support structure that helps to get you going, but it's determination along the way that keeps you moving along. I had enough of all of those to get me where I am today."

## Sources

### Periodicals

*BusinessWeek*, January 13, 2003, p. 65.
*Information Security*, February 2003, p. 64.
*InformationWeek*, December 22, 2003, p. 38.
*New York Times*, November 19, 2000, p. 4.
*San Francisco Chronicle*, January 4, 2004, p. 11.

## Online

"Digital 50—John W. Thompson," http://www.
time.com/time/digital/digital50/43.html
(August 12, 2004).

"Newsmaker Profile" *San Franciso Chronicle,* http://
www.sfgate.com/cgi- bin/article.cgi?file=/
chronicle/archive/2002/01/29/BU53763.DTL
(August 14, 2004).

*—Eve M. B. Hermann*

# Usher

## Singer and actor

**B**orn Usher Raymond IV, October 14, 1979, in Dallas, TX; son of Jonnetta Patton (a choir director and later his manager).

**Addresses:** *Record company*—Arista Records, 888 Seventh Ave., New York, NY 10019. *Website*—http://www.usherworld.com/about-biography.php.

## Career

**S**inger and actor. Released debut album, *Usher* 1994; released *My Way*, 1997; released *Live*, 1999; released *8701*, 2001; released *Confessions*, 2004. Television appearances include: *Moesha* 1997-99; *The Bold and the Beautiful*, 1998; *Promised Land*, 1999; *The Famous Jett Jackson*, 2000; *Geppetto* (movie), 2000; *Sabrina the Teenage Witch*, 2002; *The Twilight Zone*, 2002; *American Dreams*, 2002; *7th Heaven*, 2002; *Soul Food*, 2003. Film appearances include: *The Faculty*, 1998; *She's All That*, 1999; *Light It Up*, 1999; *Texas Rangers*, 2001.

**Awards:** First place, *Star Search*, 1992; favorite male singer, Blockbuster Awards, for *My Way*; pop music award for "You Make Me Wanna" from *My Way*, American Society of Composers, Authors and Publishers; best R&B/soul single award for "You Make Me Wanna" from *My Way*, Soul Train Awards, 1998; *Billboard* Artist of the Year, 1998; pop music award for "Nice & Slow" from *8701*, American Society of Composers, Authors and Publishers; pop music award for "U Got It Bad" from *8701*, American Society of Composers, Authors and Publishers;

*Fred Prouser/Landov*

Grammy Award for best male R&B performance, Recording Academy, for "U Remind Me" from *8701*, 2001; best R&B/soul album, male, for *8701*, Soul Train Awards, 2002; favorite male singer, Nickelodeon Kids' Choice Awards, 2002; Grammy Award for best male R&B performance, Recording Academy, for "U Don't Have To Call" from *8701*, 2002; best love song award, Teen Choice Awards, for "U Got It Bad" from *8701*, 2002; favorite R&B artist for *8701*, Teen Choice Awards, 2002; best R&B male artist award for *8701*, BET Awards, 2002; favorite hook up, Teen Choice Awards, for "Yeah" from *Confessions*, 2004; favorite R&B track, Teen Choice Awards, for "Yeah" from *Confessions*, 2004;

## Sidelights

**R**hythm and blues singer Usher began his career as a teen singer in the 1990s, but his career has grown to include television and film acting as well as music. The winner of Grammy Awards and a *Billboard* Artist of the Year Award, Usher has seen his albums riding high on the No. 1 spot for weeks at a time.

Born Usher Raymond IV in 1978, Usher grew up in Chattanooga, Tennessee. His father abandoned the family, but Usher's mother, Jonnetta Patton, gave him constant encouragement and support as he grew up. Usher told an *Interview* reporter, "She showed me the difference between good and evil. My dad never did. He split when I was born."

Usher also benefited from having an extended family of grandmothers and aunts. They all enjoyed R&B music, so he grew up listening to it. His first favorite song was the Jackson 5's "I Want You Back;" it inspired him to sing along. His mother, noticing his vocal talent, convinced him to join her church choir—a training ground for many well-known R&B singers. After he had honed his abilities in church, she entered him in talent contests, many of which he won.

Hoping to further nurture his abilities, his mother moved the family to Atlanta, Georgia, where many R&B singers had gotten their start. Usher continued to compete in singing contests and was selected to compete on the nationally televised show *Star Search*. He won the competition and signed a contract with LaFace Music in 1992.

At the time, the popularity of R&B was giving way to hip-hop, and one of the most well-known names in the hip-hop scene was that of Sean "Puffy" Combs, a performer and producer who had helped promote "gangsta" rap and who eventually became a multiplatinum-selling artist. Combs took Usher under his wing for a year, showing him the ropes, although Combs' style did not always feel comfortable for the young Usher. Usher told a *People* reporter, "That whole bad-boy thing, me frowning for the camera—that wasn't me." His first album, the self-titled *Usher,* sold modestly; one single, "Think of You," became a gold-selling hit, launching Usher's career.

In 1995, Usher was chosen to sing the Coca-Cola jingle in ads for the holiday season. He also joined other singers to create Black Men United, a group that sang on the soundtrack for the film *Jason's Lyric*.

Usher, wanting to take more control over his career and image, moved away from the Combs-inspired "bad boy" pose and began working with R&B producer Jermaine Dupri. He also began writing some of his own songs, working with Dupri; of the nine tracks on his second album, *My Way,,* six were cowritten with Dupri. Usher's new image paid off with *My Way,* which sold more than five million copies and appealed to listeners beyond the R&B niche, as it mixed R&B and hip-hop styles. Tracks that were especially popular included "You Make Me Wanna" and "Nice and Slow." "You Make Me Wanna" shot

up the *Billboard* charts to No. 1, staying there for eleven consecutive weeks. The album was more diverse than *Usher,* a deliberate attempt to appeal to a variety of listeners with a mix of soulful ballads and lively dance songs.

One group did not find the album particularly appealing: the critics. A *Rolling Stone* critic noted that although "You Make Me Wanna" was catchy, "Usher's voice lacks the force and nuance to make up for the thin, synthetic quality of the backing tracks. And you know there's a problem with the songwriting when you see the word 'hook' plastered over the choruses in the lyric booklet." Despite this response, listeners loved the album.

While on tour to promote the album, Usher performed before an enthusiastic audience at the prestigious Apollo Theater in Harlem. He told a reporter for *MTV News,* "When you come to the Apollo, you gotta sing, you gotta dance, you gotta give it up to the audience. They want to see that, and to get the response I got, when the song came on I came sliding out, all the audience bumrushed the stage. It's like … I think I'm a superstar." As a result of the album's success, Usher was chosen to join Combs' fall tour, as well as for performance dates supporting singers Mary J. Blige and Janet Jackson. He was also named *Billboard*'s Artist of the Year in 1998. Usher, always grateful to his mother for all her support, gave her a Mercedes 420 automobile and a Cartier watch.

Usher also began acting, appearing on the teen television shows *Moesha* and *Promised Land*. Of his appearance on *Moesha,* he told a *Jet* reporter, "I'm a natural [actor]. I have a talent to take words off paper and relate to it." After this experience, Usher wanted to move into film acting. Knowing that horror movies were popular among teens of all races, he chose to make his debut in *The Faculty,* in which he played a high-school football player possessed by aliens. Director Robert Rodriguez told a *People* reporter that for an amateur, Usher did an excellent job. "He was already way above and beyond a lot of people I have worked with who were coming in for the first time." The film was a success, and it attracted the attention of clothing designer Tommy Hilfiger, who featured members of the cast wearing his designs in his advertising. Usher was prominent in the ads, and he also argued with Hilfiger over the use of his image and his payment for it. He eventually sued Hilfiger for $1 million, claiming the company had used his image far more than he had originally agreed to, but had not paid him appropriately.

In 1998, Usher was nominated for a Grammy award for Best Male R&B Vocal Performance, and he won the award for Best R&B/Soul Single at the Soul

Train Music Awards. He also appeared on the soap opera *The Bold and the Beautiful.* In 1999, Usher appeared in the teen comedy film *She's All That* and the action movie *Light It Up,* which starred Vanessa L. Williams and Forest Whitaker. He also signed for two more films, Disney's telepic *Geppetto* and *Texas Rangers.* He told a *People* interviewer, "I've found a new love. My acting is making me want to leave my singing."

However, critics did not love his acting as much as Usher did. In the *Seattle Times,* journalist Christy Lemire commented, "*Texas Rangers* should have been put out to straight-to-video pasture," and noted that the film's shallow characterization was at fault. In the *Arizona Daily Star,* Phil Villarreal noted, "Usher? Stick to the singing. He lacks the smooth, controlled presence of an action star." Although the movie received these reviews, Miramax planned to release more films with Usher. Usher told Jenel Smith and Marilyn Beck in the Los Angeles *Daily News,* "If there was a class over at Miramax, I guess I would be the [teacher's pet]." He added that in order to play his role in *Texas Rangers,* he had to learn to handle both guns and horses. "I just had to go for it, and I did. I got to know my horse real well. He became my best friend."

In 2004, Usher's album *Confessions* started out at No. 1 on the *Billboard* charts, selling 1.1 million copies in its first week, surpassing every other debut album in the preceding two years, and eventually spending nine weeks on top of the list. The singles "Yeah," "Burn," and "Confessions, Part 2" were especially popular, riding at the number-one spot in succession, making Usher the artist with the most weeks at No. 1 in a calendar year. *Confessions* became the year's best-selling album. Usher re-released it with four new tracks, including a duet with Alicia Keys that became a hit. Usher noted that with this album, he wanted to get back to his roots in R&B, citing singer Marvin Gaye as an inspiration. "I really fell in love with his style of music and just realized how honest he was able to be through his music," he explained to Megan Leach of the Canadian *National Post.* He said of his own album, "When you go back and read through the lyrics it means something, it says something. That's what being a great R&B artist is to me. Thinking outside the box, and yet still making yourself available to a hip-hip nation." Usher explained to *Ebony* reporter Kevin Chappell, "I try to have that urban edge, but still put out real music. I listen to what the streets are saying."

In 2004, Usher performed at the MTV Video Music Awards, and he also signed with MTV Films to star in and be the executive producer of a big-screen film. Van Toffler, president of MTV, MTV2, and MTV Films told a Knight-Ridder/Tribune News Service reporter, "Usher's incredible music and acting talents combined with MTV Films' sensibility marks a perfect marriage for a feature." The film would use a soundtrack by Usher, effectively becoming a long advertisement for that album.

Usher further commercialized himself by launching the first-ever celebrity debit card, backed by Bankfirst. The card, featuring the word "success" and a photo of Usher wearing a diamond earring, was a "pre-paid" card that cost $19.95 to acquire. It gave users discounts on Usher merchandise, and was targeted to his young fans, many of whom either did not qualify for a credit card or did not have a checking account. "This is about empowering my fans," Usher told Phyllis Furman in the *Daily News,* but Furman observed it was also about making a lot of money.

In that same year, Usher was featured prominently in the gossip pages with the breakup of his two-year relationship with Rozonda "Chilli" Thomas, who performed with the R&B group TLC. He initially told Chappell in *Ebony* simply that they grew apart: "She wanted things and was moving in a direction, and I wanted things and was moving in a different direction, and we were unable to both compromise and meet each other halfway." However, when his mother and brother left the room, he admitted that he had cheated on Thomas. As a result, he said, there was little chance that they would ever get back together; they had not spoken since the breakup.

In August of 2004, Usher began a 28-city tour, traveling in a 45-foot bus outfitted with a television, DVD player, CD player, and a laptop computer, as well as five beds and a shower. Of his musical and financial success, he told a *People* reporter on the second day of the tour, "I don't believe in good luck, I believe in blessings." Whatever the source, it seems clear that his singing ability and financial savvy will continue to carry him to new heights in the music world.

## Selected discography

(Contributor) *LaFace Family Christmas,* LaFace, 1993.
(Contributor) *Poetic Justice* (soundtrack), Sony, 1993.
*Usher,* LaFace, 1994.
(Contributor) *Miss Thang,* Rowdy, 1995.
(Contributor) *Panther* (soundtrack), Mercury, 1995.
(Contributor) *Kazaam* (soundtrack), A&M, 1995.
*My Way,* LaFace, 1997.

(Contributor) *Soul Food* (soundtrack), LaFace, 1997.
*Live,* LaFace, 1999.
*8701,* Arista, 2001.
*Confessions,* Arista, 2004.

## Sources

### Books

*Contemporary Black Biography,* vol. 23, Gale Group, 1999.
*Contemporary Musicians,* vol. 23, Gale Group, 1999.

### Periodicals

*Arizona Daily Star,* December 2, 2001, p. E1.
*Billboard,* April 17, 2004, p. 72; June 26, 2004, p. 8; July 24, 2004, p. 69.
*Daily News* (Los Angeles, CA), October 6, 1999, p. L2; December 31, 1999, p. L21; July 30, 2004.

*Ebony,* June 2004, p. 170.
*Entertainment Weekly,* April 16, 2004, pp. 46-48.
*Interview,* May 1998, p. 102.
*Jet,* March 9, 1998.
Knight Ridder/Tribune News Service, July 31, 2004, p. K1614.
*People,* January 11, 1999, p. 83; April 19, 2004, pp. 67-68; August 23, 2004, p. 126.
*Rolling Stone,* December 25, 1997.
*Seattle Times,* December 4, 2001, p. E4.

### Online

"Biography," Usher World, http://www.usherworld.com/about-biography.php (October 6, 2004).
"Usher brings his Confessions to Canada for one night with Truth Tour," *National Post,* http://www.canada.com/national/nationalpost/news/artslife/story.html (October 6, 2004).

*—Kelly Winters*

# Alisa Valdes-Rodriguez

*Stephen J. Boitano/Getty Images*

## Author and journalist

**B**orn in 1969, in Albuquerque, NM; daughter of Nelson P. Valdes (a sociologist) and Maxine Conant (a poet); married Patrick Rodriguez (a writer), 1999; children: Alexander. *Education:* Graduated from the Berklee College of Music, c. 1991; Columbia University, M.A. (journalism), 1994.

**Addresses:** *Office*—St. Martin's Press, 175 Fifth Ave., New York, NY 10010.

## Career

**R**eporter, *Boston Globe,* Boston, MA, c. 1994-98; reporter, *Los Angeles Times,* Los Angeles, CA, 1998-2001; features editor, *Albuquerque Tribune,* Albuquerque, NM, 2002. Film rights to *The Dirty Girls Social Club* were optioned by Jennifer Lopez and Columbia Pictures.

## Sidelights

**A**lisa Valdes-Rodriguez's debut novel, *The Dirty Girls Social Club,* was heralded as a publishing-industry breakthrough when it appeared in 2003. The tale of six college-educated Latina women, and their career and romantic travails, prompted book-world talk that an author had finally managed to crack the popular-fiction market for Hispanic-American readers, and she was hailed as the next Terry McMillan, the best-selling writer of *Waiting to Exhale.* "This is the book I wanted to read but couldn't find," Valdes-Rodriguez told *Rocky Mountain News* writer Erika Gonzalez. "So much of what's written in English about Latinas is about us being downtrodden and struggling. I wanted to have fun."

Valdes-Rodriguez's career trajectory from journalist to author was not her first foray into the creative professions. Born in 1969 in Albuquerque, New Mexico, she was a talented tenor saxophonist in her teens, and graduated from Boston's prestigious Berklee College of Music. She sometimes points out in interviews that she was only half-Hispanic, and did not become fluent in Spanish until she took it up in her twenties. "There's a part of me that wants to vomit to be called a Latina writer," she told *Chicago Tribune* writer Patrick T. Reardon. "Why am I identified as part of a Latino movement and not by my mother's Irish background?" Her Cuban-born father was a sociologist who taught at various universities, and the family moved around often during her childhood before her parents' divorce.

After attempting to earn a living as a musician in New York City for a time, Valdes-Rodriguez enrolled in the graduate journalism program at Columbia University, finishing in 1994. She then landed a staff writing job with the *Boston Globe,* where her innate sense of justice found an outlet both in the stories she filed, and in calling attention to what she felt was the paper's biased coverage of news events involving minorities. She also sensed that African-American and Hispanic journalists were treated differently by the paper's editors, and it was only then that she started to learn the language of her paternal ancestors. "At newspapers there was always this sort of, 'we need someone to go cover this story who speaks Spanish, can you go?'" she recalled in an interview with Kristin Finan of the *Houston Chronicle*. "At the beginning I was afraid to admit that I didn't [speak Spanish] because I thought that might have been one of the main reasons they hired me."

After Boston, Valdes-Rodriguez moved on to the *Los Angeles Times* in 1998, where she covered the Spanish-language music industry. She also married and became pregnant, and she and her husband decided to move to her home state. Her letter of resignation to her *LA Times* bosses was a lengthy e-mail screed that made it onto the Internet, and gained Valdes-Rodriguez a certain measure of notoriety. In it, she excoriated the paper's editors for grouping the diverse nationalities of Central America, South America, and the Caribbean under a single umbrella term. "'Latino'—as used in The Los Angeles Times—is the most recent attempt at genocide perpetrated against the native people of the Americas," she asserted, according to a *New York Times* article by Dinitia Smith.

Not surprisingly, Valdes-Rodriguez had a difficult time finding another job in journalism thanks to that letter. She scraped by, doing freelance public-relations work for Hispanic entertainers, and had to rely on Medicaid to cover the cost of her son's delivery. But when she submitted a proposal for a nonfiction book about Hispanic pop divas, the editors who read it asked if she had written any fiction instead. Valdes-Rodriguez had been working intermittently on a manuscript for several years, and decided to leave her infant son at home with her husband and head for the local Starbucks. "The staff thought that I was strange because I was there all the time," she recalled in an interview with London *Daily Telegraph* writer Marcus Warren. "I would be there 10 to 15 hours a day for two weeks."

The submitted manuscript sparked a bidding war among publishers, who had long sought a "Latina Terry McMillan" to jump-start fiction aimed at Hispanic-American female readers. Valdes-Rodriguez earned a $475,000 advance on the book's royalties when she signed with St. Martin's Press, though that had not been the highest offer tendered. She chose St. Martin's, she told Gonzalez in the *Rocky Mountain News* article, because "they never viewed it as an ethnic book. They saw it as the next Nanny Diaries—a mainstream book with Latino characters."

*The Dirty Girls Social Club* was published to great fanfare in the spring of 2003. Its chapters chronicle the post-collegiate lives of a sextet of Latinas, all friends from their Boston University days. They are a diverse group, both in heritage, class, and professional aspirations, but manage to get together twice yearly to catch up with the "sucias," a term that, roughly translated, means fast young women. Reviews were generally mixed, as in critic Fabiola Santiago's assessment for the *Miami Herald*. She termed Valdes-Rodriguez's debut "a chatty, watered-down view of 18- to 34-year-old Latinahood and a failed attempt to dispel stereotypes (just check out the cover for plentiful Jennifer Lopez hotness). Yet there is something charming about the novel, which has the feel of a night out with the girls that's both comfortable and adventurous."

Valdes-Rodriguez's next book, *Playing with Boys*, was published by St. Martin's in 2004. This one centers around a trio of Hispanic women in the Hollywood entertainment-industry orbit whose lives intersect thanks to a screenplay in the works about Central American politics. "Once again, without resorting to didacticism," noted *Library Journal* reviewer Shelley Mosley, Valdes-Rodriguez's "novel becomes a subtle vehicle for demonstrating the rich diversity of Latina culture."

Valdes-Rodriguez's last job in journalism was as the features editor for the *Albuquerque Tribune*. She lives in the area, not far from her childhood home, with her husband Patrick Rodriguez, a screenwriter, and their son, Alexander. At work on a third novel—this one set in Miami—she is thrilled to have left the constraints of newspaper journalism behind and discovered a more creative outlet for her principles. "The process of writing is a joy," she told *Atlanta Journal-Constitution* writer Teresa K. Weaver. "I feel a little guilty when I'm doing it because I enjoy it so much."

## Selected writings

*The Dirty Girls Social Club,* St. Martin's Press (New York, NY), 2003.
*Playing with Boys,* St. Martin's Press (New York, NY), 2004.

## Sources

### Periodicals

*Atlanta Journal-Constitution,* June 23, 2003, p. D1.
*Chicago Tribune,* August 21, 2002.
*Cosmopolitan,* May 2003, p. 82.

*Daily Telegraph* (London, England), August 13, 2003.
*Detroit Free Press,* May 11, 2003.
*Entertainment Weekly,* May 16, 2003, p. 42.
*Houston Chronicle,* September 27, 2004, p. 1.
Knight-Ridder/Tribune News Service, May 14, 2003.
*Library Journal,* August 2004, p. 70.
*Miami Herald,* May 2, 2003.
*New York Times,* April 24, 2003, p. E1.

*Publishers Weekly,* April 14, 2003, p. 49; July 7, 2003, p. 17; August 30, 2004, p. 31.
*Rocky Mountain News,* June 5, 2003, p. 8D.

**Online**

*Contemporary Authors Online,* Thomson Gale, 2004.

—*Carol Brennan*

# Daniel Vasella

**Chief Executive Officer of Novartis**

*Graham Barclay/Bloomberg News/Landov*

**B**orn in 1953 in Fribourg, Switzerland; son of Oskar (a history professor) Vasella; married Anne-Laurence, 1978; children: one daughter, two sons. *Education:* University of Bern, M.D., 1979.

**Addresses:** *Office*—Novartis International AG, CH-4002 Basel, Switzerland.

## Career

**D**octor, University of Bern, 1984-88; joined Sandoz Pharma, 1988; named chief executive officer of Sandoz Pharma, 1994; named chief executive officer of Novartis, 1996; named chairman of Novartis, 1999; co-authored *Magic Cancer Bullet: How a Tiny Orange Pill is Rewriting Medical History,* 2003.

**Awards:** Named one of the world's "100 Most Influential People" by *Time,* 2004; voted Europe's most influential business leader of the last 25 years by readers of the *Financial Times;* Pharmaceutical Executive of the Year, Pharmaceutical Achievement Awards, 2004.

## Sidelights

**I**n eight years, Daniel Vasella went from being a doctor to becoming the head of Novartis, one of the world's biggest drug companies. He has managed the company with a doctor's interest in research into new treatments and a tough-minded businessman's aggressive, innovative thinking. Thanks to his leadership, Novartis has released a

drug that fights a rare cancer without hurting healthy cells, and his company has dozens of new drugs almost ready for market at a time when competitors are running low on new products. In early 2005, he led Novartis in a bold move into the generic drug market, again showing his competitive streak and calculated risk-taking.

Vasella, who was born in Switzerland in 1953, had to face illness and death at a young age. He came down with tuberculosis and meningitis as a child. When he was ten, his older sister died of cancer. Three years later, his father, Oskar, a history professor, died of complications from surgery. He says watching his sister fight her illness led to his interest in medicine, and he went to the University of Bern Medical School. (Another sister, who went to medical school with him, died in an accident in 1982.)

After getting his medical degree, Vasella worked in pathology and internal medicine, eventually becoming the University of Bern's chief resident. But he was developing an interest in business, so he left the hospital to join the drug company Sandoz Pharma, where his wife's uncle was chief executive officer. He started working at the Sandoz office in New Jersey, where he became product manager for an anti-pancreatic cancer drug. He knew that his success depended on the drug's success, so he had researchers, production chemists, and marketers work together to find new uses for the drug, instead of the usual practice of the three groups working in isolation. They discovered that it could also treat the side effects of certain cancers, and its sales skyrocketed.

Returning to Switzerland in 1993, Vasella worked in top corporate positions, using the methods he had developed with the cancer drug on all of Sandoz's drug-development efforts. He became CEO of Sandoz in 1994, and when Sandoz merged with rival Ciba-Geigy to form Novartis in 1996, Vasella was named the new company's CEO. His family ties to Sandoz made some feel he had gotten the job out of nepotism, but others disagree. "To anyone who followed the company at the time, Dan was the live wire," SG Cowen analyst Peter Laing told Unmesh Kher of *Time.* "He had the most international outlook, and there really wasn't anyone at Ciba to challenge him."

Making the new company work was difficult. Sandoz had a hierarchical leadership style that Vasella thought discouraged initiative, while the culture at Ciba seemed to discourage strong decision-making. Both companies had started off as chemical companies and gone into drug manufacturing; now, they were pharmaceutical companies that still had some chemical production business left over. Vasella reorganized the company, laying off 12,500 workers and firing several managers, and formed a venture fund that helped ex-employees start new businesses. For a while, when Vasella would travel to Novartis offices around the world, he would fire managers immediately if he did not like what they did or said, until he was told that workers had started to fear his visits. "Now I ask that they not be fired until several weeks after I come back" to Switzerland, he told the *Wall Street Journal.*

At first, success was slow to come. Novartis' sales increased only slightly in 1998 and 1999. Vasella invested in life sciences with the idea that new biotechnology would link the drug business with agricultural and nutritional products. But the life sciences market floundered. Vasella realized it and abandoned his goal. Novartis sold off its agricultural arm in 2000.

At the time, Novartis' competitors in the pharmaceutical industry dismissed it "as a sleepy European giant without the marketing and sales firepower to compete in the U.S.," wrote Kerry Capell of *BusinessWeek.* But thanks to Vasella's decision to spend heavily on research and marketing, Novartis scored a huge success when it released the cancer drug Gleevec in May of 2001.

Gleevec worked on relatively rare forms of cancer such as chronic myeloid leukemia and gastrointestinal stromal tumors. But the way it works is unique and promising. It is the first drug that had been proven to destroy a certain kind of tumor. Other cancer drugs destroy healthy cells and cancer cells alike, but Gleevec attacks the proteins that make tumors grow.

Vasella's leadership was a key ingredient in Gleevec's success. According to the magazine *Chief Executive,* after the Sandoz/Ciba-Geigy merger, Vasella talked to some Ciba-Geigy researchers, who told him about the drug compound that eventually became Gleevec. Although it seemed the drug would only appeal to a narrow market because it treated a rare disease, Vasella pushed for testing and production of it to move forward and personally answered the letters from cancer patients who asked to be included in the trials.

In 2003, Vasella told the story in a book, *Magic Cancer Bullet: How a Tiny Orange Pill is Rewriting Medical History,* co-written with Robert Slater. Clifton Leaf, a writer for *Fortune,* called the book "a heroic saga," attracted to the story of a corporate culture championing a life-saving drug. *Publishers Weekly* acknowledged it was an inspiring story, but complained that the book "reads largely as an extended press release for Novartis" because of its "repetition and stilted writing" and lack of "the details and depth of feeling needed to make that story come alive."

As CEO, Vasella is known for putting a lot of money into research and development. In 2004, Novartis was spending $3 billion on research, or 19 percent of its drug sales, compared to an industry standard of 13 to 16 percent. He moved the company's research and development headquarters from Basel, Switzerland, to Cambridge, Massachusetts, to take advantage of the Boston area's heavy concentration of medical researchers and personally recruited a top scientist from Harvard Medical School to run the lab. As a doctor, Vasella can oversee research better than other drug company CEOs, his admirers say, because he can ask his research teams complex questions.

Relying so much on research and development (as opposed to, say, acquiring other companies and their patents) is risky for a pharmaceutical company because it means betting on rare successes to come out of its labs. But so far, Vasella's approach is paying off. Novartis moves its drugs through research and development in two-thirds the time of the average drug company, in part thanks to a strategy of testing a drug on several diseases at once. It had 64 drugs in the medium or late stages of development in 2004, compared to 37 and 14 at competitors Roche and Merck, respectively.

Vasella's accomplishments are more striking in comparison to his competitors, who have struggled with decreased profits and competition from generic drugs. Novartis "has had to face many of the same issues bedeviling its peers, including expiring patents on big-selling drugs," according to the *Wall Street Journal.* "But Dr. Vasella has steered the company through these problems, in large part by jettisoning its staid Swiss culture and transforming the firm into a bare-knuckled, American-style marketing powerhouse,"—a reference to his strategy for getting company researchers and marketers to work together to create more effective marketing strategies for products. For instance, the company dropped an ineffective ad for Lamisil, Novartis' treatment for fungal infections, and created a brochure salesmen could give to doctors about the condition. Sales of Lamisil went up afterward. "I love Switzerland and I think people know that I'm patriotic," Vasella told Harris. "But this is about making decisions that are essential to the business. We are going to be as, or even more, American as any company."

Vasella's success has won him a lot of praise. In 2004, *Time* named Vasella one of the world's "100 Most Influential People," the only drug company executive on the list. Readers of the *Financial Times* selected him as the most influential business leader in Europe in the last 25 years. Capell of *Business-Week* wrote that he is "an unusual mix: an aggressive manager who still keeps something of the gentle bedside manner he developed as a general practitioner." Vasella also has a casual, calm persona; Capell described him as "an unbuttoned type who likes roaring around the Swiss countryside on his BMW bike."

To build on his achievements, Vasella moved to expand Novartis. He tripled its United States sales force to 6,200, seeing the United States—the world's most lucrative drug market—as key to the company's future. He also acquired some North American companies. He bought a majority stake in Idenix Pharmaceuticals of Cambridge, Massachusetts, which was working on new drugs to treat hepatitis B and C, for $225 million, and bought Sabex, a Canadian drug company, for more than $500 million.

Many business analysts expected Vasella to make a big move to merge with another major company, but he came back empty-handed from his hunt for a big deal. He looked longingly at Roche, also based in Basel, and began buying its stock, but Roche's CEO and the family who owns the majority stake in the company were opposed to a merger. As of early 2005, Novartis had only managed to acquire 33 percent of Roche. He also pursued a merger with French drug company Aventis, but he backed off after the French government, preferring that the company remain French, put up hurdles to a deal.

In January of 2005, as Novartis announced record profits and sales for 2004, Vasella got the drug industry's attention by speaking out about recent scandals involving other companies' patented drugs. He warned his competitors, who had been accused of not releasing enough research information about side effects, that they needed to become more open. But he also told critics of the drug industry to back off from calls to ease patent protection. That, he said, would discourage companies from researching new drugs, hurting patients in the long run.

The next month, Novartis made a bold move. It became the world's biggest maker of generic drugs by spending $8.3 billion to buy Hexal, a German company that makes generic pharmaceuticals, and Eon Labs, Hexal's United States affiliate. The generic drug market is expected to be lucrative in the next several years, as patents on many popular drugs worth tens of billions of dollars expire. Novartis says it is pursuing a third route to success, instead of focusing only on patented drugs or diversifying by going into other medical technologies, the usual strategies of major pharmaceutical companies.

Vasella, whose salary was about $2.6 million in 2004, believes Novartis has a bright future. The company predicted that by 2008 or 2009, it should have eight blockbuster drugs on the market—that is, drugs with annual sales of $1 billion or more. In early 2005, it had five. The possible future drugs include the first pill to fight multiple sclerosis, a new asthma treatment, and drugs to fight cancers and high blood pressure.

## Sources

### Periodicals

America's Intelligence Wire, February 22, 2005.
*BusinessWeek,* May 26, 2003, pp. 68-70.
*Chief Executive,* July 2004, p. 30.
*Financial Times,* January 21, 2005, p. 24; February 22, 2005, p. 28.

*Fortune,* May 12, 2003, p. 144.
*Publishers Weekly,* March 24, 2003, p. 65.
*SCRIP World Pharmaceutical News,* August 13, 2004, p. 10.
*Time,* July 29, 2002, p. B6.
*Wall Street Journal,* August 23, 2002, p. A1; June 15, 2004, p. B1.

**Online**

"Daniel Vasella, M.D," *Forbes.com,* http://www. forbes.com/finance/mktguideapps/personinfo/ FromPersonIdPersonTearsheet .jhtml?passed PersonId=213443 (February 25, 2005).

Novartis.com, http://www.novartis.com (February 27, 2005).

"Vasella, Daniel," World Economic Forum Knowledge Navigator, http:// www.weforum.org/site/ knowledgenavigator.nsf/Content/Vasella20 Daniel (February 25, 2005).

*—Erick Trickey*

# Ellen S. Vitetta

## Immunologist

**B**orn c. 1942. *Education:* Connecticut College, B.A.; New York University, M.S., 1966, Ph.D., 1968.

**Addresses:** *Home*—6914 Pemberton Dr., Dallas, TX 75230-4260. *Office*—University of Texas Southwestern Medical Center, Cancer Immunobiology Center, 6000 Harry Hines Blvd., Dallas, TX 75235-5303.

## Career

**U**niversity of Texas (UT) Southwestern Medical Center, professor of microbiology, 1976—, Immunology Graduate Program, chairperson, 1984-88; Medical Research Council, Cambridge, England, 1986; UT Southwestern Medical Center, Cancer Immunology Center, director, 1988—, Sheryle Simmons Patigian Distinguished Chair, 1989—.

**Member:** American Association of Immunologists (president), Natonal Academy of Sciences.

**Awards:** Taittinger Breast Cancer Research Award, Komen Foundation, 1983; NIH Merit Award, 1987—; Pierce Immunotoxin Award, 1988; Women's Excellence in Science Award, FASEB, 1991; Abbott Award, American Society of Microbiologists, 1992; Rosenthal Award, American Association of Cancer Research, 1995; Charlotte Friend Award, American Association of Cancer Research, 2002.

## Sidelights

**C**astor beans are used to make castor oil. When the beans are boiled down they produce ricin, a highly toxic compound. It takes only a pin point to be lethal to humans. Since it is readily available, ricin can and has been used as a biochemical weapon. However, a team of researchers led by Dr. Ellen S. Vitetta have developed a vaccine. Vitetta, an immunologist, has also found other uses for the deadly toxin that could help in the battle against cancer.

Vitetta was born around 1942. She earned her Bachelor of Arts degree from Connecticut College. She went on to receive her masters degree from New York University, where she also earned her Ph.D. in the late 1960s. In 1976, she became a professor in the microbiology department at the University of Texas (UT) Southwestern Medical Center. The invention of monoclonal antibody technology by Dr. George Kohler and Dr. Cesar Milstein in 1975 provided Vitetta with the focus of her mission. She told Ricki Lewis of the *Scientist,* "When I read their paper in 1975, a light bulb went off and I knew that targeted therapy using monoclonal antibodies was the way to go after many diseases, including cancer." It would be another eleven years before Vitetta would reach a turning point in her career.

In 1984 Vitetta became the chairperson for the Immunology Graduate Program at UT Southwestern and continued as a professor of microbiology. She served as the chair until 1988. In 1986 Vitetta took a leave of absence to work at the Medical Research Council in Cambridge, England, which was headed by Milstein. While there she studied molecular engineering of antibodies and immunotoxins. Upon her return from England, she became the director of the Cancer Immunology Center as well as the Scheryle Simmons Patigian Distinguished Chair in Cancer Immunology at UT Southwestern.

The Cancer Immunology Center's focus was on developing immunotoxins and monoclonal antibodies to destroy cancer cells and AIDS. The center had a number of breakthroughs under Vitetta's leadership. In 1997 Vitetta and her team of scientists found that chemically altered monoclonal antibodies killed cancer cells. Monoclonal antibodies are single-celled antibodies that have binding sites at the end of their two arms which could attach to cancer cells and signal them to die. The scientists combined two of the antibodies to form a dimer that had four binding sites. This would increase the effectiveness of the antibodies in destroying the cancer cells. The new dimers were used to treat patients with lymphoma or breast cancer.

In the fight against HIV, the virus that causes AIDS, highly active antiretroviral therapy was used to control the virus. In most cases, when the therapy stopped, the virus reappeared. Vitetta and her team focused on removing the dormant HIV cells. According to a press release from UT Southwestern, the scientists "joined a monoclonal antibody—an antibody made up of a protein from a single clone of cells—and a subunit of a plant toxin, ricin" to form an immunotoxin. The immunotoxin would target the dormant HIV cells and kill them. The immunotoxin also provided a bonus according to Vitetta. She stated in the press release, "In additional experiments we found that this immunotoxin could kill both latent cells and those actively cranking out the virus." The scientists used patients' cells that were grown in lab dishes. The next step is to use actual patients. Vitetta also began a study to see if immunotoxins could be used to kill cancer cells. Human trials have shown that 60 percent of the patients using the immunotoxins received partial or complete tumor reduction.

While using the immunotoxin, Vitetta and her team of scientists developed a vaccine for ricin. The vaccine named RiVax has been approved for trials on humans. According to a press release from UT Southwestern, ricin "can be administered in foods and water or sprayed as an aerosol." Victims develop fever, nausea, and abdominal pain or lung damage. The Centers for Disease Control classifies ricin as a "Category B" biological agent. The RiVax vaccine was injected into mice and the mice were given lethal doses of ricin. The mice were protected with no side effects. The trials will also be used to confirm the safety of the doses needed to induce effective antibodies in humans. DOR BioPharma, Inc. received the exclusive license to produce the vaccine.

In addition to their work with vaccines and immunotoxins, Vitetta and her team have developed a blood test that could detect genetic changes in breast cancer. In the advanced stages of breast cancer, cancer can spread to different parts of the body. The scientists have learned that circulatory cancer cells are shed from a primary tumor. The blood test was designed to detect the cancer cells. With detection, treatments can be tailor-made to slow the spread.

In addition to her groundbreaking discoveries, Vitetta is the president of the American Association of Immunologists. She is also a member of the National Academy of Sciences. She has received two awards from the American Association of Cancer Research: the Rosenthal Award in 1995, and the Charlotte Friend Award in 2002.

Vitetta credited her success with assembling a top-notch team; keeping the lab fully stocked—yet cost-effective—and keeping competition to a minimum. In addition to being an effective manager, she has also helped her team and the Cancer Immunology Center receive numerous grants to help further their studies. She also mentors, and was honored by 2004 Nobel Prize in Medicine winner Dr. Linda Buck, who publicly and privately thanked her for helping her throughout her career. Vitetta is a tireless activist for getting more women involved with science. She told Sue Goetnick Ambrose of the *Dallas Morning News,* "Quite honestly, I think that men have skills, and I think women have skills, and the challenge is to harness your skills and use them to achieve what you wish to achieve rather than putting us into boxes." She also stated to Ambrose that she believes that "women bring certain skills and personalities to science that are very valuable. They tend often to have very good skills with people, with trainees, and I think you lose that if you have a totally male population of scientists."

Vitetta has also shown herself to be an excellent teacher who uses humor and plain English to help students understand the complexities of science.

She told Ann Gibbons in *Science* that the high point of her career occurred in 1994 when 55 of her former students and postdoctoral researchers attended a barbecue to celebrate the 20th anniversary of her lab. In fact, the majority of researchers and students that have worked in her lab have continued their careers in science.

Vitetta has shown the tenacity to carry on with her research that has proven successful in eradicating several diseases. Her research has helped in the fight against biochemical warfare. No doubt she and her team will continue to make more scientific breakthroughs.

## Sources

### Books

*Marquis Who's Who*, Marquis Who's Who, 2004.

### Periodicals

*Dallas Morning News*, February 9, 2004; January 29, 2005.
*Science*, September 23, 1994, pp. 1937-38.
*Scientist*, June 24, 2002, p. 52.

### Online

"The Birth, Death and Rebirth of a Novel Disease-Fighting Tool," Illyria (Balkans) Forum, http://pub18.ezboard.com/fbalkansfrm73?page=2 (April 11, 2005).
"Chemically Altered Monoclonal Antibodies Kill Cancer Cells," Doctor's Guide, http://www.pslgroup.com/dg/2E70E.htm (April 11, 2005).
"Ellen Vitetta, PhD," UT Southwestern Medical Center, http://www8.utsouthwestern.edu/findfac/professional/0,2356,17609,00.html (April 11, 2005).
"UT Southwestern researchers kill latent HIV-infected cells using immunotoxin," EurekAlert! Public News List, http://www.eurekalert.org/pub_releases/1999-10/UoTS-USrk-141099.php (June 22, 2005).
"What is ricin?" CNN.com, http://www.cnn.com/2003/WORLD/europe/01/07/ricin.facts (May 22, 2005).

Additional information was obtained from press releases from Texas Tech University.

—*Ashyia N. Henderson*

# Pharrell Williams

## Music producer, singer, and songwriter

**B**orn April 5, 1973, in Virginia Beach, VA; son of Pharoah (a handyman) and Carolyn (a teacher) Williams.

**Addresses:** *Home*—Virginia Beach, VA. *Office*—Star Trak Entertainment, PO Box 5017, New York, NY 10185-5017. *Website*—http://www.n-e-r-d.com.

## Career

**T**eamed with Chad Hugo to form the producing duo the Neptunes while still in high school; sold first song, "Rump Shaker," to rappers Wreckx-N-Effect, 1992; produced "Tonight's the Night" for R&B group Blackstreet, 1994; began producing chart-bound songs for acts like Babyface, Nelly, Britney Spears, and Usher, 1998— formed own artistic act, N.E.R.D., early 2000s; released debut album, *In Search Of ...*, 2002.

**Awards:** Grammy Award for Producer of the Year, 2004.

## Sidelights

**B**ehind every chart-topping singer is a behind-the-scenes producer who is in charge of the creative mix that underlies each song. It does not matter how solid a song's lyrics or performer; the producer can ultimately make or break a hit. Over the past few years, Pharrell Williams has emerged as one of the most revolutionary producers of 21st century music. He is one-half of a production duo called the Neptunes; childhood friend Chad Hugo makes up the other half. As producers, the Neptunes have put their touch on more than 150 songs and generated hits in nearly every musical genre with their innovative, out-of-this-world beats. Williams and Hugo are the masterminds behind such hits as urban pop-rapper Nelly's "Hot in Herre," rapper Jay-Z's "I just Wanna Love U (Give it to Me)," R&B star Usher's "U Don't Have to Call," and pop star Britney Spears' "I'm A Slave 4 U."

At one point in 2003, 20 percent of all songs receiving air time on British radio had Williams' touch. The music industry took note and in 2004, the Neptunes walked away with the coveted producer of the year award at the Grammys. In the early 2000s, Williams and Hugo stepped out from behind the scenes and became front-stage material when they formed their own group, called N.E.R.D., which released albums in 2002 and 2004. Since then, Williams has spent a lot of time on the road touring to promote the albums.

Though Williams exudes a city-slick, tough-as-nails playboy persona by sporting "bling" (diamond jewelry), wearing his ball cap tipped to the side and dropping plenty of expletives into each conversation, he is really a nerdy suburbanite at heart. "I'm no rapper," he told *Time*'s Josh Tyrangiel. "I'm, like, a suburban kid." Williams was born on April 5, 1973, to Pharoah and Carolyn Williams and grew up in Virginia Beach, Virginia, the oldest of three boys. His father was a handyman and house painter and his mother was a teacher. Williams' success has brought him plenty of money, in stark contrast to his upbringing. He grew up in a household where paying the bills posed a problem at times. "It wasn't, like, third world poverty, but let's just say we ate a lot of pork and beans," Williams' younger brother, David Williams, told the London *Guardian*'s Paul Lester while N.E.R.D. was touring in Europe. Williams helped his parents out by buying them a house after he made it big.

Growing up, Williams' musical influences were just as diverse as the music he now produces. He listened to Michael Jackson, Stevie Wonder, and Queen and believes Axl Rose is the biggest rock star of all time. Since childhood, Williams has made a point of allowing himself to enjoy all types of music by not tying his identity to any one genre. "I love Kool Moe Dee, but I also love America," Williams told *Time*'s Tyrangiel. "And I would never let my appreciation for one kind of music keep me from listening to another."

Williams took a personal interest in music in seventh grade after his grandmother suggested he join the school band. He took her advice and chose to become a percussionist. Williams' involvement in school bands as an adolescent provided two key tools for his adult success—the ability to read music and discipline, which he learned as a member of a marching band drum line. "Being a drummer is megamacho," Williams told *People* magazine. "I'm constantly pushing myself. I got that from band camp. We were pushed on a military level."

The school band also provided a backdrop for his friendship with Hugo, a boy who attended the same Virginia Beach school for gifted children as Williams. Hugo played saxophone. They became fast pals and spent their free time experimenting with samplers and beat production. By eleventh grade, they were calling themselves the Neptunes and were discovered by a scout for music producer Teddy Riley while performing in a school talent show. Riley, who had collaborated with Michael Jackson, had a studio near their school. Riley let them work on songs and make some tracks at his studio.

In 1992, while still in high school, Williams and Hugo sold their first song, "Rump Shaker," to the rap ensemble Wreckx-N-Effect. It appeared on the group's second album, *Hard or Smooth*. The related video was wildly popular, producing a fervor that nearly matched the enthusiasm for Sir Mix-A-Lot's "Baby Got Back." Sales of the album soared and it was platinum-certified. A second big break came in 1994 when Riley had them produce the track "Tonight's the Night" for his R&B vocal group Blackstreet. In 1998, they hooked up with hardcore hip-hop rapper Noreaga to produce his single "SuperThug." The music industry took note of the Neptunes and more jobs rolled in. Soon enough, artists like Snoop Dogg were knocking at their door and Williams could concentrate on making music, a job he enjoyed more than a stint at McDonald's. Incidentally, Williams wrote and produced the popular McDonald's "I'm Lovin' It" jingle.

As the producing duo known as the Neptunes, Williams and Hugo have written songs and mapped out the beats for such artists as Janet Jackson, Babyface, Mary J. Blige, and Justin Timberlake, as well as rock acts No Doubt, Garbage, and Marilyn Manson. Songs produced by the duo often feature startling synthesizer beats and rock guitar riffs resulting in a fresh, cutting-edge style. Sometimes they include sound snippets from 1980s pop culture, such as Atari-game bleeps and early cell phone rings. Writing in the *Washington Post*, David Segal described their phenomenon this way: "In pop, every age has its sound and few producers have shaped the sound of today as much as Pharrell Williams and Chad Hugo. Their work is distinctly digital age, comprising hard, flat tones, repetitive electronic hooks and arrangements that make use of the silence between the beats." Segal described their genius as their ability to play down a track. Unlike other producers, they never add useless passages just for the sake of extending a song, or trying to create something that just is not there. "There's nothing extra on a song like [Spears'] 'Slave 4 U.' You get enough to make you dance and nothing more."

The Neptunes are such popular music-makers they command six-figure salaries to deliver a single tune and artists seem happy to cough up the money for the chance to work with the duo. Williams and Hugo view each song they produce as a fresh opportunity. They strive to give pop artists more attitude and rappers more emotional depth. "We want people to sound different," Williams told Tyrangiel in *Time*. "Taking somebody from A to B is cool, but when we produce, we want to take people from A to D, to challenge their artistic natures, their image, everything." From all accounts, they seem to be doing the job well. "Pharrell is a very sweet guy," Blige told *People*. "If he writes a song, he writes the song for you."

In 2002, the Neptunes placed five top-ten hits on the *Billboard* Hot 100 Singles chart, including Nelly's

"Hot in Herre," which peaked at number one; Usher's "U Don't Have to Call," which peaked at number three; LL Cool J's "Luv U Better," which peaked at number four; "Girlfriend," by 'N Sync featuring Nelly, which peaked at number five; and N.O.R.E.'s "Nothin'," which peaked at number ten. In 2003, Justin Timberlake's "Rock Your Body" hit number five on the chart and Jay-Z's "Excuse Me Miss" peaked at number eight. The real payoff came the following year, in 2004, when Williams and Hugo won the Grammy Award for producer of the year. In an interview with *Billboard*'s Rashaun Hall, Williams made producing sound easy, equating it to decorating a house. "You're going to need the basics—like a couch—and then you personalize it according to what your personality is."

In the early 2000s, Williams and Hugo stepped out from behind the sound boards to create their own band with pal Shae Haley, who goes by the moniker Shay. They call themselves N.E.R.D., an acronym for "No One Ever Really Dies." For the trio, N.E.R.D. is more than just a name; it is also their philosophy on life. Writing on the band's website, http://www.n-e-r-d.com, Williams explained the philosophy this way: "People's energies are made of their souls. When you die, that energy may disperse but it isn't destroyed. Energy cannot be destroyed. It can manifest in a different way but even then it's like their souls are going somewhere. If it's going to heaven or hell or even if it's going into a fog or somewhere in the atmosphere to lurk unbeknownst to itself, it's going somewhere."

N.E.R.D. released its debut album *In Search Of ...* in 2002, followed by *Fly or Die* in 2004. Ironically, songs from their albums have never been as successful as ones they have produced for other artists. N.E.R.D. members created their first album using synthesizers, then re-recorded it with a live instrumental band. The combination created a unique sound. Instead of hearing one of their legendary single-hand keyboard lines on synthesizer, the passages were played on guitar, with guitars imitating synthesizers.

On its first album, N.E.R.D. explored adolescent anxiety and awkwardness. Writing on the Virgin Records website, the trio spoke out about the content of *In Search Of ...*: "This album is like a life soundtrack. It's a diary of [stuff] we've been through over the last year or two. We're just trying to express ourselves as colorful as possible, as musical as possible." Songs include "Backseat Love," about girls who refuse to go all the way and "Lapdance," which compares politicians and strippers.

Because the tone of the songs on each album is diverse, it is tough to place N.E.R.D.'s music in any one genre. Their sound is a fusion of hip-hop, rock, jazz, and soul backed by guitars under Williams' falsetto singing. Because of this, N.E.R.D. has not seen a lot of radio airtime because DJs do not know where to place the songs. But that does not mean N.E.R.D. plans to change its ways. Speaking to the *Washington Post*'s Segal, Williams said the group would not be shoe-horned into one area. Like his song lyrics, Williams spoke in metaphor. "The music is very in-between. A Ferrari is not meant to be in suburban areas. It's meant to be in upper-echelon areas, and it's not meant to be driven around the ghetto. There are a lot of things that don't necessarily fit, but some of us don't give a [darn.] We drive our Ferraris wherever we want, and the rest of the world doesn't always understand that. I think I stay true to what I believe, and N.E.R.D. just pushes the envelope."

By forming N.E.R.D. and touring, Williams has moved from an anonymous, behind-the-scenes producer to a crowd-mobbed sex symbol. He is a predictable crowd-pleaser: slim and tattooed with a carefree style. Though papers have paired him with many women over the years, Williams is most often seen with Jade Jagger, daughter of Mick Jagger of the Rolling Stones. Beyond his sex appeal, Williams has also earned a reputation as a competent musician. He performed at the 2004 Grammy Awards alongside an all-star cast of musicians in a rendition of the Beatles classic "I Saw Her Standing There." Williams, on drums, was accompanied by Sting, Vince Gill, and Dave Matthews. The highlight, of course, was his Grammy win.

In addition to producing and writing songs, Williams has his own clothing company, called Billionaire's Boys Club (BBC). He also has a sneaker line that he named Ice Cream because "ice and cream are two things that run the world," Williams told Paul Lester in the *Guardian*. "The jewellery—the ice—the diamonds; and the cream is the cash." Williams and Hugo also have their own imprint record label through Arista, called Star Trak Entertainment. As such, they now have the opportunity to launch the careers of up-and-coming stars. As for the future, Williams has a pretty ambitious plan. "I'm going to make $500 million—that's my goal," he told *Rolling Stone*. "Of that, I'll only keep $100 million, for my family."

## Selected discography

*In Search Of ...*, Virgin Records, 2002.

*Neptunes Present: The Clones* (with other artists), Arista, 2003.

*Fly or Die*, Virgin Records, 2004.

## Sources

### Periodicals

*Billboard,* April 6, 2002, p. 28.
*Daily Telegraph* (London, England), June 5, 2004.
*New York Times,* April 17, 2004, p. B7.
*People,* October 13, 2003, p. 111; June 28, 2004, p. 115.
*Rolling Stone,* April 17, 2003, p. 75.
*Time,* August 25, 2003, p. 64.
*Washington Post,* June 6, 2004.

### Online

"Biography," N.E.R.D., http://www.n-e-r-d.com/bio.php (February 24, 2005).
"The Hit Man," *Guardian* (London, England) http://www.guardian.co.uk/arts/fridayreview/story/0,12102,1151480,00.html (February 26, 2005).
"N-E-R-D Biography," Virgin Records, http://www.virginmusic.co.nz/Biography.aspx?artist=3707 (February 26, 2005).

*—Lisa Frick*

# Judd Winick

**Cartoonist, illustrator, and author**

Born February 12, 1970, in Long Island, NY; married Pam Ling, August 26, 2001. *Education:* University of Michigan, B.A., 1992.

**Addresses:** *Home*—915 Cole St., No. 301, San Francisco, CA 94117. *Website*—http://www.frumpy.com.

## Career

Cartoonist, illustrator, and author. AIDS educator and lecturer. Participant in MTV's *The Real World,* 1994. Host of television programs, including: (with Pam Ling) *MTV Video Now What?: A Guide to Jobs, Money, and the Real World,* and *MTV's Real World-Road Rules Casting Special* and (co-host) *Best Fights of the Real World,* both 2000. Author and illustrator of cartoon strip "Nuts and Bolts," published in *Michigan Daily,* 1988-92, and *San Francisco Examiner,* 1994, and collected in *Watching the Spin-Cycle: The Nuts and Bolts,* privately printed (Ann Arbor, MI). Author and illustrator of "Road Trip" comic strip, in *ONI Double Feature;* "Frumpy the Clown," syndicated, 1996-98; "The Adventures of Barry Ween, Boy Genius," Image Comics, 1999; "Green Lantern," DC Comics; and "Exiles," Marvel Comics. Illustrator, with others, of Jamie S. Rich's *Cut My Hair,* ONI Press, 2000, and for numerous titles in the "Complete Idiot's Guide" series, Que (Indianapolis, IN). Producer and writer for cartoon *The Life and Times of Juniper Lee,* 2005.

**Awards:** Eisner Award nomination for best sequential story, for *Road Trip,* 1998; Eisner Award nominations for talent deserving wider recognition, best humor artist/writer, and best original graphic novel, for *Pedro and Me,* 1999; notable graphic novel citation, Young Adult Library Services Association (YALSA), for *The Adventures of Barry Ween, Boy Genius;* GLAAD Media Award for best comic book, Bulletin Blue Ribbon Book citation, notable graphic novel citation, YALSA, *Publishers Weekly* Best Book citation, Américas Award for Children's and Young Adult Literature, National Association of Latin American Studies Programs, all for *Pedro and Me;* Bay Area Book Reviewers' Award, 2000, and Notable Children's Book selection and Gay Lesbian, Bisexual, Transgender Roundtable Nonfiction Honor Book, American Library Association, Robert F. Sibert Informational Book Honor Award, Quick Pick for Reluctant Readers selection, YALSA, all 2001, all for *Pedro and Me.*

## Sidelights

The world became all too real for Judd Winick in 1993 as one of seven "stars" of MTV's *Real World III,* a pioneering reality-based television show. It was then that he met not only his future wife, Pam Ling, but also temporary housemate Pedro Zamora, a young man from Florida whose eventual death from AIDS would bring the tragic effects of that disease home to millions of young television viewers. Zamora, an AIDS activist, inspired Winick, a promising young cartoonist, to hit the lecture circuit for more than a year after the filming of *The Real World* to speak with young people about AIDS-related issues. In 2000 Winick published a moving and honest graphic-novel account of his friendship with Zamora, *Pedro and Me: Friendship, Loss, and What I Learned.* Additionally, Winick is also a popular author and illustrator of, among other things, the comic strip "Frumpy the Clown," which follows the trail of a chain-smoking, cynical clown who decides to move in with a typical suburban family, and "The Adventures of Barry Ween, Boy Genius," a series of comic books dealing with the misadventures of a cranky, obnoxious, brilliant, and foul-mouthed ten-year-old. Plus, *The Life and Times of Juniper Lee,* a new cartoon that Winick wrote and produced, debuted on the Cartoon Network in 2005.

Born in 1970, Winick grew up in Dix Hill, Long Island, New York, "a grumpy, quasi-budding artist kid," as he admitted to Bill Jensen in *Newsday.* Schoolwork was not his favorite pastime at Half Hollow Hills East High School; instead, young Winick took refuge in reading comics and then in creating his own. By the time he was 16, he was already a professional cartoonist, selling a single-paneled strip, "Nuts and Bolts," to Anton Publications, which published newspapers in a three-state northeastern region.

When he graduated from high school and moved on to college at the University of Michigan, Winick studied drawing and art. He also continued his "Nuts and Bolts" strip, now expanded into four panels and running five days a week in the college paper, the *Michigan Daily.* Shortly before graduation, Winick's strips were collected in a privately printed edition, *Watching the Spin-Cycle: The Nuts and Bolts,* which sold out its thousand copies in a matter of two weeks. Encouraged by such a response, Winick landed a development contract with a syndicator to develop the cartoon as a national strip, but after a year of work in Boston, the "bottom dropped out," as Winick reported on his website. "[T]he syndicate decided that they were not going to pursue 'Nuts and Bolts' for syndication and were terminating the development contract."

Out of work, Winick returned temporarily to his parents' home, commuting into New York City for occasional illustration jobs and working on a development deal with Nickelodeon on an animated series based on "Nuts and Bolts." This deal also fell through and when, in August of 1993, Winick saw a newspaper ad for auditions for MTV's *The Real World,* to be shot in San Francisco, he jumped at the chance. The six-month-long audition process included doing a video, filling out a 15-page application, having in-person interviews with the producers, and being followed around for a day by a film crew. Finally, Winick, along with six others, were chosen for the cast of the reality show in which these seven—strangers from all over the United

States—were put together in a house and filmed nonstop for half a year. One possible stumbling block came when producers asked Winick how he would feel about sharing quarters with another young man who was HIV positive. At that moment, Winick was forced to live up to his liberal PC convictions and confront the fears and ignorance they actually covered up. He told the producers there was no problem with that, but secretly he had his doubts, which he shared with friends. "Here I was, this weenie, open-minded, liberal New York Jew," Winick told Chad Jones in an *Oakland Tribune* interview. "I should have been fine with it, but I was really scared."

Winick and his fellow housemates gathered at a house on Lombard Street in San Francisco to be filmed cinema-verité style. The HIV-positive roommate turned out to be AIDS activist Pedro Zamora, a Cuban immigrant who had been diagnosed with AIDS as a teenager. Zamora wanted to be on the show to give a human face to the AIDS scourge, and he and Winick became fast friends. Together they and the others, including Asian-American medical student Pam Ling, confronted the day-to-day hassles of living together. During the filming of the show, Winick's cartoon strip, "Nuts and Bolts," was reprised in the local *San Francisco Examiner.*

Winick, who took the job on *The Real World* as a way to get free rent and live in San Francisco temporarily, quickly learned there was much more to the deal. He became known as the serious one of the group and the guy who could never get a date. This was his persona to an entire segment of Generation X viewers, the 20-something audience MTV was hoping to reach. After filming for six months in 1993, the show began airing in 1994 and became one of the most popular in the series, not least because of Zamora's medical condition. It was not long after the show went on the air that Zamora became ill from AIDS complications. Winick agreed to take over his speaking engagements until Zamora could get back on his feet, but the activist never did. In August of 1994, Zamora was put in the hospital and died the following November, shortly after the final episode of *The Real World III* appeared on television.

Following Zamora's death, Winick continued to lecture about his friend and about AIDS education and prevention. For about a year and a half he devoted most of his time to this cause. It was, Winick explained on his website, "the most fulfilling and difficult time in my life." By 1995 Winick needed to return to his cartooning career. He had, by this time, outgrown "Nuts and Bolts" and was ready to take on new challenges. Working as an illustrator, he began providing artwork for many titles in the "Complete Idiot's Guide" series, a collection of which was published as *Terminal Madness*. As a writer and illustrator, he worked on his first syndicated comic strip, "Frumpy the Clown," beginning in July of 1996. Stealing one of his favorite characters from "Nuts and Bolts," Winick gave the cynical clown a new home, with a suburban family mom, dad, children (Brad and Kim), and family dog. The children are ecstatic about their new member, Frumpy, but the parents, along with neighbors, wish only that he would go away. Winick depicts Frumpy and family embroiled in such quotidian tasks as getting the kids to school and fixing snacks, but all the while Frumpy attempts to enlighten the children about the dark truths lurking behind the bright lights of so-called reality, taking great delight in warping their young minds. Winick continued the strip for two years, with an initial syndication of 30 national papers. "Unfortunately," Winick noted on his website, "Frumpy ran into trouble." The clown's edginess ultimately cost readership in more family oriented newspapers, and eventually syndication dwindled to a trickle. Also, and more importantly, Winick found the daily grind of turning out a comic strip less creative than he had imagined. "I found daily comic strips to be limiting," he noted, "not just in length and size formats or language, but creatively. I just didn't find the strip fulfilling."

It was about this time that Winick began work on a graphic novel about his friendship with Zamora, a project that would last more than two years. Meanwhile, he also formed a relationship with ONI Press, and began work on a comic, "The Adventures of Barry Ween, Boy Genius." Barry is not your typical ten-year-old. Possessed of an IQ of 350, the youth delights in days spent on his own with the sitter heavily sedated, allowing him to work on his anti-terrorist equipment, or alternately build an atom smasher that fits under his bed. He gets into adventures with his pal Jeremy Ramirez, such as dealing with art thieves and time warps, repairing a stranded space ship of an alien on the run from intergalactic mobsters, and rescuing his buddy from the government. Popular with audiences already keen on the graphic format popularized by such works as *Maus* by Art Spiegelman, both "Barry Ween" and "Frumpy" were published in paperback collections by ONI Press. "Barry Ween" was optioned for development as an animated television series by Platinum Studios.

Throughout 1999 Winick continued work on his graphic novel *Pedro and Me*. Armistead Maupin, the San Francisco-based author of *Tales of the City*, saw an early version of the work and encouraged Win-

ick to push on and to be even more open and frank about his friendship with Zamora. Submitting the manuscript to his agent, Jill Kneerim, Winick was hopeful for early publication. But 30 publishers saw it, loved it, and failed to buy it. Then the manuscript was sent to editor Marc Aronson at Holt who was "very hands-off but provided lots of guidance," as Winick told Shannon Maughan in a *Publishers Weekly* interview. "He helped me work on the pacing, finding a moment here, a moment there, building a true beginning, middle and end." Eventually, through working with Aronson, Winick whittled down his manuscript to 180 book pages. It was also decided to target the book at a young adult audience, the population most at risk for contracting AIDS.

*Pedro and Me* tells the twin stories of both Winick and Zamora. One young man came from Cuba in the Mariel Boatlift of 1968 that saw the immigration of 125,000 refugees from Castro's Cuba. Still in his early teens, Zamora watches his mother die of skin cancer in Florida; at 17 he contracts the AIDS virus and soon thereafter becomes a major activist and AIDS educator. Meanwhile, Winick grows up safe and sound on Long Island, mowing lawns in the summer. As fellow cast members, Winick and Zamora grow to understand one another. Winick does not spare himself when he shows his own initial ignorance and fear of Zamora's disease, nor does he replay the events of *The Real World* house; rather he focuses on the friendship and what he learned from his brief time with Zamora. The story continues after the filming of *The Real World* is over, as Zamora becomes ill, and both Winick and Ling take time out from their busy lives to be with him. It ends with the emotional deathbed scene with a gathering of friends.

Reviewers and critics had high praise for Winick's book and its message. Writing in the *Advocate*, a contributor called *Pedro and Me* a "touching remembrance" and a "cathartic experience," while a reviewer for *Publishers Weekly* described the graphic novel as "powerful and captivating," and felt that it struck "just the right balance of cool and forthrightness to attract a broad cross section of teens, twenty-somethings, and beyond." The same writer noted the "deceptively simple" black and white comic-strip art that contains a "full spectrum of emotion," concluding that Winick's book was an "innovative and accessible approach" to a very difficult subject. *Booklist* contributor Stephanie Zvirin lauded the cartoonist's illustrations, noting that "facial expressions ... count most" in a book filled with "great tenderness and a keen sense of loss." In a review for *School Library Journal*, Francisca Goldsmith commented, "This is an important book for teens and the adults who care about them. Winick handles his topics with both sensitivity and a thoroughness that rarely coexist so seamlessly." *Horn Book*'s Peter D. Sieruta concluded, "In this warm and ultimately life-affirming remembrance, Winick gives the world a second chance to know Pedro and his message."

Reader response was equally positive, and Winick soon found he was once again a sought-after speaker at schools. "My hope is that people learn from Pedro the way I did," he noted in an interview for the *Advocate*, "that they have their stereotypes broken and learn about AIDS and the people who live with it—and that they are empowered by his accomplishments. Lastly, I hope they remember my friend. That's why I wrote and illustrated this in the first place."

Winick eventually moved beyond the bounds of the world he first confronted in *The Real World*. While he hoped never to forget the message Zamora gave the world about AIDS and people with AIDS, he had other creative plans in the works, including another graphic novel. In March of 2000, Winick proposed to Ling, his girlfriend of six years, by dressing up in a gorilla suit and holding a clipboard. The clipboard held a marriage proposal with a choice of two cartoon sketches of Winick, one happy for "yes" and one sad for "no"; Ling chose happy Judd. On August 26, 2001, the couple married at San Francisco's Westin St. Francis hotel in a ceremony performed by one of their friends.

Winick went on to write for many different comic book series, one of which was titled *Exiles*. The series was "an unabashed hybrid of television's time-traveling *Quantum Leap* and dimension-spanning *Sliders,* mixed in with the mythology of the X-Men," Bill Radford explained in the Knight Ridder/Tribune News Service. The heroes of the series are mutants pulled from alternate realities to work together to fix glitches in the chain of time. By fixing the problems, they save their own pasts. Starting in 2001, Winick also wrote for DC Comics' "Green Lantern" series, taking the story line in new directions, including introducing an HIV-positive character. By May of 2005, he had written many issues for the series, while also writing *Batman: As the Crow Flies, Green Arrow, The Outsiders,* another book of Barry Ween's adventures, and other projects. One of those other projects was a show for the Cartoon Network called *The Life and Times of Juniper Lee,* scheduled to debut in February of 2005. The eleven-year-old girl of the title is secretly a superhero crime fighter. According to *Children's Business*, "On any given day, she may be forced to bail on her best pal's birthday bash to corral a crew of unruly giant leprechauns or discipline a gang of troublemaking gnomes." Winick was a writer and executive producer for the cartoon.

In his talks with students, Winick encourages other budding cartoonists. "Develop a style," he tells cartoonist hopefuls on his website. "It's not necessary to be a jack of all trades. And get published! Any little paper that'll have you, or print them up yourself and give them away in comic stores. I don't believe in luck. Success comes when opportunity meets preparation."

## Selected writings

### Self-illustrated works

*Terminal Madness: The Complete Idiot's Guide Computer Cartoon Collection,* Que (Indianapolis, IN), 1997.
*The Adventures of Barry Ween, Boy Genius,* ONI Press (Portland, OR), 1999.
*The Adventures of Barry Ween, Boy Genius, 2.0,* ONI Press (Portland, OR), 2000.
*Pedro and Me: Friendship, Loss, and What I Learned,* Holt (New York, NY), 2000.
*Frumpy the Clown: Freaking out the Neighbors,* ONI Press (Portland, OR), 2001.
*Frumpy the Clown: The Fat Lady Sings,* ONI Press (Portland, OR), 2001.
*The Adventures of Barry Ween, Boy Genius, 3.0,* ONI Press (Portland, OR), 2001.
*The Adventures of Barry Ween, Boy Genius, Gorilla Warfare,* ONI Press (Portland, OR), 2002.

### Storyline writer

*Road Trip,* Oni Press, 1998.
*Green Lantern: New Journey,* Old Path, DC Comics, 2001.
*Exiles: Down the Rabbit Hole,* Marvel Comics, 2002.
*Green Lantern: Circle of Fire,* DC Comics, 2002.
*Exiles: A World Apart,* Marvel Comics, 2002.
*Star Wars: A Valentine Story,* Dark Horse Comics, 2003.
*Green Lantern: The Power of Ion,* DC Comics, 2003.
*Exiles: Out of Time,* Marvel Comics, 2003.
*Green Lantern: Brother's Keeper,* DC Comics, 2003.
*Exiles: Legacy,* Marvel Comics, 2003.
*Caper,* DC Comics, 2003.
*Blood and Water,* DC Comics, 2004.
*Outsiders: Looking for Trouble,* DC Comics, 2004.
*Exiles: Fantastic Voyage,* Marvel Comics, 2004.
*Green Arrow: Straight Shooter,* DC Comics, 2004.
*Teen Titans/Young Justice: Graduation Day,* DC Comics, 2004.
*Green Lantern: Passing the Torch,* DC Comics, 2004.
*Batman: As the Crow Flies,* DC Comics, 2004.
*Outsiders: Sum of All Evil,* DC Comics, 2004.
*Green Arrow: City Walls,* DC Comics, 2005.

## Sources

### Periodicals

*Advocate,* February 1, 2000, p. 2; September 12, 2000, p. 61.

*Billboard,* September 7, 1996, p. 100.

*Booklist,* September 15, 2000, p. 230; December 1, 2000, p. 693.

*Boston Herald,* September 5, 2000.

*Children's Business,* June/July 2004, p. 19.

*Entertainment Weekly,* July 23, 2003, p. 79; December 19, 2003.

*Horn Book,* November-December, 2000, pp. 775-76.

*InStyle,* January 15, 2002, p. 250.

Knight Ridder/Tribune News Service, August 2, 2001.

*Library Journal,* November 1, 2003, p. 63.

*Newsday,* April 16, 2000.

*Oakland Tribune,* September 6, 2000.

*Publishers Weekly,* September 11, 2000, p. 92; September 18, 2000, p. 37.

*Ross Reports Television & Film,* November 2004, p. 11.

*Sacramento Bee,* August 31, 2000.

*San Francisco Chronicle,* September 6, 2000.

*School Library Journal,* October 2000, p. 192.

*TV Guide,* July 29, 2000.

*USA Today,* September 18, 2000.

*Washington Times,* January 11, 2003, p. B2.

### Online

"The HIV-positive superhero sidekick," CNN.com, http://www.cnn.com (March 4, 2005).

# Marissa Jaret Winokur

## Actress

**B**orn February 2, 1973, in New York, NY; daughter of Michael (an architect) and Maxine (a teacher) Winokur. *Education:* Studied at the American Musical and Dramatic Academy.

**Addresses:** *Agent*—Acme Talent & Literary Agency, 6310 San Vincent Blvd., #520, Los Angeles, CA 90048.

## Career

**A**ctress on stage, including: *Grease,* touring company, 1994, New York production, 1995-98; *Hairspray,* New York, NY, 2002. Film appearances include: *Never Been Kissed,* 1999; *American Beauty,* 1999; *Scary Movie,* 2000; *Sleep Easy, Hutch Rimes,* 2000; *On Edge,* 2001; *Now You Know,* 2002. Television appearances include: *The Steve Harvey Show,* 1998; *Malibu, CA,* 1998; *Honey, I Shrunk the Kids: The TV Show,* 1999; *Felicity,* 1999; *Dharma & Greg,* 1999, 2000; *Get Real,* 2000; *Chicken Soup for the Soul,* 2000; *Moesha,* 2000; *Curb Your Enthusiasm,* 2000; *Just Shoot Me!,* 2000; *Nikki,* 2001; *The Ellen Show,* 2001; *Boston Public,* 2001; *Beautiful Girl* (movie; also producer), 2003.

**Awards:** Best actress in a musical, Antoinette Perry (Tony) Awards, American Theater Wing, for *Hairspray,* 2003; Theatre World award for best Broadway debut newcomer, for *Hairspray,* 2003.

## Sidelights

**M**arissa Jaret Winokur triumphed on Broadway in 2002 as the star of the new musical version of *Hairspray.* Winokur had been one of the first to

*AP/Wide World Photos*

audition for the role of zaftig but spirited teenager Tracy Turnblad in the stage version of the cult-classic 1988 movie, and spent two years preparing for it with voice and dance lessons. On opening night, she said in a *People* interview with Samantha Miller, "it literally took all of my energy not to burst out crying. It was the day I'd been waiting for my entire life."

Winokur had already spent much of her life dreaming of just such a Broadway debut. Born in 1973, she was the last of four children in her family, and grew up in Bedford Village, a suburb of New York City. She was enchanted by the first show she ever saw, a dinner theater production of *Meet Me in St. Louis,* which came at the impressionable age of eight. As she told Miller in *People,* "I retained the entire show. We had a porch in the backyard and I would dance around singing to the trees."

The love of theater ran deep in Winokur's family: her paternal grandfather had been a well-known Broadway accountant, while her father, an architect, would occasionally let her leave school for the day to catch a Broadway matinee in the city with him; sometimes they even stayed around and found tickets for an evening show. Once, while on a legitimate school field trip from Fox Lane High School to see Gregory Hines in *Sophisticated Ladies,* Winokur was late getting back to the bus after waiting at the stage door to meet Hines, and earned some time in detention for it.

Winokur always planned on a career in show business, though she lacked the requisite leggy-dancer physique for a musical-theater star. Plump for much of her life, she was never daunted by the extra pounds, and had been a cheerleader and captain of her soccer team in high school. After graduating from Fox Lane, she spent two years at the American Musical and Dramatic Academy in New York City, which she has hinted in one interview was a disappointing experience, and eventually landed in the touring company of *Grease* in 1994. A year later, she was given the role of Jan in the Broadway production, and held it until the show closed in 1998.

Winokur had become good friends with Lucy Lawless, one of a long line of *Grease* stage veterans, and went to Los Angeles, California, for the *Xena, Warrior Princess*'s wedding. She decided to stay for a time and audition for a few film roles, and was quickly cast in a small part in the 1999 Drew Barrymore movie *Never Been Kissed.* She also played Kevin Spacey's fast-food co-worker in the Oscar-winning *American Beauty* that same year, delivering the memorable "You are so busted" line to Annette Bening's character at the drive-through window. She also played the girl who gets stuck in a dog door in *Scary Movie.*

Winokur also did some television episodes of *The Steve Harvey Show, Felicity, Dharma & Greg,* and *Curb Your Enthusiasm.* Broadway still beckoned, however, and when she learned that there was going to be a stage version of the John Waters film *Hairspray,* she was one of the first to audition for the role that had catapulted another heavy-set actress, Ricki Lake, to stardom back in 1988. "They kept trying to get me to go away," she told *Back Stage West*'s Les Spindle about that first audition, "but I wouldn't.... Everyone in the country who weighed more than 100 pounds was coming to audition. I was cast in the workshops, which I did for 2 1/2 years, and finally they let me keep the role."

*Hairspray*'s plot revolves around teenage Tracy and her determination to appear on a local Top-40 dance show in early 1960s Baltimore. When she auditions for a spot, the other kids tease her, but she wins it anyway, and winds up helping usher the local show into the civil-rights era. Both the film and stage version featured massive hairdos, and one of Waters's

trademark gender-bending twists: Tracy's mother is played by a man in drag. Winokur trained heavily for the part, which required singing, dancing, and being onstage in nearly every scene: she took voice lessons, worked with a choreographer, and built up her stamina by running on a treadmill while singing. She wowed audiences at *Hairspray*'s brief trial run in Seattle, Washington, and did the same when it opened in August of 2002 at Broadway's Neil Simon Theater after record-setting advance ticket sales.

Critical plaudits for Broadway's newest star were enthusiastic. "Plucky, adorable, and warmer than an August day in New York, she takes the part played in the movie by Ricki Lake and makes her utterly winning," declared *Newsweek* reviewer Marc Peyser, while the *New York Times* theater critic, Ben Brantley, commended both Broadway veteran Harvey Fierstein as Edna, Tracy's mother, and Winokur, the newcomer. "Her Tracy is less visibly assured, more wistful than Ricki Lake's was in the film version, and this gives the audience a firmer grasp of empathy," wrote Brantley. "Although she sounds more like Brenda Lee than she does the frog-voiced Mr. Fierstein, Tracy is unmistakably her mother's daughter. That's a compliment."

*Hairspray* went on to win eight Antoinette Perry Awards, also known as "Tonys," for the 2002-2003 Broadway season. At the ceremony in June of 2003, it won for best musical, and Winokur nabbed the Tony for best actress in a musical. Later in 2003, she appeared in a made-for-television movie, *Beautiful Girl,* about an overweight young woman determined to win a beauty pageant's first prize. She has said that she has consciously tried to avoid being typecast because of her size. "I don't take jobs that are about the poor, pathetic fat girl," she told *New York Times* journalist Robin Pogrebin. "I think that's really important. Fortunately my agent agrees with me."

## Sources

### Books

*Contemporary Theatre, Film and Television,* vol. 30, Gale Group, 2000.

### Periodicals

*American Theatre,* July-August 2003, pp. 11-12.
*Back Stage West,* July 22, 2004, p. 10.
*Daily Variety,* August 21, 2003, p. 1.
*Dance,* December 2003, p. S20.

*Entertainment Weekly,* August 23, 2002, p. 134.
*Newsweek,* August 26, 2002, p. 52.
*New York Daily News,* August 14, 2002.
*New York Times,* August 16, 2002; August 21, 2002,
   p. E1.

*People,* September 9, 2002, p. 75.
*Time,* August 26, 2002, p. 63.

—*Carol Brennan*

# Tobias Wolff

AP/Wide World Photos

## Author and professor

**B**orn Tobias Jonathan Ansell-Wolff III, June 19, 1945, in Birmingham, AL; son of Arthur (an aeronautical engineer) and Rosemary (Loftus) Wolff; married Catherine Dolores Spohn (a clinical social worker), 1975; children: Michael, Patrick, Mary Elizabeth. *Education:* Oxford University, B.A. (with first class honors), 1972, M.A., 1975; Stanford University, M.A., 1978.

**Addresses:** *Agent*—Amanda Urban, International Creative Management, 40 West 57th St., New York, NY 10019. *Office*—Department of English, Stanford University, Stanford, CA 94305-2087.

## Career

**J**ones Lecturer in Creative Writing, Stanford University, Stanford, CA, 1975-78; Peck Professor of English, Syracuse University, Syracuse, NY, 1980-97; professor of English and Creative Writing, Stanford University, Stanford, CA, 1997—. Member of faculty at Goddard College, Plainfield, VT, and Arizona State University, Tempe. Former reporter for *Washington Post. Military service*—U.S. Army, 1964-68 (Special Forces, 1965-67); served in Vietnam; became first lieutenant.

**Member:** PEN, Associated Writing Programs.

**Awards:** Wallace Stegner fellowship in creative writing, 1975-76; National Endowment for the Arts fellowship in creative writing, 1978; Mary Roberts Rinehart grant, 1979; O. Henry short story prize, 1980; Arizona Council on the Arts and Humanities fellowship in creative writing, 1980; O. Henry short story prize, 1981; Guggenheim fellowship, 1982; St. Lawrence Award for Fiction, for *In the Garden of the North American Martyrs,* 1982; O. Henry short story prize, 1985; National Endowment for the Arts fellowship in creative writing, 1985; PEN/Faulkner Award for Fiction, for *The Barracks Thief,* 1985; Rea Award for short story, 1989; *Los Angeles Times* Book Prize for biography, for *This Boy's Life: A Memoir,* 1989; Ambassador Book Award of the English-speaking Union, for *This Boy's Life: A Memoir,* 1989; Whiting Foundation Award, 1990; Lila Wallace-*Reader's Digest* Award, 1993; Lyndhurst Foundation Award, 1994; Esquire-Volvo-Waterstone's Prize for Nonfiction (England), for *In Pharaoh's Army: Memories of the Lost War,* 1994.

## Sidelights

**A**s enthralled critics have so often observed, American author Tobias Wolff is a master storyteller. His short stories, novels, and memoirs have earned him an assortment of sought-after fellowships and grants, three O. Henry short story prizes, and the prestigious PEN/Faulkner Award for Fiction.

Much of Wolff's fiction is built from reworked recollections, and his memoirs—supposedly works of nonfiction—are embellished or edited versions of his personal history. "All my stories are in one way or another autobiographical," Wolff explained to *Contemporary Authors'* Jean W. Ross. "Sometimes they're autobiographical in the actual events which they describe, sometimes more in their depiction of a particular character. In fact, you could say that all of my characters are reflections of myself."

Wolff tries to treat his characters honestly once he has developed them. He revealed to Francine Prose in the *New York Times Magazine* that he felt an "affinity" for Raymond Carver's "standards of honesty and exactness," and his refusal "to destroy his characters with irony that proved his own virtue." Accordingly, with sparse prose, Wolff dwells on realistic, telling moments that represent or challenge the lives of his own characters. As often as not, they are left in the abyss of the daily existence in which they were introduced; they are not allowed happy endings or forced to suffer terrible, moral-proving consequences. Wolff is thus described as a realist and minimalist.

As Wolff demonstrates in his memoir, *This Boy's Life,* his childhood was difficult, but ultimately rewarding. His mother, Rosemary Loftus, was the daughter of a navy man who beat her every day. Although she provided security for Wolff, she also accepted a number of violent, unstable, or otherwise destructive men into her life. Tobias Wolff's father, Arthur Samuels Wolff, was a charming and talented liar who concocted a false history for himself and settled down with Loftus in Connecticut.

The *New York Times Magazine*'s Prose noted that Arthur Wolff was a con man who, while "charming, charismatic, endlessly inventive," was also "a forger, a passer of bad checks, a car thief, a deadbeat extraordinaire, a compulsive spender, a dandy, and a heavy drinker." His deceptions were numerous. Arthur Wolff was the son of a Jewish doctor, but he presented himself as an Episcopalian. Although he had been expelled from various boarding schools, he convinced people that he had degrees from Yale and Oxford. Wolff had also been rejected from the military because of his dental record, but he claimed he had been a fighter pilot for the Royal Air Force. "Some of Arthur Wolff's schemes worked astonishingly well," commented Prose. "Using faked credentials, he fast-talked himself into a job as an aeronautical engineer and became a top-ranking executive in the booming postwar aviation industry." Eventually, though, his slippery maneuvering resulted in multiple arrests, three jail terms, and two ruined marriages.

The elder Wolff's storytelling talents influenced Tobias. In fact, as he told *Contemporary Authors'* Ross, "Both my father and my mother were great raconteurs, and my brother is also a wonderful storyteller. It's always been the most natural kind of thing for me to do." Wolff began to write stories when he was just six years old. "I don't know exactly at what time the idea hardened in me to become a writer, but I certainly never wanted to be anything else." Rosemary left Arthur Wolff when Toby, as Tobias was called, was just five years old. Geoffrey, the couple's elder son, stayed with his father on the East Coast. Rosemary and Toby made their way to Florida, where they lived with her boyfriend, Roy. When Roy's abuse became overwhelming, Rosemary and Toby fled to Utah, where Rosemary thought that she could get rich picking up uranium. Instead, Rosemary found an office job, and her boyfriend from Florida found her. They lived together until he proposed marriage, and then she decided to flee from him once again, this time to Phoenix, Arizona. But instead of waiting for the Phoenix bus at the station, she and Toby took the bus that came before it. That bus deposited the two of them in Seattle, Washington.

After a time in Seattle, where Wolff renamed himself Jack (in honor of novelist Jack London) and made trouble at school, Rosemary married Dwight, a mechanic and house painter with three children of his own. They moved to the small town of Chinook, Washington, where Wolff was determined to work harder in school and create an entirely new reputation. Dwight's attitude and behavior, however, precluded that possibility. As Richard Eder of *Los Angeles Times Book Review* pointed out, Dwight treated Tobias "as a perpetual interloper and rival."

Dwight tormented and humiliated Wolff with continuous lectures and constant harassment. "Tobias' stepfather assigned him a battery of tedious jobs," related the *New York Times Magazine*'s Prose, "stole Tobias' paper-route earnings, [and] traded Tobias' beloved rifle for an ugly, incontinent, gun-shy hunting dog." When Wolff joined the Boy Scouts, Dwight volunteered as an assistant scoutmaster and thus extended his influence beyond his home. Incredibly, as Wolff wrote in *This Boy's Life,* Dwight once painted the interior of their entire house, including the Christmas tree and the piano, white.

It is in this environment, wrote Joel Conarroe in the *New York Times Book Review,* that Wolff "gets an informal education in humiliation, betrayal, and injustice, and learns how to fight, cheat, steal, gamble and, especially, lie." Life at home with Dwight and at Concrete High School became increasingly unbearable. Finally, at the age of 16, Wolff contacted his brother, Geoffrey, who had not even known where Wolff and his mother had been living. Geoffrey began to write to his younger brother, and Arthur Wolff invited his younger son to visit him in La Jolla, California. The day after Tobias arrived, Wolff left for a trip to Las Vegas with his girlfriend, and left Tobias alone. Later, when Tobias's brother Geoffrey arrived, Arthur had a serious nervous breakdown and was hospitalized. Tobias and Geoffrey used the time to get acquainted.

"Geoffrey was the first person I'd ever met for whom books were the only way in which you could in good conscience spend your life. I already had the notion that I wanted to be a writer, but I'd never been with people to whom books mattered, people who had a sense that this was something a sane person would want to be," Wolff told Prose in the *New York Times Magazine*. In fact, Geoffrey Wolff is an accomplished novelist as well.

Geoffrey had been to Choate and was in school at Princeton. Tobias wanted those things for himself, too, but he knew that his poor grades would not help his cause. Aware that he needed an outstanding academic record to gain acceptance to top schools, he invented one. Wolff forged his transcript and improvised enthusiastic letters of recommendation on school stationary. Noted Wolff in *This Boy's Life,* "I wrote ... in the words my teachers would have used if they had known me as I knew myself.... And on the boy who lived in their letters, the splendid phantom who carried all my hopes, it seems to me I saw, at last, my own face." Wolff's fabricated history was convincing enough to get him a scholarship to the prestigious Hill School, far from his horrible stepfather in Washington. Unfortunately, Wolff's education had not prepared for him for the rigors of scholarship at the private institution, and he was eventually expelled.

Instead of finishing high school, Wolff eventually joined the army. As he explains in his book *In Pharaoh's Army,* he became a member of the Special Forces, learned Vietnamese, and was sent to Vietnam as an adviser. After serving in the Vietnam War, he visited England. Wolff set his sights on attending Oxford University. He managed to pass the entrance tests after months of study, and, fascinated with his courses, became a serious student. He graduated with a first class honors degree and stayed at Oxford to pursue a master's degree. After a short stint working as a *Washington Post* reporter, Wolff settled in California. He supported himself with odd jobs and concentrated his efforts on his writing. Wolff's talents were recognized with a Wal-

lace Stegner Fellowship, which allowed him to write in residence at Stanford. He eventually earned another master's degree at that university.

Wolff published *Ugly Rumours* in 1975, then sold several stories to various magazines and journals. Perhaps the most notable of these stories was "Smokers," published in *Atlantic*. In 1981 he unveiled *In the Garden of the North American Martyrs.* This collection of 12 stories was received with praise and enthusiasm by critics. The characters in these collections, from a boy who lies about his family at school to a shy professor who finally manages to speak her mind, are presented within the contexts of the daily lives they have created for themselves. As Le Anne Schreiber in the *New York Times Book Review* remarked, Wolff's range in *In the Garden of the North American Martyrs* "extends from fastidious realism to the grotesque and the lyrical." She congratulated Wolff on his ability to allow his characters "scenes of flamboyant madness as well as quiet desperation."

Wolff's 1984 book *The Barracks Thief* earned the writer more praise from critics and readers alike, and was recognized as the best work of fiction with the PEN/Faulkner Award in 1985. Although, as Walter Kendrick in the *New York Times Book Review* pointed out, the character of Philip Bishop "plays a minor role in the events that give" the story its title, *The Barracks Thief* is "principally" Bishop's story. The work begins by describing Bishop's childhood, while the conclusion discusses how that childhood led to Bishop's decision to become a soldier. The core of the novella features Bishop's haunting memory of a reckless moment in his past.

The histories of Bishop, Lewis, and Hubbard, three young paratroopers, merge forever in Bishop's mind on the day in 1967 when they are ordered to guard an ammunition dump at Fort Bragg. The three soldiers perversely consider allowing a forest fire to reach the dump and explode it. Lewis later becomes a thief and is thrown out of the army, while Hubbard deserts the force. Bishop, though, goes on to become a "conscientious man, a responsible man, maybe even what you'd call a good man ... a careful man, addicted to comfort, with an eye for the safe course.... I would never do what we did that day at the ammunition dump, threatening people with rifles, nearly getting ourselves blown to pieces for the hell of it."

In the *New York Times Book Review*, Kendrick explained that the characters in *The Barracks Thief* "are portrayed with clear-eyed generosity" and that

Wolff leaves it up to his readers to decide whether it is best to live and die in "safe conventionality" or recklessness. *Times Literary Supplement* reviewer Linda Taylor observed that readers may want to take in the book "all at once—the ingenuousness of the narration and the vulnerability of the characters are disarmingly seductive."

Wolff's next book was 1985's *Back in the World.* The title alludes to the shared daydreams of American soldiers in Vietnam who told each other about what they would do when they returned home, known as "back in the world." *Back in the World,* a collection of ten short stories, presents an interpretation of what that world is like for many people. In the words of *New York Times Book Review* contributor Russell Banks, *Back in the World* reveals "the inner lives of middle-class loners in the Sun Belt ... lapsed materialists in a material world trying to ignite a spiritual flame despite being cut off from all traditional sources of the spirit—family, church, art, even politics."

*This Boy's Life: A Memoir,* released in 1989, was an autobiographical book that describes, according to Eder, how Wolff "masked and masqueraded his way through a childhood and adolescence that might otherwise have unhinged him." The story begins in 1955 with the flight of Tobias and his mother from Florida and concludes soon after his concoction of a glowing school record has won him admission to the Hill School.

According to *Publishers Weekly,* Wolff "characterizes the crew of grown-up losers with damning objectivity." Eder commented that *This Boy's Life* "is a desperate story. The desperation is conveyed in a narration that is chilly and dispassionate on the whole, vivid in detail, and enlivened by disconcerting comedy." *Times Literary Supplement* critic John Clute reminded readers that *This Boy's Life* is a story about lying, and implied that it demonstrates the benefits of stretching the truth in writing fiction. It was nominated for a National Book Critics Circle Award in 1989. The book was made into the film *This Boy's Life* in 1993, and starred Robert De Niro as Wolff's stepfather, Ellen Barkin as Wolff's mother, and Leonardo DiCaprio playing Wolff as a teenager.

The 1994 book *In Pharaoh's Army: Memories of the Lost War* was a long-awaited account of Wolff's memories of his year in Vietnam. Wolff told Ron Fletcher of *Bloomsbury Review* that he hadn't intended to write another memoir after he finished *This Boy's Life,* but a story he wrote about Vietnam was a catalyst for the generation of the memoir. He explained that to "bring out" such memories "is, in some ways, to disarm" them, and "with any luck you understand the experience better." The first version of the manuscript was a long one, and Wolff found it necessary to shorten it. "A lot of writing is recognizing what should be mentioned and what should go unsaid," he told Fletcher.

*In Pharaoh's Army* describes the author's training for the special forces and his experiences as an army adviser to a Vietnamese division in the Mekong Delta. His tour of duty is neither glorious nor exciting. While his life is threatened on occasion, he spends most of his time in a muddy village where he performs mundane jobs (like arranging the trade of a rifle for a color television for a superior officer). Wolff does not excel as a soldier. When he is ordered to lead a company on a jump, he misses the target by five miles. *Publisher's Weekly* noted that the book "records his sense of futility and growing disillusionment with the war." The book details the author's decision to leave the army and depart for San Francisco. Later, at Oxford University, his study of English literature allows him to regain his sense of direction.

Although *In Pharaoh's Army* focuses on Wolff's year as a soldier in Vietnam and its aftermath, flashbacks recall other memories and explore other experiences, including those with his father. He also remembers the year he spent in Washington, D.C., studying Vietnamese and conducting a romance (which ultimately failed) with a Russian aristocrat. *Publishers Weekly* praised *In Pharaoh's Army* and the "great candor" with which he "charts ... his evolution as a human being and a writer." The year of its release, the book was nominated for the National Book Award and received England's Esquire-Volvo-Waterstone's Prize for Nonfiction. In 1995, it was nominated for a *Los Angeles Times* Book Award.

Wolff's next book, 1996's *The Night in Question,* was a collection of 14 short stories in which the characters search for identities beneath their everyday existences. According to Jay Parini in the *New York Times Book Review,* Wolff's characters want to find "something authentic, something they can unmistakably call their own." Moral judgment is sometimes compromised in these tales. In 2003, Wolff's first full-length novel, *Old School,* was published. In the book, students at a New England boys' boarding school in the 1960s submit a piece of writing to win a private meeting with a famous author. The narrator of the novel strives to win the contest so he can meet with Ernest Hemingway. "His hunger to meet Hemingway at any cost leads to a series of shattering lessons that have as much to do with life as with literature—revelations about honesty and deception, identity and loyalty, betrayal and forgiveness, and about the crucial difference between fiction and falsehood," explained Francine Prose in *People.* The novel was nominated for a National Book Critics Circle Award for fiction in 2003, and both a *Los Angeles Times* Book Award and a PEN/Faulkner Award for Fiction in 2004.

In addition to writing his own works, Wolff has edited several short story collections featuring the work of other writers. Wolff also serves as a professor of English and creative writing at Stanford University. Working as a teacher has its advantages, Wolff told Ross in *Contemporary Authors.* "I still consider myself lucky to be in a profession where I am given a lot of time to write—a lot more than I would be in any other profession—and not only that, but where people care about writing and give you room to breathe if you're a writer; where you're with other people for whom writing is the most important thing."

Wolff also spends months writing and revising each story. He explained his need to write and rewrite in his *Contemporary Authors* interview with Ross. "Obviously by the time I come to write the last draft I know where every word is going to go, and every comma. It's in my mind from beginning to end, but there have been lots of surprises along the way that I hope the reader will feel even if I don't feel them when I'm writing the last draft."

## Selected writings

*Ugly Rumours,* Allen & Unwin (London), 1975.

*In the Garden of the North American Martyrs* (short stories), Ecco Press (New York, NY), 1981, published as *Hunters in the Snow* (also see below), J. Cape (London), 1982.

(Editor) *Matters of Life and Death: New American Stories,* Wampeter (Green Harbor, ME), 1982.

*The Barracks Thief* (novella; also see below), Ecco Press, 1984, published as *The Barracks Thief and Other Stories,* Bantam (New York, NY), 1984.

*Back in the World* (short stories; also see below), Houghton (Boston), 1985.

"The Other Miller," *The Best American Short Stories,* edited by Ann Beattie and Shannon Ravenel, Houghton, 1987.

(Editor) *A Doctor's Visit: The Short Stories of Anton Chekhov,* Bantam, 1987.

*The Stories of Tobias Wolff* (contains *Hunters in the Snow, Back in the World,* and *The Barracks Thief*), Picador (London), 1988.

"Smorgasbord," *The Best American Short Stories,* edited by Mark Helprin and Ravenel, Houghton, 1988.

*This Boy's Life: A Memoir,* Atlantic Monthly Press (New York, NY), 1989.

"Migrane," *Antaeus,* spring-autumn 1990.

"Sanity," *Atlantic,* December 1990.

(Editor) *The Picador Book of Contemporary American Stories,* Picador, 1993.

(Editor and author of introduction) *The Vintage Book of Contemporary American Short Stories,* Random House (New York, NY), 1994.

*In Pharaoh's Army: Memories of the Lost War* (memoir), Knopf (New York, NY), 1994.

(Editor) *Best American Short Stories,* Houghton, 1994.

*The Night in Question: Stories,* Knopf, 1996.

(Editor and author of introduction) *Writers Harvest 3,* Dell (New York, NY), 2000.

*Old School* (novel), Knopf, 2003.

Contributor to periodicals, including the *Atlantic, New Yorker, Granta, Story, Esquire,* and *Antaeus.*

## Sources

### Books

*Contemporary Authors,* vol. 117, Gale, 1986, pp. 494-98.

Hannah, James, *Tobias Wolff: A Study of the Short Fiction,* Twayne (Boston), 1996.

Wolff, Tobias, *The Barracks Thief,* Ecco Press, 1984.

Wolff, Tobias, *This Boy's Life: A Memoir,* Atlantic Monthly, 1989.

### Periodicals

*Bloomsbury Review,* March/April, 1995, p. 13, p. 16.

*Entertainment Weekly,* November 7, 2003, p. 38; November 21, 2003, p. 90.

*Los Angeles Times Book Review,* January 8, 1989, p. 3, p. 6.

*New York Times Book Review,* November 15, 1981; June 2, 1985, p. 42; October 20, 1985, p. 9; January 15, 1989, p. 1, p. 28; November 3, 1996.

*New York Times Magazine,* February 5, 1989, pp. 22-28.

*People,* April 26, 1993, p. 13; January 12, 2004, p. 47.

*Publishers Weekly,* December 9, 1988, p. 50; August 29, 1994, p. 55; October 13, 2003, p. 57.

*School Library Journal,* April 2004, p. 182.

*Times Literary Supplement,* November 6-12, 1987, p. 1227; May 12-18, 1989, p. 508.

### Online

"Talking with Tobias Wolff," Continuum, http://www.alumni.utah.edu/continuum/summer98/finally.html (September 29, 2004).

"Tobias Wolff," *Salon.com,* http://archive.salon.com/dec96/interview961216.html (September 29, 2004).

"Tobias Wolff," Stanford Today, http://www.stanford.edu/dept/news/stanfordtoday/ed/9809/9809fea101.shtml (September 29, 2004).

"Wolff at the door," *Guardian Unlimited,* http://books.guardian.co.uk/departments/generalfiction/story/0,6000,1130428,00.html (September 29, 2004).

# Wu Yi

**Vice-Premier of the State Council and Minister of Public Health for China**

**B**orn in November of 1938, in Wuhan, in the Hubei Province, China. *Education:* Attended Beijing National Defense Department of the Northwest Polytechnic Institute; Petroleum Institute, petroleum engineering degree, 1962.

**Addresses:** *Office*—Ministry of Health, No. 1 Xizhimen Nanlu, Beijing 100044; phone: (86-10) 6879-2114. *Office*—State Council, No. 2 Fuyoujie, Zhongnanhai, Beijing, 100017.

## Career

**T**echnician, staff member of political department, Lanzhou Oil Refinery, 1962-65; technician, Production and Technology Department of the Ministry of Petroleum Industry, 1965-67; technician, deputy chief, and chief of technology section, deputy chief engineer, and deputy director, Beijing Dongfanghong Refinery, 1967-83; deputy general manager, Party secretary, Yanshan Petrochemical Corporation, 1983-88; vice-mayor of Beijing, 1988-91; vice-minister of Foreign Economic Relations and Trade, deputy secretary of Leading Party Members' Group, 1991-93; named vice-minister of Foreign Trade and Economic Cooperation, 1991; named minister of Foreign Trade and Economic Cooperation, 1993; elected president of the China Association of Foreign-Funded Enterprises; named secretary of Leading Party Members' Group, 1993-98; alternate member of Political Bureau of CCP Central Committee, 1997-98; alternate member of Political Bureau of CCP Central Committee, State Councilor,

*Molly Riley/Reuters/Landov*

member of Leading Party Members' Group of State Council, 1998-2002; named vice-premier of the State Council and minister of Public Health, 2003.

**Awards:** Ranked second most powerful woman in the world, *Forbes*; one of the top 50 most influential people in intellectual property, *Managing Intellectual Property*, 2004.

## Sidelights

**W**u Yi (pronounced Woo Yee), a longtime public servant in China, has earned the reputation as China's Iron Lady. The name recalls the moniker given to Britain's Prime Minister Margaret Thatcher, who was known for her political influence and forceful nature. Wu has held successively higher positions within China's communist party. As minister of Foreign Trade and Economic Cooperation she negotiated with the United States on such topics as copyright protection, trade, and investment agreements. Her tough yet flexible stance in negotiations has earned her respect inside and outside China.

In 1998, Madame Wu, as she is often called, became the most powerful woman in government when she was promoted to the position of state councilor.

There are only five state councilors, which is a position that ranks just below that of vice premier—the highest position in government. In this role, she worked to promote China and gain membership into the World Trade Organization, a global trade agreement organization established in 1995. While she made great inroads into international negotiations, Wu also worked diligently to promote development within China, especially within the interior. Her goals were to grow the high tech industry while also attracting international investments. On the philanthropic front, Wu worked to develop plans that would improve living conditions for women and children in the most impoverished areas of China. In 2003, Wu was named health minister, a position for which she was well prepared. Her candidness in the face of the international health crisis created by Severe Acute Respiratory Syndrome (SARS) earned her the respect of health officials worldwide.

Wu was born in November of 1938, in Wuhan, in the Hubei Province of China. Her family was well educated and Wu studied at National Defense Department of the Northwest Polytechnic Institute and the Oil Refinery Department of the Beijing Petroleum Institute. She graduated in 1962 with an engineering degree. Her first job out of college was working for the Lanzhou Oil Refinery in the Gansu Province. Soon afterward she landed a position in the technology department of the Ministry of Petroleum Industry.

In 1967, she went to work for the Beijing Dongfanghong Refinery. She worked for the refinery for 16 years, rising in position during her tenure from technician to deputy director. In 1983, she left the Beijing Dongfanghong Refinery to become deputy general manager and Party secretary of the Yanshan Petrochemical Corporation. During this time she began to rise in the ranks of the Communist Party and in 1988 she was elected vice-mayor of Beijing. She held that position for three years. During her tenure as vice-mayor, Wu was responsible for keeping electrical-plant workers from striking in response to student deaths in Tiananmen Square.

In 1991, she claimed a position in the Foreign Trade and Economic Cooperation. She held the seat of vice-minister for two years before stepping up to the minister role. During that time she was also elected president of the China Association of Foreign-Funded Enterprises. From 1997 to 2002, she also served as an alternate or full member of China's Communist Party (CCP) Central Committee—the ruling elite of China.

Wu related in a *China Online* article that growing up she had always wanted to be a businesswoman, "My biggest wish was to become a great entrepreneur.... In an enterprise, you can develop your own thinking." A short, compact woman who always dresses well, Wu is easy to spot among the men who make up the majority of high-level positions. One characteristic that stands out prominently is her graying hair—most of the men color their hair black to cover the gray. Wu is an anomaly in many respects. She is the only woman to hold such a high ranking and not be married to another party official. Wu's busy career and dedication to China's economic future left her with little time to form a family. She explained to *China Online,* "I spent 20 years in the backwoods. When I got out, I was already too old. Plus work was hectic. So I gave up."

In April of 2003, Wu added another title to her name, that of Health Minister. During the winter months of 2003, a deadly virus was spreading through Asia and the world. Known as Severe Acute Respiratory Syndrome (SARS), the World Health Organization indicated that China was an area that was highly affected. Unfortunately, the acting health minister refused to acknowledge that China was suffering from the outbreak. Wu, who was also holding the position of Vice Premier, replaced him. She approached the situation in her usually forthright and honest manner. She was open and truthful about the virus and its spread among the Chinese population. Many people within China and internationally agreed that she was the best person for the job. Former U.S. trade representative Charlene Barshefsky explained to John Pomfret of the *Washington Post,* "If one was looking for a minister to help China regain international trust, she would be the person. Her directness undercuts the notion that there's guile or any attempt to deceive. Also, she means business."

Her actions and attitude earned her high esteem among health professionals worldwide and helped stem the spread of the potentially fatal virus. Afterward, Wu called on the Chinese government to help establish a national disease prevention and control network to deal with health crises such as SARS. The following year, Wu declared that the health ministry would begin focusing on HIV and AIDS—diseases affecting more than 800,000 people throughout the country. She initiated programs to educate people on the causes as well as ways to prevent the spread of the disease. She also launched educational programs to end discrimination and fear of HIV/AIDS sufferers by giving people factual information on how the disease cannot be spread.

In addition to her commitment to providing and improving healthcare throughout the nation, Wu continues to form trade alliances and agreements with nations worldwide. In 2004, she worked to make formal agreements with countries such as Belgium, Barbados, Finland, and Uzbekistan. Because of her work and influence, Wu has been ranked as an influential and powerful person. In July of 2004, she was named to the list of the top 50 most influential people in the area of intellectual property by *Managing Intellectual Property.* The following month *Forbes* magazine ranked her as the second most powerful woman in the world, on a list that included United States national security advisor Condoleezza Rice and U.S. senator Hillary Rodham Clinton. From all appearances she will continue to be a positive force working in China.

## Sources

### Periodicals

Agence France Presse, April 26, 2003.
*Calgary Herald,* August 24, 2004, p. A3.

Deutsche Presse-Agentur, February 26, 2004.
*Economic Times,* September 3, 2004.
*Independent* (London, England), March 1, 1998, p. 17.
*Time,* April 26, 2004, p. 56.
*Washington Post,* May 6, 2003, p. A17.
Xinhua General News Service, November 15, 2002.

### Online

"Wu Yi among Top 50 most influential figures in IP," *China Daily,* http://www.chinadaily.com.cn/english/doc/2004-07/21/content_350363.htm (November 6, 2004).
"Wu Yi: State Councilor, State Council," *China Online,* http://www.chinaonline.com/refer/bio graphies/secure/BB-REV-WuYi3.as p (November 6, 2004).

—*Eve M. B. Hermann*

# Xzibit

**Rap artist, television show host, and film actor**

**B**orn Alvin Nathaniel Joiner, January 8, 1974, in Detroit, MI; children: Tremayne (son).

**Addresses:** *Home*—Woodland Hills, CA. *Record company*—Sony BMG Music Entertainment Co., 550 Madison Ave., New York, NY 10022-3211.

## Career

**B**egan rapping in the Los Angeles hip-hop underground, 1990s; made guest appearances on albums for fellow rappers King Tee and Tha Alkaholics, mid-1990s; released first solo album, 1996; rapped on Snoop Dogg's album *Top Dogg*, 1999. Film appearances include: *The Breaks*, 1999; *Tha Eastsidaz*, 2000; *The Wash*, 2001; *8 Mile*, 2002; *Full Clip*, 2004; *xXx: State of the Union*, 2005. Television appearances include: *Cedric the Entertainer Presents*, 2003; *CSI: Miami*, 2004; *Pimp My Ride* (host), MTV, 2004—.

## Sidelights

**S**ince the release of his first solo album in 1996, Xzibit has been a leading force in keeping the hip-hop genre vibrant. The surly-tongued rapper became a hot commodity in 2004 after he began hosting an offbeat reality makeover show for MTV called *Pimp My Ride*. During the program, mechanics do more than simply make over the rusted-out cars of deserving guests—the cars end up with eye-popping paint jobs, flashy chrome rims, and car-vibrating sound systems. To use Xzibit's words, the cars are made "scrumptulescent."

*John Rogers/Getty Images*

As host of the show Xzibit flaunts his charm, tossing out witty punch lines. This charisma helped turn him into an MTV celebrity in his own right and opened the doors to a budding film career, earning him roles in several action flicks, including 2005's *xXx: State of the Union*, starring Samuel L. Jackson. Though music remains the focus of his career, Xzibit feels fortunate for the opportunity to cross over into other realms of entertainment. "There will be a day when I'm not gonna wanna get up on stage and stand in front of a crowd for 45 minutes," he told the *Daily Telegraph*'s Kathy McCabe. "This is a young man's sport. Hip-hop has done wonders for my life but I'm not gonna let hip-hop consume my life. There's other endeavours I have to achieve."

Born January 8, 1974, in Detroit, Michigan, Alvin Nathaniel Joiner—aka Xzibit—spent his early childhood in one of the city's drug- and gang-riddled neighborhoods. He said his mother, a writer, helped spark his creative side, as well as his sense of humor by having him watch such shows as *Saturday Night Live* and *The Muppet Show*. She died when he was nine. Within a year, Xzibit began rapping, mostly out of boredom; he lacked a radio, so he decided to make his own music. His father soon remarried and relocated the family to Albuquerque, New Mexico, a place the young adolescent despised. He passed his time creating song lyrics.

"I was about 13 when I started writin' my own rhymes," Xzibit told *Murder Dog,* an online rap magazine. "It was something I enjoyed [doing]. I liked to put words together, it was easy for me. I just stuck with it." Often, Xzibit would share his rhymes with classmates as they competed to see who would be the rhyme master of the day. Despite this early passion, Xzibit found plenty of time to goof around. When he was 14, Xzibit got into serious trouble with the law, was removed from his home, and placed in state custody. He also got kicked out of school for fighting and had to earn a G.E.D., or general equivalency diploma.

When Xzibit was 17, the state released him from custody and he headed west. He landed in Los Angeles and recalled that although he was starving most of the time after his arrival, he was happy to be there. The change of environment was lifesaving. Xzibit made a point of leaving his old friends and bad habits behind and set about finding a new set of friends who could inspire him to stay on a better path. Speaking to *Interview* magazine, Xzibit recounted his turnaround. "When I went out to California, I was still doing the [stuff] that saw a lot of my friends killed or put in prison. But I got a job in a car wash and just started hitting underground clubs, doing a cappella because I didn't have a track, or a DJ."

In time, Xzibit became somewhat of a celebrity in the West Coast hip-hop underground. He made connections and was invited to make a guest appearance on fellow rapper King Tee's 1995 album, *IV Life,* as well as on Tha Alkaholiks' *Coast II Coast* album. Spending time in the recording studio with other artists inspired Xzibit to push his music to a new level. "I really started getting into makin' records when I saw how it was done," Xzibit told *Murder Dog.* "When I saw the people around me goin' from step A (in the studio), to B (puttin' it together and mastering it), to C (really puttin' it out). Bein' involved in that process allowed me to wanna reach out and do that myself."

Soon enough, Xzibit signed with Loud Records. Because he had never even cut a demo, Xzibit stepped into the recording studio a complete novice. Speaking to *Murder Dog,* Xzibit acknowledged that mistakes were made on that first album, 1996's *At the Speed of Life,* although he was pleased with the effort. "I didn't know what to expect, I didn't know

what to deliver, but I put my best effort in. It made enough noise for me to come with the second and the third." One song on that first album, a track called "Paparazzi," earned Xzibit his first significant air time and mild recognition. In the song Xzibit condemns artists who use hip-hop as nothing more than a vehicle for money and fame.

Xzibit released a second album, *40 Dayz & 40 Nightz,* in 1998, but it was not until 1999, when he rapped on Snoop Dogg's LP *Top Dogg,* that hip-hop insiders really took note of his potential. Snoop Dogg's album was produced by Dr. Dre, who liked Xzibit's rock-solid delivery so much that he invited Xzibit to appear on his 2001 album as a guest musician.

The exposure Xzibit received from joining forces with Snoop Dogg and Dr. Dre broadened his fan base. He also opened for Eminem and Limp Bizkit on their 2000 tour, giving himself even more exposure. By the time Xzibit released his third solo album, *Restless,* in 2000, he had hit his stride. His first two albums were commercial failures, selling just 360,000 copies altogether. *Restless* proved to be a million-copy selling album and was certified platinum. In 2002, Xzibit released his fourth solo album, *Man Vs. Machine,* where he rails against the corporate world and other systems that tie people down. This album went gold. These albums, packed with abstract rhymes that convey powerful meaning, established Xzibit as a favorite among hardcore hip-hoppers.

Besides delivering on his albums, Xzibit delivers in concert. Fans love his lively stage performances, which run in contrast to the calm and cool presentation style of other rappers like Snoop Dogg and Dr. Dre. Xzibit is flamboyant. During performances he races his five-foot-eleven-inch buff body around stage atop a tricked-out low-rider bicycle, simultaneously spinning doughnuts and delivering his spirited rhymes without missing a beat.

In March of 2004 Xzibit began hosting *Pimp My Ride* for MTV and turned it into a hugely popular makeover show. As the title suggests, the mechanics on the show—with Xzibit leading the commentary as the master of ceremonies—spiff up dilapidated cars with over-the-top custom accessories and paint jobs. The half-hour show attracts an average of 2.6 million viewers.

In each episode a young person with an incredibly awful eyesore of a car is chosen to receive a vehicle makeover. Typically, this person depends on the car to make a living or to help others in need. The show, however, goes way beyond just fixing up cars. The mechanics at West Coast Customs, a Los Angeles-based celebrity car shop, do the makeovers. *Pimp My Ride* makeover cars have included a 1978 Cadillac DeVille, a 1986 Oldsmobile Cutlass Supreme, and a 1991 Ford Escort. On the show, luxury embellishments are a must. The mechanics have done such things as replace a dome light with a chandelier, add a plasma television, an espresso machine and a wood-paneled yoga chamber—not on the same vehicle. Once they added a bubble-blowing tailpipe to a Mustang.

The show has been a hit not only because of the extreme car makeovers, but also because Xzibit is highly entertaining. One episode featured a 19-year-old college student named Christine Allende and her 1992 Honda Civic. Allende used the car to take her 83-year-old grandmother to the doctor, the store, and to church, which was a problem because the doors were hard to open. In addition, Allende was driving on the compact spare tire and the alarm was so out of whack it went off spontaneously. In typical *Pimp My Ride* fashion, her car got a full work over, complete with purple paint and racing stripes, a rear wing, spoked wheels and a velvet and leather interior. Especially for grandma, mechanics included a seat massager and doors that flip up, like those found on a Lamborghini.

According to a write up in *AutoWeek* by Mark Vaughn, Allende got so excited after seeing the makeover that Xzibit had to remind her to breathe, then brought the show home with his antics. "It's a very touching moment here on *Pimp My Ride*," Xzibit told the audience. "But with the proper equipment, we'll get through," he said, holding a box of tissues.

Since Xzibit began hosting *Pimp my Ride,* his career has opened up. He hosted MTV's European Music Awards in November of 2004 and has had several film appearances. He filmed alongside Jennifer Aniston and Clive Owen in the thriller *Derailed,* set for release in 2005. He also made a guest appearance on the CBS series *CSI: Miami.* Speaking to Raptism.com, Xzibit noted that television acting is a challenge because "television is way different than hip hop, like you only get one chance to do it right whereas hip hop you can do it 'till you get it right; TV is kind of like you only get one chance to actually get it off."

Xzibit released a fifth album, *Weapons of Mass Destruction,* in December of 2004, in which he raps about social and political issues. He rants about President George W. Bush and the war in Iraq, tying his hardcore rap into a larger, global picture. On the album Xzibit sings about all kinds of weapons, from AK-47s and other street guns to the kind of weapons the United States was seeking in Iraq. In the track "Cold World," Xzibit draws a parallel between an American inner-city dweller battling addiction and a child living in war-torn Baghdad unable to escape U.S. bombs. He reminds listeners that, like the people in his song, they, too, have a choice in life—they can give up their problems or die with them. In "State of the Union," Xzibit rearranges one of Bush's State of the Union addresses, skillfully mixing up words here and there to produce phrases like "homicidal dictator." These global—and political—ruminations have turned Xzibit into a true crossover rapper whose music is popular with both the gangsta crowd and college-culture intellectuals.

For all his vitriolic gangsta raps, Xzibit also has a cool side—one that feels gratitude. Speaking to *Interview,* Xzibit explained that there are two types of artists. "There's a guy who really thinks he deserves everything that's happening to him and there's a guy who knows he worked [hard] and was blessed. I really feel like everything is a blessing."

Besides his gruff rapper persona and his jovial TV show demeanor, Xzibit has another side—father. His son, Tremayne, was born when Xzibit was 19. The rapper never mentions the name of Tremayne's mother but has said they broke up in 1998; they share custody. Tremayne stays with his mom during the week while attending school, then spends weekends and summers with Xzibit. "I'm learning just like he's learning," Xzibit told *Vibe*'s Benjamin Meadows-Ingram. "I just try to keep his environment stable and make him feel like he's my highest priority."

As a father Xzibit is aware that some of the lyrics and stories conveyed through hip-hop are less than life-inspiring. He has called on fellow hip-hop artists to work to remake the genre into the meaningful art form it once was. In an interview with the *Independent*'s Chris Mugan, Xzibit asked fellow rappers to place positive and sensitive messages into the mix instead of just "hooky junk-food rap." Xzibit called for a return to integrity. "We have kids that listen to hip-hop by the millions and they listen to us more than they listen to their parents, their teachers, and politicians. So if the only thing we're doing is selling them clothes and making them have sex, what are we preparing them for?"

## Selected discography

*At the Speed of Life,* Loud, 1996.
*40 Dayz & 40 Nightz,* Loud, 1998.
*Restless,* Loud, 2000.
*Man Vs. Machine,* Loud/Columbia, 2002.
*Weapons of Mass Destruction,* Sony, 2004.

## Sources

### Periodicals

*AutoWeek,* April 5, 2004, p. 30.
*Billboard,* December 18, 2004, p. 24.
*Daily Telegraph* (Sydney, Australia), March 10, 2005, p. T10.
*Independent* (London, England), December 31, 2004.
*Interview,* October 2002, p. 94.
*People,* December 20, 2004, p. 104.

*Plain Dealer* (Cleveland, OH), December 16, 2004, p. F5.
*Washington Post,* June 5, 2004, p. C1.

### Online

"Biography," Xzibit Central, http://www.xzibitcentral.com/biography.php (May 16, 2005).
"Interview with Xzibit," *Murder Dog* magazine, http://www.murderdog.com/archives/xbit/xzbit.html (May 16, 2005).
"Xzibit—Father MC," *Vibe,* http://www.vibe magazine.com/modules.php?op=modload&name=News&file=article&sid=608&mode=&order=&thold= (May 16, 2005).
"Xzibit Interview," Raptism.com, http://www.raptism.com/html/xzibitint-raptismdotcom.shtml (May 16, 2005).

*—Lisa Frick*

# Obituaries

## Alan Bates

Born Alan Arthur Bates, February 17, 1934, in Allestree, Derbyshire, England; died of pancreatic cancer, December 27, 2003, in London, England. Actor. British stage and screen veteran Alan Bates was best remembered for his quiet power in a range of supporting roles. A member of a cadre of postwar British actors who had been trained in Shakespeare but made their mark in gritty realist dramas, Bates was one of the more prolific of the bunch. Known by his shock of thick dark hair and sly smile, "his particular gift was for conveying a dangerous charm flecked with irony," *Guardian* writer Michael Billington said of Bates.

Born in 1934, Bates was the first of three sons, and grew up in the British Midlands area of Derbyshire. His father was an insurance salesperson who also played the cello, while Bates' mother was an accomplished pianist. His parents hoped he would become a concert pianist, but by the time he was eleven he had resolved to become an actor. He won a scholarship to the Royal Academy of Dramatic Arts (RADA) in London, and made his stage debut in 1955 with the Midland Theater Company. A year later, he joined the English Stage Company at the Royal Court in London, and was cast in an audacious new drama about disaffected working-class youth in Britain, *Look Back in Anger*. Bates originated the role of Cliff, the more easygoing sidekick to the lead role in John Osborne's acclaimed drama, and took it to Broadway as well in 1957. A Hollywood studio offered Bates a seven-year contract, but he declined, not wishing to map out his career that far in advance.

Bates' generation of fellow actors, who began their careers after World War II and the subsequent social upheavals, included Albert Finney, Tom Courtenay, Richard Harris, Peter O'Toole, and Oliver Reed. He studied with some at RADA, and worked with others at the Royal Court. All were eager to move British drama forward with plays like Osborne's and others, which had emerged as part of Britain's new "kitchen sink" movement. These gritty, realistic stories usually tackled social issues and cast a grim eye on the stuffy middle-class morals left over from the Victorian era. Harold Pinter's plays were also part of this postwar wave, and Bates excelled in Pinter's 1960 drama *The Caretaker* as Mick, a young man with a brain-damaged brother.

Bates also starred in the screen version of *The Caretaker,* and went on to take other notable film roles during the rest of the decade. He was Basil, the poetry-spouting British writer in *Zorba the Greek,* and appeared in the box-office smash of 1966, *Georgy Girl,* with Lynn Redgrave. In 1969, he was one of a quartet in the screen adaptation of D.H. Lawrence's novel *Women In Love,* which featured Bates and Oliver Reed in a rather famous nude wrestling match scene.

Bates made the occasional Hollywood film. He won an Academy Award nomination for his lead in the *The Fixer,* adapted from the Bernard Malamud novel about a Russian Jew unfairly accused and tortured, and also appeared as the painter who tries to capture Jill Clayburgh's heart in the 1978 film *An Unmarried Woman.* A dozen years later, he starred as Claudius alongside Mel Gibson in the 1990 Franco Zeffirelli version of *Hamlet.*

The stage, however, remained Bates' true calling. He won a Tony Award in 1972 for the title role in *Butley,* a play from Simon Gray about the psychological disintegration of a petty-minded English literature professor, and a second Tony three decades later for *Fortune's Fool,* an Ivan Turgenev play. Always choosy about his roles, he took only the film jobs that appealed to him, such as the starchy butler in *Gosford Park* in 2001, or the terrorist with designs on the Super Bowl in the 2002 Ben Affleck film *The Sum of All Fears.*

Bates stayed away from the legendary carousing and romantic entanglements for which many in his generation of British actors were known. He wed an actress, Victoria Ford, with whom he had twin sons, and rarely gave lengthy interviews. In 1990, his son Tristan died of an asthma attack in Japan at age 19, and Bates' wife died two years later. He later spoke of enduring what he called "a trough of bewilderment," according to a *Los Angeles Times* article by Susan King. "It's physical as well as an emotional loss. For a year or two, you think they are going to come through that door."

Diagnosed with pancreatic cancer in early 2003, Bates characteristically refrained from courting press attention as he underwent chemotherapy. His condition worsened in November, however, and he died at a London hospital two days after Christmas at the age of 69. He is survived by two brothers, his son, Ben, and a granddaughter. **Sources:** *Chicago Tribune,* December 29, 2003, sec. 1, p. 10; CNN.com, http://www.cnn.com/2003/SHOWBIZ/Movies/12/28/alan.bates.dead.ap/index.html (January 5, 2004); *Entertainment Weekly,* January 9, 2004, p. 18; *Guardian* (London), December 29, 2003, p. 15; *Los Angeles Times,* December 29, 2003, p. B9; *New York Times,* December 29, 2003, p. A19; *Times* (London), December 29, 2003, p. 25; *Washington Post,* December 30, 2003, p. B4.

—*Carol Brennan*

## Geoffrey Beene

Born August 30, 1927, in Haynesville, LA; died of complications from pneumonia, September 28, 2004, in New York, NY. Fashion designer. Geoffrey Beene helped define American style in women's fashion. Abandoning the rigid forms of the rather unadventurous dresses of his 1960s period, Beene went on to create pared-down, chicly simple couture that made him "the godfather of modern American minimalism," as a writer for London's *Independent,* Linda Watson, termed him. Never one to run with the fashion pack or heed the newest trends, Beene, noted the writer of his *Times* of London obituary, "wielded an unspoken but potent influence on the young that far exceeded that of his contemporaries whose heavily advertised labels are household names across the globe."

Beene was born in 1927, and grew up in Haynesville, Louisiana. He came from a family of physicians, and duly entered the medical-school curriculum at Tulane University in New Orleans. But he sketched evening dresses during class, and later admitted that he had always been entranced by design; at the age of eight, he bought a pattern for beach pajamas at the local store, brought it to his aunt, and directed her to sew them in a blue and orange floral fabric he had selected. He eventually dropped out of Tulane, not long after his class began their cadaver work, and headed to California. He had planned to enroll in college there, but instead took a job as a window-display associate at I. Magnin, a high-end retailer.

In 1947, at the age of 20, Beene moved to New York City and enrolled at the Traphagen School of Fashion. From there, he went to Paris, where he learned the art of tailoring from a master who had once worked for the renowned house of Molyneux. Back in New York City in 1951, he landed a job at a small design atelier located inside the posh Sherry-Netherland Hotel, but lost it when his sandwich dripped onto an expensive antique chair. He headed over to the less elegant world of New York's Garment District, and from 1954 to 1963 was a designer for Teal Traina, a women's clothing firm. In 1963, he launched his own company, and put his own name on the label, which was a somewhat unusual move at the time, for few American designers operated under their own name. Generally, they worked for a manufacturer, whose name was the label.

This first phase of Beene's career was marked by standard Seventh Avenue fare. "He had achieved modest success with stiff, structured dresses that had a high waistline, a paper-doll silhouette that was widely copied," wrote *New York Times* critic Anne-Marie Schiro. In 1967, he designed the wedding dress for one of the daughters of President Lyndon B. Johnson, but had a change of heart regarding his design style when an essay by the *New Yorker*'s Kennedy Fraser likened his dresses to concrete. He decided to move forward with the times, and began creating fluid, minimalist dresses that became a favorite of the fashion editors and tastemakers of Manhattan.

Beene's best work often featured undulating seams that moved with the wearer, as well as an unusual mix of fabrics. In 1974, he launched a secondary line, called Beene Bag, which made him one of the first American designers to enter the so-called "bridge" segment of the market. He was also the first American designer to show his work during Milan's fashion week in the mid-1970s, several years before the Italian city became one of the required stops for fashion-magazine editors and retail buyers on the biannual circuit of runway shows.

Beene, however, never attained the stratospheric financial success of other American designers, partly because of a long-running feud with *Women's Wear Daily,* the industry bible. It began in 1967, when he refused to provide the requested advance details of Lynda Bird Johnson's wedding dress, but he later noted that coverage of his designs was absent from *WWD* because he could not afford to buy lavish advertising space in its sister publication, *W.* Despite the freeze, Beene's runway presentations of his latest spring and autumn collections at the Pierre Hotel were well-attended affairs in the 1980s. Much of his company, it was said, was financed by his hugely popular men's fragrance, Grey Flannel, one of the few license agreements he had made.

Over the years, Beene's work remained contemporary in spirit, and even increasingly minimalist in construction. He was widely cited by a younger generation of modernist designers as an early inspiration. "The more you learn about clothes, the more you realise what has to be left off. Cut and line become increasingly important," *Independent* writer Iain R. Webb quoted him as saying. He was also known for his strong pronouncements on style and design, once asserting, for example, that "dressing for success is something unsuccessful women do," according to the *Independent*'s Watson.

Beene was a well-known figure in fashion, with his signature owlish black glasses, and was honored by his peers several times over during his career; he won several Coty awards and received awards from the Council of Fashion Designers of America four times, including one in 1998 for lifetime achievement. He lived in a duplex on New York's Upper East Side, and also had a weekend home on Long Island's Oyster Bay, where he cultivated rare orchids in an extensive greenhouse. He died on September 28, 2004, in New York City at the age of 77, of complications from pneumonia, and is survived by a sister in Texas. "Beene was a rarity," a writer for the *Times* of London declared in tribute. "Possessed of a strong intellect, an undeviating purity of vision and the painstaking obsession of the true craftsman, he was not just a fashion designer. It is more accurate to call him an industrial designer who happened to create clothes." **Sources:** *Independent* (London), September 30, 2004, p. 42; October 7, 2004, p. 15; *New York Times,* September 29, 2004, p. A23; *Times* (London), September 30, 2004, p. 66.

—*Carol Brennan*

# Elmer Bernstein

Born April 4, 1922, in New York, NY; died on August 18, 2004, in Ojai, CA. Composer. Elmer Bernstein composed more than 200 films and television programs in a career that spanned more than five decades. He was an Academy Award nominee 14 times in six consecutive decades. He finally won an Oscar in 1967 for the score to the film *Thoroughly Modern Millie.*

Bernstein's childhood was filled with creativity. Born to Ukrainian parents who were both creatively inclined (his father taught English literature and his mother was a dancer), young Bernstein took dancing lessons and played the piano. He also won prizes for some of his paintings. At age 12, he forsook his other talents, and focused on playing the piano. He won a scholarship to study with Henriette Mitchellson, who also taught at Juilliard. She recognized his talent for improvisation, and arranged for Bernstein to meet with Aaron Copland. Copland also saw the talent of the child prodigy. He arranged for Bernstein to study under Israel Citkowitz. Bernstein also attended The Walton School, and later went on to New York University.

Bernstein graduated from New York University in 1942. He joined the army, and began writing scores for propaganda films. His work for United Nations Radio was brought to the attention of a Columbia Pictures executive. The executive offered Bernstein work on two films: *Sunday's Hero,* and *Boots Malone.* His work on the movies led to another film, *Sudden Fear,* starring Joan Crawford and Jack Palance. The unusual score brought Bernstein to the attention of many in Hollywood.

In the late 1940s and early 1950s, Senator Joseph McCarthy of Wisconsin began hearings trying to locate and squash members of the American Communist Party. Many of those in the entertainment field who did have Communist leanings were blacklisted; in other words, they were barred from getting any work. Bernstein's career as a film composer was almost derailed due to a brief stint working on a left-wing newspaper. Though he was not blacklisted, he was "gray-listed," which basically meant he could get work but nothing major from the studios. His time on the gray-list was short. Director Cecil B. DeMille hired him to score just the dance scenes for the epic *The Ten Commandments;* however, the lead composer grew ill, and DeMille offered the entire film score to Bernstein.

Bernstein was offered the chance to score *The Man with the Golden Arm,* starring Frank Sinatra. While previous films had used jazz before, no one had ever written an all-jazz score. This new work took film music in a new direction, and Bernstein was praised for this effort. According to elmerbernstein. com, Jack Moffitt told the *Hollywood Reporter,* "Elmer Bernstein's historic contribution to the development of screen music should be emphasized. Until now jazz has been used as a specialty or a culmination of a plot point. It remained for Bernstein to prove that it can be used as a sustained and continuous story-telling element in underscoring the mood elements of an entire picture."

Bernstein soon became a much sought-after composer. He created jazz scores for a number of films including *The Sweet Smell of Success,* and Academy Award-nominated *Walk on the Wild Side.* However, Bernstein would not be pigeon-holed into one genre.

Bernstein was also offered the opportunity to score *To Kill A Mockingbird.* He had a little difficulty with writing the score, but soon decided to include a child-like quality to the music, since the film was about seeing adult problems through the eyes of a child. The score was nominated for an Academy Award, and won a Golden Globe. It was also one of Bernstein's favorites.

In the 1960s and early 1970s, Bernstein scored several Westerns, including a few that starred John Wayne. Also during this time, he won his first and only Oscar for the film score to *Thoroughly Modern Millie.* Many felt this was one of his less distinguished works.

In the late 1970s, Bernstein began scoring comedies. He wrote the music for *National Lampoon's Animal House, Airplane!,* and *Stripes,* all blockbusters. In the early 1980s, he also wrote the scores for *Ghostbusters* and *Trading Places,* among many other comedies. He received another Academy Award nomination for *Trading Places.*

Moving to another genre in the film industry also proved profitable for Bernstein. He scored the music for the independent film *My Left Foot.* He also began collaborating with famed director Martin Scorsese, starting with the film *The Grifters.* Bernstein had long admired the work of composer Bernard Herrmann, and when he learned that Scorsese was remaking the film *Cape Fear,* he asked for the chance to rework Herrmann's original score. Scorsese agreed, and both were able to present a work that was remarkably different from the original motion picture.

Throughout his career, Bernstein worked with a number of Hollywood's top directors, including Francis Ford Coppola, Jim Sheridan, Martha Coolidge, Al Pacino, Carl Franklin, and Todd Haynes, who directed Bernstein's fourteenth Academy Award-nominated film, 2002's *Far From Heaven.* Though prolific in the 1950s through the 1980s, work came in less and less as movie studios switched from using orchestral scores to using music that would also generate album sales. Nonetheless, Bernstein also recorded a large portion of his music on record as well as the music of other great film and television composers. Many used his music as well, particularly his theme from *The Magnificent Seven,* which was used in cigarette ads for Marlboro.

In addition to his composing, Bernstein was also an instructor at the University of Southern California's Thornton School of Music. He was vice president of the Academy of Motion Picture Arts and Sciences and president of the Composers and Lyricists Guild of America. He was also president of the Young Musicians Foundation, and a founding life member of the National Academy of Recording Arts and Sciences. He was president of the Film Music Museum, and on the board of directors at ASCAP.

In addition to being nominated 14 times for an Oscar, and winning one time, Bernstein also was nominated twice for an Emmy, winning once for his score for the television program *The Making Of The President.* He also received three nominations for Golden Globes, winning two for the films *To Kill A Mockingbird* and *Hawaii.* He received two Tony Award nominations, and won a *Downbeat* award for short film *Toccata For Toy Trains.* He also received two Western Heritage Awards for the scores for *The Hallelujah Trail* and *The Magnificent Seven.* Bernstein also received five Grammy nominations for various compositions, scores, and themes for 1993's *The Age of Innocence,* 1984's *Ghostbusters,* and 1962's *Walk on the Wild Side.*

He married Pearl Glusman in 1946; they divorced in 1965. Bernstein died on August 18, 2004, in Ojai, California; he was 82. He is survived by his second wife, Eve, their two daughters, and two sons from his first marriage. **Sources:** CNN.com, http://www. cnn.com/2004/SHOWBIZ/Music/08/19/obit.

bernstein.ap/index.html (August 19, 2004); Elmer Bernstein Website, http://www.elmerbernstein.com (May 11, 2005); *Entertainment Weekly,* September 3, 2004, p. 24; E! Online, http://www.eonline.com/ News/Items/0,1,14756,00.html?tnews (August 19, 2004); *Los Angeles Times,* August 19, 2004, p. B9; *New York Times,* August 20, 2004, p. A21; August 28, 2004, p. A32; *Times* (London), August 20, 2004, p. 32; *Washington Post,* August 20, 2004, p. B6.

*—Ashyia N. Henderson*

## Marlon Brando

Born Marlon Brando, Jr., April 3, 1924, in Omaha, NE; died of lung failure, July 1, 2004, in Los Angeles, CA. Actor. In the post World War II world of cinema, no one stood out like Marlon Brando. Projecting a raw, forceful energy from the screen, Brando created a cast of characters that tugged at viewers' heartstrings like never before. Whenever Brando inhabited a character, he went beyond simply memorizing lines and delivering them eloquently; he delved into the dark corners of humanity, literally setting his emotions free in pursuit of nailing his characters. Brando's performances set a new standard, forcing other actors to follow. Over the course of his half-century career, Brando won two Academy Awards.

Brando was born on April 3, 1924, in Omaha, Nebraska, to Marlon Sr. and Dorothy Pennebaker Brando. His dad was a cattle- and chicken-feed dealer; his mother, an aspiring actress, was a founder of the Omaha Community Playhouse. Unfortunately, they were both alcoholics. Brando's tumultuous childhood at the hands of his abusive father and frustrated mother, however, gave him an emotional base to later draw from when inhabiting his roles.

When Brando was a child, his parents separated for a while and he moved to Santa Clara, California, with his mother before a reconciliation moved them to Illinois. Brando, known as "Bud" to his family, attended high school in Libertyville, Illinois, but made such meager efforts that his father shipped him off to the Shattuck Military Academy in Minnesota. He was later expelled for insubordination.

By the early 1940s, the United States was heavily involved in World War II and most of Brando's peers headed off to the military. A bad knee kept him out of the draft. Instead, the 19-year-old Brando went to New York City to live with a sister. Another sister, Jocelyn, was living in New York, too, and was enrolled in acting classes under Stella Adler at the New School for Social Research. Adler taught her students a new approach to acting called the Method, encouraging them to develop their parts by conjuring up real emotions tucked away inside from their real-life human experiences. By 1943, Brando was taking classes there and became the definitive leader at this approach to acting. Before, actors concentrated on externalized actions; Brando, however, under Adler's direction, had learned to look inward, relying on emotion over delivery.

Brando first appeared on Broadway in 1944. He captured the attention of theatergoers three years later, in 1947, for his steadfast performance as the boorish, yet sometimes comic, Stanley Kowalski in the famed Tennessee Williams play *A Streetcar Named Desire.* He became famous for the role and continued this willingness to bare his emotions in his first film, *The Men,* released in 1950. In this film he played a hostile hospitalized paraplegic soldier trying to come to terms with his fate. The film version of *Streetcar* appeared a year later, with Brando taking up his same role, which he played to almost disturbing perfection, thus establishing himself as a major star in Hollywood.

He next played a Mexican bandit in *Viva Zapata!* in 1952 before appearing in 1953's *The Wild One,* 1954's *On the Waterfront,* and 1955's *Guys and Dolls.* Brando earned his first award in 1952, a best actor award at Cannes Film Festival, for *Viva Zapata!*. In 1954, he captured his first Oscar for his role as washed-up boxer Terry Malloy in *On the Waterfront.* In this role, Brando uttered one of Hollywood's most famous lines, "I coulda been a contender." The line was still being imitated 50 years after Brando first muttered it.

Brando was clearly the scene-stealer of the 1950s. As Neal Gabler, author of *Life the Movie,* told the *Chicago Tribune*'s Mark Caro, "Marlon Brando defined American movies in the 1950s and early 1960s. He was an attitude. Brando contained an aesthetic in the way he mumbled, the way he walked, the way he grimaced and rolled his eyes.... You only had to watch Marlon Brando, not even to hear him, to see the things that he stood for, which essentially was an antagonism to everything that was neat and straight and square."

The 1960s were filled with a string of bad films for Brando, including *Mutiny on the Bounty,* filmed on a South Seas island, which was a total flop. Producers blamed Brando's poor work habits for the movie's failure and enormous cost overruns. It was said that he put plugs in his ears so he did not have to listen to the director.

In 1972, Brando revived his career with the box office sensation *The Godfather,* under the direction of Francis Ford Coppola. Playing Don Vito Corleone, Brando once again displayed his acting genius. Delivering his lines in an abrasive whisper, he created a timeless portrait of patriarchal authority. Brando, in essence, was able to act between the lines of the script, creating one of the most tantalizing characters to ever fill the screen.

Brando won an Academy Award for the role, but did not attend the ceremony. Instead, he sent an actress who called herself Sacheen Littlefeather. She declined the Oscar on Brando's behalf, citing mistreatment of Native Americans in film, television, and real life. Another memorable 1970s role was his portrayal of the crazed Colonel Kurtz in *Apocalypse Now.*

Brando's real life was as full of blistery torment as the characters he played. He married three times and had a long-term relationship with his housekeeper. In 1990, his son, Christian, was accused of killing his sister's boyfriend, the son of a prominent Tahitian banker and politician. Christian Brando alleged that his victim had been abusing his sister, Cheyenne. Christian spent five years in prison for the crime and Cheyenne later committed suicide.

In 2001, Brando made his last film, *The Score,* playing opposite Robert De Niro in this flick about a heist. By then, Brando was considered a crazy eccentric. In the mid-1990s he ballooned to a reported 400 pounds, driven by an unstoppable love for food. There were also bizarre interview appearances, such as the time he appeared on *Larry King Live* barefoot and donning heavy makeup and red suspenders, saying he wanted to look like King. During the interview, Brando was belligerent and at the end, kissed King on the lips.

Brando died on July 1, 2004, when his lungs failed; he was 80. For years he had suffered from pulmonary fibrosis, a lung disease. Survivors include his son, Christian, from his first marriage to Welsh actress Anna Kashfi; two children, Miko and Rebecca, from his second marriage to Mexican actress Movita Castaneda; and a son, Teihotu, from his third marriage to Tarita Teriipaia. He also had several children with his housekeeper, Christina Ruiz, including Ninna Priscilla, Myles, and Timothy. He is also survived by Petra Barrett, whom he adopted in

1984. Brando may have more children but was generally tight-lipped about his domestic affairs during his lifetime. **Sources:** *Chicago Tribune,* July 3, 2004, p. 1; CNN.com, http://www.cnn.com/2004/SHOWBIZ/Movies/07/02/obit.brando/index.htm (February 28, 2005); CNN.com, http://www.cnn.com/2004/SHOWBIZ/Movies/07/07/people.brando.reut/index.html (February 28, 2005); *Entertainment Weekly,* July 16, 2004, pp. 24-36; *Los Angeles Times,* July 3, 2004, p. A1, pp. A26-27; *New York Times,* July 3, 2004, p. A1; *People,* July 19, 2004, pp. 80-86.

—Lisa Fric

# Art Carney

Born Arthur William Matthew Carney, November 4, 1918, in Mount Vernon, NY; died November 9, 2003, in Chester, CT. Actor and comedian. Art Carney is most remembered for the simple-minded, effusive, and charismatic character of Ed Norton who played a foil to Jackie Gleason's Ralph Kramden on the situation comedy *The Honeymooners.* Never formally trained, Carney was a genius of comic-timing, earning a great deal of respect and admiration from his contemporaries, including Gleason and comedian Sid Caesar. Although Carney never considered himself a comedian, he will always be regarded as one of the finest comic actors in television history.

Carney was born in Mount Vernon, New York, into a large Irish-American family. His father, Edward Michael Carney, was a newspaperman and his mother, Helen Farrell, was a former professional violinist. As the youngest of six boys, Carney developed his talents at an early age. He performed acts for his family, one of which was cleverly named "Art for Art's Sake." In elementary school and high school he won talent contests with his ability to impersonate famous people of the day.

Carney graduated from A. B. Davis High School in 1936. An audition with the Horace Heidt Orchestra landed him a role singing and doing impersonations with their traveling show. When the band landed a radio show, Carney announced for it and in 1941 he had a small role in the band's movie, *Pot O' Gold.* Not long afterward, he quit the band, supposedly because he was so drunk he could not announce for their show and he did not want to be fired.

Carney attempted to perform a solo act on vaudeville, but he learned the hard way that he was not a stand-up comedian. While unsuccessful at vaudeville, Carney continued to find small fulfilling roles in radio. In 1942, he began working on the CBS show *Report on the Nation.* His repertoire of impersonations included president Franklin Delano Roosevelt, British prime minister Winston Churchill, and commanding general Dwight D. Eisenhower.

In 1944, his stint on *Report on the Nation* was interrupted when he was sent to France after joining the Army. His tour of duty abruptly ended when shrapnel from an enemy attack shattered part of his leg. He spent nine months in the hospital and suffered from a permanent limp he spent the rest of his acting career trying to mask.

In the late 1940s and early 1950s, Carney appeared on television in small roles on shows like *Henry Morgan's Great Talent Hunt.* His trademark character, Ed Norton, was first seen on Jackie Gleason's show *Cavalcade of Stars.* When Gleason moved to CBS, Carney went with him and tried out a handful of characters, but Ed Norton, the kooky sewer worker, always seemed to capture the most attention, so much so that sewer worker associations across the country offered him honorary memberships.

Carney performed in other television shows and specials including the 1957 television movie *The Fabulous Irishman,* a 1960 production of *Our Town,* and a one-man drama called *Call Me Back.* Other dramatic series that he performed in included *Studio One, Kraft Television Theater,* and *Omnibus.* Carney also appeared on Broadway. In 1965, he played the original Felix Unger—the compulsive neat freak in the Neil Simon play *The Odd Couple.* Other Broadway credits include roles in 1957's *The Rope Dancers* and 1961's *Take Her, She's Mine,* as well as 1968's *Lovers.*

His most memorable big-screen role was in *Harry and Tonto.* At first unwilling to take a role playing someone nearly 20 years older than he was at the time, Carney relented and went on to win an Oscar for his performance. In the film he played an elderly man who travels across the country with his cat after being evicted from his apartment in New York City. Although this was his only Oscar, Carney received critical acclaim and awards throughout his career.

He appeared on *The Honeymooners* from 1951 to 1957. During that time he was awarded three Emmy Awards for Best Supporting Actor. In 1960 he won an Emmy for humor programming for his special *The Art Carney Show.* He won another Emmy in 1968 for Individual Achievement. In 1977, he was named Best Actor by the National Society of Film Critics for his role in the film *The Late Show.* In that film, he played a retired private eye opposite actress and comedienne Lily Tomlin. In 1984, he won another Emmy for his performance in the television movie *Terrible Joe Moran.*

In 1965, while starring in *The Odd Couple,* Carney and his wife of 25 years, Jean Myers, divorced. He had been a heavy drinker for years. During the run of *The Odd Couple* Carney had a breakdown and checked himself into a sanatorium to help him stop drinking. He married Barbara Isaac in 1966, but they divorced in 1976. Carney and Myers reconciled in the late 1970s and married a second time. They had three children together, Eileen, Bryan, and Paul.

Carney died on November 9, 2003; he was 85. Carney is survived by his wife, Jean, three children, six grandchildren, and one grandson. His broad range of acting abilities may have been overshadowed by the character of Ed Norton, but that fact never seemed to hinder Carney. A month before he died, the Academy of Television Arts and Sciences inducted him into their Hall of Fame. **Sources:** *Chicago Tribune,* November 12, 2003, sec. p. 11; *New York Times,* November 12, 2003, p. C13; *People,* November 26, 2003, p. 68; *Times* (London), November 13, 2003, p. 36.

—*Eve M. B. Hermann*

## Henri Cartier-Bresson

Born August 22, 1908, in Chanteloup, France; died August 3, 2004, in Lisle-sur-la-Sorgue, France. Photographer. French visionary Henri Cartier-Bresson gave the world some of the most indelible images of twentieth-century life. A pioneering photojournalist whose career emerged somewhat accidentally after a failed attempt at painting, Cartier-Bresson "insisted that photography was art as well as record," noted Val Williams in London's *Independent,* "and that neither was more important than the other. He knew the value of photography as evidence and education, that it was a way of telling us both about ourselves and about societies with which we are unfamiliar."

Born in Paris in 1908, Cartier-Bresson grew up in a well-to-do but notoriously frugal household headed by a father who ran the family's successful textile business. After a strict Roman Catholic education, he rebelled against the bourgeois conventions of his upbringing, and duly took up the study of painting in Paris. There, in the late 1920s, he fell into Surrealist circles, and cultivated friendships with a number of cutting-edge artists and writers of the era. At England's Cambridge University, he took courses in literature and art, and did a tour of duty in the French Army in the early 1930s. Upon his discharge, he headed to Africa to hunt big game. There, he contracted a deadly fever, and sent his family a postcard with instructions for his funeral. "Your grandfather finds all that too expensive," was the reply, according to the *New York Times'* Michael Kimmelman. "It would be preferable that you return first."

Cartier-Bresson made it back to France, and recuperated in the seaport city of Marseilles. There, he bought a small Leica, one of the first easily portable 35-millimeter cameras, and took his first photographs. From his Surrealist ties, he had come to understand the importance of spontaneity in art, and so he would wander the sometimes-dingy streets of Marseilles until he chanced upon the perfect scene to capture. His assured eye produced stunning images, and his work quickly gained renown across Europe thanks to gallery exhibitions. He also worked for *Ce Soir,* the French Communist newspaper. When World War II erupted, he served in a film unit of the French Army, but in June of 1940 was taken prisoner. Held for nearly three years, he escaped on his third attempt and joined the French Resistance.

After documenting the end of war in some famously compelling images, Cartier-Bresson went on to become one of the founders of the Magnum photo agency in 1947. Its photographers owned the rights to their photos, which was a novel idea at the time. Cartier-Bresson did not believe that a photograph should ever be cropped and asserted that any editing should be done just before, or as, the image was snapped.

Though his eye for composition was extraordinary, Cartier-Bresson preferred to describe the medium as the moment when the eye, the head, and the heart aligned. He traveled the world photographing events and their participants, or just ordinary individuals. Other photographers marveled at what seemed to be his extraordinary luck in getting a perfect, emotionally incisive shot, and Cartier-Bresson called this "the decisive moment," which was also the English-language title of his book, *Images a la Sauvette.* Once, his luck was tragic: he photographed Indian leader Mahatma Gandhi just 15 minutes before he was assassinated. He was granted a rare photographer's visa to visit the Soviet Union in the 1950s, and later photographed Cuba for a *Life* magazine photo essay.

Cartier-Bresson enjoyed a lengthy list of honors and retrospectives during his lifetime, but he left Magnum in 1966, and took up drawing again in his senior years. With his wife, the photographer Martine Franck, he established a foundation in Paris bearing his name, which opened in 2003. The *New York Times'* Kimmelman called some of his early images "simply among the best works of 20th-century art," while Peter Conrad's tribute in the London *Observer* contained a meditation on the author's favorite Cartier-Bresson photograph—of a little boy returning from a Paris market. "He carries two bottles of wine, cradling them as if they were his fragile twin siblings," Conrad wrote. "He beams with delight, pleased to be charged with this delicate responsibility, even more pleased to be, while the photographer is looking at him, the centre of the world."

Cartier-Bresson's first marriage, in 1937 to a Javanese dancer named Ratna Mohini, ended after 30 years. He died on August 3, 2004, at his home in Lisle-sur-la-Sorgue, in southwest France. He is survived by his wife, Martine, and their daughter, Melanie. He was 95 years old, and had retained his characteristic wit and lively spirit until the end of his life. He often joked that he had no imagination, which was why he had failed at painting and abandoned a brief fling with filmmaking in the 1930s. Taking photographs, he countered, was much easier, and he was enchanted by the Buddhist teachings he read, one of which seemed to be the driving force behind the beauty and humanity of his images. It was the tenet that "life changes every minute," he once said, according to Andrew Robinson of the *Guardian,* and "the world is born and dies every minute." **Sources:** BBC News, http://news.bbc.co.uk/1/hi/entertainment/arts/3536742.stm (May 3, 2005); *Guardian* (London), August 5, 2004, p. 27; *Independent* (London), August 5, 2004, p. 34; *New York Observer,* August 16, 2004, p. 1; *New York Times,* August 5, 2004, p. A1; *Observer* (London), August 8, 2004, p. 7.

—*Carol Brennan*

## Ray Charles

Born Ray Charles Robinson, September 23, 1930, in Albany, GA; died of liver disease, June 10, 2004, in Beverly Hills, CA. Singer. Blind from the age of seven, Ray Charles became an influential innovator of Rhythm & Blues music and an inventor of Soul, making more than 60 albums over a nearly 60-year period. With a soulful singing style that slipped effortlessly from jubilation to torment, and an energetic stage presence that included flashy suits and big dark glasses, Charles was one of the most successful recording artists of the 1950s, '60s, and '70s.

For most of his long career, Charles was considered a national treasure, and with the exception of a year-long hiatus from recording in the mid-'60s, while he kicked a drug addiction, he was seldom out of the spotlight. Releasing new albums almost every year and touring frequently, he also appeared in the cult film classic *The Blues Brothers* in 1980, and sang "America the Beautiful" at the Republican National Convention in 1984, where he was embraced by President Ronald Reagan and First Lady Nancy Reagan. He also made a series of television commercials for a brand of cola in the early 1990s. Despite suffering from severe illness in his last year, he was planning a new tour.

The younger of two brothers, Charles was born to working-class parents. His mother, Aretha, had a job in a sawmill; his father, Bailey, worked as a mechanic. Charles played music from the age of three. When he was five, he began losing his sight to glaucoma. As an immediate consequence, he was unable to save his older brother when he drowned in a tub. By age seven, he was completely blind, and his parents moved him to Greenville, Florida, to study music at the Florida School for the Blind. After his mother died when he was 15, he left school to pursue a career as a musician. At 17, he moved to Seattle, Washington, and formed his first band. Imitating the style of Nat "King" Cole, and billing himself as R.C. Robinson (to distinguish himself from the boxer "Sugar" Ray Robinson), he played regularly on the West Coast and recorded a number of singles, often as a sideman. He finally simplified his name to Ray Charles and recorded his first hit single, "Baby Let Me Hold Your Hand," in 1950. Over the next two years he moved to New Orleans, then Dallas, Atlanta, and finally Los Angeles. In 1952, he signed with Atlantic Records and formed a new band, which had a large horn section. A few years later, he added female backup singers who came to be known as the Raelettes. Charles' combination of piano and horns and his use of call-and-response interplay between himself and the Raelettes would remain fixtures of his music for decades.

As a result of 1959's landmark "What'd I Say?"—an album bursting with jubilation, rhythm, and suggestive interplay between Charles and the Raelettes—he became a hugely influential performer whose immense popularity was reflected in the charts through the 1970s with such hits as "Hit the Road Jack," "Georgia on my Mind," "Busted," "The Night Time is the Right Time," "I'm Movin' On," "Unchain My Heart," "Let's Go Get Stoned," and many more.

Though he was primarily known for popular vocals, in 1961 Charles recorded a much admired instrumental jazz album with strings entitled, "Genius+Soul=Jazz." Ever reaching "beyond the music," as jazz great Miles Davis liked to say of himself, in 1962, Charles successfully crossed over into country music with "Modern Sounds in Country and Western Music," which applied big band arrangements to country standards. Charles' enormously popular rendition of "I Can't Stop Loving You" caused the album to sell millions of copies. He remained a familiar and accepted voice in country for the next four decades. Shortly before his death, he recorded a duet with country singer Willie Nelson.

Starting in the early 1960s, Charles began recording music on his own labels, Tangerine and, later, Crossover. In 1964, he was arrested on a drugs charge and spent a year recovering from an addiction to heroin. In 1986, he was among the first recording artists to be inducted into the Rock and Roll Hall of Fame, in a decade that ironically marked his return to the country music charts. Also in 1986, he received a Kennedy Center Honor. In 1987, he was awarded a Lifetime Achievement Grammy, and in 1989, he won his 12th performance Grammy, for a duet with Chaka Khan. In 1993, President Bill Clinton awarded him the Presidential Medal for the Arts. In 2003, he published his autobiography, co-written with David Ritz, entitled, *Brother Ray: Ray Charles' Own Story.*

The year of his death saw both the release of his final album, *Genius Loves Company,* featuring duets with such friends as Nelson, B.B. King, Diana Krall, and Van Morrison, and a Hollywood biopic about his life, *Ray,* starring Jamie Foxx. His album won five Grammy Awards, including album of the year, best pop vocal album, record of the year and best pop collaboration with vocals, both for "Here We Go Again" with Norah Jones, and best gospel performance, for "Heaven Help Us All" with Gladys Knight. Charles died of liver disease on June 10, 2004, in Beverly Hills, California; he was 73. He was twice divorced and is survived by 12 children, 20 grandchildren, and five great-grandchildren. **Sources:** *Independent* (London), June 12, 2004, p. 52; *Los Angeles Times,* June 11, 2004, p. A1, p. A17; *New York Times,* June 11, 2004, p. A1.

—D. László Conhaim

# Madame Chiang Kai-shek

Born Soong Mei-ling, December 2, 1898, in Kwang-tung, China; died October 23, 2003, in New York, NY. Politician. Articulate, charismatic, and beautiful, Madame Chiang Kai-shek was the wife of Generalissimo Chiang Kai-shek, one-time president of China. Unlike most Chinese women of her day, Madame Chiang was a woman of remarkable political influence and perhaps the most powerful woman on earth during the 1940s. In 1943, she became the first Chinese person, and only the second woman, to address a joint session of the United States Congress as she sought to have the United States repeal the Chinese Exclusion Act, which had been in effect since 1882 and prohibited new Chinese immigration.

Madame Chiang was born Soong Mei-Ling on December 2, 1898, into an influential family in the Kwangtung province of China. She was educated in the United States, attending high school in Macon, Georgia, and earning a degree in English literature from Wellesley College in Massachusetts. Wellesley honored her with the school's highest distinction when she was named a Durant Scholar in her senior year. Her years in the United States and the influence of western cultures on her led her to once note, "The only thing Oriental about me is my face."

After graduating from Wellesley, she returned to China. "She was in her mid-20s and the flower of Shanghai's intellectual community when she first caught the eye of Chiang Kai-shek, then chairman of the Supreme National Defense Council," noted *Time* contributor Pico Iyer. The couple married in 1927, and Madame Chiang quickly became an influential confidante to her husband. The following year, he became president of China when the Nationalist Party rose to power after overthrowing the Qing Dynasty, the last of China's royal dynasties.

Unlike the wives of many rulers and government leaders, Madame Chiang was highly influential. She became her husband's most trusted confidante, as well as his interpreter and chief propagandist. She also converted her husband, who was a Buddhist, to Christianity. Known for her powers of persuasion, as well as her beauty, Madame Chiang once saved her husband's life when he was taken by the troops of a angry warlord. She not only persuaded the warlord to release her husband but, according to one version of the story, also got the warlord to surrender himself into their custody.

In the 1930s, Madame Chiang was a prime mover in China's New Life Movement, which focused on a moral rebirth of the Chinese people and focused on such values as dutifulness, discipline, loyalty and cleanliness. The effort garnered attention from the world press, and Madame Chiang became the movement's most eloquent and famous spokesperson.

During World War II, Madame Chiang traveled the world eliciting support for her country's battle against Japan. A report about her death on CNN.com noted, "Her husband could not speak English and hated talking with foreigners so Chiang took on the role of his spokesman, wowing world leaders and especially Washington." The story went on to note, "The American public became enamored with Madame Chiang, and her name appeared annually on the U.S. list of the ten most admired women in the world."

Although China, with the help of its allies, defeated the Japanese, the Nationalist Party's rule was to be short lived. In 1949, China underwent a communist revolution. Madame Chiang and her husband fled mainland China and settled in Taipei, Taiwan, where they remained as leaders of the Nationalist government until the Generalissimo's death in 1975.

Following her husband's death, Madame Chiang moved to the United States, where she lived in a New York City apartment and a family mansion on Long Island. Although her days as a powerful influence were largely over, she was still revered by many. When the United States broke off diplomatic ties with Taiwan in 1978 to establish stronger relations with China, Madame Chiang did not comment on the change of diplomacy.

Once called the "Empress of China" by writer Ernest Hemingway, Madame Chiang was the last surviving world figure of World War II when she died on October 23, 2003, in her apartment in New York City; she was 106. Memorial services were held at St. Bartholomew's Church in New York City. She was buried in a family cemetery in upstate New York with the stipulation that her remains will be returned to China if the country becomes democratic and reunites with Taiwan. **Sources:** *Asian Political News*, March 12, 2001; Clari News, http://quickstart.clari.net/qs_se/webnews/wed/dj/Qus-taiwan-chiang.Rbmq_DOU.html (November 13, 2003); CNN.com, http://www.cnn.com/2003/WORLD/asiapcf/east/10/24/obit.madame.chiang/

index.html (November 13, 2003); *Guardian* Newspapers, http://www.buzzle.com/editorials/11-4-2003-47260.asp (November 13, 2003); *San Francisco Chronicle,* October 25, 2003; *Time,* November 3, 2003; Wellesley College, http://www.wellesley.edu/Anniversary/chiang.html (November 13, 2003).

—*Marie Thompson*

## Alistair Cooke

Born Alfred Cooke, November 20, 1908, in Salford, England; died March 30, 2004, in New York, NY. Journalist. A figure of immense stature on both sides of the Atlantic, veteran British Broadcasting Corporation (BBC) journalist Alistair Cooke bridged two worlds: the proper English one of his birth, and that of his adopted homeland, the United States. For 58 years Cooke delivered the weekly *Letter from America* on the BBC, reporting on American news, events, and characters from a unique British perspective. His *Times* of London obituary called him a "prototype mid-Atlantic man: perceived in Britain as the best sort of sophisticated American and in the United States as the very model of an English gentleman. "

Cooke's origins, however, were less than genteel, and his transformation into the epitome of British erudition seemed a quintessentially American, rags-to-riches one. Born Alfred Cooke in 1908 in Salford, a town near Manchester, he was the son of a lay preacher and metalsmith by trade; his mother's family were of Irish Protestant origin. The family relocated to the seaside town of Blackpool in 1917, and the late entry of the United States into World War I, on the side of the British, caused a contingent of American soldiers to be billeted at the family home. The event was a pivotal one in Cooke's life, he later recalled. The seven U.S. doughboys, he once said, were "inordinately kind and outgoing and quite devoid of the joylessness that, in my view, afflicted my own countrymen," a *New York Times* article by Frank J. Prial quoted him as saying.

Cooke won a scholarship to Jesus College of Cambridge University, which carried with it a stipulation that he would enter into teaching as a profession. He was an excellent piano player and active in extracurricular drama activities, even founding a theater group that was the first at Cambridge to admit female students into its ranks. He also changed his name to the posher-sounding "Alistair" around 1930, completing his transformation, and partly avoided the teaching requirement after graduation by landing a fellowship for further study at Yale and Harvard. From there, he ventured on to Hollywood in 1934, befriending actor and director Charlie Chaplin, and then parleyed his experiences into a job as the film critic for the BBC.

Cooke came back to England for that job, with his American-born wife, Ruth Emerson, a model, but was eager to return to America. An unexpected opportunity arose with King Edward VIII's abdication crisis of 1936, when Cooke landed an assignment for NBC to broadcast reports on the royal drama and its political implications from London. He filed some 400,000 words for the radio network, and the pay netted him a small fortune that gave the Cookes the chance to permanently settle in New York City in 1937.

Cooke served as a correspondent for the *Times* of London, and took occasional BBC work during the World War II years. Wholly embracing his new home, he even became an American citizen in 1941, though his ties to England remained strong. Reporting from San Francisco on the founding of the United Nations in 1945, he was offered a post as the chief American correspondent for the *Manchester Guardian,* the newspaper that eventually became London's *Guardian* daily. He eagerly delved into all the major stories of the day, and his nonfiction account of some notorious postwar domestic espionage trials, *A Generation on Trial: U.S.A. vs. Alger Hiss,* was published by Knopf in 1950 and became a best-seller.

By then Cooke had already began his long-running *Letter from America,* which was first broadcast on the BBC on March 24, 1946. It was slated to be just a 13-week series, but his trenchant observations of American life and events, which usually clocked in between 13 and 14 minutes, proved so popular that it became the most enduring program on BBC radio as well as the longest-ever hosted by a single person in broadcast history.

The major American networks courted the elegant Brit as well, and Cooke hosted a highly regarded American documentary series called *Omnibus* that aired on CBS in the 1950s. He ventured back into television several more times, most notably with a 1972 series for NBC, *Alistair Cooke's America,* which won two Emmy Awards. A lucrative deal he inked for a companion book earned him another small fortune when it became a best-seller as well.

Cooke was also a familiar figure to American viewers of the Public Broadcasting Service (PBS) staple *Masterpiece Theatre* as its host from 1971 to 1992. The series featured lavish film adaptations of classics from British literature; Cooke wrote his scripts himself and was famous for never using a teleprompter. His introductions were such an institution unto themselves that they became the source of parodies, from *Saturday Night Live* to *Sesame Street.*

*Letter from America* ended in late February of 2004, when Cooke was finally forced to give up the assignment, which he still wrote from a manual typewriter, because of declining health. The last of its 2,869 broadcasts aired a few weeks later, and Cooke died that same month, on March 30, 2004, at the age of 95. He had lived in the same rent-controlled apartment on New York's Upper East Side for decades, but also had a summer home on Long Island with his second wife, the painter Jane Hawkes White. He is survived by their daughter and a son from his first marriage. **Sources:** BBC.com, http://news.bbc.co.uk/1/hi/entertainment/tv_and_radio/3581573.stm (February 23, 2005); *Economist,* April 3, 2004, p. 89; *Guardian* (London), March 31, 2004, p. 27; *New York Times,* March 31, 2004, p. C12; *Times* (London), March 31, 2004, p. 29.

—*Carol Brennan*

## Francis Crick

Born June 8, 1916, in Northampton, England; died of colon cancer, July 28, 2004, in San Diego, California. Scientist. Called "one of the most brilliant and influential scientists of all time," by Richard A. Murphy, the president of Salk Institute, in Patricia Sullivan's *Washington Post* article, Francis Crick discovered, along with James Watson, the double-helical structure of deoxyribonucleic acid (DNA). This one discovery has been called one of the most important in modern times. DNA, the blueprint of life, is the thing responsible for heredity. This discovery made it possible for the fields of genetic engineering and biotechnology and for most of the advances in medicine in the late 20th century and beyond.

Crick was born in Northampton, England, in 1916. The area was famous for its cobbling businesses, and Crick's father, Harry, ran a shoe factory. Crick was a curious boy and his parents bought him a children's encyclopedia when he was young that helped answer a lot of his questions. So many things were being discovered and so many questions answered as he grew up that Crick once admitted to his mother that he was afraid that by the time he grew up everything would have been discovered. He need not have worried. He attended Northampton Grammar School before going to a boarding school in London. After graduation Crick attended University College in London, earning a bachelor's degree in physics in 1937. He had just started work on a Ph.D. in physics at University College when World War II started. He joined the military and served as a scientist at the British Admiralty during the war, designing magnetic and acoustic underwater mines. When he returned to his studies he realized that he was more interested in molecular biology than physics, and he began his studies at the Cavendish Laboratory.

Crick went to Cambridge University in the early 1950s where he met James Watson. The two men discovered a shared interest in DNA and began researching together, with Crick often leading the quest. As a person, Crick was quite an individual. Mark S. Bretscher in the *Independent* said of Crick, "Francis Crick's greatest assets were his curiosity and ruthless intellect.... He could be uncharacteristically mean to a pompous speaker; his presence at meetings made sure everyone was on their toes. He had a fine sense for aesthetic elegance, reflected in his scientific discoveries and writing. His wonderful humor, accompanied by a somewhat raucous laugh, was infectious. He was a great entertainer." It was often this verve and humor that helped along the strenuous research into the obscure nature of DNA.

Scientists at the time knew that cells had a nucleus that contained DNA, but no one knew what its function was. Crick and Watson were convinced that DNA contained the clue to heredity, but that no one had proved this yet. After much research, the pair discovered the spiral ladder shape of DNA and gleaned from this discovery the information about DNA that has become the prevalent and accepted belief. The spiral staircase, they discovered, is actually made up of four different chemicals that make up the "steps" of the ladder. These steps repeat and form a pattern or code. Areas of this code form genes, which carry the blueprints for proteins. Proteins do most of the work in the body and carry out most of its functions, so basically DNA controls everything that a body is and does. The report of the double-helix form of DNA was first reported in the May 23, 1953, edition of the British journal *Nature.* Crick's wife, Odile Speed, an artist who generally painted nudes, created the first model of the DNA double-helix for the men, and Watson's sister typed up the article.

It was an amazing, life-altering discovery that since that time has been used for just about everything medical. This one discovery gave rise to the biotechnology industry. According to Sullivan in the *Washington Post,* "The discovery helped scientists understand how humans inherit traits and how that system of inheritance further explains evolution." The discovery has also led to the ability to clone animals. Crick and Watson were awarded the Nobel Prize in Medicine in 1962 for their discovery.

After the DNA discovery Crick continued his research at Cambridge University's Medical Research Council into the mid-1970s, with a focus on the genetics of viruses, protein synthesis, and embryology. In 1976 he took a one-year sabbatical at the Salk Institute for Biological Studies, which he liked so much that in 1977 he moved to La Jolla, California, to work full-time, even holding the position of president of the Salk Institute for a while. At the institute, Crick transferred his focus to the study of the brain and the nature of consciousness. He held the title of J.W. Kieckhefer distinguished professor at the institute until his death. He was also an adjunct professor at the University of California at San Diego.

While he was involved in his research and teaching, Crick was also actively publishing books about his research. In 1981 he published the book *Life Itself,* which discusses the idea that life began on Earth when microorganisms wafted in from space. It was a shocking, controversial idea and he later came to regret the book. In 1994 he published *The Astonishing Hypothesis: The Scientific Search for the Soul,* a treatise on consciousness.

After a long bout of illness, Crick died on July 28, 2004, of colon cancer in San Diego, California; he was 88. Watson, Crick's one-time partner, looked back at his friendship with Crick on the CNN website, "I will always remember Francis for his extraordinarily focused intelligence and for the many ways he showed me kindness and developed my self-confidence…. I always looked forward to being with him and speaking to him, up until the moment of his death. He will be sorely missed." During his lifetime Crick married Ruth Doreen Dodd, but the couple divorced after seven years. They had one son, Michael F. C. Crick. He married Odile Speed, a French artist, in 1949 and had two daughters, Gabrielle and Jacqueline. He is survived by his wife, three children, and four grandchildren. **Sources:** CNN.com, http://www.cnn.com/2004/TECH/science/07/29/people.crick.reut/index.html

(July 30, 2004); *Independent* (London), August 3, 2004, p. 34; *Los Angeles Times,* July 28, 2004, p. A1, p. A26; *New York Times,* July 30, 2004, p. A1, p. A13; *Washington Post,* July 30, 2004, p. A1, p. A4.

—*Catherine Victoria Donaldson*

## Gertrude Ederle

Born Gertrude Caroline Ederle, October 23, 1905, in New York, NY; died November 30, 2003, in Wyckoff, NJ. Record-setting swimmer. In 1926, American Gertrude Ederle became the first woman to swim the English Channel, and broke the previous record by some two hours despite strong winds against her. Ederle was just the sixth person to complete the 21-mile route between France and England, and set a new record time that remained for nearly a quarter-century afterward. "Ederle was a symbol of the Roaring '20s," noted *New York Times* writer Richard Severo, "a decade given as much to heroics as to materialism."

Born in 1905, Ederle grew up in the New York City area and came from a family of swimmers. Her father, a butcher who owned a meat market, first taught her how to swim by putting a rope around her waist when she was a toddler. Her parents owned a cottage in Highlands, New Jersey, and so Ederle and her siblings spent their summers swimming in the Atlantic Ocean. She had a bout with measles as a child, which caused some slight hearing loss. Doctors warned her to stay out of the water, fearing that dampness and bacteria would worsen it, but Ederle found it hard to stay dry.

Ederle emerged as a top competitive swimmer in the early 1920s, training at the Women's Swimming Association facility in Manhattan and setting new national records for her times in events. She went on to compete in the 1924 Olympics in Paris, France. When she returned home, she began training for a 1925 swim from the tip of Manhattan to Sandy Hook, New Jersey. She completed the course in seven hours, eleven minutes, and was hooked on record-setting distance swimming from then on. Later that same year she made her first attempt at swimming the English Channel, but came in after nine hours when her trainer, fearing she was in trouble when he saw her coughing, reached out from the boat to grab her. Under the rules of distance swimming, no member of her team was allowed to touch her while in the water.

Determined to try again, Ederle returned to France in August of 1926. Only five men had ever completed the route, and the media was intrigued by her moxie. Her daredevil stunt came at a time when there was tremendous bias against female athletes, based on the notion that women simply did not possess the physical strength for such challenges. On August 6, Ederle dove in just after seven a.m. off the coast of Cap Gris Nez, France, near Calais, on a morning when a red ball near the shore warned boaters of choppy seas. Over a modest swimsuit, she slathered herself in sheep grease, olive oil, and Vaseline for insulation, and gave firm instructions to her father, coach, and crew that she was not to be pulled out of the water unless she directly asked to be.

Ederle's journey was not exactly solo: alongside her training boat were two tugboats, one with her family and friends, and another filled with reporters, many of whom became seasick because of the rough waters. She plowed through the waters with an adept crawl stroke for the better part of a day. A southwest wind drove her off-course, and she actually swam the equivalent of 35 miles by the time she neared the shoreline of Kingsdown, in Kent, England. Her time was 14 hours, 31 minutes, two hours faster than the men's record. She had spurned the urgings of her coach, worried about the terrible weather conditions, to come in by calling out from the waves, "What for?"

Ederle's feat made headlines around the world. She was honored in New York City with a ticker-tape parade, and invited to the White House to meet President Calvin Coolidge, who called her "America's best girl." Nicknamed "Miss What-For," she did a stint in vaudeville and earned a reported $2,000 a week for it. She accepted the numerous speaking engagements that came her way, but turned down the countless marriage proposals that even inspired a popular song.

True to her doctors' predictions, Ederle's hearing worsened, and she faded from the public eye after appearing at the 1939 World's Fair in New York. During World War II she worked at LaGuardia airport as an aircraft instrument inspector, and taught deaf children to swim at a New York City school for the hard of hearing. She lived in Flushing, Queens, for many years, and spent her last seven in a New Jersey nursing home. She died at the age of 98 on November 30, 2003. Her record English Channel time stood until 1950, when another American woman, Florence Chadwick, bested it. Though she was a major celebrity for a few years after her 1926 feat, Ederle was modest about it, saying only when she arrived in Kent, "I knew it could be done," according to the *Times* of London. **Sources:** *Chicago Tribune,* December 1, 2003, sec. 1, p. 11; *Independent* (London), December 2, 2003, p. 18; *Los Angeles Times,* December 1, 2003, p. B9; *New York Times,* December 1, 2003, p. A23; *Times* (London), December 2, 2003, p. 33; *Washington Post,* December 3, 2003, p. B6.

—*Carol Brennan*

## Janet Frame

Born Janet Paterson Frame, August 28, 1924, in Dunedin, New Zealand; died of leukemia, January 29, 2004, in Dunedin. Author. One of New Zealand's most famous literary exports, Janet Frame searingly chronicled the sometimes-fluid border between mental illness and what society terms "normal" in her dozen novels. Her fiction was a byproduct of her own struggle: she had been hospitalized for eight years in a series of psychiatric facilities, and was saved from barbarous corrective surgery only when one of the doctors noted that she had won a literary prize for a short-story collection. She was fond of saying that writing had literally saved her life. "Writing is a boon, analgesic, and so on," Frame once asserted, according to *New York Times* obituary writer Douglas Martin. "I think it's all that matters to me. I dread emerging from it each day."

Born in 1924, Frame grew up in an impoverished household. Her father was an engineer for the railroad, and her mother had once been a maid in the household of Katherine Mansfield, one of New Zealand's most famous authors. Frame likely inherited her literary ambitions from her mother, who wrote poetry and peddled it door-to-door in their neighborhood. But it was a bleak life, and the situation was compounded by the drowning deaths of two of Frame's sisters. She emerged from adolescence a painfully shy, socially awkward young woman, but found regular refuge in her writing. Schooled at a teachers' college in Dunedin, she was expected to undergo an evaluation for her student teaching credit, but when the observer arrived to watch her in the classroom, she panicked and fled. A suicide attempt followed, but she later enrolled at the University of Otaga. There, for a psychology-class assignment, she wrote about the attempt, and school authorities became alarmed. She was forced into treatment two days later, and spent the next eight years confined to a psychiatric hospital.

Frame was diagnosed with schizophrenia, and underwent extensive electroshock treatment. A leucotomy was recommended, a surgery that would sever the connection between the brain and its prefrontal cortex. Such procedures were performed regularly between the 1930s through the '60s as a treatment for severe depression or anxiety, but sometimes rendered the patient into a near-catatonic state. A doctor at the hospital, however, saw that a collection of short stories by Frame, *The Lagoon,* had been published and even won a literary prize. She was released from care, and taken in by a well-known New Zealand writer, Frank Sargeson. He let her stay in an old Army hut on his property outside Auckland, where she wrote her first novel, 1957's *Owls Do Cry,* based on her own experiences as a shy child and a young woman undergoing psychiatric treatment.

Frame received a government grant, and used it to travel to Spain and England. She produced a number of novels in the early part of the 1960s, including *Faces in the Water,* about a woman in a psychiatric hospital. Often her fictional characters were silenced in some way, either mute or shunned by others. Of her 12 novels, "each explored a dimension of human suffering and rejection and furthered her reputation for graceful and sorrowful prose," noted Adam Bernstein in the *Washington Post.* "Frame's literary output often blended themes of fractured identity, morbidity, and caustic appraisals of modern society."

Frame was fascinated by language and its possibilities, and once recounted the genesis of one of her novels. She had gone to see a London dentist, who "was very vague," she remembered, according to her obituary in the London *Independent* newspaper by C.K. Stead. "Then he said, 'Rinse whilst I'm gone.' I hadn't heard anyone say 'whilst' and it was that word that prompted me to write the whole book."

During her time in London, she was also examined at a renowned mental-health facility, whose doctors concluded she had never suffered from schizophrenia in the first place. Her later autobiographies—beginning with *To the Is-land* in 1982 and concluding in 1985 with *The Envoy from Mirror City*—strive to explain how she came to be misdiagnosed. The middle volume, *An Angel at My Table,* was made into an acclaimed 1990 film by Jane Campion. "It's no wonder that I value writing as a way of life when it actually saved my life," she later wrote in one of her autobiographies, according to *Los Angeles Times* obituary writer Mary Rourke.

Frame was less shy later in life, but remained somewhat reclusive. In 1990, she received her country's highest honor, the Order of New Zealand. Frame died at the age of 79 in Dunedin on January 29, 2004; she had been suffering from leukemia. The woman "widely considered New Zealand's finest writer," according to Rourke, was the subject of a 2001 biography, *Wrestling with the Angel.* She had told its author, Michael King, that sometimes others suggested to her, "'Why don't you go out and mix?'" referring to her preference for isolation, and scoffed, "as if I were a pudding." **Sources:** *Independent* (London), January 30, 2004, p. 22; *Los Angeles Times,* January 31, 2004, p. B23; *New York Times,* January 30, 2004, p. A23; *Washington Post,* January 30, 2004, p. B8.

—*Carol Brennan*

## Thomas Gold

Born May 22, 1920, in Vienna, Austria; died of heart disease, June 22, 2004, in Ithaca, NY. Scientist. Through his maverick research at Cornell University, Thomas Gold first came to prominence in 1948 when he published, with fellow scientists, the now discredited "steady-state" theory, which proposed that the universe continuously creates new matter even as it loses it. The theory's eventual discrediting led to the validation of the Big Bang theory. Twenty years later, he published a paper explaining pulsars, a hitherto unexplained phenomenon detected by radio telescopes. It was received with some hostility but eventually won universal acceptance. In the 1960s, he sat on the National Aeronautic and Space Administration's (NASA) space science advisory panel. In the 1980s, he was a proponent of unmanned spaceflight. Finally, in his 1998 book, *The Deep Hot Biosphere,* he proposed that there is no such thing as "fossil" fuels, but rather that oil products were formed along with the earth and therefore exist in almost unlimited quantity. He suggested that life might be found on Mars and other planets from subterranean drilling. He was also a gifted and daring sportsman, enjoying water and downhill skiing and amateur tightrope walking. In 1964, he was elected to the Royal Astronomical Society and later to the U.S. National Academy of Sciences.

Gold was the son of a Jewish businessman in Vienna, Austria. His family moved to Berlin when he was an adolescent, and later fled to England from the Nazis. His father's gift of a watch, which Gold took apart and reassembled, led to his interest in technology. He earned a master's degree in mechanical sciences from Cambridge University with a thesis that proposed that the ear acts as an oscillator of sound. Years later it was discovered that minute hair cells working with vibrating membranes do indeed serve this function in the ear. After he was briefly interned at the start of World War II due to his Austrian origin, his degree got him a job on a top secret British radar project. During his internment, he struck up a friendship with fellow prisoner Herman Bondi, with whom he would later co-write his "steady-state" paper. He taught at Trinity College, Cambridge, from 1947 to 1951, was an assistant at the Royal Greenwich Observatory from 1952 to 1956, and then was hired by Harvard University in 1957 to teach astronomy. In 1959, he accepted a directorship in Radiophysics and Space Research at Cornell University in Ithaca, New York. There he pushed for American supremacy in the space race, and as chairman of the astronomy faculty he hired the astronomer Carl Sagan, later a famous author on cosmology and host of the popular television documentary series *Cosmos.*

Gold's "steady-state" theory on the universal continual creation of matter—which argued that the universe is infinite and its matter constantly replenished—was presented at the Royal Astronomical Society in Edinburgh in 1948 to generally skeptical peers, but it provoked fervent discussion and research into measuring microwave radiation that resulted in strengthening the Big Bang theory. In the face of mounting evidence of a violent and instantaneous creation of the universe, even Gold began to view his alternative theory as doubtful. But in 1968, his research into the slowing down of a pulsing star in the Crab Nebula gave rise to his well-received theory of spinning neutron stars. While under contract at NASA in the 1960s, he proposed that the moon had been pockmarked by meteor bombardments that accounted for its powdery surface. Fearful that a manned spacecraft might sink deep into the surface of the moon upon landing, the agency sent the unmanned Surveyor on a pre-Apollo troubleshooting mission. Though the powder's depth was found to pose no danger to spacecraft or astronauts, Gold was proved correct about its existence.

His next daring theory emerged as a result of the energy crisis of the 1970s. With an ambitious drilling project in Sweden, he sought to prove that hydrocarbons are not of biological origin and therefore could exist in huge supply in deeper subterranean depths. Gold proposed that these substances—oil, gas, and especially methane—flow from gigantic reserves toward the earth' surface, where our limited drilling capabilities are able to exploit them. The deeper we can drill, he argued, the more we will find. Though his discovery of an oily evidence was ridiculed by critics, two decades later he published

*The Deep Hot Biosphere,* a book that rehashed his theory. According to the *Washington Post,* Gold said, "Most men ... can seldom accept even the simplest and most obvious truth if it obliges them to admit the falsity of conclusions which they have delighted in explaining to colleagues, which they have proudly taught to others, and which they have woven thread by thread into the fabric of their lives."

Gold died of heart disease on June 22, 2004, in Ithaca, New York, at the age of 84. He was divorced from Merle Tuberg Gold, whom he married in 1947, and is survived by three daughters from that marriage. He is also survived by his second wife, Carvel Beyer Gold, whom he married in 1972, their daughter, and six grandchildren. **Sources:** *Independent* (London), June 29, 2004, p. 35; *Los Angeles Times,* June 26, 2004, p. B17; *New York Times,* June 24, 2004, p. A25; *Washington Post,* June 24, 2004, p. B6.

—D. László Conhaim

## Spalding Gray

Born on June 5, 1941, in Barrington, RI; went missing on January 10, 2004, confirmed dead from suicide on March 8, 2004, after his body was recovered from the East River in New York City. Author and actor. Spalding Gray detailed the minutiae of his neuroses, fears, experiences, and desires through his cutting and dry self-deprecating humor. An actor, playwright, and novelist, Gray came into his own with the 1987 film adaptation of his monologue *Swimming to Cambodia.* The spare set included Gray sitting at a table with a pitcher of water and a drinking glass with a map of Cambodia behind him while he detailed parts of his personal history with a history of the Khmer Rouge and its impact on the people of Cambodia. Author Francine Prose described the power of Gray's monologues to Bruce Weber of the *New York Times,* "He transformed darkness into dark comedy."

Gray grew up in Barrington, Rhode Island, with a lot of darkness. His family life was troubled from the beginning. His factory-worker father was an alcoholic, while his mother suffered from several nervous breakdowns. Later known for his ability to talk non-stop, Gray reportedly stopped talking for a year when he was child after the death of his dog. In 1967, at the age of 52, Gray's mother committed suicide.

After graduating from high school, Gray attended Emerson College in Boston, Massachusetts. He studied theatre and writing, and graduated in 1965. During this time, Gray began to perfect his monologue technique. He worked two jobs, one as a garbage collector and the other as night dishwasher at a restaurant. He learned how to turn the events of his daily life into entertainment by trying to make the cooks laugh.

In the late 1960s he moved to New York City and delved into experimental theater. He was a member of Performance Group as well as the co-founder of Wooster Theater Group, whose members included actors Willem Dafoe and Jill Clayburgh. During this time he wrote and debuted some of his early monologues including *Sex and Death to the Age 14, Booze, Cars and College Girls,* and *A Personal History of the American Theater.* All of his works were based on the details of his personal life and experiences, which became a hallmark of his style. Bridget Byrne reported at E! Online that Gray once said, "There's no area of my life that I haven't spoken about or confessed or discussed with someone."

Gray's first film roles were ones he later denied, contrary to his exhibitionist tendencies. For a short period of time he had roles in a few cheaply made, sexually explicit adult films. As his theater career gained momentum though, he was offered small roles in mainstream movies beginning in the 1980s. One of these was his role as a United States consul in the 1984 film *The Killing Fields.* His experiences in Thailand making the film formed the basis for the monologue *Swimming to Cambodia.* As a work of theater, *Swimming to Cambodia* won an Obie Award in 1985. Two years later it was made into the popular film directed by Jonathan Demme.

Gray was never the leading man in a film, but he made appearances in films throughout the 1990s and into the 2000s. Most of his roles cast him as a doctor or a professor, sometimes as priest or preacher. In total he appeared in 38 films, including *Beaches,* which starred Bette Midler; *The Paper,* directed by Ron Howard; and *King of the Hill,* directed by Steven Soderbergh.

All the while he continued to write. His published works included those based on his monologues like *Monster in a Box* and *It's a Slippery Slope* as well as a novel, *Impossible Vacation.* His last book, which was also a performance piece, was called *Morning, Noon and Night.* It detailed a day in the life of Gray and his family, including his three children and his wife. Veering from his normally cynical take on existence, *Morning, Noon and Night* exposed Gray's acceptance of the mundane and an almost positive outlook on life.

In 2001, Gray, who had been battling depression for years, was sent into a profound depression after a car wreck left him with a broken hip and ankle, and a fractured skull. The pain from that accident never relented; neither did Gray's depression. Even though he continued to work and perform, by 2002 he was seriously considering suicide. That year in October he was rescued from an attempt to jump from a bridge near his home. The following year he tried to jump from a ferry in New York, but was talked out of it by a friend. Five months later, on January 9, 2004, he was physically removed from a ferry by security guards. The next evening Gray missed an appointment with friends and was declared officially missing on January 11. His body was found March 8, 2004, in the East River in New York City. He was 62.

Gray is survived by his second wife, Kathie, his two sons, and a stepdaughter. As a writer and performer, Gray perfected the art of self-revelation. His ability to combine historical fact with personal idiosyncrasies created exciting and challenging theater and film experiences. Robert Falls, artistic director of the Goodman Theater in Chicago, told Chris Jones of the *Chicago Tribune,* "He was known primarily as an actor; but he was first and foremost a writer.... He influenced an enormous number of other artists and writers to use autobiography in their work."
**Sources:** *Chicago Tribune,* March 9, 2004, sec. 1, p. 5; CNN.com, http://www.cnn.com/2004/SHOWBIZ/ Movies/03/08/obit.gray/index.html (March 9, 2004); E! Online News, http://www.eonline.com/ News/Items/0,1,13655,00.html?eol.tkr (March 9, 2004); *Independent* (London), March 10, 2004, p. 34; *New York Times,* March 9, 2004, p. A1; April 14, 2004, p. C15; *Times* (London), March 10, 2004, p. 38; *Washington Post,* March 9, 2004, p. B4.

—*Eve M. B. Hermann*

## Uta Hagen

Born Uta Thyra Hagen, June 12, 1919, in Gottingen, Germany; died after complications from a stroke, January 14, 2004, in New York, NY. Actress. Veteran Broadway star Uta Hagen spent decades training subsequent generations of actors from the renowned New York City dramatic arts studio she ran with her husband. The German-born thespian electrified theatergoers with her performances in a number of outstanding dramas in the 1940s and '50s, but she was a beloved figure for her skills as a teacher and acting coach for more than 40 years as well. "I would like to disagree with George Bernard Shaw's statement that 'He who can, does. He who cannot, teaches' to express my personal belief that 'Only he who can should teach,'" she wrote in *A Challenge for the Actor*, one of the two books she wrote on the craft.

Hagen was born in 1919 in Gottingen, Germany, into a learned and culture-loving family. Her mother had trained as an opera singer, and her father was an art history professor who named her after a statue in the cathedral in Naumburg. At the age of six, she was taken to see Shaw's classic *St. Joan* in Berlin, and the experience sparked her desire for a career on the stage. A year later, her family moved to Madison, Wisconsin, when her father began teaching at the state university there. In her late teens, Hagen took a few classes there herself, and also studied acting at the Royal Academy of Dramatic Art in London, but she remained largely untrained as a performer. Her instincts for the art, however, were flawless, and enough so to impress Eva Le Gallienne, an influential actor, director, and teacher of the era. Though Hagen botched her audition, Le Gallienne cast her in a Massachusetts production of *Hamlet* as Ophelia in 1937.

Hagen won excellent reviews, and joined Le Gallienne's theater company. She moved from there to a stunning list of roles on Broadway over the next two decades, appearing in some of the best-known American dramas of the twentieth century, often in their original productions. She played Blanche DuBois in the national company tour of *A Streetcar Named Desire* in 1948, and took over from Jessica Tandy on Broadway alongside Marlon Brando. In 1951, she won her first Antoinette Perry "Tony" award for *The Country Girl*, the Clifford Odets drama.

Married to actor Jose Ferrer in the 1940s, Hagen and her husband knew actor Paul Robeson from a production of *Othello*. That connection to the outspoken Robeson, as well as her own political beliefs, landed Hagen on an unofficial Hollywood blacklist of the 1950s involving writers, directors, and actors who were suspected of harboring Communist Party sympathies. The shutout was a good thing in the end, Hagen later reflected, asserting it "kept me pure," *Los Angeles Times* writer Mike Boehm quoted her as saying. "Commercially, I was hot in the early 1950s. I might have been tempted by Hollywood. I might have gotten lost in all that crap."

Instead Hagen turned her energies to HB Studios in Greenwich Village, founded by her second husband, Herbert Berghof, whom she wed in 1951. They trained more than one generation of actors, and the list includes Lily Tomlin, Robert De Niro, Jack Lemmon, Al Pacino, and Matthew Broderick. Hagen continued to appear on Broadway, too, and originated the role of Martha in Edward Albee's 1962 drama *Who's Afraid of Virginia Woolf?*. The riveting play, centered on the combative, booze-fueled marriage of a college professor and his shrewish wife, became a classic, if not least for the play's opening line, "Jesus H. Christ," uttered by Hagen. Both she and Arthur Hill, as her husband George, won Tonys for their work. Though she was cast in the London version as well, the screen version featured Elizabeth Taylor opposite her real-life husband, Richard Burton.

Hagen did appear in a few films, including 1990's *Reversal of Fortune*, in which she played the suspicious maid of comatose Sunny von Bulow (Glenn Close). She took over HB Studios and its Playwrights Foundation after the death of her husband that year, and still appeared in the occasional stage work well into the 1990s. A longtime resident of Greenwich Village, Hagen lived in an apartment overlooking Washington Square Park, where she died on January 14, 2004, at the age of 84. Her health had declined since suffering a stroke in 2001. She is survived by a daughter, Leticia Ferrer, as well as a granddaughter and great-granddaughter. The two books on acting she authored for students also serve as her legacy. In one of them, she set forth the six fundamental questions actors must ask themselves to prepare for a role, but conceded the necessary inward scrutiny was, in the end, futile. "Nobody ever learns how," she once said of acting, according to the *Los Angeles Times* obituary. "The search for human behavior is infinite. You'll never understand it all. I think that's wonderful." **Sources:** *Chicago Tribune*, January 16, 2004, sec. 3, p. 12; CNN.com, http://www.cnn.com/2004/SHOWBIZ/Movies/01/15/obit.hagen.ap/index.html (January 16, 2004); *Independent* (London, England), January 17, 2004, p. 20; *Los Angeles Times*, January 16, 2004, p. B12; *New York Times*, January 15, 2004, p. A31; *Washington Post*, January 16, 2004, p. B7.

—*Carol Brennan*

## Carl F.H. Henry

Born Carl Ferdinand Howard Henry, January 22, 1913, in New York, NY; died of heart disease, December 7, 2003, in Watertown, WI. Theologian and author. Carl F.H. Henry, founding editor of the magazine *Christianity Today* and author or editor of more than 40 books, was often considered the most prominent American evangelical thinker of the mid-20th century. He went to college with famed evangelist Billy Graham, and teamed up with him to bring evangelical Protestantism back into the American mainstream after a period where it had turned insular. "If we see Billy Graham as the great public face and generous spirit of the evangelical movement, Carl Henry was the brains," *Christianity Today* editor David Neff told the *New York Times*' Laurie Goodstein on the occasion of Henry's death.

Henry's parents were German immigrants, his father Lutheran and his mother Roman Catholic, and they did not teach him much about religion. Later, working as a newspaper proofreader, he was struck by a co-worker's religious faith when she scolded him for taking God's name in vain. He grew curious about Christianity, and in 1933 he met an evangelist named Gene Bedford. "He told me about Christ as we drove around Long Island in my battered old Chevy," Henry told the *New York Times* in 1966, according to Goodstein. "I knelt in the back of that car and dedicated myself to Jesus Christ. Life has not been the same since."

In fall of 1935, he went to Wheaton College, where he met his wife, Helga Bender, and Graham. Henry earned a bachelor's degree in philosophy and a master's in biblical and theological studies at Wheaton, and later added a bachelor's degree in divinity and a doctorate in theology from Northern Baptist Theological Seminary and a doctorate in philosophy from Boston University. He helped found the National Association of Evangelicals and edited the books section of its magazine, *United Evangelical Action.*

Henry's career-defining year came in 1947, when he published the influential book *The Uneasy Conscience of Modern Fundamentalism* and became the first acting dean of the new Fuller Theological Seminary in Pasadena, California. His book came at a time when fundamentalist Christianity was in retreat. Fundamentalists had been responding to the early 20th century's increasing secularism and the rise of liberal Protestantism by withdrawing from the mainstream and preserving their churches. Henry's book encouraged conservative Protestants to engage in society and apply their values to issues such as racial integration, militarism, and labor and management issues. The book "came just as Billy Graham was preaching, and many people believe, as I do, that Henry and Graham, together, sparked the re-

newal of evangelicalism," Charles Colson, founder of Prison Fellowship Ministries and a former counsel to President Richard Nixon, told the *Chicago Tribune.*

Henry avoided the term fundamentalist, which he thought had developed a quarrelsome connotation, and preferred the term neo-evangelical—which means someone born again as a Christian who believes in interpreting the Bible literally and spreading the faith. In 1955, Graham decided that the newly energetic movement needed a magazine to display its intellectual ideas and counter the liberal publication *Christian Century,* and he proposed Henry as its first editor. Henry agreed, and he edited *Christianity Today* from its 1956 debut until 1968, keeping the magazine focused on ethics, theology, and insistence that the Bible is historically true. In 1957, he published another of his influential books, *Christian Personal Ethics.*

After leaving the magazine over conflicts with its board, Henry taught and gave lectures around the world and worked with Prison Fellowship Ministries and the Christian relief and development group World Vision International. In the late 1970s, he started writing his landmark six-volume work, *God, Revelation and Authority,* published in 1983. An interviewer asked him why he decided to take on such a huge writing project, and he replied, according to the *Washington Post*'s Adam Bernstein, "First, because our generation largely settles for grime when it could reach for glory; it is indifferent to spiritual value. Secondly, because God isn't bullish either on the Communist world or on the free world or on present-day America. Thirdly, because the problem of authority, which haunts all arenas of thought and life today, turns ultimately on the reality of God in His revelation."

In Henry's 1988 book *Twilight of a Great Civilization: The Drift Towards Neo-Paganism,* he criticized American society for becoming more secular. In his later years—frustrated by the scandals among popular evangelists in the 1980s, among other things—he criticized the movement he had once pushed to engage more in society for going too far in that direction and losing some of its identity.

Henry led the evangelical movement "out of the margins of social, political, and academic life ... to where today we are mainstream Protestantism, a powerful intellectual and political force," Fuller Theological Seminary President Richard J. Mouw told the *Los Angeles Times.* "Without his rigorous thought and his determined will," *Christianity*

*Today's* Neff told the same publication, "evangelicalism's premiere institutions would have been clearly second-rate."

Henry died of a heart ailment in Watertown, Wisconsin, on December 7, 2003. He is survived by his wife, his daughter, Carol; three sisters, and four grandchildren. His son, Michigan congressman Paul Henry, died in 1993. **Sources:** *Chicago Tribune,* December 11, 2003, p. S14; *Los Angeles Times,* December 10, 2003, p. B13; *New York Times,* December 13, 2003, p. A17; *Washington Post,* December 11, 2003, p. B6; *Wisconsin State Journal,* December 10, 2003, p. C3.

—*Erick Trickey*

## Syd Hoff

Born September 4, 1912, in New York, NY; died May 12, 2004, in Miami Beach, FL. Children's book author and illustrator. Syd Hoff was both author and illustrator of more than 60 children's books, including the well-loved *Danny and the Dinosaur,* a 1958 classic. A cartoonist contributor to the esteemed *New Yorker* for more than six decades, Hoff was a masterfully elegant artist who was able to capture humor in just a few quick strokes of the brush or pen. "In Hoff's simple lines, a curve can serve as a smile or a snake, they can be read by four-year-olds and yet touch adults," declared Christopher Hawtree in London's *Guardian* newspaper.

Born in 1912, Hoff was a New York City native and son of a salesman. He grew up in the Bronx, and began drawing at the age of four. When he was 16, a well-known cartoonist for the Hearst Syndicate newspaper chain, Milt Gross, visited his high school. Upon seeing Hoff's work, Gross predicted success for Hoff, telling him, "Kid, some day you'll be a great cartoonist!" according to Martin Plimmer in the *Independent.*

Taking the advice to heart, Hoff dropped out of school and managed to gain admittance to New York's National Academy of Design in order to pursue his ambition. He sold his first cartoon to the *New Yorker* two years later, in 1930, an association that would continue for the rest of his career. In 1939, he began his own comic strip for the Hearst Syndicate, about a girl called Tuffy, which had a ten-year run. His first book for children, *Muscles and Brains,* was published by Dial in 1940.

But it was *Danny and the Dinosaur,* Hoff's fourth title for young readers, that launched his career as the originator of some of the most beloved children's books of the twentieth century. When his daughter was stricken with a hip problem, she had to undergo rehabilitation therapy, and so Hoff drew fanciful stories to amuse her that became the story of a little boy and his dinosaur pet. Published by Harper in 1958, the tale centers around little Danny, who visits a natural history museum and is so entranced by the brontosaurus on display that he rides it right out of the building. *Danny and the Dinosaur* was an immense success, translated into several languages, and sold some ten million copies in Hoff's lifetime. It was also said to have single-handedly launched the entire dinosaur craze among children.

Hoff wrote and illustrated a slew of other books for young readers, often featuring gentle animals and clever boys and girls. Their sweet, gentle themes usually came to "the conclusion that although the grass may look greener outside the circus or beyond the peddler's wagon, there's no place like home," noted *New York Times* journalist Eric P. Nash. Another one of Hoff's better-known titles was *Sammy the Seal* in which a seal is released from the zoo and begins classes at the local elementary school. *Grizzwold,* dating from 1963, features a title character bear who tries to convince humans that he is not merely a man wearing a bear suit. Several other titles featured an irrepressible hen named Henrietta. Hoff even had his own television series in the 1950s, *Tales of Hoff,* a title that may have been an erudite nod to German Romantic writer E.T.A. Hoffmann and his well-known short stories, which were the basis for an 1881 opera, *Tales of Hoffmann.*

Hoff wrote short fiction himself, in the form of mystery tales for the Alfred Hitchcock and Ellery Queen publications, as well as two novels, *Gentleman Jim and the Great John L* in 1977 and *Boss Tweed and the Man Who Drew Him,* published a year later. There was another comic strip from his pen, *Laugh It Off,* which ran in American newspapers from 1958 to 1978, and he continued to produce typically witty, sophisticated fare for the *New Yorker* and *Esquire* over the course of a long career. "Hoff's cartoons captured moments of everyday absurdity," noted Plimmer in the *Independent.* "Often the gag was slight, the emphasis being the celebration of a common human trait, such as the nosiness of the woman pressing her ear against the neighbour's wall, saying to her ostensibly indifferent husband, 'Boy, have they got your number!'"

Hoff also provided reams of advice to a younger generation of illustrators and *New Yorker* aspirants, sometimes in the form of such books as *The Young Cartoonist: The ABCs Of Cartooning,* published in 1983; he also visited schools regularly. Hoff died on

May 12, 2004, in Miami Beach at the age of 91. The daughter who had been so entertained with the first "Danny" drawings, Susan, predeceased him, as did Hoff's wife, Dora, whom he married in 1937. He is survived by another daughter, Bonnie, and two grandchildren. For Hoff, the joys of life as well as its harder moments served as an infinite fount of inspiration. "Humor, for some reason, is basically sad," the *New York Times'* Nash quoted him as once writing in an essay. "The best humor has to do with events that people can identify as having happened to them, or something that has been in the subconscious." **Sources:** *Guardian* (London), July 9, 2004, p. 27; *Independent* (London), May 25, 2004, p. 35; *New York Times,* May 17, 2004, p. B7.

—*Carol Brennan*

## Rick James

Born James Ambrose Johnson, Jr. on February 1, 1948, in Buffalo, NY; died of a heart attack on August 6, 2004, in Los Angeles, CA. Singer. Rick James burst on the scene with his smash hit, "Super Freak," in the early 1980s. He later had a string of hits and some believe his record sales are responsible for keeping Motown Records solvent. He is credited with bridging the gap between funk and punk music. His sound was reminiscent of Sly Stone, Parliament, The Ramones, and Prince (whom he toured with before either was famous). According to CNN.com, James had stated, "I'm trying to change the root of funk, trying to make it more progressive, more melodic, and more lyrically structured." His rowdy image and drug habit led to his arrest for assault and eventual time in prison. After his release, he began to regain all that he lost.

James' upbringing was rough. He was one of eight children born to James and Mabel Johnson. According to James, his father was abusive and abandoned the family when James was eight. James' mother was a former dancer who worked as a housekeeper, but also was a numbers runner. Though James went to Catholic school and was an altar boy, he also committed petty theft crimes, and spent some time in juvenile detention centers. He also began doing drugs. While James was always musically inclined, it was not until he performed in a talent show in high school that he seriously considered a career in music. He formed a group called the Duprees. At the same time, he joined the Naval Reserve to avoid the draft. As he and his group gained popularity— and more importantly, gigs—he began to skip out on his naval duties. James was soon drafted, but he fled to Canada.

During his stay in Canada, he formed another group, the Mynah Birds. Members included Neil Young, Bruce Palmer, and Goldie McJohn, who would later join Steppenwolf. The group would combine both folk music and R&B. However, they never recorded an album due to James' draft evasion. The group later disbanded.

James moved to London, and joined a blues band called Main Line. His uncle was Melvin Franklin of the legendary Temptations. Franklin helped his nephew get a recording contract with Motown Records. James struck a deal with the government, and served some time in prison for draft evasion. After his release, he began to record his first album, which included the hits "You & I," and his alleged ode to marijuana, "Mary Jane." The album sold two million copies.

His third album, *Street Songs,* proved to be a cross-over success. With the Temptations on background vocals, James released "Super Freak." With lyrics that included "She's a very kinky girl/the kind you don't take home to mother," "Super Freak" quickly rose on the R&B charts, and crossed over to the pop charts. He also released "Give It To Me Baby" as a B-side, and it did well.

With the success of "Super Freak," James began to produce for other artists. He formed an all-girl band named the Mary Jane Girls. He also performed duets with R&B singer Teena Marie and Smokey Robinson. He also produced comedian Eddie Murphy's "Party All The Time," which was a hit in the mid-1980s.

James' on-stage persona was one of wild debauchery. Dressed in sequins, tight leather, high-heeled boots, and cornrows or a jheri curl, James oozed sex on stage. Offstage, he smoked marijuana and snorted cocaine. According to the *Washington Post,* he told the *Detroit News* in 2004, "The biggest mistake I made is that I tried to become my alter ego. I wanted to be Rick James, wild man, party machine, lady slayer, and the cocaine told me I could. I forgot that I was James Johnson, a nerdy kid who grew up reading *Dante's Inferno* on Saturday nights."

In the late 1980s, James' career took a nose dive. However, when rap star M.C. Hammer sampled "Super Freak" for his song "U Can't Touch This," the latter song became a huge hit. Though the usage was unauthorized, James and M.C. Hammer settled out of court and he reaped the benefits, including his first Grammy that he shared with M.C. Hammer and co-writer of "Super Freak," Alonzo Miller.

James' spiral out of control came to a head when he was charged with assault in 1991. He and his girlfriend, Tanya Hijazi, held a woman against her will, burned her with a crack pipe, and assaulted her. While on bond, he and Hijazi assaulted a second woman. He was also arrested for cocaine possession. James was convicted in 1993 and served three years. He vowed to get clean and live a more sedate life.

Upon his release, he married Hijazi. The couple had one son but later divorced. He began to resurrect his career, and released an album titled *Urban Rapsody*. Though he hated rap and sampling, James worked with Snoop Dogg as well as Bobby Womack. He began touring again in 1997, but it was cut short by a stroke, which was attributed to "rock 'n' roll neck," which is excessive twisting of the head. The following year, James underwent hip replacement surgery. He also suffered from heart problems.

James was enjoying a minor comeback, thanks to comedian Dave Chappelle, who created spoofs about the singer that aired on the Comedy Central show *Chappelle's Show*. James even showed up to play himself. He also penned his memoirs, and put in a couple of performances. There were talks of bringing his life to the big screen, with Chappelle playing the singer. In June of 2004, he received a career achievement honor from ASCAP.

James was found dead on August 6, 2004; he was 56. There was speculation that he had returned to his old ways, and a Los Angeles county coroner's report confirmed it. His death was ruled accidental but nine drugs were found in his system. However, the official cause of death was a heart attack. A memorial service was held in Los Angeles, and James was buried in his hometown. Motown founder Berry Gordy told the *Chicago Tribune* that James' "creative abilities, his instincts about music and production were just awesome.... [James was] a pioneer who took Motown in a whole new direction." In addition to his son by Hijazi, James had two other children, and two grandchildren. **Sources:** *Chicago Tribune,* August 7, 2004, sec. 2, p. 11; CNN.com, http://www.cnn.com/2004/SHOWBIZ/Music/08/06/rick.james/index.html (August 10, 2004); *Entertainment Weekly,* August 20/27, 2004, p. 22; E! Online, http://www.eonline,com/News/Items/0,1,14666,00.html?eol.tkr (August 10, 2004); http://www.eonline.com/News/Items/0,1,14949,00.html

(September 20, 2004) ; *Los Angeles Times,* August 7, 2004, p. B16; *New York Times,* August 7, 2004, p. A15; *People,* August 23, 2004, pp. 56-57; *Times* (London), August 9, 2004, p. 26; *USA Today,* http://www.usatoday.com/life/people/2004-09-16-james-obit_x.htm?csp=27&RM (September 20, 2004); *Washington Post,* August 7, 2004, p. B4.

—Ashyia N. Henderson

# Mildred Jeffrey

Born December 29, 1910, in Alton, IA; died March 24, 2004, in Detroit, MI. Labor union official. Longtime labor activist and civil-rights champion Mildred Jeffrey was a longtime Democratic Party supporter who played a key role in bringing the first woman onto the ballot of a major national political party. The 1984 Democratic vice presidential nominee, Geraldine Ferraro, was one of a long list of elected officials who credited the Detroiter with providing inspiration, advice, and immeasurable support over the years. Jeffrey, Ferraro asserted, "was a household name in the house of every feminist in this country, every woman who has looked at running for office," she told *Washington Post* reporter Adam Bernstein.

Jeffrey, whose birth name was Mildred McWilliams, was born in 1910 in Alton, Iowa, near the farm where her widowed grandmother had raised 16 children on her own. "Millie" was the first of seven children in the brood, and her mother also became head of a single-parent household when Jeffrey's father abandoned them. Her own mother was the first registered female pharmacist in the state of Iowa, but the family moved to Minneapolis for better educational opportunities. After high school, she enrolled in the University of Minnesota, and also joined a progressive branch of the local Young Women's Christian Association (YWCA) whose members worked to integrate Minneapolis restaurants.

Jeffrey graduated with a psychology degree in 1932 and went on to Bryn Mawr College in Pennsylvania, where she earned a graduate degree in social economy and social research in 1934. She took a job in Philadelphia as a union organizer for the Amalgamated Clothing Workers of America. The union sent representatives like Jeffrey undercover into garment factories, where workers toiled long hours under dangerous conditions for meager wages. Jeffrey helped organize formal groups that demanded better wages and safer workplaces from owners and management. In 1936, she and fellow Amalgamated union activist Homer Newman Jeffrey wed, and spent the next few years traveling the United States organizing plants and factories in several states.

Jeffrey's work in the labor movement brought her to Washington, D.C. during World War II, when she served as a consultant to the War Labor Board. In this capacity she came to know Walter, Victor, and Roy Reuther, the brothers who played a key role in the founding of the United Auto Workers (UAW) union. The UAW emerged as one of the most powerful and influential labor organizations in the post-World War II era, fighting for and winning major concessions from corporate giants like General Motors. The Detroit-based union pioneered many advances that became commonplace for full-time wage-earners in America, such as health-insurance coverage and annual cost-of-living increases.

In 1944, Jeffrey and her husband moved to Detroit when Victor Reuther offered her a job as head of the UAW Women's Bureau. At the time, women had taken wartime jobs in Detroit-area automotive factories, which churned out tanks and munitions for the war effort; when American men began returning from military duty, the women who had staffed the plants were forced out in large numbers. Jeffrey's office at the UAW dealt with this issue, and she went on to serve in a number of other UAW posts. As head of its community-relations office, she brought the union into the burgeoning civil-rights movement in the 1950s, and took part in civil rights marches alongside the Reverend Dr. Martin Luther King Jr. and other key figures.

Jeffrey's long record of service made her one of the senior figures among postwar liberals in America. In the early 1970s, she helped found the National Women's Political Caucus, a group that would go on to help dozens of women achieve political office. In 1975, she chaired a Democratic National Committee task force that rewrote national convention rules to ensure that half the number of delegates in attendance in 1980 would be women. It was a groundbreaking moment that altered the American political landscape.

Although Jeffrey was well-known inside Democratic, labor, and civil-rights circles, she was relatively unknown to the general public. She ran for office only once herself, for a seat on the Wayne State University Board of Governors, which she held from 1974 to 1990. Closer to home, she helped her daughter, Sharon, and some politically minded

friends find a meeting place for an anti-war group they were forming in the early 1960s on the University of Michigan campus. Jeffrey secured access to a labor-union camp on the shores of Lake Huron, about an hour outside Detroit, and the group met there and formulated the famous Port Huron Statement. Its members emerged as the Students for a Democratic Society, one of the major players in the anti-war movement during the Vietnam era.

In the run-up to the 1984 Democrat National Convention, Jeffrey gathered with other leading party figures to find a suitable running mate for the party's presidential nominee, Walter Mondale. They decided on Ferraro, a New York congresswoman who became the first woman in American history to appear on the ballot of a major political party. Though the Mondale-Ferraro ticket lost, back in Michigan Jeffrey helped a lengthy roster of women to win election by providing both concrete support and behind-the-scenes advice. "I can say with absolute conviction that without Millie Jeffrey, I would not be the first woman governor of the State of Michigan today," the *Detroit Free Press* quoted Michigan governor Jennifer Granholm as saying.

Jeffrey earned the highest civilian honor awarded to U.S. citizens, the Presidential Medal of Freedom, from President Bill Clinton in 2000. Fiercely independent despite her advanced years, she continued to live alone and drive before succumbing to a respiratory ailment on March 24, 2004, at the age of 93. Much as her grandmother and mother's formidable achievements were reflected in her own life, Jeffrey passed on her determination and spirit to a younger generation of achievers. "I believe in individual initiative," she was once quoted as saying in a documentary film, according to her *Washington Post* obituary. "In other words, that each of us has a responsibility to take some action as an individual in our own part." **Sources:** *Detroit Free Press*, March 25, 2004; *International Herald Tribune*, April 6, 2004; *Los Angeles Times*, March 29, 2004; *New York Times*, April 5, 2004; *Washington Post*, March 26, 2004.

—*Carol Brennan*

## E. Fay Jones

Born January 31, 1921, in Pine Bluff, AR; died of heart and lung failure, August 30, 2004, in Fayetteville, AR. Architect. Though E. Fay Jones was not quite a household name, most American architects and followers of Frank Lloyd Wright gave his residences and chapels outstanding praise for their beauty. Jones was one of the most highly regarded devotees of Wright, and designed a number of structures that both adhered to the master's concepts and took them to a new level of grace and simplicity.

Jones was often dubbed the "Frank Lloyd Wright" of the Ozark Mountains region, because he spent nearly all of his career in Arkansas. Born in Pine Bluff on January 31, 1921, he was christened Euine Fay Jones and grew up in El Dorado, where his parents ran a restaurant. As a youngster, he constructed elaborate treehouses out of scavenged materials, including one that boasted an actual working brick fireplace—which unfortunately could not contain a spark that burned the structure down.

Jones' passion for the architecture of Frank Lloyd Wright began at the age of 17 when he saw a short documentary film at the local cinema on Wright's masterful Johnson Wax headquarters in Racine, Wisconsin. "You gotta put yourself back to southern Arkansas in the heart of the Depression," Jones recalled in an interview with *Smithsonian* writer Andrea Oppenheimer Dean in 1991. "Here was this building that looked so futuristic, with Pyrex tubing, curving walls, light-suffused but windowless spaces, a forest of columns, and shimmering light coming through the whole thing. It reminded me of things in the comic strips. Flash Gordon and Buck Rogers."

Jones entered the University of Arkansas in 1939 as an engineering student, but his studies were interrupted by World War II, when he served in the U.S. Navy in the Pacific theater. He earned his architecture degree in 1950, and went on to take a master's in the subject from Rice University in Texas. For a time, he taught at the University of Oklahoma, and finally met Wright, still an idol to him and countless other young American architects, by chance in a Houston hotel hallway when Wright was in town for a professional honors dinner. A friendship developed, and Jones later remarked that he and Wright were exactly the same height and of Welsh heritage as well; in fact, it was Wright who told him that "Euine" was an archaic Welsh form of the name "John."

In 1953, Jones won a fellowship at Taliesin West, Wright's school in Arizona, and would spend several other stints under Wright's tutelage before the master's 1959 death. Jones eventually took a teaching position at the University of Arkansas in Fayetteville, which he held until his retirement in 1988. On the side, he built up a small but esteemed practice, taking some of his first commissions for the homes of fellow professors. His own residence, dating from 1956, gained him additional renown when it was featured in magazines that included *House Beautiful* and *Progressive Architecture.*

In all, Jones designed some 135 residences around the United States, but he created nearly three dozen chapels as well. The most famous of these is the Thorncrown Chapel outside Eureka Springs, Arkansas, which he finished in 1981. Situated on a picturesque parcel of woodland, with a spectacular mountain view, the chapel was initially the idea of the property's owner, who was unnerved by the tourists who parked on his land to appreciate the vista. Thorncrown, made of glass, stone, and wood, is just 24 feet wide, but 60 feet long, and became a major tourist destination for the region. A former architect at Jones' firm, Michael Cockram, called it "a masterpiece," he wrote in a tribute to his late boss in *Architecture Week.* "This small elegant chapel in the woods, with its lacework of trusses, is a metaphor for its place—a forest within a forest. Like any great spiritual space, Thorncrown makes a symphony of daylight. The ordered complexity of the structure refracts light in ever-changing ways."

Though Jones was sometimes referred to as the creator of an "Ozark style" of architecture, he rejected the label, noting that many of his works were located far from the Ozark region. One of those commissions, however, was never completed: Jones had been hired by pizza magnate and Frank Lloyd Wright devotee Tom Monaghan to create a lavish residence in the Ann Arbor, Michigan, area. But Monaghan, a devout Roman Catholic, had an attack of spiritual remorse over the money he was spending, and ordered construction halted in 1992 after four years.

Jones was feted with numerous professional honors over the course of his career, including more than 20 citations from the American Institute of Architects. He was presented with its top honor, the gold medal, in 1990, and a survey by AIA members the following year ranked him among top ten most influential living architects. Jones passed away on August 30, 2004, at the age of 83, survived by his wife, Mary Elizabeth, and two daughters. He had suffered from Parkinson's disease, and died of heart and lung failure. Another famous son of Arkansas, Bill Clinton, wrote about one of Jones' homes in his 2004 autobiography *My Life.* Clinton had lived in Fayetteville in the 1970s while teaching at the University of Arkansas law school, and moved into a Jones home near the campus. Clinton called it a "perfect place to live, a beautiful little house."

**Sources:** *Architecture Week,* September 15, 2004; *New York Times,* September 1, 2004, p. B7; *Smithsonian,* August 1991, p. 102; *Times* (London), September 28, 2004, p. 63.

—*Carol Brennan*

# Juliana

Born Juliana Louise Emma Marie Wilhelmina, April 30, 1909, in The Hague, Netherlands; died of pneumonia, March 20, 2004, in Baarn, Netherlands. Monarch. Princess Juliana of the Netherlands was an institution in her country, a former queen as well as queen mother, royal princess, wife and mother, and her death in March of 2004 was mourned by thousands in the progressive Western European nation. Juliana and her family were among Europe's prototypical "bicycle-riding" royals, whose relatively modest lifestyles contrasted sharply with Britain's more ceremonious House of Windsor.

Juliana inherited the throne through her bloodline. She was a descendant of William I, founder of the House of Orange, who was assassinated in 1584. Her mother was Queen Wilhelmina, who came to the throne at the age of ten; the country was governed by the Queen Dowager until Wilhelmina's eighteenth birthday in 1898. Juliana was born in 1909, Wilhelmina's only child with her husband, the former Duke of Mecklenburg-Schwerin, and grew up in the royal palaces in The Hague and Apeldoorn. Her mother was a pious and earnest woman, and Juliana was compelled to address her only as "Madame." She was said to have been a lonely child, with few playmates, and grew into a shy, plainly dressed young woman. Her mother did not allow her to wear makeup, even at the age of 18, when she was installed in the Council of State as part of her role as heir to the throne.

Juliana began to blossom when she entered Leiden University, from which she graduated with a degree in international law in 1930. She twinned her official royal duties with unofficial charity work, but she was also an avid skier, and promptly entered a whirlwind romance with a dashing German prince, Bernhard of Lippe-Biesterfeld, after the two met at the 1936 Winter Olympics in Bavaria. They were married in January of 1937, and their first child, the Princess Beatrix, was born the following year. A second daughter followed, but the couple was forced to flee with the two children when the Netherlands was invaded by Nazi Germany in 1940. Juliana settled in Canada, near a favorite cousin who was a member of the British royal family, and produced a third daughter, Margriet, during the war years. Later, Juliana sent an annual supply of famous Dutch tulips to Ottawa as thanks for its wartime hospitality.

After the war, Juliana and her family returned home, and the hardships of the postwar years were compounded by personal tragedy, when she contracted German measles during her fourth pregnancy. Daughter Marijke (later known as Princess Christina) was born nearly blind. A new era was ushered in a year later, however, when her mother chose to abdicate and Juliana became queen of the Netherlands on September 4, 1948.

Recalling her own lonely childhood, Juliana strove to provide her four daughters with as normal a life as possible. Their family home, Soestdijk Palace, was in the countryside near Baarn, and the girls attended local schools. Juliana was known to buy her clothes off the rack, and could even be spotted in the local supermarket at times. She also loved to ride her bicycle, and the family was often seen in Baarn or on streets of The Hague, like countless other Dutch citizens, doing just that. Along with the modern, modest-living royal houses of Sweden and Norway, Juliana and her family gave rise to the term "bicycle-riding" royals, those whose lifestyles were a drastic departure from that of the world's most famous monarch, Queen Elizabeth II of Britain, and her brood.

Juliana's aversion to pomp translated into one of her first decrees as queen, which abolished the curtsey rule at court. In 1949, she ended a 346-year legacy of colonial rule by severing Dutch authority over its remaining colonies in the East Indies, including Java and Sumatra. Her 32-year reign was not scandal-free, however: early on, she reportedly grew close to a psychic, who had promised to restore Princess Christina's sight and then seemingly delivered on it, and the woman had to be banished from the royal household in 1956. A more shameful episode occurred 20 years later, when Prince Bernhard was implicated in a bribery scandal involving kickbacks from the Lockheed Corporation, the American aerospace firm. Bernhard allegedly used his influence with Dutch military officials to help Lockheed land lucrative contracts, and he narrowly avoided criminal prosecution for his transgressions. Aghast when the scandal broke, Juliana offered to abdicate, but her daughter Beatrix was unwilling to accede to the throne during a time of crisis. Instead, Bernhard was instead stripped of his public offices.

Four years later, Juliana followed her mother's lead and abdicated on her 71st birthday, in April of 1980. She and Prince Bernhard remained active skiers well into the early 1990s, but her health declined and she reportedly suffered from Alzheimer's disease in her final years. She died of pneumonia on March 20, 2004, at the Soestdijk Palace; she was 94. She is survived by her four daughters and numerous grandchildren; Prince Bernhard did, as well, but he died later that year. Thousands of Dutch paid their respect to the plain, warm-hearted woman who once said she would have been a social worker had she not become queen. Her coffin lay in state at Noordeinde Palace in The Hague for a week, and then an honor guard of 9,000 lined the route from the palace to Juliana's final resting place, at a Delft cemetery next to William of Orange. **Sources:** BBC.com, http://news.bbc.co.uk/1/hi/world/europe/3580397.stm (February 23, 2005); *Guardian* (London), March 22, 2004, p. 21; *Independent* (London), March 22, 2004, p. 34; *New York Times,* March 21, 2004, p. A33; *Times* (London), March 22, 2004, p. 24.

*—Carol Brennan*

## Bob Keeshan

Born Robert J. Keeshan, June 27, 1927, in Lynbrook, NY; died after a long illness on January 23, 2004, in Windsor, VT. Television personality. Bob Keeshan spent almost four decades on the air as the gentle-voiced, grandfatherly figure of Captain Kangaroo. Like his contemporary Fred Rogers, he pioneered thoughtful children's programming in which he hoped to make the viewing audience feel as if they had a friend talking to them on the television screen. Charles Leroux of the *Chicago Tribune* described Keeshan's impact on children's television: "Ahead of his time in recognizing the importance of early learning ... [he] built confidence and intellectual development in children who were having too much fun to notice the lessons."

Born in 1927, Keeshan lived for a while on Long Island, where his father, Joseph, worked as the manager of a grocery store. Eventually his father was laid off and the family moved to Forest Hills in the Queens section of Brooklyn. In school, Keeshan was encouraged by a teacher to get into radio because of his nice voice. He is said to have produced and broadcast plays over his school's loudspeaker system. In 1943, Keeshan's mother, Margaret, died of a heart attack.

When he was a senior in high school, Keeshan went to work as a page at the NBC studios in New York City. He left work at NBC after he graduated from high school to join the Marines. The war ended soon after Keeshan entered the Marines and he returned to work at NBC. He ended up becoming the assistant to Bob Smith, who eventually created *The Howdy Doody Show.* Keeshan performed odd tasks here and there and would sometimes be called upon to appear onscreen. Eventually Keeshan was asked to don a clown costume and became the first Clarabell in the show's history. He performed as the horn-tooting, seltzer-spraying clown for about five years before he was fired from the show over a disagreement with Smith.

During his turn as Clarabell, Keeshan was also attending Fordham University. Throughout high school and after graduating, he had thought he wanted to be a lawyer. But the years of experience working with Smith taught Keeshan all he needed to know about creating quality television shows, and he eventually left Fordham to continue in television. He was not unemployed for too long before he went to ABC to star as Corny the Clown on *Time for Fun.* His stint as Corny lasted until 1955; he finished his final year on that show while at the same time appearing on *Tinker's Workshop.*

That same year, CBS offered Keeshan his own children's show, which became *Captain Kangaroo.* CNN.com reported Keeshan's reasoning for choosing the character of Captain Kangaroo, "I was impressed with the potential positive relationship between grandparents and grandchildren, so I chose an elderly character." In order to look the part of a grandfather, Keeshan, who was in his late 20s when the show started, wore a gray wig for years until his own hair turned gray. He refused to have a studio audience of children so that he could create a sense of inclusion for the children who watched his show at home. In the early years of the program, Keeshan would perform two back-to-back episodes of the show for the different time zones—one for New York audiences and then another for Midwestern audiences.

*Captain Kangaroo* ran on CBS until 1984, almost 30 years. Afterward the show moved to PBS where it ran for six years. Keeshan took his dedication to children seriously and volunteered and supported causes for health and childcare. From 1953 to 1958, he was on the board of education in West Islip, Long Island. In 1987, he co-founded Corporate Family Solutions, which provided daycare solutions for corporations. He also wrote books, including the semi-autobiographical *Growing Up Happy;* a picture book about his years as Captain Kangaroo called *Good Morning, Captain: 50 Wonderful Years with Bob Keeshan, TV's Captain Kangaroo,* and a children's book called *She Loves Me ... She Loves Me Not.* He also worked on recordings for children that introduced them to a variety of musical styles.

Throughout his career, Keeshan was recognized for his contributions to television as well as his public service. He won six Emmy Awards and three Peabody Awards. He was inducted into the Clown Hall of Fame in 1990 and the National Association of Broadcasters Hall of Fame in 1998. The American Medical Association awarded him a Distinguished Service Award in 1991 and he received a National Education Award in 1981. He earned a Kennedy Center honor in 1987.

Keeshan married his wife in 1950. They had three children and lived in Long Island, New York, for most of their lives. After his wife died in 1990, Keeshan moved to Hartford, Vermont, and dedicated himself further to children's issues while also writing. As children's programming changed, Keeshan bemoaned the increase in violent content. Dennis McLellan of the *Los Angeles Times* reported that Keeshan said, "Violence is part of life, and there is no getting away from it. But there is also gentleness in life, and this is what we have tried to stress on our shows." Keeshan died after a long illness on January 23, 2004, at the age of 76. He is survived by his three children and six grandchildren. **Sources:** *Chicago Tribune,* January 24, 2004, sec. 1, p. 1, p. 6; CNN.com, http://www.cnn.com/2004/SHOWBIZ/ TV/01/23/obit.kangaroo/index.html (January 26, 2004). *Entertainment Weekly,* February 6, 2004, p. 19; *Los Angeles Times,* January 24, 2004, p. B22; *New York Times,* January 24, 2004, p. A13; *Washington Post,* January 24, 2004, p. A1, p. A7.

—*Eve M. B. Hermann*

## Clark Kerr

Born May 17, 1911, in Stony Creek, PA; died in his sleep after suffering a fall, December 1, 2003, in El Cerrito, CA. University administrator. Clark Kerr's most significant contributions to higher education may be overshadowed in the public eye by his controversial dismissal from his position as president of the University of California system. That event is only a blip on the screen of a decades-long career studying and implementing innovative solutions to the problems facing modern universities. He created the term "multiversity," which helped described higher education as it evolved over the second half of the 20th century.

Kerr's dedication to education most surely came about because of the importance that both his par-

ents placed on learning. His mother, Caroline, refused to get married until she had worked to save enough money for her future children's college educations. When she finally married, it was to Samuel Kerr—an apple farmer with a master's degree from the University of Berlin who spoke four languages. Kerr's father always believed in diversity of opinion, questioning popular beliefs and ideas.

After graduating from high school, Kerr attended Swarthmore College where he was an active member of groups and clubs. He became captain of the debating team as well as student body president. He joined a Quaker service group called the American Friends Service Committee and spent a couple of summers educating workers and the poor on social issues. One of those summers was spent in California.

As part of a group of traveling Quakers, Kerr had fallen in love with the West Coast. He graduated from Swarthmore in 1932 and was accepted into Columbia Law School. He changed his mind and decided to pursue a master's degree in economics at Stanford University, which is located south of San Francisco. He received his master's degree in 1933 and went on to the University of California-Berkeley to pursue a Ph.D. in economics, which he earned in 1939.

During the Depression, Kerr worked for the national government as a labor negotiator on the West Coast. He honed his mediation skills during those times and emerged having assisted in 500 negotiations. Kerr went on to be a professor of labor economics at Antioch College, London School of Economics, Stanford University, and the University of Washington. In 1945, he returned to UC Berkeley as head of the Institute of Industrial Relations.

As the effects of the Cold War spread into academia, Berkeley became embroiled in controversy involving loyalty oaths. In 1949, the regents of the university wanted to fire any professors who refused to sign the loyalty oaths, which declared that you were not a Communist. Kerr, who had signed the oath, advocated for the retention of all faculty even if they refused to sign. His mediation between the faculty and the regents won him favor among the faculty.

In 1952, this favor among the faculty helped him gain the position of UC Berkeley's first chancellor. He was overwhelmingly recommended to the position by the faculty. During his tenure as chancellor he started work on the California Master Plan for

Higher Education. The goal of the master plan was to make higher education available to all who wanted it while also guaranteeing the integrity of the University of California. The plan took effect in 1960 and stated that the top eighth of the state's high school graduates automatically qualify for any of the campuses of the University of California. The top two-thirds were automatically eligible for California State University. All others were free to attend local and community colleges.

In 1958, Kerr became the 12th president of the University of California statewide system of schools. He was instrumental in creating three new UC campuses—in Irvine, San Diego, and Santa Cruz. During his presidency, Berkeley became the number-one graduate school in the United States. In 1963, he published *The Uses of the University*, in which he termed the word "multiversity" and outlined the framework for how modern universities needed to function.

In 1964, Kerr returned to the Berkeley campus from traveling and found students and protesters facing off against the university administration. The Free Speech Movement spurred controversy across the political spectrum and Kerr was asked to put a stop to it. As a trained negotiator, Kerr saw no need for violence and felt the events would pass. Criticism of his actions, or lack thereof, led him to submit his resignation in 1965. At that time, the regents refused to accept it and Kerr maintained his position as protests turned from free speech to focus on the conflict in Vietnam.

In 1966, Ronald Reagan was elected governor of California. He had made campaign promises that involved clearing Berkeley of its protesters. One of his first acts after being sworn in was to call a meeting of the Board of Regents and vote Kerr out of office. Kerr stepped down gracefully and in later years was able to joke about his tenure as president, including his abrupt firing.

Offers for jobs flooded in from across the country for Kerr, but five days later he became chair of the Carnegie Commission on Higher Education. In 1973, he became chairman of the Carnegie Council on Policy Studies in Higher Education. He worked with the Carnegie Council until he was forced to step down because he had met the mandatory retirement age. Afterward, he went on speaking tours, did some consulting, and worked on his memoirs. His memoirs, titled *The Gold and the Blue: A Personal Memoir of the University of California, 1949-1967*, were published in two volumes. *Academic Triumphs* was published in 2001, and *Political Turmoil* was released two years later.

Kerr died on December 1, 2003, in El Cerritto, California; he was 92. Kerr is survived by his wife of 69 years, Catherine; his sons, Alexander and Clark; and his daughter, Caroline. Kerr's influence on education is reflected in the mission, focus, and outreach of universities across the country. Arthur Levine, formerly of the Carnegie Council, told Tanya Schevitz of the *San Francisco Chronicle*, "There isn't anyone who had as large a role in higher education as Clark Kerr did in the post-World War II 20th century." **Sources:** *Los Angeles Times*, December 2, 2003, p. A1, p. A24; *New York Times*, December 2, 2003, p. B7; *San Francisco Chronicle*, December 2, 2003, p. A1; *Washington Post*, December 3, 2003, p. B6.

—Eve M. B. Hermann

# Dan Kiley

Born Daniel Urban Kiley, September 2, 1912, in Boston, MA; died February 21, 2004, in Charlotte, VT. Landscape architect. One of the United States' more prolific and popular landscape architects, Kiley had more than 1,000 designs in his portfolio. His designs ranged from large-scale public works like the exteriors for the Lincoln Center and the Ford Foundation Headquarters in New York City to the private garden of manufacturer J. Irwin Miller in Columbus, Indiana. Known for his pragmatism, Kiley disliked having his work analyzed for deeper meaning. Adam Bernstein reported in the *Washington Post* Kiley's response to some theories about why he designed the Miller garden the way he did, "I planted those trees to shade the west side of the house... There needed to be an allée [canopy of trees lining a walkway] there, so why avoid it?"

Growing up in Boston, Kiley had little extra money. As a teenager he entertained his dates by taking them to the Arnold Arboretum. That early experience along with his interest in golf courses culled from his work as a golf caddy led him to discover the field of landscape architecture. After he graduated from high school in 1930, Kiley became an apprentice under Boston-based landscape architect Warren H. Manning, who had worked for years with another premier landscape architect Frederick Law Olmsted—designer for Central Park in New York City. In 1936, Kiley attended the Graduate

School of Design at Harvard part- time for two years while continuing to work for Manning. Unfortunately, Kiley's ideas about design differed significantly with the focus of the Harvard curriculum.

In 1938, Manning died, leading to the closure of his firm and ending Kiley's hopes of becoming a partner. Kiley ended up moving to Washington, D.C., where he partnered with architect Louis Kahn in the U.S. Housing Authority designing housing projects. During this time Kiley worked hard to improve his skills by creating practice designs on a daily basis. He also wrote articles for *Architectural Record,* often criticizing the current trends and calling for a change in focus in landscape architecture; one that was functional and modern while also fulfilling the need of urban dwellers to experience nature.

During World War II, Kiley started out in the field artillery, but his skills were in demand by the Office of Strategic Services. He became chief of design. Working for the Office of Strategic Services gave Kiley the opportunity to design the courtroom at the Palace of Justice in Nuremburg, Germany, where the war crimes of the Nazis were tried. His stint in Europe also allowed him to tour some of the world's most historically significant sites. One of the most influential upon Kiley was the gardens of the Palace of Versailles. The symmetry and control that its designer, André Le Nôtre, created in the gardens inspired much of Kiley's subsequent work.

After the war, Kiley returned to the United States to open his own office. He tried a few different locations before settling in Charlotte, Vermont. Kiley lived on a 350-acre farm with his wife, Anne, and their eight children. The family entertained often and enjoyed the rural life replete with swimming, boating, and camping. Douglas Martin reported in the *New York Times* that Kiley once stated that he was inspired by the land around him and that he did his best work there because it made him happy.

This post-war era was the beginning of a long period of productivity and work for Kiley. He teamed with architect Eero Saarinen several times on major projects. In 1947 they worked on the Jefferson National Expansion Memorial in St. Louis—which led to the St. Louis Arch. Unfortunately, Kiley was removed from the team before the project finished and his landscape designs were not implemented. In 1955 he and Saarinen designed the Miller house and grounds. In 1963, they collaborated on the designs for Dulles Airport in Washington, D.C. His later designs included gardens for the Air Force Academy in Colorado Springs, Colorado, and the Oakland Museum in California.

Kiley never formally taught nor did he write treatises on his philosophy of design. Instead he focused on his personal designs while also mentoring inexperienced landscape architects. He was called upon by President John Kennedy to serve on his advisory council. In later years his contributions and talent were well recognized and awarded. In 1997, President Clinton awarded him the National Medal of Arts. In 2002, he was given the National Design Award for lifetime achievement by the Smithsonian's Cooper-Hewitt National Design Museum. Also in 2002, he was made an honorary Fellow of the Royal Institute of British Architects.

Kiley died on February 21, 2004, after a period of illness; he was 91. Kiley is survived by Anne, his wife of 61 years; his eight children, 19 grandchildren, and one great-grandson. His designs were a major contribution to and influence on 20th century landscape architecture. Kris Jarantoski, director of the Chicago Botanic Garden told Blair Kamin of the *Chicago Tribune,* "He had a fresh perspective for Americans on landscape architecture.... He reorganized nature." **Sources:** *Chicago Tribune,* February 26, 2004, sec. 3, p. 11; *New York Times,* February 25, 2004, p. A25; *Times* (London), March 9, 2004, p. 33; *Washington Post,* February 25, 2004, p. B26.

—Eve M. B. Hermann

## Alan King

Born Irwin Alan Kniberg, December 26, 1927, in Brooklyn, NY; died of lung cancer, May 9, 2004, in Manhattan, NY. Comedian. An acerbic, cigar-puffing wit who went from the so-called "Borscht Belt" to fame in nightclubs, on television, in the movies, and in print, Alan King bridged the Jewish humor gap between Milton Berle and Billy Crystal. His signature shtick was a cheeky rant on society, delivered in a blunt staccato to sustained laughter throughout a 60-year career. In the 1950s and '60s he was a frequent guest on the *Ed Sullivan Show* and a guest host of the *Tonight Show.* In 1972, he hosted the Academy Awards. He opened for Frank Sinatra and Judy Garland, among others, and was a popular performer in his own right at Caesar's Palace in Las Vegas and other venues across the country. King also appeared in a number of motion pictures and theatrical productions, both in comedic and dramatic roles, and produced several New York theatrical productions. In his lifetime he published five books of humor and reminiscences, and left a sixth to be published posthumously.

Comedian Jerry Stiller told CNN.com that King was "in touch with what was happening with the world, which is what made him so funny. He always talked about the annoyances of life." Stiller described him as a "Jewish Will Rogers." Among his gags was calling the Long Island Expressway "the world's largest parking lot." During the turbulent 1960s, when African-American groups were staging sit-ins for equal rights, he asked a black audience, "Why is everybody carrying on about Woolworth's? Have you ever eaten at the counter at Woolworth's? If you wanted to sit in the Colony Club I could understand." He told another audience that after he sought compensation for a robbery at his house, his insurance company explained that his policy "should have had fire or theft, not fire *and* theft."

King was born in the borough of Brooklyn in New York City to Russian immigrants Minnie and Bernard Kniberg. His father made leather handbags. By the age of eight, King was earning small change by doing impersonations on street corners. In high school he performed in school plays. When he was 14, he was a runner-up in an amateur talent radio contest whose host invited him on a nationwide tour. This led to a standup summer job at the Catskills'—"Borscht Belt"—resort Hotel Gradus. He was fired from his job for telling his audience, "When you work for Gradus, you work for gratis." But there were other resorts willing to hire him. Eventually he moved to Canada, where he worked in burlesque shows and even took up boxing. Though largely successful at both, he soon returned to New York as "Alan King," having adopted the surname of a victorious boxing opponent for his stage act. While working as a doorman at Leon and Eddie's, a 52nd street nightclub, he met the legendary Milton Berle. The older comedian quickly recognized King's promise, taking him under his wing. But rather than imitating Berle's famously goofy shtick, King began cultivating a distinctive style—that of a man angry with society, particularly with suburbia. King also admired comedian Danny Thomas and from him he learned a crucial skill—to "talk" to his audiences. "He was as much a commentator as he was a comedian," Stiller told *Entertainment Weekly*.

King became an immensely popular nightclub comic, opened around the country for singers such as Nat "King" Cole and Lena Horne, and appeared in several New York shows, including the long-running *The Impossible Years.* One of his final roles was as film producer Samuel Goldwyn in the Off Broadway production of *Mr. Goldwyn* in 2002. He also appeared in 29 films, including 1955's *Hit the Deck,* a musical starring Tony Martin; 1971's *The Anderson Tapes,* starring Sean Connery; 1980's *Just Tell Me What You Want,* in which he played the leading role; 1988's *Memories of Me,* co-starring Billy Crystal; and 1989's *Enemies, a Love Story,* directed by Paul Mazursky. In the movies he usually played serious character roles.

After a gambling addiction affected his finances in the 1960s, he branched out into producing. In New York, he produced a number of shows, including *The Lion in Winter* on Broadway and *Dinner at Eight.* In the early 1990s he hosted a popular comedian-interview program on cable television, sponsored a pro tennis tournament in Las Vegas that bore his name, and raised funds for a number of charities in the United States and Israel. He co-wrote a number of books, including *Anyone Who Owns His Own Home Deserves It; The Alan King Great Jewish Joke Book; Is Salami and Eggs Better Than Sex?; Help, I'm a Prisoner in a Chinese Bakery; Matzo Balls for Breakfast and Other Memories of Growing Up Jewish* (published posthumously), and his autobiography, *Name Dropping: The Life and Lies of Alan King.*

An avid cigar smoker, King struggled with cancer in later years, and had his jaw replaced in 1992. He died of lung cancer on May 9, 2004, in Manhattan; he was 76. He is survived by his wife of 57 years, Jeanette, two sons, and a daughter. **Sources:** *Chicago Tribune,* May 10, 2004, sec. 4, p. 11; CNN.com, http://www.cnn.com/2004/SHOWBIZ/05/09/obit.king.ap/index.html (February 10, 2005); *Entertainment Weekly,* May 21, 2004, p. 20; *Independent,* (London), May 21, 2004, p. 35; *Los Angeles Times,* May 10, 2004, p. B9; *New York Times,* May 10, 2004, p. B7; *Washington Post,* May 10, 2004, B6.

—D. László Conhaim

## Elisabeth Kübler-Ross

Born Elisabeth Kübler, July 8, 1926, in Zurich, Switzerland; died August 24, 2004, in Scottsdale, AZ. Psychiatrist and author. Early in her medical career, Elisabeth Kübler-Ross developed an interest in the way hospitals cared for dying patients. Mostly, she was alarmed that the medical community, so focused on saving lives, seemed unable to deal with those who were dying. At the time, terminally ill patients were generally ignored and left to die on their own without ever being told the entire truth of their condition.

Kübler-Ross changed all that. She befriended thousands of terminally ill patients and interviewed them personally to find out how to meet their needs. She published her findings in a 1969 best-seller titled *On Death and Dying,* which ultimately helped transform the way the medical community dealt with terminally ill patients. In the book, Kübler-Ross categorized the five stages of grief terminally ill patients go through—denial, anger, bargaining, depression, and acceptance. The book, which sold millions of copies, provided a vocabulary for doctors, patients, and families to use when discussing the process of death. In the end, her work helped spawn the hospice-care movement.

Kübler-Ross, a triplet, was born on July 8, 1926, in Zurich, Switzerland, to Ernst and Emma Villiger Kübler; she weighed just two pounds. By sixth grade, Kübler-Ross had decided to become a doctor. Her father, believing this was a foolish pursuit for a girl, tried to force her into becoming a secretary in his office supply business. Rebellious and freethinking, Kübler-Ross, just 16, left home and supported herself by working as a cook, a mason, a roofer, and assisting in an eye clinic. During this time she also became familiar with hospitals while working as a volunteer helping refugees from Germany.

After World War II came to an end in 1945, Kübler-Ross traveled across Europe helping set up first-aid clinics in war-torn countries. In her journeys, Kübler-Ross met refugees and survivors of concentration camps and visited the Majdanek death camp in Poland. Afterward, she decided to become a psychiatrist so she could help people deal with the grief of death.

Kübler-Ross graduated from Switzerland's University of Zurich medical school in 1957. There she met her future husband, a Jewish-American neuropathologist named Emanuel Ross. They married in 1958 and settled in New York City. She became a research fellow at Manhattan State Hospital and was instantly alarmed by the way doctors there treated the dying. Often, they were isolated and ignored. Kübler-Ross noticed that doctors would not even give them pain medication for fear of addiction.

Intrigued by the process of dying, Kübler-Ross began talking with the terminally ill in an attempt to understand their misery and loneliness. She was eventually given permission to care for them and offer counseling. According to the London *Independent,* Kübler-Ross berated the medical community for teaching "everything about your liver and nothing about you as a person."

In 1961, Kübler-Ross became a U.S. citizen and in 1962 she and her husband accepted teaching positions at the University of Colorado medical center in Denver. One day, when asked to fill in for a well-liked instructor, Kübler-Ross brought in a 16-year-old girl who was dying of leukemia. The students, who had never spoken with a terminally ill patient, were teary by the end of the class. Afterward, Kübler-Ross regularly offered similar lectures.

In 1965, Kübler-Ross joined the faculty at the University of Chicago medical school, where she served as an assistant professor of psychiatry. While there, some theology students asked her for help on a research project concerning death. To help with the project, she began holding intimate interviews with terminally ill patients in front of hospital staff members, medical students, and theology students. Initially, the medical community shunned her seminars but in time they became so well-attended they had to be moved to a large auditorium. Eventually, her seminar became an accredited course. Today, courses on death and dying are included in medical school curriculums.

These interviews, as well as others, became the basis for Kübler-Ross's book *On Death and Dying,* where she identified and described the five psychological stages terminally ill people go through. The book became popular beyond the medical community and helped open up discussions on death in a culture that was generally uneasy with the subject. After the book's publication, Kübler-Ross was a household name. She also advocated that the dying need respect and dignity. Her work was integral in generating the creation of the U.S. hospice system.

Kübler-Ross left the academic setting after the University of Chicago began to question the validity of her work as genuine medical research. She went into private practice and spent her time writing, speaking, and giving workshops on "Life, Death, and Transition." She began interviewing patients who had had near-death experiences and these discussions led her to an investigation of life after death. As Kübler-Ross began to explore this phenomenon and talk freely about out-of-body experiences and spirit guides, the medical community lost faith in the science of her work and her credibility waned. However, as the 20th century drew to a close in 1999, *Time* magazine named her one of the "100 Most Important Thinkers" of the century.

Throughout her career Kübler-Ross maintained a heavy travel schedule and her husband eventually left her. They divorced in the 1970s and he raised their two children. In the early 1980s, she established the Kübler-Ross Center, a healing facility, on a 300-acre farm in Virginia. Kübler-Ross also began working with AIDS patients, babies in particular. In 1985, she tried to open a home for AIDS-infected children at the center; however, nearly every adult in the area signed a petition to bar the center from opening. In 1994, the center burned in an arson-suspected fire. Kübler-Ross's life's work—her notes, journals, and photos—were lost in the blaze.

Later in life, Kübler-Ross relocated to Scottsdale, Arizona, where her son and former husband lived. In the 1990s, Kübler-Ross suffered a series of strokes that left her partially paralyzed. She continued working on books, though, and moved into a hospice in 2002.

Kübler-Ross died on August 24, 2004, of natural causes at a group home in Scottsdale, AZ; she was 78. A week before her death, Kübler-Ross had lost consciousness and suffered from infections. She is survived by her son, Kenneth; her daughter, Barbara; her sister, and two granddaughters. Her ex-husband preceded her in death. **Sources:** CNN.com, http://www.cnn.com/2004/US/Southwest/08/25/obit.kublerross.ap/index.html (August 26, 2004); *Independent* (London), August 28, 2004, p. 48; *New York Times,* August 26, 2004, p. B8; *Washington Post,* August 26, 2004, p. A1, p. A11.

*—Lisa Frick*

## Janet Leigh

Born Jeanette Helen Morrison, July 6, 1927, in Merced, California; died of an inflammation of the blood vessels, October 3, 2004, in Beverly Hills, California. Actress. Though Janet Leigh appeared in more than 60 motion pictures, she is best remembered for her role as the screaming blonde beauty knifed to death in the shower at the Bates Motel in the Alfred Hitchcock thriller *Psycho.* The shower scene remains one of the most famous murder scenes in the history of film. "That scene in *Psycho* alone established Janet as one of the stars every movie fan in the world will always remember," Paramount producer A.C. Lyles noted after her death, according to the *Los Angeles Times.*

Leigh was born in 1927 to Fred and Helen Morrison. She was an only child of wanderlust parents who switched jobs frequently, moving from city to city

and apartment to apartment. Leigh escaped her household briefly at around age 15 when she eloped, marrying a 19-year-old man named John Carlyle. The marriage, however, was soon annulled and she returned home. After high school, Leigh studied music at the College of the Pacific in Stockton, California, and married Stanley Reames, a budding bandleader and sailor.

Leigh got her start in acting after Norma Shearer, a popular MGM film star of the 1920s and '30s, saw a picture of Leigh on her father's desk at the California ski lodge where he worked as a receptionist. Shearer was taken with Leigh's sexy-yet-wholesome look and passed the picture along to an agent. Leigh, just 19, went for a screen test and was awarded a $50-a-week contract with MGM.

The studio renamed her Janet Leigh and sent her to work with a drama coach. The work paid off and Leigh earned the female lead in the 1947 Civil War-era drama *The Romance of Rosy Ridge,* playing a mountain girl. She starred opposite Van Johnson, MGM's most popular male lead of the time. The following year, she played a country girl in *The Hills of Home,* which also starred the famous collie, Lassie. She divorced Reames that same year.

One of Leigh's first hits was the 1949 literary adaptation of *Little Women,* where she played the practical sister, Meg. Co-stars included June Allyson as the tomboyish protagonist, Jo, along with Elizabeth Taylor as the selfish sister, Amy.

In 1950, Leigh met actor Tony Curtis at a Hollywood party. They married in June of 1951, becoming one of Hollywood's most famed and beloved couples of the time. Countless photos of them at work—and at play—ran in magazines regularly. They made their first film together in 1953, a biography of the famous escape artist Houdini. According to the *Independent,* a *Daily Variety* movie reviewer at the time wrote that "Paired, they are a harmonious, ingratiating team." Fans filled theaters to watch them onscreen together. They followed with the 1954 action-adventure *The Black Shield of Falworth.*

Leigh's life was forever changed after appearing in the Hitchcock classic *Psycho,* released in 1960. In the film, Leigh played Marion Crane, an office worker and embezzler on the run who makes the fatal mistake of stopping for the night at the Bates Motel only to be slashed to death in the shower. This legendary scene—among the most memorable in all of movie history—lasted just 45 seconds but made

Leigh famous for life. The scene, complete with shrill music, was shot in some 70 takes over seven days with cameras positioned at every imaginable angle. Leigh wore a flesh-colored moleskin bikini so as to appear nude. The slashing was not even shown; instead, Hitchcock built up the scene then left the scary slaying to the imagination of his viewers.

The scene, shocking for its day, has been endlessly analyzed by film scholars and parodied time and time again. Besides the shock value, the scene proved fascinating to moviegoers because Hitchcock killed off the film's biggest star just 30 minutes from its beginning. Leigh nailed the role with cameras capturing a truly terrified expression on her face the moment her character realized her gruesome death was coming. She received an Academy Award nomination for best supporting actress and won a Golden Globe.

Over the course of her career Leigh appeared in some 60 films. Among her most memorable films was *The Manchurian Candidate,* a 1962 Cold-War political thriller that also starred Frank Sinatra. Another noteworthy film was the 1958 Orson Welles classic *Touch of Evil.* In this murder saga, Leigh played the American bride of a Mexican narcotics cop played by Charlton Heston. Of her films, the National Film Registry has deemed four—*Psycho, The Manchurian Candidate, A Touch of Evil* and *The Naked Spur*—as worthy of preservation.

As Leigh's film career blossomed, her marriage began to suffer and in 1962 she and Curtis divorced. She soon married stockbroker and producer Robert Brandt and the two remained together until the end of her life. She continued to regularly make films through the 1960s. In 1963, Leigh appeared in *Bye Bye Birdie* alongside Dick Van Dyke.

One of Leigh's daughters with Tony Curtis, Jamie Lee Curtis, followed in her mother's footsteps and made a name for herself in horror flicks as well, appearing in the 1978 thriller *Halloween.* The mother-daughter duo appeared together in the horror film *The Fog* in 1980 and also in 1998's *Halloween H20: 20 Years Later.* Leigh made her final film appearance in 2000 in *A Fate Totally Worse than Death.*

Leigh wrote two novels and an autobiography titled *There Really Was a Hollywood.* In addition, she wrote an entire book on her account of the infamous shower scene that launched her career. It was called *Psycho: Behind the Scenes of the Classic Thriller.*

Leigh died of vasculitis, an inflammation of the blood vessels, on October 3, 2004, at her home in Beverly Hills. She is survived by her husband, Robert Brandt, and daughters Kelly and Jamie Lee. **Sources:** CNN.com, http://www.cnn.com/2004/SHOWBIZ/Movies/10/04/obit.leigh/index.html (October 4, 2004); *Entertainment Weekly,* October 15, 2004, p. 15; E! Online, http://www.eonline.com/News/Items/0,1,15063,00.html?eol.tkr (October 5, 2004); *Independent* (London, England), October 5, 2004, p. 32; *Los Angeles Times,* October 5, 2004, p. B10; *New York Times,* October 5, 2004, p. B8.

—*Lisa Frick*

## Edward B. Lewis

Born on May 20, 1918, in Wilkes-Barre, PA; died of prostate cancer, July 21, 2004, in Pasadena, CA. Geneticist. A youthful obsession with a simple insect led Edward B. Lewis to become one of the key scientists who deciphered the genetic code that forms all living beings. Lewis used the fruit fly to show how genes control an embryo's development, and researchers have since shown that his discovery holds true in almost every animal, including humans. He won a Nobel Prize in 1995 for his work.

Lewis was born in Wilkes-Barre, Pennsylvania, in 1918. His father was a watchmaker. He began his work on fruit flies as a high school sophomore, when he and a friend spent the school biology club's entire treasury, $4, responding to an ad in *Science* magazine selling fruit flies at the rate of 100 for $1. Fruit flies are easy creatures to study because they breed easily, have a simple structure, and go from eggs to mature flies in only ten days. Lewis and his friend would visit a school lab every day to look through newly hatched flies with a magnifying glass, searching for mutants, the keys to biology research. One mutant they found, called "held-out," is still used in genetics research.

An accomplished young flute player, Lewis went to Bucknell University for a year on a flute scholarship. But Bucknell did not offer any genetics courses, so he transferred to the University of Minnesota, where he earned a bachelor's degree in 1939. Lewis then enrolled in the California Institute of Technology (Caltech) in Pasadena, California, where received a doctorate in genetics in 1942 and a master's degree in meteorology in 1943. His career at the school was interrupted by service in the United States Army and Army Air Corps; he was stationed in Hawaii and Okinawa, worked as a meteorologist and ocean-ographer, and reached the rank of captain. He returned to Caltech in 1946, spent a year as a fellow at Cambridge University in Britain from 1947 to 1948, then spent the rest of his career at Caltech.

After the war, Lewis returned to his studies of the fruit fly. One of his supervisors, Thomas Hunt Morgan, had used fruit flies to help prove that chromosomes carry genes, which hold hereditary characteristics, a discovery that won him the Nobel Prize in 1933. But when Lewis began his work, scientists did not know much more than that about how genes worked.

Lewis reached a breakthrough when he bred two mutant flies and produced flies with four wings instead of two. That meant that a whole section of the fly's thorax had been replaced with a duplicate of the section next to it. Not only had a mutant gene caused the change, Lewis realized, but the gene must have controlled the activity of other genes to produce the second wing.

For decades, Lewis bred mutant fruit flies, until he finally identified the genes that controlled the development of each section of the fly. He surprised other scientists by showing that the genes' code was simple: the genes that control early development of the fly embryo (called homeotic genes) lined up on the chromosomes in order, just as the segments they controlled appear on the fly. That order, which scientists call the "colinearity principle," was later proven to be true in humans, mice, and other vertebrates. Lewis' work on homeotic genes, summarized in a major article in 1978, won him the 1995 Nobel Prize for Physiology or Medicine.

"It was as if he made evolution occur in real time," Dr. Gerald R. Fink, a professor of genetics at the Massachusetts Institute of Technology, told the *New York Times.* "Ed Lewis worked to use genetics to show profound evolutionary strategies. There is no more remarkable evidence of that than his fruit fly with four wings."

In the 1950s, Lewis offered another, very different contribution to science: he examined how the human body reacts to radiation from X-rays, nuclear fallout, and other sources. For his research, he examined medical records from survivors of the atomic bombs the United States dropped on the Japanese cities of Hiroshima and Nagasaki in 1945 during World War II. Lewis concluded that there is no risk-free dose of radiation, and that its effects had been underestimated. He presented his find-

ings to a Congressional committee in 1957. The effects of low-dose radiation are still controversial, and they were even more so in the 1950s, when the United States was testing nuclear weapons as a major part of its military defense. Prominent supporters of nuclear technology, such as Admiral Lewis Strauss, then-chairman of the United States' Atomic Energy Commission, attacked Lewis publicly for his findings. Hurt, Lewis left the public eye and turned back to his research.

Lewis remained a biology professor at Caltech until his 1988, and stayed active at the school as a professor emeritus after his retirement. He provided the entertainment at the Caltech dinner in honor of his Nobel prize in 1995, playing with a chamber music group in the lobby as guests arrived. He was famous on campus for the costumes he wore to the school's Halloween party; once, he came dressed as a mutant fruit fly with two tails. Lewis' schedule at Caltech remained the same until a few months before his death: he got to his office at 8 a.m. and often worked until midnight, with breaks to practice the flute from 10 to 10:30, swim in the pool, and take a mid-afternoon nap.

Lewis died of prostate cancer on July 21, 2004, in Pasadena, California; he was 86. He is survived by his wife, Pamela, an artist he met in the Caltech laboratory, and their sons, Hugh and Keith. A third son died in 1965. **Sources:** *Chicago Tribune,* July 27, 2004, sec. 2, p. 11; *Los Angeles Times,* July 23, 2004, p. B10; *New York Times,* July 26, 2004, p. A14; *Times* (London), August 3, 2004, p. 26; *Washington Post,* July 26, 2004, p. B4.

*—Erick Trickey*

# Bella Lewitzky

Born January 13, 1916, in Los Angeles, CA; died from complications of a stroke, July 16, 2004, in Pasadena, CA. Dancer and choreographer. Widely acclaimed dancer and choreographer Bella Lewitzky established her career in Los Angeles where, after developing as an artist in ensemble companies, she nurtured a prominent modern dance troupe that bore her name. She won many honors during her 60-year career, including five honorary doctorates, the *Dance Magazine* Award, a Guggenheim fellowship, the prestigious Capezio Award, the first California Governor's Award for Lifetime Achievement, and the National Medal of the Arts. She created such works as "On the Brink of Time" (1969), "Kinaesonata" (1970), and "Greening" (1976). Because her fiercely independent work was remote from the mainstream East Coast establishment, she and her productions were less famous than might be thought, considering her impressive list of honors, awards, and appointments. An ardent advocate of free artistic expression, when accepting a grant from the National Endowment for the Arts (NEA) in 1990 Lewitzky scratched out a mandatory anti-obscenity pledge. Later, she successfully sued the NEA to remove the pledge from its awards process.

The younger of two daughters of Russian immigrants, Lewitzky spent her childhood in a utopian community in the Mojave Desert until her family moved to San Bernardino, California, where she studied dance and learned to play the piano. As a teenager, she moved to Los Angeles and began taking ballet lessons. She became a devoted dancer at the age of 18 while studying under the renowned Lester Horton at the Norma Gould Studio. By age 21, she had already won widespread recognition. In 1940, she married a fellow dancer and architect, Newell Taylor Reynolds, and six years later joined efforts with him, Horton, and William Bowne to found the Dance Theatre. In that troupe, she performed works by Horton such as "Salome" (1937) and "The Beloved" (1948). But in 1951, Lewitzky left the company to found Dance Associates, which she dissolved in 1955 after the birth of her daughter. Also in 1951, she was summoned before the House Un-American Activities Committee but refused to cooperate in its efforts to identify communists in the arts.

In her early years of motherhood, she directed her professional attention toward education, becoming a highly regarded instructor at a number of institutions, including the University of Southern California, the Idyllwild School of the Arts, and the California Institute for the Arts. She also taught abroad. From 1966 to 1997, she led the acclaimed Bella Lewitzky Dance Company in Los Angeles, which toured in 43 states and 20 countries. Departing from the emphasis on ethnic dance that had characterized Horton's approach, hers had intensely feminine energy that was able to "appeal, always vehemently and often poignantly, to the emotions," wrote Martin Bernheimer in the *Los Angeles Times*. The company's New York debut at the Brooklyn Academy of Music in 1971 firmly established her as a leading national artist. According to Lewis Segal in the *Los Angeles Times*, she was called "one of America's great modern dancers" by the *New York Times*' Clive Barnes. Jack Anderson of the *New York Times* noted that fellow *Times* writer Anna Kiselgoff

referred to Lewitzky as "an extraordinary artist with an astounding mastery of technique." Lewitzky retired as a performer at the age of 62.

Vivacious and exceptionally prolific, Lewitzky created a minimum of one new production each year, directing her company until she was 80. She was noted for the motherly care she took in the welfare and livelihood of her dancers, providing them with health insurance and year-round salaries regardless of their work schedule. The choreographer Loretta Livingston, who was once a member of Lewitzky's company, told Segal that Lewitzky was "an extraordinary and rare role model, a powerful woman who was every bit as strong as the men in society." In 1997, President Bill Clinton presented her with the National Medal of the Arts in recognition of her contributions to modern American dance. She was also honored in April of 2001 at the annual Lester Horton Dance Award ceremony in Hollywood.

Lewitzky served both on the panel of the NEA and on the California Arts Council. Disheartened after 15 years trying to acquire sufficient funding for a proposed school for dance in Los Angeles—the Dance Gallery on Bunker Hill—she abandoned the project in 1992. Then, at age 83, her right leg was amputated as the result of chronic arterial disease from which she had long suffered. She and Reynolds spent their later years near their daughter, Nora Reynolds Daniel, and grandchildren in Albuquerque, New Mexico, before moving to an assisted living home in Pasadena, California. She died there on July 16, 2004, at the age of 88 from a heart attack after a stroke. She is survived by her husband, their daughter, and several grandchildren. **Sources:** *Los Angeles Times,* July 17, 2004, p. B17; *New York Times,* July 19, 2004, p. A19; *Times,* (London), July 19, 2004, p. 25; *Washington Post,* July 18, 2004, p. C9.

—D. László Conhaim

## Ratu Sir Kamisese Mara

Born Kamisese Kapaiwai Tuimacilai Mara, May 6, 1920, in Lomaloma, Fiji; died from complications of a stroke, April 18, 2004, in Suva, Fiji. Politician. As a tribal chief of the Lau Islands of eastern Fiji, Ratu Sir Kamisese Mara led his people to independence from Britain, becoming Fiji's first prime minister in 1970. During the Cold War he was an important ally of the United States, Australia, and New Zealand in the South Pacific. Considered Fiji's "founding father," Mara is credited with uniting the islands' feuding tribes toward the common goal of independence. "His leadership was marked by discipline, vision, and a keen and penetrating intellect," observed the sitting prime minister at the time of his death, according to the *Los Angeles Times.*

Belonging to an indigenous noble family in a British colonial society, Mara grew up in Vanuabalavu in the archipelago of Lau. Fiji consists of some 300 islands, its populace generally divided between Melanesian and Polynesian cultures. Mara became the tribal king of Lakemba, Lau's largest island. He studied medicine at the University of Otago in New Zealand. But prior to earning his degree, a Fijian leader, Rau Sir Lala Sukuna, recalled him to be groomed for the diplomatic service of his country. He was sent to Oxford University, where Sukuna had been the first Fijian to graduate. There, Mara learned modern history and earned a master's degree in political science; later, he studied Third World development principles at the London School of Economics. He also excelled in sports, especially in cricket. He returned home to assume various tribal and political responsibilities. In 1963, Mara founded the Alliance Party (AP), which represented multiracial interests (Fijian, European, part-European, Chinese, and Gujerati Indian), and was soon appointed to its chief magisterial position. That year, women were fully enfranchised in Fiji. In 1965, Britain granted Fiji a measure of self-government. The island's leaders, accustomed to ruling by birth-right, began to adopt the principles of elective government.

In 1970, Mara received the "Instruments of Independence" from the Prince of Wales, making Fiji a sovereign nation within the Commonwealth, and after becoming prime minister he set about forming a government that cut across race, creed, and color lines. The West looked upon his efforts favorably. For more than a decade foreign investment poured into Fiji. The economy, formerly hampered by the post-colonial caste system, made strides with strong sugar and tourism industries and by encouraging free enterprise. But while many of the middle class became rich, the poor generally remained destitute. As the disparity between the haves and the have-nots grew, racial tension increased, and Mara was accused of dynastic favoritism and corruption.

A coalition of opposition parties was formed to contest the AP, and in the general election of 1987 Mara was ousted. But the following month, Lieutenant-Colonel Sitiveni Rabuka led a successful coup attempt backed, it was alleged, by Mara's eldest son, perhaps even by Mara himself. In October of that year, Rabuka named Fiji a republic. Mara became

its first prime minister, officially to prevent further upheaval, particularly amongst rival Melanesian and ethnic Indian factions. However a new constitution was written that put the interests of ethnic Fijians over others those of other groups, earning the Great Council of Chiefs—its promulgator—the condemnation of India, Australia, and New Zealand. In 1992, heading the Fijian Political Party, Rabuka took over the role of prime minister and Mara became vice-president. Two years later, after the death of the sitting president, Mara assumed the country's presidency. In May of 2000, another coup brought Mara down, this time permanently. Along with his daughter and many others, Mara was held hostage in Parliament for 56 days by an armed gang with ties to business and the army. After they threatened his daughter's life, Mara agreed to step down and retire from public life. Shortly thereafter, one of the coup plotters, George Speight, appointed himself acting premier, and as a result the British Commonwealth suspended Fiji's membership.

Though Speight was arrested two months later at the order of the Great Council of Chiefs, he was briefly an MP in the new government, but in 2001 he was expelled for poor attendance in parliament. Speight would later be found guilty of treason and sentenced to life imprisonment.

Mara, who published a 1997 autobiography, *The Pacific Way,* suffered a stroke in 2001 and never fully recovered. He died from stroke-related complications on April 18, 2004, in Suva, Fiji, at the age of 83. His burial ceremony was a colorful affair attended by thousands and held in a mixture of Fijian and British styles: 600 soldiers carried his coffin to the burial grounds guarded by traditional warriors dressed in palm leaf skirts and wielding clubs. Mara is survived by his wife, Lady Ro Lala Mara, two sons, and three daughters. **Sources:** BBC News, http://news.bbc.co.uk/1/hi/world/asia-pacific/3680829.stm (January 2, 2005); BBC News, http://news.bbc.co.uk/1/hi/world/asia-pacific/country_profiles/1300499.stm (January 2, 2005); *Independent,* (London), April 20, 2004, p. 34; *Los Angeles Times,* April 20, 2004, p. B13; *New York Times,* April 20, 2004, p. A21; *Times* (London), April 20, 2004 p. 26; *Washington Post,* April 21, 2004, p. B6.

—D. László Conhaim

# Tug McGraw

Born Frank Edwin McGraw, August 30, 1944, in Martinez, CA; died from cancer, January 5, 2004, in

Franklin, TN. Professional baseball player. The 2004 death of retired baseball player Tug McGraw from cancer at the age of 59 stunned legions of his long-time fans. McGraw was one of the sport's most exuberant and popular figures during the 1970s and 1980s as a pitcher with the New York Mets and the Philadelphia Phillies. In 1980, he led the Phillies to their only World Series victory. McGraw's personal life was similarly mythic: late in life, he learned he was the father of a young boy, who went on to become country-music star Tim McGraw.

Born Frank Edwin McGraw in 1944, the future Major League Baseball legend grew up in Vallejo, California, where he played ball for St. Vincent Ferrer High School. His nickname dated back to infancy and his insistent feeding habits. After a stint on the team at Vallejo Junior College, he was signed to the New York Mets in 1964 as a free agent, and played with the Mets' farm team for a season. He emerged as a top-notch left-handed pitcher with a good fastball and solid curveball, but a third throw was necessary to advance him out of the minors, and so McGraw perfected the screwball pitch, which would become his trademark.

McGraw went on to help the Mets win the 1969 World Series, but it was in the build-up to the 1973 post-season that his signature phrase, "Ya gotta believe!" was coined. In August of that year, the Mets were down more than eleven games, and after a particularly bad performance, Mets chair M. Donald Grant delivered a torrid locker-room lecture to the chastened team. Coming out of the meeting, McGraw was said to have uttered the phrase, poking fun of Grant's pep talk, but his teammates burst out laughing and they went on to a winning streak that landed them in the World Series. Though the Mets lost to Oakland in seven games, "Ya gotta believe!" became the catchphrase of the season and would remain indelibly associated with McGraw's high-spirited personality.

McGraw amassed a solid record as a pitcher, though he admitted that the pressures of performing as a relief pitcher occasionally unnerved him. "Coming into a game, my knees always feel weak," he admitted to *New York Times* columnist Dave Anderson. "I have to push off the mound harder." Known for his spontaneous quips and graciousness to his fans, McGraw became one of the sport's most beloved figures of the times. "He wore his sandy hair long," noted *New York Times* writer Frank Litsky, "and with his little-boy face and boyish enthusiasm he was a crowd favorite. After a third out, he would run off the mound, slapping his glove against a thigh. After a close call, he would pat his heart." Traded to

Philadelphia in 1974, he went on to help the franchise take East Division titles in 1976, 1977, and 1978, and the National League pennant in 1980 and 1983. But it was Game Six of the Phillies' World Series race in 1980 that would define McGraw's career and make him a hero forever in his adopted hometown: in the ninth inning, with bases loaded, he struck out batter Kansas City's Willie Wilson, and the Phillies won the World Series pennant for the first time in Major League history.

The photograph taken just after that moment showed McGraw jumping off his mound, hands high in the air, and became one of the classic images in sports history. Another timeless photo was captured just seconds later, when Phillies third-base player Mike Schmidt jumped into his arms on the mound. Schmidt later said the two had planned it on their ride to Veterans Stadium that night. "Both of us knew whoever was on or near that mound for the final out would probably be on the cover of *Sports Illustrated*," Schmidt told the same publication. "Sure enough, it worked. Tug struck out Wilson and then turned to look at me at third base. Of course I came running and jumped on him."

The 1984 season was McGraw's last in baseball. He retired with a 96-92 record and a 3.14 earned-run average. He became a television reporter for a Philadelphia station, wrote three children's books, and remained a fan favorite. The father of two sons and a daughter, he belatedly discovered his fourth and oldest child after an eleven-year-old Louisiana boy came across his birth certificate. Tim Smith was an ardent baseball fan, and was stunned to find the name of one of his heroes in the space on the document that listed the father's name. Smith, who later took his father's name, was the product of a romance between McGraw and Betty Trimble that occurred during his minor-league career, and McGraw had never known of the boy's existence. McGraw and his long-lost son enjoyed a close relationship, and Tim McGraw grew up to become a country-music legend and husband of Faith Hill, another Nashville star.

McGraw was diagnosed with a brain tumor in March of 2003 while working at Phillies spring-training camp in Clearwater, Florida, as a special instructor. He underwent surgery in Tampa, after which his doctors—a team of top specialists assembled and paid for by his son, Tim—believed they had eradicated it completely, but a wait-and-see policy was in place when McGraw next appeared in public again on May 29. "I'm not fearful," McGraw told reporters in a characteristically upbeat mood, according to a Knight Ridder/Tribune News Service report by Paul Hagen. "I have confidence." He went to work on his autobiography, which carried the not-unexpected working title, *Ya Gotta Believe!*.

In September of 2003, McGraw reprised his 1980 World Series moment at the closing ceremonies at Veterans' Stadium in Philadelphia, which was slated for demolition in March of 2004. He had hoped to be there for the demolition, but on December 31, 2003, he suffered a seizure, and died six days later at a cabin in Franklin, Tennessee, near the home of his son, Tim, and family. His former Philly teammate Schmidt told *Sports Illustrated* that McGraw accepted his fate with the same attitude that had made him such a favorite among players and fans alike. "Publicly, he never let on that he had gotten a raw deal," Schmidt noted. "As he always said, 'I front-loaded my life, just like my contract.'"
**Sources:** Knight Ridder/Tribune News Service, January 5, 2004; *Los Angeles Times,* January 6, 2004; *New York Times,* January 6, 2004; January 11, 2004; *People,* January 19, 2004; *SI.com,* http://sportsillustrated.cnn.com/2004/baseball/mlb/01/05/obit.mcgraw.ap/index.htm 1 (January 7, 2004); *Times* (London), February 17, 2004.

—*Carol Brennan*

## Ann Miller

Born Johnnie Lucille Collier, April 12, 1923, in Chireno, TX; died of lung cancer on January 22, 2004, in Los Angeles, CA. Actress and dancer. Charismatic and popular, Ann Miller performed on stage and screen for more than 60 years. She made films opposite some of Hollywood's most beloved male dancers, including Gene Kelly and Fred Astaire. Though she worked hard and always gave her best in any role, she never made it to the level of leading lady until 1979 when she starred in the Broadway show *Sugar Babies* with movie legend Mickey Rooney. Richard Severo of the *New York Times* reported that she once said of the role, "I was never the star in films. I was the brassy, good-hearted showgirl.... *Sugar Babies* gave me the stardom that my soul kind of yearned for."

The first and only child of criminal lawyer John Alfred Collier and Clara Birdwell, Miller was named Johnnie at birth because her father had wanted a boy. Miller started dance classes beginning at age five after she suffered a bout of rickets; her mother

hoped it would strengthen the young girl's legs. By age ten, Miller was an accomplished tap dancer. Unfortunately, her parents divorced and Miller moved with her mother to California. It was around this time that Miller's birthdates became obscured. Birdwell was deaf and found it hard to find work, but Miller could pass for older and began dancing in nightclubs to support the two of them. Her mother started calling her Annie once they moved to California, and eventually Miller adopted the stage name Ann Miller, which she kept throughout her career.

In 1934, she was spotted at a San Francisco nightclub by actress and comedienne Lucille Ball who returned to her studio, RKO, and convinced them to give her a contract. Miller had her uncredited screen debut in the 1934 film *Anne of the Green Gables*. She had a few more small uncredited appearances before appearing as herself in the 1937 film *New Faces of 1937* alongside Ball as well as up-and-coming Hollywood stars Ginger Rogers and Katherine Hepburn. In 1938, she had a memorable role in the film *You Can't Take It With You* as a member of a freewheeling, somewhat crazy family who meets their very proper soon-to-be in-laws.

Throughout the rest of the 1930s and 1940s, she appeared in a variety of B-grade movies produced by RKO, Columbia, and Republic. Always a favorite with the critics, even when the movie was not well liked, Miller never made it to the leading role in a major Hollywood film. The closest she came was in 1948 after she signed to MGM Studios. She played the ex-girlfriend of Fred Astaire in the classic film *Easter Parade*. Miles Kreuger, president of the Institute of the American Musical, described her performance of "Shaking the Blues Away" to the *Los Angeles Times,* "It's a great solo turn where she's on the stage alone and she just uses the space wonderfully. That number captures all the essence .... of Ann Miller—the bravura tap dancing and her enormous energy and that joyous smile that was so engaging."

Unfortunately, the era of the Hollywood musical ended. Miller had memorable roles in a couple other films including 1949's *On the Town,* which starred Gene Kelly and Frank Sinatra, and 1953's *Kiss Me Kate.* By the end of the 1950s she had moved to the small screen and was making occasional appearances on television variety shows like *The Ed Sullivan Show.* She also supported herself by performing at nightclubs. In 2001, Miller returned to the big screen for a role in director David Lynch's *Mulholland Drive.* As Coco Lenoix, Miller imparted an air of old Hollywood glamour into a film that meant to expose the illusions Hollywood can create.

In 1939, she made her Broadway debut in a show called *Scandals.* Her performance earned her rave reviews, and she used that as leverage for her film career. Thirty years later she returned to Broadway for even more raves as the title character in *Mame.* In 1979, after more than 40 years in show business, Miller headlined in yet another popular Broadway show, *Sugar Babies.* The show toured for years and helped make Miller wealthy. It also earned her her only Tony nomination.

In 1998, she appeared in a production of Stephen Sondheim's *Follies* as an aging star who has the guts to go on. Her performance earned yet more rave reviews, especially for her take on "I'm Still Here," a song about surviving in show business. Angelo Del Rossi, executive producer for *Follies,* described her work ethic to the *Los Angeles Times,* "The audiences adored her.... But she wasn't someone with a star complex. She worked. She never slouched on rehearsals. She was very disciplined."

Miller was married and divorced three times. Her first marriage, to millionaire Reese Milner in 1946, ended in divorce a short time after the death of their newborn daughter. She married oilman William Moss in 1958, but divorced him shortly thereafter. Her 1961 marriage to another oilman, Arthur Cameron, was annulled. Despite being unlucky in love, Miller was financially successful. The money she made touring with *Sugar Babies* made her rich. In addition she had investments in real estates and one of the largest collections of Native American jewelry in the world.

Miller died on January 22, 2004; she was 81. As testament to her contribution to dance, the Smithsonian Institution displays her favorite tap shoes, named Moe and Joe. The director of *Mame,* John Bowab, told the *Los Angeles Times,* "She brought an aura of happiness with her to the stage.... She was funny, bright, glamorous, and she loved every minute of it." **Sources:** *Independent* (London), January 24, 2004, p. 20; *Los Angeles Times,* January 23, 2004, p. B10; *New York Times,* January 23, 2004, p. A21; *San Francisco Chronicle,* January 23, 2004, p. A2; *Washington Post,* January 23, 2004, p. B7.

—*Eve M. B. Hermann*

## Czeslaw Milosz

Born June 30, 1911, in Szetejnie, Lithuania; died August 14, 2004, in Krakow, Poland. Poet. One of the most eminent poets to emerge from Eastern Europe's troubled twentieth-century landscape, Czeslaw Milosz (pronounced CHESS-wahf MEE-wosh) fled Poland as Soviet-style communism took root there, but returned as a literary legend as he neared his eightieth birthday. Milosz's astounding output, which included volumes of verse, essays, and criticism, mark him as one of his country's most prolific chroniclers of its tragic—but ultimately triumphant—modern era, but the quality of his work made him one of Poland's rare Nobel Prize recipients in literature, which he was awarded in 1980.

Milosz was born in what is technically Lithuania, which was part of Imperial Russia at the time but included a large Polish population, which had also been subsumed into Russia's empire's borders. He was born on June 30, 1911, in the town of Szetejnie, where his Polish-speaking family was living at the time. Trouble came a few years later, when World War I broke out; Milosz's father, a civil engineer, was drafted into the tsar's army, and the family had to flee encroaching German troops a number of times. After the war, they settled in Vilnius, the Lithuanian capital which Milosz would later describe as "a city of clouds resembling Baroque architecture and of Baroque architecture like coagulated clouds" according to his *Times* of London obituary. He began writing poetry in his teens, and was fascinated by the sciences as well; he spurned both of these to study law, but won a scholarship to study literature in Paris thanks to a distant relative, Oscar Milosz, a respected poet.

Milosz's earliest verse was somewhat apocalyptic in its themes, and this type of poetry came to be grouped under the "Catastrophist" school of the 1930s. Much of the doom foretold by this generation, literary critics note, did indeed come to pass. In Poland, those horrors began in earnest with Nazi Germany's invasion in 1939; Milosz was working for Polish state radio in Warsaw at the time, and fled to Romania. He went to Vilnius—by then under Soviet occupation—and eventually returned to German-controlled Warsaw after a perilous trip. There, he worked with the anti-German resistance movement, and served as a poetry editor for an underground publisher. Some of his most moving poems, such as "A Poor Christian Looks at the Ghetto," chronicle the tragedies of this period, including the walling off of Warsaw's Jews into a ghetto, where countless died.

After World War II, Milosz worked for the Polish embassy in New York City, and was later posted to Paris. He still wrote, but was wary of the new cultural dictates from Poland's Communist regime. Artistic output, according to the party line, should conform to certain political ideals, and this included new literary works. When he learned in 1951 that he was about to be detained, he sought political asylum in France. His landmark 1953 work, *The Captive Mind,* argued that doctrinaire authoritarian regimes stifle intellectual output. In it, he provided thinly disguised case histories that recounted the brainwashing tactics used on some leading Polish cultural icons in recent years. Milosz was not hesitant about criticizing the left in the West, either: in other writings and interviews, he mocked the French left's flirtation with communism and its adoration of Soviet tyrant Josef Stalin. Some of this was retributive: he had arrived in France as a political exile, and was virtually destitute; prominent figures of the left-leaning literary world treated him coolly, and he had a difficult time finding a publisher during these years.

Milosz left France when the University of California offered him a professorship. After 1961, he taught Slavic languages and literature at the university's vibrant Berkeley campus, where his classes were popular with several generations of students. He became an American citizen, but still wrote his poems in Polish. The epic "Gdzie slonce wschodzi I kedy zapada" (From the Rising of the Sun), from 1974, is considered one of his best works, and was part of an impressive body of work that brought him the 1980 Nobel Prize in literature.

By the end of that decade, Communism in Poland had retreated, and Milosz was able to return. He was hailed as national literary icon, a voice of Poland's conscience, and spent the remainder of his years in Krakow, where he died at the age of 93 on August 14, 2004. Married twice, he was twice widowed, but sons Anthony and John Peter with first wife Janina Dluska, who endured the Warsaw Nazi occupation with him, survive him.

When he was still quite young, Milosz wrote of the fragility of life, from the vantage point of a Pole enjoying a heady sojourn in 1935 Paris. This particular poem, partly reprinted in his *Times* of London obituary, seems all the more poignant for all the near-brushes with death or oblivion that its author would subsequently endure. "Roll on, rivers; raise your hands / cities! I, a faithful son of the black earth, shall return to the black earth. / as if my life had not been, / as if not my heart, not my blood, / not my duration / had created words and songs / but an unknown, impersonal voice, / only the flapping of waves, only the choir of winds / and the autumnal sway / of the tall trees." **Sources:** *Guardian* (London), August 16, 2004, p. 17; *Independent* (London), August 16, 2004, p. 30; *New York Times,* August 15, 2004, p. A41; *Times* (London), August 16, 2004, p. 24.

*—Carol Brennan*

# Carl Mydans

Born May 20, 1907, in Boston, MA; died of heart failure, August 16, 2004, in Larchmont, NY. Photographer. Carl Mydans spent 40 years with *Life* magazine, and delivered some of the most potent images of American triumph in World War II in just one phase of his long career. Mydans snapped the iconic moment when General Douglas MacArthur purposefully strode ashore in the Philippines in 1945, and also captured the signing of Japan's surrender aboard the U.S.S. *Missouri,* among other scenes. But he also photographed the war from the viewpoint of the ordinary soldier or sailor. "Resourceful and unruffled, Mr. Mydans sent back pictures of combat that even now define how we remember World War II, Korea, and other conflicts," noted *New York Times* obituary writer Andy Grundberg.

A native of Boston, Mydans was born in 1907 into a family of second-generation Russian immigrants. He studied journalism at Boston University, where he first learned how to take and develop photographs. After he graduated in 1930, he found work as a reporter for *American Banker,* but eventually bought a 35-millimeter Contax camera, which was a competitor to the more-famous Leica brand. The Contax was small, and enabled its carrier to easily roam about and take photos with a minimum of advance preparation. He quickly mastered the camera, and began to sell his work to *Time* and other magazines.

In 1935, Mydans was hired as a photographer with a U.S. federal agency called the Resettlement Administration; it later became the Farm Security Administration. He traveled throughout New England and the South, documenting the end of a rural-based economy, and gained a measure of renown for his images of bedraggled Arkansas farmers and their families. It was the Great Depression, and the poorest of America's poor were devastated by the economic downturn. "One picture, of a Tennessee family living in a hut built on an abandoned truck chassis, portrays the misery of the times," noted Mydans' *Times* of London obituary, "as starkly as any photographs by his more celebrated contemporaries."

After a more than a year with the Farm Security Administration, Mydans was hired by *Life* magazine just before its debut issue hit newsstands in late 1936. He was only the fifth photographer on its staff, joining an impressive roster that included Alfred Eisenstaedt and Margaret Bourke-White. For one of his first assignments, he was sent to a Texas town, Freer, to document the heady oil-boom atmosphere there. In 1938, Mydans married Shelley

Smith, a *Life* staff writer whose father had established the journalism program at Stanford University. The pair would spent the remainder of their marriage working side by side.

At the onset of World War II, *Life* sent Mydans to shoot the Soviet invasion of Finland in 1939. He later roamed over to the Pacific, where he covered the Sino-Japanese War, but in the Philippines capital of Manila he and his wife were captured by incoming Japanese troops in January of 1942. They were held captive for almost two years—first in Manila, then Shanghai—and were released in a prisoner-exchange agreement. After a brief respite in New York, both Mydans and his wife returned to the combat zone, this time in Europe as the war wound to a close.

Back in the Pacific theater in mid-1945, Mydans shot the famous image of General MacArthur striding ashore. The legendary officer had declared, when the Japanese came in 1942, "I shall return," and Mydans' photograph of the formidable general immortalized that claim for posterity. Some asserted that it must have been staged, but Mydans resolutely defended the photograph as entirely spontaneous, though he did admit that MacArthur was savvy about public-relations opportunities. The general had appeared in Mydans' other memorable image from that assignment, watching with other top U.S. brass as a Japanese delegation signed the official documents of surrender on an early September day in 1945. "No one I have ever known in public life had a better understanding of the drama and power of a picture," the *Guardian*'s Christopher Reed quoted Mydans as saying about MacArthur.

Despite his two years in captivity, Mydans bore no ill will toward the Asian nation, and accepted an assignment to head Time-Life's Tokyo bureau with his wife. Time-Life was the publisher of *Time, Life* and other top magazines, which Mydans continued to provide with an array of visual stories. In 1948, he just happened to be in the city of Fukui when a massive earthquake struck; some of his shots were taken on the street while buildings were collapsing around him.

After covering the Korean War, Mydans traveled the globe for the next two decades for *Life* before the publication folded in 1972. When it was re-launched several years later, he was still listed as one of its contributing photographers. He died on August 16, 2004, of heart failure at his home in Larchmont, New York, at the age of 97. Widowed in 2002, he is survived by his daughter, Misty, a Cali-

fornia attorney; and his son, Seth, who is the *New York Times'* Asia correspondent. **Sources:** BBC News, http://news.bbc.co.uk/1/hi/entertainment/arts/3576040.stm (May 3, 2005); *Guardian* (London), August 20, 2004, p. 25; *New York Times,* August 18, 2004, p. A21; *Times* (London), August 20, 2004, p. 32.

—*Carol Brennan*

## Jack Paar

Born Jack Harold Paar, May 1, 1918, in Canton, OH; died January 27, 2004, in Greenwich, CT. Television personality, actor, and radio-show host. Jack Paar took over as host of *The Tonight Show* in 1957 and in five brilliant years revolutionized late-night television. Before Paar, most programs in that time slot featured a variety-show atmosphere, where guests came to perform various acts, comic skits, songs, and dances. Paar, however, changed all that. He required guests to do more than simply perform—he made them sit and chat while the cameras rolled, entertaining viewers with colorful dialogues. Paar also introduced the idea of the opening monologue, as well as the sofa-and-desk set still popular on late-night television. He is remembered by fans as the original "King of Late Night."

Jack Harold Paar was born May 1, 1918, in Canton, Ohio, to Howard and Lillian Paar. He grew up mostly in Michigan, though the family moved around a lot because Paar's father transferred locations frequently for his job with the New York Central Railroad.

Paar learned about misfortune early in life. When he was five, his older brother died in an accident and five years later, his best friend died. When Paar was 14, he contracted tuberculosis, which left him bed-ridden for eight months. To help pass the time during his illness, Paar tinkered with radios and other simple electronics at a bedside workbench built by his father. He also spent a lot of time reading about historical figures. As Paar began to recover, he took a job with a railroad crew to help strengthen his body.

During childhood, Paar also had to overcome a stuttering problem. To improve his speech, Paar said he spent many hours reading aloud with buttons in his mouth. Paar wrestled in high school but never graduated, dropping out to take a job announcing station breaks at a local radio station. Radio suited him well and Paar worked his way up through the ranks, becoming a fairly well-known comic disc jockey. He spent time in small radio stations in Youngstown (Ohio), Indianapolis, Pittsburgh, Cleveland, and Buffalo.

After the United States became involved in World War II, Paar joined the Army and was assigned to a special services unit whose mission was to entertain the troops stationed in the South Pacific. Working as a stand-up comic for the Army, Paar hit his stride as he dashed off joke after joke that tickled the soldiers, most often at the expense of the officers. According to the *Los Angeles Times,* Paar once told an officer who was talking during the show, "Lieutenant, a man with your IQ should have a low voice, too." His Army antics caught the eye of war correspondent Sidney Carroll, who wrote a rave review of Paar for *Esquire* magazine, earning him national exposure.

Paar left the Army in 1946 and took his act to Hollywood, where he landed roles as minor characters in several films. He played the part of Marilyn Monroe's boyfriend in the 1951 comedy *Love Nest.* He also appeared in 1950's *Walk Softly, Stranger,* and 1953's *Down Among the Sheltering Palms.* Paar also tried his hand at television, hosting a couple of failed television game shows and quiz shows. His only real success during this period came in 1947, when he was chosen as the summer replacement for Jack Benny's wildly popular Sunday evening radio show. In 1954, Paar replaced Walter Cronkite as host of CBS's *The Morning Show* in an attempt to grab viewers from NBC's *The Today Show.* The show did not attract enough sponsors, so Paar left.

Paar's big break came in 1957, when he took over from Steve Allen as host of *The Tonight Show.* Allen had favored sketch comedy, but the quick-witted Paar turned the program into a talk show. Paar became famous for the incredulous anecdotes he told about his family and his life, which he always introduced with his famous catch phrase, "I kid you not."

From his set, Paar helped launch the careers of dozens of unknowns like Bill Cosby, Carol Burnett, and Woody Allen. Intrigued by the personalities of the day, Paar brought in a range of guests, from pianist-composer Oscar Levant to 1960 presidential hopefuls John F. Kennedy and Richard Nixon. Actress Judy Garland was often in the mix. Paar also took his audience outside the studio. He traveled to Cuba to interview Fidel Castro and to Africa to speak

with medical missionary Albert Schweitzer. During the time Paar hosted the show, it became known as *The Jack Paar Tonight Show.*

Paar could be charming and sentimental, but also edgy and unpredictable. Sometimes he cried; other times he blew up. In 1960, Paar left the show for a month when NBC censored a segment about a toilet. According to the *Los Angeles Times,* Paar returned four weeks later, opening with, "As I was saying before I was interrupted."

Paar left the show in 1962, much to the dismay of his fans. He was replaced by Johnny Carson, who stayed for nearly 30 years. Next, Paar hosted a prime-time interview program for three more seasons before retiring. In summing up Paar's career, Ron Simon of the Museum of Television and Radio told the *Times* of London, "Anyone who saw him when he was in his prime knew he was a great television original. You never knew what was going to happen.... He was the catalyst for ways the talk show would go."

After Paar left television, he kept his life mostly out of the public eye. He died on January 27, 2004; he was 85. Paar's health had been declining in the months prior to his death. A year earlier, he had suffered a stroke. Paar had been previously married and divorced twice to a pianist named Irene. He is survived by his second wife, Miriam Wagner Paar, whom he married in October of 1943; his daughter, Randy; and a grandson. **Sources:** *Chicago Tribune,* January 28, 2004, sec. 1, p. 11; CNN.com, http://www.cnn.com/2004/SHOWBIZ/TV/01/27/obit.paar.ap/index.html (January 28, 2004); *Los Angeles Times,* January 28, 2004, p. B10; *New York Times,* January 28, 2004, p. A21; *Times* (London), February 5, 2004, p. 40; *Washington Post,* January 28, 2004, p. B6.

—Lisa Frick

## John Pople

Born John Anthony Pople, October 31, 1925, in Burnham-on-Sea, Somerset, England; died of liver cancer, March 15, 2004, in Chicago, IL. Mathematician and chemist. Sir John A. Pople was a brilliant British mathematician who gained notoriety for being one of the first researchers to realize the role computers could play in the field of science. Pople wrote a computer program that could predict the shifting structure of molecules in chemical reactions, thus allowing scientists to study matter without labs. His program is widely used in chemical research from pharmaceuticals to plastics. For this breakthrough, Pople was awarded the 1998 Nobel Prize in chemistry. His work so altered the field of science that Queen Elizabeth II made him a Knight of the British Empire in 2003.

Pople (pronounced POPE-el) was born October 31, 1925, in the small English resort town of Burnham-on-Sea in Somerset. His father owned a clothing shop and his mother served as a tutor to the area's wealthy families. She also worked as an Army librarian during World War I. Pople was born into a working-class family, but his parents made it known early on that they had high expectations and wanted him to do more with his life than simply take over the family business.

Pople's ambitious parents knew a solid education would be central to his success, but because Pople was from a working-class family, he was not allowed to enroll at the prep school in Burnham. Pople ended up attending school 30 miles away in Bristol. Getting there required dedication. Every day, Pople biked two miles, rode the train 25 miles, and walked another mile just to get to school. There were other impediments as well. By 1940, Britain was heavily involved in World War II and the shipping port of Bristol was frequently bombed by enemy raids. Pople passed burning buildings and unexploded bombs on his way to school. Because of the bombings, classes were held in deep underground bunkers.

By the age of 12, Pople had developed a fondness for mathematics. He rescued a calculus book from the trash and read it cover to cover. Teachers soon recognized Pople's talents and coached him at his level, helping him earn a math scholarship to Cambridge University's Trinity College in 1943. Like other gifted young men of the time, Pople was allowed to enroll in college instead of entering the army like most others. He was the first member of his family to attend college. Students with high potential, however, were pushed to finish their schooling in two years instead of the standard three so they could join radar and nuclear weapons research projects to help with the war. Pople finished the requirements for his mathematics degree in May of 1945, just as the war in Europe was ending.

Pople wanted to attend graduate school but was forced out of college by the flood of servicemen returning to the area. He took a job with the Bristol Aeroplane Company and was able to return to Cambridge in 1947 to work as a research student in mathematical sciences. He earned his doctoral degree in mathematics in 1951. During his college years, Pople took up the piano and hired Joy Bowers to instruct him. They married in 1952.

Pople worked as a research fellow and mathematics lecturer at Cambridge until 1958. That year, he became head of the physics division of England's National Physical Laboratory, located near London in Teddington. The position involved a lot of administrative work and Pople soon yearned to return to research. He quit, then traveled to the United States. In 1964, he started teaching chemical physics at Pittsburgh's Carnegie Institute of Technology, now Carnegie-Mellon University. Pople spent the rest of his life in the United States but remained a British citizen.

At Carnegie, Pople concentrated his efforts on exploring the electronic structure of molecules. He wondered if there was a way to predict how they would react to one another. By the mid-1980s, he was teaching part-time at Northwestern University in Chicago and in 1993 became a full faculty member there.

Pople's years of research culminated in a computer program called Gaussian-70, which researchers can use to study matter outside of a laboratory. He released the first version of the program in the 1970s but continually revised and updated it. Pople's program has many applications. Pharmaceutical companies use it to simulate the effects of new drugs. It can also be used to examine how pollutants like Freon affect the ozone layer. "It's literally thousands of chemists worldwide who are using the results of Pople's research," Carnegie-Mellon chemistry professor Dr. Stuart W. Staley told the *New York Times*. "It's had a tremendous impact."

For this work, Pople received the 1998 Nobel Prize in chemistry, which he shared with Australian Walter Kohn of the University of California at Santa Barbara. Over the years, he won many other awards for his research, including the American Chemical Society's Gilbert Nerton Lewis Award in 1977, the Royal Society's Davy Medal in 1988, and the Jerusalem Wolf Prize in Chemistry in 1992. Pople became a fellow of the Royal Society of London in 1961 and a fellow of the American Academy of Arts and Sciences in 1971. In 1993, he became a corresponding member of the Australian Academy of Sciences.

Pople died of liver cancer on March 15, 2004, in Chicago; he was 78. Pople is survived by his daughter, Hilary; his sons Adrian, Mark, and Andrew; eleven grandchildren, and a great-granddaughter.

His wife died of cancer in 2002. **Sources:** *Chicago Tribune,* March 19, 2004, sec. 1, p. 9; *Los Angeles Times,* March 20, 2004, p. B21; *New York Times,* March 18, 2004, p. C17; *Times* (London), March 24, 2004, p. 29.

—Lisa Frick

## Tony Randall

Born Leonard Rosenberg, February 26, 1920, in Tulsa, OK; died from complications of pneumonia, May 17, 2004, in Manhattan, NY. Actor. Best known for portraying Felix Unger, the neat-freak roommate of slob Oscar Madison in *The Odd Couple* TV series, Tony Randall enjoyed a long and varied career as an actor, stage director, and theater impresario. After his New York stage debut in 1941, he landed a number of major theatrical parts on Broadway throughout the 1940s, and in the 1950s alternated between stage and television work. An early success was his role opposite Wally Cox on the popular sitcom *Mr. Peepers* (1952-55). From the late '50s throughout much of the next decade, he famously appeared in a string of motion picture comedies, costarring with the likes of Jayne Mansfield, Doris Day, and Rock Hudson. Work in television comedies and dramas dominated his career from 1970 to the early eighties. In 1991, he founded the National Actors Theatre, and with the exception of occasional guest appearances on television and small roles in motion pictures, he devoted the rest of his life to the theater. Called "a great comedian [and] role model" in the *Los Angeles Times* by fellow sitcom actor David Hyde Pierce, Randall was one of the most familiar faces of television, film, and stage for more than 60 years.

Randall was born in Tulsa, Oklahoma, where his father was a dealer in art and antiquities. His love of theater began when as a boy he was dazzled by a touring ballet troupe. In school, his penchant for mimicry raised the ire of his teachers. One sent home a note to his parents that read, "Please stop him from making faces." Later he studied at Northwestern University in Illinois and at the Neighborhood Playhouse School of Theatre in New York. Among his instructors were the famous acting coach Sanford Meisner and the choreographer Martha Graham. In New York, he took the name Anthony Randall and soon began making use of his rich baritone voice on radio soap operas and mysteries. After his stage debut in *The Circle of Chalk* in 1941, he appeared as Eugene Marchbanks in George Bernard

Shaw's *Candida,* opposite Jane Cowl in the title role and in Emlyn William's *The Corn is Green,* opposite Ethel Barrymore.

He briefly served in the Army Signal Corps during World War II, and then returned to Broadway, appearing in numerous productions, including *Anthony and Cleopatra,* in which he appeared alongside Katherine Cornell, Charlton Heston, Eli Wallach and Maureen Stapleton.

In the 1950s, he appeared in the TV soap opera *One Man's Family* and in the classic NBC sitcom *Mr. Peepers* in which he played a major role. His film debut came in 1957 in *Oh, Men! Oh, Women!.* In that film he reprised a role he had performed on Broadway three years earlier. More significant in 1957 was his starring role in the comedy *Will Success Spoil Rock Hunter?,* opposite screen siren Jayne Mansfield. Throughout the late '50s and 1960s he appeared in a number of successful films, mostly comedies, including three with Doris Day and Rock Hudson, 1959's *Pillow Talk,* 1961's *Lover Come Back to Me,* and 1964's *Send Me No Flowers.* But he was also effective in dramas, such as Martin Ritt's 1957's *No Down Payment* in which he played an alcoholic. Randall showed his considerable range by playing all seven faces in 1964's *The 7 Faces of Dr. Lao.* He returned to Broadway in 1968 to lend his singing talents to the musical *Oh, Captain!.* In the 1970s and '80s he appeared largely on television, first in ABC's *The Odd Couple,* which remained popular in reruns, then on ABC and later CBS in *The Tony Randall Show,* and finally NBC's *Love, Sidney.* In 1991, he founded the National Actors Theater in New York with a million dollars of his own money, becoming its artistic director. Though its star-studded productions (mostly of classics) seldom elicited high praise from critics, the company survived, and among its triumphs was the Tony-award winning *M. Butterfly* in which Randall starred.

Just as *The Odd Couple* was completing its final season in 1975, Randall won an Emmy for outstanding performance in a comedy. In reference to the cancellation of the show for which he had won the award, he quipped, as quoted in the *Independent,* "I'm so happy. Now if I only had a job."

Randall was also popular on the late-night television circuit. According to *People,* show host Johnny Carson once joked that out of a total of 35,460 *Tonight Show* guests, "32,000 of them were Tony Randall." Also a frequent guest on the *Late Show with David Letterman,* he was beloved by its host: "I was lucky enough to know Tony as an actor and friend. Whenever we needed a big laugh, we would bring in Tony. He always made us better for having worked with him," Letterman said in a statement, according to the *Los Angeles Times*.

An accomplished singer in his own right, Randall was known to opera lovers for conducting intermission quizzes during Metropolitan Opera broadcasts. He was also a commentator on *Live from Lincoln Center*. Randall, who lost his first wife, Florence Gibbs, to cancer in 1992, remarried in 1995 at the age of 74. His bride, Heather Harlan, an assistant at the National Actors Theatre, was just 24 years old. Three years later they had their first of two children.

Randall died on May 17, 2004, in New York City, from complications of pneumonia; he was 84. He is survived by his wife, Heather, and their son and daughter. **Sources:** *Independent,* (London), May 20, 2004, p. 41; *Los Angeles Times,* May 19, 2004, p. B12; *New York Times,* May 19, 2004, p. A22; *People,* May 31, 2004, pp. 68-70; *Washington Post,* May 19, 2004, B5.

—*D. László Conhaim*

## Ronald Reagan

Born Ronald Wilson Reagan, February 6, 1911, in Tampico, IL; died of pneumonia, June 5, 2004, in Los Angeles, CA. Politician. Called "the Great Communicator," Ronald Reagan rose from humble beginnings to fame as a B-grade Hollywood star, later cementing his public image as a television host and spokesperson for General Electric, and finally achieving the highest offices of government, first as a two-term Governor of California, and later as a two-term President of the United States. He overcame emotional trials in his boyhood to become an unabashed optimist in public life, though his political detractors would accuse him of whitewashing and being soft on details. An accomplished lifeguard and athlete as a youth, he brought vigor and dedication to his roles in Hollywood and politics, finally squaring off against—and coming to surprising agreements with—Soviet premier Mikhail Gorbachev during the thawing of the Cold War. Though he came to be known reverently as "Mr. President," and before that "Governor," enduring nicknames such as "Ronnie," "Dutch," and "the Gipper" conveyed his trademark affability.

After winning roles as an actor in high school— where his performance as a student was lackluster—and graduating from college, Reagan went on to become a radio sports announcer, and, after a successful audition for Warner Bros., a contract player. His first film role was that of a news reporter in 1937's *Love is on the Air*. In all, he would make 50 feature films from the late 1930s through the mid-'60s, including *Knute Rockne All American, King's Row, That Hagan Girl, The Hasty Heart, Bedtime for Bonzo, Hellcats of the Navy,* and *The Killers*. He also performed on radio and television. In the 1950s, he was the host of TV's popular General Electric Theater and also a spokesperson for its sponsor. From 1947 to 1952, and from 1959-60, he was President of the Screen Actors Guild. In 1966, he was first elected to the California governorship, and in 1970 reelected. In 1976, he ran unsuccessfully for the Republican Party nomination for President, but in 1980, after a successful second attempt to win his party's nomination, he defeated Democratic incumbent Jimmy Carter decisively. In 1984, he was reelected in a landslide victory over his Democratic challenger, former Vice President Walter Mondale.

Born in a small apartment in Tampico, Illinois, to John Edward Reagan, an Irish Roman Catholic, and Nelle Clyde Wilson Reagan, a Scottish-Irish Protestant, Ronald Reagan was the youngest of two boys. His brother, Neil, who performed in several films in the 1940s, died in 1996. At the time of Reagan's birth, his alcoholic and always struggling father sold shoes in Tampico's general store, but he eventually moved the family to Dixon, Illinois. Meanwhile his mother, a devout Christian who sometimes worked retail jobs, took pains to raise her boys to live productive and temperate lives, baptizing them, enrolling them in Bible study at the local church, and directing young Ronald in church plays. In high school, "Dutch," as he came to be known from a nickname given to him by his father, played football, basketball and track, and, in an early sign of his promise as a leader, became president of the student council. Summers he worked as a lifeguard. Later, at Eureka College, he excelled in football, became captain of the swim team, and president of the student body.

After his graduation in 1932, Reagan found sports announcing jobs on radio stations in Davenport and Des Moines, Iowa. Five years later, during a trip to California with the Chicago Cubs, a friend arranged a screen test for him at Warner Bros. studios. He was signed to a seven-year contract starting at $200 a week.

While Reagan became a certifiable star of the silver screen, he never reached A-list status, making mostly low budget action pictures, romantic comedies, and the occasional western. Still, he did win a few parts alongside big stars, such as Humphrey Bogart, Bette Davis, and Lionel Barrymore. An early success, 1942's *King's Row,* in which he played an amputee, provided him with a dramatic role in the film he considered his best. It also provided him with the title of his 1965 autobiography, *Where's the rest of me?.* His most famous role was opposite a chimpanzee in 1951's *Bedtime for Bonzo.*

In 1940, he wed actress Jane Wyman, with whom he had a daughter, Maureen. They also adopted a son, Michael. In 1948, Wyman divorced Reagan, telling the court, "there was nothing common between us...," according to the *New York Times.* Maureen Reagan died of cancer in 2001.

From 1947 to 1952, and again in 1959, he presided over the Screen Actors Guild. During the House Un-American Activities Committee's witch-hunting of suspected communists in Hollywood, Reagan refused to name names, but evidence has come to light that he secretly did just that to the Federal Bureau of Investigation. While Guild president, he met actress Nancy Davis when she complained to his office that her name had wrongfully appeared on the blacklist. They were married in 1952.

As his career as an actor waned, he became increasingly active in politics, first as a Democrat, then as a conservative Republican. As governor of California from 1967 to 1975, he increased the number of the state's functionaries by 34,000. In contrast to his later platform as President, he also raised taxes and signed a bill into law that effectively allowed abortion on demand.

Reagan's legacy as President of the United States, from 1981 to 1989, was garlanded by such successes as the fall of the Berlin Wall, the liberation of Grenada, the stifling of Colonel Qaddafi of Libya, and the signing of the Intermediate-Range Nuclear Forces Treaty with the Soviet Union. But there were low points too. In 1981, he survived an assassination attempt, but his press secretary was paralyzed by a stray bullet; in 1983, a terrorist bombing of a barracks in Beirut, Lebanon, cost the lives of 241 U.S. marines; and in 1986, news broke of a conspiracy within his administration by which the profits from illegal arms sales to Iran, in exchange for the release of American hostages in Lebanon, had been diverted to fund the Contra rebels in Nicaragua, whose guerrilla fighters Reagan likened to America's founding fathers. Though he avoided impeachment, Reagan's legacy was seriously tarnished. While his economic policies reinvigorated the economy, and crucial tax reform was passed under

his watch, he spent liberally on defense. His deficit spending in the arms race tripled the size of the national debt and made the United States into the largest debtor nation.

Three years after the end of his second term as president, Reagan announced that he had been diagnosed with Alzheimer's disease and quietly retired from public view. He lived another ten years, until his death at age 93 on June 5, 2004, in Los Angeles, California. He is survived by his wife, Nancy; his daughter, Patti; and sons Ron Jr. and Michael. **Sources:** CNN.com, http://www.cnn.com/SPECIALS/2004/reagan/stories/bio.part.one/index.html (January 10, 2005); CNN.com, http://www.cnn.com/SPECIALS/2004/reagan/stories/bio.part.two/index.html (January 10, 2005); CNN.com, http://www.cnn.com/SPECIALS/2004/reagan/stories/bio.part.three/index.html (January 10, 2005); CNN.com, http://www.cnn.com/SPECIALS/2004/reagan/stories/bio.part.four/index.html (January 10, 2005); Internet Movie Database, http://www.imdb.com/name/nm0001654/ (January 18, 2005); *New York Times,* June 6, 2004, p. A1; *People,* June 21, 2004, pp. 92-105; *Washington Post,* June 6, 2004, p. A1, p. A28.

—D. László Conhaim

# William Victor Roth

Born William Victor Roth Jr., July 22, 1921, in Great Falls, MT; died of heart failure, December 13, 2003, in Washington, DC. U.S. congressman and attorney. Delaware's former senator, William V. Roth Jr., passed away at age 82 in 2003, but his legacy survives in the popular Individual Retirement Account, or IRA, that bears his name. The five-term Republican also held the record as the longest-serving state-elected official in Delaware history.

Roth was born in 1921, in Montana cattle country. His parents moved from Great Falls to the state capital of Helena, where his father managed a brewery. Roth's mother liked to visit the Montana capitol building to listen to the political debates on the floor during sessions, and often took her young son with her. After graduating from the University of Oregon in 1943, Roth enlisted in the U.S. Army at the height of World War II, and served as a military intelligence officer in the South Pacific. He earned a Bronze Star for his service, but also benefited from the historic GI Bill, which provided college tuition aid for returning war veterans. Roth earned business and law degrees from Harvard University, and moved to Wilmington, Delaware, to become an attorney with a chemical company there. He eventually opened a law practice and became active in state Republican politics.

Roth lost his first bid for political office when he was narrowly defeated for the lieutenant governor's slot in 1960, but he became the state GOP chair a year later. In 1966, he ousted a Democrat incumbent in the U.S. House of Representatives, in part by exposing his opponent's less-than-stellar legislative attendance record. He quickly made his mark on Capitol Hill by compiling a list of all sources of government aid—programs, grants and other types of assistance—which he found by combing through the federal budget. The results were published in the Congressional Record in 1968, and annually thereafter as the Catalog of Federal Domestic Assistance, informally known as the "Roth Catalog."

Roth's name would also be appended to two significant legislative victories after he moved on to a seat in the U.S. Senate in 1970. He later teamed with a young House Republican named Jack Kemp on a tax cut proposal that languished until a newly elected Republican president, Ronald Reagan, championed it. The former California governor had campaigned on a promise to cut federal taxes, and the Kemp-Roth Act, passed by Congress in 1981, became one of the hallmarks of the Reagan Administration's supply-side economic strategy. Roth and Kemp's package reduced tax rates on the theory that higher taxes were discouraging investment, and perhaps even work itself. The resulting cuts were said to have ushered in a economic revitalization boom in the 1980s via new business investment, but were also blamed for large budget deficits during Reagan era.

Roth gained prominence as chair of the Senate Government Affairs Committee in the early 1980s. He was responsible for the infamous report revealing that defense contractors were gouging the Pentagon to the tune of $640 toilet seats and $9,600 wrenches sold to the U.S. Navy. Of the toilet seat, its maker argued that it was designed to meet the tough requirements for Navy aircraft, which included being "lightweight, corrosive resistant ... and sufficiently durable to withstand repeated usage" according to the New York Times. Roth responded to such claims, according to the newspaper, by pointing out, "You can go into a mobile home and see something not much different." In a 1983 stunt, he decorated a Christmas tree with nuts and bolts that, if purchased at prices charged to the Pentagon, racked up a total price tag of $101,000. "It costs us $110 to buy the same parts at local hardware stores and supply houses," the Chicago Tribune's Randall Chase quoted him as saying.

Roth was a prominent Delaware official whose high marks from constituents crossed party lines. He often campaigned with his attention-getting Saint Bernard hounds, which served to soften a demeanor that was said to be a bit taciturn. His most enduring political legacy, however, came with the Roth IRA, which was part of Congress's Taxpayer Relief Act of 1997. The Roth individual retirement account differed from the standard IRA, in which taxes came due when the IRA reached maturity. In the Roth IRA, deposits were made from after-tax income, but the earnings were never taxed.

That same year, as chair of the Senate Finance Committee, Roth organized hearings to investigate abuses by the Internal Revenue Service. Reports had surfaced that IRS employees had access to the tax files of friends, families, and even celebrities, and the hearings also called the IRS to task for wrongful harassment of taxpayers over delinquent bills that were in error. Some Democrats called the hearings grandstanding, but a General Accounting Office report issued at the same time of Roth's hearings also documented numerous flaws in IRS record-keeping. "The agency as a whole does not enjoy the confidence of the American public," Roth said, according to his Los Angeles Times obituary. From the experience he even authored a 1999 book, The Power to Destroy, the cover of which declared, "How the IRS Became America's Most Powerful Agency, How Congress Is Taking Control and What You Can Do to Protect Yourself under the New Law."

In 2000, Roth made his bid for a sixth Senate term, but the popular incumbent faced an equally popular opponent, former Delaware Governor Thomas Carper. Carper was 53, and though Roth's 79 years were not a campaign issue outright, he collapsed twice during the campaign, once in front of television cameras. A check-up revealed an inner-ear problem that affected his balance, but the damage was done, and Carper beat him by eleven percentage points. The former legislator remained active, serving as co-chair of the U.S.-E.U.-Slovakia Action Commission, but died suddenly at the age of 82 after collapsing at his daughter's home in Washington, D.C. on December 13, 2003. The cause was heart failure. He is survived by his wife, Jane Richards Roth, a U.S. Court of Appeals judge in Philadelphia;

and two children. **Sources:** *Chicago Tribune,* December 15, 2003; *Los Angeles Times,* December 15, 2003; *New York Times,* December 15, 2003; *Times* (London), December 30, 2003; *Washington Post,* December 15, 2003.

—Carol Brennan

## Francesco Scavullo

Born January 16, 1921, in New York, NY; died of heart failure, January 6, 2004, in New York, NY. Fashion photographer. The fashion world's Francesco Scavullo was indelibly associated with the unapologetically seductive portraits that adorned the cover of *Cosmopolitan* magazine for more than 30 years. The covers epitomized the "Cosmo Girl" archetype, and made Scavullo one of the most sought-after photographers in fashion journalism. His meticulously perfected lighting techniques and talent for styling a scene were so trademark that they even became an industry-insider verb, "Scavullo-ize."

Scavullo was born on January 16, 1921, in New York. His family was living on Staten Island at the time, but later moved to Manhattan when his father's business fortunes improved after he bought the old Central Park Casino supper club. The first photographs Scavullo took were of his sisters, which became the first examples of what was known as the "Scavulloization" of a model—he styled their hair and experimented with their makeup to make them look as glamorous as possible. "I definitely wanted to make everyone look like a movie star," he once said, according to *Independent* journalist Val Williams. "I was always looking at my mother's fashion magazines."

Scavullo's father wanted him enter the restaurant business. Through family connections, a job was secured for him at the posh Colony restaurant, but Scavullo proved to be such a terrible busboy that the chefs actually chased him out the door one night. He found a job working in a photography studio that did catalog work, which was more to his liking, and from there had a trial run at *Vogue.* One of the world's top fashion photographers of the era, Horst P. Horst, hired him as an assistant. His first real break came when he styled a famous 1943 photograph of Lauren Bacall for *Harper's Bazaar,* and the smoldering noir mood of the photo virtually launched the actress's career, and Scavullo's as well.

Scavullo began gaining an increasing number of magazine jobs, including a 1948 cover of *Seventeen.* His father, finally impressed by his son's choice of career, bought him a four-story carriage house in Manhattan that he could use as his home and studio. From there Scavullo worked steadily, but it was his association with *Cosmopolitan* that proved the most lucrative of his assignments. He began shooting its covers in 1965, just after it came under a new and daring editor, Helen Gurley Brown, who turned the newsstand stalwart into a magazine for the new, income-earning, sexually liberated young woman of the era. Inside its pages, the content tackled provocative subject matter, while the full-torso shot on the cover, with a sauciness bordering on the aggressive, conveyed a frank and unapologetic sexuality.

By then Scavullo had perfected his innovative lighting techniques, some of which he had borrowed from the movie business: he used white umbrellas and muslin sheets to eradicate glare, and in close-up shots he sometimes framed faces with large sheets of cardboard, which made the skin glow. He was a favorite of many models, and in turn helped launch the careers of many new faces. During the 1970s, when fashion dissolved into a looser, less posed and more sexually provocative look, Scavullo shot thousands of pages for the likes of *Vogue* and *Harper's Bazaar,* and worked with designers as well. The controversial photographs of a young Brooke Shields in the 1970s, which caused a stir for their sexual content, were the work of Scavullo, whom the model-actress called "Uncle Frankie."

Scavullo both photographed and socialized with a heady A-list of celebrities in his day, including Andy Warhol and the Studio 54 crowd. He did formal portraits and also specialized in enamel-on-canvas photo silkscreens. There were several gallery shows of his work over the years, and he wrote a number of lushly illustrated tomes. Yet behind the scenes, Scavullo suffered from manic depression, which went undiagnosed until the early 1980s. He was a consummate professional on the job, however, rarely displaying a bad temper with his clients, who recalled him as soothing and genial, but he was known to walk out of a shoot at times if he was perturbed.

Scavullo was briefly married in the 1950s, but met his partner, Sean M. Byrnes, when he hired him as a stylist in 1972. Though he had suffered from heart problems over the years, Scavullo was still working on the day he died, readying for an assignment. He died of heart failure at his Manhattan home on January 6, 2004, at the age of 82. He later said that his manic depression had actually helped his career, the echo of many creative types. "When I'm manic, everything is intensified," he wrote in one of his books, according to *New York Times* writer Enid Nemy. "It's exciting and scary—my creativity peaks, my mind races, I work through the depressions photographing intensely. It's like singing over a cold for an opera singer." **Sources:** CNN.com, http://www.cnn.com/2004/SHOWBIZ/books/01/07/obit.scavullo.ap/index.html (January 8, 2004); *Entertainment Weekly,* January 23/30, 2004, p. 17; *Guardian* (London), January 13, 2004, p. 27; *Independent* (London), January 13, 2004, p. 18; *New York Times,* January 7, 2004, p. C12; *People,* January 19, 2004, pp. 110-111.

—Carol Brennan

## Paul Simon

Born Paul Martin Simon, November 29, 1928, in Eugene, OR; died after undergoing heart surgery, December 9, 2003, in Springfield, IL. United States senator. Paul Simon, who spent 12 years as a United States senator from Illinois and ran for president in 1988, earned a reputation for honesty, fiscal responsibility, and a belief that government can improve people's lives. The son of missionaries, he fought against corruption as a newspaper editor, then was elected to the Illinois legislature, where he got the nickname "Reverend." His bow ties and horn-rimmed glasses became symbols of his forthrightness, helping create an image that may have hurt his presidential campaign but brought him immense respect. "I never served with anybody else who voted his conscience every time," Dale Bumpers (D-Arkansas), another former senator, told the *New York Times.*

Simon was born on November 29, 1928, to Reverend Martin and Ruth Simon. Both Lutheran missionaries, they had returned from China and settled in Eugene, Oregon, while Ruth was pregnant. They instilled a social conscience in their son. Later in life, Simon recalled his father opposing the internment of Japanese Americans on the West Coast during World War II, an unpopular stance that embarrassed his teenage son, though he later decided his father was right.

Simon enrolled in the University of Oregon at age 16, then transferred to Dana College in Nebraska, about the same time his parents moved to Illinois. He was elected Dana College's student body presi-

dent and helped create a racially integrated admissions policy for the school. He left college at 19 when the Lions Club of Troy, Illinois, convinced him to buy the town newspaper and use it to fight local gambling interests. He exposed illegal casinos and brothels, and testified before the Senate Crime Investigating Committee in 1951. Though the gambling rings had bought off legislators in both political parties, reformers in the Democratic Party convinced Simon to run for the Illinois House in 1954.

He won a seat in the House, and joined with other reformers to pass an open meetings law and rewrite adoption and penal laws. He released his personal financial records to prove his honesty, long before it was common for politicians to do so. He married a fellow legislator, Jeanne Hurley of Wilmette, in 1960, and they went to the Democratic National Convention for their honeymoon.

In 1964, Simon wrote "A Study In Corruption," an article for *Harper's* magazine, that alleged several fellow Illinois legislators were bought off by organized crime and the racing industry or extorted bribes from special interest groups. That made him a lot of enemies in the legislature—but he had powerful friends, too. Mayor Richard Daley of Chicago helped Simon become the Democratic candidate for lieutenant governor in 1968, and he won. But when he tried to move up to governor in 1972, he lost in the Democratic primary after being attacked for his tax reform plan, which would have raised one tax while cutting another. He bounced back quickly, though: after spending some time teaching journalism, he ran for U.S. Congress in 1974 and won.

Among his fellow congressmen, Simon was not very popular; he finished third when he ran for chairman of the House Budget Committee. But he spoke out on education issues such as literacy programs and college loans and championed political morality. "The path upwards in politics is a slippery, stumbling one for both the officeholder and the public," he wrote in his 1984 book, *The Glass House,* according to Ray Long in the *Chicago Tribune.* "But unless there are those willing to tread the slippery path, willing to stumble, willing to expose themselves, warts and all, willing to give the nation something good and noble toward which to strive, we will follow the downward path...."

In 1984, he became a star in the Democratic Party when he challenged incumbent Illinois Republican senator Charles Percy and won—in a year that brought a Republican landslide in most of the country. In the Senate, he was a strong liberal, believing in government social programs. "Government is not the enemy," Simon said, according to CNN.com. "Government is simply a tool that can be used wisely or unwisely." But he also supported a balanced-budget amendment to the Constitution at a time when many liberal Democrats felt that eliminating the country's large budget deficit would keep them from providing enough social spending.

Simon took that mix of government activism and pay-as-you-go caution into the 1988 presidential race, where he failed to excite people. He did fairly well in the early Iowa caucus and New Hampshire primary, but the only primary he won was in his home state, and he dropped out, short on campaign money. During the campaign, his bow tie and proper manner seemed to attract the most attention, and he played with his public image, appearing on the TV show *Saturday Night Live* with the singer Paul Simon in a comedy routine where both pretended to be confused about who was supposed to be the guest host.

After leaving the presidential race, Simon continued his work in the Senate for eight more years, winning reelection easily in 1990. He kept supporting a balanced-budget amendment and the North American Free Trade Agreement.

When Simon retired in 1996, almost every member of the Senate, including conservatives, wore a bow tie in tribute to him. Dick Durbin, a fellow Democrat and former aide of Simon's, succeeded him in the Senate. Simon became director of a public policy institute named after himself at Southern Illinois University. During his life he wrote 22 books, including his autobiography which was published in 1999. His first wife, Jeanne, died in 2000, and he married Patricia Derge, a former high school government teacher, in 2001.

In early December of 2003, Simon endorsed presidential candidate Howard Dean—another fiscally responsible liberal—from his hospital bed in Springfield, Illinois, just before undergoing heart surgery. He died on December 9, 2003, due to complications from the surgery. He is survived by his second wife, Patricia; his daughter, Sheila; his son, Martin; and six grandchildren. **Sources:** *Chicago Tribune,* December 10, 2003, sec. 1, p. 1, p. 6; *CNN.com,* http://www.cnn.com/2003/ALLPOLITICS/12/09/simon.obit.ap/index.html (December 12, 2003); *Independent,* December 11, 2003, p. 22; *Los Angeles Times,* December 10, 2003, p. B12; *New York Times,* December 10, 2003, p. A29; *Washington Post,* December 10, 2003, p. B6.

—*Erick Trickey*

## Margaret Thaler Singer

Born July 29, 1921, in Denver, CO; died of pneumonia, November 23, 2003, in Berkeley, CA. Psychologist and college professor. Clinical psychologist Margaret Thaler Singer was a leading expert on cults and their peculiar hold on members for three decades before her death in 2003. The Berkeley, California, researcher sought to raise public awareness about the dangers of such groups as the Reverend Sun Myung Moon's Unification Church and the Church of Scientology. She warned that groups that engage in coercive behavior to obtain and keep members were more pervasive a threat than commonly believed. "The public takes care of their fear by thinking only crazies and stupid people wind up in cults," an article by *Lancet* writer Ivan Oransky quoted her as saying. "I've interviewed more than 4,000 ex-cult members. There's no one type of person who is vulnerable."

Singer was a native of Denver, Colorado, where her father was the chief engineer at the city's U.S. Mint. Born in 1921, she was an accomplished cellist as a young woman, and played with the Denver Civic Symphony during her years at the University of Denver. After earning an undergraduate degree in speech, she received a master's in speech pathology, and went on to finish a doctorate in clinical psychology in 1943. She first worked in the psychiatry department of the University of Colorado School of Medicine for eight years before joining the Walter Reed Army Institute of Research in Washington, D.C.

At the highly regarded Army hospital, Singer was fascinated by the U.S. soldiers who had been captured by North Koreans or Chinese during the Korean War. When they were released, some returned with a vitriolic aversion to America. Singer began conducting research into the techniques used to cause such change, which she continued after taking an adjunct professorship at the University of California at Berkeley in 1958. She was also a trained family therapist.

In the 1960s, the Berkeley campus and nearby Bay Area was a hotbed of political activism and counterculture, but the movement drew unsavory types as well. Singer began to hear from parents whose children had suddenly disappeared, and connected the phenomenon to a rise in nontraditional, quasi-religious groups that were gaining ground on the fringes of hippie culture. "A sudden change of personality, a new way of talking ... and then they would disappear," Singer recalled in a *San Francisco Chronicle* interview with Steve Rubenstein. One of the first targets in her fight against cults was

Synanon, a California group that gained a measure of fame in the 1960s for its work as a substance-abuse rehabilitation facility. She also began to investigate the practices of the Unification Church, which had attracted record numbers of idealistic young people in the 1970s.

Singer first entered the limelight when she testified at the 1976 trial of California newspaper heiress Patty Hearst, who had been kidnapped by a leftist political group called the Symbionese Liberation Army and then took part in a bank heist caught on film. Singer delivered expert testimony on how brainwashing techniques involving isolation and the threat of physical harm could lead anyone to adopt a value system that was at odds with long-held beliefs. The judge presiding over the case, however, disqualified her testimony on the basis that cult psychology was too new a field for someone to qualify as an expert.

Singer went on to conduct further research on cults such as the People's Temple in Jonestown, Guyana, the Branch Davidians of Waco, Texas, and the Californian group Heaven's Gate, each of which dissolved in tragic, headline-grabbing mass deaths. She wrote dozens of articles that appeared in professional journals, as well as the books *Cults in Our Midst: The Hidden Menace in Our Everyday Lives,* and *Crazy Therapies,* which warned of the cultish aspects of some New Age behavioral fads.

Later in life, Singer also conducted research on scam artists who preyed on the elderly. It was her own advancing age of 75 that spurred her to do so. "I am a good example of a tough old bird who wants to help the other old birds see to it their roofs and swings and cages don't get stolen," the *Lancet* obituary quoted her as saying. One of the last major legal actions she took part in involved a Federal Bureau of Investigation probe into wrongdoing at the National Aeronautics and Space Administration (NASA) agency. She testified at the 1996 Houston, Texas, proceedings, and asserted that the confessions of the 13 defendants had been coerced. They had been taken to a mysterious warehouse, for example, warned about the danger of asking for a lawyer, and told that only by informing on others could they avoid trouble for themselves. "It is my opinion that psychological techniques were used on these NASA 13 that are forbidden in the ordinary legal world we live in and are forbidden in the Geneva Convention and the terms of international warfare," *Houston Chronicle* journalist Eric Hanson quoted Singer as saying.

Singer was the target of periodic threats and harassment. Interviewed by a newspaper in 2002, she recounted an episode in which someone was leaving threatening letters in her mailbox in the middle of the night. Singer stayed up late, and when the culprit returned to leave another, she confronted him from a window. "I've got a shotgun up here with a spray pattern that'll put a three-foot hole in you, sonny," a writer for London's *Guardian* newspaper, Christopher Reed, quoted her as telling the man. "So you'd better get off my porch or you'll be sorry! And tell your handlers not to send you back." The threats stopped.

In addition to her high-profile work on cults, Singer was also an authority on schizophrenia, and was nominated twice for a Nobel Prize for her research. With her physics-professor husband, Jerome, she held a regular Tuesday-night table at a Berkeley restaurant. She died of pneumonia on November 23, 2003, at the age of 82. She is survived by her husband, a son, and a daughter. "My mom spent her whole life assisting other people—victims, parents, or lawyers—and often for free," her son, Sam Singer, told the *San Francisco Chronicle.* "Nothing gave her greater joy than helping to get someone unscrewed up." **Sources:** *Guardian* (London), December 2, 2003; *Houston Chronicle,* December 20, 1996; *Lancet,* January 31, 2004; *Los Angeles Times,* November 28, 2003; *New York Times,* December 7, 2003; *Publishers Weekly,* March 6, 1995; *San Francisco Chronicle,* November 25, 2003; *Washington Post,* December 1, 2003.

—Carol Brennan

## Warren Spahn

Born April 23, 1921, in Buffalo, NY; died November 24, 2003, in Broken Arrow, OK. Professional baseball player. Warren Spahn was a remarkable left-handed pitcher who won more games than any other left-hander in the history of major league baseball. He had a long career spent almost exclusively with the Braves team. His approach to pitching involved a signature style and absolute precision.

Spahn's father had played semi-pro baseball at one point, but by the time Spahn was born he was selling wallpaper. The elder Spahn had hopes for his son and set out to make him a professional player. He created a space for Spahn to practice and taught him a unique method of pitching. A Spahn pitch involved a grand movement of his leading leg that obstructed the view of his mitt and placement of the ball that was so precise that catchers loved working with him.

Spahn was signed to the Braves in 1940. At the time the Braves were located in Boston, Massachusetts. He started out in the minor divisions of the Braves team, eventually making his major league debut in 1942. He spent only a season and a half playing with the Braves before he was drafted into the Army. He served in Europe for three years and returned to the Braves in 1946.

Spahn's years in the Army were not lost years. He played a role in some of the war's most decisive battles. He fought at the Battle of the Bulge, a harsh battle that waged in the middle of winter. He was also present at the battle in Remagen, Germany, over the last bridge standing over the Rhine. His service in the Army earned him a Bronze Star, a Purple Heart, a battlefield commission, and a presidential citation. He also returned with an outlook on life that helped him succeed in his baseball career.

After facing freezing temperatures and battles in Europe, Spahn never considered his job as pitcher difficult. He won his first game at the age of 25, and would go on to set records as well as help form the backbone of a highly successful team. Starting in 1947, Spahn would win at least 14 games per season for the next 16 years. In 13 of those seasons he pitched more than 20 wins; six of those seasons were consecutive. In 1963, his last good year, Spahn pitched 23 winning games.

From 1949 to 1952, Spahn was the National League leader in strikeouts. His 63 shutouts is the National League record for a left-hander. He also holds the left-hander's record for innings pitched at 5,243 2/3. As a left-hander he also pitched more winning games than any other left-hander in the history of major league baseball with a total of 363 wins. He led or tied eight times for most victories in the National League and led the league three times in strikeouts and earned-run average.

Not only was Spahn an excellent pitcher, he could hit the ball as well. In 1958, he had a batting average of .333. In his career he hit 35 home runs, which is the National League record for home runs by a pitcher. His skill as a baseball player helped his team win the National League pennant in 1948, 1957, and 1958. In 1957, he led his team to defeat the New York Yankees in the World Series. That same year he won the Cy Young award for Outstanding Pitcher.

In 1960, when Spahn was 39, he pitched his first no-hitter against the Philadelphia Phillies. In that game he struck out 15 hitters and walked two. The following spring, just days after his 40th birthday, Spahn pitched his second no-hitter against San Francisco. In August of 1961, Spahn would have the most personally satisfying game of his life. In a 2-1 win against the Chicago Cubs, he pitched his 300th winning game. Mike Kupper of the *Los Angeles Times* reported Spahn's feelings about that game, "It was really a big thrill—the thrill of my life. Winning the pennant and the World Series … was the big thing from a team basis. But this had to be the biggest personally."

Within three years of these accomplishments, Spahn was finished in major league baseball. His 23 wins in 1963 were followed in 1964 by a 6-13 season. The Braves traded him to the New York Mets who kept him for a short time before trading him to the San Francisco Giants. He left the major leagues soon afterward but continued to pitch in minor leagues and in Mexico. At age 47, he pitched his last game.

Baseball was Spahn's life and he played the game until he could play no longer. In testament to the high esteem in which he was held by members of the baseball community, he was elected to the Hall of Fame in 1973, the first year he was eligible. In 1999, the Braves inducted him into their team's Hall of Fame and in 2003 erected a bronze statue of him at their field in Atlanta, Georgia.

Spahn's wife, LoRene, died in 1978. Spahn died on November 24, 2003, at his home in Broken Arrow, Oklahoma, from natural causes. He was 82. He is survived by his son, Greg, and two granddaughters. Known for his easygoing attitude and fondness for practical jokes off the field, Spahn was a meticulous, precise, and hard-working player on the field. **Sources:** *Los Angeles Times,* November 25, 2003, p. B13; *New York Times,* November 25, 2003, p. A27; *Washington Post,* November 25, 2003, p. B6.

—*Eve M. B. Hermann*

## Stephen Sprouse

Born in 1953, in Ohio; died of heart failure, March 4, 2004, in New York, NY. Fashion designer. Twenty years after Stephen Sprouse's debut as a fashion designer on New York runways, street culture was regularly invoked as an inspiration at the most luxe of design ateliers. Yet back in 1983, when Sprouse's spray-paint-derived Day-Glo colors took their cue from the subway graffiti that once plagued the New York underground, his vision was light-years ahead. The exuberant designer was a fixture in the New York spheres of music and art as well as fashion, and was a longtime contributor to *Interview*, the magazine founded by his friend and role model, Andy Warhol. *Interview* eulogized Sprouse as "a perfect embodiment of the cultural renaissance of the times, when the barriers separating high and low, uptown and downtown, and fashion and art— once as solid and redoubtable as the Berlin Wall— came crashing down and everything from painting to politics came together."

Sprouse was born in Ohio, but grew up in Columbus, Indiana, a semi-rural area. He was entranced by fashion at an early age, and was sketching outfits at the age of nine. His father, a onetime Air Force officer who became a small-appliance business owner, even took him to New York City and introduced him to well-known designers when he was barely in his teens. "I feel lucky that my parents were understanding," Sprouse told *People* in 1984. "They could have kicked me out on the football field with my brother."

Sprouse was able to land summer jobs on Seventh Avenue, the epicenter of the fashion industry in New York, when he was still in his teens. Formal schooling, however, eluded him: he left the prestigious Rhode Island School of Design after just three months when he was offered a job in New York City with Halston, one of the leading American ready-to-wear designers at the time. He spent three years with the firm, but left in order to explore his creative energies on his own. He dabbled in painting, photography, silkscreen prints, and even hand-colored images with the help of a Xerox machine.

By the mid-1970s Sprouse was working as a band photographer, and as the New York music scene segued from glam rock to the punk scene, Sprouse was living and socializing in the thick of it. He had an apartment in the Bowery, a rather seedy part of Lower Manhattan at the time that was generally home to the near-destitute, and wound up living in the same building as Blondie lead singer Deborah Harry. The clothes he began making for her stage shows were some of his first ready-to-wear pieces. "I've always liked music, art, and fashion," he told *New York Times* writer Lynda Richardson in 2001. "They all go off to different forks in the road, but they lead to one another."

A loan from Sprouse's ever-supportive family launched his business in earnest, and his first two collections caused a sensation. Some deployed a graffiti print that came thanks to his friend, the tagger-turned-artist Keith Haring, but Sprouse's interest in the printed word came partially as a result of his habit of scribbling phone numbers and reminder notes on his arm in felt-tip pen. He claimed once that he was so nervous when his first collection was about to go down the runway that he wrote the Lord's Prayer backward on his models' clothing. The items—miniskirts and punk-inspired frocks and coats, an updated motorcycle jacket— had a 1960s Pop-Art feel, but with New Wave updating. Sprouse was also fond of the dazzling fluorescent colors favored by subway taggers, and such hot pinks and neon oranges quickly filtered down to mainstream fashion. Though he showed just a few collections on the New York runways during this brief zenith, the clothes were an instant hit and usually sold out in stores within a matter of days.

Sprouse failed to find a good set of business mentors, and struggled for the remainder of his career. After failing to present a collection in 1986, he ventured into retail in 1987, but the New York and Los Angeles venues were shuttered a year later. "It happened so fast. I was in my own little vacuum. I trusted everyone, and then a wall went up," his obituary by *WWD* writer Lisa Lockwood quoted him as saying. The 1990s were marked by a series of struggles and small successes: he did a line in 1992 exclusively for haute-New York retailer Bergdorf Goodman, and another in 1995 for Barneys New York. He presented a collection at the 1997 New York Fashion Week, and scored a hit in 2000 with the signature graffiti-print limited edition handbag line for Louis Vuitton, a company whose creative director, Marc Jacobs, was an old pal from the punk-rock era. Sprouse's last venture was a special line for Target in 2002 with his exuberant signature graffiti print.

Sprouse had been diagnosed with lung cancer, and was hospitalized not long after he returned from a trip to South America in early 2004. He died of heart failure at the age of 50 on March 4, 2004, in New York City. He is survived by his mother, brother, niece, and three nephews. **Sources:** *Chicago Tribune,* March 8, 2004, sec. 4, p. 11; *Contemporary Fashion,* second ed., St. James Press, 2002; *Interview,* July 2002, p. 25; May 2004, p. 50; *New York Times,* August 22, 2001, p. B2; March 5, 2004, p. A21; *People,* May 28, 1984, p. 96; *Time,* October 29, 1984, p. 83; *Washington Post,* March 7, 2004, p. C12; *WWD,* March 8, 2004, p. 9;

—*Carol Brennan*

# Boris Trajkovski

Born June 25, 1956, in Strumica, Yugoslavia; died in a plane crash, February 26, 2004, near Stolac, Bosnia-Herzegovina. President of Macedonia. In two great moments of crisis, Boris Trajkovski, president of the small Balkan nation of Macedonia, defined his career and his country's future. When hundreds of thousands of ethnic Albanians fled the Kosovo war and overwhelmed Macedonia in 1999, Trajkovski, then deputy foreign minister, insisted that the refugees be allowed to stay. Two years later, as president, Trajkovski made peace with ethnic Albanian guerillas fighting government forces, avoiding a full-fledged war. In 2004, he died in a plane crash, and all sides in his divided country mourned.

Trajkovski was born in Strumica, Macedonia, in 1956, when it was part of Communist-era Yugoslavia. He graduated from Skopje University in 1980 with a law degree and also studied in the United States. He worked in commercial and employment law. In 1992, not long after Macedonia gained independence from Yugoslavia, Trajkovski joined a traditionally nationalist political party, the Macedonian Internal Revolutionary Organization, and became a part-time adviser to its leader on foreign policy.

Ethnic divisions in Macedonia define much of its politics. An Orthodox Christian majority dominates the country (and Trajkovski's political party), but an ethnic Albanian, Muslim minority makes up about 25 percent of the population, and there are smaller minority groups. Trajkovski, a member of Macedonia's small Methodist Church, was never a strong nationalist and was a moderate within his party—all of which help explain his public stances, his political appeal, and his success.

After Trajkovski's party won the 1998 elections (in coalition with an ethnic Albanian party), Trajkovski was named deputy foreign minister. Soon the war in the nearby Yugoslav province of Kosovo made Trajkovski prominent outside his country. In early 1999, ethnic Albanian civilians began fleeing brutal treatment by Yugoslav government forces in Kosovo. The nations of the North Atlantic Treaty Organization (NATO) began bombing Yugoslavia in hopes of stopping the crackdown, but the bombings prompted even more Albanians to flee. Hundreds of thousands went to Macedonia.

Unprepared, the Macedonian government asked other nations to fly the refugees elsewhere. Hard-liners in the Orthodox majority, afraid the refugees would change the country's ethnic balance, wanted them removed or refused entry. But Trajkovski insisted that Macedonia should allow the refugees in. NATO troops and refugee agencies built camps in Macedonia for the refugees to stay in until the war ended. Trajkovski's talent for conciliatory politics also helped calm Macedonians who worried that allowing NATO troops into the country might bring military retaliation from Yugoslavia.

Grateful ethnic Albanians in Macedonia rewarded Trajkovski by supporting his campaign for president in late 1999. He was considered a long shot, but his Methodist faith and stance on the refugee issue made him an attractive middle ground in the eternal tension between Orthodox ethnic Macedonians and Muslim ethnic Albanians. He won 52 percent of the vote and was sworn in as president in December of 1999 at age 43. Since the prime minister holds a lot of power in Macedonia, and the president has limited powers, Trajkovski was not expected to make too many vital decisions. He seemed more valuable to his party as a modern, pro-Western diplomat.

But in 2001, when Macedonia faced its greatest crisis since its independence, Trajkovski "almost single-handedly prevented the tiny Balkan nation [from] veering into a full-blown civil war," the *Times* of London noted after he died. Hard-liners in Trajkovski's party pressured him to pre-emptively attack ethnic Albanian guerrillas who were planning a revolt. The guerrillas wanted Albanian to become an official language of Macedonia and wanted more ethnic Albanians allowed into Macedonia's army, police, and educational system. Trajkovski denounced the guerrillas as terrorists, and Macedonian forces attacked them. The guerrillas responded by starting their uprising and laying siege to Tetovo, Macedonia's second largest city. In June, they took over Aracinovo, a suburb of the capital, Skopje. About 250 people were killed in the fighting.

To keep the country united, Trajkovski had formed a government coalition of national unity that included his party, its main opposition, and two ethnic Albanian parties in May. In June, Trajkovski proposed a peace plan that gave the Albanians some of the rights they demanded. With NATO and the European Union pressuring the government, both sides signed a deal in August of 2003 that called for the guerrillas to give up their arms, gave ethnic Albanians more rights in schools, and allowed Albanian lawmakers to speak Albanian in parliament.

The deal was risky for Trajkovski. After American peacekeeping troops escorted guerrillas out of Aracinovo, angry, armed Orthodox hard-liners took over part of the presidential palace. But Trajkovski deployed his diplomatic skills and calm to great effect. He got the hard-liners to back down by making a "typically conciliatory speech to the nation," as the *Times* of London described it. "There was little doubt in the minds of Western observers ... that Trajkovski, by his courage and force of character, had prevented a fifth Balkan war that might have dragged in Bulgaria and Albania and possibly even ... Greece and Turkey."

Diplomacy and conciliation remained themes during the rest of Trajkovski's time in office. After his party lost parliamentary elections in 2002, he managed to get along well with Branco Crvenkovski, the new prime minister from the winning Social Democratic party. He also worked hard to integrate Macedonia with the rest of Europe. One of his last acts as president was signing his country's formal application for membership in the European Union.

Trajkovski was flying to an international investment conference in Mostar, Bosnia, on February 26, 2004, when his small plane crashed in a fog in a mountainous area still filled with mines from the 1992-95 Bosnian war. Trajkovski and the eight others in the plane died in the crash. Explosives experts had to clear a path to the wreck. When his funeral was held in Skopje in early March, officials from more than 60 countries attended, and tens of thousands of Macedonians lined the streets. Crvenkovski, the prime minister, was elected to replace Trajkovski as president that April. Trajkovski is survived by his wife, son, and daughter; he was 47. **Sources:** *Financial Times,* April 15, 2004, p. 10; *Independent* (London), Feb. 27, 2004, p. 42; *New York Times,* Feb. 27, 2004, p. A4; Feb. 28, 2004, p. A4; March 6, 2004, p. A4; *Times* (London), Feb. 28, 2004, p. 48; *Washington Post,* Feb. 28, 2004, p. A18.

—*Erick Trickey*

## Peter Ustinov

Born Peter Alexander Ustinov, April 16, 1921, in London, England; died of heart failure, March 28, 2004, in Genolier, Switzerland. Actor and writer. Cosmopolitan, erudite, and in possession of seemingly boundless stores of wit, actor Peter Ustinov had a prolific, and prolifically diverse, career. Ustinov was a veteran of stage and film whose screen appearances included the slave-revolt drama *Spartacus,* but he was also an accomplished playwright, director, author, and even goodwill ambassador for

UNICEF. He continued taking new roles even in his early eighties, and with characteristic wit reportedly told his agent in that he hoped to keep working until the day he died, "as long as I can be guaranteed that I won't know in advance when it's going to happen," the *Independent's* Tom Vallance quoted him as saying.

Born in 1921 to parents who were both of half-Russian heritage, Ustinov was descended from true White Russian stock, including an ancestor had owned Imperial Russia's largest caviar fishery. Ustinov's parents, however, lived a more modest existence: his father worked as a journalist in London, and his mother was a painter. A precocious child, Ustinov discovered his talent for voices and accents when he began mimicking his parents' friends at an early age. He was sent to an elite prep school in London, but disliked the stuffy British atmosphere. One of the teachers delivered an early review on a report card, noting that the boy "shows great originality which must be curbed at all costs," according to the *Independent's* Vallance.

After dropping out of school at the age of 16, Ustinov took acting classes at the London Theater Studio and began writing plays. His first work was produced on the London stage in 1942, when he was just 21. He made his film debut in some wartime comedies that poked fun at Nazi Germany, Britain's arch-enemy at the time, and enlisted in the British Army in 1942. He was bypassed for officers' school, and later made light of another one of his official assessments: "On no account must this man be put in charge of others," a report stated, according to the *New York Times.*

After the war, Ustinov made a better impression as the Roman Emperor Nero in the 1951 epic *Quo Vadis,* which earned him an Oscar nomination. Still an active playwright, his 1953 comedy *The Love of Four Colonels* was named the best play of the year in the New York Drama Critics Circle awards. He continued to divide his time between acting and writing, and won his first Academy Award as best supporting actor for his role as a lovestruck slave dealer in the 1961 Stanley Kubrick classic *Spartacus.* He was more proud of his next achievement, however: a 1962 film adaptation of the Herman Melville classic *Billy Budd,* for which he wrote the screenplay, directed, and appeared in as well. A second Oscar statue came in 1965 for his portrayal of a bumbling jewel thief in the heist caper *Topkapi.*

The plays Ustinov wrote were produced in London, New York, Paris, and Berlin, and he sometimes directed them as well as various operas. He also authored such novels as 1960's *The Loser,* as well as short stories that appeared in the *Atlantic Monthly.* He had a long-running newspaper column, and penned a 1977 memoir, *Dear Me.* Later screen roles included a turn as famed fictional Detective Hercule Poirot in *Death on the Nile,* a 1978 film, and *Appointment With Death* a decade later.

Deeply interested in his Russian heritage, Ustinov traveled to the Soviet Union, and filmed two travel specials for television, *Peter Ustinov on Russia* in 1987 and *Ustinov Aboard the Orient Express* five years later. Still a talented mimic, he did voice work for animated features, and was most notably the voice of Babar the Elephant for many years.

Since the late 1960s he had served as a goodwill ambassador for UNICEF, and used his position as an advocate for impoverished children around the world. He continued working well into what were, ostensibly, his retirement years, with a supporting role in a 2003 film about religious leader Martin Luther as one of his last roles. Of that experience, he told one interviewer it helped him to understand why life expectancy in the sixteenth century was so short. It was, the *New York Times* quoted him as saying, "because having to dress up in curtains, which press the human body in all sorts of places where it's not usually pressed, was real agony."

Though Ustinov had mixed feelings about his British citizenship, and liked to poke fun at the still somewhat stuffy national character, he was knighted in 1991. He spent much of his time on the Continent, however, either at his estate in Switzerland with a vineyard that produced some 4,000 bottles annually, or on a boat he moored off the coast of Spain. Tending to be on the portly side, he suffered from diabetes and heart problems in his later years, and died of heart failure on March 28, 2004, at a clinic near Lake Geneva, Switzerland; he was 82. Perhaps not unsurprisingly, the witty bon vivant and father of four had been married three times, lastly to Helen du Lau d'Allemans in 1972, of whom he told one interviewer, "she has made me into something approaching the man I once hoped to be, privately and secretly," according to Vallance's tribute in the *Independent.* He is survived by his wife and four children. **Sources:** *Daily Variety,* March 30, 2004, p. 2; *Guardian* (London), March 30, 2004, p. 3; *Independent* (London), March 30, 2004, p. 34; *New York Times,* March 30, 2004, p. C14.

—*Carol Brennan*

## Fred L. Whipple

Born November 5, 1906, in Red Oak, IA; died August 30, 2004, in Cambridge, MA. Astrophysicist. Fred L. Whipple "was one of those rare individuals who affected our lives in many ways," Charles Alcock, director of the Harvard-Smithsonian Center for Astrophysics, was quoted as having said to Thomas H. Maugh II and Alan Zarembo in the *Los Angeles Times.* Whipple was a pioneer in the field of astrophysics and was best known as the man who proposed the dirty snowball theory to explain the makeup of comets. His legacy also included the Whipple shield, a shield still used in the making of spacecraft in the 21st century, to keep meteors from destroying crafts sent into space.

Born in 1906 to farmers, Whipple had no intentions as a youth of becoming an astronomer. Instead he wanted to be a professional tennis player. His dreams were shattered, however, when he caught polio, which left him in no shape to play sports professionally. The Whipples moved to Los Angeles when young Fred was 15. There he attended Long Beach High School before he went on to the University of California, Los Angeles, where he received his bachelor's degree in mathematics in 1927. It was a class he took during his undergraduate studies that turned him toward a career in astronomy. Such was his interest that Whipple went on to the University of California at Berkeley to get a Ph.D. in astronomy in 1931. While finishing up his Ph.D. Whipple helped to map the orbit of the planet Pluto, which at the time had just been discovered. After his graduation he accepted a position at Harvard University. He started out as an instructor, then moved on to the positions of lecturer in 1938, associate professor in 1945, and professor in 1950.

During World War II Whipple invented a device to aid Allied planes. The device, which basically dropped bits of aluminum from a plane, fooled enemy radar into thinking that there were a larger number of planes flying than were actually there, making it impossible for them to tell where the real planes were. It worked very well. In 1946 he invented something that later became known as the Whipple Shield. There were already discussions of future space flights and one of the problems facing scientists was the idea of meteors hitting the space crafts and injuring them. The Whipple Shield, a thin outer skin of metal, served as a bumper, disintegrating any meteors, leaving only vapor to hit the spacecraft. It was still in use in 2005.

Whipple made his name, however, as a pioneer who proposed the dirty snowball theory for the substance of comets. Comets had perplexed scientists since they were first discovered, but it was not until Whipple proposed his theory in 1950—the idea that comets consisted of ice and rock, rather than sand held together by gravity as had been previously thought, or rocks thrown out into space by volcanoes on Saturn or Jupiter—that scientists really began to understand the comets' nature. The theory helped explain why some comets arrived earlier or later at certain destinations than predictions said they would. This was because as comets got closer to the sun, the light vaporized ice in the comet's nucleus. This too would explain why there were jets, or tails, shooting out from the comets; they were the particles that had been vaporized by the sun's rays. These tails, in turn, would act like jets, either speeding up or slowing down the comet, depending on the direction the tail was pointed in— either toward or away from the line of travel. Whipple theorized this, amazingly enough, with very little data to go on. As Mike Lecar, an astrophysicist at Whipple's old stomping grounds said to Maugh and Zarembo in the *Los Angeles Times,* "Unlike other great physicists, he had uncommon common sense.... He just looked at things with a fresh eye." Whipple's theories were proven correct in 1986 when the European Space Agency's Giotto spacecraft took close-up photos of Haley's comet. In the 1950s Whipple's advice on scientific things was sought after and he became a consultant to *Collier's* magazine for articles about space exploration, along with his rocket scientist friends Willy Ley and Wernher von Braun. Also, in 1955 Whipple became the director of the Smithsonian Astrophysical Observatory in Cambridge.

In 1963 President John F. Kennedy gave Whipple an award for distinguished public service for a project that Whipple had invented using a network of cameras to track the Soviet Union's new Sputnik satellite. Whipple also arranged another type of observation group, consisting of amateur astronomers. He foresaw the coming satellite age, and set up America to be in a position to observe and guard against it. When Sputnik was eventually launched, America was the only country able to watch and track the satellite, and only because of Whipple's work.

Whipple continued as the director of the Smithsonian Astrophysical Observatory until 1973. At that point the Observatory merged with the Harvard Observatory and was renamed the Harvard-Smithsonian Center for Astrophysics. He retired from Harvard in 1977, although he biked to the center six days a week until he was 90. He also wrote a standard textbook for his field called *Earth, Moon, and Planets,* and has been credited with the discovery of six comets. According to Adam Bernstein in

the *Washington Post,* "An observatory in Arizona and an asteroid were named in his honor." He received many awards and was seen on postage stamps in Mauritania in 1986 and St. Vincent in 1994. He was also a member of the Royal Society of Arts in London.

In 1999 Whipple was asked to take part in the National Aeronautics and Space Administration's comet nucleus tour (CONTOUR) group. He was the oldest man ever to accept such an assignment. The spacecraft that was designed is scheduled to meet up with Comet Schwassmann-Wachmann 3 in June of 2006. His fellow designers were saddened because Whipple did not live long enough to see this happen, as Whipple died on August 30, 2004, in Cambridge, Massachusetts; he was 97. He married Dorothy Woods Whipple in 1928, and the couple had one son, Earle Raymond, before they were divorced. He married Babette Samuelson Whipple in 1946, and Whipple is survived by her, his son, and two daughters, Sandra and Laura, from his second marriage. **Sources:** CNN.com, http://www.cnn.com/2004/TECH/space/08/31/obit.whipple.ap/index.html (August 31, 2004); *Daily Telegraph* (London), September 1, 2004; *Los Angeles Times,* September 1, 2004, p. B8; *New York Times,* August 31, 2004, p. C15; *Washington Post,* September 1, 2004, p. B5.

—*Catherine Victoria Donaldson*

## Paul Winfield

Born May 22, 1941, in Los Angeles, CA; died March 7, 2004 in Los Angeles, CA. Actor. Paul Winfield was a versatile actor, equally at home on the stage, in films, and on television. Winfield was nominated for an Oscar in 1972 for his role in the movie *Sounder,* and he won acclaim for his portrayal of Rev. Martin Luther King in a 1978 television miniseries. Although he never achieved superstar status, Winfield had a successful and varied career that spanned more than three decades and included scores of distinguished performances and memorable roles. So prolific was his output in the 1970s that according to the *Times* of London, *People* magazine dubbed him "the most ubiquitous black TV/movie actor of the decade."

Paul Edward Winfield was born in Los Angeles and raised by his mother, Lois Edwards, a single parent and professional labor organizer working in the garment industry. Winfield's stepfather, who Edwards married when Winfield was eight, was a construction worker and city trash collector. In an era of aggressive school desegregation, Winfield was bused to the predominantly white Manual Arts High School, where he quickly excelled in drama and music. He was chosen best actor for three years running in an annual drama competition for high school students in Southern California. Winfield was offered a drama scholarship to Yale, but he felt intimidated and instead opted to enroll at the University of Portland. Portland was the first of four colleges Winfield attended. He never received a degree, however, dropping out of the University of California at Los Angeles just six credits shy of graduation. His lack of a degree did not stop him from serving as an artist-in-residence at Stanford University and the University of Hawaii in 1964 and 1965.

In 1966 Winfield was signed as a contract player by Columbia Pictures. Shortly after that, actor/director Burgess Meredith cast him in two stage plays written by Amiri Baraka. That work captured the attention of Sidney Poitier, who gave Winfield his first role in a movie, *The Lost Man,* in 1969. Around the same time, Winfield was making his first mark on the small screen as well. In 1968 he landed the role of Diahann Carroll's boyfriend on the situation comedy *Julia,* in which Carroll played a nurse raising her son alone after her husband was killed in Vietnam.

In 1972 Winfield was nominated for an Oscar—making him only the third African American so honored—for his role as the father in the film *Sounder.* While he worked regularly in film and television from that point on, the publicity he received from his Oscar nomination did not translate into instant stardom, a fact the *Washington Post,* as quoted in the *New York Times,* later attributed to "the industry's fickle interest in black actors and stories." He found himself cast in supporting roles like Jim in a 1974 remake of *Huckleberry Finn.* Winfield's personal life had some bumps as well. His 18-month relationship with *Sounder* co-star Cicely Tyson had stalled around this time. While working in Mississippi, Winfield was charged with marijuana possession. He pleaded no contest and was fined $11,000.

As the 1970s progressed, however, Winfield's roles began to improve. His portrayal of Martin Luther King, Jr. in the 1978 miniseries *King* earned him an Emmy nomination for best actor. Another Emmy nomination, this one for best supporting actor, followed in 1979 for his role as a college chancellor in *Roots: The Next Generation.* By this time, the offers were arriving in quick succession. In 1982, Winfield played a Starfleet commander in the film *Star Trek II: The Wrath of Khan.* Two years later he appeared in the Arnold Schwarzenegger vehicle *The Terminator.* One of his best-known roles of the 1980s was Gabriel Grimes, the lead character in the made-for-television film *Go Tell It on the Mountain,* an adaptation of the semi-autobiographical novel of that title by James Baldwin.

Winfield's television career remained in high gear over the next several years. He appeared in dozens of network shows, including *L.A. Law, Wiseguy, The Charmings,* and *Family Matters.* As he aged, Winfield increasingly landed roles as authority figures. His 1990 portrayal of a wise-but-sarcastic judge in the feature film *Presumed Innocent* won rave reviews. A similar role—a judge involved in a school desegregation case on the television series *Picket Fences*—resulted in an Emmy for best supporting actor in 1995. Another high-profile role that year was that of promoter Don King in an HBO film about boxer Mike Tyson. He also had a recurring role on the series *Touched by an Angel* during the mid-1990s. Winfield remained active on the stage as well during this phase of his career, appearing with Denzel Washington in the Broadway play *Checkmates.*

One of Winfield's chief assets was his voice, which he lent to a number of projects in which he did not appear visually. These included the 1994 PBS documentary *Baseball,* the PBS children's series *The Magic School Bus,* and *City Confidential,* a 1998 crime documentary series on the A&E cable network.

Winfield was a huge fan of pug dogs. He had seven pet pugs in his Los Angeles home, and hundreds of ceramic and bronze pug figures. Winfield never married. He died of a heart attack in Los Angeles at the age of 62 on March 7, 2004. He is survived by his sister, Patricia Wilson. **Sources:** *New York Times,* March 9, 2004, p. C17; *Times* (London), March 17, 2004, p. 36; *Washington Post,* March 11, 2004, p. B6.

*—Robert Jacobson*

# Cumulative Nationality Index

This index lists all newsmakers alphabetically under their respective nationalities. Indexes in softbound issues allow access to the current year's entries; indexes in annual hardbound volumes are cumulative, covering the entire *Newsmakers* series.

Listee names are followed by a year and issue number; thus **1996**:3 indicates that an entry on that individual appears in both 1996, Issue 3, and the 1996 cumulation. For access to newsmakers appearing earlier than the current softbound issue, see the previous year's cumulation.

**AFGHAN**
Karzai, Hamid **2002**:3

**ALGERIAN**
Zeroual, Liamine **1996**:2

**AMERICAN**
Aaliyah **2001**:3
Abbey, Edward
  Obituary **1989**:3
Abbott, George
  Obituary **1995**:3
Abbott, Jim **1988**:3
Abdul, Paula **1990**:3
Abercrombie, Josephine **1987**:2
Abernathy, Ralph
  Obituary **1990**:3
Abraham, S. Daniel **2003**:3
Abraham, Spencer **1991**:4
Abrams, Elliott **1987**:1
Abramson, Lyn **1986**:3
Abzug, Bella **1998**:2
Achtenberg, Roberta **1993**:4
Ackerman, Will **1987**:4
Acuff, Roy
  Obituary **1993**:2
Adair, Red **1987**:3
Adams, Patch **1999**:2
Adams, Scott **1996**:4
Addams, Charles
  Obituary **1989**:1
Adu, Freddy **2005**:3
Affleck, Ben **1999**:1
Agassi, Andre **1990**:2
Agatston, Arthur **2005**:1
Agee, Tommie
  Obituary **2001**:4
Agnew, Spiro Theodore
  Obituary **1997**:1
Aguilera, Christina **2000**:4
Aiello, Danny **1990**:4
Aikman, Troy **1994**:2
Ailes, Roger **1989**:3
Ailey, Alvin **1989**:2
  Obituary **1990**:2
Ainge, Danny **1987**:1

Akers, John F. **1988**:3
Akers, Michelle **1996**:1
Akin, Phil
  Brief Entry **1987**:3
Alba, Jessica **2001**:2
Albee, Edward **1997**:1
Albert, Marv **1994**:3
Albert, Stephen **1986**:1
Albom, Mitch **1999**:3
Albrecht, Chris **2005**:4
Albright, Madeleine **1994**:3
Alda, Robert
  Obituary **1986**:3
Alexander, Jane **1994**:2
Alexander, Jason **1993**:3
Alexander, Lamar **1991**:2
Alexie, Sherman **1998**:4
Ali, Laila **2001**:2
Ali, Muhammad **1997**:2
Alioto, Joseph L.
  Obituary **1998**:3
Allaire, Paul **1995**:1
Allard, Linda **2003**:2
Allen, Bob **1992**:4
Allen, Debbie **1998**:2
Allen, Joan **1998**:1
Allen, John **1992**:1
Allen, Mel
  Obituary **1996**:4
Allen, Ray **2002**:1
Allen, Steve
  Obituary **2001**:2
Allen, Tim **1993**:1
Allen, Woody **1994**:1
Allen Jr., Ivan
  Obituary **2004**:3
Alley, Kirstie **1990**:3
Allred, Gloria **1985**:2
Alter, Hobie
  Brief Entry **1985**:1
Altman, Robert **1993**:2
Altman, Sidney **1997**:2
Alvarez, Aida **1999**:2
Ambrose, Stephen **2002**:3
Ameche, Don
  Obituary **1994**:2

Amory, Cleveland
  Obituary **1999**:2
Amos, Tori **1995**:1
Amos, Wally **2000**:1
Amsterdam, Morey
  Obituary **1997**:1
Anastas, Robert
  Brief Entry **1985**:2
Ancier, Garth **1989**:1
Anderson, Gillian **1997**:1
Anderson, Harry **1988**:2
Anderson, Laurie **2000**:2
Anderson, Marion
  Obituary **1993**:4
Anderson, Poul
  Obituary **2002**:3
Andreessen, Marc **1996**:2
Andrews, Lori B. **2005**:3
Andrews, Maxene
  Obituary **1996**:2
Angelos, Peter **1995**:4
Angelou, Maya **1993**:4
Angier, Natalie **2000**:3
Aniston, Jennifer **2000**:3
Annenberg, Walter **1992**:3
Anthony, Earl
  Obituary **2002**:3
Anthony, Marc **2000**:3
Antonini, Joseph **1991**:2
Applegate, Christina **2000**:4
Applewhite, Marshall Herff
  Obituary **1997**:3
Arad, Avi **2003**:2
Archer, Dennis **1994**:4
Arden, Eve
  Obituary **1991**:2
Aretsky, Ken **1988**:1
Arison, Ted **1990**:3
Arkoff, Samuel Z.
  Obituary **2002**:4
Arledge, Roone **1992**:2
Arlen, Harold
  Obituary **1986**:3
Arman **1993**:1
Armstrong, C. Michael **2002**:1
Armstrong, Henry
  Obituary **1989**:1

Bloch, Henry **1988**:4
Bloch, Ivan **1986**:3
Block, Herbert
  Obituary **2002**:4
Bloodworth-Thomason,
  Linda **1994**:1
Bloomberg, Michael **1997**:1
Blume, Judy **1998**:4
Bly, Robert **1992**:4
Blyth, Myrna **2002**:4
Bochco, Steven **1989**:1
Boggs, Wade **1989**:3
Bogosian, Eric **1990**:4
Bohbot, Michele **2004**:2
Boiardi, Hector
  Obituary **1985**:3
Boies, David **2002**:1
Boitano, Brian **1988**:3
Bolger, Ray
  Obituary **1987**:2
Bollinger, Lee C. **2003**:2
Bolton, Michael **1993**:2
Bombeck, Erma
  Obituary **1996**:4
Bonds, Barry **1993**:3
Bonet, Lisa **1989**:2
Bonilla, Bobby **1992**:2
Bon Jovi, Jon **1987**:4
Bonner, Robert **2003**:4
Bono, Sonny **1992**:2
  Obituary **1998**:2
Bontecou, Lee **2004**:4
Boone, Mary **1985**:1
Booth, Shirley
  Obituary **1993**:2
Bopp, Thomas **1997**:3
Bose, Amar
  Brief Entry **1986**:4
Bosworth, Brian **1989**:1
Botstein, Leon **1985**:3
Boudreau, Louis
  Obituary **2002**:3
Bowe, Riddick **1993**:2
Bowles, Paul
  Obituary **2000**:3
Bowman, Scotty **1998**:4
Boxcar Willie
  Obituary **1999**:4
Boxer, Barbara **1995**:1
Boyer, Herbert Wayne **1985**:1
Boyington, Gregory 'Pappy'
  Obituary **1988**:2
Boyle, Gertrude **1995**:3
Boyle, Lara Flynn **2003**:4
Boyle, Peter **2002**:3
Boynton, Sandra **2004**:1
Bradford, Barbara Taylor **2002**:4
Bradley, Bill **2000**:2
Bradley, Todd **2003**:3
Bradley, Tom
  Obituary **1999**:1
Bradshaw, John **1992**:1
Brady, Sarah and James S. **1991**:4
Brady, Tom **2002**:4
Braff, Zach **2005**:2
Brando, Marlon
  Obituary **2005**:3
Brandy **1996**:4
Braun, Carol Moseley **1993**:1
Bravo, Ellen **1998**:2
Bravo, Rose Marie **2005**:3
Braxton, Toni **1994**:3

Brazile, Donna **2001**:1
Breathed, Berkeley **2005**:3
Bremen, Barry **1987**:3
Bremer, L. Paul **2004**:2
Brennan, Edward A. **1989**:1
Brennan, Robert E. **1988**:1
Brennan, William
  Obituary **1997**:4
Brenneman, Amy **2002**:1
Breyer, Stephen Gerald
  **1994**:4 **1997**:2
Bridges, Lloyd
  Obituary **1998**:3
Brinkley, David
  Obituary **2004**:3
Bristow, Lonnie **1996**:1
Brite, Poppy Z. **2005**:1
Brockovich-Ellis, Erin **2003**:3
Brokaw, Tom **2000**:3
Bronfman, Edgar, Jr. **1994**:4
Bronson, Charles
  Obituary **2004**:4
Brooks, Albert **1991**:4
Brooks, Diana D. **1990**:1
Brooks, Garth **1992**:1
Brooks, Gwendolyn **1998**:1
  Obituary **2001**:2
Brooks, Mel **2003**:1
Brower, David **1990**:4
Brown, Bobbi **2001**:4
Brown, Dan **2004**:4
Brown, Dee
  Obituary **2004**:1
Brown, Edmund G., Sr.
  Obituary **1996**:3
Brown, J. Carter
  Obituary **2003**:3
Brown, James **1991**:4
Brown, Jerry **1992**:4
Brown, Jim **1993**:2
Brown, John Seely **2004**:1
Brown, Judie **1986**:2
Brown, Les **1994**:3
Brown, Les
  Obituary **2001**:3
Brown, Paul
  Obituary **1992**:1
Brown, Ron
  Obituary **1996**:4
Brown, Ron **1990**:3
Brown, Willie **1996**:4
Brown, Willie L. **1985**:2
Browner, Carol M. **1994**:1
Browning, Edmond
  Brief Entry **1986**:2
Bryant, Kobe **1998**:3
Brynner, Yul
  Obituary **1985**:4
Buchanan, Pat **1996**:3
Buck, Linda **2004**:2
Buckley, Betty **1996**:2
Buckley, Jeff
  Obituary **1997**:4
Buffett, Jimmy **1999**:3
Buffett, Warren **1995**:2
Bullock, Sandra **1995**:4
Bundy, McGeorge
  Obituary **1997**:1
Bundy, William P.
  Obituary **2001**:2
Bunshaft, Gordon **1989**:3
  Obituary **1991**:1

Burck, Wade
  Brief Entry **1986**:1
Burger, Warren E.
  Obituary **1995**:4
Burk, Martha **2004**:1
Burnett, Carol **2000**:3
Burnison, Chantal Simone **1988**:3
Burns, Charles R.
  Brief Entry **1988**:1
Burns, Edward **1997**:1
Burns, George
  Obituary **1996**:3
Burns, Ken **1995**:2
Burns, Robin **1991**:2
Burr, Donald Calvin **1985**:3
Burroughs, William S. **1994**:2
Burroughs, William S.
  Obituary **1997**:4
Burrows, James **2005**:3
Burstyn, Ellen **2001**:4
Burton, Tim **1993**:1
Burum, Stephen H.
  Brief Entry **1987**:2
Buscaglia, Leo
  Obituary **1998**:4
Buscemi, Steve **1997**:4
Busch, August A. III **1988**:2
Busch, August Anheuser, Jr.
  Obituary **1990**:2
Busch, Charles **1998**:3
Bush, Barbara **1989**:3
Bush, George W., Jr. **1996**:4
Bush, Jeb **2003**:1
Bush, Millie **1992**:1
Bushnell, Candace **2004**:2
Bushnell, Nolan **1985**:1
Buss, Jerry **1989**:3
Butcher, Susan **1991**:1
Butler, Brett **1995**:1
Butler, Octavia E. **1999**:3
Butterfield, Paul
  Obituary **1987**:3
Bynes, Amanda **2005**:1
Caan, James **2004**:4
Caen, Herb
  Obituary **1997**:4
Caesar, Adolph
  Obituary **1986**:3
Cage, John
  Obituary **1993**:1
Cage, Nicolas **1991**:1
Cagney, James
  Obituary **1986**:2
Cain, Herman **1998**:3
Calhoun, Rory
  Obituary **1999**:4
Caliguiri, Richard S.
  Obituary **1988**:3
Callaway, Ely
  Obituary **2002**:3
Calloway, Cab
  Obituary **1995**:2
Calloway, D. Wayne **1987**:3
Cameron, David
  Brief Entry **1988**:1
Cammermeyer, Margarethe **1995**:2
Campanella, Roy
  Obituary **1994**:1
Campbell, Bebe Moore **1996**:2
Campbell, Ben Nighthorse **1998**:1
Campbell, Bill **1997**:1

Canfield, Alan B.
  Brief Entry **1986**:3
Cantrell, Ed
  Brief Entry **1985**:3
Caplan, Arthur L. **2000**:2
Capriati, Jennifer **1991**:1
Caras, Roger
  Obituary **2002**:1
Caray, Harry **1988**:3
  Obituary **1998**:3
Carcaterra, Lorenzo **1996**:1
Card, Andrew H., Jr. **2003**:2
Carey, Drew **1997**:4
Carey, Mariah **1991**:3
Carey, Ron **1993**:3
Carlin, George **1996**:3
Carlisle, Belinda **1989**:3
Carlson, Richard **2002**:1
Carmona, Richard **2003**:2
Carnahan, Jean **2001**:2
Carnahan, Mel
  Obituary **2001**:2
Carney, Art
  Obituary **2005**:1
Carpenter, Mary-Chapin **1994**:1
Carradine, John
  Obituary **1989**:2
Carson, Ben **1998**:2
Carson, Lisa Nicole **1999**:3
Carter, Amy **1987**:4
Carter, Benny
  Obituary **2004**:3
Carter, Billy
  Obituary **1989**:1
Carter, Chris **2000**:1
Carter, Gary **1987**:1
Carter, Jimmy **1995**:1
Carter, Joe **1994**:2
Carter, Nell
  Obituary **2004**:2
Carter, Ron **1987**:3
Carter, Rubin **2000**:3
Carter, Vince **2001**:4
Caruso, David **1994**:3
Carver, Raymond
  Obituary **1989**:1
Carvey, Dana **1994**:1
Case, Steve **1995**:4 **1996**:4
Casey, William
  Obituary **1987**:3
Cash, Johnny **1995**:3
Cash, June Carter
  Obituary **2004**:2
Cassavetes, John
  Obituary **1989**:2
Castelli, Leo
  Obituary **2000**:1
Castillo, Ana **2000**:4
Catlett, Elizabeth **1999**:3
Cattrall, Kim **2003**:3
Caulfield, Joan
  Obituary **1992**:1
Cavazos, Lauro F. **1989**:2
Caviezel, Jim **2005**:3
Cerf, Vinton G. **1999**:2
Chabon, Michael **2002**:1
Chaing Kai-Shek, Madame
  Obituary **2005**:1
Chamberlain, Wilt
  Obituary **2000**:2
Chamberlin, Wendy **2002**:4

Chancellor, John
  Obituary **1997**:1
Chaney, John **1989**:1
Channing, Stockard **1991**:3
Chapman, Tracy **1989**:2
Chappell, Tom **2002**:3
Chappelle, Dave **2005**:3
Charles, Ray
  Obituary **2005**:3
Charron, Paul **2004**:1
Chase, Chevy **1990**:1
Chast, Roz **1992**:4
Chastain, Brandi **2001**:3
Chatham, Russell **1990**:1
Chaudhari, Praveen **1989**:4
Chavez, Cesar
  Obituary **1993**:4
Chavez, Linda **1999**:3
Chavez-Thompson, Linda **1999**:1
Chavis, Benjamin **1993**:4
Cheadle, Don **2002**:1
Cheatham, Adolphus 'Doc'
  Obituary **1997**:4
Cheek, James Edward
  Brief Entry **1987**:1
Chenault, Kenneth I. **1999**:3
Cheney, Dick **1991**:3
Cheney, Lynne V. **1990**:4
Cher **1993**:1
Chia, Sandro **1987**:2
Chihuly, Dale **1995**:2
Chiklis, Michael **2003**:3
Child, Julia **1999**:4
Chittister, Joan D. **2002**:2
Chizen, Bruce **2004**:2
Cho, Margaret **1995**:2
Chouinard, Yvon **2002**:2
Christopher, Warren **1996**:3
Chu, Paul C.W. **1988**:2
Chung, Connie **1988**:4
Chyna **2001**:4
Cisneros, Henry **1987**:2
Claiborne, Liz **1986**:3
Clancy, Tom **1998**:4
Clark, J. E.
  Brief Entry **1986**:1
Clark, Jim **1997**:1
Clark, Marcia **1995**:1
Clark, Mary Higgins **2000**:4
Clarke, Richard A. **2002**:2
Clarke, Stanley **1985**:4
Clarkson, Kelly **2003**:3
Clarkson, Patricia **2005**:3
Clavell, James
  Obituary **1995**:1
Clay, Andrew Dice **1991**:1
Cleaver, Eldridge
  Obituary **1998**:4
Clemens, Roger **1991**:4
Clements, George **1985**:1
Cleveland, James
  Obituary **1991**:3
Cliburn, Van **1995**:1
Clinton, Bill **1992**:1
Clinton, Hillary Rodham **1993**:2
Clooney, George **1996**:4
Clooney, Rosemary
  Obituary **2003**:4
Close, Glenn **1988**:3
Clyburn, James **1999**:4
Cobain, Kurt
  Obituary **1994**:3

Coburn, James
  Obituary **2004**:1
Coca, Imogene
  Obituary **2002**:2
Cochran, Johnnie **1996**:1
Coco, James
  Obituary **1987**:2
Codrescu, Andreá **1997**:3
Coen, Joel and Ethan **1992**:1
Coffin, William Sloane, Jr. **1990**:3
Cohen, William S. **1998**:1
Colasanto, Nicholas
  Obituary **1985**:2
Colby, William E.
  Obituary **1996**:4
Cole, Johnetta B. **1994**:3
Cole, Kenneth **2003**:1
Cole, Natalie **1992**:4
Coleman, Dabney **1988**:3
Coleman, Sheldon, Jr. **1990**:2
Coles, Robert **1995**:1
Collier, Sophia **2001**:2
Collins, Albert
  Obituary **1994**:2
Collins, Billy **2002**:2
Collins, Cardiss **1995**:3
Collins, Eileen **1995**:3
Collins, Kerry **2002**:3
Colwell, Rita Rossi **1999**:3
Combs, Sean 'Puffy' **1998**:4
Commager, Henry Steele
  Obituary **1998**:3
Como, Perry
  Obituary **2002**:2
Condit, Phil **2001**:3
Condon, Richard
  Obituary **1996**:4
Conigliaro, Tony
  Obituary **1990**:3
Connally, John
  Obituary **1994**:1
Connelly, Jennifer **2002**:4
Conner, Dennis **1987**:2
Connerly, Ward **2000**:2
Connick, Harry, Jr. **1991**:1
Conrad, Pete
  Obituary **2000**:1
Convy, Bert
  Obituary **1992**:1
Conyers, John, Jr. **1999**:1
Cook, Robin **1996**:3
Cooke, Alistair
  Obituary **2005**:3
Coolio **1996**:4
Cooper, Alexander **1988**:4
Cooper, Chris **2004**:1
Cooper, Cynthia **1999**:1
Cooper, Stephen F. **2005**:4
Coors, William K.
  Brief Entry **1985**:1
Copeland, Al **1988**:3
Copland, Aaron
  Obituary **1991**:2
Copperfield, David **1986**:3
Coppola, Carmine
  Obituary **1991**:4
Coppola, Francis Ford **1989**:4
Coppola, Sofia **2004**:3
Corbett, John **2004**:1
Corea, Chick **1986**:3
Cornwell, Patricia **2003**:1
Corwin, Jeff **2005**:1

Cosby, Bill **1999**:2
Cosell, Howard
  Obituary **1995**:4
Costas, Bob **1986**:4
Costner, Kevin **1989**:4
Couples, Fred **1994**:4
Couric, Katherine **1991**:4
Courier, Jim **1993**:2
Cousteau, Jean-Michel **1988**:2
Covey, Stephen R. **1994**:4
Cowley, Malcolm
  Obituary **1989**:3
Cox, Courteney **1996**:2
Cox, Richard Joseph
  Brief Entry **1985**:1
Cozza, Stephen **2001**:1
Craig, James **2001**:1
Cram, Donald J.
  Obituary **2002**:2
Crandall, Robert L. **1992**:1
Craven, Wes **1997**:3
Crawford, Broderick
  Obituary **1986**:3
Crawford, Cheryl
  Obituary **1987**:1
Crawford, Cindy **1993**:3
Cray, Robert **1988**:2
Cray, Seymour R.
  Brief Entry **1986**:3
  Obituary **1997**:2
Crenna, Richard
  Obituary **2004**:1
Crichton, Michael **1995**:3
Cronkite, Walter Leland **1997**:3
Crosby, David **2000**:4
Crothers, Scatman
  Obituary **1987**:1
Crow, Sheryl **1995**:2
Crowe, Cameron **2001**:2
Cruise, Tom **1985**:4
Crumb, R. **1995**:4
Cruz, Nilo **2004**:4
Cruzan, Nancy
  Obituary **1991**:3
Crystal, Billy **1985**:3
Cugat, Xavier
  Obituary **1991**:2
Culkin, Macaulay **1991**:3
Cunningham, Merce **1998**:1
Cunningham, Michael **2003**:4
Cunningham, Randall **1990**:1
Cunningham, Reverend William
  Obituary **1997**:4
Cuomo, Mario **1992**:2
Curran, Charles E. **1989**:2
Curren, Tommy
  Brief Entry **1987**:4
Curry, Ann **2001**:1
Curtis, Ben **2004**:2
Curtis, Jamie Lee **1995**:1
Cusack, John **1999**:3
Cyrus, Billy Ray **1993**:1
Dafoe, Willem **1988**:1
Dahmer, Jeffrey
  Obituary **1995**:2
Daily, Bishop Thomas V. **1990**:4
D'Alessio, Kitty
  Brief Entry **1987**:3
Daly, Carson **2002**:4
D'Amato, Al **1996**:1
Damon, Johnny **2005**:4
Damon, Matt **1999**:1

Danes, Claire **1999**:4
Daniels, Faith **1993**:3
Daniels, Jeff **1989**:4
Danticat, Edwidge **2005**:4
Danza, Tony **1989**:1
D'Arby, Terence Trent **1988**:4
Darden, Christopher **1996**:4
Daschle, Tom **2002**:3
Davenport, Lindsay **1999**:2
David, George **2005**:1
David, Larry **2003**:4
Davis, Angela **1998**:3
Davis, Bette
  Obituary **1990**:1
Davis, Eric **1987**:4
Davis, Geena **1992**:1
Davis, Miles
  Obituary **1992**:2
Davis, Noel **1990**:3
Davis, Paige **2004**:2
Davis, Patti **1995**:1
Davis, Sammy, Jr.
  Obituary **1990**:4
Davis, Terrell **1998**:2
Day, Dennis
  Obituary **1988**:4
Day, Pat **1995**:2
Dean, Howard **2005**:4
Dean, Laura **1989**:4
Dearden, John Cardinal
  Obituary **1988**:4
DeBartolo, Edward J., Jr. **1989**:3
DeCarava, Roy **1996**:3
De Cordova, Frederick **1985**:2
Dees, Morris **1992**:1
DeGeneres, Ellen **1995**:3
de Kooning, Willem **1994**:4
  Obituary **1997**:3
De La Hoya, Oscar **1998**:2
Delany, Sarah
  Obituary **1999**:3
de la Renta, Oscar **2005**:4
DeLay, Tom **2000**:1
Dell, Michael **1996**:2
DeLuca, Fred **2003**:3
De Matteo, Drea **2005**:2
de Mille, Agnes
  Obituary **1994**:2
Deming, W. Edwards **1992**:2
  Obituary **1994**:2
Demme, Jonathan **1992**:4
De Niro, Robert **1999**:1
Dennehy, Brian **2002**:1
Dennis, Sandy
  Obituary **1992**:4
Denver, John
  Obituary **1998**:1
de Passe, Suzanne **1990**:4
Depp, Johnny **1991**:3
Dern, Laura **1992**:3
Dershowitz, Alan **1992**:1
Desormeaux, Kent **1990**:2
Destiny's Child **2001**:3
Deutch, John **1996**:4
Devine, John M. **2003**:2
DeVita, Vincent T., Jr. **1987**:3
De Vito, Danny **1987**:1
Diamond, I.A.L.
  Obituary **1988**:3
Diamond, Selma
  Obituary **1985**:2
Diaz, Cameron **1999**:1

DiBello, Paul
  Brief Entry **1986**:4
DiCaprio, Leonardo Wilhelm **1997**:2
Dickerson, Nancy H.
  Obituary **1998**:2
Dickey, James
  Obituary **1998**:2
Dickinson, Brian **1998**:2
Dickinson, Janice **2005**:2
Diebenkorn, Richard
  Obituary **1993**:4
Diemer, Walter E.
  Obituary **1998**:2
Diesel, Vin **2004**:1
DiFranco, Ani **1997**:1
Diggs, Taye **2000**:1
Diller, Barry **1991**:1
Diller, Elizabeth and Ricardo
  Scofidio **2004**:3
Dillon, Matt **1992**:2
DiMaggio, Joe
  Obituary **1999**:3
Di Meola, Al **1986**:4
Dinkins, David N. **1990**:2
Disney, Lillian
  Obituary **1998**:3
Disney, Roy E. **1986**:3
Divine
  Obituary **1988**:3
Dixie Chicks **2001**:2
Dr. Demento **1986**:1
Dr. Dre **1994**:3
Doherty, Shannen **1994**:2
Dolan, Terry **1985**:2
Dolan, Tom **2001**:2
Dolby, Ray Milton
  Brief Entry **1986**:1
Dole, Bob **1994**:2
Dole, Elizabeth Hanford **1990**:1
Dolenz, Micky **1986**:4
Donahue, Tim **2004**:3
Donahue, Troy
  Obituary **2002**:4
Donghia, Angelo R.
  Obituary **1985**:2
Donnellan, Nanci **1995**:2
Dorati, Antal
  Obituary **1989**:2
Dorris, Michael
  Obituary **1997**:3
Dorsey, Thomas A.
  Obituary **1993**:3
Doubleday, Nelson, Jr. **1987**:1
Douglas, Buster **1990**:4
Douglas, Marjory Stoneman **1993**:1
  Obituary **1998**:4
Douglas, Michael **1986**:2
Dove, Rita **1994**:3
Dowd, Maureen Brigid **1997**:1
Downey, Bruce **2003**:1
Downey, Morton, Jr. **1988**:4
Dravecky, Dave **1992**:1
Drescher, Fran **1995**:3
Drexler, Clyde **1992**:4
Drexler, Millard S. **1990**:3
Dreyfuss, Richard **1996**:3
Drysdale, Don
  Obituary **1994**:1
Duarte, Henry **2003**:3
Dubrof, Jessica
  Obituary **1996**:4
Duchovny, David **1998**:3

Dudley, Jane
Obituary **2002**:4
Duff, Hilary **2004**:4
Duffy, Karen **1998**:1
Dukakis, Michael **1988**:3
Dukakis, Olympia **1996**:4
Duke, David **1990**:2
Duke, Doris
Obituary **1994**:2
Duke, Red
Brief Entry **1987**:1
Duncan, Tim **2000**:1
Duncan, Todd
Obituary **1998**:3
Dunham, Carroll **2003**:4
Dunlap, Albert J. **1997**:2
Dunne, Dominick **1997**:1
Dunst, Kirsten **2001**:4
Dupri, Jermaine **1999**:1
Durocher, Leo
Obituary **1992**:2
Durrell, Gerald
Obituary **1995**:3
Duval, David **2000**:3
Duvall, Camille
Brief Entry **1988**:1
Duvall, Robert **1999**:3
Dykstra, Lenny **1993**:4
Dylan, Bob **1998**:1
Earle, Sylvia **2001**:1
Earnhardt, Dale
Obituary **2001**:4
Earnhardt, Dale, Jr. **2004**:4
Eastwood, Clint **1993**:3
Eaton, Robert J. **1994**:2
Eazy-E
Obituary **1995**:3
Ebert, Roger **1998**:3
Ebsen, Buddy
Obituary **2004**:3
Eckert, Robert A. **2002**:3
Eckstine, Billy
Obituary **1993**:4
Edelman, Marian Wright **1990**:4
Ederle, Gertrude
Obituary **2005**:1
Edmonds, Kenneth 'Babyface'
**1995**:3
Edwards, Bob **1993**:2
Edwards, Harry **1989**:4
Eggers, Dave **2001**:3
Ehrlichman, John
Obituary **1999**:3
Eilberg, Amy
Brief Entry **1985**:3
Eisenman, Peter **1992**:4
Eisenstaedt, Alfred
Obituary **1996**:1
Eisner, Michael **1989**:2
Elders, Joycelyn **1994**:1
Eldridge, Roy
Obituary **1989**:3
Elfman, Jenna **1999**:4
Ellerbee, Linda **1993**:3
Elliott, Missy **2003**:4
Ellis, Perry
Obituary **1986**:3
Ellison, Larry **2004**:2
Ellison, Ralph
Obituary **1994**:4
Ellroy, James **2003**:4
Elway, John **1990**:3

Eminem **2001**:2
Engelbreit, Mary **1994**:3
Engibous, Thomas J. **2003**:3
Engler, John **1996**:3
Englund, Richard
Obituary **1991**:3
Engstrom, Elmer W.
Obituary **1985**:2
Ensler, Eve **2002**:4
Ephron, Henry
Obituary **1993**:2
Ephron, Nora **1992**:3
Epps, Omar **2000**:4
Epstein, Jason **1991**:1
Epstein, Theo **2003**:4
Erdrich, Louise **2005**:3
Ertegun, Ahmet **1986**:3
Ervin, Sam
Obituary **1985**:2
Esiason, Boomer **1991**:1
Estefan, Gloria **1991**:4
Estes, Pete
Obituary **1988**:3
Estevez, Emilio **1985**:4
Estrich, Susan **1989**:1
Etheridge, Melissa **1995**:4
Evanovich, Janet **2005**:2
Evans, Dale
Obituary **2001**:3
Evans, Janet **1989**:1
Evans, Joni **1991**:4
Evans, Nancy **2000**:4
Evans, Robert **2004**:1
Eve **2004**:3
Evers-Williams, Myrlie **1995**:4
Ewing, Patrick **1985**:3
Eyler, John. H., Jr. **2001**:3
Factor, Max
Obituary **1996**:4
Fagan, Garth **2000**:1
Fairbanks, Douglas, Jr.
Obituary **2000**:4
Fairstein, Linda **1991**:1
Falconer, Ian **2003**:1
Falkenberg, Nanette **1985**:2
Fallon, Jimmy **2003**:1
Faludi, Susan **1992**:4
Fanning, Dakota **2005**:2
Fanning, Shawn **2001**:1
Farley, Chris
Obituary **1998**:2
Farmer, James
Obituary **2000**:1
Farrakhan, Louis **1990**:4
Farrell, Perry **1992**:2
Farrell, Suzanne **1996**:3
Farrow, Mia **1998**:3
Fast, Howard
Obituary **2004**:2
Faubus, Orval
Obituary **1995**:2
Fauci, Anthony S. **2004**:1
Faulkner, Shannon **1994**:4
Favre, Brett Lorenzo **1997**:2
Favreau, Jon **2002**:3
Fawcett, Farrah **1998**:4
Fehr, Donald **1987**:2
Feinstein, Dianne **1993**:3
Feld, Eliot **1996**:1
Feld, Kenneth **1988**:2
Feldman, Sandra **1987**:3
Feldshuh, Tovah **2005**:3

Fell, Norman
Obituary **1999**:2
Fender, Leo
Obituary **1992**:1
Fenley, Molissa **1988**:3
Fenwick, Millicent H.
Obituary **1993**:2
Fernandez, Joseph **1991**:3
Ferraro, Geraldine **1998**:3
Ferrell, Trevor
Brief Entry **1985**:2
Ferrell, Will **2004**:4
Fertel, Ruth **2000**:2
Fetchit, Stepin
Obituary **1986**:1
Fey, Tina **2005**:3
Fieger, Geoffrey **2001**:3
Field, Patricia **2002**:2
Field, Sally **1995**:3
Fielder, Cecil **1993**:2
Fields, Debbi **1987**:3
Fields, Evelyn J. **2001**:3
Fierstein, Harvey **2004**:2
Filo, David and Jerry Yang **1998**:3
Finley, Karen **1992**:4
Fiorina, Carleton S. **2000**:1
Fireman, Paul
Brief Entry **1987**:2
Firestone, Roy **1988**:2
Fish, Hamilton
Obituary **1991**:3
Fishburne, Laurence **1995**:3
Fisher, Carrie **1991**:1
Fisher, Mary **1994**:3
Fisher, Mel **1985**:4
Fitzgerald, A. Ernest **1986**:2
Fitzgerald, Ella
Obituary **1996**:4
Flanders, Ed
Obituary **1995**:3
Flatley, Michael **1997**:3
Fleischer, Ari **2003**:1
Fleiss, Mike **2003**:4
Fleming, Art
Obituary **1995**:4
Fleming, Claudia **2004**:1
Fleming, Renee **2001**:4
Flockhart, Calista **1998**:4
Flood, Curt
Obituary **1997**:2
Florio, James J. **1991**:2
Flutie, Doug **1999**:2
Flynn, Ray **1989**:1
Flynt, Larry **1997**:3
Foley, Thomas S. **1990**:1
Folkman, Judah **1999**:1
Fomon, Robert M. **1985**:3
Fonda, Bridget **1995**:1
Foote, Shelby **1991**:2
Forbes, Malcolm S.
Obituary **1990**:3
Forbes, Steve **1996**:2
Ford, Faith **2005**:3
Ford, Harrison **1990**:2
Ford, Henry II
Obituary **1988**:1
Ford, Tennessee Ernie
Obituary **1992**:2
Ford, Tom **1999**:3
Ford, William Clay, Jr. **1999**:1
Foreman, Dave **1990**:3
Foreman, George **2004**:2

Forsythe, William **1993**:2
Foss, Joe **1990**:3
Fosse, Bob
    Obituary **1988**:1
Fossey, Dian
    Obituary **1986**:1
Foster, David **1988**:2
Foster, Jodie **1989**:2
Foster, Phil
    Obituary **1985**:3
Foster, Sutton **2003**:2
Foster, Tabatha
    Obituary **1988**:3
Foster, Vincent
    Obituary **1994**:1
Fox, Matthew **1992**:2
Fox, Vivica **1999**:1
Foxworthy, Jeff **1996**:1
Foxx, Jamie **2001**:1
Foxx, Redd
    Obituary **1992**:2
France, Johnny
    Brief Entry **1987**:1
Franciscus, James
    Obituary **1992**:1
Frank, Barney **1989**:2
Frank, Robert **1995**:2
Franken, Al **1996**:3
Frankenheimer, John
    Obituary **2003**:4
Frankenthaler, Helen **1990**:1
Franklin, Aretha **1998**:3
Franklin, Melvin
    Obituary **1995**:3
Franks, Tommy **2004**:1
Franz, Dennis **1995**:2
Franzen, Jonathan **2002**:3
Fraser, Brendan **2000**:1
Fraser, Claire M. **2005**:2
Frazier, Charles **2003**:2
Freeh, Louis J. **1994**:2
Freeman, Cliff **1996**:1
Freeman, Morgan **1990**:4
Freleng, Friz
    Obituary **1995**:4
Friedan, Betty **1994**:2
Friend, Patricia A. **2003**:3
Frist, Bill **2003**:4
Fudge, Ann **2000**:3
Fulbright, J. William
    Obituary **1995**:3
Fulghum, Robert **1996**:1
Funt, Allen
    Obituary **2000**:1
Furman, Rosemary
    Brief Entry **1986**:4
Furyk, Jim **2004**:2
Futrell, Mary Hatwood **1986**:1
Futter, Ellen V. **1995**:1
Gabor, Eva
    Obituary **1996**:1
Gacy, John Wayne
    Obituary **1994**:4
Gaines, William M.
    Obituary **1993**:1
Gale, Robert Peter **1986**:4
Galindo, Rudy **2001**:2
Gallagher, Peter **2004**:3
Gallo, Robert **1991**:1
Galvin, John R. **1990**:1
Galvin, Martin
    Brief Entry **1985**:3

Gandolfini, James **2001**:3
Gandy, Kim **2002**:2
Ganzi, Victor **2003**:3
Garbo, Greta
    Obituary **1990**:3
Garcia, Andy **1999**:3
Garcia, Cristina **1997**:4
Garcia, Jerry **1988**:3
    Obituary **1996**:1
Garcia, Joe
    Brief Entry **1986**:4
Gardner, Ava Lavinia
    Obituary **1990**:2
Gardner, David and Tom **2001**:4
Gardner, Randy **1997**:2
Garner, Jennifer **2003**:1
Garnett, Kevin **2000**:3
Garofalo, Janeane **1996**:4
Garr, Teri **1988**:4
Garrison, Jim
    Obituary **1993**:2
Garson, Greer
    Obituary **1996**:4
Garzarelli, Elaine M. **1992**:3
Gates, Bill **1993**:3 **1987**:4
Gates, Robert M. **1992**:2
Gathers, Hank
    Obituary **1990**:3
Gault, Willie **1991**:2
Gebbie, Kristine **1994**:2
Geffen, David **1985**:3 **1997**:3
Gehry, Frank O. **1987**:1
Geisel, Theodor
    Obituary **1992**:2
Gellar, Sarah Michelle **1999**:3
Geller, Margaret Joan **1998**:2
George, Elizabeth **2003**:3
Gephardt, Richard **1987**:3
Gerba, Charles **1999**:4
Gerberding, Julie **2004**:1
Gere, Richard **1994**:3
Gergen, David **1994**:1
Gerstner, Lou **1993**:4
Gertz, Alison
    Obituary **1993**:2
Gerulaitis, Vitas
    Obituary **1995**:1
Getz, Stan
    Obituary **1991**:4
Giamatti, A. Bartlett **1988**:4
    Obituary **1990**:1
Giannulli, Mossimo **2002**:3
Gibson, Althea
    Obituary **2004**:4
Gibson, Kirk **1985**:2
Gibson, William Ford, III **1997**:2
Gifford, Kathie Lee **1992**:2
Gilbert, Walter **1988**:3
Gilford, Jack
    Obituary **1990**:4
Gill, Vince **1995**:2
Gillespie, Dizzy
    Obituary **1993**:2
Gillespie, Marcia **1999**:4
Gillett, George **1988**:1
Gilruth, Robert
    Obituary **2001**:1
Gingrich, Newt **1991**:1 **1997**:3
Ginsberg, Allen
    Obituary **1997**:3
Ginsburg, Ruth Bader **1993**:4

Gish, Lillian
    Obituary **1993**:4
Giuliani, Rudolph **1994**:2
Glaser, Elizabeth
    Obituary **1995**:2
Glass, David **1996**:1
Glass, Philip **1991**:4
Glasser, Ira **1989**:1
Glaus, Troy **2003**:3
Gleason, Jackie
    Obituary **1987**:4
Glenn, John **1998**:3
Gless, Sharon **1989**:3
Glover, Danny **1998**:4
Glover, Savion **1997**:1
Gobel, George
    Obituary **1991**:4
Gober, Robert **1996**:3
Goetz, Bernhard Hugo **1985**:3
Goizueta, Roberto **1996**:1
    Obituary **1998**:1
Gold, Thomas
    Obituary **2005**:3
Goldberg, Gary David **1989**:4
Goldberg, Leonard **1988**:4
Goldberg, Whoopi **1993**:3
Goldblum, Jeff **1988**:1 **1997**:3
Golden, Thelma **2003**:3
Goldhaber, Fred
    Brief Entry **1986**:3
Goldman, William **2001**:1
Goldman-Rakic, Patricia **2002**:4
Goldwater, Barry
    Obituary **1998**:4
Gomez, 'Lefty'
    Obituary **1989**:3
Gooden, Dwight **1985**:2
Gooding, Cuba, Jr. **1997**:3
Goodman, Benny
    Obituary **1986**:3
Goodman, John **1990**:3
Goody, Joan **1990**:2
Goody, Sam
    Obituary **1992**:1
Gorder, Genevieve **2005**:4
Gordon, Dexter **1987**:1 **1990**:4
Gordon, Gale
    Obituary **1996**:1
Gordon, Jeff **1996**:1
Gordon, Michael **2005**:1
Gore, Albert, Jr. **1993**:2
Gore, Albert, Sr.
    Obituary **1999**:2
Gore, Tipper **1985**:4
Goren, Charles H.
    Obituary **1991**:4
Gorman, Leon
    Brief Entry **1987**:1
Gossett, Louis, Jr. **1989**:3
Gould, Chester
    Obituary **1985**:2
Gould, Gordon **1987**:1
Gould, Stephen Jay
    Obituary **2003**:3
Grace, J. Peter **1990**:2
Grace, Topher **2005**:4
Graden, Brian **2004**:2
Grafton, Sue **2000**:2
Graham, Bill **1986**:4
    Obituary **1992**:2
Graham, Billy **1992**:1
Graham, Donald **1985**:4

Graham, Heather **2000**:1
Graham, Katharine Meyer **1997**:3
 Obituary **2002**:3
Graham, Lauren **2003**:4
Graham, Martha
 Obituary **1991**:4
Gramm, Phil **1995**:2
Grammer, Kelsey **1995**:1
Granato, Cammi **1999**:3
Grange, Red
 Obituary **1991**:3
Grant, Amy **1985**:4
Grant, Cary
 Obituary **1987**:1
Grant, Charity
 Brief Entry **1985**:2
Grant, Rodney A. **1992**:1
Graves, Michael **2000**:1
Graves, Nancy **1989**:3
Gray, Hanna **1992**:4
Gray, John **1995**:3
Gray, Macy **2002**:1
Gray, Spalding
 Obituary **2005**:2
Graziano, Rocky
 Obituary **1990**:4
Green, Richard R. **1988**:3
Greenberg, Hank
 Obituary **1986**:4
Greenberg, Robert **2003**:2
Green Day **1995**:4
Greene, Brian **2003**:4
Greenspan, Alan **1992**:2
Gregorian, Vartan **1990**:3
Gregory, Cynthia **1990**:2
Gregory, Dick **1990**:3
Grier, Pam **1998**:3
Griffey, Ken Jr. **1994**:1
Griffith, Melanie **1989**:2
Griffiths, Martha
 Obituary **2004**:2
Grisham, John **1994**:4
Grodin, Charles **1997**:3
Groening, Matt **1990**:4
Gross, Terry **1998**:3
Grove, Andrew S. **1995**:3
Grucci, Felix **1987**:1
Gruden, Jon **2003**:4
Grusin, Dave
 Brief Entry **1987**:2
Guccione, Bob **1986**:1
Guccione, Bob, Jr. **1991**:4
Guest, Christopher **2004**:2
Guggenheim, Charles
 Obituary **2003**:4
Gumbel, Bryant **1990**:2
Gumbel, Greg **1996**:4
Gund, Agnes **1993**:2
Gunn, Hartford N., Jr.
 Obituary **1986**:2
Guyer, David
 Brief Entry **1988**:1
Gwynn, Tony **1995**:1
Gyllenhaal, Jake **2005**:3
Haas, Robert D. **1986**:4
Hackett, Buddy
 Obituary **2004**:3
Hackman, Gene **1989**:3
Hackney, Sheldon **1995**:1
Hagelstein, Peter
 Brief Entry **1986**:3

Hagen, Uta
 Obituary **2005**:2
Hagler, Marvelous Marvin **1985**:2
Hahn, Jessica **1989**:4
Hair, Jay D. **1994**:3
Ha Jin **2000**:3
Hakuta, Ken
 Brief Entry **1986**:1
Haldeman, H. R.
 Obituary **1994**:2
Hale, Alan **1997**:3
Hale, Clara
 Obituary **1993**:3
Haley, Alex
 Obituary **1992**:3
Hall, Anthony Michael **1986**:3
Hall, Arsenio **1990**:2
Hall, Gus
 Obituary **2001**:2
Halston
 Obituary **1990**:3
Hamilton, Margaret
 Obituary **1985**:3
Hamilton, Scott **1998**:2
Hamm, Mia **2000**:1
Hamm, Paul **2005**:1
Hammer, Armand
 Obituary **1991**:3
Hammer, Jan **1987**:3
Hammer, M. C. **1991**:2
Hammond, E. Cuyler
 Obituary **1987**:1
Hammond, John
 Obituary **1988**:2
Hampton, Lionel
 Obituary **2003**:4
Hanauer, Chip **1986**:2
Hancock, Herbie **1985**:1
Handler, Daniel **2003**:3
Handler, Ruth
 Obituary **2003**:3
Hanks, Tom **1989**:2 **2000**:2
Hanna, William
 Obituary **2002**:1
Hannah, Daryl **1987**:4
Hardaway, Anfernee **1996**:2
Harden, Marcia Gay **2002**:4
Haring, Keith
 Obituary **1990**:3
Harker, Patrick T. **2001**:2
Harkes, John **1996**:4
Harmon, Mark **1987**:1
Harmon, Tom
 Obituary **1990**:3
Harriman, Pamela **1994**:4
Harriman, W. Averell
 Obituary **1986**:4
Harris, Barbara **1996**:3
Harris, Barbara **1989**:3
Harris, E. Lynn **2004**:2
Harris, Ed **2002**:2
Harris, Emmylou **1991**:3
Harris, Katherine **2001**:3
Harris, Patricia Roberts
 Obituary **1985**:2
Harris, Thomas **2001**:1
Harry, Deborah **1990**:1
Hart, Mary
 Brief Entry **1988**:1
Hart, Melissa Joan **2002**:1
Hart, Mickey **1991**:2

Hartman, Phil **1996**:2
 Obituary **1998**:4
Harvard, Beverly **1995**:2
Harvey, Paul **1995**:3
Harwell, Ernie **1997**:3
Haseltine, William A. **1999**:2
Hassenfeld, Stephen **1987**:4
Hastert, Dennis **1999**:3
Hatch, Orin G. **2000**:2
Hatch, Richard **2001**:1
Hatcher, Teri **2005**:4
Hatem, George
 Obituary **1989**:1
Hawk, Tony **2001**:4
Hawke, Ethan **1995**:4
Hawkins, Jeff and
 Donna Dubinsky **2000**:2
Hawkins, Screamin' Jay
 Obituary **2000**:3
Hawn, Goldie Jeanne **1997**:2
Hayes, Helen
 Obituary **1993**:4
Hayes, Isaac **1998**:4
Hayes, Robert M. **1986**:3
Hayes, Woody
 Obituary **1987**:2
Hayse, Bruce **2004**:3
Hayworth, Rita
 Obituary **1987**:3
Headroom, Max **1986**:4
Healey, Jack **1990**:1
Healy, Bernadine **1993**:1
Healy, Timothy S. **1990**:2
Heard, J.C.
 Obituary **1989**:1
Hearst, Randolph A.
 Obituary **2001**:3
Heat-Moon, William Least **2000**:2
Heche, Anne **1999**:1
Heckerling, Amy **1987**:2
Heckert, Richard E.
 Brief Entry **1987**:3
Hefner, Christie **1985**:1
Heid, Bill
 Brief Entry **1987**:2
Heifetz, Jascha
 Obituary **1988**:2
Heinz, H.J.
 Obituary **1987**:2
Heinz, John
 Obituary **1991**:4
Helgenberger, Marg **2002**:2
Heller, Joseph
 Obituary **2000**:2
Heller, Walter
 Obituary **1987**:4
Helms, Bobby
 Obituary **1997**:4
Helms, Jesse **1998**:1
Helmsley, Leona **1988**:1
Heloise **2001**:4
Helton, Todd **2001**:1
Hemingway, Margaux
 Obituary **1997**:1
Henderson, Rickey **2002**:3
Hennessy, John L. **2002**:2
Henning, Doug
 Obituary **2000**:3
Henry, Carl F.H.
 Obituary **2005**:1
Hensel Twins **1996**:4
Henson, Brian **1992**:1

Henson, Jim **1989**:1
  Obituary **1990**:4
Hepburn, Katharine **1991**:2
Hernandez, Willie **1985**:1
Hero, Peter **2001**:2
Hershey, Barbara **1989**:1
Hershiser, Orel **1989**:2
Herzog, Doug **2002**:4
Heston, Charlton **1999**:4
Hewitt, Jennifer Love **1999**:2
Hewlett, William
  Obituary **2001**:4
Highsmith, Patricia
  Obituary **1995**:3
Hilbert, Stephen C. **1997**:4
Hilfiger, Tommy **1993**:3
Hill, Anita **1994**:1
Hill, Faith **2000**:1
Hill, George Roy
  Obituary **2004**:1
Hill, Grant **1995**:3
Hill, Lauryn **1999**:3
Hill, Lynn **1991**:2
Hillegass, Clifton Keith **1989**:4
Hills, Carla **1990**:3
Hines, Gregory **1992**:4
Hinton, Milt
  Obituary **2001**:3
Hirschhorn, Joel
  Brief Entry **1986**:1
Hirt, Al
  Obituary **1999**:4
Hiss, Alger
  Obituary **1997**:2
Hoff, Syd
  Obituary **2005**:3
Hoffa, Jim, Jr. **1999**:2
Hoffman, Abbie
  Obituary **1989**:3
Hoffman, Dustin **2005**:4
Hoffs, Susanna **1988**:2
Hogan, Ben
  Obituary **1997**:4
Hogan, Hulk **1987**:3
Holbrooke, Richard **1996**:2
Holden, Betsy **2003**:2
Holl, Steven **2003**:1
Holmes, John C.
  Obituary **1988**:3
Holtz, Lou **1986**:4
Holyfield, Evander **1991**:3
Hooker, John Lee **1998**:1
  Obituary **2002**:3
hooks, bell **2000**:2
Hootie and the Blowfish **1995**:4
Hope, Bob
  Obituary **2004**:4
Horne, Lena **1998**:4
Horner, Jack **1985**:2
Hornsby, Bruce **1989**:3
Horovitz, Adam **1988**:3
Horowitz, Paul **1988**:2
Horowitz, Vladimir
  Obituary **1990**:1
Horrigan, Edward, Jr. **1989**:1
Horwich, Frances
  Obituary **2002**:3
Houseman, John
  Obituary **1989**:1
Houston, Cissy **1999**:3
Houston, Whitney **1986**:3
Howard, Desmond Kevin **1997**:2

Howard, Ron **1997**:2
Howser, Dick
  Obituary **1987**:4
Hubbard, Freddie **1988**:4
Hudson, Kate **2001**:2
Hudson, Rock
  Obituary **1985**:4
Huerta, Dolores **1998**:1
Hughes, Cathy **1999**:1
Hughes, Karen **2001**:2
Hughes, Mark **1985**:3
Hughes, Sarah **2002**:4
Hughley, D.L. **2001**:1
Huizenga, Wayne **1992**:1
Hull, Jane Dee **1999**:2
Hullinger, Charlotte
  Brief Entry **1985**:1
Hundt, Reed Eric **1997**:2
Hunt, Helen **1994**:4
Hunter, Catfish
  Obituary **2000**:1
Hunter, Holly **1989**:4
Hunter, Howard **1994**:4
Hunter, Madeline **1991**:2
Hurt, William **1986**:1
Huston, Anjelica **1989**:3
Huston, John
  Obituary **1988**:1
Hutton, Timothy **1986**:3
Hwang, David Henry **1999**:1
Hyatt, Joel **1985**:3
Hyde, Henry **1999**:1
Hynde, Chrissie **1991**:1
Iacocca, Lee **1993**:1
Ice Cube **1999**:2
Ice-T **1992**:3
Ifill, Gwen **2002**:4
Iglesias, Enrique **2000**:1
Ilitch, Mike **1993**:4
Immelt, Jeffrey R. **2001**:2
Imus, Don **1997**:1
Inatome, Rick **1985**:4
Indigo Girls **1994**:4
Ingersoll, Ralph II **1988**:2
Inkster, Juli **2000**:2
Inman, Bobby Ray **1985**:1
Ireland, Patricia **1992**:2
Irvin, Michael **1996**:3
Irwin, Bill **1988**:3
Irwin, Hale **2005**:2
Irwin, James
  Obituary **1992**:1
Isaacson, Portia
  Brief Entry **1986**:1
Isaacson, Walter **2003**:2
Ito, Lance **1995**:3
Iverson, Allen **2001**:4
Ives, Burl
  Obituary **1995**:4
Ivins, Molly **1993**:4
Jackson, Alan **2003**:1
Jackson, Bo **1986**:3
Jackson, Cordell **1992**:4
Jackson, Janet **1990**:4
Jackson, Jesse **1996**:1
Jackson, Jesse, Jr. **1998**:3
Jackson, Michael **1996**:2
Jackson, Phil **1996**:3
Jackson, Samuel L. **1995**:4
Jackson, Thomas Penfield **2000**:2
Jacobs, Joe **1994**:1
Jacobs, Marc **2002**:3

Jacuzzi, Candido
  Obituary **1987**:1
Jahn, Helmut **1987**:3
James, Etta **1995**:2
James, Jesse **2004**:4
James, Rick
  Obituary **2005**:4
Jamison, Judith **1990**:3
Janklow, Morton **1989**:3
Janney, Allison **2003**:3
Janzen, Daniel H. **1988**:4
Jarmusch, Jim **1998**:3
Jarrett, Keith **1992**:4
Jarvik, Robert K. **1985**:1
Jay, Ricky **1995**:1
Jeffords, James **2002**:2
Jeffrey, Mildred
  Obituary **2005**:2
Jemison, Mae C. **1993**:1
Jen, Gish **2000**:1
Jenkins, Sally **1997**:2
Jennings, Waylon
  Obituary **2003**:2
Jeter, Derek **1999**:4
Jewel **1999**:2
Jillian, Ann **1986**:4
Jobs, Steve **2000**:1
Joel, Billy **1994**:3
Joffrey, Robert
  Obituary **1988**:3
Johansson, Scarlett **2005**:4
John, Daymond **2000**:1
Johnson, Abigail **2005**:3
Johnson, Betsey **1996**:2
Johnson, Beverly **2005**:2
Johnson, Diane **2004**:3
Johnson, Don **1986**:1
Johnson, Earvin 'Magic' **1988**:4
Johnson, Jimmy **1993**:3
Johnson, Kevin **1991**:1
Johnson, Keyshawn **2000**:4
Johnson, Larry **1993**:3
Johnson, Michael **2000**:1
Johnson, Philip **1989**:2
Johnson, Randy **1996**:2
Johnson, Robert L. **2000**:4
Jolie, Angelina **2000**:2
Jones, Arthur A. **1985**:3
Jones, Bill T. **1991**:4
Jones, Cherry **1999**:3
Jones, Chuck **2001**:2
Jones, E. Fay
  Obituary **2005**:4
Jones, Edward P. **2005**:1
Jones, Etta
  Obituary **2002**:4
Jones, Gayl **1999**:4
Jones, Jerry **1994**:4
Jones, Marion **1998**:4
Jones, Norah **2004**:1
Jones, Quincy **1990**:4
Jones, Sarah **2005**:2
Jones, Tommy Lee **1994**:2
Jong, Erica **1998**:3
Jonze, Spike **2000**:3
Jordan, Barbara
  Obituary **1996**:3
Jordan, Charles M. **1989**:4
Jordan, James
  Obituary **1994**:1
Jordan, King **1990**:1
Jordan, Michael **1987**:2

Jordan, Vernon, Jr. 2002:3
Jorgensen, Christine
    Obituary 1989:4
Jovovich, Milla 2002:1
Joyner, Florence Griffith 1989:2
    Obituary 1999:1
Joyner-Kersee, Jackie 1993:1
Judd, Ashley 1998:1
Judge, Mike 1994:2
Judkins, Reba
    Brief Entry 1987:3
Junck, Mary E. 2003:4
Jurgensen, Karen 2004:3
Justin, John Jr. 1992:2
Justiz, Manuel J. 1986:4
Kael, Pauline 2000:4
    Obituary 2002:4
Kahane, Meir
    Obituary 1991:2
Kahn, Madeline
    Obituary 2000:2
Kallen, Jackie 1994:1
Kamali, Norma 1989:1
Kamen, Dean 2003:1
Kandel, Eric 2005:2
Kanokogi, Rusty
    Brief Entry 1987:1
Kapor, Mitch 1990:3
Karan, Donna 1988:1
Kasem, Casey 1987:1
Kashuk, Sonia 2002:4
Kaskey, Ray
    Brief Entry 1987:2
Kassebaum, Nancy 1991:1
Kathwari, M. Farooq 2005:4
Katz, Alex 1990:3
Katz, Lillian 1987:4
Katzenberg, Jeffrey 1995:3
Kaufman, Charlie 2005:1
Kaufman, Elaine 1989:4
Kavner, Julie 1992:3
Kaye, Danny
    Obituary 1987:2
Kaye, Nora
    Obituary 1987:4
Kaye, Sammy
    Obituary 1987:4
Kazan, Elia
    Obituary 2004:4
Keating, Charles H., Jr. 1990:4
Keaton, Diane 1997:1
Keaton, Michael 1989:4
Keeshan, Bob
    Obituary 2005:2
Keitel, Harvey 1994:3
Keith, Brian
    Obituary 1997:4
Keith, Louis 1988:2
Kelleher, Herb 1995:1
Kelley, DeForest
    Obituary 2000:1
Kelley, Virginia
    Obituary 1994:3
Kelly, Ellsworth 1992:1
Kelly, Gene
    Obituary 1996:3
Kelly, Jim 1991:4
Kelly, Patrick
    Obituary 1990:2
Kelly, R. 1997:3
Kelly, William R.
    Obituary 1998:2

Kemp, Jack 1990:4
Kemp, Jan 1987:2
Kemp, Shawn 1995:1
Kendricks, Eddie
    Obituary 1993:2
Kennedy, John F., Jr. 1990:1
    Obituary 1999:4
Kennedy, Rose
    Obituary 1995:3
Kennedy, Weldon 1997:3
Kenny G 1994:4
Keno, Leigh and Leslie 2001:2
Kent, Corita
    Obituary 1987:1
Keough, Donald Raymond 1986:1
Keplinger, Dan 2001:1
Kerkorian, Kirk 1996:2
Kerr, Clark
    Obituary 2005:1
Kerr, Jean
    Obituary 2004:1
Kerr, Walter
    Obituary 1997:1
Kerrey, Bob 1986:1 1991:3
Kerrigan, Nancy 1994:3
Kerry, John 2005:2
Kesey, Ken
    Obituary 2003:1
Kessler, David 1992:1
Ketcham, Hank
    Obituary 2002:2
Kevorkian, Jack 1991:3
Keyes, Alan 1996:2
Kidd, Jason 2003:2
Kid Rock 2001:1
Kilborn, Craig 2003:2
Kilby, Jack 2002:2
Kiley, Dan
    Obituary 2005:2
Kilmer, Val 1991:4
Kilts, James M. 2001:3
Kimsey, James V. 2001:1
King, Alan
    Obituary 2005:3
King, Bernice 2000:2
King, Coretta Scott 1999:3
King, Don 1989:1
King, Larry 1993:1
King, Mary-Claire 1998:3
King, Stephen 1998:1
Kingsborough, Donald
    Brief Entry 1986:2
Kingsley, Patricia 1990:2
Kingsolver, Barbara 2005:1
Kinison, Sam
    Obituary 1993:1
Kiraly, Karch
    Brief Entry 1987:1
Kirk, David 2004:1
Kissinger, Henry 1999:4
Kissling, Frances 1989:2
Kistler, Darci 1993:1
Kite, Tom 1990:3
Klass, Perri 1993:2
Klein, Calvin 1996:2
Kline, Kevin 2000:1
Kloss, Henry E.
    Brief Entry 1985:2
Kluge, John 1991:1
Knievel, Robbie 1990:1
Knight, Bobby 1985:3
Knight, Philip H. 1994:1

Knight, Ted
    Obituary 1986:4
Knight, Wayne 1997:1
Knowles, John
    Obituary 2003:1
Koch, Bill 1992:3
Koch, Jim 2004:3
Kohnstamm, Abby 2001:1
Koogle, Tim 2000:4
Koons, Jeff 1991:4
Koontz, Dean 1999:3
Koop, C. Everett 1989:3
Kopits, Steven E.
    Brief Entry 1987:1
Koplovitz, Kay 1986:3
Kopp, Wendy 1993:3
Koppel, Ted 1989:1
Kordich, Jay 1993:2
Koresh, David
    Obituary 1993:4
Kornberg, Arthur 1992:1
Kors, Michael 2000:4
Kostabi, Mark 1989:4
Kovacevich, Dick 2004:3
Kozinski, Alex 2002:2
Kozol, Jonathan 1992:1
Kramer, Larry 1991:2
Kramer, Stanley
    Obituary 2002:1
Krantz, Judith 2003:1
Kravitz, Lenny 1991:1
Krim, Mathilde 1989:2
Kroc, Ray
    Obituary 1985:1
Krol, John
    Obituary 1996:3
Kroll, Alexander S. 1989:3
Krone, Julie 1989:2
Kruk, John 1994:4
Krzyzewski, Mike 1993:2
Kubler-Ross, Elisabeth
    Obituary 2005:4
Kubrick, Stanley
    Obituary 1999:3
Kudrow, Lisa 1996:1
Kulp, Nancy
    Obituary 1991:3
Kunitz, Stanley J. 2001:2
Kunstler, William
    Obituary 1996:1
Kunstler, William 1992:3
Kuralt, Charles
    Obituary 1998:3
Kurzban, Ira 1987:2
Kurzweil, Raymond 1986:3
Kushner, Tony 1995:2
Kutcher, Ashton 2003:4
Kwoh, Yik San 1988:2
Kyser, Kay
    Obituary 1985:3
Lachey, Nick and
    Jessica Simpson 2004:4
LaDuke, Winona 1995:2
Laettner, Christian 1993:1
Lafley, A. G. 2003:4
LaFontaine, Pat 1985:1
Lagasse, Emeril 1998:3
Lahiri, Jhumpa 2001:3
Lahti, Christine 1988:2
Laimbeer, Bill 2004:3
Lake, Ricki 1994:4
Lalas, Alexi 1995:1

Lamb, Wally **1999**:1
Lamour, Dorothy
  Obituary **1997**:1
L'Amour, Louis
  Obituary **1988**:4
Lancaster, Burt
  Obituary **1995**:1
Land, Edwin H.
  Obituary **1991**:3
Lander, Toni
  Obituary **1985**:4
Landers, Ann
  Obituary **2003**:3
Landon, Alf
  Obituary **1988**:1
Landon, Michael
  Obituary **1992**:1
Landrieu, Mary L. **2002**:2
Landry, Tom
  Obituary **2000**:3
Lane, Burton
  Obituary **1997**:2
Lane, Nathan **1996**:4
Lang, Eugene M. **1990**:3
Lange, Jessica **1995**:4
Lange, Liz **2003**:4
Langer, Robert **2003**:4
Langevin, James R. **2001**:2
Langston, J. William
  Brief Entry **1986**:2
Lanier, Jaron **1993**:4
Lansbury, Angela **1993**:1
Lansdale, Edward G.
  Obituary **1987**:2
Lansing, Sherry **1995**:4
Lanza, Robert **2004**:3
LaPaglia, Anthony **2004**:4
Lardner Jr., Ring
  Obituary **2001**:2
Larroquette, John **1986**:2
Larson, Jonathan
  Obituary **1997**:2
LaSalle, Eriq **1996**:4
Lauder, Estee **1992**:2
Lauper, Cyndi **1985**:1
Lauren, Ralph **1990**:1
Lawless, Lucy **1997**:4
Lawrence, Martin **1993**:4
Laybourne, Geraldine **1997**:1
Lazarus, Charles **1992**:4
Lazarus, Shelly **1998**:3
Lear, Frances **1988**:3
Leary, Denis **1993**:3
Leary, Timothy
  Obituary **1996**:4
LeBlanc, Matt **2005**:4
Lederman, Leon Max **1989**:4
Lee, Brandon
  Obituary **1993**:4
Lee, Chang-Rae **2005**:1
Lee, Henry C. **1997**:1
Lee, Pamela **1996**:4
Lee, Peggy
  Obituary **2003**:1
Lee, Spike **1988**:4
Leguizamo, John **1999**:1
Lehane, Dennis **2001**:4
Leibovitz, Annie **1988**:4
Leigh, Janet
  Obituary **2005**:4
Leigh, Jennifer Jason **1995**:2
Lelyveld, Joseph S. **1994**:4

Lemmon, Jack **1998**:4
  Obituary **2002**:3
Lemon, Ted
  Brief Entry **1986**:4
LeMond, Greg **1986**:4
Leno, Jay **1987**:1
Leonard, Elmore **1998**:4
Leonard, Sugar Ray **1989**:4
Lerner, Michael **1994**:2
Lerner, Sandy **2005**:1
Leslie, Lisa **1997**:4
Letterman, David **1989**:3
Levin, Gerald **1995**:2
Levine, Arnold **2002**:3
Levine, James **1992**:3
Levinson, Barry **1989**:3
Levitt, Arthur **2004**:2
Lewis, Edward B.
  Obituary **2005**:4
Lewis, Edward T. **1999**:4
Lewis, Henry
  Obituary **1996**:3
Lewis, Huey **1987**:3
Lewis, John
  Obituary **2002**:1
Lewis, Juliette **1999**:3
Lewis, Loida Nicolas **1998**:3
Lewis, Ray **2001**:3
Lewis, Reggie
  Obituary **1994**:1
Lewis, Reginald F. **1988**:4
  Obituary **1993**:3
Lewis, Richard **1992**:1
Lewis, Shari **1993**:1
  Obituary **1999**:1
LeWitt, Sol **2001**:2
Lewitzky, Bella
  Obituary **2005**:3
Leyland, Jim **1998**:2
Liberace
  Obituary **1987**:2
Libeskind, Daniel **2004**:1
Lichtenstein, Roy **1994**:1
  Obituary **1998**:1
Lieberman, Joseph **2001**:1
Lightner, Candy **1985**:1
Liguori, Peter **2005**:2
Lilly, John C.
  Obituary **2002**:4
Liman, Arthur **1989**:4
Limbaugh, Rush **1991**:3
Lin, Maya **1990**:3
Lincoln, Blanche **2003**:1
Lindbergh, Anne Morrow
  Obituary **2001**:4
Lindros, Éric **1992**:1
Lindsay, John V.
  Obituary **2001**:3
Lines, Ray **2004**:1
Ling, Bai **2000**:3
Ling, Lisa **2004**:2
Lipinski, Tara **1998**:3
Lipkis, Andy
  Brief Entry **1985**:3
Lipsig, Harry H. **1985**:1
Lipton, Martin **1987**:3
Lithgow, John **1985**:2
Little, Cleavon
  Obituary **1993**:2
Liu, Lucy **2000**:4
LL Cool J **1998**:2
Lobell, Jeanine **2002**:3

Locklear, Heather **1994**:3
Lodge, Henry Cabot
  Obituary **1985**:1
Loewe, Frederick
  Obituary **1988**:2
Lofton, Kenny **1998**:1
Logan, Joshua
  Obituary **1988**:4
Lohan, Lindsay **2005**:3
Long, Nia **2001**:3
Long, Shelley **1985**:1
Longo, Robert **1990**:4
Lopes, Lisa
  Obituary **2003**:3
Lopez, George **2003**:4
Lopez, Jennifer **1998**:4
Lopez, Nancy **1989**:3
Lord, Bette Bao **1994**:1
Lord, Jack
  Obituary **1998**:2
Lord, Winston
  Brief Entry **1987**:4
Lords, Traci **1995**:4
Lott, Trent **1998**:1
Louganis, Greg **1995**:3
Louis-Dreyfus, Julia **1994**:1
Love, Courtney **1995**:1
Love, Susan **1995**:2
Loveless, Patty **1998**:2
Lovett, Lyle **1994**:1
Lovley, Derek **2005**:3
Lowe, Edward **1990**:2
Lowe, Rob **1990**:4
Lowell, Mike **2003**:2
Loy, Myrna
  Obituary **1994**:2
Lucas, George **1999**:4
Lucci, Susan **1999**:4
Luce, Clare Boothe
  Obituary **1988**:1
Lucid, Shannon **1997**:1
Lucke, Lewis **2004**:4
Ludlum, Robert
  Obituary **2002**:1
Lukas, D. Wayne **1986**:2
Lupino, Ida
  Obituary **1996**:1
Lutz, Robert A. **1990**:1
Lynch, David **1990**:4
Lyne, Susan **2005**:4
Lynn, Loretta **2001**:1
Mac, Bernie **2003**:1
MacCready, Paul **1986**:4
MacDonald, Laurie and Walter
  Parkes **2004**:1
MacDowell, Andie **1993**:4
MacKinnon, Catharine **1993**:2
MacMurray, Fred
  Obituary **1992**:2
MacNelly, Jeff
  Obituary **2000**:4
MacRae, Gordon
  Obituary **1986**:2
Macy, William H. **1999**:3
Madden, John **1995**:1
Maddux, Greg **1996**:2
Madonna **1985**:2
Maglich, Bogdan C. **1990**:1
Magliozzi, Tom and Ray **1991**:4
Maguire, Tobey **2002**:2
Maher, Bill **1996**:2
Mahony, Roger M. **1988**:2

Maida, Adam Cardinal **1998**:2
Mailer, Norman **1998**:1
Majerle, Dan **1993**:4
Malkovich, John **1988**:2
Malloy, Edward 'Monk' **1989**:4
Malone, John C. **1988**:3 **1996**:3
Malone, Karl **1990**:1 **1997**:3
Maltby, Richard, Jr. **1996**:3
Mamet, David **1998**:4
Mancini, Henry
  Obituary **1994**:4
Mankiller, Wilma P.
  Brief Entry **1986**:2
Mann, Sally **2001**:2
Mansfield, Mike
  Obituary **2002**:4
Mansion, Gracie
  Brief Entry **1986**:3
Manson, Marilyn **1999**:4
Mantegna, Joe **1992**:1
Mantle, Mickey
  Obituary **1996**:1
Mapplethorpe, Robert
  Obituary **1989**:3
Maraldo, Pamela J. **1993**:4
Maravich, Pete
  Obituary **1988**:2
Marchand, Nancy
  Obituary **2001**:1
Marcus, Stanley
  Obituary **2003**:1
Marier, Rebecca **1995**:4
Marin, Cheech **2000**:1
Marineau, Philip **2002**:4
Maris, Roger
  Obituary **1986**:1
Marky Mark **1993**:3
Marriott, J. Willard
  Obituary **1985**:4
Marriott, J. Willard, Jr. **1985**:4
Marsalis, Branford **1988**:3
Marsalis, Wynton **1997**:4
Marshall, Penny **1991**:3
Marshall, Susan **2000**:4
Marshall, Thurgood
  Obituary **1993**:3
Martin, Billy **1988**:4
  Obituary **1990**:2
Martin, Casey **2002**:1
Martin, Dean
  Obituary **1996**:2
Martin, Dean Paul
  Obituary **1987**:3
Martin, Judith **2000**:3
Martin, Lynn **1991**:4
Martin, Mary
  Obituary **1991**:2
Martin, Steve **1992**:2
Martinez, Bob **1992**:1
Marvin, Lee
  Obituary **1988**:1
Mas Canosa, Jorge
  Obituary **1998**:2
Master P **1999**:4
Masters, William H.
  Obituary **2001**:4
Matalin, Mary **1995**:2
Mathews, Dan **1998**:3
Mathis, Clint **2003**:1
Matlin, Marlee **1992**:2
Matlovich, Leonard P.
  Obituary **1988**:4

Matthau, Walter **2000**:3
Matthews, Dave **1999**:3
Mattingly, Don **1986**:2
Matuszak, John
  Obituary **1989**:4
Mauldin, Bill
  Obituary **2004**:2
Maxwell, Hamish **1989**:4
Mayes, Frances **2004**:3
Maynard, Joyce **1999**:4
McAuliffe, Christa
  Obituary **1985**:4
McCain, John S. **1998**:4
McCall, Nathan **1994**:4
McCarron, Chris **1995**:4
McCarthy, Carolyn **1998**:4
McCarthy, Jenny **1997**:4
McCartney, Bill **1995**:3
McCartney, Linda
  Obituary **1998**:4
McCloskey, J. Michael **1988**:2
McCloskey, James **1993**:1
McCloy, John J.
  Obituary **1989**:3
McColough, C. Peter **1990**:2
McConaughey, Matthew David
  **1997**:1
McCourt, Frank **1997**:4
McCrea, Joel
  Obituary **1991**:1
McDermott, Alice **1999**:2
McDonald, Camille **2004**:1
McDonnell, Sanford N. **1988**:4
McDonough, William **2003**:1
McDormand, Frances **1997**:3
McDougall, Ron **2001**:4
McDuffie, Robert **1990**:2
McElligott, Thomas J. **1987**:4
McEntire, Reba **1987**:3 **1994**:2
McFarlane, Todd **1999**:1
McFerrin, Bobby **1989**:1
McGillis, Kelly **1989**:3
McGinley, Ted **2004**:4
McGowan, William **1985**:2
McGowan, William G.
  Obituary **1993**:1
McGraw, Phil **2005**:2
McGraw, Tim **2000**:3
McGraw, Tug
  Obituary **2005**:1
McGreevey, James **2005**:2
McGruder, Aaron **2005**:4
McGuire, Dorothy
  Obituary **2002**:4
McGwire, Mark **1999**:1
McIntyre, Richard
  Brief Entry **1986**:2
McKee, Lonette **1996**:1
McKenna, Terence **1993**:3
McKinney, Cynthia A. **1997**:1
McKinney, Stewart B.
  Obituary **1987**:4
McLaughlin, Betsy **2004**:3
McMahon, Jim **1985**:4
McMahon, Vince, Jr. **1985**:4
McMillan, Terry **1993**:2
McMillen, Tom **1988**:4
McMurtry, James **1990**:2
McNamara, Robert S. **1995**:4
McNealy, Scott **1999**:4
McRae, Carmen
  Obituary **1995**:2

McSally, Martha **2002**:4
McVeigh, Timothy
  Obituary **2002**:2
Meadows, Audrey
  Obituary **1996**:3
Meier, Richard **2001**:4
Meisel, Steven **2002**:4
Mellinger, Frederick
  Obituary **1990**:4
Mello, Dawn **1992**:2
Mellon, Paul
  Obituary **1999**:3
Melman, Richard
  Brief Entry **1986**:1
Meltzer, Brad **2005**:4
Mengers, Sue **1985**:3
Menninger, Karl
  Obituary **1991**:1
Menuhin, Yehudi
  Obituary **1999**:3
Merchant, Natalie **1996**:3
Meredith, Burgess
  Obituary **1998**:1
Merrick, David
  Obituary **2000**:4
Merrill, James
  Obituary **1995**:3
Merritt, Justine
  Brief Entry **1985**:3
Messing, Debra **2004**:4
Metallica **2004**:2
Mfume, Kweisi **1996**:3
Michelman, Kate **1998**:4
Michener, James A.
  Obituary **1998**:1
Mickelson, Phil **2004**:4
Midler, Bette **1989**:4
Mikulski, Barbara **1992**:4
Milano, Alyssa **2002**:3
Milbrett, Tiffeny **2001**:1
Milburn, Rodney Jr.
  Obituary **1998**:2
Milland, Ray
  Obituary **1986**:2
Millard, Barbara J.
  Brief Entry **1985**:3
Miller, Andre **2003**:3
Miller, Ann
  Obituary **2005**:2
Miller, Arthur **1999**:4
Miller, Bebe **2000**:2
Miller, Bode **2002**:4
Miller, Dennis **1992**:4
Miller, Merton H.
  Obituary **2001**:1
Miller, Nicole **1995**:4
Miller, Rand **1995**:4
Miller, Reggie **1994**:4
Miller, Roger
  Obituary **1993**:2
Miller, Sue **1999**:3
Mills, Malia **2003**:1
Mills, Wilbur
  Obituary **1992**:4
Minner, Ruth Ann **2002**:2
Minnesota Fats
  Obituary **1996**:3
Minsky, Marvin **1994**:3
Misrach, Richard **1991**:2
Mitchell, Arthur **1995**:1
Mitchell, George J. **1989**:3

Randall, Tony
Obituary 2005:3
Randi, James 1990:2
Raphael, Sally Jessy 1992:4
Rapp, C.J.
Brief Entry 1987:3
Rashad, Phylicia 1987:3
Raskin, Jef 1997:4
Rauschenberg, Robert 1991:2
Raven 2005:1
Rawlings, Mike 2003:1
Ray, James Earl
Obituary 1998:4
Raye, Martha
Obituary 1995:1
Raymond, Lee R. 2000:3
Reagan, Ronald
Obituary 2005:3
Reasoner, Harry
Obituary 1992:1
Redenbacher, Orville
Obituary 1996:1
Redfield, James 1995:2
Redford, Robert 1993:2
Redig, Patrick 1985:3
Redman, Joshua 1999:2
Redstone, Sumner 1994:1
Reed, Dean
Obituary 1986:3
Reed, Donna
Obituary 1986:1
Reed, Ralph 1995:1
Reed, Robert
Obituary 1992:4
Reese, Della 1999:2
Reeve, Christopher 1997:2
Reeves, Keanu 1992:1
Reeves, Steve
Obituary 2000:4
Regan, Judith 2003:1
Rehnquist, William H. 2001:2
Reich, Robert 1995:4
Reilly, John C. 2003:4
Reiner, Rob 1991:2
Reiser, Paul 1995:2
Remick, Lee
Obituary 1992:1
Reno, Janet 1993:3
Retton, Mary Lou 1985:2
Reubens, Paul 1987:2
Rey, Margret E.
Obituary 1997:2
Reznor, Trent 2000:2
Ribicoff, Abraham
Obituary 1998:3
Ricci, Christina 1999:1
Rice, Anne 1995:1
Rice, Condoleezza 2002:1
Rice, Jerry 1990:4
Rich, Buddy
Obituary 1987:3
Rich, Charlie
Obituary 1996:1
Richards, Ann 1991:2
Richards, Michael 1993:4
Richter, Charles Francis
Obituary 1985:4
Rickover, Hyman
Obituary 1986:4
Riddle, Nelson
Obituary 1985:4
Ridge, Tom 2002:2

Rifkin, Jeremy 1990:3
Riggio, Leonard S. 1999:4
Riggs, Bobby
Obituary 1996:2
Riley, Pat 1994:3
Riley, Richard W. 1996:3
Rimes, LeeAnn 1997:4
Riney, Hal 1989:1
Ringgold, Faith 2000:3
Ringwald, Molly 1985:4
Riordan, Richard 1993:4
Ripa, Kelly 2002:2
Ripken, Cal, Jr. 1986:2
Ripken, Cal, Sr.
Obituary 1999:4
Ritchie, Dennis and
Kenneth Thompson 2000:1
Ritter, John 2003:4
Ritts, Herb 1992:4
Rivera, Geraldo 1989:1
Rivers, Joan 2005:3
Rizzo, Frank
Obituary 1992:1
Robards, Jason
Obituary 2001:3
Robb, Charles S. 1987:2
Robbins, Harold
Obituary 1998:1
Robbins, Jerome
Obituary 1999:1
Robbins, Tim 1993:1
Roberts, Brian L. 2002:4
Roberts, Cokie 1993:4
Roberts, Doris 2003:4
Roberts, Julia 1991:3
Roberts, Steven K. 1992:1
Roberts, Xavier 1985:3
Robertson, Pat 1988:2
Robinson, David 1990:4
Robinson, Earl
Obituary 1992:1
Robinson, Frank 1990:2
Robinson, Max
Obituary 1989:2
Robinson, Sugar Ray
Obituary 1989:3
Robinson, V. Gene 2004:4
Roche, Kevin 1985:1
Rock, Chris 1998:1
Rock, John
Obituary 1985:1
Rock, The 2001:2
Rockwell, David 2003:3
Roddenberry, Gene
Obituary 1992:2
Roddick, Andy 2004:3
Rodin, Judith 1994:4
Rodman, Dennis 1991:3 1996:4
Rodriguez, Alex 2001:2
Rodriguez, Narciso 2005:1
Rodriguez, Robert 2005:1
Roedy, Bill 2003:2
Roemer, Buddy 1991:4
Rogers, Adrian 1987:4
Rogers, Fred 2000:4
Rogers, Ginger
Obituary 1995:4
Rogers, Roy
Obituary 1998:4
Rogers, William P.
Obituary 2001:4
Roker, Al 2003:1

Roker, Roxie
Obituary 1996:2
Rolle, Esther
Obituary 1999:2
Rollins, Howard E., Jr. 1986:1
Romano, Ray 2001:4
Rooney, Art
Obituary 1989:1
Roosevelt, Franklin D., Jr.
Obituary 1989:1
Rose, Axl 1992:1
Rose, Charlie 1994:2
Rose, Pete 1991:1
Rosenberg, Evelyn 1988:2
Rosenberg, Steven 1989:1
Rosendahl, Bruce R.
Brief Entry 1986:4
Rosenzweig, Ilene 2004:1
Rosgen, Dave 2005:2
Ros-Lehtinen, Ileana 2000:2
Ross, Herbert
Obituary 2002:4
Ross, Percy
Brief Entry 1986:2
Ross, Steven J.
Obituary 1993:3
Rossellini, Isabella 2001:4
Rosten, Leo
Obituary 1997:3
Roth, Philip 1999:1
Roth, William Victor, Jr.
Obituary 2005:1
Rothenberg, Susan 1995:3
Rothstein, Ruth 1988:2
Rothwax, Harold 1996:3
Rourke, Mickey 1988:4
Rouse, James
Obituary 1996:4
Rowan, Carl
Obituary 2001:2
Rowan, Dan
Obituary 1988:1
Rowe, Jack 2005:2
Rowland, Pleasant 1992:3
Rowley, Coleen 2004:2
Rowley, Cynthia 2002:1
Roybal-Allard, Lucille 1999:4
Royko, Mike
Obituary 1997:4
Rozelle, Pete
Obituary 1997:2
Rubin, Jerry
Obituary 1995:2
Rudner, Rita 1993:2
Rudnick, Paul 1994:3
Rudolph, Wilma
Obituary 1995:2
Ruehl, Mercedes 1992:4
Ruffin, David
Obituary 1991:4
Rumsfeld, Donald 2004:1
Runyan, Marla 2001:1
RuPaul 1996:1
Ruppe, Loret Miller 1986:2
Rusk, Dean
Obituary 1995:2
Russell, Keri 2000:1
Russo, Rene 2000:2
Russo, Richard 2002:3
Rutan, Burt 1987:2
Ryan, Meg 1994:1
Ryan, Nolan 1989:4

Ryder, Winona **1991**:2
Saberhagen, Bret **1986**:1
Sachs, Jeffrey D. **2004**:4
Safire, William **2000**:3
Sagal, Katey **2005**:2
Sagan, Carl
    Obituary **1997**:2
Sagansky, Jeff **1993**:2
St. James, Lyn **1993**:2
Sajak, Pat
    Brief Entry **1985**:4
Salerno-Sonnenberg, Nadja **1988**:4
Salk, Jonas **1994**:4
    Obituary **1995**:4
Salzman, Mark **2002**:1
Sample, Bill
    Brief Entry **1986**:2
Sampras, Pete **1994**:1
Sanchez, Loretta **2000**:3
Sanders, Barry **1992**:1
Sanders, Bernie **1991**:4
Sanders, Deion **1992**:4
Sandler, Adam **1999**:2
Sanger, Steve **2002**:3
Saporta, Vicki
    Brief Entry **1987**:3
Sapphire **1996**:4
Saralegui, Cristina **1999**:2
Sarandon, Susan **1995**:3
Sarazen, Gene
    Obituary **1999**:4
Satcher, David **2001**:4
Satriani, Joe **1989**:3
Savage, Fred **1990**:1
Savalas, Telly
    Obituary **1994**:3
Sawyer, Diane **1994**:4
Scalia, Antonin **1988**:2
Scardino, Marjorie **2002**:1
Scavullo, Francesco
    Obituary **2005**:1
Schaap, Dick
    Obituary **2003**:1
Schaefer, William Donald **1988**:1
Schank, Roger **1989**:2
Scheck, Barry **2000**:4
Schembechler, Bo **1990**:3
Schenk, Dale **2002**:2
Schiavo, Mary **1998**:2
Schilling, Curt **2002**:3
Schlessinger, David
    Brief Entry **1985**:1
Schlessinger, Laura **1996**:3
Schmidt, Eric **2002**:4
Schmidt, Mike **1988**:3
Schnabel, Julian **1997**:1
Schneider, Rob **1997**:4
Schoenfeld, Gerald **1986**:2
Scholz, Tom **1987**:2
Schott, Marge **1985**:4
Schroeder, Barbet **1996**:1
Schroeder, William J.
    Obituary **1986**:4
Schultes, Richard Evans
    Obituary **2002**:1
Schultz, Howard **1995**:3
Schulz, Charles
    Obituary **2000**:3
Schulz, Charles M. **1998**:1
Schumacher, Joel **2004**:3
Schuman, Patricia Glass **1993**:2
Schwab, Charles **1989**:3

Schwartz, David **1988**:3
Schwarzenegger, Arnold **1991**:1
Schwarzkopf, Norman **1991**:3
Schwimmer, David **1996**:2
Schwinn, Edward R., Jr.
    Brief Entry **1985**:4
Scorsese, Martin **1989**:1
Scott, Gene
    Brief Entry **1986**:1
Scott, George C.
    Obituary **2000**:2
Scott, Randolph
    Obituary **1987**:2
Sculley, John **1989**:4
Seacrest, Ryan **2004**:4
Sears, Barry **2004**:2
Sebold, Alice **2005**:4
Secretariat
    Obituary **1990**:1
Sedaris, David **2005**:3
Sedelmaier, Joe **1985**:3
Segal, Shelli **2005**:3
Seger, Bob **1987**:1
Seidelman, Susan **1985**:4
Seidenberg, Ivan **2004**:1
Seinfeld, Jerry **1992**:4
Selena
    Obituary **1995**:4
Selig, Bud **1995**:2
Semel, Terry **2002**:2
Serrano, Andres **2000**:4
Sevareid, Eric
    Obituary **1993**:1
Sevigny, Chloe **2001**:4
Shabazz, Betty
    Obituary **1997**:4
Shaich, Ron **2004**:4
Shakur, Tupac
    Obituary **1997**:1
Shalala, Donna **1992**:3
Shalikashvili, John **1994**:2
Shandling, Garry **1995**:1
Sharkey, Ray
    Obituary **1994**:1
Sharpe, Sterling **1994**:3
Sharpton, Al **1991**:2
Shaw, Carol **2002**:1
Shaw, William **2000**:3
Shawn, Dick
    Obituary **1987**:3
Shawn, William
    Obituary **1993**:3
Shea, Jim, Jr. **2002**:4
Sheedy, Ally **1989**:1
Sheehan, Daniel P. **1989**:1
Sheen, Charlie **2001**:2
Sheen, Martin **2002**:1
Sheffield, Gary **1998**:1
Sheindlin, Judith **1999**:1
Shepard, Alan
    Obituary **1999**:1
Shepard, Sam **1996**:4
Shepherd, Cybill **1996**:3
Sherman, Cindy **1992**:3
Sherman, Russell **1987**:4
Shields, Brooke **1996**:3
Shields, Carol
    Obituary **2004**:3
Shilts, Randy **1993**:4
    Obituary **1994**:3
Shimomura, Tsutomu **1996**:1
Shirley, Donna **1999**:1

Shocked, Michelle **1989**:4
Shoemaker, Bill
    Obituary **2004**:4
Shore, Dinah
    Obituary **1994**:3
Shreve, Anita **2003**:4
Shriver, Maria
    Brief Entry **1986**:2
Shue, Andrew **1994**:4
Shula, Don **1992**:2
Shyamalan, M. Night **2003**:2
Sidney, Ivan
    Brief Entry **1987**:2
Sidransky, David **2002**:4
Siebert, Muriel **1987**:2
Sigmund, Barbara Boggs
    Obituary **1991**:1
Silber, John **1990**:1
Silverman, Jonathan **1997**:2
Silvers, Phil
    Obituary **1985**:4
Silverstein, Shel
    Obituary **1999**:4
Silverstone, Alicia **1997**:4
Simmons, Adele Smith **1988**:4
Simmons, Russell and
    Kimora Lee **2003**:2
Simmons, Ruth **1995**:2
Simon, Lou Anna K. **2005**:4
Simon, Paul
    Obituary **2005**:1
Simon, Paul **1992**:2
Simone, Nina
    Obituary **2004**:2
Simpson, Wallis
    Obituary **1986**:3
Sinatra, Frank
    Obituary **1998**:4
Sinclair, Mary **1985**:2
Singer, Isaac Bashevis
    Obituary **1992**:1
Singer, Margaret Thaler
    Obituary **2005**:1
Singleton, John **1994**:3
Sinise, Gary **1996**:1
Sirica, John
    Obituary **1993**:2
Siskel, Gene
    Obituary **1999**:3
Skaist-Levy, Pam and
    Gela Taylor **2005**:1
Skelton, Red
    Obituary **1998**:1
Skinner, B.F.
    Obituary **1991**:1
Skinner, Sam **1992**:3
Slater, Christian **1994**:1
Slater, Rodney E. **1997**:4
Slick, Grace **2001**:2
Slotnick, Barry
    Brief Entry **1987**:4
Smale, John G. **1987**:3
Smigel, Robert **2001**:3
Smiley, Jane **1995**:4
Smith, Anna Deavere **2002**:2
Smith, Buffalo Bob
    Obituary **1999**:1
Smith, Emmitt **1994**:1
Smith, Frederick W. **1985**:4
Smith, Howard K.
    Obituary **2003**:2
Smith, Jack **1994**:3

Thurmond, Strom
  Obituary **2004**:3
Tiffany **1989**:1
Tillman, Robert L. **2004**:1
Tillstrom, Burr
  Obituary **1986**:1
Tilly, Jennifer **1997**:2
Tisch, Laurence A. **1988**:2
Tito, Dennis **2002**:1
TLC **1996**:1
Tom and Ray Magliozzi **1991**:4
Tomei, Marisa **1995**:2
Tompkins, Susie
  Brief Entry **1987**:2
Tone-Loc **1990**:3
Toomer, Ron **1990**:1
Toone, Bill
  Brief Entry **1987**:2
Torme, Mel
  Obituary **1999**:4
Torre, Joseph Paul **1997**:1
Totenberg, Nina **1992**:2
Tower, John
  Obituary **1991**:4
Townsend, Kathleen Kennedy
  **2001**:3
Trask, Amy **2003**:3
Traub, Marvin
  Brief Entry **1987**:3
Travis, Randy **1988**:4
Travolta, John **1995**:2
Treybig, James G. **1988**:3
Tribe, Laurence H. **1988**:1
Tritt, Travis **1995**:1
Trotman, Alex **1995**:4
Trotter, Charlie **2000**:4
Troutt, Kenny A. **1998**:1
Trudeau, Garry **1991**:2
Truitt, Anne **1993**:1
Trump, Donald **1989**:2
Tsongas, Paul Efthemios
  Obituary **1997**:2
Tucci, Stanley **2003**:2
Tucker, Chris **1999**:1
Tucker, Forrest
  Obituary **1987**:1
Tully, Tim **2004**:3
Tune, Tommy **1994**:2
Ture, Kwame
  Obituary **1999**:2
Turlington, Christy **2001**:4
Turner, Janine **1993**:2
Turner, Kathleen **1985**:3
Turner, Lana
  Obituary **1996**:1
Turner, Ted **1989**:1
Turner, Tina **2000**:3
Turturro, John **2002**:2
Tutwiler, Margaret **1992**:4
Twitty, Conway
  Obituary **1994**:1
Twombley, Cy **1995**:1
Tyler, Anne **1995**:4
Tyler, Liv **1997**:2
Tyler, Richard **1995**:3
Tyner, Rob
  Obituary **1992**:2
Tyson, Don **1995**:3
Tyson, Laura D'Andrea **1994**:1
Tyson, Mike **1986**:4
Udall, Mo
  Obituary **1999**:2

Union, Gabrielle **2004**:2
Unitas, Johnny
  Obituary **2003**:4
Unz, Ron **1999**:1
Updike, John **2001**:2
Upshaw, Dawn **1991**:2
Upshaw, Gene **1988**:1
Urich, Robert **1988**:1
  Obituary **2003**:3
Usher **2005**:1
Vagelos, P. Roy **1989**:4
Valdes-Rodriguez, Alisa **2005**:4
Valente, Benita **1985**:3
Valvo, Carmen Marc **2003**:4
Van Duyn, Mona **1993**:2
Van Dyken, Amy **1997**:1
Van Halen, Edward **1985**:2
Vanilla Ice **1991**:3
Van Sant, Gus **1992**:2
Van Slyke, Andy **1992**:4
Varney, Jim
  Brief Entry **1985**:4
  Obituary **2000**:3
Varone, Doug **2001**:2
Vaughan, Sarah
  Obituary **1990**:3
Vaughan, Stevie Ray
  Obituary **1991**:1
Vaughn, Mo **1999**:2
Vaughn, Vince **1999**:2
Veeck, Bill
  Obituary **1986**:1
Vega, Suzanne **1988**:1
Venter, J. Craig **2001**:1
Ventura, Jesse **1999**:2
Venturi, Robert **1994**:4
Verdi-Fletcher, Mary **1998**:2
Verdon, Gwen
  Obituary **2001**:2
Vickrey, William S.
  Obituary **1997**:2
Vidal, Gore **1996**:2
Vieira, Meredith **2001**:3
Vincent, Fay **1990**:2
Vinton, Will
  Brief Entry **1988**:1
Violet, Arlene **1985**:3
Vischer, Phil **2002**:2
Vitale, Dick **1988**:4 **1994**:4
Vitetta, Ellen S. **2005**:4
Vitousek, Peter **2003**:1
Vogel, Paula **1999**:2
Voight, Jon **2002**:3
Vonnegut, Kurt **1998**:4
von Trapp, Maria
  Obituary **1987**:3
vos Savant, Marilyn **1988**:2
Vreeland, Diana
  Obituary **1990**:1
Wachner, Linda **1988**:3 **1997**:2
Waddell, Thomas F.
  Obituary **1988**:2
Wagner, Catherine F. **2002**:3
Waitt, Ted **1997**:4
Waldron, Hicks B. **1987**:3
Walgreen, Charles III
  Brief Entry **1987**:4
Walker, Alice **1999**:1
Walker, Jay **2004**:2
Walker, Junior
  Obituary **1996**:2
Walker, Kara **1999**:2

Walker, Nancy
  Obituary **1992**:3
Wallace, Ben **2004**:3
Wallace, George
  Obituary **1999**:1
Wallace, Irving
  Obituary **1991**:1
Wallis, Hal
  Obituary **1987**:1
Walsh, Bill **1987**:4
Walters, Barbara **1998**:3
Walton, Sam **1986**:2
  Obituary **1993**:1
Wang, An **1986**:1
  Obituary **1990**:3
Wang, Vera **1998**:4
Wapner, Joseph A. **1987**:1
Ward, Sela **2001**:3
Warhol, Andy
  Obituary **1987**:2
Warner, Kurt **2000**:3
Warren, Robert Penn
  Obituary **1990**:1
Washington, Alonzo **2000**:1
Washington, Denzel **1993**:2
Washington, Grover, Jr. **1989**:1
Washington, Harold
  Obituary **1988**:1
Wasserman, Lew
  Obituary **2003**:3
Wasserstein, Wendy **1991**:3
Waterman, Cathy **2002**:2
Waters, John **1988**:3
Waters, Maxine **1998**:4
Watkins, Sherron **2003**:1
Watson, Elizabeth **1991**:2
Watterson, Bill **1990**:3
Wattleton, Faye **1989**:1
Watts, J.C. **1999**:2
Wayans, Damon **1998**:4
Wayans, Keenen Ivory **1991**:1
Wayne, David
  Obituary **1995**:3
Weaver, Sigourney **1988**:3
Webb, Wellington E. **2000**:3
Webber, Chris **1994**:1
Weber, Pete **1986**:3
Wegman, William **1991**:1
Weicker, Lowell P., Jr. **1993**:1
Weil, Andrew **1997**:4
Weill, Sandy **1990**:4
Weinstein, Bob and Harvey **2000**:4
Weintraub, Jerry **1986**:1
Weitz, Bruce **1985**:4
Welch, Bob **1991**:3
Welch, Jack **1993**:3
Wells, David **1999**:3
Wells, Linda **2002**:3
Wells, Mary
  Obituary **1993**:1
Wells, Sharlene
  Brief Entry **1985**:1
Wellstone, Paul
  Obituary **2004**:1
Welty, Eudora
  Obituary **2002**:3
Wenner, Jann **1993**:1
West, Cornel **1994**:2
West, Dorothy **1996**:1
West, Dottie
  Obituary **1992**:2
Wexler, Nancy S. **1992**:3

Travers, P.L.
 Obituary **1996**:4
Tyler, Richard **1995**:3
Webb, Karrie **2000**:4

**AUSTRIAN**
 Brabeck-Letmathe, Peter **2001**:4
 Brandauer, Klaus Maria **1987**:3
 Djerassi, Carl **2000**:4
 Drucker, Peter F. **1992**:3
 Falco
  Brief Entry **1987**:2
 Frankl, Viktor E.
  Obituary **1998**:1
 Hrabal, Bohumil
  Obituary **1997**:3
 Jelinek, Elfriede **2005**:3
 Lamarr, Hedy
  Obituary **2000**:3
 Lang, Helmut **1999**:2
 Lorenz, Konrad
  Obituary **1989**:3
 Perutz, Max
  Obituary **2003**:2
 Porsche, Ferdinand
  Obituary **1998**:4
 Pouillon, Nora **2005**:1
 Puck, Wolfgang **1990**:1
 Strobl, Fritz **2003**:3
 von Karajan, Herbert
  Obituary **1989**:4
 von Trapp, Maria
  Obituary **1987**:3

**BANGLADESHI**
 Nasrin, Taslima **1995**:1

**BELGIAN**
 Henin-Hardenne, Justine **2004**:4
 Hepburn, Audrey
  Obituary **1993**:2
 von Furstenberg, Diane **1994**:2

**BOLIVIAN**
 Sanchez de Lozada, Gonzalo **2004**:3

**BOSNIAN**
 Izetbegovic, Alija **1996**:4

**BRAZILIAN**
 Cardoso, Fernando Henrique **1996**:4
 Castaneda, Carlos
  Obituary **1998**:4
 Collor de Mello, Fernando **1992**:4
 Fittipaldi, Emerson **1994**:2
 Ronaldo **1999**:2
 Salgado, Sebastiao **1994**:2
 Senna, Ayrton **1991**:4
  Obituary **1994**:4
 Silva, Luiz Inacio Lula da **2003**:4
 Xuxa **1994**:2

**BRITISH**
 Adamson, George
  Obituary **1990**:2
 Baddeley, Hermione
  Obituary **1986**:4
 Beckett, Wendy (Sister) **1998**:3
 Branson, Richard **1987**:1

Chatwin, Bruce
 Obituary **1989**:2
Cleese, John **1989**:2
Cummings, Sam **1986**:3
Dalton, Timothy **1988**:4
Davison, Ian Hay **1986**:1
Day-Lewis, Daniel **1989**:4 **1994**:4
Dench, Judi **1999**:4
Egan, John **1987**:2
Eno, Brian **1986**:2
Ferguson, Sarah **1990**:3
Fiennes, Ranulph **1990**:3
Foster, Norman **1999**:4
Gift, Roland **1990**:2
Goodall, Jane **1991**:1
Hamilton, Hamish
 Obituary **1988**:4
Harrison, Rex
 Obituary **1990**:4
Hawking, Stephen W. **1990**:1
Hockney, David **1988**:3
Hoskins, Bob **1989**:1
Hounsfield, Godfrey **1989**:2
Howard, Trevor
 Obituary **1988**:2
Ireland, Jill
 Obituary **1990**:4
Knopfler, Mark **1986**:2
Laing, R.D.
 Obituary **1990**:1
Lawrence, Ruth
 Brief Entry **1986**:3
Leach, Robin
 Brief Entry **1985**:4
Lennox, Annie **1985**:4 **1996**:4
Livingstone, Ken **1988**:3
Lloyd Webber, Andrew **1989**:1
Macmillan, Harold
 Obituary **1987**:2
MacMillan, Kenneth
 Obituary **1993**:2
Maxwell, Robert **1990**:1
Michael, George **1989**:2
Milne, Christopher Robin
 Obituary **1996**:4
Moore, Henry
 Obituary **1986**:4
Murdoch, Iris
 Obituary **1999**:4
Norrington, Roger **1989**:4
Oldman, Gary **1998**:1
Olivier, Laurence
 Obituary **1989**:4
Philby, Kim
 Obituary **1988**:3
Rattle, Simon **1989**:4
Redgrave, Vanessa **1989**:2
Rhodes, Zandra **1986**:2
Roddick, Anita **1989**:4
Runcie, Robert **1989**:4
 Obituary **2001**:1
Saatchi, Charles **1987**:3
Steptoe, Patrick
 Obituary **1988**:3
Stevens, James
 Brief Entry **1988**:1
Thatcher, Margaret **1989**:2
Tudor, Antony
 Obituary **1987**:4
Ullman, Tracey **1988**:3

Wilson, Peter C.
 Obituary **1985**:2
Wintour, Anna **1990**:4

**BRUNEI**
 Bolkiah, Sultan Muda
  Hassanal **1985**:4

**BULGARIAN**
 Christo **1992**:3
 Dimitrova, Ghena **1987**:1

**BURMESE**
 Suu Kyi, Aung San **1996**:2

**CAMBODIAN**
 Lon Nol
  Obituary **1986**:1
 Pol Pot
  Obituary **1998**:4

**CANADIAN**
 Altman, Sidney **1997**:2
 Arbour, Louise **2005**:1
 Atwood, Margaret **2001**:2
 Barenaked Ladies **1997**:2
 Black, Conrad **1986**:2
 Bouchard, Lucien **1999**:2
 Bourassa, Robert
  Obituary **1997**:1
 Bourque, Raymond Jean **1997**:3
 Burr, Raymond
  Obituary **1994**:1
 Campbell, Kim **1993**:4
 Campbell, Neve **1998**:2
 Campeau, Robert **1990**:1
 Candy, John **1988**:2
  Obituary **1994**:3
 Carrey, Jim **1995**:1
 Cavanagh, Tom **2003**:1
 Cerovsek, Corey
  Brief Entry **1987**:4
 Cherry, Don **1993**:4
 Chretien, Jean **1990**:4 **1997**:2
 Christensen, Hayden **2003**:3
 Coffey, Paul **1985**:4
 Copps, Sheila **1986**:4
 Cronenberg, David **1992**:3
 Cronyn, Hume
  Obituary **2004**:3
 Dewhurst, Colleen
  Obituary **1992**:2
 Dion, Celine **1995**:3
 Eagleson, Alan **1987**:4
 Ebbers, Bernie **1998**:1
 Egoyan, Atom **2000**:2
 Erickson, Arthur **1989**:3
 Fonyo, Steve
  Brief Entry **1985**:4
 Foster, David **1988**:2
 Fox, Michael J. **1986**:1 **2001**:3
 Frank, Robert **1995**:2
 Frye, Northrop
  Obituary **1991**:3
 Fuhr, Grant **1997**:3
 Garneau, Marc **1985**:1
 Gatien, Peter
  Brief Entry **1986**:1
 Giguere, Jean-Sebastien **2004**:2
 Gilmour, Doug **1994**:3
 Graham, Nicholas **1991**:4

Palmer, Robert
  Obituary **2004**:4
Park, Nick **1997**:3
Patten, Christopher **1993**:3
Penrose, Roger **1991**:4
Pleasence, Donald
  Obituary **1995**:3
Pople, John
  Obituary **2005**:2
Porter, George
  Obituary **2003**:4
Princess Margaret, Countess of
  Snowdon
  Obituary **2003**:2
Pullman, Philip **2003**:2
Queen Elizabeth the Queen Mother
  Obituary **2003**:2
Redgrave, Lynn **1999**:3
Reisz, Karel
  Obituary **2004**:1
Richards, Keith **1993**:3
Ritchie, Guy **2001**:3
Roth, Tim **1998**:2
Saatchi, Maurice **1995**:4
Sacks, Oliver **1995**:4
Schlesinger, John
  Obituary **2004**:3
Scott, Ridley **2001**:1
Seal **1994**:4
Seymour, Jane **1994**:4
Smith, Paul **2002**:4
Smith, Zadie **2003**:4
Springer, Jerry **1998**:4
Springfield, Dusty
  Obituary **1999**:3
Stewart, Patrick **1996**:1
Sting **1991**:4
Stoppard, Tom **1995**:4
Strummer, Joe
  Obituary **2004**:1
Sullivan, Andrew **1996**:1
Taylor, Elizabeth **1993**:3
Taylor, Graham **2005**:3
Thompson, Emma **1993**:2
Tilberis, Elizabeth **1994**:3
Trotman, Alex **1995**:4
Uchida, Mitsuko **1989**:3
Ustinov, Peter
  Obituary **2005**:3
Ware, Lancelot
  Obituary **2001**:1
Watson, Emily **2001**:1
Westwood, Vivienne **1998**:3
Wiles, Andrew **1994**:1
Wilkinson, Tom **2003**:2
Wilmut, Ian **1997**:3
Winslet, Kate **2002**:4

**FIJI ISLANDER**
Mara, Ratu Sir Kamisese
  Obituary **2005**:3
Singh, Vijay **2000**:4

**FILIPINO**
Aquino, Corazon **1986**:2
Lewis, Loida Nicolas **1998**:3
Macapagal-Arroyo, Gloria **2001**:4
Marcos, Ferdinand
  Obituary **1990**:1
Natori, Josie **1994**:3

Ramos, Fidel **1995**:2
Salonga, Lea **2003**:3

**FINNISH**
Kekkonen, Urho
  Obituary **1986**:4
Ollila, Jorma **2003**:4
Torvalds, Linus **1999**:3

**FRENCH**
Adjani, Isabelle **1991**:1
Agnes B **2002**:3
Arnault, Bernard **2000**:4
Baulieu, Etienne-Emile **1990**:1
Becaud, Gilbert
  Obituary **2003**:1
Besse, Georges
  Obituary **1987**:1
Binoche, Juliette **2001**:3
Bourgeois, Louise **1994**:1
Brando, Cheyenne
  Obituary **1995**:4
Calment, Jeanne
  Obituary **1997**:4
Cardin, Pierre **2003**:3
Cartier-Bresson, Henri
  Obituary **2005**:4
Chagall, Marc
  Obituary **1985**:2
Chirac, Jacques **1995**:4
Colbert, Claudette
  Obituary **1997**:1
Cousteau, Jacques-Yves
  Obituary **1998**:2
Cousteau, Jean-Michel **1988**:2
Cresson, Edith **1992**:1
Delors, Jacques **1990**:2
Deneuve, Catherine **2003**:2
Depardieu, Gerard **1991**:2
Dubuffet, Jean
  Obituary **1985**:4
Duras, Marguerite
  Obituary **1996**:3
Fekkai, Frederic **2003**:2
Gaultier, Jean-Paul **1998**:1
Godard, Jean-Luc **1998**:1
Grappelli, Stephane
  Obituary **1998**:1
Guillem, Sylvie **1988**:2
Indurain, Miguel **1994**:1
Klarsfeld, Beate **1989**:1
Kouchner, Bernard **2005**:3
Lacroix, Christian **2005**:2
Lefebvre, Marcel **1988**:4
Malle, Louis
  Obituary **1996**:2
Mercier, Laura **2002**:2
Mitterrand, Francois
  Obituary **1996**:2
Nars, Francois **2003**:1
Petrossian, Christian
  Brief Entry **1985**:3
Picasso, Paloma **1991**:1
Ponty, Jean-Luc **1985**:4
Prost, Alain **1988**:1
Rampal, Jean-Pierre **1989**:2
Reza, Yasmina **1999**:2
Rothschild, Philippe de
  Obituary **1988**:2
Rykiel, Sonia **2000**:3

Simone, Nina
  Obituary **2004**:2
Starck, Philippe **2004**:1
Tautou, Audrey **2004**:2
Thom, Rene
  Obituary **2004**:1
Thomas, Michel **1987**:4
Ungaro, Emanuel **2001**:3
Villechaize, Herve
  Obituary **1994**:1
Xenakis, Iannis
  Obituary **2001**:4

**GERMAN**
Barbie, Klaus
  Obituary **1992**:2
Becker, Boris
  Brief Entry **1985**:3
Beuys, Joseph
  Obituary **1986**:3
Blobel, Gunter **2000**:4
Boyle, Gertrude **1995**:3
Brandt, Willy
  Obituary **1993**:2
Breitschwerdt, Werner **1988**:4
Casper, Gerhard **1993**:1
Dietrich, Marlene
  Obituary **1992**:4
Etzioni, Amitai **1994**:3
Fischer, Joschka **2005**:2
Frank, Anthony M. **1992**:1
Graf, Steffi **1987**:4
Grass, Gunter **2000**:2
Gursky, Andreas **2002**:2
Hahn, Carl H. **1986**:4
Hess, Rudolph
  Obituary **1988**:1
Honecker, Erich
  Obituary **1994**:4
Kiefer, Anselm **1990**:2
Kinski, Klaus **1987**:2
  Obituary **1992**:2
Klarsfeld, Beate **1989**:1
Klemperer, Werner
  Obituary **2001**:3
Kohl, Helmut **1994**:1
Krogner, Heinz **2004**:2
Lagerfeld, Karl **1999**:4
Max, Peter **1993**:2
Mengele, Josef
  Obituary **1985**:2
Mutter, Anne-Sophie **1990**:3
Newton, Helmut **2002**:1
Nuesslein-Volhard, Christiane **1998**:1
Pfeiffer, Eckhard **1998**:4
Pilatus, Robert
  Obituary **1998**:3
Polke, Sigmar **1999**:4
Rey, Margret E.
  Obituary **1997**:2
Richter, Gerhard **1997**:2
Sander, Jil **1995**:2
Schily, Otto
  Brief Entry **1987**:4
Schrempp, Juergen **2000**:2
Schroder, Gerhard **1999**:1
Schumacher, Michael **2005**:2
Tillmans, Wolfgang **2001**:4

Werner, Ruth
Obituary **2001**:1
Witt, Katarina **1991**:3
Zetsche, Dieter **2002**:3

## GHANIAN
Annan, Kofi **1999**:1
Chambas, Mohammed ibn **2003**:3
Kufuor, John Agyekum **2005**:4

## GREEK
Huffington, Arianna **1996**:2
Papandreou, Andrea
Obituary **1997**:1

## GUATEMALAN
Berger, Oscar **2004**:4
Menchu, Rigoberta **1993**:2

## GUINEA-BISSAUNI
Makeba, Miriam **1989**:2
Ture, Kwame
Obituary **1999**:2

## HAITIAN
Aristide, Jean-Bertrand **1991**:3
Cedras, Raoul **1994**:4
Danticat, Edwidge **2005**:4
Preával, Reneá **1997**:2

## HONG KONGER
Chow Yun-fat **1999**:4
Lee, Martin **1998**:2

## HUNGARIAN
Dorati, Antal
Obituary **1989**:2
Fodor, Eugene
Obituary **1991**:3
Gabor, Eva
Obituary **1996**:1
Grove, Andrew S. **1995**:3
Polgar, Judit **1993**:3
Solti, Georg
Obituary **1998**:1

## ICELANDIC
Bjork **1996**:1
Finnbogadóttir, Vigdiás
Brief Entry **1986**:2

## INDIAN
Chopra, Deepak **1996**:3
Devi, Phoolan **1986**:1
Obituary **2002**:3
Durrell, Gerald
Obituary **1995**:3
Gandhi, Indira
Obituary **1985**:1
Gandhi, Rajiv
Obituary **1991**:4
Gandhi, Sonia **2000**:2
Gowda, H. D. Deve **1997**:1
Iyengar, B.K.S. **2005**:1
Mahesh Yogi, Maharishi **1991**:3
Mehta, Zubin **1994**:3
Mother Teresa **1993**:1
Obituary **1998**:1
Musharraf, Pervez **2000**:2

Narayan, R.K.
Obituary **2002**:2
Nooyi, Indra **2004**:3
Prowse, Juliet
Obituary **1997**:1
Rajneesh, Bhagwan Shree
Obituary **1990**:2
Ram, Jagjivan
Obituary **1986**:4
Rao, P. V. Narasimha **1993**:2
Rushdie, Salman **1994**:1
Sharma, Nisha **2004**:2
Vajpayee, Atal Behari **1998**:4
Wahid, Abdurrahman **2000**:3

## INDONESIAN
Habibie, Bacharuddin Jusuf **1999**:3
Megawati Sukarnoputri **2000**:1
Megawati Sukarnoputri **2002**:2

## IRANIAN
Ebadi, Shirin **2004**:3
Khatami, Mohammed **1997**:4
Khomeini, Ayatollah Ruhollah
Obituary **1989**:4
McCourt, Frank **1997**:4
Rafsanjani, Ali Akbar
Hashemi **1987**:3
Schroeder, Barbet **1996**:1

## IRAQI
Hussein, Saddam **1991**:1
Kamel, Hussein **1996**:1
Saatchi, Maurice **1995**:4

## IRISH
Adams, Gerald **1994**:1
Ahern, Bertie **1999**:3
Beckett, Samuel Barclay
Obituary **1990**:2
Bono **1988**:4
Branagh, Kenneth **1992**:2
Brosnan, Pierce **2000**:3
Byrne, Gabriel **1997**:4
de Valois, Dame Ninette
Obituary **2002**:1
Enya **1992**:3
Farrell, Colin **2004**:1
Geldof, Bob **1985**:3
Heaney, Seamus **1996**:2
Herzog, Chaim
Obituary **1997**:3
Hume, John **1987**:1
Huston, John
Obituary **1988**:1
Jordan, Neil **1993**:3
McGuinness, Martin **1985**:4
Neeson, Liam **1993**:4
O'Connor, Sinead **1990**:4
O'Sullivan, Maureen
Obituary **1998**:4
Power, Samantha **2005**:4
Robinson, Mary **1993**:1
Trimble, David **1999**:1
U **2002**:4

## ISRAELI
Arens, Moshe **1985**:1
Arison, Ted **1990**:3
Barak, Ehud **1999**:4

Begin, Menachem
Obituary **1992**:3
Herzog, Chaim
Obituary **1997**:3
Levinger, Moshe **1992**:1
Levy, David **1987**:2
Mintz, Shlomo **1986**:2
Netanyahu, Benjamin **1996**:4
Peres, Shimon **1996**:3
Rabin, Leah
Obituary **2001**:2
Rabin, Yitzhak **1993**:1
Obituary **1996**:2
Shcharansky, Anatoly **1986**:2

## ITALIAN
Agnelli, Giovanni **1989**:4
Armani, Giorgio **1991**:2
Bartoli, Cecilia **1994**:1
Benetton, Luciano **1988**:1
Benigni, Roberto **1999**:2
Berio, Luciano
Obituary **2004**:2
Berlusconi, Silvio **1994**:4
Capra, Frank
Obituary **1992**:2
Cavalli, Roberto **2004**:4
Ciampi, Carlo Azeglio **2004**:3
Clemente, Francesco **1992**:2
Coppola, Carmine
Obituary **1991**:4
Dolce, Domenico and Stefano
Gabbana **2005**:4
Fabio **1993**:4
Fano, Ugo
Obituary **2001**:4
Fellini, Federico
Obituary **1994**:2
Ferrari, Enzo **1988**:4
Ferretti, Alberta **2004**:1
Ferri, Alessandra **1987**:2
Fo, Dario **1998**:1
Gardenia, Vincent
Obituary **1993**:2
Gassman, Vittorio
Obituary **2001**:1
Gucci, Maurizio
Brief Entry **1985**:4
Lamborghini, Ferrucio
Obituary **1993**:3
Leone, Sergio
Obituary **1989**:4
Masina, Giulietta
Obituary **1994**:3
Mastroianni, Marcello
Obituary **1997**:2
Michelangeli, Arturo Benedetti
**1988**:2
Montand, Yves
Obituary **1992**:2
Pavarotti, Luciano **1997**:4
Pozzi, Lucio **1990**:2
Prada, Miuccia **1996**:1
Rizzoli, Paola **2004**:3
Rosso, Renzo **2005**:2
Sinopoli, Giuseppe **1988**:1
Staller, Ilona **1988**:3
Tomba, Alberto **1992**:3
Versace, Donatella **1999**:1
Versace, Gianni
Brief Entry **1988**:1
Obituary **1998**:2

Zanardi, Alex **1998**:2
Zeffirelli, Franco **1991**:3

**JAMAICAN**
Marley, Ziggy **1990**:4
Tosh, Peter
Obituary **1988**:2

**JAPANESE**
Akihito, Emperor of Japan **1990**:1
Ando, Tadao **2005**:4
Aoki, Rocky **1990**:2
Doi, Takako
Brief Entry **1987**:4
Hirohito, Emperor of Japan
Obituary **1989**:2
Honda, Soichiro
Obituary **1986**:1
Hosokawa, Morihiro **1994**:1
Isozaki, Arata **1990**:2
Itami, Juzo
Obituary **1998**:2
Katayama, Yutaka **1987**:1
Koizumi, Junichiro **2002**:1
Kurosawa, Akira **1991**:1
Obituary **1999**:1
Kutaragi, Ken **2005**:3
Masako, Crown Princess **1993**:4
Matsuhisa, Nobuyuki **2002**:3
Mitarai, Fujio **2002**:4
Miyake, Issey **1985**:2
Miyazawa, Kiichi **1992**:2
Mori, Yoshiro **2000**:4
Morita, Akio **1989**:4
Morita, Akio
Obituary **2000**:2
Murakami, Takashi **2004**:2
Nagako, Empress Dowager
Obituary **2001**:1
Nomo, Hideo **1996**:2
Obuchi, Keizo
Obituary **2000**:4
Obuchi, Keizo **1999**:2
Oe, Kenzaburo **1997**:1
Sasakawa, Ryoichi
Brief Entry **1988**:1
Shimomura, Tsutomu **1996**:1
Suzuki, Ichiro **2002**:2
Suzuki, Sin'ichi
Obituary **1998**:3
Takada, Kenzo **2003**:2
Takei, Kei **1990**:2
Takeshita, Noboru
Obituary **2001**:1
Tanaka, Tomoyuki
Obituary **1997**:3
Taniguchi, Yoshio **2005**:4
Toyoda, Eiji **1985**:2
Uchida, Mitsuko **1989**:3
Yamamoto, Kenichi **1989**:1

**JORDANIAN**
Abdullah II, King **2002**:4
al-Abdullah, Rania **2001**:1
Hussein I, King **1997**:3
Obituary **1999**:3

**KENYAN**
Kibaki, Mwai **2003**:4
Maathai, Wangari **2005**:3
Moi, Daniel arap **1993**:2

**KOREAN**
Chung Ju Yung
Obituary **2002**:1
Lee Jong-Wook **2005**:1
Kim Dae Jung **1998**:3
Kim Il Sung
Obituary **1994**:4
Kim Jong Il **1995**:2
Pak, Se Ri **1999**:4
Roh Moo-hyun **2005**:1

**LATVIAN**
Baryshnikov, Mikhail Nikolaevich
**1997**:3

**LEBANESE**
Berri, Nabih **1985**:2
Jumblatt, Walid **1987**:4
Sarkis, Elias
Obituary **1985**:3

**LIBERIAN**
Doe, Samuel
Obituary **1991**:1

**LIBYAN**
Qaddhafi, Muammar **1998**:3

**LITHUANIAN**
Landsbergis, Vytautas **1991**:3
Milosz, Czeslaw
Obituary **2005**:4

**MACEDONIAN**
Trajkovski, Boris
Obituary **2005**:2

**MADAGASCAN**
Ravalomanana, Marc **2003**:1

**MALAWI**
Banda, Hastings **1994**:3

**MALAYSIAN**
Ngau, Harrison **1991**:3
Yeoh, Michelle **2003**:2

**MEXICAN**
Alvarez Bravo, Manuel
Obituary **2004**:1
Catlett, Elizabeth **1999**:3
Colosio, Luis Donaldo **1994**:3
Esquivel, Juan **1996**:2
Felix, Maria
Obituary **2003**:2
Fox, Vicente **2001**:1
Garcia, Amalia **2005**:3
Graham, Robert **1993**:4
Hayek, Salma **1999**:1
Kahlo, Frida **1991**:3
Paz, Octavio **1991**:2

Salinas, Carlos **1992**:1
Santana, Carlos **2000**:2
Tamayo, Rufino
Obituary **1992**:1
Zedillo, Ernesto **1995**:1

**MOROCCAN**
King Hassan II
Obituary **2000**:1

**MOZAMBICAN**
Chissano, Joaquim **1987**:4
Dhlakama, Afonso **1993**:3
Machel, Samora
Obituary **1987**:1

**NAMIBIAN**
Nujoma, Sam **1990**:4

**NEW ZEALANDER**
Campion, Jane **1991**:4
Castle-Hughes, Keisha **2004**:4
Crowe, Russell **2000**:4
Frame, Janet
Obituary **2005**:2
Jackson, Peter **2004**:4
Shipley, Jenny **1998**:3

**NICARAGUAN**
Astorga, Nora **1988**:2
Cruz, Arturo **1985**:1
Obando, Miguel **1986**:4
Robelo, Alfonso **1988**:1

**NIGERAN**
Abacha, Sani **1996**:3
Babangida, Ibrahim Badamosi
**1992**:4
Obasanjo, Olusegun **2000**:2
Okoye, Christian **1990**:2
Olajuwon, Akeem **1985**:1
Sade **1993**:2
Saro-Wiwa, Ken
Obituary **1996**:2

**NORWEGIAN**
Brundtland, Gro Harlem **2000**:1
Cammermeyer, Margarethe **1995**:2
Olav, King of Norway
Obituary **1991**:3

**PAKISTANI**
Bhutto, Benazir **1989**:4
Zia ul-Haq, Mohammad
Obituary **1988**:4

**PALESTINIAN**
Arafat, Yasser **1989**:3 **1997**:3
Freij, Elias **1986**:4
Habash, George **1986**:1
Husseini, Faisal **1998**:4
Nidal, Abu **1987**:1
Sharon, Ariel **2001**:4
Terzi, Zehdi Labib **1985**:3

**PANAMANIAN**
Blades, Ruben **1998**:2

**PERUVIAN**
Fujimori, Alberto **1992**:4
Perez de Cuellar, Javier **1991**:3
Testino, Mario **2002**:1

**POLISH**
Begin, Menachem
Obituary **1992**:3
Eisenstaedt, Alfred
Obituary **1996**:1
John Paul II, Pope **1995**:3
Kieslowski, Krzysztof
Obituary **1996**:3
Kosinski, Jerzy
Obituary **1991**:4
Masur, Kurt **1993**:4
Niezabitowska, Malgorzata **1991**:3
Rosten, Leo
Obituary **1997**:3
Sabin, Albert
Obituary **1993**:4
Singer, Isaac Bashevis
Obituary **1992**:1
Walesa, Lech **1991**:2

**PORTUGUESE**
Saramago, Jose **1999**:1

**PUERTO RICAN**
Alvarez, Aida **1999**:2
Del Toro, Benicio **2001**:4
Ferrer, Jose
Obituary **1992**:3
Julia, Raul
Obituary **1995**:1
Martin, Ricky **1999**:4
Novello, Antonia **1991**:2
Trinidad, Felix **2000**:4

**ROMANIAN**
Ceausescu, Nicolae
Obituary **1990**:2
Codrescu, Andreá **1997**:3

**RUSSIAN**
Brodsky, Joseph
Obituary **1996**:3
Gorbachev, Raisa
Obituary **2000**:2
Gordeeva, Ekaterina **1996**:4
Grinkov, Sergei
Obituary **1996**:2
Kasparov, Garry **1997**:4
Kasyanov, Mikhail **2001**:1
Konstantinov, Vladimir **1997**:4
Kournikova, Anna **2000**:3
Lapidus, Morris
Obituary **2001**:4
Lebed, Alexander **1997**:1
Primakov, Yevgeny **1999**:3
Putin, Vladimir **2000**:3
Safin, Marat **2001**:3
Sarraute, Nathalie
Obituary **2000**:2
Schneerson, Menachem Mendel
**1992**:4
Obituary **1994**:4
Sharapova, Maria **2005**:2
Titov, Gherman
Obituary **2001**:3

**RWANDAN**
Kagame, Paul **2001**:4

**SALVADORAN**
Duarte, Jose Napoleon
Obituary **1990**:3

**SCOTTISH**
Coldplay **2004**:4
Connery, Sean **1990**:4
Ferguson, Craig **2005**:4
McGregor, Ewan **1998**:2
Ramsay, Mike **2002**:1
Rowling, J.K. **2000**:1

**SENEGALESE**
Senghor, Leopold
Obituary **2003**:1

**SOMALIAN**
Iman **2001**:3

**SOUTH AFRICAN**
Barnard, Christiaan
Obituary **2002**:4
Blackburn, Molly
Obituary **1985**:4
Buthelezi, Mangosuthu Gatsha **1989**
:3
Coetzee, J. M. **2004**:4
de Klerk, F.W. **1990**:1
Duncan, Sheena
Brief Entry **1987**:1
Fugard, Athol **1992**:3
Hani, Chris
Obituary **1993**:4
Makeba, Miriam **1989**:2
Mandela, Nelson **1990**:3
Mandela, Winnie **1989**:3
Matthews, Dave **1999**:3
Mbeki, Thabo **1999**:4
Oppenheimer, Harry
Obituary **2001**:3
Paton, Alan
Obituary **1988**:3
Ramaphosa, Cyril **1988**:2
Sisulu, Walter
Obituary **2004**:2
Slovo, Joe **1989**:2
Suzman, Helen **1989**:3
Tambo, Oliver **1991**:3
Theron, Charlize **2001**:4
Treurnicht, Andries **1992**:2
Woods, Donald
Obituary **2002**:3

**SOVIET**
Asimov, Isaac
Obituary **1992**:3
Chernenko, Konstantin
Obituary **1985**:1
Dalai Lama **1989**:1
Dubinin, Yuri **1987**:4
Dzhanibekov, Vladimir **1988**:1
Erte
Obituary **1990**:4
Federov, Sergei **1995**:1
Godunov, Alexander
Obituary **1995**:4
Gorbachev, Mikhail **1985**:2

Grebenshikov, Boris **1990**:1
Gromyko, Andrei
Obituary **1990**:2
Karadzic, Radovan **1995**:3
Milosevic, Slobodan **1993**:2
Molotov, Vyacheslav Mikhailovich
Obituary **1987**:1
Nureyev, Rudolf
Obituary **1993**:2
Sakharov, Andrei Dmitrievich
Obituary **1990**:2
Smirnoff, Yakov **1987**:2
Vidov, Oleg **1987**:4
Yeltsin, Boris **1991**:1
Zhirinovsky, Vladimir **1994**:2

**SPANISH**
Almodovar, Pedro **2000**:3
Banderas, Antonio **1996**:2
Blahnik, Manolo **2000**:2
Calatrava, Santiago **2005**:1
Carreras, Jose **1995**:2
Cela, Camilo Jose
Obituary **2003**:1
Chillida, Eduardo
Obituary **2003**:4
Cruz, Penelope **2001**:4
Dali, Salvador
Obituary **1989**:2
de Pinies, Jamie
Brief Entry **1986**:3
Domingo, Placido **1993**:2
Juan Carlos I **1993**:1
Lopez de Arriortua, Jose Ignacio
**1993**:4
Miro, Joan
Obituary **1985**:1
Moneo, Jose Rafael **1996**:4
Montoya, Carlos
Obituary **1993**:4
Samaranch, Juan Antonio **1986**:2
Segovia, Andreás
Obituary **1987**:3
Wences, Senor
Obituary **1999**:4

**SRI LANKAN**
Bandaranaike, Sirimavo
Obituary **2001**:2
Ondaatje, Philip Michael **1997**:3
Wickramasinghe, Ranil **2003**:2

**SUDANESE**
Turabi, Hassan **1995**:4

**SWEDISH**
Bergman, Ingmar **1999**:4
Cardigans, The **1997**:4
Carlsson, Arvid **2001**:2
Garbo, Greta
Obituary **1990**:3
Hallstrom, Lasse **2002**:3
Lindbergh, Pelle
Obituary **1985**:4
Lindgren, Astrid
Obituary **2003**:1
Olin, Lena **1991**:2
Palme, Olof
Obituary **1986**:2
Persson, Stefan **2004**:1

# Cumulative Occupation Index

This index lists all newsmakers alphabetically by their occupations or fields of primary activity. Indexes in softbound issues allow access to the current year's entries; indexes in annual hardbound volumes are cumulative, covering the entire *Newsmakers* series.

Listee names are followed by a year and issue number; thus **1996**:3 indicates that an entry on that individual appears in both 1996, Issue 3, and the 1996 cumulation. For access to newsmakers appearing earlier than the current softbound issue, see the previous year's cumulation.

**ART AND DESIGN**
Adams, Scott **1996**:4
Addams, Charles
 Obituary **1989**:1
Agnes B **2002**:3
Allard, Linda **2003**:2
Alvarez Bravo, Manuel
 Obituary **2004**:1
Anderson, Laurie **2000**:2
Ando, Tadao **2005**:4
Arman **1993**:1
Armani, Giorgio **1991**:2
Ashwell, Rachel **2004**:2
Aucoin, Kevyn **2001**:3
Avedon, Richard **1993**:4
Azria, Max **2001**:4
Badgley, Mark and
 James Mischka **2004**:3
Baldessari, John **1991**:4
Banks, Jeffrey **1998**:2
Barbera, Joseph **1988**:2
Barks, Carl
 Obituary **2001**:2
Barnes, Ernie **1997**:4
Barry, Lynda **1992**:1
Bean, Alan L. **1986**:2
Beene, Geoffrey
 Obituary **2005**:4
Beuys, Joseph
 Obituary **1986**:3
Bird, Brad **2005**:4
Blahnik, Manolo **2000**:2
Blass, Bill
 Obituary **2003**:3
Bohbot, Michele **2004**:2
Bontecou, Lee **2004**:4
Boone, Mary **1985**:1
Botero, Fernando **1994**:3
Bourgeois, Louise **1994**:1
Bowie, David **1998**:2
Boynton, Sandra **2004**:1
Breathed, Berkeley **2005**:3
Brown, Bobbi **2001**:4
Brown, J. Carter
 Obituary **2003**:3
Bunshaft, Gordon **1989**:3
 Obituary **1991**:1

Calatrava, Santiago **2005**:1
Cameron, David
 Brief Entry **1988**:1
Campbell, Ben Nighthorse **1998**:1
Campbell, Naomi **2000**:2
Cardin, Pierre **2003**:3
Cartier-Bresson, Henri
 Obituary **2005**:4
Castelli, Leo
 Obituary **2000**:1
Catlett, Elizabeth **1999**:3
Cavalli, Roberto **2004**:4
Chagall, Marc
 Obituary **1985**:2
Chalayan, Hussein **2003**:2
Chast, Roz **1992**:4
Chatham, Russell **1990**:1
Chia, Sandro **1987**:2
Chihuly, Dale **1995**:2
Chillida, Eduardo
 Obituary **2003**:4
Christo **1992**:3
Claiborne, Liz **1986**:3
Clemente, Francesco **1992**:2
Cole, Kenneth **2003**:1
Cooper, Alexander **1988**:4
Crumb, R. **1995**:4
Dali, Salvador
 Obituary **1989**:2
Davis, Paige **2004**:2
DeCarava, Roy **1996**:3
de Kooning, Willem **1994**:4
 Obituary **1997**:3
de la Renta, Oscar **2005**:4
Diebenkorn, Richard
 Obituary **1993**:4
Diller, Elizabeth and
 Ricardo Scofidio **2004**:3
Dolce, Domenico and
 Stefano Gabbana **2005**:4
Donghia, Angelo R.
 Obituary **1985**:2
Duarte, Henry **2003**:3
Dubuffet, Jean
 Obituary **1985**:4
Dunham, Carroll **2003**:4
Eisenman, Peter **1992**:4

Eisenstaedt, Alfred
 Obituary **1996**:1
Ellis, Perry
 Obituary **1986**:3
Engelbreit, Mary **1994**:3
Erickson, Arthur **1989**:3
Erte
 Obituary **1990**:4
Eve **2004**:3
Fekkai, Frederic **2003**:2
Ferretti, Alberta **2004**:1
Field, Patricia **2002**:2
Finley, Karen **1992**:4
Fisher, Mary **1994**:3
Ford, Tom **1999**:3
Foster, Norman **1999**:4
Frank, Robert **1995**:2
Frankenthaler, Helen **1990**:1
Freud, Lucian **2000**:4
Frieda, John **2004**:1
Gaines, William M.
 Obituary **1993**:1
Galliano, John **2005**:2
Gaultier, Jean-Paul **1998**:1
Gehry, Frank O. **1987**:1
Giannulli, Mossimo **2002**:3
Gober, Robert **1996**:3
Golden, Thelma **2003**:3
Goody, Joan **1990**:2
Gorder, Genevieve **2005**:4
Gordon, Michael **2005**:1
Gould, Chester
 Obituary **1985**:2
Graham, Nicholas **1991**:4
Graham, Robert **1993**:4
Graves, Michael **2000**:1
Graves, Nancy **1989**:3
Greenberg, Robert **2003**:2
Groening, Matt **1990**:4
Guccione, Bob **1986**:1
Gund, Agnes **1993**:2
Gursky, Andreas **2002**:2
Hadid, Zaha **2005**:3
Halston
 Obituary **1990**:3
Handford, Martin **1991**:3

Wilson, Peter C.
  Obituary **1985**:2
Winick, Judd **2005**:3
Wintour, Anna **1990**:4
Witkin, Joel-Peter **1996**:1
Yamasaki, Minoru
  Obituary **1986**:2

## BUSINESS

Abraham, S. Daniel **2003**:3
Ackerman, Will **1987**:4
Agnelli, Giovanni **1989**:4
Ailes, Roger **1989**:3
Akers, John F. **1988**:3
Akin, Phil
  Brief Entry **1987**:3
Albrecht, Chris **2005**:4
Allaire, Paul **1995**:1
Allard, Linda **2003**:2
Allen, Bob **1992**:4
Allen, John **1992**:1
Alter, Hobie
  Brief Entry **1985**:1
Alvarez, Aida **1999**:2
Ames, Roger **2005**:2
Amos, Wally **2000**:1
Ancier, Garth **1989**:1
Andreessen, Marc **1996**:2
Annenberg, Walter **1992**:3
Antonini, Joseph **1991**:2
Aoki, Rocky **1990**:2
Arad, Avi **2003**:2
Aretsky, Ken **1988**:1
Arison, Ted **1990**:3
Arledge, Roone **1992**:2
Armstrong, C. Michael **2002**:1
Arnault, Bernard **2000**:4
Ash, Mary Kay **1996**:1
Ashwell, Rachel **2004**:2
Aurre, Laura
  Brief Entry **1986**:3
Ballmer, Steven **1997**:2
Banks, Jeffrey **1998**:2
Barad, Jill **1994**:2
Barksdale, James L. **1998**:2
Barrett, Craig R. **1999**:4
Bauer, Eddie
  Obituary **1986**:3
Beals, Vaughn **1988**:2
Becker, Brian **2004**:4
Beene, Geoffrey
  Obituary **2005**:4
Beers, Charlotte **1999**:3
Ben & Jerry **1991**:3
Benetton, Luciano **1988**:1
Berlusconi, Silvio **1994**:4
Besse, Georges
  Obituary **1987**:1
Bezos, Jeff **1998**:4
Bieber, Owen **1986**:1
Bikoff, James L.
  Brief Entry **1986**:2
Black, Carole **2003**:1
Black, Cathleen **1998**:4
Black, Conrad **1986**:2
Bloch, Henry **1988**:4
Bloch, Ivan **1986**:3
Bloomberg, Michael **1997**:1
Bohbot, Michele **2004**:2
Boiardi, Hector
  Obituary **1985**:3

Bolkiah, Sultan Muda
  Hassanal **1985**:4
Bond, Alan **1989**:2
Bose, Amar
  Brief Entry **1986**:4
Boyer, Herbert Wayne **1985**:1
Boyle, Gertrude **1995**:3
Boynton, Sandra **2004**:1
Brabeck-Letmathe, Peter **2001**:4
Bradley, Todd **2003**:3
Branson, Richard **1987**:1
Bravo, Ellen **1998**:2
Bravo, Rose Marie **2005**:3
Breitschwerdt, Werner **1988**:4
Brennan, Edward A. **1989**:1
Brennan, Robert E. **1988**:1
Bronfman, Edgar, Jr. **1994**:4
Brooks, Diana D. **1990**:1
Brown, John Seely **2004**:1
Brown, Tina **1992**:1
Buffett, Jimmy **1999**:3
Buffett, Warren **1995**:2
Burnison, Chantal Simone **1988**:3
Burns, Robin **1991**:2
Burr, Donald Calvin **1985**:3
Busch, August A. III **1988**:2
Busch, August Anheuser, Jr.
  Obituary **1990**:2
Bushnell, Nolan **1985**:1
Buss, Jerry **1989**:3
Cain, Herman **1998**:3
Callaway, Ely
  Obituary **2002**:3
Calloway, D. Wayne **1987**:3
Campeau, Robert **1990**:1
Canfield, Alan B.
  Brief Entry **1986**:3
Carter, Billy
  Obituary **1989**:1
Case, Steve **1995**:4 **1996**:4
Chalayan, Hussein **2003**:2
Chappell, Tom **2002**:3
Charron, Paul **2004**:1
Chenault, Kenneth I. **1999**:3
Chizen, Bruce **2004**:2
Chouinard, Yvon **2002**:2
Chung Ju Yung
  Obituary **2002**:1
Claiborne, Liz **1986**:3
Clark, Jim **1997**:1
Cole, Kenneth **2003**:1
Coleman, Sheldon, Jr. **1990**:2
Collier, Sophia **2001**:2
Combs, Sean 'Puffy' **1998**:4
Condit, Phil **2001**:3
Cooper, Alexander **1988**:4
Cooper, Stephen F. **2005**:4
Coors, William K.
  Brief Entry **1985**:1
Copeland, Al **1988**:3
Covey, Stephen R. **1994**:4
Cox, Richard Joseph
  Brief Entry **1985**:1
Craig, James **2001**:1
Craig, Sid and Jenny **1993**:4
Crandall, Robert L. **1992**:1
Crawford, Cheryl
  Obituary **1987**:1
Cray, Seymour R.
  Brief Entry **1986**:3
  Obituary **1997**:2
Cummings, Sam **1986**:3

D'Alessio, Kitty
  Brief Entry **1987**:3
David, George **2005**:1
Davis, Crispin **2004**:1
Davison, Ian Hay **1986**:1
DeBartolo, Edward J., Jr. **1989**:3
de la Renta, Oscar **2005**:4
Dell, Michael **1996**:2
DeLuca, Fred **2003**:3
Deming, W. Edwards **1992**:2
  Obituary **1994**:2
de Passe, Suzanne **1990**:4
Devine, John M. **2003**:2
Diemer, Walter E.
  Obituary **1998**:2
DiFranco, Ani **1997**:1
Diller, Barry **1991**:1
Disney, Lillian
  Obituary **1998**:3
Disney, Roy E. **1986**:3
Dolby, Ray Milton
  Brief Entry **1986**:1
Dolce, Domenico and
  Stefano Gabbana **2005**:4
Donahue, Tim **2004**:3
Doubleday, Nelson, Jr. **1987**:1
Downey, Bruce **2003**:1
Drexler, Millard S. **1990**:3
Drucker, Peter F. **1992**:3
Dunlap, Albert J. **1997**:2
Dupri, Jermaine **1999**:1
Dyson, James **2005**:4
Eagleson, Alan **1987**:4
Eaton, Robert J. **1994**:2
Ebbers, Bernie **1998**:1
Eckert, Robert A. **2002**:3
Egan, John **1987**:2
Eisner, Michael **1989**:2
Ellis, Perry
  Obituary **1986**:3
Ellison, Larry **2004**:2
Engibous, Thomas J. **2003**:3
Engstrom, Elmer W.
  Obituary **1985**:2
Epstein, Jason **1991**:1
Ertegun, Ahmet **1986**:3
Estes, Pete
  Obituary **1988**:3
Evans, Nancy **2000**:4
Eyler, John. H., Jr. **2001**:3
Factor, Max
  Obituary **1996**:4
Fekkai, Frederic **2003**:2
Feld, Kenneth **1988**:2
Fender, Leo
  Obituary **1992**:1
Ferrari, Enzo **1988**:4
Ferretti, Alberta **2004**:1
Fertel, Ruth **2000**:2
Fields, Debbi **1987**:3
Fiorina, Carleton S. **2000**:1
Fireman, Paul
  Brief Entry **1987**:2
Fisher, Mel **1985**:4
Fleming, Claudia **2004**:1
Flynt, Larry **1997**:3
Fodor, Eugene
  Obituary **1991**:3
Fomon, Robert M. **1985**:3
Forbes, Malcolm S.
  Obituary **1990**:3

Cumulative Occupation Index

Vagelos, P. Roy **1989**:4
Vasella, Daniel **2005**:3
Veeck, Bill
   Obituary **1986**:1
Versace, Donatella **1999**:1
Versace, Gianni
   Brief Entry **1988**:1
   Obituary **1998**:2
Vinton, Will
   Brief Entry **1988**:1
Vischer, Phil **2002**:2
von Furstenberg, Diane **1994**:2
Wachner, Linda **1988**:3 **1997**:2
Waitt, Ted **1997**:4
Waldron, Hicks B. **1987**:3
Walgreen, Charles III
   Brief Entry **1987**:4
Walker, Jay **2004**:2
Walton, Sam **1986**:2
   Obituary **1993**:1
Wang, An **1986**:1
   Obituary **1990**:3
Ware, Lancelot
   Obituary **2001**:1
Watkins, Sherron **2003**:1
Weill, Sandy **1990**:4
Weinstein, Bob and Harvey **2000**:4
Weintraub, Jerry **1986**:1
Welch, Jack **1993**:3
Westwood, Vivienne **1998**:3
Whitman, Meg **2000**:3
Whittle, Christopher **1989**:3
Williams, Edward Bennett
   Obituary **1988**:4
Williams, Lynn **1986**:4
Wilson, Jerry
   Brief Entry **1986**:2
Wilson, Peter C.
   Obituary **1985**:2
Wintour, Anna **1990**:4
Wolf, Stephen M. **1989**:3
Woodcock, Leonard
   Obituary **2001**:4
Woodruff, Robert Winship
   Obituary **1985**:1
Wrigley, William, Jr. **2002**:2
Wynn, Stephen A. **1994**:3
Yamamoto, Kenichi **1989**:1
Yetnikoff, Walter **1988**:1
Zagat, Tim and Nina **2004**:3
Zamboni, Frank J.
   Brief Entry **1986**:4
Zanker, Bill
   Brief Entry **1987**:3
Zetcher, Arnold B. **2002**:1
Zetsche, Dieter **2002**:3
Ziff, William B., Jr. **1986**:4
Zuckerman, Mortimer **1986**:3

## DANCE

Abdul, Paula **1990**:3
Acosta, Carlos **1997**:4
Ailey, Alvin **1989**:2
   Obituary **1990**:2
Allen, Debbie **1998**:2
Astaire, Fred
   Obituary **1987**:4
Baryshnikov, Mikhail Nikolaevich
   **1997**:3
Bennett, Michael
   Obituary **1988**:1

Bissell, Patrick
   Obituary **1988**:2
Bocca, Julio **1995**:3
Campbell, Neve **1998**:2
Cunningham, Merce **1998**:1
Davis, Sammy, Jr.
   Obituary **1990**:4
Dean, Laura **1989**:4
de Mille, Agnes
   Obituary **1994**:2
de Valois, Dame Ninette
   Obituary **2002**:1
Dudley, Jane
   Obituary **2002**:4
Englund, Richard
   Obituary **1991**:3
Fagan, Garth **2000**:1
Farrell, Suzanne **1996**:3
Feld, Eliot **1996**:1
Fenley, Molissa **1988**:3
Ferri, Alessandra **1987**:2
Flatley, Michael **1997**:3
Fonteyn, Margot
   Obituary **1991**:3
Forsythe, William **1993**:2
Fosse, Bob
   Obituary **1988**:1
Garr, Teri **1988**:4
Glover, Savion **1997**:1
Godunov, Alexander
   Obituary **1995**:4
Graham, Martha
   Obituary **1991**:4
Gregory, Cynthia **1990**:2
Guillem, Sylvie **1988**:2
Herrera, Paloma **1996**:2
Hewitt, Jennifer Love **1999**:2
Hines, Gregory **1992**:4
Jackson, Janet **1990**:4
Jamison, Judith **1990**:3
Joffrey, Robert
   Obituary **1988**:3
Jones, Bill T. **1991**:4
Kaye, Nora
   Obituary **1987**:4
Keeler, Ruby
   Obituary **1993**:4
Kelly, Gene
   Obituary **1996**:3
Kistler, Darci **1993**:1
Lander, Toni
   Obituary **1985**:4
Lewitzky, Bella
   Obituary **2005**:3
MacMillan, Kenneth
   Obituary **1993**:2
Madonna **1985**:2
Marshall, Susan **2000**:4
Miller, Ann
   Obituary **2005**:2
Miller, Bebe **2000**:2
Mitchell, Arthur **1995**:1
Morris, Mark **1991**:1
Murray, Arthur
   Obituary **1991**:3
North, Alex **1986**:3
Nureyev, Rudolf
   Obituary **1993**:2
Parker, Sarah Jessica **1999**:2
Parsons, David **1993**:4
Perez, Rosie **1994**:2

Prowse, Juliet
   Obituary **1997**:1
Rauschenberg, Robert **1991**:2
Renvall, Johan
   Brief Entry **1987**:4
Robbins, Jerome
   Obituary **1999**:1
Rogers, Ginger
   Obituary **1995**:4
Stroman, Susan **2000**:4
Takei, Kei **1990**:2
Taylor, Paul **1992**:3
Tharp, Twyla **1992**:4
Tudor, Antony
   Obituary **1987**:4
Tune, Tommy **1994**:2
Varone, Doug **2001**:2
Verdi-Fletcher, Mary **1998**:2
Verdon, Gwen
   Obituary **2001**:2
Whelan, Wendy **1999**:3

## EDUCATION

Abramson, Lyn **1986**:3
Alexander, Lamar **1991**:2
Bakker, Robert T. **1991**:3
Bayley, Corrine
   Brief Entry **1986**:4
Billington, James **1990**:3
Bollinger, Lee C. **2003**:2
Botstein, Leon **1985**:3
Bush, Millie **1992**:1
Campbell, Bebe Moore **1996**:2
Casper, Gerhard **1993**:1
Cavazos, Lauro F. **1989**:2
Cheek, James Edward
   Brief Entry **1987**:1
Cheney, Lynne V. **1990**:4
Clements, George **1985**:1
Cole, Johnetta B. **1994**:3
Coles, Robert **1995**:1
Commager, Henry Steele
   Obituary **1998**:3
Curran, Charles E. **1989**:2
Davis, Angela **1998**:3
Delany, Sarah
   Obituary **1999**:3
Deming, W. Edwards **1992**:2
   Obituary **1994**:2
Dershowitz, Alan **1992**:1
Dove, Rita **1994**:3
Drucker, Peter F. **1992**:3
Edelman, Marian Wright **1990**:4
Edwards, Harry **1989**:4
Etzioni, Amitai **1994**:3
Feldman, Sandra **1987**:3
Fernandez, Joseph **1991**:3
Folkman, Judah **1999**:1
Fox, Matthew **1992**:2
Fulbright, J. William
   Obituary **1995**:3
Futrell, Mary Hatwood **1986**:1
Futter, Ellen V. **1995**:1
Ghali, Boutros Boutros **1992**:3
Giamatti, A. Bartlett **1988**:4
   Obituary **1990**:1
Goldhaber, Fred
   Brief Entry **1986**:3
Gray, Hanna **1992**:4
Green, Richard R. **1988**:3
Gregorian, Vartan **1990**:3
Gund, Agnes **1993**:2

Hackney, Sheldon **1995**:1
Hair, Jay D. **1994**:3
Harker, Patrick T. **2001**:2
Hayakawa, Samuel Ichiye
  Obituary **1992**:3
Healy, Bernadine **1993**:1
Healy, Timothy S. **1990**:2
Heaney, Seamus **1996**:2
Heller, Walter
  Obituary **1987**:4
Hennessy, John L. **2002**:2
Hill, Anita **1994**:1
Hillegass, Clifton Keith **1989**:4
Horwich, Frances
  Obituary **2002**:3
Hunter, Madeline **1991**:2
Janzen, Daniel H. **1988**:4
Jones, Edward P. **2005**:1
Jordan, King **1990**:1
Justiz, Manuel J. **1986**:4
Kandel, Eric **2005**:2
Kemp, Jan **1987**:2
Kerr, Clark
  Obituary **2005**:1
King, Mary-Claire **1998**:3
Kopp, Wendy **1993**:3
Kozol, Jonathan **1992**:1
Lagasse, Emeril **1998**:3
Lamb, Wally **1999**:1
Lang, Eugene M. **1990**:3
Langston, J. William
  Brief Entry **1986**:2
Lawrence, Ruth
  Brief Entry **1986**:3
Laybourne, Geraldine **1997**:1
Leach, Penelope **1992**:4
Lee, Chang-Rae **2005**:1
Lerner, Michael **1994**:2
Levine, Arnold **2002**:3
MacKinnon, Catharine **1993**:2
Malloy, Edward 'Monk' **1989**:4
Marier, Rebecca **1995**:4
McAuliffe, Christa
  Obituary **1985**:4
McCall Smith, Alexander **2005**:2
McMillan, Terry **1993**:2
Morrison, Toni **1998**:1
Mumford, Lewis
  Obituary **1990**:2
Nemerov, Howard
  Obituary **1992**:1
Nye, Bill **1997**:2
O'Keefe, Sean **2005**:2
Owens, Delia and Mark **1993**:3
Pagels, Elaine **1997**:1
Paglia, Camille **1992**:3
Paige, Rod **2003**:2
Parizeau, Jacques **1995**:1
Peter, Valentine J. **1988**:2
Riley, Richard W. **1996**:3
Rodin, Judith **1994**:4
Rosendahl, Bruce R.
  Brief Entry **1986**:4
Rowland, Pleasant **1992**:3
Scheck, Barry **2000**:4
Schuman, Patricia Glass **1993**:2
Shalala, Donna **1992**:3
Sherman, Russell **1987**:4
Silber, John **1990**:1
Simmons, Adele Smith **1988**:4
Simmons, Ruth **1995**:2
Simon, Lou Anna K. **2005**:4

Singer, Margaret Thaler
  Obituary **2005**:1
Smoot, George F. **1993**:3
Sowell, Thomas **1998**:3
Spellings, Margaret **2005**:4
Spock, Benjamin **1995**:2
  Obituary **1998**:3
Steele, Shelby **1991**:2
Swanson, Mary Catherine **2002**:2
Tannen, Deborah **1995**:1
Thiebaud, Wayne **1991**:1
Thomas, Michel **1987**:4
Tilghman, Shirley M. **2002**:1
Tribe, Laurence H. **1988**:1
Tyson, Laura D'Andrea **1994**:1
Unz, Ron **1999**:1
Van Duyn, Mona **1993**:2
Vickrey, William S.
  Obituary **1997**:2
Warren, Robert Penn
  Obituary **1990**:1
West, Cornel **1994**:2
Wexler, Nancy S. **1992**:3
Wiesel, Elie **1998**:1
Wigand, Jeffrey **2000**:4
Wiles, Andrew **1994**:1
Wilson, Edward O. **1994**:4
Wilson, William Julius **1997**:1
Wolff, Tobias **2005**:1
Wu, Harry **1996**:1
Zanker, Bill
  Brief Entry **1987**:3
Zigler, Edward **1994**:1

## FILM

Abbott, George
  Obituary **1995**:3
Adjani, Isabelle **1991**:1
Affleck, Ben **1999**:1
Aiello, Danny **1990**:4
Alda, Robert
  Obituary **1986**:3
Alexander, Jane **1994**:2
Alexander, Jason **1993**:3
Allen, Debbie **1998**:2
Allen, Joan **1998**:1
Allen, Woody **1994**:1
Alley, Kirstie **1990**:3
Almodovar, Pedro **2000**:3
Altman, Robert **1993**:2
Ameche, Don
  Obituary **1994**:2
Anderson, Judith
  Obituary **1992**:3
Andrews, Julie **1996**:1
Aniston, Jennifer **2000**:3
Applegate, Christina **2000**:4
Arad, Avi **2003**:2
Arden, Eve
  Obituary **1991**:2
Arkoff, Samuel Z.
  Obituary **2002**:4
Arlen, Harold
  Obituary **1986**:3
Arnaz, Desi
  Obituary **1987**:1
Arnold, Tom **1993**:2
Arquette, Patricia **2001**:3
Arquette, Rosanna **1985**:2
Arthur, Jean
  Obituary **1992**:1

Ashcroft, Peggy
  Obituary **1992**:1
Astaire, Fred
  Obituary **1987**:4
Astin, Sean **2005**:1
Astor, Mary
  Obituary **1988**:1
Atkinson, Rowan **2004**:3
Autry, Gene
  Obituary **1999**:1
Aykroyd, Dan **1989**:3 **1997**:3
Bacall, Lauren **1997**:3
Backus, Jim
  Obituary **1990**:1
Bacon, Kevin **1995**:3
Baddeley, Hermione
  Obituary **1986**:4
Bailey, Pearl
  Obituary **1991**:1
Bakula, Scott **2003**:1
Baldwin, Alec **2002**:2
Bale, Christian **2001**:3
Ball, Alan **2005**:1
Ball, Lucille
  Obituary **1989**:3
Banderas, Antonio **1996**:2
Banks, Tyra **1996**:3
Barker, Clive **2003**:3
Barkin, Ellen **1987**:3
Barr, Roseanne **1989**:1
Barrymore, Drew **1995**:3
Baryshnikov, Mikhail Nikolaevich
  **1997**:3
Basinger, Kim **1987**:2
Bassett, Angela **1994**:4
Bateman, Jason **2005**:3
Bateman, Justine **1988**:4
Bates, Alan
  Obituary **2005**:1
Bates, Kathy **1991**:4
Baxter, Anne
  Obituary **1986**:1
Beals, Jennifer **2005**:2
Beatty, Warren **2000**:1
Belushi, Jim **1986**:2
Benigni, Roberto **1999**:2
Bening, Annette **1992**:1
Bennett, Joan
  Obituary **1991**:2
Bergen, Candice **1990**:1
Bergman, Ingmar **1999**:4
Bernardi, Herschel
  Obituary **1986**:4
Bernhard, Sandra **1989**:4
Bernsen, Corbin **1990**:2
Berry, Halle **1996**:2
Bialik, Mayim **1993**:3
Bigelow, Kathryn **1990**:4
Binoche, Juliette **2001**:3
Birch, Thora **2002**:4
Bird, Brad **2005**:4
Black, Jack **2002**:3
Blades, Ruben **1998**:2
Blanc, Mel
  Obituary **1989**:4
Blanchett, Cate **1999**:3
Bloom, Orlando **2004**:2
Bogosian, Eric **1990**:4
Bolger, Ray
  Obituary **1987**:2
Bonet, Lisa **1989**:2
Bonham Carter, Helena **1998**:4

Booth, Shirley
  Obituary **1993**:2
Bowie, David **1998**:2
Boyle, Lara Flynn **2003**:4
Boyle, Peter **2002**:3
Braff, Zach **2005**:2
Branagh, Kenneth **1992**:2
Brandauer, Klaus Maria **1987**:3
Brando, Marlon
  Obituary **2005**:3
Bridges, Lloyd
  Obituary **1998**:3
Bronson, Charles
  Obituary **2004**:4
Brooks, Albert **1991**:4
Brooks, Mel **2003**:1
Brosnan, Pierce **2000**:3
Brown, James **1991**:4
Brown, Jim **1993**:2
Brynner, Yul
  Obituary **1985**:4
Buckley, Betty **1996**:2
Bullock, Sandra **1995**:4
Burnett, Carol **2000**:3
Burns, Edward **1997**:1
Burns, George
  Obituary **1996**:3
Burns, Ken **1995**:2
Burr, Raymond
  Obituary **1994**:1
Burstyn, Ellen **2001**:4
Burton, Tim **1993**:1
Burum, Stephen H.
  Brief Entry **1987**:2
Buscemi, Steve **1997**:4
Bynes, Amanda **2005**:1
Byrne, Gabriel **1997**:4
Caan, James **2004**:4
Caesar, Adolph
  Obituary **1986**:3
Cage, Nicolas **1991**:1
Cagney, James
  Obituary **1986**:2
Caine, Michael **2000**:4
Calhoun, Rory
  Obituary **1999**:4
Campbell, Naomi **2000**:2
Campbell, Neve **1998**:2
Campion, Jane **1991**:4
Candy, John **1988**:2
  Obituary **1994**:3
Capra, Frank
  Obituary **1992**:2
Carey, Drew **1997**:4
Carlin, George **1996**:3
Carney, Art
  Obituary **2005**:1
Carradine, John
  Obituary **1989**:2
Carrey, Jim **1995**:1
Carson, Lisa Nicole **1999**:3
Caruso, David **1994**:3
Carvey, Dana **1994**:1
Cassavetes, John
  Obituary **1989**:2
Castle-Hughes, Keisha **2004**:4
Cattrall, Kim **2003**:3
Caulfield, Joan
  Obituary **1992**:1
Cavanagh, Tom **2003**:1
Caviezel, Jim **2005**:3
Chan, Jackie **1996**:1

Channing, Stockard **1991**:3
Chappelle, Dave **2005**:3
Chase, Chevy **1990**:1
Cheadle, Don **2002**:1
Chen, Joan **2000**:2
Cher **1993**:1
Chiklis, Michael **2003**:3
Chow Yun-fat **1999**:4
Christensen, Hayden **2003**:3
Clarkson, Patricia **2005**:3
Clay, Andrew Dice **1991**:1
Cleese, John **1989**:2
Close, Glenn **1988**:3
Coburn, James
  Obituary **2004**:1
Coco, James
  Obituary **1987**:2
Coen, Joel and Ethan **1992**:1
Colbert, Claudette
  Obituary **1997**:1
Coleman, Dabney **1988**:3
Connelly, Jennifer **2002**:4
Connery, Sean **1990**:4
Connick, Harry, Jr. **1991**:1
Cooper, Chris **2004**:1
Coppola, Carmine
  Obituary **1991**:4
Coppola, Francis Ford **1989**:4
Coppola, Sofia **2004**:3
Corbett, John **2004**:1
Cosby, Bill **1999**:2
Costner, Kevin **1989**:4
Cox, Courteney **1996**:2
Craven, Wes **1997**:3
Crawford, Broderick
  Obituary **1986**:3
Crenna, Richard
  Obituary **2004**:1
Crichton, Michael **1995**:3
Cronenberg, David **1992**:3
Cronyn, Hume
  Obituary **2004**:3
Crothers, Scatman
  Obituary **1987**:1
Crowe, Cameron **2001**:2
Crowe, Russell **2000**:4
Cruise, Tom **1985**:4
Cruz, Penelope **2001**:4
Crystal, Billy **1985**:3
Culkin, Macaulay **1991**:3
Curtis, Jamie Lee **1995**:1
Cusack, John **1999**:3
Cushing, Peter
  Obituary **1995**:1
Dafoe, Willem **1988**:1
Dalton, Timothy **1988**:4
Damon, Matt **1999**:1
Danes, Claire **1999**:4
Daniels, Jeff **1989**:4
Danza, Tony **1989**:1
David, Larry **2003**:4
Davis, Bette
  Obituary **1990**:1
Davis, Geena **1992**:1
Davis, Sammy, Jr.
  Obituary **1990**:4
Day, Dennis
  Obituary **1988**:4
Day-Lewis, Daniel **1989**:4 **1994**:4
De Cordova, Frederick **1985**:2
DeGeneres, Ellen **1995**:3
Del Toro, Benicio **2001**:4

De Matteo, Drea **2005**:2
Demme, Jonathan **1992**:4
Dench, Judi **1999**:4
Deneuve, Catherine **2003**:2
De Niro, Robert **1999**:1
Dennehy, Brian **2002**:1
Dennis, Sandy
  Obituary **1992**:4
Depardieu, Gerard **1991**:2
Depp, Johnny **1991**:3
Dern, Laura **1992**:3
De Vito, Danny **1987**:1
Diamond, I.A.L.
  Obituary **1988**:3
Diamond, Selma
  Obituary **1985**:2
Diaz, Cameron **1999**:1
DiCaprio, Leonardo Wilhelm **1997**:2
Diesel, Vin **2004**:1
Dietrich, Marlene
  Obituary **1992**:4
Diggs, Taye **2000**:1
Diller, Barry **1991**:1
Dillon, Matt **1992**:2
Disney, Roy E. **1986**:3
Divine
  Obituary **1988**:3
Doherty, Shannen **1994**:2
Donahue, Troy
  Obituary **2002**:4
Douglas, Michael **1986**:2
Drescher, Fran **1995**:3
Dreyfuss, Richard **1996**:3
Driver, Minnie **2000**:1
Duchovny, David **1998**:3
Duff, Hilary **2004**:4
Duffy, Karen **1998**:1
Dukakis, Olympia **1996**:4
Dunst, Kirsten **2001**:4
Duvall, Robert **1999**:3
Eastwood, Clint **1993**:3
Ebsen, Buddy
  Obituary **2004**:3
Egoyan, Atom **2000**:2
Eisner, Michael **1989**:2
Elliott, Denholm
  Obituary **1993**:2
Ephron, Henry
  Obituary **1993**:2
Ephron, Nora **1992**:3
Epps, Omar **2000**:4
Estevez, Emilio **1985**:4
Evans, Robert **2004**:1
Eve **2004**:3
Everett, Rupert **2003**:1
Fairbanks, Douglas, Jr.
  Obituary **2000**:4
Fallon, Jimmy **2003**:1
Fanning, Dakota **2005**:2
Farley, Chris
  Obituary **1998**:2
Farrell, Colin **2004**:1
Farrow, Mia **1998**:3
Favreau, Jon **2002**:3
Fawcett, Farrah **1998**:4
Feldshuh, Tovah **2005**:3
Felix, Maria
  Obituary **2003**:2
Fell, Norman
  Obituary **1999**:2
Fellini, Federico
  Obituary **1994**:2

Kasem, Casey **1987**:1
Katzenberg, Jeffrey **1995**:3
Kaufman, Charlie **2005**:1
Kavner, Julie **1992**:3
Kaye, Danny
 Obituary **1987**:2
Kazan, Elia
 Obituary **2004**:4
Keaton, Diane **1997**:1
Keaton, Michael **1989**:4
Keeler, Ruby
 Obituary **1993**:4
Keitel, Harvey **1994**:3
Keith, Brian
 Obituary **1997**:4
Kelly, Gene
 Obituary **1996**:3
Kidman, Nicole **1992**:4
Kilmer, Val **1991**:4
King, Alan
 Obituary **2005**:3
King, Stephen **1998**:1
Kinski, Klaus **1987**:2
 Obituary **1992**:2
Kline, Kevin **2000**:1
Knight, Wayne **1997**:1
Knightley, Keira **2005**:2
Kramer, Larry **1991**:2
Kramer, Stanley
 Obituary **2002**:1
Kubrick, Stanley
 Obituary **1999**:3
Kulp, Nancy
 Obituary **1991**:3
Kurosawa, Akira **1991**:1
 Obituary **1999**:1
Kutcher, Ashton **2003**:4
Lahti, Christine **1988**:2
Lake, Ricki **1994**:4
Lamarr, Hedy
 Obituary **2000**:3
Lamour, Dorothy
 Obituary **1997**:1
Lancaster, Burt
 Obituary **1995**:1
Lane, Nathan **1996**:4
Lange, Jessica **1995**:4
Lansbury, Angela **1993**:1
Lansing, Sherry **1995**:4
LaPaglia, Anthony **2004**:4
Lardner Jr., Ring
 Obituary **2001**:2
Larroquette, John **1986**:2
Law, Jude **2000**:3
Lawless, Lucy **1997**:4
Lawrence, Martin **1993**:4
Leary, Denis **1993**:3
LeBlanc, Matt **2005**:4
Lee, Ang **1996**:3
Lee, Brandon
 Obituary **1993**:4
Lee, Pamela **1996**:4
Lee, Spike **1988**:4
Leguizamo, John **1999**:1
Leigh, Janet
 Obituary **2005**:4
Leigh, Jennifer Jason **1995**:2
Lemmon, Jack **1998**:4
 Obituary **2002**:3
Leno, Jay **1987**:1
Leone, Sergio
 Obituary **1989**:4

Levinson, Barry **1989**:3
Levy, Eugene **2004**:3
Lewis, Juliette **1999**:3
Lewis, Richard **1992**:1
Li, Jet **2005**:3
Liberace
 Obituary **1987**:2
Ling, Bai **2000**:3
Lithgow, John **1985**:2
Little, Cleavon
 Obituary **1993**:2
Liu, Lucy **2000**:4
LL Cool J **1998**:2
Lloyd Webber, Andrew **1989**:1
Locklear, Heather **1994**:3
Loewe, Frederick
 Obituary **1988**:2
Logan, Joshua
 Obituary **1988**:4
Lohan, Lindsay **2005**:3
Long, Nia **2001**:3
Long, Shelley **1985**:1
Lopez, Jennifer **1998**:4
Lord, Jack
 Obituary **1998**:2
Lords, Traci **1995**:4
Louis-Dreyfus, Julia **1994**:1
Lovett, Lyle **1994**:1
Lowe, Rob **1990**:4
Loy, Myrna
 Obituary **1994**:2
Lucas, George **1999**:4
Luhrmann, Baz **2002**:3
Lupino, Ida
 Obituary **1996**:1
Lynch, David **1990**:4
Lyne, Adrian **1997**:2
Mac, Bernie **2003**:1
MacDonald, Laurie and
 Walter Parkes **2004**:1
MacDowell, Andie **1993**:4
MacMurray, Fred
 Obituary **1992**:2
MacRae, Gordon
 Obituary **1986**:2
Macy, William H. **1999**:3
Madonna **1985**:2
Maguire, Tobey **2002**:2
Maher, Bill **1996**:2
Malkovich, John **1988**:2
Malle, Louis
 Obituary **1996**:2
Mamet, David **1998**:4
Mancini, Henry
 Obituary **1994**:4
Mandel, Howie **1989**:1
Mantegna, Joe **1992**:1
Marin, Cheech **2000**:1
Markle, C. Wilson **1988**:1
Marsalis, Branford **1988**:3
Marshall, Penny **1991**:3
Martin, Dean
 Obituary **1996**:2
Martin, Dean Paul
 Obituary **1987**:3
Martin, Steve **1992**:2
Marvin, Lee
 Obituary **1988**:1
Masina, Giulietta
 Obituary **1994**:3
Mastroianni, Marcello
 Obituary **1997**:2

Matlin, Marlee **1992**:2
Matthau, Walter **2000**:3
Matuszak, John
 Obituary **1989**:4
McConaughey, Matthew David
 **1997**:1
McCrea, Joel
 Obituary **1991**:1
McDormand, Frances **1997**:3
McDowall, Roddy
 Obituary **1999**:1
McGillis, Kelly **1989**:3
McGinley, Ted **2004**:4
McGregor, Ewan **1998**:2
McGuire, Dorothy
 Obituary **2002**:4
McKee, Lonette **1996**:1
McKellen, Ian **1994**:1
McLaren, Norman
 Obituary **1987**:2
Meadows, Audrey
 Obituary **1996**:3
Meredith, Burgess
 Obituary **1998**:1
Messing, Debra **2004**:4
Midler, Bette **1989**:4
Milano, Alyssa **2002**:3
Milland, Ray
 Obituary **1986**:2
Miller, Ann
 Obituary **2005**:2
Milligan, Spike
 Obituary **2003**:2
Minghella, Anthony **2004**:3
Minogue, Kylie **2003**:4
Mirren, Helen **2005**:1
Mitchum, Robert
 Obituary **1997**:4
Molina, Alfred **2005**:3
Montand, Yves
 Obituary **1992**:2
Montgomery, Elizabeth
 Obituary **1995**:4
Moore, Clayton
 Obituary **2000**:3
Moore, Demi **1991**:4
Moore, Dudley
 Obituary **2003**:2
Moore, Julianne **1998**:1
Moore, Mandy **2004**:2
Moore, Mary Tyler **1996**:2
Moore, Michael **1990**:3
Morita, Noriyuki 'Pat' **1987**:3
Mortensen, Viggo **2003**:3
Mos Def **2005**:4
Moss, Carrie-Anne **2004**:3
Murphy, Brittany **2005**:1
Murphy, Eddie **1989**:2
Murray, Bill **2002**:4
Myers, Mike **1992**:3 **1997**:4
Nance, Jack
 Obituary **1997**:3
Neeson, Liam **1993**:4
Nelson, Harriet
 Obituary **1995**:1
Nelson, Rick
 Obituary **1986**:1
Nelson, Willie **1993**:4
Newman, Paul **1995**:3
Newton-John, Olivia **1998**:4
Nichols, Mike **1994**:4
Nicholson, Jack **1989**:2

Nolan, Lloyd
  Obituary **1985**:4
Nolte, Nick **1992**:4
North, Alex **1986**:3
Northam, Jeremy **2003**:2
Norton, Edward **2000**:2
O'Connor, Donald
  Obituary **2004**:4
O'Donnell, Rosie **1994**:3
Oldman, Gary **1998**:1
Olin, Ken **1992**:3
Olin, Lena **1991**:2
Olivier, Laurence
  Obituary **1989**:4
Olmos, Edward James **1990**:1
O'Sullivan, Maureen
  Obituary **1998**:4
Ovitz, Michael **1990**:1
Paar, Jack
  Obituary **2005**:2
Pacino, Al **1993**:4
Page, Geraldine
  Obituary **1987**:4
Pakula, Alan
  Obituary **1999**:2
Paltrow, Gwyneth **1997**:1
Pantoliano, Joe **2002**:3
Park, Nick **1997**:3
Parker, Mary-Louise **2002**:2
Parker, Sarah Jessica **1999**:2
Parker, Trey and Matt Stone **1998**:2
Parks, Bert
  Obituary **1992**:3
Pascal, Amy **2003**:3
Patrick, Robert **2002**:1
Paxton, Bill **1999**:3
Payne, Alexander **2005**:4
Peck, Gregory
  Obituary **2004**:3
Peete, Holly Robinson **2005**:2
Penn, Sean **1987**:2
Perez, Rosie **1994**:2
Perkins, Anthony
  Obituary **1993**:2
Perry, Luke **1992**:3
Perry, Matthew **1997**:2
Pesci, Joe **1992**:4
Peters, Bernadette **2000**:1
Peterson, Cassandra **1988**:1
Pfeiffer, Michelle **1990**:2
Phifer, Mekhi **2004**:1
Phillips, Julia **1992**:1
Phoenix, Joaquin **2000**:4
Phoenix, River **1990**:2
  Obituary **1994**:2
Picasso, Paloma **1991**:1
Pinchot, Bronson **1987**:4
Pinkett Smith, Jada **1998**:3
Pitt, Brad **1995**:2
Pleasence, Donald
  Obituary **1995**:3
Plimpton, George
  Obituary **2004**:4
Poitier, Sidney **1990**:3
Portman, Natalie **2000**:3
Potts, Annie **1994**:1
Preminger, Otto
  Obituary **1986**:3
Presley, Pricilla **2001**:1
Preston, Robert
  Obituary **1987**:3

Price, Vincent
  Obituary **1994**:2
Prince **1995**:3
Prinze, Freddie, Jr. **1999**:3
Prowse, Juliet
  Obituary **1997**:1
Pryor, Richard **1999**:3
Puzo, Mario
  Obituary **2000**:1
Quaid, Dennis **1989**:4
Queen Latifah **1992**:2
Quinn, Anthony
  Obituary **2002**:2
Radner, Gilda
  Obituary **1989**:4
Raimi, Sam **1999**:2
Randall, Tony
  Obituary **2005**:3
Raven **2005**:1
Raye, Martha
  Obituary **1995**:1
Reagan, Ronald
  Obituary **2005**:3
Redford, Robert **1993**:2
Redgrave, Lynn **1999**:3
Redgrave, Vanessa **1989**:2
Reed, Donna
  Obituary **1986**:1
Reese, Della **1999**:2
Reeve, Christopher **1997**:2
Reeves, Keanu **1992**:1
Reeves, Steve
  Obituary **2000**:4
Reilly, John C. **2003**:4
Reiner, Rob **1991**:2
Reiser, Paul **1995**:2
Reisz, Karel
  Obituary **2004**:1
Reitman, Ivan **1986**:3
Remick, Lee
  Obituary **1992**:1
Reuben, Gloria **1999**:4
Reubens, Paul **1987**:2
Ricci, Christina **1999**:1
Richards, Michael **1993**:4
Riddle, Nelson
  Obituary **1985**:4
Ringwald, Molly **1985**:4
Ritchie, Guy **2001**:3
Ritter, John **2003**:4
Robards, Jason
  Obituary **2001**:3
Robbins, Jerome
  Obituary **1999**:1
Robbins, Tim **1993**:1
Roberts, Doris **2003**:4
Roberts, Julia **1991**:3
Rock, Chris **1998**:1
Rodriguez, Robert **2005**:1
Rogers, Ginger
  Obituary **1995**:4
Rogers, Roy
  Obituary **1998**:4
Roker, Roxie
  Obituary **1996**:2
Rolle, Esther
  Obituary **1999**:2
Rollins, Howard E., Jr. **1986**:1
Ross, Herbert
  Obituary **2002**:4
Roth, Tim **1998**:2
Rourke, Mickey **1988**:4

Rowan, Dan
  Obituary **1988**:1
Rudner, Rita **1993**:2
Rudnick, Paul **1994**:3
Ruehl, Mercedes **1992**:4
RuPaul **1996**:1
Rush, Geoffrey **2002**:1
Russo, Rene **2000**:2
Ryan, Meg **1994**:1
Ryder, Winona **1991**:2
Sagal, Katey **2005**:2
Salonga, Lea **2003**:3
Sandler, Adam **1999**:2
Sarandon, Susan **1995**:3
Savage, Fred **1990**:1
Savalas, Telly
  Obituary **1994**:3
Schlesinger, John
  Obituary **2004**:3
Schneider, Rob **1997**:4
Schroeder, Barbet **1996**:1
Schumacher, Joel **2004**:3
Schwarzenegger, Arnold **1991**:1
Schwimmer, David **1996**:2
Scorsese, Martin **1989**:1
Scott, George C.
  Obituary **2000**:2
Scott, Randolph
  Obituary **1987**:2
Scott, Ridley **2001**:1
Seidelman, Susan **1985**:4
Sevigny, Chloe **2001**:4
Seymour, Jane **1994**:4
Shaffer, Paul **1987**:1
Sharkey, Ray
  Obituary **1994**:1
Shawn, Dick
  Obituary **1987**:3
Sheedy, Ally **1989**:1
Sheen, Martin **2002**:1
Shepard, Sam **1996**:4
Shields, Brooke **1996**:3
Shore, Dinah
  Obituary **1994**:3
Short, Martin **1986**:1
Shue, Andrew **1994**:4
Shyamalan, M. Night **2003**:2
Silverman, Jonathan **1997**:2
Silvers, Phil
  Obituary **1985**:4
Silverstone, Alicia **1997**:4
Sinatra, Frank
  Obituary **1998**:4
Singleton, John **1994**:3
Sinise, Gary **1996**:1
Siskel, Gene
  Obituary **1999**:3
Slater, Christian **1994**:1
Smirnoff, Yakov **1987**:2
Smith, Kevin **2000**:4
Smith, Will **1997**:2
Smits, Jimmy **1990**:1
Snipes, Wesley **1993**:1
Sobieski, Leelee **2002**:3
Soderbergh, Steven **2001**:4
Sondheim, Stephen **1994**:4
Sorkin, Aaron **2003**:2
Sorvino, Mira **1996**:3
Sothern, Ann
  Obituary **2002**:1
Southern, Terry
  Obituary **1996**:2

Spacek, Sissy **2003**:1
Spacey, Kevin **1996**:4
Spade, David **1999**:2
Spader, James **1991**:2
Spheeris, Penelope **1989**:2
Spielberg, Steven **1993**:4 **1997**:4
Stack, Robert
  Obituary **2004**:2
Staller, Ilona **1988**:3
Stallone, Sylvester **1994**:2
Steel, Dawn **1990**:1
  Obituary **1998**:2
Stefani, Gwen **2005**:4
Steiger, Rod
  Obituary **2003**:4
Stevenson, McLean
  Obituary **1996**:3
Stewart, Jimmy
  Obituary **1997**:4
Stewart, Patrick **1996**:1
Stiles, Julia **2002**:3
Stiller, Ben **1999**:1
Sting **1991**:4
Stone, Oliver **1990**:4
Stone, Sharon **1993**:4
Stoppard, Tom **1995**:4
Streep, Meryl **1990**:2
Streisand, Barbra **1992**:2
Strummer, Joe
  Obituary **2004**:1
Studi, Wes **1994**:3
Styne, Jule
  Obituary **1995**:1
Susskind, David
  Obituary **1987**:2
Sutherland, Kiefer **2002**:4
Swank, Hilary **2000**:3
Tanaka, Tomoyuki
  Obituary **1997**:3
Tandy, Jessica **1990**:4
  Obituary **1995**:1
Tarantino, Quentin **1995**:1
Tautou, Audrey **2004**:2
Taylor, Elizabeth **1993**:3
Taylor, Lili **2000**:2
Theron, Charlize **2001**:4
Thiebaud, Wayne **1991**:1
Thompson, Emma **1993**:2
Thompson, Fred **1998**:2
Thornton, Billy Bob **1997**:4
Thurman, Uma **1994**:2
Tilly, Jennifer **1997**:2
Tomei, Marisa **1995**:2
Travolta, John **1995**:2
Tucci, Stanley **2003**:2
Tucker, Chris **1999**:1
Tucker, Forrest
  Obituary **1987**:1
Turner, Janine **1993**:2
Turner, Kathleen **1985**:3
Turner, Lana
  Obituary **1996**:1
Turturro, John **2002**:2
Tyler, Liv **1997**:2
Ullman, Tracey **1988**:3
Union, Gabrielle **2004**:2
Urich, Robert **1988**:1
  Obituary **2003**:3
Usher **2005**:1
Ustinov, Peter
  Obituary **2005**:3
Vanilla Ice **1991**:3

Van Sant, Gus **1992**:2
Vardalos, Nia **2003**:4
Varney, Jim
  Brief Entry **1985**:4
  Obituary **2000**:3
Vaughn, Vince **1999**:2
Ventura, Jesse **1999**:2
Vidal, Gore **1996**:2
Vidov, Oleg **1987**:4
Villechaize, Herve
  Obituary **1994**:1
Vincent, Fay **1990**:2
Voight, Jon **2002**:3
Walker, Nancy
  Obituary **1992**:3
Wallis, Hal
  Obituary **1987**:1
Warhol, Andy
  Obituary **1987**:2
Washington, Denzel **1993**:2
Wasserman, Lew
  Obituary **2003**:3
Waters, John **1988**:3
Watson, Emily **2001**:1
Wayans, Damon **1998**:4
Wayans, Keenen Ivory **1991**:1
Wayne, David
  Obituary **1995**:3
Weaver, Sigourney **1988**:3
Wegman, William **1991**:1
Weinstein, Bob and Harvey **2000**:4
Weintraub, Jerry **1986**:1
Whitaker, Forest **1996**:2
Wiest, Dianne **1995**:2
Wilder, Billy
  Obituary **2003**:2
Wilkinson, Tom **2003**:2
Williams, Robin **1988**:4
Williams, Treat **2004**:3
Williams, Vanessa L. **1999**:2
Willis, Bruce **1986**:4
Wilson, Owen **2002**:3
Winfield, Paul
  Obituary **2005**:2
Winfrey, Oprah **1986**:4 **1997**:3
Winger, Debra **1994**:3
Winokur, Marissa Jaret **2005**:1
Winslet, Kate **2002**:4
Witherspoon, Reese **2002**:1
Wolfman Jack
  Obituary **1996**:1
Wong, B.D. **1998**:1
Woo, John **1994**:2
Wood, Elijah **2002**:4
Woods, James **1988**:3
Wyle, Noah **1997**:3
Wynn, Keenan
  Obituary **1987**:1
Xzibit **2005**:4
Yeoh, Michelle **2003**:2
Young, Loretta
  Obituary **2001**:1
Young, Robert
  Obituary **1999**:1
Zanuck, Lili Fini **1994**:2
Zeffirelli, Franco **1991**:3
Zellweger, Renee **2001**:1
Zemeckis, Robert **2002**:1
Zeta-Jones, Catherine **1999**:4
Zucker, Jerry **2002**:2

## LAW

Abzug, Bella **1998**:2
Achtenberg, Roberta **1993**:4
Allred, Gloria **1985**:2
Andrews, Lori B. **2005**:3
Angelos, Peter **1995**:4
Archer, Dennis **1994**:4
Astorga, Nora **1988**:2
Babbitt, Bruce **1994**:1
Bailey, F. Lee **1995**:4
Baker, James A. III **1991**:2
Bikoff, James L.
  Brief Entry **1986**:2
Blackmun, Harry A.
  Obituary **1999**:3
Boies, David **2002**:1
Bradley, Tom
  Obituary **1999**:1
Brennan, William
  Obituary **1997**:4
Breyer, Stephen Gerald
  **1994**:4 **1997**:2
Brown, Willie **1996**:4
Brown, Willie L. **1985**:2
Burger, Warren E.
  Obituary **1995**:4
Burnison, Chantal Simone **1988**:3
Campbell, Kim **1993**:4
Cantrell, Ed
  Brief Entry **1985**:3
Casey, William
  Obituary **1987**:3
Casper, Gerhard **1993**:1
Clark, Marcia **1995**:1
Clinton, Bill **1992**:1
Clinton, Hillary Rodham **1993**:2
Cochran, Johnnie **1996**:1
Colby, William E.
  Obituary **1996**:4
Cuomo, Mario **1992**:2
Darden, Christopher **1996**:4
Dees, Morris **1992**:1
del Ponte, Carla **2001**:1
Dershowitz, Alan **1992**:1
Deutch, John **1996**:4
Dole, Elizabeth Hanford **1990**:1
Dukakis, Michael **1988**:3
Eagleson, Alan **1987**:4
Ehrlichman, John
  Obituary **1999**:3
Ervin, Sam
  Obituary **1985**:2
Estrich, Susan **1989**:1
Fairstein, Linda **1991**:1
Fehr, Donald **1987**:2
Fieger, Geoffrey **2001**:3
Florio, James J. **1991**:2
Foster, Vincent
  Obituary **1994**:1
France, Johnny
  Brief Entry **1987**:1
Freeh, Louis J. **1994**:2
Fulbright, J. William
  Obituary **1995**:3
Furman, Rosemary
  Brief Entry **1986**:4
Garrison, Jim
  Obituary **1993**:2
Ginsburg, Ruth Bader **1993**:4
Giuliani, Rudolph **1994**:2
Glasser, Ira **1989**:1

Gore, Albert, Sr.
  Obituary **1999**:2
Grisham, John **1994**:4
Harvard, Beverly **1995**:2
Hayes, Robert M. **1986**:3
Hill, Anita **1994**:1
Hills, Carla **1990**:3
Hirschhorn, Joel
  Brief Entry **1986**:1
Hoffa, Jim, Jr. **1999**:2
Hyatt, Joel **1985**:3
Ireland, Patricia **1992**:2
Ito, Lance **1995**:3
Janklow, Morton **1989**:3
Kennedy, John F., Jr. **1990**:1
  Obituary **1999**:4
Kennedy, Weldon **1997**:3
Kunstler, William
  Obituary **1996**:1
Kunstler, William **1992**:3
Kurzban, Ira **1987**:2
Lee, Henry C. **1997**:1
Lee, Martin **1998**:2
Lewis, Loida Nicolas **1998**:3
Lewis, Reginald F. **1988**:4
  Obituary **1993**:3
Lightner, Candy **1985**:1
Liman, Arthur **1989**:4
Lipsig, Harry H. **1985**:1
Lipton, Martin **1987**:3
MacKinnon, Catharine **1993**:2
Marshall, Thurgood
  Obituary **1993**:3
McCloskey, James **1993**:1
Mitchell, George J. **1989**:3
Mitchell, John
  Obituary **1989**:2
Mitchelson, Marvin **1989**:2
Morrison, Trudi
  Brief Entry **1986**:2
Nader, Ralph **1989**:4
Napolitano, Janet **1997**:1
Neal, James Foster **1986**:2
O'Connor, Sandra Day **1991**:1
O'Leary, Hazel **1993**:4
O'Steen, Van
  Brief Entry **1986**:3
Panetta, Leon **1995**:1
Pirro, Jeanine **1998**:2
Powell, Lewis F.
  Obituary **1999**:1
Puccio, Thomas P. **1986**:4
Quayle, Dan **1989**:2
Raines, Franklin **1997**:4
Ramaphosa, Cyril **1988**:2
Ramo, Roberta Cooper **1996**:1
Rehnquist, William H. **2001**:2
Reno, Janet **1993**:3
Rothwax, Harold **1996**:3
Scalia, Antonin **1988**:2
Scheck, Barry **2000**:4
Schily, Otto
  Brief Entry **1987**:4
Sheehan, Daniel P. **1989**:1
Sheindlin, Judith **1999**:1
Sirica, John
  Obituary **1993**:2
Skinner, Sam **1992**:3
Slater, Rodney E. **1997**:4
Slotnick, Barry
  Brief Entry **1987**:4
Souter, David **1991**:3

Starr, Kenneth **1998**:3
Steinberg, Leigh **1987**:3
Stern, David **1991**:4
Stewart, Potter
  Obituary **1986**:1
Strauss, Robert **1991**:4
Tagliabue, Paul **1990**:2
Thomas, Clarence **1992**:2
Thompson, Fred **1998**:2
Tribe, Laurence H. **1988**:1
Vincent, Fay **1990**:2
Violet, Arlene **1985**:3
Wapner, Joseph A. **1987**:1
Watson, Elizabeth **1991**:2
White, Byron
  Obituary **2003**:3
Williams, Edward Bennett
  Obituary **1988**:4
Williams, Willie L. **1993**:1
Wilson, Bertha
  Brief Entry **1986**:1

**MUSIC**
Aaliyah **2001**:3
Abdul, Paula **1990**:3
Ackerman, Will **1987**:4
Acuff, Roy
  Obituary **1993**:2
Aguilera, Christina **2000**:4
Albert, Stephen **1986**:1
Allen, Peter
  Obituary **1993**:1
Ames, Roger **2005**:2
Amos, Tori **1995**:1
Anderson, Marion
  Obituary **1993**:4
Andrews, Julie **1996**:1
Andrews, Maxene
  Obituary **1996**:2
Anthony, Marc **2000**:3
Arlen, Harold
  Obituary **1986**:3
Arnaz, Desi
  Obituary **1987**:1
Arrau, Claudio
  Obituary **1992**:1
Arrested Development **1994**:2
Ashanti **2004**:1
Astaire, Fred
  Obituary **1987**:4
Autry, Gene
  Obituary **1999**:1
Backstreet Boys **2001**:3
Badu, Erykah **2000**:4
Baez, Joan **1998**:3
Bailey, Pearl
  Obituary **1991**:1
Baker, Anita **1987**:4
Barenboim, Daniel **2001**:1
Bartoli, Cecilia **1994**:1
Basie, Count
  Obituary **1985**:1
Battle, Kathleen **1998**:1
Beastie Boys, The **1999**:1
Becaud, Gilbert
  Obituary **2003**:1
Beck **2000**:2
Bee Gees, The **1997**:4
Benatar, Pat **1986**:1
Bennett, Tony **1994**:4
Berio, Luciano
  Obituary **2004**:2

Berlin, Irving
  Obituary **1990**:1
Bernhard, Sandra **1989**:4
Bernstein, Elmer
  Obituary **2005**:4
Bernstein, Leonard
  Obituary **1991**:1
Berry, Chuck **2001**:2
Bjork **1996**:1
Blades, Ruben **1998**:2
Blakey, Art
  Obituary **1991**:1
Blige, Mary J. **1995**:3
Bolton, Michael **1993**:2
Bon Jovi, Jon **1987**:4
Bono **1988**:4
Bono, Sonny **1992**:2
  Obituary **1998**:2
Borge, Victor
  Obituary **2001**:3
Botstein, Leon **1985**:3
Bowie, David **1998**:2
Bowles, Paul
  Obituary **2000**:3
Boxcar Willie
  Obituary **1999**:4
Boyz II Men **1995**:1
Brandy **1996**:4
Branson, Richard **1987**:1
Braxton, Toni **1994**:3
Brooks, Garth **1992**:1
Brown, James **1991**:4
Brown, Les
  Obituary **2001**:3
Buckley, Jeff
  Obituary **1997**:4
Buffett, Jimmy **1999**:3
Bush, Kate **1994**:3
Butterfield, Paul
  Obituary **1987**:3
Cage, John
  Obituary **1993**:1
Calloway, Cab
  Obituary **1995**:2
Cardigans, The **1997**:4
Carey, Mariah **1991**:3
Carlisle, Belinda **1989**:3
Carpenter, Mary-Chapin **1994**:1
Carreras, Jose **1995**:2
Carter, Benny
  Obituary **2004**:3
Carter, Nell
  Obituary **2004**:2
Carter, Ron **1987**:3
Cash, Johnny **1995**:3
Cash, June Carter
  Obituary **2004**:2
Cerovsek, Corey
  Brief Entry **1987**:4
Chapman, Tracy **1989**:2
Charles, Ray
  Obituary **2005**:3
Cheatham, Adolphus 'Doc'
  Obituary **1997**:4
Cher **1993**:1
Clapton, Eric **1993**:3
Clarke, Stanley **1985**:4
Clarkson, Kelly **2003**:3
Cleveland, James
  Obituary **1991**:3
Cliburn, Van **1995**:1

Seger, Bob **1987**:1
Segovia, Andreás
 Obituary **1987**:3
Selena
 Obituary **1995**:4
Serkin, Rudolf
 Obituary **1992**:1
Shaffer, Paul **1987**:1
Shakira **2002**:3
Shakur, Tupac
 Obituary **1997**:1
Sherman, Russell **1987**:4
Shocked, Michelle **1989**:4
Shore, Dinah
 Obituary **1994**:3
Simmons, Russell and
 Kimora Lee **2003**:2
Simon, Paul **1992**:2
Simone, Nina
 Obituary **2004**:2
Sinatra, Frank
 Obituary **1998**:4
Sinopoli, Giuseppe **1988**:1
Smith, Kate
 Obituary **1986**:3
Smith, Will **1997**:2
Snider, Dee **1986**:1
Snoop Doggy Dogg **1995**:2
Snow, Hank
 Obituary **2000**:3
Solti, Georg
 Obituary **1998**:1
Sondheim, Stephen **1994**:4
Spears, Britney **2000**:3
Spector, Phil **1989**:1
Springfield, Dusty
 Obituary **1999**:3
Staples, Roebuck 'Pops'
 Obituary **2001**:3
Stefani, Gwen **2005**:4
Stern, Isaac
 Obituary **2002**:4
Sting **1991**:4
Strait, George **1998**:3
Streisand, Barbra **1992**:2
Strummer, Joe
 Obituary **2004**:1
Styne, Jule
 Obituary **1995**:1
Sun Ra
 Obituary **1994**:1
Suzuki, Sin'ichi
 Obituary **1998**:3
Tan Dun **2002**:1
Tesh, John **1996**:3
Thomas, Michael Tilson **1990**:3
Tiffany **1989**:1
TLC **1996**:1
Tone-Loc **1990**:3
Torme, Mel
 Obituary **1999**:4
Tosh, Peter
 Obituary **1988**:2
Travis, Randy **1988**:4
Tritt, Travis **1995**:1
Tune, Tommy **1994**:2
Turner, Tina **2000**:3
Twain, Shania **1996**:3
Twitty, Conway
 Obituary **1994**:1
Tyner, Rob
 Obituary **1992**:2

U **2002**:4
Uchida, Mitsuko **1989**:3
Ullman, Tracey **1988**:3
Upshaw, Dawn **1991**:2
Usher **2005**:1
Valente, Benita **1985**:3
Van Halen, Edward **1985**:2
Vanilla Ice **1991**:3
Vaughan, Sarah
 Obituary **1990**:3
Vaughan, Stevie Ray
 Obituary **1991**:1
Vega, Suzanne **1988**:1
Vollenweider, Andreas **1985**:2
von Karajan, Herbert
 Obituary **1989**:4
von Trapp, Maria
 Obituary **1987**:3
Walker, Junior
 Obituary **1996**:2
Washington, Grover, Jr. **1989**:1
Wasserman, Lew
 Obituary **2003**:3
Weintraub, Jerry **1986**:1
Wells, Mary
 Obituary **1993**:1
West, Dottie
 Obituary **1992**:2
White, Barry
 Obituary **2004**:3
Williams, Joe
 Obituary **1999**:4
Williams, Pharrell **2005**:3
Williams, Vanessa L. **1999**:2
Willis, Bruce **1986**:4
Wilson, Brian **1996**:1
Wilson, Carl
 Obituary **1998**:2
Wilson, Cassandra **1996**:3
Winans, CeCe **2000**:1
Winston, George **1987**:1
Winter, Paul **1990**:2
Womack, Lee Ann **2002**:1
Wynette, Tammy
 Obituary **1998**:3
Wynonna **1993**:3
Xenakis, Iannis
 Obituary **2001**:4
Xzibit **2005**:4
Yankovic, 'Weird Al' **1985**:4
Yankovic, Frank
 Obituary **1999**:2
Yearwood, Trisha **1999**:1
Yoakam, Dwight **1992**:4
Young, Neil **1991**:2
Zappa, Frank
 Obituary **1994**:2
Zevon, Warren
 Obituary **2004**:4
Zinnemann, Fred
 Obituary **1997**:3
Zwilich, Ellen **1990**:1

**POLITICS AND
GOVERNMENT--FOREIGN**
Abacha, Sani **1996**:3
Abdullah II, King **2002**:4
Adams, Gerald **1994**:1
Ahern, Bertie **1999**:3
Akihito, Emperor of Japan **1990**:1
al-Abdullah, Rania **2001**:1
al-Assad, Bashar **2004**:2

Albright, Madeleine **1994**:3
Amin, Idi
 Obituary **2004**:4
Annan, Kofi **1999**:1
Aquino, Corazon **1986**:2
Arafat, Yasser **1989**:3 **1997**:3
Arens, Moshe **1985**:1
Arias Sanchez, Oscar **1989**:3
Aristide, Jean-Bertrand **1991**:3
Assad, Hafez
 Obituary **2000**:4
Assad, Hafez al- **1992**:1
Assad, Rifaat **1986**:3
Astorga, Nora **1988**:2
Babangida, Ibrahim Badamosi
 **1992**:4
Balaguer, Joaquin
 Obituary **2003**:4
Banda, Hastings **1994**:3
Bandaranaike, Sirimavo
 Obituary **2001**:2
Barak, Ehud **1999**:4
Barbie, Klaus
 Obituary **1992**:2
Begin, Menachem
 Obituary **1992**:3
Berger, Oscar **2004**:4
Berlusconi, Silvio **1994**:4
Berri, Nabih **1985**:2
Bhutto, Benazir **1989**:4
Blair, Tony **1996**:3 **1997**:4
Bolkiah, Sultan Muda Hassanal
 **1985**:4
Bouchard, Lucien **1999**:2
Bourassa, Robert
 Obituary **1997**:1
Brandt, Willy
 Obituary **1993**:2
Brundtland, Gro Harlem **2000**:1
Buthelezi, Mangosuthu Gatsha
 **1989**:3
Campbell, Kim **1993**:4
Cardoso, Fernando Henrique **1996**:4
Castro, Fidel **1991**:4
Ceausescu, Nicolae
 Obituary **1990**:2
Cedras, Raoul **1994**:4
Chaing Kai-Shek, Madame
 Obituary **2005**:1
Chambas, Mohammed ibn **2003**:3
Chen Shui-bian **2001**:2
Chernenko, Konstantin
 Obituary **1985**:1
Chiluba, Frederick **1992**:3
Chissano, Joaquim **1987**:4
Chretien, Jean **1990**:4 **1997**:2
Ciampi, Carlo Azeglio **2004**:3
Collor de Mello, Fernando **1992**:4
Colosio, Luis Donaldo **1994**:3
Copps, Sheila **1986**:4
Cresson, Edith **1992**:1
Cruz, Arturo **1985**:1
Dalai Lama **1989**:1
Deby, Idriss **2002**:2
de Hoop Scheffer, Jaap **2005**:1
de Klerk, F.W. **1990**:1
Delors, Jacques **1990**:2
Deng Xiaoping **1995**:1
 Obituary **1997**:3
de Pinies, Jamie
 Brief Entry **1986**:3

Robinson, Mary **1993**:1
Roh Moo-hyun **2005**:1
Saleh, Ali Abdullah **2001**:3
Salinas, Carlos **1992**:1
Sanchez de Lozada, Gonzalo **2004**:3
Sarkis, Elias
   Obituary **1985**:3
Saro-Wiwa, Ken
   Obituary **1996**:2
Savimbi, Jonas **1986**:2 **1994**:2
Schily, Otto
   Brief Entry **1987**:4
Schroder, Gerhard **1999**:1
Sharon, Ariel **2001**:4
Shipley, Jenny **1998**:3
Silva, Luiz Inacio Lula da **2003**:4
Simpson, Wallis
   Obituary **1986**:3
Sisulu, Walter
   Obituary **2004**:2
Slovo, Joe **1989**:2
Staller, Ilona **1988**:3
Strauss, Robert **1991**:4
Suu Kyi, Aung San **1996**:2
Suzman, Helen **1989**:3
Takeshita, Noboru
   Obituary **2001**:1
Tambo, Oliver **1991**:3
Terzi, Zehdi Labib **1985**:3
Thaksin Shinawatra **2005**:4
Thatcher, Margaret **1989**:2
Trajkovski, Boris
   Obituary **2005**:2
Treurnicht, Andries **1992**:2
Trimble, David **1999**:1
Trudeau, Pierre
   Obituary **2001**:1
Tudjman, Franjo
   Obituary **2000**:2
Tudjman, Franjo **1996**:2
Turabi, Hassan **1995**:4
Uribe, Alvaro **2003**:3
Vajpayee, Atal Behari **1998**:4
Vander Zalm, William **1987**:3
Wahid, Abdurrahman **2000**:3
Walesa, Lech **1991**:2
Wei Jingsheng **1998**:2
Werner, Ruth
   Obituary **2001**:1
Wickramasinghe, Ranil **2003**:2
William, Prince of Wales **2001**:3
Wilson, Bertha
   Brief Entry **1986**:1
Wu Yi **2005**:2
Ye Jianying
   Obituary **1987**:1
Yeltsin, Boris **1991**:1
Zedillo, Ernesto **1995**:1
Zeroual, Liamine **1996**:2
Zhao Ziyang **1989**:1
Zhirinovsky, Vladimir **1994**:2
Zia ul-Haq, Mohammad
   Obituary **1988**:4
Chirac, Jacques **1995**:4

## POLITICS AND GOVERNMENT--U.S.
Abraham, Spencer **1991**:4
Abrams, Elliott **1987**:1
Abzug, Bella **1998**:2
Achtenberg, Roberta **1993**:4
Agnew, Spiro Theodore
   Obituary **1997**:1

Ailes, Roger **1989**:3
Albright, Madeleine **1994**:3
Alexander, Lamar **1991**:2
Alioto, Joseph L.
   Obituary **1998**:3
Allen Jr., Ivan
   Obituary **2004**:3
Alvarez, Aida **1999**:2
Archer, Dennis **1994**:4
Ashcroft, John **2002**:4
Aspin, Les
   Obituary **1996**:1
Atwater, Lee **1989**:4
   Obituary **1991**:4
Babbitt, Bruce **1994**:1
Baker, James A. III **1991**:2
Baldrige, Malcolm
   Obituary **1988**:1
Banks, Dennis J. **1986**:4
Barry, Marion **1991**:1
Barshefsky, Charlene **2000**:4
Beame, Abraham
   Obituary **2001**:4
Begaye, Kelsey **1999**:3
Bennett, William **1990**:1
Benson, Ezra Taft
   Obituary **1994**:4
Bentsen, Lloyd **1993**:3
Berger, Sandy **2000**:1
Berle, Peter A.A.
   Brief Entry **1987**:3
Biden, Joe **1986**:3
Bonner, Robert **2003**:4
Bono, Sonny **1992**:2
   Obituary **1998**:2
Boxer, Barbara **1995**:1
Boyington, Gregory 'Pappy'
   Obituary **1988**:2
Bradley, Bill **2000**:2
Bradley, Tom
   Obituary **1999**:1
Brady, Sarah and James S. **1991**:4
Braun, Carol Moseley **1993**:1
Brazile, Donna **2001**:1
Bremer, L. Paul **2004**:2
Brennan, William
   Obituary **1997**:4
Brown, Edmund G., Sr.
   Obituary **1996**:3
Brown, Jerry **1992**:4
Brown, Ron
   Obituary **1996**:4
Brown, Ron **1990**:3
Brown, Willie **1996**:4
Brown, Willie L. **1985**:2
Browner, Carol M. **1994**:1
Buchanan, Pat **1996**:3
Bundy, McGeorge
   Obituary **1997**:1
Bundy, William P.
   Obituary **2001**:2
Bush, Barbara **1989**:3
Bush, George W., Jr. **1996**:4
Bush, Jeb **2003**:1
Caliguiri, Richard S.
   Obituary **1988**:3
Campbell, Ben Nighthorse **1998**:1
Campbell, Bill **1997**:1
Card, Andrew H., Jr. **2003**:2
Carey, Ron **1993**:3
Carmona, Richard **2003**:2
Carnahan, Jean **2001**:2

Carnahan, Mel
   Obituary **2001**:2
Carter, Billy
   Obituary **1989**:1
Carter, Jimmy **1995**:1
Casey, William
   Obituary **1987**:3
Cavazos, Lauro F. **1989**:2
Chamberlin, Wendy **2002**:4
Chavez, Linda **1999**:3
Chavez-Thompson, Linda **1999**:1
Cheney, Dick **1991**:3
Cheney, Lynne V. **1990**:4
Christopher, Warren **1996**:3
Cisneros, Henry **1987**:2
Clark, J. E.
   Brief Entry **1986**:1
Clinton, Bill **1992**:1
Clinton, Hillary Rodham **1993**:2
Clyburn, James **1999**:4
Cohen, William S. **1998**:1
Collins, Cardiss **1995**:3
Connally, John
   Obituary **1994**:1
Conyers, John, Jr. **1999**:1
Cuomo, Mario **1992**:2
D'Amato, Al **1996**:1
Daschle, Tom **2002**:3
Dean, Howard **2005**:4
DeLay, Tom **2000**:1
Dinkins, David N. **1990**:2
Dolan, Terry **1985**:2
Dole, Bob **1994**:2
Dole, Elizabeth Hanford **1990**:1
Dukakis, Michael **1988**:3
Duke, David **1990**:2
Ehrlichman, John
   Obituary **1999**:3
Elders, Joycelyn **1994**:1
Engler, John **1996**:3
Ervin, Sam
   Obituary **1985**:2
Estrich, Susan **1989**:1
Falkenberg, Nanette **1985**:2
Farmer, James
   Obituary **2000**:1
Farrakhan, Louis **1990**:4
Faubus, Orval
   Obituary **1995**:2
Feinstein, Dianne **1993**:3
Fenwick, Millicent H.
   Obituary **1993**:2
Ferraro, Geraldine **1998**:3
Fish, Hamilton
   Obituary **1991**:3
Fitzgerald, A. Ernest **1986**:2
Fleischer, Ari **2003**:1
Florio, James J. **1991**:2
Flynn, Ray **1989**:1
Foley, Thomas S. **1990**:1
Forbes, Steve **1996**:2
Foster, Vincent
   Obituary **1994**:1
Frank, Anthony M. **1992**:1
Frank, Barney **1989**:2
Franks, Tommy **2004**:1
Frist, Bill **2003**:4
Fulbright, J. William
   Obituary **1995**:3
Galvin, John R. **1990**:1
Garrison, Jim
   Obituary **1993**:2

Suarez, Xavier
  Brief Entry **1986**:2
Sullivan, Louis **1990**:4
Sununu, John **1989**:2
Swift, Jane **2002**:1
Taylor, Maxwell
  Obituary **1987**:3
Tenet, George **2000**:3
Thomas, Clarence **1992**:2
Thomas, Edmond J. **2005**:1
Thomas, Helen **1988**:4
Thompson, Fred **1998**:2
Thurmond, Strom
  Obituary **2004**:3
Tower, John
  Obituary **1991**:4
Townsend, Kathleen Kennedy
  **2001**:3
Tsongas, Paul Efthemios
  Obituary **1997**:2
Tutwiler, Margaret **1992**:4
Tyson, Laura D'Andrea **1994**:1
Udall, Mo
  Obituary **1999**:2
Ventura, Jesse **1999**:2
Violet, Arlene **1985**:3
Wallace, George
  Obituary **1999**:1
Washington, Harold
  Obituary **1988**:1
Waters, Maxine **1998**:4
Watts, J.C. **1999**:2
Webb, Wellington E. **2000**:3
Weicker, Lowell P., Jr. **1993**:1
Wellstone, Paul
  Obituary **2004**:1
Whitman, Christine Todd **1994**:3
Whitmire, Kathy **1988**:2
Wilder, L. Douglas **1990**:3
Williams, Anthony **2000**:4
Williams, G. Mennen
  Obituary **1988**:2
Wilson, Pete **1992**:3
Yard, Molly **1991**:4
Young, Coleman A.
  Obituary **1998**:1
Zech, Lando W.
  Brief Entry **1987**:4
Zerhouni, Elias A. **2004**:3
Zinni, Anthony **2003**:1

**RADIO**
Albert, Marv **1994**:3
Albom, Mitch **1999**:3
Ameche, Don
  Obituary **1994**:2
Autry, Gene
  Obituary **1999**:1
Backus, Jim
  Obituary **1990**:1
Barber, Red
  Obituary **1993**:2
Becker, Brian **2004**:4
Bell, Art **2000**:1
Blanc, Mel
  Obituary **1989**:4
Campbell, Bebe Moore **1996**:2
Caray, Harry **1988**:3
  Obituary **1998**:3
Cherry, Don **1993**:4
Codrescu, Andreá **1997**:3

Cosell, Howard
  Obituary **1995**:4
Costas, Bob **1986**:4
Crenna, Richard
  Obituary **2004**:1
Day, Dennis
  Obituary **1988**:4
Dr. Demento **1986**:1
Donnellan, Nanci **1995**:2
Durrell, Gerald
  Obituary **1995**:3
Edwards, Bob **1993**:2
Fleming, Art
  Obituary **1995**:4
Ford, Tennessee Ernie
  Obituary **1992**:2
Gobel, George
  Obituary **1991**:4
Goodman, Benny
  Obituary **1986**:3
Gordon, Gale
  Obituary **1996**:1
Graham, Billy **1992**:1
Granato, Cammi **1999**:3
Grange, Red
  Obituary **1991**:3
Greene, Lorne
  Obituary **1988**:1
Gross, Terry **1998**:3
Harmon, Tom
  Obituary **1990**:3
Harvey, Paul **1995**:3
Harwell, Ernie **1997**:3
Hill, George Roy
  Obituary **2004**:1
Hope, Bob
  Obituary **2004**:4
Houseman, John
  Obituary **1989**:1
Hughes, Cathy **1999**:1
Imus, Don **1997**:1
Ives, Burl
  Obituary **1995**:4
Kasem, Casey **1987**:1
Keyes, Alan **1996**:2
King, Larry **1993**:1
Kyser, Kay
  Obituary **1985**:3
Leávesque, Reneá
  Obituary **1988**:1
Limbaugh, Rush **1991**:3
Magliozzi, Tom and Ray **1991**:4
Milligan, Spike
  Obituary **2003**:2
Nelson, Harriet
  Obituary **1995**:1
Olson, Johnny
  Obituary **1985**:4
Osgood, Charles **1996**:2
Paar, Jack
  Obituary **2005**:2
Paley, William S.
  Obituary **1991**:2
Parks, Bert
  Obituary **1992**:3
Porter, Sylvia
  Obituary **1991**:4
Quivers, Robin **1995**:4
Raphael, Sally Jessy **1992**:4
Raye, Martha
  Obituary **1995**:1

Reagan, Ronald
  Obituary **2005**:3
Riddle, Nelson
  Obituary **1985**:4
Roberts, Cokie **1993**:4
Saralegui, Cristina **1999**:2
Schlessinger, Laura **1996**:3
Seacrest, Ryan **2004**:4
Sedaris, David **2005**:3
Sevareid, Eric
  Obituary **1993**:1
Shore, Dinah
  Obituary **1994**:3
Smith, Buffalo Bob
  Obituary **1999**:1
Smith, Kate
  Obituary **1986**:3
Stern, Howard **1988**:2 **1993**:3
Swayze, John Cameron
  Obituary **1996**:1
Tom and Ray Magliozzi **1991**:4
Totenberg, Nina **1992**:2
Wolfman Jack
  Obituary **1996**:1
Young, Robert
  Obituary **1999**:1

**RELIGION**
Abernathy, Ralph
  Obituary **1990**:3
Altea, Rosemary **1996**:3
Applewhite, Marshall Herff
  Obituary **1997**:3
Aristide, Jean-Bertrand **1991**:3
Beckett, Wendy (Sister) **1998**:3
Benson, Ezra Taft
  Obituary **1994**:4
Bernardin, Cardinal Joseph **1997**:2
Berri, Nabih **1985**:2
Browning, Edmond
  Brief Entry **1986**:2
Burns, Charles R.
  Brief Entry **1988**:1
Carey, George **1992**:3
Chavis, Benjamin **1993**:4
Chittister, Joan D. **2002**:2
Chopra, Deepak **1996**:3
Clements, George **1985**:1
Cleveland, James
  Obituary **1991**:3
Coffin, William Sloane, Jr. **1990**:3
Cunningham, Reverend William
  Obituary **1997**:4
Curran, Charles E. **1989**:2
Daily, Bishop Thomas V. **1990**:4
Dalai Lama **1989**:1
Dearden, John Cardinal
  Obituary **1988**:4
Dorsey, Thomas A.
  Obituary **1993**:3
Eilberg, Amy
  Brief Entry **1985**:3
Farrakhan, Louis **1990**:4
Fox, Matthew **1992**:2
Fulghum, Robert **1996**:1
Graham, Billy **1992**:1
Grant, Amy **1985**:4
Hahn, Jessica **1989**:4
Harris, Barbara **1996**:3
Harris, Barbara **1989**:3
Healy, Timothy S. **1990**:2

Henry, Carl F.H.
  Obituary **2005**:1
Huffington, Arianna **1996**:2
Hume, Basil Cardinal
  Obituary **2000**:1
Hunter, Howard **1994**:4
Irwin, James
  Obituary **1992**:1
Jackson, Jesse **1996**:1
John Paul II, Pope **1995**:3
Jumblatt, Walid **1987**:4
Kahane, Meir
  Obituary **1991**:2
Khomeini, Ayatollah Ruhollah
  Obituary **1989**:4
Kissling, Frances **1989**:2
Koresh, David
  Obituary **1993**:4
Krol, John
  Obituary **1996**:3
Lefebvre, Marcel **1988**:4
Levinger, Moshe **1992**:1
Mahesh Yogi, Maharishi **1991**:3
Mahony, Roger M. **1988**:2
Maida, Adam Cardinal **1998**:2
Malloy, Edward 'Monk' **1989**:4
McCloskey, James **1993**:1
Mother Teresa **1993**:1
  Obituary **1998**:1
Obando, Miguel **1986**:4
O'Connor, Cardinal John **1990**:3
O'Connor, John
  Obituary **2000**:4
Perry, Harold A.
  Obituary **1992**:1
Peter, Valentine J. **1988**:2
Rafsanjani, Ali Akbar Hashemi
  **1987**:3
Rahman, Sheik Omar Abdel- **1993**:3
Rajneesh, Bhagwan Shree
  Obituary **1990**:2
Reed, Ralph **1995**:1
Reese, Della **1999**:2
Robertson, Pat **1988**:2
Robinson, V. Gene **2004**:4
Rogers, Adrian **1987**:4
Runcie, Robert **1989**:4
  Obituary **2001**:1
Schneerson, Menachem Mendel
  **1992**:4
  Obituary **1994**:4
Scott, Gene
  Brief Entry **1986**:1
Sharpton, Al **1991**:2
Shaw, William **2000**:3
Smith, Jeff **1991**:4
Spong, John **1991**:3 **2001**:1
Stallings, George A., Jr. **1990**:1
Swaggart, Jimmy **1987**:3
Taylor, Graham **2005**:3
Turabi, Hassan **1995**:4
Violet, Arlene **1985**:3
Wildmon, Donald **1988**:4
Williamson, Marianne **1991**:4
Youngblood, Johnny Ray **1994**:1

**SCIENCE**
  Abramson, Lyn **1986**:3
  Adams, Patch **1999**:2
  Adamson, George
    Obituary **1990**:2
  Agatston, Arthur **2005**:1

Allen, John **1992**:1
Altman, Sidney **1997**:2
Atkins, Robert C.
  Obituary **2004**:2
Bakker, Robert T. **1991**:3
Ballard, Robert D. **1998**:4
Barnard, Christiaan
  Obituary **2002**:4
Baulieu, Etienne-Emile **1990**:1
Bayley, Corrine
  Brief Entry **1986**:4
Bean, Alan L. **1986**:2
Beattie, Owen
  Brief Entry **1985**:2
Berkley, Seth **2002**:3
Berle, Peter A.A.
  Brief Entry **1987**:3
Berman, Jennifer and Laura **2003**:2
Bettelheim, Bruno
  Obituary **1990**:3
Blobel, Gunter **2000**:4
Bloch, Erich **1987**:4
Boyer, Herbert Wayne **1985**:1
Bristow, Lonnie **1996**:1
Brown, John Seely **2004**:1
Buck, Linda **2004**:2
Burnison, Chantal Simone **1988**:3
Carlsson, Arvid **2001**:2
Carson, Ben **1998**:2
Cerf, Vinton G. **1999**:2
Chaudhari, Praveen **1989**:4
Chu, Paul C.W. **1988**:2
Coles, Robert **1995**:1
Collins, Eileen **1995**:3
Colwell, Rita Rossi **1999**:3
Comfort, Alex
  Obituary **2000**:4
Conrad, Pete
  Obituary **2000**:1
Cousteau, Jacques-Yves
  Obituary **1998**:2
Cousteau, Jean-Michel **1988**:2
Cram, Donald J.
  Obituary **2002**:2
Cray, Seymour R.
  Brief Entry **1986**:3
  Obituary **1997**:2
Crick, Francis
  Obituary **2005**:4
Davis, Noel **1990**:3
DeVita, Vincent T., Jr. **1987**:3
Diemer, Walter E.
  Obituary **1998**:2
Djerassi, Carl **2000**:4
Douglas, Marjory Stoneman **1993**:1
  Obituary **1998**:4
Downey, Bruce **2003**:1
Duke, Red
  Brief Entry **1987**:1
Durrell, Gerald
  Obituary **1995**:3
Earle, Sylvia **2001**:1
Fang Lizhi **1988**:1
Fano, Ugo
  Obituary **2001**:4
Fauci, Anthony S. **2004**:1
Fields, Evelyn J. **2001**:3
Fiennes, Ranulph **1990**:3
Fisher, Mel **1985**:4
Fossey, Dian
  Obituary **1986**:1

Foster, Tabatha
  Obituary **1988**:3
Fraser, Claire M. **2005**:2
Futter, Ellen V. **1995**:1
Gale, Robert Peter **1986**:4
Gallo, Robert **1991**:1
Garneau, Marc **1985**:1
Geller, Margaret Joan **1998**:2
Gerba, Charles **1999**:4
Gerberding, Julie **2004**:1
Gilbert, Walter **1988**:3
Gilruth, Robert
  Obituary **2001**:1
Glenn, John **1998**:3
Gold, Thomas
  Obituary **2005**:3
Goldman-Rakic, Patricia **2002**:4
Goodall, Jane **1991**:1
Gould, Gordon **1987**:1
Gould, Stephen Jay
  Obituary **2003**:3
Greene, Brian **2003**:4
Hagelstein, Peter
  Brief Entry **1986**:3
Hair, Jay D. **1994**:3
Hale, Alan **1997**:3
Hammond, E. Cuyler
  Obituary **1987**:1
Haseltine, William A. **1999**:2
Hatem, George
  Obituary **1989**:1
Hawking, Stephen W. **1990**:1
Healy, Bernadine **1993**:1
Ho, David **1997**:2
Horner, Jack **1985**:2
Horowitz, Paul **1988**:2
Hounsfield, Godfrey **1989**:2
Hoyle, Sir Fred
  Obituary **2002**:4
Irwin, James
  Obituary **1992**:1
Jacobs, Joe **1994**:1
Janzen, Daniel H. **1988**:4
Jarvik, Robert K. **1985**:1
Jemison, Mae C. **1993**:1
Jorgensen, Christine
  Obituary **1989**:4
Kandel, Eric **2005**:2
Keith, Louis **1988**:2
Kessler, David **1992**:1
Kevorkian, Jack **1991**:3
King, Mary-Claire **1998**:3
Klass, Perri **1993**:2
Koop, C. Everett **1989**:3
Kopits, Steven E.
  Brief Entry **1987**:1
Kornberg, Arthur **1992**:1
Krim, Mathilde **1989**:2
Kubler-Ross, Elisabeth
  Obituary **2005**:4
Kwoh, Yik San **1988**:2
Laing, R.D.
  Obituary **1990**:1
Langer, Robert **2003**:4
Langston, J. William
  Brief Entry **1986**:2
Lanza, Robert **2004**:3
Leakey, Mary Douglas
  Obituary **1997**:2
Leakey, Richard **1994**:2
Lederman, Leon Max **1989**:4
LeVay, Simon **1992**:2

Levine, Arnold **2002**:3
Lewis, Edward B.
  Obituary **2005**:4
Lilly, John C.
  Obituary **2002**:4
Lorenz, Konrad
  Obituary **1989**:3
Love, Susan **1995**:2
Lovley, Derek **2005**:3
Lucid, Shannon **1997**:1
Maglich, Bogdan C. **1990**:1
Marsden, Brian **2004**:4
Masters, William H.
  Obituary **2001**:4
McIntyre, Richard
  Brief Entry **1986**:2
Menninger, Karl
  Obituary **1991**:1
Minsky, Marvin **1994**:3
Montagu, Ashley
  Obituary **2000**:2
Morgentaler, Henry **1986**:3
Moss, Cynthia **1995**:2
Mullis, Kary **1995**:3
Ngau, Harrison **1991**:3
Nielsen, Jerri **2001**:3
Novello, Antonia **1991**:2
Nuesslein-Volhard, Christiane **1998**:1
Nye, Bill **1997**:2
O'Keefe, Sean **2005**:2
Ornish, Dean **2004**:2
Owens, Delia and Mark **1993**:3
Patton, John **2004**:4
Pauling, Linus
  Obituary **1995**:1
Penrose, Roger **1991**:4
Perutz, Max
  Obituary **2003**:2
Peterson, Roger Tory
  Obituary **1997**:1
Pinker, Steven A. **2000**:1
Plotkin, Mark **1994**:3
Pople, John
  Obituary **2005**:2
Porco, Carolyn **2005**:4
Porter, George
  Obituary **2003**:4
Pough, Richard Hooper **1989**:1
Profet, Margie **1994**:4
Prusiner, Stanley **1998**:2
Quill, Timothy E. **1997**:3
Radecki, Thomas
  Brief Entry **1986**:2
Redenbacher, Orville
  Obituary **1996**:1
Redig, Patrick **1985**:3
Richter, Charles Francis
  Obituary **1985**:4
Rifkin, Jeremy **1990**:3
Rizzoli, Paola **2004**:3
Rock, John
  Obituary **1985**:1
Rosenberg, Steven **1989**:1
Rosendahl, Bruce R.
  Brief Entry **1986**:4
Rosgen, Dave **2005**:2
Sabin, Albert
  Obituary **1993**:4
Sacks, Oliver **1995**:4
Sagan, Carl
  Obituary **1997**:2

Sakharov, Andrei Dmitrievich
  Obituary **1990**:2
Salk, Jonas **1994**:4
  Obituary **1995**:4
Schank, Roger **1989**:2
Schenk, Dale **2002**:2
Schroeder, William J.
  Obituary **1986**:4
Schultes, Richard Evans
  Obituary **2002**:1
Sears, Barry **2004**:2
Shepard, Alan
  Obituary **1999**:1
Shimomura, Tsutomu **1996**:1
Shirley, Donna **1999**:1
Sidransky, David **2002**:4
Singer, Margaret Thaler
  Obituary **2005**:1
Skinner, B.F.
  Obituary **1991**:1
Smoot, George F. **1993**:3
Soren, David
  Brief Entry **1986**:3
Spelke, Elizabeth **2003**:1
Spergel, David **2004**:1
Spock, Benjamin **1995**:2
  Obituary **1998**:3
Steger, Will **1990**:4
Steptoe, Patrick
  Obituary **1988**:3
Sullivan, Louis **1990**:4
Szent-Gyoergyi, Albert
  Obituary **1987**:2
Thom, Rene
  Obituary **2004**:1
Thompson, Lonnie **2003**:3
Thompson, Starley
  Brief Entry **1987**:3
Thomson, James **2002**:3
Toone, Bill
  Brief Entry **1987**:2
Tully, Tim **2004**:3
Vagelos, P. Roy **1989**:4
Venter, J. Craig **2001**:1
Vickrey, William S.
  Obituary **1997**:2
Vitetta, Ellen S. **2005**:4
Waddell, Thomas F.
  Obituary **1988**:2
Weil, Andrew **1997**:4
Wexler, Nancy S. **1992**:3
Whipple, Fred L.
  Obituary **2005**:4
Whitson, Peggy **2003**:3
Wigand, Jeffrey **2000**:4
Wigler, Michael
  Brief Entry **1985**:1
Wiles, Andrew **1994**:1
Wilmut, Ian **1997**:3
Wilson, Edward O. **1994**:4
Woodwell, George S. **1987**:2
Yeager, Chuck **1998**:1
Yen, Samuel **1996**:4
Zech, Lando W.
  Brief Entry **1987**:4

## SOCIAL ISSUES
Abbey, Edward
  Obituary **1989**:3
Abernathy, Ralph
  Obituary **1990**:3
Ali, Muhammad **1997**:2

Allred, Gloria **1985**:2
Amory, Cleveland
  Obituary **1999**:2
Anastas, Robert
  Brief Entry **1985**:2
Andrews, Lori B. **2005**:3
Arbour, Louise **2005**:1
Aristide, Jean-Bertrand **1991**:3
Baez, Joan **1998**:3
Baird, Bill
  Brief Entry **1987**:2
Baldwin, James
  Obituary **1988**:2
Ball, Edward **1999**:2
Banks, Dennis J. **1986**:4
Bayley, Corrine
  Brief Entry **1986**:4
Beal, Deron **2005**:3
Bellamy, Carol **2001**:2
Ben & Jerry **1991**:3
Bergalis, Kimberly
  Obituary **1992**:3
Berresford, Susan V. **1998**:4
Biehl, Amy
  Obituary **1994**:1
Blackburn, Molly
  Obituary **1985**:4
Block, Herbert
  Obituary **2002**:4
Bly, Robert **1992**:4
Bradshaw, John **1992**:1
Brady, Sarah and James S. **1991**:4
Bravo, Ellen **1998**:2
Breathed, Berkeley **2005**:3
Bristow, Lonnie **1996**:1
Brockovich-Ellis, Erin **2003**:3
Brooks, Gwendolyn **1998**:1
  Obituary **2001**:2
Brower, David **1990**:4
Brown, Jim **1993**:2
Brown, Judie **1986**:2
Burk, Martha **2004**:1
Bush, Barbara **1989**:3
Cammermeyer, Margarethe **1995**:2
Caplan, Arthur L. **2000**:2
Caras, Roger
  Obituary **2002**:1
Carter, Amy **1987**:4
Carter, Rubin **2000**:3
Chavez, Cesar
  Obituary **1993**:4
Chavez-Thompson, Linda **1999**:1
Chavis, Benjamin **1993**:4
Cleaver, Eldridge
  Obituary **1998**:4
Clements, George **1985**:1
Clinton, Hillary Rodham **1993**:2
Coffin, William Sloane, Jr. **1990**:3
Cole, Johnetta B. **1994**:3
Coles, Robert **1995**:1
Connerly, Ward **2000**:2
Coors, William K.
  Brief Entry **1985**:1
Corwin, Jeff **2005**:1
Cozza, Stephen **2001**:1
Crisp, Quentin
  Obituary **2000**:3
Cruzan, Nancy
  Obituary **1991**:3
Davis, Angela **1998**:3
Dees, Morris **1992**:1

Sidney, Ivan
  Brief Entry **1987**:2
Sinclair, Mary **1985**:2
Singer, Margaret Thaler
  Obituary **2005**:1
Slotnick, Barry
  Brief Entry **1987**:4
Slovo, Joe **1989**:2
Smith, Samantha
  Obituary **1985**:3
Snyder, Mitch
  Obituary **1991**:1
Spong, John **1991**:3 **2001**:1
Steele, Shelby **1991**:2
Steinem, Gloria **1996**:2
Steptoe, Patrick
  Obituary **1988**:3
Stevens, Eileen **1987**:3
Stevens, James
  Brief Entry **1988**:1
Strong, Maurice **1993**:1
Strummer, Joe
  Obituary **2004**:1
Sullivan, Leon
  Obituary **2002**:2
Sullivan, Louis **1990**:4
Summers, Anne **1990**:2
Suu Kyi, Aung San **1996**:2
Sweeney, John J. **2000**:3
Szent-Gyoergyi, Albert
  Obituary **1987**:2
Tafel, Richard **2000**:4
Tambo, Oliver **1991**:3
Tannen, Deborah **1995**:1
Terry, Randall **1991**:4
Thomas, Clarence **1992**:2
Ture, Kwame
  Obituary **1999**:2
Unz, Ron **1999**:1
Verdi-Fletcher, Mary **1998**:2
Vitousek, Peter **2003**:1
Waddell, Thomas F.
  Obituary **1988**:2
Wattleton, Faye **1989**:1
Wei Jingsheng **1998**:2
Wells, Sharlene
  Brief Entry **1985**:1
West, Cornel **1994**:2
White, Ryan
  Obituary **1990**:3
Whitestone, Heather **1995**:1
Wigand, Jeffrey **2000**:4
Wildmon, Donald **1988**:4
Williams, Hosea
  Obituary **2001**:2
Williamson, Marianne **1991**:4
Willson, S. Brian **1989**:3
Wilmut, Ian **1997**:3
Wilson, William Julius **1997**:1
Wolf, Naomi **1994**:3
Woodruff, Robert Winship
  Obituary **1985**:1
Wu, Harry **1996**:1
Yard, Molly **1991**:4
Yokich, Stephen P. **1995**:4
Youngblood, Johnny Ray **1994**:1
Zamora, Pedro
  Obituary **1995**:2
Zech, Lando W.
  Brief Entry **1987**:4
Zigler, Edward **1994**:1

## SPORTS

Abbott, Jim **1988**:3
Abercrombie, Josephine **1987**:2
Adu, Freddy **2005**:3
Agassi, Andre **1990**:2
Agee, Tommie
  Obituary **2001**:4
Aikman, Troy **1994**:2
Ainge, Danny **1987**:1
Akers, Michelle **1996**:1
Albert, Marv **1994**:3
Albom, Mitch **1999**:3
Ali, Laila **2001**:2
Ali, Muhammad **1997**:2
Allen, Mel
  Obituary **1996**:4
Allen, Ray **2002**:1
Alter, Hobie
  Brief Entry **1985**:1
Angelos, Peter **1995**:4
Anthony, Earl
  Obituary **2002**:3
Aoki, Rocky **1990**:2
Armstrong, Henry
  Obituary **1989**:1
Armstrong, Lance **2000**:1
Ashe, Arthur
  Obituary **1993**:3
Austin, 'Stone Cold' Steve **2001**:3
Axthelm, Pete
  Obituary **1991**:3
Azinger, Paul **1995**:2
Babilonia, Tai **1997**:2
Baiul, Oksana **1995**:3
Baker, Kathy
  Brief Entry **1986**:1
Barkley, Charles **1988**:2
Barnes, Ernie **1997**:4
Baumgartner, Bruce
  Brief Entry **1987**:3
Becker, Boris
  Brief Entry **1985**:3
Beckham, David **2003**:1
Bell, Ricky
  Obituary **1985**:1
Belle, Albert **1996**:4
Benoit, Joan **1986**:3
Bias, Len
  Obituary **1986**:3
Bird, Larry **1990**:3
Blair, Bonnie **1992**:3
Bledsoe, Drew **1995**:1
Boggs, Wade **1989**:3
Boitano, Brian **1988**:3
Bonds, Barry **1993**:3
Bonilla, Bobby **1992**:2
Bosworth, Brian **1989**:1
Boudreau, Louis
  Obituary **2002**:3
Bourque, Raymond Jean **1997**:3
Bowe, Riddick **1993**:2
Bowman, Scotty **1998**:4
Bradman, Sir Donald
  Obituary **2002**:1
Brady, Tom **2002**:4
Bremen, Barry **1987**:3
Brown, Jim **1993**:2
Brown, Paul
  Obituary **1992**:1
Bryant, Kobe **1998**:3
Busch, August Anheuser, Jr.
  Obituary **1990**:2

Buss, Jerry **1989**:3
Butcher, Susan **1991**:1
Callaway, Ely
  Obituary **2002**:3
Campanella, Roy
  Obituary **1994**:1
Canseco, Jose **1990**:2
Capriati, Jennifer **1991**:1
Caray, Harry **1988**:3
  Obituary **1998**:3
Carter, Gary **1987**:1
Carter, Joe **1994**:2
Carter, Rubin **2000**:3
Carter, Vince **2001**:4
Chamberlain, Wilt
  Obituary **2000**:2
Chaney, John **1989**:1
Chastain, Brandi **2001**:3
Chen, T.C.
  Brief Entry **1987**:3
Cherry, Don **1993**:4
Chyna **2001**:4
Clemens, Roger **1991**:4
Coffey, Paul **1985**:4
Collins, Kerry **2002**:3
Conigliaro, Tony
  Obituary **1990**:3
Conner, Dennis **1987**:2
Cooper, Cynthia **1999**:1
Copeland, Al **1988**:3
Cosell, Howard
  Obituary **1995**:4
Costas, Bob **1986**:4
Couples, Fred **1994**:4
Courier, Jim **1993**:2
Cunningham, Randall **1990**:1
Curren, Tommy
  Brief Entry **1987**:4
Curtis, Ben **2004**:2
Damon, Johnny **2005**:4
Danza, Tony **1989**:1
Davenport, Lindsay **1999**:2
Davis, Eric **1987**:4
Davis, Terrell **1998**:2
Day, Pat **1995**:2
DeBartolo, Edward J., Jr. **1989**:3
De La Hoya, Oscar **1998**:2
Desormeaux, Kent **1990**:2
DiBello, Paul
  Brief Entry **1986**:4
DiMaggio, Joe
  Obituary **1999**:3
Dolan, Tom **2001**:2
Donnellan, Nanci **1995**:2
Doubleday, Nelson, Jr. **1987**:1
Douglas, Buster **1990**:4
Dravecky, Dave **1992**:1
Drexler, Clyde **1992**:4
Drysdale, Don
  Obituary **1994**:1
Duncan, Tim **2000**:1
Durocher, Leo
  Obituary **1992**:2
Duval, David **2000**:3
Duvall, Camille
  Brief Entry **1988**:1
Dykstra, Lenny **1993**:4
Eagleson, Alan **1987**:4
Earnhardt, Dale
  Obituary **2001**:4
Earnhardt, Dale, Jr. **2004**:4

Ederle, Gertrude
  Obituary **2005**:1
Edwards, Harry **1989**:4
Elway, John **1990**:3
Epstein, Theo **2003**:4
Esiason, Boomer **1991**:1
Evans, Janet **1989**:1
Ewing, Patrick **1985**:3
Faldo, Nick **1993**:3
Favre, Brett Lorenzo **1997**:2
Federer, Roger **2004**:2
Federov, Sergei **1995**:1
Fehr, Donald **1987**:2
Ferrari, Enzo **1988**:4
Fielder, Cecil **1993**:2
Fiennes, Ranulph **1990**:3
Firestone, Roy **1988**:2
Fittipaldi, Emerson **1994**:2
Flood, Curt
  Obituary **1997**:2
Flutie, Doug **1999**:2
Foreman, George **2004**:2
Foss, Joe **1990**:3
Freeman, Cathy **2001**:3
Fuhr, Grant **1997**:3
Furyk, Jim **2004**:2
Galindo, Rudy **2001**:2
Garcia, Joe
  Brief Entry **1986**:4
Gardner, Randy **1997**:2
Garnett, Kevin **2000**:3
Gathers, Hank
  Obituary **1990**:3
Gault, Willie **1991**:2
Gerulaitis, Vitas
  Obituary **1995**:1
Giamatti, A. Bartlett **1988**:4
  Obituary **1990**:1
Gibson, Althea
  Obituary **2004**:4
Gibson, Kirk **1985**:2
Giguere, Jean-Sebastien **2004**:2
Gilmour, Doug **1994**:3
Glaus, Troy **2003**:3
Gomez, 'Lefty'
  Obituary **1989**:3
Gooden, Dwight **1985**:2
Gordeeva, Ekaterina **1996**:4
Gordon, Jeff **1996**:1
Graf, Steffi **1987**:4
Granato, Cammi **1999**:3
Grange, Red
  Obituary **1991**:3
Graziano, Rocky
  Obituary **1990**:4
Greenberg, Hank
  Obituary **1986**:4
Gretzky, Wayne **1989**:2
Griffey, Ken Jr. **1994**:1
Grinkov, Sergei
  Obituary **1996**:2
Gruden, Jon **2003**:4
Gumbel, Greg **1996**:4
Gwynn, Tony **1995**:1
Hagler, Marvelous Marvin **1985**:2
Hamilton, Scott **1998**:2
Hamm, Mia **2000**:1
Hamm, Paul **2005**:1
Hanauer, Chip **1986**:2
Hardaway, Anfernee **1996**:2
Harkes, John **1996**:4

Harmon, Tom
  Obituary **1990**:3
Harwell, Ernie **1997**:3
Hasek, Dominik **1998**:3
Hawk, Tony **2001**:4
Hayes, Woody
  Obituary **1987**:2
Helton, Todd **2001**:1
Hempleman-Adams, David **2004**:3
Henderson, Rickey **2002**:3
Henin-Hardenne, Justine **2004**:4
Hernandez, Willie **1985**:1
Hershiser, Orel **1989**:2
Hewitt, Lleyton **2002**:2
Hextall, Ron **1988**:2
Hill, Grant **1995**:3
Hill, Lynn **1991**:2
Hingis, Martina **1999**:1
Hogan, Ben
  Obituary **1997**:4
Hogan, Hulk **1987**:3
Holtz, Lou **1986**:4
Holyfield, Evander **1991**:3
Howard, Desmond Kevin **1997**:2
Howser, Dick
  Obituary **1987**:4
Hughes, Sarah **2002**:4
Hull, Brett **1991**:4
Hunter, Catfish
  Obituary **2000**:1
Indurain, Miguel **1994**:1
Inkster, Juli **2000**:2
Irvin, Michael **1996**:3
Irwin, Hale **2005**:2
Ivanisevic, Goran **2002**:1
Iverson, Allen **2001**:4
Jackson, Bo **1986**:3
Jackson, Phil **1996**:3
Jagr, Jaromir **1995**:4
Jenkins, Sally **1997**:2
Jeter, Derek **1999**:4
Johnson, Earvin 'Magic' **1988**:4
Johnson, Jimmy **1993**:3
Johnson, Kevin **1991**:1
Johnson, Keyshawn **2000**:4
Johnson, Larry **1993**:3
Johnson, Michael **2000**:1
Johnson, Randy **1996**:2
Jones, Jerry **1994**:4
Jones, Marion **1998**:4
Jordan, Michael **1987**:2
Joyner, Florence Griffith **1989**:2
  Obituary **1999**:1
Joyner-Kersee, Jackie **1993**:1
Kallen, Jackie **1994**:1
Kanokogi, Rusty
  Brief Entry **1987**:1
Kasparov, Garry **1997**:4
Kelly, Jim **1991**:4
Kemp, Jack **1990**:4
Kemp, Jan **1987**:2
Kemp, Shawn **1995**:1
Kerrigan, Nancy **1994**:3
Kidd, Jason **2003**:2
King, Don **1989**:1
Kiraly, Karch
  Brief Entry **1987**:1
Kite, Tom **1990**:3
Klima, Petr **1987**:1
Knievel, Robbie **1990**:1
Knight, Bobby **1985**:3
Koch, Bill **1992**:3

Konstantinov, Vladimir **1997**:4
Kournikova, Anna **2000**:3
Kroc, Ray
  Obituary **1985**:1
Krone, Julie **1989**:2
Kruk, John **1994**:4
Krzyzewski, Mike **1993**:2
Kukoc, Toni **1995**:4
Laettner, Christian **1993**:1
LaFontaine, Pat **1985**:1
Laimbeer, Bill **2004**:3
Lalas, Alexi **1995**:1
Landry, Tom
  Obituary **2000**:3
Lemieux, Claude **1996**:1
Lemieux, Mario **1986**:4
LeMond, Greg **1986**:4
Leonard, Sugar Ray **1989**:4
Leslie, Lisa **1997**:4
Lewis, Lennox **2000**:2
Lewis, Ray **2001**:3
Lewis, Reggie
  Obituary **1994**:1
Leyland, Jim **1998**:2
Lindbergh, Pelle
  Obituary **1985**:4
Lindros, Eric **1992**:1
Lipinski, Tara **1998**:3
Lofton, Kenny **1998**:1
Lopez, Nancy **1989**:3
Louganis, Greg **1995**:3
Lowell, Mike **2003**:2
Lukas, D. Wayne **1986**:2
MacArthur, Ellen **2005**:3
Madden, John **1995**:1
Maddux, Greg **1996**:2
Majerle, Dan **1993**:4
Malone, Karl **1990**:1 **1997**:3
Mantle, Mickey
  Obituary **1996**:1
Maradona, Diego **1991**:3
Maravich, Pete
  Obituary **1988**:2
Maris, Roger
  Obituary **1986**:1
Martin, Billy **1988**:4
  Obituary **1990**:2
Martin, Casey **2002**:1
Mathis, Clint **2003**:1
Mattingly, Don **1986**:2
Matuszak, John
  Obituary **1989**:4
McCarron, Chris **1995**:4
McCartney, Bill **1995**:3
McGraw, Tug
  Obituary **2005**:1
McGwire, Mark **1999**:1
McMahon, Jim **1985**:4
McMahon, Vince, Jr. **1985**:4
Messier, Mark **1993**:1
Mickelson, Phil **2004**:4
Milbrett, Tiffeny **2001**:1
Milburn, Rodney Jr.
  Obituary **1998**:2
Miller, Andre **2003**:3
Miller, Bode **2002**:4
Miller, Reggie **1994**:4
Minnesota Fats
  Obituary **1996**:3
Monaghan, Tom **1985**:1
Monk, Art **1993**:2
Montana, Joe **1989**:2

Bloom, Orlando **2004**:2

Bochco, Steven **1989**:1

Bolger, Ray
  Obituary **1987**:2

Bonet, Lisa **1989**:2

Bono, Sonny **1992**:2
  Obituary **1998**:2

Booth, Shirley
  Obituary **1993**:2

Boyle, Lara Flynn **2003**:4

Boyle, Peter **2002**:3

Bradshaw, John **1992**:1

Braff, Zach **2005**:2

Brandy **1996**:4

Brenneman, Amy **2002**:1

Bridges, Lloyd
  Obituary **1998**:3

Brinkley, David
  Obituary **2004**:3

Brokaw, Tom **2000**:3

Bronson, Charles
  Obituary **2004**:4

Brooks, Mel **2003**:1

Brosnan, Pierce **2000**:3

Brown, Les **1994**:3

Buckley, Betty **1996**:2

Bullock, Sandra **1995**:4

Burnett, Carol **2000**:3

Burnett, Mark **2003**:1

Burns, George
  Obituary **1996**:3

Burns, Ken **1995**:2

Burr, Raymond
  Obituary **1994**:1

Burrows, James **2005**:3

Butler, Brett **1995**:1

Bynes, Amanda **2005**:1

Caan, James **2004**:4

Caine, Michael **2000**:4

Calhoun, Rory
  Obituary **1999**:4

Campbell, Neve **1998**:2

Campion, Jane **1991**:4

Candy, John **1988**:2
  Obituary **1994**:3

Carey, Drew **1997**:4

Carlin, George **1996**:3

Carney, Art
  Obituary **2005**:1

Carrey, Jim **1995**:1

Carson, Lisa Nicole **1999**:3

Carter, Chris **2000**:1

Carter, Nell
  Obituary **2004**:2

Caruso, David **1994**:3

Carvey, Dana **1994**:1

Cassavetes, John
  Obituary **1989**:2

Cattrall, Kim **2003**:3

Caulfield, Joan
  Obituary **1992**:1

Cavanagh, Tom **2003**:1

Caviezel, Jim **2005**:3

Chancellor, John
  Obituary **1997**:1

Channing, Stockard **1991**:3

Chappelle, Dave **2005**:3

Chase, Chevy **1990**:1

Chavez, Linda **1999**:3

Cher **1993**:1

Cherry, Don **1993**:4

Chiklis, Michael **2003**:3

Child, Julia **1999**:4

Cho, Margaret **1995**:2

Chow Yun-fat **1999**:4

Christensen, Hayden **2003**:3

Chung, Connie **1988**:4

Clarkson, Kelly **2003**:3

Clarkson, Patricia **2005**:3

Clay, Andrew Dice **1991**:1

Cleese, John **1989**:2

Clooney, George **1996**:4

Close, Glenn **1988**:3

Coca, Imogene
  Obituary **2002**:2

Coco, James
  Obituary **1987**:2

Colasanto, Nicholas
  Obituary **1985**:2

Coleman, Dabney **1988**:3

Connery, Sean **1990**:4

Convy, Bert
  Obituary **1992**:1

Cook, Peter
  Obituary **1995**:2

Cooke, Alistair
  Obituary **2005**:3

Cooper, Chris **2004**:1

Copperfield, David **1986**:3

Coppola, Francis Ford **1989**:4

Corbett, John **2004**:1

Corwin, Jeff **2005**:1

Cosby, Bill **1999**:2

Cosell, Howard
  Obituary **1995**:4

Costas, Bob **1986**:4

Couric, Katherine **1991**:4

Cousteau, Jacques-Yves
  Obituary **1998**:2

Cowell, Simon **2003**:4

Cox, Courteney **1996**:2

Cox, Richard Joseph
  Brief Entry **1985**:1

Crawford, Broderick
  Obituary **1986**:3

Crawford, Cindy **1993**:3

Crawford, Michael **1994**:2

Crenna, Richard
  Obituary **2004**:1

Crichton, Michael **1995**:3

Cronkite, Walter Leland **1997**:3

Crothers, Scatman
  Obituary **1987**:1

Crystal, Billy **1985**:3

Curry, Ann **2001**:1

Curtis, Jamie Lee **1995**:1

Cushing, Peter
  Obituary **1995**:1

Dalton, Timothy **1988**:4

Daly, Carson **2002**:4

Damon, Matt **1999**:1

Danes, Claire **1999**:4

Daniels, Faith **1993**:3

Daniels, Jeff **1989**:4

Danza, Tony **1989**:1

David, Larry **2003**:4

Davis, Bette
  Obituary **1990**:1

Davis, Geena **1992**:1

Davis, Paige **2004**:2

Davis, Sammy, Jr.
  Obituary **1990**:4

Day, Dennis
  Obituary **1988**:4

De Cordova, Frederick **1985**:2

DeGeneres, Ellen **1995**:3

De Matteo, Drea **2005**:2

Depardieu, Gerard **1991**:2

Depp, Johnny **1991**:3

De Vito, Danny **1987**:1

Dewhurst, Colleen
  Obituary **1992**:2

Diamond, Selma
  Obituary **1985**:2

DiCaprio, Leonardo Wilhelm **1997**:2

Dickerson, Nancy H.
  Obituary **1998**:2

Dickinson, Janice **2005**:2

Diller, Barry **1991**:1

Disney, Roy E. **1986**:3

Doherty, Shannen **1994**:2

Dolenz, Micky **1986**:4

Douglas, Michael **1986**:2

Downey, Morton, Jr. **1988**:4

Drescher, Fran **1995**:3

Duchovny, David **1998**:3

Duff, Hilary **2004**:4

Duffy, Karen **1998**:1

Dukakis, Olympia **1996**:4

Duke, Red
  Brief Entry **1987**:1

Durrell, Gerald
  Obituary **1995**:3

Duvall, Robert **1999**:3

Eastwood, Clint **1993**:3

Ebert, Roger **1998**:3

Ebsen, Buddy
  Obituary **2004**:3

Eisner, Michael **1989**:2

Elfman, Jenna **1999**:4

Ellerbee, Linda **1993**:3

Elliott, Denholm
  Obituary **1993**:2

Engstrom, Elmer W.
  Obituary **1985**:2

Evans, Dale
  Obituary **2001**:3

Eve **2004**:3

Fallon, Jimmy **2003**:1

Fanning, Dakota **2005**:2

Farley, Chris
  Obituary **1998**:2

Fawcett, Farrah **1998**:4

Feldshuh, Tovah **2005**:3

Fell, Norman
  Obituary **1999**:2

Ferguson, Craig **2005**:4

Ferrell, Will **2004**:4

Ferrer, Jose
  Obituary **1992**:3

Fey, Tina **2005**:3

Field, Sally **1995**:3

Finney, Albert **2003**:3

Firestone, Roy **1988**:2

Fishburne, Laurence **1995**:3

Fisher, Carrie **1991**:1

Flanders, Ed
  Obituary **1995**:3

Fleiss, Mike **2003**:4

Fleming, Art
  Obituary **1995**:4

Flockhart, Calista **1998**:4

Fonda, Bridget **1995**:1

Ford, Faith **2005**:3

Ford, Tennessee Ernie
  Obituary **1992**:2

Ward, Sela **2001**:3
Washington, Denzel **1993**:2
Wasserman, Lew
  Obituary **2003**:3
Wayans, Damon **1998**:4
Wayans, Keenen Ivory **1991**:1
Wayne, David
  Obituary **1995**:3
Weitz, Bruce **1985**:4
Whitaker, Forest **1996**:2
White, Jaleel **1992**:3
Whittle, Christopher **1989**:3
Wilkinson, Tom **2003**:2
Williams, Robin **1988**:4
Williams, Treat **2004**:3
Williams, Vanessa L. **1999**:2
Willis, Bruce **1986**:4
Wilson, Flip
  Obituary **1999**:2
Winfield, Paul
  Obituary **2005**:2
Winfrey, Oprah **1986**:4 **1997**:3
Winger, Debra **1994**:3
Winokur, Marissa Jaret **2005**:1
Wolfman Jack
  Obituary **1996**:1
Wong, B.D. **1998**:1
Woods, James **1988**:3
Wright, Steven **1986**:3
Wyle, Noah **1997**:3
Wynn, Keenan
  Obituary **1987**:1
Xuxa **1994**:2
Xzibit **2005**:4
Yetnikoff, Walter **1988**:1
York, Dick
  Obituary **1992**:4
Young, Robert
  Obituary **1999**:1
Youngman, Henny
  Obituary **1998**:3
Zahn, Paula **1992**:3
Zamora, Pedro
  Obituary **1995**:2
Zeta-Jones, Catherine **1999**:4
Zucker, Jeff **1993**:3

**THEATER**
Abbott, George
  Obituary **1995**:3
Adjani, Isabelle **1991**:1
Albee, Edward **1997**:1
Alda, Robert
  Obituary **1986**:3
Alexander, Jane **1994**:2
Alexander, Jason **1993**:3
Allen, Joan **1998**:1
Allen, Peter
  Obituary **1993**:1
Ameche, Don
  Obituary **1994**:2
Andrews, Julie **1996**:1
Angelou, Maya **1993**:4
Arden, Eve
  Obituary **1991**:2
Ashcroft, Peggy
  Obituary **1992**:1
Atkinson, Rowan **2004**:3
Aykroyd, Dan **1989**:3 **1997**:3
Bacall, Lauren **1997**:3
Bacon, Kevin **1995**:3

Baddeley, Hermione
  Obituary **1986**:4
Bailey, Pearl
  Obituary **1991**:1
Ball, Alan **2005**:1
Barkin, Ellen **1987**:3
Barry, Lynda **1992**:1
Bassett, Angela **1994**:4
Bates, Alan
  Obituary **2005**:1
Bates, Kathy **1991**:4
Becker, Brian **2004**:4
Beckett, Samuel Barclay
  Obituary **1990**:2
Belushi, Jim **1986**:2
Bening, Annette **1992**:1
Bennett, Joan
  Obituary **1991**:2
Bennett, Michael
  Obituary **1988**:1
Bernardi, Herschel
  Obituary **1986**:4
Bernhard, Sandra **1989**:4
Bernstein, Leonard
  Obituary **1991**:1
Bishop, Andre **2000**:1
Blackstone, Harry Jr.
  Obituary **1997**:4
Blanchett, Cate **1999**:3
Bloch, Ivan **1986**:3
Bloom, Orlando **2004**:2
Bogosian, Eric **1990**:4
Bolger, Ray
  Obituary **1987**:2
Bonham Carter, Helena **1998**:4
Booth, Shirley
  Obituary **1993**:2
Bowie, David **1998**:2
Branagh, Kenneth **1992**:2
Brandauer, Klaus Maria **1987**:3
Brando, Marlon
  Obituary **2005**:3
Brooks, Mel **2003**:1
Brynner, Yul
  Obituary **1985**:4
Buckley, Betty **1996**:2
Bullock, Sandra **1995**:4
Burck, Wade
  Brief Entry **1986**:1
Burr, Raymond
  Obituary **1994**:1
Busch, Charles **1998**:3
Byrne, Gabriel **1997**:4
Caan, James **2004**:4
Caesar, Adolph
  Obituary **1986**:3
Cagney, James
  Obituary **1986**:2
Caine, Michael **2000**:4
Candy, John **1988**:2
  Obituary **1994**:3
Carney, Art
  Obituary **2005**:1
Carrey, Jim **1995**:1
Carson, Lisa Nicole **1999**:3
Carter, Nell
  Obituary **2004**:2
Cassavetes, John
  Obituary **1989**:2
Caulfield, Joan
  Obituary **1992**:1
Cavanagh, Tom **2003**:1

Caviezel, Jim **2005**:3
Channing, Stockard **1991**:3
Clarkson, Patricia **2005**:3
Close, Glenn **1988**:3
Coco, James
  Obituary **1987**:2
Connery, Sean **1990**:4
Convy, Bert
  Obituary **1992**:1
Cook, Peter
  Obituary **1995**:2
Cooper, Chris **2004**:1
Coppola, Carmine
  Obituary **1991**:4
Costner, Kevin **1989**:4
Crawford, Broderick
  Obituary **1986**:3
Crawford, Cheryl
  Obituary **1987**:1
Crawford, Michael **1994**:2
Crisp, Quentin
  Obituary **2000**:3
Cronyn, Hume
  Obituary **2004**:3
Cruz, Nilo **2004**:4
Culkin, Macaulay **1991**:3
Cusack, John **1999**:3
Cushing, Peter
  Obituary **1995**:1
Dafoe, Willem **1988**:1
Dalton, Timothy **1988**:4
Daniels, Jeff **1989**:4
Davis, Paige **2004**:2
Day-Lewis, Daniel **1989**:4 **1994**:4
Dee, Janie **2001**:4
Dench, Judi **1999**:4
De Niro, Robert **1999**:1
Dennis, Sandy
  Obituary **1992**:4
Depardieu, Gerard **1991**:2
Dern, Laura **1992**:3
De Vito, Danny **1987**:1
Dewhurst, Colleen
  Obituary **1992**:2
Diggs, Taye **2000**:1
Douglas, Michael **1986**:2
Dukakis, Olympia **1996**:4
Duncan, Todd
  Obituary **1998**:3
Duvall, Robert **1999**:3
Ebsen, Buddy
  Obituary **2004**:3
Elliott, Denholm
  Obituary **1993**:2
Ephron, Henry
  Obituary **1993**:2
Fawcett, Farrah **1998**:4
Feld, Kenneth **1988**:2
Feldshuh, Tovah **2005**:3
Ferguson, Craig **2005**:4
Ferrer, Jose
  Obituary **1992**:3
Fiennes, Ralph **1996**:2
Fierstein, Harvey **2004**:2
Finney, Albert **2003**:3
Fishburne, Laurence **1995**:3
Fisher, Carrie **1991**:1
Flanders, Ed
  Obituary **1995**:3
Flockhart, Calista **1998**:4
Fo, Dario **1998**:1
Ford, Faith **2005**:3

Fosse, Bob
  Obituary **1988**:1
Foster, Sutton **2003**:2
Freeman, Morgan **1990**:4
Fugard, Athol **1992**:3
Gabor, Eva
  Obituary **1996**:1
Gallagher, Peter **2004**:3
Gardenia, Vincent
  Obituary **1993**:2
Garr, Teri **1988**:4
Geffen, David **1985**:3 **1997**:3
Gere, Richard **1994**:3
Gielgud, John
  Obituary **2000**:4
Gilford, Jack
  Obituary **1990**:4
Gleason, Jackie
  Obituary **1987**:4
Glover, Danny **1998**:4
Glover, Savion **1997**:1
Gobel, George
  Obituary **1991**:4
Goldberg, Whoopi **1993**:3
Goldblum, Jeff **1988**:1 **1997**:3
Gossett, Louis, Jr. **1989**:3
Grammer, Kelsey **1995**:1
Grant, Cary
  Obituary **1987**:1
Grant, Hugh **1995**:3
Gray, Spalding
  Obituary **2005**:2
Greene, Graham **1997**:2
Gregory, Dick **1990**:3
Gyllenhaal, Jake **2005**:3
Hagen, Uta
  Obituary **2005**:2
Hall, Anthony Michael **1986**:3
Hamilton, Margaret
  Obituary **1985**:3
Harris, Richard
  Obituary **2004**:1
Harrison, Rex
  Obituary **1990**:4
Havel, Vaclav **1990**:3
Hawke, Ethan **1995**:4
Hayes, Helen
  Obituary **1993**:4
Hennessy, Jill **2003**:2
Henning, Doug
  Obituary **2000**:3
Hepburn, Katharine **1991**:2
Hill, George Roy
  Obituary **2004**:1
Hines, Gregory **1992**:4
Hoffman, Dustin **2005**:4
Hopkins, Anthony **1992**:4
Horne, Lena **1998**:4
Hoskins, Bob **1989**:1
Houseman, John
  Obituary **1989**:1
Houston, Cissy **1999**:3
Humphries, Barry **1993**:1
Hunt, Helen **1994**:4
Hunter, Holly **1989**:4
Hurt, William **1986**:1
Hwang, David Henry **1999**:1
Irons, Jeremy **1991**:4
Irwin, Bill **1988**:3
Itami, Juzo
  Obituary **1998**:2

Ives, Burl
  Obituary **1995**:4
Jackman, Hugh **2004**:4
Jackson, Samuel L. **1995**:4
Janney, Allison **2003**:3
Jay, Ricky **1995**:1
Jillian, Ann **1986**:4
Johansson, Scarlett **2005**:4
Jones, Cherry **1999**:3
Jones, Sarah **2005**:2
Jones, Tommy Lee **1994**:2
Julia, Raul
  Obituary **1995**:1
Kahn, Madeline
  Obituary **2000**:2
Kavner, Julie **1992**:3
Kaye, Danny
  Obituary **1987**:2
Kaye, Nora
  Obituary **1987**:4
Kazan, Elia
  Obituary **2004**:4
Keeler, Ruby
  Obituary **1993**:4
Keitel, Harvey **1994**:3
Kerr, Jean
  Obituary **2004**:1
Kilmer, Val **1991**:4
King, Alan
  Obituary **2005**:3
Kinski, Klaus **1987**:2
  Obituary **1992**:2
Kline, Kevin **2000**:1
Kramer, Larry **1991**:2
Kushner, Tony **1995**:2
Lahti, Christine **1988**:2
Lane, Burton
  Obituary **1997**:2
Lane, Nathan **1996**:4
Lange, Jessica **1995**:4
Lansbury, Angela **1993**:1
Larson, Jonathan
  Obituary **1997**:2
Lawless, Lucy **1997**:4
Leary, Denis **1993**:3
Leigh, Jennifer Jason **1995**:2
Lithgow, John **1985**:2
Little, Cleavon
  Obituary **1993**:2
Lloyd Webber, Andrew **1989**:1
Loewe, Frederick
  Obituary **1988**:2
Logan, Joshua
  Obituary **1988**:4
Lord, Jack
  Obituary **1998**:2
MacRae, Gordon
  Obituary **1986**:2
Macy, William H. **1999**:3
Maher, Bill **1996**:2
Malkovich, John **1988**:2
Maltby, Richard, Jr. **1996**:3
Mamet, David **1998**:4
Mantegna, Joe **1992**:1
Marshall, Penny **1991**:3
Martin, Mary
  Obituary **1991**:2
McDormand, Frances **1997**:3
McDowall, Roddy
  Obituary **1999**:1
McGillis, Kelly **1989**:3
McGregor, Ewan **1998**:2

McKee, Lonette **1996**:1
McKellen, Ian **1994**:1
Merrick, David
  Obituary **2000**:4
Messing, Debra **2004**:4
Midler, Bette **1989**:4
Minghella, Anthony **2004**:3
Mirren, Helen **2005**:1
Molina, Alfred **2005**:3
Montand, Yves
  Obituary **1992**:2
Montgomery, Elizabeth
  Obituary **1995**:4
Moore, Dudley
  Obituary **2003**:2
Moore, Mary Tyler **1996**:2
Mos Def **2005**:4
Moss, Carrie-Anne **2004**:3
Neeson, Liam **1993**:4
Newman, Paul **1995**:3
Nichols, Mike **1994**:4
Nolan, Lloyd
  Obituary **1985**:4
Nolte, Nick **1992**:4
North, Alex **1986**:3
Northam, Jeremy **2003**:2
Nunn, Trevor **2000**:2
O'Donnell, Rosie **1994**:3
Oldman, Gary **1998**:1
Olin, Ken **1992**:3
Olin, Lena **1991**:2
Olivier, Laurence
  Obituary **1989**:4
Osborne, John
  Obituary **1995**:2
O'Sullivan, Maureen
  Obituary **1998**:4
Pacino, Al **1993**:4
Page, Geraldine
  Obituary **1987**:4
Papp, Joseph
  Obituary **1992**:2
Parks, Suzan-Lori **2003**:2
Paulsen, Pat
  Obituary **1997**:4
Peck, Gregory
  Obituary **2004**:3
Penn, Sean **1987**:2
Penn & Teller **1992**:1
Perkins, Anthony
  Obituary **1993**:2
Peters, Bernadette **2000**:1
Pfeiffer, Michelle **1990**:2
Picasso, Paloma **1991**:1
Pinchot, Bronson **1987**:4
Pleasence, Donald
  Obituary **1995**:3
Poitier, Sidney **1990**:3
Preminger, Otto
  Obituary **1986**:3
Preston, Robert
  Obituary **1987**:3
Price, Vincent
  Obituary **1994**:2
Prince, Faith **1993**:2
Quaid, Dennis **1989**:4
Radner, Gilda
  Obituary **1989**:4
Randall, Tony
  Obituary **2005**:3
Rashad, Phylicia **1987**:3

Raye, Martha
  Obituary **1995**:1
Redford, Robert **1993**:2
Redgrave, Lynn **1999**:3
Redgrave, Vanessa **1989**:2
Reeves, Keanu **1992**:1
Reilly, John C. **2003**:4
Reitman, Ivan **1986**:3
Reza, Yasmina **1999**:2
Richards, Michael **1993**:4
Ritter, John **2003**:4
Robbins, Jerome
  Obituary **1999**:1
Roberts, Doris **2003**:4
Roker, Roxie
  Obituary **1996**:2
Rolle, Esther
  Obituary **1999**:2
Rudner, Rita **1993**:2
Rudnick, Paul **1994**:3
Ruehl, Mercedes **1992**:4
Salonga, Lea **2003**:3
Sarandon, Susan **1995**:3
Schoenfeld, Gerald **1986**:2
Schwimmer, David **1996**:2
Scott, George C.
  Obituary **2000**:2
Seymour, Jane **1994**:4
Shaffer, Paul **1987**:1
Shawn, Dick
  Obituary **1987**:3
Shepard, Sam **1996**:4
Short, Martin **1986**:1
Silvers, Phil
  Obituary **1985**:4
Sinise, Gary **1996**:1
Slater, Christian **1994**:1
Smith, Anna Deavere **2002**:2
Snipes, Wesley **1993**:1
Sondheim, Stephen **1994**:4
Spacey, Kevin **1996**:4
Steiger, Rod
  Obituary **2003**:4
Stewart, Jimmy
  Obituary **1997**:4
Stewart, Patrick **1996**:1
Stiller, Ben **1999**:1
Sting **1991**:4
Stoppard, Tom **1995**:4
Streep, Meryl **1990**:2
Streisand, Barbra **1992**:2
Stritch, Elaine **2002**:4
Styne, Jule
  Obituary **1995**:1
Susskind, David
  Obituary **1987**:2
Tandy, Jessica **1990**:4
  Obituary **1995**:1
Taylor, Elizabeth **1993**:3
Taylor, Lili **2000**:2
Thompson, Emma **1993**:2
Tomei, Marisa **1995**:2
Tucci, Stanley **2003**:2
Tune, Tommy **1994**:2
Ullman, Tracey **1988**:3
Urich, Robert **1988**:1
  Obituary **2003**:3
Ustinov, Peter
  Obituary **2005**:3
Vardalos, Nia **2003**:4
Vogel, Paula **1999**:2

Walker, Nancy
  Obituary **1992**:3
Washington, Denzel **1993**:2
Wasserstein, Wendy **1991**:3
Wayne, David
  Obituary **1995**:3
Weaver, Sigourney **1988**:3
Weitz, Bruce **1985**:4
Wences, Senor
  Obituary **1999**:4
Whitaker, Forest **1996**:2
Whitehead, Robert
  Obituary **2003**:3
Wiest, Dianne **1995**:2
Wilkinson, Tom **2003**:2
Williams, Treat **2004**:3
Willis, Bruce **1986**:4
Winfield, Paul
  Obituary **2005**:2
Winokur, Marissa Jaret **2005**:1
Wong, B.D. **1998**:1
Woods, James **1988**:3
Worth, Irene
  Obituary **2003**:2
Wyle, Noah **1997**:3
Youngman, Henny
  Obituary **1998**:3
Zeffirelli, Franco **1991**:3

**WRITING**
Adams, Douglas
  Obituary **2002**:2
Adams, Scott **1996**:4
Albom, Mitch **1999**:3
Alexie, Sherman **1998**:4
Amanpour, Christiane **1997**:2
Ambler, Eric
  Obituary **1999**:2
Ambrose, Stephen **2002**:3
Amis, Kingsley
  Obituary **1996**:2
Amory, Cleveland
  Obituary **1999**:2
Anderson, Poul
  Obituary **2002**:3
Angelou, Maya **1993**:4
Angier, Natalie **2000**:3
Asimov, Isaac
  Obituary **1992**:3
Atkins, Robert C.
  Obituary **2004**:2
Atwood, Margaret **2001**:2
Axthelm, Pete
  Obituary **1991**:3
Bacall, Lauren **1997**:3
Bakker, Robert T. **1991**:3
Baldwin, James
  Obituary **1988**:2
Ball, Edward **1999**:2
Baraka, Amiri **2000**:3
Barber, Red
  Obituary **1993**:2
Barker, Clive **2003**:3
Barry, Dave **1991**:2
Barry, Lynda **1992**:1
Beckett, Samuel Barclay
  Obituary **1990**:2
Bloodworth-Thomason, Linda
  **1994**:1
Blume, Judy **1998**:4
Bly, Robert **1992**:4
Blyth, Myrna **2002**:4

Bombeck, Erma
  Obituary **1996**:4
Bowles, Paul
  Obituary **2000**:3
Boynton, Sandra **2004**:1
Bradford, Barbara Taylor **2002**:4
Bradshaw, John **1992**:1
Branagh, Kenneth **1992**:2
Breathed, Berkeley **2005**:3
Brite, Poppy Z. **2005**:1
Brodsky, Joseph
  Obituary **1996**:3
Brokaw, Tom **2000**:3
Brooks, Gwendolyn **1998**:1
  Obituary **2001**:2
Brown, Dan **2004**:4
Brown, Dee
  Obituary **2004**:1
Brown, Tina **1992**:1
Buffett, Jimmy **1999**:3
Burgess, Anthony
  Obituary **1994**:2
Burroughs, William S. **1994**:2
Burroughs, William S.
  Obituary **1997**:4
Buscaglia, Leo
  Obituary **1998**:4
Busch, Charles **1998**:3
Bush, Millie **1992**:1
Bushnell, Candace **2004**:2
Butler, Octavia E. **1999**:3
Byrne, Gabriel **1997**:4
Caen, Herb
  Obituary **1997**:4
Campbell, Bebe Moore **1996**:2
Caplan, Arthur L. **2000**:2
Carcaterra, Lorenzo **1996**:1
Carey, George **1992**:3
Carlson, Richard **2002**:1
Carver, Raymond
  Obituary **1989**:1
Castaneda, Carlos
  Obituary **1998**:4
Castillo, Ana **2000**:4
Cela, Camilo Jose
  Obituary **2003**:1
Chabon, Michael **2002**:1
Chatwin, Bruce
  Obituary **1989**:2
Chavez, Linda **1999**:3
Cheney, Lynne V. **1990**:4
Child, Julia **1999**:4
Chopra, Deepak **1996**:3
Clancy, Tom **1998**:4
Clark, Mary Higgins **2000**:4
Clavell, James
  Obituary **1995**:1
Cleaver, Eldridge
  Obituary **1998**:4
Codrescu, Andreá **1997**:3
Coetzee, J. M. **2004**:4
Cole, Johnetta B. **1994**:3
Coles, Robert **1995**:1
Collins, Billy **2002**:2
Collins, Jackie **2004**:4
Comfort, Alex
  Obituary **2000**:4
Condon, Richard
  Obituary **1996**:4
Cook, Robin **1996**:3
Cornwell, Patricia **2003**:1
Cosby, Bill **1999**:2

# Cumulative Subject Index

This index lists all newsmakers by subjects, company names, products, organizations, issues, awards, and professional specialties. Indexes in softbound issues allow access to the current year's entries; indexes in annual hardbound volumes are cumulative, covering the entire *Newsmakers* series.

Listee names are followed by a year and issue number; thus **1996**:3 indicates that an entry on that individual appears in both 1996, Issue 3, and the 1996 cumulation. For access to newsmakers appearing earlier than the current softbound issue, see the previous year's cumulation.

## Advertising
Ailes, Roger **1989**:3
Beers, Charlotte **1999**:3
Freeman, Cliff **1996**:1
Kroll, Alexander S. **1989**:3
Lazarus, Shelly **1998**:3
McElligott, Thomas J. **1987**:4
Ogilvy, David
  Obituary **2000**:1
O'Steen, Van
  Brief Entry **1986**:3
Peller, Clara
  Obituary **1988**:1
Proctor, Barbara Gardner **1985**:3
Riney, Hal **1989**:1
Saatchi, Charles **1987**:3
Saatchi, Maurice **1995**:4
Sedelmaier, Joe **1985**:3
Vinton, Will
  Brief Entry **1988**:1
Whittle, Christopher **1989**:3

## AFL-CIO
See: American Federation of Labor and Congress of Industrial Organizations

## African National Congress [ANC]
Buthelezi, Mangosuthu Gatsha **1989**:3
Hani, Chris
  Obituary **1993**:4
Mandela, Nelson **1990**:3
Mbeki, Thabo **1999**:4
Sisulu, Walter
  Obituary **2004**:2
Slovo, Joe **1989**:2
Tambo, Oliver **1991**:3

## Agriculture
Davis, Noel **1990**:3

## AIDS
See: Acquired Immune Deficiency Syndrome

## AIDS Coalition to Unleash Power [ACT-UP]
Kramer, Larry **1991**:2

## AIM
See: American Indian Movement
Peltier, Leonard **1995**:1

## A.J. Canfield Co.
Canfield, Alan B.
  Brief Entry **1986**:3

## ALA
See: American Library Association

## Albert Nipon, Inc.
Nipon, Albert
  Brief Entry **1986**:4

## Alcohol abuse
Anastas, Robert
  Brief Entry **1985**:2
Bradshaw, John **1992**:1

Lightner, Candy **1985**:1
MacRae, Gordon
  Obituary **1986**:2
Mantle, Mickey
  Obituary **1996**:1
Welch, Bob **1991**:3

## ALL
See: American Life League

## Alternative medicine
Jacobs, Joe **1994**:1
Weil, Andrew **1997**:4

## Alvin Ailey Dance Theatre
Jamison, Judith **1990**:3

## AMA
See: American Medical Association

## Amazon.com, Inc.
Bezos, Jeff **1998**:4

## American Academy and Institute of Arts and Letters
Brooks, Gwendolyn **1998**:1
  Obituary **2001**:2
Cunningham, Merce **1998**:1
Dickey, James
  Obituary **1998**:2
Foster, Norman **1999**:4
Graves, Michael **2000**:1
Mamet, David **1998**:4
Roth, Philip **1999**:1
Vonnegut, Kurt **1998**:4
Walker, Alice **1999**:1
Wolfe, Tom **1999**:2

## American Airlines
Crandall, Robert L. **1992**:1

## American Ballet Theatre [ABT]
Bissell, Patrick
  Obituary **1988**:2
Bocca, Julio **1995**:3
Englund, Richard
  Obituary **1991**:3
Feld, Eliot **1996**:1
Ferri, Alessandra **1987**:2
Godunov, Alexander
  Obituary **1995**:4
Gregory, Cynthia **1990**:2
Herrera, Paloma **1996**:2
Kaye, Nora
  Obituary **1987**:4
Lander, Toni
  Obituary **1985**:4
Parker, Sarah Jessica **1999**:2
Renvall, Johan
  Brief Entry **1987**:4
Robbins, Jerome
  Obituary **1999**:1
Tudor, Antony
  Obituary **1987**:4

## American Book Awards
Alexie, Sherman **1998**:4
Baraka, Amiri **2000**:3
Child, Julia **1999**:4

Erdrich, Louise **2005**:3
Kissinger, Henry **1999**:4
Walker, Alice **1999**:1
Wolfe, Tom **1999**:2

## American Civil Liberties Union [ACLU]
Abzug, Bella **1998**:2
Glasser, Ira **1989**:1

## American Express
Chenault, Kenneth I. **1999**:3
Weill, Sandy **1990**:4

## American Federation of Labor and Congress of Industrial Organizations [AFL-CIO]
Chavez-Thompson, Linda **1999**:1
Sweeney, John J. **2000**:3

## American Indian Movement [AIM]
Banks, Dennis J. **1986**:4

## American Library Association [ALA]
Blume, Judy **1998**:4
Heat-Moon, William Least **2000**:2
Schuman, Patricia Glass **1993**:2
Steel, Danielle **1999**:2

## American Life League [ALL]
Brown, Judie **1986**:2

## American Medical Association [AMA]
Bristow, Lonnie **1996**:1

## Amer-I-can minority empowerment program
Brown, Jim **1993**:2

## American Museum of Natural History
Futter, Ellen V. **1995**:1

## American Music Awards
Ashanti **2004**:1
Badu, Erykah **2000**:4
Boyz II Men **1995**:1
Brooks, Garth **1992**:1
Cole, Natalie **1992**:4
Franklin, Aretha **1998**:3
Jackson, Alan **2003**:1
Jackson, Michael **1996**:2
Jewel **1999**:2
Loveless, Patty **1998**:2
McEntire, Reba **1987**:3 **1994**:2
Newton-John, Olivia **1998**:4
Parton, Dolly **1999**:4
Spears, Britney **2000**:3
Strait, George **1998**:3
Turner, Tina **2000**:3
Yoakam, Dwight **1992**:4

## American Power Boat Association [APBA]
Copeland, Al **1988**:3
Hanauer, Chip **1986**:2

## America Online [AOL]
Case, Steve **1995**:4 **1996**:4
Kimsey, James V. **2001**:1

King, Mary-Claire **1998**:3
Krim, Mathilde **1989**:2
Love, Susan **1995**:2
Rosenberg, Steven **1989**:1
Szent-Gyoergyi, Albert
  Obituary **1987**:2
Wigler, Michael
  Brief Entry **1985**:1

**Cannes Film Festival**
Brando, Marlon
  Obituary **2005**:3
Egoyan, Atom **2000**:2
Hou Hsiao-hsien **2000**:2
Mirren, Helen **2005**:1
Smith, Kevin **2000**:4

**Carnival Cruise Lines**
Arison, Ted **1990**:3

**Car repair**
Magliozzi, Tom and Ray **1991**:4

**Cartoons**
Addams, Charles
  Obituary **1989**:1
Barbera, Joseph **1988**:2
Barry, Lynda **1992**:1
Blanc, Mel
  Obituary **1989**:4
Chast, Roz **1992**:4
Disney, Roy E. **1986**:3
Freleng, Friz
  Obituary **1995**:4
Gaines, William M.
  Obituary **1993**:1
Gould, Chester
  Obituary **1985**:2
Groening, Matt **1990**:4
Judge, Mike **1994**:2
MacNelly, Jeff
  Obituary **2000**:4
Mauldin, Bill
  Obituary **2004**:2
Parker, Trey and Matt Stone **1998**:2
Schulz, Charles
  Obituary **2000**:3
Schulz, Charles M. **1998**:1
Spiegelman, Art **1998**:3
Tartakovsky, Genndy **2004**:4
Trudeau, Garry **1991**:2
Watterson, Bill **1990**:3

**Catholic Church**
Beckett, Wendy (Sister) **1998**:3
Bernardin, Cardinal Joseph **1997**:2
Burns, Charles R.
  Brief Entry **1988**:1
Clements, George **1985**:1
Cunningham, Reverend William
  Obituary **1997**:4
Curran, Charles E. **1989**:2
Daily, Bishop Thomas V. **1990**:4
Dearden, John Cardinal
  Obituary **1988**:4
Fox, Matthew **1992**:2
Healy, Timothy S. **1990**:2
Hume, Basil Cardinal
  Obituary **2000**:1
John Paul II, Pope **1995**:3
Kissling, Frances **1989**:2

Krol, John
  Obituary **1996**:3
Lefebvre, Marcel **1988**:4
Mahony, Roger M. **1988**:2
Maida, Adam Cardinal **1998**:2
Obando, Miguel **1986**:4
O'Connor, Cardinal John **1990**:3
O'Connor, John
  Obituary **2000**:4
Peter, Valentine J. **1988**:2
Rock, John
  Obituary **1985**:1
Stallings, George A., Jr. **1990**:1

**CAT Scanner**
Hounsfield, Godfrey **1989**:2

**Cattle rustling**
Cantrell, Ed
  Brief Entry **1985**:3

**Caviar**
Petrossian, Christian
  Brief Entry **1985**:3

**CBC**
See: Canadian Broadcasting Corp.

**CBS, Inc.**
Cox, Richard Joseph
  Brief Entry **1985**:1
Cronkite, Walter Leland **1997**:3
Moonves, Les **2004**:2
Paley, William S.
  Obituary **1991**:2
Reasoner, Harry
  Obituary **1992**:1
Sagansky, Jeff **1993**:2
Tellem, Nancy **2004**:4
Tisch, Laurence A. **1988**:2
Yetnikoff, Walter **1988**:1

**CDF**
See: Children's Defense Fund

**Center for Equal Opportunity**
Chavez, Linda **1999**:3

**Centers for Living**
Williamson, Marianne **1991**:4

**Central America**
Astorga, Nora **1988**:2
Cruz, Arturo **1985**:1
Obando, Miguel **1986**:4
Robelo, Alfonso **1988**:1

**Central Intelligence Agency [CIA]**
Carter, Amy **1987**:4
Casey, William
  Obituary **1987**:3
Colby, William E.
  Obituary **1996**:4
Deutch, John **1996**:4
Gates, Robert M. **1992**:2
Inman, Bobby Ray **1985**:1
Tenet, George **2000**:3

**Centurion Ministries**
McCloskey, James **1993**:1

**Cesar Awards**
Adjani, Isabelle **1991**:1
Deneuve, Catherine **2003**:2
Depardieu, Gerard **1991**:2
Tautou, Audrey **2004**:2

**Chanel, Inc.**
D'Alessio, Kitty
  Brief Entry **1987**:3
Lagerfeld, Karl **1999**:4

**Chantal Pharmacentical Corp.**
Burnison, Chantal Simone **1988**:3

**Charlotte Hornets basketball team**
Bryant, Kobe **1998**:3
Johnson, Larry **1993**:3
Mourning, Alonzo **1994**:2

**Chef Boy-ar-dee**
Boiardi, Hector
  Obituary **1985**:3

**Chess**
Kasparov, Garry **1997**:4
Polgar, Judit **1993**:3

**Chicago Bears football team**
McMahon, Jim **1985**:4
Payton, Walter
  Obituary **2000**:2

**Chicago Bulls basketball team**
Jackson, Phil **1996**:3
Jordan, Michael **1987**:2
Kukoc, Toni **1995**:4
Pippen, Scottie **1992**:2

**Chicago Blackhawks**
Hasek, Dominik **1998**:3

**Chicago Cubs baseball team**
Caray, Harry **1988**:3
  Obituary **1998**:3
Sosa, Sammy **1999**:1

**Chicago, Ill., city government**
Washington, Harold
  Obituary **1988**:1

**Chicago White Sox baseball team**
Caray, Harry **1988**:3
  Obituary **1998**:3
Leyland, Jim **1998**:2
Thomas, Frank **1994**:3
Veeck, Bill
  Obituary **1986**:1

**Child care**
Hale, Clara
  Obituary **1993**:3
Leach, Penelope **1992**:4
Spock, Benjamin **1995**:2
  Obituary **1998**:3

**Children's Defense Fund [CDF]**
Clinton, Hillary Rodham **1993**:2
Edelman, Marian Wright **1990**:4

**Chimpanzees**
Goodall, Jane **1991**:1

**Choreography**
Abdul, Paula **1990**:3
Ailey, Alvin **1989**:2
Obituary **1990**:2
Astaire, Fred
Obituary **1987**:4
Bennett, Michael
Obituary **1988**:1
Cunningham, Merce **1998**:1
Dean, Laura **1989**:4
de Mille, Agnes
Obituary **1994**:2
Feld, Eliot **1996**:1
Fenley, Molissa **1988**:3
Forsythe, William **1993**:2
Fosse, Bob
Obituary **1988**:1
Glover, Savion **1997**:1
Graham, Martha
Obituary **1991**:4
Jamison, Judith **1990**:3
Joffrey, Robert
Obituary **1988**:3
Jones, Bill T. **1991**:4
Lewitzky, Bella
Obituary **2005**:3
MacMillan, Kenneth
Obituary **1993**:2
Mitchell, Arthur **1995**:1
Morris, Mark **1991**:1
Nureyev, Rudolf
Obituary **1993**:2
Parsons, David **1993**:4
Ross, Herbert
Obituary **2002**:4
Takei, Kei **1990**:2
Taylor, Paul **1992**:3
Tharp, Twyla **1992**:4
Tudor, Antony
Obituary **1987**:4
Tune, Tommy **1994**:2
Varone, Doug **2001**:2

**Christian Coalition**
Reed, Ralph **1995**:1

**Christic Institute**
Sheehan, Daniel P. **1989**:1

**Chrysler Motor Corp.**
Eaton, Robert J. **1994**:2
Iacocca, Lee **1993**:1
Lutz, Robert A. **1990**:1

**CHUCK**
See: Committee to Halt Useless
College Killings

**Church of England**
Carey, George **1992**:3
Runcie, Robert **1989**:4
Obituary **2001**:1

**Church of Jesus Christ of Latter-Day
Saints**
See: Mormon Church

**CIA**
See: Central Intelligence Agency

**Cincinatti Bengals football team**
Esiason, Boomer **1991**:1

**Cincinnati Reds baseball team**
Davis, Eric **1987**:4
Rose, Pete **1991**:1
Schott, Marge **1985**:4

**Cinematography**
Burum, Stephen H.
Brief Entry **1987**:2
Markle, C. Wilson **1988**:1
McLaren, Norman
Obituary **1987**:2

**Civil rights**
Abernathy, Ralph
Obituary **1990**:3
Abzug, Bella **1998**:2
Allen Jr., Ivan
Obituary **2004**:3
Allred, Gloria **1985**:2
Aquino, Corazon **1986**:2
Baldwin, James
Obituary **1988**:2
Banks, Dennis J. **1986**:4
Blackburn, Molly
Obituary **1985**:4
Buthelezi, Mangosuthu Gatsha
**1989**:3
Chavez, Linda **1999**:3
Chavis, Benjamin **1993**:4
Clements, George **1985**:1
Connerly, Ward **2000**:2
Davis, Angela **1998**:3
Dees, Morris **1992**:1
Delany, Sarah
Obituary **1999**:3
Duncan, Sheena
Brief Entry **1987**:1
Farmer, James
Obituary **2000**:1
Faubus, Orval
Obituary **1995**:2
Glasser, Ira **1989**:1
Griffiths, Martha
Obituary **2004**:2
Harris, Barbara **1989**:3
Healey, Jack **1990**:1
Hoffman, Abbie
Obituary **1989**:3
Hume, John **1987**:1
Jordan, Vernon, Jr. **2002**:3
King, Bernice **2000**:2
King, Coretta Scott **1999**:3
Kunstler, William **1992**:3
Makeba, Miriam **1989**:2
Mandela, Winnie **1989**:3
Marshall, Thurgood
Obituary **1993**:3
McGuinness, Martin **1985**:4
Pendleton, Clarence M.
Obituary **1988**:4

Ram, Jagjivan
Obituary **1986**:4
Shabazz, Betty
Obituary **1997**:4
Sharpton, Al **1991**:2
Shcharansky, Anatoly **1986**:2
Simone, Nina
Obituary **2004**:2
Slovo, Joe **1989**:2
Stallings, George A., Jr. **1990**:1
Steele, Shelby **1991**:2
Sullivan, Leon
Obituary **2002**:2
Suzman, Helen **1989**:3
Ture, Kwame
Obituary **1999**:2
Washington, Harold
Obituary **1988**:1
West, Cornel **1994**:2
Williams, G. Mennen
Obituary **1988**:2
Williams, Hosea
Obituary **2001**:2
Wu, Harry **1996**:1

**Civil War**
Foote, Shelby **1991**:2

**Claymation**
Park, Nick **1997**:3
Vinton, Will
Brief Entry **1988**:1

**Cleveland Ballet Dancing Wheels**
Verdi-Fletcher, Mary **1998**:2

**Cleveland Browns football team**
Brown, Jim **1993**:2

**Cleveland Cavaliers basketball team**
Wilkens, Lenny **1995**:2

**Cleveland city government**
Stokes, Carl
Obituary **1996**:4

**Cleveland Indians baseball team**
Belle, Albert **1996**:4
Boudreau, Louis
Obituary **2002**:3
Greenberg, Hank
Obituary **1986**:4
Lofton, Kenny **1998**:1
Veeck, Bill
Obituary **1986**:1

**Cliff's Notes**
Hillegass, Clifton Keith **1989**:4

**Climatology**
Thompson, Starley
Brief Entry **1987**:3

**Clio Awards**
Proctor, Barbara Gardner **1985**:3
Riney, Hal **1989**:1
Rivers, Joan **2005**:3
Sedelmaier, Joe **1985**:3

Travis, Randy **1988**:4
Twitty, Conway
    Obituary **1994**:1
Womack, Lee Ann **2002**:1
Wynette, Tammy
    Obituary **1998**:3
Wynonna **1993**:3
Yearwood, Trisha **1999**:1

**Creation Spirituality**
Altea, Rosemary **1996**:3
Fox, Matthew **1992**:2

**Creative Artists Agency**
Ovitz, Michael **1990**:1

**CSICOP**
See: Committee for the Scientific
    Investigation of Claims of the
    Paranormal

**Cy Young Award**
Clemens, Roger **1991**:4
Hernandez, Willie **1985**:1
Hershiser, Orel **1989**:2
Johnson, Randy **1996**:2
Maddux, Greg **1996**:2
Palmer, Jim **1991**:2
Saberhagen, Bret **1986**:1

**Daimler-Benz AG [Mercedes-Benz]**
Breitschwerdt, Werner **1988**:4

**DaimlerChrysler Corp.**
Schrempp, Juergen **2000**:2
Zetsche, Dieter **2002**:3

**Dallas Cowboys football team**
Aikman, Troy **1994**:2
Irvin, Michael **1996**:3
Johnson, Jimmy **1993**:3
Jones, Jerry **1994**:4
Landry, Tom
    Obituary **2000**:3
Smith, Emmitt **1994**:1

**Doubleday Mystery Guild**
Grafton, Sue **2000**:2

**Dance Theatre of Harlem**
Fagan, Garth **2000**:1
Mitchell, Arthur **1995**:1

**Datsun automobiles**
See: Nissan Motor Co.

**Dell Computer Corp.**
Dell, Michael **1996**:2

**DEC**
See: Digital Equipment Corp.

**Democratic National Committee [DNC]**
Brown, Ron
    Obituary **1996**:4
Brown, Ron **1990**:3
Dean, Howard **2005**:4
Waters, Maxine **1998**:4

**Denver Broncos football team**
Barnes, Ernie **1997**:4
Davis, Terrell **1998**:2
Elway, John **1990**:3

**Department of Commerce**
Baldrige, Malcolm
    Obituary **1988**:1
Brown, Ron
    Obituary **1996**:4

**Department of Education**
Cavazos, Lauro F. **1989**:2
Riley, Richard W. **1996**:3

**Department of Defense**
Cohen, William S. **1998**:1
Perry, William **1994**:4

**Department of Energy**
O'Leary, Hazel **1993**:4

**Department of Health, Education, and Welfare [HEW]**
Harris, Patricia Roberts
    Obituary **1985**:2
Ribicoff, Abraham
    Obituary **1998**:3

**Department of Health and Human Services [HHR]**
Kessler, David **1992**:1
Sullivan, Louis **1990**:4

**Department of Housing and Urban Development [HUD]**
Achtenberg, Roberta **1993**:4
Harris, Patricia Roberts
    Obituary **1985**:2
Kemp, Jack **1990**:4
Morrison, Trudi
    Brief Entry **1986**:2

**Department of the Interior**
Babbitt, Bruce **1994**:1

**Department of Labor**
Dole, Elizabeth Hanford **1990**:1
Martin, Lynn **1991**:4

**Department of State**
Christopher, Warren **1996**:3
Muskie, Edmund S.
    Obituary **1996**:3

**Department of Transportation**
Dole, Elizabeth Hanford **1990**:1
Schiavo, Mary **1998**:2

**Depression**
Abramson, Lyn **1986**:3

**Desilu Productions**
Arnaz, Desi
    Obituary **1987**:1
Ball, Lucille
    Obituary **1989**:3

**Detroit city government**
Archer, Dennis **1994**:4
Maida, Adam Cardinal **1998**:2
Young, Coleman A.
    Obituary **1998**:1

**Detroit Lions football team**
Ford, William Clay, Jr. **1999**:1
Sanders, Barry **1992**:1
White, Byron
    Obituary **2003**:3

**Detroit Pistons basketball team**
Hill, Grant **1995**:3
Laimbeer, Bill **2004**:3
Rodman, Dennis **1991**:3 **1996**:4
Thomas, Isiah **1989**:2
Vitale, Dick **1988**:4 **1994**:4
Wallace, Ben **2004**:3

**Detroit Red Wings hockey team**
Bowman, Scotty **1998**:4
Federov, Sergei **1995**:1
Ilitch, Mike **1993**:4
Klima, Petr **1987**:1
Konstantinov, Vladimir **1997**:4
Yzerman, Steve **1991**:2

**Detroit Tigers baseball team**
Fielder, Cecil **1993**:2
Gibson, Kirk **1985**:2
Greenberg, Hank
    Obituary **1986**:4
Harwell, Ernie **1997**:3
Hernandez, Willie **1985**:1
Ilitch, Mike **1993**:4
Monaghan, Tom **1985**:1
Schembechler, Bo **1990**:3

**Digital Equipment Corp. [DEC]**
Olsen, Kenneth H. **1986**:4

**Diets**
Agatston, Arthur **2005**:1
Atkins, Robert C.
    Obituary **2004**:2
Gregory, Dick **1990**:3
Ornish, Dean **2004**:2
Powter, Susan **1994**:3
Sears, Barry **2004**:2

**Dilbert cartoon**
Adams, Scott **1996**:4

**Dinosaurs**
Bakker, Robert T. **1991**:3
Barney **1993**:4
Crichton, Michael **1995**:3
Henson, Brian **1992**:1

**Diplomacy**
Abrams, Elliott **1987**:1
Albright, Madeleine **1994**:3
Astorga, Nora **1988**:2
Baker, James A. III **1991**:2
Begin, Menachem
    Obituary **1992**:3
Berri, Nabih **1985**:2
Carter, Jimmy **1995**:1

Cray, Seymour R.
  Brief Entry **1986**:3
  Obituary **1997**:2
Cummings, Sam **1986**:3
Dell, Michael **1996**:2
DiFranco, Ani **1997**:1
Ertegun, Ahmet **1986**:3
Garcia, Joe
  Brief Entry **1986**:4
Gates, Bill **1993**:3 **1987**:4
Gatien, Peter
  Brief Entry **1986**:1
Gillett, George **1988**:1
Graham, Bill **1986**:4
  Obituary **1992**:2
Guccione, Bob **1986**:1
Haney, Chris
  Brief Entry **1985**:1
Herrera, Carolina **1997**:1
Hilbert, Stephen C. **1997**:4
Honda, Soichiro
  Obituary **1986**:1
Hughes, Mark **1985**:3
Hyatt, Joel **1985**:3
Ilitch, Mike **1993**:4
Inatome, Rick **1985**:4
Isaacson, Portia
  Brief Entry **1986**:1
Jacuzzi, Candido
  Obituary **1987**:1
Jones, Arthur A. **1985**:3
Katz, Lillian **1987**:4
Kerkorian, Kirk **1996**:2
Kingsborough, Donald
  Brief Entry **1986**:2
Knight, Philip H. **1994**:1
Koplovitz, Kay **1986**:3
Kurzweil, Raymond **1986**:3
Mahesh Yogi, Maharishi **1991**:3
Markle, C. Wilson **1988**:1
Marriott, J. Willard
  Obituary **1985**:4
McGowan, William **1985**:2
McIntyre, Richard
  Brief Entry **1986**:2
Melman, Richard
  Brief Entry **1986**:1
Monaghan, Tom **1985**:1
Moody, John **1985**:3
Morgan, Dodge **1987**:1
Murdoch, Rupert **1988**:4
Murray, Arthur
  Obituary **1991**:3
Olsen, Kenneth H. **1986**:4
Paulucci, Jeno
  Brief Entry **1986**:3
Penske, Roger **1988**:3
Pocklington, Peter H. **1985**:2
Radocy, Robert
  Brief Entry **1986**:3
Roberts, Xavier **1985**:3
Roddick, Anita **1989**:4
Sasakawa, Ryoichi
  Brief Entry **1988**:1
Schlessinger, David
  Brief Entry **1985**:1
Smith, Frederick W. **1985**:4
Tanny, Vic
  Obituary **1985**:3
Thalheimer, Richard
  Brief Entry **1988**:3
Thomas, Michel **1987**:4

Tompkins, Susie
  Brief Entry **1987**:2
Trump, Donald **1989**:2
Trump, Ivana **1995**:2
Turner, Ted **1989**:1
Waitt, Ted **1997**:4
Wilson, Jerry
  Brief Entry **1986**:2
Wilson, Peter C.
  Obituary **1985**:2
Wynn, Stephen A. **1994**:3
Zanker, Bill
  Brief Entry **1987**:3

**Environmentalism**
  Ben & Jerry **1991**:3
  Brockovich-Ellis, Erin **2003**:3
  Brower, David **1990**:4
  Denver, John
    Obituary **1998**:1
  Douglas, Marjory Stoneman **1993**:1
    Obituary **1998**:4
  Foreman, Dave **1990**:3
  Gore, Albert, Jr. **1993**:2
  Hair, Jay D. **1994**:3
  Hayse, Bruce **2004**:3
  Korchinsky, Mike **2004**:2
  Maathai, Wangari **2005**:3
  McDonough, William **2003**:1
  Ngau, Harrison **1991**:3
  Plotkin, Mark **1994**:3
  Puleston, Dennis
    Obituary **2002**:2
  Strong, Maurice **1993**:1
  Strummer, Joe
    Obituary **2004**:1
  Vitousek, Peter **2003**:1

**Environmental Protection Agency [EPA]**
  Browner, Carol M. **1994**:1

**EPA**
  See: Environmental Protection
  Agency

**Episcopal Church**
  Browning, Edmond
    Brief Entry **1986**:2
  Harris, Barbara **1996**:3
  Harris, Barbara **1989**:3
  Spong, John **1991**:3 **2001**:1

**Espionage**
  Philby, Kim
    Obituary **1988**:3

**Esprit clothing**
  Krogner, Heinz **2004**:2
  Tompkins, Susie
    Brief Entry **1987**:2

**Essence magazine**
  Gillespie, Marcia **1999**:4
  Lewis, Edward T. **1999**:4
  Taylor, Susan L. **1998**:2

**Estee Lauder**
  Burns, Robin **1991**:2
  Lauder, Estee **1992**:2

**Ethnobotany**
  Plotkin, Mark **1994**:3

**European Commission**
  Delors, Jacques **1990**:2

**Euthanasia**
  Cruzan, Nancy
    Obituary **1991**:3
  Humphry, Derek **1992**:2
  Kevorkian, Jack **1991**:3

**Excel Communications**
  Troutt, Kenny A. **1998**:1

**Exploration**
  Ballard, Robert D. **1998**:4
  Fiennes, Ranulph **1990**:3
  Hempleman-Adams, David **2004**:3
  Steger, Will **1990**:4

**ExxonMobil Oil**
  Raymond, Lee R. **2000**:3

**Fabbrica Italiana Automobili Torino SpA [Fiat]**
  Agnelli, Giovanni **1989**:4

**Faith Center Church**
  Scott, Gene
    Brief Entry **1986**:1

**Fallon McElligott**
  McElligott, Thomas J. **1987**:4

**Famous Amos Chocolate Chip Cookies**
  Amos, Wally **2000**:1

**Fashion**
  Agnes B **2002**:3
  Allard, Linda **2003**:2
  Armani, Giorgio **1991**:2
  Avedon, Richard **1993**:4
  Bacall, Lauren **1997**:3
  Badgley, Mark and
    James Mischka **2004**:3
  Banks, Jeffrey **1998**:2
  Beene, Geoffrey
    Obituary **2005**:4
  Benetton, Luciano **1988**:1
  Blahnik, Manolo **2000**:2
  Blass, Bill
    Obituary **2003**:3
  Bohbot, Michele **2004**:2
  Bravo, Rose Marie **2005**:3
  Cameron, David
    Brief Entry **1988**:1
  Cardin, Pierre **2003**:3
  Cavalli, Roberto **2004**:4
  Chalayan, Hussein **2003**:2
  Charron, Paul **2004**:1
  Claiborne, Liz **1986**:3
  Cole, Kenneth **2003**:1
  Crawford, Cindy **1993**:3
  D'Alessio, Kitty
    Brief Entry **1987**:3
  de la Renta, Oscar **2005**:4
  Dickinson, Janice **2005**:2

Schmidt, Eric **2002**:4
Taylor, Jeff **2001**:3

**Investment banking**
Fomon, Robert M. **1985**:3

**IOC**
See: International Olympic
Committee

**IRA**
See: Irish Republican Army

**Irish Northern Aid Committee
[NORAID]**
Galvin, Martin
Brief Entry **1985**:3

**Irish Republican Army [IRA]**
Adams, Gerald **1994**:1
Galvin, Martin
Brief Entry **1985**:3
McGuinness, Martin **1985**:4

**Jacuzzi Bros., Inc.**
Jacuzzi, Candido
Obituary **1987**:1

**Jaguar Cars PLC**
Egan, John **1987**:2

**Jane magazine**
Pratt, Jane **1999**:1

**Jewish Defense League**
Kahane, Meir
Obituary **1991**:2

**Joffrey Ballet**
Joffrey, Robert
Obituary **1988**:3

**Jolt Cola**
Rapp, C.J.
Brief Entry **1987**:3

**Joe Boxer Corp.**
Graham, Nicholas **1991**:4

**Judo**
Kanokogi, Rusty
Brief Entry **1987**:1

**Juno Awards**
Lavigne, Avril **2005**:2
McLachlan, Sarah **1998**:4
Sainte-Marie, Buffy **2000**:1

**Justin Industries**
Justin, John Jr. **1992**:2

**Kansas City Chiefs football team**
Okoye, Christian **1990**:2
Thomas, Derrick
Obituary **2000**:3

**Kansas City Royals baseball team**
Howser, Dick
Obituary **1987**:4
Jackson, Bo **1986**:3
Saberhagen, Bret **1986**:1

**Kelly Services**
Kelly, William R.
Obituary **1998**:2

**Khmer Rouge**
Lon Nol
Obituary **1986**:1

**Kitty Litter**
Lowe, Edward **1990**:2

**Kloss Video Corp.**
Kloss, Henry E.
Brief Entry **1985**:2

**K Mart Corp.**
Antonini, Joseph **1991**:2
Stewart, Martha **1992**:1

**Kraft General Foods**
Fudge, Ann **2000**:3
Holden, Betsy **2003**:2

**Ku Klux Klan**
Duke, David **1990**:2

**Labor**
Bieber, Owen **1986**:1
Carey, Ron **1993**:3
Eagleson, Alan **1987**:4
Fehr, Donald **1987**:2
Feldman, Sandra **1987**:3
Hoffa, Jim, Jr. **1999**:2
Huerta, Dolores **1998**:1
Kielburger, Craig **1998**:1
Martin, Lynn **1991**:4
Nussbaum, Karen **1988**:3
Presser, Jackie
Obituary **1988**:4
Ramaphosa, Cyril **1988**:2
Rothstein, Ruth **1988**:2
Saporta, Vicki
Brief Entry **1987**:3
Steinberg, Leigh **1987**:3
Upshaw, Gene **1988**:1
Williams, Lynn **1986**:4

**Labour Party (Great Britain)**
Blair, Tony **1996**:3 **1997**:4
Jenkins, Roy Harris
Obituary **2004**:1
Livingstone, Ken **1988**:3
Maxwell, Robert **1990**:1

**Ladies Professional Golf Association
[LPGA]**
Baker, Kathy
Brief Entry **1986**:1
Inkster, Juli **2000**:2
Lopez, Nancy **1989**:3
Pak, Se Ri **1999**:4
Sorenstam, Annika **2001**:1

Webb, Karrie **2000**:4
Whaley, Suzy **2003**:4

**Language instruction**
Thomas, Michel **1987**:4

**Lasers**
Gould, Gordon **1987**:1
Hagelstein, Peter
Brief Entry **1986**:3

**Law enforcement**
Cantrell, Ed
Brief Entry **1985**:3
France, Johnny
Brief Entry **1987**:1
Harvard, Beverly **1995**:2
Rizzo, Frank
Obituary **1992**:1
Watson, Elizabeth **1991**:2
Williams, Willie L. **1993**:1

**Learning Annex**
Zanker, Bill
Brief Entry **1987**:3

**Lear's magazine**
Lear, Frances **1988**:3

**Lego toy system**
Kristiansen, Kjeld Kirk **1988**:3

**Lenin Peace Prize**
Kekkonen, Urho
Obituary **1986**:4

**Lettuce Entertain You Enterprises, Inc.**
Melman, Richard
Brief Entry **1986**:1

**Leukemia research**
Gale, Robert Peter **1986**:4

**Levi Strauss & Co.**
Haas, Robert D. **1986**:4
Marineau, Philip **2002**:4

**Liberal Democratic Party (Japan)**
Miyazawa, Kiichi **1992**:2

**Liberal Party (Canada)**
Chretien, Jean **1990**:4 **1997**:2
Peterson, David **1987**:1

**Liberal Party (South Africa)**
Paton, Alan
Obituary **1988**:3

**Library of Congress**
Billington, James **1990**:3
Dickey, James
Obituary **1998**:2
Van Duyn, Mona **1993**:2

**Likud Party (Israel)**
Netanyahu, Benjamin **1996**:4

**National Endowment for the Arts**
Alexander, Jane **1994**:2
Alexie, Sherman **1998**:4
Anderson, Laurie **2000**:2
Bishop, Andre **2000**:1
Brooks, Gwendolyn **1998**:1
Obituary **2001**:2
Castillo, Ana **2000**:4
Cruz, Nilo **2004**:4
Erdrich, Louise **2005**:3
Fagan, Garth **2000**:1
Jones, Gayl **1999**:4
Lewitzky, Bella
Obituary **2005**:3
Marshall, Susan **2000**:4
Miller, Bebe **2000**:2
Oates, Joyce Carol **2000**:1
Parks, Suzan-Lori **2003**:2
Reeve, Christopher **1997**:2
Ringgold, Faith **2000**:3
Serrano, Andres **2000**:4
Wagner, Catherine F. **2002**:3
Wolff, Tobias **2005**:1

**National Endowment for the Humanities [NEH]**
Cheney, Lynne V. **1990**:4
Hackney, Sheldon **1995**:1

**National Federation for Decency**
Wildmon, Donald **1988**:4

**National Football League [NFL]**
Favre, Brett Lorenzo **1997**:2
Flutie, Doug **1999**:2
Howard, Desmond Kevin **1997**:2
Moss, Randy **1999**:3
Shula, Don **1992**:2
Tagliabue, Paul **1990**:2

**National Football League Players Association**
Upshaw, Gene **1988**:1

**National Hockey League Players Association [NHLPA]**
Bourque, Raymond Jean **1997**:3
Eagleson, Alan **1987**:4
Fuhr, Grant **1997**:3

**National Hot Rod Association [NHRA]**
Muldowney, Shirley **1986**:1

**National Institute of Education**
Justiz, Manuel J. **1986**:4

**National Institutes of Health [NIH]**
Healy, Bernadine **1993**:1
Jacobs, Joe **1994**:1
Zerhouni, Elias A. **2004**:3

**National Organization for Women [NOW]**
Abzug, Bella **1998**:2
Friedan, Betty **1994**:2
Gandy, Kim **2002**:2
Ireland, Patricia **1992**:2
Yard, Molly **1991**:4

**National Park Service**
Mott, William Penn, Jr. **1986**:1

**National Public Radio [NPR]**
Codrescu, Andreá **1997**:3
Edwards, Bob **1993**:2
Gross, Terry **1998**:3
Magliozzi, Tom and Ray **1991**:4
Maynard, Joyce **1999**:4
Roberts, Cokie **1993**:4
Tom and Ray Magliozzi **1991**:4
Totenberg, Nina **1992**:2

**National Restaurant Association**
Cain, Herman **1998**:3

**National Rifle Association [NRA]**
Foss, Joe **1990**:3
Helms, Jesse **1998**:1
Heston, Charlton **1999**:4

**National Science Foundation [NSF]**
Bloch, Erich **1987**:4
Colwell, Rita Rossi **1999**:3
Geller, Margaret Joan **1998**:2

**National Security Agency**
Inman, Bobby Ray **1985**:1

**National Union for the Total Independence of Angola [UNITA]**
Savimbi, Jonas **1986**:2 **1994**:2

**National Union of Mineworkers [NUM]**
Ramaphosa, Cyril **1988**:2

**National Wildlife Federation [NWF]**
Hair, Jay D. **1994**:3

**Native American issues**
Banks, Dennis J. **1986**:4
Begaye, Kelsey **1999**:3
Brown, Dee
Obituary **2004**:1
Campbell, Ben Nighthorse **1998**:1
Castaneda, Carlos
Obituary **1998**:4
Grant, Rodney A. **1992**:1
Greene, Graham **1997**:2
LaDuke, Winona **1995**:2
Mankiller, Wilma P.
Brief Entry **1986**:2
Peltier, Leonard **1995**:1
Sidney, Ivan
Brief Entry **1987**:2
Studi, Wes **1994**:3

**NATO**
See: North Atlantic Treaty Organization

**Nautilus Sports/Medical Industries**
Jones, Arthur A. **1985**:3

**Navajo Nation**
Begaye, Kelsey **1999**:3

**Nazi Party**
Hess, Rudolph
Obituary **1988**:1
Klarsfeld, Beate **1989**:1
Mengele, Josef
Obituary **1985**:2

**NBC Television Network**
Brokaw, Tom **2000**:3
Curry, Ann **2001**:1
Gumbel, Greg **1996**:4
Tartikoff, Brandon **1985**:2
Obituary **1998**:1

**NCPAC**
See: National Conservative Political Action Committee

**NCTV**
See: National Coalition on Television Violence

**NDP**
See: New Democratic Party (Canada)

**NEA**
See: National Education Association

**Nebraska state government**
Kerrey, Bob **1986**:1 **1991**:3
Orr, Kay **1987**:4

**Nebula Awards**
Asimov, Isaac
Obituary **1992**:3
Brooks, Mel **2003**:1

**Negro American League**
Pride, Charley **1998**:1

**NEH**
See: National Endowment for the Humanities

**Netscape Communications Corp.**
Andreessen, Marc **1996**:2
Barksdale, James L. **1998**:2
Clark, Jim **1997**:1

**Neurobiology**
Goldman-Rakic, Patricia **2002**:4
Kandel, Eric **2005**:2
LeVay, Simon **1992**:2
Tully, Tim **2004**:3

**New Democratic Party (Canada) [NDP]**
Lewis, Stephen **1987**:2
McLaughlin, Audrey **1990**:3

**New England Patriots football team**
Bledsoe, Drew **1995**:1
Brady, Tom **2002**:4

**Newfoundland provincial government**
Peckford, Brian **1989**:1

**New Hampshire state government**
Sununu, John **1989**:2

**New Jersey Devils hockey team**
Lemieux, Claude **1996**:1

**New Orleans Saints football team**
Williams, Ricky **2000**:2

**New York City Ballet**
Kistler, Darci **1993**:1
Whelan, Wendy **1999**:3

**New York City Board of Education**
Green, Richard R. **1988**:3

**New York City government**
Dinkins, David N. **1990**:2
Fairstein, Linda **1991**:1
Giuliani, Rudolph **1994**:2
Kennedy, John F., Jr. **1990**:1
Obituary **1999**:4

**New Yorker magazine**
Brown, Tina **1992**:1
Chast, Roz **1992**:4
Hoff, Syd
Obituary **2005**:3
Shawn, William
Obituary **1993**:3
Steig, William
Obituary **2004**:4

**New York Giants football team**
Collins, Kerry **2002**:3
Taylor, Lawrence **1987**:3

**New York Islanders hockey team**
LaFontaine, Pat **1985**:1

**New York Knicks basketball team**
Bradley, Bill **2000**:2
Ewing, Patrick **1985**:3
McMillen, Tom **1988**:4
Riley, Pat **1994**:3
Sprewell, Latrell **1999**:4

**New York Mets baseball team**
Agee, Tommie
Obituary **2001**:4
Bonilla, Bobby **1992**:2
Carter, Gary **1987**:1
Doubleday, Nelson, Jr. **1987**:1
Gooden, Dwight **1985**:2
McGraw, Tug
Obituary **2005**:1
Piazza, Mike **1998**:4
Ryan, Nolan **1989**:4

**New York Philharmonic Orchestra**
Masur, Kurt **1993**:4

**New York Public Library**
Gregorian, Vartan **1990**:3
Healy, Timothy S. **1990**:2

**New York Rangers hockey team**
Messier, Mark **1993**:1

**New York City public schools**
Fernandez, Joseph **1991**:3

**New York State Government**
Cuomo, Mario **1992**:2
Florio, James J. **1991**:2
Pataki, George **1995**:2
Rothwax, Harold **1996**:3

**New York Stock Exchange**
Fomon, Robert M. **1985**:3
Phelan, John Joseph, Jr. **1985**:4
Siebert, Muriel **1987**:2

**New York Times**
Dowd, Maureen Brigid **1997**:1
Lelyveld, Joseph S. **1994**:4
Sulzberger, Arthur O., Jr. **1998**:3

**New York Titans football team**
Barnes, Ernie **1997**:4

**New York Yankees baseball team**
DiMaggio, Joe
Obituary **1999**:3
Gomez, 'Lefty'
Obituary **1989**:3
Howser, Dick
Obituary **1987**:4
Jeter, Derek **1999**:4
Mantle, Mickey
Obituary **1996**:1
Maris, Roger
Obituary **1986**:1
Martin, Billy **1988**:4
Obituary **1990**:2
Mattingly, Don **1986**:2
Steinbrenner, George **1991**:1
Torre, Joseph Paul **1997**:1
Wells, David **1999**:3

**NFL**
See: National Football League

**NHLPA**
See: National Hockey League
Players Association

**NHRA**
See: National Hot Rod Association

**NIH**
See: National Institutes of Health

**Nike, Inc.**
Hamm, Mia **2000**:1
Knight, Philip H. **1994**:1 9 to 5
Bravo, Ellen **1998**:2
Nussbaum, Karen **1988**:3

**Nissan Motor Co.**
Katayama, Yutaka **1987**:1

**No Limit (record label)**
Master P **1999**:4

**Nobel Prize**
Altman, Sidney **1997**:2
Arias Sanchez, Oscar **1989**:3
Beckett, Samuel Barclay
Obituary **1990**:2
Begin, Menachem
Obituary **1992**:3
Blobel, Gunter **2000**:4
Carlsson, Arvid **2001**:2
Cela, Camilo Jose
Obituary **2003**:1
Coetzee, J. M. **2004**:4
Cram, Donald J.
Obituary **2002**:2
Crick, Francis
Obituary **2005**:4
Ebadi, Shirin **2004**:3
Fo, Dario **1998**:1
Gao Xingjian **2001**:2
Garcia Marquez, Gabriel **2005**:2
Grass, Gunter **2000**:2
Heaney, Seamus **1996**:2
Hounsfield, Godfrey **1989**:2
Jelinek, Elfriede **2005**:3
Kandel, Eric **2005**:2
Kilby, Jack **2002**:2
Kissinger, Henry **1999**:4
Kornberg, Arthur **1992**:1
Lederman, Leon Max **1989**:4
Lewis, Edward B.
Obituary **2005**:4
Lorenz, Konrad
Obituary **1989**:3
Menchu, Rigoberta **1993**:2
Milosz, Czeslaw
Obituary **2005**:4
Morrison, Toni **1998**:1
Mother Teresa **1993**:1
Obituary **1998**:1
Mullis, Kary **1995**:3
Nuesslein-Volhard, Christiane **1998**:1
Oe, Kenzaburo **1997**:1
Pauling, Linus
Obituary **1995**:1
Paz, Octavio **1991**:2
Perutz, Max
Obituary **2003**:2
Pople, John
Obituary **2005**:2
Porter, George
Obituary **2003**:4
Prusiner, Stanley **1998**:2
Sakharov, Andrei Dmitrievich
Obituary **1990**:2
Saramago, Jose **1999**:1
Singer, Isaac Bashevis
Obituary **1992**:1
Suu Kyi, Aung San **1996**:2
Szent-Gyoergyi, Albert
Obituary **1987**:2
Trimble, David **1999**:1
Walesa, Lech **1991**:2
Wiesel, Elie **1998**:1

**NORAID**
See: Irish Northern Aid Committee

**North Atlantic Treaty Organization [NATO]**
de Hoop Scheffer, Jaap **2005**:1
Galvin, John R. **1990**:1

**NOW**
See: National Organization for Women

**NRA**
See: National Rifle Association

**NRC**
See: Nuclear Regulatory Commission

**NPR**
See: National Public Radio
Tom and Ray Magliozzi **1991**:4

**NSF**
See: National Science Foundation

**Nuclear energy**
Gale, Robert Peter **1986**:4
Hagelstein, Peter
Brief Entry **1986**:3
Lederman, Leon Max **1989**:4
Maglich, Bogdan C. **1990**:1
Merritt, Justine
Brief Entry **1985**:3
Nader, Ralph **1989**:4
Palme, Olof
Obituary **1986**:2
Rickover, Hyman
Obituary **1986**:4
Sinclair, Mary **1985**:2
Smith, Samantha
Obituary **1985**:3
Zech, Lando W.
Brief Entry **1987**:4

**Nuclear Regulatory Commission [NRC]**
Zech, Lando W.
Brief Entry **1987**:4

**NUM**
See: National Union of Mineworkers

**NWF**
See: National Wildlife Federation

**Oakland A's baseball team**
Canseco, Jose **1990**:2
Caray, Harry **1988**:3
Obituary **1998**:3
Stewart, Dave **1991**:1
Welch, Bob **1991**:3
Zito, Barry **2003**:3

**Oakland Raiders football team**
Matuszak, John
Obituary **1989**:4
Trask, Amy **2003**:3
Upshaw, Gene **1988**:1

**Obie Awards**
Albee, Edward **1997**:1
Baldwin, Alec **2002**:2
Bergman, Ingmar **1999**:4
Close, Glenn **1988**:3
Coco, James
Obituary **1987**:2
Daniels, Jeff **1989**:4
Dewhurst, Colleen
Obituary **1992**:2
Diller, Elizabeth and
Ricardo Scofidio **2004**:3
Dukakis, Olympia **1996**:4
Duvall, Robert **1999**:3
Ensler, Eve **2002**:4
Fierstein, Harvey **2004**:2
Fo, Dario **1998**:1
Fugard, Athol **1992**:3
Gray, Spalding
Obituary **2005**:2
Hoffman, Dustin **2005**:4
Hurt, William **1986**:1
Hwang, David Henry **1999**:1
Irwin, Bill **1988**:3
Kline, Kevin **2000**:1
Leguizamo, John **1999**:1
Miller, Arthur **1999**:4
Pacino, Al **1993**:4
Parks, Suzan-Lori **2003**:2
Shepard, Sam **1996**:4
Streep, Meryl **1990**:2
Tune, Tommy **1994**:2
Turturro, John **2002**:2
Vogel, Paula **1999**:2
Washington, Denzel **1993**:2
Woods, James **1988**:3

**Occidental Petroleum Corp.**
Hammer, Armand
Obituary **1991**:3

**Oceanography**
Cousteau, Jacques-Yves
Obituary **1998**:2
Cousteau, Jean-Michel **1988**:2
Fisher, Mel **1985**:4

**Office of National Drug Control Policy**
Bennett, William **1990**:1
Martinez, Bob **1992**:1

**Ogilvy & Mather Advertising**
Lazarus, Shelly **1998**:3

**Ohio State University football team**
Hayes, Woody
Obituary **1987**:2

**Oil**
Adair, Red **1987**:3
Aurre, Laura
Brief Entry **1986**:3
Hammer, Armand
Obituary **1991**:3
Jones, Jerry **1994**:4

**Olympic games**
Abbott, Jim **1988**:3
Ali, Muhammad **1997**:2
Armstrong, Lance **2000**:1

Baiul, Oksana **1995**:3
Baumgartner, Bruce
Brief Entry **1987**:3
Benoit, Joan **1986**:3
Blair, Bonnie **1992**:3
Boitano, Brian **1988**:3
Bradley, Bill **2000**:2
Conner, Dennis **1987**:2
Davenport, Lindsay **1999**:2
De La Hoya, Oscar **1998**:2
DiBello, Paul
Brief Entry **1986**:4
Dolan, Tom **2001**:2
Drexler, Clyde **1992**:4
Eagleson, Alan **1987**:4
Edwards, Harry **1989**:4
Evans, Janet **1989**:1
Ewing, Patrick **1985**:3
Freeman, Cathy **2001**:3
Gault, Willie **1991**:2
Graf, Steffi **1987**:4
Granato, Cammi **1999**:3
Grinkov, Sergei
Obituary **1996**:2
Hamilton, Scott **1998**:2
Hamm, Mia **2000**:1
Hamm, Paul **2005**:1
Holyfield, Evander **1991**:3
Hughes, Sarah **2002**:4
Johnson, Michael **2000**:1
Jordan, Michael **1987**:2
Joyner, Florence Griffith **1989**:2
Obituary **1999**:1
Joyner-Kersee, Jackie **1993**:1
Kerrigan, Nancy **1994**:3
Kiraly, Karch
Brief Entry **1987**:1
Knight, Bobby **1985**:3
Laettner, Christian **1993**:1
LaFontaine, Pat **1985**:1
Lalas, Alexi **1995**:1
Leonard, Sugar Ray **1989**:4
Leslie, Lisa **1997**:4
Lewis, Lennox **2000**:2
Lindbergh, Pelle
Obituary **1985**:4
Lipinski, Tara **1998**:3
Louganis, Greg **1995**:3
Milbrett, Tiffeny **2001**:1
Milburn, Rodney Jr.
Obituary **1998**:2
Miller, Bode **2002**:4
Retton, Mary Lou **1985**:2
Rudolph, Wilma
Obituary **1995**:2
Runyan, Marla **2001**:1
Samaranch, Juan Antonio **1986**:2
Shea, Jim, Jr. **2002**:4
Street, Picabo **1999**:3
Strobl, Fritz **2003**:3
Strug, Kerri **1997**:3
Summitt, Pat **2004**:1
Swoopes, Sheryl **1998**:2
Thomas, Debi **1987**:2
Thompson, John **1988**:3
Tomba, Alberto **1992**:3
Van Dyken, Amy **1997**:1
Waddell, Thomas F.
Obituary **1988**:2
Witt, Katarina **1991**:3
Woodard, Lynette **1986**:2
Yamaguchi, Kristi **1992**:3

**Planned Parenthood Federation of America**
Maraldo, Pamela J. **1993**:4
Wattleton, Faye **1989**:1

**Playboy Enterprises**
Hefner, Christie **1985**:1
Ingersoll, Ralph II **1988**:2
Melman, Richard
Brief Entry **1986**:1

**Pleasant Company**
Rowland, Pleasant **1992**:3

**PLO**
See: Palestine Liberation
Organization

**PMRC**
See: Parents' Music Resource Center

**Poetry**
Angelou, Maya **1993**:4
Bly, Robert **1992**:4
Brooks, Gwendolyn **1998**:1
Obituary **2001**:2
Burroughs, William S.
Obituary **1997**:4
Codrescu, Andreá **1997**:3
Collins, Billy **2002**:2
Dickey, James
Obituary **1998**:2
Dove, Rita **1994**:3
Dylan, Bob **1998**:1
Ginsberg, Allen
Obituary **1997**:3
Heaney, Seamus **1996**:2
Hughes, Ted
Obituary **1999**:2
Jewel **1999**:2
Jones, Sarah **2005**:2
Kunitz, Stanley J. **2001**:2
Milligan, Spike
Obituary **2003**:2
Milosz, Czeslaw
Obituary **2005**:4
Mortensen, Viggo **2003**:3
Nemerov, Howard
Obituary **1992**:1
Paz, Octavio **1991**:2
Sapphire **1996**:4
Senghor, Leopold
Obituary **2003**:1
Van Duyn, Mona **1993**:2
Walker, Alice **1999**:1

**Polaroid Corp.**
Land, Edwin H.
Obituary **1991**:3

**Pole vaulting**
Olson, Billy **1986**:3

**Pop art**
Castelli, Leo
Obituary **2000**:1
Lichtenstein, Roy **1994**:1
Obituary **1998**:1
Richter, Gerhard **1997**:2

Warhol, Andy
Obituary **1987**:2

**Popular Front for the Liberation of Palestine [PFLP]**
Habash, George **1986**:1

**Pornography**
Flynt, Larry **1997**:3

**Portland, Ore., city government**
Clark, J. E.
Brief Entry **1986**:1

**Portland Trail Blazers basketball team**
Drexler, Clyde **1992**:4
Wilkens, Lenny **1995**:2

**POWER**
See: People Organized and Working
for Economic Rebirth

**President's Council for Physical Fitness**
Schwarzenegger, Arnold **1991**:1

**Presidential Medal of Freedom**
Annenberg, Walter **1992**:3
Cagney, James
Obituary **1986**:2
Cheek, James Edward
Brief Entry **1987**:1
Copland, Aaron
Obituary **1991**:2
Cronkite, Walter Leland **1997**:3
Ellison, Ralph
Obituary **1994**:4
Fulbright, J. William
Obituary **1995**:3
Kissinger, Henry **1999**:4
Luce, Clare Boothe
Obituary **1988**:1
Ormandy, Eugene
Obituary **1985**:2
Rickover, Hyman
Obituary **1986**:4
Rumsfeld, Donald **2004**:1
Salk, Jonas **1994**:4
Obituary **1995**:4
Sinatra, Frank
Obituary **1998**:4
Smith, Kate
Obituary **1986**:3
Strauss, Robert **1991**:4
Wasserman, Lew
Obituary **2003**:3

**Primerica**
Weill, Sandy **1990**:4

**Princeton, N.J., city government**
Sigmund, Barbara Boggs
Obituary **1991**:1

**Pritzker Prize**
Ando, Tadao **2005**:4
Bunshaft, Gordon **1989**:3
Obituary **1991**:1
Foster, Norman **1999**:4
Hadid, Zaha **2005**:3

Johnson, Philip **1989**:2
Koolhaas, Rem **2001**:1
Pritzker, A.N.
Obituary **1986**:2
Roche, Kevin **1985**:1
Venturi, Robert **1994**:4

**Procter & Gamble Co.**
Lafley, A. G. **2003**:4
Smale, John G. **1987**:3

**Proctor & Gardner Advertising, Inc.**
Proctor, Barbara Gardner **1985**:3

**Professional Bowlers Association [PBA]**
Weber, Pete **1986**:3

**Professional Golfers Association [PGA]**
Azinger, Paul **1995**:2
Chen, T.C.
Brief Entry **1987**:3
Couples, Fred **1994**:4
Curtis, Ben **2004**:2
Furyk, Jim **2004**:2
Irwin, Hale **2005**:2
Norman, Greg **1988**:3
Peete, Calvin **1985**:4
Sarazen, Gene
Obituary **1999**:4
Singh, Vijay **2000**:4
Stewart, Payne
Obituary **2000**:2
Strange, Curtis **1988**:4
Weir, Mike **2004**:1

**Professional Flair**
Verdi-Fletcher, Mary **1998**:2

**Progress and Freedom Foundation**
Huffington, Arianna **1996**:2

**Project Head Start**
Zigler, Edward **1994**:1

**Promise Keepers**
McCartney, Bill **1995**:3

**Psychedelic drugs**
Castaneda, Carlos
Obituary **1998**:4
Leary, Timothy
Obituary **1996**:4
McKenna, Terence **1993**:3

**Psychiatry**
Bettelheim, Bruno
Obituary **1990**:3
Coles, Robert **1995**:1
Frankl, Viktor E.
Obituary **1998**:1
Laing, R.D.
Obituary **1990**:1
Menninger, Karl
Obituary **1991**:1

**Psychology**
Pinker, Steven A. **2000**:1

Melman, Richard
  Brief Entry **1986**:1
Petrossian, Christian
  Brief Entry **1985**:3
Pouillon, Nora **2005**:1
Puck, Wolfgang **1990**:1
Shaich, Ron **2004**:4
Thomas, Dave **1986**:2 **1993**:2
  Obituary **2003**:1
Zagat, Tim and Nina **2004**:3

**Retailing**
  Bravo, Rose Marie **2005**:3
  Charron, Paul **2004**:1
  Drexler, Millard S. **1990**:3
  Marcus, Stanley
    Obituary **2003**:1
  Persson, Stefan **2004**:1

**Reuben Awards**
  Gould, Chester
    Obituary **1985**:2
  Schulz, Charles
    Obituary **2000**:3

**Revlon, Inc.**
  Duffy, Karen **1998**:1
  Perelman, Ronald **1989**:2

**Rhode Island state government**
  Violet, Arlene **1985**:3

**Richter Scale**
  Richter, Charles Francis
    Obituary **1985**:4

**Ringling Brothers and Barnum & Bailey Circus**
  Burck, Wade
    Brief Entry **1986**:1
  Feld, Kenneth **1988**:2

**RJR Nabisco, Inc.**
  Horrigan, Edward, Jr. **1989**:1

**Robotics**
  Kwoh, Yik San **1988**:2

**Rock Climbing**
  Hill, Lynn **1991**:2

**Rockman**
  Scholz, Tom **1987**:2

**Roller Coasters**
  Toomer, Ron **1990**:1

**Rolling Stone magazine**
  Wenner, Jann **1993**:1

**Rotary engine**
  Yamamoto, Kenichi **1989**:1

**Running**
  Benoit, Joan **1986**:3
  Joyner, Florence Griffith **1989**:2
    Obituary **1999**:1

Knight, Philip H. **1994**:1
Zatopek, Emil
  Obituary **2001**:3

**Russian Federation**
  Putin, Vladimir **2000**:3
  Yeltsin, Boris **1991**:1

**SADD**
  See: Students Against Drunken Driving

**Sailing**
  Alter, Hobie
    Brief Entry **1985**:1
  Conner, Dennis **1987**:2
  Koch, Bill **1992**:3
  Morgan, Dodge **1987**:1
  Turner, Ted **1989**:1

**St. Louis Blues hockey team**
  Fuhr, Grant **1997**:3
  Hull, Brett **1991**:4

**St. Louis Browns baseball team**
  Veeck, Bill
    Obituary **1986**:1

**St. Louis Cardinals baseball team**
  Busch, August A. III **1988**:2
  Busch, August Anheuser, Jr.
    Obituary **1990**:2
  Caray, Harry **1988**:3
    Obituary **1998**:3
  McGwire, Mark **1999**:1
  Pujols, Albert **2005**:3

**St. Louis Rams football team**
  Warner, Kurt **2000**:3

**San Antonio Spurs basketball team**
  Duncan, Tim **2000**:1
  Robinson, David **1990**:4

**San Antonio, Tex., city government**
  Cisneros, Henry **1987**:2

**San Diego Chargers football team**
  Barnes, Ernie **1997**:4
  Bell, Ricky
    Obituary **1985**:1
  Unitas, Johnny
    Obituary **2003**:4

**San Diego Padres baseball team**
  Dravecky, Dave **1992**:1
  Gwynn, Tony **1995**:1
  Kroc, Ray
    Obituary **1985**:1
  Sheffield, Gary **1998**:1

**San Francisco city government**
  Alioto, Joseph L.
    Obituary **1998**:3
  Brown, Willie **1996**:4

**San Francisco 49ers football team**
  DeBartolo, Edward J., Jr. **1989**:3
  Montana, Joe **1989**:2
  Rice, Jerry **1990**:4
  Walsh, Bill **1987**:4
  Young, Steve **1995**:2

**San Francisco Giants baseball team**
  Bonds, Barry **1993**:3
  Dravecky, Dave **1992**:1

**SANE/FREEZE**
  Coffin, William Sloane, Jr. **1990**:3

**Save the Children Federation**
  Guyer, David
    Brief Entry **1988**:1

**SBA**
  See: Small Business Administration

**Schottco Corp.**
  Schott, Marge **1985**:4

**Schwinn Bicycle Co.**
  Schwinn, Edward R., Jr.
    Brief Entry **1985**:4

**Science fiction**
  Anderson, Poul
    Obituary **2002**:3
  Asimov, Isaac
    Obituary **1992**:3
  Butler, Octavia E. **1999**:3
  Kelley, DeForest
    Obituary **2000**:1
  Lucas, George **1999**:4
  Sterling, Bruce **1995**:4

**Sculpture**
  Beuys, Joseph
    Obituary **1986**:3
  Bontecou, Lee **2004**:4
  Botero, Fernando **1994**:3
  Bourgeois, Louise **1994**:1
  Chia, Sandro **1987**:2
  Chillida, Eduardo
    Obituary **2003**:4
  Christo **1992**:3
  Dubuffet, Jean
    Obituary **1985**:4
  Dunham, Carroll **2003**:4
  Gober, Robert **1996**:3
  Graham, Robert **1993**:4
  Graves, Nancy **1989**:3
  Kaskey, Ray
    Brief Entry **1987**:2
  Kelly, Ellsworth **1992**:1
  Kiefer, Anselm **1990**:2
  Lin, Maya **1990**:3
  Moore, Henry
    Obituary **1986**:4
  Murakami, Takashi **2004**:2
  Nevelson, Louise
    Obituary **1988**:3
  Ono, Yoko **1989**:2
  Puryear, Martin **2002**:4

Raimondi, John
  Brief Entry **1987**:4
Rauschenberg, Robert **1991**:2
Rosenberg, Evelyn **1988**:2
Tamayo, Rufino
  Obituary **1992**:1
Truitt, Anne **1993**:1

**SDLP**
  See: Social Democratic and Labour
  Party

**Seagram Co.**
  Bronfman, Edgar, Jr. **1994**:4

**Seattle Mariners baseball team**
  Griffey, Ken Jr. **1994**:1
  Johnson, Randy **1996**:2
  Suzuki, Ichiro **2002**:2

**Seattle Seahawks football team**
  Bosworth, Brian **1989**:1

**Seattle Supersonics basketball team**
  Kemp, Shawn **1995**:1
  Wilkens, Lenny **1995**:2

**Sears, Roebuck & Co.**
  Brennan, Edward A. **1989**:1

**Second City comedy troupe**
  Aykroyd, Dan **1989**:3 **1997**:3
  Belushi, Jim **1986**:2
  Candy, John **1988**:2
    Obituary **1994**:3
  Fey, Tina **2005**:3
  Levy, Eugene **2004**:3
  Radner, Gilda
    Obituary **1989**:4
  Short, Martin **1986**:1

**Sedelmaier Film Productions**
  Sedelmaier, Joe **1985**:3

**Seismology**
  Richter, Charles Francis
    Obituary **1985**:4

**Senate Armed Services Committee**
  Cohen, William S. **1998**:1
  Goldwater, Barry
    Obituary **1998**:4
  McCain, John S. **1998**:4
  Nunn, Sam **1990**:2
  Tower, John
    Obituary **1991**:4

**Sharper Image, The**
  Thalheimer, Richard
    Brief Entry **1988**:3

**Shiites**
  Berri, Nabih **1985**:2
  Khomeini, Ayatollah Ruhollah
    Obituary **1989**:4
  Rafsanjani, Ali Akbar Hashemi
    **1987**:3

**ShoWest Awards**
  Driver, Minnie **2000**:1
  Swank, Hilary **2000**:3
  Yeoh, Michelle **2003**:2

**Shubert Organization**
  Schoenfeld, Gerald **1986**:2

**Sierra Club**
  McCloskey, J. Michael **1988**:2

**Sinn Fein**
  Adams, Gerald **1994**:1
  McGuinness, Martin **1985**:4

**Skiing**
  DiBello, Paul
    Brief Entry **1986**:4
  Miller, Bode **2002**:4
  Street, Picabo **1999**:3
  Strobl, Fritz **2003**:3
  Tomba, Alberto **1992**:3

**Sled dog racing**
  Butcher, Susan **1991**:1

**Small Business Administration [SBA]**
  Alvarez, Aida **1999**:2

**Smith College**
  Simmons, Ruth **1995**:2

**Smoking**
  Horrigan, Edward, Jr. **1989**:1
  Maxwell, Hamish **1989**:4

**So So Def Recordings, Inc.**
  Dupri, Jermaine **1999**:1

**Soccer**
  Adu, Freddy **2005**:3
  Akers, Michelle **1996**:1
  Beckham, David **2003**:1
  Chastain, Brandi **2001**:3
  Harkes, John **1996**:4
  Lalas, Alexi **1995**:1
  Maradona, Diego **1991**:3
  Mathis, Clint **2003**:1
  Ronaldo **1999**:2

**Social Democratic and Labour Party [SDLP]**
  Hume, John **1987**:1

**Socialism**
  Castro, Fidel **1991**:4
  Sanders, Bernie **1991**:4

**Socialist Party (France)**
  Cresson, Edith **1992**:1

**Softball**
  Stofflet, Ty
    Brief Entry **1987**:1

**Soloflex, Inc.**
  Wilson, Jerry
    Brief Entry **1986**:2

**Sony Corp.**
  Kutaragi, Ken **2005**:3
  Morita, Akio **1989**:4
  Morita, Akio
    Obituary **2000**:2
  Mottola, Tommy **2002**:1

**Sotheby & Co.**
  Brooks, Diana D. **1990**:1
  Wilson, Peter C.
    Obituary **1985**:2

**South West African People's Organization [SWAPO]**
  Nujoma, Sam **1990**:4

**Southwest Airlines**
  Kelleher, Herb **1995**:1

**Southern Baptist Convention**
  Rogers, Adrian **1987**:4

**Soviet-American relations**
  Chernenko, Konstantin
    Obituary **1985**:1
  Dubinin, Yuri **1987**:4
  Dzhanibekov, Vladimir **1988**:1
  Gale, Robert Peter **1986**:4
  Gorbachev, Mikhail **1985**:2
  Grebenshikov, Boris **1990**:1
  Gromyko, Andrei
    Obituary **1990**:2
  Hammer, Armand
    Obituary **1991**:3
  Harriman, W. Averell
    Obituary **1986**:4
  Putin, Vladimir **2000**:3
  Sakharov, Andrei Dmitrievich
    Obituary **1990**:2
  Smith, Samantha
    Obituary **1985**:3
  Vidov, Oleg **1987**:4

**Speed skating**
  Blair, Bonnie **1992**:3

**Spin magazine**
  Guccione, Bob, Jr. **1991**:4

**Spinal-cord injuries**
  Reeve, Christopher **1997**:2

**Starbucks Coffee Co.**
  Schultz, Howard **1995**:3

**Strategic Defense Initiative**
  Hagelstein, Peter
    Brief Entry **1986**:3

**Stroh Brewery Co.**
  Stroh, Peter W. **1985**:2

**Students Against Drunken Driving [SADD]**
  Anastas, Robert
    Brief Entry **1985**:2
  Lightner, Candy **1985**:1

**Submarines**
  Rickover, Hyman
    Obituary **1986**:4
  Zech, Lando W.
    Brief Entry **1987**:4

**Sun Microsystems, Inc.**
  McNealy, Scott **1999**:4

**Sunbeam Corp.**
Dunlap, Albert J. **1997**:2

**Suicide**
Applewhite, Marshall Herff
Obituary **1997**:3
Dorris, Michael
Obituary **1997**:3
Hutchence, Michael
Obituary **1998**:1
Quill, Timothy E. **1997**:3

**Sundance Institute**
Redford, Robert **1993**:2

**Sunshine Foundation**
Sample, Bill
Brief Entry **1986**:2

**Superconductors**
Chaudhari, Praveen **1989**:4
Chu, Paul C.W. **1988**:2

**Supreme Court of Canada**
Wilson, Bertha
Brief Entry **1986**:1

**Surfing**
Curren, Tommy
Brief Entry **1987**:4

**SWAPO**
See: South West African People's
Organization

**Swimming**
Ederle, Gertrude
Obituary **2005**:1
Evans, Janet **1989**:1
Van Dyken, Amy **1997**:1

**Tampa Bay Buccaneers football team**
Bell, Ricky
Obituary **1985**:1
Gruden, Jon **2003**:4
Johnson, Keyshawn **2000**:4
Testaverde, Vinny **1987**:2
Williams, Doug **1988**:2
Young, Steve **1995**:2

**Tandem Computers, Inc.**
Treybig, James G. **1988**:3

**Teach for America**
Kopp, Wendy **1993**:3

**Tectonics**
Rosendahl, Bruce R.
Brief Entry **1986**:4

**Teddy Ruxpin**
Kingsborough, Donald
Brief Entry **1986**:2

**Tele-Communications, Inc.**
Malone, John C. **1988**:3 **1996**:3

**Televangelism**
Graham, Billy **1992**:1
Hahn, Jessica **1989**:4
Robertson, Pat **1988**:2

Rogers, Adrian **1987**:4
Swaggart, Jimmy **1987**:3

**Temple University basketball team**
Chaney, John **1989**:1

**Tennis**
Agassi, Andre **1990**:2
Ashe, Arthur
Obituary **1993**:3
Becker, Boris
Brief Entry **1985**:3
Capriati, Jennifer **1991**:1
Courier, Jim **1993**:2
Davenport, Lindsay **1999**:2
Federer, Roger **2004**:2
Gerulaitis, Vitas
Obituary **1995**:1
Gibson, Althea
Obituary **2004**:4
Graf, Steffi **1987**:4
Henin-Hardenne, Justine **2004**:4
Hewitt, Lleyton **2002**:2
Hingis, Martina **1999**:1
Ivanisevic, Goran **2002**:1
Kournikova, Anna **2000**:3
Navratilova, Martina **1989**:1
Pierce, Mary **1994**:4
Riggs, Bobby
Obituary **1996**:2
Roddick, Andy **2004**:3
Sabatini, Gabriela
Brief Entry **1985**:4
Safin, Marat **2001**:3
Sampras, Pete **1994**:1
Seles, Monica **1991**:3
Sharapova, Maria **2005**:2
Williams, Serena **1999**:4
Williams, Venus **1998**:2

**Test tube babies**
Steptoe, Patrick
Obituary **1988**:3

**Texas Rangers baseball team**
Rodriguez, Alex **2001**:2
Ryan, Nolan **1989**:4

**Texas State Government**
Bush, George W., Jr. **1996**:4
Richards, Ann **1991**:2

**Therapeutic Recreation Systems**
Radocy, Robert
Brief Entry **1986**:3

**Timberline Reclamations**
McIntyre, Richard
Brief Entry **1986**:2

**Time Warner Inc.**
Ho, David **1997**:2
Levin, Gerald **1995**:2
Ross, Steven J.
Obituary **1993**:3

**TLC Beatrice International**
Lewis, Loida Nicolas **1998**:3

**TLC Group L.P.**
Lewis, Reginald F. **1988**:4
Obituary **1993**:3

**Today Show**
Couric, Katherine **1991**:4
Gumbel, Bryant **1990**:2
Norville, Deborah **1990**:3

**Tony Awards**
Abbott, George
Obituary **1995**:3
Alda, Robert
Obituary **1986**:3
Alexander, Jane **1994**:2
Alexander, Jason **1993**:3
Allen, Debbie **1998**:2
Allen, Joan **1998**:1
Bacall, Lauren **1997**:3
Bailey, Pearl
Obituary **1991**:1
Bates, Alan
Obituary **2005**:1
Bennett, Michael
Obituary **1988**:1
Bloch, Ivan **1986**:3
Booth, Shirley
Obituary **1993**:2
Brooks, Mel **2003**:1
Brynner, Yul
Obituary **1985**:4
Buckley, Betty **1996**:2
Burnett, Carol **2000**:3
Carter, Nell
Obituary **2004**:2
Channing, Stockard **1991**:3
Close, Glenn **1988**:3
Crawford, Cheryl
Obituary **1987**:1
Crawford, Michael **1994**:2
Cronyn, Hume
Obituary **2004**:3
Dench, Judi **1999**:4
Dennis, Sandy
Obituary **1992**:4
Dewhurst, Colleen
Obituary **1992**:2
Fagan, Garth **2000**:1
Ferrer, Jose
Obituary **1992**:3
Fiennes, Ralph **1996**:2
Fierstein, Harvey **2004**:2
Fishburne, Laurence **1995**:3
Flanders, Ed
Obituary **1995**:3
Fosse, Bob
Obituary **1988**:1
Foster, Sutton **2003**:2
Gleason, Jackie
Obituary **1987**:4
Glover, Savion **1997**:1
Hagen, Uta
Obituary **2005**:2
Harrison, Rex
Obituary **1990**:4
Hepburn, Katharine **1991**:2
Hines, Gregory **1992**:4
Hoffman, Dustin **2005**:4
Hwang, David Henry **1999**:1
Irons, Jeremy **1991**:4
Jackman, Hugh **2004**:4
Kahn, Madeline
Obituary **2000**:2
Keaton, Diane **1997**:1
Kline, Kevin **2000**:1
Kushner, Tony **1995**:2
Lane, Nathan **1996**:4

Lansbury, Angela **1993**:1
LaPaglia, Anthony **2004**:4
Lithgow, John **1985**:2
Mantegna, Joe **1992**:1
Matthau, Walter **2000**:3
McKellen, Ian **1994**:1
Merrick, David
  Obituary **2000**:4
Midler, Bette **1989**:4
Miller, Arthur **1999**:4
Moore, Dudley
  Obituary **2003**:2
Nichols, Mike **1994**:4
Nunn, Trevor **2000**:2
Pacino, Al **1993**:4
Papp, Joseph
  Obituary **1992**:2
Parker, Mary-Louise **2002**:2
Peters, Bernadette **2000**:1
Preston, Robert
  Obituary **1987**:3
Prince, Faith **1993**:2
Reza, Yasmina **1999**:2
Robbins, Jerome
  Obituary **1999**:1
Ruehl, Mercedes **1992**:4
Salonga, Lea **2003**:3
Sondheim, Stephen **1994**:4
Spacey, Kevin **1996**:4
Stoppard, Tom **1995**:4
Stritch, Elaine **2002**:4
Stroman, Susan **2000**:4
Styne, Jule
  Obituary **1995**:1
Tune, Tommy **1994**:2
Verdon, Gwen
  Obituary **2001**:2
Wasserstein, Wendy **1991**:3
Wayne, David
  Obituary **1995**:3
Whitehead, Robert
  Obituary **2003**:3
Winokur, Marissa Jaret **2005**:1
Wong, B.D. **1998**:1
Worth, Irene
  Obituary **2003**:2

**Toronto Blue Jays baseball team**
  Ainge, Danny **1987**:1
  Carter, Joe **1994**:2
  Wells, David **1999**:3

**Toronto Maple Leafs hockey team**
  Gilmour, Doug **1994**:3

**Tour de France**
  Armstrong, Lance **2000**:1
  Indurain, Miguel **1994**:1
  LeMond, Greg **1986**:4

**Toyota Motor Corp.**
  Toyoda, Eiji **1985**:2

**Toys and games**
  Barad, Jill **1994**:2
  Bushnell, Nolan **1985**:1
  Hakuta, Ken
    Brief Entry **1986**:1
  Haney, Chris
    Brief Entry **1985**:1
  Hassenfeld, Stephen **1987**:4

Kingsborough, Donald
  Brief Entry **1986**:2
Kristiansen, Kjeld Kirk **1988**:3
Lazarus, Charles **1992**:4
Roberts, Xavier **1985**:3
Rowland, Pleasant **1992**:3

**Toys R Us**
  Eyler, John. H., Jr. **2001**:3
  Lazarus, Charles **1992**:4

**Track and field**
  Johnson, Michael **2000**:1
  Jones, Marion **1998**:4
  Joyner, Florence Griffith **1989**:2
    Obituary **1999**:1

**Trade negotiation**
  Hills, Carla **1990**:3
  Reisman, Simon **1987**:4

**Tradex**
  Hakuta, Ken
    Brief Entry **1986**:1

**Travel**
  Arison, Ted **1990**:3
  Fodor, Eugene
    Obituary **1991**:3
  Steger, Will **1990**:4

**Treasure Salvors, Inc.**
  Fisher, Mel **1985**:4

**TreePeople**
  Lipkis, Andy
    Brief Entry **1985**:3

**Trevor's Campaign**
  Ferrell, Trevor
    Brief Entry **1985**:2

**Trivial Pursuit**
  Haney, Chris
    Brief Entry **1985**:1

**Twentieth Century-Fox Film Corp.**
  Diller, Barry **1991**:1
  Goldberg, Leonard **1988**:4

**UAW**
  See: United Auto Workers

**UFW**
  See: United Farm Workers
  Chavez, Cesar
    Obituary **1993**:4

**Ultralight aircraft**
  MacCready, Paul **1986**:4
  Moody, John **1985**:3

**UN**
  See: United Nations

**Uncle Noname (cookie company)**
  Amos, Wally **2000**:1

**UNICEF**
  Bellamy, Carol **2001**:2
  Hepburn, Audrey
    Obituary **1993**:2
  Ustinov, Peter
    Obituary **2005**:3

**Union Pacific Railroad**
  Harriman, W. Averell
    Obituary **1986**:4

**UNITA**
  See: National Union for the Total
    Independence of Angola

**United Airlines**
  Friend, Patricia A. **2003**:3
  Wolf, Stephen M. **1989**:3

**United Auto Workers [UAW]**
  Bieber, Owen **1986**:1
  Woodcock, Leonard
    Obituary **2001**:4
  Yokich, Stephen P. **1995**:4

**United Farm Workers [UFW]**
  Chavez, Cesar
    Obituary **1993**:4
  Huerta, Dolores **1998**:1

**United Federation of Teachers**
  Feldman, Sandra **1987**:3

**United Nations [UN]**
  Albright, Madeleine **1994**:3
  Annan, Kofi **1999**:1
  Arbour, Louise **2005**:1
  Astorga, Nora **1988**:2
  Bailey, Pearl
    Obituary **1991**:1
  de Pinies, Jamie
    Brief Entry **1986**:3
  Fulbright, J. William
    Obituary **1995**:3
  Ghali, Boutros Boutros **1992**:3
  Gromyko, Andrei
    Obituary **1990**:2
  Kouchner, Bernard **2005**:3
  Lewis, Stephen **1987**:2
  Lodge, Henry Cabot
    Obituary **1985**:1
  Perez de Cuellar, Javier **1991**:3
  Terzi, Zehdi Labib **1985**:3

**United Petroleum Corp.**
  Aurre, Laura
    Brief Entry **1986**:3

**United Press International [UPI]**
  Thomas, Helen **1988**:4

**United Steelworkers of America [USW]**
  Williams, Lynn **1986**:4

**University Network**
  Scott, Gene
    Brief Entry **1986**:1

**University of Chicago**
  Gray, Hanna **1992**:4

**Viacom, Inc.**
Redstone, Sumner **1994**:1

**Vietnam War**
Dong, Pham Van
Obituary **2000**:4

**Vigilantism**
Goetz, Bernhard Hugo **1985**:3
Slotnick, Barry
Brief Entry **1987**:4

**Virgin Holdings Group Ltd.**
Branson, Richard **1987**:1

**Virginia state government**
Robb, Charles S. **1987**:2
Wilder, L. Douglas **1990**:3

**Vogue magazine**
Wintour, Anna **1990**:4

**Volkswagenwerk AG**
Hahn, Carl H. **1986**:4
Lopez de Arriortua, Jose Ignacio **1993**:4

**Volleyball**
Kiraly, Karch
Brief Entry **1987**:1

**Voyager aircraft**
Rutan, Burt **1987**:2

**Vanity Fair magazine**
Brown, Tina **1992**:1

**Virtual reality**
Lanier, Jaron **1993**:4

**Wacky WallWalker**
Hakuta, Ken
Brief Entry **1986**:1

**Wall Street Analytics, Inc.**
Unz, Ron **1999**:1

**Wallyball**
Garcia, Joe
Brief Entry **1986**:4

**Wal-Mart Stores, Inc.**
Glass, David **1996**:1
Walton, Sam **1986**:2
Obituary **1993**:1

**Walt Disney Productions**
Disney, Roy E. **1986**:3
Eisner, Michael **1989**:2
Katzenberg, Jeffrey **1995**:3

**Wang Laboratories, Inc.**
Wang, An **1986**:1
Obituary **1990**:3

**War crimes**
Barbie, Klaus
Obituary **1992**:2
Hess, Rudolph
Obituary **1988**:1

Karadzic, Radovan **1995**:3
Klarsfeld, Beate **1989**:1
Mengele, Josef
Obituary **1985**:2
Milosevic, Slobodan **1993**:2

**Warnaco**
Wachner, Linda **1988**:3 **1997**:2

**Washington Bullets basketball team**
McMillen, Tom **1988**:4
O'Malley, Susan **1995**:2

**Washington, D.C., city government**
Barry, Marion **1991**:1
Williams, Anthony **2000**:4

**Washington Post**
Graham, Donald **1985**:4
Graham, Katharine Meyer **1997**:3
Obituary **2002**:3

**Washington Redskins football team**
Monk, Art **1993**:2
Rypien, Mark **1992**:3
Smith, Jerry
Obituary **1987**:1
Williams, Doug **1988**:2
Williams, Edward Bennett
Obituary **1988**:4

**Watergate**
Dickerson, Nancy H.
Obituary **1998**:2
Ehrlichman, John
Obituary **1999**:3
Ervin, Sam
Obituary **1985**:2
Graham, Katharine Meyer **1997**:3
Obituary **2002**:3
Haldeman, H. R.
Obituary **1994**:2
Mitchell, John
Obituary **1989**:2
Neal, James Foster **1986**:2
Nixon, Richard
Obituary **1994**:4
Thompson, Fred **1998**:2

**Water skiing**
Duvall, Camille
Brief Entry **1988**:1

**Wayne's World**
Myers, Mike **1992**:3 **1997**:4

**WebTV Networks Inc.**
Perlman, Steve **1998**:2

**Wendy's International**
Thomas, Dave **1986**:2 **1993**:2
Obituary **2003**:1

**Who Wants to be a Millionaire**
Philbin, Regis **2000**:2

**Windham Hill Records**
Ackerman, Will **1987**:4

**Wine making**
Lemon, Ted
Brief Entry **1986**:4
Mondavi, Robert **1989**:2
Rothschild, Philippe de
Obituary **1988**:2

**WNBA**
See: Women's National Basketball Association

**Women's National Basketball Association [WNBA]**
Cooper, Cynthia **1999**:1
Laimbeer, Bill **2004**:3
Swoopes, Sheryl **1998**:2

**Women's issues**
Allred, Gloria **1985**:2
Baez, Joan **1998**:3
Boxer, Barbara **1995**:1
Braun, Carol Moseley **1993**:1
Burk, Martha **2004**:1
Butler, Brett **1995**:1
Cresson, Edith **1992**:1
Davis, Angela **1998**:3
Doi, Takako
Brief Entry **1987**:4
Faludi, Susan **1992**:4
Faulkner, Shannon **1994**:4
Ferraro, Geraldine **1998**:3
Finley, Karen **1992**:4
Finnbogadóttir, Vigdiás
Brief Entry **1986**:2
Flynt, Larry **1997**:3
Friedan, Betty **1994**:2
Furman, Rosemary
Brief Entry **1986**:4
Grant, Charity
Brief Entry **1985**:2
Griffiths, Martha
Obituary **2004**:2
Harris, Barbara **1989**:3
Hill, Anita **1994**:1
Ireland, Jill
Obituary **1990**:4
Jong, Erica **1998**:3
Kanokogi, Rusty
Brief Entry **1987**:1
Love, Susan **1995**:2
MacKinnon, Catharine **1993**:2
Marier, Rebecca **1995**:4
Mikulski, Barbara **1992**:4
Monroe, Rose Will
Obituary **1997**:4
Morgan, Robin **1991**:1
Nasrin, Taslima **1995**:1
Nussbaum, Karen **1988**:3
Paglia, Camille **1992**:3
Profet, Margie **1994**:4
Steinem, Gloria **1996**:2
Summers, Anne **1990**:2
Wattleton, Faye **1989**:1
Wolf, Naomi **1994**:3
Yard, Molly **1991**:4

**Woods Hole Research Center**
Woodwell, George S. **1987**:2

**World Bank**
McCloy, John J.
Obituary **1989**:3
McNamara, Robert S. **1995**:4

**World Cup**
Hamm, Mia **2000**:1

**World Health Organization**
Brundtland, Gro Harlem **2000**:1

**World of Wonder, Inc.**
Kingsborough, Donald
Brief Entry **1986**:2

**World Wrestling Federation [WWF]**
Austin, 'Stone Cold' Steve **2001**:3
Chyna **2001**:4
Hogan, Hulk **1987**:3
McMahon, Vince, Jr. **1985**:4
Ventura, Jesse **1999**:2

**Wrestling**
Austin, 'Stone Cold' Steve **2001**:3
Baumgartner, Bruce
Brief Entry **1987**:3

Chyna **2001**:4
Hogan, Hulk **1987**:3
McMahon, Vince, Jr. **1985**:4
Rock, The **2001**:2
Ventura, Jesse **1999**:2

**WWF**
See: World Wrestling Federation

**Xerox**
Allaire, Paul **1995**:1
Brown, John Seely **2004**:1
McColough, C. Peter **1990**:2
Mulcahy, Anne M. **2003**:2
Rand, A. Barry **2000**:3

**Yahoo!**
Filo, David and Jerry Yang **1998**:3
Koogle, Tim **2000**:4
Semel, Terry **2002**:2

**Young & Rubicam, Inc.**
Kroll, Alexander S. **1989**:3

**Zamboni ice machine**
Zamboni, Frank J.
Brief Entry **1986**:4

**ZANU**
See: Zimbabwe African National
Union

**Ziff Corp**
Ziff, William B., Jr. **1986**:4

**Zimbabwe African National Union
[ZANU]**
Mugabe, Robert **1988**:4

# Cumulative Newsmakers Index

This index lists all newsmakers included in the entire *Newsmakers* series.

Listee names are followed by a year and issue number; thus **1996**:3 indicates that an entry on that individual appears in both 1996, Issue 3, and the 1996 cumulation.

Lauder, Estee 1908(?)- ............... **1992**:2
Lauper, Cyndi 1953- ............... **1985**:1
Lauren, Ralph 1939- ............... **1990**:1
Lavigne, Avril 1984- ............... **2005**:2
Law, Jude 1971- ............... **2000**:3
Lawless, Lucy 1968- ............... **1997**:4
Lawrence, Martin 1966(?)- ............... **1993**:4
Lawrence, Ruth
    Brief Entry ............... **1986**:3
Lawson, Nigella 1960- ............... **2003**:2
Laybourne, Geraldine 1947- ............... **1997**:1
Lazarus, Charles 1923- ............... **1992**:4
Lazarus, Shelly 1947- ............... **1998**:3
Leach, Archibald Alexander
    See Grant, Cary
Leach, Penelope 1937- ............... **1992**:4
Leach, Robin 1942(?)-
    Brief Entry ............... **1985**:4
Leakey, Mary Douglas 1913-1996
    Obituary ............... **1997**:2
Leakey, Richard 1944- ............... **1994**:2
Lear, Frances 1923- ............... **1988**:3
Leary, Denis 1958- ............... **1993**:3
Leary, Timothy 1920-1996
    Obituary ............... **1996**:4
Lebed, Alexander 1950- ............... **1997**:1
LeBlanc, Matt 1967- ............... **2005**:4
le Carre, John 1931- ............... **2000**:1
Lederman, Leon Max 1922- ............... **1989**:4
Le Duan 1908(?)-1986
    Obituary ............... **1986**:4
Le Duc Tho 1911-1990
    Obituary ............... **1991**:1
Lee, Ang 1954- ............... **1996**:3
Lee, Brandon 1965(?)-1993
    Obituary ............... **1993**:4
Lee, Chang-Rae 1965- ............... **2005**:1
Lee, Chang-Yuh
    See Lee, Henry C.
Lee, Henry C. 1938- ............... **1997**:1
Lee Jong-Wook 1945- ............... **2005**:1
Lee, Martin 1938- ............... **1998**:2
Lee, Pamela 1967(?)- ............... **1996**:4
Lee, Peggy 1920-2002
    Obituary ............... **2003**:1
Lee, Shelton Jackson
    See Lee, Spike
Lee, Spike 1957- ............... **1988**:4
Lee Teng-hui 1923- ............... **2000**:1
Lefebvre, Marcel 1905- ............... **1988**:4
Leguizamo, John 1965- ............... **1999**:1
Lehane, Dennis 1965- ............... **2001**:4
Leibovitz, Annie 1949- ............... **1988**:4
Leigh, Janet 1927-2004
    Obituary ............... **2005**:4
Leigh, Jennifer Jason 1962- ............... **1995**:2
Lelyveld, Joseph S. 1937- ............... **1994**:4
Lemieux, Claude 1965- ............... **1996**:1
Lemieux, Mario 1965- ............... **1986**:4
Lemmon, Jack 1925- ............... **1998**:4
    Obituary ............... **2002**:3
Lemon, Ted
    Brief Entry ............... **1986**:4
LeMond, Greg 1961- ............... **1986**:4
LeMond, Gregory James
    See LeMond, Greg
Lennox, Annie 1954- ............... **1985**:4 **1996**:4
Leno, James Douglas Muir
    See Leno, Jay
Leno, Jay 1950- ............... **1987**:1
Leonard, Elmore 1925- ............... **1998**:4
Leonard, Ray Charles

See Leonard, Sugar Ray
Leonard, Sugar Ray 1956- ............... **1989**:4
Leone, Sergio 1929-1989
    Obituary ............... **1989**:4
Lerner, Michael 1943- ............... **1994**:2
Lerner, Sandy 1955(?)- ............... **2005**:1
Leslie, Lisa 1972- ............... **1997**:4
Letterman, David 1947- ............... **1989**:3
LeVay, Simon 1943- ............... **1992**:2
Leávesque, Reneá
    Obituary ............... **1988**:1
Levin, Gerald 1939- ............... **1995**:2
Levine, Arnold 1939- ............... **2002**:3
Levine, James 1943- ............... **1992**:3
Levinger, Moshe 1935- ............... **1992**:1
Levinson, Barry 1932- ............... **1989**:3
Levitt, Arthur 1931- ............... **2004**:2
Levy, Burton
    See Lane, Burton
Levy, David 1938- ............... **1987**:2
Levy, Eugene 1946- ............... **2004**:3
Lewis, Edward B. 1918-2004
    Obituary ............... **2005**:4
Lewis, Edward T. 1940- ............... **1999**:4
Lewis, Henry 1932-1996
    Obituary ............... **1996**:3
Lewis, Huey 1951- ............... **1987**:3
Lewis, John 1920-2001
    Obituary ............... **2002**:1
Lewis, Juliette 1973- ............... **1999**:3
Lewis, Lennox 1965- ............... **2000**:2
Lewis, Loida Nicolas 1942- ............... **1998**:3
Lewis, Ray 1975- ............... **2001**:3
Lewis, Reggie 1966(?)-1993
    Obituary ............... **1994**:1
Lewis, Reginald F. 1942-1993 ............... **1988**:4
    Obituary ............... **1993**:3
Lewis, Richard 1948(?)- ............... **1992**:1
Lewis, Shari 1934-1998 ............... **1993**:1
    Obituary ............... **1999**:1
Lewis, Stephen 1937- ............... **1987**:2
LeWitt, Sol 1928- ............... **2001**:2
Lewitzky, Bella 1916-2004
    Obituary ............... **2005**:3
Leyland, Jim 1944- ............... **1998**:2
Li, Jet 1963- ............... **2005**:3
Liberace 1919-1987
    Obituary ............... **1987**:2
Liberace, Wladziu Valentino
    See Liberace
Libeskind, Daniel 1946- ............... **2004**:1
Lichtenstein, Roy 1923-1997 ............... **1994**:1
    Obituary ............... **1998**:1
Lieberman, Joseph 1942- ............... **2001**:1
Lightner, Candy 1946- ............... **1985**:1
Liguori, Peter 1960- ............... **2005**:2
Lilly, John C. 1915-2001
    Obituary ............... **2002**:4
Liman, Arthur 1932- ............... **1989**:4
Limbaugh, Rush ............... **1991**:3
Lin, Maya 1960(?)- ............... **1990**:3
Lincoln, Blanche 1960- ............... **2003**:1
Lindbergh, Anne Morrow 1906-2001
    Obituary ............... **2001**:4
Lindbergh, Pelle 1959-1985
    Obituary ............... **1985**:4
Lindgren, Astrid 1907-2002
    Obituary ............... **2003**:1
Lindros, Eric 1973- ............... **1992**:1
Lindsay, John V. 1921-2000
    Obituary ............... **2001**:3
Lines, Ray 1960(?)- ............... **2004**:1

Ling, Bai 1970- ............... **2000**:3
Ling, Lisa 1973- ............... **2004**:2
Lipinski, Tara 1982- ............... **1998**:3
Lipkis, Andy
    Brief Entry ............... **1985**:3
Lipsig, Harry H. 1901- ............... **1985**:1
Lipton, Martin 1931- ............... **1987**:3
Lithgow, John 1945- ............... **1985**:2
Little, Cleavon 1939-1992
    Obituary ............... **1993**:2
Liu, Lucy 1968- ............... **2000**:4
Livi, Yvo
    See Montand, Yves
Living Colour ............... **1993**:3
Livingstone, Ken 1945- ............... **1988**:3
Lizhi, Fang
    See Fang Lizhi
LL Cool J 1968- ............... **1998**:2
Lloyd Webber, Andrew 1948- ............... **1989**:1
Lobell, Jeanine 1964(?)- ............... **2002**:3
Locklear, Heather 1961- ............... **1994**:3
Lodge, Henry Cabot 1902-1985
    Obituary ............... **1985**:1
Loewe, Frederick 1901-1988
    Obituary ............... **1988**:2
Lofton, Kenny 1967- ............... **1998**:1
Lofton, Ramona
    See Sapphire
Logan, Joshua 1908-1988
    Obituary ............... **1988**:4
Lohan, Lindsay 1986- ............... **2005**:3
Long, Nia 1970- ............... **2001**:3
Long, Shelley 1950(?)- ............... **1985**:1
Longo, Robert 1953(?)- ............... **1990**:4
Lon Nol
    Obituary ............... **1986**:1
Lopes, Lisa 1971-2002
    Obituary ............... **2003**:3
Lopes, Lisa 'Left Eye'
    See TLC
Lopez, George 1963- ............... **2003**:4
Lopez, Ignacio
    See Lopez de Arriortua, Jose Ignacio
Lopez, Inaki
    See Lopez de Arriortua, Jose Ignacio
Lopez, Jennifer 1970- ............... **1998**:4
Lopez, Nancy 1957- ............... **1989**:3
Lopez de Arriortua, Jose Ignacio
    1941- ............... **1993**:4
Lord, Bette Bao 1938- ............... **1994**:1
Lord, Jack 1920-1998
    Obituary ............... **1998**:2
Lord, Winston
    Brief Entry ............... **1987**:4
Lords, Traci 1968- ............... **1995**:4
Lorenz, Konrad 1903-1989
    Obituary ............... **1989**:3
Lott, Trent 1941- ............... **1998**:1
Louganis, Greg 1960- ............... **1995**:3
Louis-Dreyfus, Julia 1961(?)- ............... **1994**:1
Love, Courtney 1964(?)- ............... **1995**:1
Love, Susan 1948- ............... **1995**:2
Loveless, Patty 1957- ............... **1998**:2
Lovett, Lyle 1958(?)- ............... **1994**:1
Lovley, Derek 1954(?)- ............... **2005**:3
Lowe, Edward 1921- ............... **1990**:2
Lowe, Rob 1964(?)- ............... **1990**:4
Lowell, Mike 1974- ............... **2003**:2
Loy, Myrna 1905-1993
    Obituary ............... **1994**:2
Lucas, George 1944- ............... **1999**:4
Lucci, Susan 1946(?)- ............... **1999**:4

Monroe, Rose Will 1920-1997
  Obituary ....................................... **1997**:4
Montagu, Ashley 1905-1999
  Obituary ....................................... **2000**:2
Montana, Joe 1956- ...................... **1989**:2
Montand, Yves 1921-1991
  Obituary ....................................... **1992**:2
Montgomery, Elizabeth 1933-1995
  Obituary ....................................... **1995**:4
Montoya, Carlos 1903-1993
  Obituary ....................................... **1993**:4
Moody, John 1943- ........................ **1985**:3
Moody, Rick 1961- ........................ **2002**:2
Moon, Warren 1956- ..................... **1991**:3
Moonves, Les 1949- ...................... **2004**:2
Moore, Archie 1913-1998
  Obituary ....................................... **1999**:2
Moore, Clayton 1914-1999
  Obituary ....................................... **2000**:3
Moore, Demi 1963(?)- .................... **1991**:4
Moore, Dudley 1935-2002
  Obituary ....................................... **2003**:2
Moore, Henry 1898-1986
  Obituary ....................................... **1986**:4
Moore, Julianne 1960- .................... **1998**:1
Moore, Mandy 1984- ..................... **2004**:2
Moore, Mary Tyler 1936- ............... **1996**:2
Moore, Michael 1954(?)- ................ **1990**:3
Moose, Charles 1953(?)- ................ **2003**:4
Moreno, Arturo 1946- ................... **2005**:2
Morgan, Claire
  See Highsmith, Patricia
Morgan, Dodge 1932(?)- ................ **1987**:1
Morgan, Robin 1941- ..................... **1991**:1
Morgentaler, Henry 1923- .............. **1986**:3
Mori, Yoshiro 1937- ...................... **2000**:4
Morissette, Alanis 1974- ................ **1996**:2
Morita, Akio 1921- ........................ **1989**:4
Morita, Akio 1921-1999
  Obituary ....................................... **2000**:2
Morita, Noriyuki 'Pat' 1932- .......... **1987**:3
Morita, Pat
  See Morita, Noriyuki 'Pat'
Moritz, Charles 1936- .................... **1989**:3
Morris, Dick 1948- ........................ **1997**:3
Morris, Doug 1938- ....................... **2005**:1
Morris, Mark 1956- ....................... **1991**:1
Morris, Nate
  See Boyz II Men
Morris, Wanya
  See Boyz II Men
Morrison, Sterling 1942-1995
  Obituary ....................................... **1996**:1
Morrison, Toni 1931- ..................... **1998**:1
Morrison, Trudi
  Brief Entry ................................... **1986**:2
Morrissey 1959- ............................ **2005**:2
Morrow, Tracey
  See Ice-T
Mortensen, Viggo 1958- ................ **2003**:3
Mosbacher, Georgette 1947(?)- ...... **1994**:2
Mos Def 1973- .............................. **2005**:4
Mosley, Walter 1952- ..................... **2003**:4
Moss, Carrie-Anne 1967- ............... **2004**:3
Moss, Cynthia 1940- ..................... **1995**:2
Moss, Kate 1974- .......................... **1995**:3
Moss, Randy 1977- ........................ **1999**:3
Mother Hale
  See Hale, Clara
Mother Teresa 1910-1997 ............... **1993**:1
  Obituary ....................................... **1998**:1

Motherwell, Robert 1915-1991
  Obituary ....................................... **1992**:1
Mott, William Penn, Jr. 1909- ........ **1986**:1
Mottola, Tommy 1949- ................... **2002**:1
Mourning, Alonzo 1970- ................ **1994**:2
Moyers, Bill 1934- ......................... **1991**:4
Moynihan, Daniel Patrick 1927-2003
  Obituary ....................................... **2004**:2
Mubarak, Hosni 1928- ................... **1991**:4
Mugabe, Robert 1924- ................... **1988**:4
Mulcahy, Anne M. 1952- ............... **2003**:2
Muldowney, Shirley 1940- ............. **1986**:1
Mullenger, Donna Belle
  See Reed, Donna
Mullis, Kary 1944- ........................ **1995**:3
Mulroney, Brian 1939- ................... **1989**:2
Mumford, Lewis 1895-1990
  Obituary ....................................... **1990**:2
Muniz, Frankie 1985- ..................... **2001**:4
Munro, Alice 1931- ........................ **1997**:1
Murakami, Takashi 1962- ............... **2004**:2
Murcia, Ann Jura Nauseda
  See Jillian, Ann
Murdoch, Iris 1919-1999
  Obituary ....................................... **1999**:4
Murdoch, Keith Rupert
  See Murdoch, Rupert
Murdoch, Rupert 1931- .................. **1988**:4
Murphy, Brittany 1977- .................. **2005**:1
Murphy, Eddie 1961- ..................... **1989**:2
Murray, Arthur 1895-1991
  Obituary ....................................... **1991**:3
Murray, Bill 1950- ......................... **2002**:4
Murrieta, Luis Donaldo Colosio
  See Colosio, Luis Donaldo
Musburger, Brent 1939- ................. **1985**:1
Museveni, Yoweri 1944- ................. **2002**:1
Musharraf, Pervez 1943- ............... **2000**:2
Muskie, Edmund S. 1914-1996
  Obituary ....................................... **1996**:3
Mutter, Anne-Sophie 1963- ........... **1990**:3
Mydans, Carl 1907-2004
  Obituary ....................................... **2005**:4
Myers, Mike 1964(?)- ......... **1992**:3 **1997**:4
Nader, Ralph 1934- ....................... **1989**:4
Nagako, Empress Dowager 1903-2000
  Obituary ....................................... **2001**:1
Nakszynski, Nikolaus Gunther
  See Kinski, Klaus
Nance, Jack 1943(?)-1996
  Obituary ....................................... **1997**:3
Napolitano, Janet 1957- ................. **1997**:1
Narayan, R.K. 1906-2001
  Obituary ....................................... **2002**:2
Nars, Francois 1959- ..................... **2003**:1
Nasreen, Taslima
  See Nasrin, Taslima
Nasrin, Taslima 1962- .................... **1995**:1
Natori, Josie 1947- ........................ **1994**:3
Natsios, Andrew 1949- ................... **2005**:1
Nauman, Bruce 1941- .................... **1995**:4
Navratilova, Martina 1956- ............ **1989**:1
Neal, James Foster 1929- .............. **1986**:2
Nechita, Alexandra 1985- .............. **1996**:4
Neeleman, David 1959- .................. **2003**:3
Neeson, Liam 1952- ....................... **1993**:4
Neiman, LeRoy 1927- .................... **1993**:3
Nelson, Harriet 1909(?)-1994
  Obituary ....................................... **1995**:1
Nelson, Rick 1940-1985
  Obituary ....................................... **1986**:4
Nelson, Willie 1933- ...................... **1993**:4

Nemerov, Howard 1920-1991
  Obituary ....................................... **1992**:1
Netanyahu, Benjamin 1949- ........... **1996**:4
Neuharth, Allen H. 1924- .............. **1986**:1
Nevelson, Louise 1900-1988
  Obituary ....................................... **1988**:3
Newhouse, Samuel I., Jr. 1927- ..... **1997**:1
New Kids on the Block ................... **1991**:2
Newkirk, Ingrid 1949- ................... **1992**:3
Newman, Arnold 1918- .................. **1993**:1
Newman, Joseph 1936- .................. **1987**:1
Newman, Paul 1925- ..................... **1995**:3
Newman, Ryan 1977- .................... **2005**:1
Newton, Helmut 1920- .................. **2002**:1
Newton, Huey 1942-1989
  Obituary ....................................... **1990**:1
Newton-John, Olivia 1948- ............ **1998**:4
Ngau, Harrison ............................. **1991**:3
Ni Bhraonain, Eithne
  See Enya
Nichols, Mike 1931- ...................... **1994**:4
Nicholson, Jack 1937- .................... **1989**:2
Nidal, Abu 1937- .......................... **1987**:1
Nielsen, Jerri 1951(?)- ................... **2001**:3
Niezabitowska, Malgorzata
  1949(?)- .................................... **1991**:3
Nipon, Albert
  Brief Entry ................................... **1986**:4
Niro, Laura
  See Nyro, Laura
Nirvana ........................................ **1992**:4
Nixon, Pat 1912-1993
  Obituary ....................................... **1994**:1
Nixon, Richard 1913-1994
  Obituary ....................................... **1994**:4
No Doubt ..................................... **1997**:3
Nol, Lon
  See Lon Nol
Nolan, Lloyd 1902-1985
  Obituary ....................................... **1985**:4
Nolte, Nick 1941- ......................... **1992**:4
Nomo, Hideo 1968- ....................... **1996**:2
Noonan, Peggy 1950- .................... **1990**:3
Nooyi, Indra 1955- ........................ **2004**:3
Norman, Greg 1955- ...................... **1988**:3
Norman, Gregory John
  See Norman, Greg
Norrington, Roger 1934- ............... **1989**:4
North, Alex 1910- ......................... **1986**:3
North, Oliver 1943- ....................... **1987**:4
Northam, Jeremy 1961- .................. **2003**:2
Norton, Edward 1969- ................... **2000**:2
Norville, Deborah 1958- ................ **1990**:3
Norwood, Brandy
  See Brandy
Notorious B.I.G. 1973(?)-1997
  Obituary ....................................... **1997**:3
Novello, Antonia 1944- .................. **1991**:2
Novoselic, Chris
  See Nirvana
Noyce, Robert N. 1927- ................. **1985**:4
'N Sync ........................................ **2001**:4
Nuesslein-Volhard, Christiane
  1942- ......................................... **1998**:1
Nujoma, Sam 1929- ....................... **1990**:4
Nunn, Sam 1938- .......................... **1990**:2
Nunn, Trevor 1940- ....................... **2000**:2
Nureyev, Rudolf 1938-1993
  Obituary ....................................... **1993**:2
Nussbaum, Karen 1950- ................ **1988**:3
Nye, Bill 1955- ............................. **1997**:2

Quinn, Martha 1959- ........................ **1986**:4
Quivers, Robin 1953(?)- ................. **1995**:4
Ra, Sun
  See Sun Ra
Rabbitt, Eddie 1941-1998
  Obituary ........................ **1998**:4
Rabin, Leah 1928-2000
  Obituary ........................ **2001**:2
Rabin, Yitzhak 1922-1995 ............. **1993**:1
  Obituary ........................ **1996**:2
Radecki, Thomas
  Brief Entry ........................ **1986**:2
Radner, Gilda 1946-1989
  Obituary ........................ **1989**:4
Radocy, Robert
  Brief Entry ........................ **1986**:3
Raffi 1948- ........................ **1988**:1
Rafsanjani, Ali Akbar Hashemi
  1934(?)- ........................ **1987**:3
Rafter, Patrick 1972- ........................ **2001**:1
Rahman, Sheik Omar Abdel-
  1938- ........................ **1993**:3
Raimi, Sam 1959- ........................ **1999**:2
Raimondi, John
  Brief Entry ........................ **1987**:4
Raines, Franklin 1949- ................. **1997**:4
Raitt, Bonnie 1949- ........................ **1990**:2
Rajneesh, Bhagwan Shree 1931-1990
  Obituary ........................ **1990**:2
Ram, Jagjivan 1908-1986
  Obituary ........................ **1986**:4
Ramaphosa, Cyril 1953- ................. **1988**:2
Ramaphosa, Matamela Cyril
  See Ramaphosa, Cyril
Ramirez, Manny 1972- ................. **2005**:4
Ramo, Roberta Cooper 1942- ........ **1996**:1
Ramone, Joey 1951-2001
  Obituary ........................ **2002**:2
Ramos, Fidel 1928- ........................ **1995**:2
Rampal, Jean-Pierre 1922- ............. **1989**:2
Ramsay, Mike 1950(?)- ................. **2002**:1
Rand, A. Barry 1944- ..................... **2000**:3
Randall, Tony 1920-2004
  Obituary ........................ **2005**:3
Randi, James 1928- ........................ **1990**:2
Rao, P. V. Narasimha 1921- ........... **1993**:2
Raphael, Sally Jessy 1943- ........... **1992**:4
Rapp, C.J.
  Brief Entry ........................ **1987**:3
Rapp, Carl Joseph
  See Rapp, C.J.
Rasa Don
  See Arrested Development
Rashad, Phylicia 1948- ................. **1987**:3
Raskin, Jef 1943(?)- ........................ **1997**:4
Rattle, Simon 1955- ........................ **1989**:4
Rauschenberg, Robert 1925- ......... **1991**:2
Ravalomanana, Marc 1950(?)- ........ **2003**:1
Raven 1985- ........................ **2005**:1
Rawlings, Mike 1954- ..................... **2003**:1
Ray, Amy
  See Indigo Girls
Ray, James Earl 1928-1998
  Obituary ........................ **1998**:4
Raye, Martha 1916-1994
  Obituary ........................ **1995**:1
Raymond, Lee R. 1930- ................. **2000**:3
Reagan, Ronald 1911-2004
  Obituary ........................ **2005**:3
Reasoner, Harry 1923-1991
  Obituary ........................ **1992**:1

Redenbacher, Orville 1907-1995
  Obituary ........................ **1996**:1
Redfield, James 1952- ..................... **1995**:2
Redford, Robert 1937- ..................... **1993**:2
Redgrave, Lynn 1943- ..................... **1999**:3
Redgrave, Vanessa 1937- ............... **1989**:2
Red Hot Chili Peppers ................. **1993**:1
Redig, Patrick 1948- ........................ **1985**:3
Redman, Joshua 1969- ..................... **1999**:2
Redstone, Sumner 1923- ............... **1994**:1
Reed, Dean 1939(?)-1986
  Obituary ........................ **1986**:3
Reed, Donna 1921-1986
  Obituary ........................ **1986**:1
Reed, Ralph 1961(?)- ..................... **1995**:1
Reed, Robert 1933(?)-1992
  Obituary ........................ **1992**:4
Reese, Della 1931- ........................ **1999**:2
Reeve, Christopher 1952- ............. **1997**:2
Reeves, Keanu 1964- ..................... **1992**:1
Reeves, Steve 1926-2000
  Obituary ........................ **2000**:4
Regan, Judith 1953- ........................ **2003**:1
Rehnquist, William H. 1924- ........ **2001**:2
Reich, Robert 1946- ........................ **1995**:4
Reid, Vernon
  See Living Colour
Reilly, John C. 1965- ..................... **2003**:4
Reiner, Rob 1947- ........................ **1991**:2
Reiser, Paul 1957- ........................ **1995**:2
Reisman, Simon 1919- ................. **1987**:4
Reisman, Sol Simon
  See Reisman, Simon
Reisz, Karel 1926-2002
  Obituary ........................ **2004**:1
Reitman, Ivan 1946- ........................ **1986**:3
Remick, Lee 1936(?)-1991
  Obituary ........................ **1992**:1
Reno, Janet 1938- ........................ **1993**:3
Renvall, Johan
  Brief Entry ........................ **1987**:4
Retton, Mary Lou 1968- ................. **1985**:2
Reuben, Gloria 1964- ..................... **1999**:4
Reubens, Paul 1952- ........................ **1987**:2
Rey, Margret E. 1906-1996
  Obituary ........................ **1997**:2
Reza, Yasmina 1959(?)- ................. **1999**:2
Reznor, Trent 1965- ........................ **2000**:2
Rhea, Caroline 1964- ..................... **2004**:1
Rhodes, Zandra 1940- ..................... **1986**:2
Ribicoff, Abraham 1910-1998
  Obituary ........................ **1998**:3
Ricci, Christina 1980- ..................... **1999**:1
Rice, Anne 1941- ........................ **1995**:1
Rice, Condoleezza 1954- ............... **2002**:1
Rice, Jerry 1962- ........................ **1990**:4
Rich, Bernard
  See Rich, Buddy
Rich, Buddy 1917-1987
  Obituary ........................ **1987**:3
Rich, Charlie 1932-1995
  Obituary ........................ **1996**:1
Richard, Maurice 1921-2000
  Obituary ........................ **2000**:4
Richards, Ann 1933- ........................ **1991**:2
Richards, Keith 1943- ..................... **1993**:3
Richards, Michael 1949(?)- ............. **1993**:4
Richter, Charles Francis 1900-1985
  Obituary ........................ **1985**:4
Richter, Gerhard 1932- ................. **1997**:2
Rickover, Hyman 1900-1986
  Obituary ........................ **1986**:4

Riddle, Nelson 1921-1985
  Obituary ........................ **1985**:4
Ridenhour, Carlton
  See Public Enemy
Ridge, Tom 1945- ........................ **2002**:2
Rifkin, Jeremy 1945- ..................... **1990**:3
Riggio, Leonard S. 1941- ............... **1999**:4
Riggs, Bobby 1918-1995
  Obituary ........................ **1996**:2
Riley, Pat 1945- ........................ **1994**:3
Riley, Richard W. 1933- ................. **1996**:3
Rimes, LeeAnn 1982- ..................... **1997**:4
Riney, Hal 1932- ........................ **1989**:1
Ringgold, Faith 1930- ..................... **2000**:3
Ringwald, Molly 1968- ................. **1985**:4
Riordan, Richard 1930- ................. **1993**:4
Ripa, Kelly 1970- ........................ **2002**:2
Ripken, Cal, Jr. 1960- ..................... **1986**:2
Ripken, Cal, Sr. 1936(?)-1999
  Obituary ........................ **1999**:4
Ripken, Calvin Edwin, Jr.
  See Ripken, Cal, Jr.
Ritchie, Dennis
  See Ritchie, Dennis and
  Kenneth Thompson
Ritchie, Dennis and
  Kenneth Thompson ................. **2000**:1
Ritchie, Guy 1968- ........................ **2001**:3
Ritter, John 1948- ........................ **2003**:4
Ritts, Herb 1954(?)- ........................ **1992**:4
Rivera, Geraldo 1943- ..................... **1989**:1
Rivers, Joan 1933- ........................ **2005**:3
Rizzo, Frank 1920-1991
  Obituary ........................ **1992**:1
Rizzoli, Paola 1943(?)- ................. **2004**:3
Robards, Jason 1922-2000
  Obituary ........................ **2001**:3
Robb, Charles S. 1939- ................. **1987**:2
Robbins, Harold 1916-1997
  Obituary ........................ **1998**:1
Robbins, Jerome 1918-1998
  Obituary ........................ **1999**:1
Robbins, Tim 1959- ........................ **1993**:1
Robelo, Alfonso 1940(?)- ............... **1988**:1
Roberts, Brian L. 1959- ................. **2002**:4
Roberts, Cokie 1943- ..................... **1993**:4
Roberts, Corinne Boggs
  See Roberts, Cokie
Roberts, Doris 1930- ..................... **2003**:4
Roberts, Julia 1967- ........................ **1991**:3
Roberts, Steven K. 1952(?)- ........... **1992**:1
Roberts, Xavier 1955- ..................... **1985**:3
Robertson, Marion Gordon
  See Robertson, Pat
Robertson, Pat 1930- ..................... **1988**:2
Robinson, David 1965- ................. **1990**:4
Robinson, Earl 1910(?)-1991
  Obituary ........................ **1992**:1
Robinson, Frank 1935- ................. **1990**:2
Robinson, Mary 1944- ..................... **1993**:1
Robinson, Max 1939-1988
  Obituary ........................ **1989**:2
Robinson, Sugar Ray 1921-1989
  Obituary ........................ **1989**:3
Robinson, V. Gene 1947- ............... **2004**:4
Roche, Eamonn Kevin
  See Roche, Kevin
Roche, Kevin 1922- ........................ **1985**:1
Rock, Chris 1967(?)- ........................ **1998**:1
Rock, John
  Obituary ........................ **1985**:1
Rock, The 1972- ........................ **2001**:2